INVENTORY   (Chapter 5)

Perpetual vs. Periodic Journal Entries (buyer)

Transaction	Perpetual	Periodic
Purchase of merchandise	Dr. Merchandise Inventory Cr. Cash or Accounts Payable	Dr. Purchases Cr. Cash or Accounts Payable
Freight on merchandise purchased (FOB shipping point)	Dr. Merchandise Inventory Cr. Cash or Accounts Payable	Dr. Freight In Cr. Cash or Accounts Payable
Return of purchased merchandise	Dr. Cash or Accounts Payable Cr. Merchandise Inventory	Dr. Cash or Accounts Payable Cr. Purchase Returns and Allowances
Paying creditors on account within discount period	Dr. Accounts Payable Cr. Merchandise Inventory Cr. Cash	Dr. Accounts Payable Cr. Purchase Discounts Cr. Cash
Adjustment of inventory in accounting records to lower physical count amount (entry is opposite for higher amount)	Dr. Cost of Goods Sold Cr. Merchandise Inventory	No entry

Perpetual vs. Periodic Journal Entries (seller)

Transaction	Perpetual	Periodic
Sale of merchandise	Dr. Cash or Accounts Receivable Cr. Sales Dr. Cost of Goods Sold Cr. Merchandise Inventory	Dr. Cash or Accounts Receivable Cr. Sales No entry
Freight on merchandise sold (FOB destination)	Dr. Freight Out Cr. Cash or Accounts Payable	Dr. Freight Out Cr. Cash or Accounts Payable
Return of sold merchandise (assuming resaleable)	Dr. Sales Returns and Allowances Cr. Cash or Accounts Receivable Dr. Merchandise Inventory Cr. Cost of Goods Sold	Dr. Sales Returns and Allowances Cr. Cash or Accounts Receivable No entry
Collection of account from customer within discount period	Dr. Cash Dr. Sales Discounts Cr. Accounts Receivable	Dr. Cash Dr. Sales Discounts Cr. Accounts Receivable

INVENTORY   (Chapter 6)

Ownership of Merchandise

General Rule: Inventory is the buyer's when received, except:	
Goods purchased in transit—FOB shipping point	–Buyer's once shipped
Goods sold in transit—FOB destination	–Buyer's until it reaches the seller's destination
Consigned goods	–Seller's (consignor) until sold
Other situations—Goods on approval	–Seller's until sold

Inventory Cost Determination Methods

1. Specific identification: Used for goods that are not ordinarily interchangeable, or goods that have been produced and segregated for specific projects
2. Cost formulas: First-in, first-out (FIFO) or Average

Guidelines for Choice of Cost Formula

1. Choose method that corresponds to physical flow of goods.
2. Report inventory cost on the statement of financial position close to inventory's recent cost.
3. Use same method for all inventories having similar nature and usage.

Financial Statement Effects of Cost Determination Methods (during period of rising prices)

	Specific Identification	FIFO	Average
Income statement			
Cost of goods sold	Variable	Lowest	Highest
Gross profit	Variable	Highest	Lowest
Profit	Variable	Highest	Lowest
Statement of financial position			
Cash (pre-tax)	Same	Same	Same
Ending inventory	Variable	Highest	Lowest
Retained earnings	Variable	Highest	Lowest

Formula for Cost of Goods Sold (periodic inventory system)

INTERNAL CONTROL AND CASH   (Chapter 7)

Control Activities

Authorization of transactions and activities
Segregation of duties
Documentation
Physical controls
Independent checks of performance
Human resource controls

Calculation of Deposits in Transit

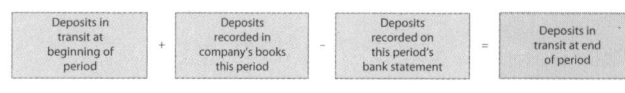

Calculation of Outstanding Cheques

Bank Reconciliation

Bank	Books
Cash balance per bank statement Add: Deposits in transit Deduct: Outstanding cheques Add (deduct): Bank errors = Adjusted cash balance per bank	Cash balance per books Add: Unrecorded credit memoranda from bank statement Deduct: Unrecorded debit memoranda from bank statement Add (deduct): Book errors = Adjusted cash balance per books

Note: 1. Errors should be offset (added or deducted) on the side that made the error.
2. Adjusting journal entries should only be made on the books side.

STOP AND CHECK: (1) Do adjusted cash balances per bank and per books agree? (2) Does adjusted cash balance equal the balance in the general ledger Cash account after all adjusting journal entries have been made?

RECEIVABLES   (Chapter 8)

Debit and Credit Card Transactions

Debit Card	Bank Credit Card	Company Credit Card
Dr. Cash Dr. Debit Card Expense Cr. Sales	Dr. Cash Dr. Credit Card Expense Cr. Sales	Dr. Credit Card Receivables Cr. Sales

Bad Debts

Transaction	Journal Entry
Record credit sales	Dr. Accounts Receivable Cr. Sales
Estimate bad debts	Dr. Bad Debts Expense Cr. Allowance for Doubtful Accounts
Write off uncollectible account	Dr. Allowance for Doubtful Accounts Cr. Accounts Receivable
Subsequent recovery	Dr. Accounts Receivable Cr. Allowance for Doubtful Accounts Dr. Cash Cr. Accounts Receivable

Notes Receivable

Honouring Notes Receivable	Dishonouring Notes Receivable (eventual collection assumed)	Dishonouring Notes Receivable (eventual collection not assumed)
Dr. Cash Cr. Notes Receivable Cr. Interest Revenue and/or Receivable	Dr. Accounts Receivable Cr. Notes Receivable Cr. Interest Revenue and/or Receivable	Dr. Allowance for Doubtful Notes Cr. Notes Receivable Cr. Interest Receivable (if any)

Steps to Manage Receivables

1. Determine to whom to extend credit
2. Establish a payment period
3. Monitor collections
4. Evaluate the liquidity of receivables
5. Accelerate cash receipts from receivables when necessary

LONG-LIVED ASSETS   (Chapter 9)

Calculation of Annual Depreciation Expense

Straight-line	$\dfrac{\text{Cost} - \text{Residual value}}{\text{Useful life (in years)}}$
Diminishing-balance	Carrying amount at beginning of year $\times$ Straight-line rate Straight-line rate = 1 ÷ Useful life (in years)
Units-of-production	$\dfrac{\text{Cost} - \text{Residual value}}{\text{Estimated total units of activity}} \times$ Units of activity during year

Note: 1. If depreciation is calculated for partial periods, the straight-line and diminishing-balance methods must be adjusted for the relevant proportion of the year. Multiply annual depreciation expense by the number of months expired in the year divided by 12 months.

2. The total depreciation for the diminishing-balance method is limited to depreciable cost (cost – residual value).

Impairment Loss

Carrying amount – Recoverable amount = Impairment loss

Dr. Impairment Loss
    Cr. Accumulated Depreciation

Disposal of Property, Plant, and Equipment

1. Update depreciation for appropriate portion of current year	Dr. Depreciation Expense Cr. Accumulated Depreciation
2. Calculate carrying amount	Cost – Accumulated depreciation = Carrying amount
3. Calculate gain or loss	Proceeds – Carrying amount = Gain (loss)
4. Record disposal	Dr. Cash (or Receivable) Dr. Accumulated Depreciation Dr. Loss (or credit Gain) Cr. Property, Plant, and Equipment

NON-CURRENT LIABILITIES   (Chapter 10)

Instalment Notes Payable—Payment Schedule

Payments	Interest Period	(A) Cash Payment	(B) Interest Expense	(C) Reduction of Principal	(D) Principal Balance
Fixed principal payments	Month	Variable B + C	$D^* \times$ Annual Interest Rate $\times \dfrac{1}{12}$	Principal balance ÷ # of months	$D^* - C$
Blended principal and interest	Month	Fixed B + C	$D^* \times$ Annual Interest Rate $\times \dfrac{1}{12}$	A – B	$D^* - C$

* From the prior period

Bonds Payable

Premium	Market interest rate < Coupon interest rate
Face Value	Market interest rate = Coupon interest rate
Discount	Market interest rate > Coupon interest rate

Amortization of Bond Premium or Discount

(1) Bond Interest Expense		(2) Bond Interest Paid		(3)
Carrying Amount of Bonds at Beginning of Period	$\times$ Market (Effective) Interest Rate	– Face Amount of Bonds	$\times$ Coupon Interest Rate	= Amortization Amount

SHAREHOLDERS' EQUITY   (Chapter 11)

Reacquisition of Shares (retired and cancelled)

Average cost of shares = Dollar amount in share account ÷ Number of shares

Below Average Cost	Above Average Cost

Dr. Common/Preferred Shares (@average cost)
    Cr. Contributed Capital—Reacquisition of Shares
    Cr. Cash (@ market price)
	Dr. Common/Preferred Shares (@ average cost)
	Dr. Contributed Capital—Reacquisition of Shares (if any)
	Dr. Retained Earnings
	    Cr. Cash (@ market price)

Comparison of Dividend Effects

	Assets	=	Liabilities	+	Shareholders' Equity Share Capital	+	Retained Earnings	Number of Shares
Cash dividend	–		NE		NE		–	NE
Stock dividend	NE		NE		+		–	+
Stock split	NE		NE		NE		NE	+

Note: "+" means increase, "–" means decrease, "NE" means no effect.

Comprehensive Income

Comprehensive income (loss)	=	Profit	+	Other comprehensive income (loss)

⇩ Retained earnings (statement of changes in equity and shareholders' equity section of statement of financial position)

⇩ Accumulated other comprehensive income (loss) (statement of changes in equity and shareholders' equity section of statement of financial position)

INVESTMENTS   (Chapter 12)

Reporting and Valuation of Investments

Statement of Financial Position Classification	Strategy	Type of Investment	Valuation Model
Short-term investments (current assets)	Non-strategic	Trading investments (debt or equity)	Fair value
Long-term investments (non-current assets)	Non-strategic	Equity investments without significant influence or control, with determinable fair values	Fair value (with option under IFRS to use fair value through OCI)
		Debt investments held to earn interest revenue	Amortized cost
	Strategic	Investments in associates (equity investments with significant influence)	Equity method (with option to use cost or fair value model under ASPE). Consolidation required if control exists (with option to use equity, cost or fair value under ASPE).

Comparison of Fair Value Model and Equity Method of Accounting for Equity Investments

Transaction	Fair Value (no significant influence)	Equity (significant influence)

Acquisition	Dr. Trading Investments
	    Cr. Cash
		Dr. Investment in Associates
		    Cr. Cash

Investee reports profit	No entry	Dr. Investment in Associates Cr. Revenue from Investment in Associates

Investee pays dividends	Dr. Cash
	    Cr. Dividend Revenue
		Dr. Cash
		    Cr. Investment in Associates

Adjustment for increase in fair value (entry is opposite for decrease)	Dr. Trading Investments Cr. Unrealized Gain on Trading Investments	No entry

Note: The unrealized gain (or loss) on trading investments is reported as other revenues and gains (or other expenses and losses) in the income statement.

Continued on EP-4 at the end of the book

www.wileyplus.com

ALL THE HELP, **RESOURCES**, AND PERSONAL **SUPPORT** YOU AND YOUR STUDENTS NEED!

www.wileyplus.com/resources

2-Minute Tutorials and all of the resources you & your students need to get started.

Student support from an experienced student user.

Collaborate with your colleagues, find a mentor, attend virtual and live events, and view resources.
www.WhereFacultyConnect.com

Pre-loaded, ready-to-use assignments and presentations. Created by subject matter experts.

Technical Support 24/7. FAQs, online chat, and phone support.
www.wileyplus.com/support

Your *WileyPLUS* Account Manager. Personal training and implementation support.

FINANCIAL ACCOUNTING

TOOLS FOR BUSINESS DECISION-MAKING

Fifth Canadian Edition

Paul D. Kimmel Ph.D., CPA
University of Wisconsin—Milwaukee, Wisconsin

Jerry J. Weygandt Ph.D., CPA
University of Wisconsin—Madison, Wisconsin

Donald E. Kieso Ph.D., CPA
Northern Illinois University, DeKalb, Illinois

Barbara Trenholm MBA, FCA
University of New Brunswick, Fredericton, New Brunswick

Wayne Irvine BComm, CFA, CA
University of Calgary, Alberta

John Wiley & Sons Canada, Ltd.

Dedicated to our families for their patience and support

Library and Archives Canada Cataloguing in Publication

Financial accounting: tools for business decision-making / Paul D. Kimmel . . . [et al.]. — 5th Canadian ed.

Includes index.
ISBN 978-1-118-02449-2

1. Accounting—Textbooks. I. Kimmel, Paul D.

HF5635.F44 2011   657'.044   C2011-903615-0

Production Credits

Acquisitions Editor: Zoë Craig
Vice President and Publisher: Veronica Visentin
Marketing Manager: Anita Osborne
Editorial Manager: Karen Staudinger
Production Manager: Tegan Wallace
Developmental Editor: Daleara Hirjikaka
Media Editor: Channade Fenandoe
Editorial Assistants: Laura Hwee and Luisa Begani
Design: Interrobang Graphic Design, Inc.
Typesetting: Thomson Digital
Cover Design: Tegan Wallace
Cover Photo: © Michael Christopher Brown/Corbis
Printing and Binding: Quad / Graphics

Printed and bound in the United States of America
2 3 4 5 QG 16 15 14 13 12

WILEY

John Wiley & Sons Canada, Ltd.
6045 Freemont Blvd.
Mississauga, Ontario L5R 4J3

Visit our website at: www.wiley.ca

Your
TEAM *FOR* SUCCESS
in Accounting

Wiley is your partner in accounting education. We want to be the publisher you think of first when it comes to quality content, reliable technology, innovative resources, professional training, and unparalleled support for your accounting classroom.

Your Wiley Accounting Team for Success has three distinctive advantages that you won't find with any other publisher:

- Author commitment
- WileyPLUS
- Wiley Faculty Network

AUTHOR COMMITMENT
A Proven Author Team of Inspired Teachers

The Team for Success authors bring years of practical and academic experience, as well as their passion for teaching, to the development of each textbook that relates accounting concepts to real-world experiences. This cohesive team brings continuity of writing style, pedagogy, and end-of-chapter material to each course from financial to intermediate accounting so you and your students can seamlessly progress from introductory through intermediate courses in accounting.

COLLABORATION.
INNOVATION. EXPERIENCE.

After decades of success as outstanding educators, Barbara Trenholm and Wayne Irvine, the authors of this book and part of the Wiley Accounting Team for Success, understand that teaching accounting goes beyond simply presenting data. The authors are truly effective because they know that teaching is about telling compelling stories in ways that make each concept come to life.

Through their textbooks, supplements, online learning tools, and classrooms, these authors have developed a comprehensive pedagogy that engages students in learning and faculty in teaching.

These authors work together throughout the entire process. The end result is a true collaboration where the authors bring their individual experience and talent to the development of every paragraph, page, and chapter, thus creating a well-rounded, thorough view on any given accounting topic.

Many Ways in One Direction

Our **Team for Success** has developed a learning system that addresses every learning style. Each year brings new insights, feedback, ideas, and improvements on how to deliver the material to every student with a passion for the subject in a format that gives them the best chance to succeed. The key to the team's approach is in understanding that, just as there are many different ways to learn, there are also many different ways to teach.

WILEYPLUS
An Experienced Team of Support Professionals

The *WileyPLUS* account managers understand the time constraints of busy faculty who want to provide the best resources available to their students with minimal frustrations and planning time. They know how intimidating a new version of software can sometimes be, so they are sure to make the transition easy and painless. Account managers act as your personal contact and expert resource for training, course set-up, and shortcuts throughout the *WileyPLUS* experience. Your success as an educator directly correlates with student success, and that's our goal. The Wiley Accounting Team for Success truly strives for YOUR success! Partner with us today!

WILEY FACULTY NETWORK
A Team of Educators Dedicated to Your Professional Development

The Wiley Faculty Network (WFN) is a global group of seasoned accounting professionals who share best practices in teaching with their peers. Our Virtual Guest Lecture Series provides the opportunity you need for professional development in an on-line environment that is relevant, convenient, and collaborative. The quality of these seminars and workshops meets the strictest standards, so we are proud to offer valuable professional development credits to attendees who require these. With a number of faculty mentors in accounting, it's easy to find help with your most challenging curriculum questions—just ask our experts!

AUTHOR TEAM

Canadian Edition

Barbara Trenholm, MBA, FCA,
is a professor emerita at the University
of New Brunswick, for which she
continues to teach locally and
internationally. Her teaching and ed-
ucational leadership has been widely
recognized. She is a recipient of the
Leaders in Management Education

Award, the Global Teaching Excellence Award, and the
University of New Brunswick's Merit Award and Dr. Allan
P. Stuart Award for Excellence in Teaching.

Professor Trenholm is an active member of the boards
of several organizations, including Atomic Energy of
Canada Limited and Plazacorp Retail Properties Ltd. She
is a member of the Institute of Corporate Directors, a past
board member of the Canadian Institute of Chartered
Accountants and the Atlantic School of Chartered
Accountancy, and past president of the New Brunswick
Institute of Chartered Accountants. She has also served as
a chair of the Canadian Institute of Chartered Accountants
Academic Research Committee, Interprovincial Education
Committee, and Canadian Institute of Chartered
Accountants/Canadian Academic Accounting Association
Liaison Committee. She has served as a member of the
Canadian Institute of Chartered Accountants Qualification
Committee, International Qualifications Appraisal
Board, and Education Reeingineering Task Force, and
the American Accounting Association's Globalization
Initiatives Task Force, in addition to numerous other com-
mittees at the international, national, and provincial levels
of the profession.

She has presented at many conferences and published
widely in the field of accounting education and standard
setting in journals including *Accounting Horizons, Journal
of the Academy of Business Education, CAmagazine, CGA
Magazine,* and *CMA Magazine.*

Wayne Irvine, CFA, CA, is a senior
instructor at the Haskayne School of
Business at the University of Calgary.
He has been the recipient of more than
ten teaching awards from university
students, CA articling students, and
the Dean of his school.

Professor Irvine began his career
with PricewaterhouseCoopers, where he worked for over
12 years as a senior manager assigned to audits of both
public and private companies. After leaving the firm, he
commenced his academic career and for the next 19 years
taught at Mount Royal University, where he was the chair
of the accounting area, and at the Haskayne School of
Business.

He teaches extensively for the CA School of Business
and has authored several case-based exams for that organization. In the past, he was also active in preparing
candidates for the Certified Management Accountants entrance exam.

Professor Irvine is a Chartered Financial Analyst charter-
holder and has been active in teaching accounting to CFA
candidates for a number of years. He is also involved in
the Director Education Program and serves in an advisory
capacity to the Institute of Corporate Directors.

U.S. Edition

Paul D. Kimmel, Ph.D., CPA, received his bachelor's
degree from the University of Minnesota and his doctor-
ate in accounting from the University of Wisconsin. He is
an Associate Professor at the University of Wisconsin—
Milwaukee, and has public accounting experience with
Deloitte & Touche (Minneapolis). He was the recipi-
ent of the UWM School of Business Advisory Council
Teaching Award, the Reggie Taite Excellence in Teaching
Award, and a three-time winner of the Outstanding
Teaching Assistant Award at the University of Wisconsin.
He is also a recipient of the Elijah Watts Sells Award for
Honorary Distinction for his results on the CPA exam.

He is a member of the American Accounting Association
and the Institute of Management Accountants and has published articles in *Accounting Review, Accounting Horizons,
Advances in Management Accounting, Managerial Finance,
Issues in Accounting Education,* and *Journal of Accounting
Education,* as well as other journals. His research interests
include accounting for financial instruments and innovation in accounting education. He has published papers and
given numerous talks on incorporating critical thinking
into accounting education, and helped prepare a catalogue
of critical thinking resources for the Federated Schools
of Accountancy.

Jerry J. Weygandt, Ph.D., CPA, is the Arthur Andersen
Alumni Emeritus Professor of Accounting at the University
of Wisconsin—Madison. He holds a Ph.D. in accounting from the University of Illinois. Articles by Professor

Weygandt have appeared in *Accounting Review, Journal
of Accounting Research, Accounting Horizons, Journal of
Accountancy,* and other academic and professional journals. These articles have examined such financial reporting

issues as accounting for price-level adjustments, pensions, convertible securities, stock option contracts, and interim reports. Professor Weygandt is author of other accounting and financial reporting books and is a member of the American Accounting Association, the American Institute of Certified Public Accountants, and the Wisconsin Society of Certified Public Accountants. He has served on numerous committees of the American Accounting Association and as a member of the editorial board of *Accounting Review*; he has also served as President and Secretary-Treasurer of the American Accounting Association. In addition, he has been actively involved with the American Institute of Certified Public Accountants and has been a member of the Accounting Standards Executive Committee of that organization. He served on the FASB task force that examined the reporting issues related to accounting for income taxes and as a trustee of the Financial Accounting Foundation. Professor Weygandt has received the Chancellor's Award for Excellence in Teaching and the Beta Gamma Sigma Dean's Teaching Award. He is on the board of directors of M&I Bank of Southern Wisconsin. He is the recipient of the Wisconsin Institute of CPA's Outstanding Educator's Award and the Lifetime Achievement Award. In 2001, he received the American Accounting Association's Outstanding Accounting Educator Award.

Donald E. Kieso, Ph.D., CPA, received his bachelor's degree from Aurora University and his doctorate in accounting from the University of Illinois. He has served as chairman of the Department of Accountancy and is currently the KPMG Emeritus Professor of Accounting at Northern Illinois University. He has public accounting experience with Price Waterhouse & Co. (San Francisco and Chicago) and Arthur Andersen & Co. (Chicago) and research experience with the Research Division of the American Institute of Certified Public Accountants. He has done post-doctorate work as a Visiting Scholar at the University of California at Berkeley and is a recipient of NIU's Teaching Excellence Award and four Golden Apple Teaching Awards. Professor Kieso is the author of other accounting and business books and is a member of the American Accounting Association, the American Institute of Certified Public Accountants, and the Illinois CPA Society. He has served as a member of the Board of Directors of the Illinois CPA Society, the AACSB's Accounting Accreditation Committees, the State of Illinois Comptroller's Commission, as Secretary-Treasurer of the Federation of Schools of Accountancy, and as Secretary-Treasurer of the American Accounting Association. Professor Kieso is currently serving on the Board of Trustees and Executive Committee of Aurora University, as a member of the Board of Directors of Kishwaukee Community Hospital, and as Treasurer and Director of Valley West Community Hospital. From 1989 to 1993, he served as a charter member of the national Accounting Education Change Commission. He is the recipient of the Outstanding Accounting Educator Award from the Illinois CPA Society, the FSA's Joseph A. Silvoso Award of Merit, the NIU Foundation's Humanitarian Award for Service to Higher Education, a Distinguished Service Award from the Illinois CPA Society, and in 2003 an honorary doctorate from Aurora University.

The Place Where Faculty Connect...

Attend

Learn from instructors around the world, as well as recognized leaders across disciplines. Join thousands of faculty just like you who participate in virtual and live events each semester. You'll connect with fresh ideas, best practices, and practical tools for a wide range of timely topics.

- **Training**
- **Virtual Guest Lectures**
- **Live Events**

View

Explore your resources and development opportunities.

- **Teaching Resources**
- **Archived Guest Lectures**
- **Recorded Presentations**
- **Learning Modules**

Collaborate

Tap into your greatest resource – your peers. Exchange ideas and teaching tools, while broadening your perspective. Whether you choose to blog, join interest groups, or connect with a mentor – you've come to the right place.

- **Connect with Colleagues**
- **Find a Mentor**
- **Interest Groups**
- **Blog**

The Wiley Faculty Network... you belong here!
Get connected at www.WhereFacultyConnect.com

WILEY

www.wileyplus.com

WileyPLUS is an innovative, on-line environment for effective teaching and learning.

FOR STUDENTS	FOR INSTRUCTORS

What do STUDENTS receive with WileyPLUS?

WileyPLUS increases confidence as it allows greater engagement, which leads to improved learning outcomes.

Design

The WileyPLUS design integrates relevant resources, including the entire digital textbook, in an easy-to-navigate framework that helps students study more effectively and ensures student engagement. Innovative features, such as a variety of self-evaluation tools, are all designed to improve time management and increase student confidence.

Engagement

WileyPLUS links all material to demonstrable study objectives and outcomes. Related media, examples, and sample practice items reinforce the study objectives. Students can assess progress and gain immediate feedback on strengths and weaknesses in order to ensure they are spending their time most effectively.

Outcomes

Throughout each study session, students can assess their progress and gain immediate feedback. WileyPLUS provides precise reporting of strengths and weaknesses, so that students are confident they are spending their time on the right things. With WileyPLUS, students always know the exact outcome of their efforts.

With increased confidence, motivation is sustained so students stay on task longer, leading to success.

What do INSTRUCTORS receive with WileyPLUS?

Support and insight into student progress

WileyPLUS provides reliable, customizable resources that reinforce course goals inside and outside of the classroom, as well as visibility into individual student progress. Pre-created materials and activities help instructors optimize their time.

For class preparation and classroom use:

- Lecture notes, PowerPoint slides, and tutorials
- Classroom response system (clicker) questions

For assignments and testing:

- Reading assignment questions (embedded with on-line text)
- Question assignments: all end-of-chapter problems and additional problems coded algorithmically with links to text

For course planning: WileyPLUS comes with a pre-created **Course Plan** designed by a subject matter expert uniquely for this course.

For progress monitoring: WileyPLUS provides instant access to reports on class performance and student use of course materials helping inform decisions and drive classroom discussions.

Experience WileyPLUS for effective teaching and learning at **www.wileyplus.com**.

Powered by proven technology, WileyPLUS has enriched the education of millions of students in over 20 countries around the world.

Our purpose in writing this text is to introduce students to accounting in a way that demonstrates how important it is to business careers and to society overall. Whether a student becomes a business owner, an employee, or an investor, understanding and being able to use accounting information is crucial. We strive to teach students what they really need to know in a way that can enhance their success with this course. To accomplish this, this text relies on a few key beliefs:

"It really matters."

Over the past decade, there has been a heightened awareness of the importance of accounting to a smoothly running economic system. Many of our feature stories, *Accounting Matters* boxes, and *Broadening Your Perspective* cases have been designed to reveal accounting's critical role in society. In short, it has never been more evident that accounting really matters!

"Don't just sit there— do something."

Students learn best when they are actively engaged. The overriding pedagogical objective of this book is to provide students with opportunities for active learning. Key concepts are presented in combination with *Do It!* examples and comprehensive *Do It!* problems, allowing students to practise techniques covered in the chapter. Technology also offers many opportunities for students to enhance their learning. Through WileyPLUS, students can access a wide array of additional practice material and learning resources to support every learning style. To understand what your learning style is, take the learning style quiz on the textbook's student companion site or on WileyPLUS and then apply the tips for your personal learning style to your studies.

"I'll believe it when I see it."

Students are most willing to commit time and energy to a topic when they believe that it is relevant to their future career. There is no better way to demonstrate relevance than to ground discussion in the real world. We do this in several ways. First, we use well-known companies such as Canadian Tire, Loblaw, lululemon, Shoppers Drug Mart, Sears, and Tim Hortons to frame our discussion of accounting issues. Second, the book employs a "macro" approach in its first two chapters, teaching students how to understand and use the real financial statements of two publicly traded companies using International Financial Reporting Standards, Eastern Platinum Limited and Anglo American Platinum Limited, before teaching students how to record transactions. Many students determine their opinion of a course during the initial weeks, and this macro approach clearly demonstrates the relevance of accounting while students are forming their first impression of the course. Finally, our *Accounting Matters* boxes and *All About You* features specifically connect accounting to business functions such as finance, marketing, and management and show uses of accounting for students both professionally and personally, regardless of whether they are concentrating their studies in the accounting field.

"You need to make a decision."

All business people must make decisions. Decision-making involves critical evaluation and analysis of the information at hand, and this takes practice. We have integrated important analytical tools throughout the book. After each new decision tool is presented, we summarize the key features of that tool in a *Decision Toolkit*. At the end of each chapter, we provide a comprehensive demonstration of an analysis of a company in *Using the Decision Toolkit*, which incorporates the decision tools presented in the chapter. The presentation of these tools throughout the book is cumulative, sequenced to take full advantage of the tools presented in earlier chapters. This sequence of decision tools culminates in a capstone analysis chapter at the end of the book.

"Dealing with change."

We have seen much change in accounting standards over the last few years. One of our objectives in this textbook is to provide students with an understanding of those concepts that are fundamental to the use of accounting. Most students will forget procedural details within a short period of time. On the other hand, concepts, if well taught, should be remembered for a lifetime. Concepts are especially important in a world that has experienced a significant change in accounting standards, with further changes yet to come. Consequently, we have added many features in this edition of the text to help students understand the conceptual similarities and differences underlying International Financial Reporting Standards (IFRS) and Accounting Standards for Private Enterprises (ASPE), the rationale for different sets of standards, and how they are likely to evolve in future to meet the differing needs of users.

TOOLS FOR STUDENT SUCCESS

Financial Accounting: Tools for Business Decision-Making, Fifth Canadian Edition, provides many proven pedagogical tools to help students learn accounting concepts and apply them to decision-making in the business world. Here are a few key features.

Learning How to Use the Text

- On the book's companion website, you will find learning strategies and tips for different learning styles, and available resources in WileyPLUS and the textbook that relate to those learning styles.
- **The Navigator** guides students through each chapter by pulling all the learning tools together into a learning system. Throughout the chapter, the Navigator prompts students to use the learning aids and to set priorities as they study.
- Marginal notes in yellow boxes in Chapter 1 explain how to use the text's learning tools to help achieve success in the course.

Understanding the Context

- **Study Objectives**, listed at the beginning of each chapter, reappear in the margins and again in the Summary of Study Objectives.
- The **Accounting Matters! Feature Story** helps students understand how the chapter topic relates to the real world of accounting and business and illustrates the necessity of sound accounting as the basis of informed decisions.
- A chapter **Preview** links the Feature Story to the major topics of the chapter and provides a road map to the chapter.
- The **Keeping an Eye on Cash** feature helps students to understand the connections between, and significance of, cash flows from operating, investing, and financing activities.

■ Keeping an Eye on Cash

We have seen that both inventory on the statement of financial position and cost of goods sold on the income statement are affected by the choice of cost determination method. It is very important to understand, however, that the choice of method does *not* affect cash flow. All three methods of cost determination—specific identification, FIFO, and average—produce exactly the same cash flow before income tax.

Why is that? Sales and purchases are not affected by the method of inventory cost determination. The only thing that is affected is the allocation of the cost of goods available for sale between the cost of goods sold and ending inventory—which does not involve cash.

- A new feature, called **Anatomy of a Fraud**, has been added to Chapter 7 to illustrate how a missing internal control can result in fraud.

ANATOMY OF A FRAUD

Sophia and Tamra are sales representatives for their company. They both travel a great deal and complete expense reports to obtain reimbursements of their travel expenses from the company. One day, Sophia realized that the accounting department would accept photocopies of invoices relating to travel. Sophia went to Tamra's desk and noticed several invoices for a trip Tamra had just taken to Calgary. Sophia photocopied the invoices and submitted them as her own expenses. She received a reimbursement cheque for these costs. She did this 18 times during the year.

> **THE MISSING CONTROL**
> *Documentation*
> The company should only accept original invoices when processing expense reimbursements.

- Differences between IFRS and ASPE are highlighted throughout the chapter with an ASPE logo where applicable.
- An **All About You** feature links some aspect of the chapter topic to a student's personal life, and often to some financial situation they are likely to face now or in the near future.

Learning the Material

- Emphasis on accounting experiences of **real companies** and business situations throughout.
- Four types of **Accounting Matters!** boxes highlight ethics, investor, management, and international perspectives. These stories provide glimpses into how real companies make decisions using accounting information and how individuals in non-accounting functions use accounting information in their decision-making.

ACCOUNTING MATTERS! *Management Perspective*

Counting Inventory That Swims

There are many challenges involved in taking a physical inventory for certain kinds of businesses. One of the more difficult types of inventory to count is at a salmon farm, where the inventory is swimming around in the ocean.

Salmon farms can be found in provinces in Atlantic Canada, as well as British Columbia, with the salmon kept in net cages in the ocean. An average salmon farm contains between 6 and 14 cages, and each cage contains from 50,000 to 80,000 fish. At Cooke Aquaculture Inc., headquartered in New Brunswick, salmon are initially counted when they are put in cages as smolts, or young salmon, from the hatchery. Every week, divers go down and count the number of fish at the bottom of the cage that have died. The remainder is the company's best estimate of what is left. Other factors, such as fish escaping or predators getting some of the fish, will reduce these estimates.

After the salmon reach about 4.5 kg, they are harvested. The actual number of salmon harvested is compared with the number estimated. The percentage differences are tracked and future estimates are adjusted for expected differences.

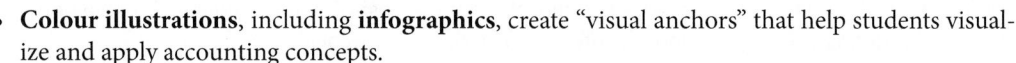

- **Colour illustrations**, including **infographics**, create "visual anchors" that help students visualize and apply accounting concepts.
- **Do It!** problems appear at key breaks called "Before You Go On . . ." in the chapter narrative. These mini demonstration problems invite students to test their understanding of the just-completed section before they proceed to the next one.
- **Financial statements** appear regularly throughout the book. Those from real companies are usually identified by a logo or have the company name highlighted in red type.
- **Accounting equation analyses** in the margin next to key journal entries reinforce understanding of the impact of an accounting transaction on the financial statements. They also report the cash effect of each transaction to reinforce understanding of the difference between **cash effects** and **accrual accounting**.
- **Helpful Hints, Alternative Terminology**, and blue-highlighted **Key Terms** help focus students on important concepts as they study the material.
- **Decision tools** useful for analyzing and solving business problems are presented and then summarized in **Decision Toolkits**.

A	=	L	+	SE
−1,000,000		−1,000,000		

↓Cash flows: − 1,000,000

Putting It Together

At the end of each chapter are several features useful for review and reference.

- **A Comparing IFRS and ASPE** summary outlines key differences between the two standards in the chapter.

comparing
IFRS and ASPE

Key Differences	International Financial Reporting Standards (IFRS)	Accounting Standards for Private Enterprises (ASPE)
Accounting standards	Publicly traded corporations must use IFRS; private corporations can choose to use IFRS or ASPE.	Private corporations can choose to use IFRS or ASPE. Once the choice is made, it must be applied consistently.
Terminology	The balance sheet is more commonly known as the statement of financial position and net income as profit under IFRS.	The statement of financial position is more commonly known as the balance sheet and profit as net income under ASPE.
Statement of changes in equity vs. statement of retained earnings	A statement of changes in equity must be presented that shows the changes in all components of shareholders' equity (e.g., share capital and retained earnings).	A statement of retained earnings is presented that shows the change in only one component–retained earnings–of shareholders' equity.

- A **Summary of Study Objectives** reviews the main points of the chapter.
- A **Glossary** of key terms gives definitions with page references to the text.
- The **Decision Toolkit—A Summary** presents in one place the decision tools used throughout the chapter.

DECISION TOOLKIT—A SUMMARY

Decision Checkpoints	Info Needed for Decision	Tools to Use for Decision	How to Evaluate Results
What is the impact of the choice of inventory cost determination method?	Are prices increasing, or are they decreasing?	Income statement and statement of financial position effects	In periods of rising prices, profit and inventory are higher under FIFO than average. FIFO results in the best measure of ending inventory on the statement of financial position. The average cost formula provides opposite results (i.e., profit and inventory are lower compared to FIFO), but can smooth the impact of changing prices. Specific identification's impact on the financial statements will vary, depending on the actual cost. This method results in the best allocation of costs to revenues on the income statement.

- A **Using the Decision Toolkit** problem asks students to apply the decision tools presented in the chapter to a company, and takes them through the problem-solving steps.
- A **Comprehensive Do It!** with an **Action Plan** gives students another opportunity to study a detailed solution to a representative problem before they do homework assignments. Additional demonstration problems are available on the companion website.
- **Self Test Questions** provide a practice test that gives students an opportunity to check their knowledge of important topics. Answers appear on the last page of each chapter. Additional assessment quizzes are available in WileyPLUS.

Developing Skills through Practice

Each chapter is supported by a full complement of assignment material:

- Questions, Brief Exercises, Exercises, two sets of Problems, and Broadening Your Perspective cases, all keyed to the Study Objectives.
- **Broadening Your Perspective** cases at the end of each chapter offer a wealth of resources for instructors who want to broaden the learning experience by bringing in more real-world decision-making, analysis, and critical thinking activities.
  - A **Financial Reporting Case** directs students to study various aspects of the recent financial statements of Eastern Platinum Limited, which are printed in Chapter 1 (in simplified form) and in Appendix A (in full).
  - A **Comparative Analysis Case** offers the opportunity to compare and contrast the financial reporting of Eastern Platinum Limited with a competitor, Anglo American Platinum Limited.
  - **Interpreting Financial Information** cases ask students to read parts of financial statements of actual companies and use the decision tools of the chapter to interpret them.
  - A **Comparing IFRS and ASPE** case requires students to compare the financial information or reporting requirements of a company that uses IFRS with one that uses ASPE.
  - **Collaborative Learning Activities** help prepare students for the business world, where they will be working with many people, by giving students practice in solving problems with colleagues. They also allow students to learn from each other.
  - **Communication Activities** provide practice in written communication, a skill much in demand among employers.
  - **Ethics Cases** ask students to analyze situations, identify the ethical issues involved, and decide on an appropriate course of action.
  - An **"All About You" Activity** offers students an opportunity to link the accounting concepts learned in the chapter to some aspect of personal finance such as applying for a student loan, protecting themselves from identity theft, and using credit cards. These topics provide great opportunities for classroom discussion.
  - A **Serial Case** in every chapter traces the growth of an entrepreneurial venture, Koebel's Family Bakery Ltd. In each chapter, students apply their newly acquired accounting skills to solve the financial accounting and reporting issues faced by this small business.
- A **Comprehensive Case** (in Chapters 3, 4, 5, 8, 9, 11, and 14) combines material from the current chapter with previous chapters so that students understand how "it all fits together."

Comprehensive Case: Chapters 1–4

Record and post transaction and adjusting journal entries; prepare adjusted trial balance and financial statements.

(SO 3, 4)

Red River Computer Consultants Ltd. commenced operations more than a year ago. At its last year end, on June 30, 2012, the company's post-closing trial balance was prepared as follows:

RED RIVER COMPUTER CONSULTANTS LTD.
Trial Balance
June 30, 2012

	Debit	Credit
Cash	$5,230	
Accounts receivable	1,200	
Supplies	690	
Accounts payable		$ 400
Unearned revenue		1,120
Common shares		3,600
Retained earnings		2,000
	$7,120	$7,120

The company underwent a major expansion in July 2012. New staff was hired and more financing was obtained. Red River plans to record and adjust its accounts monthly. It conducted the following transactions during July 2012.

July 2   Issued $50,000 of common shares for cash.
     2   Obtained a bank loan for $10,000 at 6%. Interest is payable monthly on the first day of the following month. No principal payments are required until 2014.

The fifth Canadian edition expands on our emphasis on student learning and improves upon an already successful teaching and learning package with the following additions:

The Accounting Cycle

For many students, success in an introductory accounting course hinges on developing a sound conceptual understanding of the accounting cycle. In past editions, we have received positive feedback regarding the framework that we have used to introduce the recording process in Chapter 3. In this edition, we have expanded our use of this framework to cover the entire accounting cycle in Chapters 3 and 4.

Chart of Accounts

It is important to always try to eliminate unnecessary barriers to student understanding. Sometimes, financial accounting can seem unnecessarily complicated to students—especially when using an on-line homework system—because so many similar account titles are used. In order to reduce possible confusion, and to keep students focused on those concepts that really matter, in this edition of the textbook we undertook to reduce the number of account titles used. In some chapters, we were able to cut the number of accounts used by more than half without impacting the understanding of the topic.

IFRS and ASPE

As we continue to strive to reflect the ongoing changes in the accounting environment, this edition has been rewritten to replace Canadian generally accepted accounting principles with International Financial Reporting Standards (IFRS) and Accounting Standards for Private Enterprises (ASPE). Differences between IFRS and ASPE are highlighted throughout each chapter with an ASPE logo **ASPE** where applicable. Each chapter concludes with a *Comparing IFRS and ASPE* table to provide students with a quick summary of the key distinctions between the two sets of accounting standards. End-of-chapter material has been updated to include questions, exercises, problems, and cases relevant to both sets of standards. In addition, a new case in the Broadening Your Perspective section called *Comparing IFRS and ASPE* has been added. The Serial Case has been rewritten to incorporate a small, private company using ASPE at the beginning of the text that later becomes a publicly traded company using IFRS.

Comparison Companies

This textbook is the only introductory accounting textbook to use intracompany, intercompany, and industry comparisons throughout to illustrate the application of financial accounting. In this edition, we have changed our "comparison companies" to Eastern Platinum Limited (Eastplats), a Canadian company, and Anglo American Platinum Limited (Amplats), an international company. They were chosen because they are close competitors and both report using International Financial Reporting Standards. References to these companies have been included throughout the textbook, including simplified financial statements in the chapter material where appropriate, ratio analysis, *Using the Decision Toolkit*, end-of-chapter assignments, and detailed financial statements in Appendices A and B at the end of the textbook.

Terminology

Changes in terminology were made throughout the text to be consistent with that used in the *CICA Handbook*. For example, IFRS refers to the *statement of financial position* rather than *balance sheet*, which is the current term used under ASPE. With the recent adoption of IFRS and ASPE by Canadian companies, we expect to see many examples of alternative terminology in practice. We have therefore taken steps to explain to students when different words may be used in financial reporting that convey the same meaning.

Keeping an Eye on Cash

In each chapter, we added a new feature called *Keeping an Eye on Cash*. Cash is critical to the financial health of a company and this focus on cash will increase students' ability to understand the differences between accrual-based figures and cash. It also will help students to better understand the connections between, and significance of, cash flows from operating, investing, and financing activities.

Anatomy of a Fraud

We have added a new feature, called *Anatomy of a Fraud*, in Chapter 7 to illustrate how a missing internal control can result in fraud. We believe this feature will be especially effective in demonstrating to both accounting and non-accounting students how internal controls can prevent fraud.

Comprehensive Updating

In addition to the above new features, this edition was subject to comprehensive updating to ensure that it continues to be relevant and fresh. Our textbook includes more than 300 references to real-world companies. All of the company information was updated and replaced, as necessary. In addition, more than half of the chapter-opening feature stories were replaced with new stories while the remainder were updated. More than 85% of the *Accounting Matters!* ethics, international, management, and investor perspectives are new. The *All About You* feature was updated in each chapter with new statistics and information applicable to today's student. The number of *Do It!* activities in this edition were increased by a third, and nearly half of the Do It!s are new. These activities give students an opportunity to stop and actively test their understanding of the material as they read the chapter.

All of the end-of-chapter material was carefully reviewed. Topical gaps were identified and additional material added as required. In total, 335 new questions, brief exercises, exercises, problems, and cases have been added to the end-of-chapter material. The remaining material was revised as required, with new parts added where appropriate to apply ASPE considerations or extend the problem.

KEY FEATURES OF EACH CHAPTER

Chapter 1: The Purpose and Use of Financial Statements
- Feature story is about Eastern Platinum (Eastplats) and how accounting aids decision-making
- Identifies the users and uses of financial accounting information and forms of business organization—proprietorship, partnership, private corporation, and public corporation
- Describes the business activities—financing, investing, and operating activities—that affect companies
- Explains the content, purpose, and interrelationships of each of the financial statements—income statement, statement of changes in equity, statement of financial position, and statement of cash flows
- Uses financial statements of a hypothetical company (to keep it simple), followed by those for a real company, Eastplats (to make it relevant)
- Keeping an Eye on Cash describes how each of the business activities—financing, investing, and operating activities—affects cash flow
- Comparing IFRS and ASPE summarizes key differences in choice of accounting standards, financial statement terminology, and the use of a statement of changes in equity versus a statement of changes in retained earnings
- All About You focuses on a student's personal annual report (resumé)
- Using the Decision Toolkit compares Eastern Platinum's financial statements with those of Anglo American Platinum

- *Key changes*: Expanded list of primary external users to include investors, lenders, and other creditors. Expanded discussion of the importance of ethics. Added private corporations to forms of business organizations and discussion of advantages and disadvantages of each type of organization. Added definitions for business activities and key financial terms. Replaced statement of retained earnings with statement of changes in equity for companies following IFRS; deferred illustration of statement of retained earnings in detail until Chapter 11.

Chapter 2: A Further Look at Financial Statements
- Feature story is about Plazacorp Retail Properties and the impact of its transition to IFRS
- Presents the classified statement of financial position in order of liquidity and reverse liquidity
- Applies ratio analysis to Sobeys and Loblaw (working capital, current ratio, debt to total assets, earnings per share, and price-earnings ratio)
- Describes the conceptual framework of accounting
- Keeping an Eye on Cash discusses Amazon's free cash flow
- Comparing IFRS and ASPE summarizes key differences in terminology, presentation of earnings per share, and application of the conceptual framework
- All About You introduces a personal statement of financial position
- Using the Decision Toolkit analyzes Canadian Tire's liquidity, profitability, and solvency
- *Key changes*: Changed title of chapter to better reflect revised organization and content. Repositioned financial statement and analysis sections to beginning of chapter to allow for better transition from discussion of financial statements in Chapter 1. Added definitions of assets, liabilities, and equity items. Introduced concept of reverse liquidity ordering of statement of financial position. Rewrote conceptual framework section to incorporate publication of Phase A: Objectives and Qualitative Characteristics as well as the proposed underlying assumption (going concern), elements, and measurement of the elements (historical cost and fair value). Moved discussion of free cash flow ratio in detail to Chapter 13; introduced free cash flow in brief in Keeping an Eye on Cash feature.

Chapter 3: The Accounting Information System
- Feature story is about BeaverTails and its experiences with an accounting information system
- Covers transaction analysis in five steps so that students can see the entire thought process undertaken when recording and posting transactions
- Explains the first three steps in the accounting cycle, from journalizing to posting to preparation of the trial balance

- Keeping an Eye on Cash relates cash transactions posted to the ledger to the operating, investing, and financing activities undertaken by a business
- Comparing IFRS and ASPE indicates that there are no significant differences in this chapter
- All About You discusses important personal documents and records and how to prevent identity theft
- Using the Decision Toolkit prepares a trial balance for lululemon athletica, and identifies on which financial statement each account would be presented
- *Key changes*: Basic analysis and equation analysis sections included when analyzing transactions using the expanded accounting equation.

Chapter 4: Accrual Accounting Concepts
- Feature story is about the University of Western Ontario's application of accrual accounting
- Explains revenue and expense recognition
- Emphasizes the difference between cash and accrual accounting
- Completes the accounting cycle, from adjusting entries to the closing process
- Keeping an Eye on Cash contrasts the calculation of profit and the calculation of cash flows from operating activities
- Comparing IFRS and ASPE summarizes key differences relating to frequency of adjusting entries, terminology, and closing entries related to other comprehensive income
- All About You discusses estimating and recording environmental clean-up costs
- Using the Decision Toolkit prepares a statement of financial position and closing entries for Highliner Foods
- *Key changes*: Revised revenue recognition and expense recognition criteria to be consistent with treatment under IFRS. Added more illustrations of subsequent journal entries, after adjusting entries recorded. Added a brief mention of reversing entries and expanded the discussion of closing entries to include other comprehensive income and accumulated other comprehensive income.

Chapter 5: Merchandising Operations
- Feature story is about Shoppers Drug Mart's initiatives to improve its merchandising process
- Introduces merchandising concepts using perpetual inventory system (periodic inventory system presented in an appendix)
- Explains how to record purchases and sales of merchandise
- Presents single-step and multiple-step income statements
- Applies ratio analysis to Shoppers Drug Mart and Jean Coutu (gross profit margin and profit margin)
- Keeping an Eye on Cash explains cash conversion cycle
- Comparing IFRS and ASPE summarizes key differences in the classification of expenses on the income statement

- All About You focuses on controlling cost of goods sold in the retail sector
- Using the Decision Toolkit compares Rite Aid's profitability with that of Shoppers Drug Mart and Jean Coutu
- *Key changes*: Added an explanation of operating cycles and manufacturing inventories. Illustrated how to record inventory shortages. Expanded discussion of how revenue is earned. Introduced classification of expenses by nature or function. Reclassified gains and losses on property, plant, and equipment as an operating expense. Added a full illustration of a multiple-step income statement in a periodic inventory system.

Chapter 6: Reporting and Analyzing Inventory
- Feature story is about Forzani's inventory management
- Explains how inventory quantities and ownership are determined
- Covers cost determination methods and their financial statement effects using perpetual inventory system (the periodic inventory system is presented in an appendix)
- Discusses effects of inventory errors on financial statements
- Outlines how to value and record inventory at the lower of cost and net realizable value
- Applies ratio analysis to Forzani and Dick's Sporting Goods (inventory turnover and days in inventory)
- Keeping an Eye on Cash reviews impact of choice of cost determination method on cash flow
- Comparing IFRS and ASPE indicates that there are no significant differences in this chapter
- All About You is about inventory theft and loss prevention techniques
- Using the Decision Toolkit reviews Foot Locker's inventory management and performance
- *Key changes*: Added summary section for determining ownership of goods. Separated discussion of financial statement effects of cost determination methods and inventory errors. Changed recording of lower of cost and net realizable value to direct method from allowance method.

Chapter 7: Internal Control and Cash
- Feature story is about cash control at Nick's Steakhouse and Pizza
- Explains the nature of fraud, internal control activities, and the limitations of internal control
- Provides illustrations of various types of fraud
- Identifies control activities over cash receipts and cash payments
- Discusses bank reconciliations in detail as a control feature
- Explains how cash is reported and managed
- Keeping an Eye on Cash explains how to prepare a cash budget

- Comparing IFRS and ASPE indicates that there are no significant differences in this chapter
- All About You provides information on how to prevent identity theft
- Using the Decision Toolkit reviews internal control issues at a local basketball association
- *Key changes*: Added Anatomy of a Fraud examples to provide more practical coverage of internal control activities. Covered regulatory reactions to corporate frauds. Moved coverage of bank credit cards from Chapter 8 to Chapter 7. Provided additional information on calculating outstanding cheques and deposits at the end of a period if there are outstanding amounts at the beginning of the period. Enhanced coverage of electronic funds transfers.

Chapter 8: Reporting and Analyzing Receivables
- Feature story is about Canadian Tire's receivables
- Presents the basics of accounts and notes receivable and allowance for doubtful accounts estimation based on receivables balances
- Discusses statement presentation of receivables
- Identifies various ways to manage receivables, including methods used to accelerate cash receipts
- Applies ratio analysis to Winpak (receivables turnover and average collection period)
- Keeping an Eye on Cash explains how profit does not measure cash flow and the importance of collecting receivables to cash flow
- Comparing IFRS and ASPE indicates that there are no significant differences in this chapter
- All About You covers the advantages and disadvantages of using credit cards
- Using the Decision Toolkit compares Winpak and Richards receivables management and liquidity to industry averages
- *Key changes*: Introduced concept of financial assets. Moved bank credit cards into Chapter 7; coverage of company credit cards remained in Chapter 8.

Chapter 9: Reporting and Analyzing Long-Lived Assets
- Feature story is about WestJet
- Covers the determination of the cost of property, plant, and equipment including asset retirement costs, and intangible assets
- Reviews lease or buy decisions
- Discusses the implications of alternative depreciation methods and explains the difference between these and depreciation for income tax purposes
- Explains the concept of componentization for depreciation purposes
- Introduces the revaluation and valuation models used under IFRS

- Covers disposal and retirements of property, plant, and equipment
- Explains amortization and the differences in the accounting treatment of intangibles with definite and indefinite lives
- Explains the difference between research and development costs
- Reviews the reporting of long-lived assets
- Applies ratio analysis to WestJet and Air Canada (return on assets, asset turnover, and profit margin)
- Keeping an Eye on Cash discusses depreciation as a major difference between profit and operating cash flows
- Comparing IFRS and ASPE compares differences in terminology, use of the revaluation and valuation models, and the application of impairment tests
- All About You deals with the decision to buy a new or a used car
- Using the Decision Toolkit reviews and analyzes Research In Motion's long-lived assets
- *Key changes*: Expanded coverage of asset retirement costs and explained IFRS-related terminology. Expanded coverage of componentization and explained the differences in impairment tests between IFRS and ASPE. Covered aspects of the revaluation model more fully and introduced investment properties with a brief explanation of the valuation model. Discussed the difference between research and development costs and the point at which amortization of development costs should commence.

Chapter 10: Reporting and Analyzing Liabilities
- Feature story is about Canada Post's liabilities
- Covers current liabilities, including operating lines of credit, sales taxes, property taxes, payroll, short-term notes payable, and current maturities of non-current debt
- Covers non-current liabilities, including instalment notes payable and bonds payable
- Applies effective-interest method of amortization to long-term instalment notes and bonds
- Reviews reporting and analysis of liabilities
- Applies ratio analysis to Canada Post and UPS (debt to total assets and times interest earned)
- Keeping an Eye on Cash explores cash effects of debt and the importance of meeting debt covenants
- Comparing IFRS and ASPE summarizes key differences in amortizing bond premiums and discounts and in the definition of probability used to record a contingent liability
- All About You is about student loans
- Using the Decision Toolkit compares Canada Post's liquidity and solvency with Royal Mail's

- *Key changes*: Added summary information to better distinguish between fixed principal payment and blended payment instalment notes. Deleted discussion of convertible debt. Improved explanation of how to separate current and non-current portions of debt. Added information about how to use a financial calculator and expanded discussion about using present value tables. Repositioned present value tables from chapter to Appendix C. Moved effective-interest amortization schedule into chapter from chapter appendix and added summary information about amortization of discounts and premiums. Updated and moved contingent liabilities from analysis section to financial statement presentation section and expanded discussion to distinguish between provisions and contingencies. Added a discussion about credit ratings.

Chapter 11: Reporting and Analyzing Shareholders' Equity

- Feature story is about lululemon athletica
- Discusses corporate form of organization
- Covers issues related to common and preferred shares, including reasons why companies repurchase their own shares
- Explains cash dividends, stock dividends, stock splits, and implications for analysis
- Describes the presentation of equity items in statement of financial position and statement of changes in equity (IFRS) or statement of retained earnings (ASPE)
- Applies ratio analysis to CN Railway (payout ratio and dividend yield) and to lululemon (earnings per share and return on common shareholders' equity)
- Keeping an Eye on Cash discusses how much cash is enough in order to pay a cash dividend
- Comparing IFRS and ASPE summarizes key differences in issuing shares for noncash considerations; disclosure of authorized share capital; presentation of comprehensive income, the statement of changes in equity, and statement of retained earnings; and presentation of earnings per share
- All About You is about investing in shares
- Using the Decision Toolkit compares Limited Brand's dividend record and earnings performance with lululemon's
- *Key changes*: Updated accounting for noncash consideration. Added a brief description of treasury stock in reacquisition of shares section. Added *Canada Business Corporations Act* requirement for federally incorporated corporations to meet a two-part solvency test in order to pay a dividend. Summarized corporate effects of cash dividend and clarified changes for all dividend and split effects; deleted discussion of individual effects.

Chapter 12: Reporting and Analyzing Investments

- Feature story is about Scotiabank's management of investments
- Explains why companies purchase debt and equity securities as strategic or non-strategic investments
- Describes the various valuation models for non-strategic investments: cost, fair value, and amortized cost
- Describes the accounting for strategic investments, including fair value, cost, and equity models
- Explains how investments are reported on the financial statements, including the income statement, statement of comprehensive income, statement of changes in equity, and statement of financial position
- Introduces consolidation accounting for financial reporting purposes at a conceptual level
- Keeping an Eye on Cash explains how investment-related transactions are treated on the statement of cash flows
- Comparing IFRS and ASPE explains differences in the use of the fair value through OCI model, cost model, and amortization methods for bond discounts and premiums
- All About You explains the benefits of saving and using a tax free savings account
- Using the Decision Toolkit explores the various ways of accounting for investments under both IFRS and ASPE
- *Key changes:* Chapter substantially rewritten to incorporate proposed changes to financial instruments. The coverage of available-for-sale investments was reduced while coverage of choices available under ASPE was introduced. Glossary was significantly expanded to include new terminology.

Chapter 13: Statement of Cash Flows

- Feature story is about Teck Resources' cash flows
- Explains the purpose and content of the statement of cash flows
- Describes the preparation of the operating, investing, and financing activities sections of the statement of cash flows. Splits the operating activities section into two parts, allowing instructors to use the indirect approach, the direct approach, or both
- Applies ratio analysis to Teck and Freeport-McMoRan (cash current debt coverage, cash total debt coverage, and free cash flow)
- Keeping an Eye on Cash explains cash flow effects of different phases of the corporate life cycle
- Comparing IFRS and ASPE summarizes key differences in classification of activities
- All About You is about where students spend their cash
- Using the Decision Toolkit calculates cash-based ratios and analyzes cash flows for Stantec
- *Key changes*: Renamed chapter to be consistent with IFRS terminology used for statement. Updated purpose of statement of cash flows. Added sample illustration

of statement format at beginning of chapter. Changed short-term (trading) investments to now be treated as an operating activity, not an investing activity. Expanded summaries of indirect and direct methods. Added information about effect of other comprehensive income. Detailed discussion of free cash flow measure moved to this chapter from Chapter 2.

Chapter 14: Performance Measurement
- Feature story is about PotashCorp's award-winning annual report
- Discusses sustainable income, and implications of discontinued operations and changes in accounting polices
- Demonstrates horizontal analysis, vertical analysis, and ratio analysis
- Applies ratio analysis to PotashCorp and Agrium (comprehensive analysis of all ratios)
- Discusses factors that can limit financial analysis, including alternative accounting policies, professional judgement, comprehensive income, diversification, inflation, and economic factors

- Keeping an Eye on Cash discusses analysis of the statement of cash flows
- Comparing IFRS and ASPE summarizes key differences in reporting of changes in accounting policies, earnings per share, comprehensive income, and segments
- All About You is about purchasing shares for dividend income
- Using the Decision Toolkit assesses the liquidity, profitability, and solvency of Goldcorp and Yamana Gold
- *Key changes:* Expanded presentation of discontinued operations and changes in accounting policies. Clarified allowable reasons for voluntary changes in accounting policy (rare). Added formulas for horizontal and vertical analyses. Expanded ratio analysis for competitor and industry to two years from one. Integrated comprehensive analysis of ratios, previously included in the appendix, directly in the chapter. Included a diagram and discussion of the relationship between profitability measures. Added comprehensive income and economic factors to limiting factors section.

ACKNOWLEDGEMENTS

During the course of development of the fifth Canadian edition of *Financial Accounting: Tools for Business Decision-Making*, the authors benefited from the feedback from instructors and students of financial accounting across the country. In addition, the constructive advice and attention to accuracy by the contributors to the fifth edition text and supplements provided valuable input to the development of this edition.

Reviewers

David Adams, *Ambrose University College*
Norman Betts, *University of New Brunswick*
Lindsay Brock, *Kwantlen Polytechnic University*
Liang Chen, *University of Toronto*
Judy Cumby, *Memorial University of Newfoundland*

John Currie, *Humber College and University of Guelph-Humber*
Angela Davis, *Booth University College*
Barb Edwards, *Simon Fraser University*
Mark Gandey, *Bishop's University*
Elizabeth Grasby, *University of Western Ontario*
Else Grech, *University of Toronto*
Ian Hutchinson, *Acadia University*
Linda Jin-Troendle, *Humber College*

Wasi Khan, *Seneca College*
Rafik Kurji, *Mount Royal University*
Shiraz Kurji, *Mount Royal University*
Shelley Martin, *Memorial University of Newfoundland*
George Quan Fun, *University of Toronto*
Sathees Ratnam, *University of Toronto*
Helen Vallee, *Kwantlen Polytechnic University*

Textbook Contributors

Sally Anderson, *Mount Royal University*—Broadening Your Perspective case contributor
Alison Arnot, *Amso Editorial*—Feature Story contributor

Chris Duff, *Royal Roads University*—All About You feature and Broadening Your Perspective case contributor
Julia Duff, Duff Associates Inc.—All About You feature and Broadening Your Perspective case contributor

Sandra Iacobelli, *York University*—Broadening Your Perspective case contributor
Joanne Jones, *York University*—Broadening Your Perspective case contributor

Supplement Contributors

Vida Barker, *Centennial College*—WileyPLUS contributor
Maria Belanger, *Algonquin College*—Solutions Manual author
Lindsay Brock, *Kwantlen Polytechnic University*—supplement reviewer
Angela Davis, *Booth University College*—WileyPLUS contributor
Lynn DeGrace, *McGill University*—WileyPLUS contributor
Robert Ducharme, *University of Waterloo*—Solutions Manual accuracy checker and WileyPLUS contributor
Ian Farmer—WileyPLUS accuracy checker

Rosalie Harms, *University of Winnipeg*—Solutions Manual accuracy checker
Elizabeth Hicks, *Douglas College*—Testbank author
Steven Plateo Konvalinka, *George Brown College*—WileyPLUS contributor
Cecile Laurin, *Algonquin College*—Solutions Manual author
Camillo Lento, *Lakehead University*—WileyPLUS contributor
Michelle Lum, *Wilfrid Laurier University*—Study Guide author
Richard Michalski, *McMaster University*—WileyPLUS contributor and accuracy checker

Debbie Musil, *Kwantlen Polytechnic University*—PowerPoint slides author
Marie Sinnott, *College of New Caledonia*—Solutions Manual accuracy checker
Rik Smistad, *Mount Royal University*—Solutions Manual accuracy checker
Brian Trenholm, *Tantramar Management Limited*—WileyPLUS contributor and accuracy checker
Helen Vallee, *Kwantlen Polytechnic University*—Rapid Review contributor
Kim Varey, Kim Varey Consulting—Solutions Manual accuracy checker
Amanda Wallace, *Nipissing University*—Instructors Manual author

We appreciate the exemplary support and professional commitment given us by the talented team in the Wiley Canada higher education division, including Lauren Connor, Marketing Assistant; Zoë Craig, Acquisitions Editor; Deanna Durnford, Supplements Coordinator; Channade Fenandoe, Media Editor; Daleara Hirjikaka, Developmental Editor; Aida Krneta, Marketing Manager; Karen Staudinger, Editorial Manager; Maureen Talty, General Manager, Higher Education; Luisa Begani, Laura Hwee, and Sara Tinteri, Editorial Assistants; Veronica Visentin, Vice-President and Publisher; Tegan Wallace, Production Manager; and Carolyn Wells, Vice-President, Marketing; in addition to all of Wiley's dedicated sales managers and representatives, who continue to work tirelessly to service your needs.

We also wish to thank the many people who worked behind the scenes to improve the design and accuracy of this text, including Thomson Digital, typesetter; Laurel Hyatt, copyeditor; Zofia Laubitz, proofreader; and Belle Wong, indexer.

It would not have been possible to write this text without the understanding of our employers, colleagues, students, friends, and family. Together, they provided a creative and supportive environment for our work.

We have tried our best to produce a text and supplement package that is error-free and that meets your specific needs. Suggestions and comments from users are encouraged and appreciated; please e-mail us at KimmelAuthors@gmail.com.

Barbara Trenholm and Wayne Irvine
September 2011

BRIEF CONTENTS

CONTENTS

The Purpose and Use of Financial Statements

The **Navigator** is a learning system designed to prompt you to use the learning aids in the chapter and set priorities as you study.

The Navigator
Chapter 1

- Scan *Study Objectives*
- Read *Feature Story*
- Read text and answer *Do It!s*
- Review *Comparing IFRS and ASPE*
- Review *Summary of Study Objectives*
- Review *Decision Toolkit—A Summary*
- Work *Using the Decision Toolkit*
- Work *Comprehensive Do It!*
- Answer *Self-Test Questions*
- Complete *assignments*
- Go to *WileyPLUS* for practice and tutorials

Study Objectives give you a framework for learning the specific concepts that are covered in the chapter.

study objectives

After studying this chapter, you should be able to:

1. Identify the users and uses of accounting.
2. Describe the primary forms of business organization.
3. Explain the three main types of business activity.
4. Describe the content and purpose of each of the financial statements.

the navigator

ACCOUNTING MATTERS!

The **Feature Story** helps you picture how the chapter relates to the real world of accounting and business. You will find references to the story throughout the chapter.

Vancouver Company Becomes Big Miner in South Africa

INSIDE CHAPTER

1

- Accountants are trustworthy (p. 6)

- What's in a company name? (p. 10)

- Fiscal year ends (p. 14)

- Your personal annual report (p. 26)

Vancouver-based Eastern Platinum Limited (known as Eastplats) began as Elgin Resources in the 1990s with the goal of finding platinum group metal (PGM) deposits in South Africa. At the time, it owned one property in South Africa's platinum-rich area known as the Bushveld Complex, a geological horseshoe located north of Johannesburg, where over 75% of the world's platinum is mined, explains Horng Dih Lee, Vice President, Finance, and Chief Financial Officer.

In 2005, Elgin merged with Jonpol Explorations Limited, which had another project on the Eastern Limb of this horseshoe. The company changed its name to Eastern Platinum in 2006, and became Canada's largest platinum group metals producer with the purchase of a 69% interest in Barplats Investments Limited. The result of these mergers and acquisitions was the ownership of four properties: one on the Western Limb and three on the Eastern Limb.

Along with the Barplats acquisition, the company raised $150 million in share capital, much of which was invested in refurbishing and modernizing the Crocodile River Mine on the Western Limb.

Developing these mines and refurbishing their infrastructure require a lot of resources. So in 2007, the company raised another $200 million in capital by issuing shares. "We spend a lot of money to ensure the mine operates efficiently and safely," says Mr. Lee. "A big part of the company's policy is to maintain an excellent safety record."

Eastplats is currently involved only with near-the-surface or open-pit mining projects, which are lower in operational and capital costs than the very deep underground mines. Eastplats does not have an operational smelter, so it sells platinum concentrate (not bars of platinum) to another platinum company in South Africa.

The highest demand for platinum is in the automobile industry. "Basically, if the auto industry is flourishing, then there's going to be a demand for platinum," says Mr. Lee. Not surprisingly, the company's expansion slowed during the economic downturn in 2008 and 2009. The price of platinum peaked at U.S. $2,266 per ounce in March 2008, after a steady rise from U.S. $430 per ounce in 2000. It plunged to around U.S. $800 per ounce in early 2009; however, by November 2010, it had rebounded to U.S. $1,700.

With the recovery of platinum prices in 2010, Eastplats began to go forward with its Eastern Limb development plans. It raised cash in November 2010 by issuing U.S. $345 million of new shares. "These funds will enable us to . . . double our PGM production from our 2009 levels by the end of 2012," Ian Rozier, President and CEO, said at the time.

The path Eastplats has taken has involved many decisions. Assessing when to merge with another company or acquire additional properties, deciding which companies to invest in, as well as choosing to raise money through debt or equity all require important financial decisions. Then there are decisions that executives do not control, such as investors choosing whether or not to purchase Eastplats's shares. To make any of these decisions, all parties rely on many tools—one of which is accounting.

The Accounting Matters! boxes and **All About You** feature are cross-referenced at the beginning of each chapter.

the navigator

preview of CHAPTER 1

How do you start a business like Eastplats in our chapter-opening feature story? How do you determine whether your business is making or losing money? When you need to expand your operations, where do you get money to finance the expansion—should you borrow, issue shares, or use company funds? How do you convince lenders to lend you money or investors to buy your shares? To be successful in business, countless decisions have to be made—and decisions require accounting information, as mentioned in our feature story.

The purpose of this chapter is to show you accounting's role in providing useful financial information for decision-making. The chapter is organized as follows:

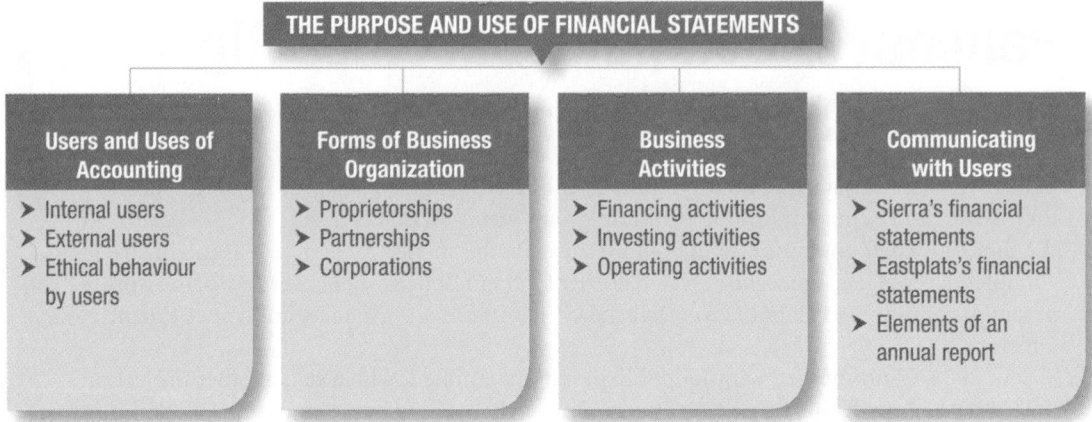

Users and Uses of Accounting

STUDY OBJECTIVE 1

Identify the users and uses of accounting.

Accounting is the information system that identifies and records the economic events of an organization, and then communicates them to a wide variety of interested users. Why does accounting matter to these users? The world's economic systems depend on highly transparent, reliable, and accurate financial reporting. Accounting has long been labelled "the language of business." That's one of the reasons why accounting has consistently ranked as one of the top career opportunities in business.

It is also one of the reasons that so many Canadians who do not plan on becoming accountants study accounting. For example, Monique Leroux, president and CEO of Desjardins Group; Elizabeth Marshall, a senator; Zarin Mehta, president and executive director of the New York Philharmonic; George Melville, chairman and owner of Boston Pizza International; Syd Pallister, president and owner of Gibbs Fishing Tackle; and Paul Sobey, president and CEO of Empire Company Limited, all have studied accounting in depth.

Whether you plan to become an accountant or not, a working knowledge of accounting will be relevant and useful in whatever role you assume as a user of accounting information. To demonstrate the value of accounting to you as an individual, each chapter includes an "All About You" feature and a related activity in the end-of-chapter material that links an accounting concept to your personal or business life.

Users of accounting information can be divided broadly into two types: internal users and external users.

> Essential terms are printed in blue when they first appear. They are listed and defined again in the glossary at the end of the chapter.

INTERNAL USERS

Internal users of accounting information plan, organize, and run companies. They work for the company. These include finance directors, marketing managers, human resource personnel, production supervisors, and company officers. All of the people studying accounting cited in the previous section would be considered internal users.

In running a business, internal users must answer many important questions, as shown in Illustration 1-1.

Finance
Is there enough cash to pay the bills?

Marketing
What price should we sell iPads
for to maximize profits?

Human Resources
How many employees can we
afford to hire this year?

Production
Which product line is the most profitable?

▶Illustration 1-1
Questions asked by internal users

To answer these and other questions, users need detailed accounting information on a timely basis; that is, it must be available when it is needed. For internal users, accounting provides a variety of internal reports including, for example, financial comparisons of operating alternatives, projections of profit from new sales campaigns, analyses of sales costs, and forecasts of cash needs. In addition, companies present summarized financial information in the form of financial statements for both internal and external use.

EXTERNAL USERS

There are several types of external users of accounting information. Investors use accounting information to make decisions to buy, hold, or sell their ownership interest. Lenders, such as bankers, use accounting information to evaluate the risks of lending money. Other creditors, such as suppliers, use accounting information to decide whether or not to grant credit (sell on account) to a customer. **Investors, lenders, and other creditors** are considered to be the primary or key external users of accounting information.

Some questions that investors, lenders, and other creditors may ask about a company are shown in Illustration 1-2.

> **Alternative terminology** notes give synonyms that you may hear or see in the workplace.

Alternative Terminology
Investors are also known as *shareholders* and *creditors* are also known as *lenders*.

Investors
Is the company earning enough to
give me a return on my investment?

Lenders and Other Creditors
Will the company be able to pay
its debts as they come due?

▶Illustration 1-2
Questions asked by external users

In addition to investors, lenders, and other creditors, there are many other external users with a variety of information needs and questions. For example, employees and labour unions want to know whether the company can provide employment opportunities and pay salaries and benefits. Customers are interested in whether a company will support its product lines and honour product warranties. Taxing authorities, such as the Canada Revenue Agency, want to know whether the company respects the tax laws. And regulatory agencies, such as provincial securities commissions that regulate companies that sell shares to the public, want to know whether the company is operating within prescribed rules.

ETHICAL BEHAVIOUR BY USERS

In order for financial information to have value to its users, whether internal or external, it must be prepared by individuals with high standards of ethical behaviour. Ethics in accounting is of the utmost importance to accountants and decision makers who rely on the financial information they produce.

Fortunately, most individuals in business are ethical. Their actions are both legal and responsible. They consider the organization's interests when they make decisions. Accountants and other professionals have extensive rules of conduct to guide their behaviour with each other and the public. In addition, many companies today have codes of conduct that outline their commitment to ethical behaviour in their internal and external relationships.

Throughout this textbook, ethical considerations will be presented to highlight the importance of ethics in financial reporting. Every chapter includes an Ethics Case in the end-of-chapter material that simulates a business situation and asks you to put yourself in the position of a key decision maker. When you analyze these and other ethical situations, you should follow the steps outlined in Illustration 1-3.

1. Recognize an ethical situation and the ethical issues involved.

Use your personal ethics or an organization's code of ethics to identify ethical situations and issues. Some business and professional organizations provide written codes of ethics for guidance in common business situations.

2. Identify and analyze the main elements in the situation.

Identify the *stakeholders*—persons or groups who may be harmed or benefited. Ask the question: What are the responsibilities and obligations of the parties involved?

3. Identify the alternatives, and weigh the impact of each alternative on various stakeholders.

Select the most ethical alternative, considering all the consequences. Sometimes there will be one right answer. Other situations involve more than one possible solution. These situations require an evaluation of each alternative and the selection of the best one.

▶Illustration 1-3
Steps used to analyze ethical situations

ACCOUNTING MATTERS!   *Ethics Perspective*

Accountants Are Trustworthy

A recent survey of more than 2,000 people revealed that accountants are viewed as trustworthy and exciting. A Harris Interactive poll for the Ajilon Professional Staffing group found that more than half (53%) of the respondents trust their accountant fully. In addition, the vast majority (88%) disagreed with the stereotype that accountants are boring. Although few (17%) of those surveyed believed that there were many job opportunities in accounting, labour data produced by the government actually indicate that the accounting profession will continue to be one of the fastest-growing fields in the next decade.

Source: "Public Appreciates Your Hard Work," *CAmagazine*, June–July 2010, p. 6

The **Accounting Matters!** **Perspectives** give examples of accounting situations from four different points of view: ethics, management, investor, and international.

Do It! exercises prompt you to stop and review the key points you have just studied before you go further in your reading of the text.

BEFORE YOU GO ON...

▶**Do It! Users of Accounting Information**

The following is a list of questions that may be asked by different users of accounting information:

1. Will I be able to obtain enough cash to finance this month's cash shortfall?

2. Will the company be able to repay my loan when it comes due?

3. What was the labour cost for the production of 1,000 board feet of lumber?

4. Will the company stay in business long enough to service the products I buy from it?

5. Will the company's share price go up or down in the near future?

(a) Identify the type of user that would most likely ask each of the above questions from the following list of possible users: chief financial officer, customers, investors, lenders, or production manager.

(b) Indicate whether the user you chose is an internal or external user.

Action Plan
- Understand the difference between internal and external users: Internal users work for the company; external users do not.

Solution

	(a) Type of User	(b) Internal or External User
1.	Chief financial officer	Internal
2.	Lenders	External
3.	Production manager	Internal
4.	Customers	External
5.	Investors	External

Forms of Business Organization

Businesses can be organized in different ways. There are three common forms of business organization: proprietorships, partnerships, and corporations.

PROPRIETORSHIPS

When you graduate, you might decide to start your own business. If you do, you may choose to set up a proprietorship. A **proprietorship** is a business owned by one person. It is often called a "sole" proprietorship because the owner has no partners.

The proprietorship form of business organization is simple to set up and gives the owner control over the business. In most cases, only a relatively small amount of money (capital) is needed to start in business as a proprietorship. The owner (the proprietor) receives any profits, suffers any losses, and is personally liable (responsible) for all debts of the business. This is known as unlimited liability.

There is no legal distinction between the business as an economic unit and the owner. Accordingly, the life of the proprietorship is limited to the life of the owner. The business profits are reported as self-employment income and taxed on the owner's personal income tax return. However, the business records of the proprietorship must be kept separate from those related to the owner's personal activities.

The separation of business and personal records is known in its simplest form as the reporting entity concept. The **reporting entity concept** requires that the economic activity that can be identified with a particular company be kept separate and distinct from the activities of the owner(s) and of all other economic entities. This concept applies not only to proprietorships, but also to partnerships and corporations, which are discussed in the next sections.

Small service businesses such as hair salons, plumbers, and mechanics are often proprietorships, as are many farms and small retail stores.

PARTNERSHIPS

Another possibility after graduating would be for you to join forces with other individuals to form a partnership. A **partnership** is a business owned by more than one person. In most

STUDY OBJECTIVE 2
Describe the primary forms of business organization.

respects, a partnership is similar to a proprietorship except that there is more than one owner. Partnerships are often formed because one person does not have enough economic resources to initiate or expand the business, or because partners bring unique skills or resources to the partnership.

Partnerships are normally formalized in a written partnership agreement that outlines the formation of the partnership, partners' contributions, how profits and losses are shared, provisions for withdrawals of assets and/or partners, dispute resolution, and partnership liquidation. Although there are advantages to working with others, there are also disadvantages. Each partner generally has unlimited liability for all debts of the partnership, even if one of the other partners created the debt. However, there are certain situations where partnerships can be formed with limited liability for selected partners.

Unlimited liability means that any of the partners can be forced to give up his or her personal assets in order to repay the partnership debt, just as can happen to an owner in a proprietorship. Assets are resources that provide future economic benefits. Examples of personal assets include cash, investments, house, furniture, car, and the like.

Similar to a proprietorship, the profits of the partnership are reported as self-employment income and taxed on each partner's personal income tax return. In addition, the reporting entity concept requires that partnership records be kept separate from each partner's personal activities.

Partnerships are typically used to organize professional service businesses, such as the practices of lawyers, doctors, architects, engineers, and accountants.

CORPORATIONS

Alternative Terminology
Shares are also known as *stock*.

As a third alternative after graduating, you might choose to form a business as a corporation. A **corporation**—like Eastplats in our opening feature story—is a business organized as a separate legal entity owned by shareholders. As an investor in a corporation, you receive shares to indicate your ownership claim. Individuals can become owners of shares (shareholders) by investing relatively small amounts of money.

Suppose you are one of Eastplats's shareholders. The amount of cash that you have in your personal bank account and the balance you owe on your personal car loan are not reported in Eastplats's financial statements. This is because, for accounting purposes, you and Eastplats are separate reporting entities under the reporting entity concept.

Since a corporation is a separate legal entity, its life is indefinite. That means it continues on regardless of who owns its shares. It is not affected by the withdrawal, death, or incapacity of an owner, as is the case in a proprietorship or partnership. Consequently, buying shares in a corporation, especially a large corporation, is often more attractive than investing in a proprietorship or partnership because shares are easier to sell. Successful corporations like Eastplats often have thousands of shareholders, and their shares are traded on organized stock exchanges, such as the Toronto Stock Exchange (TSX) in Canada.

There are other factors that need to be considered when deciding which organizational form of business to choose. These include legal liability and income tax. As we discussed above, if you choose to organize as a proprietorship or partnership, you are personally liable for all debts of the business. Corporate shareholders are not responsible for corporate debts unless they have personally guaranteed them. So most shareholders enjoy limited liability since they only risk losing the amount they have invested in the company's shares. All of these advantages taken together—indefinite life, ease of transferring ownership, limited liability—make it easier for corporations to raise capital compared with proprietorships and partnerships.

Proprietors and partners pay personal income tax on their respective shares of the profits, while corporations pay income tax as separate legal entities on any corporate profits. Corporations may also receive a more favourable income tax treatment than other forms of business organization. Because of the wide variety of income tax issues applicable to different companies, it is wise to seek expert advice on taxation matters before any form of business organization is chosen.

Although the combined number of proprietorships and partnerships in Canada is more than the number of corporations, the revenue produced by corporations is far greater. Most of the largest companies in Canada—for example, Bombardier, Loblaw, Manulife Financial, Research In Motion, and the Royal Bank—are corporations. Recently, the top 50 of Canada's largest corporations each reported annual revenues ranging from $7 billion to $40 billion.

Corporations such as these are publicly traded. That is, their shares are listed on Canadian, or other, stock exchanges. There are about 4,500 publicly traded corporations in Canada. **Public corporations** distribute their financial statements to investors, lenders, other creditors, other interested parties, and the general public. Eastplats is a public corporation. You can access its financial statements in Appendix A at the back of this textbook.

You will notice that Eastplats's financial statements are **consolidated**. This means that the financial results include not only Eastplats but also all the companies Eastplats owns or controls. For example, Eastplats controls Barplats Investments Limited. Although the financial results of these companies are consolidated (combined) for reporting purposes, individual accounting records and financial statements are also produced for each specific company. In order to accurately assess the performance and financial position of each company, it has to be possible to distinguish each company's activities from the transactions of any other company, even if the companies are related. This is another application of the reporting entity concept.

In addition to public corporations like Eastplats, there are **private corporations**. Private corporations issue shares, but they do not make them available to the general public nor are they traded on public stock exchanges. Consequently, many private corporations, especially small ones, do not have the same advantages of raising capital as do large corporations. For example, a small, local incorporated business would likely have as much difficulty in raising funds as would a proprietorship or partnership.

There are more than 2 million private corporations in Canada. Some of these are very large corporations, such as The Jim Pattison Group, McCain Foods, and the Irving Group of Companies. Like proprietorships and partnerships, these companies almost never distribute their financial statements publicly.

Because most Canadian business is transacted by corporations, this book focuses on the corporate form of organization. We will discuss the accounting for both publicly traded and private corporations in this textbook.

Generally Accepted Accounting Principles for Corporations

We mentioned above that public corporations must make their financial statements available to the public. How do they decide on the amount of financial information to disclose? In what format should financial information be presented? The answers to these questions can be found in accounting rules and practices that are recognized as a general guide for financial reporting purposes.

These rules and practices are referred to as **generally accepted accounting principles**, commonly abbreviated as GAAP. GAAP include broad policies and practices as well as rules and procedures that have substantive authoritative support and agreement about how to report economic events.

Generally accepted accounting principles are different for publicly traded and private corporations. Publicly traded corporations must use International Financial Reporting Standards (IFRS), a set of global accounting standards developed by the International Accounting Standards Board. Private corporations, whose users can have different needs than publicly traded corporations, have a choice between using IFRS or Accounting Standards for Private Enterprises (ASPE), developed by the Canadian Accounting Standards Board.

Most private corporations choose to use ASPE, although there are exceptions. For example, McCain Foods Ltd. is a private company that chose to use IFRS instead of ASPE. It felt that IFRS was a more appropriate option for it given its size and global presence, operating in 20 different countries. We will learn more about IFRS and ASPE for corporations in Chapter 2.

Proprietorships and partnerships do not have to choose between IFRS and ASPE as their statements are generally prepared only for internal use of the owners.

Alternative Terminology
Accounting principles are also commonly known as accounting standards or accounting policies.

ASPE

The **ASPE** logo indicates that there is a reporting difference for private companies following accounting standards for private enterprises, compared to those companies following IFRS.

What's in a Company Name?

How can you tell whether a company is a corporation or not? Corporations in North America are identified by "Ltd." ("Ltée" in French), "Inc.," "Corp.," or in some cases, "Co." following their names. These abbreviations can also be spelled out. In Brazil and France, the letters used are "SA" (Sôciedade Anonima, Société Anonyme); in Japan, "KK" (Kabushiki Kaisha); in the Netherlands, "NV" (Naamloze Vennootschap); in Italy, "SpA" (Società per Azioni); and in Sweden, "AB" (Aktiebolag).

In the United Kingdom, public corporations are identified by "plc" (public limited company), while private corporations are denoted by "Ltd." The same designations in Germany are "AG" (Aktiengesellschaft) for public corporations and "GmbH" (Gesellschaft mit beschränkter Haftung) for private corporations.

BEFORE YOU GO ON...

▶ Do It! Business Organizations

In choosing the right organizational form for your business, you should consider the characteristics of each. Choose from the characteristics listed below for each of ownership, liability, life, ease of raising capital, and income tax, and match the characteristic with the form of business organization—proprietorship, partnership, or corporation—they are normally associated with:

(a) Ownership: Choose among "one individual," "two or more individuals," or "many shareholders"

(b) Liability: Choose between "limited" or "unlimited"

(c) Life: Choose between "limited" or "indefinite"

(d) Ease of raising capital: Choose among "hard," "easier," or "easiest"

(e) Income tax: Choose between "paid by individual(s)" or "paid by entity"

Action Plan

• Know which organizational form best matches the type and purpose of the business, its size, and the preferences of the owner(s).

Solution

	Proprietorship	Partnership	Corporation
(a) Ownership	One individual	Two or more individuals	Many shareholders
(b) Liability	Unlimited	Unlimited	Limited
(c) Life	Limited	Limited	Indefinite
(d) Ease of raising capital	Hard	Easier	Easiest
(e) Income tax	Paid by individual	Paid by individuals (partners)	Paid by entity (corporation)

the navigator

Business Activities

STUDY OBJECTIVE 3

Explain the three main types of business activity.

All businesses are involved in three types of activity: financing, investing, and operating. For example, Eastplats needed cash in 2005 when it combined two companies—Elgin Resources and Jonpol Explorations—to form Eastern Platinum. It received $150 million of initial **financing** from shareholders to start and grow the new business, followed by another $200 million in 2007 and U.S. $345 million in 2010. The company then **invested** the cash in mineral properties and mining equipment to run the business. Once this was in place, it could begin its **operating** activities of mining and selling platinum.

Let's now look at these three types of business activity in more detail.

FINANCING ACTIVITIES

It takes money to make money. The two primary ways of raising outside funds for corporations are (1) borrowing money (debt financing) and (2) issuing (selling) shares (equity financing) in exchange for cash.

Eastplats can borrow money in a variety of ways. For example, it can take out a loan at a bank or borrow money from other lenders. The persons or companies that Eastplats owes money to are called lenders or creditors, one of the primary user groups of accounting information. Amounts owed to lenders and creditors—in the form of debt and other obligations—are called **liabilities**.

Specific names are given to different types of liabilities, depending on their source. For instance, Eastplats may have received funds from an operating line of credit with its bank. An operating line of credit is a pre-arranged bank loan for a maximum amount that allows a company to draw more money than there is on hand in its bank account. When a company uses its operating line of credit to cover cash shortfalls and overdraws its bank account, it results in a liability called **bank indebtedness**.

Eastplats may also have a short-term **loan payable** to a bank (also known as a note payable) for the money borrowed to purchase mining equipment. It may have **long-term debt**, which can include **mortgages payable**, **bonds payable**, **finance lease obligations**, and other types of debt securities borrowed for longer periods of time.

A corporation may also obtain financing by selling shares of ownership to investors. Eastplats first issued common shares in 2005 when the company was organized. **Common shares** is the term used to describe the amount paid by investors for shares of ownership in a company. Common shares are just one class or type of share capital that a company can issue.

Companies can also use cash for financing activities, such as repaying debt or repurchasing shares from investors. The claims of lenders and creditors differ from those of shareholders. If you loan money to a company, you are one of its lenders. In loaning money, you specify a repayment schedule; for example, payment at the end of each month. In addition, interest is normally added to the amount due or overdue. As a creditor, you have a legal right to be paid at the agreed time. In the event of nonpayment, you may force the company to sell assets to pay its debts.

Shareholders have no claim to corporate resources until the claims of lenders and creditors are satisfied. If you buy a company's shares instead of loaning it money, you have no legal right to expect any payments until all of its lenders and creditors are paid. Also, once shares are issued, the company has no obligation to buy them back, whereas debt obligations must be repaid.

Many companies pay shareholders a return on their investment on a regular basis, as long as there is enough cash to cover required payments to lenders and creditors. Payments to shareholders are called **dividends**.

INVESTING ACTIVITIES

After a company raises money through financing activities, it then uses that money for investing activities. Investing activities involve the purchase (or sale) of long-lived assets that a company needs in order to operate. **Assets** are resources that a company owns or controls. Every asset is capable of providing future economic benefits that can be short- or long-lived. Investing activities generally involve long-lived assets. For example, mining equipment, computers, vehicles, buildings, and land are all examples of long-lived assets that result from investing activities. Together, they are referred to as **property, plant, and equipment**.

Cash is one of the more important assets owned by Eastplats, or any other business. If a company has excess cash that it does not need for a while, it might choose to invest it in debt securities (e.g., bonds) or equity securities (e.g., shares) of other corporations or organizations—these are called **investments**. Investments can be either short- or long-term. With a few exceptions, short-term investments are generally classified as operating activities as they are incurred for the purpose of trading as part of the company's revenue-producing activities. Long-term investments are generally classified as investing activities. Many students misunderstand the term *investing activities*, thinking

Alternative Terminology
Property, plant, and equipment is also known as *capital assets* or *fixed assets*.

the term means "investments" only. However, in this context, investing activities means investing in the long-lived assets necessary to run the company and not just purchasing an investment on which to earn a return for the long-term, such as interest or dividends.

OPERATING ACTIVITIES

Alternative Terminology
Revenue is also known as *income*.

Once a business has the finances and has made the investments it needs to get started, it can begin its operations. For example, Eastplats is in the business of mining, processing, and selling platinum group metals (PGM). We call the amounts earned from the sale of these goods **revenue**. In accounting language, revenues are increases in economic benefits—normally an increase in an asset but sometimes a decrease in a liability—that result from the sale of a product or service in the normal course of business.

Revenues come from different sources and are identified by various names. For instance, Eastplats's main source of revenue is the money it earns from the sale of PGM (sold in ounces) to a local smelter and refinery. In 2010, for example, it sold 131,901 ounces at an average price of U.S. $995 per ounce. However, it also earned interest revenue on excess cash held as investments and earned rental income from residences on its mining properties. Sources of revenue that are common to many businesses are **sales revenue** (often just called "sales"), **service revenue**, **interest revenue**, and **rent revenue**.

When Eastplats sells PGM, it sells it on credit (on account), which means that it does not immediately receive all of the cash for the sale. This right to receive money in the future is called an **account receivable**. Accounts receivable are assets because they will result in a future benefit—cash—when the amounts owed are eventually collected.

We first mentioned the term *assets* in the investing activity section above. A company's long-lived assets, such as property, plant, and equipment, are purchased through investing activities. Other assets—typically with shorter lives—result from operating activities, such as short-term (trading) investments and accounts receivable. Companies also have other types of receivables, such as interest receivable, rent receivable, and income tax receivable (also known as "deferred tax assets") that is due from the federal government.

Supplies are another example of a short-term asset used in day-to-day operations, as is inventory, which is described next. Before Eastplats can sell PGM to its customers, it must first mine and process the ore. Once it is ready for future sale to customers, an asset called **inventory** is created. Eastplats's inventory consists of ore and concentrates. Concentrates is the form in which the platinum occurs when it is mined and before it is processed.

If the inventory consists of merchandise (e.g., food, clothes) for resale, it is usually known as merchandise inventory. When inventory is sold, it is no longer an asset with future benefits but an expense. More specifically, the cost of the inventory sold is an expense called **cost of goods sold**. In accounting language, **expenses** are the cost of assets that are consumed or services that are used in the process of generating revenues. As we will learn in Chapter 4, expenses are related to assets and liabilities. When an expense is incurred, an asset will decrease or a liability will increase.

There are many kinds of expenses and they are identified by various names, depending on the type of asset consumed or service used. For example, Eastplats keeps track of these types of expenses: **production costs**, **general and administrative expenses** (such as salaries, advertising, utilities, professional fees, rent, and other costs associated with running the business), **depreciation expense** and **depletion expense** (i.e., allocation of the cost of using the mine equipment and property), **finance costs** (amounts of interest paid on various debts), and **income tax**. All of these expenses are necessary to produce and sell their products.

Short-term liabilities may result from some of these expenses. This occurs, for example, when Eastplats purchases materials and supplies on credit (on account) from suppliers. The obligations to pay for these goods are called **accounts payable**. It may also have **interest payable** on the outstanding (unpaid) amounts owed to various lenders, **dividends payable** to shareholders, **salaries payable** to employees, **property tax payable** to the provincial government, and **sales tax payable** to the provincial and federal governments. **Income tax payable** (also known as "deferred tax liabilities") is an example of another liability that is payable to the government.

To determine whether it earned a profit, Eastplats compares the revenues of a period with the expenses of that same period. The goal of every business is to sell a good or service for a price that is greater than the cost of producing or purchasing the good or providing the service, plus the cost of operating the business. This means that revenues should, ideally, be greater than the expenses incurred to generate the revenue. When revenues are more than expenses, a **profit** results. Eastplats reported a profit of U.S. $9,777 thousand for the year ended December 31, 2010.

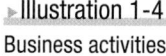

Alternative Terminology.
Profit is also commonly known as *net earnings* or *net income*.

When expenses exceed revenues, a **loss** results. Eastplats reported loss of U.S. $213,116 thousand several years ago in 2008.

To summarize, there are three types of business activities that companies engage in: (1) financing, (2) investing, and (3) operating, as shown in Illustration 1-4.

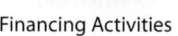

Financing Activities   Investing Activities   Operating Activities

►Illustration 1-4
Business activities

1. **Financing activities** include borrowing cash from lenders by issuing debt, or conversely, using cash to repay debt. Cash can also be raised from shareholders by issuing shares, or paid to shareholders by repurchasing shares or distributing dividends.
2. **Investing activities** include purchasing and disposing of long-lived assets such as property, plant, and equipment and purchasing and selling long-term investments.
3. **Operating activities** result from day-to-day operations and include revenues and expenses and related accounts such as receivables, supplies, inventory, and payables.

BEFORE YOU GO ON...

►Do It! Business Activities

Classify each of the following items as (a) a financing, investing, or operating activity, and (b) an asset, liability, share capital, revenue, or expense.

1. An amount paid to an employee for work performed
2. An amount earned from providing a service
3. An issue of common shares
4. A truck that is purchased
5. An amount owed to a bank

Action Plan

• Classify each item based on its economic characteristics.
• Understand the differences among financing, investing, and operating activities.
• Understand the distinctions among assets, liabilities, share capital, revenues, and expenses.

Solution

	(a)	(b)
1.	Operating activity	Expense (salary expense)
2.	Operating activity	Revenue (service revenue)
3.	Financing activity	Share capital (common shares)
4.	Investing activity	Asset (truck—property, plant, and equipment)
5.	Financing activity	Liability (bank loan payable)

the navigator

Communicating with Users

You will recall that we learned about internal and external users of accounting information earlier in this chapter. Users, especially external users, are interested in a company's assets, liabilities, shareholders' equity, revenues, and expenses. For external reporting purposes, it is customary to arrange this information in four different financial statements that are the backbone of financial reporting:

1. **Income statement**: An income statement reports revenues and expenses to show how successfully a company performed during a period of time.
2. **Statement of changes in equity**: A statement of changes in equity shows the changes in each component of shareholders' equity, as well as total equity, during a period of time.
3. **Statement of financial position**: A statement of financial position presents a picture of what a company owns (its assets), what it owes (its liabilities), and its net worth (its shareholders' equity) at a specific point in time.
4. **Statement of cash flows**: A statement of cash flows shows where a company obtained cash during a period of time and how that cash was used.

Additional information is reported in **notes to the financial statements** that are cross-referenced to the four statements. These explanatory notes clarify information presented in the financial statements and provide additional detail. They are essential to understanding a company's financial performance and position.

While the above four financial statements are the statements most commonly provided by publicly traded companies, there are other financial statements. For example, a statement of comprehensive income must be prepared when a publicly traded company reports other comprehensive income earned from certain items. In addition, private corporations prepare a statement of retained earnings instead of a statement of changes in equity. We will wait until Chapter 11 to illustrate these statements.

Financial statements are produced annually, quarterly, or monthly depending on the nature and purpose of the company. Publicly traded companies must make their financial statements available to shareholders both quarterly and annually. An accounting time period that is one year in length is called a **fiscal year**.

ACCOUNTING MATTERS!   *Management Perspective*

Fiscal Year Ends

Nearly 75% of Canadian companies use December 31 for their fiscal year end. Why does every company not use December 31 as its accounting year end? Many companies choose to end their accounting year when their inventory or operations are at a low. This is advantageous because gathering accounting information requires a lot of time and effort from managers. They would rather do it when they are not too busy operating the business. Also, inventory is easier and less costly to count when it is low. Some companies whose year ends differ from December 31 are Bombardier (January 31), Empire Company (first Saturday in May), Intrawest (June 30), CoolBrands (August 31), and Shoppers Drug Mart (last Saturday in December). Most governments in Canada use March 31 for their fiscal year end.

SIERRA'S FINANCIAL STATEMENTS

We will now look at the financial statements of a fictitious marketing agency, a service company called Sierra Corporation, to introduce you to the four primary financial statements: the income statement, statement of changes in equity, statement of financial position, and statement of cash flows.

Income Statement

The **income statement** reports the success or failure of the company's operations for a period of time—annually, quarterly, or monthly, as we mentioned in the previous section. In our example, Sierra Corporation formed the company October 1. It has been in operation for one month only, the month ended October 31, 2012, and reports its results monthly. To indicate that Sierra's income statement reports the results of operations for a period of one month, its statement is dated "Month Ended October 31, 2012."

The income statement lists the company's revenues first and then its expenses. We will learn about the order in which expenses can be listed in later chapters. For now, we have simply listed expenses in order of magnitude—that is, from the largest to the smallest. Expenses are deducted from revenues to determine profit (or loss) before income tax. Income tax expense is usually shown separately, immediately following the profit (or loss) before income tax line. Finally, profit (or loss) is determined by deducting the income tax expense. Profit is also commonly known as net income, especially by those companies following ASPE.

A sample income statement for Sierra Corporation is shown in Illustration 1-5.

Alternative Terminology
The *income statement* is also commonly known as the *statement of earnings* or *statement of profit and loss.*

ASPE

SIERRA CORPORATION Income Statement Month Ended October 31, 2012		
Revenues		
Service revenue		$10,600
Expenses		
Salaries expense	$7,200	
Supplies expense	1,500	
Rent expense	900	
Depreciation expense	83	
Insurance expense	50	
Interest expense	25	
Total expenses		9,758
Profit before income tax		842
Income tax expense		200
Profit		$ 642

Illustration 1-5
Income statement

Helpful Hint
The heading of every statement identifies the company, the type of statement, and the time period covered by the statement. Sometimes another line is added to indicate the unit of measure. When it is used, this fourth line usually indicates that the data are presented in thousands or in millions.

Note that cents are not included in the dollar figures recorded in financial statements, as illustrated here for Sierra Corporation. It is important to understand, however, that cents should be and are used in recording transactions in a company's internal accounting records. It is only for financial reporting purposes that financial statement amounts are normally rounded to the nearest dollar, thousand dollars, or million dollars, depending on the size of the company. External reporting condenses and simplifies information so that it is easier for the reader to understand.

It also really does not matter whether the data in the statements are listed in two columns, as they are for Sierra Corporation, or in one column. Companies use a variety of presentation formats, depending on their preference and what they think is easiest for the reader to understand.

Why are financial statement users interested in a company's profit? Investors are interested in a company's past profit because these numbers provide information that may help predict future profits. Investors buy and sell shares based on their beliefs about the future performance of a company. If you believe that Sierra will be even more successful in the future, and that this success will translate into a higher share price, you should buy Sierra's shares.

Like investors, lenders also use the income statement to predict the future. When a bank loans money to a company, it does this because it believes it will be repaid in the future. If it thought it was not going to be repaid, it would not loan the money. Thus, before making the loan, the bank's loan officer must try to predict whether the company will stay in business long enough, and be profitable enough, to repay the loan. Thus, reporting recurring and increasing profits will make it easier for Sierra to raise additional cash either by borrowing or by issuing shares.

Amounts received from issuing shares are not revenues, *and* **amounts paid out as dividends are not expenses**. For example, when Sierra Corporation was formed, it received $10,000 of cash from issuing common shares. This has not been reported as revenue in the income statement. In addition, Sierra paid $500 of dividends to its shareholders during the year. It has not been reported as an expense in the income statement, because it was not incurred to generate revenue. Instead, both of these transactions are reported in the statement of changes in equity, which is discussed in the next section.

DECISION TOOLKIT

 Decision Checkpoints	 Info Needed for Decision	 Tools to Use for Decision	 How to Evaluate Results
Are the company's operations profitable?	Income statement	The income statement indicates the success or failure of the company's operating activities by reporting its revenues and expenses.	If the company's revenues exceed its expenses, it will report a profit; otherwise it will report a loss.

Statement of Changes in Equity

The **statement of changes in equity** shows the changes in total shareholders' equity for the period, as well as the changes in each component of shareholders' equity, during the period. It starts with the account balances at the beginning of the period and ends with the account balances at the end of the period. The time period is the same as for the income statement—for the year, quarter, or month.

The ownership interest in a company is known as **shareholders' equity**. In its simplest form, total shareholders' equity includes (1) share capital and (2) retained earnings. It can also include other types of accounts, such as accumulated other comprehensive income, that we will discuss later.

Share capital represents amounts contributed by the shareholders in exchange for shares of ownership. If there is only one type of shares issued, it is called common shares. We will learn about another class of shares, called preferred shares, in Chapter 11. Together, these two classes of shares—common and preferred—combine to form the company's share capital.

The statement of changes in equity starts with the beginning balance of share capital—common shares, in Sierra's case. This is zero in the case of Sierra Corporation because it just commenced operations at the beginning of the month, October 1. The statement then goes on to add any changes in share capital due to new shares issued (or deduct any changes in share capital due to shares repurchased) during the period to arrive at the ending balance of share capital.

Retained earnings represent the cumulative profit that has been retained in the corporation. In other words, it is the profit that has not been paid out to shareholders that has accumulated since the company's date of incorporation. If retained earnings are negative—that is, there have been more losses than profits—it is known as a **deficit**. As we will see later in this chapter, Eastplats reports a deficit rather than a positive retained earnings balance.

In addition to showing the changes in share capital during the period, the statement of changes in equity also shows the amounts and causes of changes in retained earnings. The statement starts with the beginning balance of retained earnings. Then the profit for the period is added and dividends (if any) are deducted to calculate the retained earnings at the end of the period. If a company has a loss, it is deducted (rather than added) to arrive at the ending balance of retained earnings. Note that this statement adds both vertically (down; see "Balance, October 31" row) and horizontally (across; see "Total Equity" column).

Illustration 1-6 presents Sierra Corporation's statement of changes in equity.

► Illustration 1-6
Statement of changes in equity

SIERRA CORPORATION
Statement of Changes in Equity
Month Ended October 31, 2012

	Common Shares	Retained Earnings	Total Equity
Balance, October 1	$ 0	$ 0	$ 0
Issued common shares	10,000		10,000
Profit		642	642
Dividends		(500)	(500)
Balance, October 31	$10,000	$142	$10,142

By monitoring the statement of changes in equity for publicly traded corporations, financial statement users can evaluate the use of equity for financing purposes. From this statement, they can determine how many shares were issued during the period, or how many were repurchased. More importantly, the statement of changes in equity allows users to monitor a company's dividend payment practices. If Sierra is profitable, at the end of each period it must decide what portion of its profits to pay to shareholders through dividends. In theory, it could pay all of its current period profit, but few companies choose to do this. Why? Because they want to retain part of the profits in the business so the company can expand when it chooses to.

DECISION TOOLKIT

Decision Checkpoints	Info Needed for Decision	Tools to Use for Decision	How to Evaluate Results
Is the company expanding or contracting its share base?	Statement of changes in equity	Did the company issue or repurchase shares?	If share capital is increasing, the company may have expansion plans.
What is the company's policy on dividends and growth?	Statement of changes in equity	How much did the company pay out in dividends to shareholders?	A company looking for rapid growth will pay no, or a low, dividend.

Statement of Financial Position (Balance Sheet)

The **statement of financial position** reports assets and claims to those assets at a specific point in time. This statement is also commonly known as the balance sheet, especially for those companies following ASPE, and we will use these two terms interchangeably in this textbook.

ASPE

Claims to assets are subdivided into two categories: claims of lenders and other creditors and claims of shareholders. As noted earlier, claims of lenders and other creditors are called liabilities. Claims of shareholders, the owners of the company, are called shareholders' equity. This relationship is shown in Illustration 1-7 in a form that is known as the basic **accounting equation**.

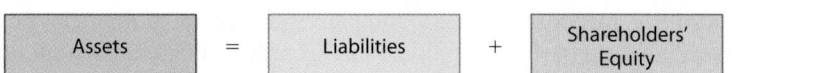

► Illustration 1-7
Basic accounting equation

The relationship is where the name *balance sheet* comes from. Assets must be in balance with the claims to the assets. The right-hand side of the equation—the liabilities and equities—also shows how the assets have been financed (through debt by borrowing from lenders or creditors or through equity by investments from shareholders or profits retained in the company).

As you can see from Sierra's statement of financial position in Illustration 1-8, assets are listed first, followed by liabilities and shareholders' equity. Sierra's assets total $21,867 and include cash, accounts receivable, supplies, prepaid insurance (insurance paid in advance but not yet used), and equipment. Of these assets, only the purchase of equipment would be presented as an investing activity in the statement of cash flows, as we will see in the next section. The other items (except for cash) are examples of assets that come from operating activities.

Sierra's liabilities total $11,725 and consist of accounts payable, salaries payable, interest payable, income tax payable, unearned revenue (cash received in advance for which the service has not yet been provided and is therefore still owed), and notes payable. Of these liabilities, only the increase in notes payable is an example of a financing activity. The other items are examples of liabilities that arose from operating activities.

Sierra's shareholders' equity consists of common shares of $10,000 and retained earnings of $142, for total shareholders' equity of $10,142. Note that Sierra's total liabilities and total shareholders' equity equal its total assets of $21,867.

► Illustration 1-8
Statement of financial position

SIERRA CORPORATION Statement of Financial Position October 31, 2012	
Assets	
Cash	$15,200
Accounts receivable	200
Supplies	1,000
Prepaid insurance	550
Equipment	4,917
Total assets	$21,867
Liabilities and Shareholders' Equity	
Liabilities	
Accounts payable	$ 2,500
Salaries payable	3,200
Interest payable	25
Income tax payable	200
Unearned revenue	800
Notes payable	5,000
Total liabilities	11,725
Shareholders' equity	
Common shares	10,000
Retained earnings	142
Total shareholders' equity	10,142
Total liabilities and shareholders' equity	$21,867

Helpful Hint
The statement of financial position is dated at a *specific point in time*. The income statement, statement of changes in equity, and statement of cash flows cover a *period of time*.

The items listed in the statement of financial position can be ordered in different ways. For example, Sierra presents its assets first, followed by liabilities and shareholders' equity. Some companies present these items in a different order, to better represent the nature of their business. For example, Anglo American Platinum Limited (Amplats), Eastplats's primary competitor, orders its balance sheet quite differently than does Sierra or Eastplats. Eastplats's and Amplats's financial statements will be discussed later in this chapter and we will learn more about how to order items within the statement of financial position in Chapter 2.

Lenders and other creditors analyze a company's statement of financial position to determine the likelihood that they will be repaid. They carefully evaluate the nature of the company's assets and liabilities. For example, does the company have assets that could easily be sold, if required, to repay its debts? Do the company's assets exceed its liabilities in both the short and long terms?

Managers use the statement of financial position to determine whether inventory is adequate to support future sales and whether cash on hand is sufficient for immediate cash needs. Managers also look at the relationship between total liabilities and shareholders' equity to determine whether they have the best proportion of debt and equity financing.

DECISION TOOLKIT

 Decision Checkpoints	 Info Needed for Decision	 Tools to Use for Decision	 How to Evaluate Results
Does the company rely mainly on debt or on equity to finance its assets?	Statement of financial position	The statement of financial position reports the company's resources and claims to those resources. There are two types of claims: liabilities and shareholders' equity.	Compare the amount of liabilities as a percentage of total assets to the amount of shareholders' equity as a percentage of total assets to determine whether the company relies more on lenders and other creditors or on shareholders for its financing.

Statement of Cash Flows

The main function of a **statement of cash flows** is to provide financial information about the cash receipts and cash payments of a business for a specific period of time. To help investors, lenders and other creditors, and others in their analysis of a company's cash position, the statement of cash flows reports the effects on cash of a company's (1) operating activities, (2) investing activities, and (3) financing activities during the period of time.

Recall from earlier in the chapter that operating activities result from transactions that create revenues and expenses. Investing activities involve the purchase or sale of long-lived resources such as property, plant, and equipment that a company needs to operate and the purchase or sale of investments in long-term securities. Financing activities involve borrowing (or repaying) long-term debt from (to) lenders and issuing shares or distributing dividends to shareholders.

Operating activities are normally presented first in the statement of cash flows, followed by either investing or financing activities. In addition, the statement shows the net increase or decrease in cash during the period, and the cash amount at the end of the period.

The statement of cash flows for Sierra, in Illustration 1-9, shows that cash increased by $15,200 during the month. This increase resulted because operating activities (services to clients) increased cash by $5,700, and financing activities increased cash by $14,500. Investing activities used $5,000 of cash for the purchase of equipment. Note that the positive numbers indicate cash inflows. Numbers in parentheses indicate cash outflows. Parentheses are often used in financial statements to indicate negative amounts.

For now, you should not worry too much about where the numbers came from. We will learn more about the preparation of the statement of cash flows in a later chapter.

▶Illustration 1-9

Statement of cash flows

SIERRA CORPORATION Statement of Cash Flows Month Ended October 31, 2012		
Operating activities		
Cash receipts from operating activities	$11,200	
Cash payments for operating activities	(5,500)	
Net cash provided by operating activities		$ 5,700
Investing activities		
Purchase of equipment	$ (5,000)	
Net cash used by investing activities		(5,000)
Financing activities		
Issue of common shares	$10,000	
Issue of notes payable	5,000	
Payment of dividend	(500)	
Net cash provided by financing activities		14,500
Net increase in cash		15,200
Cash, October 1		0
Cash, October 31		$15,200

DECISION TOOLKIT

 Decision Checkpoints	 Info Needed for Decision	 Tools to Use for Decision	 How to Evaluate Results
Does the company generate enough cash from operating activities to fund its investing activities?	Statement of cash flows	The statement of cash flows shows the amount of cash provided or used by operating activities, investing activities, and financing activities.	Compare the amount of cash provided by operating activities with the amount of cash used by investing activities. Any deficiency in cash from operating activities must be made up with cash provided by financing activities.

> You will find a section called **Keeping an Eye on Cash** in each chapter to help you understand the importance of cash.

■ Keeping an Eye on Cash

Understanding where its cash comes from and where it goes is critical for a company. The statement of cash flows provides answers to these simple but important questions: (1) Where did cash come from during the period? (2) How was cash used during the period? (3) What was the change in the cash balance during the period?

The statement of cash flows answers these questions by summarizing cash flows as operating, investing, or financing activities. A user of this statement can then determine the amount of cash provided (or used) by operating activities, the amount of cash provided (or used) for investing purposes, and the amount of cash provided (or used) by financing activities.

Operating activities are activities the company performs to generate profits. It is desirable for cash provided by operating activities to be a positive (cash provided) balance rather than using cash for operating activities. A positive source of cash from operating activities can help pay for investments to grow the business.

Investing activities include the purchase or sale of long-lived assets used in operating the business, or the purchase or sale of long-term investment securities. For most growing companies, cash is used by investing activities (a negative balance) rather than investing activities being a source of cash because growing companies purchase or replace more assets than the opposite.

Financing activities include borrowing or repaying money, issuing or repurchasing shares, and paying dividends. For most growing companies, cash is provided by financing activities (a positive balance) rather than being used for financing activities. Most growing companies have to borrow money or issue shares rather than being able to repay it. As companies mature, they are able to repay financing and this balance becomes negative (cash used) more often than positive.

Relationships between the Statements

Because the results on some statements are used as data for other statements, the statements are said to be interrelated (related to each other). These interrelationships are evident in Sierra's financial statements:

1. The statement of changes in equity depends, in part, on the results of the income statement. Sierra reported profit of $642 for the period, as shown in Illustration 1-5. This amount is added to the beginning amount of retained earnings as part of the process of determining ending retained earnings—one of the components of total shareholders' equity shown in Illustration 1-6.
2. The statement of financial position and statement of changes in equity are interrelated because the ending balances of each component of shareholders' equity—common shares, $10,000, and retained earnings, $142—as well as total shareholders' equity of $10,142 at the end of the month reported on the statement of changes in equity in Illustration 1-6 is reported in the shareholders' equity section of the statement of financial position in Illustration 1-8.

3. The statement of cash flows and the statement of financial position are also interrelated. The statement of cash flows presented in Illustration 1-9 shows how the cash account changed during the period by stating the amount of cash at the beginning of the period, the sources and uses of cash during the period, and the amount of cash at the end of the period, $15,200. The ending amount of cash shown on the statement of cash flows agrees with the amount of cash shown in the assets section of the statement of financial position shown in Illustration 1-8.

Study these interrelationships carefully. To prepare financial statements, you must understand the sequence in which these amounts are determined and how each statement affects the next. Because each financial statement depends on information contained in another statement, financial statements must be prepared in a certain order: (1) income statement; (2) statement of changes in equity; (3) statement of financial position; and (4) statement of cash flows.

EASTPLATS'S FINANCIAL STATEMENTS

The same relationships that you observed among the financial statements of Sierra Corporation can be seen in the 2010 simplified financial statements of Eastern Platinum Limited, presented in Illustration 1-10.

Eastplats's actual financial statements are presented in Appendix A at the end of the book. In Illustration 1-10, we have simplified the financial statements to assist your learning—but they may look complicated to you anyway. Do not be alarmed by this. By the end of the book, you will have a lot of experience in reading and understanding financial statements such as these, and they will no longer look so complicated.

Before examining Eastplats's statements, we need to explain a couple of points that you will note when you look at the heading of each statement:

1. The numbers are reported in thousands of dollars on Eastplats's financial statements; that is, the last three zeros (000) are omitted.
2. Eastplats reports its results in U.S. dollars rather than Canadian dollars. A number of Canadian companies report their results in U.S. dollars because they raise capital in U.S. markets or because many of their transactions occur in U.S. dollars. In such cases, the financial statements are considered to be more appropriate for the users' needs if they are prepared using U.S. dollars.
3. Eastplats's fiscal year end is December 31.

Income Statement

Take a look at the simplified version of Eastplats's income statement presented in Illustration 1-10, shown on the next page.

While Sierra is a service company, providing services to earn its revenue, Eastplats is a mining company. It explores for, mines, processes, and sells a product to earn its revenue. For 2010, Eastplats reported total revenue of U.S. $155,000 thousand. As was mentioned earlier, Eastplats reports its numbers in thousands of dollars. Thus, Eastplats' total revenue is U.S. $155,000,000 and not U.S. $155,000. Eastplats has two primary sources of revenue: one from the sales of PGM and the other from interest earned on its investments.

It then subtracts a variety of expenses related to operating the business. These expenses, totalling U.S. $147,944 thousand, include the cost of operations, general and administrative expenses, finance costs, and other expenses. Total expenses are deducted from revenue to determine profit before income tax of U.S. $8,853 thousand. Eastplats has a recovery of income tax rather than income tax expense because of prior years' losses that were carried forward to the current year. After adding the income tax recovery of U.S. $924 thousand (if the company reported an income tax expense, it would be deducted), the company reports a profit for the year of U.S. $9,777 thousand.

Statement of Changes in Equity

Eastplats presents information next about its shareholders' equity in the simplified statement of changes in equity in Illustration 1-10. This statement shows the changes in Eastplats's share capital (which it calls "issued" capital) and deficit during the period, as well as other changes that affected its shareholders' equity that we will learn about in a later chapter.

▶Illustration 1-10

Eastplats's financial statements
(in U.S. thousands)

EASTERN PLATINUM LIMITED
Income Statement
Year Ended December 31, 2010

Revenue		
Sales	$155,000	
Interest income	1,797	
Total revenue		$156,797
Expenses		
Cost of operations	$132,408	
General and administrative expenses	12,117	
Finance costs	1,807	
Other	1,612	
Total expenses		147,944
Profit before income tax		8,853
Income tax recovery		924
Profit		$ 9,777

EASTERN PLATINUM LIMITED
Statement of Changes in Equity
Year Ended December 31, 2010

	Issued Capital	Deficit	Other	Total Equity
Balance, January 1	$ 890,150	$(250,116)	$(10,522)	$ 629,512
Issued common shares	329,719			329,719
Other changes to equity			72,171	72,171
Profit		9,777		9,777
Balance, December 31	$1,219,869	$(240,339)	$ 61,649	$1,041,179

EASTERN PLATINUM LIMITED
Statement of Financial Position
December 31, 2010

Assets

Cash		$ 107,846
Short-term (non-trading) investments		242,446
Trade and other receivables		33,787
Inventories		8,832
Property, plant, and equipment		715,976
Other assets		18,088
Total assets		$1,126,975

Liabilities and Shareholders' Equity

Liabilities		
Accounts payable and accrued liabilities	$ 27,009	
Finance leases	3,211	
Deferred tax liabilities	46,642	
Other liabilities	8,934	
Total liabilities		$ 85,796
Shareholders' equity		
Share capital	$1,219,869	
Deficit	(240,339)	
Other equity items	61,649	
Total shareholders' equity		1,041,179
Total liabilities and shareholders' equity		$1,126,975

EASTERN PLATINUM LIMITED
Statement of Cash Flows
Year Ended December 31, 2010

Operating activities		
Cash receipts from operating activities	$ 150,351	
Cash payments for operating activities	(118,377)	
Cash provided by operating activities		$ 31,974
Investing activities		
Purchase of short-term (non-trading) investments	$(223,118)	
Purchase of property, plant, and equipment	(32,991)	
Purchase of other assets	(1,129)	
Cash used by investing activities		(257,238)
Financing activities		
Proceeds from common shares issued	$ 329,313	
Payment of finance leases	(2,161)	
Other	(1,291)	
Cash provided by financing activities		325,861
Increase in cash		100,597
Cash, January 1		7,249
Cash, December 31		$ 107,846

① ② ③

Find the column "Deficit" in the statement of changes in equity shown in Illustration 1-10 and look for the amount of the deficit at the beginning of the year, U.S. $250,116 thousand. This is the same amount that would be reported by Eastplats as its deficit at the end of the prior fiscal year, December 31, 2009. In Appendix A, comparative financial statements are presented for two years whereas, for simplicity, only one year has been presented here.

Profit for the year ended December 31, 2010, of U.S. $9,777 thousand is added to the beginning balance to determine the ending deficit balance at December 31, 2010, of U.S. $240,339 thousand. The profit figure was taken from Eastplats's income statement as indicated by the arrow marked with a ① in Illustration 1-10. Regardless of the order the financial statements are presented in, the income statement is always prepared first, followed by the statement of changes in equity. This is because the profit (or loss) for the period is needed to prepare the statement of changes in equity.

Statement of Financial Position

Eastplats's statement of financial position shown in Illustration 1-10 includes the types of assets mentioned in this chapter: cash; investments; accounts receivable (which it calls "trade and other" receivables); inventories; property, plant, and equipment; and other types of assets.

Similarly, its liabilities include accounts payable and accrued liabilities (we will learn about accrued liabilities in Chapter 2), amounts owed for finance leases, and deferred tax liabilities, as well as other types of liabilities.

Eastplats's statement of financial position shows that total assets equal U.S. $1,126,975 thousand and total liabilities equal U.S. $85,796 thousand at December 31, 2010. The ending balances of Eastplats's issued capital, deficit, and other items taken from the statement of changes in equity agree to the same items shown in the shareholders' equity section of the statement of financial position. Follow the arrow marked with a ② in Illustration 1-10 to confirm that the total shareholders' equity of U.S. $1,041,179 thousand reported in the statement of changes in equity as at December 31, 2010, agrees with the total shareholders' equity presented in the statement of financial position at the same date. Note also that total liabilities and total shareholders' equity equal, or agree to, total assets of U.S. $1,126,975.

You can see that Eastplats relies much more on equity financing than debt. It has very little debt and more than 12 times total shareholders' equity than it has total liabilities. As you learn more about financial statements, we will discuss how to interpret the relationships and changes in financial statement items.

Statement of Cash Flows

Eastplats's cash improved by U.S. $100,597 thousand in 2010. The reasons for the increase in cash can be determined by examining the statement of cash flows in Illustration 1-10.

Even though Eastplats reported a profit of only U.S. $9,777 thousand, it was able to generate more cash from operating activities of U.S. $31,974 thousand. This is mainly because Eastplats spent less cash paying its expenses than it received from its revenues during the year.

Eastplats used cash in its investing activities of U.S. $257,238 thousand, primarily to acquire additional short-term (non-trading) investments with some of its excess cash. It generated cash from its financing activities of U.S. $325,861 thousand, primarily from the new issue of common shares that was mentioned in the chapter-opening feature story. The net result of the sources and uses of cash during the year was an increase in cash of U.S. $100,597 thousand.

This increase in cash is added to the opening balance of U.S. $7,249 thousand to result in an ending cash balance of U.S. $107,846 thousand. Trace the ending balance of cash reported in the statement of cash flows to the ending balance reported in the statement of financial position, as indicated by the arrow marked with a ③ in Illustration 1-10.

ELEMENTS OF AN ANNUAL REPORT

Publicly traded companies must produce an **annual report** each year. The annual report is a document that includes useful nonfinancial information about the company, as well as financial information. Nonfinancial information may include the company's mission, goals and objectives, products, and people.

Financial information normally includes a management discussion and analysis (often abbreviated as MD&A), a statement of management responsibility for the financial statements, an auditors' report, the financial statements introduced in this chapter that are reported for at least two years (these are called comparative statements), notes to the financial statements, and a historical summary of key financial ratios and indicators. No analysis of a company's financial situation and prospects is complete without a review of each of these items.

BEFORE YOU GO ON...

▶ Do It! Financial Statements

CSU Corporation began operations on January 1, 2012. The following account information is available for CSU Corporation on December 31, 2012: service revenue $22,200; accounts receivable $4,000; accounts payable $2,000; rent expense $9,000; bank loan payable $5,000; common shares $10,000; equipment $16,000; insurance expense $1,000; supplies $1,800; supplies expense $200; cash $1,400; income tax expense $5,200; and dividends $600. Using this information, prepare an income statement, statement of changes in equity, statement of financial position, and statement of cash flows for the year.

For the operating activities section of the statement of cash flows, cash receipts from operating activities were $18,200 and cash payments for operating activities were $15,200. For the investing activities section, cash of $16,000 was paid for the purchase of the equipment. For the financing activities section, cash of $5,000 was received from the bank loan and $10,000 from the issue of common shares. Cash of $600 was paid for dividends.

Action Plan

- Classify each account into the following categories: revenues, expenses, dividends, assets, liabilities, and shareholders' equity.
- Report revenues and expenses for the period in the income statement.
- Show the amounts and causes of the changes in share capital and retained earnings for the period in the statement of changes in equity.
- Present assets and claims to those assets (liabilities and shareholders' equity) at a specific point in time in the statement of financial position.
- Show the changes in cash for the period, classified as operating, investing, or financing activities in the statement of cash flows.
- Remember that the income statement, statement of changes in equity, and statement of cash flows cover a period of time, while the statement of financial position is reported at a specific point in time.

Solution

See facing page.

> You will find a section called **Comparing IFRS and ASPE** at the end of each chapter to help you understand the differences in reporting for companies using IFRS, compared to those using ASPE.

comparing
IFRS and ASPE

Key Differences	International Financial Reporting Standards (IFRS)	Accounting Standards for Private Enterprises (ASPE)
Accounting standards	Publicly traded corporations must use IFRS; private corporations can choose to use IFRS or ASPE.	Private corporations can choose to use IFRS or ASPE. Once the choice is made, it must be applied consistently.
Terminology	The balance sheet is more commonly known as the statement of financial position and net income as profit under IFRS.	The statement of financial position is more commonly known as the balance sheet and profit as net income under ASPE.
Statement of changes in equity vs. statement of retained earnings	A statement of changes in equity must be presented that shows the changes in all components of shareholders' equity (e.g., share capital and retained earnings).	A statement of retained earnings is presented that shows the change in only one component—retained earnings—of shareholders' equity.

the navigator

Solution

CSU CORPORATION
Income Statement
Year Ended December 31, 2012

Revenues		
Service revenue		$22,200
Expenses		
Rent expense	$9,000	
Insurance expense	1,000	
Supplies expense	200	
Total expenses		10,200
Profit before income tax		12,000
Income tax expense		5,200
Profit		$ 6,800

CSU CORPORATION
Statement of Changes in Equity
Year Ended December 31, 2012

	Common Shares	Retained Earnings	Total Equity
Balance, January 1	$ 0	$ 0	$ 0
Issued common shares	10,000		10,000
Profit		6,800	6,800
Dividends		(600)	(600)
Balance, December 31	$10,000	$6,200	$16,200

CSU CORPORATION
Statement of Financial Position
December 31, 2012

Assets		
Cash		$ 1,400
Accounts receivable		4,000
Supplies		1,800
Equipment		16,000
Total assets		$23,200
Liabilities and Shareholders' Equity		
Liabilities		
Accounts payable		$ 2,000
Bank loan payable		5,000
Total liabilities		7,000
Shareholders' equity		
Common shares		10,000
Retained earnings		6,200
Total shareholders' equity		16,200
Total liabilities and shareholders' equity		$23,200

CSU CORPORATION
Statement of Cash Flows
Year Ended December 31, 2012

Operating activities		
Cash receipts from operating activities	$ 18,200	
Cash payments for operating activities	(15,200)	
Net cash provided by operating activities		$ 3,000
Investing activities		
Purchase of equipment	$(16,000)	
Net cash used by investing activities		(16,000)
Financing activities		
Issue of bank loan payable	$ 5,000	
Issue of common shares	10,000	
Payment of dividends	(600)	
Net cash provided by financing activities		14,400
Net increase in cash		1,400
Cash, January 1		0
Cash, December 31		$ 1,400

Helpful Hint
The arrows in this illustration show the relationships among the four financial statements.

the navigator

Your Personal Annual Report

You probably have already prepared a resumé and used it to find a job. In some ways, your resumé is like a company's annual report. Its purpose is to enable others to evaluate your past, in an effort to predict your future.

A resumé is your opportunity to create a positive first impression. It is important that it be impressive, but it should also be accurate. In order to increase their job prospects, some people are tempted to inflate their resumés by overstating the importance of some past accomplishments or positions.

Consider the skills that you have acquired from part-time or vacation employment or volunteering. These could include dealing with difficult people, improving your interpersonal skills, meeting work-related deadlines and responsibilities, mastering time management skills, and so on. Experts suggest that, while you are at school, you should use the time to build up your "human capital"; that is, to develop the job skills that will enable you to have a rewarding career that will earn you enough money to live your life.

Surveys of human resource professionals have found that an on-line profile can play an important part in the evaluation of your skills and experience. This applies to professional networks such as LinkedIn as well as social network sites, such as Facebook, MySpace, or Twitter. Your on-line profile should not conflict with your resumé and it should give a professional view of you, not be a guide to your years at school and at play.

Some Facts

- Office Team, a leading staffing firm, made the following suggestions to make the best use of network profiles:
  - Highlight your key skills and experience.
  - Limit access to pictures and any other material that could be embarrassing.
  - Keep your profile up to date and complete.
  - Include a personal photo; it can be casual, but must look professional.
- BackCheck, a Vancouver company that provides pre-employment screening for employers, has checked over 3 million resumés and found that almost one-third appeared to contain major omissions, exaggerations, or falsehoods. Human resource professionals state that the major areas in which resumés are embellished or exaggerated are education, experience, responsibilities, work dates, and salaries.
- Do not be tempted to lie on your resumé. Don't change dates, add false information, or suggest that you have graduated from school, when you have not. Potential employers can check with your university or college to confirm your qualifications and they can check with your former employers about your previous employment history. Increasingly, too, your profile on the Internet can be used to verify information on your resumé.
- One bad hiring decision can easily cost an employer a minimum of $25,000 in wasted advertising, training, compensation, and revenue for a regular worker—and $1 million or more for a bad CEO.

What Do You Think?

A company hired an individual to drive a delivery van. He was a conscientious employee and very good driver. However, he had previously been convicted of driving with a suspended licence some years ago and neglected to include this information on his resumé or tell the company before it hired him. The company found out this information several months after hiring him. Should the company suspend him from his position?

YES A person who drives for a living should act responsibly. What does it say about a company when one of its delivery persons has been convicted of a driving-related offence—even a past offence—and then lied about it by omission on his resumé?

NO He has been a reliable and conscientious employee and a good driver. The company should look only at his driving record while he worked for them.

Sources: ISB Corporate Services, "Compliance," isbcorporate.com. Robert Half, *Business Etiquette: The New Rules in a Digital Age*, 2011. D. Abma, "Online Profiles Might Replace Resumes, Survey Indicates," Postmedia, February 21, 2011. S. Hannah, "School Comes First," Canada.com, January 31, 2011. Suzanne Wintrob, "Liar, Liar, Pants on Fire," *Globe and Mail*, June 16, 2010, p. B17.

Summary of Study Objectives

1. **Identify the users and uses of accounting.** The purpose of accounting is to provide useful information for decision-making. There are two types of user groups who use accounting information: internal users and external users. Internal users work for the business and need accounting information to plan, organize, and run operations. The primary external users are investors and lenders and other creditors. Investors (existing and potential shareholders) use accounting information to help decide whether to buy, hold, or sell shares. Lenders (such as bankers) and other creditors (such as suppliers) use accounting information to evaluate the risk of loaning money or granting credit to a business. In order for financial information to have value to its users, whether internal or external, it must be prepared by individuals with high standards of ethical behaviour.

2. **Describe the primary forms of business organization.** There are three types of organizations that use accounting information: proprietorships, partnerships, and corporations. A proprietorship is a business owned by one person. A partnership is a business owned by two or more people. A corporation is a separate legal entity whose shares provide evidence of ownership.

3. **Explain the three main types of business activity.** Financing activities involve collecting the necessary funds (through debt or equity) to support the business. Investing activities involve acquiring the resources (such as property, plant, and equipment) that are needed to run the business. Operating activities involve putting the resources of the business into action to generate a profit.

4. **Describe the content and purpose of each of the financial statements.** The income statement presents the revenues and expenses of a company for a specific period of time. The statement of changes in equity summarizes the changes in shareholders' equity that have occurred for a specific period of time. The statement of financial position reports the assets, liabilities, and shareholders' equity of a business at a specific date. The statement of cash flows summarizes information about the cash inflows (receipts) and outflows (payments) for a specific period of time. Notes to the financial statements add explanatory detail where required. The financial statements are included in an annual report, along with nonfinancial and other financial information.

Glossary

Accounting The process of identifying, recording, and communicating the economic events of a business to interested users of the information. (p. 4)

Accounting equation Assets = liabilities + shareholders' equity. (p. 17)

Annual report A report prepared by management that presents financial and nonfinancial information about the company. (p. 23)

Assets The resources owned or controlled by a business that provide future economic benefits. (p. 11)

Corporation A business organized as a separate legal entity having ownership divided into transferable shares held by shareholders. (p. 8)

Deficit A negative balance in retained earnings as a result of accumulated losses from the prior and current periods exceeding the profits. (p. 16)

Dividends The distribution of retained earnings from a corporation to its shareholders, often in the form of cash. (p. 11)

Expenses The cost of assets consumed or services used in ongoing operations to generate revenue. (p. 12)

Financing activities Activities that include (1) borrowing (or repaying) cash to lenders, or (2) issuing (or reacquiring) shares or paying dividends to investors. (p. 13)

Fiscal year An accounting period that is one year long. (p. 14)

Generally accepted accounting principles (also known as standards or policies) A general guide, having substantial authoritative support, that describes how economic events should be recorded and reported for financial reporting purposes. (p. 9)

Income statement (also known as statement of earnings or statement of profit and loss) A financial statement that presents the revenues and expenses and resulting profit or loss of a company for a specific period of time. (p. 15)

Investing activities Activities that include purchasing and disposing of long-lived assets such as property, plant, and equipment and long-term investments. (p. 13)

Liabilities The debts and obligations of a business. Liabilities are claims of lenders and other creditors on the assets of a business. (p. 11)

Loss The amount by which expenses are more than revenues. (p. 13)

Operating activities   Activities that result from day-to-day operations and include revenues and expenses and related accounts such as receivables, supplies, inventory, and payables. (p. 13)

Partnership   A business owned by more than one person. (p. 7)

Profit   (also known as net income) The amount by which revenues are more than expenses. (p. 13)

Proprietorship   A business owned by one person. (p. 7)

Reporting entity concept   The concept that economic activity that can be identified with a particular company must be kept separate and distinct from the activities of the owner(s) and of all other economic entities. (p. 7)

Retained earnings   The amount of accumulated profit (less losses, if any), from the prior and current periods, that has been kept in the corporation for future use and not distributed to shareholders as dividends. (p. 16)

Revenue   (also known as income) The economic resources that result from the operating activities of a business, such as the sale of a product or provision of a service. (p. 12)

Share capital   Shares representing the ownership interest in a corporation. If only one class of shares exists, it is known as common shares. (p. 16)

Shareholders' equity   The shareholders' claim on total assets, represented by the investments of the shareholders (share capital) and undistributed earnings (retained earnings) generated by the company. (p. 16)

Statement of cash flows   A financial statement that provides information about the cash inflows (receipts) and cash outflows (payments) for a specific period of time. (p. 19)

Statement of changes in equity   A financial statement that summarizes the changes in total shareholders' equity, as well as each component of shareholders' equity, for a specific period of time. (p. 16)

Statement of financial position   (also known as balance sheet) A financial statement that reports the assets, liabilities, and shareholders' equity at a specific date. (p. 17)

DECISION TOOLKIT—A SUMMARY

Decision Checkpoints	 Info Needed for Decision	 Tools to Use for Decision	 How to Evaluate Results
Are the company's operations profitable?	Income statement	The income statement indicates the success or failure of the company's operating activities by reporting its revenues and expenses.	If the company's revenues exceed its expenses, it will report a profit; otherwise it will report a loss.
Is the company expanding or contracting its share base?	Statement of changes in equity	Did the company issue or repurchase shares?	If share capital is increasing, the company may have expansion plans.
What is the company's policy on dividends and growth?	Statement of changes in equity	How much did the company pay out in dividends to shareholders?	A company looking for rapid growth will pay no, or a low, dividend.
Does the company rely mainly on debt or on equity to finance its assets?	Statement of financial position	The statement of financial position reports the company's resources and claims to those resources. There are two types of claims: liabilities and shareholders' equity.	Compare the amount of liabilities as a percentage of total assets to the amount of shareholders' equity as a percentage of total assets to determine whether the company relies more on lenders and other creditors or on shareholders for its financing.
Does the company generate enough cash from operating activities to fund its investing activities?	Statement of cash flows	The statement of cash flows shows the amount of cash provided or used by operating activities, investing activities, and financing activities.	Compare the amount of cash provided by operating activities with the amount of cash used by investing activities. Any deficiency in cash from operating activities must be made up with cash provided by financing activities.

the navigator

Using the Decision Toolkit cases ask you to use information from financial statements to make financial decisions. Before you study the solution, we encourage you to think about how the questions related to the decision would be answered.

USING THE DECISION TOOLKIT

Anglo American Platinum Limited, commonly called Amplats, is the world's largest miner of platinum group metals. The company operates in South Africa but sells its products worldwide. It is Eastplats's number one competitor. Appendix B at the end of this textbook includes financial statements for Amplats. Assume that you are reviewing the financial information of Amplats (presented in Appendix B) and Eastplats (presented in Illustration 1-10 in this chapter) to determine which company you should invest in.

Instructions
(a) Which financial statements should you review before you invest?
(b) What should each of these financial statements tell you? Which financial statement will you likely be most interested in?
(c) Amplats reports its financial results using the South African rand (R) as its currency. Eastplats reports its financial results using U.S. dollars. Will this pose any comparison problems for you?
(d) What broad comparisons can you make between Amplats and Eastplats by reviewing their 2010 financial statements?
(e) You will notice that Amplats orders its statement of financial position differently than Eastplats. Will this affect your comparison of the two companies? If so, explain how.

Solution
(a) Before you invest, you should investigate the income statement (which Amplats calls the statement of comprehensive income), statement of financial position, statement of cash flows, and statement of changes in equity for each company. In addition, the notes to the financial statements should also be carefully reviewed.

(b) You would probably be most interested in the income statement because it shows past performance and this can give an indication of future performance. The statement of financial position reveals the company's financial position and the relationship between assets, liabilities, and shareholders' equity. The statement of cash flows reveals where the company is getting and spending its cash. Finally, the statement of changes in equity shows any changes in share capital as well as the impact that changes in current profits and dividends have on the company's retained earnings.

(c) Although the use of different currencies will affect the comparison of absolute dollar amounts (e.g., total assets of Rm 83,801 cannot be compared with total assets of U.S. $1,126,975), it will not affect the comparison of any percentages calculated for the two companies. For example, a user could compare the percentage debt is of total assets for both companies using different currencies.

    Amplats actually makes it easy to compare its financial results with those of Eastplats because it also includes supplemental information in U.S. dollar equivalents for the convenience of its users.

(d) Many interesting comparisons can be made between the two companies using the U.S. dollar financial statements. Amplats is much larger, more than 11 times the size of Eastplats based on assets. For example, Amplats has total assets of U.S. $12,690 million compared to U.S. $1,127 million for Eastplats. Amplats has total liabilities of U.S. $4,357 ($2,994 + $1,363) million, or 34% of its total assets. Eastplats has total liabilities of U.S. $86 million, a much smaller percentage—less than 8%—of its total assets. Eastplats relies much less on debt financing than does Amplats.

    Amplats's sales revenue of U.S. $6,291 million in 2010 is more than 40 times times as large as Eastplats's revenues of U.S. $155 million. Amplats reported profit of U.S. $1,384 million, compared to Eastplats's profit for the same period of U.S. $10 million.

    In 2010, Amplats generated cash from operating activities of U.S. $1,398 million, whereas Eastplats generated a much lower U.S. $32 million cash from its operating activities.

(continued)

While these comparisons are useful, these basic measures are not enough to determine whether one company will be a better investment than the other. In later chapters, you will acquire more tools to help you compare the relative profitability and financial health of these, and other, companies.

(e) You may recall that we mentioned in the chapter that companies can present the information in their statement of financial positions in different orders, depending on the needs of their users. This presentation format does not affect the comparison of the two companies because the statements still present amounts for each category (e.g., total assets, total liabilities, and total shareholders' equity), even if they are ordered differently within the statement.

the navigator

The **Comprehensive Do It!** is a final review before you begin homework. **Action Plans** give you tips about how to approach the problem, and the **Solution** provided demonstrates both the form and content of complete answers.

Comprehensive Do It!

Jeff Andringa, a former university hockey player, started Ice Camp Ltd., a hockey camp for kids from ages 8 to 18. Eventually he would like to open hockey camps nationwide. Jeff has asked you to help him prepare financial statements at the end of his first year of operations. He tells you the following facts about his business activities.

In order to get the business off the ground, he decided to incorporate and follow IFRS. He sold common shares to a few close friends and bought some of the shares himself on January 1, 2012. He initially raised $25,000 through the sale of 2,500 of these shares. In addition, the company borrowed $10,000 from a local bank. A used bus for transporting kids was purchased for $12,000 cash. Hockey nets and other miscellaneous equipment were purchased with $1,500 cash. The company earned camp tuition of $100,000 during the year but had collected only $80,000 of this amount. Thus, at the end of the year it was still owed $20,000. The company rents time at a local rink for $50 per hour. Total rink rental costs during the year were $8,000, insurance was $10,000, salaries were $20,000, administrative expenses totalled $9,000, and income tax amounted to $15,000—all of which were paid in cash. The company incurred $800 in interest expense on the bank loan, which it still owed at the end of the year.

The company paid dividends during the year of $5,000 cash. The balance in the corporate bank account at December 31, 2012, was $34,500 ($25,000 + $10,000 − $12,000 − $1,500 + $80,000 − $8,000 − $10,000 − $20,000 − $9,000 − $15,000 − $5,000). Cash payments for operating activities totalled $62,000 ($8,000 + $10,000 + $20,000 + $9,000 + $15,000).

Instructions

Prepare an income statement, statement of changes in equity, statement of financial position, and statement of cash flows for the year.

> **Action Plan**
> - On the income statement, show revenues and expenses for a period of time.
> - On the statement of changes in equity, show the changes in share capital and retained earnings for a period of time.
> - On the statement of financial position, report assets, liabilities, and shareholders' equity at a specific date.
> - On the statement of cash flows, report sources and uses of cash provided or used by operating, investing, and financing activities for a period of time.

Solution to Comprehensive Do It!

ICE CAMP LTD.
Income Statement
Year Ended December 31, 2012

Revenues		
Camp tuition revenue		$100,000
Expenses		
Salaries expense	$20,000	
Insurance expense	10,000	
Administrative expense	9,000	
Rink rental expense	8,000	
Interest expense	800	
Total expenses		47,800
Profit before income tax		52,200
Income tax expense		15,000
Profit		$ 37,200

ICE CAMP LTD.
Statement of Changes in Equity
Year Ended December 31, 2012

	Common Shares	Retained Earnings	Total Equity
Balance, January 1	$ 0	$ 0	$ 0
Issued common shares	25,000		25,000
Profit		37,200	37,200
Dividends		(5,000)	(5,000)
Balance, December 31	$25,000	$32,200	$57,200

ICE CAMP LTD.
Statement of Financial Position
December 31, 2012

Assets

Cash	$34,500
Accounts receivable	20,000
Bus	12,000
Equipment	1,500
Total assets	$68,000

Liabilities and Shareholders' Equity

Liabilities		
Interest payable		$ 800
Bank loan payable		10,000
Total liabilities		10,800
Shareholders' equity		
Common shares		25,000
Retained earnings		32,200
Total shareholders' equity		57,200
Total liabilities and shareholders' equity		$68,000

ICE CAMP LTD.
Statement of Cash Flows
Year Ended December 31, 2012

Operating activities		
Cash receipts from operating activities	$ 80,000	
Cash payments for operating activities	(62,000)	
Net cash provided by operating activities		$18,000
Investing activities		
Purchase of bus	$(12,000)	
Purchase of equipment	(1,500)	
Net cash used by investing activities		(13,500)
Financing activities		
Issue of bank loan	$ 10,000	
Issue of common shares	25,000	
Dividends paid	(5,000)	
Net cash provided by financing activities		30,000
Net increase in cash		34,500
Cash, January 1		0
Cash, December 31		$34,500

the
navigator

Self-Test Questions, Brief Exercises, Exercises, Problems: Set A, and many more components are available for practice in WileyPLUS.

Self-Test Questions

Answers are at the end of the chapter.

(SO 1)   1. Which statement about users of accounting information is *incorrect*?
(a) Management is an internal user.
(b) Investors are internal users.
(c) Lenders and other creditors are external users.
(d) The Canada Revenue Agency is an external user.

(SO 1)   2. Which of the following is *not* a step that should be used to analyze an ethical situation?
(a) Identify the main elements of the situation.
(b) Identify alternatives.
(c) Weigh impact of each alternative on various stakeholders.
(d) Choose the least expensive alternative.

(SO 2)   3. Which of the following is *not* one of the three primary forms of business organization?
(a) Proprietorship
(b) Partnership
(c) Corporation
(d) Trust

(SO 2)   4. In which of the following area(s) do corporations have an advantage over partnerships and proprietorships?
(a) Raising capital
(b) Unlimited legal life
(c) Limited liability
(d) All of the above

(SO 3)   5. Which is *not* one of the three primary business activities?
(a) Financing
(b) Planning
(c) Operating
(d) Investing

(SO 3)   6. Which of the following is *not* an example of a financing activity?
(a) Borrowing money from a bank
(b) Repaying money to a bank

(c) Selling goods on credit
(d) Paying dividends

(SO 3)   7. Operating activities include all of the following except:
(a) Purchasing goods for resale
(b) Performing services
(c) Paying employee salaries
(d) Purchasing a cash register

(SO 4)   8. Which financial statement reports assets, liabilities, and shareholders' equity?
(a) Income statement
(b) Statement of changes in equity
(c) Statement of financial position
(d) Statement of cash flows

(SO 4)   9. Financial statements must be prepared in the following order:
(a) (1) Income statement, (2) statement of cash flows, (3) statement of changes in equity, and (4) statement of financial position.
(b) (1) Statement of changes in equity, (2) income statement, (3) statement of cash flows, and (4) statement of financial position.
(c) (1) Statement of financial position, (2) income statement, (3) statement of changes in equity, and (4) statement of cash flows.
(d) (1) Income statement, (2) statement of changes in equity, (3) statement of financial position, and (4) statement of cash flows.

(SO 4)   10. As at December 31, Stoneland Corporation has assets of $3,500 and shareholders' equity of $2,000. What are the liabilities for Stoneland Corporation as at December 31?
(a) $1,500   (c) $3,500
(b) $2,000   (d) $5,500

the navigator

Questions

The financial results of real companies are included in the end-of-chapter material. These company names are shown in orange.

(SO 1)   1. What is accounting?
(SO 1)   2. Why should everyone study accounting whether they are going to be an accountant or not?
(SO 1)   3. Distinguish between internal and external users of accounting information.
(SO 1)   4. What kinds of questions might internal users of accounting information want answered? External users?

(SO 1)   5. Why are ethics as important to accountants as they are to the decision makers who rely on financial information?
(SO 1)   6. Identify an ethical dilemma that each of the following individuals might hypothetically encounter: (a) a professor at a university, (b) a cashier at Fast Food Inc., (c) a chief financial officer, and (d) a supplier of goods to a company.

(SO 2)   7. Identify the advantages and disadvantages of each of the following forms of business organization: (a) proprietorship, (b) partnership, and (c) corporation.

(SO 2)   8. Explain how the reporting entity concept applies to corporations.

(SO 2)   9. Distinguish between a public corporation and a private corporation.

(SO 2) 10. (a) Identify the financial reporting standards a public and a private corporation may use. (b) Why do you think they differ?

(SO 3) 11. Explain the following terms and give an example of each: (a) asset, (b) liability, (c) shareholders' equity, (d) revenues, and (e) expenses.

(SO 3) 12. Distinguish between operating, investing, and financing activities.

(SO 3) 13. Give two examples of each kind of business activity: (a) operating, (b) investing, and (c) financing.

(SO 3) 14. Explain why operating activities include some assets (e.g., receivables) but not others (e.g., property, plant, and equipment).

(SO 4) 15. What is a fiscal year end? Why does a company's fiscal year not always end on December 31?

(SO 4) 16. André is puzzled reading Transat A.T. (Air Transat) Inc.'s financial statements. He notices that the numbers have all been rounded to the nearest thousand. He thought financial statements

were supposed to be accurate and wonders what happened to the rest of the money. Respond to André's concern.

(SO 4) 17. The basic accounting equation is Assets = Liabilities + Shareholders' Equity. Replacing words with dollar amounts, what is Eastplats's accounting equation at December 31, 2010?

(SO 4) 18. What are the primary components explained in a statement of changes in equity? What types of items generally increase each component? What types of items generally decrease each component?

(SO 4) 19. (a) What is the purpose of the statement of cash flows? (b) What are the three main categories of activities included in the statement?

(SO 4) 20. Why is a statement of financial position prepared as at a specific point in time, while the other financial statements cover a period of time?

(SO 4) 21. How are each of the following pairs of financial statements related?
(a) Income statement and statement of changes in equity
(b) Statement of changes in equity and statement of financial position
(c) Statement of financial position and statement of cash flows

(SO 4) 22. Identify the four financial statements used by corporations using (a) IFRS and (b) ASPE.

Brief Exercises

BE1–1 The following list presents different types of evaluations made by various users of accounting information:

1. Determining if the company respected income tax regulations
2. Determining if the company pays fair wages
3. Determining if the company can pay its account
4. Determining if a marketing proposal will be cost-effective
5. Determining if the company's profit will result in a share price increase
6. Determining if the company should use debt or equity financing

(a) Beside each user of accounting information listed in the left-hand column of the table that follows, write the number of the evaluation above (1 to 6) that the user makes.

(b) Indicate if the user is internal or external. The first item has been done for you as an example.

Identify users of accounting information. (SO 1)

	(a) Type of Evaluation	(b) Type of User External
Investor	5	External
Marketing manager	_____	_____
Creditor	_____	_____
Chief financial officer	_____	_____
Canada Revenue Agency	_____	_____
Labour union	_____	_____

BE1–2 Match each of the following forms of business organization— (1) proprietorship, (2) partnership, (3) public corporation, or (4) private corporation—beside the set of characteristics that best describes it.
(a) _____ Simple to set up; founder retains control
(b) _____ Shared control; increased skills and resources
(c) _____ Easier to transfer ownership and raise funds; no personal liability
(d) _____ Separate legal entity; shares closely held

Identify forms of business organization. (SO 2)

BE1–3 Classify each item by type of business activity—operating (O), investing (I), or financing (F).
(a) _____ Cash received from customers
(b) _____ Dividends paid to shareholders
(c) _____ Common shares issued to investors

Classify items by activity. (SO 3)

(d) _____ Money borrowed from a bank
(e) _____ Purchase of an office building
(f) _____ Salaries paid

Identify business activity and effect on cash.
(SO 3)

BE1–4 For each of the following items, indicate (a) the type of business activity—operating (O), investing (I), or financing (F)—and (b) whether it increased (+), decreased (−), or had no effect (NE) on cash. The first one has been done for you as an example.

	(a) Type of Activity	(b) Cash Effect
1. Sold goods on account.	O	NE
2. Borrowed money from a bank.		
3. Purchased inventory for cash.		
4. Provided a service for cash.		
5. Paid wages in cash.		
6. Purchased a delivery truck for cash.		

Match words with descriptions.
(SO 1, 2, 3)

BE1–5 Here is a list of terms discussed in this chapter:

1. Accounts payable
2. Creditor
3. Financing activities
4. Private corporation
5. Dividends
6. Public corporation
7. Common shares
8. Accounts receivable
9. Fiscal year
10. Internal user

Match each term to the appropriate description below:
(a) _____ A company that raises money by issuing shares that are traded on a public stock exchange
(b) _____ Amounts owed to suppliers of goods
(c) _____ Someone who runs a company
(d) _____ A supplier that a company owes money to
(e) _____ Obtaining cash by borrowing money or issuing shares
(f) _____ An accounting period that is one year long
(g) _____ A company that follows Accounting Standards for Private Enterprises
(h) _____ The ownership interest of shareholders in a corporation
(i) _____ Amounts due from customers
(j) _____ Distribution of profit to shareholders

Use accounting equation.
(SO 4)

BE1–6 Use the accounting equation to determine the missing amounts below:

Assets	=	Liabilities	+	Shareholders' Equity
$75,000		(a)		$45,000
(b)		$35,000		$45,000
$90,000		$30,000		(c)

Use accounting equation.
(SO 4)

BE1–7 Use the accounting equation to answer these independent questions:
(a) The shareholders' equity of Sansom Corporation is $120,000. Its total liabilities are $55,000. What is the amount of Sansom's total assets?
(b) The liabilities of Houle Corporation are $170,000. Houle's share capital is $100,000 and its retained earnings are $90,000. What is the amount of Houle's total assets?
(c) The total assets of Pitre Limited are $150,000. Its share capital is $50,000 and its retained earnings are $25,000. What is the amount of its total liabilities?
(d) The total assets of Budovitch Inc. are $500,000 and its liabilities are equal to half its total assets. What is the amount of Budovitch's shareholders' equity?

Use accounting equation.
(SO 4)

BE1–8 At the beginning of the year, Lam Ltd. had total assets of $800,000 and total liabilities of $500,000. Use this information to answer each of the following independent parts.
(a) If Lam's total assets increased by $150,000 during the year and total liabilities decreased by $80,000, what is the amount of shareholders' equity at the end of the year?
(b) During the year, Lam's total liabilities decreased by $50,000. The company reported a profit of $50,000, sold additional shares for $75,000, and paid no dividends during the year. What is the amount of total assets at the end of the year?
(c) If Lam's total assets decreased by $80,000 during the year and shareholders' equity increased by $110,000, what is the amount of total liabilities at the end of the year?

BE1–9 Indicate which statement—income statement (IS), statement of financial position (SFP), statement of changes in equity (SCE), or statement of cash flows (SCF)—you would examine to find each of the following items:

(a) _____ Revenue earned during the year

(b) _____ Supplies on hand at the end of the year

(c) _____ Cash provided by operating activities

(d) _____ Total debt at the end of the year

(e) _____ Cash used for financing activities

(f) _____ Salaries expense for the year

(g) _____ Common shares issued during the year

Determine on which financial statement items appear.
(SO 4)

BE1–10 Indicate whether each of these items is an asset (A), a liability (L), or shareholders' equity (SE):

(a) _____ Accounts receivable

(b) _____ Salaries payable

(c) _____ Equipment

(d) _____ Office supplies

(e) _____ Common shares

(f) _____ Notes payable

(g) _____ Retained earnings

(h) _____ Cash

Identify assets, liabilities, and shareholders' equity.
(SO 4)

BE1–11 Determine whether each transaction would increase, decrease, or have no effect on each the following components found in the statement of changes in equity: share capital ($+SC$ or $-SC$), retained earnings ($+RE$ or $-RE$), total shareholders' equity ($+TSE$ or $-TSE$), or has no effect (NE) on the statement of changes in equity.

(a) _____ Profit

(b) _____ Issue of common shares

(c) _____ Repurchase of common shares

(d) _____ Dividends paid to shareholders

(e) _____ Cash

(f) _____ Loss

Determine effect of transactions on shareholders' equity.
(SO 4)

BE1–12 Identify whether a corporation that included the following statement in its financial statement package is a publicly traded corporation or a private corporation. Explain why you made the choice you did.

Determine type of corporation.
(SO 4)

CANDY CORPORATION
Statement of Retained Earnings
Year Ended April 30, 2012

Balance, May 1, 2011	$300,000
Profit	99,000
Dividends	(17,000)
Balance, April 30, 2012	$382,000

Exercises

E1–1 Roots Canada Ltd. is known around the world for its wide range of leather goods, clothing, and accessories.

Instructions

(a) Identify two internal users of Roots's accounting information. Write a question that each user might try to answer by using accounting information.

(b) Identify two external users of Roots's accounting information. Write a question that each user might try to answer by using accounting information.

Identify users and uses of accounting information.
(SO 1)

E1–2 Consider the following statements.

Identify forms of business organization.
(SO 2)

	Proprietorship	Partnership	Publicly-Traded Corporation
1. No personal liability			
2. Owner(s) pay personal income tax on company profits			
3. Generally best form of organization to raise capital			
4. Ownership indicated by shares			
5. Required to issue quarterly financial statements			
6. Owned by one person			
7. Limited life			
8. Usually easiest form of organization to set up			

Instructions

Indicate if each of the statements listed in the left-hand column of the table above is true (T) or false (F) for each of the three types of business organization: proprietorship, partnership, and a publicly traded corporation.

Identify business activity and effect on cash.
(SO 3)

E1–3   Consider the following business activities.

	(a) Type of Activity	(b) Cash Effect
1. Purchase of goods for resale	O	–
2. Purchase of equipment		
3. Borrowed money from a bank		
4. Purchase of long-term investment		
5. Sale of merchandise to customers		
6. Issue of common shares		
7. Sale of long-term investment		
8. Payment of dividends		
9. Repayment of money owed to bank		
10. Payment of interest on money borrowed from bank		

Instructions

(a) For each of the above items, indicate the type of business activity—operating (O), investing (I), or financing (F).

(b) Indicate whether each of the above items would increase (+) or decrease (−) cash. Assume all items are cash transactions. The first one has been done for you as an example.

Classify business activities.
(SO 3)

E1–4   Consider the following business activities.

	Type of Activity
1. Cash receipts from customers paying for daily ski passes	O
2. Payments made to purchase additional snow-making equipment	
3. Payments made to repair the grooming machines	
4. Receipt of funds from the bank to finance the purchase of the additional snow-making equipment	
5. Issue of shares to raise funds for a planned expansion	
6. Repayment of a portion of the loan from the bank (see #4)	
7. Payment of interest on the bank loan	
8. Payment of salaries to the employees who operate the ski lifts	
9. Receipt of a grant from the government for training a group of disabled skiers	
10. Payment of dividend to shareholders	

Instructions

Classify each of the above items by type of business activity: operating (O), investing (I), or financing (F). The first one has been done for you as an example.

Determine on which financial statement items appear.
(SO 4)

E1–5   Consider the following typical accounts and business activities.

1. _____ Cash
2. _____ Advertising expense
3. _____ Service revenue
4. _____ Common shares
5. _____ Sales
6. _____ Dividends
7. _____ Merchandise inventory
8. _____ Income tax expense
9. _____ Accounts receivable
10. _____ Interest expense
11. _____ Cash provided by operating activities
12. _____ Cash used by investing activities
13. _____ Notes payable
14. _____ Equipment
15. _____ Cash provided by financing activities

Instructions

Indicate on which statement—income statement (IS), statement of financial position (SFP), statement of changes in equity (SCE), or statement of cash flows (SCF)—you would find each of the above accounts or items.

Determine missing amounts.
(SO 4)

E1–6   Summaries of selected data from the financial statements of two corporations follow. Both companies have just completed their first year of operations:

	Lumber Inc.	Trucking Inc.
Income statement		
Total revenues	$1,000,000	$ [5]
Total expenses	[1]	250,000
Profit	150,000	50,000
Statement of changes in equity		
Total shareholders' equity, beginning of year	0	0
Issue of shares	100,000	[6]
Profit	150,000	50,000
Dividends	[2]	20,000
Total shareholders' equity, end of year	[3]	100,000

Statement of financial position

Total assets	2,000,000	500,000
Total liabilities	1,800,000	[7]
Total shareholders' equity	[4]	[8]

Instructions

Determine the missing amounts for [1] to [8]. Note that you may not be able to solve each item in numerical order.

E1–7 Summaries of selected data from the financial statements of three corporations follow:

Determine missing amounts.
(SO 4)

	Chiasson Corporation	Maxim Enterprises, Ltd.	K-Os Corporation
Beginning of year			
Total assets	$105,000	$120,000	$ [7]
Total liabilities	80,000	[4]	25,000
Total shareholders' equity	[1]	80,000	35,000
End of year			
Total assets	160,000	180,000	[8]
Total liabilities	110,000	[5]	65,000
Total shareholders' equity	[2]	110,000	[9]
Changes during year in shareholders' equity			
Issue of shares	[3]	15,000	4,000
Dividends	20,000	[6]	13,000
Total revenues	210,000	100,000	54,000
Total expenses	190,000	75,000	40,000

Instructions

Determine the missing amounts for [1] to [9].

E1–8 The following accounts and amounts (in thousands) were taken from the January 31, 2010, statement of financial position of The Forzani Group Ltd.:

Classify accounts and prepare accounting equation.
(SO 4)

_____	Accounts payable and accrued liabilities	$265,007
_____	Accounts receivable	71,544
_____	Bank indebtedness	27,932
_____	Capital assets	199,589
_____	Cash	962
_____	Goodwill and other intangibles	95,990
_____	Inventory	316,319
_____	Long-term debt	49,587
_____	Other assets	12,433
_____	Other liabilities	6,177
_____	Other shareholders' equity items	5,804
_____	Prepaid expenses	5,092
_____	Retained earnings	197,063
_____	Share capital	150,359

Instructions

(a) Classify each account as an asset (A), liability (L), or shareholders' equity (SE) item.

(b) Determine Forzani's accounting equation by calculating the amount of total assets, total liabilities, and total shareholders' equity.

E1–9 The following list of accounts, in alphabetical order, is for Aventura Inc. at November 30, 2012:

Classify accounts and prepare statement of financial position.
(SO 4)

_____	Accounts payable	$ 26,200
_____	Accounts receivable	19,500
_____	Bank loan payable	30,000
_____	Buildings	100,000
_____	Cash	20,000
_____	Common shares	20,000
_____	Equipment	30,000
_____	Income tax payable	12,000
_____	Land	50,000
_____	Merchandise inventory	18,000
_____	Mortgage payable	97,500
_____	Other payables	4,000
_____	Retained earnings	48,500
_____	Supplies	700

Instructions

(a) For each of the above accounts, identify whether it is an asset (A), liability (L), or shareholders' equity (SE) item.

(b) Prepare a statement of financial position at November 30.

Classify accounts and prepare income statement.
(SO 4)

E1–10 The following selected accounts and amounts (in millions) were taken from the February 27, 2010, financial statements of The Jean Coutu Group Inc., one of Canada's leading drugstore chains.

_____	Cost of goods sold	$2,068.9
_____	Depreciation expense	17.6
_____	Dividends	42.5
_____	Financing expenses	2.7
_____	Income tax expense	74.9
_____	Income tax payable	36.1
_____	Inventory	163.8
_____	Operating expenses	218.1
_____	Other expenses	55.2
_____	Other revenue	251.6
_____	Sales	2,298.4

Instructions

(a) For each of the above accounts, identify whether it is a revenue (R) or expense (E) or an account that is not reported on the income statement (NR).

(b) Prepare an income statement for Jean Coutu for the year ended February 27, 2010.

Prepare an income statement and statement of changes in equity.
(SO 4)

E1–11 The following information is for Kon Inc. for the year ended December 31, 2012:

Common shares, Jan. 1	$20,000
Common shares issued during year	10,000
Retained earnings, Jan. 1	58,000
Advertising expense	1,600
Dividends	5,000
Rent expense	12,400
Service revenue	61,000
Utilities expense	2,400
Salaries expense	30,000
Income tax expense	3,000

Instructions

Prepare an income statement and statement of changes in equity for the year.

Calculate profit and prepare statements of changes in equity and financial position.
(SO 4)

E1–12 Sea Surf Campground, Inc. is a public camping ground in Ocean National Park. It has the following financial information as at December 31, 2012:

Camping revenue	$168,000
Accounts payable	5,000
Bank loan payable	50,000
Cash	7,500
Equipment	119,000
Income tax expense	10,000
Dividends	12,000
Operating expenses	130,000
Supplies	2,500
Common shares, Jan. 1	30,000
Common shares issued during year	10,000
Retained earnings, Jan. 1	18,000

Instructions

(a) Determine profit for the year.

(b) Prepare a statement of changes in equity and statement of financial position for the year.

Interpret financial information.
(SO 4)

E1–13 Consider each of the following independent situations:

1. The statement of changes in equity of Yu Corporation shows dividends of $70,000, while profit for the year was $75,000.
2. The statement of cash flows for Surya Corporation shows that cash provided by operating activities was $10,000; cash used by investing activities was $100,000; and cash provided by financing activities was $120,000.

3. Naguib Ltd.'s statement of financial position reports $200,000 of total liabilities and $250,000 of shareholders' equity.
4. Rijo Inc. has total assets of $100,000 and no liabilities.

Instructions

For each company, write a brief interpretation of these financial facts. For example, you might discuss the company's financial health or what seems to be its growth philosophy.

Problems: Set A

P1-1A Financial decisions made by users often depend on one financial statement more than the others. Consider each of the following independent hypothetical situations:

Identify users and uses of financial statements.
(SO 1)

1. The South Face Inc. is considering extending credit to a new customer. The terms of the credit would require the customer to pay within 30 days of receiving goods.
2. An investor is considering purchasing the common shares of Music Online, Inc. The investor plans on holding the investment for at least five years.
3. Caisse d'Économie Base Montréal is thinking about extending a loan to a small company. The company would be required to make interest payments at the end of each month for three years, and to repay the loan at the end of the third year.
4. The chief financial officer of Tech Toy Limited is trying to determine whether the company is generating enough cash to increase the amount of dividends paid to investors in this, and future, years. He needs to be sure that Tech Toy will still have enough cash to buy equipment when needed.

Instructions

(a) Identify the key user(s) in each situation and determine whether they are internal or external users.
(b) State whether the user(s) you identified in (a) would be most interested in the income statement, statement of financial position, or statement of cash flows to make their decision. Choose only one financial statement in each case, and briefly give reasons for your choice.

P1-2A Five independent situations follow:

Determine forms of business organization.
(SO 2)

1. Three computer science professors have formed a business to expand wifi access for computers. Each has contributed an equal amount of cash and knowledge to the venture. While their plans look promising, they are concerned about the legal liabilities that their business might confront.
2. Joseph LeBlanc, a student looking for summer employment, has opened a bait shop in a small shed on a local fishing dock.
3. Robert Steven and Tom Cheng each owned a snowboard manufacturing business and have now decided to combine their businesses. They expect that in the coming year they will need funds to expand their operations.
4. Darcy Becker, Ellen Sweet, and Meg Dwyer recently graduated with business degrees, with majors in accounting. Friends since childhood, they have decided to start an accounting practice.
5. Hervé Gaudet wants to rent storage lockers in airports across the country. His idea is that customers will be able to leave their luggage at the airport if they have a long layover so they can explore the local surroundings without being burdened down with luggage. This will require the rental of space in each airport as well as hiring of employees and other operating costs.

Instructions

In each case, explain what form of organization the business is likely to take: proprietorship, partnership, private corporation, or public corporation. Give reasons for your choice.

P1-3A All businesses are involved in three types of activities: operating, investing, and financing. The names and descriptions of companies in several different industries follow:

Identify business activities.
(SO 3)

    Indigo Books & Music—book retailer
    High Liner Foods Incorporated—processor and distributor of seafood products
    Mountain Equipment Co-op—outdoor equipment retailer
    Ganong Bros. Limited—maker of candy
    Royal Bank—banking and financial service provider

Instructions

(a) For each company, provide a likely example of (1) one of its operating activities, (2) one of its investing activities, and (3) one of its financing activities.
(b) Which of the activities that you identified in (a) are common to most businesses? Which activities are not?

Classify accounts.
(SO 3, 4)

P1–4A   The following accounts have been selected from the financial statements of Maple Leaf Foods Inc.:

	(a)	(b)
Accounts payable and accrued charges	_____	_____
Accounts receivable	_____	_____
Cash	_____	_____
Common shares	_____	_____
Cost of goods sold	_____	_____
Interest expense	_____	_____
Inventories	_____	_____
Long-term debt	_____	_____
Property and equipment	_____	_____
Sales	_____	_____
Selling, general, and administrative expenses	_____	_____

Instructions
(a) Classify each account as an asset (A), liability (L), shareholders' equity (SE), revenue (R), or expense (E) item.
(b) Classify each account as being used for operating (O), investing (I), or financing (F) activities. If you believe a particular account does not fit in any of these activities, explain why.

Classify accounts.
(SO 4)

P1–5A   Slipstream Ltd. reports the following list of accounts, in alphabetical order:

	(a)	(b)
Accounts payable	_____	_____
Accounts receivable	_____	_____
Cash	_____	_____
Common shares	_____	_____
Dividends	_____	_____
Equipment	_____	_____
Income tax expense	_____	_____
Income tax payable	_____	_____
Insurance expense	_____	_____
Interest expense	_____	_____
Notes payable	_____	_____
Other payables	_____	_____
Preferred shares	_____	_____
Prepaid insurance	_____	_____
Rent expense	_____	_____
Repair and maintenance expense	_____	_____
Retained earnings	_____	_____
Salaries payable	_____	_____
Service revenue	_____	_____
Travel expense	_____	_____
Vehicles	_____	_____

Instructions
(a) Classify each account as an asset (A), liability (L), shareholders' equity (SE), revenue (R), or expense (E) item.
(b) Identify on which financial statement or statements—income statement (IS), statement of changes in equity (SCE), and/or statement of financial position (SFP)—each account would be reported.

Determine missing
amounts; answer
questions.
(SO 4)

P1–6A   Selected information (in millions) is available for Sears Canada Inc. and Canadian Tire Corporation, Limited for a recent fiscal year:

	Sears	Canadian Tire
Beginning of year		
Total assets	$ [1]	$7,784
Total liabilities	1,754	[4]
Total shareholders' equity	1,483	3,565

End of year

Total assets	3,405	[5]
Total liabilities	[2]	5,102
Total shareholders' equity	1,658	[6]
Changes during year in shareholders' equity		
Issue of shares	0	5
Dividends	0	69
Total revenues	5,201	8,687
Total expenses	[3]	8,352
Other decreases in shareholders' equity	60	148

Instructions

(a) Determine the missing amounts for [1] to [6].

(b) Which company has a higher proportion of debt financing at the end of its fiscal year? Of equity financing?

(c) Sears's year end is the last Saturday in January. Canadian Tire's year end is the last Saturday in December. How might these differing year-end dates affect your comparison in (b)?

P1–7A On June 1, 2012, One Planet Cosmetics Corp. was formed, at which time all of its opening balances were zero. Its assets, liabilities, share capital, revenues, expenses, and dividends as at June 30 follow: *Prepare financial statements.* *(SO 4)*

Cash	$ 6,000	Service revenue	$12,000
Accounts receivable	4,000	Supplies expense	1,200
Supplies	1,400	Fuel expense	800
Equipment	32,000	Advertising expense	1,500
Notes payable	14,000	Utilities expense	1,300
Accounts payable	2,300	Income tax expense	1,100
Common shares	25,000	Salaries expense	3,000
Dividends	1,000		

Instructions

(a) Prepare an income statement, statement of changes in equity, and statement of financial position for the month of June.

(b) Explain why it is necessary to prepare the financial statements in the order listed in (a).

P1–8A Selected financial information follows for Maison Corporation for the year ended December 31, 2012:   *Prepare statement of cash flows; comment on adequacy of cash.* *(SO 4)*

Cash, Jan. 1	$ 12,000
Cash dividends paid	10,000
Cash paid to purchase equipment	35,000
Cash paid to suppliers	120,000
Cash received from customers	140,000
Cash received from issue of long-term debt	20,000
Cash received from issue of shares	20,000

Instructions

(a) Prepare a statement of cash flows for Maison Corporation for the year.

(b) Comment on the adequacy of cash provided by operating activities to fund the company's investing activities and dividend payments.

P1–9A Incomplete financial statements for Baxter, Inc. follow.   *Calculate missing amounts; explain statement interrelationships.* *(SO 4)*

BAXTER, INC.
Statement of Financial Position
November 30, 2012

Assets		Liabilities and Shareholders' Equity	
Cash	$ 5,000	Liabilities	
Accounts receivable	10,000	Accounts payable	$ [3]
Land	[1]	Notes payable	50,000
Buildings	60,000	Total liabilities	84,000
Equipment	25,000	Shareholders' equity	
Total assets	$ [2]	Common shares	[4]
		Retained earnings	[5]
		Total shareholders' equity	[6]
		Total liabilities and shareholders' equity	$110,000

BAXTER, INC.
Income Statement
Year Ended November 30, 2012

Revenues	$90,000
Operating expenses	[7]
Profit before income tax	30,000
Income tax expense	6,000
Profit	$ [8]

BAXTER, INC.
Statement of Changes in Equity
Year Ended November 30, 2012

	Common Shares	Retained Earnings	Total Equity
Balance, December 1, 2011	$ 0	$ 0	$ 0
Issued common shares	12,000		[11]
Profit		[9]	[12]
Dividends		(10,000)	(10,000)
Balance, November 30, 2012	$12,000	$ [10]	$ [13]

Instructions

(a) Calculate the missing amounts for [1] to [13]. Note that you may not be able to be solve each item in numerical order.
(b) Explain (1) the sequence for preparing the financial statements, and (2) the interrelationships between the income statement, statement of changes in equity, and statement of financial position.

Prepare corrected statement of financial position; identify financial statements for ASPE.
(SO 4)

P1–10A GG Corporation was formed on July 1, 2012. It is a small private corporation, run by Guy Gélinas. On July 31, Guy prepared the following statement of financial position:

GG CORPORATION
Statement of Financial Position
July 31, 2012

Assets		Liabilities and Shareholders' Equity	
Cash	$ 20,000	Accounts payable	$ 25,000
Accounts receivable	50,000	Boat loan payable	20,000
Merchandise inventory	36,000	Common shares	59,000
Boat	24,000	Retained earnings	26,000
	$130,000		$130,000

Guy admits that his knowledge of accounting is somewhat limited and is concerned that his statement of financial position might not be correct. He gives you the following additional information:

1. The boat actually belongs to Guy Gélinas, not to GG Corporation. However, because Guy thinks he might take customers out on the boat occasionally, he decided to list it as an asset of the company. To be consistent, he also listed as a liability of the company the personal bank loan that he took out to buy the boat.
2. Included in the accounts receivable balance is $10,000 that Guy personally loaned to his brother five years ago. Guy included this in the receivables of GG Corporation so that he wouldn't forget that his brother owes him money.
3. Guy's statements didn't balance. To make them balance, he adjusted the Common Shares account until assets equalled liabilities and shareholders' equity.

Instructions

(a) Identify any corrections that should be made to the statement of financial position and explain why.
(b) Prepare a corrected statement of financial position. (*Hint*: To get the balance sheet to balance, adjust Common Shares).
(c) What other financial statements should GG Corporation prepare, assuming it follows Accounting Standards for Private Enterprises?

Problems: Set B

Identify users and uses of financial statements.
(SO 1)

P1–1B Financial decisions made by users often depend on one financial statement more than the others. Consider each of the following independent, hypothetical situations:

1. An Ontario investor is considering purchasing the common shares of Fight Fat Ltd., which operates 13 fitness centres in the Toronto area. The investor plans on holding the investment for at least three years.
2. Comeau Ltée is considering extending credit to a new customer. The terms of the credit would require the customer to pay within 45 days of receipt of the goods.

3. The chief financial officer of Private Label Corporation is trying to determine whether the company is generating enough cash to increase the amount of dividends paid to investors in this, and future, years. She needs to ensure that there will still be enough cash to expand operations when needed.

4. Drummond Bank is considering extending a loan to a small company. The company would be required to make interest payments at the end of each month for five years, and to repay the loan at the end of the fifth year.

Instructions

(a) Identify the key user(s) in each situation and determine whether they are internal or external users.

(b) State whether the user(s) you identified in (a) would be most interested in the income statement, statement of financial position, or statement of cash flows. Choose only one financial statement in each case, and briefly give reasons for your choice.

P1–2B   Five independent situations follow:

1. Dawn Addington, a student looking for summer employment, has opened a vegetable stand along a busy local highway. Each morning, she buys produce from local farmers, then sells it in the afternoon as people return home from work.

2. Joseph Counsell and Sabra Surkis each own a bike shop. They have decided to combine their businesses and try to expand their operations to include skis and snowboards. They expect that in the coming year they will need funds to expand their operations.

3. Three chemistry professors have formed a business that uses bacteria to clean up toxic waste sites. Each has contributed an equal amount of cash and knowledge to the venture. The use of bacteria in this situation is experimental, and legal obligations could result.

4. Abdur Rahim has run a successful but small cooperative health and organic food store for over five years. The increased sales at his store have made him believe that the time is right to open a chain of health and organic food stores across the country. Of course, this will require a substantial investment for inventory and property, plant, and equipment, as well as for employees and other resources. Abdur has no savings or personal assets.

5. Mary Emery, Richard Goedde, and Jigme Tshering recently graduated with law degrees. They have decided to start a law practice in their home town.

Determine forms of business organization. (SO 2)

Instructions

In each case, explain what form of organization the business is likely to take: proprietorship, partnership, private corporation, or public corporation. Give reasons for your choice.

P1–3B   All businesses are involved in three types of activities: operating, investing, and financing. The names and descriptions of companies in several different industries follow:

Identify business activities. (SO 3)

>   WestJet Airlines Ltd.—airline
>   University of Calgary Students' Union—university student union
>   Biovail Corporation—manufacturer and distributor of pharmaceutical products
>   Maple Leaf Sports & Entertainment Ltd.—owner of the Toronto Maple Leafs hockey team and Raptors basketball team
>   Grant Thornton LLP—professional accounting and business advisory firm

Instructions

(a) For each company, provide a likely example of (1) one of its operating activities, (2) one of its investing activities, and (3) one of its financing activities.

(b) Which of the activities that you identified in (a) are common to most businesses? Which activities are not?

P1–4B   Apple Inc., one of the world's top personal computing and digital media companies, details the following selected accounts in its financial statements:

Classify accounts. (SO 3, 4)

	(a)	(b)
Accounts payable		
Accounts receivable		
Cash		
Common shares		
Cost of sales		
Income tax expense		
Interest income		
Inventories		
Property, plant, and equipment		
Research and development expenses		
Sales		
Selling, general, and administrative expenses		
Short-term (trading) investments		

Instructions
(a) Classify each account as an asset (A), liability (L), shareholders' equity (SE), revenue (R), or expense (E) item.
(b) Classify each account as being used for operating (O), investing (I), or financing (F) activities. If you believe a particular account does not fit in any of these activities, explain why.

Classify accounts.
(SO 4)

P1–5B Gulfstream Inc. reports the following list of accounts, in alphabetical order:

	(a)	(b)
Accounts payable		
Accounts receivable		
Buildings		
Cash		
Common shares		
Cost of goods sold		
Dividends		
Equipment		
Income tax expense		
Income tax payable		
Interest expense		
Land		
Merchandise inventory		
Mortgage payable		
Notes payable		
Operating expenses		
Other payables		
Other revenue		
Preferred shares		
Prepaid insurance		
Retained earnings		
Salaries payable		
Sales		

Instructions
(a) Classify each account as an asset (A), liability (L), shareholders' equity (SE), revenue (R), or expense (E) item.
(b) Identify on which financial statement or statements—income statement (IS), statement of changes in equity (SCE), or statement of financial position (SFP)—each account would be reported.

Determine missing amounts; answer questions.
(SO 4)

P1–6B Selected information is available for Tim Hortons Inc. and Starbucks Corporation for a recent fiscal year:

	Tim Hortons (in CAD millions)	Starbucks (in USD millions)
Beginning of year		
Total assets	$1,993	$ [4]
Total liabilities	[1]	3,182
Total shareholders' equity	1,142	2,491
End of year		
Total assets	1,997	[5]
Total liabilities	826	2,531
Total shareholders' equity	[2]	[6]
Changes during year in shareholders' equity		
Issue (repurchase) of shares	(27)	0
Dividends	[3]	0
Total revenues	2,242	9,775
Total expenses	1,946	9,384
Other increases (decreases) in shareholders' equity	(177)	164

Instructions
(a) Determine the missing amounts for [1] to [6].
(b) Which company has the higher proportion of debt financing at the end of its fiscal year? Of equity financing?
(c) Tim Hortons' year end is the Sunday nearest to December 31. Starbucks' year end is the last Sunday in September. In addition, Tim Hortons reports its financial results in Canadian dollars and Starbucks reports in U.S. dollars. Is it appropriate to compare these two companies in (b)?

P1–7B On May 1, 2012, Aero Flying School Ltd. was formed, at which time all of its opening balances were zero. Its assets, liabilities, share capital, revenues, expenses, and dividends as at May 31 follow:

Prepare financial statements.
(SO 4)

Cash	$ 5,300	Advertising expense	$ 900
Accounts receivable	10,200	Rent expense	2,200
Equipment	60,300	Repair and maintenance expense	700
Accounts payable	2,200	Fuel expense	3,300
Bank loan payable	22,000	Insurance expense	1,400
Service revenue	12,600	Salaries expense	1,000
Interest expense	100	Income tax expense	600
Common shares	50,000	Dividends	800

Instructions
(a) Prepare an income statement, statement of changes in equity, and statement of financial position for the month of May.
(b) Explain why it is necessary to prepare the financial statements in the order listed in (a).

P1–8B Selected financial information follows for Furlotte Corporation for the year ended June 30, 2012:

Prepare statement of cash flows; comment on adequacy of cash.
(SO 4)

Cash, July 1	$ 40,000
Cash paid to suppliers	89,000
Cash paid for equipment	40,000
Repayment of long-term debt	15,000
Cash dividends paid	13,000
Cash paid for income tax	20,000
Cash received from customers	158,000

Instructions
(a) Prepare a statement of cash flows for Furlotte Corporation for the year ended June 30, 2012.
(b) Comment on the adequacy of cash provided by operating activities to fund the company's investing activities and dividend payments.

P1–9B Incomplete financial statements for Wu, Inc. follow:

Calculate missing amounts; explain statement interrelationships.
(SO 4)

WU, INC.
Statement of Financial Position
August 31, 2012

Assets		Liabilities and Shareholders' Equity	
Cash	$ [1]	Liabilities	
Accounts receivable	15,000	Accounts payable	$19,000
Land	20,000	Shareholders' equity	
Buildings	40,000	Common shares	[3]
Equipment	5,000	Retained earnings	[4]
Total assets	$ [2]	Total liabilities and shareholders' equity	$85,000

WU, INC.
Income Statement
Year Ended August 31, 2012

Service revenue	$85,000
Operating expenses	[5]
Profit before income tax	35,000
Income tax expense	9,000
Profit	$ [6]

WU, INC.
Statement of Changes in Equity
Year Ended August 31, 2012

	Common Shares	Retained Earnings	Total Equity
Balance, September 1, 2011	$25,000	$20,000	$ [9]
Issued common shares	10,000		[10]
Profit		[7]	[11]
Dividends		[8]	[12]
Balance, August 31, 2012	$35,000	$31,000	$[13]

Instructions

(a) Calculate the missing amounts [1] to [13]. Note that you may not be able to be solve each item in numerical order.

(b) Explain (1) the sequence for preparing and presenting the financial statements, and (2) the interrelationships between the income statement, statement of changes in equity, and statement of financial position.

Prepare corrected statement of financial position; identify financial statements for ASPE.
(SO 4)

P1–10B   The Independent Book Shop Ltd. was formed on April 1, 2012. It is a small private corporation, run by Joanna Kay. On April 30, Joanna prepared the following income statement:

INDEPENDENT BOOK SHOP LTD.
Income Statement
Month Ended April 30, 2012

Revenues		
Accounts receivable	$23,000	
Service revenue	41,000	
Total revenues		$64,000
Expenses		
Rent expense	$12,000	
Insurance expense	5,000	
Vacation expense	4,000	
Total expenses		21,000
Profit before income tax		85,000
Income tax expense		10,000
Profit		$95,000

Joanna admits that her knowledge of accounting is somewhat limited and is concerned that her income statement might not be correct. She gives you the following additional information:

1. Included in the Service Revenue account is $3,000 of revenue that the company expects to earn in June 2012. Joanna included it in this year's statement so she wouldn't forget about it.

2. Joanna operates her business in a converted carriage house attached to her parents' downtown home. They do not charge her anything for the use of this building, but she thinks that if she paid rent it would have cost her about $12,000 a year. She included this amount in the income statement as Rent Expense because of the "opportunity cost."

3. To reward herself after a year of hard work, Joanna took a vacation to Greece. She used personal funds to pay for the trip, but she reported it as an expense on the income statement since it was her job that made her need the vacation.

Instructions

(a) Identify any corrections that should be made to the income statement and explain why.

(b) Prepare a corrected income statement.

(c) What other financial statements should the Independent Book Shop Ltd. prepare, assuming it follows Accounting Standards for Private Enterprises?

Broadening Your Perspective

Financial Reporting and Analysis Cases

Financial Reporting: *Eastplats*

Answer questions about financial statements.
(SO 4)

BYP1–1   Actual financial statements (rather than the simplified financial statements presented in the chapter) for Eastern Platinum Limited (Eastplats) are presented in Appendix A at the end of this book.

Instructions

(a) How many pages are there in Eastplats's financial statements?

(b) What are the five financial statements that Eastplats includes in its annual report? Which ones were discussed in this chapter?

(c) Look at Eastplats's statement of financial position and identify its total assets, total liabilities, and total shareholders' equity as at (1) December 31, 2010, and (2) December 31, 2009.

(d) How much cash did Eastplats have at December 31, 2010? At December 31, 2009? Which financial statement(s) did you look at to answer this question?

(e) Look at Eastplats's income statement. Did its revenue increase or decrease between the years ended December 31, 2009 and 2010? Did its profit increase or decrease between the two years? Are its revenue and profit moving in the same direction (i.e., both increasing or both decreasing)? If not, explain why not.

(f) Look at Eastplats's statement of cash flows. How much cash did it generate from, or use for, operating activities in 2010? In 2009? Was this amount enough to cover Eastplats's investing activities in either year? (Note that Eastplats presents the operating activities section of its statement of cash flows differently than how this section was presented in the chapter. We will learn more about this in Chapter 13.)

Comparative Analysis: *Eastplats and Amplats*

BYP1–2 The financial statements of Anglo American Platinum Limited (Amplats) are presented in Appendix B following the financial statements for Eastern Platinum Limited (Eastplats) in Appendix A.

Compare financial statements. (SO 4)

Instructions

(a) Based on the information in these financial statements, determine the following for each company (in U.S. dollars for Eastplats and in the South African Rand for Amplats):
   1. Total assets, liabilities, and shareholders' equity at December 31, 2010 and 2009
   2. Revenue (use net sales revenue for Amplats) and profit for the years ended December 31, 2010 and 2009

(b) Calculate the percentage change between 2009 and 2010 for each company for the assets, liabilities, shareholders' equity, revenue and profit amounts determined in (a).

(c) What conclusions about the two companies can you draw from the data you determined in (b)?

Interpreting Financial Information

BYP1–3 Zachary Wall is thinking about expanding the product offerings in his company's automotive supply store. He would like to include tires. In deciding which product lines to carry, Zachary knows that it is important to consider many factors, including quality, performance rating, price, and warranty. However, he is also interested in investigating the financial health of the tire manufacturers and has obtained recent financial statements for The Goodyear Tire & Rubber Company ("Goodyear") and Compagnie Générale des Établissements Michelin ("Michelin").

Compare financial information from two different countries. (SO 1, 4)

As it turns out, however, Zachary is having trouble comparing the two companies' financial results. Goodyear's headquarters are in Ohio, and it reports its financial results in U.S. dollars. Michelin's headquarters are located in Clermont-Ferrand, France, and its financial statements are in euros. In addition, Michelin has ordered the accounts in its statement of financial position differently than Goodyear. Zachary is not sure how to read Michelin's statement of financial position. "I had no idea that there was more than one way to prepare a statement of financial position. How can this be useful to people outside the company?"

Instructions

(a) Who are the external users of accounting information?

(b) Zachary understands that the purpose of accounting is to provide information for decision-making. He understands that currencies change from country to country (e.g., Canadian dollars, U.S. dollars, euros), but he would like to know whether you think that basic decision-making also changes from country to country.

(c) Will Zachary be able to find the information he needs about the different tires' quality, performance rating, price, and warranty in the financial statements? If not, where might he find such information?

(d) Zachary is having difficulty comparing Michelin's statement of financial position to Goodyear's because of the different ordering used by each company in its statement. Explain to Zachary whether he should be able to compare the two statements despite their ordering.

Comparing IFRS and ASPE

BYP1–4 In Canada, accounting standards have been tailored to meet the needs of a diverse array of companies. In some sectors, companies are able to choose which set of accounting standards best suits their needs. In other sectors, such as publicly traded companies, they have no choice and are required to adopt International Financial Reporting Standards (IFRS).

Distinguish between private and public companies. (SO 1, 2)

Private companies are given a choice, and must decide which "Canadian GAAP" best meets their needs and those of their users. Private companies have a choice of two sets of accounting standards: Accounting Standards for Private Enterprises (ASPE) or IFRS.

Instructions

(a) What is the key difference between private and public companies?

(b) Who are the key users of public company financial statements? Who are the key users of private company financial statements?

(c) What is the key difference between users of private company financial statements and users of public company financial statements?

(d) Why do you think public companies do not have a choice regarding which accounting standards they use?

(e) Why do you think private companies do have a choice regarding the accounting standards they use?

Critical Thinking Cases and Activities

Collaborative Learning Activity

Identify financial and non-financial information used by sales managers.
(SO 1, 4)

BYP1–5   Financial statements aim to provide reliable information to a diverse group of users. Information must be enough for internal and external users to make decisions, but not so much that a company reveals its operating processes and competitive advantage to external users.

Instructions
With the class divided into groups, answer the following questions as if you were a regional sales manager for Metro Inc.:
(a) What information is contained in the company's financial statements that is important to the position of sales manager? Consider both a short-term and a long-term perspective in your answer.
(b) Identify several types of information that are not included in the financial statements that sales managers would use to carry out their responsibilities.

Communication Activity

Compare forms of business organization.
(SO 2)

BYP1–6   Your favourite aunt has recently passed away and left you an unexpected inheritance. You would like to open a business with the money she left you but are not quite sure which form of business organization to choose.

Instructions
(a) Identify a business that you would like to start if you received an inheritance from your aunt.
(b) Discuss the advantages and disadvantages of each form of business organization—proprietorship, partnership, private corporation, public corporation—for the type of business you identified in (a).
(c) Given the advantages and disadvantages you identified in (b), state which form of business organization you chose for your business.

Ethics Case

Discuss certification of financial statements.
(SO 1)

BYP1–7   Chief executive officers (CEOs) and chief financial officers (CFOs) of publicly traded companies are required to personally certify that their companies' financial statements and other financial information contain no untrue statements and do not leave out any important facts. Khan Corporation just hired a new management team, and its members say they are too new to the company to know whether the most recent financial reports are accurate or not. They refuse to sign the certification.

Instructions
(a) Who are the stakeholders in this situation?
(b) Should the CEO and CFO sign the certification? Explain why or why not.
(c) What are the CEO's and CFO's alternatives?

"All About You" Activity

Describe the key elements of a personal annual report.
(SO 4)

BYP1–8   Every company needs to plan in order to move forward. Its top management must consider where it wants the company to be in three to five years. Like a company, you need to think about where you want to be in three to five years and you need to start taking steps now in order to get there. With some forethought, you can help yourself avoid a bad resumé, like the one described in the "All About You" feature in this chapter.

Instructions
(a) Where would you like to be working in three to five years? Describe your plan for getting there by identifying specific steps that you need to take.
(b) In order to get the job you want, you will need a resumé. Your resumé is the equivalent of a company's annual report. It needs to provide relevant and reliable information about your past and accomplishments so that employers can decide whether to "invest" in you. Do a search on the Internet to find a good resumé format. What are the basic elements of a resumé?
(c) A company's annual report provides information about its accomplishments. In order for investors to use the annual report, the information must be reliable; that is, users must have faith that the information is accurate and believable. How can you provide assurance that the information on your resumé is reliable?

Serial Case

Identify form of business organization and accounting information.
(SO 1, 2, 3)

BYP1–9   As part of the requirements of her university entrepreneurship program, Natalie Koebel had been operating "Cookie Creations," a proprietorship, on a part-time basis. The purpose of Cookie Creations was to provide lessons to whoever wished to learn how to make cookies. For the most part, these lessons took place in people's homes, schools, and community centres. Natalie provided all of the ingredients and utensils required to make cookies. As Natalie approaches her graduation from university, she is considering other opportunities available in addition to operating Cookie Creations.

Natalie's parents, Janet and Brian Koebel, have been operating Koebel's Family Bakery Ltd., a private corporation, for a number of years. They have been overwhelmed with the demand for cupcakes. They have recently negotiated a contract with a national coffee shop to provide cupcakes on a weekly basis.

In anticipation of Natalie graduating, and in hope of spending a little more time away from the bakery, they have discussed with Natalie the possibility of her becoming one of the shareholders of Koebel's Family Bakery Ltd. In addition, Natalie would assume the full-time responsibility of administrator. Natalie could continue to provide cookie-making lessons; however, that would be done by Koebel's Family Bakery in future rather than by Natalie personally.

This **serial case** starts in this chapter and continues in each chapter of the book.

Instructions

(a) Discuss the benefits and weaknesses of each of these two forms of business organization, Cookie Creations and Koebel's Family Bakery Ltd.

(b) What form of generally accepted accounting principles do you anticipate each of these business organizations is using? Explain.

(c) As Koebel's Family Bakery begins to meet the demands of its new contractual commitment with the national coffee shop, what accounting information will Natalie need as administrator, and why? How often will she need this information?

(d) What types of users do you anticipate will use Koebel's Family Bakery's accounting information? What information will these users require?

Answers to Self-Test Questions

1. b	2. d	3. d	4. d	5. b
6. c	7. d	8. c	9. d	10. a

Remember to go back to the beginning of the chapter to check off your completed work!

←

CHAPTER 2

A Further Look at Financial Statements

study objectives

After studying this chapter, you should be able to:

1. Identify the sections of a classified statement of financial position.
2. Identify and calculate ratios for analyzing a company's liquidity, solvency, and profitability.
3. Describe the framework for the preparation and presentation of financial statements.

the navigator

Real Values and International Standards

INSIDE CHAPTER

2

- Presentation of financial statements (p. 61)
- Canada's debt to assets ratio worst in OECD (p. 66)
- Getting the numbers right (p. 72)
- Your personal statement of financial position (p. 78)

As of January 1, 2011, all public companies in Canada prepare their financial statements according to International Financial Reporting Standards (IFRS). The decision to adopt IFRS was the result of a long consultation and deliberation process on the part of the Accounting Standards Board (AcSB). "The role of accounting in the allocation of capital was the underlying driving force for the Board's decision to adopt IFRS for publicly accountable companies in Canada," says Tricia O'Malley, past Chair of the AcSB.

Like any new development, the transition to IFRS involved a lot of work and additional cost. For Plazacorp Retail Properties Ltd., the owner of shopping malls and strip plazas throughout Atlantic Canada, Quebec, and Ontario, the transition first involved getting up to speed on the significant differences between Canadian generally accepted accounting principles (GAAP) and IFRS. "Then we got an understanding of what differences were relevant to Plazacorp," says Plazacorp's Chief Financial Officer, Floriana Cipollone.

Plazacorp came up with a plan of action and prepared a timeline to tackle the IFRS change-over project since it involved not only accounting but also many of its systems and processes, including agreements with lenders and customers. The changeover plan and IFRS differences for Plazacorp were communicated regularly to the audit committee and board of directors.

One significant change for Plazacorp was that, under Canadian GAAP before the 2011 changeover to IFRS, real estate companies reported their income-producing properties (real estate assets) at historical cost in their financial statements. However, under IFRS, companies have to disclose the fair value of these assets; that is, the price they can be sold for today. "The most difficult transition issue for us has been the valuation of income-producing properties," Ms. Cipollone confirms. "This involved determining a whole process behind how best to come up with those auditable figures on a regular basis."

The benefit of the transition to IFRS for Plazacorp is the disclosure of the fair value of its income-producing properties, which Ms. Cipollone says is a more relevant measure. "Equity analysts had been calculating this for the real estate companies that they covered anyway," she points out. "Now, fair value will either be on the statement of financial position or in a note to the financial statements for real estate companies."

The move to IFRS will also improve Canadian companies' access to capital markets and hopefully lower their cost of doing business internationally. "It removed an impediment for Canadian companies to be considered by global investors," says Ms. O'Malley. After the initial transition costs, global companies will save money by having to prepare financial statements using only one set of standards.

While public companies must follow IFRS, private companies have the option of following Accounting Standards for Private Enterprises (ASPE) set by the AcSB instead. "Every time IFRS change, we'll have to think about whether, and if so how, the private enterprise standards should change," Ms. O'Malley explains. For its private enterprise standards, the AcSB will issue a single set of amendments encompassing all the changes necessary every couple of years. She stresses that, because the two sets of standards are built on the same conceptual framework, the fundamental differences between them are minimal.

the navigator

It has been a tumultuous time for companies, as well as for investors, lenders, and other creditors, over the last few years of significant accounting standard changes. Because of this, understanding the information reported in financial statements—whether prepared using Canadian generally accepted accounting principles in use until January 1, 2011, or prepared using IFRS or ASPE in use after January 1, 2011—is more important than ever before for decision makers.

In this chapter, we take a closer look at the statement of financial position and introduce some useful ways for evaluating the information provided by the financial statements. We also examine the financial reporting concepts underlying the preparation and presentation of financial statements, including those used by publicly accountable enterprises such as Plazacorp discussed in our feature story, as well as those used by private companies.

This chapter is organized as follows:

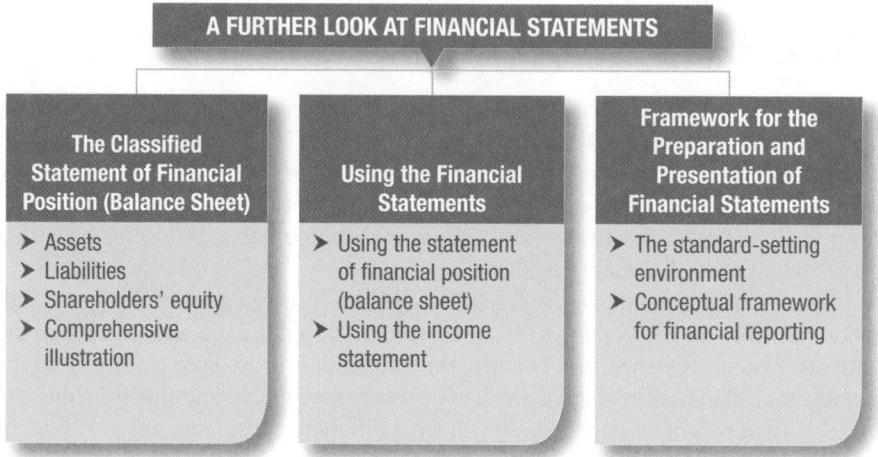

The Classified Statement of Financial Position (Balance Sheet)

STUDY OBJECTIVE 1
Identify the sections of a classified statement of financial position.

In Chapter 1, we introduced four financial statements: the statement of financial position, income statement, statement of changes in equity, and statement of cash flows. In this section, we will look at the statement of financial position in more detail and introduce standard statement classifications.

The statement of financial position, also commonly known as the balance sheet, presents a snapshot of a company's financial position—its assets, liabilities, and shareholders' equity—at a point in time. In Chapter 1, individual asset, liability, and equity items were listed in no particular order in the statement of financial position. To improve users' understanding of a company's financial position, companies group similar types of assets and similar types of liabilities together. A classified statement of financial position generally contains the standard classifications, ordered as shown in Illustration 2-1.

▶Illustration 2-1

Statement of financial position classifications

Assets	Liabilities and Shareholders' Equity
Current assets	Current liabilities
Investments	Non-current liabilities
Property, plant, and equipment	Shareholders' equity
Intangible assets	Share capital
Goodwill	Retained earnings

These classifications or groupings help readers determine such things as (1) whether the company has enough assets to pay its debts as they come due and (2) the claims of short- and long-term creditors and lenders on the company's total assets. The classifications can be ordered as shown in

Illustration 2-1 or in reverse order. In the sections that follow, we explain each of these classifications and ordering possibilities.

ASSETS

Assets are the resources that a company owns or controls that will provide future economic benefits. Assets include those resources whose benefits will be realized within one year (current assets) and those resources whose benefits will be realized over more than one year (non-current assets).

Current Assets

Current assets are assets that are expected to be converted into cash or will be sold or used up within one year of the company's financial statement date or its operating cycle, whichever is longer.

The **operating cycle** of a company is the average time it takes to go from cash to cash in producing revenue. In a merchandising business, this means the time it takes to purchase inventory, pay cash to suppliers, sell the inventory on account, and then collect cash from customers. Or, in a service business, the time it takes to pay employees, provide services on account, and then collect the cash from customers. For most businesses, the operating cycle is less than a year. But for some businesses, such as vineyards or airplane manufacturers, the operating cycle is longer than a year. For the purposes of this textbook, we will assume companies use one year to determine whether an asset is current or non-current.

Common types of current assets include:

1. Cash
2. Short-term investments
3. Accounts receivable
4. Accrued receivables
5. Notes receivable, including loans receivable
6. Merchandise inventory
7. Supplies
8. Prepaid expenses

You are already familiar with cash. We will briefly discuss each of the other common types of current assets in the above list. **Short-term investments** are investments in debt securities (e.g., bonds of another company) or equity securities (e.g., shares of another company) that are held in hopes of generating interest income and/or gains from profitable resale in the near term. These are commonly known as trading investments, which we will learn more about in Chapter 13.

Accounts receivable are amounts owed to the company by customers who purchased products or services on credit (on account). **Accrued receivables** are amounts owed to the company for interest, sales tax, rent, and like items. We will learn more about accrued receivables in Chapter 4. These and other types of receivables represent revenues earned by the company that have not yet been received in cash.

Notes receivable are amounts owed to the company by customers or others that are supported by a written promise to repay. Loans receivable are a type of note receivable. **Inventory** refers to goods held for sale to customers. This can include both "finished" and "unfinished" goods. As we saw in the case of Eastplats in Chapter 1, ore (an unfinished good) is part of its inventory and will remain so until it is processed to become a finished good. Inventory is a current asset because it will be sold and converted to cash or accounts receivable during the year. For merchandising companies like Canadian Tire, inventory consists only of finished goods such as automotive, sporting, and household goods, all ready for sale to customers, and its inventory is normally referred to as merchandise inventory.

Supplies include consumable items like office supplies (e.g., paper, toner, pens) and cleaning supplies. They are a current asset because we expect that these will be used up by the business within the year. **Prepaid expenses** represent the cost of things like rent and insurance paid in advance of use. They are current assets because they reflect unused benefits available for use during the year.

While total current assets must be disclosed, there is no prescribed order for current assets to be presented on the statement of financial position. North American companies normally list current assets in the order in which they are expected to be converted into cash; that is, in their order of liquidity. Some international companies list current assets in the reverse order of liquidity.

Current assets are shown in a simplified Illustration 2-2 for Empire Company Limited. Note that Empire calls its statement of financial position "balance sheet," as do many companies.

▶Illustration 2-2
Current assets section

EMPIRE COMPANY LIMITED Balance Sheet (partial) May 7, 2011 (in millions)	
Current assets	
Cash and cash equivalents	$ 616.9
Accounts receivable	346.6
Income tax recoverable	0.3
Inventories	906.1
Prepaid expenses	75.2
Loans and other receivables	81.7
Total current assets	2,026.8

We have already learned about most of these accounts in Chapter 1, except for "cash equivalents," which is a new term. Cash equivalents are very liquid investments in debt securities that can be easily converted into cash.

Non-Current Assets

Alternative Terminology
The terms *non-current* and *long-term* are used interchangeably in this text.

Non-current assets are not expected to be converted into cash, sold, or used up by the business within one year of the financial statement date or its operating cycle. In other words, non-current assets are everything that is not classified as a current asset.

Common types of non-current assets include:

1. Investments
2. Property, plant, and equipment
3. Intangible assets and goodwill
4. Other assets

Long-term investments include (1) multi-year investments in debt securities (e.g., loans, notes, bonds, or mortgages) that management intends to hold to earn interest, and (2) equity securities (e.g., shares) of other companies that management plans to hold for many years to generate investment revenue or for strategic reasons. These assets are classified as long-term because they are not readily marketable or expected to be converted into cash within one year. Often, long-term investments are referred to only as *investments*. If the word "investment" is used without any modifier (short- or long-term), it is assumed to be long-term. We will learn more about both short- and long-term investments in Chapter 12.

Research In Motion® reports only long-term debt investments in the partial statement of financial position shown in Illustration 2-3. In the notes to the financial statements, it describes these investments as consisting of commercial paper, treasury bills, government notes, corporate notes and bonds, asset-backed securities, as well as other types of investments.

▶Illustration 2-3
Investments section

RESEARCH IN MOTION LIMITED Balance Sheet (partial) February 27, 2010 (in USD thousands)	
Long-term investments	$958,248

Alternative Terminology
Property, plant, and equipment are sometimes called *capital assets* or *fixed assets.*

Property, plant, and equipment are tangible assets with relatively long useful lives that are currently being used in operating the business. This category includes land, buildings, equipment, and furniture.

Although the order of property, plant, and equipment items can vary among companies, these items are normally listed in the statement of financial position in their order of permanency. That is, land is usually listed first as it has an indefinite life, and is followed by the asset with the next longest useful life, normally buildings, and so on.

Most companies record their property, plant, and equipment at cost. However, as was mentioned in the feature story, some companies may choose to record these assets at fair value instead. This is known as the **revaluation model**. This is prevalent in the real estate industry but seldom applied by other industries. We will discuss the revaluation model in Chapter 9, but until then, we will assume the use of cost unless otherwise indicated.

Property, plant, and equipment, except land, have estimated useful lives over which they are expected to generate revenues. Because these assets benefit future periods, their cost is allocated over their estimated useful lives through a process called **depreciation**. Companies calculate depreciation by systematically assigning a portion of the asset's cost to expense each year (rather than expensing the full cost in the year the asset was purchased). We will learn how to calculate depreciation in Chapters 4 and 9.

Only assets with estimated useful lives are depreciated. Land also generates revenue, but its estimated useful life is considered to be infinite as land does not usually wear out or lose its value. Consequently, the cost of land is never depreciated.

Assets that are depreciated should be reported on the statement of financial position at cost less their accumulated depreciation. Accumulated depreciation shows the amount of depreciation taken so far over the *life of the asset*. It is a **contra asset account**; that is, its balance is subtracted from the balance of the asset that it relates to. The difference between cost and accumulated depreciation is referred to as the **carrying amount**, also commonly known as net book value or just simply book value.

Clothing retailer Reitmans details its property, plant, and equipment—which it calls property and equipment as it doesn't have a plant—as shown in Illustration 2-4. Reitmans uses the term *net book value* rather than *carrying amount* here, as do many companies. Note that, except for land, all of Reitmans' property and equipment are depreciated. This includes leasehold improvements, which are long-lived additions or renovations made to leased property that Reitmans rents in large shopping centres.

> Illustration 2-4
> Property, plant, and equipment section

REITMANS (CANADA) LIMITED
Balance Sheet (partial)
January 30, 2010
(in thousands)

	Cost	Accumulated Depreciation	Net Book Value
Property and equipment			
Land	$ 5,935		$ 5,935
Buildings and improvements	52,336	$ 19,499	32,837
Fixtures and equipment	177,874	97,398	80,476
Leasehold improvements	194,782	103,418	91,364
	$430,927	$220,315	$210,612

Many companies have assets that cannot be seen but are valuable. **Intangible assets** are non-current assets that do not have physical substance and that represent a privilege or a right granted to, or held by, a company. Examples of intangible assets include patents, copyrights, franchises, trademarks, trade names, and licences that give the company an exclusive right of use for a specified period of time.

Intangible assets are normally divided into two groups for accounting purposes: those with definite lives and those with indefinite lives. Similar to buildings and equipment, the cost of intangible assets with definite useful lives is allocated over these future periods. Similar to land, the cost of intangible assets with indefinite lives is not allocated over future periods.

IFRS for publicly traded companies recommends the use of the term *depreciation* to refer to the allocation of cost over the useful lives of depreciable property, plant, and equipment and the term *amortization* to refer to the allocation of the cost of certain kinds of intangible assets. In contrast, Accounting Standards for Private Enterprises recommend the use of the term *amortization* to allocate the cost of both property, plant, and equipment and intangible assets. To complicate matters further, some publicly traded companies use the terms *depreciation* and *amortization* interchangeably. We will learn more about both tangible and intangible assets in Chapter 9.

ASPE

An asset that is similar to an intangible asset and is usually discussed along with intangibles is goodwill. Goodwill results from the acquisition of another company when the price paid for the company is higher than the fair value of the purchased company's net identifiable assets. Goodwill is a calculated amount—simply the difference between the price paid for and the fair value of the assets acquired of the purchased company.

Goodwill is similar to intangible assets in that it has no physical substance but will generate future value. It differs from intangible assets in that it cannot be separated from the company and sold—it is determined in relation to the acquired company as a whole. The only way it can be sold is to sell the acquired company. Goodwill is not amortized and is reported separately from other intangibles.

Illustration 2-5 shows how Shaw Communications reports its intangible assets, which consist of broadcast rights, licences to use telecommunications spectrum, and goodwill.

Illustration 2-5
Intangible assets and goodwill section

SHAW COMMUNICATIONS INC.
Balance Sheet (partial)
August 31, 2010
(in thousands)

SHAW)

Intangibles	
Broadcast rights	$5,061,153
Spectrum licenses	190,912
Goodwill	169,143
Other intangibles	156,469

Alternative Terminology
Deferred income tax is also called *future income tax*.

Some companies also report other types of assets that don't fit neatly into any of the above classifications. These can include non-current receivables, deferred income tax assets, and property held for sale, among many other items. Deferred income tax assets represent the income tax that is expected to be recovered in a later year or years due to deductions that a company is able to take when preparing its *future* corporate income return.

Other assets are usually separately reported so that users can get a better idea of their nature and are accompanied by an explanatory note to the financial statements. Because these types of assets vary widely in practice, they are not illustrated here.

LIABILITIES

Liabilities are obligations that result from past transactions. Similar to assets, they are also classified as current (due within one year) and non-current (due after more than one year).

Current Liabilities

Current liabilities are obligations that are to be paid or settled within one year of the company's statement date or its operating cycle, whichever is longer. As with current assets, companies use a period longer than one year if their operating cycle is longer than one year. For the purposes of this textbook, we will assume an operating cycle equal to, or shorter than, one year.

Common examples of current liabilities include:

1. Bank indebtedness
2. Accounts payable
3. Accrued liabilities
4. Notes payable, including bank loans payable
5. Current maturities of long-term debt

You may recall from Chapter 1 that **bank indebtedness** is a short-term loan from a bank, typically occurring when a company uses an operating line of credit to cover cash shortfalls. **Accounts payable** represents amounts owed by the company to suppliers for purchases made on credit (account). **Accrued liabilities** are amounts owed by the company for salaries, interest, sales tax, rent, income tax, and like items. We will learn more about accrued liabilities in Chapter 4.

These and other types of receivables represent expenses incurred by the company that have not yet been paid in cash.

Notes payable are amounts owed, often to banks but also to suppliers or others, that are supported by a written promise to repay. Amounts owed to banks are usually known as bank loans payable. It is common to refer to notes and loans interchangeably, and we will do so in this text. Notes can be current or non-current. When a company has a non-current or long-term note or loan payable (for example, a five-year bank loan), a portion of the loan is often repayable each year. The portion of the payment due to be made within the current year is classified as **current maturities of long-term debt**. The remainder of the loan is classified as a non-current liability.

Similar to current assets, North American companies often list current liabilities in the order in which they are expected to be paid; that is, in their order of liquidity by due date. However, for many companies, the items in the current liabilities section are arranged according to an internal company custom rather than a prescribed rule. And some international companies list current liabilities in a reverse order of liquidity, similar to current assets.

The current liabilities section from the statement of financial position of Sears Canada is shown in Illustration 2-6.

Illustration 2-6
Current liabilities section

SEARS CANADA INC. Statement of Financial Position (partial) January 30, 2010 (in millions)	
Current liabilities	
Accounts payable	$ 647.7
Accrued liabilities	342.1
Income and other taxes payable	72.7
Principal payments on long-term obligations due within one year	314.2
Total current liabilities	1,376.7

Users of financial statements look closely at the relationship between current assets and current liabilities. This relationship is important in evaluating a company's ability to pay its current liabilities. We will talk more about this later in the chapter when we learn how to use the information in the statement of financial position.

Non-Current Liabilities

Obligations that are expected to be paid or settled after one year are classified as **non-current liabilities**, or, as they are commonly known, long-term liabilities.

Examples of non-current liabilities include:

1. Notes payable, including bank loans payable, mortgages payable, and bonds payable
2. Lease obligations
3. Pension and benefit obligations
4. Deferred income tax liabilities

We discussed notes payable in the current liability section above. **Mortgages payable** are similar to long-term notes but have property (e.g., a house or a building) pledged as security for the loan. **Bonds payable** are used by large corporations and governments to borrow large sums of money. **Lease obligations** include amounts to be paid in the future on long-term rental contracts used for equipment or other property. **Pension and benefit obligations** are amounts companies owe past and current employees for retirement benefits. **Deferred income tax liabilities** represent income tax that is expected to be payable in a later year or years when a company prepares its *future* corporate income return.

Non-current liabilities reported in the statement of financial position are normally accompanied by extensive notes to the financial statements, which include the nature of the obligation and other relevant details. For example, disclosure for long-term mortgages payable would include the maturity date, interest rate, and any security pledged to support it. Non-current liabilities will be discussed in detail in Chapter 10.

In Illustration 2-7, TELUS reported non-current liabilities, which it calls long-term liabilities, of $7,449 million on a recent statement of financial position. There is no generally prescribed order for reporting non-current liabilities.

▶ Illustration 2-7
Non-current liabilities section

TELUS CORPORATION Statement of Financial Position (partial) December 31, 2010 (in millions)	🎵 TELUS·
Long-term liabilities	
Long-term debt	$5,313
Other long-term liabilities	638
Future income taxes	1,498
	7,449

Additional detail about its liabilities was reported by TELUS in the notes to its financial statements. There it indicated that its long-term debt consisted of notes, commercial paper, debentures, and bonds, and it gave details about the amounts, interest rates, and maturity dates. Its other long-term liabilities comprise liabilities for pensions and post-retirement benefits, as well as other items.

SHAREHOLDERS' EQUITY

Shareholders' equity is divided into two parts: share capital and retained earnings. For some companies, there may also be other parts to this section, such as accumulated other comprehensive income. We will learn more about comprehensive income in later chapters.

Share Capital

Alternative Terminology
Share capital is also commonly known as *capital stock*.

As we learned in Chapter 1, shareholders purchase shares in a company by investing cash (or other assets). These investments are recorded as either common or preferred shares. If preferred shares are issued in addition to common shares, the total of all classes of shares issued is classified as, or titled, **share capital**. Quite often, companies only have one class of shares and the title is simply common shares.

Retained Earnings

The cumulative profits that have been retained for use in a company are known as **retained earnings**. Recall from Chapter 1 that the changes during the year (or period) to both share capital and retained earnings are detailed on the statement of changes in equity. The ending balances of share capital and retained earnings, determined on the statement of changes in equity, are combined and reported as shareholders' equity on the statement of financial position.

The shareholders' equity section of Danier Leather's statement of financial position (balance sheet) is shown in Illustration 2-8. In addition to share capital and retained earnings, Danier Leather also reports contributed surplus. Contributed surplus arises from the sale of shares; we will learn more about it in Chapter 11.

▶ Illustration 2-8
Shareholders' equity section

DANIER LEATHER INC. Balance Sheet (partial) June 26, 2010 (in thousands)	DANIER LEAVE ORDINARY BEHIND™
Shareholders' equity	
Share capital	$14,176
Contributed surplus	1,106
Retained earnings	39,539
	54,821

COMPREHENSIVE ILLUSTRATION

All of the standard classifications discussed above are illustrated in a comprehensive statement of financial position for a hypothetical company called Frenette Corporation in Illustration 2-9.

▶ Illustration 2-9
Classified statement of financial position in order of liquidity

FRENETTE CORPORATION
Statement of Financial Position
October 31, 2012

Assets

Current assets			
Cash		$ 6,600	
Short-term investments		2,000	
Accounts receivable		7,000	
Merchandise inventory		4,000	
Supplies		2,100	
Prepaid insurance		400	
Total current assets			$ 22,100
Long-term investments			
Debt investment		$ 2,000	
Equity investment		5,200	
Total long-term investments			7,200
Property, plant, and equipment			
Land		$40,000	
Buildings	$75,000		
Less: Accumulated depreciation	15,000	60,000	
Equipment	$24,000		
Less: Accumulated depreciation	5,000	19,000	
Total property, plant, and equipment			119,000
Goodwill			3,100
Total assets			$151,400

Liabilities and Shareholders' Equity

Liabilities			
Current liabilities			
Accounts payable		$ 2,100	
Salaries payable		1,600	
Interest payable		450	
Unearned revenue		900	
Bank loan payable		11,000	
Current portion of mortgage payable		1,000	
Total current liabilities			$ 17,050
Non-current liabilities			
Mortgage payable		$10,300	
Total non-current liabilities			10,300
Total liabilities			27,350
Shareholders' equity			
Common shares		$74,000	
Retained earnings		50,050	
Total shareholders' equity			124,050
Total liabilities and shareholders' equity			$151,400

Illustration 2-9 uses the common practice among North American companies of classifying the items on the statement of financial position in order of liquidity (from the most to the least liquid). Accounting standards do not prescribe the order in which items are presented in the statement of financial position. As was mentioned earlier in the chapter, international companies often present items in this statement using a reverse order of liquidity. Some Canadian companies, especially financial institutions and real estate companies, use this reverse-liquidity order format as well.

Statements prepared using a reverse-liquidity order usually show assets first, followed by shareholders' equity and liabilities. The assets section starts with non-current assets, followed by current assets. Non-current assets include goodwill and intangible assets; property, plant, and equipment; and long-term investments, which are normally grouped under a non-current heading. This differs from the separate disclosure of non-current assets without a heading that is more usual in North America, as we saw in Illustration 2-9. Within the current assets section, items are listed in reverse order of liquidity; that is, cash is normally shown last. Items within the property, plant, and equipment section are normally listed in order of permanency, similar to that shown in Illustration 2-9.

Shareholders' equity is shown next, followed by liabilities. Within shareholders' equity, common shares are commonly known as **ordinary shares**. The liabilities section presents non-current liabilities before current liabilities, and current liabilities are listed in reverse order of liquidity similar to current assets.

This difference in ordering assets and liabilities is summarized below:

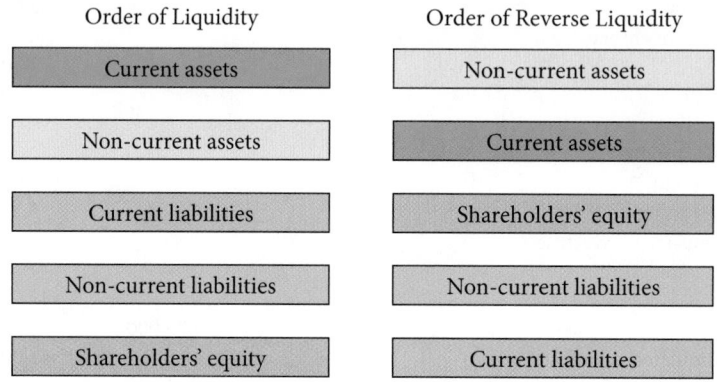

Frenette Corporation is presented again in Illustration 2-10, with its accounts reordered as commonly presented by international companies.

▸Illustration 2-10
Classified statement of financial position in reverse order of liquidity

FRENETTE CORPORATION Statement of Financial Position October 31, 2012			
Assets			
Non-current assets			
Goodwill			$ 3,100
Property, plant, and equipment			
Land		$40,000	
Buildings	$75,000		
Less: Accumulated depreciation	15,000	60,000	
Equipment	$24,000		
Less: Accumulated depreciation	5,000	19,000	
Total property, plant, and equipment			119,000
Long-term investments			
Debt investment		$2,000	
Equity investment		5,200	
Total long-term investments			7,200
Total non-current assets			129,300
Current assets			
Prepaid insurance		$ 400	
Supplies		2,100	
Merchandise inventory		4,000	
Accounts receivable		7,000	
Short-term investments		2,000	
Cash		6,600	
Total current assets			22,100
Total assets			$151,400

Shareholders' Equity and Liabilities

Shareholders' equity			
Ordinary shares		$74,000	
Retained earnings		50,050	
Total shareholders' equity			$124,050
Liabilities			
Non-current liabilities			
Mortgage payable	$10,300		
Total non-current liabilities		$10,300	
Current liabilities			
Current portion of mortgage payable	$ 1,000		
Bank loan payable	11,000		
Unearned revenue	900		
Interest payable	450		
Salaries payable	1,600		
Accounts payable	2,100		
Total current liabilities		17,050	
Total liabilities			27,350
Total shareholders' equity and liabilities			$151,400

Amplats's statement of financial position, included in Appendix B to this textbook, uses a reverse order of liquidity. You might find it helpful to take another look at this statement now.

Illustrations 2-9 and 2-10 are but two examples of differing orders that might be used in a statement of financial position. Companies are allowed to choose how to order items so they can provide information that is most useful to their users. For your assignments, it is recommended that you use the standard order used by most North American companies unless specifically instructed to do otherwise.

ACCOUNTING MATTERS!   *Investor Perspective*

Presentation of Financial Statements

The International Accounting Standards Board, along with the Financial Accounting Standards Board in the United States, are working on a joint project to fundamentally change the format of financial statements. Some of the changes propose to organize each of the financial statements in the same format to better communicate an integrated (cohesive) financial picture of a company. Information presented in the statements would separate a company's financing activities from its operating and investing activities and further separate financing activities into transactions with lenders and other creditors and with investors. This means that the statement of financial position would no longer be separated into assets, liabilities, and equity, although assets and liabilities would be separated into short- and long-term groupings within each activity classification. At the time of writing, it was anticipated that this project would be finalized late in 2011.

BEFORE YOU GO ON...

▶ Do It! Statement of Financial Position Classifications

The following selected accounts were taken from a company's statement of financial position:

_____ Accounts payable

_____ Accounts receivable

_____ Accumulated depreciation—buildings

_____ Bank loan payable (due in 6 months)

_____ Buildings

(continued)

_____ Cash
_____ Common shares
_____ Goodwill
_____ Income tax payable
_____ Interest payable
_____ Land
_____ Merchandise inventory
_____ Mortgage payable (due in 10 years)
_____ Notes receivable (due in 3 months)
_____ Retained earnings
_____ Salaries payable
_____ Sales taxes payable
_____ Short-term investments
_____ Supplies
_____ Vehicles

Classify each of the above accounts as current assets (CA), non-current assets (NCA), current liabilities (CL), non-current liabilities (NCL), or shareholders' equity (SE).

Action Plan

- Understand the differences between each broad statement classification: assets, liabilities, and shareholders' equity.
- Determine if asset and liability items are current or non-current by assessing whether the item is likely to be realized, paid, or settled within one year.

Solution

CL	Accounts payable
CA	Accounts receivable
NCA	Accumulated depreciation—buildings
CL	Bank loan payable (due in 6 months)
NCA	Buildings
CA	Cash
SE	Common shares
NCA	Goodwill
CL	Income tax payable
CL	Interest payable
NCA	Land
CA	Merchandise inventory
NCL	Mortgage payable (due in 10 years)
CA	Notes receivable (due in 3 months)
SE	Retained earnings
CL	Salaries payable
CL	Sales taxes payable
CA	Short-term investments
CA	Supplies
NCA	Vehicles

the navigator

STUDY OBJECTIVE 2

Identify and calculate ratios for analyzing a company's liquidity, solvency, and profitability.

Using the Financial Statements

In Chapter 1, we briefly discussed how the financial statements give information about a company's financial position and performance. In this chapter, we continue this discussion by showing you specific tools, such as ratio analysis, that can be used to analyze two of the financial statements—the statement of financial position and income statement—in order to make a more meaningful evaluation of a company.

Ratio analysis expresses the relationships between selected items of financial statement data. Liquidity, solvency, and profitability ratios are the three general types of ratios that are used to analyze financial statements, as shown in Illustration 2-11.

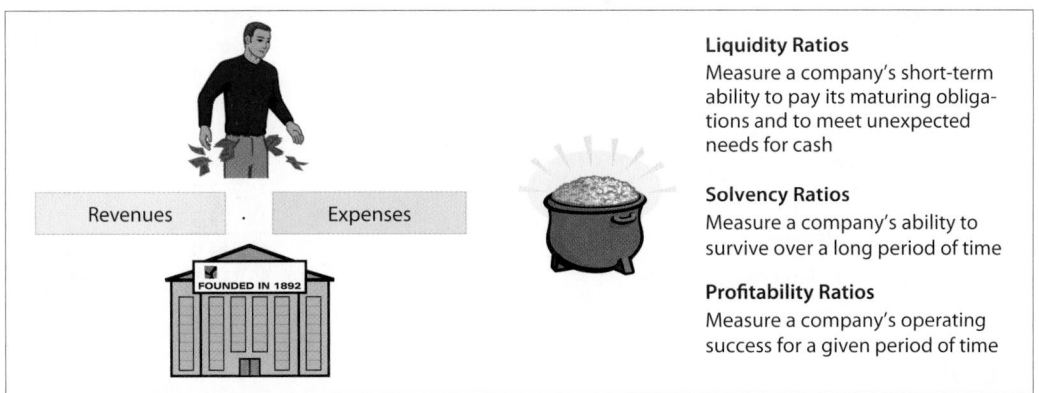

▶Illustration 2-11
Ratio classifications

Liquidity Ratios
Measure a company's short-term ability to pay its maturing obligations and to meet unexpected needs for cash

Solvency Ratios
Measure a company's ability to survive over a long period of time

Profitability Ratios
Measure a company's operating success for a given period of time

Ratios can give clues about underlying conditions that may not be easy to see when the items of a particular ratio are examined separately. Since a single ratio by itself is not very meaningful, in this and later chapters we will use the following comparisons wherever possible:

1. **Intracompany comparisons** covering two years for the same company
2. **Intercompany comparisons** based on comparisons with a competitor in the same industry
3. **Industry average comparisons** based on average ratios for particular industries

In the following sections, we will introduce some examples of liquidity, solvency, and profitability ratios, using Sobeys Inc.'s statement of financial position and income statement. Sobeys is one of Canada's top two grocery stores, with more than 1,300 food and drug stores across Canada, operating under the names Sobeys, IGA, Foodland, Price Chopper, Thrifty Foods, and Lawtons Drugs.

To broaden our analysis to include an intercompany comparison, we will then compare Sobeys' ratios for these two years with those of one of its competitors, Loblaw Companies Limited. Loblaw operates more than 1,000 grocery stores across Canada under the names Loblaws, Atlantic Superstore, No Frills, Provigo, Your Independent Grocer, and Zehrs.

Finally, we will compare ratios for Sobeys and Loblaw with industry averages for the grocery industry.

USING THE STATEMENT OF FINANCIAL POSITION (BALANCE SHEET)

You can learn a lot about a company's financial health by evaluating the relationships between its various assets and liabilities. A condensed and simplified statement of financial position for Sobeys (which it calls balance sheet), with comparative data for two fiscal years, is shown in Illustration 2-12.

▶Illustration 2-12
Sobeys' statement of financial position

SOBEYS INC. Balance Sheet May 1, 2010 and May 2, 2009 (in millions)		
	2010	2009
Assets		
Current assets	$1,640.7	$1,398.4
Loans and other receivables	74.4	69.4
Investments	48.0	48.0
Property and equipment	2,157.2	2,197.1
Intangible assets	175.3	157.7
		(continued)

Goodwill	875.7	874.5
Other assets	139.2	105.6
Total assets	$5,110.5	$4,850.7
Liabilities and Shareholders' Equity		
Liabilities		
Current liabilities	$1,658.2	$1,588.4
Long-term debt	812.5	831.6
Future tax liabilities	66.4	72.9
Other long-term liabilities	262.4	259.3
Total liabilities	2,799.5	2,752.2
Shareholders' equity		
Common shares	958.5	958.5
Retained earnings	1,273.0	1,068.2
Other equity items	79.5	71.8
Total shareholders' equity	2,311.0	2,098.5
Total liabilities and shareholders' equity	$5,110.5	$4,850.7

Liquidity

Suppose you are a supplier interested in entering into an arrangement to sell fruits and vegetables on credit to Sobeys. You would be concerned about Sobeys' liquidity—its ability to pay obligations that are expected to become due within the next year. You would use liquidity ratios to look closely at the relationship of its current assets to its current liabilities. **Liquidity ratios** measure a company's short-term ability to pay its maturing obligations and to meet unexpected needs for cash. We will look at two examples of liquidity measures in this chapter—working capital and the current ratio— and others in later chapters.

Working Capital.   One measure of liquidity is **working capital**, which is the difference between current assets and current liabilities. When working capital is positive, there is a greater likelihood that the company will be able to pay its liabilities. When working capital is negative, a company may have to borrow money; otherwise, short-term creditors may not be paid.

Illustration 2-13 shows the calculation of working capital for Sobeys for 2010 and 2009, and compares it with that of Loblaw. Note that detailed calculations are not included for either Loblaw or the industry; just the results for comparison purposes.

▸ Illustration 2-13
Working capital

WORKING CAPITAL = CURRENT ASSETS − CURRENT LIABILITIES		
($ in millions)	**2010**	**2009**
Sobeys	$1,640.7 − $1,658.2 = $(17.5)	$1,398.4 − $1,588.4 = $(190.0)
Loblaw	$736.0	$730.0
Industry average	n/a	n/a

Sobeys reported negative working capital in both 2010 and 2009, which means that its current liabilities exceeded its current assets. Its working capital did improve significantly in 2010, but it is still negative and much smaller in absolute dollars than that of Loblaw.

When industry averages are not available for the ratios that we calculate in this text, "n/a" (not available) appears.

Current Ratio.   An important liquidity ratio is the **current ratio**, which is calculated by dividing current assets by current liabilities. The current ratio is a more dependable indicator of liquidity than working capital. Two companies with the same amount of working capital may have significantly different current ratios.

The 2010 and 2009 current ratios for Sobeys, Loblaw, and the industry average are shown in Illustration 2-14.

$$\text{CURRENT RATIO} = \dfrac{\text{CURRENT ASSETS}}{\text{CURRENT LIABILITIES}}$$		
($ in millions)	2010	2009
Sobeys	$\dfrac{\$1,640.7}{\$1,658.2} = 1.0{:}1$	$\dfrac{\$1,398.4}{\$1,588.4} = 0.9{:}1$
Loblaw	1.2:1	1.2:1
Industry average	1.8:1	1.1:1

What does the ratio actually mean? The 2010 current ratio of 1.0:1 means that for every dollar of current liabilities, Sobeys has $1 of current assets. Actually Sobeys' unrounded current ratio is 0.99:1, so it has slightly fewer current assets than current liabilities. In 2009, it had $0.90 of current assets for every $1 of current liabilities. Because Sobeys' current assets increased in absolute dollars in 2010 faster than its current liabilities increased, its current ratio increased marginally from 2010 to 2009. However, when compared with Loblaw and the industry average, Sobeys' short-term liquidity is not as strong.

The current ratio is only one measure of liquidity. It does not take into account the **composition** of the current assets. For example, a satisfactory current ratio does not reveal that a portion of the current assets may be tied up in uncollectible accounts receivable or slow-moving inventory. The composition of the assets matters because a dollar of cash is more easily available to pay the bills than is a dollar of inventory. For example, suppose a company's cash balance declined while its inventory increased significantly. If inventory increased because the company was having difficulty selling it, then the current ratio would not fully reflect the reduction in the company's liquidity. We will look at these effects in more detail in later chapters.

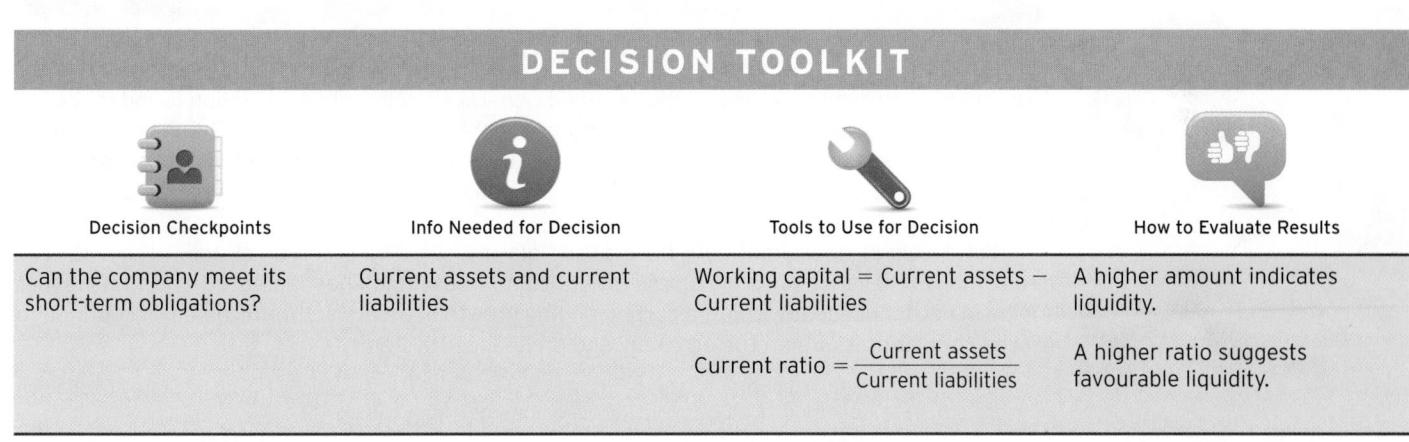

DECISION TOOLKIT

Decision Checkpoints	Info Needed for Decision	Tools to Use for Decision	How to Evaluate Results
Can the company meet its short-term obligations?	Current assets and current liabilities	Working capital = Current assets − Current liabilities	A higher amount indicates liquidity.
		Current ratio = $\dfrac{\text{Current assets}}{\text{Current liabilities}}$	A higher ratio suggests favourable liquidity.

Solvency

Now suppose that, instead of being a short-term creditor, you are interested in either buying Sobeys' shares or making a long-term loan to the company. Investors and long-term lenders are interested in a company's long-run solvency—its ability to pay interest as it comes due and to repay the face value of debt at maturity. **Solvency ratios** measure a company's ability to survive over a long period of time.

Debt to Total Assets.   The **debt to total assets** ratio is one source of information about long-term debt-paying ability. It measures the percentage of assets that is financed by lenders and other creditors rather than by shareholders. Financing provided by lenders and creditors (debt) is riskier than financing provided by shareholders (equity) because debt must be repaid at specific points in time, whether the company is performing well or not. Equity does not have to be repaid.

The debt to total assets ratio is calculated by dividing total debt (both current and non-current liabilities) by total assets. The higher the percentage of debt to total assets, the greater the risk that the company may be unable to pay its debts as they come due. The ratios of debt to total assets for Sobeys, Loblaw, and the industry average are shown in Illustration 2-15.

Illustration 2-15
Debt to total assets

DEBT TO TOTAL ASSETS $= \dfrac{\text{TOTAL LIABILITIES}}{\text{TOTAL ASSETS}}$		
($ in millions)	2010	2009
Sobeys	$\dfrac{\$2,799.5}{\$5,110.5} = 54.8\%$	$\dfrac{\$2,752.2}{\$4,850.7} = 56.7\%$
Loblaw	58.2%	58.4%
Industry average	37.9%	42.9%

The 2010 ratio of 54.8% means that approximately 55 cents of every dollar that Sobeys invested in assets was provided by its lenders and other creditors. Sobeys' ratio is improving and is better than (below) Loblaw's debt to total assets ratio, which has not changed very much over the two years. Both companies' debt to total assets ratios are higher than the industry average. The higher the ratio, the lower the equity "cushion" available to lenders and other creditors if the company becomes insolvent (unable to pay its debts). Thus, from the lenders' and other creditors' point of view, a high ratio of debt to total assets is undesirable. In other words, Sobeys' and Loblaw's solvency is less attractive to lenders and other creditors than that of their competitors, as their solvency is not as good as that of the average company in the industry.

ACCOUNTING MATTERS!   *Management Perspective*

Canada's Debt to Assets Ratio Worst in OECD

A research study commissioned by the Certified General Accountants Association found that each person in Canada would owe $41,470, if household debt were spread across all Canadians. That's two and a half times more debt than was the case two decades ago. This level of debt puts Canada at the top of the 20 largest Organisation for Economic Co-operation and Development (OECD) nations in terms of its debt to total assets ratio.

High levels of household debt have raised alarm bells. The research stated, "There is little doubt that the level of financial stress on Canadian households has increased and that further run up in household debt without a corresponding growth in assets and/or income will continue to exert a circular pressure on the economy and on financial systems."

Source: Certified General Accountants Association of Canada, "Where Is the Money Now: The State of Canadian Household Debt as Conditions for Economic Recovery Emerge," May 2010, p. 79

DECISION TOOLKIT

Decision Checkpoints	**Info Needed for Decision**	**Tools to Use for Decision**	**How to Evaluate Results**
Can the company meet its long-term obligations?	Total debt and total assets	Debt to total assets $= \dfrac{\text{Total liabilities}}{\text{Total assets}}$	A lower percentage suggests favourable solvency.

■ Keeping an Eye on Cash

In the statement of cash flows, cash provided by operating activities is intended to indicate the company's cash-generating capability. Analysts have noted, however, that cash provided by operating activities fails to take into account the fact that a company must invest in new property, plant, and equipment (capital expenditures) just to maintain its current level of operations. A company also must try to maintain dividends at current levels to satisfy investors.

A solvency measurement that offers additional insight regarding a company's cash-generating ability is free cash flow. Free cash flow describes the cash remaining from operating activities after adjusting for capital expenditures and dividends paid.

Consider the following example: Amazon.com, the world's largest on-line store, reported U.S. $3,293 million of cash provided by operating activities in a recent year. Amazon invested U.S. $373 million in capital expenditures, including capitalized expenditures related to software and website development. It chose not to pay any dividends. Its free cash flow was U.S. $2,920 million (U.S. $3,293 − U.S. $373), an increase of 114% over the prior year. The company could use this U.S. $2,920 million to purchase new assets to expand the business, to pay off debts, or to pay dividends. Amazon emphasizes the importance of free cash in its annual report: "Our financial focus is on long-term sustainable growth in free cash flow."

USING THE INCOME STATEMENT

Sobeys generates profits for its shareholders by selling groceries and other household goods. The income statement reports how successful it is at generating profit (or net earnings, as Sobeys calls it) from its sales. Illustration 2-16 shows a condensed and simplified income statement for Sobeys (which it calls statement of earnings), with comparative data for two recent fiscal years.

SOBEYS INC. Statement of Earnings Year Ended May 1, 2010 and May 2, 2009 (in millions)		
	2010	2009
Sales revenue	$15,243.0	$14,764.8
Operating expenses	14,869.5	14,432.8
Earnings before income taxes	373.5	332.0
Income tax expense	110.7	104.0
Net earnings	$ 262.8	$ 228.0

▸Illustration 2-16
Sobeys' income statement

Profitability

Existing and potential investors, lenders, and other creditors are interested in a company's profitability. **Profitability ratios** measure a company's operating success for a specific period of time. We will look at two examples of profitability ratios in this chapter: earnings per share and the price-earnings ratio.

Earnings per Share. **Earnings per share (EPS)** measures the profit earned on each common share. Accordingly, earnings per share is reported only for common shareholders. It is calculated by dividing the profit available to the common shareholders by the weighted average number of common shares.

Unless a company has preferred shares, the profit available to common shareholders will be the same as the profit reported on a company's income statement. If a company has preferred shares, preferred share dividends must be deducted from profit. We will learn more about how to calculate profit available to common shareholders and the weighted average number of shares in Chapter 11.

Shareholders usually think in terms of the number of shares they own—or plan to buy or sell— so reducing profit to a per-share amount gives a useful number for determining the investment

ASPE   return. In fact, earnings per share is such an important measure that it must be presented in the financial statements for publicly traded companies. It is the only ratio with this requirement. Private corporations reporting under Accounting Standards for Private Enterprises are not required to report earnings per share.

Sobeys is a private corporation, wholly owned by Empire Company Limited. Consequently, it does not report earnings per share information in its statements. Information is only available for Loblaw, which is a publicly traded company, in Illustration 2-17.

▶ Illustration 2-17
Earnings per share

EARNINGS PER SHARE = $\dfrac{\text{PROFIT AVAILABLE TO COMMON SHAREHOLDERS}}{\text{WEIGHTED AVERAGE NUMBER OF COMMON SHARES}}$		
	2010	2009
Sobeys	n/a	n/a
Loblaw	$2.39	$2.01
Industry average	n/a	n/a

Comparisons of earnings per share are not very meaningful among companies, because of the wide variation in the number of shares and in the financing structures. This is why there is no industry average for earnings per share in Illustration 2-17.

Price-Earnings Ratio.   Although we cannot compare earnings per share, we can use this amount to calculate the **price-earnings (P-E) ratio**, which can be compared across companies. The price-earnings ratio is a frequently quoted statistic that measures the ratio of the stock market price of each common share to its earnings per share. It is calculated by dividing the market price per share by earnings per share.

We should note that we have classified the price-earnings ratio as a profitability ratio for simplicity in this chapter. In later chapters, we will learn that the P-E ratio is not really a measure of "corporate" profitability but rather a profitability ratio used by investors for valuation purposes.

Because Sobeys' shares are 100% owned by Empire Company there is no publicly traded market for its shares. So we are able to include the price-earnings ratio for Loblaw only in this section. The market price of Loblaw's shares at year end was $33.88 and $35.23, respectively, for 2010 and 2009. This price is divided by the earnings per share amounts presented in Illustration 2-17 above to determine the price-earnings ratio presented in Illustration 2-18.

▶ Illustration 2-18
Price-earnings ratio

PRICE-EARNINGS RATIO = $\dfrac{\text{MARKET PRICE PER SHARE}}{\text{EARNINGS PER SHARE}}$		
	2010	2009
Sobeys	n/a	n/a
Loblaw	14.2 times	17.5 times
Industry average	17.2 times	15.4 times

The price-earnings ratio shows what investors expect of a company's future profitability. The ratio of the share price to profit will be higher if investors think that current profit levels will continue or increase; it will be lower if investors think that profits will decline.

From 2009 to 2010, Loblaw's earnings per share increased while its price-earnings ratio decreased. This decrease shows that investors are concerned about Loblaw's ability to increase its profitability in the future. In addition, Loblaw's price-earnings ratio declined below that of the industry in 2010, indicating that investors had more confidence in other companies than in Loblaw.

DECISION TOOLKIT

Decision Checkpoints

Info Needed for Decision

Tools to Use for Decision

How to Evaluate Results

Decision Checkpoints	Info Needed for Decision	Tools to Use for Decision	How to Evaluate Results
How does the company's profit compare with previous years?	Profit available to common shareholders and weighted average number of common shares	Earnings per share = $\dfrac{\text{Profit available to common shareholders}}{\text{Weighted average number of common shares}}$	A higher measure suggests improved performance. Values should not be compared across companies.
How does the market see the company's prospects for future profitability?	Market price per share and earnings per share	Price-earnings ratio = $\dfrac{\text{Market price per share}}{\text{Earnings per share}}$	A high ratio suggests the market expects good performance, although it may also suggest that shares are overvalued.

BEFORE YOU GO ON...

▶ Do It! Ratio Analysis

Selected financial information is available for Drummond Inc.

	2012	2011
Current assets	$ 72,000	$ 60,800
Total assets	400,000	341,000
Current liabilities	40,000	38,000
Total liabilities	180,000	150,000
Profit	90,000	40,000
Weighted average number of common shares	90,000	50,000
Market price per common share	$12	$8

Drummond has no preferred shares, so profit is equal to the profit available to common shareholders.

(a) Calculate the (1) current, (2) debt to total assets, (3) earnings per share, and (4) price-earnings ratios for each year.

(b) State whether there was an improvement or deterioration in liquidity, solvency, and profitability for Drummond in 2012.

Action Plan

- Use the formula for the current ratio: current assets ÷ current liabilities.
- Use the formula for debt to total assets: total liabilities ÷ total assets.
- Use the formula for earnings per share: profit available for common shareholders ÷ weighted average number of common shares.
- Understand that higher is better for liquidity and profitability ratios and lower is better for certain solvency ratios, like debt to total assets.

(continued)

Solution

(a)

	2012	2011
1. Current ratio	$72,000 ÷ $40,000 = 1.8:1	$60,800 ÷ $38,000 = 1.6:1
2. Debt to total assets ratio	$180,000 ÷ $400,000 = 45.0%	$150,000 ÷ $341,000 = 44.0%
3. Earnings per share	$90,000 ÷ 90,000 = $1.00	$40,000 ÷ 50,000 = $0.80
4. Price-earnings ratio	$12 ÷ $1 = 12 times	$8 ÷ $0.80 = 10 times

(b) Liquidity: The current ratio increased from 1.6:1 in 2011 to 1.8:1 in 2012. This would be viewed as an improvement, depending on how the composition of its current assets (e.g., receivables and inventories) changed.

Solvency: The debt to total assets ratio increased from 44% in 2011 to 45% in 2012. This would be viewed as a deterioration as the company has a higher debt, as a percentage of its assets, to repay in the future.

Profitability: Both the earnings per share and price-earnings ratios increased between 2011 and 2012. Both would be viewed as an improvement. Investors are viewing Drummond's potential to generate future profits favourably, as indicated by the price-earnings ratio.

Framework for the Preparation and Presentation of Financial Statements

STUDY OBJECTIVE 3

Describe the framework for the preparation and presentation of financial statements.

In Chapter 1, you learned about financial statements. In this chapter, we continued our discussion of financial statements and introduced you to some basic ways to interpret these statements. In this last section, we will discuss the framework that underlies the preparation and presentation of financial statements. It would be unwise to make decisions using financial statements without understanding the implications of this framework.

THE STANDARD-SETTING ENVIRONMENT

How do Sobeys and Loblaw decide on the type of financial information to disclose? What format should they use? How should they measure assets, liabilities, revenues, and expenses? These and all other companies get guidance from a standardized framework for the preparation and presentation of financial statements called the conceptual framework for financial reporting. Standard-setting bodies, in consultation with the accounting profession and business community, determine this framework.

According to standard setters, the **conceptual framework** is "a coherent system of interrelated objectives and fundamentals that can lead to consistent standards and that prescribes the nature, function, and limits of financial accounting statements." In other words, the conceptual framework of accounting guides decisions about what to present in financial statements, alternative ways of reporting economic events, and appropriate ways of communicating this information.

Not every country uses the same conceptual framework or set of accounting standards. They can, and do, differ significantly from country to country. This lack of uniformity has arisen over time because of differences in legal systems, in processes for developing standards, in government requirements, and in economic environments.

The International Accounting Standards Board (IASB)—the standard-setting body responsible for developing International Financial Reporting Standards—was formed to try to reduce these areas of difference and unify global standard setting. Currently, nearly 125 countries either require or permit the use of IFRS. This includes Canada, which adopted IFRS in 2011, as was mentioned in our chapter-opening feature story. Most remaining major economies have established time lines to converge with, or to make a decision to adopt, IFRS in the near future. This includes Canada's most significant trading partner, the United States, which is evaluating whether to eventually adopt IFRS as the required set of standards for U.S. publicly traded companies. In the meantime, accounting standard setters for the IASB and its U.S. equivalent, the Financial Accounting Standards Board, are working closely together to minimize the differences in their standards.

CONCEPTUAL FRAMEWORK FOR FINANCIAL REPORTING

One joint initiative between international and U.S. standard setters is a project to update and produce a common conceptual framework. We describe the following selected portions of the conceptual framework in the next sections:

- Objective of financial reporting
- Qualitative characteristics of useful financial information
- Underlying assumption
- Elements of financial statements
- Measurement of the elements of financial statements

There are other portions of the conceptual framework that will be discussed in future accounting courses. For the purpose of this financial accounting textbook, we will concentrate on the sections outlined above.

We must note that the work to update the conceptual framework is being completed in phases. At the time of writing, the first two components described above—the objective and qualitative characteristics—had been finalized. The other sections of the conceptual framework outlined above—the underlying assumption, elements of financial statements, and measurement of the elements—were still under way, with indeterminate timing about their completion. Consequently, our description of these sections is based on the framework currently published. We caution that changes to these sections are likely in future as phases are finalized.

As mentioned in our feature story, the conceptual framework is fundamentally similar for publicly traded companies in Canada reporting under IFRS and private companies reporting under ASPE. While there are some differences, the Accounting Standards Board—the Canadian accounting standard setter—has committed to update the conceptual framework for private companies to remain consistent with the IASB conceptual framework. It does not believe that the differences between publicly accountable companies and private companies justify different conceptual frameworks.

Objective of Financial Reporting

The **objective of financial reporting** is to provide financial information about a company that is useful to existing and potential investors, lenders, and other creditors in making decisions about providing resources to the company. Those decisions involve buying, selling, or holding equity and debt instruments and providing or settling loans and other forms of credit. Although a wide variety of users rely on financial reporting, investors, lenders, and other creditors are identified as the main users of financial reporting. You will recall that we discussed these, and other, users and their needs in Chapter 1.

Financial information about the company is provided by general purpose financial statements. These statements provide information about the company's economic resources and the claims against these resources. Financial statements also provide information about the effects of transactions and other events that change a company's economic resources and claims. Both types of information provide useful input for decisions made by external users about providing resources to the company.

Financial statements are prepared using the **accrual basis of accounting**. Under the accrual basis of accounting, the effects of transactions on a company's economic resources and claims are recorded in the period when a transaction occurs and not when cash is received or paid. For example, a law firm would record revenue in the accounting period when the legal services are provided to the client and not necessarily in the accounting period when the client pays for the services. We will learn about the accrual basis of accounting in the next two chapters.

Qualitative Characteristics of Useful Financial Information

The qualitative characteristics of useful financial information identify the types of information that are likely to be most useful to existing and potential investors, lenders, and other creditors in making their decisions. The qualitative characteristics are divided into those that are fundamental and those that are enhancing.

Fundamental Qualitative Characteristics. The two fundamental qualitative characteristics of useful financial information are (1) relevance and (2) faithful representation. To be useful for decision-making, information must be relevant and faithfully represent what it is supposed to represent.

Accounting information has **relevance** if it will make a difference in users' decisions. Relevant information may have predictive value, confirmatory value, or both. Financial information has **predictive value** if it helps users make predictions about future events. Financial information has **confirmatory value** if it helps users confirm or correct their previous predictions or expectations. For example, information about a company's sales for the current year can be used as a basis to help predict sales in one or more future years. It can also be compared with sales predictions that were made in past years. The results of such comparisons can help a user to confirm or correct the processes that were used to make these previous predictions.

Materiality is an important component of relevance. Information is considered material if its omission or misstatement could influence the decisions of users. Materiality and relevance are both defined in terms of what influences or makes a difference to a decision maker. A decision not to disclose certain information may be made, say, because users have no need for that kind of information (it is not relevant) or because the amounts involved are too small to make a difference (they are not material). Magnitude by itself, without regard to the nature of the item and the circumstances in which the judgement has to be made, is not generally a sufficient basis for a materiality judgement.

For accounting information to be useful, it must not only be relevant but it must represent economic reality; that is, it must be a **faithful representation** of what really exists or happened. To provide a faithful representation, information must be **complete** (nothing important was omitted), **neutral** (is not biased toward one position or another), and **free from material error**.

Complete, unbiased, and factual information that is faithfully represented is critical in financial reporting. Of course, perfection is seldom, if ever, achievable. Consequently, faithful representation does not necessarily mean accuracy in all respects. For example, as we will learn in later chapters, estimates are required in accounting and estimates may not be accurate. However, a representation of an estimate can be faithful if the amount is described as being an estimate, the nature and limitations of the estimating process are explained, and no errors have been made in the process used to develop the estimate.

 ACCOUNTING MATTERS!   *Ethics Perspective*

Getting the Numbers Right

In the early 2000s, corporate reporting scandals shocked the world, with companies like Nortel Networks Corporation making headlines when investors, lenders, and other creditors learned that financial statements are not always "faithfully represented."

In 2005, Nortel restated (revised) its financial statements for 2003, 2002, and 2001. The original results for 2003 had reported the first profitable year in seven, triggering a jump in share price and increased investor confidence. In 2004, however, Nortel revealed that there had been accounting irregularities, and that profit was overstated by up to 50%. Nortel's chief executive officer and nine senior financial officers were fired "with cause," and the share price began to drop.

But the telecommunications company's financial problems were not over. In 2006, Nortel announced that it would again restate its financial results, this time for 2003, 2004, and 2005. Still, the juggling of the numbers was not yet complete. 2007 brought another announcement of restatements to the financial results for 2004, 2005, and 2006. Class action lawsuits and legal and regulatory investigations ensued. In 2009, Nortel filed for bankruptcy protection.

Corporate scandals like the one at Nortel have made it clear that financial statements *must* get the numbers right in order to provide relevant and faithfully represented information that is useful to external users.

Enhancing Qualitative Characteristics. In addition to the two fundamental qualities of relevance and faithful representation, the conceptual framework also describes four enhancing qualities of useful information. These include (1) comparability, (2) verifiability, (3) timeliness, and (4) understandability.

In accounting, **comparability** results when users can identify and understand similarities in, and differences among, items. Consistency, although related to comparability, does not mean the same thing. Instead, consistency aids comparability when a company uses the same accounting principles and methods from year to year or when companies with similar circumstances use the same accounting principles. When a company's financial information is reported on a consistent basis, the financial statements can be used for a meaningful analysis of trends within the company. This does not mean that a company can never change from one accounting principle to another. Companies can change accounting principles, but only if the change is required by the standard setters or if the change will result in more relevant information for decision-making.

Information has **verifiability** if different knowledgeable and independent users can reach consensus that the information is faithfully represented. Verifiability can be determined by verifying an amount directly; for example, by counting cash. It can also be determined by checking the inputs to a formula and recalculating the outputs. Public accountants perform audits of financial statements to verify their accuracy.

For accounting information to be relevant, it must have **timeliness**. That is, it must be available to decision makers before it loses its ability to influence decisions. Regulators require that public companies provide their financial statements to investors within 90 days of their year end.

Information has the quality of **understandability** if it is classified, characterized, and presented clearly and concisely. Understandable information means that reasonably informed users can interpret the information and comprehend its meaning.

Applying the enhancing qualitative characteristics is an iterative process that does not have to follow a prescribed order. In addition, sometimes one enhancing qualitative characteristic may have to be given less emphasis in order to maximize another qualitative characteristic. For example, a new financial reporting standard may improve relevance or faithful representation in the longer term while comparability is sacrificed in the shorter term.

Cost Constraint on Useful Financial Reporting

The **cost constraint** is a pervasive constraint that ensures that the value of the information provided in financial reporting is greater than the cost of providing it. That is, the benefits of financial reporting information should justify the costs of providing and using it.

For example, to achieve completeness, which we discussed along with the fundamental qualitative characteristic of faithful representation, accountants could record or disclose every financial event that occurs and every uncertainty that exists. However, providing additional information increases costs, and the benefits of providing this information, in some cases, may be less than the costs.

You will recall that earlier we mentioned that the conceptual framework was fundamentally similar for publicly traded and private companies in Canada. The Accounting Standards Board decided that the application of the cost constraint would result in accounting that was largely similar for the two sectors but would appropriately address their differences.

Underlying Assumption

A key assumption—the going concern assumption—creates a foundation for the accounting process. The **going concern assumption** assumes that a company will continue in operation for the foreseeable future. Of course, some businesses do fail. However, if a business has a history of profitable operations and access to financial resources, it is reasonable to assume that it will continue operating long enough to carry out its existing objectives and commitments.

The going concern assumption has important implications in accounting. If a company is assumed to be a going concern, then reporting assets, such as land, at their cost may be more appropriate than reporting land at its fair value. We will learn about the cost and fair value bases of accounting in a later section. In addition, if a company was not a going concern, the classification of assets and liabilities as current and non-current would not matter. Labelling anything as non-current would be hard to justify.

Elements of Financial Statements

Financial statements portray the financial effects of transactions and other events by grouping them into broad categories or classes according to their economic characteristics. These broad classes are termed the **elements of financial statements**, which include **assets**, **liabilities**, **equity**, **income** (including gains), and **expenses** (including losses).

Because these elements are so important and are often interrelated, they must be precisely defined and universally measured and applied. You were briefly introduced to these definitions in Chapter 1. We will summarize them in Illustration 2-19 and will discuss these definitions in more detail in later chapters.

▶ Illustration 2-19

Elements of financial statements

Assets An asset is a resource controlled by the company as a result of past events and from which future economic benefits are expected to flow to the company.

Liabilities A liability is a present obligation of the company arising from past events, the settlement of which is expected to result in an outflow from the company of resources embodying economic benefits.

Equity Equity is the residual interest in the assets of the company after deducting all its liabilities.

Income Income includes both revenue and gains. Revenue arises in the course of the ordinary activities of the company while gains may or may not arise from ordinary activities. Income is the increase in economic benefits during the accounting period in the form of inflows or enhancements of assets or decreases of liabilities that result in increases in equity, other than those relating to contributions from equity participants.

Expenses Expenses include losses as well as those expenses that arise from ordinary activities of the company. Losses may or may not arise from ordinary activities. Expenses are decreases in economic benefits during the accounting period in the form of outflows or depletions of assets or incurrence of liabilities that result in decreases in equity, other than those relating to distributions to equity participants.

Measurement of the Elements of Financial Statements

Using the objective of financial reporting, the qualitative characteristics, and the underlying assumption described in the previous sections, standard setters have developed foundational principles that describe which, when, and how the elements of financial statements should be recognized, measured, and reported. These foundational principles are known as generally accepted accounting principles (GAAP), which were introduced to you in Chapter 1. In Canada, "generally accepted" means that these principles are widely recognized and have authoritative support through the Canadian and provincial business corporations acts and securities legislation.

Generally accepted accounting principles related to the *recognition* of the elements of financial statements will be introduced in Chapter 4. In this chapter, we introduce two *measurement* principles—historical cost and fair value. These are more commonly referred to as measurement bases rather than principles, although both terms can be, and are, used interchangeably. It is worth noting that although we discuss only two measurement principles here, a number of different measurement principles are used to different degrees and in varying combinations in financial statements.

Historical Cost. The **cost basis of accounting** states that assets and liabilities should be recorded at their cost at the time of acquisition. This is true not only at the time when the item is purchased, but also during the time that an asset or liability is held.

For example, if a company were to purchase land for $3 million, it would be recorded and reported on the statement of financial position at $3 million at the time of purchase. But what would the company do if by the end of the next year the land had increased in value to $4 million? The answer is that under historical cost the land would still be reported at $3 million. In this particular case, cost is the most **relevant** value because the land is intended for use in the business. It is not being held for resale. The land will continue to be reported at cost until either it is sold or the **going concern assumption** is no longer valid.

Fair Value. The **fair value basis of accounting** states that certain assets and liabilities should be recorded and reported at fair value (the price that would be received to sell an asset). It is worth noting that at the acquisition date, cost and fair value are generally the same. It is only as time passes that these two values diverge and fair value may become more useful than cost for certain types of assets and liabilities. For example, certain investment securities held for trading are reported at fair value because market price information is readily available for these types of assets and they are intended to be sold, in which case the fair value is more relevant for users' needs.

In choosing between cost and fair value, two fundamental qualitative characteristics that make financial information useful for decision-making are applied: relevance and faithful representation. Recall that Plazacorp's chief financial officer, Floriana Cipollone, mentioned that fair value was a more **relevant** measure for its income-producing properties in our chapter-opening feature story.

In determining which measurement principle to use, the factual nature of the cost figures must be weighed against the relevance of the fair value figures. In general, standard setters require that most assets be recorded using historical cost because fair values may not always be representationally faithful. That is, cost is the more faithful representation because it can be easily verified and is neutral. Only in situations where assets are actively traded, such as investment securities or investment properties in certain industries such as the real estate industry, is fair value basis of accounting applied. Ms. Cipollone also spoke about the importance and difficulty of obtaining the fair value of Plazacorp's investment properties in our feature story.

Summary of Conceptual Framework for Financial Reporting

As we have seen, the conceptual framework for developing sound reporting practices starts with the objective of financial reporting—providing financial information that is useful for decision-making. Financial information is provided by general purpose financial statements that are prepared using the accrual basis of accounting. Qualitative characteristics help ensure that the information provided in these statements is useful. A key assumption—the going concern assumption—underlies the preparation of financial statements. The elements of the financial statements define the main terms used in the financial statements and measurement principles describe how the elements of financial statements should be measured and reported.

Alternative Terminology
The words *principles*, *standards*, *policies*, *models*, and *bases* are used interchangeably in accounting.

The conceptual framework is summarized in Illustration 2-20:

▶Illustration 2-20
Summary of conceptual framework

Objective of Financial Reporting		

Qualitative Characteristics of Useful Financial Information		
Fundamental Qualitative Characteristics	Enhancing Qualitative Characteristics	Constraint

1. Relevance
  • Predictive value
  • Confirmatory value
  • Material
2. Faithful representation
  • Complete
  • Neutral
  • Free from material error
	1. Comparability
	2. Verifiability
	3. Timeliness
	4. Understandability
		1. Cost

Underlying Assumption—Going Concern

Elements	Measurement of the Elements
1. Assets 2. Liabilities 3. Equity 4. Revenue 5. Expenses	1. Historical cost 2. Fair value

BEFORE YOU GO ON...

▶ Do It! Conceptual Framework

The following is an alphabetized list of the qualitative characteristics, assumption, and measurement principles found in the conceptual framework for financial reporting.

1. Comparability
2. Cost constraint
3. Historical cost
4. Fair value
5. Faithful representation
6. Going concern
7. Relevance
8. Timeliness
9. Understandability
10. Verifiability

Match each item above with a description below.

(a) _____ The qualitative characteristic that the use of the same accounting principles enables evaluation of one company's results relative to another company's.

(b) _____ The qualitative characteristic for describing information that indicates the information makes a difference in a decision.

(c) _____ The measurement principle that assets are reported at the cost incurred to acquire the item.

(d) _____ The qualitative characteristic that the value of information should exceed the cost of preparing it.

(e) _____ The qualitative characteristic that presents a true and transparent picture of what really exists or happened.

(f) _____ The qualitative characteristic that information can be recalculated and determined to be without errors or omissions.

(g) _____ The qualitative characteristic that information is available before the information loses its ability to influence decisions.

(h) _____ The assumption that a company will continue to operate for the foreseeable future.

(i) _____ The qualitative characteristic that informed users are able to interpret information and comprehend its meaning.

(j) _____ The measurement principle that assets are reported at the price that would be received if the item was sold.

Action Plan

- Understand the fundamental and enhancing qualitative characteristics of accounting information:
  - Fundamental: relevance and faithful representation.
  - Enhancing: comparability, verifiability, timeliness, and understandability.
  - Constraint: cost.
- Understand the underlying assumption of the accounting process: going concern.
- Understand the choice between how the elements of financial statements are measured: historical cost or fair value.

Solution

(a) 1	(c) 3	(e) 5	(g) 8	(i) 9
(b) 7	(d) 2	(f) 10	(h) 6	(j) 4

comparing
IFRS and ASPE

Key Differences	International Financial Reporting Standards (IFRS)	Accounting Standards for Private Enterprises (ASPE)
Terminology	The term *depreciation* refers to the allocation of the cost of depreciable tangible assets over their useful lives. The term *amortization* refers to the allocation of the cost of certain kinds of intangible assets over their useful lives.	The term *amortization* is used for the allocation of the cost of both depreciable tangible assets and certain kinds of intangible assets over their useful lives.
Earnings per share	Required to present in financial statements	Not required to present in financial statements
Conceptual framework for financial reporting	Still under development	Same general framework currently under development by international and U.S. standard setters anticipated to be applied to private enterprises when complete

Your Personal Statement of Financial Position

By now, you should be comfortable with how to prepare a company's statement of financial position. Perhaps it is time to look at your personal position. Similar to a corporate statement, a personal statement of financial position reports what you own and what you owe.

What are the items of value that you own—your personal assets? Some of your assets are liquid—cash and items of value that can easily be converted to cash. Others, such as vehicles, real estate, and some types of investments, may be less liquid. Some assets, such as investments and real estate, tend to increase in value over time, thereby increasing your personal equity. Other assets, such as vehicles and furniture, tend to fall in value, thereby decreasing your personal equity.

What are the amounts you owe—your personal liabilities? These liabilities may be either current (to be repaid within 12 months) or non-current (not to be paid until more than a year from now). Student loans, vehicle loans, credit card bills, and mortgages are all examples of liabilities.

Your personal equity is the difference between your total assets and your total liabilities. A person may have a high equity position but still have financial difficulties because of a shortage of cash. You can increase your equity in various ways, including increasing your savings, decreasing your spending, and increasing the value of your investments. Your personal equity is not money that is available for use. Rather, it is an indication of your net assets (assets less liabilities) or financial position at a specific point in time.

Some Facts

- Canadians own a lot of "stuff." Statistics Canada reported that in 2009, almost all Canadian households had a refrigerator, a telephone, a colour TV, and a microwave. Over 80% of Canadian households had a washer and dryer, a computer, and owned or leased a vehicle. Over 60% of households had a dishwasher.
- In 2010, Canadian household debt, consisting of both mortgage and consumer credit, totalled $1.53 billion—equivalent to $44,500 per capita. Household net worth per capita was $181,700 or $6.2 billion in total, with a total debt to income ratio of 1.4675.
- In 2010, the savings rate of Canadians averaged 4.2%. This is a big drop from the 1990s when the rate averaged 10%. In the United States, the savings rate has increased to almost 6%.
- When times get tough, statistics indicate that Canadians reduce spending on items such as motor vehicles, furniture, clothes, appliances, and sporting equipment. They continue to spend on more essential items such as shelter, child care, and medical care.
- A recent poll by RBC found that about one-third of Canadians saved on a regular basis and just under one-third did not save because they had no money left after paying all their bills. The two most common reasons why Canadians aged 18 to 24 saved were to create an emergency fund (47% of respondents) or to travel (47%). Other reasons for savings included the purchase or renovation of a home (36%) or a car (26%). Those respondents aged 25 to 34 were less interested in travel (38%) and more focused on saving for emergency funds (53%). For Canadians aged over 50, saving for vacations, cars, and houses was less popular than saving for retirement, emergency funds, or children's education.

What Do You Think?

Should you prepare a personal statement of financial position?

YES — In order to attain your financial goals, you need to know where you are starting from. The personal statement gives a benchmark that will allow you to measure your progress toward your financial goals.

NO — Your present financial position is dramatically different from what it will look like in the future. After graduation, you will have a job, or a better job, and you will not have to pay tuition.

Sources: B. Tal, "Back to Old-Fashioned Saving," CIBC Economics, March 1, 2011. RBC, "RBC Poll, Half of Canadians Struggling to Save," October 13, 2010. Statistics Canada, *Spending Patterns in Canada, 2009.* Statistics Canada, "National Balance Sheet Accounts," *The Daily*, March 14, 2011.

Summary of Study Objectives

1. **Identify the sections of a classified statement of financial position.** In a classified statement of financial position, assets are classified as current or non-current assets. In the non-current asset category, they are further classified as investments; property, plant, and equipment; intangible assets and goodwill; and other assets. Liabilities are classified as either current or non-current. There is also a shareholders' equity section, which shows share capital and retained earnings, among other equity items if any exist.

2. **Identify and calculate ratios for analyzing a company's liquidity, solvency, and profitability.** Liquidity ratios, such as working capital and the current ratio, measure a company's short-term ability to pay its maturing obligations and meet unexpected needs for cash. Solvency ratios, such as debt to total assets, measure a company's ability to survive over a long period. Profitability ratios, such as earnings per share and the price-earnings ratio, measure a company's operating success for a specific period of time.

3. **Describe the framework for the preparation and presentation of financial statements.** The key components of the conceptual framework are (1) the objective of financial reporting; (2) qualitative characteristics of useful financial information, which include fundamental and enhancing characteristics and the cost constraint; (3) the going concern assumption underlying the accounting process; (4) elements of the financial statements; and (5) measurement of the elements of financial statements.

Glossary

Accounts payable   Amounts owed to suppliers for purchases made on credit (on account). (p. 56)

Accounts receivable   Amounts owed by customers who purchased products or services on credit (on account). (p. 53)

Accrued liabilities   Expenses incurred by the company that have not yet been paid. (p. 56)

Accrued receivables   Revenues earned by the company that have not yet been received in cash. (p. 53)

Bank indebtedness   A short-term loan up to a maximum amount pre-arranged with a bank to cover cash shortfalls. (p. 56)

Comparability   An enhancing qualitative characteristic of useful information that enables users to identify and understand similarities in, and differences among, items. (p. 73)

Conceptual framework   A coherent system of interrelated elements that guides decisions about what to present in financial statements, alternative ways of reporting economic events, and appropriate ways of communicating this information. (p. 70)

Contra asset account   An account that is offset against (reduces) an asset account on the balance sheet. (p. 55)

Cost constraint   The constraint that the costs of obtaining and providing information should not be higher than the benefits that are gained by providing it. (p. 73)

Cost basis of accounting   A measurement principle that states that assets and liabilities should be recorded and reported at their cost at the time of acquisition, as well as during the time the asset is held. (p. 75)

Current assets   Cash and other resources that it is reasonable to expect will be converted into cash, or will be sold or used up within one year of the company's financial statement date or its operating cycle, whichever is longer. (p. 53)

Current liabilities   Obligations that will be paid or settled within one year of the company's financial statement date or its operating cycle, whichever is longer. (p. 56)

Current maturities of long-term debt   The portion of a non-current or long-term loan that is repayable in the current year. (p. 57)

Current ratio   A measure of liquidity used to evaluate a company's short-term debt-paying ability. It is calculated by dividing current assets by current liabilities. (p. 64)

Debt to total assets   A measure of solvency showing the percentage of total financing that is provided by lenders and other creditors. It is calculated by dividing total liabilities by total assets. (p. 65)

Earnings per share (EPS)   A measure of profitability showing the profit earned by each common share. It is calculated by dividing profit available to common shareholders by the weighted average number of common shares. (p. 67)

Elements of financial statements   A set of definitions of basic terms in accounting, such as assets, liabilities, equity, revenues, and expenses. (p. 74)

Fair value basis of accounting   A measurement principle that states that assets should be reported at their market value (price to sell). (p. 75)

Faithful representation   A fundamental qualitative characteristic describing information that represents economic reality. It must be complete, neutral, and free from material error. (p. 72)

Going concern assumption   The assumption that the business will remain in operation for the foreseeable future. (p. 74)

Intangible assets   Assets of a long-lived nature that do not have physical substance but represent a privilege or a right granted to, or held by, a company. (p. 55)

Inventory   (also known as merchandise inventory) Goods held for sale to customers. (p. 53)

Liquidity ratios   Measures of a company's short-term ability to pay its maturing obligations and to meet unexpected needs for cash. (p. 64)

Long-term investments   (also known as investments) Investments intended to be held for many years in debt securities (e.g., loans, notes, bonds, or mortgages) to earn interest, and (2) equity securities (e.g., shares) of other corporations held to generate investment revenue or held for strategic reasons. (p. 54)

Non-current assets   (also known as long-term assets) Assets that are not expected to be converted into cash, sold, or used up by the business within one year of the statement date or its operating cycle. (p. 54)

Non-current liabilities   (also known as long-term liabilities) Obligations that are not expected to be paid or settled within one year or the company's operating cycle. (p. 57)

Notes payable   (also known as loans payable) Amounts owed to suppliers, banks, or others that are supported by a written promise to repay. (p. 57)

Notes receivable   (also known as loans receivable) Amounts owed by customers or others that are supported by a written promise to repay. (p. 53)

Objective of financial reporting   The provision of information about a company's financial position, performance, and changes in financial position that is useful to existing and potential investors, lenders, and other creditors in making decisions about providing resources to the company. (p. 71)

Operating cycle   Average time it takes to go from cash to cash in producing revenue. Can be one year or longer, depending on the type of business. (p. 53)

Prepaid expenses   Costs paid in advance of use (e.g., rent and insurance). (p. 53)

Price-earnings (P-E) ratio   A profitability measure of the ratio of the market price of each common share to the earnings per share. It reflects investors' beliefs about a company's future profit potential. (p. 68)

Profitability ratios   Measures of a company's operating success for a specific period of time. (p. 67)

Property, plant, and equipment   Tangible assets of a long-lived nature that are being used to operate the business. (p. 54)

Relevance   A fundamental qualitative characteristic describing information that makes a difference in a decision. It should have predictive value, confirmatory value, or both, and be material. (p. 72)

Short-term investments   (also known as trading investments) Investments in debt securities (e.g., bonds of another company) or equity securities (e.g., shares of another company) that are held in hopes of generating interest income and/or gains from profitable resale in the near term. (p. 53)

Solvency ratios   Measures of a company's ability to survive over a long period of time. (p. 65)

Supplies   Consumable items used in running a business, such as office and cleaning supplies. (p. 53)

Timeliness   An enhancing qualitative characteristic of useful information that means that information is available to decision-makers in time to be capable of influencing their decisions. (p. 73)

Understandability   An enhancing qualitative characteristic of useful information that means that information is clearly and concisely classified, characterized, and presented. (p. 73)

Verifiability   An enhancing qualitative characteristic of useful information that means that different knowledgeable and independent users could reach consensus, although not necessarily complete agreement, that the information is a faithful representation. (p. 73)

Working capital   A measure of liquidity used to evaluate a company's short-term debt-paying ability. It is calculated by subtracting current liabilities from current assets. (p. 64)

DECISION TOOLKIT–A SUMMARY

|
Decision Checkpoints |
Info Needed for Decision |
Tools to Use for Decision |
How to Evaluate Results |
|---|---|---|---|
| Can the company meet its short-term obligations? | Current assets and current liabilities | Working capital = Current assets − Current liabilities

$\text{Current ratio} = \dfrac{\text{Current assets}}{\text{Current liabilities}}$ | A higher amount indicates liquidity.

A higher ratio suggests favourable liquidity. |
| Can the company meet its long-term obligations? | Total debt and total assets | $\text{Debt to total assets} = \dfrac{\text{Total liabilities}}{\text{Total assets}}$ | A lower percentage suggests favourable solvency. |
| How does the company's profit compare with previous years? | Profit available to common shareholders and weighted average number of common shares | Earnings per share =
$\dfrac{\text{Profit available to common shareholders}}{\text{Weighted average number of common shares}}$ | A higher measure suggests improved performance. Values should not be compared across companies. |
| How does the market see the company's prospects for future profitability? | Market price per share and earnings per share | $\text{Price earnings ratio} = \dfrac{\text{Market price per share}}{\text{Earnings per share}}$ | A high ratio suggests the market expects good performance, although it may also suggest that shares are overvalued. |

USING THE DECISION TOOLKIT

the navigator

Canadian Tire Corporation, Limited sells a wide array of products, including casual clothing and home, car, sports, and leisure products. Condensed and simplified financial statements with comparative data for the years ended January 1, 2011 (fiscal 2010) and January 2, 2010 (fiscal 2009) are shown below.

CANADIAN TIRE CORPORATION, LIMITED Balance Sheet January 1, 2011 and January 2, 2010 (in millions)		
	2010	2009
Assets		
Current assets	$5,004.6	$5,196.2
Long-term receivables and other assets	100.9	109.9
Long-term investments	75.8	48.8
Goodwill	71.9	71.8
Intangible assets	291.1	265.4
Property and equipment	3,219.8	3,180.4
Total assets	$8,764.1	$8,872.5
Liabilities and Shareholders' Equity		
Liabilities		
Current liabilities	$2,112.1	$2,647.8
Long-term debt	1,079.4	1,101.2
Future income taxes	54.6	49.8
Other long-term liabilities	1,451.3	1,385.8
Total liabilities	4,697.4	5,184.6
Shareholders' equity		
Share capital	711.6	720.4
Other equity items	(38.4)	(46.2)
Retained earnings	3,393.5	3,013.7
Total shareholders' equity	4,066.7	3,687.9
Total liabilities and shareholders' equity	$8,764.1	$8,872.5

(continued)

CANADIAN TIRE CORPORATION, LIMITED Statement of Earnings Year Ended January 1, 2011 and January 2, 2010 (in millions)		
	2010	2009
Operating revenue	$8,980.8	$8,686.5
Total expenses	8,383.8	8,207.3
Earnings before income tax	597.0	479.2
Income tax expense	143.4	144.2
Net earnings	$ 453.6	$ 335.0

Additional information:

- Canadian Tire's profit (net earnings) is the same as its profit available to common shareholders. The weighted average number of shares was 81.6 million in 2010 and 81.7 million in 2009. The share price was $74.71 at the end of 2010, and $60.71 at the end of 2009.
- Industry averages are as follows: current ratio, 1.5:1 in 2010 and 1.8:1 in 2009; debt to total assets, 24.2% in 2010 and 37.9% in 2009; and price-earnings ratio, 34.0 times in 2010 and 17.2 times in 2009. Industry averages are not available for earnings per share.

Instructions

(a) Calculate Canadian Tire's current ratio for both fiscal years. Discuss the company's liquidity generally, and compared with the industry.

(b) Calculate Canadian Tire's debt to total assets for both fiscal years. Discuss the company's solvency generally, and compared with the industry.

(c) Calculate Canadian Tire's earnings per share and price-earnings ratio for both fiscal years. Discuss the company's profitability generally, and compared with the industry.

Solution

(a) Liquidity
Current ratio (in millions)

	Canadian Tire	Industry
2010	$5,004.6 ÷ $2,112.1 = 2.4:1	1.5:1
2009	$5,196.2 ÷ $2,647.8 = 2.0:1	1.8:1

Based on the current ratio, Canadian Tire's liquidity appears strong and improving, at 2.0:1 for 2009 and 2.4:1 for 2010. This means that Canadian Tire had at least twice as many current assets as current liabilities. This is also higher than the current ratio of its industry competitors. It is interesting that Canadian Tire's current ratio improved in 2010 while the industry average deteriorated in the same year.

(b) Solvency
Debt to total assets (in millions)

	Canadian Tire	Industry
2010	$4,697.4 ÷ $8,764.1 = 53.6%	24.2%
2009	$5,184.6 ÷ $8,872.5 = 58.4%	37.9%

Canadian Tire's solvency improved in 2010. Its debt to total assets ratio decreased from 58.4% in 2009 to 53.6% in 2010. However, its reliance on debt financing is higher (worse) than that of the industry in both years. In contrast to what we observed with the change in liquidity for Canadian Tire and the industry, the industry ratio improved in 2010 while Canadian Tire's ratio deteriorated in the same year.

(c) Profitability
Earnings per share (in millions)

	Canadian Tire	Industry
2010	$453.6 ÷ 81.6 = $5.56	n/a
2009	$335.0 ÷ 81.7 = $4.10	n/a

Price-earnings ratio

	Canadian Tire	Industry
2010	$74.71 ÷ $5.56 = 13.4 times	34.0 times
2009	$60.71 ÷ $4.10 = 14.8 times	17.2 times

Canadian Tire's profitability appears to be improving. Nonetheless, despite a significant increase in the company's earnings per share in 2010, its price-earnings ratio declined from 14.8 times in 2009 to 13.4 times in 2010. This decline likely reflects investors' concerns about Canadian Tire's ability to improve its profitability in the future. Canadian Tire's price-earnings ratio continues to fall below that of the industry average in both years. This is especially so in 2010 when the price-earnings ratios for the industry increased significantly compared to 2009 while Canadian Tire's price-earnings ratio decreased.

Comprehensive Do It!

The following accounts and amounts are taken from the financial statements of the Visentin Corporation for the year ended January 31, 2012:

Accounts payable	$ 779,000
Accounts receivable	602,000
Accumulated depreciation—buildings	150,000
Accumulated depreciation—equipment	100,000
Buildings	1,000,000
Cash	85,000
Common shares	1,500,000
Cost of goods sold	5,900,000
Depreciation expense	100,000
Dividends	37,000
Equipment	250,000
Goodwill	152,000
Income tax expense	45,000
Interest expense	42,000
Land	89,000
Long-term investments	175,000
Merchandise inventory	1,485,000
Mortgage payable (long-term)	383,000
Mortgage payable due within one year	125,000
Operating expenses	1,138,000
Prepaid expenses	78,000
Retained earnings, February 1, 2011	740,000
Sales	7,400,000
Short-term bank loan payable	1,000

Additional information:
There were no changes in common shares during the year.

Instructions
Prepare an income statement, statement of changes in equity, and statement of financial position for Visentin Corporation.

(continued)

Action Plan

- Identify which accounts should be reported on each statement. Then determine which classification each account should be reported in (e.g., in current assets, non-current assets, current liabilities, non-current liabilities, or shareholders' equity on the statement of financial position; or in revenues or expenses on the income statement).
- Prepare the statements in this order: (1) income statement, (2) statement of changes in equity, and (3) statement of financial position.
- The income statement covers a period of time. In preparing the income statement, first list revenues, and then expenses. List expenses in order of size—from largest to smallest. Report income tax expense separately.
- The statement of changes in equity covers the same period of time as the income statement. This statement calculates the ending balance in common shares by adding any changes to common shares to the opening common shares amount. The ending balance in retained earnings is calculated by adding profit (from the income statement) to, and deducting dividends from, the opening retained earnings amount.
- The statement of financial position is prepared at a specific point in time. In preparing a classified statement of financial position, list items in order of their liquidity in the current classifications and in order of their permanency in the non-current classifications.

Solution to Comprehensive Do It!

VISENTIN CORPORATION
Income Statement
Year Ended January 31, 2012

Sales		$7,400,000
Expenses		
Cost of goods sold	$5,900,000	
Operating expenses	1,138,000	
Depreciation expense	100,000	
Interest expense	42,000	
Total expenses		7,180,000
Profit before income tax		220,000
Income tax expense		45,000
Profit		$ 175,000

VISENTIN CORPORATION
Statement of Changes in Equity
Year Ended January 31, 2012

	Common Shares	Retained Earnings	Total Equity
Balance, February 1, 2011	$1,500,000	$740,000	$2,240,000
Profit		175,000	175,000
Dividends		(37,000)	(37,000)
Balance, January 31, 2012	$1,500,000	$878,000	$2,378,000

VISENTIN CORPORATION
Statement of Financial Position
January 31, 2012

Assets		
Current assets		
Cash	$ 85,000	
Accounts receivable	602,000	
Merchandise inventory	1,485,000	
Prepaid expenses	78,000	
Total current assets		$2,250,000
Investments		175,000

Property, plant, and equipment			
Land		$ 89,000	
Buildings	$1,000,000		
Less: Accumulated depreciation	(150,000)	850,000	
Equipment	$ 250,000		
Less: Accumulated depreciation	(100,000)	150,000	1,089,000
Goodwill			152,000
Total assets			$3,666,000

Liabilities and Shareholders' Equity

Liabilities		
Current liabilities		
Accounts payable	$ 779,000	
Bank loan payable	1,000	
Mortgage payable due within one year	125,000	
Total current liabilities		$ 905,000
Non-current liabilities		
Mortgage payable		383,000
Total liabilities		1,288,000
Shareholders' equity		
Common shares	$1,500,000	
Retained earnings	878,000	2,378,000
Total liabilities and shareholders' equity		$3,666,000

Self-Test, Brief Exercises, Exercises, Problems—Set A, and many more components are available for practice in WileyPLUS.

Self-Test Questions

Answers are at the end of the chapter.

(SO 1) 1. In a classified statement of financial position, assets are usually classified by North American companies in this order:
(a) current assets; investments; property, plant, and equipment; and intangible assets.
(b) current assets and current liabilities.
(c) current assets, investments, and share capital.
(d) intangible assets; property, plant, and equipment; investments; and current assets.

(SO 1) 2. In a classified statement of financial position, the following selected current assets are usually classified by North American companies in this order:
(a) accounts receivable, cash, prepaid insurance, and inventory.
(b) cash, inventory, accounts receivable, and prepaid insurance.
(c) cash, accounts receivable, merchandise inventory, and prepaid insurance.
(d) prepaid insurance, merchandise inventory, accounts receivable, and cash.

(SO 1) 3. Current assets are often listed by international companies:
(a) by importance.
(b) by permanence.
(c) by liquidity.
(d) by reverse liquidity.

(SO 2) 4. Which of the following is *not* an indicator of a company's profitability?
(a) Current ratio
(b) Earnings per share
(c) Profit
(d) Price-earnings ratio

(SO 2) 5. Which of the following measures is the best indicator of a company's ability to pay current liabilities?
(a) Price-earnings ratio
(b) Current ratio
(c) Debt to total assets
(d) Earnings per share

(SO 2)   6. Which of the following measures is the best indicator of a company's ability to survive over the long term?
(a) Price-earnings ratio
(b) Current ratio
(c) Debt to total assets
(d) Earnings per share

(SO 2)   7. The following ratios are available for Bachus Inc. and Newton Ltd.

	Current Ratio	Debt to Total Assets	Earnings per Share
Bachus	2.0:1	75.5%	$3.50
Newton	1.5:1	40.3%	$2.75

Compared with Newton, Bachus has:
(a) higher liquidity, higher solvency, and higher profitability.
(b) lower liquidity, higher solvency, and higher profitability.
(c) higher liquidity, lower solvency, and higher profitability.
(d) higher liquidity and lower solvency, but profitability cannot be compared based on the information provided.

(SO 3)   8. Which of the following is *not* a fundamental or enhancing qualitative characteristic of useful financial information?
(a) Accrual basis of accounting
(b) Relevance
(c) Faithful representation
(d) Comparability

(SO 3)   9. What accounting constraint allows a company to ignore the conceptual framework if the cost of providing the information is greater than the benefit?
(a) Comparability
(b) Verifiability
(c) Cost
(d) Relevance

(SO 3)   10. The cost basis of accounting states that:
(a) the benefits should exceed the costs of providing information.
(b) cost is more relevant than fair value.
(c) assets should be reported at their fair value.
(d) assets should be reported at their historical cost.

Questions

(SO 1)   1. What are current assets? Give four examples of current assets a company might have.

(SO 1)   2. What is meant by the term *operating cycle*?

(SO 1)   3. (a) Distinguish between current assets and non-current assets. (b) Distinguish between current assets and current liabilities.

(SO 1)   4. (a) What are current liabilities? (b) Give four examples of current liabilities a company might have.

(SO 1)   5. (a) Distinguish between current liabilities and non-current liabilities. (b) Explain how a note payable can sometimes be classified as both a current liability and a non-current liability.

(SO 1)   6. Identify the two components of shareholders' equity normally found in a corporation and indicate the purpose of each.

(SO 1)   7. Explain what it means to present a statement of financial position in order of liquidity, as is done by Eastplats and many other North American companies, compared with presenting it in an order of reverse liquidity, as is done by Amplats and many other international companies.

(SO 2)   8. Explain what each of the following classes of ratios measures and give an example of each: (a) liquidity ratios, (b) solvency ratios, and (c) profitability ratios.

(SO 2)   9. Why is the current ratio a better measure of liquidity than working capital?

(SO 2)   10. "The current ratio should not be used as the only measure of liquidity, because it does not take into account the composition of the current assets." Explain what this statement means.

(SO 2)   11. Dong Corporation has a debt to total assets ratio of 45%, while its competitor, Du Ltd., has a debt to total assets ratio of 55%. Based on this information, which company is more solvent?

(SO 2)   12. Jonathan Baird, the founder of Waterboots Inc., needs to raise $500,000 to expand his company's operations. He has been told that raising the money through debt (e.g., signing a bank loan payable) will increase the riskiness of his company much more than by raising the money through equity (issuing common shares). He doesn't understand why this is true. Explain it to him.

(SO 2)   13. Why can you compare the price-earnings ratio among different companies but not earnings per share?

(SO 2)   14. The TD Bank has a price-earnings ratio of 15, while CIBC has a price-earnings ratio of 12. Which company do investors appear to favour?

(SO 2)   15. Explain why increases in earnings per share, price-earnings, and current ratios are considered to be signs of improvement in a company's financial health, but an increase in the debt to total assets ratio is considered to be a sign of deterioration.

(SO 3)   16. (a) Describe the conceptual framework and explain how it helps financial reporting. (b) Is the conceptual framework applicable to publicly traded companies reporting using IFRS, to private companies using ASPE, or to both?

(SO 3) 17. (a) What is the objective of financial reporting? (b) Who are the main users that rely on this objective?

(SO 3) 18. Explain how the going concern assumption supports (a) the use of the cost basis of accounting, and (b) the classification of assets and liabilities as current and non-current.

(SO 3) 19. Identify and explain the two fundamental qualitative characteristics of useful financial information.

(SO 3) 20. How is materiality related to the fundamental qualitative characteristic of relevance?

(SO 3) 21. Identify and explain the four enhancing qualitative characteristics of useful financial information. Is there a prescribed order for applying these enhancing characteristics?

(SO 3) 22. Explain how the cost constraint relates to the quality of completeness.

(SO 3) 23. What are the elements of financial statements?

(SO 3) 24. Identify and explain the two principles used to measure the elements.

(SO 3) 25. Explain how the qualitative characteristics of relevance and faithful representation relate to the cost and fair value bases of accounting.

Brief Exercises

BE2–1 The following are the major statement of financial position classifications:

Classify accounts.
(SO 1)

1. Current assets
2. Long-term investments
3. Property, plant, and equipment
4. Intangible assets

5. Current liabilities
6. Non-current liabilities
7. Share capital
8. Retained earnings

Classify each of the following selected accounts by writing in the number of its appropriate classification above:

(a) _____ Accounts payable
(b) _____ Accounts receivable
(c) _____ Accumulated depreciation
(d) _____ Buildings
(e) _____ Cash
(f) _____ Patent
(g) _____ Dividends
(h) _____ Income tax payable

(i) _____ Investment in long-term bonds
(j) _____ Land
(k) _____ Merchandise inventory
(l) _____ Common shares
(m) _____ Supplies
(n) _____ Mortgage payable, due in 20 years
(o) _____ Current portion of mortgage payable

BE2–2 A list of current assets for Swann Limited includes the following: accounts receivable $14,500; cash $16,400; merchandise inventory $9,000; supplies $4,200, and prepaid insurance $3,900. Prepare the current assets section of the statement of financial position.

Prepare current assets section.
(SO 1)

BE2–3 A list of financial statement items for Shum Corporation includes the following: accumulated depreciation— buildings $33,000; accumulated depreciation—equipment $25,000; buildings $110,000; equipment $70,000; and land $65,000. Prepare the property, plant, and equipment section of the statement of financial position.

Prepare property, plant, and equipment section.
(SO 1)

BE2–4 Hirjika Inc. reports the following current and non-current liabilities: accounts payable $22,500; salaries payable $3,900; interest payable $5,200; income tax payable $6,400; mortgage payable (due within the year) $5,000; mortgage payable (due in more than one year) $50,000. Prepare the current liabilities section of the statement of financial position.

Prepare current liabilities section.
(SO 1)

BE2–5 The following is a list of current assets and current liabilities in alphabetical order. (a) In the first column, number each from 1 to 8 in the order it would appear in a statement of financial position listed in order of liquidity. (b) Repeat (a) in the second column but this time list the items in order of reverse liquidity.

Determine order of current assets and liabilities.
(SO 1)

	(a) Liquidity	(b) Reverse Liquidity
Accounts payable	_____	_____
Accounts receivable	_____	_____
Cash	_____	_____
Income tax payable	_____	_____
Merchandise inventory	_____	_____
Notes payable	_____	_____
Notes receivable	_____	_____
Short-term investments	_____	_____

Identify items affecting shareholders' equity. (SO 1)

BE2–6 For each of the following events affecting the shareholders' equity of Wu Corporation, indicate whether the event would increase share capital (+), decrease share capital (−), increase retained earnings (+), or decrease retained earnings (−). Write "NE" if there is no effect.

	Share Capital	Retained Earnings
(a) Issued common shares	_____	_____
(b) Paid a cash dividend	_____	_____
(c) Purchased merchandise inventory for cash	_____	_____
(d) Reported a profit	_____	_____
(e) Paid cash to creditors	_____	_____
(f) Reported a loss	_____	_____
(g) Issued preferred shares	_____	_____

Calculate ratios and evaluate liquidity. (SO 2)

BE2–7 Indigo Books & Music Inc. reported the following selected information for the years ended April 3, 2010, and March 28, 2009 (in thousands):

	2010	2009
Total current assets	$351,044	$335,125
Total current liabilities	244,665	248,043

(a) Calculate the working capital and current ratio for each year.
(b) Was Indigo's liquidity stronger or weaker in 2010 compared with 2009?

Calculate ratios and evaluate solvency. (SO 2)

BE2–8 Convenience store operator Alimentation Couche-Tard Inc. reported the following selected information for the years ended April 25, 2010, and April 26, 2009 (in USD millions):

	2010	2009
Current assets	$1,031.0	$ 844.5
Non-current assets	2,665.7	2,411.4
Current liabilities	882.9	789.0
Non-current liabilities	1,199.5	1,140.9

(a) Calculate the debt to total assets ratio for each year.
(b) Was the company's solvency stronger or weaker in 2010 compared with 2009?

Calculate ratios and evaluate profitability. (SO 2)

BE2–9 The following information is available for Leon's Furniture Limited for the years ended December 31 (in thousands, except for share price):

	2010	2009
Profit available to common shareholders	$63,284	$56,864
Weighted average number of common shares	70,732	70,714
Share price	$14.80	$10.50

(a) Calculate the earnings per share and the price-earnings ratio for each year.
(b) Indicate whether profitability improved or deteriorated in 2010.

Identify components of conceptual framework. (SO 3)

BE2–10 Presented below is a chart showing selected portions of the conceptual framework. Fill in the blanks from (a) to (f).

Qualitative Characteristics		Constraint	Underlying Assumption	Measurement of the Elements
Fundamental Qualitative Characteristics	Enhancing Qualitative Characteristics			
Relevance	Comparability	(d)	(e)	Cost
(a)	(b)			(f)
	Timeliness			
	(c)			

BE2–11   The following selected items relate to the qualitative characteristics of useful financial information discussed in this chapter:

Identify qualitative characteristics. (SO 3)

1. Comparability	8. Neutrality
2. Completeness	9. Predictive value
3. Confirmatory value	10. Relevance
4. Cost constraint	11. Timeliness
5. Faithful representation	12. Understandability
6. Freedom from error or bias	13. Verifiability
7. Materiality	

Match each characteristic to one of the statements below:

(a) _____ Information that has predictive value, confirmatory value, and is material is said to have this fundamental qualitative characteristic.

(b) _____ Information that is complete, neutral, and reasonably free of error is said to have this fundamental qualitative characteristic.

(c) _____ This enhancing qualitative characteristic requires that similar companies should apply the same accounting principles to similar events for successive accounting periods.

(d) _____ This quality results in information that has nothing important omitted.

(e) _____ This constraint requires that the value of the information presented should be greater than the cost of providing it.

(f) _____ Public accountants perform audits to determine this enhancing qualitative characteristic.

(g) _____ This quality requires that information cannot be selected to favour one position over another.

(h) _____ This enhancing qualitative characteristic describes information that a reasonably informed user can interpret and comprehend.

(i) _____ When information provides a basis for forecasting profits for future periods, it is said to have this quality.

(j) _____ This quality describes information that confirms or corrects users' prior expectations.

(k) _____ This enhancing qualitative characteristic requires that information must be available to decision makers before it loses its ability to influence their decisions.

(l) _____ Faithful representation means that information is complete, neutral, and this third quality.

(m) _____ This quality allows items of insignificance that would not likely influence a decision not to be disclosed.

BE2–12   For each of the situations discussed below, choose a measurement principle to use and explain why.

Identify measurement principles. (SO 3)

(a) Sosa Ltd. is a real estate company that purchases and holds land for eventual sale to developers.

(b) Mohawk Inc. is a manufacturing company that purchased land on which it plans to construct a new plant next year. It expects the value of the land to rise rapidly over the next few years.

Exercises

E2–1   The following are the major statement of financial position classifications:

Classify accounts. (SO 1)

1. Current assets	5. Current liabilities
2. Long-term investments	6. Non-current liabilities
3. Property, plant, and equipment	7. Shareholders' equity
4. Intangible assets	

Instructions
Classify each of the following selected accounts taken from TELUS Corporation's statement of financial position by writing in the number of the appropriate classification above:

(a) _____ Accounts payable and accrued liabilities

(b) _____ Accounts receivable

(c) _____ Accumulated depreciation

(d) _____ Buildings and leasehold improvements

(e) _____ Common shares

(f) _____ Current maturities of long-term debt

(g) _____ Dividends payable

(h) _____ Goodwill

(i) _____ Income and other taxes payable

(j) _____ Income and other taxes receivable

(k) _____ Inventories

(l) _____ Investments

(m) _____ Land

(n) _____ Long-term debt

(o) _____ Other long-term liabilities

(p) _____ Prepaid expenses

(q) _____ Spectrum licences [to use public frequencies]

Prepare assets section.
(SO 1)

E2-2   The assets (in thousands) that follow were taken from the December 31, 2010, balance sheet for Big Rock Brewery:

Accounts receivable	$ 1,789
Accumulated amortization—buildings	3,304
Accumulated amortization—furniture and fixtures	1,818
Accumulated amortization—production equipment	18,648
Accumulated amortization—vehicles	890
Buildings	11,879
Cash	769
Furniture and fixtures	2,328
Inventories	4,471
Land	2,516
Prepaid expenses and other	397
Production equipment	33,871
Vehicles	1,101

Instructions

Prepare the assets section of the statement of financial position.

Prepare liabilities and equity sections.
(SO 1)

E2-3   The liabilities and shareholders' equity items (in thousands) that follow were taken from the March 31, 2010, balance sheet for Saputo Inc.:

Accounts payable and accrued liabilities	$ 471,106
Bank loans payable (short-term)	61,572
Common shares	584,749
Future income taxes payable (short-term)	8,639
Future income taxes payable (long-term)	143,675
Income taxes payable	149,377
Long-term debt	380,790
Other reductions in shareholders' equity	159,524
Other long-term liabilities	9,694
Retained earnings	1,603,373

Instructions

Prepare the liabilities and shareholders' equity sections of the statement of financial position.

Prepare statement of financial position.
(SO 1)

E2-4   These items are taken from the financial statements of Summit's Bowling Alley Ltd. at December 31, 2012:

Accounts payable	$ 14,050	Income tax expense	$ 5,000
Accounts receivable	13,780	Interest expense	4,750
Accumulated depreciation—buildings	45,600	Interest payable	1,600
Accumulated depreciation—equipment	17,770	Land	54,000
Bowling revenue	73,040	Long-term investments	30,000
Buildings	128,800	Mortgage payable	95,000
Cash	15,040	Operating expenses	35,600
Common shares	50,000	Prepaid insurance	390
Depreciation expense	13,080	Retained earnings, Jan. 1	66,520
Equipment	62,400	Supplies	740

Instructions

(a) Calculate profit and the ending balance of retained earnings at December 31, 2012. It is not necessary to prepare a formal income statement or statement of changes in equity.

(b) Prepare a statement of financial position. Assume that $13,600 of the mortgage payable will be paid in 2013.

Prepare statement of financial position—reverse liquidity.
(SO 1)

E2-5   Refer to the information presented in E2-4 for Summit's Bowling Alley Ltd.

Instructions

(a) Calculate profit and the ending balance of retained earnings at December 31, 2012. It is not necessary to prepare a formal income statement or statement of changes in equity.

(b) Prepare a statement of financial position, listing items in order of reverse liquidity. Assume that $13,600 of the mortgage payable will be paid in 2013.

E2–6 These financial statement items are for Batra Corporation at year end, July 31, 2012:

Salaries expense	$44,700	Supplies expense	$ 900
Utilities expense	2,600	Dividends	12,000
Equipment	35,900	Depreciation expense	3,000
Accounts payable	4,220	Retained earnings, Aug. 1, 2011	17,940
Commission revenue	81,100	Rent expense	10,800
Rent revenue	18,500	Income tax expense	5,000
Common shares	10,000	Supplies	1,500
Cash	5,060	Short-term investments	20,000
Accounts receivable	17,100	Bank loan payable (due Dec. 31, 2012)	21,800
Accumulated depreciation—equipment	6,000	Interest expense	2,000
Interest payable	1,000		

Additional information:

Batra started the year with $6,000 of common shares and issued $4,000 more during the year.

Instructions

Prepare an income statement, statement of changes in equity, and statement of financial position for the year.

E2–7 The chief financial officer (CFO) of Padilla Corporation requested that the accounting department prepare a preliminary statement of financial position on December 20, 2012. He knows that certain debt agreements with its lenders require the company to maintain a current ratio of at least 2:1 and wants to know how the company is doing. The preliminary statement of financial position follows:

PADILLA CORPORATION
Statement of Financial Position
December 20, 2012

Assets		Liabilities		
Current assets		Current liabilities		
Cash	$ 25,000	Accounts payable	$ 20,000	
Accounts receivable	30,000	Salaries payable	10,000	$ 30,000
Prepaid insurance	5,000	Bank loan payable		80,000
Total current assets	60,000	Total liabilities		110,000
Equipment	200,000	Shareholders' equity		
Total assets	$260,000	Common shares	$100,000	
		Retained earnings	50,000	150,000
		Total liabilities and shareholders' equity		$260,000

Instructions

(a) Calculate the current ratio based on the data in the preliminary statement of financial position.

(b) Based on the results in (a), the CFO requested that $20,000 of the cash be used to pay off the balance of the accounts payable account on December 21. Calculate the current ratio after this payment is made, assuming there are no further changes to current assets and current liabilities.

(c) Is it ethical for the CFO to recommend this action?

E2–8 Safeway Inc. is a competitor of Sobeys and Loblaw, operating over 1,700 grocery and drug stores across Western Canada and in the United States. Safeway reported the following selected information (in USD millions):

	2010	2009
Current assets	$ 3,825.3	$ 3,976.2
Non-current assets	11,138.3	13,508.5
Current liabilities	4,237.8	4,499.2
Non-current liabilities	5,779.4	6,199.3

Instructions

(a) Calculate the working capital, current ratio, and debt to total assets ratio for each year.

(b) Did Safeway's liquidity and solvency improve or worsen during 2010?

(c) Using the data in the chapter, compare Safeway's liquidity and solvency with that of Sobeys, Loblaw, and the industry for 2010 and 2009.

Calculate ratios and evaluate profitability.
(SO 2)

E2-9   The following information is available for Cameco Corporation for the year ended December 31 (in thousands, except share price):

	2010	2009
Profit available for common shareholders	$514,749	$1,099,422
Weighted average number of common shares	393,169	387,956
Share price	$40.30	$33.93

Instructions

(a) Calculate the earnings per share and price-earnings ratio for each year.

(b) Based on your calculations above, how did the company's profitability change from 2009 to 2010?

Identify qualitative characteristics.
(SO 3)

E2-10   Here are some fundamental and enhancing qualitative characteristics of useful financial information:

1. Comparability	7. Neutrality
2. Completeness	8. Predictive value
3. Confirmatory value	9. Relevance
4. Faithful representation	10. Timeliness
5. Freedom from error or bias	11. Understandability
6. Materiality	12. Verifiability

Instructions

Match each characteristic to one of the following statements, using the numbers 1 to 12.

(a) _____ Accounting information cannot be selected, prepared, or presented to favour one set of interested users over another.

(b) _____ Accounting information must be available to decision makers before it loses its ability to influence their decisions.

(c) _____ Accounting information is prepared on the assumption that users have a reasonable understanding of accounting and general business and economic conditions.

(d) _____ Accounting information provides a basis to evaluate a previously made decision.

(e) _____ Accounting information includes everything it needs to.

(f) _____ Accounting information helps users make predictions about the outcome of past, present, and future events.

(g) _____ Accounting information about one company can be evaluated against the accounting information from another company.

(h) _____ Accounting information is included if its omission or misstatement could influence the economic decisions of users.

(i) _____ All the accounting information that is necessary to faithfully represent economic reality is included.

(j) _____ Accounting information can be determined to be free of material error.

(k) _____ Accounting information is included if it will make a difference in users' decisions.

(l) _____ Accounting information about a company can be confirmed by two or more users to be a faithful representation.

Identify assumption or principle.
(SO 3)

E2-11   Marietta Corp. had the following reporting issues during the year:

1. Land with a cost of $208,000 that is intended on being used by the company as a building site was reported at its fair value of $260,000.

2. A surplus parcel of land with a cost of $150,000 intended for resale in the near future is reported at its fair value of $160,000.

3. The president of Marietta, Deanna Durnford, decided it wasn't necessary to classify assets and liabilities as current and non-current as she expects to operate the company only for another 10 years.

Instructions

For each of the above situations, identify (a) the assumption or principle involved, and (b) whether it is being followed correctly or has been violated.

Problems: Set A

Classify accounts.
(SO 1)

P2-1A   You are provided with the following selected balance sheet accounts for entertainment retailer HMV Group plc:

Accumulated depreciation	Deferred income tax asset (non-current)
Cash	Deferred income tax liabilities (non-current)
Current income tax payable	Goodwill
Current income tax recoverable	Interest-bearing loans and borrowings (current)

Interest-bearing loans and borrowings (non-current)   Retained earnings
Inventories   Trade and other payables
Investments   Trade and other receivables
Ordinary shares   Trademarks
Plant, equipment, and vehicles

Instructions

Identify the balance sheet (statement of financial position) category for classifying each account. For example, accumulated depreciation should be classified as a contra asset to plant, equipment, and vehicles in the property, plant, and equipment section of HMV's balance sheet.

P2–2A   Refer to the list of balance sheet accounts presented in P2–1A for HMV Group plc.

List accounts in order of liquidity and reverse liquidity.
(SO 1)

Instructions

(a) Number the accounts from 1 to 17 as they would appear in a balance sheet presented in order of liquidity.
(b) Number the accounts from 1 to 17 as they would appear in a balance sheet presented in order of reverse liquidity.
(c) Which order do you think HMV actually uses? Does it matter which method of ordering the company uses?

P2–3A   The following items are from the assets section of WestJet Airlines Ltd.'s December 31, 2010, balance sheet (in thousands):

Prepare assets section.
(SO 1)

Accounts receivable	$ 17,518
Accumulated depreciation—aircraft	622,997
Accumulated depreciation—buildings	13,154
Accumulated depreciation—ground property and equipment	61,895
Accumulated depreciation—leasehold improvements	3,348
Accumulated depreciation—spare engines and parts	28,251
Aircraft	2,471,806
Buildings	135,817
Cash	1,187,899
Ground property and equipment	121,814
Inventory	20,181
Intangible assets	13,018
Leasehold improvements	9,965
Other assets	166,557
Prepaid expenses, deposits, and other	41,716
Spare engines and parts	106,198

Instructions

(a) Identify the balance sheet (statement of financial position) category in which each of the above items should be classified.
(b) Prepare the assets section of the balance sheet.

P2–4A   The following items are from the liability and shareholders' equity sections of WestJet Airlines Ltd.'s December 31, 2010, balance sheet (in thousands):

Prepare liabilities and equity sections.
(SO 1)

Accounts payable and accrued liabilities	$303,583
Advance ticket sales	308,022
Current portion of long-term debt	183,789
Future income tax (long-term)	337,410
Long-term debt	866,745
Other current liabilities	36,778
Other long-term liabilities	18,838
Other shareholders' equity items	52,064
Retained earnings	807,978
Share capital	647,637

Instructions

(a) Identify the balance sheet (statement of financial position) category in which each of the above items should be classified.
(b) Prepare the liabilities and equity sections of the balance sheet.
(c) If you completed P2–3A, compare the total assets in P2–3A with the total liabilities and shareholders' equity in P2–4A. Do these two amounts agree?

Prepare financial
statements; discuss
relationships.
(SO 1)

P2–5A These items are taken from the financial statements of Mbong Corporation for the year ended December 31, 2012:

Retained earnings, Jan. 1	$105,000	Depreciation expense	$ 6,200
Utilities expense	2,000	Accounts receivable	14,200
Equipment	66,000	Insurance expense	2,200
Accounts payable	8,300	Salaries expense	37,000
Buildings	72,000	Accumulated depreciation—equipment	17,600
Cash	5,200	Income tax expense	6,000
Salaries payable	3,000	Supplies	200
Common shares	34,200	Supplies expense	1,000
Dividends	5,000	Bank loan payable, due 2015	15,000
Service revenue	81,700	Short-term investments	20,000
Prepaid insurance	2,000	Accumulated depreciation—buildings	18,000
Repair and maintenance expense	2,800	Interest expense	1,500
Land	40,000	Interest revenue	500

Additional information:

1. Mbong started the year with $30,000 of common shares and issued $4,200 more during the year.
2. $1,500 of the bank loan payable is due to be repaid within the next year.

Instructions

(a) Prepare an income statement, statement of changes in equity, and statement of financial position for the year.
(b) Explain how each financial statement is related to the others.

Calculate ratios and
comment on liquidity,
solvency, and
profitability.
(SO 2)

P2–6A The financial statements of Johannsen Inc. are presented here:

JOHANNSEN INC.
Income Statement
Year Ended December 31, 2012

Sales		$2,218,500
Expenses		
Cost of goods sold	$1,012,500	
Operating expenses	906,000	
Interest expense	98,000	2,016,500
Profit before income tax		202,000
Income tax expense		42,000
Profit		$ 160,000

JOHANNSEN INC.
Statement of Financial Position
December 31, 2012

Assets

Current assets		
Cash	$ 60,100	
Short-term investments	54,000	
Accounts receivable	207,800	
Merchandise inventory	125,000	$ 446,900
Property, plant, and equipment		625,300
Total assets		$1,072,200

Liabilities and Shareholders' Equity

Current liabilities		
Accounts payable	$100,000	
Income tax payable	15,000	
Current portion of mortgage payable	27,500	$ 142,500
Mortgage payable		310,000
Total liabilities		452,500
Shareholders' equity		
Common shares	$307,630	
Retained earnings	312,070	619,700
Total liabilities and shareholders' equity		$1,072,200

Additional information:

1. Profit available to common shareholders was $160,000.
2. The weighted average number of shares was 40,000.
3. The share price at December 31 was $35.

Instructions

(a) Calculate the following values and ratios for 2012. We provide the results for 2011 for comparative purposes.
  1. Working capital (2011: $260,500)
  2. Current ratio (2011: 1.6:1)
  3. Debt to total assets (2011: 31.5%)
  4. Earnings per share (2011: $3.15)
  5. Price-earnings ratio (2011: 7.5 times)
(b) Using the information in part (a), discuss the changes in liquidity, solvency, and profitability between 2011 and 2012.

P2–7A Selected financial statement data for a recent year for Chen Corporation and Caissie Corporation, two competitors, are as follows:

Calculate ratios and comment on liquidity, solvency, and profitability.
(SO 2)

	Chen	Caissie
Sales revenue	$1,800,000	$620,000
Cost of goods sold	1,175,000	340,000
Operating expenses	283,000	98,000
Interest expense	10,000	4,000
Income tax expense	85,000	35,400
Current assets	407,200	190,400
Non-current assets	532,000	139,700
Current liabilities	166,325	133,700
Non-current liabilities	108,500	40,700
Share price	25	15
Weighted average number of common shares	76,000	62,000

Instructions

(a) Calculate working capital and the current ratio for each company. Comment on their relative liquidity.
(b) Calculate the debt to total assets ratio for each company. Comment on their relative solvency.
(c) Calculate the profit, earnings per share, and price-earnings ratio for each company. Assume that the profit you calculate equals the profit available to common shareholders. Comment on the two companies' relative profitability.

P2–8A Selected financial data for a recent year for two clothing competitors, Le Château Inc. and H&M AB, are presented here (in millions, except share price):

Calculate ratios and comment on liquidity, solvency, and profitability.
(SO 2)

	Le Château (in CAD)	H&M (in SEK, Swedish krona)
Current assets	135	36,081
Total assets	236	54,363
Current liabilities	43	11,090
Total liabilities	79	13,750
Profit available to common shareholders	30	16,384
Share price	13.82	412.30
Weighted average number of common shares	24	827

Instructions

(a) For each company, calculate the following values and ratios. Where available, industry averages are included in parentheses.
  1. Working capital (n/a)
  2. Current ratio (2.3:1)
  3. Debt to total assets (21.9%)
  4. Earnings per share (n/a)
  5. Price-earnings ratio (16.0 times)
(b) Compare the liquidity, solvency, and profitability of the two companies and their industry.
(c) Does the fact that Le Château reports its results in Canadian dollars while H&M uses Swedish krona affect your comparisons in (b)? Explain.

Comment on
liquidity, solvency,
and profitability.
(SO 2)

P2–9A   Selected ratios for Pitka Corporation are as follows:

	2012	2011	2010
Working capital	$10,000	$25,000	$35,000
Current ratio	1.1:1	1.2:1	1.2:1
Debt to total assets	34.2%	42.3%	40.0%
Earnings per share	$3.50	$3.15	$3.40
Price-earnings ratio	5.7 times	5.1 times	5.5 times

Instructions

(a) Identify if the change in each value or ratio is an improvement or deterioration between (1) 2010 and 2011, and (2) 2011 and 2012.

(b) Briefly discuss the change in Pitka's liquidity, solvency, and profitability over the three-year period.

Discuss financial
reporting objective
and qualitative
characteristics.
(SO 3)

P2–10A   A friend of yours, Ana Gehrig, recently completed an undergraduate degree in science and has just started working with a biotechnology company. Ana tells you that the company management is trying to secure new sources of financing to proceed with development of a new health care product. Ana said that her boss told her that the company must put together a report to present to potential investors.

Ana thought that the company should include in this package the detailed scientific findings related to the Phase I clinical trials for this product. She said, "I know that the biotech industry sometimes has only a 10% success rate with new products, but if we report all the scientific findings, everyone will see what a sure success this is going to be! The president was talking about the importance of following some set of international financial reporting standards. Why do we need to look at some accounting standards? What they need to realize is that we have scientific results that are quite encouraging, some of the most talented employees around, and the start of some really great customer relationships. We haven't made any sales yet, but we will. We just need the funds to get through all the clinical testing and get government approval for our product. Then these investors will be quite happy that they invested in our company early!"

Instructions

(a) What is the objective of financial reporting? Do Ana's suggestions for what should be reported to prospective investors meet the objective of financial reporting? Explain.

(b) Comment on whether what Ana proposes to report conforms, or does not conform, to the fundamental and enhancing qualitative characteristics of useful financial information.

Discuss qualitative
characteristics.
(SO 3)

P2–11A   A friend of yours, Ryan Konotopsky, has come to you looking for some answers about financial statements. Ryan tells you that he is thinking about opening a movie theatre in his home town. Before doing so, he wants to find out how much he could expect to make in sales from food concessions as opposed to ticket sales. He wants to know what portion of ticket sales he could expect for children, youths, and seniors, who pay less than adults, who pay the highest admission rate. He also wants to know how much profit he would make on ticket sales versus sales at the concession stands, and he would like to know the average wage per employee.

Ryan downloaded the financial statements of Empire Company Limited, which owns Sobeys, Canada's #2 grocery chain, and a variety of commercial and residential real estate, in addition to Empire Theatres, Canada's #2 movie exhibitor. He read through Empire's annual report and learned that Empire Theatres is just one part of the company's Investments and Other Operations division. There are food retailing and real estate divisions as well.

Ryan is disillusioned because he cannot find many details about Empire Theatres in the financial statements. He has come to you looking for explanations.

Instructions

(a) Describe the fundamental and enhancing qualitative characteristics, including the cost constraint, of useful financial information.

(b) Identify which, if any, of the characteristics you identified in (a) might explain why Ryan cannot find much information about Empire Theatres in Empire's financial statements.

Discuss measurement
principles.
(SO 3)

P2–12A   In 2011, when publicly traded companies in Canada adopted IFRS, real estate companies were given the choice of using cost or fair value to account for their real estate portfolios. This was not an easy decision for real estate companies to make as there were advantages and disadvantages to each choice. In the end, while many companies chose to revalue their real estate portfolios to fair value, others chose cost.

Instructions

(a) Identify the advantages and disadvantages of each of the two measurement principles: cost and fair value.

(b) Speculate as to why a company might choose to adopt the fair value basis of accounting for its real estate portfolio. What impact do you think this will have on the elements of its financial statements?

(c) Speculate as to why a company might choose to adopt the cost basis of accounting for its real estate portfolio. What impact do you think this will have on the elements of its financial statements?

(d) Do you believe you could effectively compare the financial statements of two competing companies using different measurement principles?

Problems: Set B

P2–1B You are provided with the following selected balance sheet accounts for L'Oréal Group SA, the world's largest beauty products company:

Classify accounts. (SO 1)

Accumulated amortization—patents and trademarks	Investments
Accumulated depreciation—industrial machinery and equipment	Land
	Marketable securities
	Non-current borrowings and debts
Bank overdraft	Ordinary shares
Cash	Patents and trademarks
Current borrowings and debts	Prepaid expenses
Goodwill	Retained earnings
Income tax payable (current)	Trade accounts payable
Industrial machinery and equipment	Trade accounts receivable
Inventories	

Instructions

Identify the balance sheet (statement of financial position) category for classifying each account. For example, accumulated amortisation should be classified as a contra asset to patents and trademarks in the intangible assets section of L'Oréal's balance sheet.

P2–2B Refer to the list of balance sheet accounts presented in P2–1B for L'Oréal Group SA.

Instructions

(a) Number the accounts from 1 to 19 as they would appear in a balance sheet presented in order of liquidity.
(b) Number the accounts from 1 to 19 as they would appear in a balance sheet presented in order of reverse liquidity.
(c) Which order do you think L'Oréal actually uses? Does it matter which method of ordering the company uses?

List accounts in order of liquidity and reverse liquidity. (SO 1)

P2–3B The following items are from the assets section of Reitmans (Canada) Limited's January 30, 2010, balance sheet (in thousands):

Prepare assets section. (SO 1)

Accounts receivable	$ 2,926
Accumulated amortization—software	7,108
Accumulated depreciation—buildings and improvements	19,499
Accumulated depreciation—fixtures and equipment	97,398
Accumulated depreciation—leasehold improvements	103,418
Buildings and improvements	52,336
Cash	228,577
Fixtures and equipment	177,874
Future income tax assets (current)	2,395
Future income tax assets (non-current)	11,466
Goodwill	42,426
Land	5,935
Leasehold improvements	194,782
Marketable securities	48,026
Merchandise inventories	63,127
Prepaid expenses	11,873
Software	17,072

Instructions

(a) Identify the balance sheet (statement of financial position) category in which each of the above assets should be classified.
(b) Prepare the assets section of the balance sheet.

P2–4B The following items are from the liability and shareholders' equity sections of Reitmans (Canada) Limited's January 30, 2010, balance sheet (in thousands):

Prepare liabilities and equity sections. (SO 1)

Accounts payable and accrued items	$ 77,766
Current portion of mortgage payable	1,300
Income taxes payable	4,677
Mortgage payable	11,431
Other long-term liabilities	26,052
Other shareholders' equity items	(1,508)
Retained earnings	480,622
Common shares	31,052

Instructions

(a) Identify the balance sheet (statement of financial position) category in which each of the above items should be classified.

(b) Prepare the liabilities and equity sections of the balance sheet.

(c) If you completed P2–3B, compare the total assets in P2–3B with the total liabilities and shareholders' equity in P2–4B. Do these two amounts agree?

Prepare financial statements; discuss relationships.
(SO 1)

P2–5B These items are taken from financial statements of Beaulieu Limited for the year ended December 31, 2012:

Cash	$ 8,000	Retained earnings, Jan. 1	$34,000
Buildings	80,000	Dividends	3,500
Accumulated depreciation—buildings	12,000	Service revenue	80,500
Accounts receivable	7,500	Depreciation expense	5,400
Prepaid insurance	250	Insurance expense	2,400
Equipment	32,000	Salaries expense	33,000
Accumulated depreciation—equipment	19,200	Utilities expense	3,700
Accounts payable	9,550	Interest expense	8,000
Salaries payable	3,000	Interest revenue	500
Common shares	20,000	Land	50,000
Income tax expense	5,000	Mortgage payable	80,000
Long-term investments	20,000		

Additional information:

1. Beaulieu started the year with $15,000 of common shares and issued $5,000 more during the year.
2. $10,000 of the mortgage payable is due to be repaid within the next year.

Instructions

(a) Prepare an income statement, statement of changes in equity, and statement of financial position for the year.

(b) Explain how each financial statement is related to the others.

Calculate ratios and comment on liquidity, solvency, and profitability.
(SO 2)

P2–6B The financial statements of Fast Corporation are presented here:

FAST CORPORATION
Income Statement
Year Ended December 31, 2012

Sales		$706,000
Expenses		
Cost of goods sold	$420,000	
Operating expenses	144,000	
Interest expense	10,000	574,000
Profit before income taxes		132,000
Income tax expense		35,400
Profit		$ 96,600

FAST CORPORATION
Statement of Financial Position
December 31, 2012

Assets

Current assets		
Cash	$ 23,100	
Short-term investments	34,800	
Accounts receivable	86,200	
Merchandise inventory	109,750	$253,850
Property, plant, and equipment		465,300
Total assets		$719,150

Liabilities and Shareholders' Equity

Current liabilities		
Accounts payable	$134,200	
Income tax payable	10,350	
Current portion of mortgage payable	12,000	$156,550
Mortgage payable		132,000
Total liabilities		288,550

Shareholders' equity
    Common shares $100,000
    Retained earnings   330,600   430,600
    Total liabilities and shareholders' equity $719,150

Additional information:

1. Profit available to common shareholders was $96,600.
2. The weighted average number of common shares was 40,000.
3. The share price at December 31 was $30.

Instructions

(a) Calculate the following values and ratios for 2012. We provide the results for 2011 for comparative purposes.
   1. Working capital (2011: $78,000)
   2. Current ratio (2011: 1.4:1)
   3. Debt to total assets (2011: 51.5%)
   4. Earnings per share (2011: $1.35)
   5. Price-earnings ratio (2011: 10.8 times)
(b) Using the information in part (a), discuss the changes in liquidity, solvency, and profitability between 2011 and 2012.

P2–7B Selected financial statement data for a recent year for Belliveau Corporation and Shields Corporation, two competitors, are as follows:

Calculate ratios and comment on liquidity, solvency, and profitability. (SO 2)

	Belliveau	Shields
Sales revenue	$450,000	$890,000
Cost of goods sold	260,000	620,000
Operating expenses	130,000	59,000
Interest expense	6,000	10,000
Income tax expense	10,000	65,000
Current assets	180,000	700,000
Non-current assets	600,000	800,000
Current liabilities	75,000	300,000
Non-current liabilities	190,000	200,000
Share price	2.50	6.00
Weighted average number of common shares	200,000	200,000

Instructions

(a) Calculate working capital and the current ratio for each company. Comment on their relative liquidity.
(b) Calculate the debt to total assets ratio for each company. Comment on their relative solvency.
(c) Calculate the profit, earnings per share, and price-earnings ratio for each company. Assume that the profit you calculate equals the profit available to common shareholders. Comment on the two companies' relative profitability.

P2–8B Selected financial data for a recent year for two discount retail chains, Walmart Stores, Inc. and Target Corporation, are presented here (in USD millions, except for share price):

Calculate ratios and comment on liquidity, solvency, and profitability. (SO 2)

	Walmart	Target
Current assets	$ 48,331	$18,424
Total assets	170,706	44,533
Current liabilities	55,561	11,327
Total liabilities	97,777	29,186
Profit available to common shareholders	14,335	2,488
Share price	53.43	48.26
Weighted average number of common shares	3,866	752

Instructions

(a) For each company, calculate the following values and ratios. Where available, industry averages have been included in parentheses.
   1. Working capital (n/a)
   2. Current ratio (1.1:1)
   3. Debt to total assets (36.3%)
   4. Earnings per share (n/a)
   5. Price-earnings ratio (14.3 times)
(b) Compare the liquidity, solvency, and profitability of the two companies and their industry.

Comment on liquidity, solvency, and profitability.
(SO 2)

P2–9B   Selected ratios for Giasson Corporation are as follows:

	2012	2011	2010
Working capital	$47,000	$53,000	$50,000
Current ratio	1.5:1	1.7:1	2.0:1
Debt to total assets	25.4%	25.5%	20.0%
Earnings per share	$0.86	$1.29	$1.00
Price-earnings ratio	4.7 times	5.1 times	5.5 times

Instructions
(a) Identify if the change in each value or ratio is an improvement or deterioration between (1) 2010 and 2011, and (2) 2011 and 2012.
(b) Briefly discuss the change in Giasson's liquidity, solvency, and profitability over the three-year period.

Discuss financial reporting objective and qualitative characteristics.
(SO 3)

P2–10B   **Bre-X Minerals Ltd.** (Bre-X), a small mining company based in Calgary, was involved in one of the biggest stock scandals in Canadian history and the biggest mining scandal of all time. The company announced in the early 1990s that it had discovered a significant gold deposit in Indonesia, after which its share price skyrocketed from pennies a share to more than $285 per share. In 1997, it was discovered that the company had tampered with samples by "salting" crushed ore with gold and that there was little, if any, gold there. Shareholders lost billions of dollars and sued the company and its management for providing misleading information.

Investors have had little luck to date in getting back their money. In 2010, the former chief geologist of Bre-X was found not guilty of insider trading and misleading investors. Some of the class action suits have collapsed and other civil suits are still proceeding slowly through the courts.

Instructions
(a) What is the objective of financial reporting? Did Bre-X's reporting meet this objective? Explain.
(b) Describe the fundamental and enhancing qualitative characteristics of useful financial information. Which of these, if any, were violated by Bre-X?

Discuss elements of financial statements.
(SO 3)

P2–11B   Assets and liabilities are critical elements of financial statements. Assets are defined as a resource that will provide future economic benefits. Three examples include:

1. Land owned by Shoppers Drug Mart
2. The BlackBerry® trademark
3. Accounts receivable

Liabilities are defined as obligations that result from past transactions. Three examples include:

1. Accounts payable
2. Unearned revenue
3. Bank loan payable

Instructions
(a) Discuss how each of the three assets listed above will provide future economic benefits.
(b) Discuss how each of the three liabilities listed above arose.

Identify measurement principles.
(SO 3)

P2–12B   The following are hypothetical situations that require the choice of one of the two measurement principles: cost or fair value.

1. You purchase your textbooks at the university bookstore to use during the term, but plan on selling them at the end of the term.
2. You purchase a new iPad and never plan on parting with it, at least not until a new model comes out.
3. You purchase software for your computer under a special deal that allows you to upgrade it whenever a new version is released.
4. You purchase a used car.
5. You purchase land, which you eventually hope to build a home on.

Instructions
(a) Identify the advantages and disadvantages of each of the two measurement principles: cost and fair value.
(b) For each of the above situations, identify which measurement principle would be the most appropriate to choose, and explain why.

Broadening Your Perspective

Financial Reporting and Analysis Cases

Financial Reporting: *Eastplats*

BYP2–1 The financial statements of Eastern Platinum Limited (Eastplats) are presented in Appendix A at the end of this book.

Instructions

(a) What were the balances of Eastplats's total current assets and total assets at December 31, 2010 and 2009?

(b) In what order are Eastplats's current assets listed? Non-current assets?

(c) What were the balances of Eastplats's total current liabilities and total liabilities at December 31, 2010 and 2009?

(d) In what order are its current liabilities listed? Non-current liabilities?

Answer questions about statement of financial position. (SO 1)

Comparative Analysis: *Eastplats and Amplats*

BYP2–2 The financial statements of Anglo American Platinum Limited (Amplats) are presented in Appendix B following the financial statements for Eastern Platinum Limited (Eastplats) in Appendix A.

Instructions

(a) For each company, calculate or find the following ratios and values for the year ended December 31, 2010. Industry averages, where available, are shown in parentheses.

1. Working capital (n/a)

2. Current ratio (2.3:1)

3. Debt to total assets (23.7%)

4. Earnings per share (n/a)

5. Price-earnings ratio (the year-end share price for Eastplats was $1.77 and R664 for Amplats) (19.7 times)

(b) Based on your findings for question (a), discuss the relative liquidity, solvency, and profitability of the two companies and their industry.

(c) Would your findings in (b) change for Amplats if you used the financial statements it presented in U.S. dollars to calculate your ratios in (a) rather than those using the South African rand (R)?

Calculate ratios and comment on liquidity, solvency, and profitability. (SO 2)

Interpreting Financial Information

BYP2–3 Thomson Reuters Corporation considers itself the world's leading provider of information. It provides electronic information and services worldwide, serving the legal, financial services, tax and accounting, health care and science, and media markets. It operates in more than 100 countries, including Canada.

One of the challenges global companies face is to make themselves attractive to investors from other countries. This is difficult to do when different accounting principles can blur the real impact of profits. For example, Thomson Reuters was an early adopter of IFRS in Canada. In its income statement for the year ended December 31, 2008, the company reported a profit of U.S. $1,321 million. Had Thomson Reuters reported under Canadian GAAP for the same year, its profit would have been U.S. $1,405 million. Had it reported under U.S. GAAP for the same year, its profit would have been U.S. $1,264 million.

Discuss impact of using different measurement principles. (SO 2, 3)

Instructions

(a) Suppose you wish to compare Thomson Reuters with a publicly traded competitor in Canada that did not choose to adopt IFRS early and reported using Canadian GAAP in 2008. How would the use of different accounting principles—IFRS and Canadian GAAP—within the same country affect your ability to compare the financial position and performance of the two companies?

(b) Suppose you wish to compare Thomson Reuters with a private company operating in Canada that reported using Accounting Standards for Private Enterprises. How would the use of different accounting principles—IFRS and ASPE—within the same country affect your ability to compare the financial position and performance of the two companies?

(c) Suppose you wish to compare Thomson Reuters with a United States–based competitor that reported using U.S. GAAP. How would the use of different accounting principles—IFRS and U.S. GAAP—within different countries affect your ability to compare the financial position and performance of the two companies?

(d) Suppose you wish to compare Thomson Reuters with a Canadian-based publicly traded competitor that also reported using IFRS. If the competitor chose to use different measurement principles than Thomson Reuters (e.g., the fair value basis of accounting rather than cost), how would the use of different principles within the same country affect your ability to compare the financial position and performance of the two companies?

Comparing IFRS and ASPE

Discuss qualitative characteristics of accounting information for private and public companies.
(SO 3)

BYP2–4   McCain Foods Limited is a large multinational private company with $6 billion in sales. It produces both frozen and non-frozen food products and makes one-third of the frozen French fries produced worldwide. It has manufacturing operations in 18 countries, sales operations in over 100 countries, and employs more than 20,000 people.

Most private companies choose to use ASPE. However, some private companies like McCain have adopted IFRS. McCain's Vice President and Corporate Controller, Richard Burton, notes that although McCain is privately held, it treats itself for reporting purposes like a public company.

Instructions

(a) McCain has numerous subsidiaries located throughout the globe. How would this type of multinational structure motivate McCain to choose IFRS?

(b) Why would users of McCain's financial statements want them prepared using IFRS? Try to relate the users' needs to the four qualitative characteristics of accounting information: relevance, faithful representation, comparability, and understandability.

(c) It is often assumed that only large private companies would choose to adopt IFRS and small companies would avoid IFRS. Why do you think that is? Can you think of reasons why a small private company would want to adopt IFRS?

Critical Thinking Cases and Activities

Collaborative Learning Activity

Obtain company information and calculate ratios.
(SO 2)

**BYP2–5   In this chapter, you have learned about the preparation of a company's financial statements. Companies that are listed on a stock exchange, such as the Toronto Stock Exchange (TSX), must make annual disclosures of financial and other information in accordance with securities legislation. These documents are available to the public, either on the company's own website or on the System for Electronic Document Analysis and Retrieval (SEDAR) website (www.sedar.com).

Instructions

With the class divided into groups, each group should pick one company that is listed on the TSX in one of the following sectors and download the relevant financial information:

- energy, oil, and gas
- financial services
- manufacturing
- real estate
- retail
- telecommunications

Answer the following questions:
(a) What does the company do?
(b) In which countries other than Canada, if any, does the company operate?
(c) Is your company subject to regulation, either federally or provincially?
(d) Does your company pay a dividend? If so, how much was paid per share to the common shareholders in the last year?
(e) Calculate or find the following ratios for the most recent year: (1) current ratio, (2) debt to total assets, (3) earnings per share, and (4) price-earnings ratio.
(f) As a group, discuss whether this is a company you would like to work for and/or invest in.
(g) Compare your findings with the other groups.

Communication Activity

Apply qualitative characteristic of relevance.
(SO 3)

**BYP2–6   You are planning to meet with a former classmate that you have not seen or communicated with for four years. You used to be good friends when you were growing up but lost touch when your friend moved away. The two of you have only one hour together to catch up on what has happened during the last four years. Therefore, you must make a decision on what needs to be covered as part of your conversation. You want to be sure to cover the important events.

Instructions

(a) Write down the key items you want to cover during your meeting.
(b) Compare the decision process you went through to determine what to include in your one-hour meeting with the fundamental qualitative characteristic of relevance.

Ethics Case

Discuss early implementation of accounting standards.
(SO 3)

**BYP2–7   When new accounting standards are issued, a required implementation date (the date when a company has to start applying the recommendation) is dictated but early implementation is also possible—even encouraged. For example, Canadian publicly traded companies were required to start using IFRS by January 1, 2011, but early adoption was permitted.

Kathy Johnston, the controller at Redondo Corporation, discussed with Redondo's vice-president of finance the possibility of implementing IFRS early. She said it would result in a much better comparison of the company's financial condition and profit with its international competitors. When the vice-president determined that early implementation would decrease reported profit for the year, he strongly discouraged Kathy from implementing IFRS until it was required.

Instructions

(a) Who are the stakeholders in this situation?

(b) What, if any, are the ethical considerations in this situation?

(c) What could Kathy gain by supporting early implementation? Who might be affected by the decision against early implementation?

"All About You" Activity

BYP2–8 As discussed in the "All About You" feature presented in this chapter, in order to evaluate your own financial situation, you need to prepare a personal statement of financial position. Assume that you have gathered the following information about your personal finances:

Amount owed on student loan (non-current)	$20,500
Balance in chequing account	1,500
Amount paid for vehicle	3,000
Student fees due in three months' time	2,300
Amount paid for laptop and accessories	750
Amount paid for clothes and furniture	4,500
Balance owed on credit cards	900
Balance owed on loan from parents (non-current)	2,400

Prepare personal statement of financial position. (SO 1)

Instructions

Prepare a personal statement of financial position using the format you have learned for a statement of financial position for a company. *Note:* Instead of shareholders' equity, use personal equity (or deficit).

Serial Case

(*Note:* This serial case was started in Chapter 1 and will continue in each chapter.)

BYP2-9 After investigating the opportunities available to her and graduating from university, Natalie chooses to become a shareholder of, and work for, Koebel's Family Bakery Ltd. She begins the process of familiarizing herself with the business operation and all of the information that is generated to enable her parents to run their business on a day-to-day basis.

Answer questions about sources of financial information. (SO 2, 3)

While at a trade show, Natalie is introduced to Gerry Richards, operations manager of Biscuits Inc., a national food retailer and publicly traded company. After much discussion, Gerry asks Natalie (acting for Koebel's Family Bakery Ltd.) to consider being Biscuits' major supplier of oatmeal chocolate chip cookies. He provides Natalie with the most recent copy of Biscuits' financial statements. He anticipates that Koebel's Family Bakery will need to provide Biscuits with approximately 1,500 dozen cookies a week. Koebel's Family Bakery is to provide a monthly invoice to Biscuits and will be paid approximately 30 days from the date the invoice is received.

Natalie is thrilled with the offer; however, she is concerned that taking on this additional contractual commitment along with the one that has just recently been negotiated for the providing of cupcakes will be too much to handle for Koebel's Family Bakery.

Instructions

Natalie has come to you for advice and asks the following questions.

(a) Biscuits has provided me with a full set of financial statements. Can you please identify each financial statement included in this package and explain what type of information each statement provides?

(b) I would like to be sure that Biscuits will be able to pay Koebel's Family Bakery's invoices. How can I determine if Biscuits has enough cash to meet its current liabilities? Are there any ratios or financial information I should look at specifically to obtain that information?

(c) Is Biscuits profitable? Are there any ratios or financial information I should look at specifically to obtain that information?

(d) Does Biscuits have any non-current debt? If so, is Biscuits able to pay off both its debt and the related interest on its debt? Are there any ratios or financial information I should look at specifically to obtain that information?

(e) If Koebel's Family Bakery were to sign a contract committing to provide 1,500 dozen cookies a week, what other factors should be considered before accepting the contract?

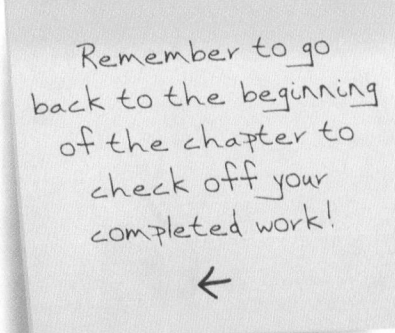

Remember to go back to the beginning of the chapter to check off your completed work!

←

Answers to Self-Test Questions

1. a	2. c	3. d	4. a	5. b
6. c	7. d	8. a	9. c	10. d

CHAPTER 3

The Accounting Information System

The Navigator
Chapter 3

- [ ] Scan *Study Objectives*
- [ ] Read *Feature Story*
- [ ] Read text and answer *Do It!s*
- [ ] Review *Comparing IFRS and ASPE*
- [ ] Review *Summary of Study Objectives*
- [ ] Review *Decision Toolkit—A Summary*
- [ ] Work *Using the Decision Toolkit*
- [ ] Work *Comprehensive Do It!*
- [ ] Answer *Self-Test Questions*
- [ ] Complete *assignments*
- [ ] Go to *WileyPLUS* for practice and tutorials

study objectives

After studying this chapter, you should be able to:

1. Analyze the effects of transactions on the accounting equation.
2. Define debits and credits and explain how they are used to record transactions.
3. Identify the basic steps in the recording process.
4. Prepare a trial balance.

the navigator

Learning to Handle the Dough

For generations, grandmothers in Grant Hooker's family would make a pastry of flattened, whole-wheat dough as special treat, called a BeaverTail®, which became a Sunday staple with Mr. Hooker's own kids during the 1970s.

In 1978, Mr. Hooker sold the family secret to the public for the first time at a music festival near Killaloe, Ontario. The crowd loved it. The delectable dough was then served up at several Ottawa Valley agricultural fairs throughout that fall. Encouraged by the enthusiasm for his treats, Mr. Hooker trademarked the name "BeaverTails" and built his own booth in Ottawa's Byward Market in 1980 to sell them full-time. However, sales weren't as swift as at the fairs.

Undaunted, Mr. Hooker secured permission to sell BeaverTails on the Rideau Canal during Ottawa's Winterlude festival. "We had lineups down the lake," he says. Within three years, BeaverTails Canada Inc. had the contract to sell all the food on the Rideau Canal and employed 450 people. The business continued to grow; BeaverTails began franchising in 1990 and now includes more than 80 outlets across Canada, with two locations in Saudi Arabia and two in Colorado's ski country.

At first, keeping track of the money was straightforward and didn't require a formal accounting system. It was merely a matter of staying on top of how much was owed to suppliers and staff, and in rent and utilities. Mr. Hooker, who has no formal business training, got along fine simply managing the chequebook.

But this changed with franchising. "We weren't just selling products to people for cash, putting the cash in the bank, and then writing cheques for what we owed," says Mr. Hooker. "We were into receivables; people owed us money." The company also had liabilities—in the form of a bank loan.

Mr. Hooker hired a firm to set up an accounting system for the business, an experience he describes as a "rude awakening" that cost him approximately $200,000. One of the accounting staff members was negligent, writing cheques for government remittances, but not sending them for fear the company's line of credit wouldn't cover them. Clearly, the company's accounts weren't balanced properly.

"I realized how much improper accounting could cost me and how, if I didn't understand accounting, I'd have to trust somebody," Mr. Hooker says. He hired another accountant to rebuild the accounting system, working closely with him to learn how it worked.

The breakthrough point for him, he says, was in understanding that "cash is a debit." Assets (from the statement of financial position) and expenses (from the income statement) have normal debit balances. Liabilities and shareholders' equity (from the statement of financial position) and revenues (from the income statement) have normal credit balances. To increase the amount in an account, an entry has to be the same sign, he adds. In other words, only debits increase debit accounts and credits increase credit accounts.

Now that he understands the basics of the accounting system, Mr. Hooker monitors it very closely. He insists his accountant provide him with "TAMFS"—timely, accurate, monthly financial statements. "That is an absolute necessity any time a business grows to where the owner puts his trust in somebody else to handle the money," he says. A lesson this entrepreneur learned the hard way.

the navigator

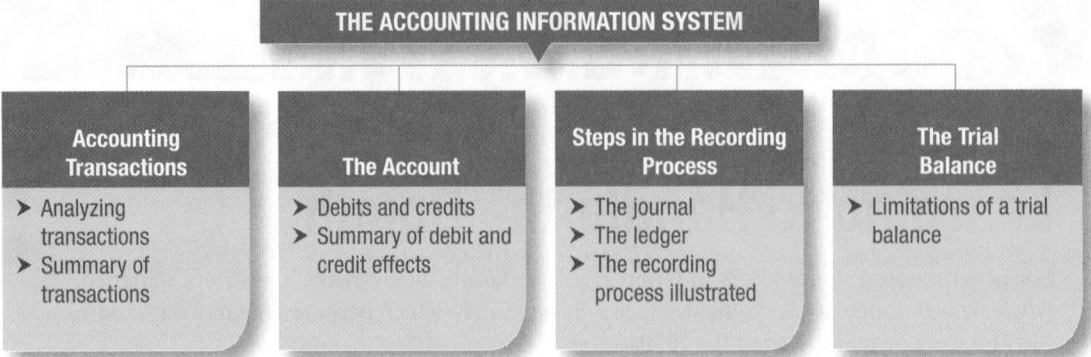

As indicated in the feature story, an accounting information system that produces timely and accurate financial information is a necessity for a company like BeaverTails. The purpose of this chapter is to explain and illustrate the features of an accounting information system. The chapter is organized as follows:

THE ACCOUNTING INFORMATION SYSTEM

Accounting Transactions	The Account	Steps in the Recording Process	The Trial Balance
➤ Analyzing transactions ➤ Summary of transactions	➤ Debits and credits ➤ Summary of debit and credit effects	➤ The journal ➤ The ledger ➤ The recording process illustrated	➤ Limitations of a trial balance

Accounting Transactions

STUDY OBJECTIVE 1

Analyze the effects of transactions on the accounting equation.

The system of collecting and processing transaction data and communicating financial information to decision-makers is known as the **accounting information system**. Accounting information systems vary widely. Some factors that shape these systems are the type of business and its transactions, the size of the company, the amount of data, and the information that management and others need. For example, as indicated in the feature story, BeaverTails did not need a formal accounting system when it first began. However, as the business and the number and type of transactions grew, an organized accounting information system became essential.

An accounting information system begins with determining what relevant transaction data should be collected and processed. Not all events are recorded and reported as accounting transactions. Only those events that cause changes in assets, liabilities, or shareholders' equity should be recorded. For example, suppose a new employee is hired. Should this event be recorded in the company's accounting records? The answer is "no." While the hiring of an employee will lead to a future accounting transaction (e.g., the payment of salary after the work has been completed), no accounting transaction has occurred at this point in time.

An **accounting transaction** occurs when assets, liabilities, or shareholders' equity items change as a result of some economic event. Illustration 3-1 summarizes the process that is used to decide whether or not to record economic events.

▶ Illustration 3-1
Transaction identification process

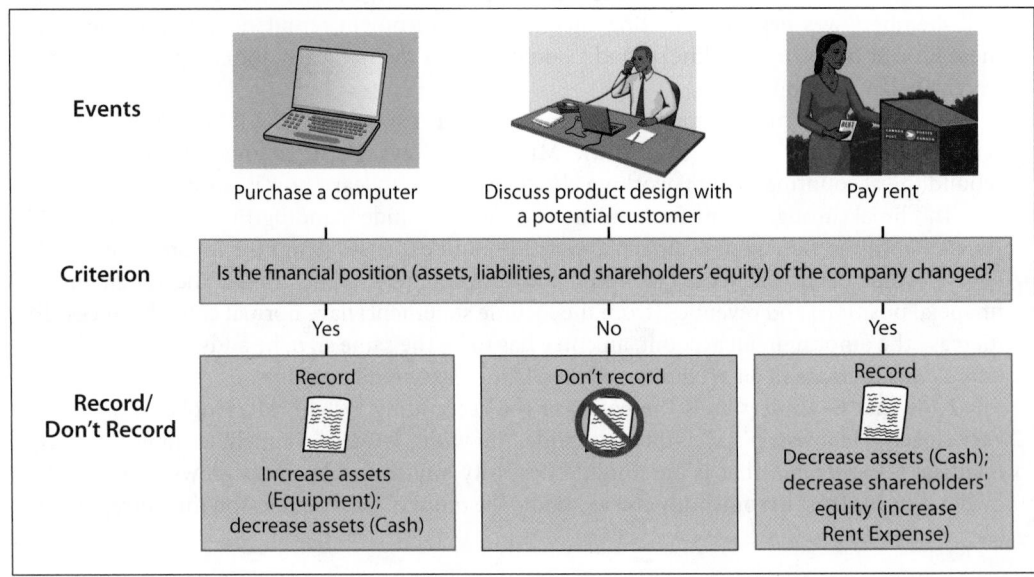

NHL Salary Caps

The NHL is a league that requires teams to maintain annual salary caps. This is done to prevent a team from paying excessive salaries and maintaining a roster of star players that always wins the Stanley Cup.

When a player is signed with a team, he is often given a signing bonus. This gives rise to a transaction that must be recorded because the team's asset accounts are affected. But what would happen if the player just signed a contract and did not get a payment? Does just the signing of the contract mean that a transaction has occurred? In this case, no; there has been no economic event that has changed the team's assets, liabilities, or equity.

ANALYZING TRANSACTIONS

In Chapter 1, you learned about the accounting equation:

$$\text{Assets} = \text{Liabilities} + \text{Shareholders' Equity}$$

In this chapter, you will learn how to analyze transactions for their effect on each component of the accounting equation—assets, liabilities, and shareholders' equity. Remember that the accounting equation must always balance, so each transaction will have a dual (double-sided) effect on the equation. For example, if an individual asset is increased, there must be either a corresponding decrease in another asset, an increase in a specific liability, and/or an increase in shareholders' equity.

Note that two or more items could be affected when analyzing the accounting equation. For example, an asset (cash) could increase by $50, a different asset (accounts receivable) could increase by $150, and shareholders' equity (sales) could increase by $200.

Chapter 1 presented the financial statements for Sierra Corporation for its first month of operations, October 2012. To illustrate the effects of economic events on the accounting equation, we will now examine some of the events that affected Sierra Corporation in its first month and were ultimately reported on its financial statements in Chapter 1 in Illustrations 1-5, 1-6, 1-8, and 1-9.

Transaction (1): Investment by Shareholders. On October 1, cash of $10,000 was invested in Sierra Corporation in exchange for 10,000 common shares. This transaction results in an equal increase in assets and shareholders' equity. There is an increase of $10,000 in the asset account Cash and an increase of $10,000 in the shareholders' equity account Common Shares.

Basic Analysis	The asset Cash is increased by $10,000, and the shareholders' equity account Common Shares is increased by $10,000.

Equation Analysis	Assets	=	Liabilities	+	Shareholders' Equity
	Cash	=			Common Shares
	(1) +$10,000	=			+$10,000

Notice that the two sides of the accounting equation remain equal. Note also that investments by shareholders are not recorded as revenue, but as share capital of the corporation.

Transaction (2): Issue of Note Payable. Also on October 1, Sierra borrowed $5,000 from Scotiabank by signing a note payable. It promised to repay the note, plus 6% interest, in three months. This transaction results in an equal increase in assets and liabilities: Cash (an asset) increases by $5,000 and the liability Notes Payable increases by $5,000. The specific effect of this transaction and the cumulative effect of the first two transactions are:

| Basic Analysis | The asset Cash is increased by $5,000, and the liability Notes Payable is increased by $5,000. |

		Assets	=	Liabilities	+	Shareholders' Equity
				Notes		Common
Equation Analysis		Cash	=	Payable	+	Shares
		$10,000				$10,000
	(2)	+5,000		+$5,000		
		$15,000	=	$5,000	+	$10,000

$15,000

Total assets are now $15,000 and shareholders' equity of $10,000 plus the new liability of $5,000 is also $15,000.

Transaction (3): Purchase of Equipment. On October 1, Sierra acquired equipment by paying $5,000 cash to Superior Equipment. This transaction resulted in an equal increase and decrease in Sierra's assets, although the composition of the assets changed. Equipment (an asset) increases by $5,000 and Cash (an asset) decreases by $5,000, as shown:

| Basic Analysis | The asset Equipment is increased by $5,000; the asset Cash is decreased by $5,000. |

		Assets			=	Liabilities	+	Shareholders' Equity
						Notes		Common
Equation Analysis		Cash	+	Equipment	=	Payable	+	Shares
		$15,000				$5,000		$10,000
	(3)	−5,000		+$5,000				
		$10,000	+	$5,000	=	$5,000	+	$10,000

$15,000 $15,000

The total assets have remained at $15,000. Liabilities plus shareholders' equity also total $15,000.

Transaction (4): Receipt of Cash in Advance from Customer. On October 2, Sierra received a $1,200 cash advance from R. Knox, a client, for advertising services that are expected to be completed before November 15. Revenue should not be recorded until the work has been performed. However, since cash was received before performing the advertising services, Sierra has a liability for the work due. We call this liability unearned revenue.

Note that the word *unearned* indicates that this is a liability account rather than a revenue account. Although many liability accounts have the word *payable* in their title, not all do. Unearned Revenue is a liability account even though the word *payable* is not used.

This transaction results in an increase to Cash (an asset) of $1,200 and an increase in Unearned Revenue (a liability) by the same amount:

| Basic Analysis | The asset Cash is increased by $1,200; the liability Unearned Revenue is increased by $1,200 because the service has not been provided yet. |

| Equation Analysis |

		Assets			=	Liabilities			+	Shareholders' Equity
						Notes		Unearned		Common
		Cash	+	Equipment	=	Payable	+	Revenue	+	Shares
		$10,000		$5,000		$5,000				$10,000
	(4)	+1,200						+$1,200		
		$11,200	+	$5,000	=	$5,000	+	$1,200	+	$10,000

$16,200 $16,200

Transaction (5): Payment of Rent. Also on October 2, Sierra Corporation paid its office rent for the month of October in cash, $900. To record this transaction, Cash is decreased by $900 and Rent

Expense is increased by $900. Rent is an expense incurred by Sierra in its effort to generate revenues. Expenses decrease retained earnings, which in turn decrease shareholders' equity. You will recall from earlier chapters that shareholders' equity consists of common shares (or share capital) and retained earnings. Retained earnings are increased by revenues and decreased by expenses and dividends.

We have expanded our accounting equation to show the detailed components of retained earnings. As there is not enough room to use specific account names for each individual revenue and expense account in this illustration, they will be summarized under the column headings Revenues (abbreviated as "Rev."), Expenses (abbreviated as "Exp."), and Dividends (abbreviated as "Div."). Revenue and dividend transactions will be added later in this section.

Basic Analysis	The expense Rent Expense is increased by $900 because the payment is only for the current month; the asset Cash is decreased by $900.

Equation Analysis

	Assets			=	Liabilities		+	Shareholders' Equity			
					Notes	Unearned		Common		Retained Earnings	
	Cash	+	Equipment	=	Payable	+ Revenue	+	Shares	+ Rev.	− Exp.	− Div.
	$11,200		$5,000		$5,000	$1,200		$10,000			
(5)	−900									−$900	
	$10,300 +		$5,000	=	$5,000 +	$1,200	+	$10,000		− $900	

$15,300 $15,300

As mentioned above, expenses reduce retained earnings and ultimately shareholders' equity. Therefore, this transaction reduces both assets and shareholders' equity by $900, keeping the equation in balance.

Transaction (6): Purchase of Insurance. On October 3, Sierra paid $600 for a one-year insurance policy effective October 1 that expires next year on September 30. This event is a transaction because one asset was exchanged for another. The asset Cash is decreased by $600. The asset Prepaid Insurance (abbreviated as "Pre. Ins.") is increased by $600 because the payment is for more than the current month. Payments of expenses that will benefit more than one accounting period are identified as prepaid expenses or prepayments. We will learn more about how to account for prepayments in the next chapter.

As shown, the balance in total assets did not change; one asset account decreased by the same amount by which another increased.

Basic Analysis	The asset Prepaid Insurance is increased by $600 because the payment extends to more than the current month; the asset Cash is decreased by $600.

Equation Analysis

	Assets					=	Liabilities		+	Shareholders' Equity			
							Notes	Unearned		Common		Retained Earnings	
	Cash	+	Pre. Ins.	+	Equipment	=	Payable	+ Revenue	+	Shares	+ Rev.	− Exp.	− Div.
	$10,300				$5,000		$5,000	$1,200		$10,000		$900	
(6)	−600		+$600										
	$9,700 +		$600	+	$5,000	=	$5,000 +	$1,200	+	$10,000		− $900	

$15,300 $15,300

Transaction (7): Hiring of New Employees. On October 4, Sierra hired four new employees to begin work on Monday, October 8. Each employee will receive a weekly salary of $500 for a five-day (Monday–Friday) workweek, payable every two weeks. Employees will receive their first paycheques on Friday, October 19. There is no effect on the accounting equation because the company's assets, liabilities, and shareholders' equity have not changed. An accounting transaction has not occurred because the employees have not yet worked; at this point, there is only an agreement that the employees will begin work on October 8. (See transaction 10 for the first payment of salaries.)

Transaction (8): Purchase of Supplies on Account.   On October 9, Sierra purchased advertising materials on account from Aero Supply Corp. for $2,500. The account is due in 30 days. This transaction is referred to as a purchase "on account" or "on credit." Instead of paying cash, the company incurs a liability, usually accounts payable, by promising to pay cash in the future.

Assets are increased by this transaction because supplies represent a resource that will be used in the process of providing services to customers. Liabilities are increased by the amount due to Aero Supply. The asset Supplies (abbreviated as "Sup.") is increased by $2,500, and the liability Accounts Payable (abbreviated as "A/P") is increased by the same amount. The Notes Payable account has also been abbreviated as "N/P" due to space limitations in the equation analysis below. The effect on the equation is:

Basic Analysis	The asset Supplies is increased by $2,500; the liability Accounts Payable is increased by $2,500.

Equation Analysis

		Assets			=		Liabilities		+	Shareholders' Equity			
								Unearned		Common		Retained Earnings	
Cash +	Sup.	+ Pre. Ins.	+ Equipment	=	A/P	+ N/P +	Revenue	+	Shares	+ Rev.	− Exp.	− Div.
$9,700		$600	$5,000			$5,000	$1,200		$10,000		$900	
(8)	+$2,500				+$2,500							
$9,700 +	$2,500 +	$600	+ $5,000	=	$2,500	+ $5,000 +	$1,200	+	$10,000		− $900	

$17,800 $17,800

Transaction (9): Services Performed on Account.   On October 13, Sierra performed $10,000 of advertising services for Copa Ltd. Sierra sent Copa a bill for these services asking for payment before the end of the month.

Companies often provide services "on account" or "on credit." Instead of receiving cash, the company receives a different type of asset, an account receivable. Accounts receivable represent the right to receive payment at a future date.

Revenue, however, is earned when services are performed. Therefore, revenue is recorded when services are performed, even though cash has not been received. As revenue increases retained earnings—a shareholders' equity account—both assets and shareholders' equity are increased by this transaction.

In this transaction, Accounts Receivable (abbreviated as "A/R") is increased by $10,000 and Service Revenue is increased by the same amount. The new balances in the equation are:

Basic Analysis	The asset Accounts Receivable is increased by $10,000. The revenue account Service Revenue is increased by $10,000.

Equation Analysis

			Assets			=		Liabilities		+	Shareholders' Equity			
									Unearned		Common		Retained Earnings	
Cash +	A/R	+ Sup.	+ Pre. Ins.	+ Equipment	=	A/P +	N/P +	Revenue	+	Shares	+	Rev.	− Exp.	− Div.
$9,700		$2,500	$600	$5,000		$2,500	$5,000	$1,200		$10,000			$900	
(9)	+$10,000											+$10,000		
$9,700 +	$10,000	+ $2,500 +	$600	+ $5,000	=	$2,500 +	$5,000 +	$1,200	+	$10,000	+	$10,000	− $900	

$27,800 $27,800

Transaction (10): Payment of Salaries. Employees worked two weeks, earning $4,000 in salaries (4 employees × $500/week × 2 weeks), and were paid on October 19. Salaries are an expense similar to rent because they are a cost of generating revenues. While the act of hiring the employees in transaction 7 did not result in an accounting transaction, the payment of the employees' salary is a transaction because assets and shareholders' equity are affected. Cash is decreased by $4,000 and Salaries Expense is increased by $4,000:

| Basic Analysis | The expense Salaries Expense is increased by $4,000; the asset Cash is decreased by $4,000. |

Equation Analysis

	Assets					=	Liabilities			+	Shareholders' Equity				
									Unearned		Common		Retained Earnings		
	Cash +	A/R +	Sup. +	Pre. Ins. +	Equipment =		A/P +	N/P +	Revenue +		Shares +	Rev. −	Exp. −	Div.	
	$9,700	$10,000	$2,500	$600	$5,000		$2,500	$5,000	$1,200		$10,000	$10,000	$900		
(10)	−4,000												−4,000		
	$5,700 +	$10,000 +	$2,500 +	$600 +	$5,000 =		$2,500 +	$5,000 +	$1,200 +		$10,000 +	$10,000 −	$4,900		

$23,800 $23,800

Transaction (11): Payment of Dividend. On October 26, Sierra paid a $500 cash dividend. Dividends are a distribution of retained earnings rather than an expense—they are not incurred to generate revenue. A cash dividend transaction reduces both Cash (asset) and Retained Earnings (shareholders' equity). Cash is decreased by $500 and Dividends is increased by $500:

| Basic Analysis | Dividends is increased by $500; the asset Cash is decreased by $500. |

Equation Analysis

	Assets					=	Liabilities			+	Shareholders' Equity				
									Unearned		Common		Retained Earnings		
	Cash +	A/R +	Sup. +	Pre. Ins. +	Equipment =		A/P +	N/P +	Revenue +		Shares +	Rev. −	Exp. −	Div.	
	$5,700	$10,000	$2,500	$600	$5,000		$2,500	$5,000	$1,200		$10,000	$10,000	$4,900		
(11)	−$500													−$500	
	$5,200 +	$10,000 +	$2,500 +	$600 +	$5,000 =		$2,500 +	$5,000 +	$1,200 +		$10,000 +	$10,000 −	$4,900 −	$500	

$23,300 $23,300

Transaction (12): Collection of Account. On October 30, Copa paid Sierra the amount owing on its account. Recall that an account receivable and the revenue from this transaction were recorded earlier in transaction 9, when the service was provided. Revenue should not be recorded again when the cash is collected. Rather, Cash is increased by $10,000 and Accounts Receivable is decreased by $10,000, bringing the balance in this account to zero. Total assets and total liabilities and shareholders' equity are unchanged, as shown:

| Basic Analysis | The asset Cash is increased by $10,000. The asset Accounts Receivable is decreased by $10,000. |

Equation Analysis

| | Assets | | | | | = | Liabilities | | | + | Shareholders' Equity | | | |
	Cash +	A/R +	Sup. +	Pre. Ins. +	Equipment =		A/P +	N/P +	Unearned Revenue +		Common Shares +	Rev. −	Exp. −	Div.
	$5,200	$10,000	$2,500	$600	$5,000		$2,500	$5,000	$1,200		$10,000	$10,000	$4,900	$500
(12)	+$10,000	−10,000												
	$15,200 +	$0 +	$2,500 +	$600 +	$5,000 =		$2,500 +	$5,000 +	$1,200 +		$10,000 +	$10,000 −	$4,900 −	$500

$23,300 = $23,300

SUMMARY OF TRANSACTIONS

The transactions of Sierra Corporation are summarized in Illustration 3-2 to show their cumulative effect on the accounting equation. The transaction number, the specific effects of the transaction, and the final balances are indicated. Remember that event 7—the hiring of employees—did not result in a transaction, so no entry is included for that event.

▶ **Illustration 3-2**
Tabular summary of transactions

| | Assets | | | | | = | Liabilities | | | + | Shareholders' Equity | | | |
	Cash +	A/R +	Sup. +	Pre. Ins. +	Equipment =		A/P +	N/P +	Unearned Revenue +		Common Shares +	Rev. −	Exp. −	Div.
(1)	+$10,000										+$10,000			
(2)	+5,000							+$5,000						
(3)	−5,000				+$5,000									
(4)	+1,200								+$1,200					
(5)	−900												−$900	
(6)	−600			+$600										
(8)			+$2,500				+$2,500							
(9)		+$10,000										+$10,000		
(10)	−4,000												−4,000	
(11)	−500													−$500
(12)	+10,000	−10,000												
	$15,200 +	$0 +	$2,500 +	$600 +	$5,000 =		$2,500 +	$5,000 +	$1,200 +		$10,000 +	$10,000 −	$4,900 −	$500

$23,300 = $23,300

The illustration demonstrates that (1) each transaction must be analyzed for its effect on the three primary components of the accounting equation (assets, liabilities, and shareholders' equity), and (2) the two sides of the equation must always be equal.

DECISION TOOLKIT

 Decision Checkpoints	 Info Needed for Decision	 Tools to Use for Decision	 How to Evaluate Results
Has an accounting transaction occurred?	Details of the event	Accounting equation	Determine the effect, if any, on assets, liabilities, and shareholders' equity.

▶Do It! Analyze Transactions

Transactions made by Virmari Corporation for the month of August follow:

1. Common shares were issued to shareholders for $25,000 cash.

2. Equipment costing $7,000 was purchased on account.

3. Services were performed for customers amounting to $8,000. Of this amount, $2,000 was received in cash and $6,000 is due on account.

4. Rent was paid for the month, $850.

5. Customers on account paid $4,000 (see transaction 3).

6. Dividends of $1,000 were paid to shareholders.

Prepare a tabular analysis that shows the effects of these transactions on the accounting equation.

Action Plan

- Analyze the effects of each transaction on the accounting equation.
- Remember that a change in an asset will require a change in another asset, a liability, or shareholders' equity in order to keep the accounting equation in balance.
- Choose an appropriate account name (not a description) and use it consistently.

Solution

| | Assets | | | = | Liabilities + | | Shareholders' Equity | | | |
| | | Accounts | | | Accounts | Common | | Retained Earnings | | |
	Cash +	Receivable +	Equipment =		Payable +	Shares +	Revenues –	Expenses –	Dividends
(1)	+$25,000					+$25,000			
(2)			+$7,000		+$7,000				
(3)	+2,000	+$6,000					+$8,000		
(4)	–850							–$850	
(5)	+4,000	–4,000							
(6)	–1,000								–$1,000
	$29,150+	$2,000 +	$7,000	=	$7,000 +	$25,000 +	$8,000 –	$850 –	$1,000

$38,150 $38,150

The Account

STUDY OBJECTIVE 2
Define debits and credits and explain how they are used to record transactions.

Instead of using a tabular summary like the one in Illustration 3-2 for Sierra Corporation, an accounting information system uses accounts. An **account** is an individual accounting record of increases and decreases in a specific asset, liability, or shareholders' equity item. For example, Sierra Corporation has separate accounts for cash, accounts receivable, accounts payable, service revenue, salaries expense, and so on.

In its simplest form, an account consists of three parts: (1) the title of the account, (2) a left or debit side, and (3) a right or credit side. Because the alignment of these parts of an account resembles the letter T, it is referred to as a **T account**. The basic form of an account is shown in Illustration 3-3.

▶Illustration 3-3
Basic form of T account

Title of Account	
Debit (Dr.) (left) side	Credit (Cr.) (right) side

The actual account form used in real life looks different from the above T account. It is designed with multiple columns to facilitate the inclusion of additional information. However, because of its simplicity, the T account is used for teaching purposes and will be used throughout this textbook to explain basic accounting relationships.

DEBITS AND CREDITS

The term **debit** means left, and the term **credit** means right. These terms are commonly abbreviated as Dr. for debit and Cr. for credit. Debits and credits are merely directional signals used in the recording process to describe where entries are made in the accounts. For example, the act of entering an amount on the left side of an account is called **debiting** the account, and making an entry on the right side is **crediting** the account. When the totals of the two sides are compared, an account will have a debit balance if the total of the debit amounts recorded exceeds the total of the credit amounts recorded. Conversely, an account will have a credit balance if the credit amounts exceed the debits.

When we record transactions, two or more accounts are affected and their balances change. We use debits and credits to explain the effect of these changes. When we record transactions, the debit movement in the accounts must equal the credit movement in the accounts. The equality of debits and credits is the basis for the **double-entry accounting system**, in which the dual (two-sided) effect of each transaction is recorded in appropriate accounts. This system provides a logical method for recording transactions and ensuring that amounts are recorded accurately. If every transaction is recorded with equal debits and credits, then the sum of all the debits to the accounts must equal the sum of all the credits.

The following diagram will help us understand how debit and credit effects apply to the accounting equation:

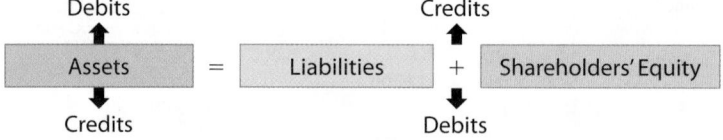

Beginning on the left-hand side of the accounting equation (asset accounts), we can see that increases in asset accounts are recorded by debits. The converse is also true: decreases in asset accounts are recorded by credits. If we cross to the right-hand side of the equation, it must follow that increases and decreases in liabilities and shareholders' equity have to be recorded opposite from increases and decreases in assets. Thus, increases in liabilities and shareholders' equity are recorded by credits and decreases by debits.

We will apply debit and credit procedures to T accounts for each component of the accounting equation—assets, liabilities, and shareholders' equity—in the following sections.

> **Helpful Hint**
> Debits and credits do not always mean "increases" and "decreases." While debits do increase certain accounts (e.g., assets), they decrease other accounts (e.g., liabilities).

Assets

If we apply the accounting equation to a T account for assets, we can see that increases in assets must be entered on the left or debit side, and decreases in assets must be entered on the right or credit side. **Asset accounts normally show debit balances**. That is, debits to a specific asset account should exceed credits to that account. It was a breakthrough for Mr. Hooker in the feature story when he learned that assets, such as cash, are normally debits.

The diagram below shows the effects that debits and credits have on asset accounts, and the accounts' normal balance:

> **Helpful Hint**
> The normal balance of an account is always on its increase side.

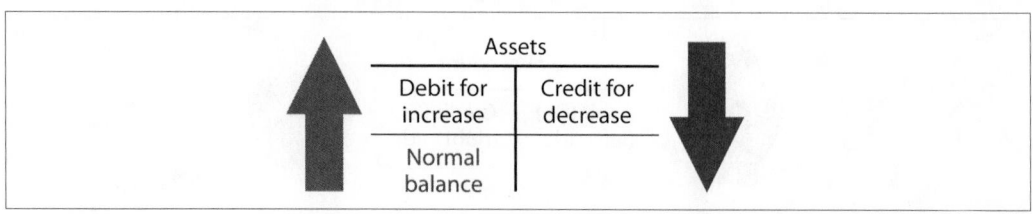

Knowing an account's normal balance may help when you are trying to identify errors. For example, a credit balance in an asset account such as Land would indicate a recording error. Occasionally, however, an abnormal balance may be correct. The Cash account, for example, will have a credit balance if a company has overdrawn its bank balance. If the Cash account has a credit balance, it is called "bank indebtedness" and reported as a current liability rather than as a current asset. We will learn more about cash and bank indebtedness in Chapter 7.

Liabilities and Shareholders' Equity

Liability and shareholders' equity accounts are increased by credits and decreased by debits. Increases are entered on the right or credit side of the T account, and decreases are entered on the left or debit side of the T account. Just as asset accounts normally show debit balances, **liability and equity accounts normally show credit balances**.

Because assets are on the opposite side of the accounting equation from liabilities and shareholders' equity, increases and decreases in assets are recorded opposite from increases and decreases in liabilities and shareholders' equity. In this way, the total amount of debits always equals the total amount of credits and the accounting equation stays in balance.

The effects that debits and credits have on liabilities and shareholders' equity and the normal balances are as follows:

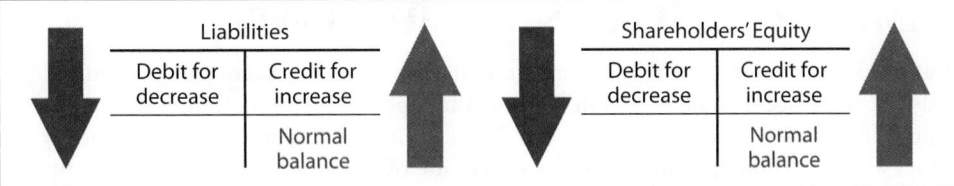

All asset and liability accounts have the same debit/credit rule procedures. That is, all asset accounts are increased by debits and decreased by credits. All liability accounts are increased by credits and decreased by debits. However, shareholders' equity consists of different components, and they do not all move in the same direction. In the following sections, we will look at how debit and credit procedures apply to each of selected equity components.

Increases in Shareholders' Equity.   Common shares and retained earnings both increase shareholders' equity. Common shares are issued in exchange for the shareholders' investments. Retained earnings are the portion of shareholders' equity that has been accumulated through the profitable operation of the company. Retained earnings are divided further into revenues and expenses (which make up profit) and dividends. Of these, revenues increase retained earnings, which then increases shareholders' equity.

The common shares, retained earnings, and revenue accounts are increased by credits and decreased by debits. The **normal balance in these accounts is a credit balance**. This, and the effects that debits and credits have on them, is shown below:

Decreases in Shareholders' Equity.   Dividends and expenses both decrease retained earnings, which then decreases shareholders' equity. Since decreases in shareholders' equity are recorded by debits, it makes sense that **dividend and expense accounts would have a normal debit balance**.

Dividends are a distribution to shareholders of retained earnings, which reduces retained earnings. If retained earnings are decreased by debits, it follows that increases in the dividends account are recorded with debits. Credits to the dividends account are unusual, but might be used to correct a dividend recorded in error, for example.

Expenses, along with revenues, combine to determine profit. Since expenses are the negative factor in the calculation of profit, and revenues are the positive factor, it is logical that the increase and decrease sides of expense accounts should be the reverse of revenue accounts. Thus, expense accounts are increased by debits and decreased by credits.

The normal balance in these accounts, and the effects that debits and credits have on them, are shown below:

SUMMARY OF DEBIT AND CREDIT EFFECTS

Illustration 3-4 summarizes the debit and credit effects on the accounting equation. It also expands the basic accounting equation to show the types of accounts that make up shareholders' equity. Assets (on the left-hand side of the accounting equation) are increased by debits. Liabilities and shareholders' equity, on the other side of the equation, are increased by credits. Recall Mr. Hooker's comment in the feature story that increases to accounts have to be of like signs, which is a way of saying that a debit will increase a debit account and a credit will increase a credit account.

As we learned above, shareholders' equity can be further divided into two components: common shares and retained earnings. Since shareholders' equity is increased by credits, both of these accounts—common shares and retained earnings—are also increased by credits.

Retained earnings can be further subdivided into dividends, and revenues and expenses (revenues and expenses combine to determine profit). Since revenues increase retained earnings and shareholders' equity, increases in revenue accounts are recorded by credits. Expenses and dividends decrease retained earnings, and thus shareholders' equity. Decreases in shareholders' equity are recorded by debits. Because expenses and dividends decrease shareholders' equity, increases in each of these accounts are recorded by debits.

The debit/credit rules and effects on each type of account are summarized in Illustration 3-4. Like the basic accounting equation, the expanded equation must always be in balance (total debits must equal total credits). Study this carefully. It will help you understand the fundamentals of the double-entry accounting system.

▶ Illustration 3-4

Summary of debit and credit rules for expanded accounting equation

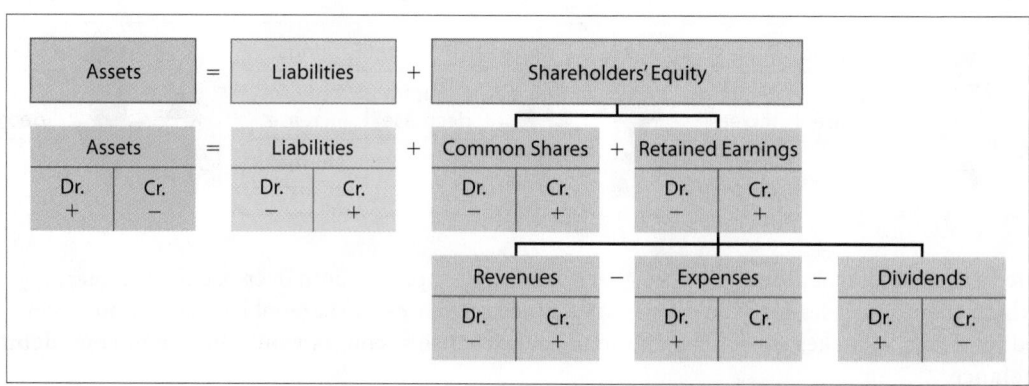

BEFORE YOU GO ON...

▶ Do It! Debits and Credits

Lin Limited has the following selected accounts:

1. Service Revenue
2. Dividends
3. Equipment
4. Accounts Receivable
5. Supplies
6. Unearned Revenue
7. Accounts Payable
8. Common Shares
9. Salaries Expense
10. Cash

(a) Indicate whether each of the above accounts is an asset, liability, or shareholders' equity account. If the account is an asset or liability, indicate its statement of financial position classification. If it is a shareholders' equity account, indicate what specific type it is (i.e., common shares, dividends, revenue, or expense).

(b) Indicate whether a debit would increase or decrease each account.

(c) Identify the normal balance.

Action Plan

- Classify each account into its place in the expanded accounting equation.
- Apply the debit and credit rules. Remember that assets are increased by debits, and liabilities and shareholders' equity are increased by credits.
- Remember that the normal balance of an account is on its increase side.

Solution

Account	(a) Classification	(b) Debit Effect	(c) Normal Balance
1. Service Revenue	Shareholders' equity (revenue)	Decrease	Credit
2. Dividends	Shareholders' equity (dividends)	Increase	Debit
3. Equipment	Assets (property, plant, and equipment)	Increase	Debit
4. Accounts Receivable	Assets (current)	Increase	Debit
5. Supplies	Assets (current)	Increase	Debit
6. Unearned Revenue	Liabilities (current)	Decrease	Credit
7. Accounts Payable	Liabilities (current)	Decrease	Credit
8. Common Shares	Shareholders' equity (common shares)	Decrease	Credit
9. Salaries Expense	Shareholders' equity (expense)	Increase	Debit
10. Cash	Assets (current)	Increase	Debit

Steps in the Recording Process

The procedures used in the recording process are part of what is called the **accounting cycle**, which consists of nine steps in total. The first three steps of the accounting cycle—called the recording process—are shown in Illustration 3-5.

In step 1, each transaction is analyzed to determine if it has an effect on the accounts. Evidence of the transaction comes from a **source document**, such as a sales slip, cheque, bill, or cash register tape. In the beginning, as described in our feature story, Grant Hooker used cheques to begin the recording process for BeaverTails. This evidence of the transaction is analyzed to determine the effect on specific accounts. Deciding whether a transaction has occurred and, if so what to record, is the most critical point in the accounting process.

STUDY OBJECTIVE 3

Identify the basic steps in the recording process.

▶Illustration 3-5
The accounting cycle—Steps 1–3

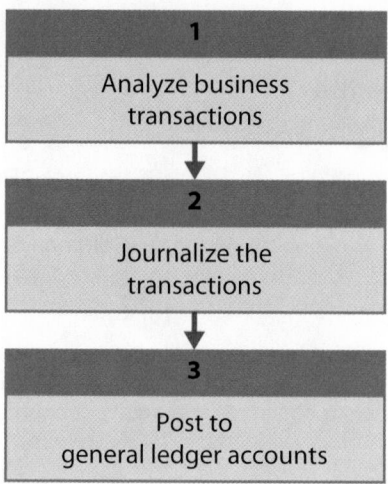

In step 2, the transaction information is recorded as a journal entry in the general journal (a book of original entry). In step 3, the information is transferred from the general journal to the appropriate accounts in the general ledger (a book of accounts). We will discuss the remaining steps of the accounting cycle later in this, and the next, chapter.

The first three steps in the accounting cycle occur repeatedly in every company, whether a manual or a computerized accounting system is used. However, the first two steps—the analysis and entering of each transaction—must be done by a person even when a computerized system is used. The basic difference between a manual and computerized system is in the last step in the recording process—transferring information (and subsequent steps that we will learn about later). In a computerized system, this step is done automatically by the computer. In order to understand how this happens, we need to understand manual approaches to the recording process, which is what we will focus on in this chapter.

ACCOUNTING MATTERS!   *Management Perspective*

Computerized Accounting Systems

Organizations of all shapes and sizes use computerized accounting systems. Cathy Love, the administrator of Bryony House, a Halifax women's shelter, agrees. "We really need our computerized system to track our accounts in detail," she says. The shelter users the popular small-business accounting software, Simply Accounting. In addition, the shelter's fundraising activities are tracked in detail using custom donation software. The shelter's staff have found that the more easily and quickly they can get the information they need, the more time they have to do their main work with the women who come for help.

THE JOURNAL

Transactions are first recorded in chronological order (i.e., by date) in a journal and then transferred to the accounts. For this reason, the journal is referred to as the book of original entry. For each transaction, the journal shows the debit and credit effects on specific accounts. Companies may use various kinds of journals, but every company has the most basic form of journal, a **general journal**.

The general journal makes several contributions to the recording process:

1. It discloses the complete effect of a transaction in one place, including an explanation and, where applicable, identification of the source document.
2. It provides a chronological record of transactions.
3. It helps to prevent and locate errors, because the debit and credit amounts for each entry can be quickly compared.

Entering transaction data in the general journal is known as **journalizing**. To illustrate the technique of journalizing, let's look at the first transaction of Sierra Corporation. On October 1, common shares were issued in exchange for $10,000 cash. In tabular equation form, this transaction appeared in our earlier discussion as follows:

Assets	=	Liabilities	+	Shareholders' Equity
Cash	=			Common Shares
(1) +$10,000	=			+$10,000

This transaction would be recorded in the general journal as follows:

GENERAL JOURNAL			
Date	Account Titles and Explanation	Debit	Credit
2012			
Oct. 1	Cash	10,000	
	Common Shares		10,000
	(Issued common shares)		

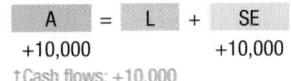

A	=	L	+	SE
+10,000				+10,000

↑ Cash flows: +10,000

> In the margins next to key journal entries are **equation analyses** that summarize the effects of the transaction on the accounting equation (A = L + SE) and cash flows.

Note the following features of the journal entry:

1. The date of the transaction is entered in the Date column.
2. The account to be debited is entered first at the left. The account to be credited is then entered on the next line, indented under the line above. The indentation differentiates debits from credits and decreases the chance of switching the debit and credit amounts by mistake.
3. The amounts for the debits are recorded in the Debit (left) column, and the amounts for the credits are recorded in the Credit (right) column.
4. A brief explanation of the transaction is given.

If a journal entry affects only two accounts, one debit and one credit, it is considered to be a simple journal entry. Some transactions use more than two accounts in journalizing. When three or more accounts are required in one journal entry, the entry is called a compound entry. Regardless of the number of accounts used in the journal entry, **the total debit and credit amounts must be equal**.

In assignments when specific account titles are given, they should be used in journalizing. When account titles are not given, you should create account titles that identify the nature and content of each account. Ambiguous or multiple account titles with similar names can lead to incorrect financial reporting. For example, a company could use any one of these account titles for recording the cost of delivery trucks: automobiles, delivery trucks, trucks, or vehicles. However, if it uses more than one of these account titles, it will not be able to easily determine the total cost of its delivery trucks.

Once the company chooses the specific account title to use (say, Vehicles), all future transactions related to that account should be recorded in the Vehicles account. Note that an account title itself should not contain explanations or descriptions (such as Vehicles Purchased). Explanations are given as a separate part of the journal entry and should not be included within the account title.

THE LEDGER

The entire group of accounts maintained by a company is referred to as the ledger. The ledger keeps all the information about changes in specific account balances in one place.

Companies may use various kinds of ledgers, but every company has a general ledger. A **general ledger** contains all the asset, liability, shareholders' equity, revenue, and expense accounts. Each account has a number so that it is easier to identify. A company can use a loose-leaf binder or card file for the ledger, with each account kept on a separate sheet or card. A column in spreadsheet software can be used as general ledger account but most companies today, use a computerized accounting system where the entries from the journal are automatically recorded a second time in the ledger by the software.

The ledger is often arranged in the order in which accounts are presented in the financial statements, beginning with the statement of financial position accounts. The asset accounts come first, followed by liability accounts, and then shareholders' equity accounts, including share capital, dividend, revenue, and expense accounts. Of course, in a computerized accounting system, the accounts can easily be rearranged in whatever order is wanted.

Most companies list their ledger accounts in a **chart of accounts.** The chart of accounts is the framework for the accounting database. It lists the accounts and the account numbers that identify where the accounts are in the ledger. The numbering system that is used to identify the accounts can be quite sophisticated or pretty simple. The chart of accounts usually starts with the statement of financial position accounts, followed by the income statement accounts. These account numbers are often referenced in both the general journal and general ledger.

The chart of accounts for Sierra Corporation is shown in Illustration 3-6, with their financial statement category indicated in the right-hand column for your information. Accounts shown in red are used in this chapter; accounts shown in black are explained in later chapters. The four-digit numbering system used allows lots of room for new accounts to be created as needed during the life of the business.

▶Illustration 3-6
Chart of accounts

SIERRA CORPORATION—CHART OF ACCOUNTS

Assets	Liabilities	Shareholders' Equity	Revenues	Expenses
1000 Cash	3000 Accounts Payable	4000 Common Shares	5000 Service Revenue	7000 Salaries Expense
1100 Accounts Receivable	3100 Salaries Payable	4500 Retained Earnings		7100 Supplies Expense
1500 Supplies	3200 Interest Payable	4600 Dividends		7500 Rent Expense
1550 Prepaid Insurance	3300 Unearned Revenue			7600 Depreciation Expense
2000 Equipment	3400 Notes Payable			8200 Insurance Expense
2010 Accumulated Depreciation—Equipment				8400 Interest Expense
				9000 Income Tax Expense

Posting

The procedure of transferring journal entries from the general journal to the general ledger accounts is called **posting.** This phase of the recording process accumulates the effects of journalized transactions in the individual accounts. Posting involves transferring information from the general journal to the general ledger. For example, the date and amount shown on the first line of a general journal entry is entered in the debit column of the appropriate account in the general ledger. The same is done for the credit side of the entry—the date and amount are entered in the credit column of the general ledger account.

Posting should be done in chronological order. That is, all the debits and credits of a journal entry should be posted before going on to the next journal entry. Posting should also be done on a timely basis—at least monthly—to ensure that the general ledger is up to date. In a computerized accounting system, posting is usually performed by software simultaneously after each journal entry is prepared.

THE RECORDING PROCESS ILLUSTRATED

The following transaction analyses show the basic steps in the recording process using the transactions for the month of October for Sierra Corporation. A basic analysis and a debit-credit analysis are done before the journalizing and posting of each transaction.

Study these transaction analyses carefully. The purpose of transaction analysis is first to identify the type of account involved and then to determine whether a debit or a credit to the account is required. You should always perform this type of analysis before preparing a journal entry. Doing so will help you understand the journal entries discussed in this chapter, as well as more complex journal entries described in later chapters.

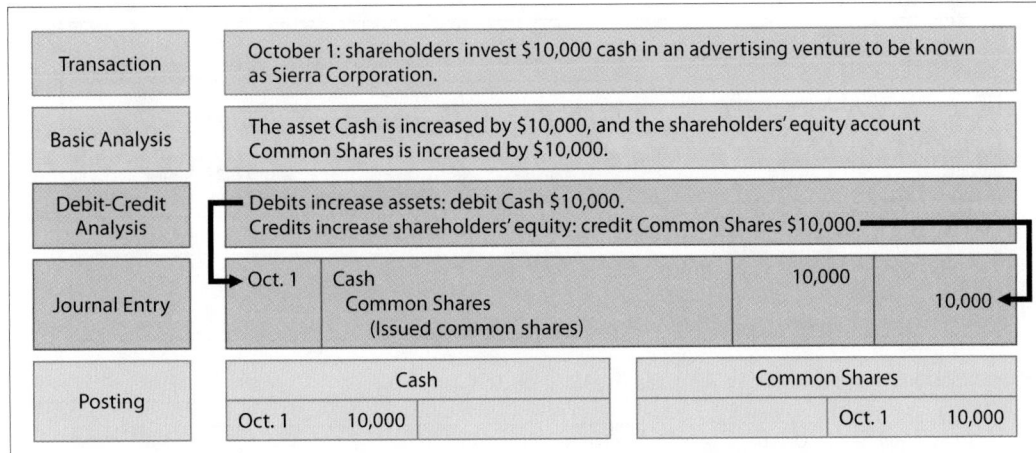

Transaction (1)
Investment by shareholders

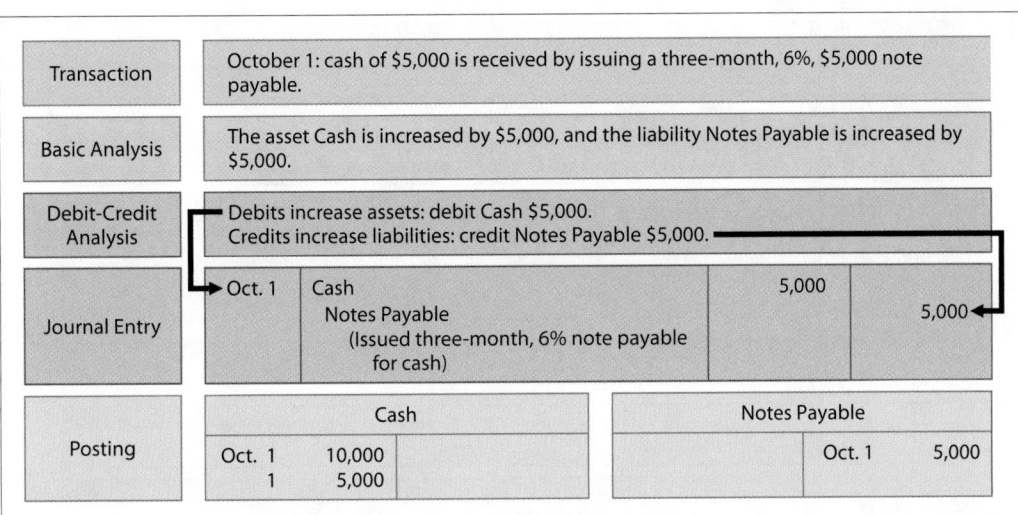

Transaction (2)
Issue of note payable

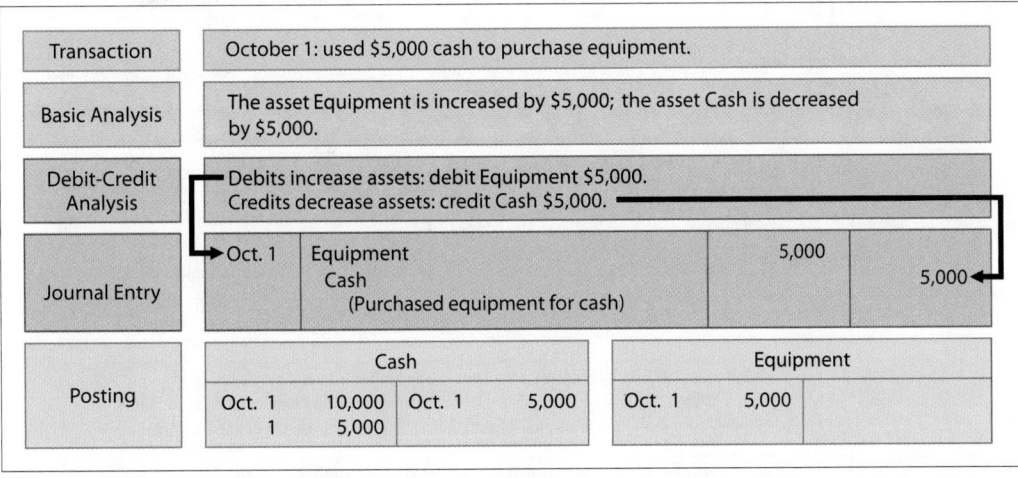

Transaction (3)
Purchase of equipment

Transaction (4)
Receipt of cash in advance from customer

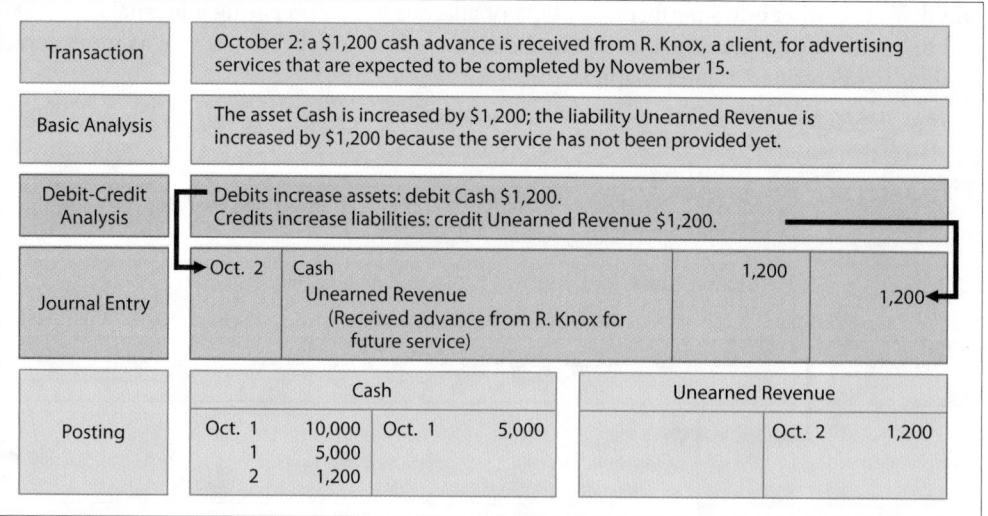

Transaction	October 2: a $1,200 cash advance is received from R. Knox, a client, for advertising services that are expected to be completed by November 15.
Basic Analysis	The asset Cash is increased by $1,200; the liability Unearned Revenue is increased by $1,200 because the service has not been provided yet.
Debit-Credit Analysis	Debits increase assets: debit Cash $1,200. Credits increase liabilities: credit Unearned Revenue $1,200.

Journal Entry	Oct. 2 Cash 1,200
	            Unearned Revenue 1,200
	            (Received advance from R. Knox for future service)

Posting

Cash			
Oct. 1	10,000	Oct. 1	5,000
1	5,000		
2	1,200		

Unearned Revenue	
	Oct. 2 1,200

Transaction (5)
Payment of rent

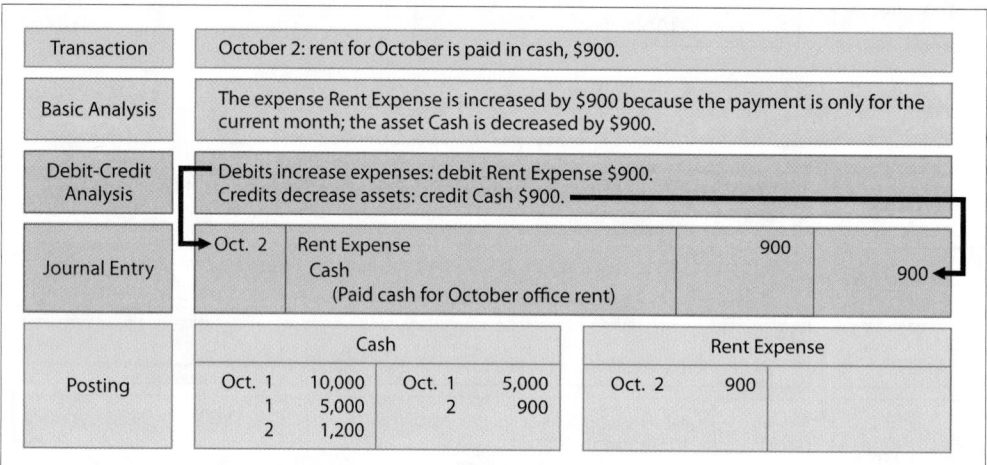

Transaction	October 2: rent for October is paid in cash, $900.
Basic Analysis	The expense Rent Expense is increased by $900 because the payment is only for the current month; the asset Cash is decreased by $900.
Debit-Credit Analysis	Debits increase expenses: debit Rent Expense $900. Credits decrease assets: credit Cash $900.

Journal Entry	Oct. 2 Rent Expense 900
	            Cash 900
	            (Paid cash for October office rent)

Posting

Cash			
Oct. 1	10,000	Oct. 1	5,000
1	5,000	2	900
2	1,200		

Rent Expense	
Oct. 2 900	

Transaction (6)
Purchase of insurance

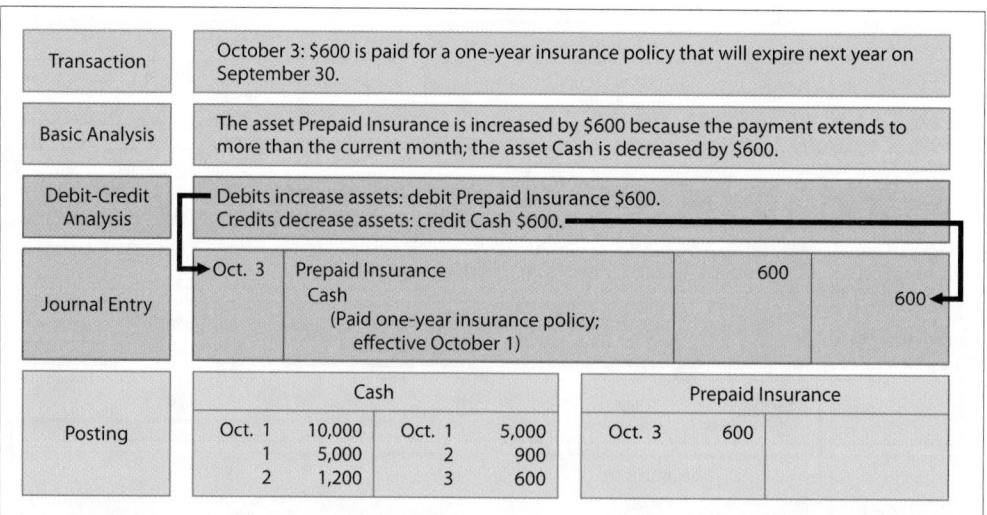

Transaction	October 3: $600 is paid for a one-year insurance policy that will expire next year on September 30.
Basic Analysis	The asset Prepaid Insurance is increased by $600 because the payment extends to more than the current month; the asset Cash is decreased by $600.
Debit-Credit Analysis	Debits increase assets: debit Prepaid Insurance $600. Credits decrease assets: credit Cash $600.

Journal Entry	Oct. 3 Prepaid Insurance 600
	            Cash 600
	            (Paid one-year insurance policy; effective October 1)

Posting

Cash			
Oct. 1	10,000	Oct. 1	5,000
1	5,000	2	900
2	1,200	3	600

Prepaid Insurance	
Oct. 3 600	

Transaction (7)
Hiring of new employees

Transaction	October 4: hired four employees to begin work on Monday, October 8. Each employee is to receive a weekly salary of $500 for a five-day workweek (Monday–Friday), payable every two weeks—first payment to be made on Friday, October 19.
Basic Analysis	An accounting transaction has not occurred. There is only an agreement that the employees will begin work on October 8. Thus, a debit-credit analysis is not needed because there is no accounting entry. (See transaction of October 19 for first entry.)

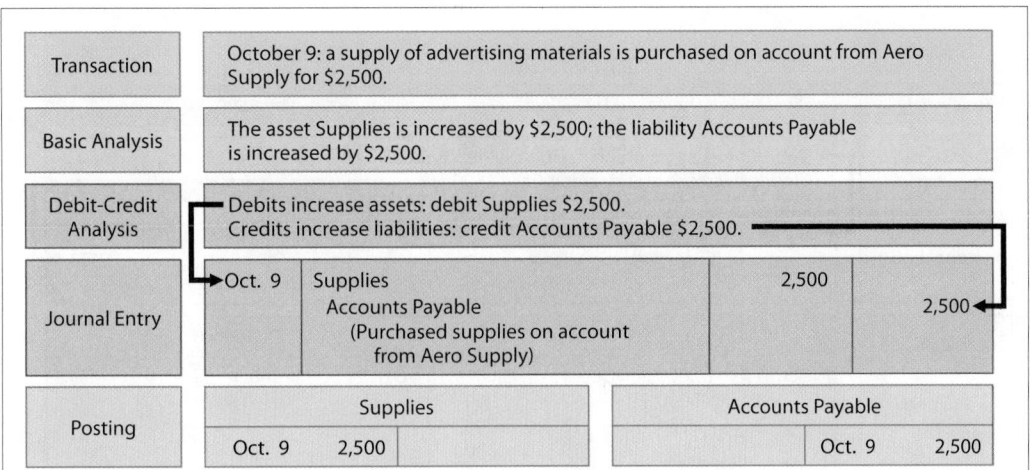

▶ Transaction (8)
Purchase of supplies on account

Transaction	October 9: a supply of advertising materials is purchased on account from Aero Supply for $2,500.		
Basic Analysis	The asset Supplies is increased by $2,500; the liability Accounts Payable is increased by $2,500.		
Debit-Credit Analysis	Debits increase assets: debit Supplies $2,500. Credits increase liabilities: credit Accounts Payable $2,500.		

Journal Entry	Oct. 9 Supplies
	        Accounts Payable
	        (Purchased supplies on account
	          from Aero Supply)
		2,500	2,500

Posting

Supplies		Accounts Payable	
Oct. 9 2,500			Oct. 9 2,500

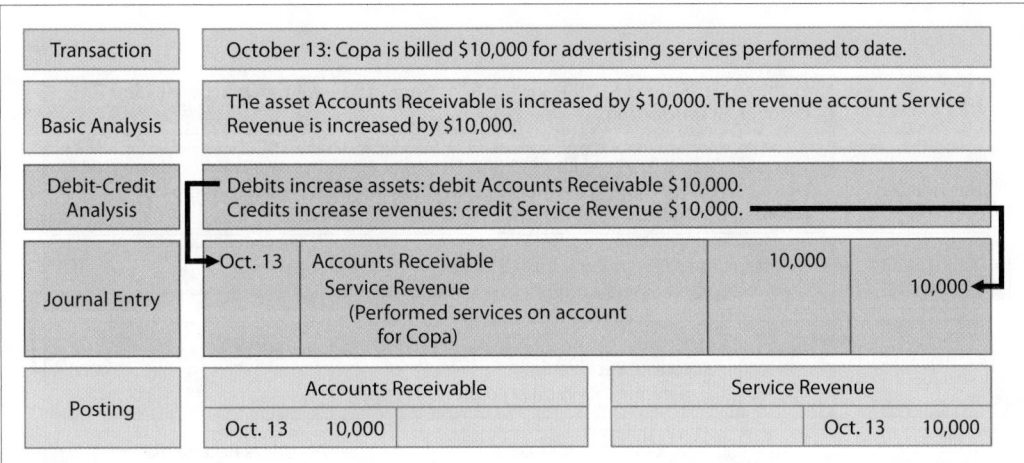

▶ Transaction (9)
Services performed on account

Transaction	October 13: Copa is billed $10,000 for advertising services performed to date.		
Basic Analysis	The asset Accounts Receivable is increased by $10,000. The revenue account Service Revenue is increased by $10,000.		
Debit-Credit Analysis	Debits increase assets: debit Accounts Receivable $10,000. Credits increase revenues: credit Service Revenue $10,000.		

Journal Entry	Oct. 13 Accounts Receivable
	        Service Revenue
	        (Performed services on account
	          for Copa)
		10,000	10,000

Posting

Accounts Receivable		Service Revenue	
Oct. 13 10,000			Oct. 13 10,000

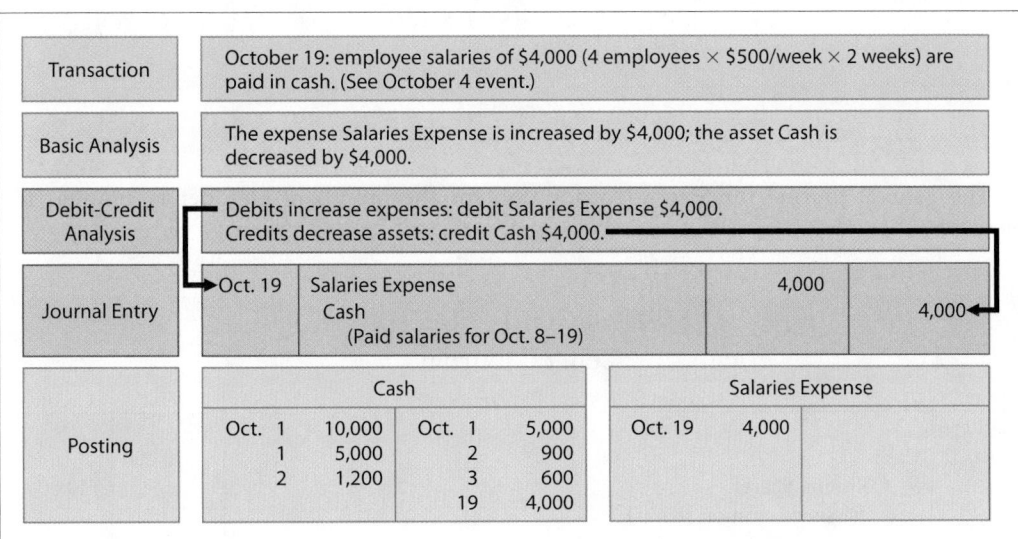

▶ Transaction (10)
Payment of salaries

Transaction	October 19: employee salaries of $4,000 (4 employees × $500/week × 2 weeks) are paid in cash. (See October 4 event.)		
Basic Analysis	The expense Salaries Expense is increased by $4,000; the asset Cash is decreased by $4,000.		
Debit-Credit Analysis	Debits increase expenses: debit Salaries Expense $4,000. Credits decrease assets: credit Cash $4,000.		

Journal Entry	Oct. 19 Salaries Expense
	        Cash
	        (Paid salaries for Oct. 8–19)
		4,000	4,000

Posting

Cash				Salaries Expense	
Oct. 1	10,000	Oct. 1	5,000	Oct. 19 4,000	
1	5,000	2	900		
2	1,200	3	600		
		19	4,000		

Transaction (11)
Payment of dividend

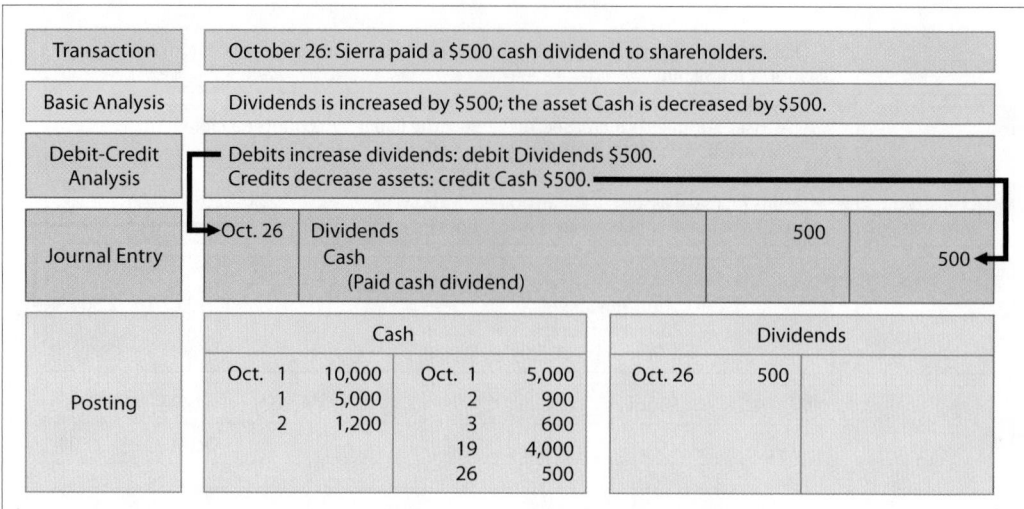

Transaction	October 26: Sierra paid a $500 cash dividend to shareholders.
Basic Analysis	Dividends is increased by $500; the asset Cash is decreased by $500.
Debit-Credit Analysis	Debits increase dividends: debit Dividends $500. Credits decrease assets: credit Cash $500.

Journal Entry	Oct. 26 Dividends 500
	          Cash 500
	          (Paid cash dividend)

Posting

Cash					Dividends		
Oct. 1	10,000	Oct. 1	5,000	Oct. 26	500		
1	5,000	2	900				
2	1,200	3	600				
		19	4,000				
		26	500				

Transaction (12)
Collection of account

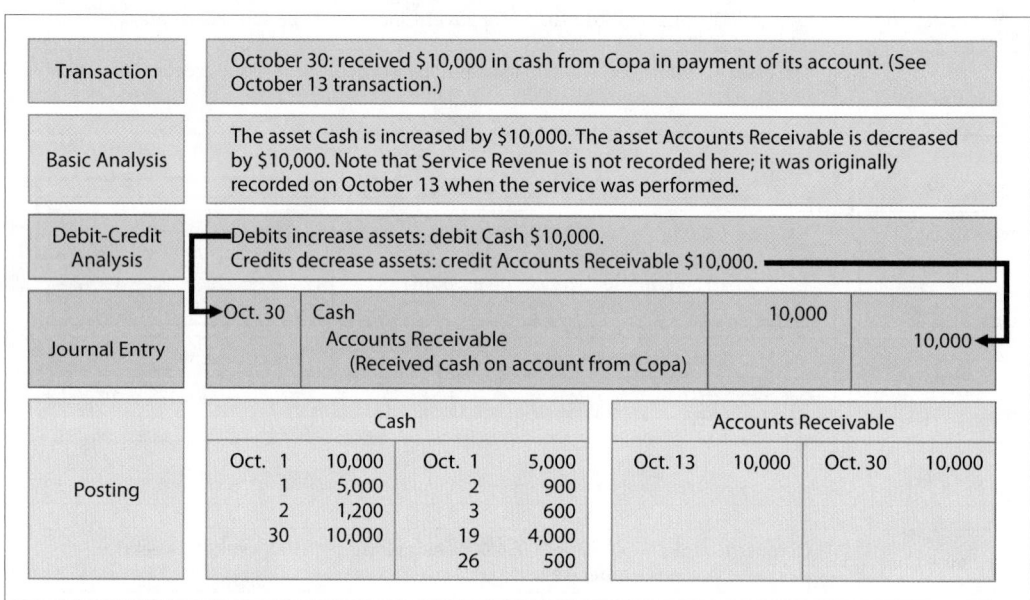

Transaction	October 30: received $10,000 in cash from Copa in payment of its account. (See October 13 transaction.)
Basic Analysis	The asset Cash is increased by $10,000. The asset Accounts Receivable is decreased by $10,000. Note that Service Revenue is not recorded here; it was originally recorded on October 13 when the service was performed.
Debit-Credit Analysis	Debits increase assets: debit Cash $10,000. Credits decrease assets: credit Accounts Receivable $10,000.

Journal Entry	Oct. 30 Cash 10,000
	          Accounts Receivable 10,000
	          (Received cash on account from Copa)

Posting

Cash					Accounts Receivable		
Oct. 1	10,000	Oct. 1	5,000	Oct. 13	10,000	Oct. 30	10,000
1	5,000	2	900				
2	1,200	3	600				
30	10,000	19	4,000				
		26	500				

The general journal for Sierra Corporation for the month of October is summarized below.

SIERRA CORPORATION
General Journal

Date	Account Titles and Explanation	Debit	Credit
2012			
Oct. 1	Cash	10,000	
	Common Shares		10,000
	(Issued common shares)		
1	Cash	5,000	
	Notes Payable		5,000
	(Issued three-month, 6% note payable for cash)		
1	Equipment	5,000	
	Cash		5,000
	(Purchased equipment for cash)		

2	Cash				1,200	
	Unearned Revenue					1,200
	(Received advance from R. Knox for future service)					
2	Rent Expense				900	
	Cash					900
	(Paid cash for October office rent)					
3	Prepaid Insurance				600	
	Cash					600
	(Paid one-year insurance policy; effective October 1)					
9	Supplies				2,500	
	Accounts Payable					2,500
	(Purchased supplies on account from Aero Supply)					
13	Accounts Receivable				10,000	
	Service Revenue					10,000
	(Performed services on account for Copa)					
19	Salaries Expense				4,000	
	Cash					4,000
	(Paid salaries for Oct. 8–19)					
26	Dividends				500	
	Cash					500
	(Paid cash dividend)					
30	Cash				10,000	
	Accounts Receivable					10,000
	(Received cash on account from Copa)					

The general ledger for Sierra Corporation follows with all balances highlighted in red.

SIERRA CORPORATION
General Ledger

		Cash						Unearned Revenue		
Oct.	1	10,000	Oct.	1	5,000			Oct.	2	1,200
	1	5,000		2	900			Bal.		1,200
	2	1,200		3	600					
	30	10,000		19	4,000			Notes Payable		
				26	500			Oct.	1	5,000
Bal.		15,200						Bal.		5,000

		Accounts Receivable						Common Shares		
Oct.	13	10,000	Oct.	30	10,000			Oct.	1	10,000
Bal.		0						Bal.		10,000

		Supplies						Dividends		
Oct.	9	2,500				Oct.	26	500		
Bal.		2,500				Bal.		500		

		Prepaid Insurance						Service Revenue		
Oct.	3	600						Oct.	13	10,000
Bal.		600						Bal.		10,000

		Equipment						Salaries Expense		
Oct.	1	5,000				Oct.	19	4,000		
Bal.		5,000				Bal.		4,000		

		Accounts Payable						Rent Expense		
			Oct.	9	2,500	Oct.	2	900		
			Bal.		2,500	Bal.		900		

■ Keeping an Eye on Cash

The Cash general ledger account shown above, and reproduced below, including transaction numbers, reflects all of the inflows and outflows of cash that occurred for Sierra Corporation during October.

		Cash						
Oct.	1	10,000	(1)	Oct.	1	5,000	(3)
	1	5,000	(2)		2	900	(5)
	2	1,200	(4)		3	600	(6)
	30	10,000	(12)		19	4,000	(10)
					26	500	(11)
Bal.		15,200					

The Cash account and the recorded cash transactions indicate why cash changed during October. However, to make this information useful for analysis, it is summarized in a statement of cash flows. As we learned in Chapter 1, the statement of cash flows classifies each transaction as an operating activity, an investing activity, or a financing activity. A user of this statement can then determine the amount of cash provided by operations, the amount of cash used for investing purposes, and the amount of cash provided by financing activities.

Operating activities are the types of activities the company performs to generate profits. Transactions 4, 5, 6, 10, and 12 relate to cash received or spent to directly support its operations.

Investing activities include the purchase or sale of long-lived assets used in operating the business, or the purchase or sale of long-term investments. Transaction 3, the purchase of equipment, is an investing activity.

The primary types of *financing activities* are borrowing (and paying back) money, issuing shares, and paying dividends. The financing activities of Sierra Corporation are transactions 1, 2, and 11.

BEFORE YOU GO ON...

▶ Do It! Record and Post Transactions

The following events occurred during the first week of business of Hair It Is, Inc., a beauty salon:

May 1   Issued common shares to shareholders for $20,000 cash.
    4   Purchased $4,800 of equipment on account (to be paid in 30 days).
    5   Interviewed three people for the position of hair stylist. Will choose one and make an offer next week.
    6   Purchased supplies for cash, $600.

(a)   Record these transactions in the general journal.
(b)   Post the journal entries to the general ledger.

Action Plan

- Understand which events (the ones with economic effects) should be recorded.
- Analyze the transactions. Determine which accounts are affected and whether the transaction increases or decreases the account.
- Record the transactions in the general journal, which provides a chronological record of the transactions.
- Posting involves transferring the journalized debits and credits to specific T accounts in the general ledger.
- Ledger accounts should be arranged in statement order.
- Determine the ending balances of each ledger account by netting (calculating the difference between) the total debits and credits.

Solution

(a)

May	1	Cash		20,000	
		Common Shares			20,000
		(Issued common shares)			
	4	Equipment		4,800	
		Accounts Payable			4,800
		(Purchased equipment on account)			
	5	No entry because no transaction occurred			
	6	Supplies		600	
		Cash			600
		(Purchased supplies)			

(b)

Cash					
May	1	20,000	May	6	600
Bal.		19,400			

Accounts Payable			
	May	4	4,800

Supplies		
May	6	600

Common Shares			
	May	1	20,000

Equipment		
May	4	4,800

The Trial Balance

As was mentioned earlier in the chapter, the basic steps of the recording process shown in the last section are the first three steps in the accounting cycle. The fourth step is to prepare a trial balance. The remaining steps (not illustrated here) will be discussed in the next chapter.

STUDY OBJECTIVE 4
Prepare a trial balance.

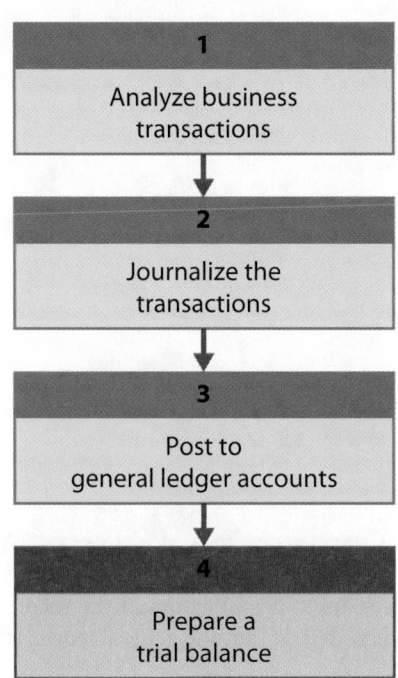

Illustration 3-7
The accounting cycle—Steps 1–4

A **trial balance** is a list of general ledger accounts and their balances at a specific time. A trial balance is prepared at the end of an accounting period, which is usually monthly, but could also be quarterly or annually. For Sierra Corporation, we have assumed that its accounting period is one month.

In the trial balance, the accounts are listed in the order in which they appear in the ledger, with debit balances listed in the left column and credit balances in the right column. The totals of the two columns must be equal.

The main purpose of a trial balance is to prove (check) that the debits equal the credits after posting. That is, the sum of the debit account balances must equal the sum of the credit account balances. If the debit and credit totals don't agree, the trial balance can uncover errors in journalizing and posting. For example, the trial balance will not balance if a debit or credit amount is unequal in a journal entry, or if the amount is transferred incorrectly to the general ledger from a journal entry. If the trial balance does not balance, then the error must be located and corrected before proceeding.

A trial balance is also useful in the preparation of financial statements, as will be explained in the next chapter. The procedure for preparing a trial balance is as follows:

1. List the account titles and their balances in the same order as the chart of accounts. Debit balances should be entered in the debit column and credit balances in the credit column.
2. Total the debit column and the credit column.
3. Ensure that the debit and credit column totals are equal (agree).

The trial balance prepared from the general ledger of Sierra Corporation shown earlier is presented below. Accounts with zero balances, such as Accounts Receivable, are normally not included in the trial balance. Note that the total debits, $28,700, equal the total credits, $28,700.

When a trial balance is first prepared, it is important to understand that the retained earnings account balance that is listed on the trial balance is not the retained earnings balance at the end of the period; rather it is the retained earnings balance at the beginning of the period. Why? Recall that retained earnings at the beginning of a period plus revenues less expenses and dividends for the period gives us retained earnings at the end of the period. If a trial balance lists revenues, expenses, and dividend account balances, the retained earnings balance has not yet been updated for these items and must therefore represent the balance in retained earnings at the beginning of the period.

Ethics Note

When they evaluate an accounting system, auditors see errors and irregularities differently. An error is the result of an unintentional mistake. As such, it is neither ethical nor unethical. An irregularity, on the other hand, is an intentional misstatement, which is generally viewed as unethical.

▶ **Illustration 3-8**
Sierra Corporation trial balance

SIERRA CORPORATION Trial Balance October 31, 2012		
	Debit	Credit
Cash	$15,200	
Supplies	2,500	
Prepaid insurance	600	
Equipment	5,000	
Accounts payable		$ 2,500
Unearned revenue		1,200
Notes payable		5,000
Common shares		10,000
Dividends	500	
Service revenue		10,000
Salaries expense	4,000	
Rent expense	900	
	$28,700	$28,700

LIMITATIONS OF A TRIAL BALANCE

Although a trial balance reveals many types of errors in the recording process, it does not prove that all transactions have been recorded or that the general ledger is correct. Errors may exist even though the trial balance column totals agree. For example, the trial balance may balance even when (1) a transaction is not journalized, (2) a correct journal entry is not posted, (3) a journal entry is posted twice, (4) incorrect accounts are used in journalizing or posting, or (5) errors that cancel each other's effect are made in recording the amount of a transaction. In other words, as long as equal debits and credits are posted, even to the wrong account or in the wrong amount, the total debits will equal the total credits. Nevertheless, despite its limitations, the trial balance is a useful screen for finding errors.

ACCOUNTING MATTERS! *Management Perspective*

"ESP" Accounting

In his autobiography, Sam Walton described the accounting information system he used when the retail empire he founded, Walmart, was just getting started. "We kept a little pigeonhole on the wall for the cash receipts and paperwork of each store. I had a blue binder ledger book for each store. . . . Then once a month, [the bookkeeper] and I would close those books—enter the merchandise, enter the sales, enter the cash, balance it, and close them.

. . . [B]ack then, we were using the ESP method, which really sped things along when it came time to close those books. It's a pretty basic method: if you can't make your books balance, you take however much they're off by and enter it under the heading ESP, which stands for Error Some Place."

Source: Sam Walton with John Huey, *Made in America: My Story*, New York: Bantam Books, 1993, pp. 67-68.

BEFORE YOU GO ON...

▶Do It! Preparing a Trial Balance

Koizumi Kollections Ltd. has the following alphabetical list of accounts and balances at July 31, 2012:

Accounts payable	$33,700	Equipment	$ 35,700
Accounts receivable	71,200	Income tax expense	12,000
Bank loan payable	49,500	Land	51,000
Building	86,500	Operating expenses	93,100
Cash	3,200	Service revenue	171,100
Common shares	99,400	Unearned revenue	3,000
Dividends	4,000		

Each of the above accounts has a normal balance. Prepare a trial balance, rearranging the accounts in normal ledger (financial statement) order:

Action Plan
- Reorder the accounts as they would normally appear in the general ledger: statement of financial position accounts are listed first (assets, liabilities, and equity), and then income statement accounts (revenues and expenses).
- Determine whether each account has a normal debit or credit balance.
- List the amounts in the appropriate debit or credit column.
- Total the trial balance columns. Total debits must equal total credits or a mistake has been made.

(continued)

Solution

KOIZUMI KOLLECTIONS LTD. Trial Balance July 31, 2012		
	Debit	Credit
Cash	$ 3,200	
Accounts receivable	71,200	
Land	51,000	
Building	86,500	
Equipment	35,700	
Accounts payable		$ 33,700
Unearned revenue		3,000
Bank loan payable		49,500
Common shares		99,400
Dividends	4,000	
Service revenue		171,100
Operating expenses	93,100	
Income tax expense	12,000	
	$356,700	$356,700

DECISION TOOLKIT

 Decision Checkpoints	 Info Needed for Decision	 Tools to Use for Decision	 How to Evaluate Results
How do you determine that debits equal credits?	All general ledger account balances	Trial balance	List the account titles and their balances, total the debit and credit columns, and verify equality.

comparing
IFRS and ASPE

Key Differences	International Financial Reporting Standards (IFRS)	Accounting Standards for Private Enterprises (ASPE)
No significant differences		

Keeping Track of Your Important Documents

In this chapter, you learned about the features of accounting information systems that help companies keep track of their important financial information. As you know, each company is an economic entity and its daily transactions create a large amount of financial information and documents. These transactions need to be recorded in records that are kept separate from the activities of the company's shareholders (owners) and all other economic entities. Although you are not a company, you are an economic entity and each day you, too, enter into a variety of economic transactions. And just as they do for companies, some of these transactions produce important financial documents that you need to keep track of.

Individuals vary in the way they keep track of this information. Some of us are meticulous with record keeping, while others pay little attention to their financial affairs. Most of us really should regularly set aside time to keep our financial records up to date and in order.

What are some of the documents and records in your life? Suppose you had five minutes to collect your most important possessions and flee to safety. Would you know where to find your vital personal papers? Are they in one place or scattered about your home?

Some Facts

- Some examples of your personal documents and records might include:
  - Identification records (birth certificate, driver's licence, passport, social insurance card, citizenship card, health card)
  - Bank account statements and loan information
  - Titles, deeds, and registrations for property and vehicles owned
  - Credit card statements and receipts
  - Insurance policies and employer benefit statements (if you have a job with benefits)
  - Income tax information (copies of past returns, assessment notices, and proof of tax payments)
- You can keep financial and personal records in filing cabinets, on your computer, or in a safety deposit box at a bank. Where to keep records depends on the characteristics of each record. Experts recommend that you do not carry all your personal identification, such as social insurance card or birth certificate, in your wallet or purse in case it is lost or stolen.
- On your computer, keep lists of the contents of your safety deposit box and contact information. You may want to print out this information and store it in your safety deposit box. You should also make a backup copy of items on your computer and store the backup off site.
- Watch out for identity theft, especially at the start of the year when income tax documents are being mailed out. Experts offer the following tips to reduce the likelihood of your being a target.
  - Pick up your mail daily.
  - Keep track of important documents.
  - Use electronic delivery of documents that contain personal information, such as your name, date of birth, and social insurance number.
  - Monitor your financial transactions regularly.
  - Check your credit report.
  - Shred documents that contain your name and address.

What Do You Think?

Do you really need to take the time to organize your financial documents?

YES Everyone engages in financial transactions each day. For a variety of reasons (such as tax reporting or job application), we need to maintain documentation of these transactions.

NO I lead a relatively uncomplicated life, and I can usually find the documents that I need when I require them.

Source: Dianne Nice, "These Simple Precautions Can Foil Identity Thieves," *Globe and Mail*, January 24, 2011, p. B12.

Summary of Study Objectives

1. **Analyze the effects of transactions on the accounting equation.** Each business transaction has a dual effect on the accounting equation. For example, if an individual asset is increased, there must be a corresponding decrease in another asset, or increase in a specific liability, or increase in shareholders' equity.

2. **Define debits and credits and explain how they are used to record transactions.** The terms *debit* and *credit* are synonymous with *left* and *right*. Assets, dividends, and expenses are increased by debits and decreased by credits. The normal balance of these accounts is a debit balance. Liabilities, common shares, retained earnings, and revenues are increased by credits and decreased by debits. The normal balance of these accounts is a credit balance.

3. **Identify the basic steps in the recording process.** The basic steps in the recording process are (a) analyzing each transaction for its effect on the accounts, (b) entering the transaction information in a general journal, and (c) transferring the information in the general journal to the appropriate accounts in the general ledger. These are also the first three steps in the accounting cycle.

4. **Prepare a trial balance.** The preparation of a trial balance is the fourth step in the accounting cycle. The trial balance is a list of accounts and their balances at a specific time. The main purpose of the trial balance is to prove the mathematical equality of debits and credits after posting. A trial balance also uncovers errors in journalizing and posting and is useful in preparing financial statements.

Glossary

Account An individual accounting record of increases and decreases in a specific asset, liability, or shareholders' equity item. (p. 113)

Accounting information system The system of collecting and processing transaction data and communicating financial information to interested parties. (p. 106)

Accounting transaction An economic event that is recorded in the financial statements because it involves an exchange that affects assets, liabilities, or shareholders' equity. (p. 106)

Chart of accounts A list of a company's accounts and account numbers that identify where the accounts are in the general ledger. (p. 120)

Credit The right side of an account. (p. 114)

Debit The left side of an account. (p. 114)

Double-entry accounting system A system that records the dual effect of each transaction in appropriate accounts. (p. 114)

General journal The book of original entry in which transactions are recorded in chronological order. (p. 118)

General ledger The book of accounts that contains a company's asset, liability, and shareholders' equity, revenue, and expense accounts. (p. 119)

Posting The procedure of transferring journal entries to the general ledger accounts. (p. 120)

T account (also known as a general ledger account) The basic form of an account, with a debit (left) side and a credit (right) side showing the effect of transactions on the account. (p. 113)

Trial balance A list of general ledger accounts and their balances at a specific time, usually at the end of the accounting period. (p. 128)

DECISION TOOLKIT—A SUMMARY

 Decision Checkpoints	 Info Needed for Decision	 Tools to Use for Decision	 How to Evaluate Results
Has an accounting transaction occurred?	Details of the event	Accounting equation	Determine the effect, if any, on assets, liabilities, and shareholders' equity.
How do you determine that debits equal credits?	All general ledger account balances	Trial balance	List the account titles and their balances, total the debit and credit columns, and verify equality.

USING THE DECISION TOOLKIT

lululemon athletica inc. is one of Canada's leading designers and suppliers of athletic wear. lululemon reports the following list of accounts, in alphabetical order. All accounts have normal balances.

LULULEMON ATHLETICA INC. List of Accounts January 30, 2011 (in USD thousands)	
Accounts payable and accrued expenses	$ 48,797
Accounts receivable	9,116
Cash and cash equivalents	316,286
Common shares and other equity	204,637
Cost of goods sold expense	316,757
Depreciation expense	24,614
Income tax expense	61,080
Income taxes payable	18,399
Intangible assets	27,112
Inventories	57,469
Long-term debt	19,645
Other assets	11,957
Other liabilities	18,168
Other revenue	2,886
Prepaid expenses	6,408
Property, plant, and equipment	70,954
Retained earnings, beginning of year	67,809
Sales revenue	711,704
Selling, general, and administrative expenses	190,292

Instructions

(a) Prepare a trial balance for lululemon, reordering the accounts in financial statement order.

(b) On the trial balance, identify on which financial statement (FS) each account should be reported. Write "SFP" beside the accounts that should be shown on the statement of financial position, "IS" beside those that should be shown on the income statement, and "SCE" beside those that should be shown on the statement of changes in equity.

Solution

LULULEMON ATHLETICA INC. Trial Balance January 30, 2011 (in USD thousands)			
	(a)		(b)
	Debit	Credit	FS
Cash and cash equivalents	$316,286		SFP
Accounts receivable	9,116		SFP
Inventories	57,469		SFP
Prepaid expenses	6,408		SFP
Property, plant, and equipment	70,954		SFP
Intangible assets	27,112		SFP
Other assets	11,957		SFP
Accounts payable and accrued liabilities		$48,797	SFP
Income taxes payable		18,399	SFP
Other liabilities		18,168	SFP

(continued)

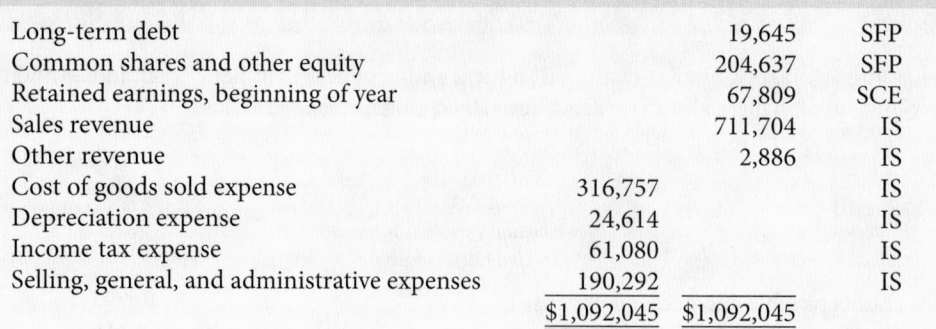

Long-term debt		19,645	SFP
Common shares and other equity		204,637	SFP
Retained earnings, beginning of year		67,809	SCE
Sales revenue		711,704	IS
Other revenue		2,886	IS
Cost of goods sold expense	316,757		IS
Depreciation expense	24,614		IS
Income tax expense	61,080		IS
Selling, general, and administrative expenses	190,292		IS
	$1,092,045	$1,092,045	

the navigator

Comprehensive Do It!

Campus Laundry Inc. opened on September 1, 2012. During the first month of operations, the following transactions occurred:

Sept. 1   Shareholders invested $20,000 cash in the business when 10,000 common shares were issued by the company.
       3   Paid $1,000 cash for rent for the month of September.
       4   Purchased washers and dryers for $25,000, paying $10,000 in cash and signing a six-month, 8%, $15,000 note payable.
       7   Paid $1,200 for a one-year insurance policy.
       15 Paid employee salaries of $2,500.
       15 Performed services on account for a nearby restaurant, $6,200.
       21 Paid a $700 cash dividend to shareholders.
       29 Cash receipts for laundry services performed throughout the month were $5,000.
       30 Paid employee salaries of $2,500.
       30 Utilities of $1,200 are owed at the end of the month.

Instructions

(a) Journalize the above transactions.
(b) Open T accounts and post the transactions.
(c) Prepare a trial balance.
(d) Prepare an income statement, statement of changes in equity, and statement of financial position.

Action Plan

- Make separate journal entries for each transaction.
- In journalizing, make sure debits equal credits.
- In journalizing, use specific account titles taken from the chart of accounts and provide an appropriate explanation of the journal entry.
- Arrange the general ledger in statement order, beginning with the statement of financial position accounts.
- Prepare a trial balance that lists accounts in the order in which they appear in the ledger.
- In the trial balance, list debit balances in the left column and credit balances in the right column. Check the accuracy of your work. Total debits must equal total credits.
- Prepare the income statement, paying attention to the order that accounts are listed in.
- Prepare the statement of changes in equity and determine how the retained earnings balance has changed during the period.
- Prepare the statement of financial position, paying attention to the categories and order in which accounts are listed. Ensure that total assets equals total liabilities plus equity.

Solution to Comprehensive Do It!

(a)

Date	Account Titles and Explanation	Debit	Credit
2012			
Sept. 1	Cash	20,000	
	Common Shares		20,000
	(Issued common shares)		
3	Rent Expense	1,000	
	Cash		1,000
	(Paid September rent)		
4	Equipment	25,000	
	Cash		10,000
	Notes Payable		15,000
	(Purchased laundry equipment for cash and six-month, 8% note payable)		
7	Prepaid Insurance	1,200	
	Cash		1,200
	(Paid one-year insurance policy)		
15	Salaries Expense	2,500	
	Cash		2,500
	(Paid salaries)		
15	Accounts Receivable	6,200	
	Service Revenue		6,200
	(To record revenue for laundry services provided)		
21	Dividends	700	
	Cash		700
	(Paid a $700 cash dividend)		
29	Cash	5,000	
	Service Revenue		5,000
	(To record collection for laundry services provided)		
30	Salaries Expense	2,500	
	Cash		2,500
	(Paid salaries)		
30	Utilities Expense	1,200	
	Accounts Payable		1,200
	(To record utilities due in October)		

(b)

Cash						Common Shares		
Sept. 1	20,000	Sept. 3	1,000				Sept. 1	20,000
29	5,000	4	10,000					
		7	1,200			Dividends		
		15	2,500		Sept. 21	700		
		21	700					
		30	2,500					
Bal.	7,100					Service Revenue		
							Sept. 15	6,200
Accounts Receivable							29	5,000
Sept. 15	6,200						Bal.	11,200

Prepaid Insurance			Salaries Expense		
Sept. 7	1,200		Sept. 15	2,500	
			30	2,500	
Equipment			Bal.	5,000	
Sept. 4	25,000				

(continued)

Accounts Payable				Utilities Expense			
	Sept.	30	1,200	Sept.	30	1,200	

Notes Payable				Rent Expense			
	Sept.	4	15,000	Sept.	3	1,000	

(c)

CAMPUS LAUNDRY INC.
Trial Balance
September 30, 2012

	Debit	Credit
Cash	$ 7,100	
Accounts receivable	6,200	
Prepaid insurance	1,200	
Equipment	25,000	
Accounts payable		$ 1,200
Notes payable		15,000
Common shares		20,000
Dividends	700	
Service revenue		11,200
Salaries expense	5,000	
Utilities expense	1,200	
Rent expense	1,000	
	$47,400	$47,400

(d)

CAMPUS LAUNDRY INC.
Income Statement
Month Ended September 30, 2012

Revenues		
Service revenue		$11,200
Expenses		
Salaries expense	$5,000	
Utilities expense	1,200	
Rent expense	1,000	7,200
Profit		$ 4,000

CAMPUS LAUNDRY INC.
Statement of Changes in Equity
Month Ended September 30, 2012

	Common Shares	Retained Earnings	Total Equity
Balance, September 1	$ 0	$ 0	$ 0
Issued common shares	20,000		20,000
Profit		4,000	4,000
Dividends		(700)	(700)
Balance, September 30	$20,000	$3,300	$23,300

CAMPUS LAUNDRY INC.
Statement of Financial Position
September 30, 2012

Assets

Current assets		
Cash	$ 7,100	
Accounts receivable	6,200	
Prepaid insurance	1,200	$14,500
Property, plant, and equipment		
Equipment		25,000
Total assets		$39,500

Liabilities and Shareholders' Equity

Current liabilities		
Accounts payable	$ 1,200	
Notes payable	15,000	$16,200
Shareholders' equity		
Common shares	$20,000	
Retained earnings	3,300	23,300
Total liabilities and shareholders' equity		$39,500

Self-Test, Brief Exercises, Exercises, Problems: Set A, and many more components are available for practice in WileyPLUS.

Self-Test Questions

Answers are at the end of the chapter.

(SO 1) 1. When cash is received in advance of performing a service, the effects on the accounting equation are:
(a) an increase in assets and a decrease in shareholders' equity.
(b) an increase in assets and an increase in shareholders' equity.
(c) an increase in assets and an increase in liabilities.
(d) an increase in liabilities and an increase in shareholders' equity.

(SO 1) 2. Shareholders' equity consists of the following:
(a) common shares, revenues, and liabilities.
(b) dividends, revenues, and assets.
(c) liabilities, common shares, and retained earnings.
(d) common shares and retained earnings.

(SO 2) 3. Which statement about an account is true?
(a) An account is an individual accounting record of increases and decreases in specific asset, liability, and shareholders' equity items.

(b) There are separate accounts for specific assets and liabilities but only one account for shareholders' equity items.
(c) The left side of an account is the credit or decrease side.
(d) The right side of an account is the debit or increase side.

(SO 2) 4. Debits:
(a) increase both assets and liabilities.
(b) decrease both assets and liabilities.
(c) increase assets and decrease liabilities.
(d) decrease assets and increase liabilities.

(SO 2) 5. Which accounts normally have debit balances?
(a) Assets, expenses, and revenues
(b) Assets, expenses, and retained earnings
(c) Assets, liabilities, and dividends
(d) Assets, dividends, and expenses

(SO 3) 6. Which of these statements about a general journal is false?
(a) It is not a book of original entry.
(b) It provides a chronological record of transactions.

(c) It helps to locate errors because the debit and credit amounts for each entry can be quickly compared.

(d) It discloses the complete effect of a transaction in one place.

(SO 3)   7. A general ledger:
(a) contains only asset and liability accounts.
(b) should show accounts in alphabetical order.
(c) is a collection of the entire group of accounts maintained by a company.
(d) provides a chronological record of transactions.

(SO 3)   8. Posting:
(a) normally occurs before journalizing.
(b) transfers general ledger transaction data to the general journal.
(c) is an optional step in the accounting cycle.
(d) transfers general journal entries to general ledger accounts.

(SO 4)   9. A trial balance:
(a) is a list of accounts with their balances at a specific time.
(b) proves that transactions have been correctly journalized.
(c) will not balance if a correct journal entry is posted twice.
(d) proves that all transactions have been recorded.

(SO 4)   10. A trial balance will not balance if:
(a) a journal entry to record a cash sale is posted twice.
(b) the purchase of supplies on account is debited to Supplies and credited to Cash.
(c) a $100 cash dividend is debited to Dividends for $1,000 and credited to Cash for $100.
(d) a $450 payment on account is debited to Accounts Payable for $45 and credited to Cash for $45.

Questions

(SO 1)   1. Why are some events recorded as accounting transactions but others are not?

(SO 1)   2. Which of the following events should be recorded in the accounting records? Explain your answer in each case.
(a) The company wins an award as one of the top 50 companies in Canada to work for.
(b) Supplies are purchased on account.
(c) An employee is terminated.
(d) The company pays a cash dividend to its shareholders.
(e) A local lawyer agrees to provide legal services to the company for the next year.

(SO 1)   3. Can a business enter into a transaction that affects only the left side of the accounting equation? If so, give an example.

(SO 1)   4. What is the effect of each of the following transactions on the accounting equation?
(a) Paid cash for janitorial services.
(b) Purchased equipment on account.
(c) Issued common shares to investors in exchange for cash.
(d) Paid an account payable.
(e) Performed services on account.

(SO 2)   5. Hiroshi Uehara, a fellow student, claims that the double-entry system means each transaction must be recorded twice. Is Hiroshi correct? Explain.

(SO 2)   6. Natalie Boudreau, an introductory accounting student, believes debit balances are favourable and credit balances are unfavourable. Is Natalie correct? Discuss.

(SO 2)   7. State the debit and credit effects and identify the normal balance for the following types of accounts: (a) assets, (b) liabilities, (c) common

shares, (d) retained earnings, (e) dividends, (f) revenues, and (g) expenses.

(SO 2)   8. For each of the following accounts, indicate (a) whether the account would have a normal debit or credit balance, and (b) the appropriate statement classification—income statement, statement of changes in equity, or statement of financial position—for each.
1. Accounts Receivable
2. Accounts Payable
3. Equipment
4. Dividends
5. Supplies
6. Service Revenue
7. Unearned Revenue
8. Income Tax Expense
9. Prepaid Rent
10. Bank Loan Payable

(SO 2)   9. Identify the two account titles that should be used to record each side of the following transactions:
(a) Cash sales
(b) Services performed on account
(c) Supplies purchased on account
(d) Collection of a customer's account
(e) Payment of an amount owing to a supplier
(f) Payment of a dividend to shareholders
(g) Payment of income taxes

(SO 2)   10. For the following transactions, indicate the account debited and the account credited:
(a) Supplies are purchased on account
(b) Cash is received on signing a note payable
(c) Employees are paid salaries in cash
(d) Cash is received from a customer in advance
(e) An expense is paid in advance

(SO 2) 11. For each account listed below, indicate whether it generally will have debit entries only, credit entries only, or both debit and credit entries:
(a) Cash
(b) Accounts Receivable
(c) Dividends
(d) Accounts Payable
(e) Service Revenue
(f) Salaries Expense

(SO 2) 12. A company received cash from a customer. It debited the Cash account. Name three credit accounts that the company might have used to record a cash receipt from a customer. Describe the circumstances where you would use each of these three accounts.

(SO 3) 13. An efficiency expert who was reviewing the steps in the accounting cycle suggested dropping the general journal and recording and summarizing transactions directly into the general ledger instead. Comment on this suggestion.

(SO 3) 14. (a) What is a general ledger? (b) In what order are accounts usually arranged in a general ledger?

(SO 3) 15. (a) What is a chart of accounts and why is it important? (b) How does numbering the accounts help?

(SO 3) 16. Arrange the following accounts in their normal order in a chart of accounts: common shares, prepaid insurance, cash, service revenue, dividends, unearned revenue, supplies, income tax expense.

(SO 3) 17. Does it matter how frequently transactions are posted from the general journal to the general ledger? Explain.

(SO 4) 18. Identify and describe the first four steps in the accounting cycle.

(SO 4) 19. (a) What is a trial balance? (b) From what source document(s) is it prepared?

(SO 4) 20. Does it matter in which order accounts are listed in the trial balance?

(SO 4) 21. On a trial balance, why does the retained earnings balance shown relate to the beginning of the period rather than the end of the period?

(SO 4) 22. What are the limitations of the trial balance?

(SO 4) 23. Two students are discussing the use of a trial balance. They wonder whether the following errors, each considered separately, would prevent the trial balance from balancing. What would you tell the students?
(a) The bookkeeper debited Supplies for $750 and debited Accounts Payable for $750 for the purchase of supplies on account.
(b) Cash collected on account was debited to Cash for $1,000, and credited to Service Revenue for $1,000.
(c) A journal entry recording the payment of dividends was posted to the general ledger as a debit to the Dividends account of $650 and a credit to the Cash account of $560.

Brief Exercises

BE3–1   Presented below are a number of economic events. Using the format shown after the transactions, indicate whether the event (including its amount) increased (+), decreased (−), or had no effect (NE) on each element of the accounting equation. The first one has been done for you as an example. *Analyze effects of transactions. (SO 1)*

1. Purchased supplies on account, $250.
2. Provided a service on account, $500.
3. Paid operating expenses, $300.
4. Issued common shares in exchange for cash, $5,000.
5. Paid a cash dividend to shareholders, $400.
6. Received cash from a customer who had previously been billed for services provided, $500 (see item 2).
7. Paid account owed to supplier, $250 (see item 1).
8. Paid for insurance in advance, $100.
9. Received cash in advance from a customer for services to be performed in the future, $300.
10. Performed the service that the customer previously paid for (see item 9).

Use the following format, in which the first one has been done for you as an example:

Trans-action	Assets	Liabilities	Shareholders' Equity			
			Common Shares	Retained Earnings		
				Revenues	Expenses	Dividends
1.	+$250	+$250	NE	NE	NE	NE

BE3–2   For each of the following accounts, indicate the (a) effect of a debit or credit on the account, (b) normal balance, and (c) appropriate statement classification—income statement, statement of changes in equity, and/or statement of financial position. *Indicate debit and credit effects. (SO 2)*

1. Accounts payable
2. Advertising expense
3. Service revenue
4. Accounts receivable
5. Unearned revenue
6. Cash

7. Dividends
8. Common shares
9. Prepaid insurance

10. Equipment
11. Retained earnings
12. Income tax expense

Match account names with transactions.
(SO 2)

BE3–3 Following is a list of account titles. Each of the transactions listed below is a cash transaction. Choose the account title that should be used to record the non-cash side of each transaction. The first one has been done for you as an example.

1. Accounts Receivable
2. Vehicles
3. Common Shares
4. Dividends
5. Interest Expense
6. Merchandise Inventory
7. Bank Loan Payable

8. Prepaid Insurance
9. Professional Fees Expense
10. Rent Expense
11. Sales
12. Unearned Revenue
13. Salaries Expense

___3___ (a) Issued common shares.
_____ (b) Repaid amount owing on bank loan payable.
_____ (c) Paid dividend.
_____ (d) Paid for accounting services.
_____ (e) Paid insurance in advance for the next year.
_____ (f) Paid interest on a bank loan.
_____ (g) Paid rent for the current month.
_____ (h) Paid salaries to employees.
_____ (i) Purchased a truck.
_____ (j) Purchased merchandise for resale.
_____ (k) Collected account due from a customer.
_____ (l) Sold merchandise inventory to a customer.
_____ (m) Received an advance as a deposit for future services from a customer.

Identify accounts to be debited and credited.
(SO 2)

BE3–4 Transactions for Ing Corporation for the month of June are presented below. Identify the accounts to be debited and credited for each transaction.

June 1 Issued common shares to shareholders in exchange for $2,500 cash.
2 Purchased equipment on account for $3,000.
3 Paid $750 to landlord for June rent.
8 Purchased supplies for $250 cash.
12 Billed J. Kronsnoble $300 for welding work done.
22 Received cash from J. Kronsnoble for work billed on June 12.
25 Hired an employee to start work on July 2.
28 Received cash of $200 from K. Jones as a deposit for welding work to be done in July.
29 Paid for equipment purchased on June 2.
30 Paid $100 for income tax.

Indicate basic debit-credit analysis.
(SO 2)

BE3–5 Riko Corporation has the following selected transactions:

1. Issued common shares to shareholders in exchange for $5,000.
2. Paid rent in advance for six months, $2,100.
3. Paid administrative assistant $500 salary.
4. Billed clients $1,200 for services provided.
5. Received $900 from clients for services provided.
6. Purchased $500 of supplies on account.
7. Paid supplier amount owing, $500.
8. Borrowed $1,000 cash by signing a note payable to a finance company.

For each transaction, indicate (a) the basic type of account debited and credited (asset, liability, shareholders' equity), (b) the specific account debited and credited (Cash, Rent Expense, Service Revenue, etc.), and (c) whether the specific account is increased or decreased to record this transaction. Use the following format, in which the first one has been done for you as an example:

	Account Debited				Account Credited		
	(a)	(b)	(c)		(a)	(b)	(c)
Trans-action	Basic Type	Specific Account	Effect		Basic Type	Specific Account	Effect
1.	Asset	Cash	Increase		Shareholders' equity	Common Shares	Increase

BE3–6 Journalize the transactions given in BE3–1.

BE3–7 Journalize the transactions for Ing Corporation given in BE3–4.

BE3–8 Using T accounts, post the journal entries in BE3–6 to the general ledger.

BE3–9 Selected transactions are presented in journal entry form below. For each entry provide an explanation of the transaction and then, using T accounts, post the journal entries to the general ledger.

Record transactions.
(SO 3)
Record transactions.
(SO 3)
Post journal entries.
(SO 3)
Post journal entries.
(SO 3)

GENERAL JOURNAL

Date	Account Titles	Debit	Credit
May 5	Accounts Receivable	3,200	
	Service Revenue		3,200
12	Cash	1,900	
	Accounts Receivable		1,900
15	Supplies	200	
	Accounts Payable		200
20	Cash	2,000	
	Service Revenue		2,000
25	Salaries Expense	2,500	
	Cash		2,500
28	Accounts Payable	200	
	Cash		200
30	Income Tax Expense	750	
	Cash		750

BE3–10 From the ledger balances given below, prepare a trial balance for Carland Inc. at June 30. All account balances are normal.

Prepare trial balance.
(SO 4)

Accounts payable	$ 3,000	Income tax expense	$ 400
Accounts receivable	4,000	Rent expense	1,000
Accumulated depreciation	3,600	Retained earnings	2,650
Cash	4,400	Salaries expense	4,000
Common shares	20,000	Service revenue	7,600
Dividends	200	Short-term investments	6,000
Equipment	17,000	Unearned revenue	150

BE3–11 Different types of posting errors are identified in the following table. For each error, indicate (a) whether the trial balance will balance, (b) the amount of the difference if the trial balance will not balance, and (c) the trial balance column that will have the larger total. Consider each error separately. Use the following form, in which error 1 is given as an example:

Identify effects of posting errors on trial balance.
(SO 4)

Error	(a) In Balance	(b) Difference	(c) Larger Column
1. A $1,200 debit to Supplies was posted as a $2,100 debit.	No	$900	Debit
2. A $1,000 credit to Cash was posted twice as two credits to Cash.			
3. A $5,000 debit to Dividends was posted to the Common Shares account.			
4. A journal entry debiting Cash and crediting Service Revenue for $2,500 was not posted.			
5. The collection of $500 cash on account was posted as a debit of $500 to Cash and a credit of $500 to Accounts Receivable.			
6. The payment of $1,000 on an account payable owed to the insurance company was posted as a debit to the Insurance Expense account. No credit was posted.			

BE3–12 An inexperienced bookkeeper prepared the following trial balance. She finished with a huge sigh of relief because she was able to balance the trial balance. (a) Is the trial balance correct? (b) If you answered "no" in (a), prepare a correct trial balance, assuming all account balances are normal.

Prepare corrected trial balance.
(SO 4)

BOURQUE LIMITED
Trial Balance
December 31, 2012

	Debit	Credit
Cash	$10,000	
Accounts receivable	6,500	
Supplies	3,500	
Accounts payable	1,500	
Unearned revenue	2,200	
Common shares	5,000	
Retained earnings	13,500	
Dividends		$ 4,500
Service revenue		20,000
Salaries expense		9,100
Office expense		4,400
Supplies expense		1,200
Travel expense		2,000
Income tax expense		1,000
	$42,200	$42,200

Exercises

Analyze effects
of transactions.
(SO 1)

E3–1   Selected transactions for Green Lawn Care Ltd. follow:

1. Issued common shares to shareholders in exchange for cash.
2. Paid monthly rent.
3. Purchased equipment on account.
4. Billed customers for services performed.
5. Paid a dividend to shareholders.
6. Received cash from customers billed in transaction 4.
7. Incurred advertising expense on account.
8. Purchased additional equipment, issuing cash and a note payable in payment.
9. Received cash from customers when service was provided.
10. Paid cash for equipment purchased in transaction 3.
11. Paid salaries to employees.
12. Paid for insurance in advance.

Instructions
Using (+) for increase, (−) for decrease, and (NE) for no effect, indicate the effect each of the transactions listed above had on the accounting equation. Use the following format, in which the first one has been done for you as an example:

				Shareholders' Equity		
					Retained Earnings	
Trans-action	Assets	Liabilities	Common Shares	Revenues	Expenses	Dividends
1.	+	NE	+	NE	NE	NE

Analyze effects
of transactions.
(SO 1)

E3–2   Wong Computer Corporation entered into these transactions during the month of May:

1. Purchased computers on account for $8,000 from Dell.
2. Paid $1,600 for rent for the month of May.
3. Provided computer services for $3,800 on account.
4. Paid Ontario Hydro $500 cash for utilities used in May.
5. Issued common shares to Li Wong in exchange for an additional $20,000 investment in the business.
6. Paid Dell for computers purchased in transaction 1.
7. Purchased a one-year accident insurance policy for $500 cash.
8. Received $3,500 cash in payment of the account in transaction 3.
9. Paid Li Wong a $500 dividend.
10. Paid income taxes of $400 for the month.

Instructions

Using (+) for increase, (−) for decrease, and (NE) for no effect, indicate the effect each of the transactions listed above had on the accounting equation and its amount. Use the following format, in which the first one has been done for you as an example:

				Shareholders' Equity			
					Retained Earnings		
Trans-			Common				
action	Assets	Liabilities	Shares	Revenues	Expenses	Dividends	
1.	+$8,000	+$8,000	NE	NE	NE	NE	

E3–3   Data for Green Lawn Care Ltd. were presented in E3–1.

Identify account names. (SO 2)

Instructions

Identify the account names that should be used to record each transaction. For example, in item #1, the accounts would be Cash and Common Shares.

E3–4   You are presented with the following alphabetical list of items, selected from the financial statements of Leon's Furniture Limited:

Identify normal balance and statement classification. (SO 2)

Accounts payable and accrued liabilities	Interest income
Accounts receivable	Inventory
Buildings	Land
Cash and cash equivalents	Equipment
Issue of common shares	Marketable securities
Cost of sales	Retained earnings, beginning of year
Customers' deposits	Salaries and commissions
Dividends	Sales
Goodwill	Dividends payable
Income taxes payable	

Instructions

(a) Identify the normal balance of each account.
(b) Indicate the financial statement—income statement, statement of changes in equity, or statement of financial position—where each account should be reported and its classification (e.g., current assets, non-current liabilities, revenues, expenses, etc.).

E3–5   Selected transactions for the Decorators Mill Ltd., an interior decorator corporation in its first month of business, are as follows:

Identify debits, credits, and normal balances. (SO 2)

March 2	Issued common shares for $11,000 cash.
4	Purchased used car for $10,000 cash, for use in business.
6	Purchased supplies on account for $600.
10	Billed customers $2,300 for services performed.
13	Paid $225 cash to advertise business opening.
25	Received $1,000 cash from customers billed on March 10.
27	Paid $500 to the supplier for the supplies purchased on March 6.
30	Received $700 cash from a customer for services to be performed in April.
31	Paid dividends of $500 to shareholders.

Instructions

For each transaction, indicate:
(a) the basic type of account debited and credited (asset, liability, shareholders' equity);
(b) the specific account debited and credited (Cash, Rent Expense, Service Revenue, etc.);
(c) whether the specific account is increased or decreased.

Use the following format, in which transaction 1 is given as an example:

	Account Debited			Account Credited		
	(a)	(b)	(c)	(a)	(b)	(c)
Trans-	Basic	Specific			Specific	
action	Type	Account	Effect	Basic Type	Account	Effect
March 2	Asset	Cash	Increase	Shareholders' equity	Common Shares	Increase

Record transactions.
(SO 3)

E3–6   Data for the Wong Computer Corporation were presented in E3–2.

Instructions
Journalize the transactions.

Record transactions.
(SO 3)

E3–7   Data for the Decorators Mill Ltd. were presented in E3–5.

Instructions
Journalize the transactions.

Analyze, record, and
post transactions.
(SO 1, 3)

E3–8   Selected transactions for the Basler Corporation during its first month in business are presented below:

Sept. 1	Issued common shares for $20,000 cash.
4	Purchased equipment for $12,000, paying $5,000 in cash and the balance by issuing a note payable.
10	Purchased $500 of supplies on account.
25	Received $4,500 cash in advance for architectural services to be provided next month.
28	Paid a $500 dividend to shareholders.
30	Paid account owing for supplies (see September 10).
30	Paid $35 interest expense on note payable.

Instructions
(a) Prepare a tabular equation analysis of the transactions as shown in the chapter.
(b) Journalize the transactions.
(c) Using T accounts, post the transactions to the general ledger.

Record transactions.
(SO 3)

E3–9   The information that follows is for Aubut Real Estate Agency Corporation:

Oct. 1	Issued common shares in exchange for $15,000 cash.
2	Hired an administrative assistant at an annual salary of $30,000. The assistant will start work on October 5.
5	Purchased furniture for $3,000, paying $500 cash and the balance on account.
6	Sold a house and lot for F. Omana. Commission due is $6,500 (not paid by Omana at this time).
9	Received $250 cash commission for renting an apartment.
15	Paid $700 for advertising costs relating to the first half of October.
24	Paid $2,500 on account for the furniture purchased on October 5.
30	Paid the administrative assistant $2,500 salary for October.
31	Received cash of $6,500 from F. Omana owed from October 6.

Instructions
Journalize the transactions.

Post journal entries
and prepare trial
balance.
(SO 3, 4)

E3–10   The journal entries for Aubut Real Estate Agency Corporation were prepared in E3–9.

Instructions
(a) Post the transactions to T accounts.
(b) Prepare a trial balance at October 31, 2012.

Post journal entries
and prepare trial
balance.
(SO 3, 4)

E3–11   Selected transactions from the general journal of Kang, Inc. are presented here:

	GENERAL JOURNAL		
Date	Account Titles	Debit	Credit
Aug. 1	Cash	3,000	
	Common Shares		3,000
7	Cash	1,800	
	Service Revenue		1,800
11	Equipment	4,000	
	Cash		1,000
	Accounts Payable		3,000
14	Accounts Receivable	1,450	
	Service Revenue		1,450
16	Cash	900	
	Unearned Revenue		900

28	Cash	700	
	Accounts Receivable		700
30	Salary Expense	2,000	
	Cash		2,000
31	Dividends	500	
	Cash		500

Instructions

(a) Prepare an explanation for each of the entries listed above.

(b) Using T accounts, post the transactions to the general ledger.

(c) Prepare a trial balance at August 31, 2012.

E3–12 Here is the general ledger for Holly Corp.:

Prepare trial balance from general ledger. (SO 4)

GENERAL LEDGER

Cash

Oct.	1	5,000	Oct.	5	400
	9	650		12	1,500
	15	5,000		16	300
	20	500		30	250
	23	2,000		30	500

Common Shares

| | | | Oct. | 1 | 5,000 |
| | | | | 23 | 2,000 |

Accounts Receivable

| Oct. | 6 | 800 | Oct. | 20 | 500 |
| | 20 | 940 | | | |

Dividends

| Oct. | 16 | 300 | | |

Supplies

| Oct. | 5 | 400 | | |

Service Revenue

			Oct.	6	800
				9	650
				20	940

Equipment

| Oct. | 2 | 2,000 | | |

Salaries Expense

| Oct. | 30 | 500 | | |

Accounts Payable

| Oct. | 12 | 1,500 | Oct. | 2 | 2,000 |
| | | | | 28 | 400 |

Advertising Expense

| Oct. | 28 | 400 | | |

Notes Payable

| | | | Oct. | 15 | 5,000 |

Rent Expense

| Oct. | 30 | 250 | | |

Instructions

(a) Prepare an explanation for each entry that was made above.

(b) Prepare a trial balance at October 31, 2012.

E3–13 The following is a list of accounts for Speedy Delivery Service, Inc. at July 31, 2012:

Prepare trial balance and financial statements. (SO 4)

Accounts payable	$ 9,500	Interest expense	$ 3,600
Accounts receivable	12,500	Bank loan payable, due 2015	39,000
Accumulated depreciation	21,400	Prepaid insurance	200
Cash	8,000	Rent expense	9,000
Common shares	38,000	Repairs and maintenance expense	5,700
Equipment	99,000	Retained earnings, Aug. 1, 2011	20,850
Depreciation expense	9,700	Salaries expense	25,000
Dividends	800	Salaries payable	800
Gas and oil expense	4,750	Service revenue	75,000
Income tax expense	4,500	Short-term investments	20,000
Insurance expense	1,800		

Additional information:

During the year, the company issued common shares for $11,000.

Instructions

(a) Prepare a trial balance.

(b) Prepare an income statement for the year ending July 31, 2012, along with a statement of changes in equity, and statement of financial position.

(c) If you did not know the retained earnings amount in the trial balance, could you have prepared the financial statements in (b)?

Analyze errors and their effects on trial balance.
(SO 4)

E3–14   The bookkeeper for Castle's Equipment Repair Corporation made these errors in journalizing and posting:

1. A credit posting of $400 to Accounts Receivable was omitted.
2. A debit posting of $750 for Prepaid Insurance was debited to Insurance Expense.
3. A collection on account of $100 was journalized and posted as a $100 debit to Cash and a $100 credit to Service Revenue.
4. A credit posting of $500 to Accounts Payable was made twice.
5. A cash purchase of supplies for $250 was journalized and posted as a $250 debit to Supplies and a $25 credit to Cash.
6. A debit of $465 to Advertising Expense was posted as $456.

Instructions

For each error, indicate

(a) whether the trial balance will balance,

(b) the amount of the difference if the trial balance will not balance, and

(c) the trial balance column that will have the larger total.

Consider each error separately. Use the following format, in which error 1 is given as an example:

	(a)	(b)	(c)
Error	In Balance	Difference	Larger Column
1.	No	$400	Debit

Problems: Set A

Analyze transactions and calculate equity balances.
(SO 1)

P3–1A   On April 1, Adventures Travel Agency, Inc. commenced operations. These transactions were completed during the month:

1. Issued common shares for $24,000 cash.
2. Obtained a bank loan for $7,000.
3. Paid $11,000 cash to buy equipment.
4. Paid $1,200 cash for April office rent.
5. Paid $1,450 for supplies.
6. Purchased $600 of advertising in the *Calgary Herald*, on account.
7. Earned $18,000 for services performed: cash of $2,000 was received from customers, and the balance of $16,000 was billed to customers on account.
8. Paid $400 dividends to shareholders.
9. Paid the utility bill for the month, $2,000.
10. Paid *Calgary Herald* the amount due in transaction 6.
11. Paid $40 of interest on the bank loan obtained in transaction 2.
12. Paid employees' salaries, $6,400.
13. Received $12,000 cash from customers billed in transaction 7.
14. Paid income tax, $3,000.

Instructions

(a) Prepare a tabular analysis of the effects of the above transactions on the accounting equation.

(b) From an analysis of the retained earnings accounts (revenues, expenses, and dividends), calculate the ending balance in Common Shares, Retained Earnings, and total Shareholders' Equity.

Analyze transactions and prepare financial statements.
(SO 1)

P3–2A   Para-Legal Services Inc. specializes in providing legal services. On July 31, 2012, the company's general ledger showed the following balances: Cash $4,000; Accounts Receivable $1,500; Supplies $500; Equipment $5,000; Accounts Payable $4,100; Common Shares $5,500; and Retained Earnings $1,400. During August, the following transactions occurred:

Aug. 3   Collected $1,200 of accounts receivable due from customers.

      5   Received $2,300 cash for issuing common shares to new investors.

      6   Paid $2,700 cash on accounts payable owing.

      7   Earned fees of $6,500, of which $3,000 is collected in cash and the remainder is due on account.

    12   Purchased additional equipment for $1,200, paying $400 in cash and the balance on account.

    14   Paid salaries, $3,500, rent, $900, and advertising expenses, $275, for the month of August.

    18   Collected the balance of the fees earned on August 7.

    20   Paid dividends of $500 to shareholders.

    24   Billed a client $1,000 for legal services provided.

    26   Received $2,000 from Laurentian Bank; the money was borrowed on a bank loan payable that is due in six months.

    27   Signed an engagement letter to provide legal services to a client in September for $4,500. The client will pay the amount owing after the work has been completed.

    28   Received the utility bill for the month of August in the amount of $275; it is not due until September 15.

    31   Paid income tax for the month, $800.

Instructions

(a) Beginning with the July 31 balances, prepare a tabular analysis of the effects of the August transactions on the accounting equation.

(b) Prepare an income statement, a statement of changes in equity, and a statement of financial position for the month.

P3–3A   You are presented with the following alphabetical list of selected items, from the financial statements of Danier Leather Inc.:

Identify normal balance and statement classification.
(SO 2)

Account	(a) Normal Balance	(b) Financial Statement	(c) Classification
Accounts payable and accrued liabilities	Credit	Statement of financial position	Current liabilities
Accounts receivable			
Accumulated depreciation			
Building			
Cash			
Common shares, beginning of year			
Computer hardware			
Cost of sales			
Depreciation expense			
Furniture and equipment			
Income tax expense			
Income taxes payable			
Interest expense			
Inventories			
Land			
Prepaid expenses			
Retained earnings, beginning of year			
Sales revenue			
Shares issued			

Instructions

For each account, indicate

(a) whether the normal balance is a debit or a credit,

(b) the financial statement where the account should be reported (e.g., statement of financial position, statement of changes in equity, or income statement), and

(c) the appropriate classification (e.g., current assets, non-current liabilities, revenues).

The first one has been done for you as an example.

P3–4A   You are presented with the following transactions for Paddick Enterprises Ltd. for the month of February:

Identify debit and credit effects and record transactions.
(SO 2, 3)

Feb. 2   Purchased supplies on account, $600.

      3   Purchased equipment for $10,000 by signing a note due in three months.

      6   Earned service revenue of $50,000. Of this amount, $30,000 was received in cash. The balance was on account.

13   Paid $1,000 in dividends to shareholders.
18   A customer paid $2,000 in advance for services to be rendered in the future.
20   Paid the amount owing for the supplies purchased on February 2.
23   Collected $20,000 of the amount owing from the February 6 transaction.
24   Paid operating expenses for the month, $22,000.
25   The services for the customer who paid in advance on February 18 were performed.
27   Recorded salaries due to employees for work performed during the month, $14,000.
28   Paid interest of $100 on the note issued on February 3.

Instructions

For each transaction, indicate
(a) the basic type of account debited and credited (asset, liability, shareholders' equity);
(b) the specific account debited and credited (Cash, Service Revenue, etc.); and
(c) whether the specific account is increased or decreased.

Use the following format, in which the first transaction is given as an example:

	Account Debited			Account Credited		
	(a)	(b)	(c)	(a)	(b)	(c)
Trans-	Basic	Specific		Basic	Specific	
action	Type	Account	Effect	Type	Account	Effect
Feb. 2	Asset	Supplies	Increase	Liability	Accounts Payable	Increase

(d) Prepare journal entries to record the above transactions.

Record transactions.
(SO 3)

P3–5A   The Funtimes Miniature Golf and Driving Range, Inc. opened on May 1. These selected events and transactions occurred during May:

May   1   Issued common shares for $120,000 cash.
      4   Purchased Henry's Golf Land for $270,000. The price consists of land $125,000; building $100,000; and equipment $45,000. Paid cash of $100,000 and signed a mortgage payable for the balance.
      4   Paid $1,500 for a one-year insurance policy; coverage commences next month.
      5   Advertised the opening of the driving range and miniature golf course, paying advertising expenses of $2,000.
      6   Purchased golf clubs and other equipment for $9,000 from Titleist Corporation.
     18   Received $8,800 from customers for golf fees earned.
     20   Paid dividends of $800 to shareholders.
     21   Paid Titleist Corporation in full for equipment purchased on May 6.
     22   Received $1,200 from a school board that paid for students' golf lessons that will be given in June.
     29   Paid $800 of interest on the mortgage payable.
     29   Paid salaries of $3,400.

Instructions

Journalize the May transactions.

Record and post transactions.
(SO 3)

P3–6A   During the first month of operations, these events and transactions occurred for Virmani Architects Inc.:

Apr.   1   Cash of $15,000 and equipment of $6,000 was invested in the company in exchange for common shares.
       1   A secretary-receptionist was hired at a monthly salary of $1,900.
       2   Paid office rent for the month, $950.
       3   Purchased architectural supplies on account from Halo Ltd., $1,750.
      10   Completed blueprints on a carport and billed client $900.
      13   Received $800 cash advance from a client for the design of a new home.
      20   Received $1,500 for services performed for a client.
      21   Received $500 from client for work completed and billed on April 10.
      23   Received April's telephone bill for $135; due May 15.
      30   Paid secretary-receptionist for the month, $1,900.
      30   Paid $1,750 to Halo Ltd. on account (see April 3 transaction).
      30   Paid $500 dividend.

Instructions

(a) Journalize the transactions.

(b) Using T accounts, post the April journal entries to the general ledger.

P3–7A The Star Theatre, Inc. is unique as it shows only triple features of sequential theme movies. As at February 29, 2012, the Star's general ledger showed Cash $15,000; Land $85,000; Buildings (concession stand, projection room, ticket booth, and screen) $77,000; Equipment $20,000; Accounts Payable $12,000; Mortgage Payable $118,000; Common Shares $40,000; and Retained Earnings $27,000. During the month of March, the following events and transactions occurred:

Record transactions, post, and prepare trial balance.
(SO 3, 4)

Mar.	2	Received three Harry Potter movies to be shown during the first three weeks of March. The film rental was $27,000. Of that amount, $10,000 was paid in cash and the remainder will be paid on March 10.
	2	Hired M. Brewer to operate concession stand. Brewer agrees to pay Star Theatre 15% of gross receipts, payable on the last day of each month, for the right to operate the concession stand.
	5	Ordered three Shrek movies, to be shown the last 10 days of March. The film rental cost is $300 per night.
	9	Received $16,300 from customers for admissions.
	12	Paid balance due on the Harry Potter movie rentals.
	13	Paid the accounts payable owing at the end of February.
	19	Paid advertising expenses, $950.
	20	Received $16,600 from customers for admissions.
	23	Received the Shrek movies and paid rental fee of $3,000 ($300 × 10 nights).
	25	Received $18,400 from customers for admissions.
	27	Paid salaries of $4,200.
	30	Received statement from M. Brewer, showing gross concession receipts of $8,600, and the balance due to Star Theatre of $1,290 for March. Brewer paid half of the balance due and will remit the remainder on April 5.
	30	Paid $1,250 of mortgage principal and $750 of interest on the mortgage.

Instructions

(a) Using T accounts, enter the beginning balances in the ledger as at February 29.

(b) Journalize the March transactions.

(c) Post the March journal entries to the ledger.

(d) Prepare a trial balance at March 31, 2012.

P3–8A Pamper Me Salon Inc.'s general ledger at April 30, 2012, included the following: Cash $7,000; Supplies $500; Equipment $24,000; Accounts Payable $2,100; Bank Loan Payable $10,000; Gift Certificates Outstanding $3,000 (this is similar to Unearned Revenue); Common Shares $5,000; and Retained Earnings $11,400. The following events and transactions occurred during May:

Record transactions, post, and prepare trial balance.
(SO 3, 4)

May	1	Paid rent for the month of May, $1,000.
	4	Paid $1,100 of the account payable at April 30.
	7	Issued gift certificates for $2,500 cash.
	8	Received $1,200 cash from customers for services performed.
	14	Paid $1,200 in salaries to employees.
	15	Received $800 in cash from customers for services performed.
	15	Customers receiving services worth $700 used gift certificates in payment.
	21	Paid the remaining accounts payable from April 30.
	22	Received $1,000 in cash from customers for services performed.
	22	Purchased supplies of $700 on account. All of these were used during the month.
	25	Received a bill for advertising for $500. This bill is due on June 13.
	25	Received and paid a utilities bill for $400.
	29	Received $700 in cash from customers for services performed.
	29	Customers receiving services worth $600 used gift certificates in payment.
	31	Interest of $50 was paid on the bank loan.
	31	Paid $1,200 in salaries to employees.

Instructions

(a) Using T accounts, enter the beginning balances in the general ledger as at April 30.

(b) Journalize the May transactions.

(c) Post the May journal entries to the general ledger.

(d) Prepare a trial balance as at May 31.

Prepare trial balance
and financial
statements.
(SO 4)

P3–9A   You are presented with the following alphabetical list of accounts and balances (in thousands) for Taggar Enterprises Inc. at June 30, 2012:

Accounts payable	$ 1,500	Income tax payable	$ 500
Accounts receivable	3,000	Interest expense	1,000
Accumulated depreciation—building	4,000	Inventories	5,100
Accumulated depreciation—equipment	1,000	Land	5,000
Building	15,000	Long-term investment	4,950
Cash	1,800	Mortgage payable, due 2014	13,750
Common shares	5,000	Operating expenses	3,300
Cost of goods sold	13,700	Prepaid insurance	900
Current portion of mortgage payable	1,250	Retained earnings, July 1, 2011	6,250
Equipment	3,000	Sales revenue	25,000
Income tax expense	1,500		

Additional information:
During the year, common shares in the amount of $2,000 were issued.

Instructions
(a) Prepare a trial balance, sorting each account balance into the debit column or the credit column.
(b) Prepare an income statement and statement of changes in equity for the year just ended, and a statement of financial position as at August 31, 2012.

Analyze errors and
effect on trial balance.
(SO 4)

P3–10A   The bookkeeper for Cater's Dance Studio Ltd. did the following in journalizing and posting:

1. A debit posting to the Interest Revenue account of $600 was omitted.
2. A credit of $500 for revenue received in advance was posted as a credit to the Unearned Service Revenue account.
3. A purchase of supplies on account of $540 was debited to Merchandise Inventory for $540 and credited to Accounts Payable for $540.
4. A credit to the Wages Payable account for $1,200 was posted as a credit to the Cash account.
5. A debit posting of $250 to the Cash account was posted twice.
6. The debit side of the entry to record the payment of $600 for dividends was posted to the Salaries Expense account.
7. The collection of an account receivable of $250 was posted as a debit to the Cash account and a credit to the Accounts Payable account.
8. The provision of services on account was debited to Accounts Receivable and credited to Service Revenue.
9. A purchase of equipment on account for $4,600 was posted as a $6,400 debit to Equipment and a $6,400 credit to Cash.
10. Rent of $1,000 for the month was paid but was neither recorded nor posted.

Instructions
(a) Indicate which of the above transactions are correct, and which are incorrect.
(b) For each error identified in (a), answer the following questions:
    1. Will the trial balance be in balance?
    2. Which account(s) will be incorrectly stated because of the error?
    3. State whether each of the incorrect account(s) you identified in (2) will be overstated or understated, and by how much.

Prepare corrected trial
balance.
(SO 4)

P3–11A   This trial balance of Cantpost Ltd. does not balance:

CANTPOST LTD.
Trial Balance
June 30, 2012

	Debit	Credit
Cash		$ 5,170
Accounts receivable	$ 3,230	
Supplies	860	
Equipment	3,000	
Accumulated depreciation	600	
Accounts payable		2,665
Unearned revenue	1,200	
Common shares		8,000
Dividends	800	
Service revenue		6,440
Salaries expense	3,400	
Office expense	910	
Income tax expense	440	
	$14,440	$22,275

Each of the listed accounts has a normal balance per the general ledger. An examination of the general ledger and general journal reveals the following errors:

1. Cash received from a customer on account was debited for $570, and Accounts Receivable was credited for the same amount. The actual collection was for $750.
2. The purchase of equipment on account for $360 was recorded as a debit to Supplies for $360 and a credit to Accounts Payable for $360.
3. Services were performed on account for a client for $890. Accounts Receivable was debited for $890 and Service Revenue was credited for $89.
4. A debit posting to Depreciation Expense of $600 was omitted.
5. A payment made by a customer on account for $206 was debited to Cash for $206 and credited to Accounts Receivable for $602.
6. A transposition (reversal of digits) error was made when copying the balance in the Salaries Expense account. The correct balance should be $4,300.
7. A payment for rent in the amount of $1,000 was neither recorded nor posted.

Instructions
Prepare the correct trial balance.

Problems: Set B

P3–1B Marty's Repair Shop, Inc. opened on May 1. A summary of the May transactions follows:

1. Issued common shares for $28,000 cash.
2. Paid $1,280 for May office rent.
3. Purchased equipment for $16,000, paying $4,000 cash and signing a note payable for the balance.
4. Purchased supplies on account, $700.
5. Received $4,200 from customers for repair services provided.
6. Paid for supplies purchased in transaction 4.
7. Paid May telephone bill of $200.
8. Provided repair services on account to customers, $3,600.
9. Paid employee salaries, $2,000.
10. Received $700 in advance for repair services to be provided next month.
11. Collected $1,600 from customers for services billed in transaction 8.
12. Paid $1,000 dividends to shareholders.
13. Paid income tax of $600.

Analyze transactions and calculate equity balances.
(SO 1)

Instructions
(a) Prepare a tabular analysis of the effects of the above transactions on the expanded accounting equation.
(b) From an analysis of the retained earnings accounts (revenues, expenses, and dividends), calculate the ending balance in Common Shares, Retained Earnings, and total Shareholders' Equity.

P3–2B The general ledger of Corso Care Corp., a veterinary company, showed the following balances on August 31, 2012: Cash $4,500; Accounts Receivable $1,800; Supplies $350; Equipment $6,500; Accounts Payable $3,200; Common Shares $2,500; and Retained Earnings $7,450. During September, the following transactions occurred:

Analyze transactions and prepare financial statements.
(SO 1)

Sept.	1	Paid the accounts payable owing at August 31.
	1	Paid $1,200 rent for September.
	3	Collected $1,450 of accounts receivable due from customers.
	4	Hired a part-time office assistant at $50 per day to start work the following week, on Monday, September 7.
	5	Received $2,300 cash for issuing common shares to new investors.
	8	Purchased additional equipment for $2,050, paying $700 in cash and the balance on account.
	14	Billed $500 for veterinary services provided.
	15	Paid $300 for advertising expenses.
	18	Collected cash for services performed on account on September 14.
	25	Received $7,500 from Canadian Western Bank; the money was borrowed on a loan payable due in nine months.
	25	Sent a statement reminding a customer that money was still owed from August.
	28	Earned revenue of $4,500, of which $3,000 was received in cash. The balance is due in October.
	29	Paid part-time office assistant $750 for working 15 days in September.

30 Incurred utility expenses for the month on account, $175.
30 Paid dividends of $1,000 to shareholders.
30 Paid income tax for the month, $550.

Instructions

(a) Beginning with the August 31 balances, prepare a tabular analysis of the effects of the September transactions on the accounting equation.

(b) Prepare an income statement, a statement of changes in equity, and a statement of financial position for the month.

Identify normal balance and statement classification.
(SO 2)

P3–3B You are presented with the following alphabetical list of items selected from the financial statements of Reitmans (Canada) Limited:

Account	(a) Normal Balance	(b) Financial Statement	(c) Classification
Accounts payable and accrued items	Credit	Statement of financial position	Current liabilities
Accounts receivable			
Depreciation expense			
Buildings and improvements			
Cash and cash equivalents			
Common shares issued during the year			
Cost of goods sold and selling, general, and administrative expenses			
Dividends			
Fixtures and equipment			
Goodwill			
Income tax expense			
Income tax payable			
Interest expense			
Investment income			
Land			
Marketable securities			
Merchandise inventories			
Prepaid expenses			
Retained earnings, beginning of year			
Sales			

Instructions

For each account, indicate

(a) whether the normal balance is a debit or a credit;

(b) the financial statement where the account should be reported (e.g., statement of financial position, income statement, or statement of changes in equity); and

(c) the appropriate classification (e.g., current assets, non-current liabilities, revenues).

The first one has been done for you as an example.

Identify debit and credit effects and record transactions.
(SO 2, 3)

P3–4B You are presented with the following transactions for Kailynn Corporation for the month of January:

Jan. 2 Issued $10,000 of common shares for cash.
      5 Provided services on account, $2,500.
      6 Obtained a bank loan for $30,000.
      7 Paid $40,000 to purchase a hybrid car.
      9 Received a $5,000 deposit from a customer for services to be provided in the future.
     12 Billed customers $20,000 for services performed during the month.
     19 Paid $500 to purchase supplies.
     20 Provided services for customers who paid in advance on January 9.
     23 Collected $5,000 owing from customers from the January 12 transaction.
     26 Received a bill for utilities of $125, due February 26.
     29 Paid rent for the month, $1,500.
     31 Paid $4,000 of salaries to employees.
     31 Paid interest of $300 on the bank loan.
     31 Paid income tax for the month, $4,000.

Instructions

For each transaction, indicate

(a) the basic type of account debited and credited (asset, liability, shareholders' equity);

(b) the specific account debited and credited (Cash, Service Revenue, etc.); and

(c) whether the specific account is increased or decreased.

Use the following format, in which the first transaction is given as an example:

	Account Debited			Account Credited		
	(1)	(2)	(3)	(1)	(2)	(3)
Trans-action	Basic Type	Specific Account	Effect	Basic Type	Specific Account	Effect
Jan. 2	Asset	Cash	Increase	Shareholders' equity	Common Shares	Increase

(d) Prepare journal entries to record the above transactions.

P3–5B The Adventure Biking Park Corp. was formed on April 1. These selected events and transactions occurred during April:

Record transactions.
(SO 3)

Apr. 1 Issued common shares for $100,000 cash.

3 Purchased an out-of-use ski hill costing $370,000, paying $60,000 cash and signing a note payable for the balance. The $370,000 purchase price consisted of land $204,000; building $121,000; and equipment $45,000.

8 Purchased advertising space of $3,800 on account.

10 Paid salaries to employees, $2,800.

13 Hired a park manager at a salary of $4,000 per month, effective May 1.

14 Paid $5,500 for a one-year insurance policy.

17 Paid $600 of dividends to shareholders.

20 Received $8,600 in cash from customers for admission fees.

30 Paid $2,800 on account for the advertising purchased on April 8.

30 Paid $1,250 of interest on the note payable.

Instructions

Journalize the April transactions.

P3–6B During the first month of operations, these events and transactions occurred for Astromech Accounting Services Inc.:

Record and post transactions.
(SO 3)

May 1 Common shares were issued for $20,000 cash and a $10,000 note receivable.

1 Paid office rent of $950 for the month.

4 A secretary-receptionist was hired at a salary of $2,000 per month. She started work the same day.

4 Purchased $750 of supplies on account from Read Supply Corp.

11 Completed an income tax assignment and billed client $2,725 for services provided.

12 Received $3,500 in advance on a management consulting engagement.

15 Received $1,350 for services completed for Arnold Corp.

20 Received $1,725 from client for work completed and billed on May 11.

22 Paid one third of balance due to Read Supply Corp.

25 Received a $275 telephone bill for May, to be paid next month.

29 Paid secretary-receptionist $2,000 salary for the month.

29 Paid monthly income tax instalment, $300.

29 Paid $250 dividend.

30 Earned interest revenue on the note received on May 1 of $75 to be received later.

Instructions

(a) Journalize the transactions.

(b) Using T accounts, post the May journal entries to the general ledger.

P3–7B On March 31, 2012, the Lake Theatre, Inc.'s general ledger showed Cash $6,000; Land $100,000; Buildings (concession stand, projection room, ticket booth, and screen) $80,000; Equipment $25,000; Accounts Payable $5,000; Mortgage Payable $125,000; Common Shares $50,000; and Retained Earnings $31,000. During the month of April, the following events and transactions occurred:

Record transactions, post, and prepare trial balance.
(SO 3, 4)

Apr.	2	Paid film rental fee of $800 on first movie.
	3	Paid advertising expenses, $620.
	3	Hired Thoms Limited to operate concession stand. Thoms agrees to pay the Lake Theatre 20% of gross concession receipts, payable monthly, for the right to operate the concession stand.
	6	Ordered two additional films at $750 each.
	11	Received $1,950 from customers for admissions.
	16	Paid $2,000 on mortgage principal. Also paid $500 in interest on the mortgage.
	17	Paid $2,800 of the accounts payable.
	20	Received one of the films ordered on April 6 and was billed $750. The film will be shown in April.
	25	Received $5,300 from customers for admissions.
	26	Paid salaries, $1,900.
	27	Prepaid $700 rental fee on special film to be run in May.
	30	Received statement from Thoms showing gross concession receipts of $2,600 and the balance due to the Lake Theatre of $520 ($2,600 × 20%) for April. Thoms paid half of the balance due and will remit the remainder on May 5.

Instructions

(a) Using T accounts, enter the beginning balances in the ledger as at March 31.
(b) Journalize the April transactions.
(c) Post the April journal entries to the ledger.
(d) Prepare a trial balance at April 30, 2012.

Record transactions, post, and prepare trial balance.
(SO 3, 4)

P3–8B   KG Spring Skating School Inc. had the following account balances as at April 30, 2012: Cash $23,000; Equipment $2,000; Accounts Payable $500; Advance Registration Fees (similar to Unearned Revenue) $17,500; Common Shares $1,000; and Retained Earnings $6,000. The following events and transactions occurred during May:

May	4	Additional registrations for the May four-week skating session were received, $5,500 cash.
	4	Paid for ice time for first two weeks of the May school, $7,200.
	9	Paid accounts payable outstanding at April 30.
	11	Booked ice with the city for the July session. It will cost $14,400.
	11	Received and paid a bill for $500 for advertising of the May skating school.
	15	Paid coaches and assistant coaches, $600.
	18	Paid for ice time for second two weeks of the May school, $7,200.
	21	Received a bill for Internet service for $100. This invoice is due on June 15.
	29	Last day of May session. All of the advance registration fees have now been earned.
	29	Paid $200 cash for supplies used immediately.
	29	Received advance registrations for the next four-week skating session in July, $2,200.
	29	Purchased gifts for volunteers who helped out during May session, $300.
	29	Paid coaches and assistant coaches, $600.

Instructions

(a) Using T accounts, enter the beginning balances in the general ledger as at April 30.
(b) Journalize the May transactions.
(c) Post the May journal entries to the general ledger.
(d) Prepare a trial balance as at May 31.

Prepare trial balance and financial statements.
(SO 4)

P3–9B   East Asian Importers Limited has the following alphabetical list of accounts and balances (in thousands) as at January 31, 2012:

Account	Amount	Account	Amount
Accounts payable	$ 46,300	Land	$ 12,500
Accounts receivable	30,200	Mortgage payable	19,150
Building	39,500	Mortgage payable due within one year	6,300
Cash	400	Merchandise inventories	74,250
Common shares	32,900	Notes payable (due 2015)	10,050
Cost of goods sold	244,200	Operating expenses	67,750
Dividends	1,850	Other assets	26,250
Equipment	10,900	Other short-term liabilities	12,200
Goodwill	7,600	Prepaid expenses	3,950
Income tax expense	12,450	Retained earnings, February 1, 2011	37,050
Interest expense	2,150	Sales	370,000

Additional information:
During the year, common shares were issued for $12,900.

Instructions

(a) Prepare a trial balance, sorting each account balance into the debit column or the credit column.

(b) Prepare an income statement and statement of changes in equity for the year just ended and the statement of financial position as at January 31, 2012.

P3–10B A first-year co-op student working for Insidz Corp. recorded the company's transactions for the month. He was a little unsure about the recording process, but he did the best he could. He had a few questions, however, about the following transactions:

Analyze errors and effect on trial balance.
(SO 4)

1. Insidz received $255 cash from a customer on account. It was recorded as a debit to Cash of $255 and a credit to Accounts Receivable of $552.
2. A service provided for cash was posted as a debit to Cash of $2,000 and a credit to Accounts Receivable of $2,000.
3. A credit of $750 for interest earned was neither recorded nor posted. The debit was recorded and posted correctly.
4. The debit to record $1,000 of dividends paid to shareholders was posted to the Salary Expense account. The credit was posted correctly.
5. Services of $325 were provided to a customer on account. The company debited Accounts Receivable for $325 and credited Service Revenue for $325.
6. A purchase of supplies for $500 on account was recorded as a debit to Supplies and a debit to Accounts Payable.
7. Insidz received advances of $500 from customers for work to be done next month. The student debited Cash for $500 but did not credit anything, as he was not sure what to credit.
8. A cash payment of $495 for salaries was recorded as a debit to Salaries Expense and a credit to Salaries Payable.
9. Insidz purchased $1,500 of equipment on account. This transaction was recorded as a $5,100 debit to Equipment and a $5,100 credit to Accounts Payable.
10. A cash payment of $850 for rent for the month was not recorded.

Instructions
(a) Indicate which of the above transactions are correct, and which are incorrect.
(b) For each error identified in (a), answer the following questions:
   1. Will the trial balance be in balance?
   2. Which account(s) will be incorrectly stated because of the error?
   3. State whether each of the incorrect account(s) you identified in (2) will be overstated or understated and by how much.

P3–11B This trial balance of Messed Up Ltd. does not balance:

Prepare corrected trial balance.
(SO 4)

MESSED UP LTD.
Trial Balance
May 31, 2012

	Debit	Credit
Cash	$ 7,376	
Accounts receivable		$ 2,630
Equipment	9,200	
Accumulated depreciation		4,200
Accounts payable		4,600
Common shares		4,250
Retained earnings		4,429
Service revenue	14,529	
Salaries expense	8,150	
Advertising expense		1,132
Depreciation expense	2,100	
Income tax expense	200	
Insurance expense	600	
	$42,155	$21,241

Your review of the ledger reveals that each account has a normal balance. You also discover the following errors:

1. Prepaid Insurance, Accounts Payable, and Income Tax Expense were each understated by $100.
2. A transposition (reversal of digits) error was made in Service Revenue. Based on the posting made, the correct balance was $14,259.
3. A debit posting to Salaries Expense of $250 was omitted.
4. A $750 dividend paid to shareholders was debited to Salaries Expense and credited to Cash.
5. A $630 purchase of supplies on account was debited to Equipment and credited to Cash.
6. A payment of $320 for advertising was debited to Advertising Expense for $32 and credit to Cash for $32.
7. A $120 collection on account was recorded as a debit to Accounts Payable and a credit to Accounts Receivable.
8. A $2,000 note payable was issued in exchange for the purchase of equipment. The transaction was neither journalized nor posted.

Instructions
Prepare the correct trial balance.

Broadening Your Perspective

Financial Reporting and Analysis Cases

Financial Reporting: *Eastplats*

Analyze the effects of transactions.
(SO 1)

BYP3–1 The financial statements of Eastern Platinum Limited (Eastplats) are presented in Appendix A at the end of this book. They contain the following selected accounts:

Trade and other receivables	Accounts payable and accrued liabilities
Inventories	Production costs
Short-term investments	Interest income
Property, plant and equipment	Depletion and depreciation

Instructions

(a) What is the increase and decrease side for each account? What is the normal balance for each account?

(b) Identify the probable other account(s) in each transaction listed below and the effect on that (those) other account(s) when:

1. Trade and other receivables are decreased.	5. Production costs are increased.
2. Inventories are increased.	6. General and administrative expense is increased.
3. Property, plant and equipment are increased.	7. Interest income is increased.
4. Accounts payable are decreased.	8. Short-term investments are increased.

Comparative Analysis: *Eastplats and Amplats*

Prepare trial balance.
(SO 4)

BYP3–2 The financial statements of Anglo American Platinum Limited (Amplats) are presented in Appendix B following the financial statements for Eastern Platinum Limited (Eastplats) in Appendix A.

Instructions

(a) Using Eastplats's statement of financial position, put the accounts and amounts provided into a trial balance format as at December 31, 2010.

(b) Using Amplats's statement of financial position, put the accounts and amounts provided into a trial balance format as at December 31, 2010.

Interpreting Financial Information

Compare presentation formats.
(SO 4)

BYP3–3 Eastern Platinum Limited, headquartered in Vancouver, and Anglo Platinum Limited (now known as Anglo American Platinum), headquartered in Johannesburg, compete internationally. The assets section for each company's statement of financial position follows:

EASTERN PLATINUM LIMITED
Statement of Financial Position (partial)
December 31, 2010
(in U.S. thousands)

Current assets:	
Cash and cash equivalents	$ 107,846
Short-term investments	242,446
Trade and other receivables	33,787
Inventories	8,832
	392,911
Non-current assets:	
Property, plant and equipment	715,976
Other assets	18,088
	734,064
Total assets	$1,126,975

ANGLO PLATINUM LIMITED
Statement of Financial Position (partial)
December 31, 2010
(in R millions)

Non-current assets:	
Property, plant and equipment	37,438
Investments	7,908
Other non-current assets	20,062
	65,408
Current assets:	
Inventories	12,558
Trade and other receivables	2,988
Other assets	313
Cash and cash equivalents	2,534
	18,393
Total assets	83,801

Instructions

(a) Which company presents its assets in the order of liquidity that most North American companies use?

(b) These companies do not present assets in the statement of financial position in the same order. Do you think that this difference would affect your interpretation of each company's liquidity relative to the other? Explain.

Comparing IFRS and ASPE

BYP3–4 Homburg Investment Inc is a real-estate development and property management company. Homburg is a publicly accountable enterprise that trades on both the Toronto Stock Exchange and the New York Stock Exchange. It holds a variety of properties in Canada, United States, and Europe. Some of its properties include residential condominiums, office buildings, industrial buildings, and shopping centres.

Understand the accounting information system. (SO 3)

First Pro Shopping Centres, which operates under the banner "Smartcentres", is also a real-estate development and property management company. First Pro is a privately held company and holds properties in all regions of Canada with a concentration in the Ontario region. It is the leader in the widespread expansion of outdoor shopping malls in Canada.

Instructions

(a) One of the companies mentioned above prepares its financial statements using International Financial Reporting Standards (IFRS) while the other uses Accounting Standards for Private Enterprises (ASPE). Which company reports under IFRS? Why?

(b) Are the users of the financials statements of each company listed above different? Do you think this influences the type of accounting standards that each company uses?

(c) In light of your answer to (b) above, which company is more likely to have a sophisticated reporting system?

(d) Could either of the companies mentioned above maintain accounting records without using a journal or a ledger? Would this be efficient?

Critical Thinking Cases and Activities

Collaborative Learning Activity

BYP3–5 A partial list of transactions for Cedar Valley Enterprises Ltd. follows:

Analyze transactions. (SO 1, 3)

	Cash	Accounts Receivable	Prepaid Advertising	Building	Office Equipment	Accounts Payable	Mortgage Payable	Common Shares	Revenue	Expenses
1.	$200,000							$200,000		
2.	−75,000			$450,000			$375,000			
3.					$15,000	$15,000				
4.		$7,500							$7,500	
5.	−2,400		$2,400							
6.			−200							$ −200
7.	−4,200						−400			−3,800
	$118,400 +	$7,500 +	$2,200 +	$450,000 +	$15,000 =	$15,000 +	$374,600 +	$200,000 +	$7,500 −	$ 4,000

$593,100

$593,100

Instructions

With the class divided into groups, do the following:

(a) Answer this question: In what ways can a spreadsheet like the one shown above serve as a journal and a ledger?

(b) Create an appropriate description for each of the above transactions.

(c) Share your answers in (b) with another group of students. If you cannot all agree on the results, share again with a second group of students.

Communication Activity

Identify accounts and steps in accounting cycle.
(SO 3)

BYP3–6 A friend of your family, Nancy Chen, has just graduated from dental school and is opening up her new practice. To do this, she has formed a corporation called Chen Dental Services Ltd. Revenues from the practice will be earned by providing dental services to individuals. Expenses will pertain to dental supplies, insurance, rent, utilities, and salaries. This is the first time that Nancy has operated a business and she needs your guidance on how to set up an accounting information system.

Instructions

Write a memo to Nancy in which you explain and illustrate the steps in the accounting cycle for this type of company. Be sure to also mention the accounts that should be set up for the company.

Ethics Case

Discuss ethical issues related to trial balance errors.
(SO 4)

BYP3–7 Ron Hollister is a member of a group of students who have been given an accounting assignment by their professor. Ron is responsible for the portion of the assignment that requires the preparation of the trial balance and the financial statements. The assignment is due within an hour and Ron is working alone. All he has to do is complete his part of the assignment and hand the entire document in for grading. He has just prepared the trial balance and found out that it does not balance. The total credits are greater than the total debits by $810.

Without telling the other members of the group, Ron forces the trial balance to balance by adding $810 to the general and administrative expense because it was the largest expense and he hoped no one would notice the difference. He wished that he had a few more hours to find out why the trial balance did not balance, but he knows he can't miss the deadline for handing in the assignment.

Instructions

(a) Who are the stakeholders in this situation?

(b) What ethical issues are involved?

(c) What are Ron's alternatives?

(d) Would your answer change if Ron was a professional accountant and was preparing financial statements for a public company?

"All About You" Activity

Discuss personal accounting system.
(SO 1, 3)

BYP3–8 In this chapter, you learned the features of accounting information systems that companies use to keep track of their important financial information. Let's now apply these same concepts to your personal financial information.

Instructions

(a) Why is it important that you develop a system to maintain and keep your personal records up to date?

(b) How would you organize such a system for yourself?

(c) What would you do if you lost your wallet with your credit cards and identification inside? (*Hint:* As a starting point, there is some very useful information on the Service Canada homepage under the "Life Events" section at www.servicecanada.gc.ca.)

Serial Case

(*Note:* This is a continuation of the serial case from Chapters 1 and 2.)

Record and post transactions; prepare trial balance.
(SO 3, 4)

BYP3–9 On June 1, 2011, Natalie becomes both a shareholder and chief administrator of operations of Koebel's Family Bakery Ltd. After much discussion with her parents, Janet and Brian, Natalie decides not to accept the Biscuits retail chain's offer to supply oatmeal chocolate chip cookies. At this point, Natalie believes that it is best to focus on providing Coffee Beans, the national coffee shop, with all of its cupcake requirements. After becoming comfortable with Coffee Beans' contractual commitment and determining the extent of oven space available, Natalie and Koebel's Family Bakery can then reconsider the Biscuits offer.

Natalie obtains a copy of Koebel's Family Bakery Ltd.'s trial balance at June 30 to become familiar with the organization's accounting records.

KOEBEL'S FAMILY BAKERY LTD.
Trial Balance
June 30, 2011

	Debit	Credit
Cash	$ 39,004	
Accounts receivable	5,900	
Merchandise inventory	16,250	
Supplies	1,875	
Prepaid insurance	12,000	
Land	100,000	
Building	165,000	
Accumulated depreciation—building		$103,125
Equipment	43,000	
Accumulated depreciation—equipment		17,200
Vehicles	55,000	
Accounts payable		3,540
Unearned revenue		100
Bank loan payable		22,500
Mortgage payable		53,200
Common shares		300
Retained earnings		66,788
Dividends	30,000	
Rent revenue		6,000
Sales		673,443
Sales returns and allowances	5,000	
Cost of goods sold	102,386	
Salaries expense	287,532	
Freight out	18,000	
Utilities expense	12,000	
Advertising expense	9,000	
Property tax expense	5,950	
Interest expense	5,299	
Income tax expense	33,000	
Total	$946,196	$946,196

While a number of transactions have already been recorded and posted for the month of June, there are other transactions listed below that have not yet been recorded in the accounting records:

June 1 Natalie cashes in a Canada Savings Bond and receives $520, which she deposits into her personal bank account.

6 A one-year insurance policy is purchased for $12,400. This policy represents property insurance on the building and equipment. (The balance in the Prepaid Insurance account represents vehicle insurance on a delivery truck, recorded in the Vehicles account, purchased on January 1.)

8 Natalie attends to the receipt of advertising supplies. 5,000 brochures were purchased on account from Nakhooda Printing for $2,500. (*Hint:* Use the Supplies account.)

15 Koebel's Family Bakery purchases baking equipment for $900 cash to accommodate the production of cupcakes. (*Hint:* Use the Equipment account.)

18 Natalie books a cookie-making class for the evening of July 5. A $100 deposit is received in advance.

20 Natalie teaches a cookie-making class that was booked over the summer months. $300 is collected in cash.

21 The first order for the preparation of 200 dozen miniature cupcakes is received from Coffee Beans. Natalie supervises the preparation of these cupcakes. She ensures that there are adequate amounts of baking ingredients on hand and that the order is appropriately filled.

22 200 dozen cupcakes are delivered to the Coffee Beans warehouse in Calgary. An invoice of $1,920 for the preparation of these cupcakes is included.

27   A $100 invoice for use of Natalie's cell phone is received. The cell phone is used exclusively for Koebel's Family Bakery's business. The invoice is for services provided in June and is due on July 15. (*Hint:* Use the Utilities Expense account.)

29   Natalie receives her first paycheque from Koebel's Family Bakery, $3,000.

29   250 dozen cupcakes are delivered to the Coffee Beans warehouse in Calgary. An invoice of $2,400 for the preparation of these cupcakes is included.

Instructions

(a) Using T accounts, enter the opening balances in the general ledger as at June 30.
(b) Journalize the above transactions.
(c) Post the journal entries to the general ledger.
(d) Prepare an updated trial balance at June 30.

Answers to Self-Test Questions

1. c	2. d	3. a	4. c	5. d
6. a	7. c	8. d	9. a	10. c

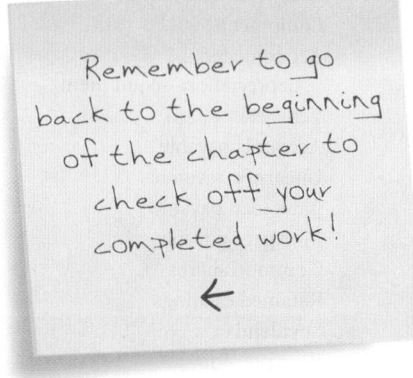

Remember to go back to the beginning of the chapter to check off your completed work!

←

Comprehensive Case: Chapters 1-3

Record and post transactions, prepare trial balance and financial statements. (SO 3, 4)

Software Advisors Limited was organized on January 1, 2012, to provide customized support to design and maintain in-home computer networks. The company does not have any full-time employees other than the principal shareholder and manager, Manroop Dhariwal. Instead it hires "consultants" to perform the work for the company. Initially, the company and the consultant split the revenue evenly. Consultants who stay with the company or who have special expertise increase their percentage of client revenue to as much as 70% of the total billing. This is an incentive for consultants to stay with the company and to develop their range of skills.

Software Advisors Limited plans to use the following chart of accounts:

1000	Cash
1100	Accounts Receivable
1200	Supplies
1300	Prepaid Insurance
1400	Prepaid Rent (security deposit)
2000	Equipment
2500	Client List
3000	Accounts Payable
3100	Bank Loan Payable
4000	Common Shares
4500	Retained Earnings
5000	Revenue—Client Services
7000	Advertising Expense
7100	Consultant Fees Expense
7200	Interest Expense
7300	Office Expense
7400	Rent Expense
7500	Telephone Expense
7600	Travel and Entertainment Expense
9000	Income Tax Expense

The company had the following transactions in the month of January:

January	2	Issued 1,000 common shares for $15 each.
	3	Borrowed $50,000 from the bank on a long-term loan.
	4	Finalized the lease and paid the first month's rent of $3,000 plus a security deposit of $3,000. The company shares office space with another business.
	5	Purchased equipment and laptops for $40,000 cash.
	10	Paid for an advertisement in a local paper, $500.
	11	Purchased supplies on account, $1,000.
	12	Took the manager of a local computer store to lunch and paid $50.
	13	Paid for several advertising spots on the local radio station, $3,000.
	16	Attended a local business fair. Paid $1,000 for promotional items and $500 for booth rental.
	17	Summarized and recorded the billings to clients for the first two weeks of January. Billings totalled $15,000. These amounts are due by the 10th of the next month.
	18	Calculated and recorded amounts payable to consultants for their work. Payments of $7,500 will be made to the consultants on the 18th of the next month.
	20	Paid $1,000 for the company's share of the current month's office administration expenses.
	23	Paid $4,000 cash for a client list from a graduate student who had a similar business and is moving out of town.
	24	Received $3,000 from clients in settlement of their accounts billed on the 17th.
	30	Paid annual insurance policy with coverage up to February 1, 2013, for $6,000.
	30	Summarized and recorded the billings to clients for the last two weeks of January. Billings totalled $18,000. These amounts are due by the 28th of the next month.
	31	Calculated and recorded amounts payable to consultants for their work. Payments of $10,000 will be made to the consultants on the 28th of the next month.
	31	Made a bank loan payment for $1,000 of which $300 related to interest and $700 to the principal.
	31	Paid $1,200 to the Canada Revenue Agency for an income tax instalment.

Instructions

(a) Journalize the January transactions.

(b) Set up T accounts and post the journal entries prepared in (a).

(c) Prepare a trial balance at January 31, 2012.

(d) Prepare an income statement, statement of changes in equity, and statement of financial position for January.

(e) Will Software Advisors Limited have enough money to pay its accounts payable in the next 30 days? Explain.

Accrual Accounting Concepts

The Navigator
Chapter 4

- Scan *Study Objectives*
- Read *Feature Story*
- Read text and answer *Do It!s*
- Review *Comparing IFRS and ASPE*
- Review *Summary of Study Objectives*
- Review *Decision Toolkit—A Summary*
- Work *Using the Decision Toolkit*
- Work *Comprehensive Do It!*
- Answer *Self-Test Questions*
- Complete *assignments*
- Go to *WileyPLUS* for practice and tutorials

the navigator

study objectives

After studying this chapter, you should be able to:

1. Explain when revenues and expenses are recognized and how this forms the basis for accrual accounting.

2. Describe the types of adjusting entries and when they are recorded and prepare adjusting entries for prepayments.

3. Prepare adjusting entries for accruals and describe how adjusting entries affect the income statement and the statement of financial position.

4. Describe the nature and purpose of the adjusted trial balance, and prepare one.

5. Prepare closing entries and a post-closing trial balance.

School's Out, Time to Balance the Books

At Western University in London, Ontario, as at campuses across the country, classes for most students start in September and end in April. Likewise, the university's fiscal year end is April 30. So essentially, the university closes its books at the same time the students do. This cohesion helps the university to satisfy the criteria needed to recognize revenues and expenses at the appropriate time when services are performed and expenses incurred, respectively.

However, many students at Western take intersession courses. They pay their course fees before the year end of April 30, but the courses don't start until May or later. "We would get intersession fees and other fees in advance of our year end, so there is a deferral there," says Carter Scott, Western's controller. The university defers the recognition of that revenue until the following accounting period, the one in which it provides the teaching services.

Another example of the deferral of revenue is the advance fees students pay for residence admission to hold their spot for the coming year. The university defers recognition of this revenue until the start of the academic year in September, when the students move into the residences.

Research activities provide another example. Western receives more than $200 million per year in external support for research projects, making research an integral part of the university's activities. "In a lot of cases, granting agencies' year ends are in March, so they send the funds in at the beginning of March," Mr. Scott points out. "For any faculty member who gets a grant, it's deferred until they start expending it, because it's restricted for that purpose. Restricted revenues for which the related expenses have not been incurred are reported as unearned revenue on the university's balance sheet." The grant money is matched against expenses incurred over the course of the research project, which could go on for years.

Expenses, too, must be recorded in the year in which they were incurred. "Post-employment benefits, at most universities, are a very large number that you accrue for," Mr. Scott explains. Other expenses that would have to be accrued at year end include vacation pay, outstanding salary for the approximately 3,500 full-time faculty and staff members, and utility bills.

Western also has a significant amount of construction projects ongoing. The construction companies usually bill around the 15th of the month after work is completed, so some of these bills will come in after the year end, Mr. Scott explains. These companies provide the university with estimates to use in its accrual process.

"Accrual accounting is considered the most appropriate method of financial reporting because revenues and expenses are recognized in the period to which they relate, regardless of whether there has been a receipt or payment of cash," Mr. Scott explains. "A more meaningful picture of financial position and operations is provided under accrual accounting than on a cash flow basis."

Recording revenues and expenses in the correct period is a challenge, but one that must be met to best reflect the various activities of a large university like Western.

the navigator

**preview of
CHAPTER** | **4**

In Chapter 3, we examined the recording process up to and including the preparation of the trial balance. Although we prepared financial statements directly from the trial balance in that chapter, additional steps are necessary to properly update the accounts before the financial statements are prepared.

In this chapter, we introduce you to the accrual accounting concepts that guide the recognition of revenue and expenses in the appropriate time period. We will also describe the remaining steps in the accounting cycle.

The chapter is organized as follows:

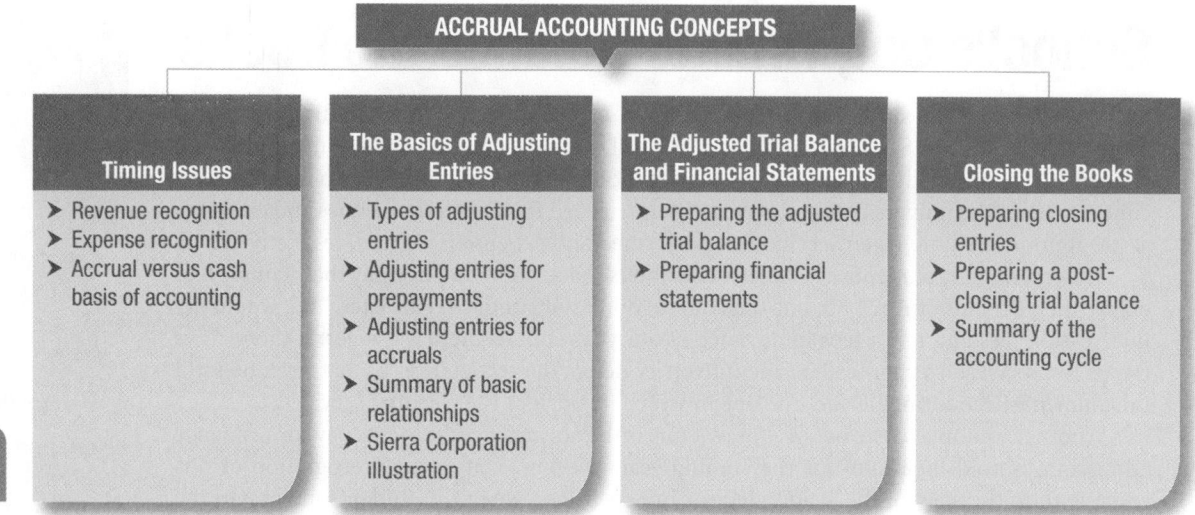

ACCRUAL ACCOUNTING CONCEPTS

Timing Issues	**The Basics of Adjusting Entries**	**The Adjusted Trial Balance and Financial Statements**	**Closing the Books**
➤ Revenue recognition ➤ Expense recognition ➤ Accrual versus cash basis of accounting	➤ Types of adjusting entries ➤ Adjusting entries for prepayments ➤ Adjusting entries for accruals ➤ Summary of basic relationships ➤ Sierra Corporation illustration	➤ Preparing the adjusted trial balance ➤ Preparing financial statements	➤ Preparing closing entries ➤ Preparing a post-closing trial balance ➤ Summary of the accounting cycle

the navigator

Timing Issues

STUDY OBJECTIVE 1

Explain when revenues and expenses are recognized and how this forms the basis for accrual accounting.

Accounting would be simple if we could wait until a company ended its operations to prepare its financial statements. As the following anecdote shows, if we waited until then we could easily determine the amount of lifetime profit earned:

> A grocery store owner from the old country kept his accounts payable on a spindle, accounts receivable on a notepad, and cash in a box. His daughter, an accountant, chided him: "I don't understand how you can run your business this way. How do you know what you've earned?"
>
> "Well," the father replied, "when I arrived in Canada 40 years ago, I had nothing but the pants I was wearing. Today your sister is a doctor, your brother is a teacher, and you are an accountant. Your mother and I have a nice car, a well-furnished house, and a cottage at the lake. We have a good business and everything is paid for. So, you add all that together, subtract the pants, and there's your profit."

Although the old grocer may be correct in his evaluation of how to calculate profit over his lifetime, most companies need more immediate feedback about how well they are doing. For example, management needs monthly reports on financial results, large corporations present quarterly and annual financial statements to shareholders, and the Canada Revenue Agency requires these businesses to file monthly sales tax reports and annual income tax returns.

Consequently, accounting divides the economic life of a business into artificial time periods. Accounting time periods are generally one month, one quarter (three months), or one year.

Many accounting transactions affect more than one of these arbitrary time periods. For example, we saw in the feature story that research grants received by faculty at Western University can span multiple years. We also saw how Western collects intersession course fees in one fiscal year but delivers the courses in the next fiscal year. Determining the amount of revenue and expenses to report in a particular accounting period can be difficult. We therefore need some standards that define when we should recognize revenues and expenses.

REVENUE RECOGNITION

Under current accounting standards, revenue is recognized or recorded when, due to ordinary activities, an increase in future economic benefits arising from an increase in an asset or a decrease in a liability has occurred. Ordinary activities could include sales, rent, interest, and other forms of revenue.

In general, **revenue recognition** occurs when the sales or performance effort is substantially complete, the amount is determinable (measurable), and collection is reasonably assured. In a merchandising company, revenue is considered to be earned when the merchandise is sold (normally at the point of sale). In a service company, revenue is considered earned at the time the service is performed.

To illustrate, assume a consulting business provides services to a client on credit after doing a thorough credit check. The services are performed in September. In October, the business sent the client an invoice, and in November, the business received payment from the client. In what month should the revenue be recorded by the consulting business? The answer is September because that was when the service was performed and consequently the revenue was earned. An asset account, Accounts Receivable, would be increased. At that time, the amount of the revenue could be measured because, even though an invoice had not been prepared, the price would have been known and agreed to by both parties. Furthermore, the revenue and any related accounts receivable are likely to be collected.

The International Accounting Standards Board has proposed a new standard for revenue recognition. This was done in consultation with the Financial Accounting Standards Board in the United States to achieve greater convergence of standards between countries. Under the proposed standard, companies would recognize revenue upon the transfer of goods or services to customers. This is a "contract" based approach rather than an "earnings" based approach. The new standard is not expected to change the way that revenues are recognized by most companies but it can give rise to significant differences for some industries, which are covered in other courses.

DECISION TOOLKIT

 Decision Checkpoints	 Info Needed for Decision	 Tools to Use for Decision	 How to Evaluate Results
At what point should the company record revenue?	Need to understand the nature of the company's business	Revenue should be recorded when earned. For a service company, revenue is earned when a service is performed. For a merchandising company, revenue is earned when the merchandise is sold.	Recognizing revenue too early overstates current period revenue; recognizing it too late understates current period revenue.

EXPENSE RECOGNITION

Expenses are recognized in the income statement when, due to an ordinary activity, there is a decrease in future economic benefits related to a decrease in an asset or an increase in a liability and this change can be measured reliably. Thus, **expense recognition** is tied to changes in assets and liabilities. Expense recognition will often coincide with revenue recognition but not always. Consider again the consulting business mentioned in the last section. During the month of September, company employees provided services to a client. Because of this the company owes these employees salaries. This obligation creates a liability, Salaries Payable, and a corresponding Salaries Expense. In this case and in the case of Western University, described in our feature story, the expenses were recognized at the same time as the revenues because the expenses were incurred at the same time and contributed to the earning of the revenue. This does not mean that revenues and expenses are always recognized at the same time. For example, if a company rented office space, each month the rent would be due and this would increase a liability (Rent Payable) and an expense (Rent Expense) even if the company earned no revenue in a particular month.

Other costs are more difficult to directly associate with revenue. For example, it is difficult to match administrative salary expense or interest expense with the revenue these help earn. Such costs are therefore expensed in the periods when the related liability arises. Other examples include costs that help generate revenue over multiple periods of time, such as the depreciation of equipment. We will learn more about allocating expenses later in this chapter.

 **ACCOUNTING MATTERS!**   *Management Perspective*

Recognizing the Cost of a Movie

Suppose you work for a movie studio. Over what period should the cost of producing a movie be expensed? It should be expensed over the economic life of the movie. But what is its economic life? The filmmaker must estimate how much revenue will be earned from box office sales, DVD sales, television and Internet royalties, and games and toys—a period that could be less than a year or many years.

Take, for example, *Harry Potter and Deathly Hallows, Part II* released by Warner Bros. It cost over U.S. $200 million to produce this film, and it more than recovered this cost by taking in U.S. $476 million in ticket sales the first weekend it was released. In fact, all of the Harry Potter movies have broken box office and product sales records. Compare this with *The Cat in the Hat*, released by Universal Studios. It cost U.S. $109 million to produce but it has only recovered U.S. $100 million to date. These situations illustrate how difficult it can be in real life for companies to properly match expenses to revenues.

DECISION TOOLKIT

 Decision Checkpoints	 Info Needed for Decision	 Tools to Use for Decision	 How to Evaluate Results
At what point should the company record expenses?	Need to understand the nature of the company's business	Expenses are recognized when assets are decreased or when liabilities are increased. Often expenses should "follow" revenues; that is, the effort (expense) should be matched with the result (revenue).	Recognizing expenses too early overstates current period expenses; recognizing them too late understates current period expenses.

ACCRUAL VERSUS CASH BASIS OF ACCOUNTING

The combined application of revenue recognition and expense recognition results in accrual basis accounting. **Accrual basis accounting means that transactions affecting a company's financial statements are recorded in the periods in which the events occur, rather than when the company actually receives or pays cash.** This means recognizing revenues when they are earned rather than when cash is received. Likewise, expenses are recognized in the period in which goods and services are used or consumed, rather than when cash is paid.

An alternative to the accrual basis is the cash basis. Under **cash basis accounting, revenue is recorded only when cash is received, and an expense is recorded only when cash is paid**. Using cash basis accounting can lead to misleading financial statements. Why? Because management can change the revenue and expenses that are reported by timing the receipt and payment of cash.

Profits can be increased by paying expenses in the following year. Profits can be lowered and income tax reduced by asking customers to pay in the following year. A cash basis income statement fails to record revenues and expenses when related assets like accounts receivable and related liabilities like accounts payable arise.

As Carter Scott, the controller of Western University in our feature story, said, "Accrual accounting is considered the most appropriate method of financial reporting because revenues and expenses are recognized in the period to which they relate, regardless of whether there has been a receipt or payment of cash. A more meaningful picture of financial position and operations is provided under accrual accounting than on a cash flow basis."

Illustration 4-1 compares accrual-based numbers and cash-based numbers, using a simple example. Suppose that you own a painting company and you paint a large building complex during year 1. In year 1, you incur and pay total expenses of $50,000, which includes the cost of the paint and your employees' salaries. You bill your customer $80,000 at the end of year 1, but you are not paid until year 2. On an accrual basis, you would report the revenue during the period when it is earned—year 1. The expenses would be recognized (recorded) in the period in which the revenues were earned. Thus, your profit for year 1 would be $30,000, and no revenue or expense from this project would be reported in year 2. The $30,000 of profit reported for year 1 provides a useful indication of the profitability of your efforts during that period.

If, instead, you were reporting on a cash basis, you would report expenses of $50,000 in year 1 and revenues of $80,000 in year 2. In year 1 there would be a loss of $50,000, while profit for year 2 would be $80,000. While total profits are the same over the two-year period ($30,000), cash basis measures are not very informative about the results of your efforts during year 1 or year 2.

Illustration 4-1
Accrual versus cash basis accounting

	Year 1		Year 2	
Activity	Purchased paint, painted building complex, paid employees		Received payment for work done in year 1	
Accrual basis	Revenue	$ 80,000	Revenue	$ 0
	Expense	50,000	Expense	0
	Profit	$ 30,000	Profit	$ 0
Cash basis	Revenue	$ 0	Revenue	$80,000
	Expense	50,000	Expense	0
	Loss	$(50,000)	Profit	$80,000

BEFORE YOU GO ON...

▶ Do It! Accrual Basis and Cash Basis Accounting

During the year ended December 31, 2012, Jomerans Corp. received $125,000 cash from customers. At December 31, 2011, customers owed Jomerans $30,000 for services provided in 2011. On December 31, 2012, customers owed Jomerans $19,500 for services provided in 2012. Calculate the revenue for 2012 using (a) the cash basis of accounting, and (b) the accrual basis of accounting.

Action Plan

- For the cash basis of accounting, revenue is equal to the cash received.
- For the accrual basis of accounting, use the proper criteria for revenue recognition. Report revenue in the period in which it is earned, not when it is collected.

(continued)

- Under the accrual basis of accounting, cash collected in 2012 for revenue earned in 2011 should not be included in the 2012 revenue.
- Under the accrual basis of accounting, amounts still owing by customers at the end of 2012 for services provided in 2012 should be included in the 2012 revenue.

Solution

(a) Revenue using the cash basis of accounting $125,000

(b)	Cash received from customers in 2012	$125,000
	Deduct: Collection of 2011 receivables	(30,000)
	Add: Amounts owing at December 31, 2012	19,500
	Revenue using the accrual basis of accounting	$114,500

The Basics of Adjusting Entries

STUDY OBJECTIVE 2

Describe the types of adjusting entries and when they are recorded and prepare adjusting entries for prepayments.

For revenues to be recorded in the period in which they are earned, and for expenses to be recorded when incurred, we may have to record **adjusting entries** to update accounts at the end of the accounting period. Adjusting entries make it possible to produce relevant financial information at the end of the accounting period. Thus, the statement of financial position reports appropriate assets, liabilities, and shareholders' equity at the statement date, and the income statement shows the proper revenues, expenses, and profit (or loss) for the period.

Adjusting entries are necessary because the trial balance—the first pulling together of the transaction data—may not contain complete and up-to-date data. This is true for several reasons:

1. Some events are not recorded daily, because it would not be useful or efficient to do so. Examples are the use of supplies and the earning of salaries by employees.
2. Some costs are not recorded during the accounting period, because these costs expire with the passage of time rather than as a result of recurring daily transactions. Examples include rent, insurance, and depreciation.
3. Some items may be unrecorded. An example is a utility service bill that will not be received until the next accounting period. The bill, however, covers services delivered in the current accounting period.

ASPE Adjusting entries are required every time financial statements are prepared, and preparing adjusting entries is often a long and detailed process. If a company is public and reporting under IFRS, quarterly financial statements must be prepared. As a result, adjusting entries will be prepared at the end of each quarter although many companies will prepare them monthly. If a company is private and reporting under ASPE, adjusting entries need to be done only annually but may be done more frequently if management wishes. Each account in the trial balance needs to be analyzed to see if it is complete and up to date, which requires an understanding of the company's operations and the interrelationship of accounts. To accumulate the adjustment data, a company may need to count its remaining supplies. It may also need to prepare supporting schedules of insurance policies, rental agreements, and other commitments.

Adjustment data are often not available until after the end of the period. For example, telephone and other bills will not be received until after the month end or year end. Carter Scott, in our feature story, notes that Western will not receive its construction bill until around May 15 for the month of April, which is after its year end. In such cases, the data are gathered as soon as possible after the end of the period and adjusting entries are made, but they are still dated as at the statement of financial position date.

TYPES OF ADJUSTING ENTRIES

Adjusting entries can be classified as either prepayments or accruals. Each of these classes has two subcategories, as follows:

Prepayments
1. **Prepaid expenses:** Expenses paid in cash and recorded as assets before they are used or consumed
2. **Unearned revenues:** Cash received and recorded as liabilities before revenue is earned

Accruals
1. **Accrued revenues:** Revenues earned but not yet received in cash or recorded
2. **Accrued expenses:** Expenses incurred but not yet paid in cash or recorded

Specific examples and explanations of each type of adjustment are provided in the following pages. Each example is based on the October 31 trial balance of Sierra Corporation, from Chapter 3, shown again here in Illustration 4-2.

▶ Illustration 4-2
Trial balance

SIERRA CORPORATION Trial Balance October 31, 2012		
	Debit	Credit
Cash	$15,200	
Supplies	2,500	
Prepaid insurance	600	
Equipment	5,000	
Accounts payable		$ 2,500
Unearned revenue		1,200
Notes payable		5,000
Common shares		10,000
Dividends	500	
Service revenue		10,000
Salaries expense	4,000	
Rent expense	900	
	$28,700	$28,700

For illustration purposes, we assume that Sierra Corporation uses an accounting period of one month. Thus, monthly adjusting entries need to be made.

ADJUSTING ENTRIES FOR PREPAYMENTS

Prepayments increase current assets such as prepaid expenses and certain types of non-current assets such as buildings and equipment. A prepayment can also be received rather than paid and in this case, a prepayment received can increase current liabilities such as unearned revenue. Adjusting entries for prepayments allocate a cost from an asset or liability account to an expense or revenue account, respectively.

This means that for prepayments made (e.g., prepaid expenses), the adjusting entry records the expense that applies to the current period and reduces the asset account that was originally recorded. This type of adjustment is necessary because the prepayment no longer has future benefit and consequently is no longer an asset—it has been used.

For prepayments received (e.g., unearned revenues), the adjusting entry records the revenue earned in the period and reduces the liability account where the unearned revenue was originally recorded. This type of adjustment is necessary because the unearned revenue is no longer owed and consequently is no longer a liability—the service has been provided and the revenue earned.

We will look at each of these types of prepayments—prepaid expenses and unearned revenues—in the next sections.

Prepaid Expenses

Costs that are paid for in cash before they are used are recorded as **prepaid expenses**. When such a cost is incurred, an asset (prepaid) account should be increased (debited)—to show the service or benefit that will be received in the future—and cash should be decreased (credited). In a few cases, the asset is purchased on account, but ultimately cash is paid.

Helpful Hint
A cost can be an asset or an expense. If the cost has future benefits (i.e., the benefits have not yet expired), it is an asset. If the cost has no future benefits (i.e., the benefits have expired), it is an expense.

Prepaid expenses are costs that expire either with the passage of time (e.g., insurance, rent, and depreciable assets) or through use (e.g., supplies). It is not practical to record the expiration of these costs on a daily basis. Instead, we record these expired costs when financial statements are prepared. At each statement date, adjusting entries are made for two purposes: (1) to record the expenses (expired costs) applicable to the current accounting period, and (2) to show the remaining amounts (unexpired costs) in the asset accounts.

Until prepaid expenses are adjusted, assets are overstated and expenses are understated. If expenses are understated, then profit and shareholders' equity will be overstated. As shown below, **an adjusting entry for prepaid expenses results in an increase (a debit) to an expense account and a decrease (a credit) to an asset account.**

Prepaid Expenses

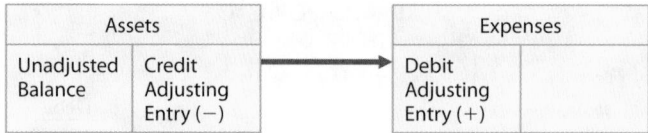

We now look in more detail at some specific types of prepaid expenses, beginning with supplies.

Supplies. The purchase of supplies, such as paper, results in an increase (a debit) to an asset account. During the accounting period, supplies are used. Rather than record supplies expense as the supplies are used, supplies expense is recognized at the end of the accounting period. At that time, the company must count the remaining supplies. The difference between the balance in the supplies (asset) account and the actual cost of supplies on hand gives the supplies used (an expense) for that period.

Recall from Chapter 3 that Sierra Corporation purchased supplies costing $2,500 on October 9. This is an example of a prepayment made on account, rather than by cash. The payment was recorded by increasing (debiting) the asset account Supplies and increasing (crediting) the liability account Accounts Payable. The Supplies account therefore shows a balance of $2,500 in the October 31 trial balance. A count at the close of business on October 31 reveals that $1,000 of supplies are still on hand. Thus, the cost of supplies used is $1,500 ($2,500 − $1,000).

The following illustration outlines the basic analysis, similar to that shown in Chapter 3, used to determine the appropriate adjusting entry to record and post:

►Adjustment (1)
Prepaid expenses—supplies

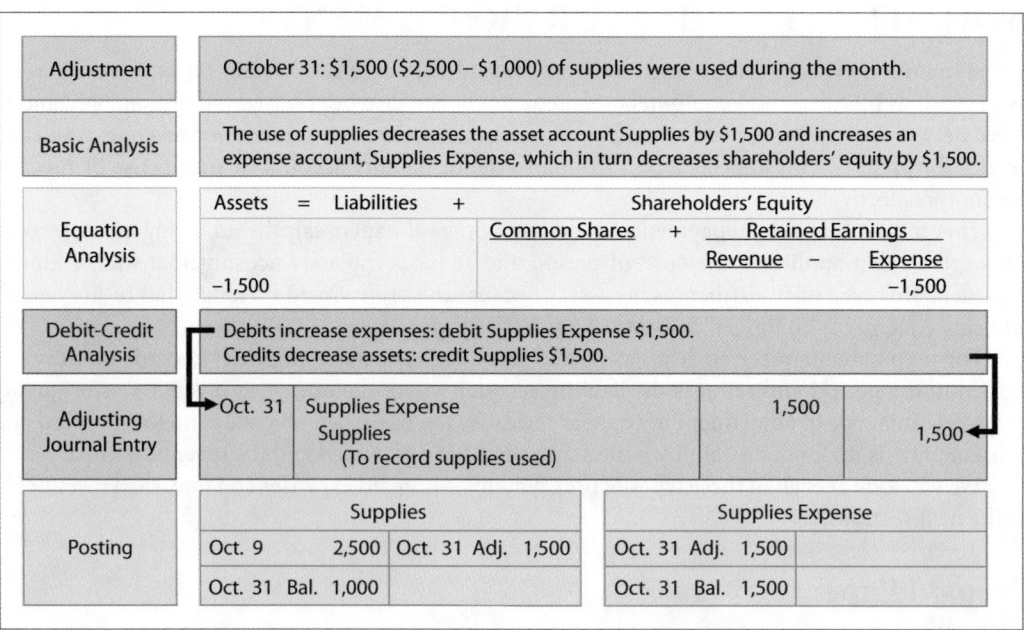

After adjustment, the asset account Supplies shows a balance of $1,000, which is equal to the cost of supplies on hand at the statement date. In addition, Supplies Expense shows a balance of $1,500, which equals the cost of supplies used in October. If the adjusting entry (abbreviated in the T account above as "Adj.") is not made, October expenses will be understated and profit overstated by $1,500. Moreover, as the accounting equation shows, both assets and shareholders' equity will be overstated by $1,500 on the October 31 statement of financial position.

Insurance. Companies purchase insurance to protect themselves from losses caused by fire, theft, and unforeseen accidents. Insurance must be paid in advance, often for one year. Insurance payments (premiums) made in advance are normally recorded in the asset account Prepaid Insurance. At the financial statement date, it is necessary to make an adjustment to increase (debit) Insurance Expense and decrease (credit) Prepaid Insurance for the cost of insurance that has expired during the period.

On October 3, Sierra Corporation paid $600 for a one-year insurance policy. Coverage began on October 1. The payment was recorded by increasing (debiting) Prepaid Insurance when it was paid. This account shows a balance of $600 in the October 31 trial balance. An analysis of the insurance policy reveals that $50 of insurance expires each month ($600 ÷ 12 months). The expiration of the prepaid insurance would be recorded as follows:

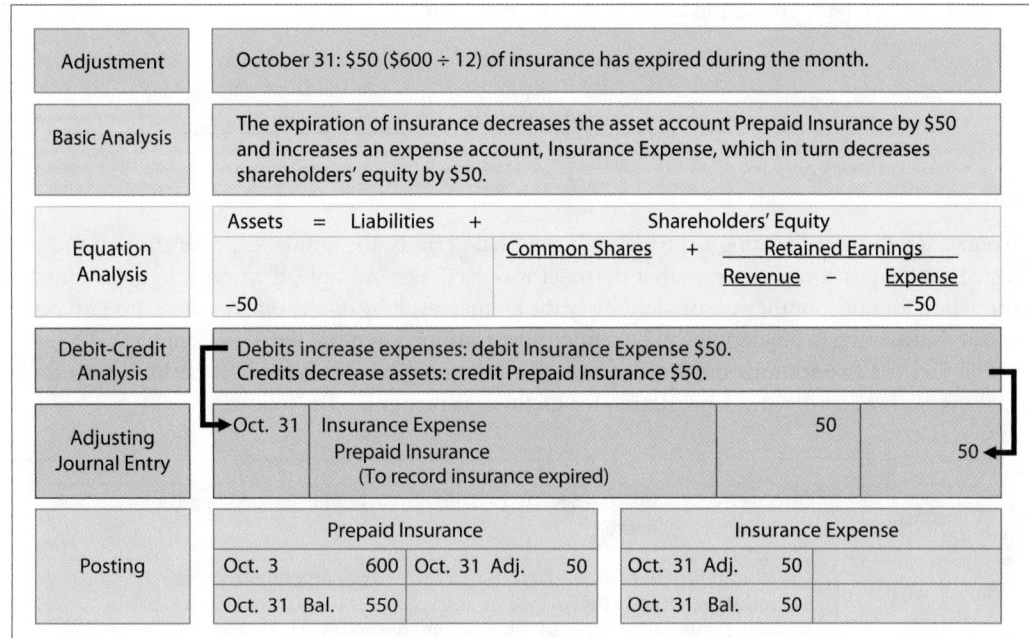

Adjustment (2)

Prepaid expenses—insurance

After adjustment, the asset Prepaid Insurance shows a balance of $550, which represents the cost that applies to the remaining 11 months of insurance coverage (11 × $50). At the same time, the balance in Insurance Expense is equal to the insurance cost that was used in October. If this adjustment is not made, October expenses will be understated and profit overstated by $50. Moreover, both assets and shareholders' equity will be overstated by $50 on the October 31 statement of financial position.

Depreciation. A company typically owns a variety of assets that have long lives, such as buildings and equipment. Each one is recorded as an asset, rather than as an expense, in the year it is acquired because these long-lived assets provide a service for many years. The period of service is called the **useful life.**

From an accounting standpoint, the acquisition of certain types of long-lived assets is essentially a long-term prepayment for services. Similar to other prepaid expenses, there is a need to recognize the cost that has been used (an expense) during the period and to report the unused cost (an asset) at the end of the period. **Depreciation** is the process of allocating the cost of a long-lived or non-current asset, such as property, plant, and equipment, to expense over its useful life. Only assets with specified useful lives are depreciated. We call them *depreciable assets*. When an asset, such as land, has an unlimited useful life, it is not depreciated.

While the term *depreciation* is normally used in relation to property, plant, and equipment, the term *amortization* is used in relation to intangible assets and *depletion* is used in relation to

ASPE

natural resources. These terms mean the same thing—the allocation of the cost of a long-lived asset to expense over its useful life. We will learn about amortizing intangible assets in Chapter 9. As was mentioned in Chapter 2, some companies use the term *amortization* in place of *depreciation*, especially private companies reporting under ASPE.

One point about depreciation is very important to understand: depreciation is an allocation concept, not a valuation concept. That is, we depreciate an asset to allocate its cost to the periods over which we use it. We are not trying to record a change in the actual value of the asset.

Calculation of Depreciation. A common practice for calculating depreciation expense for a period of time is to divide the cost of the asset by its useful life. This is known as the **straight-line method of depreciation**. Of course, at the time an asset is acquired, its useful life is not known with any certainty. It must therefore be estimated. Because of this, depreciation is an estimate rather than a factual measurement of the cost that has expired.

Sierra Corporation purchased equipment that cost $5,000 on October 1. If its useful life is expected to be five years, annual depreciation is $1,000 ($5,000 ÷ 5). Illustration 4-3 shows the formula to calculate depreciation expense in its simplest form.

> ▸ **Illustration 4-3**
> Formula for depreciation

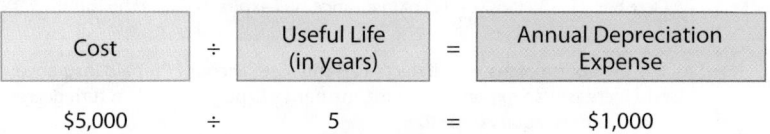

Cost	÷	Useful Life (in years)	=	Annual Depreciation Expense
$5,000	÷	5	=	$1,000

Of course, if you are calculating depreciation for partial periods, the annual expense amount must be adjusted for the portion of the year that the asset was used. For example, if we wish to determine the depreciation for one month, we would multiply the annual result by one-twelfth as there are 12 months in a year. Calculating depreciation will be refined and examined in more detail in Chapter 9.

For Sierra Corporation, depreciation on the equipment is estimated to be $83 per month ($1,000 × $\frac{1}{12}$). Accordingly, depreciation for October is recognized as follows:

> ▸ **Adjustment (3)**
> Prepaid expenses—depreciation

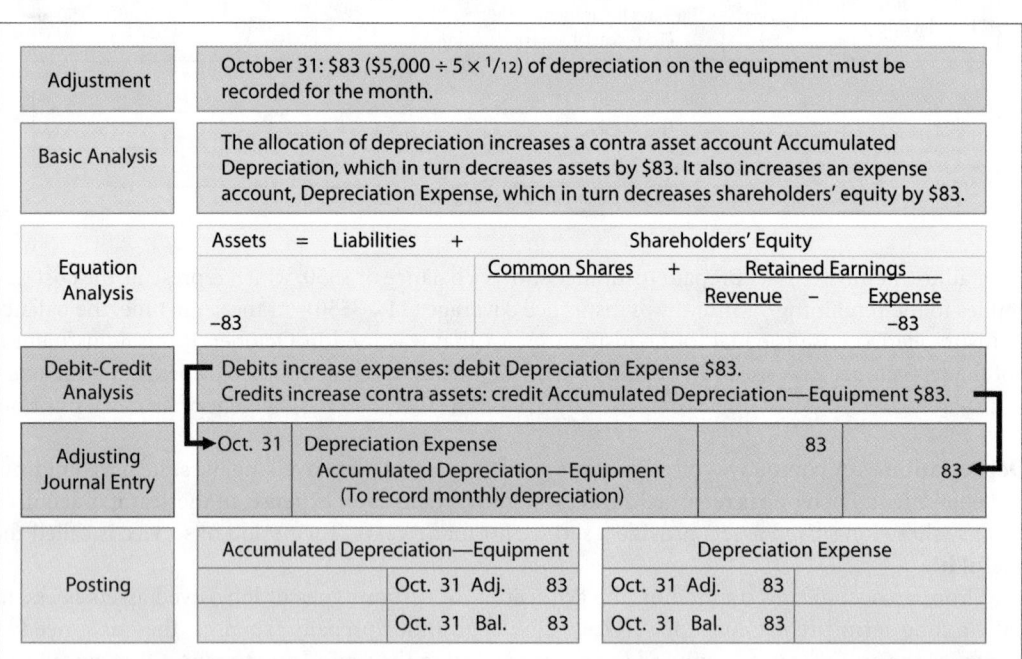

The balance in the Accumulated Depreciation account will increase by $83 each month until the asset is fully depreciated in five years. Accumulated depreciation represents the cumulative total of the depreciation expense since the asset was purchased, less any reductions when assets are sold (which we will learn about in Chapter 9).

As in the case of other prepaid expenses, if this adjusting entry is not made, total assets, shareholders' equity, and profit will all be overstated by $83 and depreciation expense will be understated by $83.

Statement Presentation.   As we learned in Chapter 2, a contra account is an account that is offset against (deducted from) a related account on the income statement or statement of financial position. Accumulated Depreciation—Equipment is a **contra asset account**. That means it is offset against an asset account, Equipment on the statement of financial position. Its normal balance is a credit—the opposite of the normal debit balance of its related account, Equipment.

    There is a simple reason for using a separate contra account instead of decreasing (crediting) Equipment: using this account discloses both the original cost of the equipment and the total estimated cost that has expired to date. This also helps separate actual amounts (cost) from estimated amounts (accumulated depreciation).

    In the statement of financial position, Accumulated Depreciation—Equipment is deducted from the related asset account as follows:

Equipment	$5,000
Less: Accumulated depreciation—equipment	83
Carrying amount	4,917

    The difference between the cost of a depreciable asset and its related accumulated depreciation is referred to as the **carrying amount** of that asset. The carrying amount is also commonly known as net book value, or simply book value. In the above illustration, the equipment's carrying amount at the statement of financial position date is $4,917. Be sure to understand that, except at acquisition, the asset's carrying amount and its fair value (the price at which it could be sold) are two different amounts. As noted earlier, the purpose of depreciation is not to state an asset's value, but to allocate its cost over time.

Unearned Revenue

Cash received before revenue is earned is recorded by increasing (crediting) a liability account for **unearned revenues**. Items like rent, magazine subscriptions, and customer deposits for future service may result in unearned revenues. Airlines, such as Air Canada, treat receipts from the sale of tickets as unearned revenue until the flight service is provided. Similarly, tuition fees received by universities before the academic session begins are considered unearned revenue, as at Western University in our feature story.

    Unearned revenues are the opposite of prepaid expenses. Indeed, unearned revenue on the books of one company is likely to be a prepaid expense on the books of the company that has made the advance payment. For example, if identical accounting periods are assumed, your landlord will have unearned rent revenue when you (the tenant) have prepaid rent.

    When a payment is received for services that will be provided in a future accounting period, Cash should be increased (debited) and Unearned Revenue (a liability) should be increased (credited) to recognize the obligation that exists. Unearned revenues are later earned when the service is provided to the customer.

    It is not practical to make daily journal entries as the revenue is earned. Instead, recognition of earned revenue is delayed until the adjustment process. At that time, an adjusting entry is then made to record the revenue that has been earned during the period and to show the liability that remains at the end of the accounting period. Typically, until the adjustment is made, liabilities are overstated and revenues are understated. If revenues are understated, then profit and shareholders' equity are also understated. As shown below, the adjusting entry for unearned revenues results in a decrease (debit) to a liability account and an increase (credit) to a revenue account.

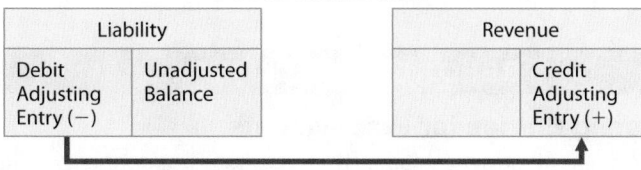

Unearned Revenue

Liability				Revenue	
Debit Adjusting Entry (−)	Unadjusted Balance				Credit Adjusting Entry (+)

    Returning to our example, we note that Sierra Corporation received $1,200 on October 2 from R. Knox for advertising services expected to be completed next month, by November 15. The payment was credited to Unearned Revenue, and this liability account shows a balance of $1,200 in

Helpful Hint
Every contra account has increases, decreases, and normal balances that are opposite to those of the account it relates to.

Alternative Terminology
Unearned revenues are also called *deferred revenues*.

the October 31 trial balance. From an evaluation of the work performed by Sierra for Knox during October, it is determined that $400 worth of work was done in October.

 Adjustment (4)
Unearned revenues

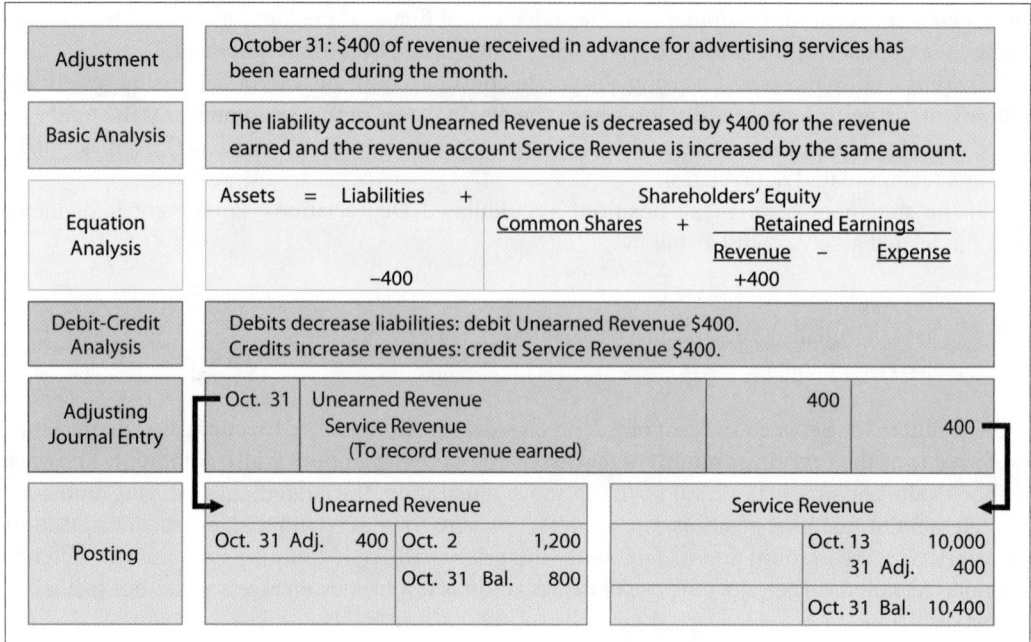

Adjustment	October 31: $400 of revenue received in advance for advertising services has been earned during the month.
Basic Analysis	The liability account Unearned Revenue is decreased by $400 for the revenue earned and the revenue account Service Revenue is increased by the same amount.

Equation Analysis

Assets	=	Liabilities	+	Shareholders' Equity		
				Common Shares	+	Retained Earnings
						Revenue – Expense
		−400				+400

Debit-Credit Analysis	Debits decrease liabilities: debit Unearned Revenue $400. Credits increase revenues: credit Service Revenue $400.

Adjusting Journal Entry

Oct. 31	Unearned Revenue	400	
	Service Revenue		400
	(To record revenue earned)		

Posting

Unearned Revenue			
Oct. 31 Adj.	400	Oct. 2	1,200
		Oct. 31 Bal.	800

Service Revenue		
	Oct. 13	10,000
	31 Adj.	400
	Oct. 31 Bal.	10,400

After adjustment, the liability Unearned Revenue shows a balance of $800, which represents the remaining advertising services expected to be performed in the future. At the same time, Service Revenue shows total revenue earned in October of $10,400. If this adjustment is not made, revenues and profit will be understated by $400 in the income statement. Moreover, liabilities will be overstated by $400 and shareholders' equity will be understated by that amount on the October 31 statement of financial position.

ACCOUNTING MATTERS!   *Investor Perspective*

Reporting Revenue in the Proper Period

Until recently, Apple Computer, Inc. was required to spread the revenues earned from iPhone sales over the two-year period following the sale of the phone. Accounting standards required this because it was argued that Apple was obligated to provide software updates after the phone was sold. Therefore, since Apple had service obligations after the initial date of sale, it was forced to spread the revenue over a two-year period. However, since the company received full payment upfront, the cash flows from iPhones significantly exceeded the revenue reported from iPhone sales in each accounting period. It also meant that the rapid growth of iPhone sales was not fully reflected in the revenue amounts reported in Apple's income statement.

A new accounting standard now enables Apple to report nearly all of its iPhone revenue at the point of sale. It has been estimated that Apple's 2009 revenues would have been about 17% higher, and earnings per share would have been almost 50% higher, if the new accounting standard had been applied in 2009.

BEFORE YOU GO ON...

▶ Do It! Adjusting Entries for Prepayments

Hammond, Inc.'s general ledger includes these selected accounts on March 31, 2012, before adjusting entries are prepared:

	Debit	Credit
Prepaid insurance	$ 3,600	
Supplies	2,800	
Equipment	24,000	
Accumulated depreciation—equipment		$5,750
Unearned revenue		9,200

An analysis of the accounts shows the following:

1. The insurance policy is a one-year policy, effective March 1, 2012.

2. Supplies on hand total $800 on March 31, 2012.

3. The equipment was purchased April 1, 2010, and is estimated to have a useful life of eight years.

4. Half of the unearned revenue was earned in March.

Prepare the adjusting entries for the month of March.

Action Plan

- Make sure you prepare adjustments for the appropriate time period.
- Adjusting entries for prepaid expenses require a debit to an expense account and a credit to an asset account.
- Adjusting entries for unearned revenues require a debit to a liability account and a credit to a revenue account.

Solution

1.	Mar. 31	Insurance Expense	300	
		Prepaid Insurance		300
		(To record insurance expired: $3,600 ÷ 12)		
2.	31	Supplies Expense	2,000	
		Supplies		2,000
		(To record supplies used: $2,800 – $800)		
3.	31	Depreciation Expense	250	
		Accumulated Depreciation—Equipment		250
		(To record monthly depreciation: $24,000 ÷ 8 × 1/12)		
4.	31	Unearned Revenue	4,600	
		Service Revenue		4,600
		(To record revenue earned: $9,200 × 1/2)		

the
navigator

ADJUSTING ENTRIES FOR ACCRUALS

The second category of adjusting entries is **accruals**. Adjusting entries for accruals are required in order to record revenues earned, or expenses incurred, in the current accounting period. Unlike prepayments, accruals have not been recognized through daily entries and thus are not yet reflected in the accounts. Until an accrual adjustment is made, the revenue account (and the related asset account), or the expense account (and the related liability account), is understated. Thus, adjusting entries for accruals will increase both a statement of financial position account and an income statement account.

There are two types of adjusting entries for accruals: accrued revenues and accrued expenses. We now look at each type in more detail.

STUDY OBJECTIVE 3

Prepare adjusting entries for accruals and describe how adjusting entries affect the income statement and the statement of financial position.

Accrued Revenues

Revenues that have been earned but not yet received in cash or recorded at the statement date need to be recorded. Revenue is therefore adjusted by the amount of this accrued revenue. **Accrued revenues** may accumulate (accrue) with the passing of time, as in the case of interest revenue, or they may result from services that have been performed but not yet billed or collected, such as fees. The former are unrecorded because, as when interest is earned, they do not involve daily transactions. The latter may be unrecorded because only a portion of the total service has been provided and the client will not be billed until the service has been completed. Therefore the recording of accrued revenue is not initiated like most revenue transactions by creating a sales invoice.

An adjusting entry is required for two purposes: (1) to show the receivable that exists at the statement of financial position date, and (2) to record the revenue that has been earned during the period. Until the adjustment is made, both assets and revenues are understated. Consequently, profit and shareholders' equity will also be understated. As shown below, **an adjusting entry for accrued revenues results in an increase (a debit) to an asset account and an increase (a credit) to a revenue account**.

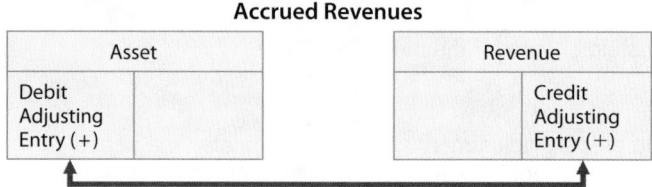

In October, Sierra Corporation earned $200 for advertising services that were not billed to clients before October 31. Because these services have not been billed, they have not yet been recorded.

Adjustment (5)
Accrued revenues—accounts receivable

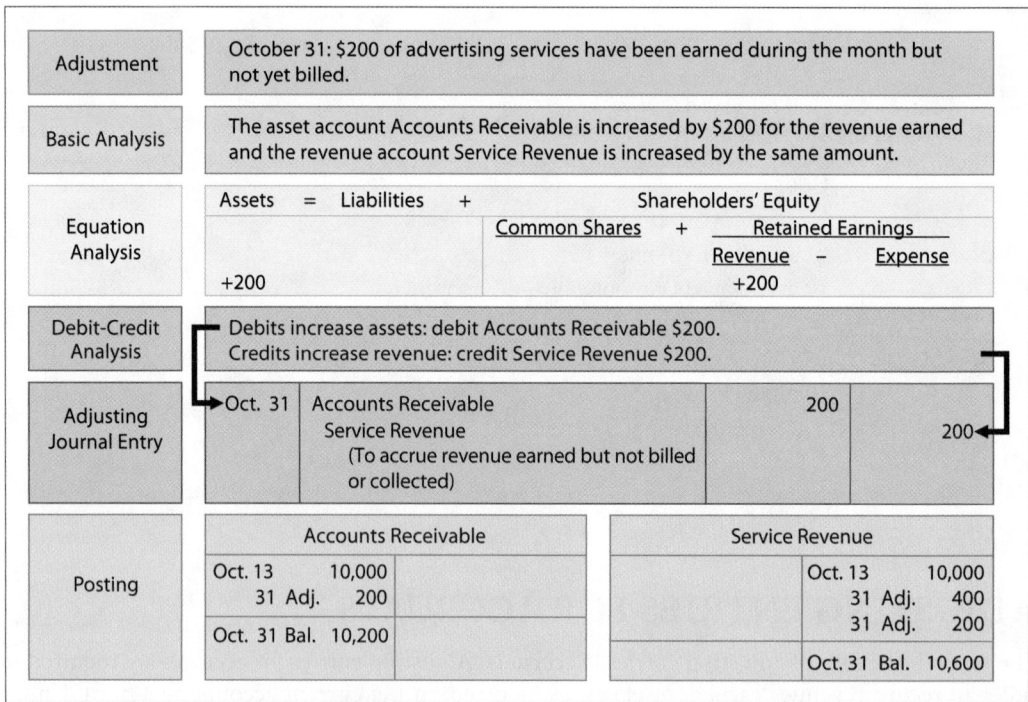

The asset Accounts Receivable shows that $10,200 is owed by clients at the statement of financial position date. The balance of $10,600 in Service Revenue represents the total revenue earned during the month. If the adjusting entry is not made, revenues and profit on the income statement, and assets and shareholders' equity on the statement of financial position, will be understated.

In the next accounting period, cash will be collected from clients for services provided in October, as well as for services provided in November. When this occurs, the entry to record the collection should recognize that $200 of the revenue was earned in October and has already been recorded in the October 31 adjusting entry and should not be re-recorded. For example, assume that $2,500 of revenue is collected from clients on November 6. Of this amount, $2,300 relates to services provided for cash in the first week of November, and $200 is for the services provided in October. The collection of cash from clients will be recorded as follows:

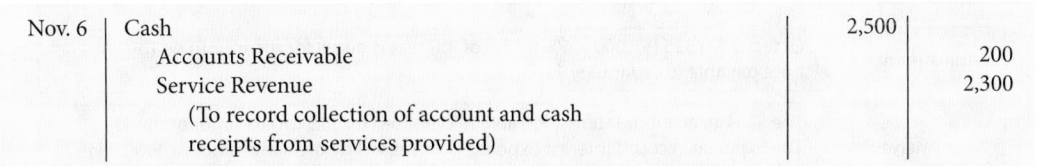

Nov. 6	Cash	2,500	
	Accounts Receivable		200
	Service Revenue		2,300
	(To record collection of account and cash receipts from services provided)		

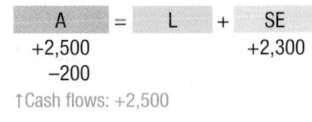

A	=	L	+	SE
+2,500				+2,300
−200				

↑Cash flows: +2,500

Some accountants prefer to reverse accrual entries at the beginning of a new accounting period rather than try to remember what entries had been made in the prior period. A reversing entry is made at the beginning of the next accounting period. It is the exact opposite of the adjusting entry made in the previous period. The accrual is reversed to ensure that revenue is not recorded a second time when the invoice is prepared. The preparation of reversing entries is an optional accounting procedure that is not a required step in the accounting cycle and will not be discussed here.

Accrued Expenses

Expenses incurred but not yet paid or recorded at the statement date need to be recorded. An expense is therefore adjusted by the amount of this accrued expense. Interest, rent, salaries, property tax, and income tax are common examples of **accrued expenses**. Accrued expenses result from the same factors as accrued revenues. In fact, an accrued expense on the books of one company is an accrued revenue to another company. For example, the $200 accrual of service revenue for Sierra Corporation discussed above is an accrued expense for the client that received the service.

Adjustments for accrued expenses are necessary to (1) record the obligations that exist at the statement of financial position date, and (2) recognize the expenses that apply to the current accounting period. Until the adjustment is made, both liabilities and expenses are understated. Consequently, profit and shareholders' equity are overstated. **An adjusting entry for accrued expenses results in an increase (debit) to an expense account and an increase (credit) to a liability account,** as follows:

Accrued Expenses

Expense		Liability	
Debit Adjusting Entry (+)		Credit Adjusting Entry (+)	

We now look in more detail at some specific types of accrued expenses, beginning with accrued interest.

Interest.   Sierra Corporation signed a three-month note payable for $5,000 on October 1. The note bears interest at an annual rate of 6%. Interest rates are always expressed in annual terms. The amount of the interest accumulation is determined by three factors: (1) the face value, or principal amount, of the note; (2) the interest rate, which is always expressed as an annual rate; and (3) the length of time that the note is outstanding (unpaid).

Interest is sometimes due monthly, and sometimes when the principal is due. In this instance, interest is due on the $5,000 note at its due date, three months in the future. The total interest due at that time will be $75 ($5,000 × 6% × $^3/_{12}$), or $25 for one month. Note that the time period is expressed as a fraction of a year.

The formula for calculating interest and how it applies to Sierra Corporation for the month of October are shown in Illustration 4-4.

Alternative Terminology
The process of accruing an expense is also referred to as accruing a payable as both are created in the same entry.

Helpful Hint
To make the illustration easier to understand, a simplified method of interest calculation is used. In reality, interest is calculated for part of a year by multiplying the annual interest amount by a ratio that uses the exact number of days in the interest period divided by the number of days in a year.

Illustration 4-4
Formula for calculating interest

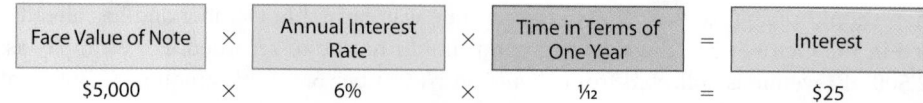

The accrual of interest at October 31 is reflected as follows:

Adjustment (6)
Accrued expenses—interest

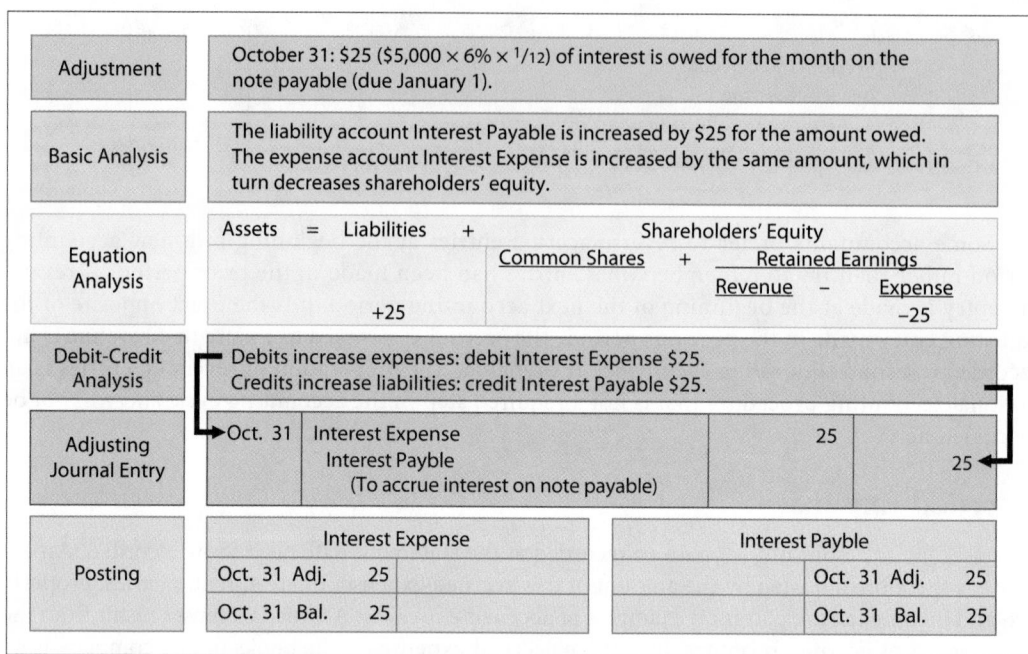

Interest Expense shows the interest charges for the month of October. The amount of interest owed at the statement date is shown in Interest Payable. It will not be paid until the note comes due on January 1, 2013. The Interest Payable account is used, instead of crediting Notes Payable, to disclose the two different types of obligations—interest and principal—in the accounts and statements. If this adjusting entry is not made, liabilities and interest expense will be understated and profit and shareholders' equity will be overstated.

Since this is a three-month note, Sierra will also need to make identical adjustments at the end of November and December to accrue for interest expense incurred in each of these months. After the three adjusting entries have been posted, the balance in Interest Payable will be $75 ($25 × 3). The following entry is made on January 1, 2013, when the note and interest are paid:

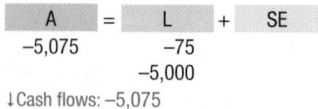

Jan. 1	Interest Payable	75	
	Note Payable	5,000	
	Cash		5,075
	(To record payment of note and interest)		

This entry does two things: (1) it eliminates the liability for Interest Payable that was recorded in the October 31, November 30, and December 31 adjusting entries; and (2) it eliminates the note payable. Notice also that the account Interest Expense is not included in this entry, because the full amount of interest incurred was accrued in previous months.

Salaries.   Some types of expenses, such as employee salaries, are paid for after the services have been performed and require an accrual adjustment when financial statements are prepared. For example, at its year end Western University, described in our feature story, accrues vacation pay and salary for approximately 3,500 faculty and staff.

At Sierra Corporation, salaries are paid every two weeks. Sierra's four employees were last paid on October 19 for the period October 8–19. The next payment of salaries will not occur until November 2. As shown on the calendar in Illustration 4-5, there are eight working days that remain unpaid for October (October 22–31).

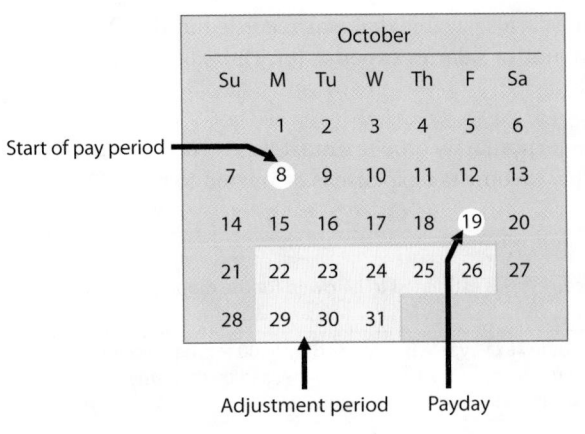

Illustration 4-5

Calendar showing Sierra Corporation's pay periods

At October 31, the salaries for these eight days (Monday, October 22, through Wednesday, October 31) represent an accrued expense and related liability for Sierra. As the four employees each receive a salary of $500 a week for a five-day workweek from Monday to Friday, or $100 a day, accrued salaries at October 31 are $3,200 (8 days × $100/day × 4 employees).

Adjustment (7)

Accrued expenses—salaries

Adjustment	October 31: $3,200 (8 × $100 × 4) of salaries have been earned by employees but not yet paid (due November 2).
Basic Analysis	The liability account Salaries Payable is increased by $3,200 for the amount owed. The expense account Salaries Expense is increased by the same amount, which in turn decreases shareholders' equity.

Equation Analysis

Assets	=	Liabilities	+	Shareholders' Equity		
				Common Shares	+	Retained Earnings
						Revenue – Expense
		+3,200				–3,200

Debit-Credit Analysis

Debits increase expenses: debit Salaries Expense $3,200.
Credits increase liabilities: credit Salaries Payable $3,200.

Adjusting Journal Entry

Oct. 31	Salaries Expense	3,200	
	Salaries Payable		3,200
	(To record accrued salaries)		

Posting

Salaries Expense			Salaries Payable	
Oct. 19	4,000			Oct. 31 Adj. 3,200
31 Adj.	3,200			Oct. 31 Bal. 3,200
Oct. 31 Bal.	7,200			

After this adjustment, the balance in Salaries Expense of $7,200 (18 days × $100/day × 4 employees) is the actual salary expense for October for the period October 8–31. The balance in Salaries Payable of $3,200 is the amount of the liability for salaries owed as at October 31. If the $3,200 adjustment for salaries is not recorded, Sierra's expenses and liabilities will be understated by $3,200. Profit and shareholders' equity will be overstated by $3,200.

At Sierra Corporation, salaries are payable every two weeks. Consequently, the next payday is November 2, when total salaries of $4,000 will again be paid. The payment consists of $3,200 of salaries payable at October 31 plus $800 of salaries expense for November 1–2 (2 days × $100/day × 4 employees). Therefore, the following entry is made on November 2:

Nov. 2	Salaries Payable (Oct. 22–31)	3,200	
	Salaries Expense (Nov. 1–2)	800	
	Cash		4,000
	(Paid salaries for Oct. 22–Nov. 2)		

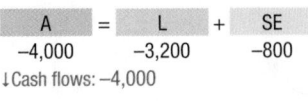

A	=	L	+	SE
–4,000		–3,200		–800

↓ Cash flows: –4,000

This entry eliminates the liability for salaries payable that was recorded in the October 31 adjusting entry and records the proper amount of salaries expense for Thursday, November 1, and Friday, November 2.

Income Tax.   For accounting purposes, corporate income tax must be accrued based on the current year's estimated profit. Sierra's monthly income tax expense is estimated to be $200.

▸Adjustment (8)
Accrued expenses—income tax

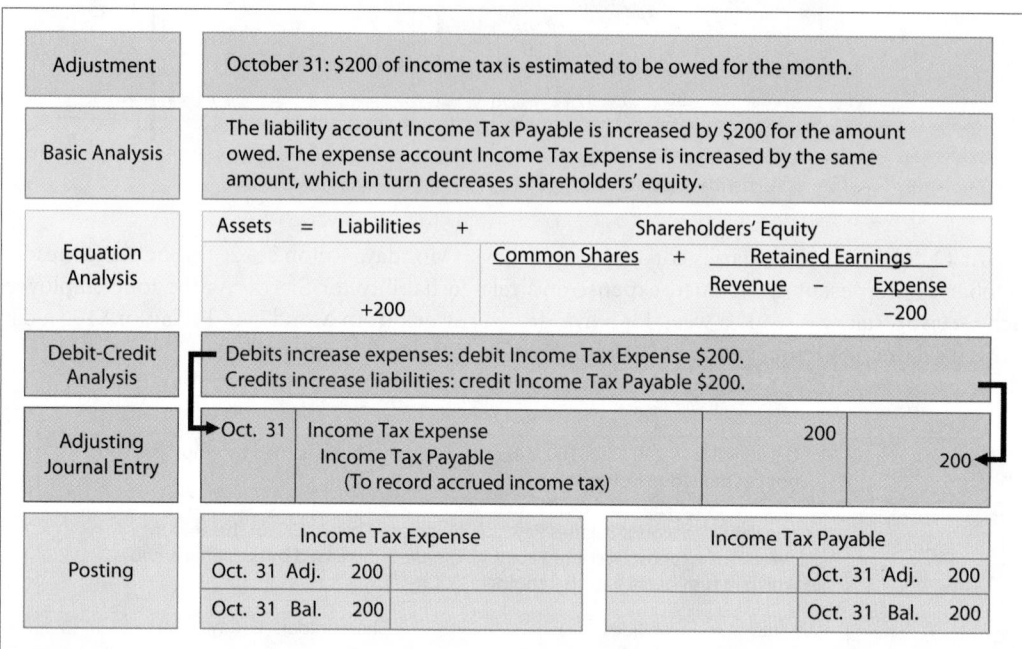

Corporations are required to pay corporate income tax in monthly instalments. The instalment payment is normally based on the income tax that was actually payable for the prior year. If the company commenced operations in the current year, as is the case with Sierra, or if there was no tax payable in the prior year, then no income tax instalment payments are required. However, the liability must still be accrued based on the current year's estimated profit.

If the adjustment for income tax is not recorded, Sierra's expenses and liabilities will be understated by $200 and its profit and shareholders' equity will be overstated by $200.

BEFORE YOU GO ON...

▸**Do It! Adjusting Entries for Accruals**

Micro Computer Services Inc. began operations on August 1, 2012, and management has decided to prepare monthly financial statements. The following information is for August:

1. Revenue earned but not yet billed or recorded for August totalled $1,100.

2. On August 1, the company borrowed $30,000 from a local bank on a one-year loan payable. The interest rate is 5% and interest is payable at maturity.

3. At August 31, the company owed its employees $800 in salaries that will be paid on September 1.

4. Estimated income tax payable for August totalled $275.

Prepare the adjusting entries needed at August 31.

Action Plan

• Remember that accruals are entries that initially record a revenue or expense; therefore, the adjustment pattern is different from the pattern for prepayments which adjust items that were recorded earlier.

- Adjusting entries for accrued revenues require a debit to a receivable account and a credit to a revenue account.
- Adjusting entries for accrued expenses require a debit to an expense account and a credit to a liability account.
- Recall that interest rates are always stated as an annual rate.

Solution

1.	Aug. 31	Accounts Receivable	1,100	
		Service Revenue		1,100
		(To accrue revenue earned but not billed or collected)		
2.	31	Interest Expense	125	
		Interest Payable		125
		(To record accrued interest: $30,000 \times 5\% \times \frac{1}{12}$)		
3.	31	Salaries Expense	800	
		Salaries Payable		800
		(To record accrued salaries)		
4.	31	Income Tax Expense	275	
		Income Tax Payable		275
		(To record accrued income taxes)		

SUMMARY OF BASIC RELATIONSHIPS

The two basic types of adjusting entries—prepayments and accruals—are summarized below. Take some time to study and analyze the adjusting entries. **Be sure to note that each adjusting entry affects one statement of financial position account and one income statement account.**

	Type of Adjustment	Reason for Adjustment	Accounts before Adjustment	Adjusting Entry
Prepayments	Prepaid expenses	Prepaid expenses, originally recorded in asset accounts, have been used.	Assets overstated; expenses understated	Dr. Expense Cr. Asset
	Unearned revenues	Unearned revenues, initially recorded in liability accounts, have been earned.	Liabilities overstated; revenues understated	Dr. Liability Cr. Revenue
Accruals	Accrued revenues	Revenues have been earned but not yet received in cash or recorded.	Assets understated; revenues understated	Dr. Asset Cr. Revenue
	Accrued expenses	Expenses have been incurred but not yet paid or recorded.	Expenses understated; liabilities understated	Dr. Expense Cr. Liability

It is important to understand that adjusting entries never involve the Cash account. In the case of prepayments, cash has already been received or paid and recorded in the original journal entry. The adjusting entry simply reallocates, or adjusts, amounts between a statement of financial position account (e.g., prepaid expenses or unearned revenues) and an income statement account (e.g., expenses or revenues). In the case of accruals, cash will be received or paid in the future and recorded then. The adjusting entry simply records the receivable or payable and the related revenue or expense.

SIERRA CORPORATION ILLUSTRATION

The journalizing and posting of the adjusting entries described in this chapter for Sierra Corporation on October 31 are summarized on the next page. As you review the general ledger, notice that the adjustments are highlighted in colour.

Note also that an account for retained earnings has been added in the general ledger. Because this is Sierra's first month of operations, there is no balance in the Retained Earnings account. Although accounts with a zero balance are not normally included in the trial balance, we have added it here to make it easier to prepare the statement of changes in equity in the next section. In addition, we will need to use this account again in the section on closing entries later in this chapter.

GENERAL JOURNAL

Date	Account Titles and Explanation	Debit	Credit
2012			
Oct. 31	Supplies Expense	1,500	
	Supplies		1,500
	(To record supplies used)		
31	Insurance Expense	50	
	Prepaid Insurance		50
	(To record insurance expired)		
31	Depreciation Expense	83	
	Accumulated Depreciation—Equipment		83
	(To record monthly depreciation)		
31	Unearned Revenue	400	
	Service Revenue		400
	(To record revenue earned)		
31	Accounts Receivable	200	
	Service Revenue		200
	(To accrue revenue earned but not billed or collected)		
31	Interest Expense	25	
	Interest Payable		25
	(To accrue interest on note payable)		
31	Salaries Expense	3,200	
	Salaries Payable		3,200
	(To record accrued salaries)		
31	Income Tax Expense	200	
	Income Tax Payable		200
	(To record accrued income tax)		

GENERAL LEDGER

	Cash						Notes Payable		
Oct.	1	10,000	Oct.	1	5,000			Oct. 1	5,000
	1	5,000		2	900			Oct. 31 Bal.	5,000
	2	1,200		3	600				
	30	10,000		19	4,000			Common Shares	
				26	500			Oct. 1	10,000
Oct.	31 Bal.	15,200						Oct. 31 Bal.	10,000

	Accounts Receivable						Retained Earnings		
Oct.	13	10,000	Oct.	30	10,000			Oct. 1	0
	31 Adj.	200						Oct. 31 Bal.	0
Oct.	31 Bal.	200							

	Supplies				Dividends		
Oct.	9	2,500	Oct 31 Adj. 1,500	Oct. 26	500		
Oct.	31 Bal.	1,000		Oct. 31 Bal.	500		

Prepaid Insurance			
Oct. 3	600	Oct 31 Adj.	50
Oct. 31 Bal.	550		

Service Revenue			
		Oct. 13	10,000
		31 Adj.	400
		31 Adj.	200
		Oct. 31 Bal.	10,600

Equipment			
Oct. 1	5,000		
Oct. 31 Bal.	5,000		

Salaries Expense			
Oct. 19	4,000		
31 Adj.	3,200		
Oct. 31 Bal.	7,200		

Accumulated Depreciation—Equipment			
		Oct. 31 Adj.	83
		Oct. 31 Bal.	83

Supplies Expense			
Oct. 31 Adj.	1,500		
Oct. 31 Bal.	1,500		

Accounts Payable			
		Oct. 9	2,500
		Oct. 31 Bal.	2,500

Rent Expense			
Oct. 2	900		
Oct. 31 Bal.	900		

Salaries Payable			
		Oct. 31 Adj.	3,200
		Oct. 31 Bal.	3,200

Depreciation Expense			
Oct. 31 Adj.	83		
Oct. 31 Bal.	83		

Income Tax Payable			
		Oct. 31 Adj.	200
		Oct. 31 Bal.	200

Insurance Expense			
Oct. 31 Adj.	50		
Oct. 31 Bal.	50		

Interest Payable			
		Oct. 31 Adj.	25
		Oct. 31 Bal.	25

Interest Expense			
Oct. 31 Adj.	25		
Oct. 31 Bal.	25		

Unearned Revenue			
Oct. 31 Adj.	400	Oct. 2	1,200
		Oct. 31 Bal.	800

Income Tax Expense			
Oct. 31 Adj.	200		
Oct. 31 Bal.	200		

The Adjusted Trial Balance and Financial Statements

After all adjusting entries have been journalized and posted, another trial balance is prepared from the general ledger accounts. This trial balance is called an **adjusted trial balance**. It shows the balances of all accounts at the end of the accounting period, including those that have been adjusted. The purpose of an adjusted trial balance is to prove the equality of the total debit balances and the total credit balances in the ledger after all adjustments have been made. Because the accounts contain all the data that are needed for financial statements, the adjusted trial balance is the main source for the preparation of financial statements.

STUDY OBJECTIVE 4
Describe the nature and purpose of the adjusted trial balance, and prepare one.

PREPARING THE ADJUSTED TRIAL BALANCE

The adjusted trial balance for Sierra Corporation presented in Illustration 4-6 has been prepared from the general ledger accounts shown in the previous section. Compare the adjusted trial balance with the unadjusted trial balance presented earlier in the chapter in Illustration 4-2. The amounts that are affected by the adjusting entries are highlighted in colour.

Illustration 4-6
Adjusted trial balance

	Debit	Credit
Cash	$15,200	
Accounts receivable	200	
Supplies	1,000	
Prepaid insurance	550	
Equipment	5,000	
Accumulated depreciation—equipment		$ 83
Accounts payable		2,500
Salaries payable		3,200
Income tax payable		200
Interest payable		25
Unearned revenue		800
Notes payable		5,000
Common shares		10,000
Retained earnings		0
Dividends	500	
Service revenue		10,600
Salaries expense	7,200	
Supplies expense	1,500	
Rent expense	900	
Depreciation expense	83	
Insurance expense	50	
Interest expense	25	
Income tax expense	200	
	$32,408	$32,408

PREPARING FINANCIAL STATEMENTS

Financial statements can be prepared directly from an adjusted trial balance. The relationships between the data in the adjusted trial balance of Sierra Corporation are presented in Illustration 4-7.

As Illustration 4-7 shows, the income statement is prepared from the revenue and expense accounts. The statement of changes in equity is prepared from the Common Shares, Retained Earnings, and Dividends accounts, and the profit (or loss) shown in the income statement. The statement of financial position is then prepared from the asset, liability, and shareholders' equity accounts. Shareholders' equity on the statement of financial position includes the ending common shares and retained earnings account balances as reported in the statement of changes in equity.

▶Illustration 4-7
Preparation of the financial statements from the adjusted trial balance

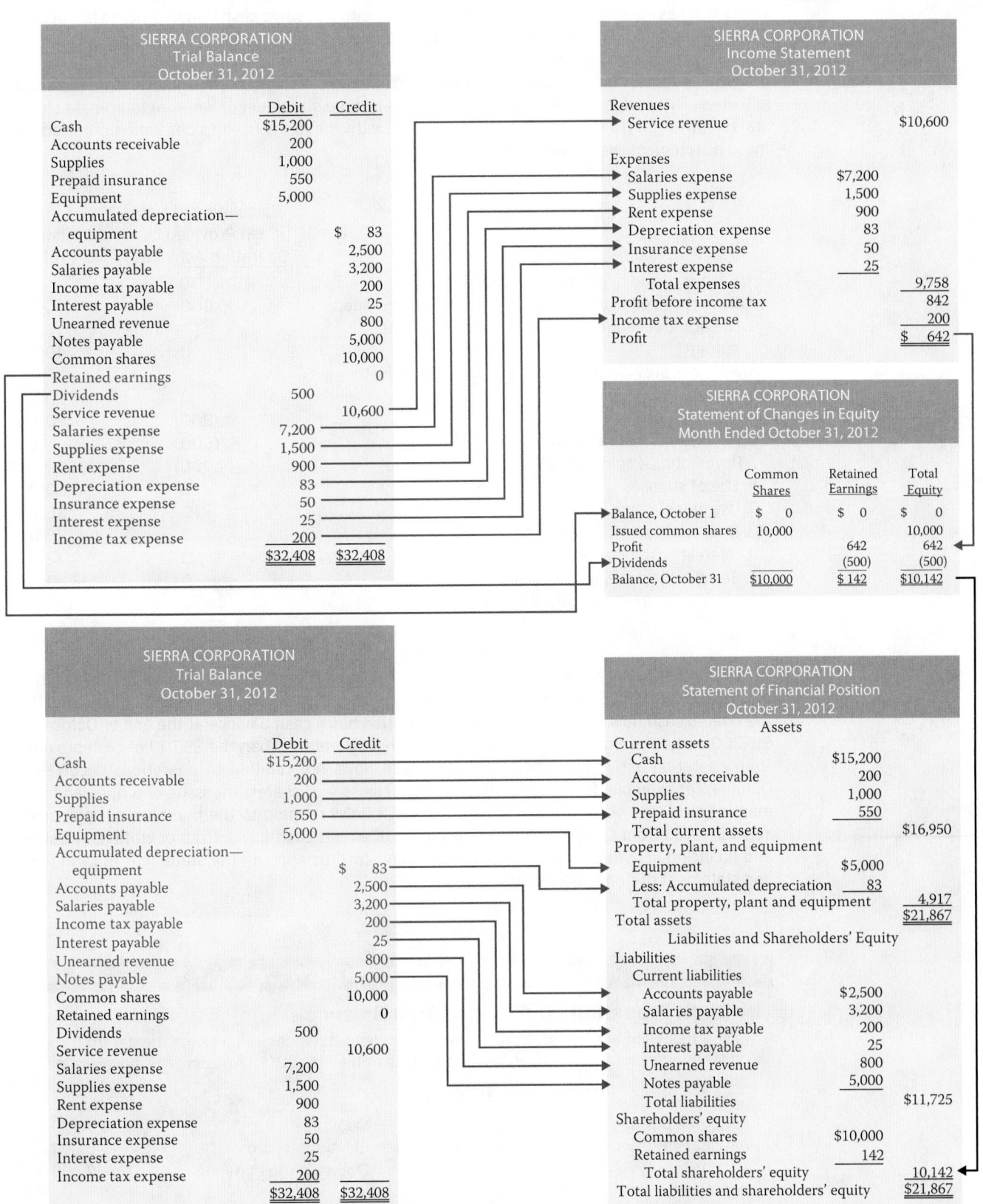

Keeping an Eye on Cash

We have just reviewed the preparation of the income statement, statement of changes in equity, and statement of financial position. However, we should not forget that a company, regardless of whether it has earned a profit or not, must operate with a positive cash flow in order to be successful. The statement of cash flows, which was introduced in Chapter 1 and will be covered in more detail in Chapter 13, allows users of the financial statements to understand whether the business is generating sufficient cash flows. One part of that statement measures cash flows from operating activities. This part is very similar to a cash basis income statement. If we were to prepare such a statement for Sierra Corporation and compare it with the items used to determine profit on the income statement, we would have the following:

	Calculation of Net Cash Provided by Operating Activities	Calculation of Profit
1. Cash received in advance from customer	$ 1,200	$ 0
2. Cash received from customers for services provided	10,000	10,000
3. Unearned revenue received in (1) that was later earned	0	400
4. Services provided on account recorded in adjusting entry	0	200
5. Payment of rent	(900)	(900)
6. Payment of insurance in advance	(600)	0
7. Payment of employee salaries	(4,000)	(4,000)
8. Use of supplies	0	(1,500)
9. Use of insurance	0	(50)
10. Depreciation	0	(83)
11. Interest cost incurred, but not paid	0	(25)
12. Salaries incurred, but not paid	0	(3,200)
13. Income tax incurred, but not paid	0	(200)
	$ 5,700	$ 642

Note that there is a difference between profit and cash flow provided by operating activities. This is very typical as a number of items in the income statement are recognized before or after the related cash flow. The reason Sierra Corporation has a cash balance at the end of October of $15,200 on its statement of financial position, which is greater than the $5,700 of cash provided from operating activities, is because other cash flows not relating to operations occurred in October. For example, financing cash flows from the sale of shares, the issue of a note, and payment of dividends occurred, as did investing cash flows relating to the purchase of equipment. You will recall from Chapter 1 that it is the total of all net cash flows—from operating, investing, and financing activities—that results in the ending cash balance on the statement of cash flows and statement of financial position.

BEFORE YOU GO ON...

▶Do It! Preparing an Adjusted Trial Balance

Listed below, in alphabetical order, are the account balances (after adjustments) from the general ledger of KS Services Limited at December 31, 2012. All accounts have normal balances.

Accounts payable	$ 4,660	Cash	$ 1,100
Accounts receivable	9,600	Common shares	5,000
Accumulated depreciation—equipment	5,200	Depreciation expense	2,600

Dividends	$ 1,000	Retained earnings	$ 3,700	
Equipment	20,800	Salaries expense	30,700	
Income tax expense	3,500	Salaries payable	710	
Interest expense	50	Service revenue	67,200	
Note payable	1,000	Supplies	180	
Other expenses	1,675	Supplies expense	475	
Rent expense	16,800	Unearned revenue	1,010	

Prepare the adjusted trial balance. Beside each account, indicate whether it should be included on the income statement (IS), statement of changes in equity (SCE), and/or statement of financial position (SFP).

Action Plan

- The title of the adjusted trial balance includes the name of the company, the type of trial balance, and the date.
- Accounts are listed in the same order as in a trial balance: assets, liabilities, shareholders' equity, revenues, and expenses. Assets and liabilities should be shown in current and non-current sections.
- Apply the normal balance rules and list the account balances in the correct columns.
- Ensure that the totals of the two columns are equal.

Solution

KS SERVICES LIMITED
Adjusted Trial Balance
December 31, 2012

	Debit	Credit	Statement
Cash	$ 1,100		SFP
Accounts receivable	9,600		SFP
Supplies	180		SFP
Equipment	20,800		SFP
Accumulated depreciation—equipment		$ 5,200	SFP
Note payable		1,000	SFP
Accounts payable		4,660	SFP
Salaries payable		710	SFP
Unearned revenue		1,010	SFP
Common shares		5,000	SFP & SCE
Retained earnings		3,700	SFP & SCE
Dividends	1,000		SCE
Service revenue		67,200	IS
Depreciation expense	2,600		IS
Rent expense	16,800		IS
Salaries expense	30,700		IS
Supplies expense	475		IS
Interest expense	50		IS
Other expenses	1,675		IS
Income tax expense	3,500		IS
	$88,480	$88,480	

the navigator

Closing the Books

In previous chapters, you learned that revenue and expense accounts and the dividends account are subdivisions of retained earnings, which is reported in the shareholders' equity section of the statement of financial position. Because revenues, expenses, and dividends relate to activities over a particular accounting period, they are considered **temporary accounts**. In contrast, all statement of financial position accounts are considered **permanent accounts** because their balances are carried forward into future accounting periods. For example, if a company has cash at the end of the year, that cash balance will also exist at the beginning of the next year, so it is a permanent account. Illustration 4-8 identifies the accounts in each category.

▸Illustration 4-8
Temporary and permanent accounts

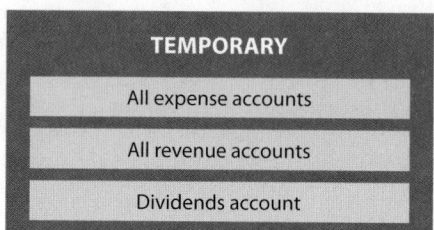
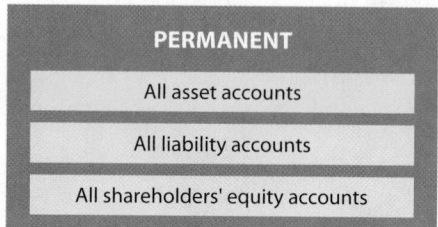

PREPARING CLOSING ENTRIES

At the end of the accounting period, the temporary account balances are transferred to the permanent shareholders' equity account Retained Earnings through the preparation of closing entries. **Closing entries** formally record in the general journal and the ledger the transfer of the balances in the revenue, expense, and dividends accounts to the Retained Earnings account thereby updating that account to its end-of-period balance. In Illustration 4-6, you will note that Retained Earnings has an adjusted balance of zero. Until the closing entries are made, the balance in Retained Earnings will be its balance at the beginning of the period. For Sierra, this is zero because it is Sierra's first year of operations. After closing entries are recorded and posted, the balance in Retained Earnings is the end-of-period balance. This ending account balance will now be the same as the balance reported at the bottom of the statement of changes in equity in the retained earnings column and on the statement of financial position in the shareholders' equity section.

In addition to updating Retained Earnings to its ending balance, closing entries produce a zero balance in each temporary account. As a result, these accounts are ready to accumulate data about revenues, expenses, and dividends for the next accounting period. Permanent accounts are not closed because the future benefits relating to assets and the obligations relating to liabilities still exist.

When closing entries are prepared, each revenue and expense account could be closed directly to Retained Earnings. This is common in computerized accounting systems where the closing process occurs automatically when it is time to start a new accounting period. For our purposes, this practice can result in too much detail in the Retained Earnings account. Accordingly, the revenue and expense accounts are first closed to another temporary account, **Income Summary**. Only the resulting total amount (profit or loss) is transferred from this account to the Retained Earnings account. Illustration 4-9 shows the closing process.

▸Illustration 4-9
Closing process

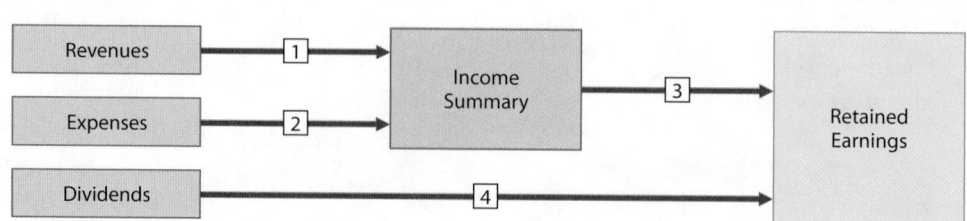

To prepare closing entries, four steps are necessary:

1. To close revenue accounts: Debit each individual revenue account for its balance, and credit Income Summary for total revenues. After this, all revenue accounts will have zero balances.
2. To close expense accounts: Debit Income Summary for total expenses, and credit each individual expense account for its balance. After this, all expense accounts will have zero balances.
3. To close Income Summary: Debit Income Summary for the balance in the account (or credit it if there is a loss), and credit (debit) Retained Earnings. After this, the Income Summary account balance is zero.
4. To close the Dividends account: Debit Retained Earnings for the balance in the Dividends account, and credit Dividends, thereby bringing the balance in this account to zero.

Do not close Dividends to the Income Summary account along with expenses. Dividends are not expenses and do not affect profit; they are a distribution of retained earnings.

Journalizing and posting closing entries is a required step in the accounting cycle. This step is done after financial statements have been prepared. Closing entries are generally recorded and posted only at the end of a company's annual accounting period.

Closing entries can be prepared directly from the general ledger or the adjusted trial balance. If we were to prepare closing entries for Sierra Corporation, we would likely use the adjusted trial balance presented earlier in the chapter in Illustration 4-6. In Sierra's case, all temporary accounts (Dividends, Service Revenue, and its seven different expense accounts) must be closed.

Even though Retained Earnings is not a temporary account, it will also be involved in the closing process. Remember that the Retained Earnings balance presented in the adjusted trial balance is the beginning balance, not the ending balance. This permanent account is not closed, but the profit (loss) and dividends for the period must be transferred into Retained Earnings through closing entries to update the account to its ending balance.

Sierra's general journal (showing the closing entries) and its general ledger (showing the posting of the closing entries) follow. In the general ledger on the following page, the notation "CE" has been used to indicate that the entry is a closing entry (CE).

GENERAL JOURNAL			
Date	Account Titles and Explanation	Debit	Credit
	Closing Entries		
2012	(1)		
Oct. 31	Service Revenue	10,600	
	Income Summary		10,600
	(To close revenue account)		
	(2)		
31	Income Summary	9,958	
	Salaries Expense		7,200
	Supplies Expense		1,500
	Rent Expense		900
	Depreciation Expense		83
	Insurance Expense		50
	Interest Expense		25
	Income Tax Expense		200
	(To close expense accounts)		
	(3)		
31	Income Summary	642	
	Retained Earnings		642
	(To close profit to retained earnings)		
	(4)		
31	Retained Earnings	500	
	Dividends		500
	(To close dividends to retained earnings)		

GENERAL LEDGER

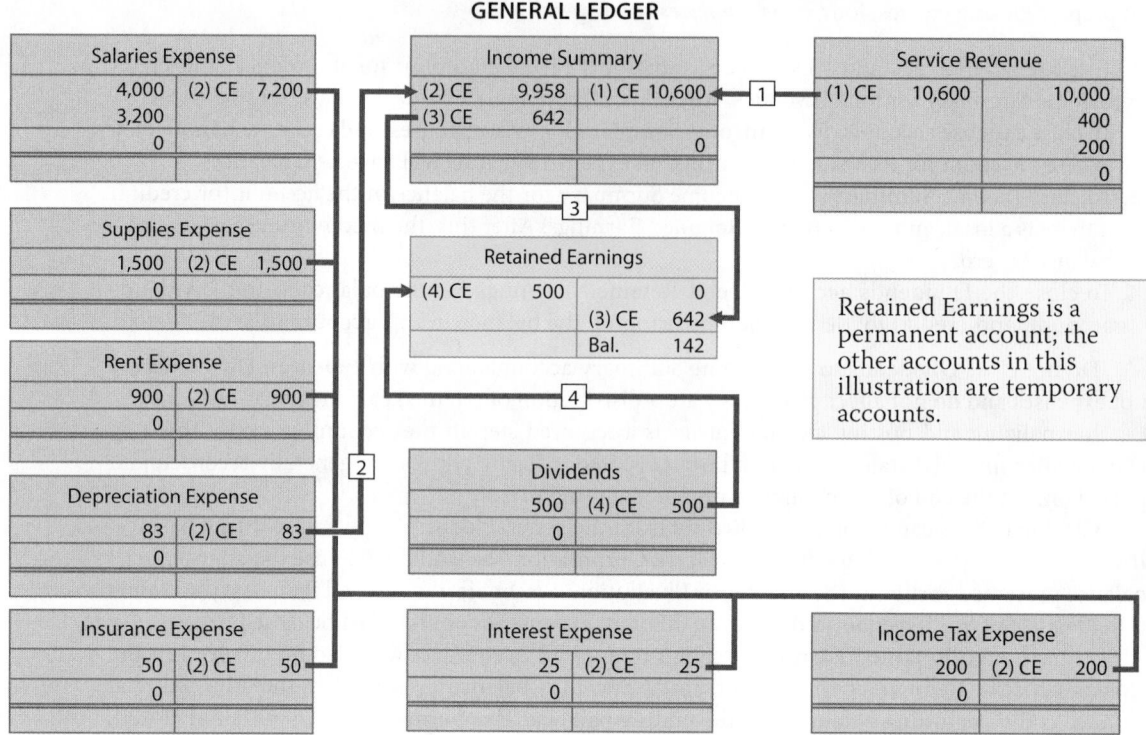

Retained Earnings is a permanent account; the other accounts in this illustration are temporary accounts.

Stop and check your work after the closing entries are posted:

1. The balance in the Income Summary account, immediately before the final closing entry to transfer the balance to the Retained Earnings account (entry 3 above), should equal the profit (or loss) reported in the income statement.
2. All temporary accounts (dividends, revenues, expenses, and income summary) should have zero balances.
3. The balance in the Retained Earnings account should equal the ending balance reported in the statement of changes in equity and statement of financial position.

ACCOUNTING MATTERS! *Management Perspective*

Closing the Books

Most companies work very hard to prepare adjusting and closing entries as soon as possible at year end so that their financial statements can be released to the public promptly. In his book *Fast Close: A Guide to Closing the Books Quickly*, author Steven Bragg advocates for companies to close their books quickly for several reasons. First of all, it gives management more time to analyze the company's performance and to share this analysis with investors, lenders, and other creditors. Second, being the first company in an industry to release financial information and trumpet its success can heighten investor interest in the company's shares, and third, it ensures that management develops efficient procedures for making accruals.

Source: Steven Bragg, Fast Close: A Guide to Closing the Books Quickly, John Wiley & Sons, Hoboken, NJ, 2009, pp. 1-2.

Other Comprehensive Income and Accumulated Other Comprehensive Income

As we know thus far, revenues and expenses are reported in the income statement. For companies reporting under IFRS, there may be some complex items that are similar to revenues and expenses but due to their nature, are not used to determine profit. Rather, they determine other comprehensive income, commonly abbreviated as OCI. Private companies reporting under ASPE do not recognize OCI. Items included in OCI are gains and losses relating to certain foreign currency transactions and certain adjustments made to reflect some assets and liabilities at their fair value. Many of the items reported in OCI will not be covered in this course. Nonetheless, you will see this balance often on the financial statements of public companies so you should have some familiarity with it.

ASPE

If a company has items that are recorded in OCI, the resulting amount would be added to profit to determine comprehensive income or total comprehensive income. For example, if Sierra Corporation had OCI of $300, this would be added to its profit of $642 to arrive at a total comprehensive income amount of $942. Comprehensive income can be reported in a combined statement of comprehensive income which includes both profit and other comprehensive income or in two separate statements: the income statement and statement of comprehensive income.

Just as revenues and expenses are closed out to Retained Earnings through the Income Summary account, OCI is closed out but not to Retained Earnings; rather it is closed out to various equity accounts that relate to each type of item that is shown in OCI. For example, if a foreign currency loss was shown in OCI, it would be closed out to a foreign currency equity account. Companies are encouraged to show each of these equity accounts separately but many combine them to form accumulated other comprehensive income (AOCI), an account reported in the statement of changes in equity and shareholders' equity section of the statement of financial position. We will learn more about items recorded in OCI in Chapters 9, 11, and 12.

PREPARING A POST-CLOSING TRIAL BALANCE

After all closing entries are journalized and posted, another trial balance, called a post-closing trial balance, is prepared from the ledger. We have learned about the unadjusted and adjusted trial balances so far. The last trial balance is the post-closing trial balance, which lists all permanent accounts and their balances after closing entries are journalized and posted. The purpose of this trial balance is to prove the equality of the permanent account balances that are carried forward into the next annual accounting period. Since all temporary accounts will have zero balances, the post-closing trial balance will contain only permanent—statement of financial position—accounts. Illustration 4-10 shows Sierra Corporation's post-closing trial balance.

SIERRA CORPORATION Post-Closing Trial Balance October 31, 2012		
	Debit	Credit
Cash	$15,200	
Accounts receivable	200	
Supplies	1,000	
Prepaid insurance	550	
Equipment	5,000	
Accumulated depreciation—equipment		$ 83
Accounts payable		2,500
Salaries payable		3,200
Income tax payable		200
Interest payable		25
Unearned revenue		800
Notes payable		5,000
Common shares		10,000
Retained earnings		142
	$21,950	$21,950

▶Illustration 4-10
Post-closing trial balance

SUMMARY OF THE ACCOUNTING CYCLE

Steps 1 to 4 of the accounting cycle were first introduced in Chapter 3. These steps and the steps introduced in this chapter are shown in Illustration 4-11. The cycle begins with the analysis of business transactions and ends with the preparation of a post-closing trial balance. The steps are done in sequence and are repeated in each accounting period.

Steps 1 to 3 may occur daily during the accounting period, as we learned in Chapter 3. Steps 4 to 7 are done on a periodic basis, such as monthly, quarterly, or annually. Steps 8 and 9, closing entries and a post-closing trial balance, are usually prepared only at the end of a company's annual accounting period.

▶ Illustration 4-11
Steps in the accounting cycle

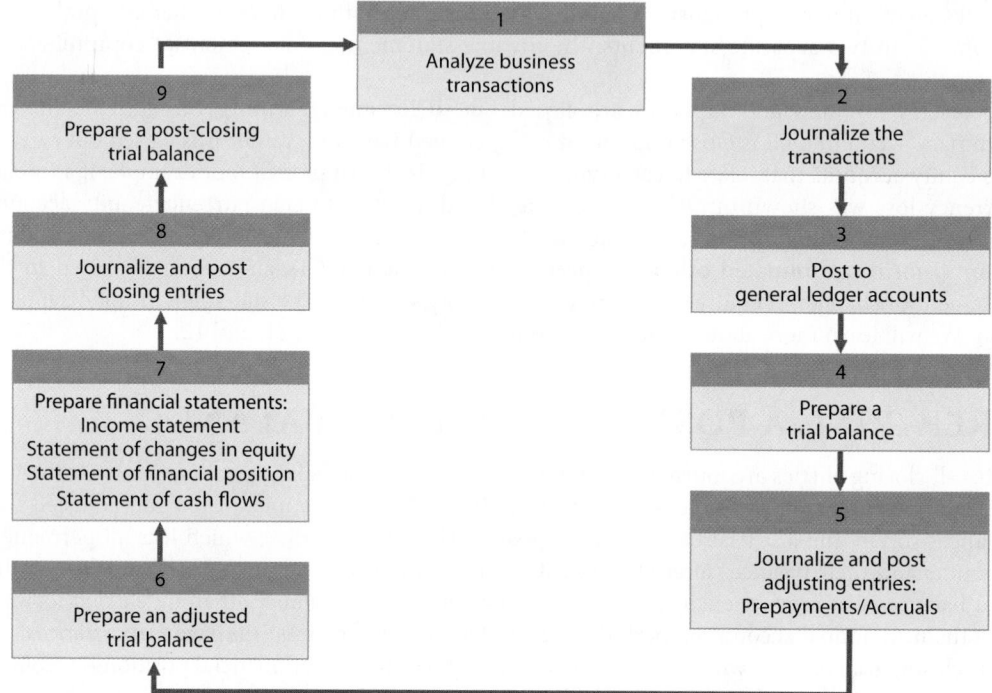

BEFORE YOU GO ON...

▶ Do It! Closing Entries

The adjusted trial balance for Nguyen Corporation shows the following selected accounts: Dividends $500; Common Shares $30,000; Retained Earnings $12,000; Service Revenue $18,000; Rent Expense $1,500; Supplies Expense $500; Salaries Expense $8,000; and Income Tax Expense $2,000. (a) Prepare the closing entries at December 31. (b) What is the balance in the Retained Earnings account after closing?

Action Plan

• Debit each individual revenue account for its balance and credit the total to the Income Summary account.
• Credit each individual expense account for its balance and debit the total to the Income Summary account.
• Stop and check your work: Does the balance in the Income Summary account equal the reported profit (loss)?
• If there is a profit, debit the balance in the Income Summary account and credit the amount to the Retained Earnings account (do the opposite if the result is a loss).
• Understand that the Retained Earnings amount on the adjusted trial balance is the balance at the beginning of the period.
• Credit the balance in the Dividends account and debit the amount to the Retained Earnings account. Do not close Dividends into the Income Summary account.

Solution

(a)

Date		Account	Debit	Credit
Dec.	31	Service Revenue	18,000	
		Income Summary		18,000
		(To close revenue account)		
	31	Income Summary	12,000	
		Rent Expense		1,500
		Supplies Expense		500
		Salaries Expense		8,000
		Income Tax Expense		2,000
		(To close expense accounts)		
	31	Income Summary	6,000	
		Retained Earnings		6,000
		(To close income summary)		
	31	Retained Earnings	500	
		Dividends		500
		(To close dividends)		

(b) Ending retained earnings is $17,500 ($12,000 + $6,000 − $500).

comparing
IFRS and ASPE

Key Differences	International Financial Reporting Standards (IFRS)	Accounting Standards for Private Enterprises (ASPE)
Frequency of adjusting entries	Public companies must release quarterly financial statements so adjusting entries have to be made at least quarterly, although many will record adjusting entries every month.	Private companies usually release financial statements to their banker, and shareholder(s), along with certain financial information to the Canada Revenue Agency on an annual basis so adjusting entries may be done only at year end, although many will record adjusting entries more frequently.
Terminology	The term *depreciation* refers to the allocation of the cost of depreciable tangible assets over their useful lives. The term *amortization* refers to the allocation of the cost of certain kinds of intangible assets over their useful lives.	The term *amortization* is used for the allocation of the cost of both depreciable tangible assets and certain kinds of intangible assets over their useful lives.
Closing entries	Other comprehensive income components are closed into accumulated other comprehensive income components.	Comprehensive income is not reported.

Are Environmental Costs a Liability?

In this chapter, you learned how to recognize revenue and expenses and how to allocate them to the appropriate accounting period. You also learned that companies, particularly public companies, must close their books quickly at the end of an accounting period and ensure they include all relevant transactions and estimates.

Many of the transactions we enter into create waste. Where does it go? What about all those outdated electronic items that are replaced by a newer, more effective models? Who pays for the mountains of waste? Old televisions and computers are loaded with lead, cadmium, mercury, and other toxic chemicals. If you have electronic equipment, you have a responsibility, and a probable cost, for disposing of it.

What about companies? Many have potential pollution or environmental-disposal problems. How do we fit these issues into the accounting equation? Are these costs and related liabilities something that companies should report? In November 2010, the Canadian Securities Administrators issued their Environmental Reporting Guidance that clarified their expectations regarding the continued disclosure of environmental matters by publicly traded companies.

Some Facts

- Almost all Canadian households have access to recycling programs. Households with curbside pickup were more likely to report that they recycled all their recyclable waste (55%) than households without curbside pickup (34%). The major reasons given for recycling were a sense of social responsibility (82%), a desire to reduce volumes of garbage sent to a landfill (75%), and a reduction in demand for raw materials (53%).
- In 2008, the latest year for which figures are available, the amount of waste created was equivalent to an average of 1,031 kilograms for each Canadian. About 25% of this was recyclable, and the rest was waste that went to a waste disposal facility. About one-third of this waste came from residential sources, the balance from non-residential. The biggest increase was in recyclables, electronic waste recycling, and plastic materials.
- Reusable shopping bags are now everywhere; for example, Loblaws has sold over 35 million of them, and Sobeys, 8 million. A recently published Statistics Canada report found that 93% of Canadian households used their own bags to carry groceries at some time and only 5% of Canadian households never used their own bags. But are reusable bags better than one-time-use plastic bags? Many of these bags are imported from China and also require significant amounts of energy in their manufacture; Sears, lululemon, and other companies have recalled their reusable bags because of unacceptable lead content.
- So how can you reduce the impact of your electronic waste? Statistics Canada has found that 36% of Canadian households have unwanted electronic devices to get rid of. Fortunately, 45% of these households took the electronics to a depot or drop-off centre, 22% of them donated or gave away the item, and only 5% of them returned the items to a retailer or supplier. Almost 30% still had the items somewhere in their household.

What Do You Think?

Should companies accrue environmental clean-up costs as liabilities on their financial statements?

YES— The Ontario Securities Commission says many public companies are providing poor disclosure of their environmental risks and liabilities. The Commission recommends that companies should put more information about their potential environmental costs and liabilities into their financial statements, including dollar valuations where possible. Investors appear to be asking for more and improved disclosure of environmental matters.

NO— The amounts are still too difficult to estimate. Reporting inaccurate estimates on the financial statements reduces their usefulness. Instead, why not charge the costs later, when the actual environmental clean-up or disposal occurs, at which time the company knows the actual cost?

Sources: Carly Weeks, "Bag Woes," *The Globe and Mail*, January 10, 2011, p. L. Statistics Canada, "Study: Recycling by Canadian Households, 2007," *The Daily*, July 7, 2010. Statistics Canada, "Waste Management Industry: Business and Government Sectors, 2008," *The Daily*, December 22, 2010. Statistics Canada, "Households and the Environment Survey, 2009," *The Daily*, March 9, 2011.

Summary of Study Objectives

1. **Explain when revenues and expenses are recognized and how this forms the basis for accrual accounting.** Revenue is recognized (recorded) when an increase in an asset or a decrease in a liability occurs. This happens when revenue is earned, regardless of when the related cash is received. Expenses are recognized (recorded) when a decrease in an asset or an increase in a liability occurs. This happens when the expense is incurred, regardless of when the related payment of cash occurs. By following revenue and expense recognition criteria, events are recorded in the period when they arise. This is known as the accrual basis of accounting, as opposed to the cash basis of accounting where events are recorded only when cash is affected.

2. **Describe the types of adjusting entries and when they are recorded and prepare adjusting entries for prepayments.** Adjusting entries for prepayments are required in order to record the portion of the prepayment that applies to the expense incurred or revenue earned in the current accounting period. Prepayments are either prepaid expenses or unearned revenues. The adjusting entry for prepaid expenses results in an increase (debit) to an expense account and a decrease (credit) to an asset account. The adjusting entry for unearned revenues results in a decrease (debit) to a liability account and an increase (credit) to a revenue account.

3. **Prepare adjusting entries for accruals and describe how adjusting entries affect the income statement and the statement of financial position.** Adjusting entries for accruals are required in order to record the revenues and expenses that apply to the current accounting period and that have not been recognized through daily entries. Accruals are either accrued revenues or accrued expenses. The adjusting entry for accrued revenues results in an increase (debit) to an asset account and an increase (credit) to a revenue account. The adjusting entry for accrued expenses results in an increase (debit) to an expense account and an increase (credit) to a liability account.

4. **Describe the nature and purpose of the adjusted trial balance, and prepare one.** An adjusted trial balance is a trial balance that shows the balances of all accounts at the end of an accounting period, including those that have been adjusted. The purpose of an adjusted trial balance is to show the effects of all financial events that have occurred during the accounting period. It also facilitates the preparation of the financial statements.

5. **Prepare closing entries and a post-closing trial balance.** One purpose of closing entries is to update the Retained Earnings account to its end-of-period balance. A second purpose is to make all temporary accounts (dividends, revenue, and expense accounts) begin the new period with a zero balance. To accomplish this, entries are made to close each individual revenue and expense account to a temporary summary account called Income Summary. The Income Summary account is then closed to the Retained Earnings account. The Dividends account is also closed to Retained Earnings. Only temporary accounts are closed. If the company has reported components of Other Comprehensive Income, these will be closed out into related equity accounts. When these equity accounts are added together, the total is called Accumulated Other Comprehensive Income.

   A post-closing trial balance lists only permanent accounts (i.e., statement of financial position accounts) and the balances that are carried forward to the next accounting period. The purpose of the post-closing trial balance, as with other trial balances, is to prove the equality of total debits and total credits.

Glossary

Accrual basis accounting An accounting basis in which transactions that change a company's financial statements are recorded in the periods in which the events occur, rather than in the periods in which the company receives or pays cash. (p. 166)

Accrued expenses Expenses incurred but not yet paid in cash that are recorded at the end of the period by an adjusting entry. (p. 177)

Accrued revenues Revenues earned but not yet received in cash that are recorded at the end of an accounting period by an adjusting entry. (p. 176)

Accumulated other comprehensive income (AOCI) The cumulative change in shareholders' equity that results from the gains and losses that bypass profit (recorded in OCI) but affect shareholders' equity. (p. 191)

Adjusted trial balance A list of accounts and their balances after all adjustments have been made. (p. 183)

Adjusting entries Journal entries made at the end of an accounting period because of the time period assumption and to ensure that the proper recognition of revenues and expenses has been adhered to. (p. 168)

Carrying amount (also known as book value) The difference between the cost of a depreciable asset and its accumulated depreciation. (p. 173)

Cash basis accounting An accounting basis in which revenue is recorded only when cash is received, and an expense is recorded only when cash is paid. (p. 166)

Closing entries   Entries at the end of an accounting period to transfer the balances of temporary accounts (revenues, expenses, and dividends) to the permanent shareholders' equity account Retained Earnings. (p. 188)

Comprehensive income   All changes in shareholders' equity during a period except those changes resulting from the sale or repurchase of shares, or from the payment of dividends. Comprehensive income includes (1) the revenues, expenses, gains, and losses included in profit; *and* (2) the gains and losses that bypass profit (recorded in OCI) but affect shareholders' equity. (p. 191)

Depreciation   (also known as amortization) The process of allocating the cost of a depreciable asset (e.g., property, plant, and equipment) over its useful life. (p. 171)

Expense recognition   The process of recording an expense when there is a decrease in future economic benefits related to a decrease in an asset or an increase in a liability in the course of ordinary activities that can be measured reliably. (p. 165)

Income summary   A temporary account used in closing revenue and expense accounts. (p. 188)

Other comprehensive income (OCI)   Gains and losses that affect shareholders' equity but are not shown in profit or loss. They relate to certain complex transactions such as revaluation adjustments for certain assets and liabilities and certain foreign currency gains and losses. (p. 191)

Permanent accounts   Statement of financial position accounts whose balances are carried forward to the next accounting period. (p. 188)

Post-closing trial balance   A list of permanent accounts and their balances after closing entries have been journalized and posted. (p. 191)

Prepaid expenses   Expenses that are generally paid in cash and recorded as assets before they are used or consumed. (p. 169)

Revenue recognition   The process whereby revenue is recorded when an increase in future economic benefits has occurred due to an increase in an asset or a reduction in a liability arising in the course of ordinary activities that can be measured reliably. (p. 165)

Straight-line method of depreciation   A depreciation method in which depreciation expense is calculated as the cost of an asset divided by its useful life. (p. 172)

Temporary accounts   Revenue, expense, and dividend accounts whose balances are transferred to Retained Earnings at the end of an accounting period. (p. 188)

Unearned revenues   Cash that is received before revenue is earned and is therefore recorded as a liability until it is earned. (p. 173)

Useful life   The length of service of a depreciable asset. (p. 171)

DECISION TOOLKIT—A SUMMARY

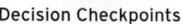 Decision Checkpoints	 Info Needed for Decision	Tools to Use for Decision	 How to Evaluate Results
At what point should the company record revenue?	Need to understand the nature of the company's business	Revenue should be recorded when earned. For a service company, revenue is earned when a service is performed. For a merchandising company, revenue is earned when the merchandise is sold.	Recognizing revenue too early overstates current period revenue; recognizing it too late understates current period revenue.
At what point should the company record expenses?	Need to understand the nature of the company's business	Expenses are recognized when assets are decreased or when liabilities are increased. Often expenses should "follow" revenues; that is, the effort (expense) should be matched with the result (revenue).	Recognizing expenses too early overstates current period expenses; recognizing them too late understates current period expenses.

the navigator

USING THE DECISION TOOLKIT

High Liner Foods Incorporated, headquartered in Lunenburg, Nova Scotia, is one of the world's largest frozen seafood processing company. A simplified version of High Liner Foods' January 1, 2011, year-end adjusted trial balance follows:

HIGH LINER FOODS INCORPORATED Adjusted Trial Balance January 1, 2011 (in thousands)		
	Debit	Credit
Cash	$ 806	
Accounts receivable	50,538	
Inventories	133,670	
Prepaid expenses	1,890	
Other current assets	3,090	
Land	2,202	
Buildings	37,099	
Computer and electronic equipment	6,040	
Machinery and equipment	69,430	
Accumulated depreciation—buildings		$ 16,662
Accumulated depreciation—computers and electronic equipment		4,375
Accumulated depreciation—machinery and equipment		34,905
Intangible assets and goodwill	64,209	
Other assets	3,360	
Bank loans (short-term)		42,423
Accounts payable and accrued liabilities		64,249
Income taxes payable		3,230
Current portion of long-term debt		5,398
Long-term debt		44,119
Other liabilities		13,432
Preferred shares		15,012
Common shares		64,551
Other shareholders' equity items	8,704	
Retained earnings, beginning of year		64,690
Dividends	11,824	
Sales		584,715
Cost of sales	466,797	
Selling, general, and administrative expenses	66,477	
Depreciation and amortization expense	8,357	
Other expenses	5,288	
Interest expense	5,237	
Other revenue		35
Income tax expense	12,778	
	$957,796	$957,796

Instructions

(a) Calculate profit for the year and retained earnings at January 1.
(b) Prepare a classified statement of financial position.
(c) Prepare the closing journal entries.

Solution

(a)

Calculation of profit:

Revenues		
Sales	$584,715	
Other revenue	35	
Total revenues	584,750	

Expenses

Cost of sales	$466,797	
Selling, general, and administrative expenses	66,477	
Depreciation expense	8,357	
Other expenses	5,288	
Interest expense	5,237	
Total expenses		552,156
Profit before income tax		32,594
Income tax expense		12,778
Profit		$ 19,816

Calculation of retained earnings:

Retained earnings, beginning of year	$ 64,690
Add: Profit	19,816
Less: Dividends	11,824
Retained earnings, end of year	$ 72,682

(b)

HIGH LINER FOODS INCORPORATED
Statement of Financial Position
January 1, 2011
(in thousands)

Assets

Current assets			
Cash			$ 806
Accounts receivable			50,538
Inventories			133,670
Prepaid expenses			1,890
Other current assets			3,090
Total current assets			189,994
Property, plant, and equipment			
Land		$ 2,202	
Buildings	$37,099		
Accumulated depreciation—buildings	16,662	20,437	
Computers and electronic equipment	$ 6,040		
Accumulated depreciation—computers and electronic equipment	4,375	1,665	
Machinery and equipment	$69,430		
Accumulated depreciation—machinery and equipment	34,905	34,525	58,829
Intangible assets and goodwill			64,209
Other assets			3,360
Total assets			$316,392

Liabilities and Shareholders' Equity

Liabilities			
Current liabilities			
Bank loans			$ 42,423
Accounts payable and accrued liabilities			64,249
Income tax payable			3,230
Current portion of long-term debt			5,398
Total current liabilities			115,300
Long-term debt			44,119
Other long-term liabilities			13,432
Total liabilities			172,851
Shareholders' equity			
Preferred shares		$15,012	
Common shares		64,551	
Other shareholders' equity items		(8,704)	
Retained earnings		72,682	
Total shareholders' equity			143,541
Total liabilities and shareholders' equity			$316,392

(continued)

(c)

Jan. 1	Sales	584,715	
	Other Revenue	35	
	Income Summary		584,750
1	Income Summary	564,934	
	Cost of Sales		466,797
	Selling, General, and Administrative Expenses		66,477
	Depreciation Expense		8,357
	Other Expenses		5,288
	Interest Expense		5,237
	Income Tax Expense		12,778
1	Income Summary	19,816	
	Retained Earnings		19,816
1	Retained Earnings	11,824	
	Dividends		11,824

the navigator

Comprehensive Do It!

The Blizzard Snow Removal Corporation in Inuvik was incorporated on October 1. At October 31, the trial balance shows the following balances for selected accounts:

Prepaid insurance	$ 1,800
Equipment	15,000
Bank loan payable	10,000
Unearned revenue	2,100
Service revenue	900

Analysis reveals the following additional data about these accounts:

1. Prepaid insurance is the cost of a one-year insurance policy, effective October 1.
2. The equipment is expected to have a useful life of five years.
3. The bank loan is payable in two years. Interest on this 6% loan is due on a monthly basis on the first day of each month.
4. Seven customers paid for the company's six-month, $300 snow removal service package beginning in October. These customers were serviced in October.
5. Snow removal services provided to other customers but not billed at October 31 totalled $1,500.
6. Income tax expense for October is estimated to be $100.

Instructions
Prepare the adjusting entries for the month of October.

> **Action Plan**
> • Note that adjustments are being made for only one month.
> • Before determining what adjustments are necessary, look at the amounts that are currently recorded in the accounts.
> • After making adjustments, check that the balances in each T account reflect what you meant them to (even when T accounts not required).
> • Show your calculations.
> • Select account titles carefully. Use existing titles wherever appropriate.

Solution to Comprehensive Do It!

GENERAL JOURNAL

Date	Account Titles and Explanation	Debit	Credit
	Adjusting Entries		
Oct. 31	Insurance Expense	150	
	Prepaid Insurance		150
	(To record insurance expired: $1,800 \times \frac{1}{12}$)		
31	Depreciation Expense	250	
	Accumulated Depreciation—Equipment		250
	(To record monthly depreciation: $15,000 \div 5 = \$3,000 \times \frac{1}{12}$)		
31	Interest Expense	50	
	Interest Payable		50
	(To accrue interest on the bank loan: $10,000 \times 6\% \times \frac{1}{12}$)		
31	Unearned Revenue	350	
	Service Revenue		350
	(To record revenue earned: $300 \div 6$ mos. $\times 7$)		
31	Accounts Receivable	1,500	
	Service Revenue		1,500
	(To accrue revenue earned but not billed or collected)		
31	Income Tax Expense	100	
	Income Tax Payable		100
	(To accrue income tax payable)		

the navigator

Self-Test, Brief Exercises, Exercises, Problems: Set A, and many more components are available for practice in WileyPLUS.

Self-Test Questions

Answers are at the end of the chapter.

(SO 1) 1. A company gave a price quote for a possible service to a client in February, performed the required service for the client in March, sent an invoice to the client in April, and received payment in May. In which month should the revenue be recognized?
(a) February
(b) March
(c) April
(d) May

(SO 1) 2. Adjusting entries are made to ensure that:
(a) expenses are recorded when they are incurred.
(b) revenues are recorded in the period in which they are earned.
(c) statement of financial position and income statement accounts have correct balances at the end of an accounting period.
(d) All of the above

(SO 2) 3. The unadjusted trial balance shows Supplies $1,350 and Supplies Expense $0. If $600 of supplies are on hand at the end of the period, the adjusting entry is:

(a) Supplies	600		
Supplies Expense		600	
(b) Supplies Expense	600		
Supplies		600	
(c) Supplies	750		
Supplies Expense		750	
(d) Supplies Expense	750		
Supplies		750	

(SO 2) 4. In August, the University of Regina received $6 million from students for tuition in advance relating to the four-month fall semester covering the period September 1 to December 31. When the cash was received, the Unearned Revenue account was credited for the full amount. What adjusting journal entry should the university record on September 30 when preparing financial statements for that month?

(a) Tuition Revenue | 1,500,000 |
Unearned Revenue | | 1,500,000

(b) Unearned Revenue | 1,500,000 |
Tuition Revenue | | 1,500,000

(c) Unearned Revenue | 4,500,000 |
Tuition Revenue | | 4,500,000

(d) Cash | 1,500,000 |
Tuition Revenue | | 1,500,000

(SO 3) 5. A bank has a three-month, $6,000 note receivable, issued on January 1 at an interest rate of 4%. Interest is due at maturity. What adjusting entry should the bank make at the end of January?

(a) Note Receivable | 20 |
Interest Revenue | | 20

(b) Interest Receivable | 60 |
Interest Revenue | | 60

(c) Cash | 20 |
Interest Revenue | | 20

(d) Interest Receivable | 20 |
Interest Revenue | | 20

(SO 3) 6. Kathy Kiska earned a salary of $400 since she was last paid in mid-September and will be paid on October 1. The adjusting entry for Kathy's employer at September 30 is:

(a) Salaries Expense | 400 |
Salaries Payable | | 400

(b) Salaries Expense | 400 |
Cash | | 400

(c) Salaries Payable | 400 |
Cash | | 400

(d) No entry is required.

(SO 4) 7. Which statement about the adjusted trial balance is *incorrect*?
(a) An adjusted trial balance proves the equality of the total debit balances and total credit balances in the ledger after all adjustments are made.
(b) The adjusted trial balance is the main source for the preparation of financial statements.
(c) The adjusted trial balance is prepared after the closing entries have been journalized and posted.
(d) The adjusted trial balance is prepared after the adjusting entries have been journalized and posted.

(SO 4) 8. The Retained Earnings balance in an unadjusted trial balance is $10,000. Profit for the period is $2,500 and dividends are $500. The Retained Earnings account balance in the adjusted trial balance will be:
(a) $9,500
(b) $10,000
(c) $12,000
(d) $12,500

(SO 5) 9. Which account will have a zero balance after closing entries have been journalized and posted?
(a) Service Revenue
(b) Supplies
(c) Unearned Revenue
(d) Accumulated Depreciation

(SO 5) 10. Which type of account will appear in the post-closing trial balance?
(a) Permanent accounts
(b) Temporary accounts
(c) Income statement accounts
(d) Cash flow statement accounts

Questions

(SO 1) 1. Why are adjusting entries needed? Include in your explanation a description of the recognition criteria that relate to adjusting the accounts.

(SO 1) 2. Tony Galego, a lawyer, accepts a legal engagement in March, does the work in April, bills the client $8,000 in May, and is paid in June. If Galego's law firm prepares monthly financial statements, when should it recognize revenue from this engagement? Why?

(SO 1) 3. In completing the engagement in question 2, Tony Galego incurs expenses that are specifically related to this engagement as follows: none in March, $4,500 in April, and none in May and June. How much expense should be deducted from revenues in the month(s) when the revenue is recognized? Why?

(SO 1) 4. The Higher Education University collects tuition in September for the fall term from registered students. The fall term runs from September to December. In what month(s) should the university recognize the revenue earned from tuition fees? Explain your reasoning.

(SO 1) 5. How does the cash basis of accounting differ from the accrual basis of accounting? Which basis gives more useful information for decision-making? Why?

(SO 2) 6. The name "prepaid expense" implies that this type of account is an expense account and belongs on an income statement. However, these accounts actually appear on the statement of financial position as assets. Explain why this is appropriate and why prepaid expense items need to be adjusted at the end of each period.

(SO 2) 7. The name "unearned revenue" implies that this type of account is a revenue account and belongs on an income statement. However, these accounts actually appear on the statement of financial position as liabilities. Explain why this is appropriate and why unearned revenue items require adjustment at the end of each period.

(SO 2) 8. "Depreciation is a process of valuation that results in the reporting of the fair value of the asset." Do you agree? Explain.

(SO 2) 9. Explain the difference between (a) depreciation expense and accumulated depreciation, and (b) cost and carrying amount.

(SO 2) 10. What is a contra asset account? Why do we use a contra asset account to record accumulated depreciation instead of directly reducing the depreciable asset account?

(SO 2, 3) 11. The trial balance of Hoi Inc. includes the statement of financial position accounts listed below. Identify the accounts that might require adjustment. For each account that requires adjustment, indicate (1) the type of adjusting entry (prepaid expenses, unearned revenues, accrued revenues, or accrued expenses) and (2) the related account in the adjusting entry.
(a) Accounts Receivable
(b) Prepaid Insurance
(c) Rent Receivable
(d) Accumulated Depreciation
(e) Interest Payable
(f) Income Tax Payable
(g) Unearned Revenue

(SO 2, 3) 12. "An adjusting entry may affect more than one statement of financial position or income statement account." Do you agree? Why or why not?

(SO 2, 3) 13. Adjusting entries for prepayments *always* include the Cash account, and adjusting entries for accruals *never* include the Cash account. Do you agree? Why or why not?

(SO 3) 14. Reactor Corp. has incurred utility costs for the month of December, but the utility company does not send out its bills until the 15th of the following month. Reactor does not plan on recording the utility costs until it receives the bill on January 15. Should Reactor record in December this cost that has been incurred but will only be billed and paid in January? Why or why not? If you believe that this cost should be recorded in December, identify the date of the entry and which accounts should be debited and credited.

(SO 4) 15. Why is it appropriate to prepare financial statements directly from an adjusted trial balance but not from an unadjusted trial balance?

(SO 2, 3, 5) 16. How do adjusting journal entries differ from transaction entries recorded on a daily basis? Although adjusting entries are usually dated on the last day of the accounting period, are they actually recorded on that day? How do closing journal entries differ from adjusting journal entries?

(SO 4, 5) 17. Explain how an unadjusted trial balance, adjusted trial balance, and post-closing trial balance differ. How often should each one be prepared?

(SO 4) 18. Why is the retained earnings balance on the unadjusted trial balance the same amount that appears on the adjusted trial balance? Why is the retained earnings balance on an adjusted trial balance different from the amount that appears on the post-closing trial balance?

(SO 4, 5) 19. What items are disclosed on a post-closing trial balance? Why are the financial statements prepared using an adjusted trial balance instead of the post-closing trial balance? If we took the account balances relating to only the statement of financial position accounts on an unadjusted trial balance, would the total of the accounts with debit balances equal the total of the accounts with credit balances? Why or why not?

(SO 5) 20. What are the two reasons for recording closing entries?

(SO 5) 21. Why is the account Dividends not closed with the expense accounts? Why is a separate closing entry required for this account?

(SO 5) 22. Identify whether the Income Summary account would be debited or credited when making each of the four closing entries, assuming the company has (a) profit for the year, and (b) a loss for the year.

(SO 5) 23. Which steps in the accounting cycle may be done daily, which steps are done on a periodic basis (monthly or quarterly), and which steps are usually done only at the company's fiscal year end?

(SO 5) 24. What are the two major components of comprehensive income? How does each component affect closing entries?

Brief Exercises

Indicate impact of transaction on cash and profit.
(SO 1)

BE4–1 Transactions that affect profit do not necessarily affect cash. Identify the impact, if any, of each of the following transactions on cash and profit. The first transaction has been completed for you as an example.

	Cash	Profit
(a) Purchased supplies for cash, $100.	−$100	$0

(b) Made an adjusting entry to record use of $75 of the supplies in (a).
(c) Performed services on account, $1,000.
(d) Received $800 from customers in payment of their accounts in (c).
(e) Purchased equipment for cash, $5,000.
(f) Made an adjusting entry to record depreciation of equipment, $1,000.
(g) Obtained a $1,000 bank loan.
(h) Made an adjusting entry to accrue interest on the loan in (g), $50.

(i) Received $500 cash for services to be provided in the future.

(j) Made an adjusting entry relating to the amount received in (i) above to show that $200 of the services had now been provided.

(k) Made an adjusting entry to record utilities incurred but not yet paid, $250.

BE4–2 Data are provided for two independent situations. Calculate the missing amount for each company.

Calculate missing data for supplies. (SO 2)

	A Ltd.	B Ltd.
Supplies on hand, beginning of year	$ 675	$ 640
Supplies purchased during the year	1,695	2,825
Supplies on hand, end of year	225	(b)
Supplies used during the year	(a)	2,715

BE4–3 Sain Advertising Ltd.'s opening trial balance on January 1 shows Supplies $1,500. On May 1, the company purchased additional supplies for $4,800 on credit. On December 31, there are $2,300 of supplies on hand.

(a) Prepare the journal entry to record the purchase of supplies on May 1.

(b) Calculate the amount of supplies used during the year.

(c) Prepare the adjusting entry required at December 31.

(d) Using T accounts, enter the opening balances in the affected accounts, post the journal entries in (a) and (c), and indicate the adjusted balance in each account.

Prepare and post transaction and adjusting entries for supplies. (SO 2)

BE4–4 On January 2, 2012, Cretien Corporation purchased a delivery truck for $40,000 cash. The company uses straight-line depreciation and estimates that the truck will have a five-year useful life. The company has a December 31 year end and adjusts its accounts annually.

(a) Prepare the journal entry to record the purchase of the delivery truck on January 2, 2012.

(b) Prepare the adjusting entries required on December 31, 2012 and 2013.

(c) Indicate the statement of financial position presentation of the delivery truck at December 31, 2012 and 2013.

(d) Indicate the income statement presentation of the depreciation expense for the years ended December 31, 2012 and 2013.

Prepare transaction and adjusting entries for depreciation; show statement presentation. (SO 2)

BE4–5 On June 1, 2012, Bere Ltd. pays $6,000 to Marla Insurance Corp. for a one-year insurance policy. Both companies have fiscal years ending December 31 and adjust their accounts annually.

(a) Record the June 1, 2012, transaction on the books of (1) Bere and (2) Marla.

(b) Calculate the amount of insurance that expired during 2012 and the unexpired cost at December 31, 2012.

(c) Prepare the adjusting entry required on December 31 by (1) Bere and (2) Marla.

(d) Post the above entries and indicate the adjusted balance in each account.

Prepare and post transaction and adjusting entries for insurance. (SO 2, 3)

BE4–6 The total weekly payroll for Classic Auto Repairs Ltd. is $5,000 ($1,000 per day). The payroll is paid every Monday for employee salaries earned during the previous five-day workweek (Monday through Friday, inclusive). Salaries were last paid on Monday, December 24. This year the company's year end, December 31, falls on a Monday. Salaries will be paid next on Monday, January 7, at which time employees will receive pay for the five days (including the New Year's holiday). Prepare the journal entries to record each of the following:

(a) Payment of the salaries on December 31

(b) The adjustment to accrue salaries at December 31

(c) Payment of the salaries on January 7

Prepare transaction and adjusting entries for salaries. (SO 3)

BE4–7 On July 1, 2012, Nakhooda Company purchased a truck for $40,000, paying $10,000 cash and signing a 6% note payable for the remainder. The note's interest and principal are due on January 1, 2013. Prepare the journal entries to record each of the following:

(a) The purchase of the truck on July 1, 2012

(b) The accrual of interest at year end, December 31, 2012, assuming interest has not previously been accrued

(c) Repayment of the interest and the note on January 1, 2013

Prepare transaction and adjusting entries for interest. (SO 3)

BE4–8 Fill in the missing amounts in the following income tax schedule for the Ducharme Corporation. Assume that 2010 was the company's first year of operations.

Determine missing amounts for income taxes. (SO 3)

	2010	2011	2012
Income tax expense	$2,600	$3,600	$ (c)
Income tax payable, end of year	(a)	500	700
Income tax paid	2,200	(b)	4,200

Prepare transaction
and adjusting entries
for accrued revenue.
(SO 3)

BE4–9   Zieborg Maintenance Corp. has a $375 monthly contract with Crispy Treat Inc. for general maintenance services. Zieborg invoices Crispy on the first of the month for services that it provided in the previous month. Crispy must then pay for these services by the 10th of the following month (i.e., the month after the month when Crispy is billed).
(a) Zieborg has a November 30 fiscal year end. Why will it need to prepare an adjusting entry on November 30?
(b) Prepare Zieborg's adjusting entry on November 30.
(c) Will Zieborg need to record a journal entry on December 1 when it invoices Crispy for services provided in November? Why or why not?
(d) Zieborg receives $375 from Crispy on January 9 for services provided in November. Prepare Zieborg's journal entry.

Determine missing
amounts.
(SO 4)

BE4–10   The unadjusted and adjusted trial balances for Oromocto Development Corporation at February 28, 2012, are as follows:

	Trial Balance		Adjusted Trial Balance	
	Debit	Credit	Debit	Credit
Cash	$ 8,000		$ 8,000	
Accounts receivable	26,000		(d)	
Supplies	(a)		1,000	
Prepaid insurance	6,000		(e)	
Equipment	22,000		22,000	
Accumulated depreciation—equipment		$ 1,000		(h)
Accounts payable		13,000		$13,000
Salaries payable		0		3,000
Income tax payable		0		(i)
Common shares		20,000		20,000
Retained earnings		(c)		21,000
Dividends	(b)		2,000	
Fees earned		30,000		32,000
Salary expense	7,000		(f)	
Rent expense	6,000		6,000	
Depreciation expense	0		(g)	
Insurance expense	0		3,500	
Supplies expense	0		4,000	
Utilities expense	2,400		2,400	
Miscellaneous expense	600		600	
Income tax expense	0		300	
Totals	$85,000	$85,000	$94,700	$94,700

The company adjusts its accounts annually. Selected data for the year-end adjustments are as follows:

1. Revenue earned but not yet billed, $2,000
2. Salaries incurred but not yet paid, $3,000
3. Depreciation expense, $4,400
4. Insurance expired, $3,500
5. Supplies used, $4,000
6. Estimated income tax expense, $300

Determine the missing amounts.

Prepare financial
statements.
(SO 4)

BE4–11   Refer to the data in BE4–10 for Oromocto Development Corporation. During the year, common shares were issued for $5,000 cash. Prepare an income statement, statement of changes in equity, and statement of financial position for the year.

Prepare closing entries.
(SO 5)

BE4–12   Refer to the data in BE4–10 for Oromocto Development Corporation. Prepare the closing journal entries.

Prepare and post
closing entries.
(SO 5)

BE4–13   The income statement for Regina Cleaning Services Ltd. for the year ended November 30 shows Salaries Expense $90,000; Repairs and Maintenance Expense $25,000; and Income Tax Expense $10,000. The statement of changes in equity shows an opening balance for Retained Earnings of $30,000, an ending balance for Retained Earnings of $55,000, and Dividends $10,000.
(a) Information provided above does not include the Cleaning Revenue account—the company's only source of revenue. Determine the amount of this revenue earned during the year.
(b) Prepare the closing journal entries.
(c) Using T accounts, post the closing entries, and determine the ending balances.

Identify post-closing
trial balance accounts.
(SO 5)

BE4–14   The following selected accounts appear in the adjusted trial balance for Atomic Energy of Canada Limited (AECL). Identify which accounts would be included in AECL's post-closing trial balance.
(a) Trade and Other Receivables
(b) Financial Expenses

(c) Intangible Assets
(d) Inventory
(e) Depreciation Expense
(f) Trade and Other Payables
(g) Cost of Sales
(h) Research and Development Expenses
(i) Accumulated Depreciation
(j) Revenue from Nuclear Laboratories

Exercises

E4-1 The following independent situations require professional judgement to determine when to recognize revenue from the transactions:

(a) WestJet Airlines sells you a non-refundable airline ticket in September for your flight home at Christmas.
(b) Leon's Furniture sells you a home theatre on a "no money down, no interest, and no payments for one year" promotional deal.
(c) The Toronto Blue Jays sell season tickets to games in the Rogers Centre on-line. Fans can purchase the tickets at any time, although the season only begins officially in April and ends in October.
(d) The RBC Financial Group loans you money in August. The loan and the interest are repayable in full in November.
(e) In August, you order a sweater from Sears using its on-line catalogue. The sweater arrives in September and you charge it to your Sears credit card. You receive and pay the Sears bill in October.

Identify point of revenue recognition. (SO 1)

Instructions
Identify when revenue should be recognized in each situation.

E4-2 In its first year of operations, Athabasca Corp. earned $52,000 in service revenue. Of that amount, $8,000 was on account and the remainder, $44,000, was collected in cash from customers.

The company incurred operating expenses of $31,000, of which $27,500 was paid in cash. At year end, $3,500 was still owing on account. In addition, Athabasca prepaid $2,000 for insurance coverage that covered the last half of the first year and the first half of the second year. Athabasca expects to owe $4,200 of income tax when it files its corporate income tax return after year end.

Calculate profit on cash and accrual bases. (SO 1)

Instructions
(a) Calculate the first year's profit under the accrual basis of accounting.
(b) Calculate the first year's profit under the cash basis of accounting.
(c) Which basis of accounting (cash or accrual) gives the most useful information for decision makers?

E4-3 Action Quest Games Inc. initially records all prepaid costs as assets and all revenue collected in advance as liabilities. The company adjusts its accounts annually. The following information is available for the year ended December 31, 2012:

1. Purchased a one-year insurance policy on June 1, for $1,800 cash.
2. Paid $6,500 on August 31 for five months' rent in advance.
3. On September 14, received $3,600 cash from a corporation to sponsor a game each month for the most improved students. The amount is to be distributed evenly over nine times of playing the game, once on the first Friday of each month starting in October. (*Hint*: Use the Unearned Revenue account.)
4. Signed a contract for cleaning services starting December 1, for $1,000 per month. Paid for the first two months on November 30.
5. On December 5, received $1,500 in advance from a gaming club. Determined that on December 31, $475 of these games had not yet been played (*Hint*: Use the Sponsorship Revenue account.).

Prepare and post transaction and adjusting entries for prepayments. (SO 2)

Instructions
(a) For each of the above transactions, prepare the journal entry to record the initial transaction.
(b) For each of the above transactions, prepare the adjusting journal entry that is required on December 31, 2012.
(c) Post the journal entries in parts (a) and (b) to T accounts and determine the final balance in each account. (*Note*: Posting to the Cash account is not required.)

E4-4 Action Quest Games Inc. owns the following long-lived assets:

Asset	Date Purchased	Cost	Estimated Useful Life
Equipment	July 1, 2010	$12,000	3 years
Vehicles	Jan. 1, 2009	28,000	7 years
Furniture	Jan. 1, 2012	10,000	5 years

Prepare adjusting entries for depreciation; calculate carrying amount. (SO 2)

Instructions

(a) Prepare depreciation adjusting entries for Action Quest Games for the year ended December 31, 2012, assuming the company adjusts its accounts annually.

(b) For each asset, calculate its accumulated depreciation and carrying amount at December 31, 2012.

Prepare adjusting and subsequent entries for accruals.
(SO 3)

E4–5   Action Quest Games Inc. has the following information available for accruals that must be recorded for the year ended December 31, 2012. The company adjusts its accounts annually.

1. The December utility bill for $425 was unrecorded on December 31. Action Quest paid the bill on January 11, 2013.
2. Action Quest is open seven days a week and employees are paid a total of $3,500 every Monday for a seven-day (Monday–Sunday) workweek. December 31, 2012, is a Monday, so employees will have worked one day (Monday, December 31) before the year end that they have not been paid for by year end. Employees will be paid next on January 7, 2013.
3. Action Quest has a 5% bank loan payable in two years to its bank for $45,000. Interest is payable on the first day of each month.
4. Action Quest receives a commission from Pizza Shop next door for all pizzas sold to customers using Action Quest's facility. The amount owing for December is $300, which Pizza Shop will pay on January 4, 2013.
5. Action Quest sold some equipment on November 1, 2012, in exchange for a 6%, $6,000 note receivable. The principal and interest are due on February 1, 2013.

Instructions

(a) For each situation, prepare the adjusting entry required at December 31, 2012. Round any calculations to the nearest dollar.

(b) For each situation, prepare the journal entry to record the subsequent cash transaction in 2013.

Prepare adjusting entries.
(SO 2, 3)

E4–6   On March 31, 2012, Easy Rental Agency Inc.'s trial balance included the following unadjusted account balances. The company's year end is December 31 and it adjusts its accounts quarterly.

	Debit	Credit
Prepaid insurance	$14,400	
Supplies	2,800	
Equipment	21,600	
Accumulated depreciation—equipment		$ 5,400
Unearned revenue		9,600
Loan payable, due December 31, 2012		20,000
Rent revenue		30,000
Salaries expense	14,000	

An analysis of the accounts shows the following:

1. The equipment, which was purchased on January 1, 2011, is estimated to have a useful life of four years.
2. One-third of the unearned rent revenue is still unearned at the end of the quarter.
3. The loan payable has an interest rate of 6%. Interest is paid monthly on the first of each following month and was last paid March 1, 2012.
4. Supplies on hand total $850 at March 31.
5. The one-year insurance policy was purchased for $14,400 on January 1, 2012.
6. Income tax is estimated to be $2,200 for the quarter.

Instructions

Prepare the quarterly adjusting entries required at March 31, 2012.

Analyze adjusted data.
(SO 2, 3, 4)

E4–7   A partial adjusted trial balance follows for Nolet Ltd. The company's fiscal year end is December 31 and it makes adjustments monthly.

<table>
<tr><td colspan="3" align="center">NOLET LTD.
Adjusted Trial Balance
January 31, 2012</td></tr>
<tr><td></td><td>Debit</td><td>Credit</td></tr>
<tr><td>Supplies</td><td>$ 700</td><td></td></tr>
<tr><td>Prepaid insurance</td><td>1,600</td><td></td></tr>
<tr><td>Equipment</td><td>7,200</td><td></td></tr>
<tr><td>Accumulated depreciation—equipment</td><td></td><td>$3,660</td></tr>
<tr><td>Income tax payable</td><td></td><td>800</td></tr>
<tr><td>Unearned revenue</td><td></td><td>750</td></tr>
<tr><td>Service revenue</td><td></td><td>2,000</td></tr>
</table>

	Debit	Credit
Depreciation expense	$ 60	
Insurance expense	400	
Supplies expense	950	
Income tax expense	1,800	

Instructions

(a) If $1,600 was received in January for services performed in January, what was the balance in Unearned Revenue at January 1?

(b) If the amount in the Depreciation Expense account is the depreciation for one month, when was the equipment purchased? Assume that there have been no purchases or sales of equipment since this original purchase.

(c) If the amount in Insurance Expense is the amount of the January 31 adjusting entry, and the original insurance premium was for one year, what was the total premium and when was the policy purchased?

(d) If the amount in Supplies Expense is the amount of the January 31 adjusting entry, and $750 of supplies were purchased in January, what was the balance in Supplies on January 1?

(e) If $2,000 of income tax was paid in January, what was the balance in Income Tax Payable at January 1?

E4–8 The unadjusted and adjusted trial balances follow for Fraser Valley Services Ltd. at the end of its fiscal year, August 31. The company adjusts its accounts annually.

Prepare adjusting entries from analysis of trial balances. (SO 2, 3, 4)

FRASER VALLEY SERVICES LTD.
Trial Balance
August 31, 2012

	Unadjusted Debit	Unadjusted Credit	Adjusted Debit	Adjusted Credit
Cash	$ 7,430		$ 7,430	
Accounts receivable	16,000		19,725	
Supplies	3,150		1,400	
Prepaid insurance	4,550		3,450	
Equipment	25,600		25,600	
Accumulated depreciation—equipment		$ 3,630		$ 5,905
Accounts payable		7,800		7,800
Salaries payable		0		2,200
Interest payable		0		1,500
Rent payable		0		1,250
Income tax payable		0		900
Unearned revenue		1,700		700
Bank loan payable, 6%, due September 1, 2012		25,000		25,000
Common shares		5,000		5,000
Retained earnings		5,400		5,400
Dividends	600		600	
Service revenue		39,550		44,275
Salaries expense	17,000		19,200	
Rent expense	13,750		15,000	
Depreciation expense	0		2,275	
Supplies expense	0		1,750	
Interest expense	0		1,500	
Insurance expense	0		1,100	
Income tax expense	0		900	
	$88,080	$88,080	$99,930	$99,930

Instructions
Prepare the adjusting entries that were made.

E4–9 The adjusted trial balance for Fraser Valley Services Ltd. is given in E4–8.

Prepare financial statements. (SO 4)

Instructions
Prepare the income statement, statement of changes in equity, and statement of financial position for the year. During the year, the company issued common shares for $1,000.

E4–10 The adjusted trial balance for Fraser Valley Services Ltd. is given in E4–8.

Prepare closing entries and post-closing trial balance. (SO 5)

Instructions
(a) Prepare the closing entries at August 31.
(b) Prepare a post-closing trial balance.

Problems: Set A

Calculate profit on cash and accrual bases. (SO 1)

P4–1A Your examination of the records of Southlake Corp. shows the company collected $187,800 in cash from customers and paid $109,400 in cash for operating costs. If Southlake followed the accrual basis of accounting, it would report the following year-end balances:

	2012	2011
Accounts receivable	$ 8,400	$ 5,400
Prepaid insurance	3,000	2,600
Accumulated depreciation	24,600	20,000
Accounts payable	3,000	4,500
Income tax payable	15,800	14,000
Unearned revenue	2,800	3,000

Instructions
(a) Determine Southlake's profit on an accrual basis for 2012.
(b) Determine Southlake's profit on a cash basis for 2012.
(c) Which method do you recommend Southlake use? Why?

Prepare transaction and adjusting entries for prepayments. (SO 2)

P4–2A Ouellette Corporation began operations on January 2. Its year end is December 31, and it adjusts its accounts annually. Selected transactions for the current year follow:

1. On January 2, purchased supplies for $4,100 cash. A physical count at December 31 revealed that $700 of supplies were still on hand.
2. Purchased a vehicle for $45,000 cash on April 1. The vehicle is estimated to have a useful life of five years.
3. Purchased a $3,780, one-year insurance policy for cash on August 1. The policy came into effect on that date.
4. Received a $1,600 advance cash payment from a client on November 9 for services to be provided in the future. As at December 31, half of these services had been completed.
5. On December 1, the company rented out excess office space for a six-month period starting on December 1 and received rent for the months of December and January amounting to $2,000 on this date.

Instructions
(a) For each of the above situations, prepare the journal entry for the original transaction.
(b) For each of the above situations, prepare any adjusting entry required at December 31.

Prepare adjusting and subsequent entries for accruals. (SO 3)

P4–3A Zheng Corporation had the following selected transactions in the month of March. The company adjusts its accounts monthly.

1. The company has an 8%, $12,000 note payable due in one year. Interest is payable the first of each month. It was last paid on March 1, and will be paid next on April 1.
2. At the end of March, the company earned $250 interest on its investments. The bank deposited this amount in Zheng's bank account on April 1.
3. Zheng has five employees who each earn $200 a day. Salaries are normally paid on Fridays for work completed Monday through Friday of the same week. Salaries were last paid on Friday, March 27, and will be paid next on Friday, April 3.
4. At the end of March, the company owed the utility company $550 and the telephone company $200 for services received during the month. These bills were paid on April 10.
5. At the end of March, Zheng has earned $3,000 that it has not yet billed. It bills its clients for fees earned on April 1. On April 30, it collects $2,000 of this amount due.

Instructions
(a) For each of the above situations, prepare the monthly adjusting journal entry required at March 31.
(b) Prepare any subsequent transaction entries that occur in the month of April.

Prepare transaction and adjusting entries. (SO 2, 3)

P4–4A The following independent events for New Age Theatre Ltd. during the year ended November 30, 2012, require a journal entry for the dates mentioned below or an adjusting journal entry, or both. The company adjusts its accounts annually.

1. On December 1, 2011, the theatre purchased vehicles for $80,000 cash. The vehicles' estimated useful life is five years.
2. On June 1, 2012, the theatre borrowed $100,000 from the Bank of Montreal at an interest rate of 6%. The principal is to be repaid in one year. The interest is payable the first of each month.
3. The theatre has eight plays each season. This year's season started in October 2012 and ends in May 2013 (one play per month). Season tickets sell for $160. On October 1, 400 season tickets were sold for the 2012–2013 season. The Theatre credited Unearned Revenue for the full amount received on October 1 and uses an Admission Revenue account to record revenue earned from season tickets.

4. Supplies on hand amounted to $1,000 at the beginning of the year. On February 17, additional Supplies were purchased for cash at a cost of $3,100. At the end of the year, a physical count showed that supplies on hand amounted to $500.

5. The New Age Theatre rents its facilities for $400 a month to a local dance club that uses the space for rehearsals. On November 2, the club's treasurer accidentally sent a cheque for only $200 for the November rent. She promised to send a cheque in December for the balance when she returned from vacation. On December 4, the theatre received a cheque for the balance owing from November plus all of December's rent.

6. The total weekly payroll is $7,000, paid every Monday for employee salaries earned during the prior seven-day week (Sunday to Saturday). Salaries were last paid (and recorded) on Monday, November 26. This year, November 30 falls on a Friday.

7. Upon reviewing its books on November 30, the theatre noted that the utility bill for the month of November had not yet been received. A call to Hydro-Québec determined that the amount owed was $1,250. The bill was paid on December 10.

Instructions
(a) Prepare the journal entry to record the original transaction for items 1, 2, 3, 4, and 5.
(b) Prepare the year-end adjusting entry required for items 1 through 7 on November 30.
(c) Record the subsequent cash transactions in December for (1) the interest paid on December 1 (item 2), (2) the cheque received on December 4 (item 5), (3) the payroll paid on December 3 (item 6), and (4) the payment of the utility bill on December 10 (item 7).

P4–5A A review of the ledger of Come-By-Chance Corporation at July 31, 2012, produces the following unadjusted data for the preparation of annual adjusting entries:

Prepare adjusting entries.
(SO 2, 3)

1. Note Receivable, July 31 unadjusted balance, $50,000: The note was issued on March 1, 2012, at an interest rate of 8%, and matures on February 28, 2013. The interest and principal are to be paid at maturity.

2. Prepaid Insurance, July 31 unadjusted balance, $11,700: The company has separate insurance policies on its building and its motor vehicles. Policy B4564 on the building was purchased on December 1, 2010, for $10,800. The policy has a term of two years. Policy A2958 on the vehicles was purchased on February 1, 2012, for $4,500. This policy has a term of 18 months.

3. Buildings, July 31 unadjusted balance, $444,000: The company owns two buildings. The first was purchased on September 1, 1998, for $252,000 and has an estimated 30-year useful life. The second was purchased on May 1, 2006, for $192,000 and has an estimated 40-year useful life.

4. Unearned Revenue, July 31 unadjusted balance, $51,000: The selling price of a magazine subscription is $50 for 12 monthly issues. A review of subscription contracts reveals the following:

Subscription Date	Number of Subscriptions
November 1, 2011	220
February 1, 2012	310
May 1, 2012	490
	1,020

5. Salaries Payable, July 31 unadjusted balance, $0: There are nine salaried employees. Salaries are paid every Monday for the previous five-day workweek (Monday to Friday). Six employees receive a salary of $625 each per week, and three employees earn $750 each per week. July 31 is a Tuesday.

Instructions
(a) Prepare a calculation to show why the unadjusted balance in the Prepaid Insurance account is $11,700 and why the unadjusted balance in the Unearned Revenue account is $51,000.
(b) Prepare the adjusting journal entries at July 31, 2012.

P4–6A During the first week of January 2012, Creative Designs Ltd. began operations. In its second year, Creative Designs approached the local bank for a $20,000 loan and was asked to submit financial statements prepared on an accrual basis. Although the company kept no formal accounting records, it did maintain a record of cash receipts and disbursements. The following information is available for the year ended December 31, 2012:

Convert profit from cash to accrual basis; prepare financial statements.
(SO 1, 2, 3, 4)

	Cash Receipts	Cash Payments
Issue of common shares	$ 20,000	
Design revenue	157,600	
Equipment		$ 35,400
Supplies		16,800
Rent		20,000
Insurance		3,840
Advertising		6,800

	Cash Receipts	Cash Payments
Salaries		$ 59,800
Telephone		1,800
Dividends		10,000
	$177,600	$154,440

Additional information:

1. Design revenue earned but not yet collected amounted to $2,400.
2. The equipment was purchased at the beginning of January and has an estimated six-year useful life.
3. Supplies on hand on December 31 were $1,260.
4. Rent payments included a $1,500 per month rental fee and a $2,000 deposit that is refundable at the end of the two-year lease.
5. The insurance was paid for a one-year period expiring on January 31, 2013.
6. Salaries earned for the last four days in December and to be paid in January 2013 amounted to $3,050.
7. At December 31, $8,000 is owed for income tax.

Instructions

(a) Calculate the cash balance at December 31, 2012.

(b) Prepare an accrual-based income statement, statement of changes in equity, and statement of financial position for the year.

Prepare and post adjusting entries; prepare adjusted trial balance.
(SO 2, 3, 4)

P4–7A The following is River Tours Limited's unadjusted trial balance at its year end, November 30. The company adjusts its accounts annually.

RIVER TOURS LIMITED
Trial Balance
November 30, 2012

	Debit	Credit
Cash	$ 3,000	
Accounts receivable	2,640	
Supplies	965	
Prepaid rent	3,600	
Prepaid insurance	7,320	
Equipment	13,440	
Accumulated depreciation—equipment		$ 3,300
Boats	140,400	
Accumulated depreciation—boats		46,800
Accounts payable		1,985
Unearned revenue		14,000
Bank loan payable, due September 1, 2015		54,000
Common shares		10,000
Retained earnings		27,225
Tour revenue		110,575
Salaries expense	69,560	
Repairs and maintenance expense	11,170	
Rent expense	10,800	
Interest expense	3,465	
Advertising expense	825	
Income tax expense	700	
	$267,885	$267,885

Additional information:

1. The insurance policy has a one-year term beginning April 2, 2012. At that time, a premium of $7,320 was paid.
2. The equipment has an estimated useful life of 8 years. The boats have an estimated useful life of 12 years.
3. A physical count shows $300 of supplies on hand at November 30.
4. The bank loan payable has a 7% interest rate. Interest is paid at the beginning of each month.
5. Deposits of $1,400 each were received for advance tour reservations from 10 school groups. At November 30, all of these deposits have been earned.
6. Employees are owed a total of $500 at November 30.
7. A senior citizens' organization that had not made an advance deposit took a river tour for $1,250. This group was not billed until December for the services provided.
8. Additional advertising costs of $260 have been incurred, but the bills have not been received by November 30.
9. On August 31, the company paid rent in advance for September, October, and November.
10. Income tax payable for the year is estimated to be an additional $4,000 beyond that recorded to date.

Instructions

(a) Prepare T accounts, and enter the trial balance amounts.
(b) Prepare and post the adjusting journal entries required at November 30.
(c) Prepare an adjusted trial balance at November 30, 2012.

P4–8A On October 31, 2012, the Alou Equipment Repair Corp.'s post-closing trial balance was as follows. The company adjusts its accounts monthly.

Complete accounting cycle through to preparation of financial statements. (SO 2, 3, 4)

	ALOU EQUIPMENT REPAIR CORP. Post-Closing Trial Balance October 31, 2012	
	Debit	Credit
Cash	$15,580	
Accounts receivable	15,820	
Supplies	4,000	
Equipment	18,000	
Accumulated depreciation—equipment		$ 3,600
Accounts payable		4,600
Salaries payable		1,000
Unearned revenue		1,000
Common shares		10,000
Retained earnings		33,200
	$53,400	$53,400

During November, the following transactions were completed:

Nov. 9   Paid $2,200 to employees for salaries due, of which $1,200 is for November salaries payable and $1,000 for October.
12   Issued common shares for $5,000.
13   Received $2,400 cash from customers in payment of accounts.
19   Received $11,400 cash for services performed in November.
20   Purchased supplies on account, $2,600.
21   Paid creditors $4,600 of accounts payable due.
23   Paid November rent, $600.
23   Paid salaries, $2,400.
27   Performed services on account, $3,800.
28   Declared and paid dividends, $500.
30   Received $1,100 from customers for services to be provided in the future.

Adjustment data for the month:

1. Supplies on hand are valued at $2,000.
2. Accrued salaries payable are $1,000.
3. The equipment has an estimated useful life of five years.
4. Unearned revenue of $800 was earned during the month.
5. Income tax payable is estimated to be $1,200.

Instructions

(a) Prepare T accounts, and enter the opening balances at November 1.
(b) Prepare and post the November transaction entries.
(c) Prepare a trial balance at November 30.
(d) Prepare and post the adjusting journal entries for the month.
(e) Prepare an adjusted trial balance at November 30.
(f) Prepare an income statement, statement of changes in equity, and statement of financial position for the month.

P4–9A Refer to the data for Alou Equipment Repair Corp. in P4–8A. Assume that Alou closes its books monthly.

Prepare and post closing entries; prepare post-closing trial balance. (SO 5)

Instructions

(a) Prepare the closing journal entries.
(b) Post the closing entries to the T accounts prepared in P4–8A.
(c) Prepare a post-closing trial balance at November 30.

P4–10A The unadjusted and adjusted trial balances of Ozaki Corp. at the end of its first quarter of operations, September 30, are as follows. The company adjusts its accounts quarterly.

Prepare adjusting entries and financial statements. (SO 2, 3, 4)

OZAKI CORP.
Trial Balance
September 30, 2012

	Unadjusted		Adjusted	
	Debit	Credit	Debit	Credit
Cash	$ 3,250		$ 3,250	
Accounts receivable	6,335		8,435	
Supplies	1,750		1,265	
Prepaid rent	1,500		0	
Equipment	15,040		15,040	
Accumulated depreciation—equipment		$ 0		$ 750
Accounts payable		4,250		4,460
Salaries payable		0		840
Interest payable		0		105
Income tax payable		0		1,000
Unearned revenue		775		550
Bank loan payable, due in 2015		7,000		7,000
Common shares		10,000		10,000
Dividends	700		700	
Commission revenue		20,160		22,485
Salaries expense	13,000		13,840	
Rent expense	0		1,500	
Depreciation expense	0		750	
Supplies expense	0		485	
Utilities expense	610		820	
Interest expense	0		105	
Income tax expense	0		1,000	
	$42,185	$42,185	$47,190	$47,190

Instructions
(a) Prepare the adjusting journal entries that were made for the quarter.
(b) Prepare an income statement, statement of changes in equity, and statement of financial position for the quarter.

Prepare closing entries and post-closing trial balance.
(SO 5)

P4–11A   The adjusted trial balance for Ozaki Corp. is presented in P4–10A. Assume that the company closes its books quarterly.

Instructions
(a) Prepare the closing journal entries.
(b) Prepare a post-closing trial balance at September 30.

Prepare and post adjusting entries; prepare adjusted trial balance and financial statements; assess financial performance.
(SO 2, 3, 4)

P4–12A   The following is the unadjusted trial balance for Rainbow Lodge Ltd. at its year end, May 31. The company adjusts its accounts monthly.

RAINBOW LODGE LTD.
Trial Balance
May 31, 2012

	Debit	Credit
Cash	$ 6,400	
Accounts receivable	11,800	
Supplies	4,880	
Prepaid insurance	4,550	
Land	106,370	
Building	168,000	
Accumulated depreciation—building		$ 16,100
Furniture	33,600	
Accumulated depreciation—furniture		12,880
Accounts payable		9,400
Unearned revenue		17,500
Mortgage payable, due in 2016		126,000
Common shares		60,000
Retained earnings		44,580
Dividends	2,000	

	Debit	Credit
Rent revenue		$200,320
Salaries expense	$ 98,700	
Utilities expense	26,600	
Interest expense	9,240	
Insurance expense	3,640	
Advertising expense	1,000	
Income tax expense	10,000	
	$486,780	$486,780

Additional information:

1. The annual insurance policy was purchased on October 1, 2011, for $10,920.
2. A count of supplies shows $1,340 of supplies on hand on May 31.
3. The building has an estimated useful life of 20 years.
4. The furniture has an estimated useful life of five years.
5. Customers must pay a $100 deposit if they want to book a room in advance during the peak period. An analysis of these bookings indicates that 175 deposits were received and credited to Unearned Revenue. By May 31, 25 of the deposits were earned.
6. On May 25, a local business contracted with Rainbow Lodge to rent one of its housekeeping units for four months, starting June 1, at a rate of $2,800 per month. An advance payment equal to one month's rent was paid on May 25 and credited to Rent Revenue.
7. On May 31, Rainbow Lodge has earned $1,780 of rent revenue from customers who are currently staying at the inn. The customers will only pay the amount owing when they check out in early June.
8. Salaries of $1,590 are unpaid at May 31.
9. The mortgage interest rate is 8%. Interest has been paid to May 1; the next payment is due June 1.
10. The May utility bill of $2,240 has not yet been recorded or paid.
11. Income taxes for the month of May are estimated to be $1,000.
12. During the month of May, $4,000 of common shares were issued.

Instructions
(a) Prepare T accounts, and enter the trial balance amounts.
(b) Prepare and post the adjusting journal entries for the month.
(c) Prepare an adjusted trial balance at May 31.
(d) Prepare an income statement, statement of changes in equity, and statement of financial position for the year.
(e) A friend of yours is considering investing in the company and asks you to comment on the company's operations and financial position. Is the company performing well or not? Does the financial position look healthy or weak? Use specific information from the financial statements to support your answer.

P4–13A Refer to the data for Rainbow Lodge Ltd. in P4–12A.

Prepare and post closing entries; prepare post-closing trial balance.
(SO 5)

Instructions
(a) Prepare the closing journal entries.
(b) Post the closing entries to the T accounts prepared in P4–12A.
(c) Prepare a post-closing trial balance at May 31.

Problems: Set B

P4–1B Your examination of the records of Northland Corp. shows the company collected $78,100 in cash from customers and paid $53,900 in cash for operating costs. If Northland followed the accrual basis of accounting, it would report the following year-end balances:

Convert profit from cash to accrual basis.
(SO 1)

	2012	2011
Accounts payable	$ 905	$ 820
Accounts receivable	1,450	1,600
Accumulated depreciation	8,625	7,500
Prepaid insurance	810	650
Unearned revenue	700	780
Income tax payable	4,600	4,035

Instructions
(a) Determine Northland's profit on a cash basis for 2012.
(b) Determine Northland's profit on an accrual basis for 2012.
(c) Which method do you recommend Northland use? Why?

Prepare transaction and adjusting entries for prepayments.
(SO 2)

P4–2B Bourque Corporation began operations on January 2. Its year end is December 31, and it adjusts its accounts annually. Selected transactions for the current year follow:

1. On January 2, purchased supplies for $2,100 cash. A physical count at December 31 revealed that $550 of supplies were still on hand.
2. Purchased equipment for $20,000 cash on March 1. The equipment is estimated to have a useful life of five years.
3. Purchased a one-year, $5,040 insurance policy for cash on June 1. The policy came into effect on that date.
4. On November 15, received a $1,275 advance cash payment from three clients for services to be provided in the future. As at December 31, work had been completed for two of the clients ($425 each).
5. On December 15, the company paid $2,500 rent in advance for the next month (January).

Instructions
(a) For each of the above situations, prepare the journal entry for the original transaction.
(b) For each of the above situations, prepare any adjusting journal entry required at December 31.

Prepare adjusting and subsequent entries for accruals.
(SO 3)

P4–3B Hangzhou Corporation had the following selected transactions in the month of November. The company adjusts its accounts monthly.

1. Hangzhou has a biweekly payroll of $6,000. Salaries are normally paid every second Monday for work completed for the two preceding weeks. Employees work a five-day week, Monday through Friday. Salaries were last paid Monday, November 23, and will be paid next on Monday, December 7.
2. The company has a 7%, $20,000 note payable due September 1 of the next year. Interest is payable the first of each month. It was last paid on November 1, and will be paid next on December 1.
3. At the end of November, Hangzhou has $1,000 of invoices that have not yet been sent to customers. It mails these invoices on December 1, and collects the amounts due on December 21.
4. At the end of November, the company earned $10 interest on the cash in its bank account. The bank deposited this amount in the company's bank account on November 30, but the company did not learn of the interest until it received its bank statement on December 4.
5. At the end of November, it was estimated that the company owed $1,000 of income tax. This amount was paid on December 18.

Instructions
(a) For each of the above situations, prepare the monthly adjusting journal entry required at November 30.
(b) Prepare any subsequent transaction entries that occur in the month of December.

Prepare transaction and adjusting entries.
(SO 2, 3)

P4–4B The following independent events for Repertory Theatre Ltd. during the year ended December 31, 2012, may require a journal entry for the dates mentioned below or an adjusting journal entry, or both. The company adjusts its accounts annually.

1. Supplies on hand amounted to $1,500 at the beginning of the year. On March 1, additional supplies were purchased for $5,250 cash. At the end of the year, a physical count showed that supplies on hand amounted to $1,500.
2. The theatre owns a truck that was purchased on January 2, 2012, for $120,000. The truck's estimated useful life is four years.
3. On June 1, the theatre borrowed $30,000 from La Caisse Populaire Desjardins at an interest rate of 6%. The principal is to be repaid in one year. The interest is paid at the beginning of each month.
4. The theatre has nine plays each season, which starts in September 2012 and ends in May 2013 (one play per month). Season tickets sell for $225. On August 21, 600 season tickets were sold for the upcoming 2012–2013 season. The theatre credited Unearned Revenue for the full amount received on August 21.
5. Every Monday, the total payroll for the theatre is $9,000 for salaries earned during a six-day workweek (Tuesday–Sunday). This year, December 31 falls on a Monday. Salaries were paid on that day.
6. Repertory Theatre rents its facilities for $600 a month to a local seniors' choir that uses the space for rehearsals. The choir's treasurer was ill during December, and on January 4, 2013, the theatre received a cheque for both the amount owing for the month of December 2012 and the rent for the month of January 2013.
7. Upon reviewing its books on December 31, the theatre noted that a telephone bill for the month of December had not yet been received. A call to Aliant determined that the telephone bill was for $1,125. The bill was paid on January 12.

Instructions
(a) Prepare the journal entry to record the original transaction for items 1, 2, 3, 4, and 5.
(b) Prepare the year-end adjusting entry required for items 1 through 7 on December 31, 2012.
(c) Record the subsequent cash transaction in January 2013 for (1) the interest paid on January 1 (item 3), (2) payment of the payroll on January 4 (item 5), (3) receipt of the rent on January 4 (item 6), and (4) payment of the telephone bill on January 12 (item 7).

P4-5B A review of the ledger of Greenberg Corporation at October 31, 2012, produces the following unadjusted data for the preparation of annual adjusting entries:

Prepare adjusting entries.
(SO 2, 3)

1. Prepaid Advertising, October 31 unadjusted balance, $14,160: This balance consists of payments on two advertising contracts. The contracts provide for advertising in two trade magazines that publish monthly, and specify that the first advertisement runs in the month following the month in which the contract is signed. In other words, if the contract is signed February 1, the first advertisement will run in the month of March. The terms of the contracts are as follows:

Contract	Signing Date	Amount	Number of Magazine Issues
A650	February 1	$ 6,240	12
B974	June 1	7,920	16
		$14,160	

2. Salaries Payable, October 31 unadjusted balance, $0: There are eight salaried employees. Salaries are paid every Friday for a five-day workweek (Monday–Friday). Six employees receive a salary of $750 each per week, and two employees earn $600 each per week. October 31 is a Wednesday.

3. Unearned Revenue, October 31 unadjusted balance, $303,000: The company began subleasing office space in its new building on September 1. At October 31, the company had the following rental contracts that are paid in full for the entire term of the lease:

Date	Term (in months)	Monthly Rent	Number of Leases	Rent Paid
Sept. 1	6	$4,500	5	$135,000
Oct. 1	6	7,000	4	168,000
				$303,000

4. Loan Payable, October 31 unadjusted balance, $90,000: This represents a one-year, 8% note issued on April 1. Interest is payable at maturity.

5. Delivery Truck, October 31 unadjusted balance, $39,000: The company owns a delivery truck, purchased for $39,000 on April 1, 2011. The truck has a five-year useful life.

Instructions
Prepare the adjusting journal entries at October 31, 2012.

P4-6B The Radical Edge Ltd., a ski tuning and repair shop, opened in November 2011. The company did not record any transactions since its opening, but carefully kept track of all its cash receipts and cash payments. The following information is available at the end of the first ski season, April 30, 2012:

Convert profit from cash to accrual basis; prepare financial statements.
(SO 1, 2, 3, 4)

	Cash Receipts	Cash Payments
Issue of common shares	$20,000	
Ski and snowboard repair services	66,500	
Repair equipment		$47,040
Rent		4,550
Insurance		2,760
Advertising		920
Utility bills		1,900
Salaries		7,200
Income tax		6,000
	$86,500	$70,370

Additional information:

1. At the end of April, customers owe The Radical Edge $1,440 for services they have received and not yet paid for.
2. The repair equipment was purchased at the beginning of November and has an estimated useful life of eight years.
3. On November 1, the company began renting space at a cost of $650 per month on a one-year lease. As required by the lease contract, the company paid the last month's (October 2012) rent in advance.
4. The insurance policy was purchased November 1 and is effective for one year.
5. At April 30, $4,240 is owed for unpaid salaries.
6. At April 30, an additional $1,200 is owed for income tax.

Instructions
(a) Calculate the cash balance at April 30, 2012.
(b) Prepare an accrual basis income statement, statement of changes in equity, and statement of financial position for the six months ended April 30, 2012.

P4-7B The following is Ortega Limo Service Ltd.'s unadjusted trial balance at its year end, December 31. The company adjusts its accounts annually.

Prepare and post adjusting entries; prepare adjusted trial balance.
(SO 2, 3, 4)

ORTEGA LIMO SERVICE LTD.
Trial Balance
December 31, 2012

	Debit	Credit
Cash	$ 5,750	
Accounts receivable	8,220	
Supplies	2,500	
Prepaid insurance	3,600	
Prepaid rent	1,150	
Vehicles	58,000	
Accumulated depreciation—vehicles		$ 14,500
Furniture	16,000	
Accumulated depreciation—furniture		4,000
Unearned revenue		3,600
Loan payable, due September 1, 2015		46,000
Common shares		5,000
Retained earnings		7,600
Dividends	3,800	
Service revenue		115,600
Salaries expense	57,000	
Fuel expense	20,075	
Rent expense	12,650	
Repairs expense	4,690	
Interest expense	2,415	
Income tax expense	450	
	$196,300	$196,300

Additional information:

1. The insurance policy has a one-year term beginning March 1.
2. A physical count of supplies at December 31 shows $570 of supplies on hand.
3. The vehicles were purchased on January 2, 2011, and have an estimated useful life of four years.
4. The furniture was purchased on July 2, 2009, and has an estimated useful life of 10 years.
5. Service revenue earned but not billed or recorded at December 31 is $1,750.
6. Interest on the 7% bank loan is paid on the first day of each quarter (January 1, April 1, July 1, and October 1).
7. One of Ortega's customers paid in advance for a six-month contract at the rate of $600 per month. The contract began on November 1 and Ortega credited Unearned Revenue at the time.
8. Drivers' salaries total $230 per day. At December 31, three days of salaries are unpaid.
9. On November 1, Ortega paid $1,150 for November and December 2012 rent in advance.
10. Income tax for the year is estimated to be $850. The company has paid $450 in income tax instalments to date.

Instructions
(a) Prepare T accounts and enter the trial balance amounts.
(b) Prepare and post the adjusting journal entries required at December 31.
(c) Prepare an adjusted trial balance at December 31, 2012.

Complete
accounting cycle
through to preparation
of financial statements.
(SO 2, 3, 4)

P4–8B   On August 31, 2012, the Rijo Equipment Repair Corp.'s post-closing trial balance was as follows. The company prepares its adjusting entries monthly.

RIJO EQUIPMENT REPAIR CORP.
Post-Closing Trial Balance
August 31, 2012

	Debit	Credit
Cash	$ 9,760	
Accounts receivable	7,440	
Supplies	1,600	
Equipment	30,000	
Accumulated depreciation—equipment		$ 3,000
Accounts payable		6,200
Salaries payable		1,400
Unearned revenue		800
Common shares		20,000
Retained earnings		17,400
	$48,800	$48,800

During September, the following transactions were completed:

Sept.	4	Paid employees $2,200 for salaries due, of which $800 was for September salaries payable and $1,400 for August.
	6	Received $2,400 cash from customers in payment of accounts.
	11	Received $8,800 cash for services performed in September.
	12	Sold common shares for $5,000.
	17	Purchased supplies on account, $2,000.
	21	Paid creditors $7,000 of accounts payable due.
	24	Paid September and October rent, $2,000 ($1,000 per month).
	25	Paid salaries, $2,200.
	26	Performed services on account, $1,600.
	27	Received $1,300 from customers for services to be provided in the future.
	28	Declared and paid a dividend, $500.
	28	Paid income tax for the month, $600.

Adjustment data for the month:

1. Supplies on hand total $1,200.
2. Accrued salaries payable are $1,600.
3. Accrued service revenue for $600.
4. The equipment has a useful life of 10 years.
5. Unearned revenue of $800 has been earned.

Instructions
(a) Prepare T accounts, and enter the opening balances at September 1.
(b) Prepare and post the September transaction entries.
(c) Prepare a trial balance at September 30.
(d) Prepare and post the adjusting journal entries for the month.
(e) Prepare an adjusted trial balance at September 30.
(f) Prepare an income statement, statement of changes in equity, and statement of financial position for the month.

P4–9B Refer to the data for Rijo Equipment Repair Corp. in P4–8B. Assume that Rijo closes its books monthly.

Instructions
(a) Prepare the closing journal entries.
(b) Post the closing entries to the T accounts prepared in P4–8B.
(c) Prepare a post-closing trial balance at September 30.

Prepare and post closing entries; prepare post-closing trial balance.
(SO 5)

P4–10B The unadjusted and adjusted trial balances for Grant Advertising Agency Limited at its year end, December 31, 2012, follow. The company adjusts its accounts annually.

Prepare adjusting entries and financial statements.
(SO 2, 3, 4)

GRANT ADVERTISING AGENCY LIMITED
Trial Balance
December 31, 2012

	Unadjusted Debit	Unadjusted Credit	Adjusted Debit	Adjusted Credit
Cash	$ 11,000		$ 11,000	
Short-term investments	10,850		10,850	
Accounts receivable	18,650		19,750	
Supplies	7,200		1,265	
Prepaid insurance	2,400		800	
Equipment	66,000		66,000	
Equipment—accumulated depreciation		$ 26,400		$ 39,600
Accounts payable		4,200		4,800
Interest payable		0		700
Salaries payable		0		1,625
Unearned revenue		7,100		6,200
Loan payable, due in 2016		10,000		10,000
Income tax payable		0		7,000
Common shares		20,000		20,000
Retained earnings		10,400		10,400
Dividends	2,000		2,000	

	Unadjusted		Adjusted	
	Debit	Credit	Debit	Credit
Advertising revenue		$ 58,600		$ 60,600
Salaries expense	$ 12,000		$ 13,625	
Depreciation expense	0		13,200	
Rent expense	6,600		7,200	
Supplies expense	0		5,935	
Insurance expense	0		1,600	
Interest expense	0		700	
Income tax expense	0		7,000	
	$136,700	$136,700	$160,925	$160,925

Additional information:
During the year, the company issued common shares for $3,000.

Instructions
(a) Prepare an income statement, statement of changes in equity, and statement of financial position for the year.
(b) Prepare the adjusting journal entries that were made for the year.

Prepare closing entries and post-closing trial balance.
(SO 5)

P4–11B   The adjusted trial balance is presented for Grant Advertising Agency Limited in P4–10B.

Instructions
(a) Prepare the closing journal entries.
(b) Prepare a post-closing trial balance at December 31.

Prepare and post adjusting entries; prepare adjusted trial balance and financial statements; assess financial performance.
(SO 2, 3, 4)

P4–12B   The following is the unadjusted trial balance for Rocky Mountain Resort Inc. at its year end, August 31. The company adjusts its accounts annually.

ROCKY MOUNTAIN RESORT INC.
Trial Balance
August 31, 2012

	Debit	Credit
Cash	$ 38,820	
Supplies	6,990	
Prepaid insurance	12,720	
Land	70,000	
Buildings	290,000	
Accumulated depreciation—buildings		$ 87,000
Furniture	57,200	
Accumulated depreciation—furniture		22,880
Accounts payable		13,000
Unearned revenue		71,000
Mortgage payable, due 2015		120,000
Common shares		40,000
Retained earnings		72,000
Dividends	10,000	
Rent revenue		497,000
Salaries expense	306,000	
Utilities expense	75,200	
Repair expense	28,250	
Interest expense	7,700	
Income tax expense	20,000	
	$922,880	$922,880

Additional information:
1. The one-year insurance policy was purchased on May 31 for $12,720.
2. A count of supplies on August 31 shows $1,380 of supplies on hand.
3. The buildings have an estimated useful life of 50 years.
4. The furniture has an estimated useful life of 10 years.
5. Customers must pay a $200 deposit if they want to book a cottage during the peak period. An analysis of these bookings indicates 355 deposits were received and credited to Unearned Revenue. Only 45 of these deposits have not been earned by August 31.
6. Salaries of $1,680 were unpaid at August 31.

7. The August utility bill of $3,120 has not yet been recorded or paid.
8. On August 25, a local business contracted with Rocky Mountain to rent one of the cottages for six months, starting October 1, at a rate of $3,000 per month. An advance payment equal to two months' (October and November) rent was received on August 31 and credited to Rent Revenue.
9. The mortgage interest rate is 7%. Interest has been paid to August 1; the next payment is due September 1.
10. In May, the company issued common shares for $5,000.
11. Income tax payable is estimated to be $2,000.

Instructions
(a) Prepare T accounts, and enter the trial balance amounts.
(b) Prepare and post the adjusting journal entries for the year.
(c) Prepare an adjusted trial balance at August 31.
(d) Prepare an income statement, statement of changes in equity, and statement of financial position for the year.
(e) A friend of yours is considering investing in the company and asks you to comment on the results of operations and financial position. Is the company performing well or not? Does the financial position look healthy or weak? Use specific information from the financial statements to support your answer.

P4–13B   Refer to the data for Rocky Mountain Resort Inc. in P4–12B.

Instructions
(a) Prepare the closing journal entries.
(b) Post the closing entries to the T accounts prepared in P4–12B.
(c) Prepare a post-closing trial balance at August 31.

Prepare and post closing entries; prepare post-closing trial balance.
(SO 5)

Broadening Your Perspective

Financial Reporting and Analysis Cases

Financial Reporting: *Eastplats*

BYP4–1   The financial statements of Eastern Platinum Limited (Eastplats) are presented in Appendix A at the end of this book.

Instructions
(a) Some companies list not only accounts payable but accrued liabilities as well in the current liabilities section of the statement of financial position. Does Eastplats do this? If so, explain the difference between these two items.
(b) In looking at the income statement, can you name two accounts that management probably recorded adjusting entries for at the end of the year?
(c) Reconstruct the summary closing journal entries prepared by Eastplats at December 31, 2010.

Analyze adjusting entries and prepare closing entries.
(SO 2, 3, 5)

Comparative Analysis: *Eastplats and Amplats*

BYP4–2   The financial statements of Anglo American Platinum Limited (Amplats) are presented in Appendix B following the financial statements for Eastern Platinum Limited (Eastplats) in Appendix A.

Instructions
(a) Eastplats has a non-current liability called Provision for Environmental Rehabilitation. Amplats has a similar account called Environmental Obligations. These accounts represent estimates of environmental clean up costs that the company will pay for later. Do you think accrual adjusting entries are made to these accounts at the end of the year? Why or why not? Is it likely that accrual entries would be made to cash accounts?
(b) Which of the following Eastplats accounts are more likely to have adjusting entries recorded in them: trade and other receivables or issued capital; accounts payable or inventories?

Identify adjusting entries.
(SO 2, 3)

Interpreting Financial Information

BYP4–3   Singapore Airlines Ltd. is one of the world's most successful airlines. An excerpt from the notes to this company's financial statements appears below.

Identify point of revenue recognition.
(SO 1)

SINGAPORE AIRLINES LIMITED
Notes to the Financial Statements

Passenger sales are recognized as operating revenue when the transportation is provided. The value of unused tickets is included as sales in advance of carriage on the statement of financial position and recognized as revenue at the end of two years.

The Company operates a frequent flyer program called "KrisFlyer" that provides travel awards to program members based on accumulated mileage. A portion of passenger revenue attributable to the award of frequent flyer benefits is deferred until they are utilized.

Cargo sales are recognized as operating revenue when the transportation is provided. The value of unused air waybills is included in current liabilities as sales in advance of carriage. The value of tickets and air waybills are recognized as revenue if unused after two years and one year, respectively.

Instructions

(a) When does this airline recognize the revenue from its ticket sales? From its cargo services? From its frequent flyer rewards?

(b) Does the timing of the receipt of cash from the sale of tickets have any effect on the recording of expenses for delivering the air transportation?

(c) When an airline ticket is sold, a portion of the price relates to future frequent flyer benefits. How is this portion recorded?

Comparing IFRS and ASPE

Compare adjusting entries, financial statements, and closing process. (SO 2, 3, 5)

BYP4–4   Homburg Invest Inc. and **First Pro Shopping Centres** are both real-estate and property management companies headquartered in Canada. However, Homburg is a public company using IFRS and First Pro is a private company using ASPE. Selected information is provided below from Homburg's statement of financial position and income statement for its most recent year:

HOMBURG INVEST INC.
Statement of Financial Position
December 31, 2010
(in thousands)

Assets	
Non-current assets	$1,832,060
Current assets	230,821
Total assets	$2,062,881
Liabilities	
Non-current liabilities	$1,515,869
Current liabilities	445,336
Total liabilities	1,961,205
Shareholders' Equity	
Deficit	(649,316)
Accumulated other comprehensive income	1,190
Share capital	701,034
Other contributed capital	48,768
Total shareholders' equity	101,676
Total liabilities and shareholders' equity	$2,062,881

HOMBURG INVEST INC.
Income Statement
Year Ended December 31, 2010
(in thousands)

Total revenue	$148,065
Property operating expenses	25,628
Cost of sale of properties developed for sale	21,369
General and administrative and other expenses	51,548
Profit from continuing operations before income tax	49,520
Income tax expense	31,197
Profit from continuing operations	18,323
Discontinued operations, net of income tax	(106,377)
Loss	$(88,054)

In addition to the above, Homburg also includes a statement of comprehensive income, statement of changes in equity, and statement of cash flows in its financial statements.

Instructions

(a) Homburg is required to release quarterly financial statements to its shareholders. First Pro only releases its financial statements annually to its bankers and for the purposes of its annual tax filings. Do you think that there will be a difference in how often the two companies prepare and record their adjusting entries? Explain.

(b) Based upon what you read in this chapter, what differences would you expect to see in First Pro's financial statements?

(c) Would you anticipate that the closing process at year end would be any different for Homburg than for First Pro?

Critical Thinking Cases and Activities

Collaborative Learning Activity

BYP4–5 If you're flying from Vancouver to Toronto with Air Canada, you can choose a Tango fare of $259 (plus taxes), a Tango Plus fare for $324 (plus taxes, etc.), or you can pay $804 (plus taxes, etc.) for a Latitude fare. Each of these fare classes has different conditions regarding refunds, altering flight dates, preflight seat selection, etc.

Identify point of revenue recognition. (SO 1)

Assume that Air Canada's management team is brainstorming its options for recognizing the revenue from the different categories of fares. One member of the management team says it should recognize the revenue as soon as the tickets are sold for the Tango-type fares because these tickets are non-cancellable and have a change fee. Passengers seldom change these fares. Another member of the management team states that revenue should be recognized when the passengers arrive at their destinations.

Instructions

After the class has been divided into groups and you have been assigned one of the fare types (Tango or Latitude), do the following:

(a) Evaluate the effect of each of the two revenue recognition options proposed by the employees on recorded revenues, expenses, and profit.

(b) Determine the point at which you think Air Canada should recognize the revenue from ticket sales. Explain why you believe your chosen point of revenue recognition is the best, referring to appropriate recognition criteria in your answer.

Communication Activity

BYP4–6 There are many people today who believe that cash flow is a better indicator of a company's future success than profit. This notion gained popularity after many reports of corporate financial scandals where management was apparently able to manipulate prepayments and accruals to influence profit.

Discuss cash and accrual bases of accounting. (SO 1)

Instructions

Write a memo discussing whether you believe cash flow is a more reliable performance measure than profit. Include in your memo the answers to the following questions:

(a) What is the difference between accrual-based profit and cash?

(b) Do you believe that it is possible for management to manipulate profit when using accrual accounting? If so, identify at least one way that management might be able to increase profit by manipulating prepayments or accruals.

(c) Do you believe that it is possible for management to manipulate profit when using cash basis accounting? If so, identify at least one way that management might be able to increase cash flow.

Ethics Case

BYP4–7 Sundream Travel Agency Ltd. is a company that sells vacation packages and has a new Chief Executive Officer (CEO) who is reviewing the draft December 31 year-end financial statements prepared by the company's controller. On these statements, the current assets total $400,000 while the current liabilities total $210,000. Several months ago, the company obtained some new bank financing that requires it to maintain a current ratio of at least 2:1. After reviewing the statements, the CEO suggests that the controller change the financial statements for two transactions.

Discuss ethics when making accruals. (SO 1, 2, 3)

The first transaction involves a vacation package that was sold to a ski club. The vacation commences in two months time, in early March, and the club has paid $12,000 in advance for the trip. Since the cash has been received, the CEO suggests that the credit relating to this transaction be shown in sales revenue.

The second transaction relates to an accrual of $3,000 for December interest expense that is not due until early January. The CEO suggests that this accrual should not be made since the interest is not due until next year.

Instructions

(a) Who are the stakeholders in this situation?

(b) How will undertaking the CEO's request have an impact on the financial statements?

(c) Is the CEO acting in an ethical manner? Why?

(d) In what way does the existence of accounting standards enhance ethical behaviour?

"All About You" Activity

Discuss personal
liabilities.
(SO 4)

BYP4–8 In the "All About You" feature in this chapter, you learned how important it is for companies to report or disclose information about all liabilities, including potential liabilities related to an environmental clean-up. There are many situations in which you will be asked to provide financial information about your own liabilities. When you take on liabilities, your creditors will want to obtain information relating to the security for their loan such as the value of your assets, along with information about your income. Sometimes you will face difficult decisions regarding what to disclose and how to disclose it. Let us assume that at the present time you own a home and have a mortgage on it.

Instructions

How would you address the following situations in reporting your financial position to the parties involved below and to your own bank where you have your mortgage?

(a) Your friend obtained a bank loan for $20,000 but in order for him to get it, you had to sign a form that guaranteed that you would make the loan payments if your friend was unable to. Your friend has made all of the payments so far, and it appears he will be able to pay in the future. Do you have a liability at this time? What information would the bank want to know about you before it will allow you to guarantee your friend's loan?

(b) The company where you work is not doing very well, and it has recently laid off employees. You are still employed, but it is quite possible that you will lose your job in the next few months.

Serial Case

(*Note:* This is a continuation of the serial case from Chapters 1 through 3.)

Prepare and post
adjusting journal
entries; prepare
adjusted trial balance.
(SO 2, 3, 4)

BYP4–9 Natalie reviews the updated trial balance prepared in Chapter 3. She recalls from her introductory accounting class that there are some adjustments that need to be prepared. She gathers up as much information as she can to enable the following adjusting journal entries to be prepared on June 30, Koebel's Family Bakery's year end:

1. A count reveals that $500 worth of advertising brochures, recorded in the Supplies account, have been distributed during the month of June.
2. Depreciation is to be recorded on the building for the year. The building was purchased 25 years ago and has an estimated useful life of 40 years.
3. Depreciation is to be recorded on the equipment for the year. The equipment was purchased two years ago at a cost of $43,000 and has an estimated useful life of five years. Recall as well that there was new baking equipment purchased on June 15 at a cost of $900. One month's depreciation is to be recorded on this equipment; its useful life is five years.
4. Depreciation is to be recorded on the delivery truck, recorded in the Vehicles account. The delivery truck was purchased on January 1 at a cost of $55,000 and has an estimated useful life of five years.
5. Interest on the bank loan and mortgage payable was last paid on June 25. Interest accrued on the five days remaining in June is $75.
6. One month's worth of the prepaid property insurance purchased for $12,400 on June 6 has expired.
7. Six months' worth of the prepaid vehicle insurance has also expired. Recall that this insurance was purchased on January 1 for $12,000.
8. At the end of June, heat and electricity on the building, $925, was owed. Amounts are to be paid by July 15. (*Hint:* Use the Utilities Expense account.)
9. During the last week of June, an unexpected order was received from Biscuits to prepare 750 dozen oatmeal chocolate chip cookies. The order was filled and an invoice was prepared, $1,400. This invoice was not included in the accounting records at June 30.
10. Salaries for employees were paid on June 30. There were two part-time employees working in the bake shop on June 30 who forgot to submit their timesheets for that day. They both worked an eight-hour shift and were paid $12 an hour.

Instructions

(a) Prepare the adjusting journal entries required at June 30.
(b) Post to the T accounts prepared in Chapter 3.
(c) Prepare an adjusted trial balance at June 30.

Answers to Self-Test Questions

1. b   2. d   3. d   4. b   5. d   6. a   7. c   8. b   9. a   10. a

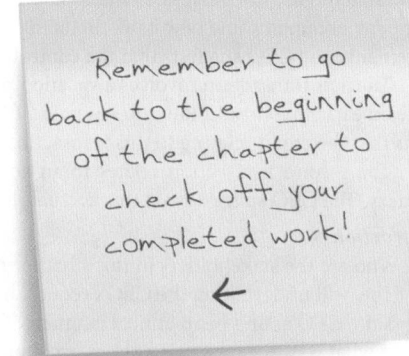

Remember to go back to the beginning of the chapter to check off your completed work!

Comprehensive Case: Chapters 1–4

Red River Computer Consultants Ltd. commenced operations more than a year ago. At its last year end, on June 30, 2012, the company's post-closing trial balance was prepared as follows:

Record and post trans-
action and adjusting
journal entries;
prepare adjusted trial
balance and financial
statements.
(SO 3, 4)

RED RIVER COMPUTER CONSULTANTS LTD.
Trial Balance
June 30, 2012

	Debit	Credit
Cash	$5,230	
Accounts receivable	1,200	
Supplies	690	
Accounts payable		$ 400
Unearned revenue		1,120
Common shares		3,600
Retained earnings		2,000
	$7,120	$7,120

The company underwent a major expansion in July 2012. New staff was hired and more financing was obtained. Red River plans to record and adjust its accounts monthly. It conducted the following transactions during July 2012.

July 2	Issued $50,000 of common shares for cash.
2	Obtained a bank loan for $10,000 at 6%. Interest is payable monthly on the first day of the following month. No principal payments are required until 2014.
3	Prepaid for a year of liability insurance coverage, $3,600.
3	Leased a vehicle for a four-year term. Paid the first month's lease payment of $600 and a security deposit of $5,000. Use the accounts Rent Expense and Prepaid Rent (long-term), respectively, to record these amounts.
3	Signed a four-year lease for office space.
3	Paid the first (July 2012) and last (June 2016) months' rent for the office, $4,000 per month, for a total payment of $8,000.
4	Purchased $3,800 of supplies for cash.
5	Purchased equipment on account, $24,000. It has a four-year useful life.
9	Visited client offices and agreed on the terms of a consulting project. Red River will invoice the client, Connor Productions, on the 20th of each month for work performed.
10	Collected $1,200 from Milani Brothers Ltd. This client was invoiced in June when the service revenue provided to them was recorded.
12	Completed services for Fitzgerald Enterprises. This client paid $1,120 in advance last month. All services relating to this payment are now completed. (*Hint*: Use the Consulting Revenue account.)
16	Met with a new client, Thunder Bay Technologies. Received $12,000 cash in advance for future work to be performed.
17	Paid semi-monthly salaries for $11,000.
18	Paid a utility bill of $400. This related to June utilities that were accrued at the end of June.
20	Invoiced Connor Productions for $18,000 of consulting fees provided on account. (*Hint*: Use the Consultant Fees Expense account.)
20	Received an invoice for routine legal advice, $2,200. The amount is not due until August 15.
23	Completed the first phase of the project for Thunder Bay Technologies. Recognized $10,000 of revenue from the cash advance previously received.
25	Received and deposited a $4,000 fee for speaking at an industry conference.
26	Received $15,000 cash from Connor Productions in partial payment of the invoice issued on July 20.
31	Prepared adjusting entries for the following: • Accrual of interest on bank loan (see July 2 transaction) • Expiry of insurance coverage (see July 3 transaction) • Supplies used, $1,250 of (see July 4 transaction) • Equipment depreciation (see July 5 transaction) • Salaries for the second half of July, $11,000, to be paid on August 1 • Estimated utilities expense for July, $800 (invoice to be received in August) • Income tax for July, $300, to be paid in August

Instructions

(a) Record the above transactions.

(b) Prepare T accounts and post the general and adjusting journal entries.

(c) Prepare an adjusted trial balance as at July 31.

(d) Prepare the (1) income statement, (2) statement of changes in equity, and (3) statement of financial position for July.

(e) Red River needs to maintain a current ratio of 2.5:1 in order to maintain its financial standing with its bankers. Calculate the current ratio. Has it achieved the 2.5-to-1 benchmark?

Merchandising Operations

study objectives

After studying this chapter, you should be able to:

1. Identify the differences between service and merchandising companies.
2. Prepare entries for purchases under a perpetual inventory system.
3. Prepare entries for sales under a perpetual inventory system.
4. Prepare a single-step and a multiple-step income statement.
5. Calculate the gross profit margin and profit margin.
6. Prepare entries for purchases and sales under a periodic inventory system and calculate cost of goods sold (Appendix 5A).

the navigator

Improved Efficiency in Merchandising

Shoppers Drug Mart's beginnings date back to 1921, when Leon Koffler opened the first two Koffler drugstores in Toronto. Mr. Koffler's son, Murray Koffler, took over the family business in 1941 at the age of 20. By the 1960s, the younger Koffler had changed the way pharmacies operated by introducing the self-serve concept and building a network of 17 drugstores called Shoppers Drug Mart, each owned by a fellow pharmacist, or what he called an "associate." His goal was to build a national network of pharmacies without sacrificing the personal service of a local community pharmacist.

Today, Shoppers Drug Mart Corporation includes more than 1,200 Shoppers Drug Mart/Pharmaprix stores in every province and two territories. The company also licenses or owns medical clinic pharmacies called Shoppers Simply Pharmacy® (Pharmaprix Simplement Santé® in Quebec), luxury beauty destinations called Murale™, medical equipment sales and services called Shoppers Home Health Care® stores, pharmaceutical distribution and patient support services called Shoppers Drug Mart Specialty Health Network Inc., and long-term-care pharmaceutical products and services called MediSystem Technologies Inc. It would seem that Mr. Koffler has exceeded his goal.

With sales of more than $10 billion in 2010, Shoppers Drug Mart is the number one provider of pharmacy products and services in Canada. For a company this size, efficient merchandising operations are essential. In 2008, Shoppers introduced a number of initiatives to help manage its cost of goods sold and improve productivity. Its Project Infinity, which was piloted in 2008, was designed to improve operational efficiency, reduce costs, and strengthen the capabilities of store management and staff. The company wanted to improve shelf maintenance, as well as properly align staff functions with a new labour scheduling tool and new standards for key activities. In-stock position improved dramatically, positively impacting sales, inventory management, and backroom efficiency. These changes also saw an improvement in customer service index scores.

With the success of Project Infinity, Shoppers launched Pharmacy Infinity. This initiative focuses on standardizing the approach to regular functions within the pharmacy and making day-to-day operations more efficient. The goal is that, with more efficient processes in place, pharmacists will have more time to deliver professional services to customers. In 2011, this project expanded to include improved technology to enhance the operating system and improve inventory management.

Shoppers is also focusing on improving the distribution of its merchandise. Although it already operated one of the leading distribution centres in Canada, it is always on the lookout for measures to streamline its distribution and transportation. In 2008, a new distribution centre in Richmond, B.C., reduced the distance travelled and costs incurred to service the stores in western Canada, while a new distribution centre in Cornwall, Ontario, completed in 2010, provides similar efficiencies in Ontario and Quebec.

All these initiatives share the goal of a more efficient merchandising process, resulting in improved inventory management and, ultimately, increased customer satisfaction.

the navigator

preview of CHAPTER | 5

The first four chapters of this text focused mostly on service companies, like the fictional Sierra Corporation. In this and the next chapter, we turn our attention to merchandising companies. Merchandising companies such as Shoppers Drug Mart buy and sell merchandise for profit rather than perform a service. In this chapter, you will learn the basics of accounting for merchandising transactions. You will also learn how to prepare and analyze the income statement for a merchandising company.

The chapter is organized as follows:

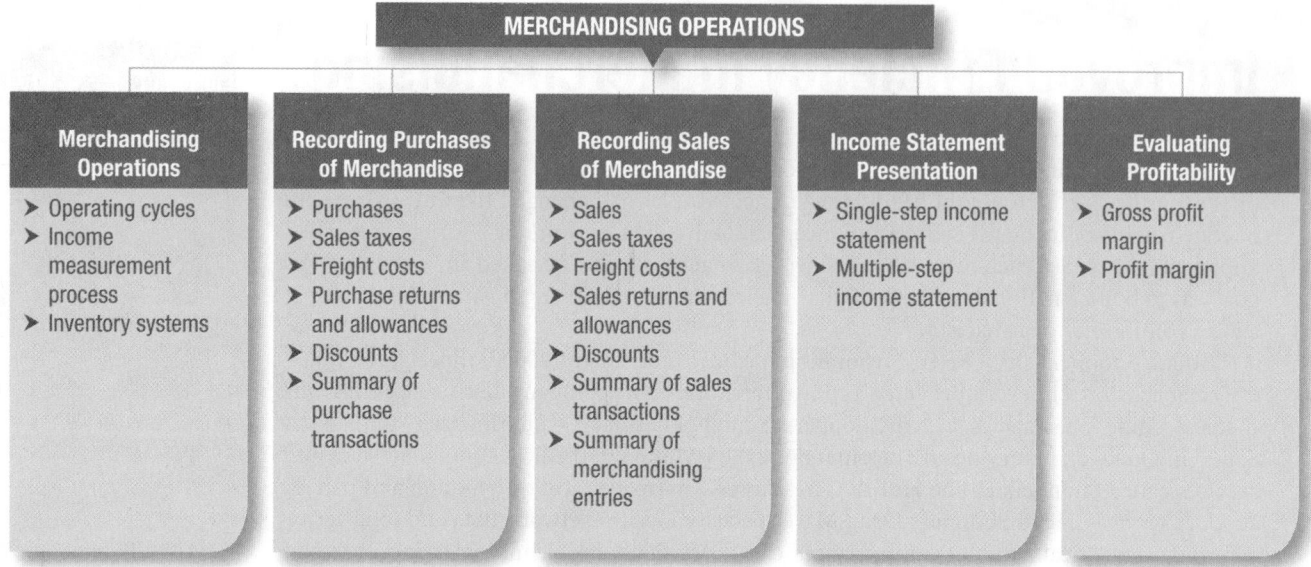

Merchandising Operations

STUDY OBJECTIVE 1

Identify the differences between service and merchandising companies.

Merchandising is one of the largest and most influential industries in Canada. For example, in a recent year, Canada exported $335 billion of merchandise and imported $365 billion.

Merchandising involves purchasing products (inventory) to resell to customers. Inventory for a merchandising company can consist of many different items. For example, in a Shoppers Drug Mart store, prescription medication, over-the-counter medication, cosmetics, and personal care products are just a few of the inventory items on hand. These items have two common characteristics: (1) they are owned by the company, and (2) they are in a form ready for sale to customers. Thus, only one inventory classification, **merchandise inventory** or just inventory, is needed to describe the many different items that make up the total inventory.

Merchandising companies that purchase and sell directly to consumers are called **retailers**. Merchandising companies that sell to retailers are known as **wholesalers**. Companies that produce goods for sale to wholesalers (or others) are called **manufacturers**.

A manufacturing company also has inventory, but differs from a merchandising company in that some of its inventory may not yet be ready for sale. Its inventory has the same first characteristic as inventory for a merchandising company: it is owned by the company. However, this inventory is not in a form ready for sale to customers, but rather is in the process of production for sale to customers.

As a result, inventory is usually classified into three categories by manufacturing companies: raw materials, work in process, and finished goods. **Raw materials** are the basic goods and materials that are on hand and will be used in production but have not yet been sent into production. **Work in process** is that portion of inventory on which production has started but is not yet complete. **Finished goods** inventory is manufactured items that are completed and ready for sale.

The accounting concepts discussed in this chapter apply to the inventory classifications of both merchandising and manufacturing companies. Our focus in this chapter is primarily on merchandising inventory. Manufacturing inventory will be discussed in more detail in a managerial accounting course.

OPERATING CYCLES

The steps in the accounting cycle for a merchandising company are the same as the steps for a service company. However, the **operating cycle**—the time it takes to go from cash to cash in producing revenues—is usually longer for a merchandising company than it is for a service company. In a service company, the company performs services for cash or on account (which eventually results in cash when the account is collected). In a merchandising company, the company first has to purchase merchandise for cash or on account, before it can sell it for cash or on account.

Illustration 5-1 contrasts the operating cycles of service and merchandising companies, assuming purchases and sales are made on account.

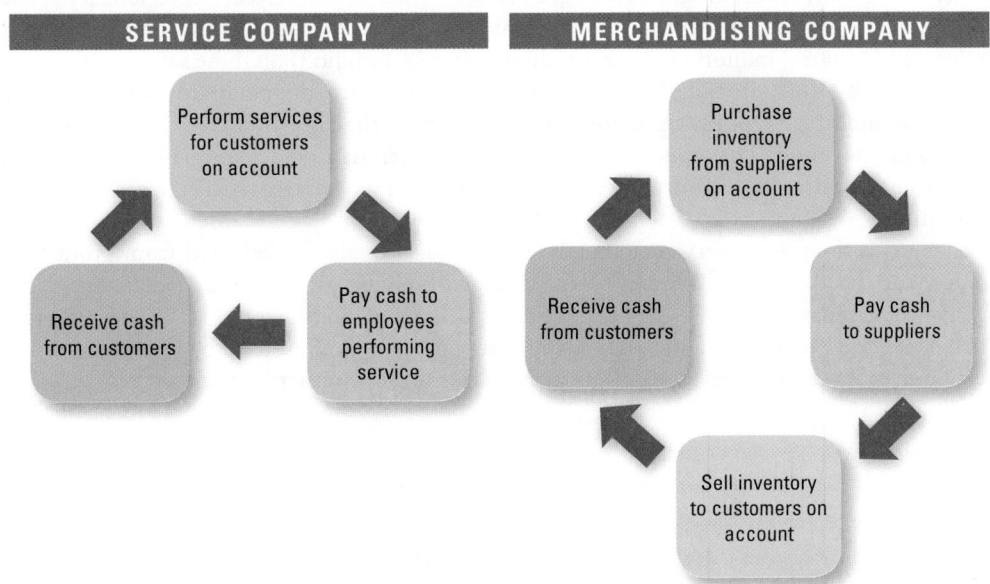

▶Illustration 5-1
Operating cycles

■ Keeping an Eye on Cash

The operating cycle for a merchandising company, as explained above, is the amount of time from the commitment of cash to buy inventory until the collection of cash resulting from the sale of inventory. In the typical course of events, a merchandising company purchases inventory on credit, increasing accounts payable. The company then sells that inventory on credit, increasing accounts receivable. Afterwards, it pays cash for its accounts payable, and collects cash from its accounts receivable. This amount of time between the outlay of cash and the collection of cash is known as the cash conversion cycle.

A short cash conversion cycle implies that the company needs to finance its inventory and accounts receivable for only a short period of time. A long cash conversion cycle indicates lower liquidity. It implies that a company must finance its inventory and accounts receivable for a longer period of time. Consequently, a shorter cash conversion cycle indicates greater liquidity.

Examples of cash conversion cycles for four competing computer companies are as follows:

Apple Inc.	22 days
Dell Inc.	38 days
IBM Corp.	59 days
Hewlett-Packard Company	63 days

INCOME MEASUREMENT PROCESS

Measuring profit for a merchandising company is basically the same as for a service company. That is, profit (or loss) results when expenses are deducted from revenues. In a merchandising company, the main source of revenue is from the sale of merchandise, which is often referred to simply as **sales revenue** or just sales. As we learned in Chapter 1, revenue is often called *income*, especially by international companies.

Unlike expenses for a service company, expenses for a merchandising company are divided into two categories: (1) cost of goods sold and (2) operating expenses. Some merchandising companies may also have other revenues and expenses, which we will learn about later in the chapter.

The **cost of goods sold** is the total cost of the merchandise that was sold during the period. This expense is directly related to the revenue that is recognized from the sale of goods. Sales revenue less the cost of goods sold is called **gross profit**. For example, as mentioned in the feature story, Shoppers Drug Mart reported sales revenue of $10,376.1 million for the year ended January 1, 2011. It cost Shoppers $6,372.4 million to purchase this merchandise to sell, so the company earned a gross profit of $4,003.7 million ($10,376.1 million – $6,372.4 million) on these sales.

Alternative Terminology
Gross profit is also called gross margin.

After gross profit is calculated, operating expenses are deducted to determine profit before income tax. **Operating expenses** are expenses that are incurred in the process of earning sales revenue. The operating expenses of a merchandising company include many of the same expenses found in a service company, such as salaries, insurance, utilities, and depreciation.

Then, as is done for a service company, income tax expense is deducted from profit before income tax to determine profit (loss). The income measurement process for a merchandising company, assuming it has no other revenues and expenses, is shown in Illustration 5-2. The items in the two blue boxes are unique to a merchandising company; they are not used by a service company. And, in a service company, revenue is known as service revenue rather than sales revenue.

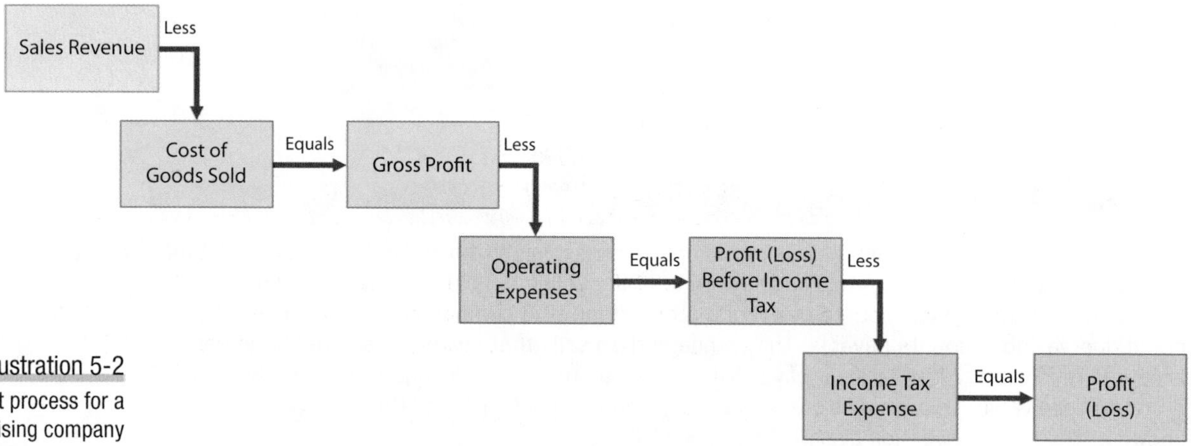

▸Illustration 5-2
Income measurement process for a merchandising company

INVENTORY SYSTEMS

A merchandising company keeps track of its inventory to determine what is available for sale (inventory) and what has been sold (cost of goods sold). The flow of costs for a merchandising company is as follows: What you have on hand at the beginning of the period plus what you purchase during the period gives you the total goods you have available for sale during the period. Or, in accounting terms, *beginning inventory* plus the *cost of goods purchased* equals the *cost of goods available for sale*. As goods are sold, they are assigned to *cost of goods sold* (we will learn how to assign these costs in Chapter 6). Those goods that are not sold by the end of the accounting period represent what's left, or in accounting terms, *ending inventory*. Ending inventory (goods not sold) is reported as merchandise inventory, a current asset on the statement of financial position. The cost of goods sold (goods sold) is reported as cost of goods sold expense on the income statement.

Illustration 5-3 describes these relationships.

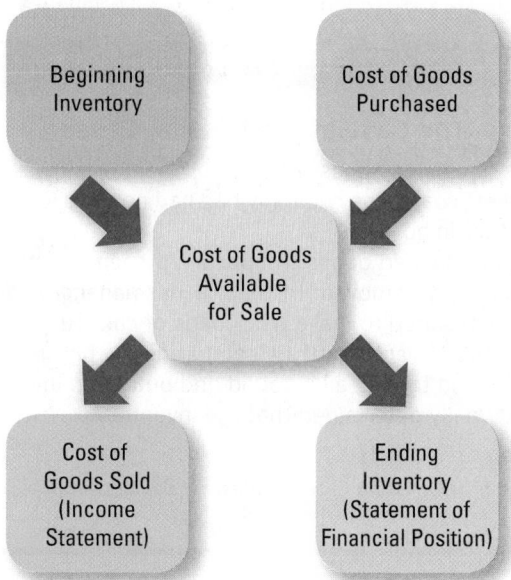

▶Illustration 5-3
Flow of costs for a merchandising company

One of two kinds of systems is used to account for inventory and the cost of goods sold: a **perpetual inventory system** or a **periodic inventory system**.

Perpetual Inventory System

In a **perpetual inventory system**, detailed records are maintained for the cost of each product that is purchased and sold. These records continuously—perpetually—show the quantity and cost of the inventory purchased, sold, and on hand. For example, a Ford auto dealership keeps separate inventory records for each automobile, truck, and van on its lot and showroom floor. Similarly, companies like Shoppers Drug Mart are able to keep a running record of prescription medication and other goods that they buy and sell by using bar codes and optical scanners.

When inventory items are purchased under a perpetual inventory system, the purchased item is recorded by debiting (increasing) the Merchandise Inventory account. When merchandise inventory is later sold, the cost of the goods that have just been sold (the original purchase cost of the merchandise) is obtained from the inventory records. This cost is transferred from the account Merchandise Inventory (an asset) to the account Cost of Goods Sold (an expense). **Under a perpetual inventory system, the cost of goods sold and the reduction in inventory—both its quantity and cost—are recorded each time a sale occurs**. As a result, the Merchandise Inventory account is always able to reflect the amount of ending inventory on hand. This helps make it possible for management to monitor merchandise availability and maintain optimum inventory levels.

Inventory is usually the largest current asset for a merchandiser. Effective control over the merchandise on hand is an important feature of a perpetual inventory system. Since the inventory records show the quantities that should be on hand, the merchandise can be counted at any time to see whether the amount actually on hand matches the inventory records. Any differences that are found can be investigated and adjusted, if required.

To adjust for any inventory shortages, the Cost of Goods Sold account would be debited and the Merchandise Inventory account credited. Although the "missing" inventory has not been sold, the Cost of Goods Sold account is debited because inventory losses are considered part of the cost of selling the goods. The missing inventory must be removed from the Merchandise Inventory account so that the account reflects the actual amount of inventory on hand.

Inventory overages are adjusted by debiting the Merchandise Inventory account and crediting the Cost of Goods Sold account. For control purposes, a physical inventory count is always taken at least once a year, and ideally more often, under the perpetual inventory system. We will learn more about counting inventory in the next chapter.

 **ACCOUNTING MATTERS!**   *Management Perspective*

The Case of the Missing Cases

Thirty-five thousand cases of canned goods—enough to fill a dozen trucks—seemingly disappeared from a warehouse on the west coast. The company had had no prior losses of this size at any of its warehouses during its century in business.

How did 35,000 cases of canned goods disappear? It seemed unlikely at the time that this amount of inventory was simply removed. Instead, a mismanaged warehouse move, software changes, and other events conspired to make truckloads of canned goods "appear to disappear." How was the "missing" inventory discovered? By comparing the physical inventory count with the perpetual inventory records and tracing all inbound and outbound inventory movements back to the original records, it was finally determined that the inventory was still there—just in a different location than expected.

Source: Paul Engle, "The Case of the Missing Cases," *Industrial Engineer,* republished June 9, 2010, originally published July 2, 2007, p. 22

Periodic Inventory System

In a **periodic inventory system**, detailed inventory records of the merchandise on hand are not kept throughout the period. As a result, **the cost of goods sold is determined only at the end of the accounting period**—that is, periodically—when a physical inventory count is done to determine the cost of the goods on hand. First, the physical inventory count determines the quantities on hand, and then costs are assigned to these quantities. As was mentioned earlier, we will learn how to assign costs to quantities in Chapter 6.

In a periodic inventory system, after the cost of the goods on hand (ending inventory) at the end of the period has been determined, we can use this information to calculate the cost of the goods that were sold during the period. To determine the cost of goods sold under a periodic inventory system, the following steps are necessary:

1. Beginning inventory: Determine the cost of goods on hand at the beginning of the accounting period (beginning inventory). Note that this is the same amount as the previous accounting period's ending inventory.
2. Cost of goods available for sale: Add the cost of goods purchased to the beginning inventory. The total is the **cost of goods available for sale** during the period.
3. Ending inventory: Determine the cost of goods on hand at the end of the accounting period (ending inventory) from the physical inventory count. Subtract the ending inventory from the cost of goods available for sale. The result is the cost of goods sold.

How do companies decide whether to use a perpetual or periodic inventory system? They compare the cost of the detailed record keeping that is required for a perpetual inventory system with the benefits of having the additional information about, and control over, their inventory. The widespread availability of computerized perpetual inventory software and optical scanners has enabled the majority of companies to adopt perpetual inventory systems at a reasonable cost and enjoy their benefits.

Some small businesses find it unnecessary or uneconomical to invest in a perpetual inventory system. Managers of these businesses can, in most cases, find other ways to control merchandise and manage day-to-day operations using a periodic inventory system.

Because the perpetual inventory system is widely used, we illustrate it in this chapter. The periodic inventory system is described in the appendix to this chapter.

BEFORE YOU GO ON...

▶ Do It! Inventory Calculations

Waterfun Corporation has 6 Bombardier GTI 130 Sea-Doos on hand on January 1 at a cost of $6,000 each. It purchased 24 more of this model of Sea-Doo during the year for a total cost of $148,800. It sold 26 GTI Sea-Doos during the year with a cost of $6,160 each and a selling price of $9,599 each. (a) Determine the following amounts in both units and dollars: (1) beginning inventory on January 1, (2) cost of goods purchased, (3) cost of goods available for sale, (4) cost of goods sold, and (5) ending inventory on December 31. (b) The company uses a perpetual inventory system and counted 4 Sea-Doos in ending inventory during a physical inventory count at year end. Does the physical inventory count agree with your calculations in (a)(5)?

Action Plan

- Remember the formula: beginning inventory + cost of goods purchased = cost of goods available for sale.
- Cost of goods available for sale – ending inventory = cost of goods sold
- The selling price affects sales revenue but not any of the inventory calculations that are carried at cost, including the cost of goods sold.

Solution

(a)

	Units		Dollars
(1) Beginning inventory	6	(6 × $6,000)	$ 36,000
(2) Cost of goods purchased	24		148,800
(3) Cost of goods available for sale	30		184,800
(4) Cost of goods sold	(26)	(26 × $6,160)	(160,160)
(5) Ending inventory	4		$ 24,640

(b) Yes, the physical inventory count of 4 units in ending inventory agrees with the calculations in (a). If it did not, the difference should be investigated and adjusted if required.

the navigator

Recording Purchases of Merchandise

Purchases of merchandise for resale are recorded in the Merchandise Inventory account. The purchase cost is increased by freight costs in certain circumstances and decreased by any purchase returns, allowances, and discounts. The net result of all of these costs is known as the **cost of goods purchased**. We will discuss each of these components of the cost of goods purchased in the next sections.

STUDY OBJECTIVE 2

Prepare entries for purchases under a perpetual inventory system.

PURCHASES

Purchases of inventory can be made for cash or credit (on account). Purchases are normally recorded by the buyer when the goods are transferred from the seller to the buyer. Every purchase should be supported by a record—whether written or electronic—that provides evidence of the transaction.

Cash purchases should be supported by a cash register receipt indicating the items purchased and amounts paid. Cash purchases are recorded by a debit (increase) to the Merchandise Inventory account and a credit (decrease) to the Cash account.

Credit purchases should be supported by a **purchase invoice** that indicates the total purchase price and other relevant information. The buyer does not prepare a separate purchase invoice. Instead, an invoice is prepared by the seller. The original copy of the invoice goes to the buyer to be used as a purchase invoice, and a copy is kept by the seller to be used as a sales invoice.

In addition, in many larger companies, when orders are placed with a supplier, credit purchases are documented by a purchase order that details the types, quantities, and agreed prices for products or services the seller will provide to the buyer. This purchase order is later matched up with the purchase invoice to ensure that what was ordered was actually received at the appropriate price.

To illustrate the recording of purchases, let's assume that PW Audio Supply, Inc. (the seller) prepares an invoice for the sale of printed circuit boards to Sauk Stereo Ltd. (the buyer) on May 4 in the amount of $3,800. The terms of the sale are 2/10, n/30, FOB shipping point. We will discuss what these terms mean in detail in the next few sections.

Sauk Stereo would make the following entry to record the purchase of merchandise:

A	=	L	+	SE
+3,800		+3,800		

Cash flows: no effect

May 4	Merchandise Inventory	3,800	
	Accounts Payable		3,800
	(To record goods purchased on account from PW Audio Supply, terms 2/10, n/30, FOB shipping point)		

Only merchandise purchased for the purpose of selling to customers is recorded in the Merchandise Inventory account. For example, Shoppers Drug Mart would record purchases of pharmacy products, health and beauty aids, household goods, and anything else it purchased for resale to customers by debiting (increasing) the Merchandise Inventory account. Purchases of assets that the company will use rather than resell, such as supplies and equipment, are recorded as increases to specific asset accounts rather than as increases to the Merchandise Inventory account. For example, Shoppers would increase the Supplies account to record the purchase of cash register receipt paper or materials that it uses to make shelf signs.

SALES TAXES

Sales taxes are collected by most merchandising and service companies on the goods they sell and the services they provide. Sales taxes in Canada include the Goods and Services Tax (GST) and the Provincial Sales Tax (PST). At the time of writing, GST was 5% and PST varied, depending on the province or territory, from 0% to 10%. In all provinces and territories except Quebec and Prince Edward Island, sales tax is charged on the selling price of the item before GST is applied, thus avoiding PST being charged on GST.

In many provinces in Canada, GST and PST have been combined into one tax called the Harmonized Sales Tax (HST). HST currently ranges from 12% to 15%.

When merchandising companies purchase goods for resale, they pay GST or HST on the cost of the goods. However, GST or HST does not form part of the cost of the merchandise because companies can get back any GST or HST they pay on purchases (by offsetting it against the GST or HST they collect from customers). Generally, retailers do not pay PST on purchases of goods for resale, as they are exempt for this purpose.

Sales taxes add much complexity to the accounting process, and not all companies and their goods and services are taxable. The accounting transactions described in this chapter are therefore presented without the added complication of sales taxes. We will learn more about sales taxes in Chapter 10.

FREIGHT COSTS

The sales/purchase invoice should indicate whether the seller or the buyer must pay the cost of transporting the goods to the buyer's place of business. Freight terms state who pays the freight charges (i.e., shipping costs) and who is responsible for the risk of damage to the merchandise during transit. Freight terms can vary, but are often expressed as either FOB shipping point or FOB destination. The letters FOB mean "free on board" until the point where ownership is transferred.

FOB shipping point means that the goods are delivered to the point of shipping (normally the seller's place of business) by the seller. The buyer pays the freight costs to get the goods from the point of shipping to the destination (normally the buyer's place of business) and is responsible for any damages that may occur along the way.

FOB destination means that the goods are delivered by the seller to their destination. The seller pays the freight to get the goods from the point of shipping to their destination and is responsible for any damages that may occur along the way.

Illustration 5-4 shows these shipping terms.

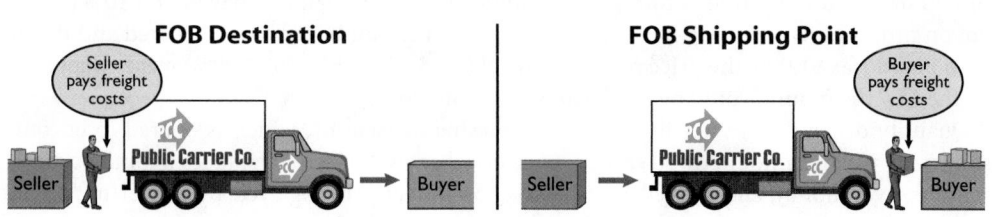

FOB Destination   **FOB Shipping Point**

▶Illustration 5-4
Freight terms

We mentioned earlier in the Purchases section that the terms of the sale of the circuit boards from PW Audio Supply to Sauk Stereo were FOB shipping point. This means that the buyer (Sauk Stereo) paid the freight charges from the shipping point (likely PW Audio Supply's place of business) to the destination (Sauk Stereo's place of business) and then debited (increased) its Merchandise Inventory account for the additional cost. Why? **The cost of inventory includes not only the purchase cost but also other costs that may be incurred in bringing inventories to their present location (e.g., shipping) and ready for sale.** As a result, any freight paid by the buyer is recorded as part of the cost of the merchandise purchased.

Assume that upon delivery of the goods on May 4, Sauk Stereo (the buyer) pays Public Carrier Co. $150 for freight charges. The entry on Sauk Stereo's books is:

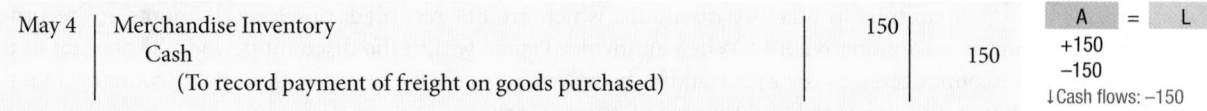

May 4	Merchandise Inventory	150	
	Cash		150
	(To record payment of freight on goods purchased)		

A	=	L	+	SE
+150				
−150				

↓Cash flows: −150

In contrast, if the freight terms had been FOB destination rather than FOB shipping point, the seller (PW Audio Supply) would have paid the freight costs. Sauk Stereo would have no entry to record and PW Audio Supply would record the freight costs it paid on outgoing merchandise as an operating expense. We will learn how to record freight costs incurred by the seller later in the chapter.

Helpful Hint
The buyer only pays freight when the shipping terms are FOB shipping point.

PURCHASE RETURNS AND ALLOWANCES

A purchaser may be dissatisfied with the merchandise received. The goods may be damaged or defective, of inferior quality, or might not fit the buyer's specifications. In such cases, the buyer may return the goods to the seller. The buyer will receive a cash refund if the purchase was made for cash. Credit is given if the purchase was made on account.

Alternatively, the buyer may choose to keep the merchandise if the seller is willing to give an allowance (deduction) from the purchase price. These types of transactions are known as **purchase returns and allowances.** In both cases, the result is a decrease in the cost of goods purchased.

Assume that Sauk Stereo returned goods costing $300 to PW Audio Supply on May 8. Because these goods were originally sold on credit, Sauk Stereo will receive a credit (rather than cash) from PW Audio Supply for the return of this merchandise. The entry by Sauk Stereo for the returned merchandise is:

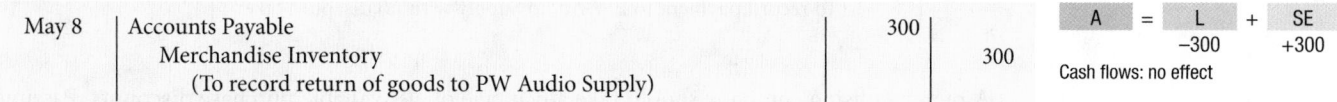

May 8	Accounts Payable	300	
	Merchandise Inventory		300
	(To record return of goods to PW Audio Supply)		

A	=	L	+	SE
		−300		+300

Cash flows: no effect

Sauk Stereo increased the Merchandise Inventory and Accounts Payable accounts when the goods were originally purchased. Sauk Stereo therefore decreases the Merchandise Inventory and Accounts Payable accounts when it returns the goods, or when it is granted an allowance.

DISCOUNTS

The terms of a purchase may include an offer of a quantity discount for a bulk purchase. A **quantity discount** gives a reduction in price according to the volume of the purchase. In other words, the larger the number of items purchased, the better the discount. **Quantity discounts are not recorded or accounted for separately**. For example, PW Audio Supply may offer a 10% price discount on orders of five or more items. So, if five printed circuit boards were ordered and the price of each board was $1,900, the price per board would be $1,710 ($1,900 × 90%) rather than $1,900. Only the $1,710 amount would be recorded by Sauk Stereo.

Quantity discounts are not the same as a **purchase discount**, which is offered to encourage customers to pay the amount owed early. A purchase discount offers advantages to both parties: the purchaser saves money, and the seller is able to shorten its operating cycle by converting accounts receivable into cash earlier.

Purchase discounts are noted on the invoice through credit terms. These terms specify the amount of the discount and the time period during which it is offered. They also indicate the date by which the purchaser is expected to pay the full invoice price. In the invoice prepared by PW Audio Supply for the sale of printed circuit boards, the credit terms were 2/10, n/30, which is read "two-ten, net thirty." This means that a 2% cash discount may be taken on the invoice price, less ("net of ") any returns or allowances, if payment is made within 10 days of the invoice date (the discount period). Otherwise, the invoice price, less any returns or allowances, is due 30 days from the invoice date.

Not every seller offers purchase discounts, although they are common in certain industries. When the seller chooses not to offer a discount for fast payment, credit terms will specify only the maximum time period for paying the balance due. For example, the period may be stated as n/30, meaning that the net amount must be paid in 30 days.

In contrast to quantity discounts, which are not recorded, purchase discounts are recorded in the accounting records. When an invoice is paid within the discount period, the amount of the discount decreases the Merchandise Inventory account. By paying within the discount period, the merchandiser has reduced the cost of its inventory.

To illustrate, assume Sauk Stereo pays the balance due of $3,500 (gross invoice price of $3,800 less purchase returns and allowances of $300) on May 14, the last day of the discount period. **Note that discounts are not taken on freight costs**. The discount is $70 ($3,500 × 2%), and the amount of cash paid by Sauk Stereo is $3,430 ($3,500 – $70). The entry to record the May 14 payment by Sauk Stereo is:

A	=	L	+	SE
−3,430		−3,500		
−70				

↓ Cash flows: −3,430

May 14	Accounts Payable	3,500	
	Cash		3,430
	Merchandise Inventory		70
	(To record payment to PW Audio Supply within discount period)		

If Sauk Stereo failed to take the discount and instead made full payment of $3,500 on June 3 (30 days after the date of sale), Sauk Stereo would make the following entry rather than the one shown above:

A	=	L	+	SE
−3,500		−3,500		

↓ Cash flows: −3,500

June 3	Accounts Payable	3,500	
	Cash		3,500
	(To record payment to PW Audio Supply with no discount taken)		

A merchandising company should take advantage of all available purchase discounts. Passing up the discount may be viewed as paying interest for use of the money. For example, if Sauk Stereo passed up the discount, it would be paying 2% for the use of $3,500 for 20 days. This equals an annual interest rate of 36.5% (2% × 365 ÷ 20). It would be better for Sauk Stereo to borrow at bank interest rates, which are substantially lower than 36.5%, than to lose the discount.

Because of the importance of taking purchase discounts, some companies prepare journal entries to track the discounts not taken, or lost. Consequently, there are other ways to record discounts than shown in this section. These will be discussed in an intermediate accounting course.

SUMMARY OF PURCHASE TRANSACTIONS

A summary of the effect of the previous purchase transactions on Merchandise Inventory is provided in the following T account (with transaction descriptions in parentheses). Sauk Stereo originally purchased $3,800 worth of inventory for resale. It paid $150 in freight charges. It then returned $300 worth of goods. Finally, it received a $70 discount off the balance owed because it paid within the discount period. This results in a balance in the Merchandise Inventory account of $3,580, as follows:

			Merchandise Inventory			
(Purchase)	May	4	3,800	May 8	300	(Purchase return)
(Freight)		4	150	14	70	(Purchase discount)
	Bal.		3,580			

The $3,580 amount in the Merchandise Inventory account represents the **cost of the goods purchased**. The cost of goods purchased includes the cost of the merchandise, increased by any freight costs incurred if the shipping terms are FOB shipping point, and decreased by any purchase returns and allowances and purchase discounts.

BEFORE YOU GO ON...

▶ Do It! Purchase Transactions

On September 2, Brighthouse Corp. buys merchandise on account from Junot Inc. for $1,500, terms 2/10, n/30, FOB shipping point. The appropriate company pays freight charges of $75 on September 4 from the point of shipping to the destination. On September 8, Brighthouse returns $200 of the merchandise to Junot. On September 11, Brighthouse pays the total amount owing. Record the transactions on Brighthouse's books.

Action Plan

- Purchases of goods for resale are recorded in the asset account Merchandise Inventory when a perpetual inventory system is used.
- Examine freight terms to determine which company pays the freight charges. Freight charges paid by the buyer increase the cost of the merchandise inventory.
- The Merchandise Inventory account is reduced by the cost of merchandise returned.
- Calculate purchase discounts using the net amount owing for purchases (purchases less any purchase returns and allowances). Do not calculate purchase discounts on freight.
- Reduce the Merchandise Inventory account by the amount of the purchase discount.

Solution

Brighthouse (Buyer)

Sept.	2	Merchandise Inventory	1,500	
		Accounts Payable		1,500
		(To record goods purchased on account from Junot, terms 2/10, n/30, FOB shipping point)		
	4	Merchandise Inventory	75	
		Cash		75
		(To record freight paid on goods purchased)		
	8	Accounts Payable	200	
		Merchandise Inventory		200
		(To record return of goods to Junot)		
	11	Accounts Payable ($1,500 – $200)	1,300	
		Merchandise Inventory ($1,300 × 2%)		26
		Cash ($1,300 – $26)		1,274
		(To record payment to Junot within discount period)		

Recording Sales of Merchandise

You will recall from Chapter 2, when we discussed the elements of the financial statements, that revenue is recorded when there is an increase or inflow of assets due to economic benefits received, or expected to be received, as a result of the performance of a service or delivery of goods. For a merchandising company, revenue is typically considered to be earned when the ownership of the merchandise is transferred from the seller to the buyer. At this point, the sales transaction is completed and the selling price is established.

We will discuss how to record sales revenue, including sales taxes, freight costs, sales returns and allowances, and sales discounts, in the next sections.

SALES

To record sales revenue, an asset (typically cash or accounts receivable) account is debited (increased) and the sales revenue account is credited (also increased). Alternatively, if a customer had previously paid in advance, a liability (unearned revenue) account is debited (decreased) and the sales revenue account credited (increased).

Similar to purchase transactions, every sales transaction—whether for cash or credit—should be supported by a record—whether written or electronic—that provides evidence of the sale. Cash register tapes provide evidence of cash sales. A **sales invoice** provides support for a credit sale.

While only one journal entry is required to record the purchase of merchandise, **two journal entries are required to record each sale in a perpetual inventory system**. The first entry records the sales revenue: Cash (or Accounts Receivable, if it is a credit sale) is increased by a debit and Sales is increased by a credit for the selling (invoice) price of the goods. The second entry records the cost of the merchandise sold: Cost of Goods Sold is increased by a debit and Merchandise Inventory is decreased by a credit for the cost of the goods. As a result, at all times Merchandise Inventory will show the amount of inventory that is (should be) on hand.

To illustrate a credit sales transaction, we will continue to use PW Audio Supply's sale of $3,800 of merchandise on May 4 to Sauk Stereo that was illustrated earlier in the purchases section. Assume the merchandise cost PW Audio Supply $2,400 when it was originally purchased. The sale is recorded as follows:

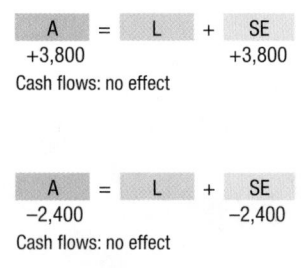

A	=	L	+	SE
+3,800				+3,800

Cash flows: no effect

May 4	Accounts Receivable	3,800	
	Sales		3,800
	(To record credit sale to Sauk Stereo, terms 2/10, n/30, FOB shipping point)		

A	=	L	+	SE
−2,400				−2,400

Cash flows: no effect

4	Cost of Goods Sold	2,400	
	Merchandise Inventory		2,400
	(To record cost of merchandise sold to Sauk Stereo)		

For internal decision-making purposes, merchandising companies may use more than one sales account. For example, PW Audio Supply may decide to keep separate sales accounts for its major product lines, rather than a single combined sales account. This enables company management to monitor sales trends more closely and respond in a more strategic way to changes in sales patterns. For example, if sales of wireless speakers are increasing while sales of powered speakers are decreasing, the company should re-evaluate both its advertising and pricing policies on each of these items to ensure that they are optimal.

On the income statement presented to external users, most merchandising companies provide only a single sales figure—the sum of all of their individual sales accounts. This is done for two reasons. First, providing detail on all of the individual sales accounts would make the income statement much longer. Second, companies generally do not want their competitors to know the details of their operating results.

We are starting to see some changes to this practice, however. A number of companies are now trying to improve the quality of their financial reporting and provide more informative disclosures. For example, General Electric Company now provides much more detail on the sources of its revenues than it did in the past.

SALES TAXES

Sales taxes are collected by merchandising companies on the goods that they sell. You will recall from earlier in the chapter that sales taxes can include GST or HST.

When a company collects sales taxes from selling a product or service, these **sales taxes are not recorded as revenue**. The sales taxes are collected on behalf of the federal and provincial governments, and must be periodically remitted to these authorities. Sales taxes that are collected from selling a product or service are recorded as a liability until they are paid to the government. Further discussion of sales taxes is deferred until Chapter 10.

FREIGHT COSTS

As discussed earlier in the chapter, freight terms on the sales invoice—FOB destination and FOB shipping point—indicate who is responsible for shipping costs. If the terms are FOB destination, the seller assumes the responsibility for getting the goods to their intended destination. Freight costs incurred by the seller on outgoing merchandise are an operating expense to the seller. These costs are debited to the account Freight Out or Delivery Expense. When the freight charges are paid by the seller, the seller will usually set a higher invoice price for the goods to cover the cost of shipping.

In PW Audio Supply's sale of electronic equipment to Sauk Stereo, the freight terms (FOB shipping point) indicate that Sauk Stereo (the buyer) must pay the cost of shipping the goods from the shipping point (likely PW Audio Supply's place of business) to their destination (Sauk Stereo's place of business). PW Audio Supply makes no journal entry to record the cost of shipping, since this cost was incurred by the buyer and not the seller.

> **Helpful Hint**
> The seller only pays freight when the shipping terms are FOB destination.

If the freight terms had been FOB destination, PW Audio Supply would have paid the freight costs and prepared a journal entry to record the cost as an operating expense, as shown below:

May 4	Freight Out	150	
	Cash		150
	(To record payment of freight on goods sold)		

A	=	L	+	SE
−150				−150

↓ Cash flows: −150

SALES RETURNS AND ALLOWANCES

We now look at the "flip side" of purchase returns and allowances, as these are recorded as **sales returns and allowances** on the books of the seller. When customers (buyers) return goods, or are given price reductions, the seller will either return cash to the buyer, or reduce the buyer's accounts receivable if the goods were originally purchased on credit.

Just as a sale requires two entries in a perpetual inventory system, so too do returns and allowances. PW Audio Supply prepares the two separate journal entries shown below to record the $300 credit for goods returned by Sauk Stereo. The first entry records a debit (increase) to the Sales Returns and Allowances account and a credit (decrease) to the Accounts Receivable account for the $300 selling price. Note that if the sales return had been for a cash sale, Cash would be credited instead of Accounts Receivable.

The Sales Returns and Allowances account is a **contra revenue account** to Sales. The normal balance of the Sales Returns and Allowances account is a debit. A contra account is used, instead of debiting the Sales account, to disclose the amount of sales returns and allowances. A debit (decrease) recorded directly to Sales would hide the percentage of total sales that ends up being lost through sales returns and allowances. It could also distort comparisons between total sales in different accounting periods.

This information is important to management. Excessive returns and allowances suggest the possibility of inferior merchandise, inefficiencies in filling orders, errors in billing customers, or mistakes in the delivery or shipment of goods.

The second journal entry required to record a sales return in a perpetual inventory system debits (increases) the Merchandise Inventory account (assuming a $140 cost) and credits (decreases) the Cost of Goods Sold account.

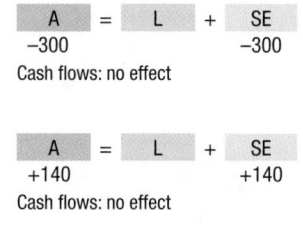

Cash flows: no effect

Cash flows: no effect

May 8	Sales Returns and Allowances	300	
	Accounts Receivable		300
	(To record return of goods by Sauk Stereo)		
8	Merchandise Inventory	140	
	Cost of Goods Sold		140
	(To record cost of merchandise returned by Sauk Stereo)		

The second entry shown above assumes that the merchandise is not damaged and is resaleable and restored to inventory. If the merchandise is not resaleable and is discarded, a second entry is not made. Since the goods are defective and cannot be resold, the seller cannot increase its Merchandise Inventory and the original cost of goods sold recorded is still the correct amount. A second entry is also not required when the seller gives the buyer an allowance. Giving a customer a sales allowance does not change the cost of the goods sold; it only changes the amount of revenue earned on the sale.

ACCOUNTING MATTERS!   *Management Perspective*

How to Make Money from Returned Goods

Returned goods can put a dent in a company's profits. When a customer returns a product, the company has to decide whether to scrap, liquidate, refurbish, return to seller, or return to stock. Calgary-based Liquidation World Inc., the largest liquidator in Canada, has made a successful business out of giving companies an opportunity to obtain some value out of unwanted products by liquidating them. It buys its merchandise from companies in Canada, the United States, the Caribbean, and the Far East and sells it in one of its nearly 100 outlets in North America at prices 30% to 70% below normal.

It is essentially a win-win situation for businesses and consumers: consumers get good value on a variety of quality goods, while manufacturers, wholesalers, and retailers have a place to dispose of unwanted merchandise.

DISCOUNTS

When quantity discounts and sales discounts are given on invoice prices, they affect the seller, as well as the buyer. No separate entry is made to record a **quantity discount**. Sales are recorded at the invoice price—whether it is the full retail price, a sale price, or a volume discount price.

Like a purchase discount, the seller may offer the buyer a cash discount for quick payment of the balance due. From the seller's point of view, this is called a **sales discount** and is offered on the invoice price less sales returns and allowances, if any.

Although no new account is added to record purchase discounts in a perpetual inventory system—the discount is recorded as a reduction in the Merchandise Inventory account—a new account, called Sales Discounts, is added to record sales discounts. Like the account for sales returns and allowances, Sales Discounts is a **contra revenue account** to Sales. Its normal balance is a debit. This account is used, instead of debiting Sales, so that management can monitor if customers are taking advantage of cash discounts.

The entry by PW Audio Supply to record the cash receipt on May 14 from Sauk Stereo within the discount period is:

May 14	Cash	3,430	
	Sales Discounts	70	
	Accounts Receivable		3,500
	(To record collection from Sauk Stereo within		
	discount period)		

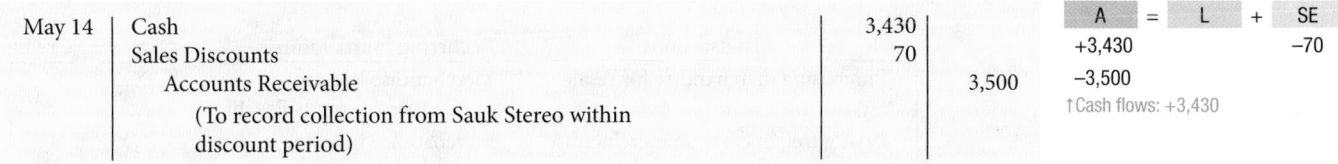

A = L + SE
+3,430   −70
−3,500
↑Cash flows: +3,430

If a customer does not take the discount, PW Audio Supply debits (increases) the Cash account for $3,500 and credits (decreases) the Accounts Receivable account for the same amount, as shown below:

June 3	Cash	3,500	
	Accounts Receivable		3,500
	(To record collection from Sauk Stereo with no		
	discount taken)		

A = L + SE
+3,500
−3,500
↑Cash flows: +3,500

SUMMARY OF SALES TRANSACTIONS

PW Audio Supply sold merchandise for $3,800, and $300 of it was later returned. A sales discount of $70 was granted as the invoice was paid within the discount period. In contrast to the purchase transactions illustrated earlier in the chapter, which affected only one account, Merchandise Inventory, sales transactions are recorded in different accounts. A summary of the effects of these transactions is provided in the following T accounts.

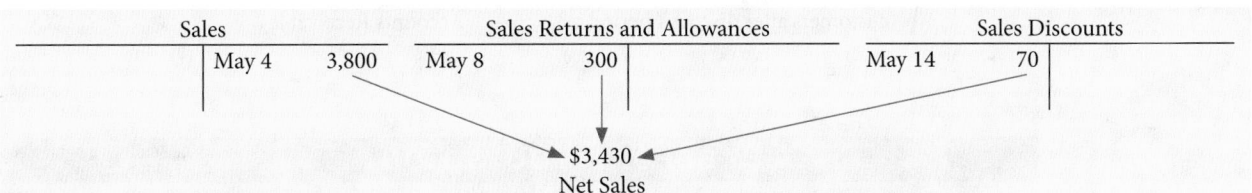

These three accounts combine to determine net sales. Illustration 5-5 shows the formula for the calculation of net sales.

Gross Sales	−	Sales Returns and Allowances	−	Sales Discounts	=	Net Sales
$3,800	−	$300	−	$70	=	$3,430

▸**Illustration 5-5**
Formula for net sales

Total sales, before deducting any sales returns and allowances and sales discounts, are known as **gross sales**. Gross sales less returns and allowances and discounts are called **net sales**. The calculation of net sales is the same whether the company uses a perpetual or a periodic inventory system. Note that freight paid by the seller is recorded as an operating expense and does not affect net sales.

SUMMARY OF MERCHANDISING ENTRIES

In the previous two sections, we have explained the journal entries made to record purchases and sales of merchandise. The following is a summary of the entries for merchandising accounts in a perpetual inventory system:

	Transactions	Recurring Journal Entries	Debit	Credit
Purchases	Purchasing merchandise for resale.	Merchandise Inventory	XX	
		Cash or Accounts Payable		XX
	Paying freight costs on merchandise purchased FOB shipping point.	Merchandise Inventory	XX	
		Cash		XX
	Receiving purchase returns or allowances from suppliers.	Cash or Accounts Payable	XX	
		Merchandise Inventory		XX
	Paying creditors on account within discount period.	Accounts Payable	XX	
		Merchandise Inventory		XX
		Cash		XX
	Paying creditors on account after discount period.	Accounts Payable	XX	
		Cash		XX
Sales	Selling merchandise to customers.	Cash or Accounts Receivable	XX	
		Sales		XX
		Cost of Goods Sold	XX	
		Merchandise Inventory		XX
	Giving sales returns or allowances to customers.	Sales Returns and Allowances	XX	
		Cash or Accounts Receivable		XX
		Merchandise Inventory	XX	
		Cost of Goods Sold		XX
	Paying freight costs on sales, FOB destination.	Freight Out	XX	
		Cash		XX
	Receiving payment on account from customers within discount period.	Cash	XX	
		Sales Discounts	XX	
		Accounts Receivable		XX
	Receiving payment on account from customers after discount period.	Cash	XX	
		Accounts Receivable		XX

BEFORE YOU GO ON...

▶ Do It! Purchase and Sales Transactions—Perpetual Inventory System

On September 4, Lalonde Ltée sells merchandise on account to Guerette Corp., terms 1/10, n/30. The selling price of the goods is $1,500, and the cost to Lalonde was $800. On September 8, goods with a selling price of $300 and a cost of $140 are returned for credit and restored to inventory. On September 13, Lalonde receives payment in full from Guerette. Record the transactions on the books of both companies, assuming a perpetual inventory system is used.

Action Plan

- Seller: Prepare two entries to record the sale of merchandise: one to record the selling price and one to record the cost of the sale. Prepare two entries to record the return of goods: one to record the selling price and one to record the cost of the return. Calculate sales discounts using the amount owing, net of any sales returns.
- Buyer: Record purchases of inventory, returned goods, and purchase discounts in one account—Merchandise Inventory. Calculate purchase discounts using the amount owing, net of any purchase returns.

Solution

Lalonde Ltée (Seller)

Sept.	4	Accounts Receivable	1,500	
		Sales		1,500
		(To record credit sale to Guerette, terms 1/10, n/30)		
	4	Cost of Goods Sold	800	
		Merchandise Inventory		800
		(To record cost of goods sold to Guerette)		
	8	Sales Returns and Allowances	300	
		Accounts Receivable		300
		(To record credit granted for receipt of returned goods from Guerette)		
	8	Merchandise Inventory	140	
		Cost of Goods Sold		140
		(To record cost of goods returned from Guerette)		
	13	Cash ($1,200 − $12)	1,188	
		Sales Discounts [($1,500 − $300) × 1%]	12	
		Accounts Receivable ($1,500 − $300)		1,200
		(To record collection from Guerette within discount period)		

Guerette Corp. (Buyer)

Sept.	4	Merchandise Inventory	1,500	
		Accounts Payable		1,500
		(To record goods purchased on account from Lalonde, terms 1/10, n/30)		
	8	Accounts Payable	300	
		Merchandise Inventory		300
		(To record return of goods to Lalonde)		
	13	Accounts Payable ($1,500 − $300)	1,200	
		Merchandise Inventory [($1,500 − $300) × 1%]		12
		Cash ($1,200 − $12)		1,188
		(To record payment to Lalonde within discount period)		

the navigator

Income Statement Presentation

Merchandisers use the classified statement of financial position introduced in Chapter 2, but add a merchandise inventory account in the current assets section of the statement. Two different forms of the income statement are widely used by merchandising companies. One is the **single-step income statement**. It has this name because only one step—subtracting total expenses (except for income tax expense) from total revenues—is required for determining profit before income tax. A second form of the income statement is the **multiple-step income statement**. This statement gets its name because it shows multiple steps in determining profit before income tax. We will look at each of these statement forms in the following sections.

STUDY OBJECTIVE 4

Prepare a single-step and a multiple-step income statement.

SINGLE-STEP INCOME STATEMENT

In a **single-step income statement**, all data are classified into two categories: (1) revenues and (2) expenses. Revenues include both operating and non-operating revenues and gains (for example, interest revenue). Expenses include cost of goods sold, operating expenses, and non-operating expenses and losses (for example, interest expense). Income tax expense is usually disclosed separately from the other expenses in a single-step income statement.

Illustration 5-6 shows a single-step income statement for PW Audio Supply, Inc., using assumed data.

▸Illustration 5-6

Single-step income statement—
perpetual inventory system

PW AUDIO SUPPLY, INC. Income Statement Year Ended December 31, 2012		
Revenues		
Net sales	$460,000	
Interest revenue	3,400	$463,400
Expenses		
Cost of goods sold	$316,000	
Salaries expense	45,000	
Rent expense	19,000	
Utilities expense	17,000	
Advertising expense	16,000	
Depreciation expense	8,000	
Freight out	7,000	
Insurance expense	2,000	
Interest expense	1,600	
Loss on sale of equipment	200	431,800
Profit before income tax		31,600
Income tax expense		6,300
Profit		$ 25,300

Cost of goods sold, interest expense, and income tax expense must be separately reported on the income statement. The remaining expenses can be included directly in the income statement, as is shown above, or can be summarized into one (or more) lines—normally called operating expenses—and detailed in the notes to the financial statements.

ASPE

Private companies following ASPE do not have to list their expenses in any particular order. Companies following IFRS must classify expenses by either their nature or function. Classifying expenses by **nature** means that expenses are reported according to their natural classification (e.g., salaries, transportation, depreciation, advertising). Illustration 5-6 shown above presents PW Audio Supply's expenses by nature.

To classify expenses by **function** means that expenses are reported according to the activity (business function) for which they were incurred (e.g., cost of goods sold, administrative, selling). Although expenses can be listed in any order within each classification, as we have done in past chapters, we have listed expenses in order of magnitude—from largest to smallest.

We should note that, while cost of goods sold is a separate account for a merchandising company using a perpetual inventory system, it can also be a functional grouping for a merchandising company using a periodic inventory system or a manufacturing company. In other words, cost of goods sold can be classified by nature or function depending on the makeup of the account. For example, when it is classified by nature for a manufacturing company, it is usually called "change in inventories of finished goods and work in process." If it is classified by function for a manufacturing company, it is called "cost of goods sold."

Administrative expenses relate to general operating activities such as management, accounting, and legal matters. **Selling expenses** are associated with making sales. They include advertising expenses as well as the expenses of completing the sale, such as delivery and shipping expenses.

Companies can choose between classifying expenses by nature or function, depending on whichever provides information that is more relevant. If a company chooses to present its expenses by function, it must also disclose additional information on the nature of certain expenses such as depreciation and employee benefits expense.

The single-step income statement is the form we have used in the text so far. There are two main reasons for using the single-step form: (1) a company does not realize any profit until total revenues exceed total expenses, so it makes sense to divide the statement into these categories; and (2) the single-step form is simple and easy to read.

About one third of Canadian companies use the single-step form of income statement. The multiple-step form is much more prevalent, as it is used by two thirds of Canadian companies. We will learn why in the next section.

MULTIPLE-STEP INCOME STATEMENT

The **multiple-step income statement** is so named because it shows several steps in determining profit (or loss). It is often considered more useful because it highlights the components of profit separately. Shoppers Drug Mart, our feature company in this chapter, uses the multiple-step form of income statement.

The multiple-step income statement shows five main steps:

1. Net sales: Sales returns and allowances and sales discounts are subtracted from gross sales to determine net sales.
2. Gross profit: Cost of goods sold is subtracted from net sales to determine gross profit.
3. Profit from operations: Operating expenses are deducted from gross profit to determine profit from operations.

} Operating Activities

4. Non-operating activities: The results of activities that are not related to operations are added (as other revenues and gains) or subtracted (as other expenses and losses) to determine profit before income tax.
5. Profit: Income tax expense is subtracted from profit before income tax to determine profit (loss).

The first three steps involve the company's principal operating activities. The fourth step distinguishes between **operating and non-operating activities**, and is only necessary if the company has non-operating activities. The last step is the same step shown in a single-step statement. We will now look more closely at the components of a multiple-step income statement.

Net Sales

The multiple-step income statement for a merchandising company begins by presenting sales revenues. The two contra revenue accounts, Sales Returns and Allowances and Sales Discounts, are deducted from gross sales in the income statement to arrive at net sales. The sales revenues section of the income statement for PW Audio Supply, using assumed data, is as follows:

Sales revenues		
Sales		$480,000
Less: Sales returns and allowances	$12,000	
Sales discounts	8,000	20,000
Net sales		460,000

This presentation shows the key aspects of the company's main revenue-producing activities. Many companies condense this information and report only the net sales figure in their income statement.

Gross Profit

Earlier in the chapter, you learned that the cost of goods sold is deducted from net sales to determine **gross profit**. Based on the sales data presented above (net sales of $460,000) and an assumed cost of goods sold amount of $316,000, the gross profit for PW Audio Supply is $144,000, calculated as follows:

Net sales	$460,000
Cost of goods sold	316,000
Gross profit	144,000

It is important to understand what gross profit is—and what it is not. Gross profit represents the **merchandising profit** of a company. Because operating expenses have not been deducted, it is *not* a measure of the overall profit of a company. Nevertheless, management and other users closely watch the amount and trend of gross profit. We will learn how to express gross profit as a rate in the next section and compare this rate on an intracompany, intercompany, and industry basis to determine the effectiveness of a company's purchasing and pricing policies.

Profit from Operations

Profit from operations, or the results of the company's normal operating activities, is calculated by subtracting operating expenses from gross profit.

At PW Audio Supply, assumed operating expenses total $114,200 and have been classified by nature rather than by function, as shown below. You will recall our discussion in the single-step income statement section about classifying operating expenses by either nature or function. This is required whether a company uses the single- or multiple-step format.

After subtracting operating expenses from gross profit, PW Audio Supply's profit from operations is determined to be $29,800, as shown below:

Gross profit		$144,000
Operating expenses		
Salaries expense	$45,000	
Rent expense	19,000	
Utilities expense	17,000	
Advertising expense	16,000	
Depreciation expense	8,000	
Freight out	7,000	
Insurance expense	2,000	
Loss on sale of equipment	200	114,200
Profit from operations		29,800

Reporting profit from operations as a separate number from overall profit helps users in understanding the profitability of the company's continuing operations or typical business activities.

Non-Operating Activities

Non-operating activities consist of other revenues and gains, as well as other expenses and losses, that are unrelated to the company's main operations.

Examples of other revenues include interest revenue, rent revenue (if the company's main activity is not rentals), and investment revenue. In addition, gains that are infrequent or unusual are normally reported in this section. Examples of other expenses include finance (interest) costs. Losses that are infrequent and unusual are also reported in this section.

When a company has non-operating activities, they are presented in the income statement right after "profit from operations." The distinction between operating and non-operating activities is crucial to many external users of financial data. Profit from operations is viewed as sustainable and therefore long-term, and non-operating activities are viewed as nonrecurring and therefore short-term. When forecasting next year's income, analysts put the most weight on this year's profit from operations as it has more **predictive value** and they put less weight on this year's non-operating activities.

PW Audio Supply's non-operating activities, using assumed data, are presented below. Depending on whether the non-operating activities result in a net increase (other revenues and gains exceed other expenses and losses) or net decrease (other expenses and losses exceed other revenues and gains), they are added to or deducted from the profit from operations. The result is profit before income tax.

Profit from operations		$29,800
Other revenues and gains		
Interest revenue	$3,400	
Other expenses and losses		
Interest expense	1,600	1,800
Profit before income tax		31,600

If there are no non-operating activities, profit from operations will be the same as profit before income tax.

Profit

Profit is the final outcome of all the company's operating and non-operating activities. PW Audio Supply's profit is $25,300 after deducting its income tax expense of $6,300:

Profit before income tax	$31,600
Income tax expense	6,300
Profit	$25,300

In Illustration 5-7, we bring together all the steps above in a comprehensive multiple-step income statement for PW Audio Supply. Note that the profit in Illustrations 5-7 (multiple-step) and 5-6 (single-step) are the same. The differences between the two income statements are the amount of detail displayed and the order of presentation.

Illustration 5-7
Multiple-step income statement—perpetual inventory system

PW AUDIO SUPPLY, INC.
Income Statement
Year Ended December 31, 2012

Sales revenue		
Sales		$480,000
Less: Sales returns and allowances	$12,000	
Sales discounts	8,000	20,000
Net sales		460,000
Cost of goods sold		316,000
Gross profit		144,000
Operating expenses		
Salaries expense	$45,000	
Rent expense	19,000	
Utilities expense	17,000	
Advertising expense	16,000	
Depreciation expense	8,000	
Freight out	7,000	
Insurance expense	2,000	
Loss on sale of equipment	200	114,200
Profit from operations		29,800
Other revenues and gains		
Interest revenue	$ 3,400	
Other expenses and losses		
Interest expense	1,600	1,800
Profit before income tax		31,600
Income tax expense		6,300
Profit		$ 25,300

BEFORE YOU GO ON...

▶Do It! Multiple-Step Income Statement Amounts

Abela Corporation reported the following selected information:

Administrative expenses	$100,000
Cost of goods sold	619,000
Income tax expense	11,500
Interest expense	2,000
Rent revenue	18,000
Sales	910,000
Sales returns and allowances	85,000
Sales discounts	15,000
Selling expenses	61,000

Calculate the following amounts for Abela Corporation: (a) net sales, (b) gross profit, (c) profit from operations, (d) profit before income tax, and (e) profit.

Action Plan

- Recall the formula for net sales: Sales – sales returns and allowances – sales discounts.
- Recall the formula for gross profit: Net sales – cost of goods sold.
- Separate relevant accounts into operating (selling and administrative expenses) and non-operating (other revenues and gains and other expenses and losses).
- Recall the formula for profit from operations: Gross profit – operating expenses.
- Recall the formula for profit before income tax: Profit from operations + other revenue and gains – other expenses and losses.
- Recall the formula for profit: Profit before income tax – income tax expense.

Solution

(a) Net sales: $910,000 – $85,000 – $15,000 = $810,000

(b) Gross profit: $810,000 (from (a)) – $619,000 = $191,000

(c) Profit from operations: $191,000 (from (b)) – ($100,000 + $61,000) = $30,000

(d) Profit before income tax: $30,000 (from (c)) + $18,000 – $2,000 = $46,000

(e) Profit: $46,000 (from (d)) – $11,500 = $34,500

the navigator

Evaluating Profitability

In Chapter 2, we learned about two profitability ratios: earnings per share and the price-earnings ratio. We add two more examples of profitability ratios in this chapter: the gross profit margin and profit margin, which take into account the impact of inventory. Inventory has a significant effect on a company's profitability because cost of goods sold is usually the largest expense on a merchandising company's income statement.

GROSS PROFIT MARGIN

When a company's gross profit is expressed as a percentage, this number is called the **gross profit margin**. It is calculated by dividing the amount of gross profit by net sales. For PW Audio Supply, the gross profit margin is 31.3% ($144,000 ÷ $460,000). The gross profit *margin* is generally considered more informative than the gross profit *amount* because the margin expresses a more meaningful relationship between gross profit and net sales. For example, a gross profit amount of $1 million may sound impressive, but if it is the result of sales of $100 million, the company's gross profit margin is only 1%.

In the following illustration, we will calculate the gross profit margin for Shoppers Drug Mart, and its largest competitor, Jean Coutu. As we learned in our chapter-opening feature story, Shoppers is the No. 1 pharmacy chain in Canada. Jean Coutu is No. 2. The gross profit margin for Shoppers, Jean Coutu, and their industry for two recent fiscal years is presented in Illustration 5-8.

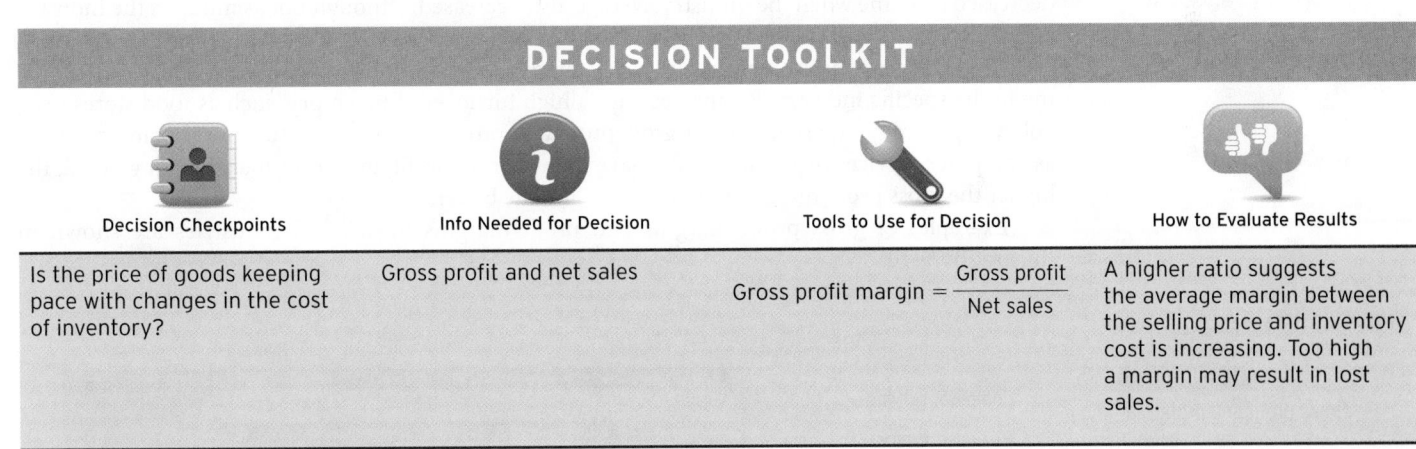

Illustration 5-8
Gross profit margin

GROSS PROFIT MARGIN $= \dfrac{\text{GROSS PROFIT}}{\text{NET SALES}}$		
($ in millions)	2010	2009
Shoppers Drug Mart	$\dfrac{(\$10{,}376.1 - \$6{,}372.4)}{\$10{,}376.1} = 38.6\%$	$\dfrac{(\$9{,}985.6 - \$6{,}238.2)}{\$9{,}985.6} = 37.5\%$
Jean Coutu	10.0%	9.0%
Industry average	24.0%	23.9%

Shoppers' gross profit margin improved in 2010 from 37.5% to 38.6%. Jean Coutu's gross profit margin, although significantly lower than Shoppers', also increased in 2010.

At first glance, it might seem surprising that Jean Coutu has a much lower gross profit margin than Shoppers and the industry average. This can be partially explained by the differing product mixes for each company. Jean Coutu sells more prescription drugs in its pharmacies than does Shoppers and less general merchandise. The general merchandise has a higher gross profit margin than pharmacy products. In addition, as mentioned in the feature story, Shoppers has instituted operational efficiencies to reduce costs and improve inventory management. It has seen dramatic results from this initiative in recent years.

DECISION TOOLKIT

Decision Checkpoints	Info Needed for Decision	Tools to Use for Decision	How to Evaluate Results
Is the price of goods keeping pace with changes in the cost of inventory?	Gross profit and net sales	Gross profit margin $= \dfrac{\text{Gross profit}}{\text{Net sales}}$	A higher ratio suggests the average margin between the selling price and inventory cost is increasing. Too high a margin may result in lost sales.

PROFIT MARGIN

Like gross profit, profit is often expressed as a percentage of sales. The **profit margin** measures the percentage of each dollar of sales that results in profit. It is calculated by dividing profit by net sales for the period.

What is the difference between gross profit margin and profit margin? Gross profit margin indicates how much higher the selling price is than the cost of goods sold. Profit margin indicates how well the selling price covers all expenses (including the cost of goods sold). A company can improve its profit margin by increasing its gross profit margin or by controlling its operating expenses (and non-operating activities), or by doing both.

Profit margins for Shoppers Drug Mart and Jean Coutu, and the industry average, are presented in Illustration 5-9.

▸Illustration 5-9
Profit margin

PROFIT MARGIN $= \dfrac{\text{PROFIT}}{\text{NET SALES}}$		
($ in millions)	2010	2009
Shoppers Drug Mart	$\dfrac{\$590.7}{\$10,376.1} = 5.7\%$	$\dfrac{\$584.9}{\$9,985.6} = 5.9\%$
Jean Coutu	4.9%	(55.9)%
Industry average	2.2%	3.0%

Shoppers generated 5.7 cents on each dollar of sales in 2010. Its profit margin remained relatively unchanged in 2010, declining marginally from 5.9% to 5.7%. Although its gross profit margin increased, its profit declined because of higher increases in its operating expenses.

How does Shoppers compare with its competitors? Its profit margin is higher than that of Jean Coutu and that of its industry competitors. Jean Coutu had a significant loss in 2009, primarily due to its ownership interest in Rite Aid Corporation, a U.S. pharmaceutical chain. If the effects of the Rite Aid loss are not included, Jean Coutu actually would have reported a profit margin of 9.2% rather than a negative profit margin of (55.9)%. It is noteworthy that Shoppers' profit margin decreased at a time when the industry average also decreased, although not as much as the industry average.

Both the gross profit margin and profit margin are **profitability measures** that vary according to the specific industry. Businesses with a high turnover of inventory, such as food stores (e.g., Sobeys), generally experience lower gross profit and profit margins. Low-turnover businesses, such as computer services (e.g., Microsoft), have higher gross profit and profit margins. In general, the higher the gross profit margin and profit margin, the better.

Examples of gross profit margins and profit margins by selected industries are shown in Illustration 5-10.

▸Illustration 5-10
Gross profit and profit margins by industry

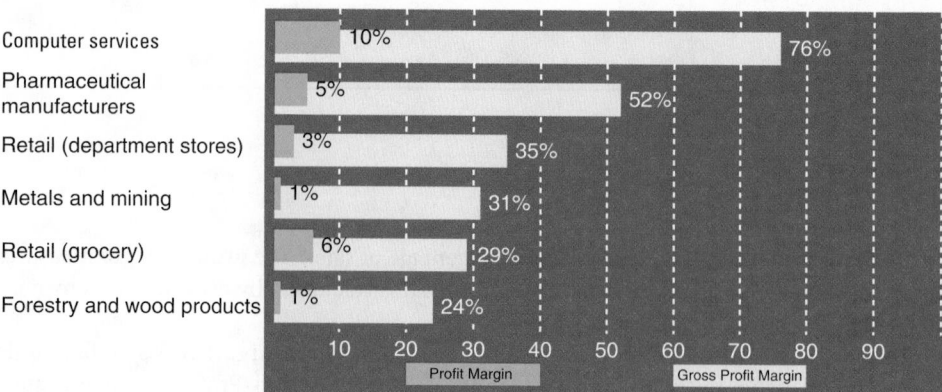

Industry	Profit Margin	Gross Profit Margin
Computer services	10%	76%
Pharmaceutical manufacturers	5%	52%
Retail (department stores)	3%	35%
Metals and mining	1%	31%
Retail (grocery)	6%	29%
Forestry and wood products	1%	24%

ACCOUNTING MATTERS!   *Management Perspective*

Determining the Cost of an iPad

It is important for companies to pay close attention to their costs, as cost is one of the biggest drivers of profitability. Research firm iSuppli estimates that the cost of manufacturing each of Apple's wildly profitable 16-GB iPads with wi-fi is U.S. $260. This includes U.S. $251 in parts like the user interface, glass display, battery, and memory in addition to manufacturing costs of U.S. $9. This means that Apple is most likely generating a gross profit of U.S. $239 for an iPad that sells for U.S. $499. This translates into a gross profit margin of 48%.

That doesn't mean that Apple is making 48% of profit, of course. There are development costs, marketing, and other operating expenses to take into account before arriving at its profit margin. Nonetheless, its profitability would appear to be healthy based on these estimates and the number of iPads that have been sold to date.

Source: Andrew Vanacore, "Research Firm Puts $499 iPad Costs at $259.60," *The Globe and Mail*, April 7, 2010, p. B2

DECISION TOOLKIT

Decision Checkpoints	Info Needed for Decision	Tools to Use for Decision	How to Evaluate Results
Is the company maintaining an adequate margin between sales and expenses?	Profit and net sales	$$\text{Profit margin} = \frac{\text{Profit}}{\text{Net sales}}$$	A higher ratio suggests a favourable return on each dollar of sales.

BEFORE YOU GO ON...

▶Do It! Calculate and Evaluate Profitability

Sports-R-Us Corporation reported the following information:

($ in thousands)	2012	2011
Net sales	$1,347	$1,331
Cost of goods sold	863	853
Operating expenses	439	407
Income tax expense	15	24

(a) Calculate the gross profit margin and profit margin for each of 2011 and 2012.
(b) Did Sports-R-Us's profitability improve or decline in 2012?

Action Plan
- Calculate gross profit and profit.
- Calculate the gross profit margin by dividing gross profit by net sales.
- Calculate the profit margin by dividing profit by net sales.
- A higher gross profit margin and profit margin indicate improved profitability.

Solution ($ in thousands)
(a) Gross profit
2012: $1,347 − $863 = $484
2011: $1,331 − $853 = $478

(continued)

(a) Profit
2012: $1,347 − $863 − $439 − $15 = $30
2011: $1,331 − $853 − $407 − $24 = $47

	2012	2011
Gross profit margin	$\dfrac{\$484}{\$1,347} = 35.9\%$	$\dfrac{\$478}{\$1,331} = 35.9\%$
Profit margin	$\dfrac{\$30}{\$1,347} = 2.2\%$	$\dfrac{\$47}{\$1,331} = 3.5\%$

(b) Sports-R-Us's gross profit margin remained unchanged in 2012. However, its profit margin declined. It appears that the company has good control of its cost of goods sold but needs to review its operating expenses, which appear to have increased faster than sales.

the navigator

APPENDIX 5A—PERIODIC INVENTORY SYSTEM

STUDY OBJECTIVE 6

Prepare entries for purchases and sales under a periodic inventory system and calculate cost of goods sold.

As described in this chapter, there are two basic systems of accounting for inventory: (1) the perpetual inventory system and (2) the periodic inventory system. In the chapter, we focused on accounting for inventory in a perpetual system. In this appendix, we discuss and illustrate the periodic system.

One key difference between the two systems is the point at which the cost of goods sold is calculated. In a periodic inventory system, revenues from the sale of merchandise are recorded when sales are made, in the same way as in a perpetual inventory system. However, on the date of sale, the cost of the merchandise sold is not recorded in a periodic inventory system. While the *cost of goods sold is determined each time a sale is made in a perpetual inventory system, cost of goods sold is only determined at the end of each period in a periodic inventory system.*

There are other differences between the perpetual and periodic inventory systems. Under a perpetual inventory system, the Merchandise Inventory asset account is adjusted for each transaction that affects inventory (such as freight costs paid by the buyer, purchase returns and allowances, and purchase discounts). Consequently, the Merchandise Inventory account shown in the trial balance in a perpetual inventory system represents the ending inventory balance. On the other hand, a periodic inventory system uses different accounts for each transaction, as summarized below. In addition, the accounts used in a periodic inventory system are temporary expense accounts rather than a permanent asset account (Merchandise Inventory) as is used in a perpetual inventory system. Consequently, the Merchandise Inventory account shown in the trial balance in a periodic inventory system represents the beginning inventory balance, or ending balance from the prior period.

	Perpetual Inventory System	Periodic Inventory System
Purchases of merchandise	Merchandise Inventory	Purchases
Freight costs paid by buyer	Merchandise Inventory	Freight In
Purchase returns and allowances	Merchandise Inventory	Purchase Returns and Allowances
Purchase discounts	Merchandise Inventory	Purchase Discounts

To illustrate the recording of merchandise transactions under a periodic inventory system, we will use purchase and sale transactions between PW Audio Supply, Inc. (the seller) and Sauk Stereo Ltd. (the buyer), as illustrated for the perpetual inventory system earlier in this chapter. You will recall that PW Audio Supply sold printed circuit boards to Sauk Stereo on May 4 in the amount of $3,800. The terms of the sale are 2/10, n/30, FOB shipping point.

RECORDING PURCHASES OF MERCHANDISE

Sauk Stereo records the $3,800 purchase of merchandise from PW Audio Supply on May 4 as follows:

May 4	Purchases	3,800	
	Accounts Payable		3,800
	(To record goods purchased on account from PW Audio Supply, terms 2/10, n/30, FOB shipping point)		

A = L + SE
+3,800 −3,800
Cash flows: no effect

Purchases is a temporary expense account reported on the income statement. Its normal balance is a debit.

Freight Costs

The freight terms for Sauk Stereo's purchase of merchandise are FOB shipping point, which means that the buyer pays the freight costs. Upon delivery of the goods, Sauk Stereo pays Public Carrier Co. $150 for freight charges on its purchases from PW Audio Supply. The entry on Sauk Stereo's books is as follows:

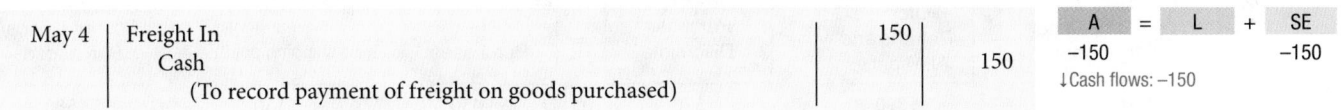

May 4	Freight In	150	
	Cash		150
	(To record payment of freight on goods purchased)		

A = L + SE
−150 −150
↓Cash flows: −150

Like Purchases, Freight In is a temporary expense account whose normal balance is a debit. Just as freight was part of the cost of the merchandise inventory in a perpetual inventory system, **freight is part of the cost of goods purchased** in a periodic inventory system. The cost of goods purchased includes any freight charges incurred in bringing the goods to the buyer. As a result, freight in is added to net purchases to determine the cost of goods purchased.

Freight costs are not subject to purchase discounts. Purchase discounts apply on the invoice cost of the merchandise, less any purchase returns and allowances, which are discussed next.

Purchase Returns and Allowances

When $300 of merchandise is returned to PW Audio Supply, Sauk Stereo prepares the following entry to recognize the return:

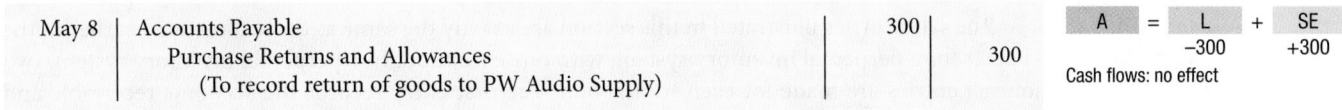

May 8	Accounts Payable	300	
	Purchase Returns and Allowances		300
	(To record return of goods to PW Audio Supply)		

A = L + SE
−300 +300
Cash flows: no effect

Purchase Returns and Allowances is a temporary account whose normal balance is a credit. It is a **contra expense account** whose balance is subtracted from the Purchases account.

Purchase Discounts

Recall that the invoice terms were 2/10, n/30. On May 14, Sauk Stereo pays the balance due on account to PW Audio Supply of $3,500 ($3,800 − $300), less the 2% cash discount allowed by PW Audio Supply for payment within 10 days. Note that freight costs are not subject to a purchase discount. Purchase discounts apply on the invoice cost of the merchandise purchased, less any returns. In this case, the purchase discount is $70, calculated as follows: ($3,800 − $300) × 2% = $70.

The payment and discount are recorded by Sauk Stereo as follows:

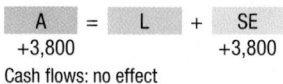

May 14	Accounts Payable ($3,800 – $300)		3,500	
	Cash			3,430
	Purchase Discounts ($3,500 × 2%)			70
	(To record payment to PW Audio Supply within discount period)			

A = L + SE
−3,430 −3,500 +75
↓Cash flows: −3,430

Purchase Discounts is a temporary account whose normal balance is a credit. Like Purchase Returns and Allowances, it is a contra expense account subtracted from the Purchases account.

As was mentioned earlier, a temporary expense account is used in each of the above transactions to record purchases of merchandise instead of the Merchandise Inventory account that is used in a perpetual inventory system. The Purchases and Freight In accounts were debited rather than Merchandise Inventory in the first two entries, and Purchase Returns and Allowances and Purchase Discounts were credited in the last two entries rather than Merchandise Inventory. These temporary accounts are needed for calculating the cost of goods purchased at the end of the period.

The difference between purchases of merchandise, less returns and allowances and discounts, is commonly known as **net purchases**. Net purchases combined with any freight costs determine the cost of goods purchased, as shown in Illustration 5A-1.

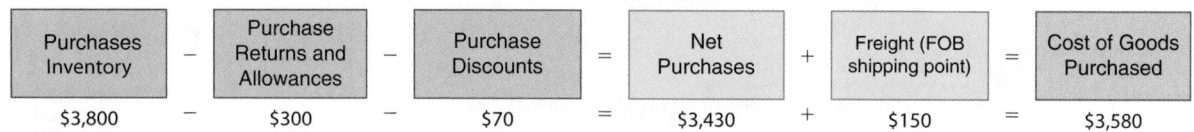

Purchases Inventory	−	Purchase Returns and Allowances	−	Purchase Discounts	=	Net Purchases	+	Freight (FOB shipping point)	=	Cost of Goods Purchased
$3,800	−	$300	−	$70	=	$3,430	+	$150	=	$3,580

▶Illustration 5A-1
Formula for cost of goods purchased

Note that the cost of goods purchased, $3,580, is the same in a periodic inventory system as it is in a perpetual inventory system, as shown on p. 231.

RECORDING SALES OF MERCHANDISE

The sale of $3,800 of merchandise to Sauk Stereo on May 4 is recorded by the seller, PW Audio Supply, as follows:

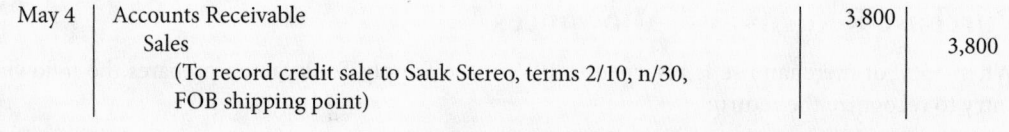

May 4	Accounts Receivable		3,800	
	Sales			3,800
	(To record credit sale to Sauk Stereo, terms 2/10, n/30, FOB shipping point)			

A = L + SE
+3,800   +3,800
Cash flows: no effect

The sales entries illustrated in this section are exactly the same as those illustrated earlier in the chapter for a perpetual inventory system, with one exception. In a perpetual inventory system, two journal entries are made for each transaction. The first entry records the accounts receivable and sales revenue, as illustrated above. The second journal entry records the cost of the sale by transferring the inventory to the Cost of Goods Sold account.

In a periodic inventory system, there is only one journal entry made at the time of the sale (the entry to record the sales revenue). The cost of the sale is not recorded. Instead, as discussed earlier, the cost of goods sold is determined by calculation at the end of the period.

Freight Costs

Freight costs incurred by the seller on outgoing merchandise are an operating expense to the seller. There is no distinction in accounting for these costs between a perpetual and periodic inventory system. Under both systems, these costs are debited to the Freight Out or Delivery Expense account.

You will recall that Sauk Stereo (the buyer) paid the shipping costs in our sales illustration, so no journal entry is required by PW Audio Supply (the seller) at this point.

Sales Returns and Allowances

When Sauk Stereo returns merchandise on May 8, PW Audio Supply records the $300 sales return as follows:

May 8	Sales Returns and Allowances	300	
	Accounts Receivable		300
	(To record return of goods by Sauk Stereo)		

A = **L** + **SE**
−300   −300
Cash flows: no effect

Just as we observed that only one entry is needed when sales are recorded in a periodic inventory system, one entry is also all that is needed to record a return. In a perpetual inventory system, two entries are needed to record the sales return and its cost.

Sales Discounts

On May 14, PW Audio Supply receives a payment of $3,430 [($3,800 − $300) × (100% − 2%] on account from Sauk Stereo. PW Audio Supply records the collection of Sauk Stereo's account receivable in full as follows:

May 14	Cash	3,430	
	Sales Discounts ($3,500 × 2%)	70	
	Accounts Receivable ($3,800 − $300)		3,500
	(To record collection from Sauk Stereo within		
	discount period)		

A = **L** + **SE**
+3,430   −70
−3,500
↑Cash flows: +3,430

All of the above accounts combine to determine net sales. The formula for net sales was shown in Illustration 5-5 in the chapter, and has been reproduced here for convenience.

Gross Sales	−	Sales Returns and Allowances	−	Sales Discounts	=	Net Sales
$3,800	−	$300	−	$70	=	$3,430

▶ **Illustration 5A-2**
Formula for net sales

COMPARISON OF ENTRIES—PERPETUAL VS. PERIODIC

The periodic inventory system's entries for purchases and sales are shown in Illustration 5A-3 next to those that were illustrated earlier in the chapter under the perpetual inventory system. Having these entries side by side should help you compare the differences. The entries that are different in the two inventory systems are highlighted in red.

▶ **Illustration 5A-3**
Comparison of entries under perpetual and periodic inventory systems

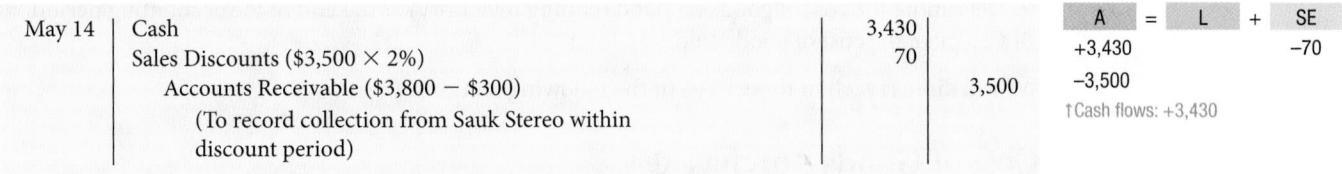
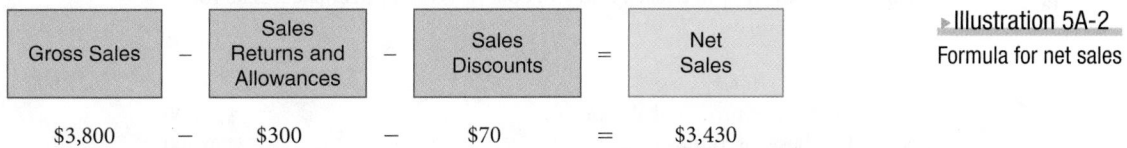

ENTRIES ON SAUK STEREO'S BOOKS (BUYER)					
Transaction	Perpetual Inventory System			Periodic Inventory System	
May 4 Purchase of merchandise on credit	Merchandise Inventory	3,800		Purchases	3,800	
	Accounts Payable		3,800	Accounts Payable		3,800
4 Freight costs on purchases	Merchandise Inventory	150		Freight In	150	
	Cash		150	Cash		150
8 Purchase returns and allowances	Accounts Payable	300		Accounts Payable	300	
	Merchandise Inventory		300	Purchase Returns and Allowances		300
14 Payment on account with a discount	Accounts Payable	3,500		Accounts Payable	3,500	
	Cash		3,430	Cash		3,430
	Merchandise Inventory		70	Purchase Discounts		70

		ENTRIES ON PW AUDIO SUPPLY'S BOOKS (SELLER)					
	Transaction	Perpetual Inventory System			Periodic Inventory System		
May 4	Sale of merchandise on credit	Accounts Receivable	3,800		Accounts Receivable	3,800	
		Sales		3,800	Sales		3,800
		Cost of Goods Sold	2,400		No entry		
		Merchandise Inventory		2,400			
8	Return of merchandise sold	Sales Returns and Allowances	300		Sales Returns and Allowances	300	
		Accounts Receivable		300	Accounts Receivable		300
		Merchandise Inventory	140		No entry		
		Cost of Goods Sold		140			
14	Cash received on account with a discount	Cash	3,430		Cash	3,430	
		Sales Discounts	70		Sales Discounts	70	
		Accounts Receivable		3,500	Accounts Receivable		3,500

CALCULATING COST OF GOODS SOLD

As was mentioned earlier, calculating the cost of goods sold is different in a periodic inventory system than in a perpetual inventory system. In a periodic inventory system, there is no running account (continuous updating) of changes in cost of goods sold and inventory as there is in a perpetual inventory system. The cost of goods sold for the period and the balance in ending inventory are calculated at the end of the period.

To calculate the cost of goods sold in a periodic inventory, three steps are required:

1. Calculate the cost of goods purchased.
2. Determine the cost of goods on hand (ending inventory) at the end of the accounting period.
3. Calculate the cost of goods sold.

We will discuss each of these steps in the following sections.

Cost of Goods Purchased

Earlier in this appendix, we used four accounts—Purchases, Freight In, Purchase Returns and Allowances, and Purchase Discounts—to record the purchase of inventory. These four accounts combine to determine the cost of goods purchased. Using assumed data for PW Audio Supply, the calculation of net purchases and the cost of goods purchased is as follows:

Purchases		$325,000
Less: Purchase returns and allowances	$10,400	
Purchase discounts	6,800	17,200
Net purchases		307,800
Add: Freight in		12,200
Cost of goods purchased		320,000

Cost of Goods on Hand

To determine the cost of the inventory on hand, PW Audio Supply must take a physical inventory. Taking a physical inventory involves these procedures:

1. Count the units on hand for each item of inventory.
2. Apply unit costs to the total units on hand for each item of inventory (we will learn more about how to do this in the next chapter).
3. Total the costs for each item of inventory to determine the total cost of goods on hand.

The total cost of goods on hand is known as the ending inventory. PW Audio Supply's physical inventory count on December 31, 2012, determines that the cost of its goods on hand, or ending inventory, is $40,000. This ending inventory amount will be used to calculate the cost of goods sold, as shown in the next section. Ending inventory is subsequently recorded in the Merchandise Inventory account as part of the closing process (not illustrated here).

Cost of Goods Sold

There are two steps in calculating the cost of goods sold:

1. Add the cost of goods purchased to the cost of goods on hand at the beginning of the period (beginning inventory). The result is the cost of goods available for sale.
2. Subtract the cost of goods on hand at the end of the period (ending inventory) from the cost of goods available for sale. The result is the cost of goods sold.

The ending inventory at December 31, 2012, was given above as $40,000. We will assume that PW Audio Supply's ending inventory at December 31, 2011 (which is the same as its beginning inventory at January 1, 2012) is $36,000. Using this information and the cost of goods purchased determined above, we can determine PW Audio Supply's cost of goods available for sale and the cost of goods sold as follows:

Merchandise inventory, January 1			$ 36,000
Purchases		$325,000	
Less: Purchase returns and allowances	$10,400		
Purchase discounts	6,800	17,200	
Net purchases		307,800	
Add: Freight in		12,200	
Cost of goods purchased			320,000
Cost of goods available for sale			356,000
Merchandise inventory, December 31			40,000
Cost of goods sold			316,000

In summary, the cost of goods purchased is added to the beginning inventory to determine the cost of goods available for sale. Ending inventory is then deducted from the cost of goods available for sale to determine the cost of goods sold. In other words, what you have on hand at the beginning of the period, plus what you purchase during the period, gives you the total goods available for sale during the period. Subtract what you have not sold, and you are left with the amount that must have been sold.

Illustration 5A-4 presents this as a formula and inserts the relevant data for PW Audio Supply.

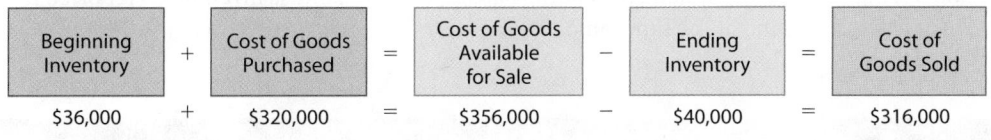

▶ Illustration 5A-4
Formula for cost of goods sold

Once cost of goods sold is calculated in a periodic inventory system, gross profit, operating expenses, non-operating items, profit before income tax, and profit are reported in a multiple-step or single-step income statement in the same way as they are in a perpetual inventory system. The only reporting difference in a multiple-step income statement is that the cost of goods sold section has more detail in a periodic inventory system than in a perpetual inventory system (see red highlighted area), where only one line is reported for the cost of goods sold. Compare the following illustration with the multiple-step income statement shown in Illustration 5-7 for a perpetual inventory system.

▶ Illustration 5A-5
Multiple-step income statement—periodic inventory system

PW AUDIO SUPPLY, INC. Income Statement Year Ended December 31, 2012			
Sales revenue			
Sales			$480,000
Less: Sales returns and allowances		$12,000	
Sales discounts		8,000	20,000
Net sales			460,000

(*continued*)

Cost of goods sold			
Merchandise inventory, January 1		$ 36,000	
Purchases	$325,000		
Less: Purchase returns and allowances	10,400		
Purchase discounts	6,800		
Net purchases	307,800		
Add: Freight in	12,200		
Cost of goods purchased		320,000	
Cost of goods available for sale		356,000	
Merchandise inventory, December 31		40,000	
Cost of goods sold			316,000
Gross profit			144,000
Operating expenses			
Salaries expense		$ 45,000	
Rent expense		19,000	
Utilities expense		17,000	
Advertising expense		16,000	
Depreciation expense		8,000	
Freight out		7,000	
Insurance expense		2,000	
Loss on sale of equipment		200	114,200
Profit from operations			29,800
Other revenues and gains			
Interest revenue		$ 3,400	
Other expenses and losses			
Interest expense		1,600	1,800
Profit before income tax			31,600
Income tax expense			6,300
Profit			$ 25,300

Using the periodic inventory system does not affect the content of the statement of financial position. As in the perpetual system, the ending balance of merchandise inventory is reported in the current assets section, and at the same amount.

BEFORE YOU GO ON...

▶ Do It! Purchase and Sales Transactions—Periodic Inventory System

On September 4, Lalonde Ltée sells merchandise on account to Guerette Corp., terms 1/10, n/30. The selling price of the goods is $1,500. On September 8, goods with a selling price of $300 are returned for credit and restored to inventory. On September 13, Lalonde receives payment in full from Guerette. Record the transactions on the books of both companies, assuming a periodic inventory system is used.

Action Plan

- Seller: Prepare only one entry to record the sale and do not record the cost of the sale. Prepare only one entry to record the return of goods and do not record the cost of the return. Calculate sales discounts using the amount owing, net of any sales returns.
- Buyer: Record purchases of inventory, returned goods, and purchase discounts in separate accounts. Calculate purchase discounts using the amount owing, net of any purchase returns.

Solution

Lalonde Ltée (Seller)

Sept.	4	Accounts Receivable	1,500	
		Sales		1,500
		(To record credit sale to Guerette, terms 1/10, n/30)		
	8	Sales Returns and Allowances	300	
		Accounts Receivable		300
		(To record credit granted for receipt of returned goods from Guerette)		
	13	Cash ($1,200 – $12)	1,188	
		Sales Discounts [($1,500 – $300) × 1%]	12	
		Accounts Receivable ($1,500 – $300)		1,200
		(To record collection from Guerette within discount period)		

Guerette Corp. (Buyer)

Sept.	4	Purchases	1,500	
		Accounts Payable		1,500
		(To record goods purchased on account from Lalonde, terms 1/10, n/30)		
	8	Accounts Payable	300	
		Purchase Returns and Allowances		300
		(To record return of goods to Lalonde)		
	13	Accounts Payable ($1,500 – $300)	1,200	
		Purchase Discounts [($1,500 – $300) × 1%]		12
		Cash ($1,200 – $12)		1,188
		(To record payment to Lalonde within discount period)		

comparing
IFRS and ASPE

Key Differences	International Financial Reporting Standards (IFRS)	Accounting Standards for Private Enterprises (ASPE)
Income statement	Expenses must be classified by nature or by function.	Expenses can be classified in any manner the company finds useful.

More About Shopping

In this chapter, you have learned about merchandising companies and how to complete the accounting transactions that give managers the information they need to run a successful business. From your own experiences, you will have noticed that the retail business is constantly changing. Brand-new stores open, or old stores reopen in new locations or under a new name. Sometimes stores go out of business altogether. One of the major problems facing the Canadian retail sector is the need to control the cost of goods sold. In an increasingly competitive environment, it is difficult to raise retail prices. So for retailers to make a profit, they need to focus on controlling their cost of goods sold and keeping operating expenses at a minimum.

Some Facts

- Retailing is big business in Canada. The retail sector grew at a much faster rate than the Canadian economy in the past five years. In 2010, the retail sector represented about 6.2% of Canada's gross domestic product.
- A recent international survey of retail CFOs reported that
  - 22% had reduced expenditure on advertising and marketing but only 7% considered that this had hurt traffic or sales.
  - 33% of retailers did not have an e-commerce site.
  - 35% of respondents stated that their e-commerce sales were growing faster than overall sales, but that it was difficult to allocate costs accurately between on-line and other retail sales, so that measures like gross profit margin and profit margin by selling platform were not always reliable.
- Canadians spent over $16 billion on-line in 2010 buying goods and services (including travel) from Canadian and foreign websites. This number is expected to double by 2015 as consumers become more comfortable buying on-line. Major impediments to this increase include high shipping costs and consumer reluctance to purchase products sight unseen.
- Extended warranties are offered by many retailers on all kinds of merchandise, not just expensive appliances or electronics. Usually these are very profitable for retailers as the cost of repairs and replacement costs are often well below the price of the extended warranty. As a consumer, an extended warranty might be worth it to you if your credit card doesn't offer an extended warranty or the manufacturer's warranty requires items to be shipped away. Studies in the United States have found that consumers are more likely to purchase extended warranties on items that give them pleasure rather than items that are useful (which often have higher failure rates).
- Chain stores are taking an increasing portion of the Canadian retail market, rising from a 39% market share in 1999 to a 47% share in 2008. Chain stores are in all retail categories, but they predominate in the clothing, department, and general merchandising categories. In 2008, chain stores reported a higher profit margin than non-chain stores.

What Do You Think?

With the growth in number and profitability of chain-owned stores, should you support a locally owned store to help it survive or should you always go to the cheapest store, even if it is a chain-owned store?

YES—It's important to support local businesses. I like the personal service and the choice and the fact that the store employs local people and the profits stay in my community.

NO—With the pressure on my personal budget, I have to find the cheapest stores and the best deals.

Sources: PricewaterhouseCoopers, "The New Retail Priorities for 2011: Results of PwC's Retail CFO Survey," www.pwc.com/ca/en/retail-consulting/cfo-survey.jhtml, accessed March 7, 2011. J. Grau, "Canada Retail Ecommerce Forecast: Measured Growth Ahead," eMarketer, February 2011. M. Walcoff, "Wal-Mart, Target Drive Canada's Retail Stocks to Six-Year Low," Bloomberg, February 17, 2011. Dakshana Bascaramurty, "Warranties: Have They Extended Their Reach?", *Globe and Mail*, February 15, 2011, p. L1. Marina Strauss, "Canadian Tire Relaunching E-commerce Site," *Globe and Mail*, February 23, 2011. Statistics Canada, "Gross Domestic Product," *The Daily*, February 28, 2011.

Summary of Study Objectives

1. **Identify the differences between service and merchandising companies.** A service company performs services. It has service or fee revenue and operating expenses. A merchandising company sells goods. It has sales revenue, cost of goods sold, and gross profit in addition to operating expenses. Both types of company may also report non-operating items and each would report income tax expense.

2. **Prepare entries for purchases under a perpetual inventory system.** The Merchandise Inventory account is debited for all purchases of merchandise, and for freight costs if they are paid by the buyer (shipping terms FOB shipping point). It is credited for purchase discounts, and purchase returns and allowances.

3. **Prepare entries for sales under a perpetual inventory system.** When inventory is sold, two entries are required: (1) Accounts Receivable (or Cash) is debited and Sales is credited for the selling price of the merchandise, and (2) Cost of Goods Sold is debited and Merchandise Inventory is credited for the cost of inventory items sold. Contra revenue accounts are used to record sales returns and allowances and sales discounts. Two journal entries are also required for sales returns so that both the selling price and the cost of the returned merchandise are recorded. Freight costs paid by the seller (shipping terms FOB destination) are recorded as an operating expense.

4. **Prepare a single-step and a multiple-step income statement.** In a single-step income statement, all data (except for income tax expense) are classified under two categories—revenues or expenses—and profit before income tax is determined in one step. Income tax expense is separated from the other expenses and reported separately after profit before income tax to determine profit (loss).

   A multiple-step income statement shows several steps in determining profit. Step 1 deducts sales returns and allowances and sales discounts from gross sales to determine net sales. Step 2 deducts the cost of goods sold from net sales to determine gross profit. Step 3 deducts operating expenses (which can be classified by nature or by function) from gross profit to determine profit from operations. Step 4 adds or deducts any non-operating items to determine profit before income tax. Finally, step 5 deducts income tax expense to determine profit (loss).

5. **Calculate the gross profit margin and profit margin.** The gross profit margin, calculated by dividing gross profit by net sales, measures the gross profit earned for each dollar of sales. The profit margin, calculated by dividing profit by net sales, measures the profit earned for each dollar of sales. Both are measures of profitability that are closely watched by management and other interested parties.

6. **Prepare entries for purchases and sales under a periodic inventory system and calculate cost of goods sold (Appendix 5A).** Unlike recording purchases in a perpetual inventory system, in a periodic inventory system separate temporary accounts are used to record (1) purchases, (2) purchase returns and allowances, (3) purchase discounts, and (4) freight costs that are paid by the buyer (shipping terms FOB shipping point). The formula for cost of goods purchased is as follows: Purchases − purchase returns and allowances − purchase discounts = net purchases; and net purchases + freight in = cost of goods purchased.

   As in a perpetual inventory system, temporary accounts are used to record (1) sales, (2) sales returns and allowances, and (3) sales discounts. However, in a periodic inventory system, only one journal entry is made to record a sale of merchandise as the cost of goods sold is not recorded throughout the period as it is in a perpetual inventory system. Instead, the cost of goods sold is determined only at the end of the period.

   To determine the cost of goods sold, first calculate the cost of goods purchased, as indicated above. Then, calculate the cost of goods sold as follows: Beginning inventory + cost of goods purchased = cost of goods available for sale; and cost of goods available for sale − ending inventory = cost of goods sold.

Glossary

Contra expense account An account that is offset against (reduces) an expense account on the income statement. Examples include purchase returns and allowances and purchase discounts. (p. 253)

Contra revenue account An account that is offset against (reduces) a revenue account on the income statement. Examples include sales returns and allowances and sales discounts. (p. 239)

Cost of goods available for sale The sum of beginning inventory and the cost of goods purchased. (p. 232)

Cost of goods purchased The sum of net purchases and freight in. (p. 233)

Cost of goods sold The total cost of merchandise sold during the period. In a perpetual inventory system, it is calculated and recorded for each sale. In a periodic inventory system, it is calculated at the end of the accounting period by deducting ending inventory from the cost of goods available for sale. (p. 230)

FOB (free on board) destination Freight terms indicating that the seller will pay for the shipping costs of the goods until they arrive at their destination (normally the buyer's place of business). (p. 235)

FOB (free on board) shipping point   Freight terms indicating that the seller is responsible for the goods only until they reach their shipping point (normally the seller's place of business). The buyer will pay for the shipping costs of the goods from the shipping point until they arrive at their destination. (p. 234)

Function   A method of organizing expenses on the income statement by way of the activity (business function) for which they were incurred (e.g., cost of goods sold, administrative, selling). (p. 244)

Gross profit   Sales revenue less cost of goods sold. (p. 230)

Gross profit margin   Gross profit expressed as a percentage of sales. It is calculated by dividing gross profit by net sales. (p. 248)

Gross sales   Total sales before deducting any sales returns and allowances and sales discounts. (p. 241)

Multiple-step income statement   An income statement that shows several steps to determine profit or loss. (p. 245)

Nature   A method of organizing expenses on the income statement by way of their natural classification (e.g., salaries, transportation, depreciation, advertising). (p. 244)

Net purchases   Purchases less purchase returns and allowances and purchase discounts. (p. 254)

Net sales   Gross sales less sales returns and allowances and sales discounts. (p. 241)

Non-operating activities   Other revenues and gains, and other expenses and losses, that are unrelated to the company's main operations. (p. 246)

Operating expenses   Expenses incurred in the process of earning sales revenue. They are deducted from gross profit to arrive at profit from operations. (p. 230)

Periodic inventory system   An inventory system in which detailed records are not maintained and the ending inventory and cost of goods sold are determined only at the end of the accounting period. (p. 232)

Perpetual inventory system   A detailed inventory system in which the quantity and cost of each inventory item is maintained. The records continuously show the inventory that should be on hand and the cost of the items sold. (p. 231)

Profit from operations   The results of a company's normal operating activities. It is calculated as gross profit less operating expenses. (p. 246)

Profit margin   Profit expressed as a percentage of net sales. It is calculated by dividing profit by net sales. (p. 249)

Purchase discount   A price reduction, based on the invoice price less any returns and allowances, claimed by a buyer for early payment of a credit purchase. (p. 236)

Purchase returns and allowances   A return of goods for cash or credit, or a deduction granted by the seller on the selling price of unsatisfactory merchandise. (p. 235)

Quantity discount   A price reduction that reduces the invoice price and is given to the buyer for volume purchases. (p. 236)

Sales discount   A price reduction that is based on the invoice price less any returns and allowances and is given by a seller for early payment of a credit sale. (p. 240)

Sales returns and allowances   A return of goods or reduction in price of unsatisfactory merchandise. (p. 239)

Sales revenue   The main source of revenue in a merchandising company. (p. 230)

Single-step income statement   An income statement that shows only one step (revenues less expenses) in determining profit (or loss). (p. 243)

DECISION TOOLKIT—A SUMMARY

Decision Checkpoints	 Info Needed for Decision	 Tools to Use for Decision	 How to Evaluate Results
Is the price of goods keeping pace with changes in the cost of inventory?	Gross profit and net sales	$$\text{Gross profit margin} = \frac{\text{Gross profit}}{\text{Net sales}}$$	A higher ratio suggests the average margin between the selling price and inventory cost is increasing. Too high a margin may result in lost sales.
Is the company maintaining an adequate margin between sales and expenses?	Profit and net sales	$$\text{Profit margin} = \frac{\text{Profit}}{\text{Net sales}}$$	A higher ratio suggests a favourable return on each dollar of sales.

USING THE DECISION TOOLKIT

Rite Aid Corporation is the third-largest drugstore in the United States. In 2007, Rite Aid purchased more than 1,850 Brooks and Eckerd drugstores from Jean Coutu. Jean Coutu currently has a 27.5% ownership interest in Rite Aid. The following selected information is available for Rite Aid:

(in USD millions)	2010	2009
Net sales	$25,569	$26,185
Cost of goods sold	18,845	19,254
Loss	(507)	(2,915)

Instructions

(a) Rite Aid is much larger than Shoppers Drug Mart and Jean Coutu. Can a comparison of the financial results of these three companies be meaningful?

(b) Calculate the gross profit margin and profit margin for Rite Aid for 2010 and 2009.

(c) Using the ratios calculated in (b), compare the gross profit margin and profit margin with that of Shoppers, Jean Coutu, and their industry found in Illustrations 5-8 and 5-9 in the chapter.

Solution

(a) It does not matter that Rite Aid is larger than Shoppers and Jean Coutu. Ratio analysis puts each company's financial information into the same perspective for a comparison. It is the relationship between the figures that is meaningful.

(b) Gross profit margin:

(in USD millions)	2010	2009
Rite Aid	$\dfrac{(\$25{,}569 - \$18{,}845)}{\$25{,}569} = 26.3\%$	$\dfrac{(\$26{,}185 - \$19{,}254)}{\$26{,}185} = 26.5\%$
Shoppers Drug Mart	38.6%	37.5%
Jean Coutu	10.0%	9.0%
Industry average	24.0%	23.9%

Profit margin:

(in USD millions)	2010	2009
Rite Aid	$\dfrac{\$(507)}{\$25{,}569} = (2.0)\%$	$\dfrac{\$(2{,}915)}{\$26{,}185} = (11.1)\%$
Shoppers Drug Mart	5.7%	5.9%
Jean Coutu	4.9%	(55.9)%
Industry average	2.2%	3.0%

(c) Rite Aid's gross profit margin deteriorated marginally at a time when Shoppers', Jean Coutu's, and the industry's gross profit margins were all improving. Shoppers' gross profit margin is significantly better than that of Jean Coutu and its industry counterparts, indicating that it either has higher prices and/or better control of its cost of goods sold.

Rite Aid's profit margin improved in 2010—even though it is still a negative number—as did Jean Coutu's profit margin. In contrast, Shoppers' profit margin deteriorated in 2010, despite its superior and improving gross profit margin. The industry average also declined during this same period, due, in part, to a challenging economic environment. Rite Aid's and Jean Coutu's improving profit margins could be an indication that they have improved control of their operating expenses in the current year more than Shoppers and the industry were able to.

the navigator

Comprehensive Do It! #1

(Perpetual Inventory System)

The adjusted trial balance at December 31, 2012, for Dykstra Inc. follows on the next page:

Instructions

Assuming Dykstra uses a perpetual inventory system, prepare a multiple-step income statement, statement of changes in equity, and statement of financial position for the year.

(*continued*)

DYKSTRA INC.
Adjusted Trial Balance
December 31, 2012

	Debit	Credit
Cash	$ 4,500	
Accounts receivable	11,100	
Merchandise inventory	29,000	
Prepaid insurance	2,500	
Land	150,000	
Buildings	500,000	
Accumulated depreciation—buildings		$ 40,000
Equipment	95,000	
Accumulated depreciation—equipment		18,000
Accounts payable		10,600
Property tax payable		4,000
Bank loan payable—short-term		25,000
Mortgage payable—current portion		21,000
Mortgage payable—non-current		530,000
Common shares		70,000
Retained earnings		61,000
Dividends	10,000	
Sales		536,800
Sales returns and allowances	6,700	
Sales discounts	5,000	
Cost of goods sold	363,400	
Administrative expenses	111,500	
Selling expenses	19,600	
Interest expense	4,600	
Interest revenue		2,500
Income tax expense	6,000	
	$1,318,900	$1,318,900

Additional information:
Dykstra issued $5,000 of common shares during the year.

Action Plan
- Prepare the income statement in steps:
  1. Sales less sales returns and allowances and sales discounts equals net sales.
  2. Net sales less cost of goods sold equals gross profit.
  3. Gross profit less operating expenses (classified by function in this case as selling and administrative expenses) is profit from operations.
  4. Profit from operations plus non-operating revenues and gains or minus expenses and losses equals profit before income tax.
- Merchandise inventory is a current asset in the classified statement of financial position.

Solution to Comprehensive Do It! #1 (Perpetual Inventory System)

DYKSTRA INC.
Income Statement
Year Ended December 31, 2012

Sales		$536,800
Less: Sales returns and allowances	$ 6,700	
Sales discounts	5,000	11,700
Net sales		525,100
Cost of goods sold		363,400
Gross profit		161,700
Operating expenses		
Administrative expenses	$111,500	
Selling expenses	19,600	131,100

Profit from operations		$ 30,600
Other revenues and gains		
Interest revenue	$ 2,500	
Other expenses and losses		
Interest expense	4,600	2,100
Profit before income tax		28,500
Income tax expense		6,000
Profit		$ 22,500

DYKSTRA INC.
Statement of Changes in Equity
Year Ended December 31, 2012

	Common Shares	Retained Earnings	Total Equity
Balance, January 1	$65,000	$61,000	$126,000
Issue of common shares	5,000		5,000
Profit		22,500	22,500
Dividends		(10,000)	(10,000)
Balance, December 31	$70,000	$73,500	$143,500

DYKSTRA INC.
Statement of Financial Position
December 31, 2012

Assets

Current assets			
Cash		$ 4,500	
Accounts receivable		11,100	
Merchandise inventory		29,000	
Prepaid insurance		2,500	
Total current assets			$ 47,100
Property, plant, and equipment			
Land		$150,000	
Buildings	$500,000		
Less: Accumulated depreciation	40,000	460,000	
Equipment	$ 95,000		
Less: Accumulated depreciation	18,000	77,000	
Total property, plant, and equipment			687,000
Total assets			$734,100

Liabilities and Shareholders' Equity

Liabilities			
Current liabilities			
Accounts payable		$ 10,600	
Property tax payable		4,000	
Bank loan payable		25,000	
Mortgage payable—current portion		21,000	
Total current liabilities			$ 60,600
Non-current liabilities			
Mortgage payable			530,000
Total liabilities			590,600
Shareholders' equity			
Common shares	$ 70,000		
Retained earnings	73,500		143,500
Total liabilities and shareholders' equity			$734,100

Comprehensive Do It! #2

(Periodic Inventory System—Appendix 5A)

DYKSTRA INC.		
Adjusted Trial Balance		
December 31, 2012		
	Debit	Credit
Cash	$ 4,500	
Accounts receivable	11,100	
Merchandise inventory, January 1	25,000	
Prepaid insurance	2,500	
Land	150,000	
Buildings	500,000	
Accumulated depreciation—buildings		$ 40,000
Equipment	95,000	
Accumulated depreciation—equipment		18,000
Accounts payable		10,600
Property tax payable		4,000
Bank loan payable—short-term		25,000
Mortgage payable—current portion		21,000
Mortgage payable—non-current		530,000
Common shares		70,000
Retained earnings		61,000
Dividends	10,000	
Sales		536,800
Sales returns and allowances	6,700	
Sales discounts	5,000	
Purchases	370,000	
Purchase returns and allowances		15,000
Purchase discounts		5,000
Freight in	17,400	
Administrative expenses	111,500	
Selling expenses	19,600	
Interest expense	4,600	
Interest revenue		2,500
Income tax expense	6,000	
	$1,338,900	$1,338,900

Additional information:

A physical inventory count on December 31 determined that ending inventory was $29,000.

Instructions

Assuming Dykstra uses a periodic inventory system, prepare a multiple-step income statement for the year.

Action Plan

- Recall that the merchandise inventory included in the trial balance is the *beginning* inventory amount in a periodic inventory system, whereas it is the *ending* inventory amount in a perpetual inventory system.
- Prepare the income statement in steps:
  1. Sales less sales returns and allowances and sales discounts equals net sales.
  2. Recall the following formulas to calculate cost of goods sold: purchases – purchase returns and allowances – purchase discounts = net purchases + freight in = cost of goods purchased. Beginning inventory + cost of goods purchased = cost of goods available for sale. Cost of goods sold = cost of goods available for sale – ending inventory.
  3. Net sales less cost of goods sold equals gross profit.
  4. Profit from operations plus non-operating revenues and gains or minus expenses and losses equals profit before income tax.

Solution to Comprehensive Do It! #2 (Periodic Inventory System)

DYKSTRA INC.
Income Statement
Year Ended December 31, 2012

Sales			$536,800
Less: Sales returns and allowances		$ 6,700	
Sales discounts		5,000	11,700
Net sales			525,100
Cost of goods sold			
Merchandise inventory, Jan. 1		$ 25,000	
Purchases	$370,000		
Less: Purchase returns and allowances	$15,000		
Purchase discounts	5,000	20,000	
Net purchases		350,000	
Add: Freight in		17,400	
Cost of goods purchased		367,400	
Cost of goods available for sale		392,400	
Merchandise inventory, Dec. 31		29,000	
Cost of goods sold			363,400
Gross profit			161,700
Operating expenses			
Administrative expenses		$111,500	
Selling expenses		19,600	131,100
Profit from operations			30,600
Other revenues and gains			
Interest revenue		$ 2,500	
Other expenses and losses			
Interest expense		4,600	2,100
Profit before income tax			28,500
Income tax expense			6,000
Profit			$ 22,500

Note that Dykstra's statement of changes in equity and statement of financial position are the same as those presented in the Comprehensive Do It! #1 using the perpetual inventory system.

Self-Test, Brief Exercises, Exercises, Problems: Set A, and many more components are available for practice in WileyPLUS.

Note: All questions, exercises, and problems below with an asterisk (*) relate to material in Appendix 5A.

Self-Test Questions

Answers are at the end of the chapter.

(SO 1)   1. Which of the following statements is true?
  (a) The operating cycle for a merchandising company is usually longer than that of a service company.
  (b) Cost of goods available for sale equals the total of cost of goods purchased and ending inventory.

  (c) A merchandising company usually has three different types of inventory: raw materials, work in process, and finished goods.
  (d) It is not necessary to perform a physical inventory count in a perpetual inventory system.

(SO 2) 2. A $750 purchase of merchandise inventory is made on June 12, terms 2/10, n/30. On June 16, merchandise costing $50 is returned. What amount will be paid if payment is made in full on June 21? On July 11?
(a) $630 and $700
(b) $686 and $700
(c) $700 and $750
(d) $735 and $750

(SO 2) 3. Enrage Inc. purchased merchandise for $310 on May 12, terms 1/10, n/30, FOB shipping point. On May 12, freight costs of $25 were also paid by the company. On May 15, Enrage returned merchandise costing $10. On May 21, the company paid the amount owing. What is the ending balance in the Merchandise Inventory account related to these transactions, if Enrage uses a perpetual inventory system?
(a) $300.00
(b) $321.75
(c) $322.00
(d) $325.00

(SO 2, 3) 4. When goods are shipped with the freight terms FOB shipping point in a perpetual inventory system:
(a) the buyer pays the freight costs and debits Merchandise Inventory.
(b) the buyer pays the freight costs and debits Freight In.
(c) the seller pays the freight costs and debits Cost of Goods Sold.
(d) the seller pays the freight costs and debits Freight Out.

(SO 3) 5. To record the sale of goods for cash in a perpetual inventory system:
(a) only one journal entry is necessary to record the cost of goods sold and reduction of inventory.
(b) only one journal entry is necessary to record the receipt of cash and the sales revenue.
(c) two journal entries are necessary: one to record the receipt of cash and sales revenue, and one to record the cost of the goods sold and reduction of inventory.
(d) two journal entries are necessary: one to record the receipt of cash and reduction of inventory, and one to record the cost of the goods sold and sales revenue.

(SO 3) 6. Which of the following is a contra revenue account that normally has a debit balance?
(a) Sales
(b) Sales Returns and Allowances

(c) Cost of Goods Sold
(d) Freight Out

(SO 4) 7. Net sales are $400,000; cost of goods sold is $310,000; selling expenses are $10,000; administrative expenses are $50,000; other revenue and gains is $10,000; and income tax expense is $8,000. What is the gross profit?
(a) $12,000
(b) $30,000
(c) $32,000
(d) $90,000

(SO 4) 8. Which of the following appears on both a single-step and multiple-step income statement?
(a) Gross profit
(b) Profit from operations
(c) Merchandise inventory
(d) Profit before income tax

(SO 5) 9. Which of the following would affect the gross profit margin?
(a) An increase in interest expense
(b) A decrease in depreciation expense
(c) An increase in cost of goods sold
(d) An increase in freight out

(SO 5) 10. Net sales are $400,000; cost of goods sold is $310,000; operating expenses are $60,000; other revenue and gains is $10,000; and income tax expense is $8,000. What are the gross profit margin and profit margin?
(a) 7.5% and 8.0%
(b) 8.0% and 22.5%
(c) 22.5% and 8.0%
(d) 25.0% and 8.0%

(SO 6) *11. When goods are purchased for resale by a company using a periodic inventory system:
(a) purchases are debited to Merchandise Inventory.
(b) purchases are debited to Purchases.
(c) purchases are debited to Cost of Goods Sold.
(d) freight costs are debited to Purchases.

(SO 6) *12. Beginning inventory is $60,000; purchases are $400,000; purchase returns and allowances are $25,000; freight in is $5,000; and ending inventory is $50,000. What is the cost of goods sold under a periodic inventory system?
(a) $380,000
(b) $390,000
(c) $435,000
(d) $440,000

Questions

(SO 1) 1. Is there any difference between the types and classifications of inventory held by a merchandising company and a manufacturing company? Explain.

(SO 1) 2. What is meant by the term *operating cycle*? Why is the normal operating cycle for a merchandising company likely to be longer than that of a service company?

(SO 1) 3. (a) Explain the income measurement process in a merchandising company. (b) How does income measurement differ between a merchandising company and a service company?

(SO 1) 4. Suppose you are starting a company that sells used clothes. What factors would you consider in determining whether to use a perpetual or periodic inventory system?

(SO 1) 5. Song Yee wonders why a physical inventory count is necessary in a perpetual inventory system. After all, the accounting records show how much inventory is on hand. Explain why a physical inventory count is required in a perpetual inventory system.

(SO 2) 6. Why are purchases of merchandise for resale not recorded in the same account as purchases of other items, such as supplies or equipment? Would it not be better to use one account to record all these purchases?

(SO 2) 7. Butler's Roofing Ltd. received an invoice for a purchase of merchandise for $10,000, terms 1/10, n/30. It will have to borrow from its bank at 6% in order to pay the invoice within the 10-day discount period. Should it take advantage of the cash discount offered or not? Explain, with calculations.

(SO 2, 3) 8. Inventory was purchased on credit in April and paid for in May. It was sold in June. In which month should the company record the sale as revenue and in which month should the company record the cost of goods sold as expense?

(SO 2, 3) 9. Distinguish between FOB shipping point and FOB destination. What freight term will result in a debit to Merchandise Inventory by the buyer? A debit to Freight Out by the seller?

(SO 2, 3) 10. Explain why purchase returns are credited directly to the Merchandise Inventory account but sales returns are not debited directly to the Sales account.

(SO 2, 3) 11. Distinguish between a quantity discount, a purchase discount, and a sales discount. Explain how each kind of discount is recorded.

(SO 3) 12. If merchandise is returned and restored to inventory, the Cost of Goods Sold account is credited. However, if merchandise is returned but not restored to inventory (because it is not resaleable), Cost of Goods Sold is not credited. Why not?

(SO 3) 13. As the end of Agnew Inc.'s fiscal year approached, it became clear that the company had excess inventory. Belden Glass, the head of marketing and sales, ordered his sales staff to "add 20% more units to each order that you ship. The customers can always ship the extra back next year if they decide they don't want it. We've got to do it to meet this year's sales goal." Discuss the implications of Belden's order.

(SO 4) 14. Distinguish between a single-step and a multiple-step income statement for a merchandising company.

(SO 4) 15. Which type of income statement—single-step or multiple-step—does Eastplats use? You can find its financial statements in Appendix A at the back of this textbook.

(SO 4) 16. What is the difference between classifying expenses in an income statement by nature or by function? Does this classification apply only to a single-step income statement, a multiple-step income statement, or both?

(SO 4) 17. Shoppers Drug Mart's biggest competitor, after Jean Coutu, is the Katz Group. Its Canadian stores include Rexall Drug Stores, Guardian, Medicine Shoppe, and Pharma Plus Drugmart, among others. Katz is a private company, while Shoppers and Jean Coutu are publicly traded companies. How might Katz's expenses reported on its income statement differ from those presented by Shoppers and Jean Coutu?

(SO 4) 18. Why is interest expense reported as a non-operating expense and not as an operating expense on a multiple-step income statement?

(SO 4) 19. Longwell Corp. announced that its profit for the current fiscal year increased by $15 million, or 20%, compared with the previous year. Further inspection of its income statement revealed that the company reported a $20-million gain as "Other Revenues and Gains" from the sale of one of its factories. Discuss the implications of Longwell's announcement in terms of its predictive value.

(SO 5) 20. How do the gross profit margin and profit margin differ?

(SO 5) 21. What factors affect a company's gross profit margin; that is, what can cause the gross profit margin to increase and what can cause it to decrease?

(SO 5) 22. Identify two types of companies that you would expect to have a high gross profit margin and two types of companies that you would expect to have a low gross profit margin.

(SO 6) *23. Distinguish between the journal entries in a periodic inventory system and a perpetual inventory system (a) made by the buyer, and (b) made by the seller.

(SO 6) *24. Identify the accounts that are added to or deducted from purchases in a periodic inventory system to determine the cost of goods purchased. For each account, indicate (a) whether its balance is added or deducted and (b) what its normal balance is.

(SO 6) *25. How is the cost of goods sold calculated and recorded in a periodic inventory system? In a perpetual inventory system?

(SO 6) *26. What differences would be found on an income statement prepared for a company using a periodic inventory system, compared with a company using a perpetual inventory system?

Brief Exercises

Compare operating cycles.
(SO 1)

BE5–1   The operating cycles of three different companies are shown below.

Company	Operating Cycle (in days)
A	98
B	67
C	35

(a) Which company has the most efficient operating cycle? (b) Identify which of the three companies is most likely a service company, a merchandising company, and a manufacturing company.

Determine missing amounts for income measurement process.
(SO 1)

BE5–2   Selected information from the income measurement process for a service company and a merchandising company is shown below.

Company	Sales or Service Revenue	Cost of Goods Sold	Gross Profit	Operating Expenses	Profit before Income Tax	Income Tax Expense	Profit
A	$100	$ 0	$ 0	$65	$[1]	$9	$[2]
B	100	[3]	60	[4]	35	[5]	26

(a) Determine the missing amounts [1] through [5]. (b) Identify which of the two companies—A or B—is a service company and which is a merchandising company. Explain why you made the choices you did.

Determine missing amounts for inventory.
(SO 2)

BE5–3   The following Merchandise Inventory T account is available for a company that uses a perpetual inventory system:

Merchandise Inventory

Balance, beg. of Year 1	[1]		
Purchases	[2]	Purchase returns	1,000
Freight	500	Purchase discounts	100
		Cost of goods sold	8,000
Balance, end of Year 1 (beg. of Year 2)	[3]		
Purchases	10,720	Purchase returns	200
Freight	600	Purchase discounts	[4]
		Cost of goods sold	[5]
Balance, end of Year 2	6,000		

In Year 1, the cost of goods purchased was $9,500 and the cost of goods available for sale was $12,000. In Year 2, the cost of goods purchased was $11,000 and the cost of goods available for sale was $15,000. Use this information to determine missing items [1] through [5]. *Note:* You may not be able to solve these in numerical order.

Record purchase and sale transactions.
(SO 2, 3)

BE5–4   On August 24, Pocras Corporation purchased merchandise on account from Wydell Inc. The selling price of the goods is $900 and the cost of goods sold is $590. Both companies use perpetual inventory systems. Record the above transactions on the books of both companies.

Record purchase transactions.
(SO 2)

BE5–5   Prepare the journal entries to record the following purchase transactions in Xiaoyan Ltd.'s books. Xiaoyan uses a perpetual inventory system.

Jan. 2 Xiaoyan purchased $10,000 of merchandise from Feng Corp., terms 1/10, n/30, FOB destination.
      5 The appropriate company paid freight costs of $150.
      6 Xiaoyan returned $1,000 of the merchandise purchased on January 2, because it was not needed.
     11 Xiaoyan paid the balance owed to Feng.

Record sales transactions.
(SO 2)

BE5–6   Refer to BE5–5 and prepare the journal entries to record the following sales transactions in Feng Corp.'s books. Feng uses a perpetual inventory system.

Jan. 2 Feng sold $10,000 of merchandise to Xiaoyan Ltd., terms 1/10, n/30, FOB destination. The cost of the merchandise sold was $7,500.
      5 The appropriate company paid freight costs of $150.
      6 Xiaoyan returned $1,000 of the merchandise purchased from Feng on January 2, because it was not needed. The cost of the merchandise returned was $750, and it was restored to inventory.
     11 Feng received the balance due from Xiaoyan.

BE5–7 Saguenay Limited reports the following information: sales $650,000; sales returns and allowances $25,000; sales discounts $55,000; cost of goods sold $320,000; administrative expenses $100,000; selling expenses $25,000; other revenues and gains $20,000; other expenses and losses $30,000; and income tax expense $25,000. Assuming Saguenay uses a multiple-step income statement, calculate the following: (a) net sales, (b) gross profit, (c) profit from operations, (d) profit before income tax, and (e) profit.

Calculate amounts from income statement.
(SO 4)

BE5–8 Explain where each of the following items would appear on (a) a single-step income statement and (b) a multiple-step income statement where expenses are classified by nature: depreciation expense, cost of goods sold, freight out, income tax expense, interest expense, interest revenue, rent revenue, salaries expense, sales, sales discounts, and sales returns and allowances.

Identify placement of items on income statement.
(SO 4)

BE5–9 A company presented its expenses in its income statement using the following format:

Sales revenue	$x
Cost of goods sold	x
Gross profit	x
Administrative expenses	x
Selling expenses	x
Profit from operations	x
Other revenue and gains	x
Profit before income tax	x
Income tax expense	x
Profit	x

Identify classification of expenses on income statement.
(SO 4)

(a) Is this company using a single- or multiple-step form of income statement? (b) Is it classifying its expenses by nature or by function? Explain.

BE5–10 In 2012, Modder Corporation reported net sales of $250,000, cost of goods sold of $137,500, operating expenses of $50,000, and income tax expense of $20,000. In 2011, it reported net sales of $200,000, cost of goods sold of $114,000, operating expenses of $40,000, other revenues and gains of $10,000, and income tax expense of $15,000. (a) Calculate the gross profit margin and profit margin for each year. (b) Comment on Modder's changing profitability.

Calculate profitability ratios and comment.
(SO 5)

BE5–11 In fiscal 2010, The Forzani Group Ltd. reported sales revenue of $1,358.3 million, cost of goods sold of $864.0 million, and profit of $28.8 million. In fiscal 2009, it reported sales revenue of $1,346.8 million, cost of goods sold of $863.2 million, and profit of $15.1 million. (a) Calculate the gross profit margin and profit margin for each year. (b) Comment on Forzani's changing profitability.

Calculate profitability ratios and comment.
(SO 5)

*BE5–12 From the information in BE5–5, prepare the journal entries to record the purchase transactions on Xiaoyan Ltd.'s books, assuming a periodic inventory system is used instead of a perpetual inventory system.

Record purchase transactions.
(SO 6)

*BE5–13 From the information in BE5–6, prepare the journal entries to record the sales transactions on Feng Corp.'s books, assuming a periodic inventory system is used instead of a perpetual inventory system.

Record sales transactions.
(SO 6)

*BE5–14 Bassing Corp. uses a periodic inventory system and reports the following information: sales $750,000; sales returns and allowances $75,000; sales discounts $25,000; purchases $425,000; purchase returns and allowances $11,000; purchase discounts $9,000; freight in $10,000; freight out $18,000; beginning inventory $60,000; and ending inventory $100,000. Assuming Bassing uses a multiple-step income statement, calculate (a) net sales, (b) net purchases, (c) cost of goods purchased, (d) cost of goods sold, and (e) gross profit.

Calculate amounts from income statement.
(SO 6)

*BE5–15 Haida Corporation reported the following selected data for the year ended December 31, 2012: purchases $130,000; purchase returns and allowances $4,400; purchase discounts $13,600; freight in $3,500; freight out $7,500; beginning inventory $70,000; and ending inventory $80,000. (a) Prepare the cost of goods sold section for Haida in a multiple-step income statement. (b) Explain how the remainder of Haida's income statement would differ, if at all, if it used a perpetual inventory system.

Prepare cost of goods sold section.
(SO 6)

Exercises

E5–1 Listed below are selected companies, accompanied by a brief description of their business:

1. Toys' R Us, Inc. sells toys.
2. Deloitte LLP is an accounting firm.
3. Atlantic Grocery Distributors Ltd. distributes food products.

Distinguish between service and merchandising companies.
(SO 1)

Instructions

(a) Identify whether the primary type of business for each of the above companies is as a service company, merchandiser (retailer) company, or merchandiser (wholesaler) company.

(b) Comment on how the operating cycles and income measurement processes of each of the above companies might differ, if at all.

Identify debit and credit effects of inventory transactions.
(SO 2, 3)

E5–2 Listed below are selected examples of transactions related to the purchase and sale of merchandise inventory. Assume a perpetual inventory system is in use.

1. Purchase of $2,500 of inventory for cash.
2. Purchase of $4,000 of inventory on account, terms 1/10, n/30.
3. Payment of $250 cash for freight on purchase of inventory (FOB shipping point).
4. Return of $500 of inventory to seller for credit on account.
5. Payment of amount owed ($3,500) for purchase of inventory, terms 1/10, n/30, within discount period. *Note:* The $3,500 does not include the purchase discount. You will have to calculate this amount.
6. Sale of inventory on account, terms n/30. Selling price $5,000; cost of sale $2,000.
7. Payment of $300 cash for freight on sale of inventory (FOB destination).
8. Return of unwanted inventory from buyer for credit on account. Selling price $1,000; cost of sale $400. Goods restored to inventory for future resale.
9. Return of damaged inventory from buyer for cash. Selling price $750; cost of sale $300. Goods not resaleable are discarded.
10. Receipt of payment ($4,000) from customer on account, terms n/30.

Instructions

For each of the above transactions, indicate: (a) the basic type (e.g., asset, liability, revenue, expense) of each account to be debited and credited; (b) the specific name of the account(s) to debit and credit (e.g., Merchandise Inventory); and (c) whether each account is increased (+) or decreased (–) and by what amount. The first one has been done for you as an example.

	Account Debited			Account Credited		
	(a)	(b)	(c)	(a)	(b)	(c)
	Basic Type of Account	Specific Account	Amount	Basic Type of Account	Specific Account	Amount
1.	Asset	Merchandise Inventory	+$2,500	Asset	Cash	–$2,500

Record and post purchase and sales transactions.
(SO 2, 3)

E5–3 On September 1, the beginning of its fiscal year, Campus Office Supply Ltd. had an inventory of 10 calculators at a cost of $20 each. The company uses a perpetual inventory system. During September, the following transactions occurred:

Sept. 2 Purchased 75 calculators for $20 each from Digital Corp. on account, terms n/30.
      10 Returned two calculators to Digital for $40 credit because they did not meet specifications.
      11 Sold 26 calculators for $30 each to Campus Book Store, terms n/30.
      14 Granted credit of $30 to Campus Book Store for the return of one calculator that was not ordered. The calculator was restored to inventory.
      21 Sold 30 calculators for $30 each to Student Card Shop, terms 1/10, n/30.
      29 Paid Digital the amount owing.
      30 Received payment in full from the Student Card Shop.

Instructions

(a) Record the September transactions.

(b) Create T accounts for the Merchandise Inventory and Cost of Goods Sold accounts. Post the opening balance and the September transactions.

(c) Determine the ending balances in both dollars and quantities.

Record purchase transactions.
(SO 2)

E5–4 Olaf Corp. uses a perpetual inventory system. The company had the following inventory transactions in April:

April 3 Purchased merchandise from DeVito Ltd. for $28,000, terms 1/10, n/30, FOB shipping point.
      6 The appropriate company paid freight costs of $700 on the merchandise purchased on April 3.
      7 Purchased supplies on account for $5,000.
      8 Returned damaged merchandise to DeVito and was given a purchase allowance of $3,500. The merchandise was repaired by DeVito and returned to inventory for future resale.
      30 Paid the amount due to DeVito in full.

Instructions
(a) Record the above transactions in Olaf's books.
(b) Assume that Olaf paid the balance due to DeVito on April 12 instead of April 30. Prepare the journal entry to record this payment on Olaf's books.

E5–5 Refer to the information in E5–4 for Olaf Corp. and the following additional information:

1. The cost of the merchandise sold on April 3 was $19,000.
2. The cost of the merchandise returned on April 8 was $2,300.
3. DeVito uses a perpetual inventory system.

Record sales transactions.
(SO 3)

Instructions
(a) Record the transactions in the books of DeVito.
(b) Assume that DeVito received the balance due from Olaf on April 12 instead of April 30. Prepare the journal entry to record this collection on DeVito's books.

E5–6 The following merchandise transactions occurred in December. Both companies use a perpetual inventory system.

Record purchase and sales transactions; calculate gross profit.
(SO 2, 3)

Dec. 3	Pippen Ltd. sold $9,000 of merchandise to Thomas Corp., terms 2/10, n/30, FOB shipping point. The cost of the merchandise sold was $5,000.
7	Shipping costs of $225 were paid by the appropriate company.
8	Thomas returned unwanted merchandise to Pippen. The returned merchandise has a sales price of $600, and a cost of $325. It was restored to inventory.
11	Pippen received the balance due from Thomas.

Instructions
(a) Record the above transactions in the books of Pippen Ltd.
(b) Record the above transactions in the books of Thomas Corp.
(c) Calculate the gross profit earned by Pippen on the above transactions.

E5–7 The following list of accounts is from the adjusted trial balance for Swirsky Corporation:

Classify accounts.
(SO 4)

Accounts payable	Equipment	Prepaid insurance
Accounts receivable	Income tax expense	Property tax payable
Accumulated depreciation	Interest expense	Salaries payable
Administrative expenses	Interest payable	Sales
Buildings	Land	Sales discounts
Cash	Merchandise inventory	Sales returns and allowances
Common shares	Mortgage payable	Unearned revenue

Instructions
For each account, identify whether it should be reported on the statement of financial position or income statement. Also specify where the account should be classified. For example, Accounts Payable would be classified under current liabilities on the statement of financial position.

E5–8 The following selected accounts from the Blue Door Corporation's general ledger are presented below for the year ended December 31, 2012:

Prepare income statement.
(SO 4)

Advertising expense	$ 55,000	Interest revenue	$ 30,000
Common shares	250,000	Merchandise inventory	67,000
Cost of goods sold	1,085,000	Rent revenue	24,000
Depreciation expense	125,000	Retained earnings	535,000
Dividends	150,000	Salaries expense	675,000
Freight out	25,000	Sales	2,400,000
Income tax expense	70,000	Sales discounts	8,500
Insurance expense	15,000	Sales returns and allowances	41,000
Interest expense	70,000	Unearned revenue	8,000

Instructions
(a) Prepare a single-step income statement.
(b) Prepare a multiple-step income statement.
(c) Are the expenses classified by nature or function in the list of accounts above? Explain.

Determine missing amounts and calculate profitability ratios.
(SO 4, 5)

E5–9 Income statement information is presented here for two companies:

	Young Ltd.	Rioux Ltée
Sales	$99,000	$ [6]
Sales returns and allowances	[1]	5,000
Net sales	89,000	100,000
Cost of goods sold	58,750	[7]
Gross profit	[2]	40,000
Operating expenses	19,500	[8]
Profit from operations	[3]	18,000
Other revenues and gains	750	0
Other expenses and losses	0	2,000
Profit before income tax	[4]	[9]
Income tax expense	2,300	[10]
Profit	[5]	12,800

Instructions
(a) Calculate the missing amounts for [1] to [10].
(b) Calculate the gross profit margin and profit margin for each company.

Prepare income statement, calculate profitability ratios, and comment.
(SO 4, 5)

E5–10 Memories Corporation reported the following condensed income statement data (in thousands) for the year ended August 31, 2012:

Administrative expenses	$ 515
Cost of goods sold	3,100
Income tax expense (30%)	428
Net sales	5,450
Other expenses and losses	210
Selling expenses	200

Instructions
(a) Prepare a multiple-step income statement.
(b) Are the expenses classified by nature or function in the list of accounts above?
(c) Calculate the gross profit margin and profit margin.
(d) Assume the marketing department has presented a plan to increase selling expenses (primarily advertising costs) from $200,000 to $300,000. It expects this plan to result in an increase in both net sales and cost of goods sold of 25%. Redo part (c) with these revised numbers and comment on whether this plan has merit. Assume an income tax rate of 30%.

Calculate profitability ratios and comment.
(SO 5)

E5–11 Best Buy Co., Inc. reported the following selected information for its three most recent fiscal years (in USD millions):

	2010	2009	2008
Net sales	$49,694	$45,015	$40,023
Cost of goods sold	37,534	34,017	30,477
Profit from operations	2,235	1,870	2,161
Profit	1,317	1,003	1,407

Instructions
(a) Calculate the gross profit margin and profit margin for Best Buy for each of the three years.
(b) Comment on whether the ratios have improved or deteriorated over the last three years.
(c) Recalculate the profit margin for the three years using profit from operations instead of profit. Does this result in a different trend than you saw in (a)? If yes, what might be the reason for this change?

Record purchase and sales transactions.
(SO 6)

*E5–12 Data for Olaf Corp. and DeVito Ltd. are presented in E5–4 and E5–5.
Instructions
Repeat the requirements for E5–4 and E5–5, assuming a periodic inventory system is used instead of a perpetual inventory system.

Record purchase and sales transactions.
(SO 2, 3, 6)

*E5–13 Duvall Ltd. and Pele Ltd. incurred the following merchandise transactions in June.

June 10   Duvall sold $5,000 of merchandise to Pele, terms 1/10, n/30, FOB shipping point. The merchandise cost Duvall $3,000 when it was originally purchased.
     11   Freight costs of $250 were paid by the appropriate company.

12 Duvall received damaged goods returned by Pele for credit. The goods were originally sold for $500; the cost of the returned merchandise was $300. The merchandise was not returned to inventory.

19 Duvall received full payment from Pele.

Instructions

(a) Prepare journal entries for each transaction in the books of Duvall Ltd., assuming (1) a perpetual inventory system is used, and (2) a periodic inventory system is used.

(b) Prepare journal entries for each transaction for Pele Ltd., assuming (1) a perpetual inventory system is used, and (2) a periodic inventory system is used.

*E5–14   Below are the cost of goods sold sections for the most recent two years for two companies using a periodic inventory system:

Determine missing amounts.
(SO 6)

	Company 1		Company 2	
	Year 1	Year 2	Year 1	Year 2
Beginning inventory	$ 200	$ [5]	$1,000	$ [14]
Purchases	1,500	[6]	[10]	8,550
Purchase returns and allowances	50	100	200	400
Purchase discounts	30	50	150	100
Net purchases	[1]	1,800	7,210	[15]
Freight in	130	[7]	[11]	550
Cost of goods purchased	[2]	[8]	7,800	[16]
Cost of goods available for sale	[3]	2,300	[12]	[17]
Ending inventory	[4]	350	1,250	1,500
Cost of goods sold	1,480	[9]	[13]	[18]

Instructions

Fill in the numbered blanks to complete the cost of goods sold sections.

*E5–15   The following selected information is presented for Okanagan Corporation for the year ended February 29, 2012. Okanagan uses a periodic inventory system.

Prepare income statement.
(SO 6)

Accounts receivable	$ 25,000	Merchandise inventory, Feb. 29, 2012	$ 61,000
Administrative expenses	83,000	Purchases	210,000
Common shares	85,000	Purchase discounts	30,000
Dividends	42,000	Purchase returns and allowances	16,000
Freight in	6,500	Sales	335,000
Income tax expense	6,900	Sales discounts	21,000
Insurance expense	10,000	Sales returns and allowances	12,000
Interest expense	6,000	Selling expenses	7,000
Merchandise inventory, Mar. 1, 2011	42,000	Unearned revenue	4,500

Instructions

Prepare a multiple-step income statement.

Problems: Set A

P5–1A   The Breeze Hair Salon Inc. commenced operations six months ago. The salon's main business is hair styling, colouring, and other hair treatment services. The salon also purchases and sells all of the products it uses, plus hair accessories such as hair extensions and jewellery. The sale of the products, while secondary to the salon's main business, still constitutes a significant amount of revenue. Most sales are paid by the salon's customers with cash, or paid for by debit and credit cards, which are considered to be equivalent to cash.

Identify appropriate inventory system.
(SO 1)

The salon purchases its products from a local wholesaler, on credit terms of n/30 days. Normally, the salon purchases a two-month supply of products at a time. Karen, the manager of the salon, is not comfortable with a high level of accounts payable so the salon pays the wholesaler much earlier than 30 days if it has cash on hand.

When the salon's accounting system was set up, a perpetual inventory system was established to track the products sold. Staff have been complaining to Karen that it is time-consuming to scan each product sold. Both the staff and customers are finding the additional time it takes to scan products to be frustrating, especially when the salon is busy.

Karen had a physical inventory count performed after the salon's first six months of operations. When the quantities of merchandise determined at the physical count were compared with the quantities per the perpetual system, there were a number of discrepancies.

Karen has noticed that the salon often runs out of the more popular products. She also noticed that while some items sell fast, others seem to collect dust. To get rid of these slow-moving products, the salon has to mark down the selling prices of its products, which is affecting the company's cash flow and gross profit.

Instructions

(a) Explain to Karen what an operating cycle is and why the salon is having problems with its cash flow and gross profit.

(b) Make a recommendation about what inventory system the salon should use and explain why.

Record purchase and sales transactions.
(SO 1, 2, 3)

P5–2A   Phantom Book Warehouse Ltd. distributes hardcover books to retail stores. At the end of May, Phantom's inventory consists of 140 books purchased at $16 each. Phantom uses a perpetual inventory system.

During the month of June, the following merchandise transactions occurred:

June 1   Purchased 160 books on account for $16 each from Reader's World Publishers, terms n/30.
  3   Sold 120 books on account to The Book Nook for $20 each, with a cost of $16, terms 2/10, n/30.
  5   Received a $160 credit for 10 books returned to Reader's World Publishers.
  8   Sold 125 books on account to Read-A-Lot Bookstore for $20 each, with a cost of $16, terms 2/10, n/30.
  9   Issued a $100 credit memorandum to Read-A-Lot Bookstore for the return of five damaged books. The books were determined to be no longer saleable and were destroyed.
  11   Purchased 110 books on account for $15 each from Read More Publishers, terms n/30.
  12   Received payment in full from The Book Nook.
  17   Received payment in full from Read-A-Lot Bookstore.
  22   Sold 100 books on account to Reader's Bookstore for $22 each, with an average cost of $15.29, terms 2/10, n/30.
  25   Granted Reader's Bookstore a $330 credit for 15 returned books. These books were restored to inventory.
  29   Paid Reader's World Publishers in full.

Instructions

(a) Is the Phantom Book Warehouse a retailer or a wholesaler? Explain.

(b) Record the June transactions for Phantom. (Record transactions to the nearest cent.)

(c) Create a T account for the Merchandise Inventory account. Post the opening balance and June transactions, and calculate the June 30 balance in the account.

(d) Determine the number of books Phantom has on hand on June 30. What is the average cost of these books on June 30? (*Hint:* Divide the ending balance in the Merchandise Inventory account calculated in (c) and divide it by the number of books on hand at June 30. Round your answer to the nearest cent.)

Record purchase and sales transactions.
(SO 2, 3)

P5–3A   Presented here are selected transactions for Norlan Inc. during September of the current year. Norlan uses a perpetual inventory system.

Sept. 2   Purchased equipment on account for $25,000, terms n/30, FOB destination.
  3   Freight charges of $625 were paid by the appropriate party on the September 2 purchase of equipment.
  4   Purchased merchandise on account from Hillary Corp. at a cost of $65,000, terms 1/15, n/30, FOB shipping point.
  5   Purchased supplies for $4,000 cash.
  7   Freight charges of $1,600 were paid by the appropriate party on the September 4 purchase of merchandise.
  8   Returned damaged goods costing $5,000 that were originally purchased from Hillary on September 4. Received a credit on account.
  9   Sold merchandise costing $15,000 to Fischer Limited for $20,000 on account, terms 2/10, n/30, FOB destination.
  10   Freight charges of $375 were paid by the appropriate party on the September 9 sale of merchandise.
  17   Received the balance due from Fischer.
  18   Paid Hillary the balance due.
  20   Purchased merchandise for $6,000 cash.
  22   Sold inventory costing $20,000 to Waldo Inc. for $27,000 on account, terms n/30, FOB shipping point.
  23   Freight charges of $500 were paid by the appropriate party on the September 22 sale of merchandise.
  28   Waldo returned merchandise sold for $10,000 that cost $7,500. The merchandise was restored to inventory.

Instructions

(a) Record the September transactions on Norlan's books.
(b) Assume that Norlan did not take advantage of the 1% purchase discount offered by Hillary Corp. and paid Hillary on Oct. 3 instead of September 18. Record the entry that Norlan would make on Oct. 3 and determine the cost of missing this purchase discount to Norlan.

P5–4A At the beginning of the current golf season, on April 1, 2012, the general ledger of Thousand Oaks Golf Shop showed Cash $3,500; Merchandise Inventory $1,500; Common Shares $3,000; and Retained Earnings $2,000. Thousand Oaks Golf Shop uses a perpetual inventory system.

Record and post purchase and sales transactions; prepare trial balance.
(SO 2, 3)

The following transactions occurred in April:

Apr. 3 Purchased golf bags, clubs, and balls on account from Balata Corp. for $2,700, terms 1/10, n/30, FOB shipping point.
6 Freight of $70 was paid by the appropriate party on the April 3 purchase from Balata.
9 Received a $150 purchase allowance from Balata for returned merchandise.
10 Sold merchandise on account to members for $2,950, terms n/30. The cost of the merchandise sold was $1,770.
12 Paid Balata in full.
14 Received payments on account from members, $1,250.
16 Purchased golf shoes, sweaters, and other accessories on account from Arrow Sportswear Limited for $770, terms 2/10, n/30.
17 Received a $75 credit from Arrow Sportswear for returned merchandise.
20 Sold merchandise on account to members for $1,890, terms n/30. The cost of the merchandise sold was $1,130.
24 Paid Arrow Sportswear in full.
27 Granted a $50 sales allowance to a member for soiled clothing. No merchandise was returned.

Instructions

(a) Prepare T accounts and enter the opening balances.
(b) Record and post the April transactions for Thousand Oaks Golf Shop. Round all calculations to the nearest dollar.
(c) Prepare a trial balance as at April 30, 2012.

P5–5A Eagle Hardware Store Ltd. completed the following merchandising transactions in the month of May 2012. At the beginning of May, Eagle's ledger showed Cash $7,000; Accounts Receivable $1,500; Merchandise Inventory $3,500; Common Shares $8,000; and Retained Earnings $4,000. Eagle Hardware uses a perpetual inventory system.

Record and post transactions and prepare partial financial statements.
(SO 2, 3, 4)

May 1 Purchased merchandise on account from Depot Wholesale Supply Ltd. for $5,800, terms 1/10, n/30, FOB shipping point.
3 Freight charges of $145 were paid by the appropriate party on the merchandise purchased on May 1.
4 Sold merchandise on account to Shep Ltd. for $3,500, terms 2/10, n/30, FOB destination. The cost of the merchandise was $2,100.
7 Freight charges of $90 were paid by the appropriate party on the May 4 sale.
8 Received a $200 credit from Depot Wholesale Supply when merchandise was returned.
9 Paid Depot Wholesale Supply in full.
11 Purchased supplies for $400 cash.
14 Received payment in full from Shep Ltd. for merchandise sold on account on May 4.
15 Collected $1,000 of the accounts receivable outstanding at the beginning of the month. All accounts were originally sold on terms of n/30, with no sales discounts.
18 Purchased merchandise from Harlow Distributors Inc. for $2,000, terms n/30, FOB destination.
21 Freight of $50 was paid by the appropriate party on the May 18 purchase of merchandise.
22 Sold merchandise to various customers for $6,500 cash. The cost of the merchandise was $3,900.
29 Paid a $100 cash refund to customers for returned merchandise. The cost of the returned merchandise was $60. It was restored to inventory.
31 A physical inventory count was taken and determined that there was $5,100 of inventory on hand. Prepare any adjustment required.

Instructions

(a) Prepare T accounts and enter the opening balances.
(b) Record and post the May transactions for Eagle Hardware Store.
(c) Prepare a partial multiple-step income statement for the month ended May 31, 2012, through to gross profit.
(d) Prepare the current assets section of the statement of financial position as at May 31, 2012.

Prepare single- and multiple-step income statements.
(SO 4)

P5–6A The adjusted trial balance of Club Canada Wholesale Inc. contained the following accounts at December 31, the company's year end:

CLUB CANADA WHOLESALE INC.
Adjusted Trial Balance
December 31, 2012

	Debit	Credit
Cash	$ 8,875	
Accounts receivable	17,600	
Notes receivable	30,000	
Merchandise inventory	92,400	
Supplies	3,780	
Land	72,000	
Buildings	197,000	
Accumulated depreciation—buildings		$ 93,575
Equipment	83,500	
Accumulated depreciation—equipment		33,400
Accounts payable		57,500
Unearned revenue		7,550
Income tax payable		3,500
Mortgage payable		86,000
Common shares		20,000
Retained earnings		139,675
Sales		922,360
Sales returns and allowances	17,745	
Sales discounts	4,615	
Cost of goods sold	692,100	
Administrative expenses	116,115	
Selling expenses	5,900	
Interest expense	8,830	
Interest revenue		2,400
Income tax expense	15,500	
	$1,365,960	$1,365,960

Instructions
(a) Prepare a single-step income statement.
(b) Prepare a multiple-step income statement.
(c) Compare the two statements and comment on the usefulness of each one.
(d) Are the expenses in the statements classified by nature or by function? Explain.

Record and post adjusting entries; prepare adjusted trial balance and financial statements.
(SO 4)

P5–7A The unadjusted trial balance of Mesa Inc., at the company's year end of December 31 follows:

MESA INC.
Trial Balance
December 31, 2012

	Debit	Credit
Cash	$ 17,000	
Accounts receivable	31,700	
Merchandise inventory	28,750	
Supplies	2,940	
Prepaid insurance	3,000	
Land	30,000	
Buildings	150,000	
Accumulated depreciation—buildings		$ 24,000
Equipment	45,000	
Accumulated depreciation—equipment		18,000
Accounts payable		33,735
Unearned revenue		4,000
Mortgage payable		147,100
Common shares		13,000
Retained earnings		31,425
Dividends	2,000	

	Debit	Credit
Sales		265,770
Sales returns and allowances	2,500	
Sales discounts	3,275	
Cost of goods sold	171,225	
Salaries expense	30,950	
Utilities expense	5,100	
Interest expense	8,090	
Income tax expense	5,500	
	$537,030	$537,030

Additional information and adjustment data:

1. The 12-month insurance policy was purchased and was effective February 1, 2012.
2. There was $750 of supplies on hand on December 31.
3. Depreciation expense for the year is $6,000 for the buildings and $4,500 for the equipment.
4. Salaries of $750 are accrued and unpaid at December 31.
5. Accrued interest expense at December 31 is $735.
6. Unearned revenue of $975 is still unearned at December 31. On the sales revenue that was earned, the cost of goods sold was $2,000.
7. Of the mortgage payable, $9,800 is payable next year.
8. Income tax of $500 is due and unpaid.
9. A physical count of inventory indicates $23,800 on hand at December 31.
10. Common shares of $3,000 were issued during the year.

Instructions
(a) Prepare T accounts and enter the trial balance amounts.
(b) Record and post the adjusting entries, assuming the company adjusts its accounts annually.
(c) Prepare an adjusted trial balance at December 31, 2012.
(d) Prepare a multiple-step income statement, statement of changes in equity, and statement of financial position for the year.

P5–8A Data for Club Canada Wholesale Inc. are presented in P5–6A.

Calculate profitability ratios and comment. (SO 5)

Instructions
(a) Calculate the profit margin and gross profit margin.
(b) The vice-president of marketing and director of human resources have proposed that the company would change its compensation of the sales force to a commission basis rather than paying a fixed salary. Given the increased incentive, they expect net sales to increase by 15%. They estimate that gross profit will increase by $27,000, operating expenses by $13,500, and income tax expense by $2,700. Net non-operating expense is not expected to change. Calculate the expected new gross profit and profit amounts. (*Hint*: You do not need to prepare a formal income statement.)
(c) Calculate the revised gross profit margin and profit margin, using the information you calculated in (b). Comment on the effect that this plan would have on profitability and evaluate the merit of this proposal.

P5–9A Psang Inc. purchases all merchandise inventory on credit and uses a perpetual inventory system. The Accounts Payable account is used for recording merchandise inventory purchases only; all other current liabilities are accrued in separate accounts.

Calculate missing amounts and assess profitability. (SO 4, 5)

You are provided with the following selected information for the most recent three years:

	2012	2011	2010
Income statement data			
Net sales	$86,000	$ [5]	$96,900
Cost of goods sold	25,500	27,000	[9]
Gross profit	[1]	61,500	69,300
Operating expenses	35,100	[6]	43,500
Income tax expense	6,350	6,120	6,450
Profit	$ [2]	$14,500	$ [10]
Statement of financial position data			
Merchandise inventory	$ [3]	$14,700	$11,000
Accounts payable	[4]	4,600	6,500
Additional information			
Purchase of merchandise inventory on account	$24,000	$ [7]	$25,900
Cash payments to suppliers	22,000	[8]	25,000

Instructions

(a) Calculate the missing amounts for items [1] through [10]. (*Hint:* You will find it helpful to prepare summary journal entries and T accounts for Merchandise Inventory and Accounts Payable to solve for items 3, 4, 7, and 8.)

(b) Calculate the gross profit margin and profit margin for each year.

(c) Net sales declined over the three-year period. Does this mean that profitability should also have declined over the same period? Refer to the gross profit margin and profit margin to explain and support your answer.

Calculate ratios and comment.
(SO 5)

P5–10A The following selected information is available for **Danier Leather Inc.** for three fiscal years (in thousands):

	2010	2009	2008
Current assets	$ 54,836	$ 48,056	$ 49,853
Current liabilities	17,958	10,967	11,205
Net sales	164,217	162,106	163,550
Cost of goods sold	77,438	88,589	87,365
Profit (loss)	7,219	(2,309)	12,892

Instructions

(a) Calculate the current ratio, gross profit margin, and profit margin for each year.

(b) Comment on whether the ratios have improved or deteriorated over the three years.

(c) Compare the 2010 ratios calculated in (a) with the following industry averages: current ratio 3.4:1; gross profit margin 49.2%; and profit margin 9.8%. Are Danier Leather's ratios better or worse than those of its industry?

Record purchase and sales transactions; discuss inventory systems.
(SO 1, 6)

*P5–11A Data for Phantom Book Warehouse Ltd. are presented in P5–2A.

Instructions

(a) Record the June transactions on Phantom Book Warehouse's books, assuming it uses a periodic inventory system instead of a perpetual inventory system.

(b) Identify the advantages and disadvantages of Phantom Book Warehouse using a periodic inventory system instead of a perpetual inventory system.

Record purchase and sales transactions.
(SO 6)

*P5–12A Data for Norlan Inc. are presented in P5–3A.

Instructions

(a) Record the September transactions on Norlan's books, assuming it uses a periodic inventory system instead of a perpetual inventory system.

(b) Assume that Norlan did not take advantage of the 1% purchase discount offered by Hillary Corp. and paid Hillary on Oct. 3 instead of September 18. Record the entry that Norlan would make on Oct. 3 and determine the cost of missing this purchase discount to Norlan.

Record and post purchase and sales transactions; prepare trial balance.
(SO 6)

*P5–13A Data for the Thousand Oaks Golf Shop are presented in P5–4A.

Instructions

(a) Prepare T accounts and enter the opening balances.

(b) Record and post the April transactions for Thousand Oaks Golf Shop, assuming it uses a periodic inventory system instead of a perpetual inventory system. Round all calculations to the nearest dollar.

(c) Prepare a trial balance as at April 30, 2012.

Prepare partial income statement; calculate gross profit.
(SO 5, 6)

*P5–14A You have been provided with the following selected accounts for Feisty Ltd. for the year ended April 30, 2012:

Inventory, May 1, 2011	$ 600,000	Interest expense	$ 30,000
Purchases	5,900,000	Interest income	20,000
Accounts receivable	780,000	Accounts payable	600,000
Sales	9,300,000	Administrative expenses	810,000
Purchase discounts	40,000	Selling expenses	150,000
Freight in	120,000	Cash	160,000
Land	900,000	Common shares	200,000
Sales returns and allowances	250,000		

Feisty conducted a physical inventory count on April 30, 2012. Inventory on hand at that date was determined to be $700,000.

Instructions

(a) Prepare a partial multiple-step income statement for the year ended April 30, 2012, through to gross profit.

(b) Calculate the gross profit margin. If the industry average gross profit margin is 30%, how does Feisty's gross profit margin compare?

*P5–15A Tater Tot Ltd.'s adjusted trial balance amounts appear in alphabetical order as follows on December 31, 2012, the end of its fiscal year:

Prepare financial statements.
(SO 6)

Accounts payable	$ 86,300	Land	$ 75,000
Accounts receivable	44,200	Merchandise inventory, Jan. 1, 2012	40,500
Accumulated		Mortgage payable	125,000
depreciation—buildings	51,800	Prepaid insurance	2,400
Accumulated		Property tax payable	4,800
depreciation—equipment	42,900	Purchases	401,600
Administrative expenses	180,900	Purchase discounts	22,500
Buildings	190,000	Purchase returns and allowances	6,400
Cash	17,000	Retained earnings	68,600
Common shares	75,000	Salaries payable	3,500
Dividends	8,000	Sales	637,000
Equipment	110,000	Sales discounts	15,000
Freight in	5,600	Sales returns and allowances	8,000
Income tax expense	16,000	Selling expenses	7,500
Interest expense	10,400	Unearned revenue	8,300

Additional information:

1. Tater Tot uses a periodic inventory system.
2. A physical inventory count determined that merchandise inventory on December 31, 2012, was $72,600.
3. Of the mortgage payable, $12,500 is due in the next year.
4. Common shares of $25,000 were issued during the year.

Instructions
Prepare a multiple-step income statement, statement of changes in equity, and statement of financial position for the year.

Problems: Set B

P5–1B The Fashion Palace Inc. sells a variety of home decorating merchandise, including pictures, small furniture items, dishes, candles, and area rugs. The company uses a periodic inventory system and counts inventory once a year. Most customers use the option to purchase on account and many take more than a month to pay. The company does not have any specific credit terms for its regular customers.

Identify appropriate inventory system.
(SO 1)

The general manager of The Fashion Palace, Rebecca Sherstabetoff, believes the company needs a bank loan because the accounts payable have to be paid long before the accounts receivable are collected. The bank manager is willing to give The Fashion Palace a loan but wants monthly financial statements.

Rebecca has also noticed that, while some of the company's merchandise sells very quickly, other items do not. Sometimes she wonders just how long some of those older items have been in stock. She has also noticed that the company seems to run out of some merchandise items on a regular basis. And she is wondering how she is going to find someone with the time to count the inventory every month so that monthly financial statements can be prepared for the bank. She has come to you for help.

Instructions
(a) Explain to Rebecca what an operating cycle is and why the company is having problems paying its bills.
(b) Make a recommendation about what inventory system the company should use and explain why.

P5–2B Travel Warehouse Ltd. distributes suitcases to retail stores. At the end of June, Travel Warehouse's inventory consisted of 25 suitcases purchased at $40 each. Travel Warehouse uses a perpetual inventory system. During the month of July, the following merchandising transactions occurred:

Record purchase and sales transactions.
(SO 1, 2, 3)

July 2 Purchased 50 suitcases on account for $40 each from Trunk Manufacturers Ltd., terms 1/10, n/30.
  3 Received a $200 credit from Trunk Manufacturers after returning five suitcases because they were damaged.
  6 Sold 40 suitcases on account to Satchel World Inc. for $75 each, with a cost of $40, terms 1/15, n/30.
  7 Issued a $375 credit for five suitcases returned by Satchel World because they were the wrong model. The suitcases were returned to inventory.
  9 Sold five suitcases—this time the right model number—on account to Satchel World Inc. for $80 each, with a cost of $40, terms 1/15, n/30.
  11 Paid Trunk Manufacturers the balance owing.

13 Sold 25 suitcases on account to The Going Concern, Limited for $80 each, with a cost of $40, terms 1/15, n/30.

16 Purchased 60 suitcases on account for $3,000 from Holiday Manufacturers, terms n/30.

17 Issued a $160 credit for two suitcases returned by The Going Concern because they were damaged. These suitcases were not restored to inventory.

20 Received payment in full from Satchel World for all transactions.

27 Received payment in full from The Going Concern.

Instructions

(a) Is Travel Warehouse a retailer or a wholesaler? Explain.

(b) Record the July transactions for Travel Warehouse. (Record transactions to the nearest cent.)

(c) Create a T account for the Merchandise Inventory account. Post the opening balance and July transactions, and calculate the July 31 balance in the account.

(d) Determine the number of suitcases Travel Warehouse has on hand on July 31. What is the average cost of these suitcases on July 31? (*Hint:* Divide the ending balance in the Merchandise Inventory account calculated in (c) and divide it by the number of suitcases on hand at July 31. Round your answer to the nearest cent.)

Record purchase and sales transactions.
(SO 2, 3)

P5–3B Presented here are selected transactions for Shaoshi Inc. during October of the current year. Shaoshi uses a perpetual inventory system.

Oct. 1 Purchased merchandise on account from Micron Ltd. at a cost of $65,000, terms 1/15, n/30, FOB shipping point.

1 Freight charges of $1,600 were paid by the appropriate party on the October 1 purchase of merchandise.

5 Returned for credit $7,000 of damaged goods purchased from Micron on October 1.

8 Sold the remaining merchandise purchased from Micron to Guidant Corp. for $100,000 on account, with a cost of $59,600, terms 2/10, n/30, FOB destination.

9 Freight charges of $2,300 were paid by the appropriate party on the October 8 sale of merchandise.

10 Guidant returned damaged merchandise that was purchased on October 8 for a $4,000 credit on account. The merchandise originally cost $2,384 and was not restored to inventory.

12 Purchased supplies for $5,000 cash.

15 Purchased merchandise for $7,500 cash.

17 Received the balance owing from Guidant.

20 Purchased equipment on account for $45,000.

28 Sold merchandise for $30,000 on account to Deux Ltée, terms 2/10, n/30, FOB shipping point. The merchandise had a cost of $18,000.

29 Freight charges of $750 were paid by the appropriate party on the October 28 sale of merchandise.

30 Paid Micron the balance owing.

31 Deux returned some of the merchandise that was purchased on October 28 for a $5,000 credit on account. The merchandise originally cost $3,000 and was restored to inventory.

Instructions

(a) Record the October transactions on Shaoshi's books.

(b) Assume that Shaoshi took advantage of the 1% purchase discount offered by Micron Ltd. and paid Micron on October 14 rather than October 30. Record the entry that Shaoshi would make on October 14 and determine the cost of missing this purchase discount to Shaoshi.

Record and post purchase and sales transactions; prepare trial balance.
(SO 2, 3)

P5–4B At the beginning of the current tennis season, on April 1, 2012, the general ledger of Kicked-Back Tennis Shop showed Cash $4,000; Merchandise Inventory $2,700; Common Shares $3,000; and Retained Earnings $3,700. Kicked-Back Tennis Shop uses a perpetual inventory system.

The following transactions occurred in April:

Apr. 2 Purchased racquets and balls from Roberts Inc. for $2,460, terms 2/10, n/30, FOB shipping point.

3 The appropriate party paid $60 freight on the purchase from Roberts on April 2.

7 Received credit of $55 from Roberts for a damaged racquet that was returned.

11 Paid Roberts in full.

13 Purchased tennis shoes from Niki Sports Ltd. for $460 cash, FOB shipping point.

16 The appropriate party paid $12 freight on the purchase from Niki on April 13.

17 Purchased supplies for $650 cash from Discount Supplies Limited.

18 Received a $55 cash refund from Niki Sports for damaged merchandise that was returned.

20 Sold merchandise to members for $3,400 on account, terms n/30. The cost of the merchandise was $2,040.

21 Some of the merchandise purchased on April 20, with a sales price of $500 and a cost of $300, was returned by members. It was restored to inventory.

23   Sold merchandise to members for $2,800, terms n/30. The cost of the merchandise was $1,680.

25   Received cash payments on account from members, $4,000.

28   Granted a $75 sales allowance on account to a member for slightly torn tennis clothing. No merchandise was returned.

30   Purchased equipment for use in the business from DomCo Ltd. for $1,800, terms n/30.

Instructions

(a) Prepare T accounts and enter the opening balances.

(b) Record and post the April transactions for Kicked-Back Tennis. Round all calculations to the nearest dollar.

(c) Prepare a trial balance as at April 30, 2012.

P5–5B   Nisson Distributing Ltd. completed the following merchandising transactions in the month of April 2012. At the beginning of April, Nisson's general ledger showed Cash $4,000; Accounts Receivable $3,500; Merchandise Inventory $2,500; Common Shares $5,000; and Retained Earnings $5,000. Nisson uses a perpetual inventory system.

Record and post transactions and prepare partial financial statements.
(SO 2, 3, 4)

Apr. 2   Purchased merchandise on account from Kai Supply Corp. for $8,900, terms 1/15, n/30, FOB shipping point.

3   The appropriate party paid $225 freight on the April 2 purchase from Kai Supply.

5   Sold $11,600 of merchandise on account to Kananaskis Supply Ltd., terms 2/10, n/30, FOB destination. The cost of the merchandise was $7,540.

9   The appropriate party paid $290 freight on the April 5 sale of merchandise to Kananaskis Supply.

10   Issued a $1,580 credit for merchandise returned by Kananaskis Supply. The merchandise originally cost $1,030 and was returned to inventory.

11   Purchased merchandise on account from Pigeon Distributors Limited for $4,200, terms 1/10, n/30, FOB destination.

12   The appropriate party paid $100 freight on the April 11 purchase from Pigeon Distributors.

13   Received a $300 credit for merchandise returned to Pigeon Distributors.

16   Received the balance owing from Kananaskis Supply.

17   Paid Kai Supply in full.

20   Paid Pigeon Distributors in full.

23   Sold merchandise for $6,400 cash. The cost of the merchandise was $5,200.

24   Made a $400 cash refund for damaged merchandise returned from the April 23 purchase. The cost of the merchandise returned was $260 and it was not restored to inventory.

27   Purchased merchandise from Tipsea Inc. for $6,100 cash.

30   Received a $500 refund for merchandise that was returned to Tipsea from the April 27 cash purchase.

Instructions

(a) Prepare T accounts and enter the opening balances.

(b) Record and post the April transactions for Nisson.

(c) Prepare a partial multiple-step income statement for the month ended April 30, 2012, through to gross profit.

(d) Prepare the current assets section of the statement of financial position as at April 30, 2012.

P5–6B   The adjusted trial balance of Poorten Wholesale Ltd. contained the following accounts at November 30, the company's fiscal year end:

Prepare single- and multiple-step income statements.
(SO 4)

POORTEN WHOLESALE LTD.
Adjusted Trial Balance
November 30, 2012

	Debit	Credit
Cash	$ 25,100	
Accounts receivable	35,700	
Notes receivable	25,000	
Merchandise inventory	45,200	
Supplies	1,500	
Land	60,000	
Buildings	102,000	
Accumulated depreciation—buildings		$ 17,000
Equipment	48,000	
Accumulated depreciation—equipment		24,000
Accounts payable		48,500

	Debit	Credit
Income tax payable		15,500
Unearned revenue		3,000
Mortgage payable		51,000
Common shares		30,000
Retained earnings		90,000
Sales		850,300
Sales returns and allowances	4,200	
Sales discounts	3,750	
Cost of goods sold	547,500	
Administrative expenses	170,670	
Selling expenses	43,100	
Interest expense	3,700	
Interest revenue		1,620
Income tax expense	15,500	
	$1,130,920	$1,130,920

Instructions

(a) Prepare a single-step income statement.

(b) Prepare a multiple-step income statement.

(c) Compare the two statements and comment on the usefulness of each one.

(d) Are the expenses in the statements classified by nature or by function? Explain.

Record and post adjusting entries; prepare adjusted trial balance and financial statements.

(SO 4)

P5–7B The unadjusted trial balance of Fashion Centre Ltd. contained the following accounts at November 30, the company's fiscal year end:

FASHION CENTRE LTD.
Trial Balance
November 30, 2012

	Debit	Credit
Cash	$ 22,000	
Accounts receivable	30,600	
Merchandise inventory	27,500	
Supplies	1,650	
Prepaid insurance	1,800	
Long-term investments	37,000	
Equipment	26,800	
Accumulated depreciation—equipment		$ 10,720
Leasehold improvements	42,000	
Accumulated depreciation—leasehold improvements		8,400
Accounts payable		34,400
Unearned revenue		3,000
Bank loan payable		35,000
Common shares		50,000
Retained earnings		30,000
Dividends	10,000	
Sales		248,500
Sales returns and allowances	4,600	
Sales discounts	4,520	
Cost of goods sold	157,000	
Salaries expense	32,600	
Rent expense	13,850	
Interest expense	4,000	
Advertising expense	2,100	
Income tax expense	2,000	
	$420,020	$420,020

Additional information and adjustment data:

1. The 12-month insurance policy was purchased on August 1.
2. There is $950 of supplies on hand at November 30.
3. Depreciation expense for the year is $5,360 on the equipment, and $4,200 on the leasehold improvements.

4. Salaries of $1,210 are unpaid at November 30.
5. Accrued interest expense at November 30 is $175.
6. Of the unearned revenue, $2,400 has been earned by November 30. The cost of goods sold incurred in earning this sales revenue is $1,560.
7. Of the bank loan payable, $5,000 is to be paid in the next year; the remainder is long-term.
8. Income tax of $1,100 is due and unpaid.
9. A physical count of inventory indicates $25,000 on hand at November 30.
10. Common shares of $5,000 were issued during the year.

Instructions
(a) Prepare T accounts and enter the trial balance amounts.
(b) Record and post the adjusting entries, assuming the company adjusts its accounts annually.
(c) Prepare an adjusted trial balance at November 30, 2012.
(d) Prepare a multiple-step income statement, statement of changes in equity, and statement of financial position for the year.

P5-8B Data for Poorten Wholesale Ltd. are presented in P5-6B.

Calculate profitability ratios and comment. (SO 5)

Instructions
(a) Calculate the profit margin and gross profit margin.
(b) The vice-president of marketing and director of human resources have proposed that the company would change its compensation of the sales force to a commission basis rather than paying a fixed salary. Given the increased incentive, they expect net sales to increase by 10%. They estimate that gross profit will increase by $30,000, operating expenses by $16,000, and income tax expense by $2,000. Net non-operating expense is not expected to change. Calculate the expected new gross profit and profit amounts. (*Hint*: You do not need to prepare a formal income statement.)
(c) Calculate the revised gross profit margin and profit margin, using the information you calculated in (b). Comment on the effect that this plan would have on profitability and evaluate the merit of this proposal.

P5-9B MacLean Corp. purchases all merchandise inventory on credit and uses a perpetual inventory system. The Accounts Payable account is used for recording merchandise inventory purchases only; all other current liabilities are accrued in separate accounts.

Calculate missing amounts and assess profitability. (SO 4, 5)

You are provided with the following selected information for the most recent three years:

	2012	2011	2010
Income statement data			
Net sales	$ [1]	$227,600	$219,500
Cost of goods sold	145,400	[5]	133,500
Gross profit	84,300	80,100	[9]
Operating expenses	[2]	47,000	[10]
Income tax expense	8,000	6,000	7,000
Profit	$ 36,300	$ [6]	$ 30,000
Statement of financial position data			
Merchandise inventory	$ [3]	$ 14,700	$ 10,000
Accounts payable	25,000	[7]	20,000
Additional information			
Purchase of merchandise inventory on account	$141,000	$ [8]	$132,000
Cash payments to suppliers	[4]	160,000	127,000

Instructions
(a) Calculate the missing amounts for items [1] through [10]. (*Hint*: You will find it helpful to prepare summary journal entries and T accounts for Merchandise Inventory and Accounts Payable to solve for items 3, 4, 7, and 8.)
(b) Calculate the gross profit margin and profit margin for each year.
(c) Sales increased over the three-year period. Does this mean that profitability should also have increased in the same period? Refer to the gross profit margin and profit margin to explain and support your answer.

P5-10B The following selected information is available for **AB Volvo**, headquartered in Sweden, for three fiscal years (in SEK [Swedish krona] millions):

Calculate ratios and comment. (SO 5)

	2010	2009	2008
Current assets	147,139	154,945	176,038
Current liabilities	124,059	122,581	155,257
Net sales	264,749	218,361	304,642
Cost of goods sold	201,797	186,167	238,928
Profit (loss)	11,212	(14,685)	10,016

Instructions

(a) Calculate the current ratio, gross profit margin, and profit margin for each year.

(b) Comment on whether the ratios have improved or deteriorated over the three years.

(c) Compare the 2010 ratios calculated in (a) with the following industry averages: current ratio 1.6:1; gross profit margin 17.5%; and profit margin 3.4%. Are Volvo's ratios better or worse than those of its industry?

Record purchase and sales transactions; discuss inventory systems.
(SO 1, 6)

*P5–11B   Data for Travel Warehouse Ltd. are presented in P5–2B.

Instructions

(a) Record the July transactions on Travel Warehouse's books, assuming it uses a periodic inventory system instead of a perpetual inventory system. (Record transactions to the nearest cent.)

(b) Identify the advantages and disadvantages of Travel Warehouse using a periodic inventory system instead of a perpetual inventory system.

Record purchase and sales transactions.
(SO 6)

*P5–12B   Data for Shaoshi Inc. are presented in P5–3B.

Instructions

(a) Record the October transactions on Shaoshi's books, assuming it uses a periodic inventory system instead of a perpetual inventory system.

(b) Assume that Shaoshi took advantage of the 1% purchase discount offered by Micron Ltd. and paid Micron on October 14 rather than October 30. Record the entry that Shaoshi would make on October 14 and determine the cost of missing this purchase discount to Shaoshi.

Record and post purchase and sales transactions; prepare trial balance.
(SO 6)

*P5–13B   Data for Kicked-Back Tennis Shop are presented in P5–4B.

Instructions

(a) Prepare T accounts and enter the opening balances.

(b) Record and post the April transactions for Kicked-Back Tennis Shop, assuming it uses a periodic inventory system instead of a perpetual inventory system. Round all calculations to the nearest dollar.

(c) Prepare a trial balance as at April 30, 2012.

Prepare partial income statement; calculate gross profit.
(SO 5, 6)

*P5–14B   You have been provided with the following selected accounts for Sparkles Inc. for the year ended June 30, 2012:

Inventory, July 1, 2011	$ 260,000	Sales discounts	$ 50,000
Purchases	3,140,000	Interest expense	10,000
Accounts receivable	330,000	Interest revenue	20,000
Sales	3,900,000	Accounts payable	270,000
Purchase returns and allowances	120,000	Selling expenses	60,000
Freight in	40,000	Cash	250,000
Administrative expenses	370,000	Common shares	150,000
Land	700,000		

Sparkles conducted a physical inventory count on June 30, 2012. Inventory on hand at that date was determined to be $300,000.

Instructions

(a) Prepare a partial multiple-step income statement for the year ended June 30, 2012, through to gross profit.

(b) Calculate the gross profit margin. If the industry average gross profit margin is 26%, how does Sparkles' gross profit margin compare?

Prepare financial statements.
(SO 6)

*P5–15B   The Goody Shop Ltd.'s adjusted trial balance amounts appear in alphabetical order as follows on November 30, 2012, the end of its fiscal year:

Administrative expenses	$218,100	Equipment	$ 57,000
Accounts payable	32,310	Freight in	5,060
Accounts receivable	13,770	Income tax expense	10,000
Accumulated depreciation—buildings	61,200	Income tax payable	6,000
Accumulated depreciation—equipment	19,880	Insurance expense	12,000
Buildings	175,000	Interest expense	11,315
Cash	8,500	Land	85,000
Common shares	26,000	Merchandise inventory, Dec. 1, 2011	34,360
Dividends	5,000	Mortgage payable	106,000

Prepaid insurance	$ 4,500	Salaries payable	$ 8,500
Property tax payable	3,500	Sales	989,000
Purchases	684,700	Sales discounts	15,000
Purchase discounts	16,000	Sales returns and allowances	10,000
Purchase returns and allowances	3,315	Selling expenses	8,200
Retained earnings	82,800	Unearned revenue	3,000

Additional information:

1. The Goody Shop uses a periodic inventory system.
2. A physical inventory count determined that merchandise inventory on November 30, 2012, was $37,350.
3. Of the mortgage payable, $5,300 is due in the next year.
4. Common shares of $25,000 were issued during the year.

Instructions

Prepare a multiple-step income statement, statement of changes in equity, and statement of financial position for the year.

Broadening Your Perspective

Financial Reporting and Analysis Cases

Financial Reporting: *Eastplats*

BYP5–1 The financial statements of Eastern Platinum Limited (Eastplats) are presented in Appendix A at the end of this book.

Instructions

(a) Is Eastplats a service company, merchandising company, or manufacturing company? Explain.
(b) Does Eastplats classify its operating expenses on its income statement by nature or by function? Explain.
(c) Are any non-operating revenues and gains or expenses and losses included in Eastplats's income statement? If so, identify the accounts included.
(d) Using "mine operating earnings" as the equivalent of gross profit, calculate Eastplats's gross profit margin for 2010 and 2009.
(e) Calculate Eastplats's profit margin for 2010 and 2009.
(f) Comment on the trend in Eastplats's gross profit margin and profit margin.

Answer questions about income statement; calculate profitability ratios and comment.
(SO 1, 4, 5)

Comparative Analysis: *Eastplats and Amplats*

BYP5–2 The financial statements of Anglo American Platinum Limited (Amplats) are presented in Appendix B following the financial statements for Eastern Platinum Limited (Eastplats) in Appendix A.

Instructions

(a) Determine the following values for each company for 2010 and 2009:
   1. Percentage change in net sales revenue for Amplats and revenue for Eastplats from 2009 to 2010
   2. Percentage change in operating profit from 2009 to 2010
   3. Gross profit margin (use "gross profit on metal sales" for Amplats and "mine operating earnings" for Eastplats)
   4. Profit margin
(b) What conclusions about the relative profitability of the two companies can be drawn from these data?

Calculate profitability ratios and comment.
(SO 5)

Interpreting Financial Information

BYP5–3 Anheuser-Busch InBev (AB-InBev) SA/NV and SABMiller plc are two of the world's largest brewers. Below are selected financial data for AB-InBev and SABMiller (both in USD millions) for a recent year.

Calculate ratios and comment.
(SO 5)

	AB-InBev	SABMiller
Sales	$ 36,758	$18,020
Cost of goods sold	17,198	4,565
Profit	5,877	2,081
Current assets	10,853	3,895
Total assets	112,525	37,504
Current liabilities	14,254	5,977
Total liabilities	79,354	16,905

Instructions

(a) Calculate the gross profit margin for each company. The industry average is 53.6%. Discuss their relative profitability and ability to control their cost of goods sold compared with each other, and with their industry.

(b) Calculate the profit margin for each company. The industry average is 10.8%. Discuss their relative profitability and ability to control their operating expenses compared with each other, and with their industry.

(c) Calculate the current ratio and the debt to total assets ratio for each company. The industry averages are 1.0:1 and 51.5%, respectively. Discuss their relative liquidity and solvency compared with each other, and with their industry.

(d) AB-InBev is headquartered in Belgium. SABMiller is headquartered in London, England. Why do you think that both companies, reporting in accordance with IFRS, are using U.S. dollars as their reporting currency?

Comparing IFRS and ASPE

Compare income statement formats and ratios. (SO 4, 5)

BYP5-4 Country Coffee Limited is a restaurant chain specializing in fresh, ready-to-serve coffee. Country Coffee is owned by its sole founder, who began the chain over 20 years ago. Today the business has expanded to 25 corporate locations and 30 franchise locations across Canada.

Country Coffee faces fierce competition from various other chains specializing in coffee. Happy Coffee Inc. is a major competitor that has successfully built a chain of over 500 restaurants. Happy Coffee enjoys strong brand recognition and customer loyalty in the Canadian market.

The founder of Country Coffee would like to compare his chain's results with those of Happy Coffee. Happy Coffee is publicly traded and prepares its financial statements in accordance with IFRS whereas Country Coffee uses ASPE. The following are condensed versions of income statements for Happy Coffee and Country Coffee for the year ended December 31, 2012:

HAPPY COFFEE INC.
Income Statement
Year Ended December 31, 2012
(in millions)

Revenues		
Sales		$2,536
Expenses		
Cost of goods sold	$1,619	
General and administrative expenses	417	2,036
Profit from operations		500
Other expenses and losses		
Interest expense		24
Profit before income tax		476
Income tax expense		95
Profit		$ 381

COUNTRY COFFEE LIMITED
Income Statement
Year Ended December 31, 2012
(in millions)

Revenues		
Sales		$84
Expenses		
Cost of goods sold	$30	
Rent	15	
Salaries	10	
Depreciation	9	
Utilities	3	
Advertising	2	
Insurance	1	70

Profit from operations	14
Other expenses and losses	
Interest expense	1
Profit before income tax	13
Income tax expense	3
Profit	$10

Instructions

(a) What is the main difference between the income statement presentation of Country Coffee and of Happy Coffee?

(b) Are these two formats acceptable under both ASPE and IFRS? Which of these methods requires a greater degree of judgement? Which of these two formats do you prefer and why?

(c) How will this difference affect the comparability of the two income statements?

(d) Will the use of different presentation formats impact the comparability of the gross profit margin and the profit margins of Country Coffee and Happy Coffee? Why or why not?

(e) What options does Country Coffee have if it wants to improve the comparability of its financial results with those of Happy Coffee?

Critical Thinking Cases and Activities

Collaborative Learning Activity

BYP5–5 Coho Brakes and Auto Parts Limited is a distribution company whose mobile sales force covers large territories of automotive repair shops and automobile dealerships. The company's partial income statement is as follows:

Determine cost of sales returns and errors.
(SO 2, 4)

Coho Brakes and Auto Parts Limited Income Statement (partial) Year Ended March 31, 2012	
Sales	$25,000,000
Less: Sales returns	3,000,000
Net sales	22,000,000
Cost of goods sold	13,585,000
Gross profit	8,415,000
Operating expenses	7,500,000
Profit before income tax	915,000

Coho's manager is concerned that, while sales have been increasing steadily, profits have not. Sales returns of 12% of sales are much greater than the industry average of 8.5%. Upon further investigation, it was determined that the company's process of manually recording customer order data is producing a large number of order errors. As these errors are caused by Coho's sales staff, Coho absorbs the handling costs of sales returns. The problem is made worse because many products have been customized and cannot be resold. The following is an estimate of the cost of these order-processing errors:

Sales returns	$3,000,000	
Percentage of products that are not resaleable	45%	
Sales value of unsaleable products	1,350,000	
Average cost as a percentage of sales	70%	
Cost of unsaleable products		$ 945,000
Additional operating expenses		150,000
Total estimated costs		$1,095,000

Coho is investigating a mobile electronic order system that would cost the company $200,000 for its first year of operations but would reduce the percentage of returned sales to a figure in line with the industry average (8.5%).

Instructions

With the class divided into groups, do the following:

(a) Review the calculation of the cost of order-processing errors. Recalculate the estimated cost assuming the electronic order system (with 8.5% returns) was purchased. Should the electronic order system be purchased?

(b) Consider the impact on customer relationships if Coho continues to use its current manual order management system. Would you recommend a change in system even if the financial analysis completed in question (a) is negative?

Communication Activity

Discuss when to record purchase and sales transactions.
(SO 2, 3)

BYP5–6   Consider the following events:

Sept. 23	Dexter Maersk decides to buy a custom-made snowboard and calls the Great Canadian Snowboard Corporation to inquire about its products.
28	Dexter asks Great Canadian Snowboard to manufacture a custom board for him.
Oct. 3	The company sends Dexter a purchase order to fill out, which he immediately completes, signs, and sends back with a required 25% down payment.
7	Great Canadian Snowboard receives Dexter's purchase order and down payment, and begins working on the board.
Dec. 31	Great Canadian Snowboard has its fiscal year end. At this time, Dexter's board is 75% completed.
Jan. 28	The company completes the snowboard for Dexter and notifies him that he can take delivery.
Feb. 3	Dexter picks up his snowboard from the company and takes it home.
4	Dexter tries the snowboard out and likes it so much that he carves his initials in it.
21	Great Canadian Snowboard bills Dexter for the cost of the snowboard, less the 25% down payment.
28	The company receives partial payment (another 25%) from Dexter.
Mar. 18	The company receives payment of the remaining amount due from Dexter.

Instructions
(a) In a memo to the president of Great Canadian Snowboard, a publicly-traded company, outline the alternatives for how, and recommend when, the company should record the sales revenue and cost of goods sold related to the snowboard.
(b) If Dexter had not been required to make a down payment with his purchase order, would your answer to part (a) be different?

Ethics Case

Discuss ethics of timing purchase discounts.
(SO 2)

BYP5–7   Rita Pelzer was just hired as the assistant controller of Zaz Stores Ltd., a retail company. Among other things, the payment of all invoices is centralized in one of the departments Rita will manage. Her main responsibilities are to maintain the company's credit rating by paying all bills when they are due and to take advantage of all cash discounts.

Jamie Caterino, the former assistant controller, who has been promoted to controller, is training Rita in her new duties. He instructs Rita that she is to continue the practice of preparing all cheques for the amount due less the discount and to date the cheques the last day of the discount period. "But," Jamie continues, "we always hold the cheques at least four days beyond the discount period before mailing them. That way we get another four days of interest on our money. Most of our creditors need our business and don't complain. And, if they scream about our missing the discount period, we blame it on Canada Post. We've only lost one discount out of every hundred we take that way. I think everybody does it. By the way, welcome to our team!"

Instructions
(a) What are the ethical considerations in this case?
(b) Which stakeholders are harmed or benefited?
(c) Should Rita continue the practice started by Jamie? Does she have any choice?

"All About You" Activity

Discuss recognition of revenue, gross profit margin, and profit margin.
(SO 3, 5)

BYP5–8   Suppose that after you graduate with a business degree, you take a job as a manager at a bookstore called McNally Robinson Booksellers. The bookstore has expanded rapidly in order to compete with Indigo Books & Music Inc. and Amazon.ca.

Instructions
(a) McNally Robinson Booksellers has begun selling gift cards for its books and providing Reader Reward cards because it hopes that people with these cards will be less likely to return their purchase than if someone had given them a book as a gift. At what point should the revenue from the gift cards and reward cards be recognized? Should the revenue be recognized at the time the gift card is sold or Reader Reward card issued, or should it be recognized when the card or reward is redeemed?
(b) McNally Robinson Booksellers is much smaller than Indigo but would still like to compare its gross profit margin and profit margin with Indigo's. Would a comparison of the financial results of these two companies be meaningful?
(c) McNally Robinson Booksellers is concerned with its gross profit margin. It believes it is lower than it should be. What steps can management take to improve its gross profit margin?

Serial Case

(*Note:* This is a continuation of the serial case from Chapters 1 through 4.)

BYP5–9   Natalie and her parents, Janet and Brian, are anxious to examine and analyze the updated financial statements. Natalie has obtained a copy of the financial statements of a major competitor, a public company, and has been able to determine a number of their ratios: the current ratio is 2:1, the gross profit margin is 75%, and the profit margin is 15%.

Record and post adjusting journal entries; prepare an adjusted trial balance and financial statements; calculate ratios and comment. (SO 4, 5)

The following information represents additional adjustment data that must be recorded to enable the preparation of Koebel's year-end financial statements.

1. Koebel's uses a perpetual inventory system. A physical count of inventory indicates $18,125 on hand at June 30.
2. Of the bank loan payable, $7,500 is to be paid in the next year; the remainder is non-current.
3. Of the mortgage payable, $5,000 is to be paid in the next year; the remainder is non-current.
4. Natalie estimates that an additional $937 of corporate income tax is owed at June 30.

Instructions

(a) Record any required adjusting entries from the above data.
(b) Post to the T accounts updated in Chapter 4.
(c) Prepare an adjusted trial balance at June 30.
(d) Prepare a multiple-step income statement for the year ended June 30.
(e) Calculate the ending retained earnings for the year.
(f) Prepare a statement of financial position as at June 30.
(g) Calculate the current ratio, gross profit margin, and profit margin for the year. Compared with Koebel's major competitor, are Koebel's Family Bakery's ratios better or worse? Why do you expect there is a difference between Koebel's Family Bakery's ratios and those of its major competitor?

Answers to Self-Test Questions

1. a	2. b	3. b	4. a	5. c	6. b
7. d	8. d	9. c	10. c	*11. b	*12. b

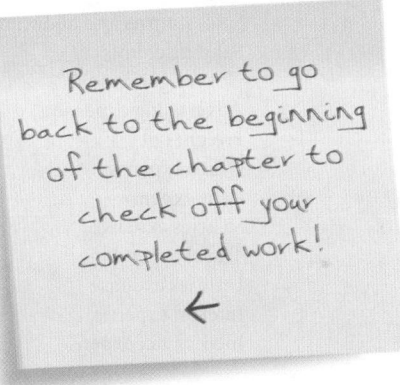

Remember to go back to the beginning of the chapter to check off your completed work!

Comprehensive Case: Chapters 3–5

Record and post general, adjusting, and closing entries; prepare trial balances and financial statements.
(SO 2, 3, 4)

Heritage Furniture Limited reports the following information for the 11 months of the year in its February 29, 2012, trial balance:

HERITAGE FURNITURE LIMITED
Trial Balance
February 29, 2012

	Debit	Credit
Cash	$ 65,000	
Accounts receivable	350,000	
Merchandise inventory	2,750,000	
Supplies	7,500	
Prepaid rent	5,000	
Equipment	145,000	
Accumulated depreciation—equipment		$ 29,000
Accounts payable		1,550,000
Unearned revenue		35,000
Bank loan payable—long-term		450,000
Common shares		200,000
Retained earnings		550,500
Dividends	50,000	
Sales		5,479,400
Sales returns and allowances	107,000	
Sales discounts	65,000	
Cost of goods sold	3,843,900	
Advertising expense	75,000	
Freight out	180,000	
Office expense	26,000	
Rent expense	55,000	
Salaries expense	360,000	
Travel expense	12,500	
Utilities expense	20,000	
Interest expense	27,000	
Income tax expense	150,000	
	$8,293,900	$8,293,900

Heritage Furniture incurred the following transactions for the month of March. The company uses a perpetual inventory system.

March 1 Received $125,000 on account from a major customer.

2 Paid a supplier an amount owing of $200,000, taking the full discount, terms 2/10, n/30.

5 Purchased merchandise from a supplier, $300,000, terms 2/10, n/30, FOB destination.

6 Recorded cash sales, $285,000. The cost of goods sold for these sales was $200,000.

7 Returned scratched merchandise to the supplier from the March 5 purchase, $25,000.

8 The appropriate company paid freight for the March 5 purchase, $7,500.

9 Sold $200,000 of merchandise on account, terms 2/10, n/30, FOB destination. The cost of goods sold was $140,000.

9 The appropriate company paid freight for the March 9 sale, $5,000.

12 Ordered custom merchandise for a local designer totalling $50,000. Received $12,500 as a deposit.

13 Accepted returned merchandise from the sale on March 9, $20,000. The cost of the goods returned to inventory was $14,000.

14 Paid for the merchandise purchased on March 5, net of merchandise returns on March 7.

16 Paid salaries of $45,000.

19 Received payment of merchandise sold on March 9, net of merchandise returns on March 13.

20 Recorded cash sales, $255,000. The cost of goods sold for these sales was $179,000.

27 Paid salaries of $50,000.

30 Paid rent, $5,000.

Adjustment and additional data:

1. Accrued $10,000 for utilities, $10,000 for salaries, and $9,000 for interest on the bank loan.
2. Recorded depreciation on equipment, which has an expected useful life of 10 years.
3. Recorded an additional $50,000 of income tax payable.
4. Common shares of $1,000 were issued during the year.
5. $45,000 of the bank loan is due to be repaid in the next year.

Instructions

(a) Prepare T accounts and enter the opening balances.
(b) Record and post the March transactions on Heritage Furniture's books.
(c) Prepare a trial balance as at March 31, 2012.
(d) Record and post adjusting entries for the year ended March 31, 2012, assuming adjusting entries are made annually.
(e) Prepare an adjusted trial balance as at March 31, 2012.
(f) Prepare a multiple-step income statement, statement of changes in equity, and statement of financial position for the year ended March 31, 2012.
(g) Prepare and post closing entries.
(h) Prepare a post-closing trial balance as at March 31, 2012.

Reporting and Analyzing Inventory

the navigator

study objectives

After studying this chapter, you should be able to:

1. Describe the steps in determining inventory quantities.

2. Apply the methods of cost determination—specific identification, FIFO, and average—under a perpetual inventory system.

3. Explain the financial statement effects of the inventory cost determination methods.

4. Identify the effects of inventory errors on the financial statements.

5. Demonstrate the presentation and analysis of inventory.

6. Apply the inventory cost formulas—FIFO and average—under a periodic inventory system (Appendix 6A).

Inventory Is Not an Easy Game at Forzani

INSIDE CHAPTER

6

- Counting inventory that swims (p. 297)
- The case of the missing gold (p. 313)
- You have to be fast! (p. 318)
- Retail fraud—an inside or outside job? (p. 323)

Calgary-based Forzani Group Ltd. kicked off in 1974 when Calgary Stampeder John Forzani and three of his teammates launched Forzani's Locker Room, a small retail operation that sold athletic footwear. Forzani, purchased by Canadian Tire in 2011, operates a number of stores from coast to coast, under the following corporate and franchise banners: Sport Chek, Atmosphere, Sport Mart, National Sports, Hockey Experts, Sports Experts, Intersport, Tech Shop/Pegasus, Nevada Bob's Golf, S3, Athletes World, Econosports, and Fitness Source. These stores include a comprehensive assortment of brand-name and private-brand products. In addition, the company's Sport Chek banner also offers an on-line catalogue of more than 9,000 products. Together, the Forzani Group has lots and lots of inventory—all requiring strict inventory management.

Forzani's inventory management group, which includes planners, buyers, and allocators, keeps track of the inventory at each store. All store transactions from its point of sale system are interfaced nightly to the company's central inventory management system, called the Portfolio Merchandise Management (PMM) System, which adjusts the records of the inventory for each store. Forzani uses the information in the PMM System to purchase, receive, and distribute inventory. The inventory purchased is shipped to a central warehouse, which distributes it to each store. Inventory is replenished at the stores through twice-weekly deliveries.

The inventory management group uses historical trends, including the inventory turnover ratio, as well as future market trends to determine what to buy and what to stock. The inventory turnover ratio also helps track each company's inventory sell-through rates and manage its aging inventories.

The stores do a physical count of inventory at least once a year. A third party, along with store staff, does the physical count to ensure it is unbiased. The company's external and internal auditors are also present during some counts. All counts are blind counts, meaning the counter does not know the number of items that have been recorded in inventory, and each item is scanned individually from the item ticket. Goods in transit are not included in the inventory count; instead, Forzani's PMM System creates a count "freeze file" that includes only on-hand inventory. The company compares this freeze file with the third-party count file and adjustments are later made as required to include any goods in transit belonging to the company.

All Forzani stores use the perpetual inventory method to track inventory. When the warehouse receives a product, it uses the number of units received at the purchase order cost, together with the on-hand quantity recorded in the PMM System and its current cost, to determine the new average cost.

Inventory is valued at the lower of cost and net realizable value. Using the average cost formula, cost includes invoice cost, duties, freight, and distribution costs. Net realizable value is defined as the expected selling price. Included within the cost of goods sold are charges to inventory made throughout the year, including the disposal of obsolete and damaged products, inventory shrinkage, and permanent markdowns to net realizable values.

Needless to say, the Forzani group of stores requires a number of essential systems and complex processes, without which it would not be able to manage its inventory efficiently and effectively.

the navigator

preview of
CHAPTER | 6

In the previous chapter, we discussed the accounting for merchandise transactions. In this chapter, we first explain the procedures for determining inventory quantities. We then discuss the three cost determination methods for assigning amounts to the cost of goods sold and the cost of inventory on hand: the specific identification method and the two cost formulas: first-in, first-out (FIFO) and average. We also discuss the effects of each of these cost determination methods and of inventory errors on a company's financial statements. We conclude by first discussing how to present inventory on the financial statements and then introducing a new liquidity measure called inventory turnover, which is used to analyze inventory.

The chapter is organized as follows:

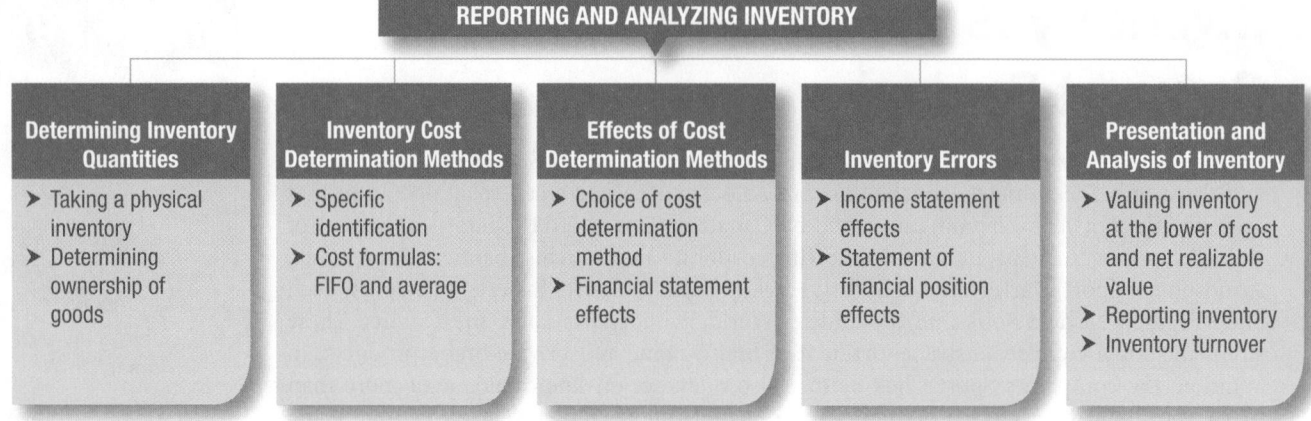

Determining Inventory Quantities

STUDY OBJECTIVE 1

Describe the steps in determining inventory quantities.

Whether they are using a perpetual inventory system or a periodic one, all companies need to determine their inventory quantities at the end of each accounting period by physically counting their inventory (i.e., a count of all of the inventory on hand).

Recall from Chapter 5 that in a perpetual inventory system the accounting records continuously—perpetually—show the quantity of inventory that *should* be on hand, not what necessarily *is* on hand. Even if the accounting records are continuously updated, companies that use a perpetual inventory system must still take a physical inventory at year end for two purposes: (1) to check the accuracy of their perpetual inventory records and (2) to determine the amount of inventory lost due to shrinkage or theft.

In a periodic inventory system, inventory quantities are not updated on a continuous basis. Companies that use a periodic inventory system must therefore take a physical inventory to determine the ending inventory (inventory on hand) at the end of each accounting period. Once the ending inventory amount is determined, this amount is then used to calculate the cost of goods sold for the period.

Determining inventory quantities, whether in a perpetual or periodic inventory system, involves two steps: (1) taking a physical inventory of goods on hand and (2) determining the ownership of goods.

TAKING A PHYSICAL INVENTORY

Taking a physical inventory involves actually counting, weighing, or measuring each kind of inventory on hand. In many companies, taking an inventory is a formidable task. For example, sports retailers such as Forzani, mentioned in our chapter-opening feature story, have thousands of different inventory items. An inventory count is generally more accurate when a limited number of, or no, goods are being sold or received during the counting. Consequently, companies often take inventory when the business is slow or when it is closed. For example, Forzani's year end is January 31—after the holiday sales and returns and when inventories are normally at their lowest level.

To make fewer errors in taking the inventory, a company should ensure that it has a good system of internal control. **Internal control** is a process designed to help an organization achieve reliable financial reporting, effective and efficient operations, and compliance with relevant laws and regulations. Specific control procedures are outlined to apply the internal control process to each aspect of an organization's financial reporting system (e.g., inventory).

Some internal control procedures for counting inventory include the following:

1. The counting should be done by employees who do not have responsibility for the custody or record-keeping of the inventory.
2. Each counter should establish the validity of each inventory item. This means checking that the items actually exist, how many there are of them, and what condition they are in.
3. There should be a second count by another employee or auditor. Counting should take place in teams of two.
4. Prenumbered inventory tags should be used to ensure that all inventory items are counted and that none are counted more than once.

Forzani, as discussed in our feature story, has strong internal controls over its physical inventory count with the use of a third party and blind counts. We will learn more about internal controls in Chapter 7.

After the physical inventory is taken, the quantity of each kind of inventory is listed on inventory summary sheets. Unit costs are then applied to the quantities in order to determine the total cost of the inventory. This will be explained later in the chapter when we discuss the methods of inventory cost determination.

ACCOUNTING MATTERS! *Management Perspective*

Counting Inventory That Swims

There are many challenges involved in taking a physical inventory for certain kinds of businesses. One of the more difficult types of inventory to count is at a salmon farm, where the inventory is swimming around in the ocean.

Salmon farms can be found in provinces in Atlantic Canada, as well as British Columbia, with the salmon kept in net cages in the ocean. An average salmon farm contains between 6 and 14 cages, and each cage contains from 50,000 to 80,000 fish. At Cooke Aquaculture Inc., headquartered in New Brunswick, salmon are initially counted when they are put in cages as smolts, or young salmon, from the hatchery. Every week, divers go down and count the number of fish at the bottom of the cage that have died. The remainder is the company's best estimate of what is left. Other factors, such as fish escaping or predators getting some of the fish, will reduce these estimates.

After the salmon reach about 4.5 kg, they are harvested. The actual number of salmon harvested is compared with the number estimated. The percentage differences are tracked and future estimates are adjusted for expected differences.

DETERMINING OWNERSHIP OF GOODS

When we take a physical inventory, we need to consider the ownership of goods. To determine who owns what inventory, two questions must be answered: (1) Do all of the goods included in the count belong to the company? (2) Does the company own any goods that were not included in the count?

Goods in Transit

Goods in transit at the end of the period (on board a truck, train, ship, or plane) make determining ownership a bit more complicated. The company may have purchased goods that have not yet been received, or it may have sold goods that have not yet been delivered. To arrive at an accurate count, ownership of these goods must be determined.

The rule to follow is straightforward. **Goods in transit should be included in the inventory of the company that has legal title to the goods.** As we learned in Chapter 5, legal title, or ownership, is determined by the terms of the sale. If the shipping terms are FOB shipping point, the buyer has legal title to the goods while they are in transit. If the shipping terms are FOB destination, the seller has legal title to the goods while they are in transit. These terms are important in determining the exact date when a purchase or sale should be recorded and what items should be included in inventory, even if the items are not physically present at the time of the inventory count.

The following table summarizes when ownership (legal title) passes while goods are in transit. The boxes with text in red normally require an adjustment of the inventory count (1) for goods that the buyer may not have yet received that have been shipped FOB shipping point so they are not included in the inventory count, and (2) for goods that the seller does not have on hand because they have been shipped FOB destination so they are not included in the inventory count.

Shipping Terms	Buyer	Seller
FOB shipping point	Inventory belongs to buyer once shipped	Inventory belongs to the seller until it is shipped
FOB destination	Inventory belongs to the buyer once it reaches its destination	Inventory belongs to the seller until it reaches the buyer's destination

Consigned Goods

In some lines of business, it is customary to hold goods belonging to other parties and sell them, for a fee, without ever taking ownership of the goods. These are called **consigned goods**. Under a consignment arrangement, the holder of the goods (called the *consignee*) does not own the goods. Ownership remains with the shipper of the goods (called the *consignor*) until the goods are actually sold to a customer. Because consigned goods are not owned by the consignee, they should not be included in the consignee's physical inventory count. Conversely, the consignor should include in its inventory any of its merchandise that is being held by the consignee.

For example, artists often display their paintings and other works of art at galleries on consignment. In such cases, the art gallery does not take ownership of the art—it still belongs to the artist. Therefore, if an inventory count is taken, any art on consignment should not be included in the art gallery's inventory. When the art sells, the gallery then takes a commission and pays the artist the remainder. Many craft stores, second-hand clothing stores, used sporting goods stores, and antique dealers sell goods on consignment to keep their inventory costs down and to avoid the risk of purchasing an item they will not be able to sell.

Other Situations

Sometimes goods are not physically on the premises because they have been taken home *on approval* by a customer. Goods on approval should be added to the physical inventory count because they still belong to the seller. The customer will either return the item or decide to buy it at some point in the future.

In other cases, goods are sold but the seller is holding them for alteration, or until they are picked up or delivered to the customer. These goods should not be included in the physical count, because legal title to ownership has passed to the customer. Damaged or unsaleable goods should also be separated from the physical count, and any loss should be recorded.

Summary

You will recall from Chapter 5 that purchases of merchandise should be recorded when ownership (title) of the merchandise passes from the seller to the buyer. In practice, however, purchases are usually recorded when the merchandise is received because it is difficult for the buyer to identify exactly when the title legally passes to the buyer. That is why companies like Forzani do not include goods in transit in their inventory count. Instead, adjustments are required when the inventory count is done to update both the quantities and amounts of unrecorded purchases and sales that are in transit, on consignment, or for other reasons should be included (or not included) in the company's inventory account at the end of the accounting period.

Illustration 6-1 summarizes the general guidelines for determining whether the seller or the buyer owns, and therefore should report, an item as inventory.

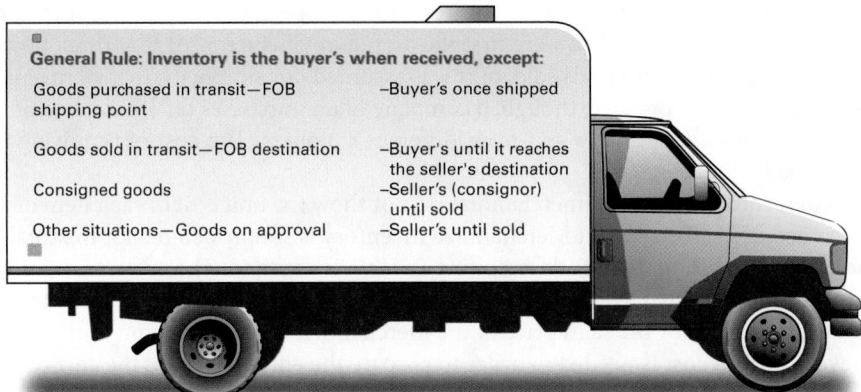

General Rule: Inventory is the buyer's when received, except:

Goods purchased in transit—FOB shipping point	–Buyer's once shipped
Goods sold in transit—FOB destination	–Buyer's until it reaches the seller's destination
Consigned goods	–Seller's (consignor) until sold
Other situations—Goods on approval	–Seller's until sold

▶Illustration 6-1
Rules of ownership

BEFORE YOU GO ON....

▶Do It! Rules of Ownership

The Too Good to Be Threw Corporation completed its inventory count at year end, August 31. It arrived at a total inventory amount of $200,000 after counting everything currently on hand in its warehouse. How will the following additional information affect the inventory count and cost?

1. Goods costing $15,000 and held on consignment for another company were included in the inventory.

2. Purchased goods of $10,000 were in transit as at August 31 (terms FOB shipping point) and not included in the count.

3. Inventory sold for $18,000 that cost $12,000 when purchased was in transit as at August 31 (terms FOB destination) and not included in the count.

Action Plan

- Apply the rules of ownership to goods held on consignment:
  - Goods held on consignment for another company are not included in inventory.
  - Goods held on consignment by another company are included in inventory.
- Apply the rules of ownership to goods in transit:
  - FOB shipping point: Goods sold or purchased and shipped FOB shipping point belong to the buyer after they have been shipped.
  - FOB destination: Goods sold or purchased and shipped FOB destination belong to the seller until they reach their destination.

Solution

Original count	$200,000
1. Consigned goods	(15,000)
2. Goods in transit (FOB shipping point)	10,000
3. Goods in transit (FOB destination)	12,000
Adjusted count	$207,000

the navigator

Inventory Cost Determination Methods

STUDY OBJECTIVE 2

Apply the methods of cost determination—specific identification, FIFO, and average—under a perpetual inventory system.

The physical inventory count we discussed in the last section determines the quantities on hand. Companies must then apply unit costs to the quantities to determine the total cost of the inventory before the physical count data can be compared with the perpetual inventory records at the end of the period. How do we determine what unit cost to apply?

And, a related question, how do we determine what cost to apply when we record the cost of merchandise sold in the accounting records throughout the period? The journal entries related to purchases and sales of merchandise were first illustrated in Chapter 5. At that time, however, you were either told the cost of the goods sold, or it was assumed, for simplicity, that all inventory items had the same unit cost. In practice, though, a company often purchases different items of inventory at different costs on different dates and from different suppliers. The cost of acquiring inventory therefore normally does change.

Entries to record purchases of merchandise do not show the unit cost of each item of merchandise that was acquired. The account Merchandise Inventory is simply debited for the total cost paid for all the units together, and Cash or Accounts Payable is credited. The entry to record the sales price is also not directly affected by the unit cost. Cash or Accounts Receivable is debited and the Sales account is credited for the sales price of the merchandise sold, not its unit cost.

However, the unit cost is needed in order to prepare the entry to record the cost of goods sold and remove the cost of the items sold from inventory. Because units of the same inventory item are typically purchased at different prices, it is necessary to determine which unit costs to use in the calculation of the cost of the goods sold. One method—specific identification—uses the actual physical flow of the goods to determine cost. We will look at this method next.

SPECIFIC IDENTIFICATION

The **specific identification method** tracks the actual physical flow of the goods in a perpetual inventory system. Each item of inventory is marked, tagged, or coded with its specific unit cost so that, at any point in time, the cost of the ending inventory and the cost of the goods sold can be determined.

Assume, for example, that Jaguar Canada buys three different cars at a cost of $77,200 for an XK coupe, $82,500 for an XK convertible, and $70,400 for an XJ saloon. During the month, two cars are then sold at the selling price of $96,500 for the XK coupe and $88,000 for the XJ saloon. At December 31, the XK convertible is still on hand. The cost of goods sold is therefore $147,600 ($77,200 + $70,400) and the ending inventory is $82,500. This determination is possible because it was easy to track the actual physical flow of these three inventory items.

▶ Illustration 6-2
Specific identification

Specific identification is appropriate and required for goods that are not ordinarily interchangeable, and for goods that are produced and segregated for specific projects. It is used most often in situations involving a relatively small number of costly items that are easily distinguishable (e.g., by their physical characteristics, serial numbers, or special markings). Examples include some types of jewellery, art work, pianos, and automobiles. Specific identification is also suitable for many types of special orders.

While specific identification works well when a company sells high-unit-cost items that can be clearly identified from purchase through to sale, there are also disadvantages to using this method. Not surprisingly, it can be time-consuming and expensive to apply and not practical in many situations. According to *Financial Reporting in Canada*, about 4% of Canadian companies use the specific identification method of cost determination.

Another disadvantage of this method is that it may allow management to manipulate profit. To see how, assume that Jaguar Canada also sells automobile parts. It has 15 fuel pumps in stock, for which it paid between $235 and $275 when they were purchased. They sell for $500. If the company wanted to maximize its profit just before its year end, management could choose to sell the units with the lowest cost ($235) to deduct from revenues ($500). Or, it could minimize profit by selecting the highest-cost ($275) fuel pumps to sell.

The requirement that the specific identification method be used only for goods that are not ordinarily interchangeable is an attempt to ensure that management does not use this method to manage profit. Consequently, companies like Jaguar Canada use the specific identification method to track the cost of their automobile inventory while using another method (FIFO in Jaguar Canada's case) to determine the cost of their parts inventory.

COST FORMULAS: FIFO AND AVERAGE

Because the specific identification method is only suitable for certain kinds of inventories, other methods of cost determination, known as cost formulas, are available to choose from. Two common inventory cost formulas are:

1. First-in, first-out (FIFO), where the cost of the first item purchased is considered to be the cost of the first item sold
2. Average, where the cost is determined using a weighted average of the cost of the items purchased

FIFO and average are known as "cost formulas" because they assume a flow of costs that may not be the same as the actual physical flow of the goods, unlike the specific identification method.

While specific identification is normally used only in a perpetual inventory system, FIFO and average can be used in both the perpetual and periodic inventory systems. Recall from Chapter 5 that a key difference between these two inventory systems is when the cost of goods available for sale (beginning inventory plus the cost of goods purchased) is allocated to the cost of goods sold and ending inventory.

Under a perpetual inventory system, the cost of goods available for sale is allocated to the cost of goods sold as each item is sold. Under a periodic inventory system, the allocation is made only at the end of the period, with the cost of goods sold then calculated by deducting the ending inventory from the cost of goods available for sale.

Similar to the structure of Chapter 5, the perpetual inventory system will be used to illustrate the FIFO and average cost inventory formulas in the main body of the chapter. The chapter appendix explains how FIFO and average cost are determined in a periodic inventory system.

To illustrate the application of FIFO and average in a perpetual inventory system, we will assume that Wynneck Electronics Ltd. has the following information for one of its products, the Astro Condenser, as shown in Illustration 6-3.

▸Illustration 6-3
Inventory data for Astro Condensers

WYNNECK ELECTRONICS LTD. Astro Condensers					
Date	Explanation	Units	Unit Cost	Total Cost	Balance in Units
Jan. 1	Beginning inventory	100	$10	$ 1,000	100
Apr. 15	Purchases	200	11	2,200	300
May 1	Sales	(150)			150
Aug. 24	Purchases	300	12	3,600	450
Sept. 10	Sales	(400)			50
Nov. 27	Purchases	400	13	5,200	450
		450		$12,000	

Perpetual Inventory System—First-In, First-Out (FIFO)

The **first-in, first-out (FIFO) cost formula** assumes that the earliest (oldest) goods purchased are the first ones to be sold. This does not necessarily mean that the oldest units are in fact sold first, only that the cost of the oldest units is recognized first. Although the cost formula chosen by a company does not have to match the actual physical movement of merchandise, it should correspond as closely as possible. FIFO generally does match because it is good business practice to sell the oldest units first.

To illustrate the application of FIFO in a perpetual inventory system, we will use the information for the Astro Condenser shown in Illustration 6-3 to prepare a perpetual inventory schedule. Perpetual inventory schedules start with inventory on hand at the beginning of the year for each product. The schedule is updated for the quantity and cost of merchandise purchased and sold throughout the year.

For example, we note in Illustration 6-3 that there were 100 units of merchandise on hand at the beginning of the year and that 200 units of additional merchandise were purchased on April 15. This results, as of April 15, in 300 units available for sale at a total cost of $3,200 ($1,000 + $2,200). Of these, 100 units have a cost of $10 each and 200 units a cost of $11 each, as shown in the partial inventory schedule below:

Date	Purchases			Cost of Goods Sold			Balance		
	Units	Cost	Total	Units	Cost	Total	Units	Cost	Total
Jan. 1							100	$10	$1,000
Apr. 15	200	$11	$2,200				100	10	} 3,200
							200	11	

On May 1, the date of the first sale, we must apply FIFO to determine whether the 150 units that were sold cost $10, $11, or a mix of both amounts. The cost must be determined on this date so that the Cost of Goods Sold account can be debited and the Merchandise Inventory account credited for the cost of this sale. Note that the sale must also be recorded on this same date, by debiting Cash or Accounts Receivable and crediting Sales. Although the sales price is required to record this entry, the above table does not include information about the sales price as this is not needed to determine the *cost* of the goods sold or the *cost* of the ending inventory.

Under FIFO, the cost of the oldest goods on hand before each sale is allocated to the cost of goods sold. Accordingly, the cost of goods sold on May 1 is assumed to consist of all 100 units of the January 1 beginning inventory and 50 units of the items purchased on April 15. This leaves 150 units of the April 15 purchase at a cost of $11 per unit remaining in ending inventory. In the illustration below, we have added this information (highlighted in red) to the inventory schedule that we started above.

Date	Purchases			Cost of Goods Sold			Balance		
	Units	Cost	Total	Units	Cost	Total	Units	Cost	Total
Jan. 1							100	$10	$1,000
Apr. 15	200	$11	$ 2,200				100	10	} 3,200
							200	11	
May 1				100	$10	} $1,550	150	11	1,650
				50	11				

After additional purchases are made on August 24, the cost of goods available for sale on this date now consists of 150 units at $11 and 300 units at $12, or 450 units costing $5,250 in total, as shown below in the continuation of the perpetual inventory schedule:

	Purchases			Cost of Goods Sold			Balance		
Date	Units	Cost	Total	Units	Cost	Total	Units	Cost	Total
Jan. 1							100	$10	$1,000
Apr. 15	200	$11	$ 2,200				100	10	
							200	11	3,200
May 1				100	$10	$1,550	150	11	1,650
				50	11				
Aug. 24	300	12	3,600				150	11	
							300	12	5,250

On September 10, when 400 units are sold, the cost of goods sold is assumed to consist of the remaining units purchased on April 15 (150 units at a cost of $11 per unit), and 250 of the units purchased on August 24 at a cost of $12 per unit. This leaves 50 units in ending inventory at a cost of $12 per unit, or $600 in total, as shown below:

	Purchases			Cost of Goods Sold			Balance		
Date	Units	Cost	Total	Units	Cost	Total	Units	Cost	Total
Jan. 1							100	$10	$1,000
Apr. 15	200	$11	$ 2,200				100	10	
							200	11	3,200
May 1				100	$10	$1,550	150	11	1,650
				50	11				
Aug. 24	300	12	3,600				150	11	
							300	12	5,250
Sept. 10				150	11	4,650	50	12	600
				250	12				

After a purchase of 400 units on November 27, the ending inventory consists of 450 units, of which 50 units cost $12 from the August 24 purchase and 400 units cost $13 from the November 27 purchase. This transaction is included below in Illustration 6-4, completing the inventory schedule shown in sections above.

	Purchases			Cost of Goods Sold			Balance		
Date	Units	Cost	Total	Units	Cost	Total	Units	Cost	Total
Jan. 1							100	$10	$1,000
Apr. 15	200	$11	$ 2,200				100	10	
							200	11	3,200
May 1				100	$10	$1,550	150	11	1,650
				50	11				
Aug. 24	300	12	3,600				150	11	
							300	12	5,250
Sept. 10				150	11	4,650	50	12	600
				250	12				
Nov. 27	400	13	5,200				50	12	
							400	13	5,800
	900		$11,000	550		$6,200			

Illustration 6-4
Perpetual inventory schedule—FIFO

Check: $6,200 + $5,800 = $12,000 ($1,000 + $11,000)

As at November 27, the total cost of goods sold is $6,200 and the ending inventory is $5,800. A useful check against calculation errors is to check whether the total of the cost of goods sold and ending inventory equals the total cost of goods available for sale of $12,000 (beginning inventory of $1,000 + purchases of $11,000).

In summary, FIFO assumes that the first goods purchased are the first ones sold. The cost formula always indicates the order of selling. As a result, FIFO assumes that the last goods purchased are still in ending inventory.

Whether a periodic or perpetual inventory system is used, FIFO will always result in the same cost of goods sold and ending inventory amounts. The same costs will always be first in, and therefore first out, whether the costs are allocated throughout the accounting period as in the perpetual inventory system or at the end of the accounting period as in the periodic inventory system. The periodic inventory system using FIFO is demonstrated in Appendix 6A.

Perpetual Inventory System—Average

The **average cost formula** recognizes that it is not possible to measure a specific physical flow of inventory when the goods available for sale are homogeneous or nondistinguishable. Consider, for example, a fuel storage tank at a gas station. When the tank is refilled with gas that costs more than the gas that is currently in the tank, the gas mixes. As the gas is being sold, it is impossible to tell which batch of gas at which cost is being pumped and which batch of gas at which cost remains in the tank.

Under the average cost formula, the allocation of the cost of goods available for sale between cost of goods sold and ending inventory is made based on the weighted average unit cost of the merchandise. The formula and calculation of the **weighted average unit cost** are given in Illustration 6-5.

▸Illustration 6-5
Calculation of weighted average unit cost

Note that the weighted average unit cost is *not* calculated by taking a simple average of the costs of each purchase, but by weighting the quantities purchased at each unit cost. This is done by dividing the cost of goods available for sale by the units available for sale at the date of each purchase. Consequently, a new average is calculated, or "moves," after each purchase (or purchase return). Because of this, this cost formula is commonly known as the **moving average cost formula** in a perpetual inventory system.

We will use the same information provided in Illustration 6-3 for Wynneck Electronics to prepare a perpetual inventory schedule using the average cost formula so that you can compare the similarities and differences between the FIFO and average cost formulas. In the partial perpetual inventory schedule below, note that the beginning inventory of $1,000 and the April 15 purchase of $2,200 combine to total 300 units available for sale at a total cost of $3,200 ($1,000 + $2,200).

Using the formula shown in Illustration 6-5, the **weighted average unit cost** on April 15 is $10.67 ($3,200 ÷ 300) (highlighted in red in the table below). Accordingly, the unit cost of the 150 units sold on May 1 is shown at $10.67, and the total cost of goods sold is $1,600. This unit cost is used in costing the units sold until another purchase (or a purchase return) is made, and a new unit cost must then be calculated.

Date	Purchases			Cost of Goods Sold			Balance		
	Units	Cost	Total	Units	Cost	Total	Units	Cost	Total
Jan. 1							100	$10.00	$1,000.00
Apr. 15	200	$11.00	$2,200.00				300	10.67	3,200.00
May 1				150	$10.67	$1,600.00	150	10.67	1,600.00

On August 24, after 300 units are purchased for $3,600, a total of 450 units costing $5,200 ($1,600 + $3,600) are on hand. This results in a new average cost per unit of $11.56 ($5,200 ÷ 450). This new cost is used to calculate the cost of the September 10 sale and the units still on hand after the sale, as shown in the continuation of the inventory schedule below:

Date	Purchases			Cost of Goods Sold			Balance		
	Units	Cost	Total	Units	Cost	Total	Units	Cost	Total
Jan. 1							100	$10.00	$1,000.00
Apr. 15	200	$11.00	$2,200.00				300	10.67	3,200.00
May 1				150	$10.67	$1,600.00	150	10.67	1,600.00
Aug. 24	300	12.00	3,600.00				450	11.56	5,200.00
Sept. 10				400	11.56	4,622.22	50	11.56	577.78

A new unit cost will be calculated again after the November 27 purchase of 400 units for $5,200. After this purchase, there are 450 units on hand with a total cost of $5,777.78 ($577.78 + $5,200). This results in a new average cost of $12.84 ($5,777.78 ÷ 450), which will be used until another purchase is made (in the following year, in Wynneck's case).

These transactions, which complete the perpetual inventory schedule for the average cost formula, are shown in Illustration 6-6 below.

Date	Purchases			Cost of Goods Sold			Balance		
	Units	Cost	Total	Units	Cost	Total	Units	Cost	Total
Jan. 1							100	$10.00	$1,000.00
Apr. 15	200	$11.00	$ 2,200.00				300	10.67	3,200.00
May 1				150	$10.67	$1,600.00	150	10.67	1,600.00
Aug. 24	300	12.00	3,600.00				450	11.56	5,200.00
Sept. 10				400	11.56	4,622.22	50	11.56	577.78
Nov. 27	400	13.00	5,200.00				450	12.84	5,777.78
	900		$11,000.00	550		$6,222.22			

▶Illustration 6-6
Perpetual inventory schedule—average

Check: $6,222.22 + $5,777.78 = $12,000 ($1,000 + $11,000)

As at November 27, therefore, the total cost of goods sold is $6,222.22 and the total ending inventory is $5,777.78. The total of these amounts should agree with the cost of goods available for sale, $12,000 ($6,222.22 + $5,777.78). This is a useful check, or proof, of the accuracy of your calculations.

In practice, average unit costs may be rounded to the nearest cent, or even to the nearest dollar. This illustration used the exact unit cost amounts in its calculations, as would a computerized schedule, even though the unit costs have been rounded to the nearest digit for presentation in Illustration 6-6. However, it is important to remember that this is a method of allocating costs and not a method to track actual costs. Using four digits, or even cents, suggests a false level of accuracy.

In summary, this cost formula uses the average cost of the goods that are available for sale to determine the cost of goods sold and ending inventory. When a perpetual inventory system is used, the average unit cost is determined after each purchase (or purchase return). When a periodic inventory system is used, the average unit cost is determined once at the end of the accounting period. Because of the different times when the average unit cost is determined in a perpetual and periodic inventory system, different amounts can result for the cost of goods sold and ending inventory in each system when using the average cost formula. The use of the average cost formula in a periodic inventory system will be explained in Appendix 6A.

BEFORE YOU GO ON...

▶Do It! Cost Formulas—Perpetual System

The inventory records of Ag Implement Inc. show the following data for the month of March:

Date		Explanation	Units	Unit Cost	Total Cost
Mar.	1	Beginning inventory	4,000	$3	$12,000
	10	Purchase	6,000	4	24,000
	19	Sale	(8,000)		
	22	Purchase	5,000	5	25,000
	28	Sale	(5,500)		
			1,500		$61,000

(continued)

Determine the cost of goods sold and ending inventory under a perpetual inventory system using the (a) FIFO and (b) average cost formulas.

Action Plan

- For FIFO, allocate the first costs to the cost of goods sold at the date of each sale. The latest costs will be allocated to the goods on hand (ending inventory).
- For average, determine the weighted average unit cost (cost of goods available for sale ÷ number of units available for sale) after each purchase. Multiply this cost by the number of units sold to determine the cost of goods sold, and by the number of units on hand to determine the cost of ending inventory.
- Prove that the cost of goods sold and ending inventory equals the cost of goods available for sale.

Solution

(a) FIFO—Perpetual

Date	Purchases			Cost of Goods Sold			Balance		
	Units	Cost	Total	Units	Cost	Total	Units	Cost	Total
Mar. 1							4,000	$3	$12,000
10	6,000	$4	$24,000				4,000	3	} 36,000
							6,000	4	
19				4,000	$3	} $28,000	2,000	4	8,000
				4,000	4				
22	5,000	5	25,000				2,000	4	} 33,000
							5,000	5	
28				2,000	4	} 25,500	1,500	5	7,500
				3,500	5				
	11,000		$49,000	13,500		$53,500			

Check: $53,500 + $7,500 = $61,000 ($12,000 + $49,000)

(b) Average—Perpetual

Date	Purchases			Cost of Goods Sold			Balance		
	Units	Cost	Total	Units	Cost	Total	Units	Cost	Total
Mar. 1							4,000	$3.00	$12,000
10	6,000	$4	$24,000				10,000	3.60	36,000
19				8,000	$3.60	$28,800	2,000	3.60	7,200
22	5,000	5	25,000				7,000	4.60	32,200
28				5,500	4.60	25,300	1,500	4.60	6,900
	11,000		$49,000	13,500		$54,100			

Check: $54,100 + $6,900 = $61,000 ($12,000 + $49,000)

Effects of Cost Determination Methods

STUDY OBJECTIVE 3

Explain the financial statement effects of the inventory cost determination methods.

Each of the cost determination methods—specific identification, FIFO, and average—is acceptable for use by both publicly traded companies and private companies. However, there are guidelines that limit the choice of the method by management. We will discuss guidelines that influence the choice of the appropriate cost determination method and the impact these choices can have on the financial statements in the sections that follow.

CHOICE OF COST DETERMINATION METHOD

If companies have goods that are not ordinarily interchangeable, or goods that have been produced and segregated for specific projects, they must use the specific identification method to determine the cost of their inventory. Otherwise, they can choose to use either FIFO or average.

How should a company choose between FIFO and average? It should consider the following guidelines in making its choice:

1. Choose a method that corresponds as closely as possible to the physical flow of goods.
2. Report an inventory cost on the statement of financial position that is close to the inventory's recent cost.
3. Use the same method for all inventories having a similar nature and usage in the company.

According to *Financial Reporting in Canada*, about 36% of Canadian companies use the FIFO cost formula. Jean Coutu, Magna International, Maple Leaf Foods, and Saputo are examples of companies that use FIFO to determine the cost of their inventories. About 55% of Canadian companies use the average cost formula. For example, Forzani (as well as its parent company Canadian Tire), Loblaw, and Sears Canada use average to determine the cost of their inventories.

About 25% of Canadian companies use more than one method of inventory cost determination. Companies can use more than one method if they have different types of inventory. Finning International, for example, uses the specific identification method to account for its equipment inventory and the average cost formula to account for its inventory of parts and supplies. And a small number of companies, about 5%, use other methods that are not discussed in this textbook.

After a company chooses a method of determining the cost of its inventory, that method should be used consistently from one period to the next. You will recall, from Chapter 2, that **comparability** of financial statements over successive time periods is an important enhancing characteristic of accounting information. Using FIFO in one year and average in the next year would make it difficult to compare the profit for the two years.

This is not to say that a company can never change from one method to another. However, a change in the method of cost determination can only occur if the nature and use of the inventory changes and a different method would result in a more reliable and more relevant presentation in the financial statements. Such a change is unusual with respect to inventories. We will learn more about changing accounting policies in Chapter 14.

FINANCIAL STATEMENT EFFECTS

Inventory affects both the statement of financial position and the income statement since ending inventory is included as a current asset on the statement of financial position and cost of goods sold is included on the income statement. Cost of goods sold also affects gross profit and profit, which in turn will affect retained earnings in the statement of changes in equity as well as in the shareholders' equity section of the statement of financial position. We will look at the impact of inventory on both the income statement and the statement of financial position in the next two sections.

Income Statement Effects

To understand the impact of the FIFO and average cost formulas on the income statement, we will now examine their effects on Wynneck Electronics Ltd. The condensed income statements in Illustration 6-7 use the amounts we determined for cost of goods sold after applying the FIFO and average cost formulas earlier in the chapter. This illustration also assumes that Wynneck sold its 550 units for $11,500, had operating expenses of $2,000, and is subject to an income tax rate of 30%.

▶ Illustration 6-7
Comparative effects of inventory cost formulas

WYNNECK ELECTRONICS LTD. Condensed Income Statements		
	FIFO	Average
Sales	$11,500	$11,500
Cost of goods sold	6,200	6,222
Gross profit	5,300	5,278
Operating expenses	2,000	2,000
Profit before income tax	3,300	3,278
Income tax expense (30%)	990	983
Profit	$ 2,310	$ 2,295

The sales and operating expense figures are the same under both FIFO and average. But the costs of goods sold amounts are different. This difference is because of the unit costs that are allocated under each cost formula. Each dollar of difference in cost of goods sold results in a corresponding dollar difference in profit before income tax. For Wynneck, there is a $22 difference between the FIFO and average amounts for cost of goods sold. A fixed percentage (30%) applied to determine income tax expense results in a difference in profit between the two formulas of $15.

In periods of changing prices, the choice of inventory cost formula can have a significant impact on profit. In a period of inflation (rising prices), as is the case for Wynneck, FIFO produces higher profit because the lower unit costs of the first units purchased are deducted from sales revenue. As Illustration 6-7 shows, FIFO reports the highest profit ($2,310) and average the lowest ($2,295). This difference is not very large for Wynneck, because prices are changing slowly. The more prices change, the larger this difference will be.

If prices are falling, the results from the use of FIFO and average are reversed: FIFO will report the lowest profit and average the highest. If prices are stable, both cost formulas will report the same results.

Compared with FIFO, average will result in more recent costs being reflected in the cost of goods sold. This will better identify or match current costs with current revenues and result in a better measurement of profit on the income statement. Of course, the specific identification method provides the best match of costs and revenues, as it exactly matches each cost with the revenue it generates.

Statement of Financial Position Effects

One advantage of FIFO is that the costs allocated to ending inventory will approximate the inventory items' current (replacement) cost. For example, for Wynneck, 400 of the 450 units in the ending inventory are costed under FIFO at the higher November 27 unit cost of $13. Since management needs to replace inventory when it is sold, a value that approximates the replacement cost is helpful for decision-making. That is why one of the guidelines in choosing an inventory cost formula is to "report an inventory cost on the statement of financial position that is close to the inventory's recent cost." FIFO provides a better ending inventory value on the statement of financial position than does average.

By extension, one limitation of average is that in a period of inflation the average cost formula results in older costs being included in ending inventory. For example, the average cost of Wynneck's ending inventory, $12.84, includes the $10 unit cost of the beginning inventory as well as the cost of some of its earlier purchases. The understatement becomes greater over extended periods of inflation if the inventory includes goods that were purchased in one or more earlier accounting periods.

Summary of Advantages and Effects of Cost Determination Methods

The advantages of each of the three major cost determination methods are summarized below in Illustration 6-8.

Specific Identification	FIFO	Average
• Exactly matches costs and revenues on the income statement.	• Ending inventory on the statement of financial position includes the most current costs (closest to replacement cost).	• Cost of goods sold on the income statement includes more current costs than FIFO.
• Tracks the actual physical flow.	• Approximates the physical flow of most retailers.	• Smooths the effects of price changes by assigning all units the same average cost.

▶Illustration 6-8
Advantages of cost determination methods

The key financial statement differences that will result from using the three different cost determination methods during a period of rising prices are summarized in Illustration 6-9. These effects will be the inverse if prices are falling, and the same for all three methods if prices are constant. In all cases, it does not matter whether a company uses the perpetual or periodic inventory system.

	Specific Identification	FIFO	Average
Income statement			
Cost of goods sold	Variable	Lowest	Highest
Gross profit	Variable	Highest	Lowest
Profit	Variable	Highest	Lowest
Statement of financial position			
Cash (pre-tax)	Same	Same	Same
Ending inventory	Variable	Highest	Lowest
Retained earnings	Variable	Highest	Lowest

▶Illustration 6-9
Summary of financial statement effects of cost determination methods (during a period of rising prices)

It is also worth remembering that all three methods will give exactly the same result over the life cycle of the business or its product. That is, the allocation between the cost of goods sold and ending inventory may vary annually, but it will produce the same cumulative results over time. Although much has been written about the impact of the choice of inventory cost determination method on a variety of performance measures, in reality there is little real economic distinction among the methods over time.

■ Keeping an Eye on Cash

We have seen that both inventory on the statement of financial position and cost of goods sold on the income statement are affected by the choice of cost determination method. It is very important to understand, however, that the choice of method does *not* affect cash flow. All three methods of cost determination—specific identification, FIFO, and average—produce exactly the same cash flow before income tax.

Why is that? Sales and purchases are not affected by the method of inventory cost determination. The only thing that is affected is the allocation of the cost of goods available for sale between the cost of goods sold and ending inventory—which does not involve cash.

Let's consider this further. When a company records its sales, it uses the same selling price regardless of whether it uses specific identification, FIFO, or average. It doesn't change its selling price based on its cost determination method. So cash receipts from cash sales, or collections of sales on account, are unchanged.

When a company records purchases of its merchandise for resale, it pays the same for the merchandise regardless of its method of cost determination. So cash payments for purchases, or payments on account, are unchanged.

Cost of goods sold is recorded by debiting the Cost of Goods Sold account and crediting the Merchandise Inventory account in a perpetual inventory system. There is no cash involved in this entry. The only accounts affected by the choice of cost determination method are inventory and retained earnings (and related amounts such as current assets, total assets, and total shareholders' equity) on the statement of financial position and cost of goods sold (and related amounts such as gross profit, profit before income tax, income tax, and profit) on the income statement.

DECISION TOOLKIT

Decision Checkpoints	Info Needed for Decision	Tools to Use for Decision	How to Evaluate Results
What is the impact of the choice of inventory cost determination method?	Are prices increasing, or are they decreasing?	Income statement and statement of financial position effects	In periods of rising prices, profit and inventory are higher under FIFO than average. FIFO results in the best measure of ending inventory on the statement of financial position. The average cost formula provides opposite results (i.e., profit and inventory are lower compared to FIFO), but can smooth the impact of changing prices. Specific identification's impact on the financial statements will vary, depending on the actual cost. This method results in the best allocation of costs to revenues on the income statement.

BEFORE YOU GO ON...

▶Do It! Cost Formula Effects on Income Statements

On July 31, UFirst Inc. had the following merchandise transactions:

July	1	Beginning inventory, 2 units @ $75 each
	7	Purchases, 4 units @ $80 each
	19	Sales, 5 units @ $180 each
	25	Purchases, 6 units @ $100 each

(a) Calculate UFirst's cost of goods sold and ending inventory for the month of July assuming the use of (1) FIFO, and (2) average in a perpetual inventory system.
(b) Prepare comparative income statements for each cost formula, assuming operating expenses of $300 and an income tax rate of 25%.

Action Plan

- Recall that FIFO allocates the earliest costs to the cost of goods sold at the date of each sale.
- Recall that average uses a weighted average unit cost to determine the cost of goods sold at the date of each sale. For average, use unrounded numbers in your calculations but round to the nearest cent for presentation purposes in an inventory schedule.
- In preparing comparative income statements, note that while the cost of goods sold will change between formulas, the sales figure does not.

Solution

(a) (1) FIFO

Date	Purchases			Cost of Goods Sold			Balance		
	Units	Cost	Total	Units	Cost	Total	Units	Cost	Total
July 1							2	$75	$150
7	4	$80	$320				2	75	} 470
							4	80	
19				2	$75	} $390	1	80	80
				3	80				
25	6	100	600				1	80	} 680
							6	100	

Check: $390 + $680 = $1,070 ($150 + $320 + $600)

(a) (2) Average

Date	Purchases			Cost of Goods Sold			Balance		
	Units	Cost	Total	Units	Cost	Total	Units	Cost	Total
July 1							2	$75.00	$150.00
7	4	$80.00	$320.00				6	78.33	470.00
19				5	$78.33	$391.67	1	78.33	78.33
25	6	100.00	600.00				7	96.91	678.33

Check: $391.67 + $678.33 = $1,070 ($150 + $320 + $600)

(b)

UFIRST INC. Condensed Income Statements		
	FIFO	Average
Sales (5 × $180)	$900	$900
Cost of goods sold	390	392
Gross profit	510	508
Operating expenses	300	300
Profit before income tax	210	208
Income tax expense (25%)	52	52
Profit	$158	$156

Inventory Errors

Unfortunately, errors occasionally occur in accounting for inventory. In some cases, errors are caused by failure to count or price the inventory correctly. Errors can also occur because companies do not properly recognize the transfer of legal title to goods that are in transit or for a wide variety of other reasons.

All errors should be investigated as the effect of an error on the financial statements can be pervasive. Recall that the Merchandise Inventory and Cost of Goods Sold accounts are affected by the following transactions:

STUDY OBJECTIVE 4
Identify the effects of inventory errors on the financial statements.

Merchandise Inventory				Cost of Goods Sold	
Beginning inventory Cost of goods purchased	Cost of goods sold		→	Cost of goods sold	
Ending inventory					

Because both accounts are affected by inventory errors, both the income statement (through cost of goods sold) and the statement of financial position (through inventory) are affected. In the following sections, we will show how these statements are affected.

INCOME STATEMENT EFFECTS

We have learned that the cost of goods available for sale (beginning inventory + cost of goods purchased) is allocated to the cost of goods sold and ending inventory. Consequently, if there is an error in either beginning inventory or cost of goods purchased, then the cost of goods sold will be similarly affected.

The overall effects of inventory errors on the current year's income statement is summarized below in Illustration 6-10. Note that the effect of inventory errors on income tax, which can be complicated, have been ignored for simplicity.

▶Illustration 6-10
Effects of inventory errors on income statement

Nature of Error	Net Sales −	Cost of Goods Sold =	Gross Profit −	Operating Expenses =	Profit Before Income Tax
Understate beginning inventory or cost of goods purchased	NE	U	O	NE	O
Overstate beginning inventory or cost of goods purchased	NE	O	U	NE	U

U = Understatement   O = Overstatement   NE = No Effect

As shown on the first line of Illustration 6-10, if beginning inventory is understated or if the cost of goods purchased is understated (assuming no offsetting errors have occurred), then cost of goods sold will be understated. Gross profit is also affected. Because cost of goods sold is deducted from net sales, an understatement in cost of goods sold will produce an overstatement (the opposite effect) in gross profit. Assuming there are no errors in operating expenses, then profit before income tax will be affected by the inventory error in the same amount and direction as gross profit.

As you know, the ending inventory of one period automatically becomes the beginning inventory of the next period. Consequently, **an error in the ending inventory of the current period will have a reverse effect on profit of the next accounting period** if it is not found and corrected.

To illustrate, assume that ending inventory in 2011 is understated by $3,000. The Merchandise Inventory account has been reproduced below using both the incorrect ending inventory figure ($12,000) and the correct inventory figure ($15,000).

Incorrect Inventory Amount				Correct Inventory Amount			
Merchandise Inventory				Merchandise Inventory			
2011				**2011**			
Beg. inv.	20,000	Cost of goods sold	48,000	Beg. inv.	20,000	Cost of goods sold	45,000
Purchases	40,000			Purchases	40,000		
End. inv.	12,000			End. inv.	15,000		
2012				**2012**			
Purchases	68,000	Cost of goods sold	57,000	Purchases	68,000	Cost of goods sold	60,000
End. inv.	23,000			End. inv.	23,000		

Because of the $3,000 understatement in ending inventory at the end of 2011 ($12,000 instead of $15,000), cost of goods sold is overstated by $3,000 ($48,000 instead of $45,000). In addition, because the inventory balance was wrong at the end of 2011, it is also wrong at the beginning of 2012. The effects of this error on the costs assigned to the goods sold continue for a second year, where cost of goods sold is now understated by $3,000 ($57,000 instead of $60,000). Assuming the ending inventory is calculated correctly at the end of the second year, 2012, this error stops now but it has had a two-year effect, as shown in Illustration 6-11.

Illustration 6-11
Effects of inventory errors on income statement for two years

SAMPLE COMPANY Income Statements				
	2011		2012	
	Incorrect	Correct	Incorrect	Correct
Sales	$80,000	$80,000	$90,000	$90,000
Cost of goods sold	48,000	45,000	57,000	60,000
Gross profit	32,000	35,000	33,000	30,000
Operating expenses	10,000	10,000	20,000	20,000
Profit before income tax	22,000	25,000	13,000	10,000

($3,000) $3,000

Profit understated   Profit overstated

The combined profit before income tax for two years is correct because the errors cancel each other out.

In this illustration, the understatement of ending inventory results, in the same year, in an overstatement of the cost of goods sold and an understatement of gross profit and profit before income tax. It also results in an understatement of the cost of goods sold in 2012 and an overstatement of gross profit and profit before income tax.

Over the two years, total profit before income tax is correct because the errors offset each other. Notice that total profit using incorrect data is $35,000 ($22,000 + $13,000), which is the same as the total profit of $35,000 ($25,000 + $10,000) using correct data.

STATEMENT OF FINANCIAL POSITION EFFECTS

The effect of ending inventory errors on the statement of financial position can be calculated by using the basic accounting equation: Assets = liabilities + shareholders' equity. Errors in the ending inventory have the effects shown in Illustration 6-12.

Illustration 6-12
Effects of inventory errors on statement of financial position

Ending Inventory Error	Assets	=	Liabilities	+	Shareholders' Equity
Overstated	O		NE		O
Understated	U		NE		U

U = Understatement   O = Overstatement   NE = No Effect

If there are errors in profit, as we discussed in the previous section, then shareholders' equity will be affected by the same amount since profit is closed into the Retained Earnings account, which is part of shareholders' equity. Consequently, an error in ending inventory affects both the asset account Merchandise Inventory and the shareholders' equity account Retained Earnings. As we did in the section on income statement effects, we have ignored any effects on the Income Tax Payable account for simplicity.

The effect of an error in ending inventory on the next period on the income statement was shown in Illustration 6-11. Recall that if the error is not corrected, the combined total profit for the two periods would be correct. In the example, therefore, the assets and shareholders' equity reported on the statement of financial position at the end of 2012 will be correct.

 **ACCOUNTING MATTERS!** *Ethics Perspective*

The Case of the Missing Gold

The case of $17 million of missing gold at the Royal Canadian Mint was all about accounting errors and miscalculations and not about a Hollywood-style theft, as it was first assumed. After a 14-month search, the RCMP and external auditors concluded that the Mint double-counted some gold bullion it sold, and also underestimated the shrinkage of the gold during processing. "The good news is that there's no theft at the Mint. The bad news is that the Mint can't count," said Liberal MP Bonnie Crombie.

(continued)

Actions to prevent this situation from recurring include doubling the physical inventory count of gold from two to four times a year, as well as implementing processing, accounting, and security recommendations put forward by the external auditors.

Source: "Miscalculations Responsible for 'Missing Gold,'" *The Globe and Mail*, December 22, 2009, p. A7.

BEFORE YOU GO ON...

▶ Do It! Inventory Errors

On July 31, Zhang Inc. counted $600,000 of inventory. This count did not include $90,000 of goods in transit that were purchased on July 29 on account and shipped to Zhang FOB shipping point. Zhang recorded the purchase on August 3 when the goods were received. (a) Determine the correct July 31 inventory amount. (b) Identify any accounts that are in error at July 31, and state the amount and direction (e.g., understated or overstated) of the error. You can ignore income tax effects. (c) Prepare the journal entry(ies) to correct any errors identified in (b).

Action Plan

- Use the income statement relationships to determine the error's impact on income statement accounts.
- Use the accounting equation to determine the error's impact on statement of financial position accounts.

Solution

(a) The inventory count should have included the goods in transit and the purchase should have been recorded in July instead of August. The correct amount of inventory on July 31 was $690,000 ($600,000 + $90,000).

(b) <u>Income statement accounts</u>: Because these inventory items were not sold, there is no error in cost of goods sold or related income statement accounts.
<u>Statement of financial position accounts</u>: Merchandise Inventory and Accounts Payable are both understated (U) by $90,000. The accounting equation shows the impact:

Assets	=	Liabilities	+	Shareholders' equity
U $90,000	=	U $90,000	+	no effect

(c) July 31   Merchandise Inventory   90,000
           Accounts Payable   90,000
                (To record merchandise received on August 3,
                FOB shipping point)

   Aug. 3   Accounts Payable   90,000
           Merchandise Inventory   90,000
                (To reverse journal entry recording merchandise received
                on August 3; should have been recorded July 31)

the navigator

Presentation and Analysis of Inventory

STUDY OBJECTIVE 5

Demonstrate the presentation and analysis of inventory.

Presenting inventory appropriately on the financial statements is important for merchandising companies because inventory is usually the largest current asset (merchandise inventory) on the statement of financial position and the largest expense (cost of goods sold) on the income statement. For example, Forzani, introduced in our feature story, reported inventory of $316 million in 2010, which accounted for 80% of its total current assets. Forzani's cost of goods sold of $864 million amounts to 65% of total expenses on its income statement.

In addition, these reported numbers are critical for analyzing a company's effectiveness in managing its inventory. In the next sections, we will discuss issues that are related to the presentation and analysis of inventory.

VALUING INVENTORY AT THE LOWER OF COST AND NET REALIZABLE VALUE

Before presenting inventory on the financial statements, we must first ensure that it is properly valued. While we hope that we can sell our merchandise for more than we paid for it, in some cases this is not possible. For example, inventory may be damaged, partially obsolete, or less popular with time. The prices of seasonal goods can drop dramatically with a change in season—few people want to buy a snow blower in the summer months. And, in some industries, such as the commodities industry, prices are significantly affected by changes in supply and demand.

For example, in a recent year, purchasing managers at Ford decided to make a large purchase of palladium, a precious metal used in vehicle emission devices. They made this large purchase because they feared a future shortage. The shortage did not materialize, and by the end of the year, the price of palladium had plummeted. Ford's inventory was then worth $1 billion less than its original cost. Do you think Ford's inventory should have been stated at cost or at its $1 billion lower fair value?

As you probably reasoned, when this situation occurs, the cost basis of accounting is no longer followed. **Assets should not be carried in excess of amounts expected to be realized from their sale or use.** Consequently, when the net realizable (fair) value of inventory is lower than its cost, inventory is written down to its net realizable value. This is called the **lower of cost and net realizable value (LCNRV)** rule. For a merchandising company, **net realizable value (NRV)** is the selling price, less any costs required to make the goods ready for sale.

Alternative Terminology
Lower of cost and net realizable value is also called *lower of cost and market*.

The lower of cost and net realizable value rule is applied to the inventory at the end of the accounting period and results in an adjusting journal entry if NRV is lower than cost. To apply this rule, the following steps must be followed:

1. Determine the cost of the inventory, using specific identification, FIFO, or average.
2. Determine the net realizable value of the inventory.
3. Compare the two values—cost and net realizable value—determined in steps 1 and 2. Determine if net realizable value is lower than cost.
4. If net realizable value is lower than cost, adjust and report inventory on the financial statements at NRV rather than cost.

To illustrate the application of the LCNRV rule, assume that at March 31, 2012, New-2-You Autos Limited has the following inventory of used motor vehicles with costs and net realizable values as indicated:

	Cost	NRV	LCNRV
Vehicle A	$16,000	$15,500	$15,500
Vehicle B	14,500	15,300	14,500
Vehicle C	14,800	14,500	14,500
Vehicle D	13,200	14,800	13,200
Vehicle E	11,500	11,400	11,400
Total inventory	$70,000	$71,500	$69,100

In the above example, we compare the cost of each used motor vehicle with its net realizable value and choose the lower amount. The lower of these two amounts, or LCNRV, is listed in the third column. For example, the NRV of $15,500 is the lower amount for Vehicle A, whereas the cost of $14,500 is the lower amount for Vehicle B. This comparison would continue for the remaining vehicles (C through E) in inventory until the total value using the lower of cost and NRV rule, or $69,100, has been determined.

The lower of cost and net realizable value rule should be applied to individual inventory items, rather than total inventory. In certain cases, it can be applied to groups of similar items. This may be the case with items of inventory relating to the same product line that have similar purposes or uses.

After the lower of cost and net realizable value has been determined—whether using individual inventory items or groups of inventory—the next step is to use the net realizable value, if it is lower than cost at the end of the accounting period, to adjust and report inventory. If New-2-You Autos uses a perpetual inventory system, an adjusting journal entry is required to write the inventory down by $900 ($70,000 – $69,100) as follows:

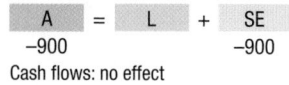

A   =   L   +   SE
−900   −900
Cash flows: no effect

Mar. 31	Cost of Goods Sold	900	
	Merchandise Inventory		900
	(To record decline in inventory value from original cost of $70,000 to net realizable value of $69,100)		

The Cost of Goods Sold account is directly debited in the above entry for the loss, even though no merchandise was sold. This is because a decline in the value of inventory is considered to be an overall cost of buying and selling merchandise, and is therefore reported as the cost of goods sold rather than as a non-operating "other expenses and losses" item. The Merchandise Inventory account is credited directly also to reflect the net realizable value of the inventory. There are other acceptable methods of recording a decline in inventory value, which will be discussed in an intermediate accounting course.

When the circumstances that previously caused inventories to be written down below cost no longer exist, or when there is clear evidence of an increase in net realizable value because of changed economic circumstances, the amount of the writedown is reversed. This occurs, for example, when an item of inventory that is carried at net realizable value, because its selling price had declined, is still on hand in a subsequent period and its selling price has increased.

It is not usual for inventory reversals to happen. Most companies will sell their inventory at a reduced price rather than keep it in stock and hope for a recovery in value. Nonetheless, it can happen. For example, Thailand's Sahaviriya Steel Industries recorded a 4.7-billion-Baht (equivalent to approximately $158 million CAD) reversal of an inventory loss following a surge in commodity prices in 2009. In such cases, a reversal of the writedown will result in an increase in inventory and a reduction in cost of goods sold in the period in which the reversal occurs. In no circumstances can a reversal be greater than the original writedown, which would result in an inventory valuation above its original cost.

REPORTING INVENTORY

Ending inventory is reported in the current assets section of the statement of financial position at its lower of cost and net realizable value. Most companies don't separately disclose the cost and net realizable value of their inventory—they simply state that it is recorded at the lower of cost and net realizable value. For example, Forzani, our feature story company, discloses the following in the notes to its financial statements:

> Inventory is valued at the lower of laid-down cost and net realizable value. Laid-down cost is determined using the weighted average cost method and includes invoice cost, duties, freight, and distribution costs. Net realizable value is defined as the expected selling price.

In addition to the basis of valuation, the following information related to inventory should also be disclosed in the financial statements or the notes to the statements: (1) the total amount of inventory; (2) the cost of goods sold; (3) the method of cost determination (specific identification, FIFO, or average); and (5) the amount of any writedown to net realizable value or reversals of previous writedowns, including the reason why the writedown was reversed.

There are no significant differences at the introductory accounting level in the valuation or reporting of inventory between publicly traded companies reporting under IFRS and private companies reporting under ASPE. There are a few specific differences regarding specialized types of inventories that will be covered in an intermediate accounting course.

INVENTORY TURNOVER

A delicate balance must be kept between having too little inventory and too much inventory. Two ratios to help a company manage its inventory levels are the inventory turnover and days in inventory ratios.

The **inventory turnover** ratio measures the number of times, on average, that inventory is sold ("turned over") during the period. It is calculated as the cost of goods sold divided by the average inventory. Whenever a ratio compares a statement of financial position figure (e.g., inventory) with an income statement figure (e.g., cost of goods sold), the statement of financial position figure must be averaged. Averages for statement of financial position figures are determined by adding the beginning and ending balances together and then dividing the result by two. Averages are used to ensure that the statement of financial position figures (which represent end-of-period amounts) cover the same period of time as the income statement figures (which represent amounts for the entire period).

A complement to the inventory turnover ratio is the **days in inventory** ratio. It converts the inventory turnover into a measure of the average age of the inventory. It is calculated as 365 days divided by the inventory turnover ratio.

In our feature story, we noted that efficient and effective inventory management was critical for Forzani. We will illustrate the calculation of the inventory turnover and days in inventory ratios for Forzani for three recent fiscal years using the following data (in thousands):

	2010	2009	2008
Cost of goods sold	$864,004	$863,239	$852,608
Inventory	316,319	291,497	319,445

Using these data, Illustration 6-13 presents the inventory turnover and days in inventory ratios for Forzani. We also include, for comparison purposes, the ratios for Dick's Sporting Goods, Inc., a large sporting goods chain in the United States (detailed calculations omitted), and their industry.

$$\text{INVENTORY TURNOVER} = \frac{\text{COST OF GOODS SOLD}}{\text{AVERAGE INVENTORY}}$$

$$\text{DAYS IN INVENTORY} = \frac{\text{365 DAYS}}{\text{INVENTORY TURNOVER}}$$

($ in thousands)		2010	2009
Forzani	Inventory turnover	$\dfrac{\$864,004}{(\$316,319 + \$291,497) \div 2}$ = 2.8 times	$\dfrac{\$863,239}{(\$291,497 + \$319,445) \div 2}$ = 2.8 times
	Days in inventory	$\dfrac{365}{2.8}$ = 130 days	$\dfrac{365}{2.8}$ = 130 days
Dick's Sporting Goods	Inventory turnover	3.7 times	3.4 times
	Days in inventory	100 days	107 days
Industry average	Inventory turnover	4.7 times	4.5 times
	Days in inventory	77 days	81 days

► Illustration 6-13
Inventory turnover and days in inventory

In general, the higher the inventory turnover and the lower the days in inventory ratios, the better. The ratios in Illustration 6-13 show that Forzani's inventory turnover remained unchanged between 2009 and 2010, at a time when both Dick's Sporting Goods and the industry averages improved. Dick's Sporting Goods is much better at turning over its inventory than Forzani. In addition, Dick's Sporting Goods has much lower days in inventory ratio than that of Forzani, whose inventory is, on average, in stock for 130 days. Overall, this suggests that Dick's is more efficient in its inventory management than its Canadian competitor, although less so than the industry overall.

Both the inventory turnover and days in inventory ratios are liquidity ratios. Along with the current ratio, which was introduced in Chapter 2, these ratios are important in evaluating a company's liquidity; i.e., its ability to pay obligations that are expected to come due in the next year. Inventory is a significant component of the current ratio and a high level of inventory will result in a high current ratio. But if the inventory is not turning over very quickly, this will result in an "artificially" high current ratio.

Consequently, the current ratio should never be interpreted on its own. It should always be interpreted along with the inventory turnover ratio, as a high current ratio could mean good liquidity, or it could be artificially inflated by slow-moving inventory. Slow-moving inventory results in higher balances in the inventory account, which could also lead to excessive carrying costs (e.g., for interest, storage, insurance, and taxes) or obsolete inventory.

 **ACCOUNTING MATTERS!**   *Management Perspective*

You Have to Be Fast!

Montreal-based Aldo Group Inc. is a $1.5-billion-a-year international shoe company, with 1,600 stores in 60 countries and one of the most successful shoe retailers in the world.

Recently, the company launched a fast-fashion project it called "Project Sunshine" to sharpen its buying and inventory management. The head office now gets hourly sales and inventory turnover data, allowing it to make faster decisions about restocking top sellers or ditching losers. The speedy updates have shaved the time it takes to get shoes on the shelf by as much as 30%.

It now takes 5 to 12 weeks to get shoes to its stores, compared with an industry average of 17 weeks. "You have to be fast . . .," says Aldo Bensadoun, the company's founder.

Source: Marina Strauss, "Aldo's Global Footprint," *The Globe and Mail*, September 4, 2010, p. B1.

DECISION TOOLKIT

Decision Checkpoints	**Info Needed for Decision**	**Tools to Use for Decision**	**How to Evaluate Results**
How long is an item in inventory?	Cost of goods sold; beginning and ending inventory	$$\text{Inventory turnover} = \frac{\text{Cost of goods sold}}{\text{Average inventory}}$$ $$\text{Days in inventory} = \frac{365 \text{ days}}{\text{Inventory turnover}}$$	A higher inventory turnover or lower number of days in inventory suggests efficiency, and that management is reducing the amount of inventory on hand relative to sales.

BEFORE YOU GO ON...

▶ Do It! Lower of Cost and Net Realizable Value

E-Efficiency Inc. sells three different types of home heating stoves (wood, gas, and pellet). The cost and net realizable value of its inventory of stoves are as follows at March 31, the company's year end:

	Cost	NRV
Wood	$250,000	$280,000
Gas	84,000	79,000
Pellet	112,000	101,000
Total inventory	$446,000	$460,000

(a) What amount should E-Efficiency report for its inventory on its statement of financial position? (b) Prepare any journal entry required to record the inventory at its proper value.

Action Plan
- Compare the cost and NRV. Choose the lower value.
- Prepare a journal entry, if required, to adjust cost to net realizable value if it is lower.

Solution

(a)

	Cost	NRV	LCNRV
Wood	$250,000	$280,000	$250,000
Gas	84,000	79,000	79,000
Pellet	112,000	101,000	101,000
Total inventory	$446,000	$460,000	$430,000

E-Efficiency should report its inventory at the lower of cost and net realizable value of $430,000.

(b)

Mar.	31	Cost of Goods Sold ($446,000 − $430,000)	16,000	
		Merchandise Inventory		16,000
		(To record decline in inventory value from original cost of $446,000 to net realizable value of $430,000)		

APPENDIX 6A—INVENTORY COST FORMULAS IN PERIODIC SYSTEMS

Both of the inventory cost formulas—FIFO and average—described in the chapter for a perpetual inventory system may be used in a periodic inventory system. To show how to use each cost formula in a periodic system, we will use the data below for Wynneck Electronics' Astro Condenser.

STUDY OBJECTIVE 6

Apply the inventory cost formulas—FIFO and average—under a periodic inventory system.

WYNNECK ELECTRONICS LTD. Astro Condensers				
Date	Explanation	Units	Unit Cost	Total Cost
Jan. 1	Beginning inventory	100	$10	$ 1,000
Apr. 15	Purchase	200	11	2,200
Aug. 24	Purchase	300	12	3,600
Nov. 27	Purchase	400	13	5,200
	Total	1,000		$12,000

These data are the same as those shown earlier in the chapter, except that the sales information has been omitted. In the periodic inventory system, we ignore the different dates of each of the sales. Instead we make the allocation **at the end of a period** and assume that the entire pool of costs is available for allocation at that time.

Wynneck Electronics had a total of 1,000 units available for sale during the period. The total cost of these units was $12,000. A physical inventory count at the end of the year determined that 450 units remained on hand. Using these data, Illustration 6A-1 shows the formula for calculating cost of goods sold that we first learned in Chapter 5.

Beginning Inventory	+	Cost of Goods Purchased	=	Cost of Goods Available for Sale	−	Ending Inventory	=	Cost of Goods Sold
100 units	+	900 units	=	1,000 units	−	450 units	=	550 units
$1,000	+	$11,000	=	$12,000	−	?	=	?

Illustration 6A-1
Formula for cost of goods sold

If we apply this formula to the unit numbers, we can determine that 550 units must have been sold during the year. The total cost (or "pool of costs") of the 1,000 units available for sale was $12,000. However, we don't know yet how much of the cost of goods available for sale to allocate to ending inventory and to cost of goods sold. We will demonstrate the allocation of this pool of costs using FIFO and average in the next sections. In a periodic inventory system, the cost formulas are applied to the ending inventory, which is then deducted from the cost of goods available for sale to calculate the cost of goods sold.

PERIODIC SYSTEM—FIRST-IN, FIRST-OUT (FIFO)

Similar to perpetual FIFO, the cost of the oldest goods on hand is allocated to the cost of goods sold. This means that the cost of the most recent purchases is assumed to remain in ending inventory. The allocation of the cost of goods available for sale at Wynneck Electronics under FIFO is shown in Illustration 6A-2.

Illustration 6A-2
Periodic system—FIFO

COST OF GOODS AVAILABLE FOR SALE					
Date		Explanation	Units	Unit Cost	Total Cost
Jan.	1	Beginning inventory	100	$10	$ 1,000
Apr.	15	Purchase	200	11	2,200
Aug.	24	Purchase	300	12	3,600
Nov.	27	Purchase	400	13	5,200
		Total	1,000		$12,000

STEP 1: ENDING INVENTORY				STEP 2: COST OF GOODS SOLD	
Date	Units	Unit Cost	Unit Total		
Nov. 27	400	$13	$5,200	Cost of goods available for sale	$12,000
Aug. 24	50	12	600	Less: Ending inventory	5,800
Total	450		$5,800	Cost of goods sold	$ 6,200

Helpful Hint
Note the sequencing of the allocation: (1) Calculate ending inventory, and (2) determine cost of goods sold.

The cost of the ending inventory is determined by taking the unit cost of the most recent purchase and working backward until all units of ending inventory have been costed. In this example, the last purchase was 400 units at $13 on November 27. The remaining 50 units are costed at the price of the second most recent purchase, $12, on August 24.

Once the cost of the ending inventory is determined, the cost of goods sold is calculated by subtracting the ending inventory (the cost of the units not sold) from the cost of all goods available for sale (the pool of costs).

The cost of goods sold can also be separately calculated or proven as shown below. To determine the cost of goods sold, simply start at the first item of beginning inventory and count forward until the total number of units sold (550) is reached. Note that of the 300 units purchased on August 24, only 250 units are assumed sold. This agrees with our calculation of the cost of the ending inventory, where 50 of these units were assumed unsold and thus included in ending inventory.

Date		Units	Unit Cost	Total Cost of Goods Sold
Jan.	1	100	$10	$1,000
Apr.	15	200	11	2,200
Aug.	24	250	12	3,000
Total		550		$6,200

Because of the potential for calculation errors, we recommend that the cost of goods sold amounts be separately calculated and proven in your assignments. The cost of goods sold and ending inventory totals can then be compared with the cost of goods available for sale to check the accuracy of the calculations. It would be as follows for Wynneck: $6,200 + $5,800 = $12,000. You will recall that we also did a similar check of our numbers under the perpetual inventory system.

Although the calculation format may differ, the results under FIFO in a periodic inventory system are the **same as in a perpetual inventory system** (see Illustration 6-4 where, similarly, the ending inventory is $5,800 and the cost of goods sold is $6,200). Under both inventory systems, the first costs in are the ones assigned to cost of goods sold.

PERIODIC SYSTEM—AVERAGE

The weighted average cost is calculated in the same manner as we calculated it in a perpetual inventory system: by dividing the cost of goods available for sale by the units available for sale. The key difference between the two cost formulas is that this calculation is done after each purchase (or purchase return) in a perpetual inventory system. In a periodic inventory system, it is done only at the end of the period, as shown in Illustration 6A-3.

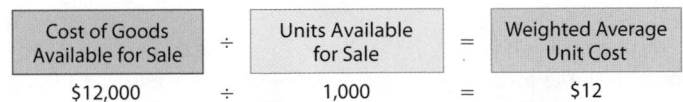

Cost of Goods Available for Sale	÷	Units Available for Sale	=	Weighted Average Unit Cost
$12,000	÷	1,000	=	$12

▶Illustration 6A-3
Calculation of weighted average unit cost

The weighted average unit cost, $12 in this case, is then applied to the units on hand to determine the cost of the ending inventory. The allocation of the cost of goods available for sale at Wynneck Electronics using the average cost formula is shown in Illustration 6A-4.

▶Illustration 6A-4
Periodic system—Average

COST OF GOODS AVAILABLE FOR SALE				
Date	Explanation	Units	Unit Cost	Total Cost
Jan. 1	Beginning inventory	100	$10	$ 1,000
Apr. 15	Purchase	200	11	2,200
Aug. 24	Purchase	300	12	3,600
Nov. 27	Purchase	400	13	5,200
	Total	1,000		$12,000

STEP 1: ENDING INVENTORY	STEP 2: COST OF GOODS SOLD	
$12,000 ÷ 1,000 = $12	Cost of goods available for sale	$12,000
	Less: Ending inventory	5,400
	Cost of goods sold	$ 6,600

Units	Unit Cost	Total Cost
450	$12	$5,400

We can verify the cost of goods sold under the average cost formula by multiplying the units sold by the weighted average unit cost (550 × $12 = $6,600). And, again, we can prove our calculations by ensuring that the total of the cost of goods sold and ending inventory equals the cost of goods available for sale ($6,600 + $5,400 = $12,000).

The results from applying the average cost formula under the periodic inventory system should be compared with Illustration 6-6 shown earlier in the chapter, which presents the results from applying the average cost formula under a perpetual inventory system. Notice that under a periodic inventory system the ending inventory of $5,400 and cost of goods sold of $6,600 are not the same as the values calculated under a perpetual inventory system even though the average cost formula was used for both systems. This is because in a perpetual system a new (moving) average is calculated with each purchase or purchase return. In a periodic system, the same weighted average is used to calculate the cost of goods sold for all the units sold during the period.

BEFORE YOU GO ON...

▶Do It! Cost Formulas—Periodic System

The accounting records of Baker's Dozen Company show the following data:

April	1	Beginning inventory	4,000 units at $3
	12	Purchases	6,000 units at $4
	26	Sales	8,000 units at $8

Determine (a) the cost of goods available for sale, and (b) the cost of goods sold and ending inventory under a periodic inventory system using (1) FIFO, and (2) average.

Action Plan

- Ignore the selling price in allocating cost.
- Calculate the number of units available for sale, cost of goods available for sale, and the ending inventory in units.
- Determine the cost of ending inventory first. Calculate cost of goods sold by subtracting ending inventory from the cost of goods available for sale for each cost formula.
- Understand the difference between FIFO and average.
- Check your work: Prove the cost of goods sold separately and then check that cost of goods sold plus ending inventory equals the cost of goods available for sale.

Solution

(a) Total units available for sale = 4,000 + 6,000 = 10,000
    Cost of goods available for sale = (4,000 × $3) + (6,000 × $4) = $36,000
    Ending inventory = 4,000 + 6,000 − 8,000 = 2,000 units

(b) (1) FIFO

Ending inventory	Units	Unit Cost	Total Cost
Apr. 12	2,000	$4	$8,000

Cost of goods sold: $36,000 − $8,000 = $28,000

Proof of cost of goods sold:

	Units	Unit Cost	Total Cost
Apr. 1	4,000	$3	$12,000
Apr. 12	4,000	4	16,000
	8,000		$28,000

Check: $28,000 + $8,000 = $36,000

(b) (2) Average

Weighted average unit cost: $36,000 ÷ 10,000 = $3.60
Ending inventory: 2,000 × $3.60 = $7,200
Cost of goods sold: $36,000 − $7,200 = $28,800
Proof of cost of goods sold: 8,000 × $3.60 = $28,800
Check: $28,800 + $7,200 = $36,000

comparing
IFRS and ASPE

Key Differences	International Financial Reporting Standards (IFRS)	Accounting Standards for Private Enterprises (ASPE)
No significant differences		

Retail Fraud—An Inside or Outside Job?

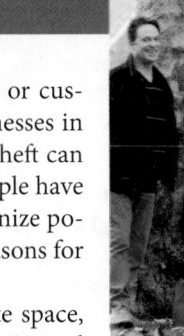

Inventory theft is a huge problem for businesses, whether it is committed by employees or customers. Findings from a recent Statistics Canada survey indicated that 57% of retail businesses in Canada had been subject to some form of retail fraud in the past 12 months. Employee theft can be reduced by running thorough background checks on prospective employees. Some people have a tendency to steal from the get-go, so it is important for a business that is hiring to scrutinize potential employees' resumés to look for lack of references, gaps in employment, or vague reasons for leaving a previous job.

One of the biggest problems for clothing retailers is that the fitting room is a private space, offering opportunities for theft by dishonest customers. Technology, such as Fitting Room Central developed in Westmount, Quebec, can help a retailer control the fitting room environment in a passive way without customers feeling as though they are being watched.

Using Fitting Room Central software, a store clerk scans the tag on each garment taken into the fitting room so the information on the items, including colour and size, is automatically captured. The Fitting Room Central software solution uses a touch screen and a bar code scanner at the entrance to the fitting room area. Sales associates use the software to check customers into the fitting room and manage the flow of customer traffic. The associates assign each customer their own fitting room, and record which items are being tried on. The result is a reduction in inventory loss, as well as access to key information about the customer's fitting room experience.

Some Facts

- A Statistics Canada survey on fraud in business found that 57% of retail businesses had experienced some kind of fraud in the past year. Of these frauds, 19% were committed by employees and the remainder by non-employees. The most common type of fraud committed by employees was asset misappropriation while the most common type of non-employee fraud was return fraud.
- Fraud is expensive for businesses. About 80% of retail businesses had lost $20,000 or less due to fraud, but 2% of businesses had lost over $100,000. Costs of fraud included the cost of inventory stolen, plus other indirect costs such as the time taken to resolve issues and funds expended on additional security and fraud detection. Retailers cited the impact of fraud on client/customer relationships, the need for amended procedures, and negative staff morale as some of the non-monetary impacts of fraud.
- Sometimes there's an innocent reason for an inventory shortage. The partners at The Moose Bar in Vancouver were constantly finding shortages in the inventory of spirits. They tended the bar themselves so they couldn't blame the shortage on staff. An independent audit revealed that the shot glasses they used were too big, pouring a U.S. fluid ounce (30 millilitres) rather than the imperial (Canadian) ounce (28 millilitres). This had resulted in overpouring liquor by 7% more than expected. Their solution was to have a special imperial shot glass manufactured. It poured exactly the right amount and the inventory error was eliminated.

What Do You Think?

Suppose you own a number of specialty boutiques selling mid-level, as well as expensive, locally sourced designer clothing and accessories. You have been experiencing significant losses of accessories at your stores. You suspect that it is a combination of employee and customer theft. Assuming it would be cost-effective, would you install video cameras to monitor both employees and customers?

YES—Most employees and customers are honest. However, some will steal if they are given the opportunity. Management has a responsibility to employ reasonable, cost-effective approaches to safeguard company assets.

NO—The use of video technology to monitor employees and customers sends a message of distrust. You may alienate your employees. Cameras might also reduce the welcoming atmosphere for your customers, who might find the cameras offensive.

Sources: A. Taylor-Butts and S. Perreault, "Fraud Against Businesses in Canada," Statistics Canada, December 2009. Adam McDowell, "A Few Nanolitres Short of a Shot," *National Post*, March 5, 2011, p. WP7. W. Ashworth, "Retail Returns Spell Disaster for Investors," Investopedia, April 26, 2010.

Summary of Study Objectives

1. **Describe the steps in determining inventory quantities.** The steps are (1) taking a physical inventory of goods on hand and (2) determining the ownership of goods in transit, on consignment, and in similar situations.

2. **Apply the methods of cost determination—specific identification, FIFO, and average—under a perpetual inventory system.** Costs are allocated to the cost of goods sold account each time that a sale occurs in a perpetual inventory system. The cost is determined by specific identification or by one of two cost formulas: first-in, first-out (FIFO) and average.

   Specific identification is used for goods that are not ordinarily interchangeable. This method tracks the actual physical flow of goods, allocating the exact cost of each merchandise item to cost of goods sold and ending inventory.

   The FIFO cost formula assumes a first-in, first-out cost flow for sales. Cost of goods sold consists of the cost of the earliest goods purchased. Ending inventory consists of the cost of the most recent goods purchased.

   The average cost formula is used for goods that are homogeneous or non-distinguishable. Under average, a new weighted (moving) average unit cost is calculated after each purchase or purchase return and applied to the number of units sold (and indirectly to the number of units remaining in ending inventory).

3. **Explain the financial statement effects of the inventory cost determination methods.** Specific identification results in an exact match of costs and revenues on the income statement. When prices are rising, the average cost formula results in a higher cost of goods sold and lower profit than FIFO. Average therefore results in a better allocation on the income statement of more current (recent) costs with current revenues than does FIFO. In the statement of financial position, FIFO is considered to be better because it results in an ending inventory that is closest to current (replacement) value. All three methods result in the same cash flow before income tax.

4. **Identify the effects of inventory errors on the financial statements.** Ignoring the effects of income tax, an error in beginning inventory will have a reverse effect on profit in the current year (e.g., an overstatement of inventory results in an understatement of profit). An error in ending inventory will have a similar effect on profit (e.g., an overstatement of inventory results in an overstatement of profit). If ending inventory errors are not corrected in the following fiscal year, their effect on profit for that year is reversed, and total profit for the two years will be correct.

   In the statement of financial position, ending inventory errors will have the same effects on total assets and total shareholders' equity (e.g., an overstatement of inventory results in an overstatement of assets and shareholders' equity), and no effect on liabilities (ignoring income taxes).

5. **Demonstrate the presentation and analysis of inventory.** Inventory is valued at the lower of its cost and net realizable value, which results in the recording of an increase in cost of goods sold and reduction in inventory when the net realizable value is less than cost. This writedown is reversed if the net realizable value of the inventory increases, but the value of the inventory can never be recorded above the original cost.

   Ending inventory is reported as a current asset on the statement of financial position at the lower of cost and net realizable value. Cost of goods sold is reported as an expense on the income statement.

   The inventory turnover ratio is a measure of liquidity. It is calculated by dividing the cost of goods sold by average inventory. It can be converted to days in inventory by dividing 365 days by the inventory turnover ratio. In general, a higher inventory turnover and lower days in inventory ratio is desired.

6. **Apply the inventory cost formulas—FIFO and average—under a periodic inventory system (Appendix 6A).** Under the FIFO cost formula, the cost of the most recent goods purchased is allocated to ending inventory. Cost of goods sold is calculated by deducting ending inventory from the cost of goods available for sale (or proven by applying the cost of the earliest goods on hand to determine the cost of goods sold).

   Under the average cost formula, the total cost of goods available for sale during the period is divided by the units available for sale during the same period to calculate a weighted average cost per unit. This unit cost is then applied to the number of units remaining in inventory to calculate the ending inventory. Cost of goods sold is calculated by deducting ending inventory from the cost of goods available for sale (or proven by applying the unit cost to the units sold to determine the cost of goods sold).

   Each of these cost formulas is applied in the same cost flow order as in a perpetual inventory system. The main difference is that in a perpetual inventory system the cost formula is applied at the date of each sale to determine the cost of goods sold. In a periodic inventory system, the cost formula is applied only at the end of the period.

Glossary

Average cost formula An inventory cost formula that assumes that the goods available for sale are homogeneous or non-distinguishable. The cost of goods sold and ending inventory are determined using an average cost, calculated by dividing the cost of the goods available for sale by the units available for sale. (p. 304)

Consigned goods Goods shipped by a consignor, who retains ownership, to a party called the consignee, who holds the goods for sale. (p. 298)

Days in inventory A liquidity measure of the average number of days that inventory is held. It is calculated as 365 days divided by the inventory turnover ratio. (p. 317)

First-in, first-out (FIFO) cost formula An inventory cost formula that assumes that the costs of the earliest (oldest) goods acquired are the first to be recognized as the cost of goods sold. The costs of the latest goods acquired are assumed to remain in ending inventory. (p. 302)

Internal control A process designed to help an organization achieve reliable financial reporting, effective and efficient operations, and compliance with relevant laws and regulations. (p. 297)

Inventory turnover A liquidity measure of the number of times, on average, that inventory is sold during the period. It is calculated by dividing the cost of goods sold by the average inventory. Average inventory is calculated by adding the beginning and ending inventory balances and dividing the result by two. (p. 317)

Lower of cost and net realizable value (LCNRV) A basis for stating inventory at the lower of its original cost and its net realizable value at the end of the period. (p. 315)

Net realizable value (NRV) The selling price of an inventory item, less any costs required to make the item saleable. (p. 315)

Specific identification method An inventory costing method used when goods are distinguishable and not ordinarily interchangeable. It follows the actual physical flow of goods, and individual items are specifically costed to arrive at the cost of goods sold and cost of the ending inventory. (p. 300)

Weighted average unit cost The average cost of inventory weighted by the number of units purchased at each unit cost. It is calculated as the cost of goods available for sale divided by the number of units available for sale. (p. 304)

DECISION TOOLKIT—A SUMMARY

Decision Checkpoints	Info Needed for Decision	Tools to Use for Decision	How to Evaluate Results
What is the impact of the choice of inventory cost determination method?	Are prices increasing, or are they decreasing?	Income statement and statement of financial position effects	In periods of rising prices, profit and inventory are higher under FIFO than average. FIFO results in the best measure of ending inventory on the statement of financial position. The average cost formula provides opposite results (i.e., profit and inventory are lower compared to FIFO), but can smooth the impact of changing prices. Specific identification's impact on the financial statements will vary, depending on the actual cost. This method results in the best allocation of costs to revenues on the income statement.
How long is an item in inventory?	Cost of goods sold; beginning and ending inventory	$$\text{Inventory turnover} = \frac{\text{Cost of goods sold}}{\text{Average inventory}}$$ $$\text{Days in inventory} = \frac{365 \text{ days}}{\text{Inventory turnover}}$$	A higher inventory turnover or lower days in inventory suggests efficiency, and that management is reducing the amount of inventory on hand relative to sales.

USING THE DECISION TOOLKIT

Foot Locker, Inc. is a leading retailer of athletic shoes and apparel, with about 3,500 stores in more than 20 countries in North America and Europe, as well as Australia and New Zealand. It is one of Forzani's and Dick's Sporting Goods' key competitors, even though it focuses more heavily on athletic footwear than the other two companies.

Selected financial information for Foot Locker (in U.S. millions) for three recent fiscal years follows:

	2010	2009	2008
Cost of goods sold	$3,522	$3,777	$4,017
Merchandise inventory	1,037	1,120	1,281
Current assets	1,772	1,764	2,063
Current liabilities	433	418	511

Selected industry data:

	2010	2009
Inventory turnover	4.7 times	4.5 times
Days in inventory	77 days	81 days
Current ratio	2.3:1	2.3:1

Instructions

(a) Foot Locker uses the first-in, first-out inventory cost formula for its international inventories and a different cost formula (called last-in, first-out, which is acceptable for use only in the United States) for its U.S. inventories. With respect to its international inventories, assume prices have risen over the last two years. If Foot Locker had used the average cost formula instead of FIFO, would its cost of goods sold and its inventory values have been higher or lower than currently reported?

(b) Do each of the following:
1. Calculate the inventory turnover and days in inventory for 2010 and 2009.
2. Calculate the current ratio for each of 2010 and 2009.
3. Evaluate Foot Locker's inventory management and overall liquidity over the most recent two years and in comparison with its industry.

Solution

(a) If Foot Locker used the average cost formula rather than FIFO during a period of rising prices, its cost of goods sold would be higher and its inventory lower than currently reported.

(b) (in U.S. millions)

1.

	2010	2009
Inventory turnover	$\dfrac{\$3,522}{(\$1,037 + \$1,120) \div 2} = 3.3$ times	$\dfrac{\$3,777}{(\$1,120 + \$1,281) \div 2} = 3.1$ times
Days in inventory	$\dfrac{365 \text{ days}}{3.3} = 111$ days	$\dfrac{365 \text{ days}}{3.1} = 118$ days

2.

	2010	2009
Current ratio	$1,772 \div $433 = 4.1:1	$1,764 \div $418 = 4.2:1

3. Foot Locker's inventory turnover and days in inventory ratios improved marginally in fiscal 2010, although they remain below the industry averages. This means that Foot Locker has more inventory on hand and is not selling it as fast as its competitors. It is interesting that its inventory turnover improved while its current ratio declined from 4.2:1 to 4.1:1 between 2009 and 2010. Despite this small drop, its current ratio is still very strong and significantly above that of its industry counterparts.

the navigator

Comprehensive Do It! #1

(Perpetual Inventory System)

Englehart Ltd. uses a perpetual inventory system. The company has the following inventory data available for the month of March:

Date		Explanation	Units	Unit Cost/Price	Total Cost
Mar.	1	Beginning inventory	200	$4.30	$ 860
	10	Purchase	500	4.50	2,250
	15	Sale	(500)	9.00	
	20	Purchase	400	4.75	1,900
	25	Sale	(400)	9.00	
	30	Purchase	300	5.00	1,500
			500		$6,510

Instructions

Determine the cost of goods sold for March and the cost of the ending inventory at March 31 using (a) FIFO and (b) average. (For average, use unrounded numbers in your calculations but round to the nearest cent for presentation purposes in your answer.)

Action Plan

- In a perpetual system, cost of goods sold is determined at the date of each sale. Inventory records maintain running balances of the ending inventory on hand.
- For FIFO, allocate the first costs to the cost of goods sold at each sale date.
- For average, calculate the weighted average unit cost (the cost of goods available for sale ÷ the number of units available for sale) after each purchase. Multiply the unit cost by the number of units sold to determine the cost of goods sold.
- Check your work: Prove that the cost of goods sold plus the ending inventory equals the cost of goods available for sale.

Solution to Comprehensive Do It! #1 (Perpetual Inventory System)

(a) FIFO

Date	Purchases			Cost of Goods Sold			Balance		
	Units	Cost	Total	Units	Cost	Total	Units	Cost	Total
Mar. 1							200	$4.30	$ 860
10	500	$4.50	$2,250				200	4.30	} 3,110
							500	4.50	
15				200	$4.30	} $2,210	200	4.50	900
				300	4.50				
20	400	4.75	1,900				200	4.50	} 2,800
							400	4.75	
25				200	4.50	} 1,850	200	4.75	950
				200	4.75				
30	300	5.00	1,500				200	4.75	} 2,450
							300	5.00	
	1,200		$5,650	900		$4,060			

Check: $4,060 + $2,450 = $6,510 ($860 + $5,650)

(continued)

(b) Average

Date	Purchases			Cost of Goods Sold			Balance		
	Units	Cost	Total	Units	Cost	Total	Units	Cost	Total
Mar. 1							200	$4.30	$ 860.00
10	500	$4.50	$2,250.00				700	4.44	3,110.00
15				500	$4.44	$2,221.43	200	4.44	888.57
20	400	4.75	1,900.00				600	4.65	2,788.57
25				400	4.65	1,859.05	200	4.65	929.52
30	300	5.00	1,500.00				500	4.86	2,429.52
	1,200		$5,650.00	900		$4,080.48			

Check: $4,080.48 + $2,429.52 = $6,510 ($860 + $5,650)

Comprehensive Do It! #2

(Periodic Inventory System—Appendix 6A)

Englehart Ltd. uses a periodic inventory system. The company has the following inventory data available for the month of March:

Date	Explanation	Units	Unit Cost	Total Cost
Mar. 1	Beginning inventory	200	$4.30	$ 860
10	Purchase	500	4.50	2,250
20	Purchase	400	4.75	1,900
30	Purchase	300	5.00	1,500
		1,400		$6,510

The physical inventory count on March 31 shows 500 units on hand.

Instructions

Determine the cost of the ending inventory at March 31 and the cost of goods sold for March using (a) FIFO and (b) average.

Action Plan
- In a periodic inventory system, ending inventory is determined at the end of the period. Ending inventory is then subtracted from the cost of goods available for sale to determine the cost of goods sold.
- For FIFO, allocate the latest costs to the goods on hand.
- For average, calculate the weighted average unit cost (the cost of goods available for sale ÷ the number of units available for sale). Multiply this cost by the number of units on hand to determine the ending inventory.
- Check your work: Prove the cost of goods sold separately and then check that the cost of goods sold plus ending inventory equals the cost of goods available for sale.

Solution to Comprehensive Do It! #2 (Periodic Inventory System—Appendix 6A)

(a) FIFO

		Units	Unit Cost	Total Cost
Ending inventory				
Mar.	30	300	$5.00	$1,500
	20	200	4.75	950
		500		$2,450

Cost of goods sold: $6,510 – $2,450 = $4,060

Proof of cost of goods sold:

		Units	Unit Cost	Total Cost
Mar.	1	200	$4.30	$ 860
	10	500	4.50	2,250
	20	200	4.75	950
		900		$4,060

Check: $4,060 + $2,450 = $6,510

(b) Average

Weighted average unit cost: $6,510 ÷ 1,400 = $4.65
Ending inventory: 500 × $4.65 = $2,325
Cost of goods sold: $6,510 – $2,325 = $4,185
Proof of cost of goods sold: 900 × $4.65 = $4,185
Check: $4,185 + $2,325 = $6,510

Self-Test, Brief Exercises, Exercises, Problems: Set A, and many more components are available for practice in WileyPLUS.

Note: All questions, exercises, and problems below with an asterisk (*) relate to material in Appendix 6A.

Self-Test Questions

Answers are at the end of the chapter.

(SO 1)   1. A physical inventory count is normally taken:
(a) in a periodic inventory system.
(b) in a perpetual inventory system.
(c) at the end of the company's fiscal year.
(d) All of the above

(SO 1)   2. As a result of a physical inventory count, Railway Ltd. determined that it had inventory of $180,000 on hand at December 31. This count did not take into consideration the following: (1) Rogers Consignment Inc. currently has goods costing $35,000 on its sales floor that belong to Railway but are being sold on consignment by Rogers. The selling price of these goods is $50,000. (2) Railway purchased $13,000 of goods that were shipped on December 27, FOB destination, that are expected to be received by Railway on January 3. What is the correct amount of inventory that Railway should report on December 31?
(a) $180,000
(b) $215,000
(c) $228,000
(d) $230,000

(SO 2)   3. The specific identification method should only be used if the inventory consists of:
(a) homogeneous, nondistinguishable goods.
(b) non-interchangeable, distinguishable goods.
(c) high-priced, low-volume goods.
(d) low-priced, high-volume goods.

(SO 2)   4. Mayerthorpe Inc. uses a perpetual inventory system and has the following beginning inventory, purchases, and sales in March:

		Units	Unit Cost	Total Cost
March 1	Beginning inventory	10,000	$ 9	$ 90,000
9	Purchase	12,000	10	120,000
12	Sale	(20,000)		
18	Purchase	7,000	11	77,000

What is the weighted average cost per unit after the last purchase on March 18? (Round the average unit cost to the nearest cent.)
(a) $9.55
(b) $9.90
(c) $10.00
(d) $10.67

(SO 2)   5. Based on the data in question 4, what is the cost of goods sold using the FIFO cost formula for the month of March?
(a) $95,000
(b) $97,000
(c) $190,000
(d) $192,000

(SO 3)   6. In periods of declining prices, the average cost formula will produce:
(a) higher profit than FIFO.
(b) the same profit as FIFO.
(c) higher cash than FIFO.
(d) lower profit than FIFO.

(SO 4)   7. Lavigne Ltd.'s ending inventory is understated by $4,000. The effects of this error on the current

year's cost of goods sold and profit before income taxes, respectively, are:
(a) an understatement and an overstatement.
(b) an overstatement and an understatement.
(c) an overstatement and an overstatement.
(d) an understatement and an understatement.

(SO 4)   8. Hall Corporation overstated its inventory by $15,000 at December 31, 2011. It did not correct the error in 2011 or 2012. As a result, Hall's shareholders' equity was:
(a) overstated at December 31, 2011, and understated at December 31, 2012.
(b) overstated at December 31, 2011, and properly stated at December 31, 2012.
(c) understated at December 31, 2011, and understated at December 31, 2012.
(d) overstated at December 31, 2011, and overstated at December 31, 2012.

(SO 5)   9. Avonlea Corp. had inventory at a cost of $5,000 and a net realizable value of $4,750 at the end of Year 1. At the end of Year 2, it had inventory at a cost of $6,000 and a net realizable value of $6,500. The amounts that should be reported for inventory at the end of Year 1 and Year 2, respectively, are:
(a) $5,000 and $6,000.
(b) $5,000 and $6,500.
(c) $4,750 and $6,000.
(d) $4,750 and $6,500.

(SO 5)   10. If a company's cost of goods sold is $120,000, its beginning inventory is $15,000, and its ending inventory is $25,000, what are its inventory turnover and days in inventory?
(a) 0.2 times and 1,825 days
(b) 4.8 times and 76 days
(c) 6 times and 61 days
(d) 8 times and 46 days

(SO 6) *11. Kam Ltd. has the following units and costs, and uses a periodic inventory system:

		Units	Unit Cost	Total Cost
Jan.	1 Beginning inventory	8,000	$11	$ 88,000
June	19 Purchase	13,000	12	156,000
Nov.	9 Purchase	5,000	13	65,000
		26,000		$309,000

If 9,000 units are on hand at December 31, what is the cost of the ending inventory using the FIFO cost formula?
(a) $100,000
(b) $113,000
(c) $196,000
(d) $209,000

(SO 6) *12. Based on the data in question 11, what is the cost of goods sold (rounded to the nearest thousand dollars) using the average cost formula?
(a) $105,000
(b) $107,000
(c) $202,000
(d) $204,000

Questions

(SO 1)   1. Your friend Tom Wetzel has been hired to help take the physical inventory in Kikujiro's Hardware Store. Explain to Tom how to do this job, giving him specific instructions for determining the inventory quantities that Kikujiro's has legal title over.

(SO 1)   2. What is internal control? How does it apply to taking a physical inventory count?

(SO 1)   3. Janine Ltd. ships merchandise to Fastrak Corporation on December 30. The merchandise reaches Fastrak on January 5. Indicate the terms of sale (i.e., FOB shipping point or FOB destination) that will result in the goods being included in (a) Janine's December 31 inventory and (b) Fastrak's December 31 inventory.

(SO 1)   4. Explain whether each of the following should be included in the inventory of Kingsway Inc.:
(a) consigned goods held by a craft shop for sale on Kingsway's behalf, (b) goods taken home on approval by a Kingsway customer, (c) goods sold but held for alteration by Kingsway.

(SO 2)   5. Why is specific identification used only in a perpetual inventory system and not in a periodic inventory system?

(SO 2)   6. Distinguish between the three methods of determining cost for inventories: specific identification, FIFO, and average. Give an example of a type of inventory for which each method might be used.

(SO 2)   7. Which of the three inventory cost determination methods assumes that goods available for sale are identical? Which assumes that the first goods purchased are the first to be sold? Which matches the actual physical flow of merchandise?

(SO 2)   8. Explain why a new weighted average unit cost must be calculated after each purchase in the average cost formula in a perpetual inventory system but not after each sale.

(SO 3)   9. What are the guidelines that a company should consider when choosing among the three methods of determining cost for inventories: specific identification, FIFO, and average cost formulas?

(SO 3)   10. Identify the advantages of each of the three cost determination methods: specific identification, FIFO, and average.

(SO 3)   11. Which inventory cost formula—FIFO or average—provides the better measure of cost of goods sold on the income statement? The better measure of ending inventory on the statement of financial position? Explain.

(SO 3)   12. Compare the financial effects of using the FIFO and average inventory cost formulas during a period of declining prices on (a) cash (pre-tax), (b) ending inventory, (c) cost of goods sold, (d) profit, and (e) retained earnings.

(SO 4)   13. If an error in ending inventory in one year will have the reverse effect in the following year, will

(SO 4) 14. Mila Ltd.'s ending inventory at December 31, 2011, was understated by $5,000. Assuming that this error is not detected, what effect will it have on (a) 2011 profit before income tax, (b) 2011 retained earnings, (c) 2011 total shareholders' equity, (d) 2012 profit before income tax, (e) 2012 retained earnings, and (f) 2012 total shareholders' equity?

(SO 4) 15. A customer took merchandise home on approval before deciding whether or not to purchase it. The clerk recorded this as a sale on the cash register and this transaction was recorded by the company accountant. Accounts Receivable was debited and Sales credited, and Cost of Goods Sold was debited and Merchandise Inventory was credited. What overall effect will this error have on the components of the accounting equation—assets, liabilities, and shareholders' equity—assuming (a) the customer decides to keep the merchandise, and (b) the customer decides to return the merchandise? Assume the books are not closed before the customer makes a decision.

(SO 5) 16. Explain the meaning of (a) cost, (b) net realizable value, and (c) when the lower of cost and net realizable value rule should be used to value inventory.

(SO 5) 17. Why is the Cost of Goods Sold account debited in the journal entry to record a decline in inventory value under the lower of cost and net realizable value rule even though no merchandise has been sold?

(SO 5) 18. Eastern Platinum Limited reports inventories of U.S. $8,832 thousand on its December 31, 2010, statement of financial position. Review the notes to Eastplats's financial statements (specifically Note 4 (m), Summary of Significant Accounting Policies) to determine what cost formula Eastplats uses and whether it uses the lower of cost and net realizable value rule.

(SO 5) 19. Identify the differences, if any, in the valuation and reporting of inventory between publicly traded companies reporting under IFRS and private companies reporting under ASPE.

(SO 5) 20. Would an increase in the days in inventory ratio from one year to the next be viewed as an improvement or a deterioration in how efficiently a company manages its inventory?

(SO 5) 21. What are the consequences for a company when its inventory turnover ratio is (a) too high and (b) too low?

(SO 6) *22. Your classmate does not understand the difference between the perpetual and periodic inventory systems. "The same cost formulas are used in both systems," he says, "and a physical inventory count is required in both systems. So what's the difference?" Explain to your confused classmate how the perpetual and periodic inventory systems differ.

(SO 6) *23. In a periodic inventory system, the ending inventory is counted and costed. This number is then used to calculate cost of goods sold. Emad asks, "Why can't you apply the cost formula to determine the cost of goods sold first instead of going through all of these steps?"

(SO 6) *24. Explain why, when a company uses the periodic inventory system, its results under the FIFO cost formula are the same as they would be in a perpetual inventory system.

(SO 6) *25. Explain why, when a company uses the periodic inventory system, its results under the average cost formula are *not* the same as they would be in a perpetual inventory system.

Brief Exercises

BE6–1 Helgeson Inc. identifies the following items as possibly belonging in its physical inventory count. For each item, indicate whether or not it should be included in the inventory.
(a) Goods shipped on consignment by Helgeson to another company
(b) Goods held on consignment by Helgeson from another company
(c) Goods sold to a customer, but being held for customer pickup
(d) Goods in transit to Helgeson from a supplier, shipped FOB destination
(e) Goods in transit to a customer, shipped FOB destination

Identify items in inventory.
(SO 1)

BE6–2 The Village Hat Shop Limited counted the entire inventory in its store on August 31 and arrived at a total inventory cost of $66,000. The count included $6,000 of inventory held on consignment for a local designer; $500 of inventory that was being held for customers who were deciding if they actually wanted to purchase the merchandise; and $1,000 of inventory that had been sold to customers but was being held for alterations. There were two shipments of inventory received on September 1. The first shipment cost $5,000. It had been shipped on August 29, terms FOB destination. The second shipment cost $3,750, plus freight charges of $250. It had been shipped on August 28, terms FOB shipping point. Neither of these shipments was included in the August 31 count. Calculate the correct cost of the inventory on August 31.

Calculate inventory cost.
(SO 1)

BE6–3 On January 3, Piano Corp. purchased three portable electronic keyboards for $400 each. On January 20, it purchased two more of the same model keyboards for $500 each. During the month, it sold two keyboards; one was purchased on January 3 and the other was purchased on January 20. (a) Calculate the cost of goods sold and ending inventory for the month using specific identification. (b) Explain how management could manipulate profit, if it wished to, using this method.

Apply specific identification.
(SO 2)

Apply perpetual FIFO.
(SO 2)

BE6–4   Akshay Limited uses the FIFO cost formula in a perpetual inventory system. Fill in the missing amounts for items [1] to [11] in the following perpetual inventory schedule:

Date	Purchases Units	Cost	Total	Cost of Goods Sold Units	Cost	Total	Balance Units	Cost	Total
Apr. 1							10	$16	$160
6	15	$14	$210				[1]	[2]	[3]
9				20	[4]	[5]	[6]	[7]	[8]
14	20	13	260				[9]	[10]	[11]

Apply perpetual average.
(SO 2)

BE6–5   Akshay Limited uses the average cost formula in a perpetual inventory system. Fill in the missing amounts for items [1] to [11] in the following perpetual inventory schedule. (Round the average unit cost to the nearest cent.)

Date	Purchases Units	Cost	Total	Cost of Goods Sold Units	Cost	Total	Balance Units	Cost	Total
Apr. 1							10	$16.00	$160.00
6	15	$14.00	$210.00				[1]	[2]	[3]
9				20	[4]	[5]	[6]	[7]	[8]
14	20	13.00	260.00				[9]	[10]	[11]

Apply perpetual FIFO and average.
(SO 2)

BE6–6   Battery Limited uses a perpetual inventory system. The inventory records show the following data for its first month of operations:

Date	Explanation	Units	Unit Cost	Total Cost	Balance in Units
Aug. 2	Purchase	250	$7	$1,750	250
3	Purchase	400	7	2,800	650
10	Sale	(300)			350
15	Purchase	325	8	2,600	675
20	Purchase return	(50)			625
25	Sale	(325)			300

Calculate the cost of goods sold and ending inventory using (a) the FIFO cost formula, and (b) the average cost formula. (For average, use unrounded numbers in your calculations but round to the nearest cent for presentation purposes in your answer.)

Identify inventory cost formulas.
(SO 3)

BE6–7   Interactive.com just started business and is trying to decide which inventory cost formula—FIFO or average—to use. Assuming prices are falling, as they often do in the information technology sector, answer the following questions for Interactive.com:
(a) Which formula will result in the higher ending inventory? Will this formula also result in an ending inventory value that is closer to replacement cost? Explain.
(b) Which formula will result in the higher cost of goods sold? Will this formula also result in the most current cost of goods sold matched against revenue? Explain.
(c) What guidelines are important for Interactive.com to consider as it tries to select the most appropriate inventory cost formula?

Determine effect of inventory error.
(SO 4)

BE6–8   DuPlessis Corporation incorrectly recorded $25,000 of goods held on consignment for another company as a purchase during the year ended December 31, 2011. The physical inventory count agreed with the perpetual inventory accounting records at year end. What effect, if any, will this error have on total assets, liabilities, and shareholders' equity at December 31, 2011, assuming the error is not detected before year end?

Determine effect of inventory error for two years.
(SO 4)

BE6–9   In its year-end physical inventory count, Tire Track Corporation forgot to count tires it had stored outside its warehouse in a trailer. As a result, ending inventory was understated by $7,000. Assuming that this error was not subsequently discovered and corrected, what is the impact of this error on assets, liabilities, and shareholders' equity at the end of the current year? At the end of the next year?

Determine LCNRV valuation.
(SO 5)

BE6–10   Hawkeye Video Centre Ltd. accumulates the following cost and net realizable value data at December 31:

Inventory Categories	Cost	NRV
Camcorders	$11,000	$10,200
Cameras	9,000	9,500
DVD players	14,000	12,800

Calculate the lower of cost and net realizable value for Hawkeye's inventory.

BE6–11 The cost of Piper Music Inc.'s inventory at December 31, 2011, is $54,700. Its net realizable value on the same date is $52,500. (a) Prepare the adjusting journal entry required, if any, to record the decline in value of the inventory, assuming Piper Music uses a perpetual inventory system. (b) If Piper Music has the same inventory on hand at December 31, 2012, with a net realizable value of $55,000, what amount should it report its inventory at on that date?

Record LCNRV valuation.
(SO 5)

BE6–12 The following information (in U.S. millions) is available for Limited Brands, Inc., the parent company of Victoria's Secret, La Senza, and Bath & Body Works, among other companies:

Calculate inventory turnover and days in inventory.
(SO 5)

	2010	2009	2008
Inventory	$1,037	$1,182	$ 1,251
Net sales	8,632	9,043	10,134
Cost of goods sold	5,604	6,037	6,625

(a) Calculate the inventory turnover and days in inventory ratios for 2010 and 2009. (b) Did Limited Brands' inventory management improve or deteriorate in 2010?

*BE6–13 In its first month of operations, Quilt Inc. made three purchases of merchandise in the following sequence: (1) 250 units @ $6 each, (2) 200 units @ $8 each, and (3) 300 units @ $7 each. A physical inventory count determined that there were 400 units on hand at the end of the month. Assuming Quilt uses a periodic inventory system, calculate the cost of the ending inventory and cost of goods sold using (a) FIFO and (b) average. (For average, use unrounded numbers in your calculations but round to the nearest cent for presentation purposes in your answer.)

Apply periodic FIFO and average.
(SO 6)

*BE6–14 G-Mac Corporation reports the following inventory data for the month of January:

Apply periodic FIFO.
(SO 6)

Date		Explanation	Units	Unit Cost	Total Cost
Jan	1	Beginning inventory	10	$3.00	$ 30
	15	Purchase	12	3.50	42
	27	Purchase	13	4.00	52
			35		$124

A physical inventory count determined that there were 10 units on hand at the end of January. (a) Calculate the cost of the ending inventory and cost of goods sold under FIFO, assuming G-Mac uses a periodic inventory system. (b) Would your answers differ if G-Mac used a perpetual inventory system?

*BE6–15 At the beginning of the year, Seller Ltd. had 700 units with a cost of $4 per unit in its beginning inventory. The following inventory transactions occurred during the month of January:

Record transactions under perpetual and periodic FIFO.
(SO 2, 6)

Jan. 3   Sold 500 units on account for $6 each.
       9   Purchased 1,000 units on account for $4 per unit.
      15   Sold 800 units for cash at $8 each.

Prepare journal entries assuming that Seller Ltd. uses FIFO (a) under a perpetual inventory system and (b) under a periodic inventory system.

Exercises

E6–1 Shippers Ltd. had the following inventory situations to consider at January 31, its year end:

Identify items in inventory.
(SO 1)

1. Goods held on consignment for Boxes Unlimited since December 22
2. Goods shipped on consignment to Rinehart Holdings Ltd. on January 5
3. Goods that are still in transit and were shipped to a customer FOB destination on January 29
4. Freight costs due on goods in transit from item 3 above
5. Goods that are still in transit and were shipped to a customer FOB shipping point on January 29
6. Goods that are still in transit and were purchased FOB destination from a supplier on January 25
7. Goods that are still in transit and were purchased FOB shipping point from a supplier on January 25

Instructions
Identify which of the above items should be included in inventory. If an item should not be included in inventory, state where it should be recorded.

E6–2 Gatineau Bank is considering giving Novotna Corporation a short-term bank loan. Before doing so, it decides that further discussions with Novotna's accountant may be desirable. One area of particular concern is the inventory account,

Determine correct inventory amount.
(SO 1)

which according to a recent physical inventory count, has a balance of $285,000 at December 31. This count agreed with the accounting records. Discussions with the accountant reveal the following:

1. Novotna sold goods costing $35,000 to India-based Moghul Company, FOB destination, on December 28. The goods are not expected to arrive in India until January 12. The goods were not included in the physical inventory count, because they were not in the warehouse.
2. The physical inventory count did not include goods costing $95,000 that were shipped to Novotna, FOB shipping point, on December 27 and were still in transit at year end.
3. Novotna received goods costing $28,000 on January 2. The goods were shipped FOB shipping point on December 26 by Cellar Corp. The goods were not included in the physical inventory count.
4. Novotna sold goods costing $49,000 to United Kingdom–based Sterling of Britain Ltd., FOB shipping point, on December 30. The goods were received by Sterling on January 8. They were not included in Novotna's physical inventory count.
5. On December 31, Schiller Corporation had $30,500 of goods held on consignment for Novotna. The goods were not included in the physical inventory count.
6. Included in the physical inventory count were $15,000 of parts for outdated products that the company had not been able to sell. It is unlikely that these obsolete parts will have any other use.

Instructions
(a) Determine the correct inventory amount on December 31.
(b) Explain why having an accurate inventory count is important to the bank in assessing whether to give Novotna a short-term bank loan or not.

Answer questions about specific identification.
(SO 2, 3)

E6–3   On December 1, Discount Electronics Ltd. has three home entertainment systems left in stock. The purchase dates, serial numbers, and cost of each of the three systems are as follows:

Date		Serial Number	Cost
Oct.	1	#1012	$900
Nov.	1	#1045	840
	30	#1056	780

All three systems are priced to sell at $1,300. By December 31, two systems had been sold and one system remained in inventory.

Instructions
(a) Explain how Discount Electronics would use specific identification to determine the cost of goods sold and the cost of the ending inventory.
(b) Explain how Discount Electronics could manipulate its profit using specific identification by "selectively choosing" which home entertainment system to sell to the two customers in the month of December. What would Discount Electronics' cost of goods sold and gross profit be if the company wished to minimize profit? To maximize profit? Ignore income tax.
(c) What guidelines should Discount Electronics consider when deciding whether to use specific identification or one of the cost formulas to determine the cost of its inventory?

Apply perpetual FIFO.
(SO 2)

E6–4   Outdoor Experience Ltd. uses a perpetual inventory system and has a beginning inventory, as at June 1, of 200 tents. This consists of 50 tents at a cost of $200 and 150 tents at a cost of $225. During June, the company had the following purchases and sales of tents:

	Purchases		Sales	
Date	Units	Unit Cost	Units	Unit Price
June 9			120	$320
12	350	$205		
16			280	320
21	300	210		
24			375	330

Instructions
(a) Determine the cost of goods sold and the cost of the ending inventory using the FIFO cost formula.
(b) Calculate Outdoor Experience's gross profit and gross profit margin for the month of June.
(c) Is the gross profit determined in part (b) higher or lower than it would be if Outdoor Experience had used the average cost formula? Explain.

Apply perpetual average.
(SO 2)

E6–5   Basis Furniture Ltd. uses a perpetual inventory system and has a beginning inventory, as at June 1, of 500 bookcases at a cost of $125 each. During June, the company had the following purchases and sales of bookcases:

	Purchases		Sales	
Date	Units	Unit Cost	Units	Unit Price
June 6	1,200	$127		
10			1,000	$200
14	1,800	128		
16			1,600	205
26	1,000	129		

Instructions

(a) Determine the cost of goods sold and the cost of the ending inventory using the average cost formula. (Use unrounded numbers in your calculations but round to the nearest cent for presentation purposes in your answer.)
(b) Calculate Basis Furniture's gross profit and gross profit margin for the month of June.
(c) Is the gross profit determined in part (b) higher or lower than it would be if Basis Furniture had used the FIFO cost formula? Explain.

E6–6 Lakshmi Ltd. uses the perpetual inventory system and reports the following inventory transactions for the month of June:

Apply perpetual FIFO and average; compare effects.
(SO 2, 3)

Date	Explanation	Units	Unit Cost	Total Cost
June 1	Inventory	150	$5	$ 750
12	Purchase	230	6	1,380
15	Sale	(250)		
16	Purchase	450	7	3,150
23	Purchase	150	8	1,200
27	Sale	(570)		

Instructions

(a) Determine the cost of goods sold and the cost of the ending inventory using (1) FIFO and (2) average. (For average, use unrounded numbers in your calculations but round to the nearest cent for presentation purposes in your answer.)
(b) Which cost formula results in the higher cost of goods sold? Why?
(c) Which cost formula results in the higher profit? Why?
(d) Which cost formula results in the higher ending inventory? Why?
(e) Which cost formula results in the higher pre-tax cash flow? Why?

E6–7 Gill Inc. is trying to determine whether to use the FIFO or average cost formula. The accounting records show the following selected inventory information:

Apply perpetual FIFO and average; compare effects.
(SO 3)

	Purchases			Cost of Goods Sold			Balance		
Date	Units	Cost	Total	Units	Cost	Total	Units	Cost	Total
Apr. 1	7,000	$ 8	$ 56,000				7,000	$8	$56,000
9	18,000	10	180,000				[1]	[2]	[3]
14				20,000	[4]	[5]	[6]	[7]	[8]

The company accountant has prepared the following partial income statement to help management understand the financial statement impact of each cost formula.

	FIFO	Average
Sales	$484,000	$484,000
Cost of goods sold	_____	_____
Gross profit	_____	_____
Operating expenses	100,000	100,000
Profit before income tax	_____	_____
Income tax expense (30%)	_____	_____
Profit	_____	_____

Instructions

(a) Fill in the missing amounts [1] to [8] in the perpetual inventory schedule shown above, assuming the use of the FIFO cost formula.
(b) Fill in the missing amounts [1] to [8] in the perpetual inventory schedule shown above, assuming the use of the average cost formula. (Round the average unit cost to the nearest cent.)
(c) Fill in the missing information in the blanks shown in the income statements above.

(d) Explain whether the comparative profits of each cost formula determined in (b) will be expected to increase, decrease, or not change if (1) costs fall, and (2) costs remain stable.

(e) Identify the advantages of each cost formula.

Determine effects of inventory errors for two years.
(SO 4)

E6–8 Seles Hardware Limited reported the following amounts for its cost of goods sold and merchandise inventory:

	2012	2011
Cost of goods sold	$168,000	$154,000
Ending inventory	37,000	30,000

Seles made two errors: (1) ending inventory for 2012 was overstated by $2,000 and (2) ending inventory for 2011 was understated by $4,000.

Instructions

(a) Calculate the correct ending inventory and cost of goods sold amounts for each year.

(b) Describe the impact of the error on (1) cost of goods sold, (2) profit before income tax, (3) assets, (4) liabilities, and (5) total shareholders' equity for each of the two years.

(c) Explain why it is important that Seles Hardware correct these errors as soon as they are discovered.

Correct partial income statements and calculate gross profit.
(SO 4)

E6–9 Aruba Inc. reported the following partial income statement data for the years ended December 31, 2012 and 2011:

	2012	2011
Sales	$265,000	$250,000
Cost of goods sold	205,000	194,000
Gross profit	60,000	56,000

Merchandise inventory was reported in the current assets section of the statement of financial position at $44,000, $52,000, and $49,000 at the end of 2010, 2011, and 2012, respectively. The ending inventory amounts for 2010 and 2012 are correct. However, the ending inventory at December 31, 2011, is understated by $8,000.

Instructions

(a) Prepare correct income statements for 2011 and 2012 through to gross profit.

(b) What is the cumulative effect of the inventory error on total gross profit for these two years?

(c) Calculate the gross profit margin for each of these two years, before and after the correction.

Record LCNRV valuation.
(SO 5)

E6–10 Cody Camera Shop Ltd. reports the following cost and net realizable value information for its inventory at December 31:

	Units	Unit Cost	Unit NRV
Cameras:			
Sony	4	$175	$160
Canon	8	150	152
Light Meters:			
Gossen	12	135	139
Seconic	10	115	110

Instructions

(a) Determine the lower of cost and net realizable value of the ending inventory.

(b) Prepare the adjusting journal entry required, if any, to record the lower of cost and net realizable value of the inventory assuming Cody Camera Shop uses a perpetual inventory system.

Calculate inventory turnover, days in inventory, and gross profit margin.
(SO 5)

E6–11 The following information is available for Gildan Activewear Inc., headquartered in Montreal, for three recent fiscal years (in U.S. thousands):

	2010	2009	2008
Inventory	$ 332,542	$ 301,867	$ 316,172
Net sales	1,311,463	1,038,319	1,249,711
Cost of sales	947,206	807,986	911,242

Instructions

(a) Calculate the inventory turnover, days in inventory, and gross profit margin for 2009 and 2010.

(b) Based on the ratios calculated in (a), did Gildan's liquidity and profitability improve or deteriorate in 2010?

Determine effect of cost formulas on liquidity.
(SO 3, 5)

E6–12 The following comparative cost formula information is available for Kingswood Limited:

	Average Inventory	Cost of Goods Sold
FIFO	$222,500	$750,000
Average	227,500	735,000

Kingswood's current assets are $450,000, exclusive of inventory. Its current liabilities are $350,000.

Instructions

(a) Calculate Kingswood's inventory turnover ratio assuming (1) FIFO and (2) average is used to determine the cost of the ending inventory.

(b) Calculate Kingswood's current ratio assuming (1) FIFO, and (2) average is used to determine the cost of the ending inventory.

(c) Does one cost formula result in better liquidity than the other for Kingswood? Explain.

*E6–13 Mawmey Inc. uses a periodic inventory system. Its records show the following for the month of May, with 20 units on hand at May 31:

Apply periodic FIFO and average.
(SO 6)

Date		Explanation	Units	Unit Cost	Total Cost
May	1	Beginning inventory	30	$ 9	$270
	12	Purchase	45	11	495
	14	Purchase	15	12	180
		Total	90		$945

Instructions

Determine the cost of the ending inventory and cost of goods sold using (a) FIFO and (b) average. (For average, use unrounded numbers in your calculations but round to the nearest cent for presentation purposes in your answer.)

*E6–14 Lakshmi Ltd. reports the following inventory transactions in a periodic inventory system for the month of June. A physical inventory count determined that 225 units were on hand at the end of the month.

Apply periodic FIFO and average.
(SO 6)

Date		Explanation	Units	Unit Cost	Total Cost
June	1	Beginning inventory	150	$5	$ 750
	12	Purchase	230	6	1,380
	16	Purchase	450	7	3,150
	23	Purchase	150	8	1,200

Instructions

(a) Determine the cost of the ending inventory and cost of goods sold using (1) FIFO and (2) average. (For average, use unrounded numbers in your calculations but round to the nearest cent for presentation purposes in your answer.)

(b) For part 2 of instruction (a), explain why the average unit cost is not $6.50 [($5 + $6 + $7 + $8) ÷ 4].

(c) How do the results for instruction (a) differ from E6–6, where the same information was used in a perpetual inventory system?

*E6–15 Powder, Inc. sells an Xpert snowboard that is popular with snowboard enthusiasts. The following information shows Powder's purchases and sales of Xpert snowboards during November:

Apply perpetual and periodic FIFO and average.
(SO 2, 6)

Date		Transaction	Units	Unit Cost	Unit Sales Price
Nov.	1	Beginning inventory	30	$295	
	5	Purchase	25	300	
	12	Sale	(42)		$460
	19	Purchase	40	305	
	22	Sale	(50)		470
	25	Purchase	30	310	
			33		

Instructions

(a) Determine the cost of goods sold and ending inventory using (1) FIFO and (2) average, assuming Powder uses a perpetual inventory system. (For average, use unrounded numbers in your calculations but round to the nearest cent for presentation purposes in your answer.)

(b) Determine the cost of goods sold and ending inventory using (1) FIFO and (2) average, assuming Powder uses a periodic inventory system. (For average, use unrounded numbers in your calculations but round to the nearest cent for presentation purposes in your answer.)

*E6–16 Refer to the data provided for Powder, Inc. in E6–15.

Record transactions in perpetual and periodic inventory systems.
(SO 2, 6)

Instructions

(a) Prepare journal entries to record purchases and sales for Powder in a perpetual inventory system using (1) FIFO and (2) average.

(b) Prepare journal entries to record purchases and sales for Powder in a periodic inventory system using (1) FIFO and (2) average.

Problems: Set A

Identify items in
inventory.
(SO 1)

P6–1A   Kananaskis Limited is trying to determine the amount of its ending inventory as at February 28, the company's year end. The accountant counted everything in the warehouse in early March, which resulted in an ending inventory amount of $75,000. However, the accountant was not sure how to treat the following transactions, so he did not include them in the count. He has asked for your help in determining whether or not the following transactions should be included in inventory:

1. Feb 1   Kananaskis shipped $900 of inventory on consignment to Banff Corporation. By February 28, Banff had sold half of this inventory for Kananaskis.
2. 15   Kananaskis received $400 of inventory on consignment from Craft Producers Ltd. By February 28, Kananaskis had not sold any of this inventory.
3. 19   Kananaskis was holding merchandise that had been sold to a customer on February 19 but needed alteration before the customer would take possession. The merchandise cost $490 and alterations cost $60. The customer plans to pick up the merchandise on March 2 after the alterations are complete.
4. 23   Kananaskis shipped goods FOB shipping point to a customer. The merchandise cost $280. Freight of $35 was paid by the appropriate party. The receiving report indicates that the goods were received by the customer on March 2.
5. 24   Kananaskis purchased goods FOB shipping point from a supplier. The merchandise cost $375. Freight of $40 was paid by the appropriate party. The goods were shipped by the supplier on February 26 and received by Kananaskis on March 3.
6. 25   Kananaskis purchased goods FOB destination from a supplier. The merchandise cost $750. Freight of $75 was paid by the appropriate party. The goods were shipped by the supplier on February 27 and received by Kananaskis on March 4.
7. 27   Kananaskis shipped goods FOB destination costing $950 to a customer. Freight of $100 was paid by the appropriate party. The receiving report indicates that the goods were received by the customer on March 7.
8. Mar. 5   Kananaskis had $630 of inventory isolated in the warehouse. The inventory is designated for a customer who has requested that the goods not be shipped until March 5.

Instructions

(a) For each of the above situations, specify whether the item should be included in ending inventory, and if so, at what amount. For each item that is not included in ending inventory, indicate who owns it and what account, if any, it should have been recorded in.

(b) How much is the revised ending inventory amount?

Apply specific
identification.
(SO 2)

P6–2A   Dean's Sales Ltd., a small Ford dealership, has provided you with the following information with respect to its vehicle inventory for the month of April. The company uses the specific identification method.

Date	Explanation	Model	Serial #	Unit Cost/Price
April 1	Beg. inventory	Focus	C81362	$22,000
		Mustang	G62313	27,000
		Flex	X3892	29,000
		F-150	F1883	23,000
		F-150	F1921	27,000
8	Sales	Focus	C81362	24,000
		Mustang	G62313	30,000
12	Purchases	Mustang	G71811	28,000
		Mustang	G71891	26,000
		Flex	X4212	28,000
		Flex	X4214	29,000
		Escape	E21202	27,000
18	Sales	Mustang	G71891	31,000
		Flex	X3892	32,000
		F-150	F1921	30,500
		Escape	E21202	30,000
23	Purchases	Focus	C81528	25,000
		Escape	E28268	28,000

Instructions

(a) Determine the cost of goods sold and ending inventory for the month of April.

(b) Determine the gross profit for the month of April.

(c) Discuss whether the specific identification method is likely the most appropriate method of cost determination for Dean's Sales.

P6-3A Sandoval Skateshop Ltd. reports the following inventory transactions for its Knife series skateboards for the month of April. The company uses a perpetual inventory system.

Apply perpetual FIFO and answer questions about effects.
(SO 2, 3)

Date		Explanation	Units	Unit Cost	Total Cost
Apr.	1	Beg. inventory	30	$50	$1,500
	6	Purchase	15	45	675
	9	Sale	(35)		
	14	Purchase	20	40	800
	20	Sale	(25)		
	28	Purchase	20	35	700

Instructions

(a) Determine the cost of goods sold and cost of ending inventory using FIFO.

(b) Assume that Sandoval wants to change to the average cost formula. What guidelines must it consider before making this change?

(c) If the company does change to the average cost formula and prices continue to fall, would you expect the cost of goods sold and ending inventory amounts to be higher or lower than these amounts under FIFO?

P6-4A Information for Sandoval Skateshop Ltd. is presented in P6–3A. Assume the same inventory data and that the company uses the perpetual inventory system.

Apply perpetual average and discuss errors.
(SO 2, 4)

Instructions

(a) Determine the cost of goods sold and cost of ending inventory using average. (Use unrounded numbers in your calculations but round to the nearest cent for presentation purposes in your answer.)

(b) When the company counted its inventory at the end of April, it counted only 24 skateboards on hand. What journal entry, if any, should the company make to record this shortage?

(c) If the company had not discovered this shortage, identify what accounts would be overstated or understated and by what amount.

P6-5A Save-Mart Centre Inc. began operations on July 1 and uses a perpetual inventory system. During July, the company had the following purchases and sales for one of its products:

Apply perpetual FIFO and average; compare effects.
(SO 2, 3)

Date		Purchases		Sales	
	Units	Unit Cost	Units	Unit Price	
July 1	6	$ 90			
3			4	$200	
8	5	100			
13			4	225	
15	3	105			
20			3	240	
27			2	245	

Instructions

(a) Determine the cost of goods sold and cost of ending inventory using (1) FIFO and (2) average. (For average, use unrounded numbers in your calculations but round to the nearest cent for presentation purposes in your answer.)

(b) What guidelines should Save-Mart consider in choosing between the FIFO and average cost formulas?

(c) Which cost formula produces the higher gross profit and profit?

(d) Which cost formula produces the higher ending inventory valuation?

(e) Which cost formula produces the higher pre-tax cash flow?

P6-6A You are provided with the following information for Amelia Inc., which purchases its inventory from a supplier for cash. Returns are usually not damaged and are immediately restored to inventory for resale. Amelia uses the average cost formula in a perpetual inventory system. Increased competition has recently reduced the price of the product.

Record transactions using perpetual average; apply LCNRV.
(SO 2, 5)

Date		Explanation	Units	Unit Cost/Price
July	1	Beginning inventory	25	$10
	6	Purchase	55	11
	8	Sale	(70)	15
	10	Sales return	15	15
	15	Purchase	60	9
	16	Purchase return	(10)	9
	20	Sale	(55)	12
	27	Purchase	10	7

Instructions

(a) Prepare all journal entries for the month of July for Amelia, the buyer. (Use unrounded numbers in your calculations but round to the nearest cent for presentation purposes in your answer.)

(b) Determine the ending inventory amount for Amelia.

(c) On July 31, Amelia learns that the product has a net realizable value of $10 per unit. What amount should ending inventory be valued at on the July 31 statement of financial position?

Determine effects of inventory error for two years.
(SO 4, 5)

P6–7A In its physical inventory count at its February 28, 2011, year end, The Orange Sprocket Corporation included inventory that was being held for another company to sell on consignment. The merchandise was sold in the next year and inventory was correctly stated at February 29, 2012.

Instructions

Ignoring income tax, indicate the effect of this error (overstated, understated, or no effect) on the following:

(a) Cash at the end of 2011 and 2012
(b) The cost of goods sold for each of 2011 and 2012
(c) Profit for each of 2011 and 2012
(d) Retained earnings at the end of 2011 and 2012
(e) Ending inventory at the end of 2011 and 2012
(f) The gross profit margin for each of 2011 and 2012
(g) The inventory turnover ratio for each of 2011 and 2012

Determine effects of inventory errors for multiple years.
(SO 4, 5)

P6–8A The records of Kmeta Inc. show the following data for the years ended July 31:

	2012	2011	2010
Income statement:			
Sales	$340,000	$320,000	$300,000
Cost of goods sold	233,000	220,000	209,000
Operating expenses	68,000	64,000	64,000
Statement of financial position:			
Merchandise inventory	40,000	40,000	24,000

After the company's July 31, 2012, year end, the accountant discovers two errors:

1. Ending inventory on July 31, 2010, was actually $33,000, not $24,000. Kmeta had goods held on consignment at another company that were not included in the inventory account.

2. A purchase of merchandise on account for $5,000 was recorded as a purchase in July 2011 (fiscal 2011) and included in the $40,000 2011 ending inventory balance. It should have been recorded as a purchase in August 2011 (fiscal 2012). The ending inventory of $40,000 was correct at the end of July 2012.

Instructions

(a) For each of the three years, prepare both incorrect and corrected income statements through to profit before income tax.

(b) What is the combined (total) impact of these errors on retained earnings (ignoring any income tax effects) for the three years before correction? After correction?

(c) Calculate both the incorrect and corrected inventory turnover ratios for 2012 and 2011.

Determine and record LCNRV.
(SO 5)

P6–9A Tascon Corporation sells coffee beans, which are sensitive to price fluctuations. The following inventory information is available for this product at December 31, 2011:

Coffee Bean	Units	Unit Cost	Net Realizable Value
Coffea Arabica	13,000 bags	$5.60	$5.55
Coffea Robusta	5,000 bags	3.40	3.50

Instructions

(a) Calculate Tascon's inventory at the lower of cost and net realizable value.

(b) Prepare any journal entry required to record the LCNRV, assuming that Tascon uses a perpetual inventory system.

(c) Assume that Tascon still holds this inventory a year later and that it has recovered its decline in value; that is, the coffee's net realizable value exceeds its cost. Should Tascon carry its inventory at December 31, 2012, at cost, net realizable value, or some other value? Explain.

Record and present LCNRV valuation for multiple periods.
(SO 5)

P6–10A You have been provided with the following information regarding Love Paper Ltd.'s inventory for June, July, and August.

	Paper Inventory (in tonnes)	Cost/Tonne	NRV/Tonne
June 30	6,000	$790	$850
July 31	6,700	850	815
August 31	5,500	815	790

Instructions

(a) Calculate the cost and net realizable value of Love Paper's paper inventory at (1) June 30, (2) July 31, and (3) August 31.

(b) Prepare any journal entry necessary to record the LCNRV of the paper inventory at (1) June 30, (2) July 31, and (3) August 31. Assume that Love Paper uses a perpetual inventory system.

(c) Are there any differences in recording LCNRV for companies reporting using ASPE rather than IFRS?

P6–11A The following information is available for The Coca-Cola Company (in U.S. millions):

Calculate ratios and comment on liquidity. (SO 5)

	2010	2009	2008
Cost of goods sold	$12,693	$11,088	$11,374
Inventories	2,650	2,354	2,187
Current assets	21,579	17,551	12,176
Current liabilities	18,508	13,721	12,988

In the notes to its financial statements, Coca-Cola disclosed that it uses the FIFO and average cost formulas to determine the cost of its inventory.

The industry averages for the inventory turnover, days in inventory, and current ratios are as follows:

	2010	2009
Inventory turnover	7.5 times	7.1 times
Days in inventory	49 days	51 days
Current ratio	1.3:1	1.4:1

Instructions

(a) Calculate Coca-Cola's inventory turnover, days in inventory, and current ratios for 2010 and 2009. Comment on the company's liquidity over the two years, and in comparison with the industry.

(b) What might be the reason that Coca-Cola uses more than one cost formula to determine the cost of its inventory?

P6–12A The following information is available for Tim Hortons Inc. and Starbucks Corporation, and their industry, for a recent year:

Compare ratios; comment on liquidity and profitability. (SO 5)

	Tim Hortons	Starbucks	Industry Average
Inventory turnover	24.8 times	7.2 times	34.7 times
Current ratio	1.4:1	1.3:1	1.0:1
Gross profit margin	27.6%	58.0%	36.9%
Profit margin	14.1%	7.9%	2.8%

Instructions

(a) Comment on the liquidity of the two companies in comparison with each other, and the industry.

(b) Comment on the profitability of the two companies in comparison with each other, and the industry.

(c) It would appear from the above ratios that Tim Hortons and Starbucks are following different pricing and product strategies. Based on these ratios, comment on whether it appears that Starbucks' strategy is working or not.

*P6–13A Kane Ltd. had a beginning inventory on January 1 of 25 units of product SXL at a cost of $160 per unit. During the year, purchases were as follows:

Apply periodic FIFO and average. (SO 6)

	Units	Unit Cost	Total Cost
Mar. 15	70	$150	$10,500
July 20	50	145	7,250
Sept. 4	45	135	6,075
Dec. 2	10	125	1,250

Kane uses a periodic inventory system. At the end of the year, a physical inventory count determined that there were 20 units on hand.

Instructions

(a) Determine the cost of goods available for sale.

(b) Determine the cost of the ending inventory and the cost of the goods sold using (1) FIFO and (2) average. (For average, round the average unit cost to the nearest cent.)

*P6–14A Data for Kane Ltd. are presented in P6–13A. Assume that Kane sold product SXL for $200 per unit during the year.

Prepare partial financial statements and assess effects. (SO 5, 6)

Instructions

(a) Prepare a partial income statement through to gross profit for each of the two cost formulas: (1) FIFO and (2) average.

(b) Show how inventory would be reported in the current assets section of the statement of financial position for (1) FIFO and (2) average.

(c) Which cost formula results in the lower inventory amount for the statement of financial position? The lower gross profit amount for the income statement?

Apply perpetual and periodic FIFO.
(SO 2, 6)

*P6–15A   You are provided with the following information about Lynk Inc.'s inventory for the month of June:

Date		Description	Units	Unit Cost
June	1	Beginning inventory	25	$60
	4	Purchase	90	62
	10	Sale	(80)	
	18	Purchase	35	64
	19	Purchase return	(5)	64
	25	Sale	(50)	
	26	Sales return	5	
	28	Purchase	20	65

Instructions

(a) Calculate the cost of ending inventory and cost of goods sold using FIFO in (1) a periodic inventory system, and (2) a perpetual inventory system.

(b) Compare your results for parts 1 and 2 of instruction (a), commenting particularly on any differences or similarities between the two inventory systems.

Apply perpetual and periodic average.
(SO 2, 6)

*P6–16A   You are provided with the following information about Apple River Inc.'s inventory for the month of November:

Date		Description	Units	Unit Cost
Nov.	1	Beginning inventory	100	$20
	4	Purchase	500	21
	11	Sale	(450)	
	16	Purchase	750	22
	20	Sale	(800)	
	27	Purchase	600	23

Instructions

(a) Calculate the ending inventory and cost of goods sold using the average cost formula in (1) a perpetual inventory system, and (2) a periodic inventory system. (Use unrounded numbers in your calculations but round to the nearest cent for presentation purposes in your answer.)

(b) Compare your results for parts 1 and 2 of instruction (a), commenting specifically on any differences or similarities between the two inventory systems.

Problems: Set B

Identify items in inventory.
(SO 1)

P6–1B   Banff Limited is trying to determine the value of its ending inventory as at February 28, the company's year end. The accountant counted everything that was in the warehouse in early March, which resulted in an ending inventory amount of $56,000. However, the accountant was not sure how to treat the following transactions, so she did not include them in the count, with the exception of item 8. She has asked for your help in determining whether or not the following transactions should be included in inventory:

1. Feb. 1   Banff received $900 of inventory on consignment from Kananaskis Limited. By February 28, Banff had sold half of this inventory for Kananaskis.

2.   5   Banff shipped $600 of inventory on consignment to a Jasper craft shop. By February 28, the craft shop had sold half of this inventory for Banff.

3.   20   Banff purchased goods FOB shipping point from a supplier. The merchandise cost $750. Freight of $75 was paid by the appropriate party. The goods were shipped by the supplier on February 22 and received by Banff on March 1.

4.   23   Banff shipped goods FOB shipping point to a customer. The merchandise cost $800. Freight of $80 was paid by the appropriate party. The receiving report indicates that the goods were received by the customer on March 1.

5. 24 Banff purchased goods FOB destination from a supplier. The merchandise cost $350. Freight of $35 was paid by the appropriate party. The goods were shipped by the supplier on February 26 and received by Banff on March 2.

6. 25 Banff shipped goods FOB destination to a customer. The merchandise cost $400. Freight of $45 was paid by the appropriate party. The receiving report indicates that the goods were received by the customer on March 3.

7. 27 A customer took goods home "on approval" from Banff. The merchandise cost Banff $650. The customer is going to let Banff know whether it wants the merchandise before March 4.

8. 28 Banff had damaged goods set aside in the warehouse because they were not saleable. These goods were included in the inventory count at their original cost of $400.

Instructions

(a) For each of the above situations, specify whether the item should be included in ending inventory, and if so, at what amount. For each item that is not included in ending inventory, indicate who owns it and what account, if any, it should have been recorded in.

(b) How much is the revised ending inventory amount?

P6–2B The Piano Studio Ltd. has provided you with the following information with respect to its piano inventory for the month of August. The company uses the specific identification method.

Apply specific identification.
(SO 2)

Date	Explanation	Supplier	Serial #	Unit Cost/Price
August 1	Beg. inventory	Yamaha	YH6318	$1,500
		Suzuki	SZ5716	1,100
		Suzuki	SZ5828	1,600
		Kawai	KG1268	1,500
		Kawai	KG1520	600
		Steinway	ST8411	2,600
		Steinway	ST0944	2,200
10	Sales	Suzuki	SZ5828	2,700
		Kawai	KG1520	1,000
15	Purchases	Yamaha	YH4418	1,300
		Yamaha	YH5632	1,600
18	Sales	Yamaha	YH4418	2,100
		Steinway	ST0944	3,700
22	Purchases	Suzuki	SZ6132	1,800
		Suzuki	SZ6148	1,600
26	Sales	Suzuki	SZ6132	2,900
		Yamaha	YH6318	2,500
		Yamaha	YH5632	2,600

Instructions

(a) Determine the cost of goods sold and ending inventory for the month of August.

(b) Determine the gross profit for the month of August.

(c) Discuss whether the specific identification method is likely the most appropriate method of cost determination for the Piano Studio.

P6–3B BigFishTackle Co. Ltd. reports the following inventory transactions for its classic fly fishing rods for the month of April. The company uses a perpetual inventory system.

Apply perpetual FIFO and compare effects.
(SO 2, 3)

Date	Explanation	Units	Unit Cost	Total Cost
Apr. 1	Beg. inventory	40	$330	$13,200
6	Purchase	25	340	8,500
9	Sale	(45)		
14	Purchase	30	345	10,350
20	Sale	(40)		
28	Purchase	20	350	7,000

Instructions

(a) Determine the cost of goods sold and cost of ending inventory using FIFO.

(b) Assume that BigFishTackle wants to change to the average cost formula. What guidelines must it consider before making this change?

(c) If the company does change to the average cost formula and prices continue to rise, would you expect the cost of goods sold and ending inventory amounts to be higher or lower than these amounts under FIFO?

Apply perpetual average and discuss errors.
(SO 2, 4)

P6–4B Information for BigFishTackle Co. Ltd. is presented in P6–3B. Assume the same inventory data and that the company uses the perpetual inventory system.

Instructions

(a) Determine the cost of goods sold and cost of ending inventory using average. (Use unrounded numbers in your calculations but round to the nearest cent for presentation purposes in your answer.)

(b) When the company counted its inventory at the end of April, it counted only 29 rods on hand. What journal entry, if any, should the company make to record this shortage?

(c) If the company had not discovered this shortage, identify what accounts would be overstated or understated and by what amount.

Apply perpetual FIFO and average; compare effects.
(SO 2, 3)

P6–5B Family Appliance Mart Ltd. began operations on May 1 and uses a perpetual inventory system. During May, the company had the following purchases and sales for one of its products:

	Purchases		Sales	
Date	Units	Unit Cost	Units	Unit Price
May 1	110	$19		
6	140	22		
11			200	$35
14	80	23		
21			100	40
27	50	25		

Instructions

(a) Determine the cost of goods sold and cost of ending inventory using (1) FIFO and (2) average. (For average, use unrounded numbers in your calculations but round to the nearest cent for presentation purposes in your answer.)

(b) What guidelines should Family Appliance Mart consider in choosing between the FIFO and average cost formulas?

(c) Which cost formula produces the higher gross profit and profit?

(d) Which cost formula produces the higher ending inventory valuation?

(e) Which cost formula produces the higher pre-tax cash flow?

Record transactions using perpetual FIFO; apply LCNRV.
(SO 2, 5)

P6–6B You are provided with the following information for G Inc., which purchases its inventory from a supplier on account. Returns are usually not damaged and are immediately restored to inventory for resale. G Inc. uses the FIFO cost formula in a perpetual inventory system. Decreased competition has recently increased the price of the product.

Date	Description	Units	Unit Price
Oct. 1	Beginning inventory	60	$14
5	Purchase	100	13
8	Sale	(130)	20
10	Sales return	20	20
15	Purchase	35	12
16	Purchase return	(5)	12
20	Sale	(50)	16
26	Purchase	15	11

Instructions

(a) Prepare all journal entries for the month of October for G Inc., the buyer.

(b) Determine the ending inventory amount for G Inc.

(c) On October 31, G Inc. learns that the product has a net realizable value of $10 per unit. What amount should ending inventory be valued at on the October 31 statement of financial position?

Determine effects of inventory error for two years.
(SO 4, 5)

P6–7B In its physical inventory count at its March 31, 2011, year end, Backspring Corporation excluded inventory that was being held on consignment for Backspring by another company. The merchandise was sold in the next year and the inventory was correctly stated at March 31, 2012.

Instructions

Ignoring income tax, indicate the effect of this error (overstated, understated, or no effect) on the following:

(a) Cash at the end of 2011 and 2012

(b) The cost of goods sold for each of 2011 and 2012

(c) Profit for each of 2011 and 2012

(d) Retained earnings at the end of 2011 and 2012

(e) Ending inventory at the end of 2011 and 2012

(f) The gross profit margin for each of 2011 and 2012

(g) The days in inventory ratio for each of 2011 and 2012

P6-8B The records of Pelletier Inc. show the following data for the years ended July 31:

Determine effects of inventory errors for multiple years. (SO 4, 5)

	2012	2011	2010
Income statement:			
Sales	$320,000	$312,000	$300,000
Cost of goods sold	187,000	203,000	170,000
Operating expenses	52,000	52,000	50,000
Statement of financial position:			
Merchandise inventory	37,000	24,000	37,000

After the company's July 31, 2012, year end, the controller discovers two errors:

1. Ending inventory at the end of 2010 was actually $27,000, not $37,000. Pelletier included goods held on consignment for another company that were mistakenly included in the 2010 inventory account.
2. A purchase of merchandise on account for $5,000 was recorded as a purchase in August 2011 (fiscal 2012) and included in the $37,000 2012 ending inventory balance. It should have been recorded as a purchase in July 2011 (fiscal 2011) and included in the 2011 inventory. The ending inventory of $37,000 was correct at the end of July 2012.

Instructions
(a) For each of the three years, prepare both the incorrect and corrected income statements through to profit before income tax.
(b) What is the combined (total) impact of the errors on retained earnings (ignoring any income tax effects) for the three years before correction? After correction?
(c) Calculate both the incorrect and corrected inventory turnover ratios for each of 2012 and 2011.

P6-9B Flin Flon Limited sells three products whose prices are sensitive to price fluctuations. The following inventory information is available for these products at March 31, 2011:

Determine and record LCNRV. (SO 5)

Product	Units	Unit Cost	Net Realizable Value
A	25	$ 7	$ 7
B	30	6	8
C	60	11	10

Instructions
(a) Calculate Flin Flon's inventory at the lower of cost and net realizable value.
(b) Prepare any journal entry required to record the LCNRV, assuming that Flin Flon uses a perpetual inventory system.
(c) Assume that Flin Flon still holds product C a year later and that it has recovered its decline in value and that the net realizable value of product C is now $11. Should Flin Flon carry its inventory of product C at March 31, 2012, at cost, net realizable value, or some other value? Explain.

P6-10B You have been provided with the following information regarding R-Steel Inc.'s inventory for March, April, and May.

Record and present LCNRV valuation for multiple periods. (SO 5)

	Steel Inventory (in tonnes)	Cost/Tonne	NRV/Tonne
March 31	3,000	$725	$740
April 30	2,500	715	710
May 31	2,800	725	725

Instructions
(a) Calculate the cost and net realizable value of R-Steel's inventory at (1) March 31, (2) April 30, and (3) May 31.
(b) Prepare any journal entry required to record the LCNRV of the steel inventory at (1) March 31, (2) April 30, and (3) May 31. Assume that R-Steel uses a perpetual inventory system.
(c) Are there any differences in recording LCNRV for companies reporting using ASPE rather than IFRS?

P6-11B The following information is available for **PepsiCo, Inc.** (in U.S. millions):

Calculate ratios and comment on liquidity. (SO 5)

	2010	2009	2008
Cost of goods sold	$26,575	$20,099	$20,351
Inventories	3,372	2,618	2,522
Current assets	17,569	12,571	10,806
Current liabilities	15,892	8,756	8,787

In the notes to its financial statements, PepsiCo disclosed that it uses the FIFO and average cost formulas to determine the cost of 90% of its inventory, and another method that is not materially different from FIFO to account for the remainder.

The industry averages for the inventory turnover, days in inventory, and current ratios are as follows:

	2010	2009
Inventory turnover	7.5 times	7.1 times
Days in inventory	49 days	51 days
Current ratio	1.3:1	1.4:1

Instructions

(a) Calculate PepsiCo's inventory turnover, days in inventory, and current ratios for 2010 and 2009. Comment on the company's liquidity over the two years, and in comparison with the industry.

(b) What might be the reason that PepsiCo uses more than one cost formula to determine the cost of its inventory?

Compare ratios; comment on liquidity and profitability.
(SO 5)

P6–12B Indigo Books & Music Inc. is Canada's top bookstore, operating under the Indigo, Chapters, and World's Biggest Bookstore banners. Its top competitor is Amazon.com, Inc. The following information is available for these two competitors, and their industry, for a recent year:

	Indigo	Amazon.com	Industry Average
Inventory turnover	4.2 times	13.6 times	4.5 times
Current ratio	1.4:1	1.3:1	1.5:1
Gross profit margin	7.0%	22.6%	31.9%
Profit margin	3.3%	3.8%	1.5%

Instructions

(a) Comment on the liquidity of the two companies in comparison with each other, and the industry.

(b) Comment on the profitability of the two companies in comparison with each other, and the industry.

(c) It would appear from the above ratios that Indigo Books & Music and Amazon.com are following very different pricing and product strategies. Based on these ratios, comment on whether it appears that Amazon.com's strategy is working or not.

Apply periodic FIFO and average.
(SO 6)

*P6–13B Steward Inc. had a beginning inventory on January 1 of 200 units of product MLN at a cost of $9 per unit. During the year, purchases were as follows:

		Units	Unit Cost	Total Cost
Feb.	20	600	$10	$6,000
May	5	500	12	6,000
Aug.	12	600	11	6,600
Dec.	8	300	13	3,900

Steward uses a periodic inventory system. At the end of the year, a physical inventory count determined that there were 300 units on hand.

Instructions

(a) Determine the cost of goods available for sale.

(b) Determine the cost of the ending inventory and the cost of goods sold using (1) FIFO and (2) average. (For average, round the average unit cost to the nearest cent.)

Prepare partial financial statements and assess effects.
(SO 5, 6)

*P6–14B Data for Steward Inc. are presented in P6–13B. Assume that Steward sold product MLN for $20 per unit during the year.

Instructions

(a) Prepare a partial income statement through to gross profit for each of the two cost formulas: (1) FIFO and (2) average.

(b) Show how inventory would be reported in the current assets section of the statement of financial position for (1) FIFO and (2) average.

(c) Which cost formula results in the higher inventory amount for the statement of financial position? The higher gross profit amount on the income statement?

Apply perpetual and periodic FIFO.
(SO 2, 6)

*P6–15B You are provided with the following information about Bear River Inc.'s inventory for the month of May:

Date	Description	Units	Unit Cost
May 1	Beginning inventory	15,000	$2.30
6	Purchase	40,000	2.35
11	Sale	(30,000)	
14	Purchase	50,000	2.40
21	Sale	(65,000)	
27	Purchase	40,000	2.45

Instructions

(a) Calculate the ending inventory and cost of goods sold using FIFO in (1) a perpetual inventory system, and (2) a periodic inventory system.

(b) Compare your results for parts 1 and 2 of instruction (a), commenting specifically on any differences or similarities between the two inventory systems.

*P6–16B You are provided with the following information about Lahti Inc.'s inventory for the month of October.

Apply perpetual and periodic average.
(SO 2, 6)

Date	Description	Units	Unit Cost
Oct. 1	Beginning inventory	50	$24
9	Purchase	125	26
12	Purchase return	(10)	26
15	Sale	(150)	
16	Sales return	5	
20	Purchase	70	27
29	Sale	(55)	

Instructions

(a) Calculate the cost of ending inventory and cost of goods sold using average in (1) a perpetual inventory system, and (2) a periodic inventory system. (Use unrounded numbers in your calculations but round to the nearest cent for presentation purposes in your answer.)

(b) Compare your results for parts 1 and 2 of instruction (a), commenting specifically on any differences or similarities between the two inventory systems.

Broadening Your Perspective

Financial Reporting and Analysis Cases

Financial Reporting: *Eastplats*

BYP6–1 The financial statements of Eastern Platinum Limited (Eastplats) are presented in Appendix A at the end of this book.

Answer questions about inventories.
(SO 3, 5)

Instructions

(a) What amounts did Eastplats report for total inventories in its statement of financial position at the end of 2010 and 2009?

(b) Calculate the change in the dollar amount of total inventories between 2010 and 2009 and the percentage change. Next calculate inventory as a percentage of current assets for each of the two years. Comment on the results.

(c) Eastplats uses the average cost formula. What guidelines do you think influenced Eastplats's choice of cost formula?

(d) Refer to Note 8, Inventories to the financial statements. Did Eastplats write down its inventories to net realizable value in either 2010 or 2009? If so, reproduce the journal entry that Eastplats likely made.

Comparative Analysis: *Eastplats and Amplats*

BYP6–2 The financial statements of Anglo American Platinum Limited (Amplats) are presented in Appendix B following the financial statements for Eastern Platinum Limited (Eastplats) in Appendix A.

Calculate liquidity ratios and comment.
(SO 5)

Instructions

(a) Calculate the current ratio for each company for 2010.

(b) Calculate the inventory turnover and days in inventory ratios for each company for 2010. (Use "cost of operations" as equivalent to cost of goods sold for Eastplats.)

(c) The 2010 industry average for the current ratio was 2.3:1; the inventory turnover was 3.0 times; and the days in inventory was 122 days. What conclusions about each company's liquidity in 2010 can you draw based on your results in (a) and (b) and the industry averages?

Interpreting Financial Information

BYP6–3 The following information is from the December 31 financial statements of Japan-based Canon Inc. (in millions of yen) and U.S.-based competitor Eastman Kodak Company (in U.S. millions):

Discuss cost formulas and LCNRV; calculate ratios and comment.
(SO 3, 5)

	Canon (JPY millions)		Eastman Kodak (U.S. millions)	
	2010	2009	2010	2009
Inventories	¥ 384,777	¥ 373,241	$ 696	$ 679
Cost of sales	1,923,813	1,781,808	5,236	5,838

Additional information comes from the notes to the financial statements:

CANON	EASTMAN KODAK
Note 1. Basis of presentation and significant accounting policies	*Note 1. Summary of significant accounting policies*
Inventories are stated at the lower of cost or market value. Cost is determined principally by the average method for domestic inventories and principally by the first-in, first-out method for overseas inventories.	Inventories are stated at the lower of cost or market. The cost of all the Company's inventories is determined by either the first-in, first-out or average cost method, which approximates current cost.

Instructions

(a) What is the likely reason that Canon and Kodak use two different cost formulas to account for their inventories? In particular, what is the probable reason for Canon to be using different methods to account for its domestic and overseas inventories?

(b) What does the statement "stated at the lower of cost and market value" in the notes to the financial statements mean?

(c) Calculate the inventory turnover and days in inventory ratios of the two companies for 2010. Comment on your findings.

Comparing IFRS and ASPE

Compare effects of different inventory systems and formulas. (SO 1, 2, 3)

BYP6-4 Gibson Lumber Limited is a small sawmill operation, servicing Atlantic Canada. It is a privately traded company, using ASPE. Gibson does not have a sophisticated costing system for its inventory. It estimates the cost of its inventory using the periodic average cost formula and performs a physical count at year end. The physical count is also performed using estimation techniques, such as measuring the piles of finished lumber and scaling the log piles.

Global Lumber Inc., an international lumber company, is a publicly traded company using IFRS that has just expanded into Atlantic Canada. It has a sophisticated inventory system including bar codes on each piece of lumber produced, along with detailed records of production costs. It uses the FIFO cost formula under a perpetual inventory system.

Lumber prices are controlled by a commodity market and have been increasing slightly over the past year.

Instructions

(a) Are there any specific differences related to the use of the two different accounting standards—ASPE and IFRS—financial analysts should consider when evaluating the management of inventory by Gibson and Global?

(b) Would the use of the two different inventory systems—periodic and perpetual—affect the comparison of the financial statements of each company? If so, explain how.

(c) Would the use of the two different cost formulas—average and FIFO—affect the comparison of the financial statements of each company? If so, explain how.

Critical Thinking Cases and Activities

Collaborative Learning Activity

Identify items in inventory and inventory errors; calculate and evaluate inventory turnover. (SO 1, 4)

BYP6-5 Megabôite Distributors Limited is reviewing its year-end inventory calculations. It uses the FIFO cost formula in a perpetual inventory system.

The company had $4.7 million of inventory at the beginning of the year and $5.5 million at the end of the year. During the year, it purchased $46.2 million of inventory.

The following items are unresolved and have not yet been reflected in the figures above:

1. Shipping logs show $1,850,000 of goods in transit to customers, shipped FOB shipping point.
2. Shipping logs show $1.6 million of goods in transit to customers, shipped FOB destination.
3. The showroom contains $450,000 of a supplier's customized products held on consignment.
4. Electronic equipment included in ending inventory is recorded at a cost of $350,000. The manufacturer has discontinued these models of equipment so their sales value has been greatly reduced. The net realizable value of this equipment is $150,000.
5. A new clerk in the wireless products department calculated FIFO incorrectly for some of the inventory. The ending inventory was determined to have a FIFO cost of $257,000 but it should have been $527,000.

Instructions

With the class divided into groups, do the following:

(a) Calculate the original (uncorrected) cost of goods sold for the year. Discuss each of the five unresolved items and determine the effect of each error on the reported cost of goods sold and ending inventory balances. Compare your corrected cost of goods sold and ending inventory figures with those of another group. Reconcile any differences.

(b) The industry's average inventory turnover is 10 times per year. Calculate Megabôite's inventory turnover (1) before any corrections, and (2) after the corrections you determined in (a). How does the corrected inventory turnover compare with the industry average?

(c) When you are reporting your results on inventory turnover to Megabôite's management team, the VP Sales states, "I don't care about inventory turnover numbers. As long as I meet my sales targets, we'll be profitable." Evaluate this statement. What is the relationship between inventory turnover and profit?

Communication Activity

BYP6–6   Some retailers, including teen clothier Abercrombie & Fitch Co., started building up inventories in anticipation of the back-to-school rush and a more upbeat mood in the fall of 2010. At the beginning of 2010, some retailers were caught with not enough merchandise on hand when consumers stepped up their spending after a year of economic uncertainty. Other retailers, including TJX Cos. Inc., which runs discounters Winners and Home Sense, cut inventory before the fall of 2010 to minimize markdowns as they anticipated further economic uncertainty in the minds of consumers.

Discuss inventory policies and impact on profitability. (SO 1, 5)

Instructions

Write a memo comparing the two different strategies of each of these groups of retailers—those that were stocking up for fall like Abercrombie & Fitch and those that were cutting back like TJX. Include in your memo the advantages and disadvantages of each strategy and the likely impact on the gross profit and inventory turnover ratios.

Ethics Case

BYP6–7   You are provided with the following information for Swag Diamonds Ltd. Swag only carries one brand and size of diamond—all are identical. Each batch of diamonds purchased is carefully coded and marked with its purchase cost.

Apply specific identification and average; answer questions. (SO 2, 3)

Mar. 1	Beginning inventory is 140 diamonds at a cost of $500 per diamond.
3	Purchased 200 diamonds at a cost of $540 each.
5	Sold 170 diamonds for $800 each.
10	Purchased 340 diamonds at a cost of $570 each.
25	Sold 500 diamonds for $850 each.

Instructions

(a) Assuming that Swag Diamonds uses the specific identification cost determination method, do the following:
   1. Show how Swag Diamonds could maximize its gross profit for the month by selecting which diamonds to sell on March 5 and March 25.
   2. Show how Swag Diamonds could minimize its gross profit for the month by selecting which diamonds to sell on March 5 and March 25.

(b) Who are the stakeholders in this situation? Is there anything unethical in choosing which diamonds to sell in a month?

(c) Assuming that Swag Diamonds uses a perpetual inventory system and the average cost formula, how much gross profit would Swag Diamonds report? (Round the average unit cost to the nearest cent—two decimal places.)

(d) Which method of cost determination—specific identification or average—should Swag Diamonds select? Explain.

"All About You" Activity

BYP6–8   In the "All About You" feature in this chapter, you learned about retail theft and fraud. Suppose, after graduating, that you accept a job as a manager for a retail store that sells high-end and mid-level cameras and photographic equipment. The equipment is purchased from other countries and is subject to currency fluctuation.

Identify internal controls; adjust inventory; discuss method of cost determination. (SO 1, 3)

Instructions

(a) Based on what you have learned about internal control in this chapter, identify any internal control measures that you think should be in place in your store to safeguard the inventory.

(b) Assume the store uses a perpetual inventory system. At year end, a physical inventory count determines that the physical count differs from the inventory account balance on your books. Identify any accounts that would be affected by an adjusting journal entry to update the inventory value.

(c) Given that the value of the store inventory varies according to the value of the Canadian dollar, what method of cost determination would you recommend the store use? Why?

Serial Case

(*Note:* This is a continuation of the serial case from Chapters 1 through 5.)

Apply perpetual
FIFO and average;
compare effects.
(SO 2, 3)

BYP6-9   The manager of Kzinski Supply Corp. has approached Koebel's Family Bakery to become the exclusive Canadian distributor of deluxe European mixers. Koebel's will pay Kzinski for its purchases of mixers in Canadian dollars. However, Kzinski uses euros as its primary currency, which means that the purchase price converted to Canadian dollars will change each time a mixer is purchased. The current cost of a mixer is $550 and Koebel's would propose to sell each mixer for $1,050. Natalie, Janet, and Brian believe that the mixers are top of the line and that, because these mixers are not available in Canada, many of their customers would be interested in purchasing this product.

Natalie believes that at the beginning of each month there should be at least three mixers in inventory. It takes approximately three weeks for the mixers to come from Europe and it is best to have an adequate supply of mixers on hand ready to be sold.

Currently, all inventory at Koebel's is accounted for using the average cost formula in a perpetual inventory system. Natalie remembers that there is another cost formula, FIFO, that can be used to determine the cost of inventory. Because this is a new type of inventory, she wonders if FIFO would make the accounting a little easier and better reflect ending inventory and cost of goods sold.

The following transactions occur between the months of July and September 2011:

July	5	Three deluxe mixers are purchased on account and received from Kzinski Supply for $1,650 ($550 each), FOB destination, terms n/30.
	14	One deluxe mixer is sold for $1,050 cash.
	25	Amounts owing to Kzinski Supply from the July 5 purchase are paid.
August	2	One deluxe mixer is purchased on account and received from Kzinski Supply for $568, FOB destination, terms n/30.
	29	Two deluxe mixers are sold for a total of $2,100 cash.
	30	Amounts owing to Kzinski Supply from the August 2 purchase are paid.
September	6	Three deluxe mixers are purchased on account and received from Kzinski Supply for $1,692 ($564 each), FOB destination, terms n/30.
	13	Three mixers are sold on account for a total of $3,150.
	28	Amounts owing to Kzinski Supply from the September 6 purchase are paid.
October	4	Three deluxe mixers are purchased on account and received from Kzinski Supply for $1,722 ($574 each), FOB destination, terms n/30.
	25	One deluxe mixer is sold for $1,050 cash.

Instructions

(a) Prepare a perpetual inventory schedule, assuming use of the FIFO cost formula.
(b) Using the information you prepared in (a), prepare journal entries to record each transaction.
(c) Prepare a perpetual inventory schedule, assuming use of the average cost formula.
(d) Using the information you prepared in (c), prepare journal entries to record each transaction.
(e) Calculate and compare the gross profit margin, assuming the use of the (1) FIFO, and (2) average cost formula.
(f) What guidelines should Natalie consider when deciding which inventory cost formula to use?

Answers to Self-Test Questions

1. d   2. b   3. b   4. d   5. c   6. a
7. b   8. b   9. c   10. c   *11. b   *12. c

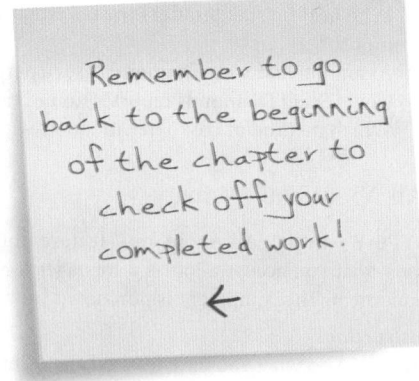

Remember to go back to the beginning of the chapter to check off your completed work!

Internal Control and Cash

The Navigator
Chapter 7

- ☐ Scan *Study Objectives*
- ☐ Read *Feature Story*
- ☐ Read text and answer *Do It!s*
- ☐ Review *Comparing IFRS and ASPE*
- ☐ Review *Summary of Study Objectives*
- ☐ Review *Decision Toolkit—A Summary*
- ☐ Work *Using the Decision Toolkit*
- ☐ Work *Comprehensive Do It!*
- ☐ Answer *Self-Test Questions*
- ☐ Complete assignments
- ☐ Go to *WileyPLUS* for practice and tutorials

study objectives

After studying this chapter, you should be able to:

1. Explain the activities that help achieve internal control and prevent fraud.
2. Apply control activities to cash receipts and payments.
3. Prepare a bank reconciliation.
4. Explain the reporting and management of cash.

the navigator

Controlling Cash at Nick's

Nick Petros, the founder of Nick's Steakhouse and Pizza in Calgary, came to Canada from Greece at age 17 with no money and speaking no English. For 25 years, he worked his way up the ranks in the restaurant industry, as a dishwasher, busboy, waiter, maître d', and then manager. In 1979, he combined his industry experience with a collection of his mother's homemade recipes to open his own restaurant. Nick's youngest child, Mark, and his wife, Michelle, took over the business in 2000.

Located across the street from McMahon Stadium, home to the CFL's Calgary Stampeders, Nick's has become a Calgary family tradition. The restaurant has 72 full- and part-time employees including servers, bartenders, and delivery drivers. Over the course of a busy Friday or Saturday evening, up to 11 servers and three bartenders serve as many as 1,200 people in the 7,000-square-foot (650-square-metre) restaurant and bar. Mark Petros says his point-of-sale (POS) system helps him keep track of the orders, inventory, and money.

After taking a table's order, servers enter the items they require into one of six computer terminals located throughout the restaurant. The computer is preprogrammed with the price of each item and the server simply presses a labelled button, for example, "Caesar salad" or "lasagna," to enter an order. The POS system sends the order information to the bar, salad station, or line cooks and uses the information to track inventory. The servers collect payment from their tables. At the end of a shift, the POS system provides an employee report that itemizes the credit card, debit card, and cash sales that the server owes.

The bartenders and servers have a cash float of $400. The hosting staff also has a float to use for pickup orders and in case the servers need change for large bills. Mr. Petros explains, "When an employee with a float starts the shift, he or she makes sure that the cash on hand is equal to the float plus any orders taken so far that day. At the end of their shift, the same calculation is done to see if it balances out, or else they are responsible for the missing money."

Similarly, before the bartenders start their shift, they have to count the beer in the fridges and note the levels in partially full bottles of alcohol. Everything must correspond to the POS system. For example, if three beers are missing from the fridge, three beers should have been entered in the system. If they weren't, the bartender is responsible.

"There's never a discrepancy," says Mr. Petros. If there ever is one, he adds, it's easy to find the problem, usually an error in pushing a button or entering information.

While cash is an obvious concern for internal control, Mr. Petros estimates that, at most, 10% of sales are paid for in cash, with the majority of customers paying by credit or debit card. Mr. Petros makes a cash deposit at the bank every day.

While there are fewer cash transactions than in the past, cash control remains crucial to a business like Nick's Steakhouse and Pizza. Fortunately, with a system in place and the help of the latest technology, cash can be controlled reliably.

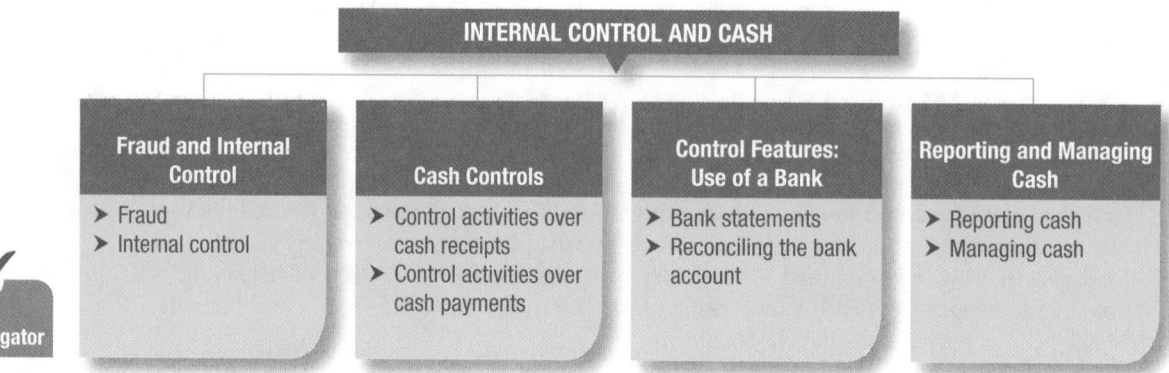

preview of
CHAPTER   7

Cash is the lifeblood of any company. Large and small companies alike must guard it carefully. Even companies that are successful in every other way can go bankrupt if they fail to manage their cash well. Managers must know both how to use cash efficiently and how to control it, as described in the feature story. In this chapter, we explain the essential features of an internal control system and describe how these controls apply to cash receipts and cash payments. We then explain how cash is reported in the financial statements, and describe ways to manage and monitor cash.

The chapter is organized as follows:

INTERNAL CONTROL AND CASH

Fraud and Internal Control	Cash Controls	Control Features: Use of a Bank	Reporting and Managing Cash
➤ Fraud ➤ Internal control	➤ Control activities over cash receipts ➤ Control activities over cash payments	➤ Bank statements ➤ Reconciling the bank account	➤ Reporting cash ➤ Managing cash

the navigator

Fraud and Internal Control

STUDY OBJECTIVE 1

Explain the activities that help achieve internal control and prevent fraud.

According to recent research by the Association of Certified Fraud Examiners, companies world-wide lose an estimated 5% of revenues annually due to fraudulent activities committed by their own employees. This translates to a projected global fraud loss of more than $2.9 trillion in revenue. The association found that most of the fraud was committed by the accounting department or management.

In the following sections of this chapter, we will learn about fraud and internal controls that can be put in place to help prevent and detect fraud.

FRAUD

Fraud is an intentional act to misappropriate (steal) assets or misstate financial statements. In the past decade, fraud has caused the high-profile collapse of many companies in North America. In Canada, one of the most significant corporate failures involved Garth Drabinsky and Myron Gottlieb, who were found guilty of fraud in 2009 for their role in misstating the financial statements of Livent Inc. They recorded expenses as assets, overstated the useful lives of assets to reduce depreciation expense, and recorded revenues that did not exist. In the United States, a number of corporations, including Enron Corporation and WorldCom Corporation, collapsed after management tried to conceal debt and record assets with little value. Another large fraud in the United States was perpetrated by former stockbroker Bernard Madoff, who defrauded investors of billions of dollars in what has been described as the biggest financial fraud in history.

ACCOUNTING MATTERS!   *Ethics Perspective*

The Madoff Fraud

No recent fraud has generated more interest and rage than the one perpetrated by Bernard Madoff. He was an elite New York investment fund manager who was highly regarded by securities regulators as well as his clients. Investors flocked to Madoff because he delivered steady returns of between 10% and 15%, no matter whether the market was going up or going down. However, for many years, he did not actually invest the cash that people gave to him. Instead, he was running a Ponzi scheme: he paid returns to existing investors using cash received from new investors. As long as the size of his investment fund continued to grow from new investments at a rate that exceeded the amounts that he needed to pay out in returns, Madoff was able to operate his fraud smoothly. To conceal his misdeeds, he fabricated false investment statements that were provided to investors. In addition, Madoff hired an auditor who never verified the accuracy of the investment records but automatically issued unqualified opinions each year. Madoff was the auditor's only client. In the end, investors, many of which were charitable organizations, lost more than U.S. $65 billion. Madoff was sentenced to a jail term of 150 years.

Regulatory Reaction to Fraud

In the United States, Congress reacted to accounting scandals by passing the *Sarbanes-Oxley Act* (SOX), which requires public companies to maintain adequate systems of internal controls and to have senior company officers sign certifications to that effect. Furthermore, independent auditors are required to express an opinion on the effectiveness of the internal controls. In Canada, the *Canada Business Corporations Act* has always required companies to maintain an adequate system of internal control. Nonetheless, Canada adopted provisions similar to SOX except for the requirement to have an audit report on internal controls. All provincial securities commissions, with the exception of British Columbia's, also adopted a regulation called *National Instrument 52-109*, which requires the CEO and CFO of public corporations to certify the effectiveness of a company's internal controls. They are also required to report any internal control weaknesses in the Management Discussion and Analysis (MD&A) section of the company's annual report.

INTERNAL CONTROL

Internal control is the most effective way to prevent fraud. You were first introduced to the need for internal control in Chapter 6. As mentioned in that chapter, **internal control** consists of all the related methods and measures adopted within a company to help it achieve reliable financial reporting, effective and efficient operations, and compliance with relevant laws and regulations. Internal controls are also used to prevent errors, which give rise to unintentional misstatements in the financial statements.

Good internal control systems have the five primary components listed here:

- **Control environment:** It is the responsibility of management to make it clear that the organization values integrity, and that unethical activity will not be tolerated (often referred to as "setting the tone at the top").
- **Risk assessment:** Companies must identify and analyze the various factors that create risk for the business and determine how to manage these risks.
- **Control activities:** To reduce the occurrence of fraud, management must design policies and procedures to address the specific risks faced by the company.
- **Information and communication:** The system must capture and communicate all pertinent information both down and up the organization and communicate it to appropriate external parties.
- **Monitoring:** Internal control systems must be monitored periodically for their adequacy. Significant deficiencies need to be reported to management and the board of directors.

Control Activities

Each of the five components of an internal control system is important. However, we will now focus on one of these components in particular: control activities. These form the backbone of a company's efforts to address the risks it faces.

The specific control activities that are used by a company will vary depending on management's assessment of these risks. This assessment is also heavily influenced by the size and nature of the company. Control activities that apply to most companies include the following:

- Authorization of transactions and activities
- Segregation of duties
- Documentation

- Physical controls
- Independent checks of performance
- Human resource controls

Each of these control activities is explained in the following sections.

Authorization of Transactions and Activities. An essential characteristic of internal control is the assignment of responsibility to specific employees. This control activity is most effective when **only one person is authorized to perform a specific task**.

To illustrate, assume that the cash on hand at the end of the day is $10 short of the cash rung up on the cash register. If only one person has operated the register, we know very easily who is responsible for the shortfall. If two or more individuals have used the same register, it may be impossible to determine who is responsible for the error unless each person is given a separate cash drawer or has their own employee report, as is done at Nick's Steakhouse and Pizza described in the feature story.

Establishing responsibility is significantly easier when there is a system for proper authorization. For example, the automated systems that are used by companies typically require passwords to ensure that only authorized personnel access the system. They also enable the company to assign responsibility for certain functions to a specific employee. This is the case at Nick's, where each employee has their own number to access the point-of-sale system. Another example of assigning responsibility is the common practice of not allowing cashiers to reverse their own entry errors. A supervisor must insert a key or type a password to authorize the correction.

In addition, it is important that policies be established by the right individuals or departments. For example, the person responsible for establishing policies for making credit sales should be the vice-president of finance, not the vice-president of sales, who may be motivated to maximize sales—even to customers with poor credit ratings—in order to maximize sales commissions. The policies that are established also typically require written credit approval for sales transactions above a certain value. For example, sales on account amounting to more than $1,000 would require written credit approval.

> **Anatomy of a Fraud** boxes are introduced in this chapter to illustrate how the lack of specific internal controls can result in real-world frauds.

ANATOMY OF A FRAUD

Marie St. Claire was the office manager at a medium-sized wholesaling business in Montreal. When her boss retired, Marie was asked to take on some of his responsibilities, which included the approval of all accounts payable invoices for payments. Realizing that no one would question her authority, Marie incorporated two businesses: one that performed office cleaning duties and another that performed courier services. She then printed up invoices from these two companies addressed to her employer. She approved the invoices for payment and just waited for the cheques to be mailed to a post office box number that she put on the invoices.

> **THE MISSING CONTROL**
>
> *Authorization of Transactions and Activities*
> Marie was allowed to authorize transactions by herself with no one verifying whether the expenditure was reasonable or within company policies.

Segregation of Duties. Segregation of duties is essential in a system of internal control because the responsibility for related activities should be assigned to different individuals. **When the same individual is responsible for related activities, the potential for errors and irregularities is increased.** In general, the following categories of activities should be separated from one another: authorization of transactions and activities (which was covered above), recording of transactions, and custody of assets.

As an example, consider what could happen if all purchasing activities were carried out by the same individual. That person could receive a bribe (a kickback) to buy merchandise at an inflated price from a dishonest supplier. The employee could record the transaction and approve payment without ever being discovered. They could also make up fictitious invoices from a company they created, record the invoices, and approve them for payment. If the employee has access to the merchandise, they could approve the purchase of merchandise and then steal it. When the responsibilities for approving orders and payments, receiving, and recording are assigned to different individuals, the risk of such abuses is much lower.

Just as purchase activities must be segregated, the same is true for sales-related activities such as approving credit for customers, shipping goods, and preparing and recording invoices. For example, a salesperson could make sales at unauthorized prices to increase sales commissions, a shipping clerk could ship goods to himself or herself, or a billing clerk could understate the amount billed for sales made to friends and relatives. These abuses are less likely to occur when the sales tasks are divided: salespersons make the sale only after another employee checks the customer's credit, shipping department employees ship the goods based on the sales order, and billing department employees prepare the sales invoice after comparing the sales order with the report of goods shipped.

Smaller organizations that have fewer employees and mostly cash sales find it harder to segregate duties. Nick's, which was mentioned in our feature story, segregates duties by ensuring that servers don't have access to bar or food inventory. Having more than one bartender with control of the bar inventory, however, weakens the segregation of duties, as it becomes harder to assign responsibility for an irregularity. A control to compensate for this weakness is a point-of-sale system that tracks the amount of inventory on hand, which can then be compared with inventory counts later. Furthermore, such a system has sales prices preprogrammed into cash registers and this decreases the risk of an employee undercharging a friend, for example. In small businesses, it is important that the owner and manager be actively involved in the business, as they provide the oversight needed to ensure that controls are not violated. For example, the owner can make bank deposits to minimize the opportunity for employees to misappropriate cash.

In summary, segregation of duties means that responsibilities should be divided up so that one person cannot both commit a fraud and cover it up. If this cannot be fully achieved, supervision by the owner of the business may be necessary. In addition, the work of one employee should be verified by another to help ensure the accuracy of accounting records.

ANATOMY OF A FRAUD

Tim Chan worked as the warehouse manager at a food wholesaling business in Victoria. The company implemented a new perpetual inventory system for the first time that provided management with the amount of inventory that should always be on hand. Once a month, inventory was counted and compared with the perpetual inventory records to identify spoilage. Almost every day, Tim would steal some of the inventory and hide it in his truck when no one was watching. He was in charge of investigating any differences between amounts counted and on hand in the inventory system. For shortages relating to the products he had stolen, he approved these differences, stating that they were normal spoilage.

THE MISSING CONTROL

Segregation of Duties
Tim had access to assets but was also allowed to approve adjustments to the accounting records, which enabled him to hide his thefts.

Documentation. Documents provide evidence that transactions and events have occurred. At Nick's, the point-of-sale system and employee reports provide documentation for the sale and the amount of cash received. Similarly, in other businesses a shipping document indicates that goods have been shipped and a sales invoice indicates that the customer has been billed for the goods. By adding a signature (or initials) to a document, it also becomes possible to identify the individual who is responsible for the transaction or event.

Procedures should be established for documents even if they are in electronic format. First, whenever possible, documents should be prenumbered and all documents should be accounted for. Prenumbering helps prevent a transaction from being recorded more than once or, conversely, from not being recorded at all. Second, documents that are source documents (the original receipts) for accounting entries should be promptly forwarded to the accounting department to help ensure timely recording of the transaction. This control contributes to the accuracy and reliability of the accounting records.

ANATOMY OF A FRAUD

Sophia and Tamra are sales representatives for their company. They both travel a great deal and complete expense reports to obtain reimbursements of their travel expenses from the company. One day, Sophia realized that the accounting department would accept photocopies of invoices relating to travel. Sophia went to Tamra's desk and noticed several invoices for a trip Tamra had just taken to Calgary. Sophia photocopied the invoices and submitted them as her own expenses. She received a reimbursement cheque for these costs. She did this 18 times during the year.

> **THE MISSING CONTROL**
>
> *Documentation*
> The company should only accept original invoices when processing expense reimbursements.

Physical Controls.   Physical controls can be used to safeguard assets and enhance the reliability of accounting records. Physical controls include the controls shown in Illustration 7-1. In addition to those shown, a company should ensure that assets are adequately insured.

▶ Illustration 7-1
Physical controls

Safes, vaults, and safety deposit boxes for cash and business papers

Locked warehouses and storage cabinets for inventories and records

Computer facilities that require a password, fingerprint or eyeball scan.

Alarms to prevent break-ins

Television monitors and garment sensors to deter theft

Time clocks for recording time worked

ANATOMY OF A FRAUD

Monique and Chantal are roommates who both work at a local bar. Sometimes they work the same shift. When employees begin their shift, they are supposed to swipe their employee cards at a time clock to register the time they arrived at work. Employees must do the same when they leave at the end of their shift. Quite often, Monique, who spends a lot of time with her boyfriend, will arrive at the bar late. If Chantal knows that Monique will be late, she will swipe Monique's card along with her own card. Sometimes, Chantal leaves the bar early because she has a job at the library. Rather than swiping her card when she leaves early, Chantal asks Monique to swipe her card for her later in the evening. They have been swiping each other's cards for more than eight months.

> **THE MISSING CONTROL**
>
> *Physical Controls*
> Time clocks should be placed where they can be easily observed to prevent employees from "punching in or out" with someone else's time card.

Independent Checks of Performance.   The four control activities that we just discussed—authorization of transactions and activities, segregation of duties, documentation, and physical controls—must be reviewed independently and frequently. Independent review is necessary because employees can forget or intentionally fail to follow internal controls, or they might become careless if there is no one to observe and evaluate their performance. These reviews should take place internally and externally, as described below.

Internal Reviews.   Independent internal reviews are especially useful in comparing accounting records with existing assets to ensure that nothing has been stolen. The beer count at the beginning of each shift by the bartender in the feature story about Nick's Steakhouse and Pizza is an example. Another example is the reconciliation by an independent person of the cash balance per books with the cash balance per bank. We will learn more about bank reconciliations later in this chapter.

For independent internal reviews to be beneficial, three measures are recommended:

1. The review should be done periodically and sometimes on a surprise basis.
2. The review should be done by an employee who is independent of the personnel responsible for the information.
3. Discrepancies and exceptions should be reported to a management-level employee who can take appropriate corrective action.

In large companies, control activities such as independent reviews are often monitored by internal auditors. **Internal auditors** are company employees who evaluate the effectiveness of the company's system of internal control. They periodically review the activities of departments and individuals to determine whether prescribed internal controls are being followed.

If a company lists its shares on a public stock exchange in Canada, a management report addressed to shareholders is included in the annual report that explains that management is responsible for the system of internal controls. In addition to this, the CEO and CFO must provide certification regarding the effectiveness of internal controls.

External Reviews.   It is useful to contrast independent *internal* reviews with independent *external* reviews. An important type of external review is conducted by the external auditors. **External auditors**, in contrast to internal auditors, are independent of the company. They are professional accountants hired by a company to report on whether or not the company's financial statements fairly present its financial position and results of operations.

All public companies, including Eastplats, are required to have an external audit. A copy of Eastplats's auditors' report is included in Appendix A. As you will see in the report, external auditors plan and perform an audit to obtain reasonable assurance that the financial statements do not have any significant errors.

In addition, as part of the company's governance processes, the independent audit committee of the board of directors is responsible for reviewing the company's internal control systems to ensure that they are adequate to result in fair, complete, and accurate financial reporting.

ANATOMY OF A FRAUD

When Lara Rooprai began working at Moose Jaw Movers Limited, she was made the custodian of a petty cash fund that consisted of a metal box and $100 cash. She was told that she could spend the cash for office-related expenses and that, when the fund ran low, she could replenish it by submitting any invoices that she had paid with petty cash to her boss, Sarah Rafiq. After getting the fund replenished several times during her first month of employment, Sarah decided that she didn't want Lara bothering her so often so she increased the fund to $5,000 and warned Lara that she would inspect the petty cash box frequently. Eight months went by and Sarah never inspected the fund. During this period, Lara "borrowed" more than $3,000 cash and opened a brokerage account to play the stock market.

(continued)

> **THE MISSING CONTROL**
>
> *Independent Verification*
> Sarah should have performed surprise counts of the petty cash fund to ensure that the funds were not used inappropriately.

Human Resource Controls.   Control measures in this area can include the following:

1. **Conduct thorough background checks.** Many believe that the most important and inexpensive measure any company can take to reduce employee theft and fraud is for the human resources department to conduct thorough background checks. For example, Loblaw weeds out prospective employees with criminal records in an effort to reduce the number of items vanishing from its stores. After the company introduced this policy, 7.5% of job applicants were eliminated.

2. **Bonding of employees who handle cash.** Bonding means having insurance protection against theft of assets by dishonest employees. This is often referred to as "fidelity" insurance. Fidelity insurance contributes to the safeguarding of cash in two ways. First, the insurance company carefully screens all individuals before adding them to the policy and may reject risky applicants. Second, bonded employees know that the insurance company will vigorously prosecute all offenders so they have an incentive to act honestly. Common fidelity insurance claims arise from employee dishonesty, embezzlement, forgery, robbery, safe burglary, computer fraud, wire transfer fraud, counterfeiting, and other criminal acts.

3. **Rotating employees' duties and requiring employees to take vacations.** These measures are designed to deter employees from attempting any thefts, since they will not be able to permanently conceal their improper actions, especially if the company has difficulty segregating duties. For example, if a manager can approve both the hiring of staff and the hours worked by staff, then requiring that manager to take a vacation will allow their replacement to determine if any fictitious employees are on the payroll. Many employee thefts have been discovered when the employee was on vacation or assigned to a new position.

ANATOMY OF A FRAUD

Tom Rollins is the supervisor of the payroll department for a company that operates a number of drilling rigs in the Estevan area of Saskatchewan. He has the ability to approve staff hiring and salary levels, to set employees up in the accounting system, to enter information relating to hours worked, and to sign payroll cheques. Tom is a very popular employee who has been with the company for over 20 years. He has resisted requests to pay employee salaries directly through the bank, preferring instead to hand out paycheques every two weeks to each employee. He has never taken a vacation since he was promoted to his present position nearly five years ago. One afternoon, just after the payroll cheques were printed but not yet signed by Tom, he collapsed from a mild heart attack. While Tom recuperated at home, his boss signed all of the payroll cheques and then distributed them to employees. She noticed, however, that there was a cheque for an employee she did not recognize. When she checked the records, she found that the employee had been on the payroll for almost five years. Later investigation revealed that the unknown employee was Tom's ex-wife in Vancouver.

> **THE MISSING CONTROL**
>
> *Human Resources*
> If Tom had been required to take a vacation more frequently, such a fraud might have been prevented or detected sooner.

Limitations of Internal Control

No matter how well it is designed and operated, a company's system of internal control can only provide **reasonable assurance** that assets are properly safeguarded and that the accounting records are reliable. The concept of reasonable assurance is based on the belief that the costs of establishing control activities should not be more than their expected benefit.

To illustrate, consider shoplifting losses in retail stores. Such losses could be completely eliminated by having a security guard stop and search customers as they leave the store. Store managers have concluded, however, that the cost of doing so, along with the negative effects on the goodwill of customers, outweighs the benefits achieved of reduced theft. Instead, stores have attempted to "control" shoplifting losses by using less costly procedures such as (1) posting signs saying, "We reserve the right to inspect all packages" and "All shoplifters will be prosecuted," (2) using hidden TV cameras and store detectives to monitor customer activity, and (3) using sensor equipment at exits.

The human element is an important factor in every system of internal control. A good system can become ineffective as a result of lack of training, employee fatigue, carelessness, or indifference. For example, a receiving clerk may not bother to count goods received or just "fudge" the count, resulting in the wrong amount of inventory being added to the records.

Occasionally, two or more individuals may work together to get around prescribed control activities. Such collusion can significantly lessen the effectiveness of internal control because it eliminates the protection expected from segregating the employees' duties. If a supervisor and a cashier collaborate to understate cash receipts and steal the shortfall, the system of internal control may be defeated (at least in the short run).

The size of the business may impose limitations on internal control. In a small company, for example, it may be difficult to apply segregation of duties and independent internal verification because of the small number of employees. In situations such as this, it is often necessary for the owner or management to assume the responsibility of performing or supervising incompatible functions. For example, at a small gas station, it is not unusual for a cashier to receive the cash and also prepare and make the night deposit at the bank. If the cash register tape is not locked, so that the cashier could tamper with the sales recorded in the cash register, it may be necessary for the owner to do the nightly bank deposits.

DECISION TOOLKIT

Decision Checkpoints	 Info Needed for Decision	 Tools to Use for Decision	 How to Evaluate Results
Are the company's financial statements supported by adequate internal controls?	Auditor's report, statement of management responsibility, management discussion and analysis	Control activities include (1) authorizing transactions and activities, (2) segregating duties, (3) documenting transactions, (4) employing physical controls, (5) independently checking performance, and (6) applying human resource controls.	If there is any indication that these or other controls are lacking, the financial statements could contain errors.

BEFORE YOU GO ON...

▶Do It! Control Activities

In each of the following situations, identify the appropriate control activity and state whether it has been supported or violated:

(a) The purchasing department orders, receives, and pays for merchandise.

(b) All cheques are prenumbered and accounted for.

(c) The internal auditor performs surprise cash counts.

(*continued*)

(d) Extra cash is kept locked in a safe that can only be accessed by the head cashier.

(e) Each cashier has their own cash drawer.

(f) The company's controller received a plaque for distinguished service because he had not taken a vacation in five years.

Action Plan

- Understand each of the control activities: authorization of transactions and activities, segregation of duties, documentation, physical controls, independent checks of performance, and human resource controls.

Solution

(a) Violation of segregation of duties

(b) Support of documentation procedures

(c) Support of independent performance checks

(d) Support of physical controls

(e) Support of authorization of transactions and activities

(f) Violation of human resource controls (employees should take vacations)

Cash Controls

STUDY OBJECTIVE 2

Apply control activities to cash receipts and payments.

Because cash is easily concealed and transported, it is highly susceptible to theft. The Association of Certified Fraud Examiners reports that cash is the asset targeted for theft 85% of the time. In addition, because of the large volume of cash transactions, errors may easily occur in recording these transactions. To safeguard cash and to ensure the accuracy of the accounting records, effective control activities are essential.

Before we apply the control activities we learned in the last section to cash, let's first look at what cash is, and is not. **Cash** consists of coins, currency (paper money), cheques, money orders, and money on hand or on deposit in a bank or similar depository. The general rule is that if the bank will accept it for deposit, it is cash.

Cash does *not* include postdated cheques (cheques payable in the future), stale-dated cheques (that will not be honoured because they are more than six months old), or returned cheques (cheques lacking sufficient funds). Because postage stamps or IOUs from employees are not the current medium of exchange or acceptable at face value on deposit, they are not considered cash either.

You may wonder if debit and credit cards are, or are not, cash. The answer is: "It depends." Debit card transactions and bank credit card transactions, such as VISA and MasterCard, are considered cash but nonbank credit card transactions, such as Sears are not. Debit and credit cards are used far more frequently than cash today, as Mark Petros mentioned in the chapter opening feature story. Because of the frequency of debit and credit card use today, it will be helpful to pause briefly here and explain how they work.

When a debit card sale occurs, the bank immediately transfers funds from the customer's account so the company can record such a sale with a debit to cash. Because there is no uncertainty as to whether the cash will be received, companies are willing to pay a bank charge for this. To illustrate, suppose that on March 21, 100 debit card sales transactions totalled $1,800. The bank charges $0.20 for each transaction. The journal entry to record these sales would be:

Mar. 21	Debit Card Expense (100 × $0.20)	20	
	Cash	1,780	
	Sales		1,800
	(To record debit card sales)		

A credit card sale is similar to a debit card sale as the payment will be immediately transferred into the company's account. With a credit card sale, the credit card company is lending the customer these funds and faces the risk that the customer may not pay promptly for these borrowed amounts. Consequently, the fee charged for processing a credit card transaction is usually higher than that charged for a debit card and is typically based on a percentage of the value of the sale, rather than a flat fee for the transaction. For example, if we assume that the bank charges a 2.5% fee for a sale of $1,800 we would record:

Mar. 21	Credit Card Expense ($1,800 × 2.5%)	45	
	Cash	1,755	
	Sales		1,800
	(To record credit card sales)		

CONTROL ACTIVITIES OVER CASH RECEIPTS

Cash receipts come from a variety of sources: cash sales; collections on account from customers by receiving cheques in the mail; the receipt of interest, rents, and dividends; investments by shareholders; bank loans; and proceeds from the sale of assets. As might be expected, the internal control procedures relating to cash receipts will vary from one company to another depending on the nature of their business. To illustrate some of these control activities, we will cover ones used in a typical retail store.

Over-the-Counter Receipts

As we saw with Nick's Steakhouse and Pizza in our feature story, most retailers receive payment with cash, credit cards, or debit cards. Staff members who operate cash registers are given a float to make change for customers who pay cash. All sales must be entered into the register through point-of-sale software, which not only records the sale at the proper price but updates inventory records at the same time. Often the sale can be recorded simply by scanning the bar code on merchandise.

At the end of a shift, staff members must ensure that the cash in the register is equal to the float plus the cash sales that were recorded on the system. A supervisor rather than a cashier should access the system to determine the amount and type of sales recorded at that register so that cashiers cannot understate the sales reported if they have taken any cash. Employees must also ensure that the receipts are on hand for sales made by debit or credit cards and that these match sales that were recorded with this type of payment.

Let's assume that an employee steals the cash received from a customer and does not record the sale in the cash register. How will this theft be detected? After all, the cash collected from sales in the cash register will still equal the sales recorded. In this case, detection of the theft can occur if inventory is counted. The count results will reveal a lower amount of inventory on hand than is shown in the point-of-sale system. This is why Nick's in our feature story counts inventory so frequently. Some companies also ensure that security cameras are used to monitor staff to ensure that all sales are recorded in the system.

Generally, internal control over cash receipts is more effective when **cash receipts are deposited intact into the bank account on a daily basis or are made by electronic funds transfer**. Bank deposits should be made by an authorized employee, such as the head cashier or general manager.

Mail-In Receipts

Although the use of cheques has diminished, recent statistics from the Canadian Payments Association indicate that, although 15% of all payments are done with cheques, they represent 55% of the value of all banking transactions. This makes sense as companies don't want to pay service charges on large-value transactions. For example, when you buy a new car, the dealer will want to receive a cheque, not your credit card.

When a cheque is received in the mail, it is usually accompanied by a remittance advice, which is the detachable part of the sales invoice that customers are asked to send back with their cheque. Mailroom clerks will send the remittance advices to the accountants responsible for recording cash receipts while sending the cheques to someone who will deposit them at the bank. The person making the bank deposit should have no record-keeping duties. In this way, accountants cannot intercept a cheque and record its receipt to cover up the theft. The person making the bank deposit will receive a bank-stamped deposit slip. On a daily basis, an independent employee can then compare the amount of cash deposited per the deposit slip with the amount of cash receipts recorded that day to ensure that funds deposited were also recorded.

Electronic Receipts

Electronic funds transfer (EFT) is a way of transferring money electronically from one bank account directly to another without any paper money changing hands. Debit and credit card transactions, mentioned above, are examples of electronic funds transfers. Another example is when customers use on-line banking to pay their accounts. When a customer pays his or her account, the cash is instantly transferred from the customer's bank account to the company's bank account.

EFT transactions can be processed through intermediaries on the Internet. One such example is e-mailing funds through Interac e-Transfer. Another way to receive an electronic payment is through the use of prepaid smart cards. These cards require no credit approval and can be scanned more quickly than debit or credit cards at the point of sale. The most successful launch of a smart card was the Octopus card used on the Hong Kong mass transit system. It worked so well that dozens of other businesses began to accept it. The information stored on these cards can also be stored on smart phones. Starbucks and other retailers now accept payment in this way from customers' cell phones. Although convenient, some authorities are worried that this method of payment allows criminals to "wash" cash received from illegal activities into the legitimate banking system.

Electronic funds transfers normally result in better internal control since no cash or cheques are handled by company employees. This does not mean that the opportunities for fraud are eliminated. For example, without proper authorization and segregation of duties, an employee might be able to redirect electronic collections into a personal bank account and conceal the theft with fraudulent accounting entries. Illustration 7-2 shows how the control activities explained earlier apply to cash receipts.

▶ Illustration 7-2

Application of control activities to cash receipts

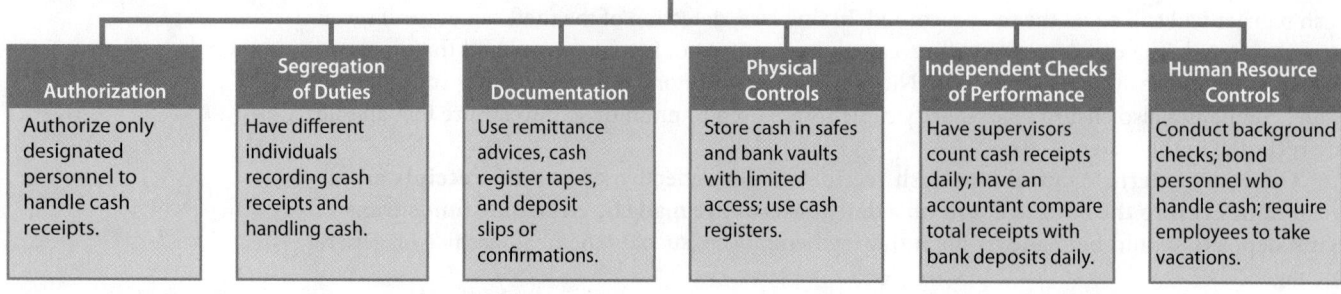

Control Activities over Cash Receipts

Authorization	Segregation of Duties	Documentation	Physical Controls	Independent Checks of Performance	Human Resource Controls
Authorize only designated personnel to handle cash receipts.	Have different individuals recording cash receipts and handling cash.	Use remittance advices, cash register tapes, and deposit slips or confirmations.	Store cash in safes and bank vaults with limited access; use cash registers.	Have supervisors count cash receipts daily; have an accountant compare total receipts with bank deposits daily.	Conduct background checks; bond personnel who handle cash; require employees to take vacations.

CONTROL ACTIVITIES OVER CASH PAYMENTS

Cash is disbursed for a variety of reasons, such as to pay expenses, to settle liabilities, or to purchase assets. Generally, control activities over cash payments are more effective when **payments are made by cheque or by electronic funds transfer, rather than in cash**. Other control procedures (such as petty cash funds, which are not discussed here) are put in place for the few payments that cannot be made by cheque (e.g., for postage).

Good control for cheques includes having them signed by at least two authorized employees. The cheque signer(s) should carefully review the supporting documentation for the payment before signing the cheque. There should be a clear segregation of duties between the cheque-signing function and the accounts payable function to ensure that accountants cannot record invoices to companies they control and then sign cheques to pay these invoices. Cheques should be pre-numbered and all cheque numbers must be accounted for in the payment and recording process. Cheques should never be pre-signed and blank cheques and cheque-signing machines should be safeguarded.

Payments can also be made electronically. For example, when a company pays its employees' salaries using a direct deposit option, the cash is instantly transferred from the company's bank account to each employee's bank account. As we discussed in the cash receipts section, as long as there is proper authorization and segregation of duties, the use of EFT for cash payments will result in better internal control. The control activities applied to cash payments are shown in Illustration 7-3.

▶ **Illustration 7-3**

Application of control activities to cash payments

Control Activities over Cash Payments

Authorization	Segregation of Duties	Documentation	Physical Controls	Independent Checks of Performance	Human Resource Controls
Authorize only designated personnel to sign cheques or approve electronic payments.	Have different individuals approve and make payments; ensure cheque signers do not record cash payments.	Use prenumbered cheques and account for them in sequence; ensure each cheque has an approved invoice.	Store cash in safes and bank vaults with limited access; restrict access to blank cheques and signing machines; use electronic payments when possible.	Compare cheques with invoices; reconcile the bank statement monthly.	Conduct background checks; bond personnel who handle cash; require employees to take vacations.

ACCOUNTING MATTERS! *Management Perspective*

E-Mail Money Transfers

In Canada, 24 banks and credit unions offer Interac e-Transfer. To use this feature, you log on to your bank's website, click on the Interac e-Transfer link, and fill in the amount to be transferred, the recipient's e-mail address, and a security question. With Interac e-Transfer, the money comes right out of your account and is transferred to the recipient as soon as he or she opens a notification e-mail and follows a few simple steps. First, the recipient chooses their bank from a list of financial institutions. The recipient is then sent to their bank's website, where they log in, answer the security question, and complete the deposit.

Some 10.7 million money transfers were processed in 2009, up from 4 million in 2006. But the buzz on e-mail money transfers is minimal. Cost may be a factor. Some banks have a banking service package that includes one or two of these transactions per month, but otherwise you'll pay $1.50 for each one.

Source: Rob Carrick, "E-Mail Money Transfer Is the Better Way," *The Globe and Mail*, September 10, 2010, p. B19.

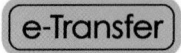

Previously INTERAC®
Email Money Transfer

BEFORE YOU GO ON...

▶ Do It! Control Activities over Cash Receipts

At Hamburger Heaven Restaurant, two cash registers are shared by six employees working behind the counter. The owner says, "In an ideal situation, one person would be designated to ring in orders for each cash register, but when we get swamped, we all have to work together to keep things running smoothly." The prices of most items are preprogrammed into the cash register. At the end of the day, each register generates a sales report and one of the employees will count the cash in both registers, and after subtracting the float, will compare the total with the sales report. Then the employee puts the cash in a drawer in the office.

Identify any violations of control activities over cash receipts at this restaurant.

Action Plan

- Understand the application of each of the control activities to cash receipts: authorization of transactions and activities, segregation of duties, documentation, physical controls, independent checks of performance, and human resource controls.

Solution

Because more than one person can use the same cash register, the authorization of transactions and activities control has been violated. If there is a cash shortage in the register at the end of the day, it will not be possible to determine who is responsible for it.

Segregation of duties has also been violated. Staff members who ring up the sale on the cash register and have access to cash should not be the ones to check the cash receipts against the sales report. They could choose to not ring up a sale and pocket the cash instead.

Finally, physical controls are weak because cash should be deposited in a bank promptly, preferably as a night deposit.

Control Features: Use of a Bank

STUDY OBJECTIVE 3

Prepare a bank reconciliation.

The use of a bank contributes significantly to good internal control over cash. A company can control its cash by using a bank to safeguard its cash, cheques received and written, and electronic funds received and paid. The use of a bank minimizes the amount of currency that must be kept on hand. In addition, control is strengthened because a second record is maintained of all bank transactions by the bank, which can then be compared to the company's records. The asset account Cash, maintained by the company (called the depositor), is the opposite of the bank's liability account for each depositor but both records will record the same transactions. It should be possible to **reconcile these accounts**—make them agree—at any time.

BANK STATEMENTS

Each month, the bank sends the company a bank statement showing the company's bank transactions and balances. For example, in Illustration 7-4, the statement for Laird Ltd. shows the following: (1) dates, (2) a description of each transaction, (3) the amounts deducted (debited) from the bank account (e.g., cheques and other payments), (4) the amounts added (credited) to the bank account (e.g., deposits and other receipts), and (5) the account balance after each transaction.

At first glance, it may appear that the debits and credits reported on the bank statement are backward. How can amounts deducted from a bank account, like a cheque, be a debit? And how can amounts added to a bank account, like a deposit, be a credit? Debits and credits are not really backward. To the company, Cash is an asset account. Assets are increased by debits (e.g., for cash receipts) and decreased by credits (e.g., for cash payments). To the bank, the cash in the company's bank account is a liability account—an amount it must repay upon request. Liabilities are increased by credits and decreased by debits. When a company deposits money into its bank account, the bank's liability to the company increases. That is why the bank shows deposits as credits. When a company writes a cheque or makes an electronic payment, the bank pays out this amount and decreases (debits) its liability to the company.

Helpful Hint

Bank	Company
Credit	Debit
Debit	Credit

Amounts Deducted from a Bank Account (Debits)

Amounts deducted from a bank account include cheques and other payments. A cheque is a written order signed by an employee with signing authority that instructs the bank to pay a specific sum of money to a designated recipient (payee).

How do payments made by a company actually flow through the banking system? When cheques, debit cards, and pre-authorized or other payments occur, they may result in one financial institution owing money to another. For example, if a company (the payor) writes a cheque to a supplier (the payee), the payee deposits the cheque in its own bank account.

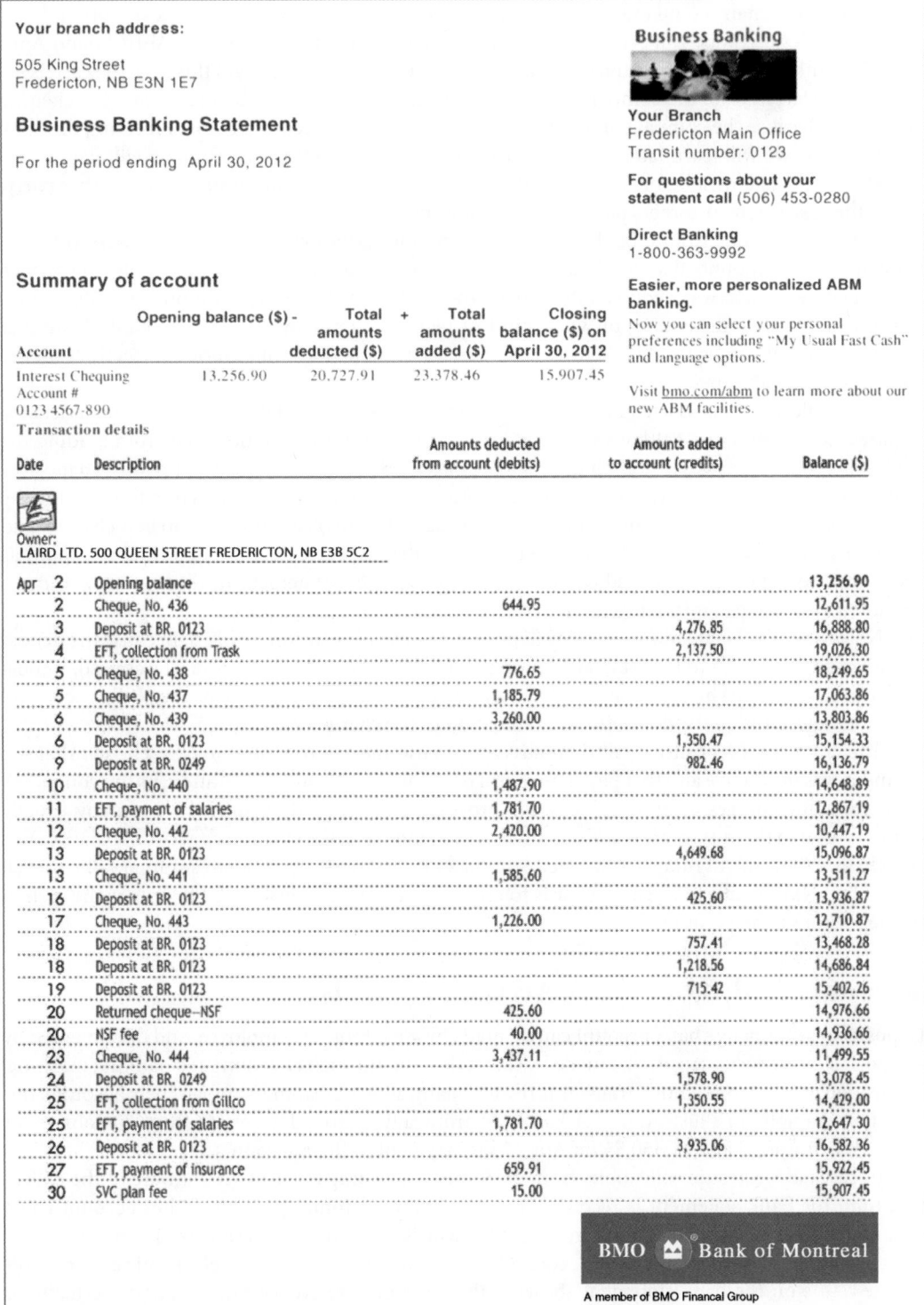

▶ Illustration 7-4

Bank statement

When the cheque is deposited, it is sent to a regional data centre for processing, usually the same day. When the cheque arrives at the centre, it is "presented" to the payor's financial institution, where it is determined whether the cheque will be honoured or returned (for example, for insufficient funds, which we will learn about shortly, or a stop payment order). This process is automated and happens very quickly. In most cases, the cheque will clear the company's bank account before the next day. **Clearing** is the term used when a cheque or deposit is accepted by the bank.

Other disbursements may appear on the bank statement, such as payments using electronic funds transfers. For example, pre-authorized payments relating to loans and insurance paid on a recurring basis are often made electronically. In Illustration 7-4, the notation "EFT, payment of insurance" tells us that on April 27 Laird paid its insurance using electronic funds transfer.

In addition, many companies pay their employees' salaries using a direct deposit option. Laird pays its salaries this way. You can see the notation "EFT, payment of salaries" on April 11 and April 25 in the bank statement in Illustration 7-4. When employee salaries are paid this way, the cash is instantly transferred from the company's bank account to each employee's bank account. No cheques are issued. Because the company initiated the transaction, it can record it before receiving the bank statement. As we will learn later when we discuss deposits, sometimes a company will have to receive the bank statement before recording the transaction because it was initiated by another party; this is the case when customers pay their account electronically.

Other deductions from a bank account can include service charges and fees assessed by the bank and other amounts that are deducted from the depositor's account. For example, the service (SVC) plan fee of $15 was deducted directly by the bank from Laird's account on April 30. Service charges vary widely depending on what kind of plan the company has with its bank. Note that banks do not bill companies for their fees. Rather, the bank deducts this amount directly from the company's bank account.

The bank statement is accompanied by a **debit memorandum (DM)** when additional detail is required about amounts that have been deducted by the bank that are not clear from reading the bank statement. For example, a debit memorandum is used by the bank when a previously deposited customer's cheque bounces (is not honoured) because of insufficient funds. When this occurs, the customer's bank marks the cheque an **NSF (not sufficient funds) cheque**, or **returned cheque**, and it is returned to the depositor's bank. The bank then debits (decreases) the depositor's account as shown by the notation, "Returned cheque—NSF" on the bank statement in Illustration 7-4 in the amount of $425.60 on April 20.

Note that this cheque was previously deposited by the company on April 16. Because the deposit was credited (added) to the bank account on April 16 and the cheque was not honoured, it must be debited (deducted) by the bank (see April 20 transaction). The bank returns the NSF cheque and debit memorandum to the depositor as notification of the charge.

The company (depositor) will then advise the customer who wrote the NSF cheque that the payment was ineffective and that payment is still owed on the account. In addition, as the company's bank generally charges a service charge for processing a returned cheque, the company usually passes this on to the customer by adding the charged amount to the customer's account balance. You can see that the Bank of Montreal charged Laird a $40 NSF fee on April 20. In summary, the overall effect of an NSF cheque to the depositor is to create an account receivable and to reduce the cash in the depositor's bank account.

Amounts Added to a Bank Account (Credits)

Deposits to a company's bank account can be made by an authorized employee, and documented by a deposit slip. Deposits can also be made by direct deposit, through an automated banking machine, or through an electronic funds transfer if the company allows customers to pay their accounts on-line. For example, in Illustration 7-4 Laird electronically collected amounts from customers for $2,137.50 on April 4 and $1,350.55 on April 25 in payment of their accounts.

In cases of electronic collections from customers, the company is often unaware of the collection until the bank statement is received. Why? When a customer pays his or her account using on-line banking or other electronic means, the cash is instantly transferred from the customer's bank account to the company's bank account. The primary evidence of these electronic cash receipts will be a line on the bank statement showing the amount, a reference number, and the name or account number of the person paying. Consequently, electronic receipts such as these are normally recorded directly from the bank statement.

In some cases, companies also earn interest on their bank account, although this is not usual for chequing accounts. No separate notification is given for these amounts either. Other deposits to the bank account sometimes include supporting documentation known as **credit memoranda (CM)**. Credit memoranda are used to identify note collections, for example, and certain other amounts added to the depositor's account.

In summary, **debit memoranda result in debits on the bank's books and credits on the company's books. Credit memoranda result in credits on the bank's books and debits on the company's books.**

RECONCILING THE BANK ACCOUNT

Although the bank and the company keep independent records of the company's chequing account, you might assume that the balances in both sets of records will always agree. In fact, the two balances are seldom the same because many transactions are not recorded at the same time on both records. It is therefore necessary to identify any differences between the bank statement and the company's accounting records whenever the bank statement is received and ensure that the reasons for the differences are acceptable. Reconciling the bank account is the process used to determine whether these differences are acceptable or not.

The lack of agreement between the balances has two causes:

1. **Time lags** that prevent one of the parties from recording the transaction in the same period as the other party
2. **Errors** by either party in recording transactions

Except in electronic banking transactions, time lags occur often. For example, several days may pass between the time a company mails a supplier a cheque and the date the supplier presents the cheque to the bank for payment. Cheques recorded by a company that have not yet cleared (been paid by) the bank are called **outstanding cheques**.

Similarly, when a company uses the bank's night depository to make its deposits, there will be a difference of one day (or more, if holidays intervene) between the time the receipts are recorded by the company and the time they are recorded by the bank. Deposits recorded by the company that have not yet been recorded by the bank are called **deposits in transit**.

Errors can also occur. How often errors occur depends on how effectively the company and bank have implemented internal controls. Bank errors are infrequent. However, either party could accidentally record a $450 cheque as $45 or $540. In addition, the bank might mistakenly charge a cheque to the wrong account if the code is missing or if the cheque cannot be scanned. Direct deposits and electronic funds transfers also depend on the correct account being keyed into the system.

ACCOUNTING MATTERS!   *Management Perspective*

Bank Errors

Bank errors may not occur as frequently as company errors, but they can still happen. Scotiabank's discount brokerage arm accidentally put $171 million of somebody else's money into a Toronto doctor's Scotiabank account. It took four months to find and correct the error. The red-faced bank admitted that many things went wrong—from posting the error to mistakes in reversals. And there are many more stories about banks making mistakes. However, they usually involve misplaced debits and rarely amounts as high as this.

Reconciliation Procedures

To get the most benefit from bank reconciliations, they should be prepared by an employee who has no other responsibilities related to cash. When the control activity of segregation of duties is not followed in preparing the reconciliation, cash embezzlements may go unnoticed. For example, a cashier who prepares the reconciliation can steal cash and hide the theft by misstating amounts on the reconciliation. In this way, the bank account would appear to reconcile with the company records and the theft would not be detected.

In reconciling the bank account, it is customary to reconcile the balance per the bank and the balance per the books to their adjusted (correct) cash balances. Both the books and the bank balance are likely to change as a result of the reconciliation process. The reconciliation is usually divided into two sections: one relating to the bank statement balance and one relating to the book balance. The starting point when preparing the reconciliation is to enter the balance per bank (found on the bank statement) and the balance per books (found in the Cash account in the general ledger) on the reconciliation. Adjustments are then made to each balance so that any unrecorded transactions are accounted for, as shown in Illustration 7-5.

▶ **Illustration 7-5**

Bank reconciliation procedures

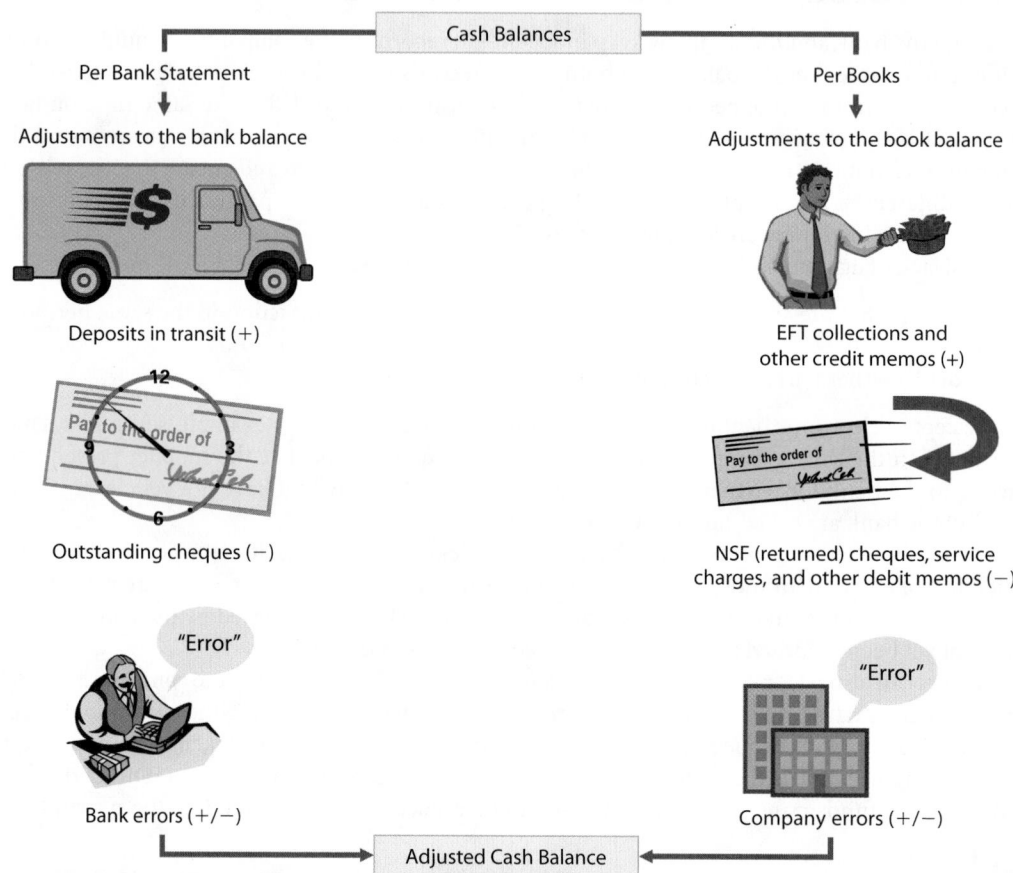

The following steps reveal the major reconciling items that cause the difference between the two balances:

Reconciling Items per Bank.   On the bank side of the reconciliation, the items to reconcile are deposits in transit (amounts added), outstanding cheques (amounts deducted), and bank errors (if any). By adjusting the bank balance for these items, we are bringing that balance up to date.

1. **Deposits in transit (+).** Compare the individual deposits on the bank statement with (1) the deposits in transit from the preceding bank reconciliation and (2) the deposits recorded in the books. Deposits in transit are already recorded on the company's books but have not yet been recorded by the bank because it does not know about them yet. Therefore, they must be added to the balance per bank in the reconciliation process.

   Before determining the deposits in transit for the current period, you must check whether all deposits in transit that are outstanding from a prior period have cleared. For example, assume that Laird Ltd. used a night deposit slot to deposit $2,201.40 on Monday, April 30.

The bank will not receive or record this deposit until Tuesday, May 1. This amount would be treated as a deposit in transit at the end of April and would be added to the balance per bank in the reconciliation process. However, this outstanding deposit will clear the bank in May and will therefore no longer be a deposit in transit at the end of May. As at the end of May, this amount will have been recorded by both the company and the bank. The relationship between deposits in transit, deposits shown on the bank statement, and deposits recorded by the company is shown below:

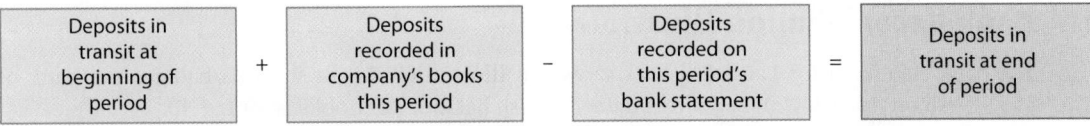

2. **Outstanding cheques (−).** Compare the paid cheques shown on the bank statement or returned with the bank statement with (a) cheques outstanding from the preceding bank reconciliation and (b) cheques issued by the company. Outstanding cheques are already recorded on the company's books but have not yet cleared the bank account. Therefore, they must be deducted from the balance per bank in the reconciliation process.

   Note that an outstanding cheque from a prior period means that the cheque was deducted from the books in the prior period, but not paid by the bank in the same period. If such a cheque was paid by the bank in the current period, the cheque is no longer outstanding and will not be listed as a reconciling item on the reconciliation. If the cheque has still not been presented to the bank for payment, it will continue to be outstanding. The relationship between outstanding cheques and cheques shown on the bank statement and recorded by the company is shown below:

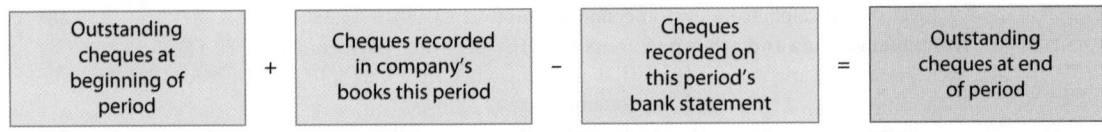

3. **Bank errors (+/−).** Note any errors made by the bank that have been discovered in the previous steps. For example, if the bank processed a deposit of $1,693 as $1,639 in error, the difference of $54 ($1,693 − $1,639) is added to the balance per bank on the bank reconciliation.

   Errors can be made by either party (the company or the bank) and can be in any direction (increases or decreases). Errors made by the bank should be included as reconciling items in determining the adjusted cash balance per bank. Errors made by the company should be included as reconciling items per books, as we will discuss in the next section.

Reconciling Items per Books. Reconciling items on the book side relate to amounts not yet recorded on the company's books and include adjustments from credit memoranda and other deposits (amounts added), debit memoranda and other payments (amounts deducted), and company errors (if any).

1. **Credit memoranda and other deposits (+).** Compare the credit memoranda and other deposits on the bank statement with the company records. Any unrecorded amounts should be added to the balance per books. For example, if the bank statement shows electronic funds transfers from customers paying their accounts on-line, unless they had previously been recorded by the company, these amounts will be added to the balance per books on the bank reconciliation to update the company's records so that they will agree with the bank's records.

2. **Debit memoranda and other payments (−).** Similarly, any unrecorded debit memoranda or other payments should be deducted from the balance per books. For example, if the bank statement shows bank service charges, this amount is deducted from the balance per books on the bank reconciliation to make the company's records agree with the bank's records. Normally, electronic payments will already have been recorded by the company. However, if this has not been the case, then these payments must be deducted from the balance per books on the bank reconciliation to make the company's records agree with the bank's records.

3. **Book errors (+/−).** Note any errors made by the depositor that have been discovered in the previous steps. For example, if a paid cheque written by the company for $1,226 was mistakenly recorded by the company as $1,262, the error of $36 ($1,262 − $1,226) is added to the balance per books. The error of $36 is added to the balance per books because the company reduced the balance per books by $36 too much when it recorded the cheque as $1,262 instead of $1,226. Make sure that you include only errors made by the company, not the bank, as reconciling items in determining the adjusted cash balance per books.

Bank Reconciliation Illustrated

The bank statement for Laird Ltd. was shown in Illustration 7-4. It shows a balance per bank of $15,907.45 on April 30, 2012. On this date, the cash balance per books is $9,161.40.

From the steps described above, the following reconciling items for the bank can be determined:

1. **Deposits in transit (+):** After comparing the deposits recorded in the books with the deposits listed in the bank statement, it was determined that the April 30 deposit of $2,201.40 was not recorded by the bank until May 1. $2,201.40
2. **Outstanding cheques (−):** After comparing the cheques recorded in the books with the cheques listed in the bank statement, it was determined that three cheques were outstanding: No. 445, $3,000.00; No. 446, $1,401.30; and No. 447, $1,502.70.   5,904.00
3. **Bank errors (+/−):** None

Reconciling items per books are as follows:

1. **Credit memoranda and other deposits (+):** Unrecorded receipts on April 4 and 25 determined from the bank statement are as follows:
   Electronic receipts from customers on account: $2,137.50 + $1,350.55 $3,488.05
2. **Debit memoranda and other payments (−):** The electronic payments on April 11, 25, and 27 were previously recorded by the company when they were initiated. Unrecorded charges determined from the bank statement are as follows:
   Returned cheque plus NSF fee on April 20 ($425.60 + $40)   465.60
   Bank service charges on April 30   15.00
3. **Company errors (+):** Cheque No. 443 was correctly written by Laird for $1,226 and was correctly paid by the bank on April 17. However, it was recorded as $1,262 on Laird's books.   36.00

The bank reconciliation follows:

LAIRD LTD.
Bank Reconciliation
April 30, 2012

Cash balance per bank statement		$15,907.45
Add: Deposits in transit		2,201.40
		18,108.85
Less: Outstanding cheques		
No. 445	$3,000.00	
No. 446	1,401.30	
No. 447	1,502.70	5,904.00
Adjusted cash balance per bank		$12,204.85
Cash balance per books		$ 9,161.40
Add: Electronic payments by customers on account		
Trask	$2,137.50	
Gillco	1,350.55	
Error in recording cheque No. 443 ($1,262 − $1,226)	36.00	3,524.05
		12,685.45
Less: Returned (NSF) cheque plus service charge ($425.60 + $40)	$ 465.60	
Bank service charge	15.00	480.60
Adjusted cash balance per books		$12,204.85

Bank Reconciliation Journal Entries

The bank reconciliation shown above is only the first step in the reconciliation process. The reconciliation is not complete until the company books are adjusted to agree with the adjusted (correct) cash balance. Each reconciling item that arises from determining the adjusted cash balance per books must be recorded by the depositor. If these items are not journalized and posted, the Cash account will not show the correct balance.

The adjusting entries for Laird Ltd.'s bank reconciliation on April 30 are as follows:

Electronic Payments on Account. A payment of an account by a customer is recorded in the same way, whether the cash is received through the mail or electronically. The entry is:

Apr. 30	Cash	3,488.05	
	Accounts Receivable—Trask		2,137.50
	Accounts Receivable—Gillco		1,350.55
	(To record electronic collection of accounts)		

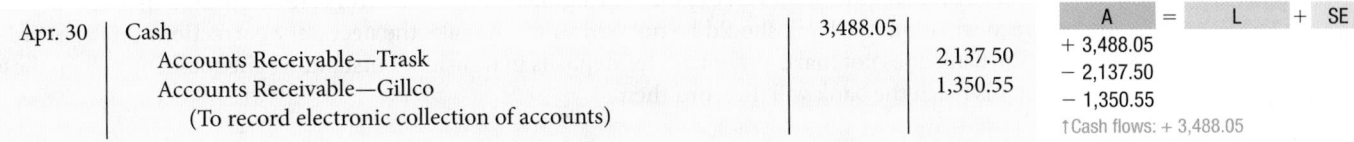

A = L + SE
+ 3,488.05
− 2,137.50
− 1,350.55
↑Cash flows: + 3,488.05

In some cases, the company will have already recorded these transactions. Some companies monitor their bank account on-line daily in order to track changes in their account. Other companies, such as Laird, wait until the bank statement is received to record transactions such as these.

Book Error. An examination of the general journal shows that the incorrectly recorded cheque, No. 443, was a payment on account to a supplier. The correcting entry is:

Apr. 30	Cash	36.00	
	Accounts Payable		36.00
	(To correct error in recording cheque No. 443)		

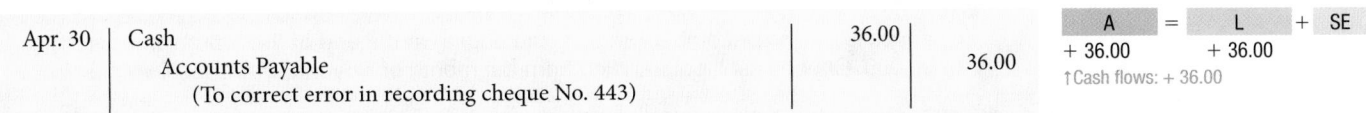

A = L + SE
+ 36.00 + 36.00
↑Cash flows: + 36.00

NSF Cheque. As indicated earlier, a cheque returned for not sufficient funds (NSF) along with the related service charge becomes an account receivable to the depositor. This charge will be passed on to the customer by adding it to the customer's account balance. The entry is:

Apr. 30	Accounts Receivable ($425.60 + $40)	465.60	
	Cash		465.60
	(To re-establish accounts receivable for NSF cheque, and		
	related service charge)		

A = L + SE
+ 465.60
− 465.60
↓Cash flows: − 465.60

Bank Service Charges. Bank service charges are normally debited to the expense account Bank Charges. The entry is:

Apr. 30	Bank Charges Expense	15.00	
	Cash		15.00
	(To record bank service charge)		

A = L + SE
+ 15.00
− 15.00
↓Cash flows: − 15.00

All of the entries above could also be combined into one compound entry. Our presentation assumes that all adjustments are made at the end of the month. In practice, a company may also make journal entries during the month as it receives information from the bank regarding its account, or as the company checks its bank account balances on-line.

After the entries are posted, the Cash account will appear as in the T account that follows. The adjusted cash balance in the ledger should agree with the adjusted cash balance per books in the bank reconciliation shown earlier.

		Cash				
Apr. 30	Bal.	9,161.40	Apr. 30			465.60
30		3,488.05	30			15.00
30		36.00				
Apr. 30	Bal.	12,204.85				

What entries does the bank make? **The bank cannot correct your errors on its books and you cannot correct the bank's errors on your books.** If any bank errors are discovered in preparing the reconciliation, the bank should be notified so it can make the necessary corrections on its records. The bank does not make any entries for deposits in transit or outstanding cheques. Only when these items reach the bank will it record them.

BEFORE YOU GO ON...

▶ Do It! Bank Reconciliation

The Cash account of the Oakville Athletic Association showed a balance of $32,666 on December 31. The bank statement as at that date showed a balance of $36,168. After comparing the bank statement with the company records, the following information was determined.

1. Deposits in transit as at December 31 amounted to $7,286.

2. Cheques issued in December but still outstanding at the end of the month amounted to $6,000. Cheques still outstanding from the month of November totalled $560.

3. The bank made a mistake in recording a U.S. dollar payment received from a customer, overstating the Canadian funds received by $56.

4. Electronic receipts from customers in payment of their accounts totalled $4,699. These receipts have not yet been recorded by the company.

5. The company made an error in recording a customer's deposit in payment of its account. The company recorded the collection of the account as $209, when it should have been $290. The bank correctly recorded the deposit as $290.

6. The bank returned an NSF cheque in the amount of $478 that Oakville had deposited on December 20. The cheque was a payment on a customer's account.

7. The bank debited Oakville's account for bank service charges of $130. Of this amount, $45 was for processing the NSF cheque (see item 6 above) and $85 was for the rental of a safety deposit box.

Prepare a bank reconciliation and any required journal entries for Oakville at December 31.

Action Plan

- Prepare the bank reconciliation in two sections: one for the bank and one for the company.
- Determine which reconciling items each side knows about and adjust the other side accordingly.
- Be careful when you determine the direction of an error correction.
- Prepare journal entries only for the book side, not the bank side.
- The adjusted cash balances must agree with each other when complete, and with the general ledger account after the journal entries are posted.

Solution

OAKVILLE ATHLETIC ASSOCIATION
Bank Reconciliation
December 31

Cash balance per bank statement		$36,168
Add: Deposits in transit		7,286
		43,454
Less: Outstanding cheques ($6,000 + $560)	$6,560	
Error correction relating to U.S. dollar receipts	56	6,616
Adjusted cash balance per bank		$36,838
Cash balance per books		$32,666
Add: Electronic receipts from customers on account	$4,699	
Deposit error correction ($290 − $209)	81	4,780
		37,446
Less: NSF cheque ($478 + $45)	$ 523	
Bank service charges	85	608
Adjusted cash balance per books		$36,838

Dec. 31	Cash	4,699	
	Accounts Receivable		4,699
	(To record electronic receipts on account)		
31	Cash ($290 − $209)	81	
	Accounts Receivable		81
	(To correct deposit error)		
31	Accounts Receivable ($478 + $45)	523	
	Cash		523
	(To re-establish accounts receivable for NSF cheque and related service charge)		
31	Bank Charges Expense	85	
	Cash		85
	(To record bank service charges)		

Check:

Cash

Dec. 31	Bal.	32,666		Dec. 31		523
31		4,699		31		85
31		81				
Dec. 31	Bal.	36,838				

the navigator

Reporting and Managing Cash

Corporate management must perform a difficult balancing act to properly manage cash. On one hand, it is critical to ensure that enough cash is available to pay bills as they come due, to buy goods, and to take advantage of opportunities as they present themselves. On the other hand, cash itself is an unproductive asset unless it is invested in other assets (e.g., investments; inventory; and property, plant, and equipment). Too much cash on hand may indicate that management is not maximizing its return on assets. So it is critical that management know at all times exactly how much cash there is, and how much cash is needed to fund future plans. In the next two sections, we will look at how cash is reported and will identify ways to manage and monitor cash.

STUDY OBJECTIVE 4

Explain the reporting and management of cash.

REPORTING CASH

Cash is reported in two different financial statements: the statement of financial position and the statement of cash flows. The statement of financial position reports the amount of cash available at a specific point in time. The statement of cash flows shows the sources and uses of cash during a period of time. These two statements are linked because the ending cash amount reported on the statement of cash flows agrees with the cash amount reported on the statement of financial position. The statement of cash flows was introduced in Chapter 1 and will be discussed in detail in Chapter 13.

Because it is the most liquid asset owned by a company, cash is listed first in the current assets section of the statement of financial position, although the reverse order of liquidity can be used under IFRS. Many companies combine cash with cash equivalents. **Cash equivalents** are short-term, highly liquid (easily sold) investments that are subject to an insignificant risk of changes in value. Generally, only debt investments due within three months qualify by this definition.

Some companies may be in a cash deficit or overdraft position at year end. Bank overdrafts occur when a cheque is written for more than the amount in the bank account. This, in effect, is a short-term loan from the bank. Most companies have overdraft protection up to a certain amount with their banks. In an overdraft situation, the cash account will show a credit balance in the general ledger and is reported as a current liability called **bank indebtedness**. Bank overdrafts that are repayable on demand and are an integral part of a company's cash management practices are also included in (deducted from) cash and cash equivalents.

In addition, rather than having term loans with fixed payment dates, some companies have a credit facility (operating line of credit) with their bank. This is similar to having a chequing account with an ability to have a very large overdraft. The bank calculates interest on the outstanding balance of the facility and the company can draw or borrow up to the limit of the facility or pay it down whenever it chooses to. Because there is no fixed date to repay the line, it is considered a cash equivalent like a bank overdraft.

A joint financial statement presentation project currently under way by the International Accounting Standards Board and the Financial Accounting Standards Board to improve the presentation of information in the financial statements proposes that cash equivalents *not* be combined with cash in the statement of financial position in future, but rather reported with other short-term investments. While no decision has been reached to date on this issue, this is a change that we may very well see in the near future.

A company may have cash that is not available for general use because it is restricted for a special purpose. For example, landfill companies are often required to maintain a fund of restricted cash to ensure that they will have adequate resources to cover closing and cleanup costs at the end of a landfill site's useful life. Cash that has a restricted use should be reported separately on the statement of financial position as **restricted cash**. If the restricted cash is expected to be used within the next year, the amount should be reported as a current asset. When this is not the case, the restricted funds should be reported as a non-current asset.

In making loans to depositors, banks commonly require borrowers to maintain minimum cash balances. These minimum balances, called **compensating balances**, provide the bank with support for the loans. They are a form of restriction on the use of cash. Similar to other restricted cash, compensating balances are reported as a non-current asset.

Illustration 7-6 shows how Tim Hortons presents restricted cash.

▶ **Illustration 7-6**
Presentation of cash

TIM HORTONS INC.
Statement of Financial Position (partial)
January 2, 2011
(in thousands)

Current assets	
Cash and cash equivalents	$574,354
Restricted cash and cash equivalents	67,110

In the notes to its financial statement, Tim Hortons states that restricted cash and cash equivalents relate to the company's Tim Card® cash card program. This amount represents cash loaded on the cards by customers, less any redemptions. The balance is restricted because it cannot be used for any purpose other than to settle obligations under the cash card program.

MANAGING CASH

Many companies struggle, not because they cannot generate sales, but because they cannot manage their cash. A real-life example of this is a clothing manufacturing company owned by Sharon McCollick. McCollick gave up a stable, high-paying marketing job to start her own company. Soon she had more clothing orders than she could fill. Yet she found herself on the brink of financial disaster: her company could generate sales, but it was not collecting cash fast enough to support its operations. To survive, a business must have cash.

To understand cash management, consider the operating cycle of Sharon McCollick's clothing manufacturing company. First, it purchases cloth. Let's assume that it purchases the cloth on credit provided by the supplier, so the company owes its supplier money. Next, employees make the cloth into clothing. Now the company also owes its employees money. Then, it sells the clothing to retailers, on credit. McCollick's company will have no money to pay suppliers or employees until it collects money from its customers.

Ensuring that a company has sufficient cash to meet its needs is one of the greatest challenges its faces as it deals with the ebb and flow of cash. Any company can improve its chances of having adequate cash by following basic principles of cash management:

1. **Increase the speed of collection on receivables.** Money owed to Sharon McCollick by her customers is money that she needs as soon as possible. The faster customers pay her, the faster she can use those funds. Thus, rather than have an average collection period of 30 days, she may want an average collection period of 20 days. However, any attempt to force her customers to pay earlier must be carefully weighed against the possibility that she may anger or alienate them. Perhaps her competitors are willing to provide a 30-day grace period. As noted in Chapter 5, a common way to encourage customers to pay more quickly is to offer cash discounts for early payments under such terms as 2/10, n/30.

2. **Keep inventory levels low.** Maintaining a large inventory of cloth and finished clothing is costly. It ties up large amounts of cash to carry the inventory, as well as warehouse space. In addition, inventory can quickly become obsolete if it is held for a long period. Many companies routinely use techniques to reduce their inventory on hand, thus conserving their cash. Of course, if McCollick has inadequate inventory, she will lose sales. The proper level of inventory is an important decision, as we learned in Chapter 6.

3. **Delay payment of liabilities.** By keeping track of when bills are due, McCollick's company can avoid paying bills too early. Let's say her supplier allows 30 days for payment. If she pays in 10 days, she has lost the use of cash for 20 days. Therefore, she should use the full payment period, but she should not "stretch" payment past the point that could damage her credit rating (and future borrowing ability).

4. **Plan the timing of major expenditures.** To maintain operations or to grow, all companies must make major expenditures that normally require some form of outside financing. In order to increase the likelihood of obtaining outside financing, McCollick should carefully consider the timing of major expenditures in light of her company's operating cycle. If at all possible, the expenditure should be made when the firm normally has excess cash—usually during the off-season when inventory is low.

5. **Invest idle cash.** Cash on hand earns nothing. Excess cash should be invested, even if it is only overnight. Many businesses, such as McCollick's clothing company, are seasonal. During her slow season, if she has excess cash, she should invest it. To avoid an immediate cash crisis, however, it is very important that these investments be liquid and risk-free. A liquid investment has a market in which someone is always willing to buy or sell the investment. A risk-free investment means there is no concern that the party will default on its promise to pay its principal and interest.

For example, using excess cash to purchase shares in a small company because you heard that it was probably going to increase in value in the near term is inappropriate. First, the shares of small companies are often illiquid. Second, if the shares suddenly decrease in value, you might be forced to sell them at a loss in order to pay your bills as they come due.

A common liquid, risk-free investment (albeit at a lower rate of interest) is treasury bills or money-market funds.

6. **Prepare a cash budget.** A cash budget is a critical tool, showing anticipated cash flows over a one- or two-year period. It can show when additional financing will be necessary well before the actual need arises. Conversely, it can indicate when excess cash will be available for the repayment of debts, for investments, or for other purposes.

Because cash is so vital to a company, applying these principles of cash management to plan the company's cash needs is essential for any business. The six principles of cash management are summarized in Illustration 7-7.

Illustration 7-7

Principles of cash management

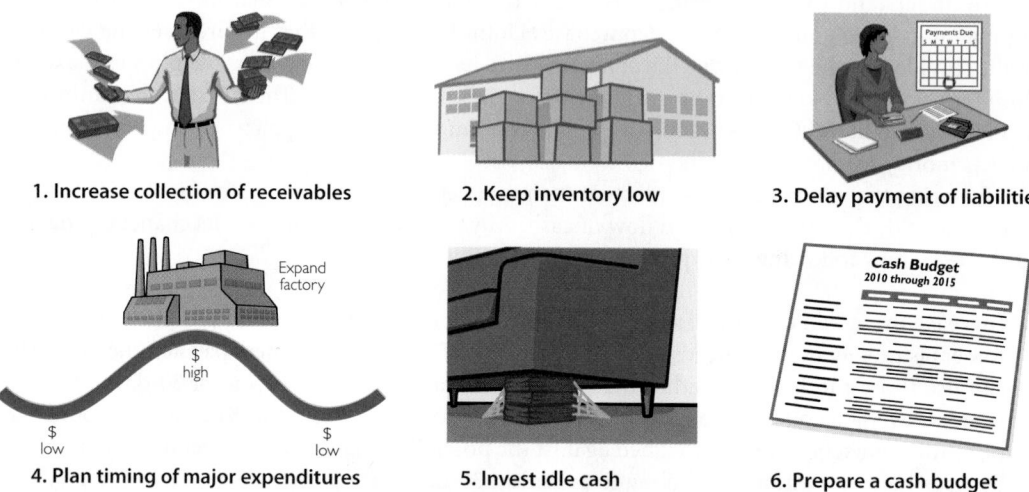

1. **Increase collection of receivables**   2. **Keep inventory low**   3. **Delay payment of liabilities**

4. **Plan timing of major expenditures**   5. **Invest idle cash**   6. **Prepare a cash budget**

▄ Keeping an Eye on Cash

Because cash is so vital to a company, planning the company's cash needs is a key business activity that can be accomplished by preparing a cash budget. A cash budget generally contains three sections—cash receipts, cash disbursements, and financing—and the beginning and ending cash balances, as shown below.

HAYES LIMITED Cash Budget Year Ended December 31, 2012				
	Quarter			
	1	2	3	4
Beginning cash balance	$ 38,000	$ 25,500	$ 15,000	$ 15,000
Add: Cash receipts				
Collections from customers	168,000	198,000	228,000	258,000
Sale of securities	2,000	0	0	0
Total receipts	170,000	198,000	228,000	258,000
Total available cash	208,000	223,500	243,000	273,000
Less: Cash disbursements				
Inventory	23,200	27,200	31,200	35,200
Salaries	62,000	72,000	82,000	92,000
Selling and administrative expenses (excluding depreciation)	94,300	99,300	104,300	109,300
Purchase of truck	0	30,000	0	0
Income tax expense	3,000	3,000	3,000	3,000
Interest expense	0	0	1,400	1,000
Total disbursements	182,500	231,500	221,900	240,500

(continued)

Excess (deficiency) of available cash over disbursements	25,500	(8,000)	21,100	32,500
Financing				
Add: Borrowings	0	23,000	0	0
Less: Repayments	0	0	6,100	16,900
Ending cash balance	$ 25,500	$ 15,000	$ 15,000	$ 15,600

The cash receipts section includes expected receipts from the company's principal source(s) of cash, such as cash sales and collections from customers on credit sales. This section also shows anticipated receipts of interest and dividends, and proceeds from planned sales of investments; property, plant, and equipment; and the company's shares.

The cash disbursements section shows expected payments for inventory, labour, and selling and administrative expenses. It also includes projected payments for income tax; dividends; investments; and property, plant, and equipment. Note that it does not include depreciation since depreciation expense does not use cash.

The financing section shows expected borrowings and repayments of borrowed funds plus interest. Financing is needed when there is a cash deficiency or when the cash balance is less than management's minimum required balance. Companies must prepare multi-period cash budgets in sequence because the ending cash balance of one period becomes the beginning cash balance for the next period.

Notice how Hayes's budget indicates that the company will need $23,000 of financing in the second quarter to maintain a minimum cash balance of $15,000. Since there is an excess of available cash over disbursements at the end of the third and fourth quarters, Hayes will repay a portion ($6,100) of the borrowing in the third quarter and the remainder ($16,900) in the fourth quarter.

BEFORE YOU GO ON...

▶ Do It! Cash Budget

Georgian Bay Resorts Limited wants to maintain a minimum monthly cash balance of $15,000. At the beginning of March, the cash balance is $16,500, expected cash receipts for March are $210,000, and cash disbursements are expected to be $220,000. How much cash, if any, must the company borrow to maintain the desired minimum monthly balance?

Action Plan

- Prepare a cash budget by first listing the cash balance at the beginning of the period.
- Add to the opening cash balance the amount of expected cash receipts for the period to determine total available cash.
- Subtract disbursements to determine excess or deficiency of cash.
- Compare the excess or deficiency with the desired minimum cash to determine borrowing needs.

Solution

Beginning cash balance	$ 16,500
Add: Cash receipts for March	210,000
Total available cash	226,500
Less: Cash disbursements for March	220,000
Excess of available cash over cash disbursements	6,500
Financing	
Add: Borrowings	8,500
Ending cash balance	$ 15,000

To maintain the desired minimum cash balance of $15,000, Georgian Bay Resorts must borrow $8,500 of cash.

DECISION TOOLKIT

Decision Checkpoints	 Info Needed for Decision	 Tools to Use for Decision	 How to Evaluate Results
Is all of the company's cash available for general use?	Statement of financial position and notes to financial statements	Does the company report any cash as being restricted?	A restriction on the use of cash limits management's ability to use those resources for general obligations. This should be considered when assessing liquidity.
Is the company able to manage its cash effectively?	Terms of collection/ payment for receivables and payables, inventory turnover rate, length of operating cycle, and cash budget (typically available only to management)	Assess the collection period, inventory on hand, when bills are paid, and whether cash discounts are available and taken. A cash budget can determine when additional cash is needed or is available for investment.	If receivables and inventory are not being sold and collected on a timely basis, liquidity is affected. Assess the cash budget for the reasonableness of its projections.

Comparing
IFRS and ASPE

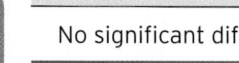

Key Differences	International Financial Reporting Standards (IFRS)	Accounting Standards for Private Enterprises (ASPE)
No significant differences.		

Protecting Yourself from Identity Theft

In April 2011, potentially millions of people were affected by a security breach at Epsilon, the largest distributor of permission-based e-mails. The company produces over 40 billion marketing e-mails on behalf of 2,500 different businesses, including banks, retailers, and even the company that offers the SAT reasoning test for post-secondary admission. More than 2% of Epsilon's customers, including Canadians, had their names and e-mail addresses stolen.

Security breaches like these can result in "identity theft." Personal information such as your name, date of birth, address, credit card number, social insurance number, and other identification can be used to steal money from your existing accounts, open new financial accounts, make purchases, or even obtain employment.

Are you a victim? The signs can be many, but indications that your identity is being used include the following:

- A creditor informs you that an application for credit was received with your name and address, which you did not apply for.
- Telephone calls or letters state that you have been approved or denied credit by a creditor that you never applied to.
- You receive credit card statements or other bills in your name, which you did not apply for.
- You no longer receive credit card statements or you notice that not all of your mail is delivered.
- A collection agency informs you that it is collecting for a defaulted account established with your identity, yet you never opened the account.

The identity thieves are not likely to go away, so what can you do to protect yourself? One obvious measure is to remember your personal identification number or password. If you must write it down, do not carry it on a piece of paper hidden in your purse or wallet that could be easily found. Also, many of the common-sense controls discussed in this chapter can be implemented in your personal life.

Up-to-date tips on preventing identity theft and protecting personal privacy can be found on the website of the Canadian Anti-Fraud Centre (Phonebusters) and the Office of the Privacy Commissioner of Canada.

Some Facts

- In 2010, there were 71.3 million credit cards in circulation in Canada, generating a net retail volume of $279.8 billion at 1.2 million merchant outlets. According to the RCMP, total credit card fraud amounted to $358 million in 2009. The biggest losses were due to counterfeiting ($159 million) and fraudulent e-commerce, telephone, and mail purchases ($140 million).
- You can protect yourself from on-line identity theft by restricting who sees your personal information. Scam artists often use friends' lists to reach potential victims because spam e-mails from friends are often opened and answered.
- Protecting customer information is just one of many internal controls that companies implement. In publicly traded companies, chief executive officers and chief financial officers must sign certifications stating that internal controls are effective. Therefore, management teams must establish and maintain systems of internal controls to help protect a company from both internal and external thieves.

What Do You Think?

More and more personal business transactions are being completed by Internet, including bill payments, travel reservations, and on-line purchasing. Do you feel there are sufficient internal controls to protect any information you provide via the Internet from identity theft?

YES—There are additional security checks such as personal identification numbers built into these services.

NO—Even the best security system does not detect every kind of intruder.

Sources: Royal Canadian Mounted Police, "Credit Card Fraud," www.rcmp-grc.gc.ca/scams-fraudes/cc-fraud-fraude-eng.htm, accessed March 9, 2011. Canadian Bankers Association, "Credit Cards: Statistics and Facts," www.cba.ca/contents/files/statistics/stat_faststat_2009_en.pdf, accessed March 9, 2011. "ID Theft Down 28 Percent in US in 2010: Survey," *National Post*, February 9, 2011. Canadian Anti-Fraud Centre website, www.antifraudcentre-centreantifraude.ca, accessed March 9, 2011. "For Fraudsters, Online Networking Isn't Social," *Globe and Mail*, March 22, 2011, p. FP4. Gillian Shaw, "Massive Internet Security Breach Spills Over to Affect Canadians," *Vancouver Sun*, April 5, 2011, p. D2.

Summary of Study Objectives

1. **Explain the activities that help achieve internal control and prevent fraud.** Fraud is an intentional act to misappropriate assets or misstate financial statements that can be prevented through the use of internal controls. Internal control systems have the following components: the control environment, risk assessment, control activities, information and communication, and monitoring. Control activities include the authorization of transactions and activities, segregation of duties, documentation, physical controls, independent performance checks, and human resource controls.

2. **Apply control activities to cash receipts and payments.** Control activities over cash receipts include (a) designating only personnel such as cashiers to handle cash; (b) assigning the duties of receiving cash, recording cash, and having custody of cash to different individuals; (c) obtaining remittance advices for mail receipts, cash register tapes for over-the-counter receipts, and deposit slips or confirmations for bank deposits; (d) using company safes and bank vaults to store cash, with access limited to authorized personnel, and using cash registers in executing over-the-counter receipts; (e) depositing all cash intact daily in the bank account or using EFT; (f) making independent daily counts of register receipts and daily comparisons of total receipts with total deposits; and (g) conducting background checks, bonding personnel who handle cash, and requiring employees to take vacations.

   Control activities over cash payments include (a) making all payments by cheque or by EFT; (b) having only specified individuals authorized to sign cheques; (c) assigning to different individuals the duties of approving items for payment, paying the items, and recording the payments; (d) using prenumbered cheques and accounting for all cheques; (e) storing each cheque in a safe or vault with access restricted to authorized personnel, and using electronic methods to print amounts on cheques; (f) comparing each cheque or EFT with the approved invoice before initiating payment, and making monthly reconciliations of bank and book balances; and (g) conducting background checks, bonding personnel who handle cash, and requiring employees to take vacations.

3. **Prepare a bank reconciliation.** In reconciling the bank account, it is customary to reconcile the balance per books and the balance per bank to their adjusted balances. Reconciling items for the bank include deposits in transit, outstanding cheques, and any errors made by the bank. Reconciling items for the books include unrecorded amounts added to or deducted from the bank account and any errors made by the company. Adjusting entries must be made for all items required to reconcile the balance per books to the adjusted cash balance.

4. **Explain the reporting and management of cash.** Cash is usually listed first in the current assets section of the statement of financial position. Cash restricted for a special purpose is reported separately as a current asset or as a non-current asset, depending on when the cash is expected to be used. Compensating balances are a form of restriction on the use of cash and are reported as a non-current asset.

   The six principles of cash management are to (a) accelerate the collection of receivables, (b) keep inventory levels low, (c) delay the payment of liabilities, (d) plan the timing of major expenditures, (e) invest idle cash, and (f) prepare a cash budget.

Glossary

Cash Resources that consist of coins, currency, cheques, money orders, debit card slips, and bank credit card slips that are acceptable at face value on deposit in a bank or similar institution. (p. 362)

Cash equivalents Short-term, highly liquid investments that can be easily sold, net of any bank overdrafts repayable on demand. (p. 376)

Compensating balance A minimum cash balance required by a bank in support of a bank loan. (p. 376)

Credit memoranda (CM) Supporting documentation for increases (additions) that appear on a bank statement, such as maturing loans. (p. 369)

Debit memoranda (DM) Supporting documentation for charges (deductions) that appear on a bank statement, such as NSF cheques. (p. 368)

Deposits in transit Amounts deposited and recorded by the depositor that have not yet been recorded by the bank. (p. 369)

Electronic funds transfer (EFT) The system of transferring money electronically from one bank account directly to another without any paper money changing hands. (p. 364)

Fraud An intentional act to misappropriate (steal) assets or misstate financial statements. (p. 354)

NSF (not sufficient funds) cheque (also known as a returned cheque) A cheque that is not paid by a bank, because there are insufficient funds in the bank account of the customer who wrote the cheque. (p. 368)

Outstanding cheques Cheques issued and recorded by a company that have not yet been paid (cleared) by the bank. (p. 369)

Restricted cash Cash that is not available for general use, but instead is restricted for a particular purpose. (p. 376)

DECISION TOOLKIT–A SUMMARY

Decision Checkpoints	Info Needed for Decision	Tools to Use for Decision	How to Evaluate Results
Are the company's financial statements supported by adequate internal controls?	Auditor's report, statement of management responsibility, management discussion and analysis	Control activities include (1) authorizing transactions and activities, (2) segregating duties, (3) documenting transactions, (4) employing physical controls, (5) independently checking performance, and (6) applying human resource controls.	If there is any indication that these or other controls are lacking, the financial statements could contain errors.
Is all of the company's cash available for general use?	Statement of financial position and notes to financial statements	Does the company report any cash as being restricted?	A restriction on the use of cash limits management's ability to use those resources for general obligations. This should be considered when assessing liquidity.
Is the company able to manage its cash effectively?	Terms of collection/payment for receivables and payables, inventory turnover rate, length of operating cycle, and cash budget (typically available only to management)	Assess the collection period, inventory on hand, when bills are paid, and whether cash discounts are available and taken. A cash budget can determine when additional cash is needed or is available for investment.	If receivables and inventory are not being sold and collected on a timely basis, liquidity is affected. Assess the cash budget for the reasonableness of its projections.

USING THE DECISION TOOLKIT

Sparks Basketball (SB) is a not-for-profit organization whose main purpose is to promote healthy living through sports activity. Its members are basketball associations throughout the province, for which SB provides a variety of services. These services include insurance coverage, the organization of provincial tournaments, and discounts from sponsor organizations. It is a volunteer organization with an independent board of directors, and one paid position—that of executive director. While the executive director was on parental leave, this position was filled by SB's vice-president of finance, John Stevens.

Unfortunately, some financial irregularities occurred while Mr. Stevens was acting as executive director. As the acting executive director, Mr. Stevens was responsible for paying invoices, making deposits, signing cheques along with SB's president, completing the bank reconciliation, and preparing financial statements for the annual general meeting.

An irregularity arose when it was discovered that the president's signature had been forged on several cheques. It was also determined that Mr. Stevens handled all deposits and cash payments by himself for a national basketball tournament hosted by SB. He had promised to have an independent treasurer for the tournament but did not get one. He also coached a basketball team in a nearby city, and had full access to the team's bank account. During this time, to save on bank fees, Mr. Stevens had also stopped having the bank return SB's cancelled cheques.

A forensic accountant was brought in to investigate further. He discovered many problems. The financial records were a mess, and there was almost no paper trail for many of the expenditures that were made. There were instances of "double dipping"—where one individual was reimbursed several times for the same expense claim. There were also several cheques made out to the team coached by Mr. Stevens. There was even a cheque where the payee's name had been scratched out and Mrs. Stevens' name was inserted.

Instructions
(a) Identify the main weakness in control activities at Sparks Basketball.
(b) Discuss what steps should be taken to ensure that this situation does not happen again.
(c) Discuss the trade-off between implementing an extensive internal control system and the cost of having such a system for a volunteer organization that has limited funds.

(continued)

Solution

(a) The main control weakness at SB was the lack of segregation of duties. While the executive director was on parental leave, one person was responsible for all financial matters. There was also no review of Mr. Stevens' work, enabling him to make fraudulent transactions without anyone knowing about them.

(b) SB should require proper segregation of duties. Although it is often difficult to have proper segregation of duties in a not-for-profit organization such as this, at least two people should be involved in all financial transactions. SB should require monthly bank reconciliations to be prepared by someone other than the executive director. The cancelled cheques should be returned each month so that they can be reviewed as well. In addition, independent checks of performance could be done by having someone from the board of directors review transactions and financial statements regularly.

(c) Implementation of extensive control systems can be expensive. Not-for-profit organizations must carefully choose what control measures are most important for their specific needs. However, the value of some control activities, such as segregation of duties, often offsets the cost, as it would have for SB. In addition, the organization should use as many free controls as it can. Examples include proper screening of possible volunteers and employees, written policies for how transactions should be processed, and a requirement that employees and volunteers sign a formal statement of ethical guidelines.

the navigator

Comprehensive Do It!

The Winnipeg Arts Society reports the following condensed information from its general ledger Cash account and bank statement at June 30:

Cash					
June	1	Bal.	34,080		
June deposits			34,000	June cheques written	39,520
June	30	Bal.	28,560		

WINNIPEG ARTS SOCIETY
Bank Statement
June 30

	Amounts Deducted (Debits)	Amounts Added (Credits)	Balance
Opening balance, June 1			35,380
Deposits		30,496	65,876
Cheques cleared	36,200		29,676
EFT, insurance payment	1,000		28,676
NSF cheque ($310 + $40 service charge)	350		28,326
Service charge	24		28,302
EFT, collection from Zukata		70	28,372

Additional information:

1. There was a deposit in transit of $1,200 at May 30, the preceding month, that cleared the bank in June.

2. There were $1,500 of outstanding cheques at the end of May.

3. The EFT payment for insurance is a pre-authorized monthly payment, which has already been recorded.

4. The NSF cheque was for $310, from Massif Corp., a customer, in payment of its account. The bank charged a $40 processing fee.

5. The EFT collection of $70 was incorrectly deposited by the bank to the society's account. It should have been deposited to the Winnipeg Arts Council account, a different organization with a similar name.

Instructions

(a) Prepare a bank reconciliation at June 30.

(b) Prepare the entries required by the reconciliation.

Action Plan

- To determine the deposits in transit at the end of June, compare the deposits on the bank statement (adjusted for any deposits in transit at the end of May) with the deposits recorded in the books in June. Recall the formula that deposits in transit at the beginning of the period + deposits recorded in the company's books this period − deposits recorded on this period's bank statement = deposits in transit at end of period.
- To determine the outstanding cheques at the end of June, compare the cheques that cleared the bank statement (adjusted for any cheques outstanding at the end of May) with the cheques recorded in the books in June. Recall the formula that outstanding cheques at the beginning of the period + cheques recorded in the company's books this period − cheques recorded on this period's bank statement = outstanding cheques at end of period.
- Identify any items recorded by the bank but not by the company as reconciling items per books (except for bank errors).
- Notify the bank of any bank errors. You cannot correct the bank errors on your own company's books.
- All the journal entries should be based on the reconciling items per books.
- After posting the reconciling items, make sure the Cash ledger account balance agrees with the adjusted cash balance per books.

Solution to Comprehensive Do It!

(a)

WINNIPEG ARTS SOCIETY
Bank Reconciliation
June 30

Cash balance per bank statement		$28,372
Add: Deposits in transit ($1,200 + $34,000 − $30,496)		4,704
		33,076
Less: Outstanding cheques ($1,500 + $39,520 − $36,200)	$4,820	
Bank deposit error	70	4,890
Adjusted cash balance per bank		$28,186
Cash balance per books		$28,560
Less: NSF cheque ($310 + $40)	$ 350	
Bank service charge	24	374
Adjusted cash balance per books		$28,186

(b)

June 30	Accounts Receivable		350	
	Cash			350
	(To re-establish accounts receivable for Massif Corp. for NSF cheque and related service charge)			
30	Bank Charges Expense		24	
	Cash			24
	(To record bank service charges)			

Check:

Cash

June 30	Bal.	28,560	June 30		350
			30		24
June 30	Bal.	28,186			

the navigator

Self-Test, Brief Exercises, Exercises, Problems—Set A, and many more components are available for practice in WileyPLUS.

Self-Test Questions

Answers are at the end of the chapter.

(SO 1)   1. Which of the following is not one of the five primary components of internal control?
   (a) Control environment
   (b) Size of business
   (c) Risk assessment
   (d) Control activities

(SO 1)   2. Control activities do not include:
   (a) authorization of transactions and activities
   (b) documentation
   (c) cost-benefit constraints
   (d) independent checks of performance

(SO 2)   3. Which of the following items in a cash drawer at November 30 is not cash?
   (a) Debit card slips from sales to customers
   (b) Unsubmitted bank credit card slips from sales to customers
   (c) A customer cheque dated December 1
   (d) A customer cheque dated November 28

(SO 2)   4. Permitting only designated personnel, such as cashiers, to handle cash receipts is an application of which of the following control activities?
   (a) Segregation of duties
   (b) Authorization of transactions and activities
   (c) Independent checks of performance
   (d) Human resource controls

(SO 2)   5. The use of prenumbered cheques in disbursing cash is an example of which of the following control activities?
   (a) Authorization of transactions and activities
   (b) Segregation of duties
   (c) Physical controls
   (d) Documentation

(SO 3)   6. Davis Corporation had cheques outstanding totalling $5,400 on its June bank reconciliation. In July, Davis Corporation issued cheques totalling $38,900. The July bank statement shows that $26,300 in cheques cleared the bank in July.

What is the amount of outstanding cheques on Davis's July bank reconciliation?
   (a) $5,400
   (b) $7,200
   (c) $12,600
   (d) $18,000

(SO 3)   7. Terriault Ltée reports an ending cash balance per books of $4,100 at the end of the month and $5,000 on its bank statement. Reconciling items include deposits in transit of $2,500, outstanding cheques of $3,500, and service charges of $100. What is the company's adjusted cash balance?
   (a) $3,900
   (b) $4,000
   (c) $4,100
   (d) $5,000

(SO 3)   8. Which of the following items on a bank reconciliation would require an adjusting entry on the company's books?
   (a) An error by the bank
   (b) Outstanding cheques
   (c) A bank service charge
   (d) A deposit in transit

(SO 4)   9. Which statement correctly describes the reporting of cash?
   (a) Restricted cash is listed as the first current asset because it cannot be spent immediately
   (b) Restricted cash funds can be combined with cash
   (c) Cash is listed as the most liquid asset in the current assets section
   (d) Compensating balances are reported as a current liability

(SO 4)   10. The principles of cash management do not include:
   (a) accelerating the collection of receivables
   (b) accelerating the payment of liabilities
   (c) keeping inventory low
   (d) investing idle cash

Questions

(SO 1)   1. Explain how the certification of financial statements by a company's CEO and CFO helps prevent fraud.

(SO 1)   2. Identify and describe the five primary components of a good internal control system.

(SO 1)   3. Identify the six control activities that apply to most companies.

(SO 1)   4. How do documentation procedures contribute to good internal control?

(SO 1) 5. Matt Tau is questioning the need for independent checks of performance if the company also segregates duties. What do you think about this?

(SO 1) 6. When faced with labour shortages and high staff turnover, most retail stores do not bother with criminal record checks when hiring employees. Explain what internal control activity is missing from this practice and what kind of problems this could result in.

(SO 1) 7. Kim is trying to design internal control activities so that there is no possibility of errors or theft. Explain to Kim why this may be impractical, and even impossible.

(SO 2) 8. Explain how electronic funds transfers can result in better internal control.

(SO 2) 9. In the corner grocery store, all the clerks make change out of the same cash register drawer. Is this a violation of an internal control activity? Explain.

(SO 2) 10. Dent Department Stores Ltd. has just installed new electronic cash registers with scanners in its stores. How do these cash registers improve control activities over cash receipts?

(SO 2) 11. "To have maximum control over cash payments, all payments should be made by cheque." Is this true? Explain.

(SO 2) 12. At a dental office, the receptionist schedules appointments and can cancel them. She also collects payment from patients (about 10% of them pay cash) and maintains all of the accounting records for the practice. Comment on whether these arrangements could give rise to fraud.

(SO 2) 13. Watch Central Ltd. is a small retail store. One of its employees, Wanda, is responsible for ordering the merchandise, receiving the goods, and paying for the goods. Describe the various ways Wanda could commit a fraud with this arrangement.

(SO 2, 3) 14. Who should be responsible for preparing a bank reconciliation? Why?

(SO 3) 15. "The use of a bank contributes significantly to good internal control over cash." Is this true? Explain.

(SO 3) 16. Paul Pascal is confused about the lack of agreement between the cash balance per books and the balance per bank. Explain the possible causes for the lack of agreement to Paul, and give an example of each cause.

(SO 3) 17. Kari Mora asks for your help concerning an NSF cheque. Explain to Kari (a) what an NSF cheque is, (b) how it is treated in a bank reconciliation, and (c) whether it will require an adjusting entry and, if an adjusting entry is required, what accounts are typically debited and credited.

(SO 3) 18. The Diable Corporation wrote cheque #2375 for $1,325 on March 16. At March 31, the cheque had not cleared the company's bank account and was correctly listed as an outstanding cheque on the March 31 bank reconciliation. If the cheque has still not cleared the bank account on April 30, should it be included in the April bank reconciliation or not? Explain.

(SO 3) 19. Explain why electronic payments appearing on a bank statement are often recorded by a company immediately but electronic receipts are not.

(SO 3) 20. Sam Wing is an accounting clerk who has stolen $1,700 in cash from the company he works for. He prepares the bank reconciliation each month. When he performs the reconciliation this month, he knows that the adjusted cash balance will be $1,700 lower than the adjusted bank balance because of his theft. He therefore decides to falsify the amount of outstanding cheques. Why would he do this and would he overstate or understate the amount?

(SO 4) 21. What is restricted cash? What are compensating balances? How should these items be reported on the statement of financial position?

(SO 4) 22. Describe the six principles of cash management.

(SO 4) 23. At the end of its first quarter in the 2011 fiscal year, Commercial Solutions Inc. had an undrawn line of credit facility that allowed the company to borrow up to $16 million and pay it down whenever it wants to. How should this line of credit be reported on the statement of financial position?

(SO 4) 24. McDonald's Corporation usually has a cash balance that represents about 5% of its total assets. Microsoft Corporation, on the other hand, has a cash balance that is roughly 40% of total assets. Why do you think Microsoft maintains a higher amount of cash?

(SO 4) 25. Explain the three major elements of a cash budget and the reasons why a company needs to prepare a cash budget.

Brief Exercises

BE7–1 Gina Milan is the new manager of Plenty Parking Ltd., a parking garage. She has heard about internal control but is not clear about its importance for the company. Explain to Gina the six control activities, and give her an example of an application of each control for Plenty Parking.

Identify control activities.
(SO 1)

BE7–2 Match each of the following control activities with its appropriate description.

1. Authorization of transactions and activities
2. Segregation of duties
3. Documentation
4. Physical controls
5. Independent checks of performance
6. Human resource controls

Match control activities.
(SO 1)

(a) _____ All transactions should include original, detailed receipts.
(b) _____ Undeposited cash should be stored in the company safe.
(c) _____ Employees must take their full vacation allotment each year.
(d) _____ Surprise cash counts are performed.
(e) _____ Responsibility for related activities should be assigned to specific employees.
(f) _____ Cheque signers are not allowed to record cash transactions.

Identify control activities for cash receipts.
(SO 1, 2)

BE7–3 Tene Ltd. has the following internal controls over cash receipts. Identify the control activity that is applicable to each procedure.

1. All over-the-counter receipts are recorded on cash registers.
2. All cashiers are bonded.
3. Daily cash counts are made by the head cashier.
4. The duties of receiving cash, recording cash, and maintaining custody of cash are assigned to different individuals.
5. Only cashiers may operate cash registers.
6. All cash is deposited intact in the bank account every day.

Identify control activities for cash payments.
(SO 1, 2)

BE7–4 Rolling Hills Ltd. has the following internal controls over cash payments. Identify the control activity that is applicable to each procedure.

1. Company cheques are prenumbered.
2. The bank statement is reconciled monthly by the assistant controller.
3. Blank cheques are stored in a safe in the controller's office.
4. Both the controller and the assistant controller are required to sign cheques or authorize electronic payments.
5. Cheque signers are not allowed to record cash payments.
6. All payments are made by cheque or electronic transfer.

Record debit and credit card transactions.
(SO 2)

BE7–5 Bergio Bar & Grill has had $5,300 of sales today. Of these, $2,700 were paid by 62 customers with their debit cards, $900 was paid by customers with cash, and the rest was paid with credit cards. The company's credit card service fees are 2% while the fee for debit cards is $0.15 per transaction. Record three journal entries, one for each type of sale that was made by the company today.

Identify location of items in bank reconciliation.
(SO 3)

BE7–6 For each of the items in the following list, identify where it is included on a bank reconciliation. Next to each item write "bank +" for an increase in the bank balance; "bank −" for a decrease in the bank balance; "book +" for an increase in the book balance; "book −" for a decrease in the book balance; or "NA" for not applicable, to indicate that the item is not included in the bank reconciliation.

_____ 1. Bank service charges
_____ 2. An EFT collection on account
_____ 3. Outstanding cheques from the current month
_____ 4. Outstanding cheques from a prior month that are still outstanding
_____ 5. Outstanding cheques from a prior month that are no longer outstanding
_____ 6. A bank error in recording a company cheque made out for $200 as $290
_____ 7. A bank credit memorandum for interest earned on an investment
_____ 8. A company error in recording a $1,280 deposit as $1,680
_____ 9. A bank debit memorandum for an NSF cheque
_____ 10. A deposit in transit from the current month
_____ 11. A company error in recording a cheque made out for $630 as $360
_____ 12. A bank error in recording a $2,575 deposit as $2,755

Identify entries required for bank reconciliation.
(SO 3)

BE7–7 Using the data in BE7–6, indicate (a) the items that will result in an adjustment to the depositor's records and (b) why the other items do not require adjustment.

Analyze deposits in transit.
(SO 3)

BE7–8 For the months of January and February, Raymonde Ltd. recorded cash deposits in its books of $5,000 and $5,600, respectively. For the same two months, the bank reported deposits totalling $4,000 and $4,600, respectively. Assuming that there were no deposits in transit at the beginning of January, what was the amount of deposits in transit at the end of January and at the end of February?

Analyze outstanding cheques.
(SO 3)

BE7–9 In the month of November, its first month of operations, Jayasinghe Inc. wrote cheques in the amount of $12,600. In December, cheques in the amount of $9,500 were written. In November, $11,100 of these cheques were presented to the bank for payment and $9,900 in December. What is the amount of outstanding cheques at the end of November and at the end of December?

BE7–10   Kashechewan Inc. mistakenly recorded a cheque as $68 that was written for $86. In addition, the company noticed the bank had mistakenly deducted a cheque for $125 from its bank account that was written by another company. (a) Explain how each of these errors should be treated on the bank reconciliation. (b) Identify any entries required on Kashechewan's books to correct these errors.

Analyze errors.
(SO 3)

BE7–11   At July 31, Southco Limited had an unadjusted cash balance of $16,320. An examination of the July bank statement shows a balance of $15,840 on July 31; outstanding cheques $2,300; deposits in transit $4,300; EFT collections on account $1,960 that were not yet recorded on the books; NSF cheque $290; NSF fee $80; and bank services charges $70. Prepare a bank reconciliation at July 31.

Prepare bank reconciliation.
(SO 3)

BE7–12   Using the data in BE7–11, prepare the adjusting entries required on July 31 for Southco Limited.

Prepare entries for bank reconciliation.
(SO 3)

BE7–13   Ouellette Ltée reports the following items: cash in bank $17,500; payroll bank account $6,000; cash register floats $500; short-term investments consisting of term deposits with maturity dates of less than 90 days $5,000; and cash restricted for plant expansion $25,000. Ouellette also maintains a $5,000 compensating bank balance in a separate bank account. Determine which accounts described above would be considered cash, cash equivalents, or other items to be reported on the statement of financial position.

Report cash.
(SO 4)

BE7–14   Evergreen Inc. owns these assets at the statement of financial position date:

Cash in bank—savings account	$12,000
Cash on hand	1,700
Income tax refund due from CRA	2,000
Cash in bank—chequing account	24,000
Bank credit card slips	5,000
Debit card slips	2,400
Postdated cheques	1,000

Calculate cash.
(SO 4)

(a) What amount should be reported as cash in the statement of financial position? (b) For any item not included in (a), identify where it should be reported.

BE7–15   Identify and discuss the likely cash management issues faced by the following businesses:
(a) Vancouver Canucks hockey team
(b) WestJet Airlines Ltd.
(c) Memorial University Bookstore
(d) Tim Hortons
(e) Pillar 'N Pine Christmas Tree Farm

Identify cash management issues.
(SO 4)

BE7–16   Currently, Riley Architects Ltd. has cash of $4,400. In the next month, the company expects to earn revenues of $80,000 and collect 90% of these revenues. The company also expects to incur and pay expenses of $42,000 and to purchase equipment for $40,000. Prepare a cash budget for the month and determine if the company needs to seek any financing from a bank before the end of the month.

Prepare cash budget.
(SO 4)

Exercises

E7–1   Each of the following situations describes an instance of fraud:

1. A bartender sells drinks to customers and when they pay cash, he does not record the sale at the cash register and keeps the cash.
2. A bartender knows that there is a special on vodka tonight so he brings his own bottle of vodka to the bar. When a customer orders vodka and pays cash, the bartender pours the vodka from his own bottle, does not record the sale at the cash register, and keeps the cash.
3. The receptionist at a spa enters all appointments into a computerized schedule. After their appointment, the client pays the receptionist for the service received. For about half of the customers who pay with cash, the receptionist keeps the amount and deletes any record of the appointment from the schedule. The receptionist makes the bank deposits and records all sales in the accounting system.
4. The receptionist at a law firm has a key to a cabinet where company cheques are stored. She takes a cheque from the cabinet, makes it payable to herself, and forges the signature of the firm's managing partner on the cheque. She opens the mail every day and when the bank statement is received, she performs the bank reconciliation. She covers the theft by understating the amount of outstanding cheques on the bank reconciliation.

Identify control activities to detect and prevent fraud.
(SO 1)

Instructions

(a) Is it possible to detect these types of fraud? Why or why not?

(b) Identify a control activity or activities that could help prevent each instance of fraud described above.

Identify control activities. (SO 1)

E7–2 The following situations suggest either a strength or weakness in an internal control activity:

1. At Tingley's, Iryna and Inder work alternate lunch hours. Normally, Iryna works the cash register at the checkout counter, but during her lunch hour Inder takes her place. They both use the same cash drawer and jointly count cash at the end of the day.
2. The Do It Corporation accepts both cash and credit cards for its sales. Due to new privacy legislation that requires credit card information to be shredded within three months, it shreds all credit card slips after they are processed.
3. The mail clerk at Genesis Legal Services Inc. prepares a daily list of all cash receipts. The cash receipts are forwarded to a staff accountant, who deposits the cash in the company's bank account. The list is sent to the accounts receivable clerk for recording.
4. The Candy Store can only afford a part-time bookkeeper. The bookkeeper's responsibilities include making the bank deposit, recording transactions, and reconciling the bank statement.
5. The Decorator Shoppe counts inventory at the end of each month. Two staff members count the inventory together. It is then priced and totalled by the accounting department and reconciled to the perpetual inventory records. Any variances are investigated.

Instructions

(a) State whether each situation above is a control strength or weakness.

(b) For each weakness, suggest an improvement.

Identify control activities for cash receipts. (SO 1, 2)

E7–3 The following control activities are used at Tolan Ltd. for over-the-counter cash receipts:

1. Cashiers are experienced, so they are not bonded.
2. All over-the-counter receipts are received by one of three clerks. The clerks share a cash register with a single cash drawer.
3. To minimize the risk of robbery, cash in excess of $100 is stored in an unlocked strongbox in the stockroom until it is deposited in the bank.
4. At the end of each day, the total receipts are counted by the cashier on duty and reconciled to the cash register total.
5. The company accountant makes the bank deposit and then records the day's receipts.
6. If a customer has the exact change and does not want a receipt, the sale is not entered in the cash register. The money is kept in a loose change box.

Instructions

(a) For each of the above situations, explain the weakness and identify the control activity that is violated.

(b) For each weakness, suggest an improvement.

Identify control activities for cash payments. (SO 1, 2)

E7–4 The following control activities are used in Sheera's Boutique Shoppe Ltd. for cash payments:

1. Blank cheques are stored in an unmarked envelope on a shelf behind the cash register.
2. The store manager personally approves all payments before signing cheques or initiating an EFT payment.
3. When the store manager goes away for an extended period of time, she pre-signs cheques to be used in her absence.
4. The company cheques are not prenumbered.
5. The company accountant prepares the bank reconciliation and reports any discrepancies to the store manager.

Instructions

(a) For each of the above situations, explain the weakness and identify the control activity that is violated.

(a) For each weakness, suggest an improvement.

Record debit and credit card transactions. (SO 2)

E7–5 During the first day of February, Peter's Burger Palace had 109 sales transactions. Of these, 62 sales totalling $3,200 were made to customers using debit cards, 43 sales totalling $3,800 were made to customers using credit cards, while the remaining sales were collected by receiving $542 cash. The bank charges a fee of 2% of credit card sales and $0.15 to process each debit card transaction.

Instructions

Record the journal entries that the company will make pertaining to the above transactions.

Indicate effect of items in bank reconciliation. (SO 3)

E7–6 Ten items that may or may not be involved in the bank reconciliation process for April are listed in the table shown below:

| | | Bank | | Books | | |
	Item	Add (Credit)	Deduct (Debit)	Add (Debit)	Deduct (Credit)	Adjusting Entry Required
1.	Deposits in transit at end of April	✓				No
2.	Deposits in transit at the beginning of April that cleared the bank in April					

3. Outstanding cheques at end of April				
4. Outstanding cheques at the beginning of April that cleared the bank in April				
5. Cheque written for $250 recorded in error as $520 on the books				
6. Deposit of $400 made in error by the bank to the company's account				
7. Bank service charges				
8. EFT, collection on account				
9. NSF cheque received from customer				
10. Interest earned on bank account				

Instructions
Complete the table shown above, identifying where each item should be included on a bank reconciliation prepared for the month of April. Insert a check mark (✓) in the appropriate column indicating whether the item should be added to, or deducted from, the bank or the books. If the item should not be included in the bank reconciliation, write "NA" for not applicable. Finally, indicate whether the item will require an adjusting entry on the company books by writing "yes" or "no" in the last column. The first item has been done for you as an example.

E7–7 The cash records of Lejeune Inc. show the following situations:

Calculate deposits in transit and outstanding cheques. (SO 3)

Deposits in transit

1. The June 30 bank reconciliation indicated that deposits in transit total $2,000. During July, the general ledger account Cash shows deposits of $14,750, but the bank statement indicates that only $15,820 in deposits were received during the month.
2. In August, deposits per bank statement totalled $22,500 and deposits per books were $22,900.

Outstanding cheques

1. The June 30 bank reconciliation reported outstanding cheques of $570. During July, the Lejeune books show that $18,200 of cheques were issued. The bank statement showed that $17,200 of cheques cleared the bank in July.
2. In August, cash payments per books were $22,700 and cheques clearing the bank were $23,520.

Instructions
(a) What were the deposits in transit at July 31 and at August 31?
(b) What were the outstanding cheques at July 31 and at August 31?

E7–8 On April 30, the bank reconciliation of Frobisher Limited shows a deposit in transit of $2,874. A list of cash deposits recorded by the bank and the company in the month of May follows:

Calculate deposits in transit. (SO 3)

		FROBISHER LIMITED Bank Statement (partial) Amounts Added to Account (Credits)			FROBISHER LIMITED Cash Account (partial) Deposits Made (debits)	
Date		Description	Amount	Date		Amount
May	1	Deposit	$2,874	May 7		$4,510
	8	Deposit	4,510	14		6,436
	15	Deposit	6,436	19		1,908
	20	Deposit	1,908	28		3,062
	25	EFT, collection from customer	2,596	31		3,784
	29	Deposit	3,062			

Instructions
(a) List the deposits in transit at May 31.
(b) List other items that must be included in the bank reconciliation. Describe the impact of each on the reconciliation.

E7–9 At April 30, the bank reconciliation of Frobisher shows three outstanding cheques: No. 254, $1,120; No. 255, $1,600; and No. 257, $820. A list of cheques recorded by the bank and the company in the month of May follows:

Calculate outstanding cheques. (SO 3)

	FROBISHER LIMITED	
	Bank Statement (partial)	
	Amounts Deducted from Account (debits)	

Date		Cheque No.	Amount
May	2	254	$1,120
	4	257	820
	12	258	318
	17	259	550
	20	260	1,000
	29	263	1,680
	30	262	1,500
	31	Service charge	108

	FROBISHER LIMITED	
	Cash Account (partial)	
	Cheques Written (Credits)	

Date		Cheque No.	Amount
May	2	258	$ 318
	5	259	550
	10	260	1,000
	15	261	1,734
	22	262	1,500
	24	263	880
	29	264	1,300

Additional information:

1. The bank did not make any errors.
2. The company made one error.

Instructions

(a) List the outstanding cheques at May 31.
(b) List other items that must be included in the bank reconciliation. Describe the impact of each on the reconciliation.

Prepare bank reconciliation and adjusting entries. (SO 3)

E7–10   Refer to the data presented in E7–8 and E7–9. On May 31, Frobisher Limited had an unadjusted cash balance of $10,218 in the general ledger. The bank statement showed a balance of $12,756 on May 31.

Instructions

(a) Prepare the bank reconciliation on May 31.
(b) Prepare any adjusting journal entries required from the reconciliation. Assume that the EFT collection from a customer on May 25 shown in E7–8 has not yet been recorded.

Prepare bank reconciliation and adjusting entries. (SO 3)

E7–11   The following information is for Neopolitan Ltd. in July:

1. Cash balance per bank, July 31, $8,833
2. Cash balance per books, July 31, $7,190
3. Bank service charge, $24
4. Deposits in transit, $1,575
5. Electronic receipts from customers in payment of their accounts, $883
6. Outstanding cheques, $2,449
7. Cheque #373 was correctly written and recorded by the company as $672. The bank deducted $762 from the company's account in error. The cheque was written for the purchase of office supplies.

Instructions

(a) Prepare the bank reconciliation on July 31.
(b) Prepare any adjusting journal entries required from the reconciliation.

Calculate amounts for bank reconciliation. (SO 3)

E7–12   The following information is for Hudson Corporation.

HUDSON CORPORATION	
Bank Reconciliation	
August 31	

	$41,720
Add: Deposits in transit	6,740
	48,460
Less: Outstanding cheques	13,760
Adjusted cash balance per bank	$34,700

Additional information:

1. The September bank statement shows the following selected items:

Amounts Deducted from Account (Debits)		Amounts Added to Account (Credits)	
NSF cheque: J. Hower	$ 820	EFT collections	$3,650
Bank service charge, NSF cheque	80		
Bank service charge	50		
EFT payments	1,800		

2. In September, the company wrote and recorded cheques totalling $127,492.

3. In September, $133,574 of cheques cleared the bank.
4. In September, deposits per bank statement (excluding the EFT collections listed in point 1 of this list) were $125,578.
5. In September, the company recorded deposits totalling $128,658.

Instructions

(a) Calculate the unadjusted balance in the Cash account on September 30.
(b) Calculate the unadjusted balance in the bank account on September 30.
(c) Calculate the deposits in transit at September 30.
(d) Calculate the outstanding cheques at September 30.
(e) Calculate the adjusted cash balance per bank at September 30.
(f) Prepare any adjusting journal entries required from the reconciliation.

E7–13 A new accountant at La Maison Ltée is trying to identify which of the following amounts should be reported as cash or cash equivalents in the year-end statement of financial position, as at April 30:

Calculate cash.
(SO 4)

1. Currency and coin totalling $87 in a locked box used for incidental cash transactions
2. A $10,000 guaranteed investment certificate, due the next month, May 31
3. April-dated cheques worth $300 that La Maison has received from customers but not yet deposited
4. An $85 cheque received from a customer in payment of its April account, but postdated to May 1
5. A balance of $2,575 in the Royal Bank chequing account
6. A balance of $4,000 in the Royal Bank savings account
7. Prepaid postage of $75 in the postage meter
8. A $50 IOU from the company receptionist
9. Cash register floats of $250
10. Over-the-counter receipts for April 30 consisting of $550 of currency and coin, $185 of cheques from customers, $685 of debit card slips, and $755 of bank credit card slips. These amounts were processed by the bank on May 1

Instructions

(a) What amount should La Maison report as its cash balance at April 30? What would be reported as a cash equivalent?
(b) In which financial statement(s) and in what account(s) should the items not included in (a) be reported?

E7–14 Tory, Hachey, and Wedunn, three young lawyers who have joined together to open a law practice, are struggling to manage their cash flow. They have not yet built up enough clientele and revenues to support the cost of running their legal practice. Initial costs, such as advertising and renovations to the premises, all result in outgoing cash flow at a time when little is coming in! Tory, Hachey, and Wedunn have not had time to establish a billing system since most of their clients' cases have not yet reached the courts and the lawyers did not think it would be right to bill them until "results were achieved." Unfortunately, Tory, Hachey, and Wedunn's suppliers do not feel the same way. Their suppliers expect them to pay their accounts payable within a few weeks of receiving their bills. So far, there has not even been enough money to pay the three lawyers, and they are not sure how long they can keep practising law without getting some money into their pockets!

Discuss cash management.
(SO 4)

Instructions

Provide suggestions for Tory, Hachey, and Wedunn to improve their cash management practices.

Problems: Set A

P7–1A Red River Theatre has a cashier's booth located near the theatre entrance. There are two cashiers: one works from 1 p.m. to 5 p.m., the other from 5 p.m. to 9 p.m. Each cashier is bonded. The cashiers receive cash from customers and operate a machine that ejects serially numbered tickets. The rolls of tickets are inserted and locked into the machine by the theatre manager at the beginning of each cashier's shift.

Identify control activities over cash receipts.
(SO 1, 2)

After purchasing a ticket, which costs a different amount depending on the day of the week and the customer's age group, the customer takes the ticket to an usher stationed at the entrance to the theatre lobby, a few metres from the cashier's booth. The usher tears the ticket in half, admits the customer, and returns the ticket stub to the customer. The other half of the ticket is dropped into a locked box by the usher.

At the end of each cashier's shift, the theatre manager removes the ticket rolls from the machine and makes a cash count. The cash count sheet is initialled by the cashier. At the end of the day, the manager deposits the total receipts in a bank night deposit slot. In addition, the manager sends copies of the deposit slip and the initialled cash count sheets to the head cashier for verification and to the accounting department for comparison to sales records. Receipts from the first shift are stored in a safe located in the manager's office.

Instructions

(a) Identify the control activities and their application to cash receipts at the theatre.
(b) If the usher and cashier decided to collaborate to steal cash, what actions might they take?

Identify control weaknesses over cash payments.
(SO 1, 2)

P7–2A   High Tech Inc. commenced operations recently. The company shares are jointly owned by two friends from university, John Deol and Rehana Gerdman. John and Rehana have developed a new software application to track shipping. The two friends spend most of their time on the development of new products and the marketing of the current product.

John and Rehana hired Fred Glass to be High Tech's controller. Fred has been given overall responsibility for the books and records of High Tech so that John and Rehana can spend their time on development and marketing.

Fred has one assistant, Asmaa. Both Fred and Asmaa have the authority to order goods for High Tech. Asmaa can approve invoices for payment up to $5,000. Fred can approve any invoice for payment. Fred, John, and Rehana are all signing officers on the company's bank account. Only one of the three signing officers needs to sign a cheque under $20,000. For cheques greater than $20,000, two signing officers must sign. Unsigned cheques are kept in the company safe. Fred is responsible for preparing the monthly bank reconciliations and making any necessary journal entries.

Instructions
(a) Identify the control weaknesses over the cash payments.
(b) Explain the problems that could occur as a result of these weaknesses.
(c) List the improvements in control activities that should be considered by High Tech.

Identify control weaknesses.
(SO 1, 2)

P7–3A   Each of the following independent situations has one or more control activity weaknesses:

1. Board Riders Ltd. is a small snowboarding club that offers specialized coaching for teenagers who want to improve their skills. Group lessons are offered every day. Members who want a lesson pay a $25 fee directly to the instructor at the start of the lesson that day. Most members pay cash. At the end of the lesson, the instructor reports the number of students and turns over the cash to the office manager.
2. Coloroso Agency Corp. offers parenting advice to young single mothers. Most of the agency's revenues are from government grants. The general manager is responsible for all of the accounting work, including approving invoices for payment, preparing and posting all entries into the accounting system, and preparing bank reconciliations.
3. At Nexus Corporation, each salesperson is responsible for deciding on the correct credit policies for his or her customers. For example, the salesperson decides if Nexus should sell to the customer on credit and how high the credit limit should be. Salespeople receive a commission based on their sales.
4. Algorithm Limited is a software company that employs many computer programmers. The company uses accounting software that was created by one of the employees. In order to be more flexible and share the workload, all of the programmers have access to the accounting software program in case changes are needed.
5. The warehouse manager at Orange Wing Distributors Ltd. is well known for running an efficient, cost-saving operation. He has eliminated the requirement for staff to create receiving reports and purchase orders because it was taking staff too long to prepare them.

Instructions
(a) Identify the control weakness(es) in each of the above situations.
(b) Explain the problems that could occur as a result of these weaknesses.
(c) Make recommendations for correcting each situation.

Identify control weaknesses over cash receipts and payments.
(SO 1, 2)

P7–4A   Cedar Grove High School wants to raise money for a new sound system for its auditorium. The main fundraising event is a dance at which the famous disc jockey Obnoxious Al will play rap music. Roger DeMaster, the music teacher, has been given the responsibility for coordinating the fundraising efforts. This is Roger's first experience with fundraising. He decides to put the Student Representative Council (SRC) in charge of the event.

Roger had 500 unnumbered tickets printed for the dance. He left the tickets in a locked box on his desk and told the SRC students to take as many tickets as they thought they could sell for $20 each. To ensure that no extra tickets would be floating around, he told the students to get rid of any unsold tickets. When the students received payment for the tickets, they were to bring the cash back to Roger, and he would put it in the locked box on his desk.

Some of the students were responsible for decorating the gymnasium for the dance. Roger gave each of them a key to the locked box and told them that if they took money out to purchase materials, they should put a note in the box saying how much they took and what it was used for. After two weeks, the locked box appeared to be getting full, so Roger asked Praveen Patel to count the money, prepare a deposit slip, and deposit the money in a bank account Roger had opened.

The day of the dance, Roger wrote a cheque from the account to pay Obnoxious Al. Al, however, said that he accepted only cash and did not give receipts. Having no alternative, Roger took $500 out of the locked box and gave it to Al. At the dance, Roger had Sara Wu working at the entrance to the gymnasium, collecting tickets from students and selling tickets to those who had not prepurchased them. Roger estimated that 400 students attended the dance.

The following day, Roger closed out the bank account, which had $750 in it, and gave that amount plus the $1,800 in the locked box to Principal Orlowski. Principal Orlowski seemed surprised that, after generating roughly $8,000 (400 tickets @ $20) in sales, the dance netted only $2,550 in cash. Roger did not know how to respond.

Instructions
(a) Identify the weaknesses in control activities over cash receipts and payments and explain their implications.
(b) List the improvements in internal controls that the school should consider.

P7–5A On July 31, Beaupré Ltd. had a cash balance of $14,786. The statement from the Caisse Populaire on that date showed a balance of $19,988. A comparison of the bank statement with the Cash account revealed the following:

1. The bank statement included a bank service charge of $100.
2. The bank statement included two electronic collections from customers on account: $4,062 from D. Bouchard and $48 from A. Tremblay. These were not previously recorded.
3. The July 31 cash receipts of $2,786 were not included in the bank deposits for July. These receipts were deposited by the company in a night deposit vault on July 31.
4. Company cheque #2480 for $1,170, issued to J. Gauthier, a creditor, cleared the bank in July and was incorrectly entered in the general journal on July 10 as $1,710.
5. A deposit of $1,800 made by another company was incorrectly added to Beaupré's account by the Caisse Populaire.
6. Salaries of $4,000 were paid electronically during the month. These have already been recorded by the company.
7. Cheques outstanding on June 30 totalled $1,844. Of these, $1,378 worth cleared the bank in July. There were $2,892 of cheques written in July that were still outstanding July 31.
8. On July 31, the bank statement showed a returned (NSF) cheque for $1,640 received by the company from a customer on account. In addition, the bank charged an $80 processing fee for this transaction.

Prepare bank reconciliation and adjusting entries. (SO 3)

Instructions
(a) Prepare the bank reconciliation on July 31.
(b) Prepare any adjusting journal entries required from the reconciliation.

P7–6A The bank portion of last month's bank reconciliation for Yap Ltd. at February 28 was as follows:

Prepare bank reconciliation and adjusting entries. (SO 3)

YAP LTD.
Bank Reconciliation
February 28

Cash balance per bank		$14,368
Add: Deposits in transit		2,530
		16,898
Less: Outstanding cheques		
#3451	$2,260	
#3470	1,535	
#3471	845	4,640
Adjusted cash balance		$12,258

The adjusted cash balance per bank agreed with the cash balance per books at February 28. The March bank statement showed the following:

YAP LTD.
Bank Statement
March 31

Date		Description	Amounts Deducted from Account (Debits)	Amounts Added to Account (Credits)	Balance
Feb.	28	Opening balance			14,368
Mar.	1	Cheque, No. 3451	2,260		12,108
	1	Deposit		2,530	14,638
	2	Cheque, No. 3471	845		13,793
	4	Deposit		1,212	15,005
	7	Deposit		550	15,555
	9	Cheque, No. 3472	1,427		14,128
	10	Returned cheque—NSF, R. Aubut	550		13,578
	10	NSF fee	40		13,538
	15	EFT, loan payment	1,062		12,476
	19	Cheque, No. 3473	1,641		10,835
	24	Cheque, No. 3474	2,130		8,705
	26	Deposit		2,567	11,272
	31	EFT, collection on account from M. Boudreault		230	11,502
	31	SVC plan fee	49		11,453

Yap's cash receipts and payments for the month of March showed the following:

Cash Receipts			Cash Payments		
Date		Amount	Date	Number	Amount
Mar. 4		$1,221	Mar. 7	3472	$1,427
7		550	15	3473	1,461
26		2,567	22	3474	2,130
31		1,025	29	3475	487
		$5,363			$5,505

Additional information:

1. The company made an error in recording the March 4 deposit. The error related to a cash sale.
2. The EFT loan payment should have been recorded by the company on March 15, but this entry was missed. The payment included $62 of interest and a $1,000 payment on the loan principal.
3. The bank made an error processing cheque #3473.
4. The EFT collections were not previously recorded.

Instructions

(a) Calculate the unadjusted cash balance per books at March 31, prior to reconciliation.
(b) What is the amount of the deposits in transit at March 31?
(c) What is the amount of the outstanding cheques at March 31?
(d) Prepare the bank reconciliation at March 31.
(e) Prepare any adjusting journal entries required from the reconciliation.

Prepare bank reconciliation and adjusting entries. (SO 3)

P7–7A The bank portion of the bank reconciliation for Hamptons Limited at October 31 is shown here:

HAMPTONS LIMITED
Bank Reconciliation
October 31

Cash balance per bank		$24,890
Add: Deposits in transit		3,060
		27,950
Less: Outstanding cheques		
#2472	$1,440	
#2473	1,690	
#2474	1,008	4,138
Adjusted cash balance		$23,812

The adjusted cash balance per bank agreed with the cash balance per books at October 31. The November bank statement showed the following:

HAMPTONS LIMITED
Bank Statement
November 30

Date		Description	Amounts Deducted from Account (Debits)	Amounts Added to Account (Credits)	Balance
Oct.	31				24,890
Nov.	1	Cheque, No. 2472	1,440		23,450
	1	Deposit		3,060	26,510
	2	Cheque, No. 2473	1,690		24,820
	3	Deposit		2,424	27,244
	4	Cheque, No. 2475	3,282		23,962
	7	Deposit		1,980	25,942
	8	Cheque, No. 2476	5,660		20,282
	10	Cheque, No. 2477	1,200		19,082
	14	Deposit		5,150	24,232
	15	Cheque, No. 2478	3,500		20,732
	15	EFT, salaries	6,400		14,332
	20	Deposit		5,890	20,222
	25	Returned cheque—NSF, Giasson Developments	500		19,722
	25	NSF fee	80		19,642
	26	Cheque, No. 2479	1,390		18,252

27	Deposit		3,300	21,552
28	EFT, collection of note receivable and interest		5,008	26,560
30	Cheque, No. 2481	1,152		25,408
30	EFT, salaries	6,400		19,008
30	SVC plan fee	50		18,958

The cash records per books for November showed the following:

Cash Receipts				Cash Payments		
Date		Amount		Date	Number	Amount
Nov.	3	$ 2,424		Nov. 1	2475	$ 3,282
	7	1,980		2	2476	4,760
	12	5,150		2	2477	1,200
	20	5,908		8	2478	3,500
	27	3,300		15	2479	1,390
	30	2,676		15	EFT, salaries	6,400
		$21,438		18	2480	1,224
				20	2481	1,152
				29	2482	1,660
				30	EFT, salaries	6,400
						$30,968

Additional information:

1. The EFT collections were not previously recorded. The collection of the note on November 28 was for $4,400, plus $608 interest. Interest was not previously accrued.
2. EFT payments are recorded when they occur.
3. The bank did not make any errors.
4. Two errors were made by the company: one in recording a cheque and one in recording a cash receipt. The correction of any errors in the recording of cheques should be made to Accounts Payable. The correction of any errors in the recording of cash receipts should be made to Accounts Receivable.

Instructions

(a) Calculate the unadjusted cash balance per books as at November 30, prior to reconciliation.
(b) Prepare the bank reconciliation at November 30.
(c) Prepare any adjusting journal entries required from the reconciliation.

P7–8A Tarika Ltd. is a profitable small business. It has not, however, given much consideration to internal control. For example, in an attempt to keep clerical and office expenses to a minimum, the company has combined the jobs of cashier and bookkeeper. As a result, Rob Tang handles all cash receipts, keeps the accounting records, and prepares the monthly bank reconciliations.

Prepare bank reconciliation and identify weaknesses in control activities. (SO 1, 3)

The balance per bank statement on October 31 was $19,460. Outstanding cheques at that time were #782 for $114, #783 for $160, #784 for $267, #789 for $171, #791 for $325, and #792 for $173. There were no deposits in transit. Included with the bank statement was a $299 electronic collection on account from a customer.

The company's general ledger showed the Cash account with a balance of $19,640. The balance included undeposited cash on hand. Because of the lack of internal controls, Tang took all of the undeposited receipts, which were recorded on the company's books, for his personal use. He then prepared the following bank reconciliation to hide his theft of cash:

TARIKA LTD.
Bank Reconciliation
October 31

Cash balance per books		$19,640
Less: EFT, collection from customer		299
Adjusted cash balance per books		$19,341
Cash balance per bank statement		$19,460
Less: Outstanding cheques		
#782	$11	
#783	16	
#784	26	
#789	17	
#791	32	
#792	17	119
Adjusted cash balance per bank		$19,341

Instructions

(a) Identify the errors in the above bank reconciliation.

(b) Prepare a correct bank reconciliation.

(c) Identify how much Tang stole for personal use. (*Hint:* The theft is the difference between the adjusted balance per books before the theft and the adjusted balance per bank.)

(d) Indicate the various ways that Tang tried to hide the theft and the dollar amount for each method.

(e) What control activities were violated in this case?

Calculate cash.
(SO 4)

P7–9A A first-year co-op student is trying to determine the amount of cash that should be reported on a company's statement of financial position. The following information was provided to the student at year end:

1. Cash on hand in the cash registers totals $5,000.
2. The balance in the commercial bank savings account is $100,000 and in the commercial bank chequing account, $25,000. The company also has a U.S. bank account, which contains the equivalent of $45,000 Canadian at year end.
3. A special bank account holds $150,000 in cash that is restricted for equipment replacement.
4. Amounts due from employees (travel advances) total $12,000.
5. Short-term investments held by the company include $32,000 in a term deposit maturing in 120 days, a Government of Canada bond for $75,000 that falls due in 30 days, and $40,000 in shares of Shoppers Drug Mart.
6. The company has a supply of unused postage stamps totalling $150.
7. The company has $1,750 of NSF cheques from customers that were returned by the bank. NSF fees charged by the bank for processing these cheques totalled $80.
8. The company keeps $5,000 as a compensating balance in a special account.

Instructions

(a) Determine which items listed above would be included in cash and which would be included in cash equivalents on the year-end statement of financial position.

(b) Identify where any items that were not reported in cash or in cash equivalents in (a) should be reported.

Discuss reporting of cash.
(SO 4)

P7–10A Wilfrid Laurier University reports the following selected information (in thousands) in its April 30, 2010, financial statements:

	2010	2009
Cash and short-term deposits	$41,817	$31,525
Restricted cash	5,350	3,100
Cash provided by operating activities	26,325	12,800

Additional information:

Cash was restricted for the funding of post-retirement benefits.

Instructions

(a) Explain the difference between cash and short-term deposits. Why are they combined for reporting purposes?

(b) In which section of the statement of financial position would the restricted cash most likely be reported? Explain.

(c) How is it possible that Wilfrid Laurier University has $41,817 thousand of cash and short-term deposits at the end of fiscal 2010 but generated only $26,325 thousand of cash flow from operating activities in the same year?

Recommend cash management improvements.
(SO 4)

P7–11A Bev's Design Services Ltd. commenced operations approximately nine months ago. Bev, the sole shareholder and designer, organizes the hall and table decorations for a variety of functions. Bev has completed 15 contracts so far and, with wedding season coming up, has 20 more signed contracts. However, the company has no cash in its bank account and Bev has had to loan the business money from her personal funds.

For each signed contract, the company requires a $50 non-refundable deposit. The balance of the payment is due three weeks following the function. For the weddings Bev has serviced, payment has been made on average five weeks after the function. All the decorations must be purchased about two months before the function or once the contract has been signed, whichever is earlier. The company pays for the decorations at the time of purchase. Recently, the company has learned that it can apply for an account, which will permit it to pay 30 days after purchase.

Instructions

Identify ways the company can improve its cash management practices.

Prepare cash budget.
(SO 4)

P7–12A Jill Narremk is just about to take over the operation of a small coffee shop on March 1. The current owner of the shop will sell Jill the furniture and equipment currently there for $15,000 and $20,000, respectively. The furniture and equipment have no residual value and will be used for five more years. Jill and two assistants will be the only employees working at the shop. The shop will be open 26 days per month for 10 hours per day. Jill believes that she will serve about 300 customers each day with an average sale of $4 each in March but she thinks that the number of customers will increase by 5% per month because of her friendly approach when dealing with customers. Half of the customers are expected to pay with debit cards and the bank charges her $0.20 for each debit card transaction. Her assistants will be paid $15 per hour for 8 hours per day each and she hopes to be paid a $5,000 salary each month. Jill is assuming the lease for the premises from the current owner, who is paying $6,000 rent per month. This also includes rent for the debit card equipment. She estimates her monthly utilities at $1,200, monthly supplies at $500, and her food and coffee costs to be one-third of her sales. She will order inventory almost daily and pay for it immediately. Jill is going to pay the $35,000 for the furniture and equipment using a $40,000 loan from her father. The extra $5,000 she has received from him will be used to buy inventory and supplies. He is wondering if she can start paying him back at the end of April. He would like her to give him $1,500 per month.

Instructions

(a) Prepare a cash budget for March and April.
(b) Based on your budget, determine if Jill can pay her father the $1,500 per month that he wants.

Problems: Set B

P7–1B You are asked to join the board of trustees of a local church to help with the control activities for the offerings collection made at weekly services. At a meeting of the board of trustees, you learn the following:

Identify control weaknesses over cash receipts.
(SO 1, 2)

1. The board of trustees has delegated responsibility for the financial management and audit of the financial records to the finance committee. This group prepares the annual budget and approves major payments but is not involved in collections or record keeping. No audit has been done in recent years, because the same trusted employee has kept church records and served as financial secretary for 15 years. The church does not carry any fidelity insurance.
2. The collection at the weekly service is taken by a team of ushers who volunteer to serve for one month. The ushers take the collection plates to a basement office at the back of the church. They hand their plates to the head usher and return to the church service. After all plates have been turned in, the head usher counts the cash collected in them. The head usher then places the cash in the church safe along with a note that includes the amount counted. The safe is unlocked because no one can remember the combination, and after all, it is in a church.
3. The morning after the service, the financial secretary goes to the safe and recounts the collection. The secretary withholds $200 to pay for cash purchases for the week, and deposits the remainder of the collection in the bank. To facilitate the deposit, church members who contribute by cheque are asked to make their cheques payable to "Cash."
4. Each month, the financial secretary reconciles the bank statement and submits a copy of the reconciliation to the board of trustees. The reconciliations have rarely revealed any bank errors and have never shown any errors per books.

Instructions

(a) Identify the weaknesses in control activities in the handling of collections.
(b) List the improvements in control activities that should be recommended for (1) the head usher, (2) the ushers, (3) the financial secretary, and (4) the finance committee.

P7–2B Segal Office Supply Limited recently changed its control activities over cash payments. The new activities include the following features:

Identify control activities over cash payments.
(SO 1, 2)

1. All cheques are prenumbered and written by an electronic cheque-writing system.
2. Before a cheque or electronic payment can be issued, each invoice must have the approval of Cindy van Bommel, the purchasing agent, and Ray Mills, the receiving department supervisor.
3. Cheques must be signed by either controller François Montpetit or assistant controller Mary Nishiyama. Before signing a cheque, the signer is expected to compare the amount of the cheque with the amount on the invoice.
4. After signing a cheque, the signer stamps the invoice "Paid" and writes in the date, cheque number, and amount of the cheque. The paid invoice is then sent to the accounting department for recording.
5. Blank cheques are stored in a safe in the controller's office. The combination to the safe is known only to the controller and assistant controller.
6. Each month, the bank statement is reconciled by a staff accountant who does not record payments.

Instructions

Identify the control activities by category and explain how they are applied to cash payments at Segal Office Supply.

P7–3B Each of the following independent situations has a control activity weakness:

Identify control weakness.
(SO 1, 2)

1. Rowena's Cleaning Service Inc. provides home cleaning services for a large number of clients who all pay cash. Rowena collects the cash and keeps it in the glove compartment of her car until the end of the week when she has time to count it and prepare a bank deposit.
2. Hornet's Convenience Store Limited sells a variety of items, including cigarettes, non-alcoholic beverages, and snack foods. A long-term employee is responsible for ordering all merchandise, checking all deliveries, and approving invoices for payment.

3. At Ye Olde Ice Cream Shoppe Ltd., there are three sales clerks on duty during busy times. All three of them use the same cash drawer.

4. Most customers at Better Used Car dealership use the option to pay for their vehicles in 24 equal payments over two years. These customers send the company cheques or cash each month. The office manager opens the mail each day, makes a bank deposit with the cash and cheques received in the mail that day, and prepares and posts a journal entry in the accounting records.

5. Jimmy's Truck Parts Ltd. employs sales staff who visit current and prospective customers. The sales staff will keep product samples in their vehicles so they can demonstrate the product to the customers. If a customer has a large order, the order is e-mailed to the warehouse. The warehouse then ships the product to the customer on account. If a customer wishes to purchase one or two sample items, the salesperson can sell these for cash or on account. To obtain more inventory, the salespeople go to the warehouse and restock the vehicle themselves.

Instructions
(a) Identify the control weakness(es) in each of the above situations.
(b) Explain the problems that could occur as a result of these weaknesses.
(c) Make recommendations for correcting each situation.

Identify control weaknesses over cash receipts and payments. (SO 1, 2)

P7–4B The president of a registered charity, the Helping Elderly Low-Income People Foundation (HELP), approaches you for help on a special project to set up the charity's accounting system. HELP is a relatively new organization that is regulated by both the federal and provincial governments. The organization is required to maintain current financial records for the public to scrutinize. In other words, the records must be available to anyone who is interested in reviewing them. It is now the end of the charity's first fiscal year, and HELP has come to you with a shoebox of receipts and bank statements. You notice that the bank statements are still in their envelopes—they have not been opened.

The charity's revenue is mostly from donations. A van driver takes volunteers around the city and they go door to door asking for donations. The volunteers give a donation receipt for amounts over $20. Since volunteering takes a lot of time, the charity has many short-term volunteers and anyone is welcome to be one.

Two car companies generously donated vans to the organization. The van drivers are paid $50 a day, which they take from the donations. Drivers keep a summary of the total donations collected by the volunteers, and at the end of the day the drivers take the money to a bank and deposit it. Drivers also pay for their gas out of the donated funds.

HELP also held a fundraising dance last month. The president said he was disappointed with the project, though, because it did not bring in much money. To keep costs down, the president made the dance tickets by photocopying tickets and cutting them up. He gave them out to volunteers to sell for $25 each. He estimates that he printed 500 tickets, but can only account for about $5,000 (200 tickets @ $25) of revenues given in by his volunteers.

Instructions
(a) Identify the weaknesses in control activities over cash receipts and payments.
(b) List the improvements in control activities that should be considered by HELP.

Prepare bank reconciliation and adjusting entries. (SO 3)

P7–5B On May 31, O'Hearn Limited had a cash balance per books of $13,400. The bank statement from Community Bank on that date showed a balance of $15,230. A comparison of the bank statement with the company's Cash account revealed the following:

1. The bank statement included a bank service charge of $80.

2. The bank statement included two electronic collections from customers on account: $4,110 received from C. Campbell and $78 received from R. Pokoj. These were not previously recorded.

3. Cash sales of $1,672 on May 12 were deposited in the bank. The journal entry and the deposit slip were incorrectly made out and recorded by O'Hearn for $1,712. The bank detected the error and credited O'Hearn for the correct amount.

4. Outstanding cheques at April 30 totalled $2,900. Of these, $2,240 worth cleared the bank in May. There were $1,892 of cheques written in May that were still outstanding on May 31.

5. On May 18, the company issued cheque #1181 for $1,370 to a creditor in payment of its account. The cheque, which cleared the bank in May, was incorrectly journalized and posted by O'Hearn as being for $1,136.

6. Included with the cancelled cheques was a cheque issued by O'Bearne Inc. for $1,200 that was incorrectly charged to O'Hearne by the bank.

7. On May 31, the bank statement showed a returned (NSF) cheque for $1,350 issued by a customer in payment of its account. In addition, the bank charged an $80 processing fee for this transaction.

8. The May 31 deposit of $1,926 was not included in the deposits on the May bank statement. The deposit had been placed in the bank's night deposit vault on May 31.

Instructions
(a) Prepare the bank reconciliation on May 31.
(b) Prepare any adjusting journal entries required from the reconciliation.

P7–6B   The bank portion of last month's bank reconciliation showed the following for River Adventures Ltd.:

Prepare bank reconciliation and adjusting entries. (SO 3)

RIVER ADVENTURES LTD.
Bank Reconciliation
April 30

Cash balance per bank		$9,009
Add: Deposits in transit		846
		9,855
Less: Outstanding cheques		
#533	$279	
#541	363	
#555	79	721
Adjusted cash balance		$9,134

The adjusted cash balance per bank agreed with the cash balance per books at April 30. The May bank statement showed the following:

RIVER ADVENTURES LTD.
Bank Statement
May 31

Date		Description	Amounts Deducted from Account (Debits)	Amounts Added to Account (Credits)	Balance
Apr.	30	Opening balance			9,009
May	1	Deposit		846	9,855
	3	Cheque, No. 541	363		9,492
	4	Cheque, No. 533	279		9,213
	5	Cheque, No. 556	223		8,990
	6	Cheque, No. 557	1,800		7,190
	6	Deposit		1,250	8,440
	7	Cheque, No. 558	934		7,506
	8	Deposit		975	8,481
	10	Cheque, No. 559	1,650		6,831
	15	Deposit		426	7,257
	18	EFT, collection on account from A. Osborne		650	7,907
	19	Cheque, No. 561	799		7,108
	20	Cheque, No. 562	2,045		5,063
	21	EFT, collection on account from P. Lau		1,222	6,285
	23	Cheque, No. 563	2,487		3,798
	25	Deposit		980	4,778
	28	Deposit		1,771	6,549
	28	Returned cheque—NSF, R. Lajeunesse	440		6,109
	28	NSF fee	40		6,069
	30	EFT, prepaid insurance payment	578		5,491
	31	SVC plan fee	25		5,466

River Adventures' cash receipts and payments for the month of May showed the following:

Cash Receipts			Cash Payments		
Date		Amount	Date	Number	Amount
May	6	$1,250	May 4	556	$ 223
	8	975	5	557	1,800
	15	426	7	558	943
	25	890	7	559	1,650
	28	1,771	10	560	890
	31	1,286	15	561	799
		$6,598	17	562	2,045
			22	563	2,487
			31	564	950
					$11,787

Additional information:

1. The bank made an error when processing cheque #558.
2. The EFT collections were not previously recorded.
3. The company made an error in recording the May 25 deposit that related to a cash sale.
4. Because the EFT for prepaid insurance payment occurred near the end of the month, it has not been recorded yet.

Instructions

(a) Calculate the unadjusted cash balance per books at May 31, prior to reconciliation.
(b) What is the amount of the deposits in transit at May 31?
(c) What is the amount of the outstanding cheques at May 31?
(d) Prepare the bank reconciliation on May 31.
(e) Prepare any adjusting journal entries required from the reconciliation.

Prepare bank reconciliation and adjusting entries.
(SO 3)

P7–7B   The bank portion of the bank reconciliation for Racine Limited at November 30 is shown here:

RACINE LIMITED
Bank Reconciliation
November 30

Cash balance per bank		$14,368
Add: Deposits in transit		2,530
		16,898
Less: Outstanding cheques		
#3451	$2,260	
#3471	845	
#3474	1,050	4,155
Adjusted cash balance		$12,743

The adjusted cash balance per bank agreed with the cash balance per books at November 30. The December bank statement showed the following:

RACINE LIMITED
Bank Statement
December 31

Date		Description	Amounts Deducted from Account (Debits)	Amounts Added to Account (Credits)	Balance
Nov.	30	Opening balance			14,368
Dec.	1	Deposit		2,530	16,898
	1	Cheque, No. 3451	2,260		14,638
	2	Cheque, No. 3471	845		13,793
	3	Deposit		1,212	15,005
	4	Cheque, No. 3475	1,641		13,364
	7	EFT, salaries	1,427		11,937
	8	Cheque, No. 3476	1,300		10,637
	10	Cheque, No. 3477	2,130		8,507
	15	Cheque, No. 3479	3,080		5,427
	15	EFT, collection on account, R Nishimura		3,145	8,572
	17	Deposit		2,945	11,517
	21	EFT, salaries	1,427		10,090
	24	Returned cheque—NSF, Hilo Holdings	987		9,103
	24	NSF fee	40		9,063
	25	Deposit		2,567	11,630
	27	Cheque, No. 3480	600		11,030
	27	Cheque, No. 3482	1,140		9,890
	30	Deposit		1,025	10,915
	30	Cheque, No. 3481	475		10,440
	31	SVC plan fee	45		10,395

The cash records per books for December showed the following:

Cash Receipts			Cash Payments		
Date		Amount	Date	Number	Amount
Dec. 1		$1,212	Dec. 1	3475	$ 1,641
17		2,954	2	3476	1,300
27		2,567	2	3477	2,130
30		1,025	4	3478	538
31		1,197	7	EFT, salaries	1,427
		$8,955	8	3479	3,080
			10	3480	600
			20	3481	475
			21	EFT, salaries	1,427
			22	3482	1,140
			30	3483	1,390
					$15,148

Additional information:

1. The EFT collections were not previously recorded.
2. EFT payments are recorded when they occur.
3. The bank did not make any errors.
4. One error was made by the company. The correction of any errors in recording cheques should be made to Accounts Payable. The correction of any errors in recording cash receipts should be made to Accounts Receivable.

Instructions
(a) Calculate the unadjusted cash balance per books at December 31, prior to reconciliation.
(b) Prepare the bank reconciliation on December 31.
(c) Prepare any adjusting journal entries required from the reconciliation.

P7–8B   Giant Inc. is a profitable small business. It has not, however, given much consideration to internal control. For example, in an attempt to keep clerical and office expenses to a minimum, the company has combined the jobs of cashier and bookkeeper. As a result, Karen Kilgora handles all cash receipts, keeps the accounting records, and prepares the monthly bank reconciliations.

Prepare bank reconciliation and identify weaknesses in control activities.
(SO 1, 3)

The balance per bank statement on November 30 was $13,655. Outstanding cheques were #62 for $127, #83 for $180, #84 for $253, and #86 for $190. There was one deposit in transit for $4,040. Included in the bank statement was a notification about a $225 electronic collection on account from a customer.

The company's general ledger showed the Cash account with a balance of $17,341. The balance included undeposited cash on hand. Because of the lack of internal controls, Kilgora took all of the undeposited receipts, which were recorded on the company's books, for her personal use. She then prepared the following bank reconciliation to hide her theft of cash:

GIANT INC.
Bank Reconciliation
November 30

Cash balance per books		$17,341
Less: EFT, collection from customer		225
Adjusted cash balance per books		$17,116
Cash balance per bank statement		$13,655
Add: Deposit in transit		4,040
		17,695
Less: Outstanding cheques		
#62	$127	
#83	108	
#84	235	
#86	109	579
Adjusted cash balance per bank		$17,116

Instructions
(a) Identify the errors in the above bank reconciliation.
(b) Prepare a correct bank reconciliation.
(c) Identify how much Kilgora stole for personal use. (*Hint*: The theft is the difference between the adjusted balance per books before the theft and the adjusted balance per bank.)
(d) Indicate the various ways that Kilgora tried to hide the theft and the dollar amount for each method.
(e) What control activities were violated in this case?

Calculate cash.
(SO 4)

P7–9B   A new accounting student has been asked to determine the balance that should be reported as cash as at December 31 for one of the firm's clients. The following information is available:

1. Cash on hand in the cash registers on December 31 totals $1,600. Of this amount, $500 is kept on hand as a cash float.
2. At December 31, the company has debit card slips in the cash register totalling $500.
3. At December 31, the company has MasterCard credit card slips in the cash register totalling $975.
4. The balance in the bank chequing account at December 31 is $7,460.
5. Short-term investments include $5,000 in a Government of Ontario bond that falls due in 80 days.
6. The company sold $250 of merchandise to a customer late in the day on December 31. The customer had forgotten her wallet and promised to pay the amount on January 2.
7. The company has a U.S. dollar bank account. At December 31, its U.S. funds were the equivalent of $2,241 Canadian.
8. In order to hook up utilities, the company is required to deposit $1,000 in trust with Ontario One.
9. The amount in item 8. above must remain on deposit until a satisfactory credit history has been established. The company expects to have this deposit back within the year.

Instructions
(a) Determine which items listed above would be included in cash and which would be included in cash equivalents on the year-end statement of financial position.
(b) Identify where any items that were not reported in cash or in cash equivalents in (a) should be reported.

Discuss reporting of
cash.
(SO 4)

P7–10B   Boardwalk Real Estate Investment Trust reports the following selected information (in thousands) in its December 31, 2010, financial statements:

	2010	2009
Cash and cash equivalents	$228,086	$190,325
Segregated tenants' security deposits	11,987	12,917
Cash provided by operating activities	134,079	133,419

Additional information:

1. Cash and cash equivalents comprise cash in the bank, cash on hand, and instruments with maturity dates of three months or less when acquired.
2. Segregated tenants' security deposits are held on behalf of tenants and are returned at the end of a lease if the apartment rented to the tenant is undamaged.

Instructions
(a) Why do you think that the security deposits are not included in cash and cash equivalents?
(b) How is it possible that Boardwalk has $228,086 thousand of cash and cash equivalents at the end of 2010 but generated only $134,079 thousand of cash from operating activities in the same year?

Recommend cash
management
improvements.
(SO 4)

P7–11B   Jackie Ledbetter started a business, Jackie's Designs Inc., on the completion of her interior design courses eight months ago. Jackie has been fortunate in that the company has already completed six contracts and has four more signed contracts and meetings with prospective customers. A number of the prospective customers are referrals from the six contracts she has already completed.

Jackie is having difficulty understanding why her business has no cash in the bank since it has been so successful. You asked her to explain the terms of the contracts and her system for purchases.

A contract is signed once the customer and Jackie agree on the work to be done. There is no deposit on signing the contract. The contract price is a flat fee for Jackie's work and cost plus a percentage for all items purchased by the company. The fee for Jackie's work is due once the contract is completed. The amount for items purchased by the company is due three weeks after the items are delivered to the customer, in case the customer wants to return them. To date, an average contract takes four months to complete.

The company does not have a formalized system for purchases. If a customer agrees that they would like to purchase certain items, Jackie will purchase the items when she finds them. Generally, she uses cash to pay for the items at the time of purchase. The items are then delivered to the customer within a week.

Instructions
Identify ways the company can improve its cash management practices.

Prepare cash budget.
(SO 4)

P7–12B   Strathcona Caterers Limited has the following projected income statement for the first two months of 2012.

	January	February
Sales	$110,000	$140,000
Cost of food and beverages sold	30,000	42,000
Salary expense	25,000	36,000
Other operating expenses	40,000	50,000

Realizing that an income statement does not measure cash flows, Strathcona's manager has asked you to prepare a cash budget for January and February. The company usually pays all of the salaries and other operating costs each month but will only collect cash from customers of $90,000 in January and $120,000 in February. Furthermore, the company's food suppliers allow the company some credit so payments for food and beverage costs in January will be $23,000 and $36,000, respectively. At the beginning of January, the company had $10,000 of cash on hand. The company would like to buy some equipment for $17,000 in January and plans to sell some investments for $10,000 in February.

Instructions

(a) Prepare a cash budget for the company for January and February.
(b) Based on your budget, determine if the company needs to obtain a loan from the bank in January and whether it can repay any of the loan in February.

Broadening Your Perspective

Financial Reporting and Analysis Cases

Financial Reporting: *Eastplats*

BYP7–1 The financial statements of Eastern Platinum Limited (Eastplats) are presented in Appendix A. At the front of the appendix is a report from the company's independent auditors.

Discuss internal control responsibilities. (SO 1)

Instructions

(a) Does the report indicate who is responsible for the internal controls maintained by the company?
(b) What is the auditors' responsibility with regard to internal control?
(c) Does the auditor express an opinion on the company's internal controls? If so, what is it?

Comparative Analysis: *Eastplats and Amplats*

BYP7–2 The financial statements of Anglo American Platinum Limited (Amplats) are presented in Appendix B following the financial statements for Eastern Platinum Limited (Eastplats) in Appendix A.

Discuss internal controls and cash and cash equivalents. (SO 1, 4)

Instructions

(a) In Amplats's auditors' report, who is responsible for the company's internal controls?
(b) Which company has the larger amount of cash and equivalents relative to its total assets?
(c) The cash and equivalents on the 2010 statement of financial position of Eastplats have increased considerably since 2009. By looking at the statement of cash flows, what is the major reason for this increase?

Interpreting Financial Information

BYP7–3 Selected account balances follow for Ryanair Holdings plc, a discount airline that operates primarily in Europe:

Discuss reporting of cash and investments. (SO 4)

RYANAIR HOLDINGS PLC	
Statement of Financial Position (partial)	
September 30, 2010	
(in millions of euros)	
Assets	
Non-current assets	
Property, plant, and equipment	€4,685
Long-term investments	166
Other	63
Total non-current assets	4,914
Current assets	
Other	201
Restricted cash	61
Financial assets: cash > 3 months	1,028
Cash and equivalents	1,936
Total current assets	3,226
Total assets	€8,140

Instructions

(a) What is meant by restricted cash?
(b) What are cash and cash equivalents?
(c) Why does the company show separately the financial assets that relate to cash deposits maturing after three months?
(d) Why do you think long-term investments are shown separately as non-current?
(e) What percentage of the 2010 total assets is represented by short-term investments?

Comparing IFRS and ASPE

Understand control activities and management's internal control responsibilities.
(SO 1)

BYP7–4   **Nick's Steakhouse and Pizza**, described in the opening feature story of this chapter, is a privately held family-run restaurant located in Calgary.

Prime Restaurants Inc. (PRI) is a Canadian public company that operates two leading brands of casual dining restaurants, East Side Mario's and Casey's restaurants, along with pubs and Belgian-style brasseries called Bier Markt.

Service Inspired Restaurants (SIR) is a privately held Canadian company that owns and operates a diverse range of full-service restaurants that include Alice Fazooli's and the Loose Moose Tap & Grill.

Since Nick's, PRI, and SIR are all in the same industry, they have much in common. However, they are also very different. For instance, Nick's is an owner-operated single location, whereas both PRI and SIR have multiple locations and multiple owners. On the other hand, Nick's and SIR are both private companies so they follow ASPE while PRI is a public company that follows IFRS.

Instructions

(a) Do you think that, when a company chooses a particular set of accounting standards to use, this has any impact on its internal controls? If so, how?
(b) Which two companies do you think have the more similar control systems: Nick's and SIR or SIR and PRI? Why?
(c) Because PRI is a public company, management is required to perform an annual in-depth evaluation of PRI's internal controls over financial reporting. PRI must state in its annual report that the evaluation was performed as well as the CEO and CFO's conclusion on the effectiveness of internal controls. If there were any material weaknesses, this must be reported along with how management plans to fix these weaknesses. Why do you think public companies are required to report on the effectiveness of their internal controls?
(d) In its annual report for the year ended January 2, 2011, PRI reported that an evaluation of internal controls was performed and that its controls were effective. What does this information tell a financial statement user about PRI?

Critical Thinking Cases and Activities

Collaborative Learning Activity

Identify control strengths and weaknesses.
(SO 1, 2)

BYP7–5   In your past or current employment and personal experiences, there have been countless situations in which cash was received and disbursed.

Instructions
With the class divided into groups, do the following:
(a) Think of a few such situations. Identify the strengths and weaknesses in internal control used for cash receipts in the situations you have chosen.
(b) Identify the strengths and weaknesses in internal control used for cash disbursements in the chosen situations.

Communication Activity

Identify control weaknesses.
(SO 1, 2)

BYP7–6   Raymond Chow was an entrepreneur who built up a successful construction company. His wife, Sheila, performed all of the accounting functions for the company until she became ill and Raymond hired Claudia Chen as his full-time accountant. She opened the mail, made bank deposits, signed cheques, reconciled bank accounts, and authorized electronic funds transfers. She also prepared invoices to customers and recorded all of the company's journal entries in a computerized software program that she had on her laptop. After working for the company for six months, Claudia failed to show up at work. Upon further investigation, Raymond found that Claudia had stripped all of the cash out of the company. He was forced to declare bankruptcy.

Instructions
Write a letter to Raymond explaining how weaknesses in control activities over cash allowed the bankruptcy to occur. Suggest possible techniques that Claudia used to defraud the company.

Ethics Case

BYP7-7   Banks charge fees of up to $45 for bounced cheques; that is, NSF cheques that exceed the balance in the payor's account. It has been estimated that processing bounced cheques costs a bank less than $5 per cheque. Thus, the profit margin on bounced cheques is high. Recognizing this, banks process cheques from largest to smallest within the same date range. By doing this, they maximize the number of cheques that bounce if a customer overdraws an account.

Discuss ethical issues related to processing cheques. (SO 3)

Instructions

(a) Who are the stakeholders in this case?

(b) Freeman Corp. had a balance of $1,500 in its chequing account on a day when the bank received the following five cheques for processing against that account:

Cheque Number	Amount
3150	$ 35
3158	1,510
3162	400
3165	890
3169	180

      Assuming a $45 fee is charged by the bank, how much fee revenue would the bank generate if it processed cheques (1) from largest to smallest and (2) from smallest to largest?

(c) Do you think that processing cheques from largest to smallest is an ethical business practice?

(d) Besides ethical issues, what else must a bank consider in deciding whether to process cheques from largest to smallest?

(e) If you were managing a bank, what policy would you adopt on bounced cheques?

"All About You" Activity

BYP7-8   The "All About You" feature in this chapter indicates potential security risks that may arise in banking, e-commerce, and other situations.

Discuss ways to prevent identity theft. (SO 1)

Instructions

(a) Go to the Canadian Anti-Fraud Centre's website www.antifraudcentre-centreantifraude.ca. What do the terms "phishing," "pharming," and "spoofing" mean? What are some of the tips on how to spot and avoid these scams?

(b) Go to the website of the Office of the Privacy Commissioner of Canada www.priv.gc.ca. What are three things that it recommends you can do to address concerns about social networking and personal information?

(c) Is it safe to pay bills on-line? What control activities can a company put in place to make a consumer feel safe in paying bills on-line? Would companies pay bills on-line? If so, what safeguards would companies want in place to ensure the safety of their electronic bill payments?

Serial Case

(Note: This is a continuation of the serial case from Chapters 1 through 6).

BYP7-9   Natalie is learning how Koebel's Family Bakery accumulates accounting information. Because Janet and Brian are always busy in the bakery, the accounting for all transactions, especially cash, is sometimes neglected. Because Natalie has taken a few accounting courses, she would like to take a more active role in ensuring that there are effective controls in place at the bakery.

Identify control strengths and weaknesses. (SO 1, 2)

    Janet, Brian, and Natalie discuss the accounting process that currently takes place and the following issues come up:

1. There are two employees who work behind the counter and look after customers. There is only one cash register. Each employee has their own password. A customer will come into the bakery, have a look at what baked goods are available behind the counter, and order what they would like from one of the employees. The employee will pull the inventory off the shelf and proceed to the cash register. After inputting a password, the employee will record what has been sold. The cash register calculates the amount owing, records how the customer has paid, and prints a receipt. Sometimes, when the bakery is very busy, the employee will not have a chance to log off a transaction before moving on to the next customer. This will sometimes result in difficulty tracking which sale was made by which employee.

2. A summary of cash, credit card, and debit card receipts is printed daily. Janet or Brian attempts to reconcile daily the summary of receipts to cash deposited. (The deposit is done nightly by Janet or Brian.) Lately, the reconciliation is being done once a week and done all at once. Because of the difficulty with passwords, it is difficult to determine who has made the error in processing a sale. Once they have finished reconciling, Janet or Brian enters the amounts into the accounting records.

3. Inventory is usually counted at the end of the day to determine what needs to be available for sale in the bakery at the start of the next day.

4. A work schedule is made at the start of each month and all overtime must be approved by either Janet or Brian. Lately, additional hours are being worked by all staff because of the additional work required to make cupcakes. When Janet completes the payroll, she attempts to reconcile the monthly schedule to the hours worked by each of the staff members. Because Janet and Brian are not writing down which employee was authorized to work overtime, it is difficult to determine whether the overtime was in fact authorized.

5. Cupcakes shipped to Coffee Beans coffee shops are invoiced when the shipment is completed. The invoices are manually prepared by date. A photocopy is made to enable the invoices to be entered in the accounting records.

6. Purchases of inventory occur when one of the bakers alerts Janet or Brian that a particular product is running low. Sometimes this will result in overpurchasing if either Janet or Brian has already recognized a shortage of a particular type of inventory and not told the other that the purchase has already been made.

Instructions

(a) Identify to Natalie the strengths in Koebel's system of internal control. For each strength identified, describe the control activity that is being addressed.

(b) Identify to Natalie the weaknesses in Koebel's system of internal control, and for each weakness identified, suggest an improvement. As well, for each weakness identified, describe the control activity that is violated.

Answers to Self-Test Questions

1. b   2. c   3. c   4. b   5. d
6. d   7. b   8. c   9. c   10. b

Remember to go back to the beginning of the chapter to check off your completed work!

←

Reporting and Analyzing Receivables

the navigator

study objectives

After studying this chapter, you should be able to:

1. Explain how accounts receivable are recognized and valued in the accounts.

2. Explain how notes receivable are recognized and valued in the accounts.

3. Explain the statement presentation of receivables.

4. Apply the principles of sound accounts receivable management.

Varying Degrees of Credit

Receivables are generally a company's third-largest asset, after its property, plant, and equipment and inventory. For large retail operations like Canadian Tire, it is essential to monitor the collections of receivables on an ongoing basis.

"The major receivables would fall into three broad buckets," explains Huw Thomas, Canadian Tire's Executive Vice President, Financial Strategy and Performance. First, there is the Canadian Tire credit card, issued to some 4.6 million customers, 1.8 million of whom are actively using it in any given month. Second are the receivable accounts created by the 470 separate dealers across the country that buy merchandise from the company. The third category is vendor receivables, which would be money due from vendors in support of various programs such as product launches or new store openings.

The largest receivable amount is Canadian Tire's credit card program, which represents about $4 billion in receivables. The criteria for issuing a card are similar to any credit card program, says Mr. Thomas. Customers apply for new accounts, usually through the hostess program, where someone in the store will invite you to apply. The company assesses applications, does a credit score, and decides whether to issue a card and at what credit limit. It then manages the account, updating the credit score and adjusting the limit, when appropriate.

The credit card processing is outsourced to a company that handles credit card accounts for many companies. Canadian Tire also has a large call centre that deals with customer service collections—although certain collections are outsourced to collection agencies. The decision on when to send the account to the outside agency depends on the individual account, says Mr. Thomas. "You have a whole series of different strategies depending on how big the balance might be, what the past non-payment history has been, etc."

Still, despite efforts to collect its credit card accounts, Canadian Tire writes off well over $200 million per year in bad debts. "Whenever you lend money to anybody, you're always into a risk-reward balance," says Mr. Thomas.

Fortunately, the company's other receivable buckets carry virtually no bad debts. Canadian Tire essentially acts as a wholesaler, where dealers acquire from Canadian Tire all the merchandise they sell. "At any point in time, there are hundreds of millions of dollars outstanding based on monies that they owe to us for product that we've shipped to them," explains Mr. Thomas. Canadian Tire has a dedicated system that tracks shipments to each store, immediately recording the receivable and billing the dealer for the amount owed. "It's very unusual for a dealer to go into a position where they can't repay the monies that are owed to us," says Mr. Thomas. "Similarly, it's very unusual not to collect amounts that would be due from vendors because we typically owe them money as well."

So, for a large retail operation like Canadian Tire, it pays to have its receivables in more than one bucket.

the navigator

As indicated in our feature story, the management of receivables is important for any company that sells on credit, as Canadian Tire does. In this chapter, we will learn how companies estimate, record, and then in some cases collect their uncollectible accounts. We will also discuss how receivables are reported on the financial statements and how they are managed.

The chapter is organized as follows:

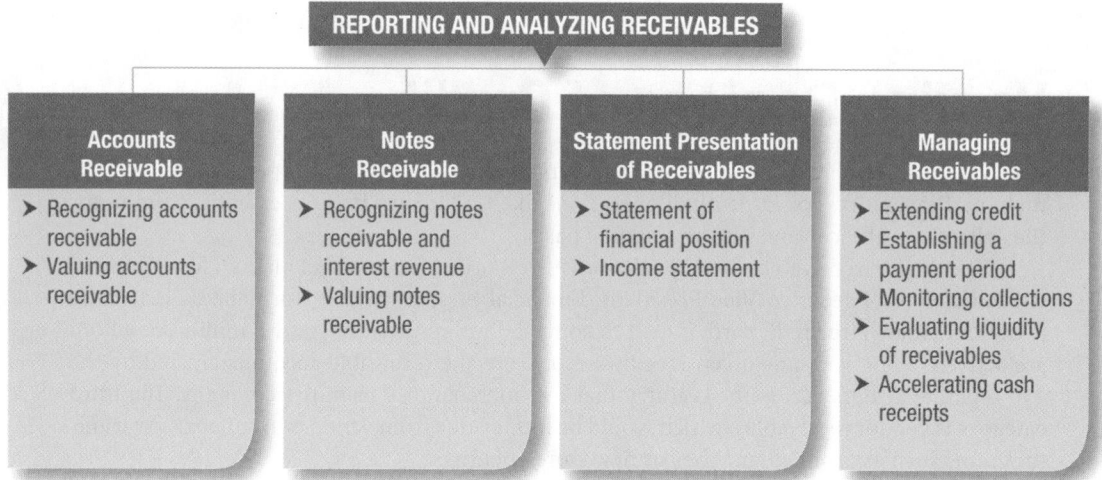

Accounts Receivable

The term *receivables* refers to amounts that are due to a business from its customers or other entities. Receivables are claims that are expected to be collected in cash, and they are frequently classified as (1) accounts receivable, (2) notes receivable, and (3) other receivables. Receivables, along with certain types of investments, are considered **financial assets**. These assets represent a contractual right to receive cash or another financial asset. We will learn more about financial assets in Chapter 12.

Accounts receivable are amounts owed by customers on account. They result from the sale of goods and services. Receivables are generally expected to be collected within 30 days or so, and are classified as current assets. They are usually the most significant type of claim held by a company.

Notes receivable are claims where formal instruments of credit—a written promise to repay—are issued as evidence of the debt. The credit instrument normally requires the debtor to pay interest and is for time periods of 30 days or longer. Notes receivable may be either current assets or non-current assets, depending on their due dates. Notes and accounts receivable that result from sales transactions are often called **trade receivables**.

Other receivables include interest receivable, loans to company officers, advances to employees, and recoverable sales tax and income tax. Canadian Tire also has dealer receivables, vendor receivables, and credit card receivables.

You will recall that in Chapter 7 we learned that, when a customer uses a bank credit card to make a purchase, we record such a transaction as a cash sale because we know that the bank will honour the credit card receipt as cash. However, if the company sponsors its own credit card, as Canadian Tire in our feature story does, such a sale is considered a credit sale, with a debit being recorded to Credit Card Receivables rather than Cash. Companies sponsor their own credit cards as it allows them to track the credit history of their customers, to earn interest revenue from overdue accounts, and to integrate this information with loyalty programs that accumulate "points" or other benefits for frequent shoppers.

We will focus our discussion in this section on accounts receivable, examining two accounting problems (1) recognizing accounts receivable and (2) valuing accounts receivable. We will discuss notes and other types of receivables later in the chapter.

RECOGNIZING ACCOUNTS RECEIVABLE

The first step in recognizing an account receivable is straightforward. For a service company, a receivable is recorded when a service is provided on account. For a merchandising company, a receivable is recorded at the point of sale of merchandise on account. Recall that we learned about revenue recognition criteria in Chapter 4. Revenue (and any related receivable) should be recognized when the sales effort is substantially complete. This normally occurs either when the service is performed or when goods are delivered at the point of sale. In addition, collection must be reasonably certain and measurable. This will be discussed in the next section.

Receivables are created by services or sales on account and reduced when cash is collected or when the customer takes advantage of a sales discount or returns the product (a sales return). The seller may offer terms, such as providing a discount, that encourage early payment. If the buyer chooses to pay within the discount period, the seller's account receivable is reduced in full by the amount of cash received plus the amount of the sales discount. Finally, the buyer might find some of the goods unacceptable and choose to return them. This also results in a reduction of the account receivable. For example, if $100 of merchandise purchased on account is returned, the seller reduces the account receivable by $100 when the returned merchandise is received. We learned about the entries required to record sales discounts and sales returns in Chapter 5. You may find it helpful to return to Chapter 5 to review these topics.

Accounts Receivable Subsidiary Ledger

In Chapter 3, we learned about the general ledger. Using the Accounts Receivable account in the general ledger works well for companies that do not have many customer accounts. Imagine what would happen, however, if a company like Canadian Tire recorded the account receivable for each of its customers in only one general ledger account. If it did, it would be very difficult to determine the balance owed by any one customer at a specific point in time.

Instead, companies like Canadian Tire use a subsidiary ledger in addition to the general ledger. A **subsidiary ledger** is a group of accounts that share a common characteristic (e.g., they are all receivable accounts). Unlike the general ledger, which has a single account for receivables, the subsidiary ledger has a receivable account for each customer. The total of all balances in the customer accounts in the subsidiary ledger should equal the total balance in the general ledger receivable account. This equality occurs because, when receivables transactions are recorded in the subsidiary ledgers on a customer-by-customer basis, summaries of these transactions are recorded in the general ledger. In this way, the subsidiary ledger provides supporting detail to the general ledger, freeing it from excessive detail. In addition to accounts receivable, other accounts that are supported by subsidiary ledgers include inventory (to track inventory quantities and balances), accounts payable (to track individual creditor balances), and payroll (to track individual employee pay records).

In the case of an accounts receivable subsidiary ledger, it contains a separate account for each individual customer; for example, a separate one for Adert Limited, Bortz Corporation, Mr. B. Carl, and so on. The general ledger contains only one receivables account—Accounts Receivable—which acts as a control account to the subsidiary ledger. A **control account** is a general ledger account that summarizes the subsidiary ledger data. At all times, the control account balance must equal the total of all the individual customer receivable balances in the subsidiary ledger.

Under this system of control and subsidiary accounts, each journal entry that affects accounts receivable must therefore be posted twice: once to the subsidiary ledger account and once to the general ledger control account. Normally, entries to the subsidiary ledger are posted immediately. Depending on the accounting software that is used, entries recorded to the general ledger may be summarized totals of the entries made to the subsidiary accounts.

To illustrate the use of ledgers and subsidiary ledgers, consider this example. Kinholm Limited had the following transactions during its first month of operations:

Credit Sales			Cash Collections		
Jan. 5	Sych Ltd.	$12,000	Jan. 16	Sych Ltd.	$9,000
9	Downey Inc.	5,000	22	Downey Inc.	3,500
13	Pawlak Corp.	6,000	28	Pawlak Corp.	6,000

The company has established an account for each customer in an accounts receivable subsidiary ledger. After recording transactions in the journal, Kinholm will also record (or post) the entry in the related account in the subsidiary ledger as follows:

Accounts Receivable Subsidiary Ledger

Sych Ltd.

Jan.	5	12,000	Jan.	16	9,000
Bal.		3,000			

Downey Inc.

Jan.	9	5,000	Jan.	22	3,500
Bal.		1,500			

Pawlak Corp.

Jan.	13	6,000	Jan.	28	6,000
Bal.		0			

The company must also post these transactions to the general ledger. Kinholm does this on a monthly basis. Notice that the debit of $23,000 to the general ledger Accounts Receivable account represents the total of all debits made to customer accounts in the subsidiary ledger in January. Likewise, the credit entry of $18,500 represents the total of all credits made to customer accounts in the subsidiary ledger in January. Because of this, the sum of all customer account balances in the subsidiary ledger is equal to the balance in the Accounts Receivable general ledger account at the end of January.

Accounts Receivable Subsidiary Ledger

Sych Ltd.

Jan.	5	12,000	Jan.	16	9,000
Bal.		3,000			

Downey Inc.

Jan.	9	5,000	Jan.	22	3,500
Bal.		1,500			

Pawlak Corp.

Jan.	13	6,000	Jan.	28	6,000
Bal.		0			

General Ledger

Accounts Receivable

Jan.	31	23,000[a]	Jan.	31	18,500[b]
Bal.		4,500			

[a]$12,000 + $5,000 + $6,000 = $23,000
[b]$9,000 + $3,500 + $6,000 = $18,500

Interest Revenue

At the end of each month, a company can use the subsidiary ledger to easily determine the transactions in each customer's account and then send the customer a statement of transactions that occurred that month. If the customer does not pay in full within a specified period of time (usually 30 days), an interest (financing) charge may be added to the balance due.

When financing charges are added, the seller recognizes interest revenue and increases the account receivable amount owed by the customer. This can be a substantial amount for some service and merchandising companies.

VALUING ACCOUNTS RECEIVABLE

Once receivables are recorded in the accounts, we need to determine the amount that they should be reported at in the financial statements. Although each customer must satisfy the seller's credit requirements before the credit sale is approved, inevitably some accounts receivable become uncollectible. For example, a corporate customer may not be able to pay because of a decline in sales due to a downturn in the economy. Similarly, individuals may be laid off from their jobs or faced with unexpected bills and find themselves unable to pay.

Credit losses from uncollectible receivables are debited to an account called Bad Debts Expense. Note that this new account, Bad Debts Expense, is used instead of debiting a contra sales account as we did for sales returns and allowances. An expense account is used because the responsibilities for granting credit and collecting accounts are normally separated from sales and marketing. You will recall from Chapter 7 that establishing responsibility to authorize transactions and activities is an important feature of a good internal control system.

Bad debts expense is considered a normal occurrence arising from the risk of having credit sales and it has an affect on the valuation of accounts receivable. The key issue in valuing accounts receivable is when to recognize these expenses. If the company waits until it knows for sure that the specific account will not be collected, it could end up recording the bad debts expense in a different period than when the revenue was recorded.

Consider the following example. In 2011, Quick Buck Computer Limited decides it could increase its revenues by offering computers to students without requiring any money down, and with no credit approval process. The promotion is a success and the company sells 100,000 computers with a selling price of $800 each. This increases Quick Buck Computer's receivables and revenues by $80 million. The 2011 statement of financial position and income statement look wonderful. Unfortunately, during 2012, nearly 40% of the student customers default on their accounts. This makes the 2012 statement of financial position and income statement look terrible. Illustration 8-1 shows that the promotion in 2011 was not such a great success after all.

Year 2011	Year 2012
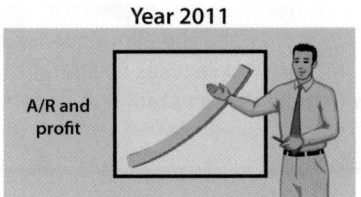	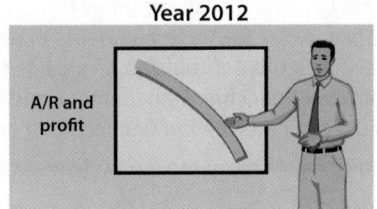
Huge sales promotion. Accounts receivable and sales increase dramatically.	Customers default on amounts owed; accounts receivable plummet. Bad debts expense increases dramatically.

► Illustration 8-1
Effects of mismatching bad debts

If bad debts expense is recorded only when customers default, no attempt is made to match this expense to sales revenues in the income statement. Recall that accrual accounting requires expenses to be reported in the same period as the sales they helped generate. Quick Buck Computer Limited's income statement is skewed with an overstatement of profit in 2011 and an understatement of profit in 2012 because of mismatched sales and bad debts expense.

In addition, accounts receivable in the statement of financial position are not reported at the amount actually expected to be collected at the end of 2011. Consequently, Quick Buck Computer's receivables are overstated in 2011, misrepresenting its statement of financial position.

The allowance method offers a solution to this problem. The **allowance method** of accounting for bad debts estimates the uncollectible accounts at the end of each period and shows this estimate in Allowance for Doubtful Accounts, which is a contra asset account with a credit balance that is shown below Accounts Receivable. This allowance is an estimate of the amount of receivables that are expected to become uncollectible in the future.

A contra account is used instead of a direct credit to Accounts Receivable for two reasons. First, we do not know which individual customers will not pay. If the company uses a subsidiary ledger, we are unable to credit specific customer accounts to show they are uncollectible. We are also unable to credit the control account itself as this would mean that its balance would not equal the sum of all customer accounts in the subsidiary ledger. Second, the balance in Allowance for

Doubtful Accounts is just an estimate. A contra account helps to separate estimates from actual amounts, such as those found in Accounts Receivable.

The Accounts Receivable balance less the Allowance for Doubtful Accounts equals the **net realizable value** or collectible portion of these accounts. The allowance has a credit balance and, when it is increased, the offsetting debit is recorded in Bad Debts Expense. Because these adjustments are made at the end of the period, the bad debts expense is recorded in the same period as the related sales.

The allowance method is required for financial reporting purposes. It has three essential features:

1. **Recording estimated uncollectible accounts:** The amount of uncollectible accounts receivable is estimated by ensuring that the balance in Allowance for Doubtful Accounts is equal to the estimate of uncollectible accounts. Any increase to the allowance balance is also recorded in Bad Debts Expense so that it can be recorded in the same period that the related revenue was earned.
2. **Recording the write-off of an uncollectible account:** Actual uncollectibles are written off at the time the specific account is determined to be uncollectible. This will cause a reduction in accounts receivable because the account is not collectible. It will also cause a reduction in the allowance for doubtful accounts, because the account is no longer doubtful.
3. **Recording the recovery of an uncollectible account:** When an account that was previously written off is later collected, the original write-off is reversed and the collection is recorded. Note that neither the write-off nor the subsequent recovery affects the income statement.

ACCOUNTING MATTERS! *Ethics Perspective*

Estimating the Allowance for Doubtful Accounts

It is during the time when a company experiences a downturn and finds it increasingly difficult to collect its receivables that investors expect management to properly indicate the seriousness of this problem in the financial statements. This is done by recording an appropriate allowance for doubtful accounts. However, it is at these times that management faces the strongest pressure to understate this allowance. Why? Because bad debts expense diminishes profits and the allowance for doubtful accounts reduces the net realizable value of receivables, which in turn reduces collateral that could be used for bank financing. Management must therefore withstand the temptation to understate the estimates used in determining uncollectible accounts.

Recording Estimated Uncollectible Accounts

To illustrate the allowance method, assume that Abrams Furniture Ltd. has net credit sales of $1.2 million in 2012. Of this amount, $200,000 remains uncollected at December 31. The credit manager estimates (using techniques we will discuss shortly) that bad debts expense is $10,000. The adjusting entry to record the bad debts expense for the year is:

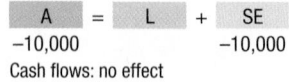

A	=	L	+	SE				
−10,000				−10,000	Dec. 31	Bad Debts Expense	10,000	
Cash flows: no effect						Allowance for Doubtful Accounts		10,000
						(To record estimate of uncollectible accounts)		

Bad debts expense is reported in the income statement as an operating expense. It is recorded in 2012 because that is the year when the related sales were recorded.

The balance in Allowance for Doubtful Accounts is deducted from Accounts Receivable in the current assets section of the statement of financial position. Assuming that Abrams Furniture Ltd. has an opening balance of $1,000 in Allowance for Doubtful Accounts, the bad debts expense would increase this balance by the end of the year to $11,000 ($1,000 + $10,000) and this would be reported as follows:

Accounts receivable	$200,000
Less: Allowance for doubtful accounts	11,000
Net realizable value	$189,000

The $189,000 represents the expected net realizable value of the accounts receivable at the statement date. This can be represented by the formula shown in Illustration 8-2.

Accounts Receivable	−	Allowance for Doubtful Accounts	=	Net Realizable Value
$200,000	−	$11,000	=	$189,000

▶Illustration 8-2
Formula for calculating net realizable value

Estimating the Allowance. For Abrams Furniture above, we simply gave the amount of the expected uncollectibles for the current period ($10,000). In actual practice, however, companies calculate an estimate of their likely uncollectible accounts. While there are several acceptable ways to estimate uncollectible accounts, most companies use a percentage of their outstanding receivables to determine the allowance for doubtful accounts.

Under the **percentage of receivables basis**, management estimates what percentage of receivables is likely to be uncollectible. This percentage can be assigned to receivables in total or stratified (divided further) by the ages of the receivables. Stratifying the percentage classifies customer balances by the length of time they have been unpaid, which can improve the reliability of the estimate. Because of its emphasis on time, using stratification is called **aging the accounts receivable**.

After the accounts are classified by age, the expected allowance amount for doubtful accounts is determined by applying percentages, based on past experience, to the totals of each category. The longer a receivable is past due, the less likely it is to be collected. As a result, the estimated percentage of uncollectible debts increases as the number of days past due increases. An aging schedule for Abrams Furniture is shown in Illustration 8-3. Note the increasing uncollectible percentages from 2% to 50%.

		Number of Days Outstanding				
Customer	Total	0–30	31–60	61–90	91–120	Over 120
Adert Limited	$ 6,800	$ 3,800	$ 3,000			
Bortz Corporation	12,200	8,700	3,500			
B. Carl	9,400	6,400	3,000			
Diker Furnishings Ltd.	36,600	22,400	8,600	$ 4,000	$1,600	
T. Ebbet	2,500					$2,500
Others	132,500	70,200	23,300	34,000	5,000	
	$200,000	$111,500	$41,400	$38,000	$6,600	$2,500
Estimated percentage uncollectible		2%	5%	10%	25%	50%
Total estimated allowance for doubtful accounts	$ 11,000	$ 2,230	$ 2,070	$ 3,800	$1,650	$1,250

▶Illustration 8-3
Aging schedule

The $11,000 total is the amount of existing receivables that is expected to become uncollectible in the future. This amount is also the required balance in Allowance for Doubtful Accounts at the statement of financial position date. Note that this is the amount of the balance in the account, and not the amount of the adjustment required. **The amount of the bad debts adjusting entry is the difference between the required balance and the existing balance in the allowance account.** If the trial balance shows Allowance for Doubtful Accounts with a credit balance of $1,000, then an adjusting entry for the difference between this existing balance and the desired balance of $11,000, which is $10,000 ($11,000 − $1,000), is recorded as follows:

Dec. 31	Bad Debts Expense	10,000	
	Allowance for Doubtful Accounts		10,000
	(To record estimate of uncollectible accounts)		

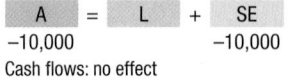

A	=	L	+	SE
−10,000				−10,000

Cash flows: no effect

After the adjusting entry is posted, the accounts of Abrams Furniture will show the following:

Bad Debts Expense				Allowance for Doubtful Accounts			
Dec. 31.	Adj.	10,000		Jan. 1	Bal.	1,000
				Dec. 31	Adj.	10,000
				Dec. 31	Bal.	11,000

Occasionally, the allowance account will have a debit balance before the adjustment. This occurs when write-offs during the year exceed previous estimates for bad debts. (We will discuss write-offs in the next section.) If there is an opening debit balance, the debit balance is added to the required balance when the adjusting entry is made. That is, if there had been a $1,000 debit balance in Abrams Furniture's allowance account before adjustment, the adjusting entry would have been for $12,000 to arrive at a credit balance in the allowance account of $11,000.

Recording the Write-Off of an Uncollectible Account

Companies use various methods of collecting past-due accounts, such as letters, phone calls, collection agencies, and legal action. In the feature story, Canadian Tire has a call centre that deals with some overdue accounts and it outsources other cases to a collection agency. When all ways of collecting a past-due account have been tried and collection appears unlikely, the account should be written off and removed from the allowance because there is no longer any doubt about its collection. Canadian Tire writes off any credit card receivables that are 180 days past due.

To prevent premature or unauthorized write-offs, each write-off should be formally approved in writing by authorized management personnel. To adhere to the appropriate internal control activity, authorization to write off accounts should not be given to someone who also has daily responsibilities related to cash or receivables, in order to prevent them from misappropriating the cash receipt and writing off the account to hide the theft.

To illustrate a receivables write-off, assume that on March 1, 2013, Abrams Furniture's vice-president of finance authorizes a write-off of the $2,500 balance owed by T. Ebbet, a customer. The entry to record the write-off is:

A	=	L	+	SE
+2,500				
−2,500				

Cash flows: no effect

Mar. 1	Allowance for Doubtful Accounts	2,500	
	Accounts Receivable—T. Ebbet		2,500
	(Write-off of T. Ebbet account)		

Bad Debts Expense is not increased (debited) when the write-off occurs. **Under the allowance method, every accounts receivable write-off entry is debited to the allowance account and not to Bad Debts Expense.** A debit to Bad Debts Expense would be incorrect because the expense was already recognized when the adjusting entry that estimated the allowance balance was recorded last year.

Notice that the entry to record the write-off of an uncollectible account reduces both Accounts Receivable and Allowance for Doubtful Accounts. After posting, using an assumed Accounts Receivable opening balance of $227,500, the general ledger accounts will appear as follows:

Accounts Receivable						Allowance for Doubtful Accounts			
Feb. 28	Bal.	227,500	Mar. 1	2,500	Mar. 1	2,500	Jan. 1	Bal.	11,000
Mar. 1	Bal.	225,000					Mar. 1	Bal.	8,500

A write-off affects only statement of financial position accounts and reduces both Accounts Receivable and Allowance for Doubtful Accounts equally. Net realizable value on the statement of financial position remains the same, as shown below:

	Before Write-Off	After Write-Off
Accounts receivable	$227,500	$225,000
Less: Allowance for doubtful accounts	11,000	8,500
Net realizable value	$216,500	$216,500

As mentioned earlier, the allowance account can sometimes end up with a debit balance after a write-off of an uncollectible account. This occurs if the write-offs during the period exceed the opening balance. This is only a temporary situation: it will be corrected when the adjusting entry for estimated uncollectible accounts is made at the end of the period.

Recording the Recovery of an Uncollectible Account

Occasionally, a company collects from a customer after the account has been written off as uncollectible. Two entries are required to record the recovery of a bad debt: (1) the entry made in writing off the account is reversed to reinstate the customer's account; and (2) the collection is recorded in the usual way.

To illustrate, assume that on July 1, T. Ebbet's fortunes have changed and he now wants to restore his credit with Abrams Furniture. In order to do so, he has to pay the $2,500 amount that had been written off on March 1. The entries are as follows:

		(1)		
July 1	Accounts Receivable—T. Ebbet		2,500	
	Allowance for Doubtful Accounts			2,500
	(To reverse write-off of T. Ebbet account)			

		(2)		
1	Cash		2,500	
	Accounts Receivable—T. Ebbet			2,500
	(To record collection from T. Ebbet)			

A	=	L	+	SE
+2,500				
−2,500				

Cash flows: no effect

A	=	L	+	SE
+2,500				
−2,500				

↑Cash flows: +2,500

Note that the recovery of a bad debt, like the write-off of a bad debt, affects only statement of financial position accounts. The net effect of the two entries is an increase (a debit) to Cash and an increase (a credit) to Allowance for Doubtful Accounts for $2,500. Accounts Receivable is debited and later credited in a second entry, as shown above, for two reasons. First, the company should reverse the write-off as soon as the receivable is considered collectible. Second, T. Ebbet did pay, and the accounts receivable account in the subsidiary (and general) ledger should show this collection as it will need to be considered for future credit purposes.

ACCOUNTING MATTERS!   *Ethics Perspective*

Social Media and Debt Collection

When a company writes off an account receivable, it may also sell the receivable to a collection agency for a very small fraction of its value. Collection agencies go to great lengths to collect amounts owed. Recently, a court ruled that debt collectors had violated a woman's privacy rights when a collection agency sent messages to her and her family on the Facebook networking site to have her call the agency about the debt.

The woman's lawyer said, "It's the beginning of an epidemic," calling it, "another weapon" debt collectors can use. In another case, a man was befriended on Facebook by a young woman in a bikini. The woman turned out to be a debt collector, something the man realized only when the "friend" posted a message on his wall: "Pay your debts, you deadbeat."

Source: Tamara Lush, "Agency Prohibited from Using Facebook to Collect Debt," Associated Press, March 9, 2011.

Summary of Allowance Method

In summary, there are three types of transactions when accounts receivable are valued using the allowance method:

1. Estimated uncollectible accounts receivable are recorded at the end of the period by debiting Bad Debts Expense and crediting Allowance for Doubtful Accounts. The amount to record can

be determined by using a percentage of total receivables, or an aging schedule. This entry is an adjusting entry that is made at the end of the period.

2. Actual uncollectibles, or write-offs, are then debited to Allowance for Doubtful Accounts and credited to Accounts Receivable. This entry is not an adjusting entry and is recorded as soon as it can be determined that collection of an account is unlikely.

3. Later recoveries, if any, are recorded in two separate entries. The first reverses the write-off by debiting Accounts Receivable and crediting Allowance for Doubtful Accounts. The second records the normal collection of the account by debiting Cash and crediting Accounts Receivable.

These entries are summarized and illustrated in the following T accounts:

Accounts Receivable		Allowance for Doubtful Accounts	
Beginning balance	Collections	Write-offs	Beginning balance
Credit sales	Write-offs		Bad debt adjustment
Subsequent recoveries			Subsequent recoveries
Ending balance			Ending balance

DECISION TOOLKIT

 Decision Checkpoints	 Info Needed for Decision	 Tools to Use for Decision	 How to Evaluate Results
Is the amount of past-due accounts increasing? Which accounts require management's attention?	List of outstanding receivables and their due dates	Prepare an aging schedule showing the receivables in various stages: outstanding 0–30 days, 31–60 days, 61–90 days, 91–120 days, and over 120 days.	Accounts in the older categories require follow-up: letters, phone calls, e-mails, and possible renegotiations of terms.

BEFORE YOU GO ON...

▶ Do It! Bad Debts

A partially prepared aging schedule for Chang Wholesalers Corporation at its year end, December 31, follows:

	Total	Number of Days Outstanding			
		0–30	31–60	61–90	Over 90
Accounts receivable	$460,000	$200,000	$120,000	$100,000	$40,000
Estimated percentage uncollectible		2%	5%	10%	20%

Complete the aging schedule and prepare the required journal entry to record the estimated bad debts expense at December 31. Assume that prior to performing the above calculations, Allowance for Doubtful Accounts had a credit balance of $8,000.

Action Plan

- Apply percentages to outstanding receivables in each age category to determine the total estimated allowance for doubtful accounts.
- Determine the difference between the desired balance in the allowance account estimated above and the current balance in that account. Be alert to the possibility that the current balance could be either a debit or a credit while the desired balance will always be a credit.

Notes Receivable

Credit may also be granted in exchange for a formal credit instrument known as a promissory note. A **promissory note** is a written promise to pay a specified amount of money on demand (i.e., as soon as the payee demands repayment) or at a definite time. Promissory notes may be used (1) when individuals and companies lend or borrow money, (2) when the amount of the transaction and the length of the credit period exceed normal limits, and (3) in settlement of accounts receivable.

In a promissory note, the party making the promise to pay is called the maker; the party who will be paid is called the payee. For the maker of the note, the note would be classified as a note payable. For the payee of the note, the note would be classified as a note receivable. The promissory note details the names of the maker and the payee, the principal or face value of the loan, the loan period, the interest rate, and whether interest is payable monthly or at maturity (the note's due date) along with the principal amount. Other details might include whether any security is pledged as collateral for the loan and what happens if the maker defaults (does not pay).

A note receivable is a formal promise to pay an amount that bears interest from the time it is issued until it is due. An account receivable is an informal promise to pay that bears interest only after its due date. Because it is less formal, it does not have as strong a legal claim as a note receivable. Most accounts receivable are due within a short period of time, usually 30 days, whereas notes receivable can be due over a longer period.

There are also similarities between notes and accounts receivable. Both are credit instruments. Both can be sold to another party. And, as you will learn in the next section, both are valued at their net realizable value. The basic issues in accounting for notes receivable are the same as those for accounts receivable: (1) recognizing notes receivable and (2) valuing notes receivable.

> **STUDY OBJECTIVE 2**
> Explain how notes receivable are recognized and valued in the accounts.

RECOGNIZING NOTES RECEIVABLE AND INTEREST REVENUE

To illustrate the basic accounting for notes receivable, we will assume that on May 1, Tabusintac Inc. (the payee) accepts a note receivable in exchange for an account receivable from Raja Ltd. (the maker). The note is for $10,000, with 6% interest due in four months, on September 1.

We record this entry as follows for the receipt of the note by Tabusintac:

May 1	Notes Receivable—Raja	10,000	
	Accounts Receivable—Raja		10,000
	(To record acceptance of Raja note)		

A = L + SE
+10,000
−10,000
Cash flows: no effect

If a note is exchanged for cash, the entry is a debit to Notes Receivable and a credit to Cash in the amount of the loan.

The note receivable is recorded at its principal value, the value shown on the face of the note. No interest revenue is reported when the note is accepted, because, as we learned in Chapter 4, interest revenue is not earned until time passes. Interest is calculated as follows:

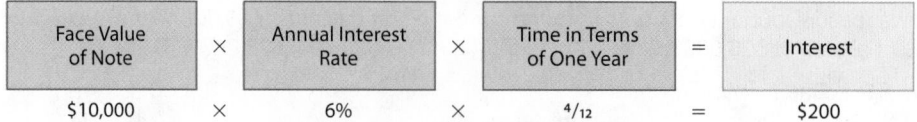

Face Value of Note	$\times$	Annual Interest Rate	$\times$	Time in Terms of One Year	$=$	Interest
$10,000	$\times$	6%	$\times$	4/12	$=$	$200

The interest rate specified on the note is an **annual** rate of interest. The time factor in the calculation represents the fraction of the year that the note is outstanding. As we did in past chapters, for simplicity we will continue to assume that interest is calculated in months, rather than days.

It is important to know that the calculation of interest as shown above applies only to short-term notes receivable with interest due at maturity. Notes that have a maturity date beyond one year from the statement of financial position date would be classified as long-term. Long-term notes generally are repayable in instalments rather than at maturity. Although not as common, short-term notes can also be repaid in instalments rather than at maturity. The interest calculations for instalment notes use a method to determine interest revenue called the effective-interest method. This method will be introduced in Chapter 10.

Interest on the Raja note will total $50 ($10,000 $\times$ 6% $\times$ $^{1}/_{12}$) a month, or $200 for the four-month period. This interest will be recorded as interest revenue for Tabusintac and interest expense for Raja. If Tabusintac's year end was May 31, the following adjusting journal entry would be required to accrue interest for the month of May:

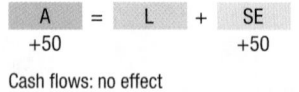

A = L + SE
+50   +50
Cash flows: no effect

May 31	Interest Receivable		50	
	Interest Revenue			50
	(To accrue interest on Raja note receivable)			

Note that while interest on an overdue account receivable is debited to Accounts Receivable, interest on a note receivable is *not* debited to the Notes Receivable account. Instead, a separate account for the interest receivable is used. Since the note is a formal credit instrument, its recorded principal must remain unchanged. In addition, it is useful for a company to track how much interest it is earning from notes receivable.

Notes are normally held to their maturity date, at which time the principal plus accrued interest is due. This is known as honouring (collecting) the note. In some situations, the maker of the note defaults and an appropriate adjustment must be made. This is known as dishonouring (not collecting) the note.

Honouring of Notes Receivable

A note is said to be honoured when it is paid in full at its maturity date. If Raja pays its note when it is due on September 1, the maturity date, the entry by Tabusintac to record the collection is:

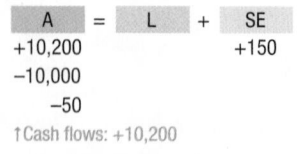

A = L + SE
+10,200   +150
−10,000
−50
↑Cash flows: +10,200

Sept. 1	Cash		10,200	
	Notes Receivable—Raja			10,000
	Interest Receivable			50
	Interest Revenue			150
	(To record collection of Raja note and interest)			

Recall that one month of interest, $50, was previously accrued on May 31. Consequently, only three months of interest revenue relating to June, July, and August—$150 ($10,000 $\times$ 6% $\times$ $^{3}/_{12}$)—is recorded in the period subsequent to May 31.

Dishonouring of Notes Receivable

A **dishonoured note** is a note that is not paid in full at maturity. A dishonoured note receivable is no longer negotiable. However, the payee still has a claim against the maker of the note for both the principal and any unpaid interest. Therefore, the Notes Receivable account balance and related interest are usually transferred to an account receivable by debiting Accounts Receivable for the total of the principal amount of the note and the interest due.

As shown below, the journal entry to record this is identical to the one above where the note was honoured, except that the debit to Cash would instead be made to the Accounts Receivable account:

Sept. 1	Accounts Receivable	10,200	
	Notes Receivable—Raja		10,000
	Interest Receivable		50
	Interest Revenue		150
	(To record dishonoured Raja note; eventual		
	collection expected)		

A	=	L	+	SE
+10,200				+150
−10,000				
−50				

Cash flows: no effect

If there is no hope of collection, the principal and any accrued interest should be written off. No interest revenue would be recorded, because collection will not occur. The entry to write off the amount is:

Sept. 1	Allowance for Doubtful Accounts (Notes)	10,050	
	Notes Receivable—Raja		10,000
	Interest Receivable		50
	(To write off dishonoured Raja note)		

A	=	L	+	SE
+10,200				+150
−10,000				
−50				

Cash flows: no effect

VALUING NOTES RECEIVABLE

Like accounts receivable, notes receivable are reported at their **net realizable value**. Each note must be analyzed to determine its probability of collection. If circumstances suggest that eventual collection is in doubt, bad debts expense and an allowance for doubtful accounts (notes) must be recorded in the same way they are recorded for accounts receivable. Many companies use just the one account, Allowance for Doubtful Accounts, for all trade receivables, which would include both accounts receivable and notes receivable.

BEFORE YOU GO ON...

▶ **Do It! Notes Receivable**

Sampson Stores Ltd. accepts from Shiraz Corp. a three-month, 6%, $6,800 note dated May 10 in settlement of Shiraz's overdue account.

(a) What journal entries would be made by Sampson on May 10 and on August 10, the maturity date, assuming Shiraz pays the note and interest in full at that time and no interest was previously accrued?

(b) What entry would be made on August 10 if Shiraz could not pay the note but the note is still expected to be collected in the future?

Action Plan

- Calculate the accrued interest. The formula is: face value × annual interest rate × time in terms of one year.
- If the note is honoured, record the collection of the note and any interest earned. Use separate accounts for the principal amount of the note and the interest.
- If the note is dishonoured, record the transfer of the note and any interest earned to an accounts receivable account if eventual collection is expected or to an allowance account if collection is not expected.

(continued)

Solution

(a) Note honoured:

May 10	Notes Receivable—Shiraz	6,800	
	Accounts Receivable—Shiraz		6,800
	(To replace account receivable with a 6% note receivable, due August 10)		
Aug. 10	Cash	6,902	
	Notes Receivable—Shiraz		6,800
	Interest Revenue ($6,800 × 6% × $^3/_{12}$)		102
	(To record collection of Shiraz note and interest)		

(b) Note dishonoured but collection in future is still likely:

Aug. 10	Accounts Receivable—Shiraz	6,902	
	Notes Receivable—Shiraz		6,800
	Interest Revenue ($6,800 × 6% × $^3/_{12}$)		102
	(To record dishonoured Shiraz note; eventual collection expected)		

the navigator

Statement Presentation of Receivables

STUDY OBJECTIVE 3

Explain the statement presentation of receivables.

Each of the major types of receivables should be identified in the statement of financial position or in the notes to the financial statements. In addition, related revenue and expense accounts are reported in the income statement, as discussed in the following sections.

STATEMENT OF FINANCIAL POSITION

Short-term receivables are reported in the current assets section of the statement of financial position, following cash and short-term investments if items are presented from most to least liquid. Although only the net realizable value of receivables must be disclosed, it is helpful to report both the gross amount of receivables and the allowance for doubtful accounts either in the statement or in the notes to the financial statements.

Illustration 8-4 shows the presentation of receivables for Shaw Communications, which provides television, Internet, and other media services to customers.

Illustration 8-4
Presentation of receivables

SHAW COMMUNICATIONS INC.
Notes to the Financial Statements (partial)
August 31, 2010
(in thousands)

SHAW

Note 3: Accounts Receivable

	2010	2009
Subscriber and trade receivables	$209,817	$204,786
Due from officers and employees	148	843
Due from related parties	1,689	682
Miscellaneous receivables	3,730	5,333
	215,384	211,644
Less: Allowance for doubtful accounts	18,969	17,161
	$196,415	$194,483

In note 3, Shaw discloses the components of its receivables. Notice how the Allowance for Doubtful Accounts increased from approximately $17 million in 2009 to almost $19 million in

2010. The net realizable value of the accounts receivable of $196 million in 2010 and $194 million in 2009 was reported in the current assets section of Shaw's statement of financial position.

INCOME STATEMENT

Income statement accounts related to receivables can include the revenue generated from sales or services on account, in addition to bad debts expense and interest revenue. Bad debts expense would be reported in the operating expense section of the income statement and interest revenue in the non-operating section.

Shaw reported, on its income statement, bad debts expense of $34 million. If we take the balance in the allowance at the beginning of 2010 of $17 million and add the bad debts expense of $34 million, one would expect that the allowance balance should be $51 million. However, by the end of 2010, the allowance balance is only $19 million. Why? Because the company wrote off receivables of $32 million during the year.

BEFORE YOU GO ON...

▶ Do It! Statement Presentation

Beau Resources Limited uses the accounts that are listed below. For each of the accounts listed, state if the account is a current asset (CA) or a non-current asset (NCA) reported on the statement of financial position, or if it is reported on the income statement (IS). Also state if the item is a contra account (C). If the item does not pertain to any of the above categories, state that it is not applicable (NA).

- Accumulated depreciation
- Allowance for doubtful accounts
- Bad debts expense
- Cash
- Credit card expense
- Credit card receivables
- Debit card expense
- Dividends
- Furniture
- Income tax expense
- Income tax payable
- Income tax receivable
- Intangible assets
- Merchandise inventory
- Notes receivable due in 120 days
- Prepaid expenses
- Sales
- Sales discounts
- Short-term investments
- Trade receivables

Action Plan

- Remember that current assets are turned into cash or used up within one year or operating cycle.
- Contra accounts offset other accounts and when applied against the related account, reduce it to a net balance.

Solution

Accumulated depreciation	NCA, C
Allowance for doubtful accounts	CA, C

(continued)

Bad debts expense	IS
Cash	CA
Credit card expense	IS
Credit card receivables	CA
Debit card expense	IS
Dividends	NA
Furniture	NCA
Income tax expense	IS
Income tax payable	NA
Income tax receivable	CA
Intangible assets	NCA
Inventory	CA
Notes receivable due in 120 days	CA
Prepaid expenses	CA
Sales	IS
Sales discounts	IS, C
Short-term investments	CA
Trade receivables	CA

the navigator

Managing Receivables

STUDY OBJECTIVE 4

Apply the principles of sound accounts receivable management.

There are five steps in managing accounts receivable:

1. Determine who to extend credit to.
2. Establish a payment period.
3. Monitor collections.
4. Evaluate the liquidity of receivables.
5. Accelerate cash receipts from receivables when necessary.

EXTENDING CREDIT

A critical part of managing receivables is determining who should receive credit and who should not. Many companies increase sales by being generous with their credit policy, but they may end up extending credit to risky customers who do not pay. If the credit policy is too tight, the company will lose sales. If it is too loose, it may sell to those who will pay either very late or not at all.

Certain steps can be taken to help minimize losses if credit standards are relaxed. Risky customers might be required to provide letters of credit or guarantees. Then, if the customer does not pay, the person or company that provided the guarantee will pay. Particularly risky customers might be required to pay a deposit in advance or cash on delivery.

In addition, companies should ask potential customers for references from banks and suppliers to determine their payment history. It is important to check these references on potential new customers and to periodically check the financial health of existing customers. Many resources are available for investigating customers. For example, to aid in lending decisions, companies such as Equifax provide credit opinions on companies around the world.

ESTABLISHING A PAYMENT PERIOD

Companies that extend credit should determine a required payment period and inform their customers about it. Normally, this period would be similar to the period used by competitors. If the period is shorter than a competitor's, sales could be lost. If the period is longer, the slower receipt of cash from customers may require the company to carry higher levels of debt.

MONITORING COLLECTIONS

An accounts receivable aging schedule should be prepared and reviewed often. Almost all accounting software programs can generate an aged listing at any time. In addition to its use in estimating the allowance for doubtful accounts, the aging schedule helps estimate the timing of future cash inflows when preparing a cash budget. It also provides information about the company's overall collection experience, and it identifies problem accounts. As we learned in our feature story, Canadian Tire uses a variety of different strategies to deal with its problem accounts depending on how big the balance might be, what the payment history has been, and so on.

Credit risk increases during periods of economic downturn. Credit policies and collection experience must always be monitored not only in comparison with past experience, but also in light of current economic conditions. Canadian Tire notes in its financial statements that its collection experience was negatively affected in 2009 as a result of a more challenging economic environment and rising unemployment levels. It noted some improvement in 2010.

Credit risk is especially important when a company has a high level of receivables from few customers. If a company sells services or products to only a few customers, it has a **concentration of credit risk** and it is required to discuss this risk in the notes to its financial statements because the company's financial health could weaken. An excerpt from the credit risk note from the financial statements of Canadian Tire is shown in Illustration 8-5.

CANADIAN TIRE LIMITED
Notes to the Financial Statements (partial)
January 1, 2011

▶Illustration 8-5
Concentration of credit risk

Note 19: Financial Instruments
Credit risk The Company's exposure to concentrations of credit risk is limited. Accounts receivable are primarily from Dealers spread across Canada who individually, generally comprise less than one percent of the total balance outstanding. Similarly, loans receivable are generated by credit card, personal loan and line of credit customers, a large and geographically dispersed group.

As the note states, Canadian Tire does not believe it has any significant concentration of credit risk.

DECISION TOOLKIT

Decision Checkpoints	Info Needed for Decision	Tools to Use for Decision	How to Evaluate Results
Is the company's credit risk increasing?	Customer account balances and due dates	Accounts receivable aging schedule	Calculate and compare the percentage of receivables overdue in each age classification.
Does the company have significant concentrations of credit risk?	Note to the financial statements on concentrations of credit risk	If risky credit customers are identified, the financial health of those customers should be evaluated to gain an independent assessment of the potential for a material credit loss.	If a material loss appears likely, the potential negative impact of that loss on the company should be carefully evaluated, as well as the adequacy of the allowance for doubtful accounts.

EVALUATING LIQUIDITY OF RECEIVABLES

Investors and managers keep a watchful eye on the relationship between sales, accounts receivable, and cash collections. If sales increase, then accounts receivable are also expected to increase. However, if accounts receivable rise faster than sales, this may be an indication of collection problems. Perhaps the company increased its sales by loosening its credit policy, and these receivables may be difficult or impossible to collect. Such receivables are considered less liquid. Recall that liquidity is measured by how quickly certain assets can be converted to cash.

The ratio that is used to assess the liquidity of receivables is the **receivables turnover** ratio. This ratio measures the number of times, on average, that receivables are collected during the year. The receivables turnover is calculated by dividing net credit sales by the average gross accounts receivable during the year.

Unfortunately, companies seldom report the amount of net credit sales in their financial statements. In such instances, net sales (including both cash and credit sales) can be used as a substitute. In addition, because some companies do not publicly report their gross accounts receivable, net accounts receivable must be used. As long as one consistently chooses the same components of a ratio, the resulting ratio will be useful for comparisons.

A popular variant of the receivables turnover is to convert it into an **average collection period** in terms of days. This is done by dividing 365 days by the receivables turnover. Alternatively, it can be calculated by dividing accounts receivable by the average amount of net credit sales per day. The average collection period is frequently used to assess the effectiveness of a company's credit and collection policies. The general rule is that the collection period should not greatly exceed the credit term period (i.e., the time allowed for payment).

Ratios such as the ones introduced above are not just used to measure the speed at which receivables are collected. They can also be used to detect error. For example, if an accountant inappropriately recorded revenue too early, this would cause an overstatement in revenue and accounts receivable. An astute analyst could speculate that such an error had arisen by noticing that there was an unexplained drop in the receivables turnover ratio.

Canadian Tire does not report its allowance account separately. So we will use the following data (in U.S. thousands) for Winpak Ltd., a Winnipeg-based packaging maker, to illustrate the calculation of the receivables turnover. We have assumed that all sales are credit sales for the purpose of this illustration.

	2010	2009	2008
Net sales	$579,441	$505,991	$512,037
Accounts receivable (gross)	79,375	72,115	66,233

The receivables turnover and average collection period for Winpak Ltd. are shown in Illustration 8-6, along with comparative industry data.

▶ **Illustration 8-6**
Receivables turnover

$$\text{RECEIVABLES TURNOVER} = \frac{\text{NET CREDIT SALES}}{\text{AVERAGE GROSS ACCOUNTS RECEIVABLE}}$$

$$\text{AVERAGE COLLECTION PERIOD} = \frac{365\ \text{DAYS}}{\text{RECEIVABLES TURNOVER}}$$

	Ratio	2010	2009
Winpak	Receivables turnover	$\dfrac{\$579,441}{(\$79,375 + \$72,115) \div 2} = 7.6$ times	$\dfrac{\$505,991}{(\$72,115 + \$66,233) \div 2} = 7.3$ times
	Average collection period	$\dfrac{365\ \text{days}}{7.6\ \text{times}} = 48$ days	$\dfrac{365\ \text{days}}{7.3\ \text{times}} = 50$ days
Industry Average	Receivables turnover	8.2 times	8.7 times
	Average collection period	45 days	42 days

Winpak's receivables turnover was 7.6 times in 2010, with an average collection period of 48 days. This was a slight improvement from its 2009 collection period of 50 days. Despite this improvement, the company is somewhat slower than its peers at collecting receivables.

The receivables turnover is an important component of a company's overall liquidity. Ideally, it should be analyzed along with other information about a company's liquidity, including the current ratio and inventory turnover. Recall from earlier chapters that the receivables turnover and inventory turnover can distort a company's current ratio. In general, the faster the turnover, the more reliable the current ratio is for assessing liquidity.

DECISION TOOLKIT

 **Decision Checkpoints**	 **Info Needed for Decision**	 **Tools to Use for Decision**	 **How to Evaluate Results**
Are collections being made in a timely fashion?	Net credit sales and average gross accounts receivable balance	Receivables turnover = $\dfrac{\text{Net credit sales}}{\text{Average gross accounts receivable}}$ Average collection period = $\dfrac{\text{365 days}}{\text{Receivables turnover}}$	The average collection period should be consistent with corporate credit policy. An increase may suggest a decline in customers' financial health.

ACCELERATING CASH RECEIPTS

Normally, receivables are simply collected in cash and then removed from the books. However, as credit sales and receivables grow in size and significance, waiting for receivables to be collected within the normal collection period can result in increased costs and delays in being able to use the cash that has not yet been received. Two typical ways to accelerate the receipt of cash from receivables are to use the receivables to secure a loan and to sell the receivables.

Loans Secured by Receivables

One of the most common ways to speed up cash flow from receivables is to borrow money from a bank by using receivables as collateral. While this does have a cost (interest has to be paid to the bank on the loan), the cash is available for the company to use earlier and the loan can be repaid as the receivables are collected. Generally, banks are willing to provide financing for up to 75% of receivables that are less than 90 days old. Quite often, these arrangements occur through a credit facility or operating line of credit, which we were introduced to in Chapter 7.

■ Keeping an Eye on Cash

A company can have strong sales and profits but still have great difficulty paying its liabilities because of poor collection of receivables. For example, assume that a bank has given your new consulting business an operating line of credit of $20,000 and you have used $15,000 of it to pay for rent, damage deposits, and equipment. After the first month of business, you have earned $18,000 of consulting revenue but have collected only $2,000 cash from your clients. You have to pay your employees tomorrow and you owe them $9,000 for the salaries incurred this month. Although your profit this month is quite healthy ($18,000 - $9,000 - some other expenses), you only have $2,000 in the bank (the amount collected from clients) and you can only borrow another $5,000 from the bank to meet your payroll. Many businesses in this situation are forced to close because their employees leave and they cannot collect their receivables any faster. Many times the shortage comes as a surprise and management does not have time to develop solutions to the problem. Businesses should always remember that profit does not measure cash flow and that they always need to find ways to deal with times when liquidity is tight.

Sale of Receivables

Companies also frequently sell their receivables to another company for cash, thereby shortening the cash-to-cash operating cycle. There are three reasons for the sale of receivables:

1. Due to the size of the business, it may make sense to establish a financing subsidiary that buys the accounts receivable from the company. In this way, the company's statement of financial position will appear more liquid due to the absence of the receivables.
2. Selling receivables provides a source of immediate cash flow for the company.
3. It allows the company to save costs relating to the monitoring and collection of receivables.

Two types of sales known as securitization and factoring are covered below.

Securitization of Receivables.   A common way to accelerate receivables collection is to transfer receivables to investors in return for cash through a process called **securitization**. In certain cases, this transfer is treated as a sale of receivables; in other cases, it is treated as a secured loan. Companies such as Canadian Tire regularly securitize some of their receivables to speed up collection. For the year ended January 1, 2011, Canadian Tire securitized $265 million of its accounts receivable relating to credit cards.

Factoring Receivables.   Another way to accelerate receivables collection is by sale to a factor. A **factor** is a finance company or bank that buys receivables from businesses for a fee. If the customer does not pay, normally the company is responsible for reimbursing the factor for the uncollected amounts.

The differences between securitization and factoring are that securitization involves many investors, the cost is lower, the receivables are of a higher quality, and the seller usually continues to have some involvement with (e.g., responsibility to collect) the receivables. In factoring, the sale is usually to only one company, the cost is higher, the receivables quality is lower, and the seller does not normally have any involvement with the receivables. These topics will be covered in more detail in an intermediate accounting course.

 **ACCOUNTING MATTERS!**   *Management Perspective*

Target Plans Sale of Receivables

In 2011, U.S. discount department store chain Target Corp. began to pursue the sale of its U.S. $6.7-billion credit-card receivables portfolio, as it also disclosed plans to expand into Canada with the purchase of Zellers stores. Target planned to spend about $1 billion revamping many Zellers stores to carry its distinctive logo and look, with a few tweaks to accommodate Canadian tastes.

Target had wanted to sell the receivables of its credit card business for some time but was hampered by the card operation's condition and the lack of a well-capitalized buyer. Target said it liked the idea of freeing up the receivables, which are listed as assets on its balance sheet, so that it could use cash from the sale of receivables for other investments, like the Zellers purchase.

Source: Karen Talley, Dow Jones Newswires, "Target Is Entering Canada, Selling Card Receivables," January 13, 2011.

BEFORE YOU GO ON...

▶Do It! Managing Receivables

The Halifax Discount Store (HDS) Ltd. specializes in selling products at discounted prices. Customers can buy products with cash, bank credit cards, or the company's new HDS credit card. The HDS card was introduced six months ago and has helped increase sales considerably. Anyone is eligible to receive an HDS credit card as long as they have valid identification and are over the age of 18. Cardholders have up to four months before they are required to pay any amounts due. HDS has a large outstanding bank loan that has grown this year. The company is concerned that the bank will raise interest rates if the receivables turnover falls any further than it has this past year. Consequently, management is looking at ways to speed up the collection of cash and would like you to discuss steps that can be taken to manage receivables more effectively. Management would also like to know if ratio analysis is useful for a company like this.

Action Plan

Assess the steps this company should take in managing its receivables by reviewing the following five steps: (a) determining who to extend credit to, (b) establishing a payment period, (c) monitoring collections, (d) evaluating the liquidity of receivables, and (e) accelerating cash receipts.

Solution

(a) **Extending credit.** The HDS credit card should not be given to just anyone over the age of 18 years. Credit-granting policies similar to those used by banks when issuing credit cards should be used by the company. Although sales have increased due to issuing this new card, it is likely that bad debts expense has increased even more.

(b) **Payment period.** Allowing HDS cardholders to pay after four months is a credit policy that is too loose. It has slowed the collection of receivables and this in turn has probably caused the company to seek more bank financing to meet cash requirements no longer being met by prompt customer collections.

(c) **Monitor collections.** On a monthly basis, management should review the age of the HDS credit card accounts and identify those cardholders who did not pay on time to determine if their receivables are collectible. It is likely that there are many overdue accounts given the ease with which these cards were issued, which makes frequent monitoring of collections even more important.

(d) **Evaluate liquidity.** The receivables turnover ratio and collection period should be determined and evaluated each month. Management is unaware of these ratios. Had they been calculated and analyzed each month, the company's liquidity issues might have been avoided.

(e) **Accelerate cash receipts.** The company could take a number of steps to improve the collection of receivables. These include factoring receivables, replacing the company credit card with a bank credit card, or changing the terms on the HDS card. The advantage of the first two options is the immediate receipt of cash but the disadvantage is the fee that will be paid to the factor and the bank credit card company and the lost interest revenue that could be earned on the HDS card. Although changing the terms of the HDS card will not bring any immediate cash to the company, it may reduce the level of bad debts in the future and still provide a source of interest revenue on overdue accounts as long as they are collectible. Management will have to calculate the effect of these advantages and disadvantages and consider the effect on the timing of cash flows. The company should discuss these options with the bank to ensure that it realizes that steps are being taken to remedy the liquidity problem.

comparing

IFRS and ASPE

Key Differences	International Financial Reporting Standards (IFRS)	Accounting Standards for Private Enterprises (ASPE)
No significant differences.		

Should You Be Carrying Plastic?

Smart businesspeople carefully consider their use of credit. They evaluate who they lend to, and how they finance their own operations. They know that being overextended on credit can destroy their business.

Individuals need to evaluate their personal credit positions using the same thought processes as businesspeople and consider carefully if they need a credit card and when to use it. The misuse of credit cards brings financial hardship to many Canadians each year. The best way to avoid credit problems is to be disciplined when using credit cards or not to have them at all. Reduce the number of credit cards you carry and do not accept all the tempting credit card offers that come to you via e-mail and regular mail.

Credit cards can make your life easier, as long as they are used properly. They certainly have advantages: (1) they provide interest-free loans on the purchase of goods as long as you pay your bill in full before the end of the grace period; (2) monthly credit card statements provide records of all transactions, payments, and returns; and (3) fraud protection with zero liability is available for the consumer in cases of fraud. However, credit cards also have disadvantages: (1) if you do not pay your bill in full each month, you can expect to pay a very high interest rate on the unpaid balance; and (2) credit cards are so easy to use that you might start buying items without really thinking about whether you really need them—and can afford them.

Credit scoring is a system used by lenders and others to assess the credit risk of prospective borrowers, and is used most often when an individual applies for a credit card, automobile loan, or home mortgage. Your credit score is a judgement about your financial health at a specific point in time. It indicates the risk you represent for lenders compared with other consumers. Lenders must decide on the lowest score you can have before they consider it is no longer wise to lend money to you. They can also use your score to set the interest rate you will pay.

Some Facts

- The Canadian Bankers Association reported that, in 2010, 65% of Canadian households paid off their cards in full each month. This percentage did not vary by income; high-income households were just as likely as low-income households to pay their card balances. Credit cards accounted for about 3% of household debt.
- At the end of 2010, 0.3% of credit cards were delinquent, i.e., the borrowers had not paid their credit card balances. The average credit card debt was $3,709. The average Canadian had 1.75 credit cards in their wallet.
- Fastsigns, a business in Surrey, B.C., estimates that the cost of processing an average retail sale of $375 with a debit card transaction is around 10 cents, but a credit card transaction can cost as much as $9.30 to process.
- Some people choose premium credit cards because of the additional perks that come with them, including extra rewards and points that can be used for travel or other purchases. The credit card companies and banks charge retailers additional fees to process these premium cards in excess of those charged for standard gold or platinum cards. Businesses are currently prohibited from charging consumers a surcharge to use their credit cards.

What Do You Think?

Should you go plastic-free and get rid of your credit card?

YES—Credit cards encourage unnecessary, spontaneous expenditures. The interest rates on credit cards are very high, so I don't want to end up in debt.

NO—Credit cards are a necessity for transactions in today's economy. In fact, many transactions are difficult or impossible to carry out without a credit card. People should learn to use credit cards responsibly.

Sources: Rita Trichur, "Feeling the Credit Card Squeeze on Profits," *The Globe and Mail,* February 9, 2011, p. B4.TransUnion, "Delinquency Rates and Past Due Balances Decrease Across All Provinces; Outlook for Canada Improving Through 2010," http://newsroom-en.transunion.ca, accessed March 10, 2011. Canadian Bankers Association, "Credit Cards: Statistics and Facts," www.cba.ca, accessed May 9, 2011.

Summary of Study Objectives

1. Explain how accounts receivable are recognized and valued in the accounts. Accounts receivable arising from sales or services on credit are recorded at the invoice price. Receivables are reduced by sales returns and allowances. Sales discounts also reduce the amount received on accounts receivable. When interest is charged on a past-due receivable, this interest is added to the accounts receivable balance and is recognized as interest revenue.

The allowance method, using a percentage of receivables, is used to match bad debts expense against sales, in the period in which the sales occurred. A percentage of total receivables, or an aging schedule applying percentages to different categories of receivables, is used to estimate the allowance for doubtful accounts. The allowance is deducted from the receivables balance to report accounts receivable at their net realizable value on the statement of financial position.

2. Explain how notes receivable are recognized and valued in the accounts. Notes receivable are recorded at their principal or face value. Interest is earned from the date the note is issued until it matures and is recorded in a separate interest receivable account. Like accounts receivable, notes receivable are also reported at their net realizable value.

Notes can be held to maturity, at which time the principal plus any unpaid interest is due and the note is removed from the accounts. In some situations, the maker of the note dishonours the note (defaults). If eventual collection is expected, an account receivable replaces the note receivable and any unpaid interest. If the amount is not expected to be repaid, the note is written off.

3. Explain the statement presentation of receivables. Each major type of receivable should be identified in the statement of financial position or in the notes to the financial statements. It is desirable to report the gross amount of receivables and allowance for doubtful accounts. Bad debts expense is reported in the income statement as an operating expense, and interest revenue is shown in the non-operating section of the statement.

4. Apply the principles of sound accounts receivable management. To properly manage receivables, management must (a) determine who to extend credit to, (b) establish a payment period, (c) monitor collections, (d) evaluate the liquidity of receivables by calculating the receivables turnover and average collection period, and (e) accelerate cash receipts from receivables when necessary.

Glossary

Aging the accounts receivable The analysis of customer balances by the length of time they have been unpaid. (p. 417)

Allowance method A method of accounting for bad debts that involves estimating uncollectible accounts at the end of each period. (p. 415)

Average collection period The average amount of time that a receivable is outstanding. It is calculated by dividing 365 days by the receivables turnover. (p. 428)

Concentration of credit risk The threat of non-payment from a single customer or class of customers that could hurt the company's financial health. (p. 427)

Control account An account in the general ledger that summarizes the details for a subsidiary ledger and controls it. (p. 413)

Dishonoured note A note that is not paid in full at maturity. (p. 422)

Factor A finance company or bank that buys receivables from businesses for a fee. (p. 430)

Financial assets Investments and receivables that have a contractual right to receive cash or another financial asset. (p. 412)

Net realizable value The difference between gross receivables and the allowance for doubtful accounts. Net realizable value measures the net amount expected to be received in cash. (p. 416)

Percentage of receivables basis A percentage relationship established by management between the amount of receivables and the expected losses from uncollectible accounts. (p. 417)

Promissory note A written promise to pay a specified amount of money on demand or at a definite time. (p. 421)

Receivables turnover A measure of the liquidity of receivables. It is calculated by dividing net credit sales by the average gross accounts receivable and is expressed as the number of times per year that the accounts receivable could be collected. (p. 428)

Securitization The transfer of assets such as receivables to a company that issues securities and uses the receivables as collateral. (p. 430)

Subsidiary ledger A group of accounts that provide details of a control account in the general ledger. (p. 413)

Trade receivables Notes and accounts receivable that result from sales transactions. (p. 412)

DECISION TOOLKIT—A SUMMARY

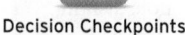

Decision Checkpoints	Info Needed for Decision	Tools to Use for Decision	How to Evaluate Results
Is the amount of past-due accounts increasing? Which accounts require management's attention?	List of outstanding receivables and their due dates	Prepare an aging schedule showing the receivables in various stages: outstanding 0-30 days, 31-60 days, 61-90 days, 91-120 days, and over 120 days.	Accounts in the older categories require follow-up: letters, phone calls, e-mails, and possible renegotiations of terms.
Is the company's credit risk increasing?	Customer account balances and due dates	Accounts receivable aging schedule	Calculate and compare the percentage of receivables overdue in each age classification.
Does the company have significant concentrations of credit risk?	Note to the financial statements on concentrations of credit risk	If risky credit customers are identified, the financial health of those customers should be evaluated to gain an independent assessment of the potential for a material credit loss.	If a material loss appears likely, the potential negative impact of that loss on the company should be carefully evaluated, as well as the adequacy of the allowance for doubtful accounts.
Are collections being made in a timely fashion?	Net credit sales and average gross accounts receivable balance	$$\text{Receivables turnover} = \frac{\text{Net credit sales}}{\text{Average gross accounts receivable}}$$ $$\text{Average collection period} = \frac{365 \text{ days}}{\text{Receivables turnover}}$$	The average collection period should be consistent with corporate credit policy. An increase may suggest a decline in customers' financial health.

the navigator

USING THE DECISION TOOLKIT

Richards Packaging Income Fund competes with Winpak. Selected financial information for this company (in thousands) is shown below and can be compared with Winpak's corresponding account balances shown earlier:

	2010	2009
Net sales	$179,010	$189,112
Accounts receivable (gross)	19,112	19,216

Instructions

Calculate Richards' receivables turnover and average collection period for 2010. Assume that all sales are made on credit. Comment on the company's accounts receivable management and liquidity compared with that of Winpak and that of the industry.

Solution

(in thousands)	Richards	Winpak	Industry
Receivables turnover	$\dfrac{\$179,010}{(\$19,112 + \$19,216) \div 2} = 9.3$ times	7.6 times	8.2 times
Average collection period	$\dfrac{365 \text{ days}}{9.3 \text{ times}} = 39$ days	48 days	45 days

Based on the above information, Richards has a higher receivables turnover and a shorter collection period than both Winpak and the industry. As this means that the company collects its receivables faster, it can more readily pay down any bank loans and keep its debt levels lower if it wishes to.

the navigator

Comprehensive Do It!

Presented here are selected transactions for Shawinigan Distributors Ltd.:

Mar. 1   Sold $40,000 of merchandise to Anderson Ltd., terms 2/10, n/30.

     11   Received payment in full from Anderson for balance due.

     12   Accepted Dieppe Ltd.'s four-month, 6%, $40,000 note for a balance due from a February transaction (not shown here). Interest is payable at maturity.

     13   Made Shawinigan Distributors Ltd. credit card sales for $26,400.

     15   Made Visa credit card sales totalling $13,400. A 3% service fee is charged by Visa.

Apr. 13   Received collections of $16,400 on Shawinigan credit card sales and added interest charges of 18% per annum (1.5% per month) to the remaining balances.

May 10   Wrote off as uncollectible $32,000 of accounts receivable.

June 30   The balance in Accounts Receivable is $400,000. Using an aging schedule, uncollectible accounts are estimated to be $40,000. At June 30, the credit balance in the allowance account before adjustment is $7,000.

July 12   Collected Dieppe note (see March 12 transaction).

     16   One of the accounts receivable written off in May was received in full, $8,000.

Instructions

Record the above transactions.

Action Plan

- Record accounts receivable at the invoice price.
- Recognize that sales returns and allowances and cash discounts reduce the amount received on accounts receivable.
- Record a credit card expense when bank credit cards are used, but not when company credit cards are used.
- Calculate interest by multiplying the interest rate by the face value, adjusting for the portion of the year that has passed.
- Consider any existing balance in the allowance account when making the adjustment for uncollectible accounts.
- Record write-offs of accounts receivable only in statement of financial position accounts.

Solution to Comprehensive Do It!

Mar. 1	Accounts Receivable—Anderson	40,000	
	Sales		40,000
	(To record sales on account)		
11	Cash	39,200	
	Sales Discounts (2% × $40,000)	800	
	Accounts Receivable—Anderson		40,000
	(To record collection of account receivable)		
12	Notes Receivable—Dieppe	40,000	
	Accounts Receivable—Dieppe		40,000
	(To record acceptance of Dieppe note)		
13	Credit Card Receivables	26,400	
	Sales		26,400
	(To record company credit card sales)		

(continued)

Mar. 15	Cash		12,998	
	Credit Card Expense (3% × $13,400)		402	
	Sales			13,400
	(To record Visa credit card sales)			
Apr. 13	Cash		16,400	
	Credit Card Receivables			16,400
	(To record collection of accounts receivable)			
	Accounts Receivable [($26,400 − $16,400) × 18% × $^1/_{12}$]		150	
	Interest Revenue			150
	(To record interest charges on overdue receivables)			
May 10	Allowance for Doubtful Accounts		32,000	
	Accounts Receivable			32,000
	(To record write-off of accounts receivable)			
June 30	Bad Debts Expense ($40,000 − $7,000)		33,000	
	Allowance for Doubtful Accounts			33,000
	(To record estimate of uncollectible accounts)			
July 12	Cash		40,800	
	Notes Receivable—Dieppe			40,000
	Interest Revenue ($40,000 × 6% × $^4/_{12}$)			800
	(To record collection of note receivable)			
16	Accounts Receivable		8,000	
	Allowance for Doubtful Accounts			8,000
	(To reverse write-off of account receivable)			
	Cash		8,000	
	Accounts Receivable			8,000
	(To record collection of account receivable)			

Self-Test, Brief Exercises, Exercises, Problems: Set A, and many more components are available for practice in WileyPLUS.

Self-Test Questions

Answers are at the end of the chapter.

(SO 1)   1. A receivable that is evidenced by a formal instrument and that normally requires the payment of interest is:
(a) an account receivable.
(b) a trade receivable.

(c) a note receivable.
(d) a classified receivable.

(SO 1)   2. Sanderson Corporation has a debit balance of $5,000 in its Allowance for Doubtful Accounts before any adjustments are made. Based on an aging of its accounts receivable at the end of the period, the company estimates that $60,000 of its receivables are uncollectible at the end of the period. The adjusting journal entry that would be recorded for bad debts expense at the end of this period would be:

| (a) | Bad Debts Expense | 55,000 | |
| | Accounts Receivable | | 55,000 |

| (b) | Bad Debts Expense | 55,000 | |
| | Allowance for Doubtful Accounts | | 55,000 |

| (c) | Bad Debts Expense | 65,000 | |
| | Allowance for Doubtful Accounts | | 65,000 |

| (d) | Bad Debts Expense | 60,000 | |
| | Allowance for Doubtful Accounts | | 60,000 |

(SO 1) 3. On January 1, 2012, Allowance for Doubtful Accounts had a credit balance of $9,000. During 2012, $15,000 of uncollectible accounts receivable were written off. Aging indicates that uncollectible accounts are $10,000 at the end of 2012. What is the required adjustment in Bad Debts Expense at December 31, 2012?
(a) $1,000
(b) $4,000
(c) $10,000
(d) $16,000

(SO 1) 4. On December 31, 2012, Allowance for Doubtful Accounts had a credit balance of $20,000, compared with a credit balance of $14,000 at the end of 2011. During 2012, $15,000 of uncollectible accounts receivable were written off. What was the bad debts expense recorded by the company for the year ended December 31, 2012?
(a) $6,000
(b) $15,000
(c) $20,000
(d) $21,000

(SO 2) 5. Mackenzie Ltd. accepts a three-month, 6%, $2,000 promissory note in settlement of Pandher Ltd.'s account. The entry to record this transaction on Mackenzie's books is:

| (a) | Notes Receivable | 2,030 | |
| | Accounts Receivable | | 2,030 |

| (b) | Notes Receivable | 2,000 | |
| | Accounts Receivable | | 2,000 |

| (c) | Notes Receivable | 2,000 | |
| | Sales | | 2,000 |

| (d) | Notes Receivable | 2,120 | |
| | Accounts Receivable | | 2,120 |

(SO 2) 6. Schlicht Corp. holds Oleniuk Inc.'s four-month, 9%, $10,000 note. The entry made by Schlicht Corp. when the note is collected, assuming no interest has previously been recorded, is:

| (a) | Cash | 10,300 | |
| | Notes Receivable | | 10,300 |

| (b) | Cash | 10,000 | |
| | Notes Receivable | | 10,000 |

(c)	Accounts Receivable	10,300	
	Notes Receivable		10,300
	Interest Revenue		300

(d)	Cash	10,300	
	Notes Receivable		10,000
	Interest Revenue		300

(SO 3) 7. Accounts and notes receivable are reported in the assets section of the statement of financial position at their:
(a) net realizable value.
(b) invoice cost.
(c) lower of cost and net realizable value.
(d) carrying amount.

(SO 4) 8. The principles of sound accounts receivable management do not include:
(a) instituting a "cash only" policy.
(b) establishing a payment period.
(c) monitoring collections.
(d) evaluating the liquidity of receivables.

(SO 4) 9. Abdel-Razek Corporation had net credit sales during the year of $800,000 and cost of goods sold of $500,000. The balance in Accounts Receivable at the beginning of the year was $100,000, and at the end of the year it was $150,000. What were the receivables turnover and average collection period ratios, respectively?
(a) 4.0 and 91 days
(b) 5.3 and 69 days
(c) 6.4 and 57 days
(d) 8.0 and 46 days

(SO 4) 10. New Millennium Retailers Corp. has managed to shorten the amount of time that it takes to collect its receivables. Because of this:
(a) The receivables turnover ratio will rise and the average collection period will fall.
(b) The receivables turnover ratio will fall and the average collection period will fall.
(c) The receivables turnover ratio will rise and the average collection period will rise.
(d) The receivables turnover ratio will fall and the average collection period will rise.

Questions

(SO 1)   1. (a) What are the three major types of receivables?
(b) Where is each type of receivable generally classified on a statement of financial position? (c) Why are receivables considered to be financial assets?

(SO 1)   2. (a) When should a receivable be recorded for a service company? For a merchandising company? (b) Explain how your answer relates to the concept of accrual accounting.

(SO 1)   3. Canadian Tire accepts its own company credit card, bank credit cards, and debit cards. What are the advantages of accepting each type of card? Explain how the accounting differs for sales of each type.

(SO 1)   4. What are the advantages of using an accounts receivable subsidiary ledger? Describe the relationship between the general ledger control account and the subsidiary ledger.

(SO 1)   5. (a) Under what circumstances is interest normally recorded for an account receivable? (b) When interest is recorded, is Accounts Receivable or Interest Receivable debited? Explain.

(SO 1)   6. (a) What is the purpose of the account Allowance for Doubtful Accounts? (b) Although the normal balance of this account is a credit balance, it can sometimes have a debit balance. Explain how and when this can happen.

(SO 1)   7. The Allowance for Doubtful Accounts is just one example of a contra account. (a) Name another contra asset account and its related asset account. (b) Name two contra revenue accounts and their related revenue accounts.

(SO 1)   8. Why is the bad debts expense that is reported in the income statement usually not the same amount as the allowance for doubtful accounts amount reported in the statement of financial position?

(SO 1)   9. Soo Eng cannot understand why the net realizable value does not change when an uncollectible account is written off under the allowance method. Clarify this for Soo Eng.

(SO 1)   10. When an account receivable that was previously written off is later collected, two separate journal entries are usually made rather than one compound journal entry. Explain why.

(SO 1, 2)   11. (a) How are accounts receivable and notes receivable alike? (b) How do they differ?

(SO 2)   12. Danielle does not understand why a note receivable is not immediately recorded at its maturity value (principal plus interest), rather than its principal

value. After all, you know you are going to collect both the principal and the interest and you know how much each will be. Clarify this for Danielle.

(SO 2)   13. Explain how recording interest revenue differs for accounts receivable and notes receivable.

(SO 2)   14. What is the difference between honouring a note receivable at maturity and dishonouring a note at maturity?

(SO 2)   15. How would the entries differ if a note receivable were dishonoured and eventual collection was expected compared with a situation where eventual collection was not expected?

(SO 2)   16. Athabasca Ltd. has several dozen notes receivable. It expects approximately 10% of these notes to be uncollectible. How should these estimated notes be accounted for?

(SO 3)   17. Saucier Ltd. has accounts receivable, notes receivable due in three months, notes receivable due in two years, an allowance for doubtful accounts, sales tax (GST) recoverable, and income tax receivable. How should the receivables be reported on the statement of financial position?

(SO 4)   18. What are the five steps in good receivables management?

(SO 4)   19. What is meant by a concentration of credit risk?

(SO 4)   20. Canam Group Inc.'s receivables turnover was 3.7 times in 2010 and 6.3 times in 2009. Has Canam's receivables management improved or worsened?

(SO 4)   21. The president of Ho Inc. proudly announces that her company has improved its liquidity since its current ratio has increased substantially. (a) Does an increase in the current ratio always indicate improved liquidity? (b) What other ratio or ratios might you review to determine whether or not the increase in the current ratio indicates an improvement in financial health?

(SO 4)   22. Why should a company not want to have a receivables turnover that is significantly higher than that of its competitors? Why would it not want a receivables turnover that is significantly lower than that of its competitors?

(SO 4)   23. During the year ended December 31, 2009, Canadian National Railway Company transferred accounts receivable of $2 million to an independent trust in a transaction known as securitization. In 2010, this was not done. (a) Why might a company like Canadian National securitize its receivables? (b) Why would it cease doing so?

Brief Exercises

Identify types of receivables.
(SO 1)

BE8–1   Presented below are six receivables trans actions. For each transaction, indicate whether the receivables should be reported as accounts receivable, notes receivable, or other receivables on a statement of financial position.
(a) Advanced $10,000 to an employee.
(b) Estimated $5,000 of income tax to be refunded.

(c) Received a promissory note of $5,000 for services performed.

(d) Sold merchandise on account to a customer for $6,000.

(e) Sales tax (HST) of $2,500 is recoverable at the end of the quarter.

(f) Extended a customer's account for six months by accepting a note in exchange for the amount owed on the account.

BE8–2 Record the following transactions on the books of Essex Corp., which uses a perpetual inventory system:

(a) On July 1, Essex Corp. sold merchandise on account to Cambridge Inc. for $42,000, terms 2/10, n/30. The cost of the merchandise sold was $30,000.

(b) On July 8, Cambridge returned merchandise worth $7,200 to Essex. Its original cost was $4,320. The merchandise was restored to inventory.

(c) On July 10, Cambridge paid for the merchandise.

(d) Assume now that Cambridge did not pay on July 10, as indicated in transaction (c). At the end of August, Essex added one month's interest to Cambridge's account for the overdue receivable. Essex charges 24% per year on overdue accounts.

Record receivables transactions. (SO 1)

BE8–3 An Ultramar gas station accepted a Visa card in payment of a $100 gas bill. The bank charges a 2.5% fee. What entry should the Ultramar gas station make to record the sale? How would this entry be different if payment had been made with an Ultramar credit card instead of a Visa card?

Record credit card sales. (SO 1)

BE8–4 At December 31, Canton Imports Ltd. estimates that 4% of total accounts receivable will become uncollectible. Accounts receivable are $600,000 at the end of the year. Allowance for Doubtful Accounts has a credit balance of $3,600 prior to recording any year-end adjusting entries.

(a) Prepare the adjusting journal entry to record bad debts expense at December 31.

(b) Assuming that Allowance for Doubtful Accounts had a debit balance of $4,000 instead of a credit balance of $3,600, how would the journal entry recorded in (a) above change?

Record bad debts. (SO 1)

BE8–5 Refer to BE8–4 and assume that Canton Imports Ltd. decides to refine its estimate of uncollectible accounts by preparing an aging schedule. Complete the following schedule and prepare the adjusting journal entry at December 31 to record bad debts expense, assuming that the allowance account has a credit balance of $3,600.

Complete aging schedule and record bad debts. (SO 1)

Number of Days Outstanding	Accounts Receivable	Estimated Percentage Uncollectible	Estimated Allowance
0–30 days	$368,000	1%	
31–60 days	120,000	4%	
61–90 days	72,000	10%	
Over 90 days	40,000	20%	
Total	$600,000		

BE8–6 At the end of 2011, Searcy Corp. has accounts receivable of $600,000 and an allowance for doubtful accounts of $36,000. On January 24, 2012, Searcy learns that its $8,000 receivable from Hutley Inc. is not collectible. Management authorizes a write-off.

(a) Prepare the journal entry to record the write-off.

(b) What is the net realizable value of the accounts receivable (1) before the write-off and (2) after the write-off?

Record write-off, and compare net realizable value. (SO 1)

BE8–7 Assume the same information as in BE8–6, but that on March 4, 2012, Searcy Corp. receives payment in full of $8,000 from Hutley Inc., after the write-off. Prepare the required journal entry (entries) to record this transaction.

Record recovery of bad debts. (SO 1)

BE8–8 Data on three promissory notes follow. Determine the missing amounts.

Calculate interest. (SO 2)

Date of Note	Term in Months	Principal	Interest Rate	Total Interest	Interest Revenue to Record for Year Ended December 31
Apr. 1	3	$1,800,000	10%	(c)	$45,000
July 2	6	168,000	(b)	$ 6,720	(d)
Nov. 1	12	(a)	6%	25,200	(e)

BE8–9 On January 10, 2012, Kuril Ltd. sold merchandise on account to R. James for $48,000, terms n/30. The merchandise originally cost $32,000. On February 1, R. James gave Kuril a five-month, 7% note in settlement of this account. On July 1, R. James paid the note and accrued interest. Prepare the journal entries for Kuril to record the above transactions. Kuril has an April 30 year end and adjusts its accounts annually.

Record receivables transactions. (SO 1)

Record note receivable transactions.
(SO 2)

BE8–10 Stratus Ltd. sells merchandise inventory on April 1, 2012, to Red River Enterprises for a 12-month, 9%, $10,000 note, with interest due at maturity. The company uses a perpetual inventory system and the cost of the inventory sold was $6,000. Stratus has a December 31 year end and adjusts its accounts annually. Prepare the journal entries that Stratus will record with regard to this note from April 1, 2012, until the note matures on March 31, 2013.

Record note payable transactions.
(SO 2)

BE8–11 Using the same information from BE8–10 above, prepare the journal entries that Red River Enterprises will record regarding the issue of the note and the receipt of the merchandise inventory. Red River, however, has a September 30 year end and adjusts its accounts annually.

Record note receivable transactions.
(SO 2)

BE8–12 Xavier Limited accepts a three-month, 6%, $40,000 note receivable in settlement of an account receivable on April 1, 2012. Interest is due at maturity.
(a) Prepare the journal entries required by Xavier Limited to record the issue of the note on April 1, and the settlement of the note on July 1, assuming the note is honoured. No interest has previously been accrued. Round your answers to the nearest dollar.
(b) Repeat part (a) assuming that the note is dishonoured, but eventual collection is expected.
(c) Repeat part (a) assuming that the note is dishonoured and eventual collection is not expected.

Prepare current assets section.
(SO 3)

BE8–13 Prepare the current assets section of the statement of financial position for Nias Corporation, which reported the following selected items at February 28, 2012:

Accounts payable	$938,000	Notes receivable—due November 1, 2012	$300,000
Accounts receivable	470,000	Notes receivable—due April 1, 2015	400,000
Allowance for doubtful accounts	30,000	Prepaid expenses	58,000
Bad debts expense	24,000	Recoverable sales taxes	38,000
Cash	150,000	Short-term investments	330,000
Merchandise inventory	380,000	Unearned revenue	5,000

Calculate ratios.
(SO 4)

BE8–14 The financial statements of Maple Leaf Foods Inc. report net sales of $4,968.2 million for the year ended December 31, 2010. Accounts receivable were $189.2 million at the beginning of the year, and $84.1 million at the end of the year. Calculate Maple Leaf's receivables turnover and average collection period.

Exercises

Record receivables and payables transactions.
(SO 1)

E8–1 On January 6, Compton Limited sold merchandise on account to Singh Inc. for $24,000, terms 2/10, n/30. The merchandise originally cost Compton $16,000. On January 15, Singh paid the amount due. Both Compton and Singh use a perpetual inventory system.

Instructions
(a) Prepare the entries on Compton Limited's books to record the sale and related collection.
(b) Prepare the entries on Singh Inc.'s books to record the purchase and related payment.

Record receivables transactions; post to subsidiary and general ledgers.
(SO 1)

E8–2 The transactions that follow were for Discovery Sports Ltd. with its customers during the company's first month of business:

Feb. 2	Sold $1,140 of merchandise to Andrew Noren on account, terms n/30.
4	Andrew Noren returned for credit $140 of the merchandise purchased on February 2.
5	Sold $760 of merchandise to Dong Corporation on account, terms 2/10, n/30.
8	Sold $842 of merchandise to Michael Collins for cash.
10	Sold $920 of merchandise to Rafik Kurji, who paid with his Visa card. Visa charges a 2% service fee.
14	Dong Corporation paid its account in full.
17	Andrew Noren purchased an additional $696 of merchandise on account, terms n/30.
22	Sold $1,738 of merchandise to Batstone Corporation, terms 2/10, n/30.
28	Andrew Noren paid $1,000 on account.

Instructions
(a) Prepare the journal entries to record each of the above transactions. Round your answers to the nearest dollar.
(b) Set up T accounts for the Accounts Receivable control account and for the Accounts Receivable subsidiary ledger accounts. Post the journal entries to these accounts.
(c) Prepare a list of customers and the balances of their accounts from the subsidiary ledger. Prove that the total of the subsidiary ledger balances is equal to the control account balance.

E8-3 Chinook Limited's general ledger reports a balance in Accounts Receivable of $360,000 at the end of December.

Record bad debts.
(SO 1)

Instructions

(a) Assuming that Allowance for Doubtful Accounts has a credit balance of $4,400 and that uncollectible accounts are determined to be $36,000 by aging the accounts, record the adjusting entry at December 31.

(b) Assuming the same information as in (a) except that uncollectible accounts are expected to be 9% of the accounts receivable, record the adjusting entry at December 31.

(c) Assuming the same information as in (a) except that the Allowance for Doubtful Accounts has a debit balance of $2,400, record the adjusting entry at December 31.

E8-4 Gemini Ltd. has accounts receivable of $370,000 at March 31, 2012. An analysis of the accounts shows these amounts:

Prepare aging schedule, record bad debts, and discuss implications.
(SO 1)

Month of Sale	2012	2011
March	$260,000	$300,000
February	50,400	32,000
January	34,000	9,600
October–December	25,600	4,400
	$370,000	$346,000

Credit terms are 2/10, n/30. At March 31, 2012, there is an $8,800 credit balance in the allowance account before adjustment. The company estimates its uncollectible accounts as follows:

Number of Days Outstanding	Estimated Percentage Uncollectible
0–30	2%
31–60	10%
61–90	30%
Over 90	50%

Instructions

(a) Prepare an aging schedule to determine the total estimated uncollectibles at March 31, 2012.

(b) Prepare the adjusting entry at March 31, 2012, to record bad debts expense.

(c) Discuss the implications of the changes in the age of receivables from 2011 to 2012.

E8-5 On December 31, 2011, when its Allowance for Doubtful Accounts had a debit balance of $2,000, Ceja Corp. estimated that $16,800 of its accounts receivable would become uncollectible, and it recorded the bad debts adjusting entry. On May 11, 2012, Ceja determined that Robert Worthy's account was uncollectible and wrote off $1,900. On November 12, 2012, Worthy paid the amount previously written off.

Record bad debts transactions.
(SO 1)

Instructions

Prepare the required journal entries to record each of the above transactions.

E8-6 During its first year of operations, which ended on December 31, 2011, Fort Nelson Resources Ltd. determined that customers owing the company $12,000 would not be able to pay and wrote off these accounts. By the end of the year, the company had $1.7 million of accounts receivable and estimated that 10% of these were doubtful of collection. In 2012, the company wrote off accounts receivable amounting to $14,000. By December 31, 2012, the company had accounts receivable of $2.1 million and estimated doubtful accounts at 10% of outstanding accounts receivable.

Record bad debts transactions and assess policy.
(SO 1)

Instructions

(a) Prepare the journal entries that Fort Nelson Resources would record in 2011.

(b) Prepare the journal entries that Fort Nelson Resources would record in 2012.

(c) Assess whether the company's policy of estimating doubtful accounts at 10% of outstanding receivables is appropriate.

E8-7 At the beginning of March, Paragon Limited, which records adjusting entries at the end of each month, had accounts receivable of $30,000 and an allowance for doubtful accounts of $5,000. During March, the company had credit sales of $40,000 and collected $35,000 from customers. At the end of March, the balance in accounts receivable was $32,000 while the allowance for doubtful accounts had a balance of $4,500. No accounts that were written off during the month were subsequently recovered.

Determine missing amounts; record bad debts transactions.
(SO 1)

Instructions

(a) Determine the journal entry that would have been made by Paragon to write off uncollectible receivables during March.

(b) Determine the journal entry that would be made by the company to record bad debts expense for the month of March.

Record notes receivable transactions.
(SO 2)

E8–8   Passara Supply Corp. has the following selected transactions for notes receivable:

Nov. 1   Loaned $48,000 cash to A. Bouchard on a one-year, 8% note.
Dec. 1   Sold goods to Wright, Inc., receiving a two-month, 6%, $8,400 note. The goods cost $5,000.
    15   Received a six-month, 7%, $16,000 note on account from Aquilina Corporation.
    31   Accrued interest on all notes receivable at year end. Interest is due at maturity.
Feb. 1   Collected the amount owing on the Wright note.

Instructions
Record the above transactions for Passara Supply Corp. Round your answers to the nearest dollar.

Record notes receivable transactions.
(SO 2)

E8–9   The following selected transactions for notes receivable are for Acre Limited:

May 1   Received a six-month, 5%, $12,000 note on account from Blackstone Limited. Interest is due at maturity.
June 30   Accrued interest on the Blackstone note on this date, which is Acre's year end.
July 31   Lent $10,000 cash to an employee, Noreen Wong, issuing a three-month, 7% note. Interest is due at the end of each month.
Aug. 31   Received the interest due from Ms. Wong.
Sept. 30   Received the interest due from Ms. Wong.
Oct. 31   Received payment in full for the employee note from Ms. Wong.
Nov. 1   Wrote off the Blackstone note as Blackstone defaulted. Future payment is not expected.

Instructions
Record the above transactions for Acre Limited. Round your answers to the nearest dollar.

Show statement presentation.
(SO 3)

E8–10   Deere & Company had the following balances in its short-term receivable accounts at October 31, 2010 (in U.S. millions): Allowance for Doubtful Trade and Notes Receivables $71; Allowance for Doubtful Financing Receivables $225; Financing Receivables $20,875; Other Receivables $925.6; and Trade Accounts and Notes Receivable $3,535.2.

Instructions
(a) Show the presentation of Deere & Company's receivables in the current assets section of its statement of financial position at October 31.
(b) The balance in the Allowance for Doubtful Financing Receivables at the beginning of the year was U.S. $239 million while Bad Debts Expense for this type of receivable was U.S. $102 million. What was the amount of financing receivables that the company wrote off during the year?

Discuss concentration of credit risk.
(SO 4)

E8–11   Refer to E8–10. Deere & Company reports in the notes to its financial statements that its trade accounts and notes receivable have significant concentrations of credit risk in the agricultural, commercial, consumer, construction, and forestry sectors. However, it does not believe that it has a significant concentration of credit risk on a geographic basis.

Instructions
Should readers of Deere & Company's financial statements be concerned about its credit risk? Why or why not?

Calculate and evaluate ratios.
(SO 4)

E8–12   The following information (in millions) was taken from the December 31 financial statements of Canadian National Railway Company (CN):

	2010	2009	2008
Accounts receivable, gross	$ 796	$ 831	$ 939
Allowance for doubtful accounts	21	34	26
Accounts receivable, net	775	797	913
Revenues	8,297	7,367	8,482
Total current assets	1,590	1,490	1,149
Total current liabilities	1,906	1,237	1,958

Instructions
(a) For 2010 and 2009, calculate CN's current ratio, receivables turnover, and average collection period.
(b) Comment on any improvement or deterioration in CN's liquidity and management of its accounts receivable.

Problems: Set A

P8–1A At January 1, 2012, Underwood Imports Inc. reported the following on its statement of financial position:

Accounts receivable	$1,990,000
Allowance for doubtful accounts	124,000

During 2012, the company had the following summary transactions for receivables:

1. Sales on account, $5,200,000
2. Sales returns and allowances, $80,000
3. Collections of accounts receivable, $5,400,000
4. Interest added to overdue accounts, $400,000
5. Write-offs of accounts receivable deemed uncollectible, $150,000
6. Recovery of accounts previously written off as uncollectible, $60,000

Instructions

(a) Prepare the journal entries to record each of the summary transactions.
(b) Enter the January 1 balances in Accounts Receivable and Allowance for Doubtful Accounts, post the entries to the two accounts, and determine the balances.
(c) Prepare the journal entry to record bad debts expense at December 31, assuming that the aging of the accounts receivable indicates that the amount for estimated uncollectible accounts is $100,000.
(d) Determine the net realizable value of the accounts receivable as at December 31.
(e) Show the statement of financial position presentation of the receivables as at December 31.
(f) Show the income statement presentation of any income statement accounts for the year ended December 31.

Record receivables and bad debts transactions; show statement presentation.
(SO 1, 3)

P8–2A At the beginning of the current period, Azim Enterprises Ltd. had balances in Accounts Receivable of $1,600,000 and in Allowance for Doubtful Accounts of $88,000 (credit). During the period, Azim had net credit sales of $3,800,000 and collections of $4,084,000. It wrote off accounts receivable of $116,000. However, an $8,000 account written off as uncollectible was recovered before the end of the current period. Uncollectible accounts are estimated to total $72,000 at the end of the period.

Record receivables and bad debts transactions; show statement presentation.
(SO 1, 3)

Instructions

(a) Prepare the entries to record sales and collections during the period.
(b) Prepare the entry to record the write-off of uncollectible accounts during the period.
(c) Prepare the entries to record the recovery of the uncollectible account during the period.
(d) Prepare the entry to record bad debts expense for the period.
(e) Determine the ending balances in Accounts Receivable and Allowance for Doubtful Accounts.
(f) Show the statement of financial position presentation of the receivables at the end of the period.

P8–3A Wilton Corporation reported the following information in its general ledger at December 31:

Determine missing amounts.
(SO 1)

Accounts Receivable				Sales	
Beg. bal.	18,000				60,000
	(a)	56,000			
End. bal.	(b)				

Allowance for Doubtful Accounts			Bad Debts Expense	
		1,800	(e)	
	1,000	(c)		
End. bal.		(d)		

All sales were on account. At the end of the year, uncollectible accounts were estimated to total $2,000 based on an aging schedule.

Instructions

Using your knowledge of receivables transactions, determine the missing amounts. (*Hint*: You may not be able to solve the above items in alphabetical order. In addition, you may find it helpful to reconstruct the journal entries.)

P8–4A Here is information for Zeus Ltd. for the 2012 calendar year:

Calculate bad debts amounts.
(SO 1)

Total credit sales	$6,600,000
Accounts receivable at December 31	2,500,000
Accounts receivable written off during year	96,000
Accounts receivable later recovered (after write-off but before year end)	16,000

At the end of the year, uncollectible accounts were estimated to total $104,000 based on an aging schedule.

Instructions

(a) What amount of bad debts expense will Zeus record if Allowance for Doubtful Accounts has an opening credit balance of $40,000 on January 1?

(b) Assume the same facts as in (a) except that there is a $20,000 opening credit balance in Allowance for Doubtful Accounts. What amount of bad debts expense will Zeus record?

(c) What are the advantages of using the allowance method of reporting bad debts expense?

Prepare aging schedule and record bad debts transactions.
(SO 1)

P8–5A The following selected information is from Rigibuctou Company's aging schedule to estimate uncollectible accounts receivable at year end:

	Total	Number of Days Outstanding			
		0–30	31–60	61–90	Over 90
Accounts receivable	$520,000	$240,000	$120,000	$100,000	$60,000
Estimated percentage uncollectible		1%	5%	10%	25%

The unadjusted balance in Allowance for Doubtful Accounts is a credit of $20,000.

Instructions

(a) Complete the aging schedule and calculate the estimated allowance for doubtful accounts from the above information.

(b) Prepare the adjusting journal entry to record the bad debts using the information determined in (a). Would your journal entry be different if the unadjusted balance in Allowance for Doubtful Accounts were a debit of $20,000?

(c) In the following year, $4,000 of the outstanding receivables is determined to be specifically uncollectible. Prepare the journal entry to write off the uncollectible amount.

(d) Rigibuctou subsequently collects $1,700 of the $4,000 that was determined to be uncollectible in (c). Prepare the journal entries to restore the account receivable and record the collection.

(e) Explain why using the allowance method provides more relevant financial information.

(f) Comment on how your answers in (a) to (d) would change if the company used a percentage of total accounts receivable of 5%, rather than aging the accounts.

(g) What are the advantages to the company of aging the accounts receivable rather than applying a percentage to total accounts receivable?

Prepare aging schedule; record bad debts transactions.
(SO 1)

P8–6A An aging analysis of Yamoto Limited's accounts receivable at December 31, 2012 and 2011, showed the following:

Number of Days Outstanding	Estimated Percentage Uncollectible	December 31	
		2012	2011
0–30 days	3%	$300,000	$320,000
31–60 days	6%	64,000	114,000
61–90 days	12%	86,000	76,000
Over 90 days	24%	130,000	50,000
Total		$580,000	$560,000

1. At December 31, 2011, the unadjusted balance in Allowance for Doubtful Accounts was a credit of $9,000.
2. In 2012, $42,000 of accounts were written off as uncollectible and $3,000 of accounts previously written off were recovered.

Instructions

(a) Prepare an aging schedule to calculate the estimated uncollectible accounts at December 31, 2011 and 2012. Comment on the results.

(b) Record the adjusting entry relating to bad debts on December 31, 2011.

(c) Record the write-off of uncollectible accounts in 2012.

(d) Record the collection of accounts previously written off in 2012.

(e) Prepare the adjusting entry relating to bad debts on December 31, 2012.

(f) Calculate the net realizable value of Yamoto's accounts receivable at December 31, 2011 and 2012.

(g) Do you think that Yamoto was conservative when estimating bad debts expense? Explain.

Record receivables transactions.
(SO 1, 2)

P8–7A The following selected transactions occurred for Bleumortier Corporation. The company has a March 31 year end and adjusts accounts annually.

Jan. 5   Sold $18,000 of merchandise to Brooks Limited, terms n/30. The cost of goods sold was $12,000.

Feb. 1   Bleumortier has introduced its own credit card. Morgan Ltd. used the card to buy merchandise for $6,000 that cost Bleumortier $4,000. Interest on unpaid balances after 30 days is charged at 18% per annum (1.5% per month).

2	Accepted a four-month, 6%, $18,000 promissory note from Brooks for the balance due. Interest is payable at maturity. (See January 5 transaction.)
3	Sold $13,400 of merchandise costing $8,800 to Gauthier Company and accepted Gauthier's two-month, 6% note in payment. Interest is payable at maturity.
26	Sold $8,000 of merchandise to Mathias Corp., terms n/30. The cost of the merchandise sold was $5,400.
Mar. 6	Sold $4,000 of merchandise that cost $3,000 to Superior Limited. Superior paid using a bank credit card that has a 3% fee.
31	Accepted a two-month, 7%, $8,000 note from Mathias for the balance due. Interest is payable at maturity. (See February 26 transaction.)
31	Adjusted any accrued interest at year end on notes and credit card receivables.
Apr. 1	Collected full payment from Morgan Ltd.
3	Collected the Gauthier note in full. (See February 3 transaction.)
May 31	The Mathias note of March 31 is dishonoured. It is expected that Mathias will eventually pay the amount owed.
June 1	Collected the Brooks note in full. (See February 2 transaction.)

Instructions

Record the transactions. Round your answers to the nearest dollar.

P8–8A On November 1, 2012, Sokos Company accepted a three-month, 6%, $40,000 note from a customer in settlement of the customer's account. Interest is due on the first day of each month, starting December 1. The company's year end is December 31.

Record notes receivable transactions.
(SO 2)

Instructions

(a) Prepare all journal entries for Sokos over the term of the note. Assume that the customer settles the note in full on the maturity date.

(b) Assume that instead of honouring the note at maturity, the customer dishonours it. Prepare the necessary journal entry at the maturity date, February 1, 2013, assuming that eventual collection of the note is (1) expected, and (2) not expected.

P8–9A Canadian Tire Corporation, Limited reports the following asset accounts (in millions) at December 29, 2010:

Prepare assets section.
(SO 3)

Accounts receivable, net	$ 662.3	Land	$ 785.8
Accumulated depreciation—buildings	960.2	Long-term receivables and other assets	100.9
Accumulated depreciation—furniture		Merchandise inventories	901.5
and equipment	488.2	Other current assets	72.4
Accumulated depreciation—other	201.8	Other long-term investments	75.8
Buildings	2,734.0	Other property, plant, and equipment	613.4
Cash and cash equivalents	554.3	Prepaid expenses and deposits	37.6
Furniture and equipment	736.8	Short-term investments	195.9
Goodwill	71.9	Short-term loans receivable	2,481.2
Income taxes recoverable	99.4		
Intangible assets	291.1		

Instructions

Prepare the assets section of Canadian Tire's statement of financial position.

P8–10A The table below shows, for the three wholesale companies listed, the collection period in days over a three-year period:

Analyze receivables collections.
(SO 4)

	2012	2011	2010
Pacific Enterprises Ltd.	25	42	33
Atlantic Limited	36	49	29
Northwest Inc.	11	37	32

Instructions

(a) What company had the best receivables turnover ratio in 2010?

(b) In which year did the industry suffer a recession in which customers underwent financial hardship?

(c) One of the companies was investigated in 2012 for improperly recording sales relating to 2013 in 2012. Which company was this most likely to be?

(d) Which company most likely factored its receivables? In what year?

(e) Following the recession, one of the companies that did not factor receivables tightened its credit-granting policies. Which company most likely did this?

Calculate and evaluate ratios.
(SO 4)

P8–11A Presented here is selected information from the 2010 financial statements of Nike, Inc. (in U.S. $ millions) and Adidas AG (in euro millions):

	Nike	Adidas
Net sales	$19,014	€11,990
Allowance for doubtful accounts, beginning of year	111	124
Allowance for doubtful accounts, end of year	117	127
Accounts receivable (gross), beginning of year	2,884	1,553
Accounts receivable (gross), end of year	2,766	1,794

Instructions

(a) Calculate the receivables turnover and average collection period for both companies, assuming all sales are credit sales. The industry average for the receivables turnover was 7.2 times and the average collection period was 51 days.

(b) Comment on the difference in the two companies' collection experiences.

Evaluate liquidity.
(SO 4)

P8–12A The following selected ratios are available for Pampered Pets Inc. for the most recent three years:

	2012	2011	2010
Current ratio	2.6:1	2.4:1	2.1:1
Receivables turnover	8.2 times	7.4 times	6.7 times
Inventory turnover	9.9 times	8.7 times	7.5 times

Instructions

(a) Is Pampered Pets' liquidity improving or worsening? Explain.

(b) Do changes in turnover ratios affect profitability? Explain.

(c) Do changes in turnover ratios affect cash flow? Explain.

(d) Identify any steps that the company may wish to take in order to improve its management of receivables and inventory.

Problems: Set B

Record receivables and bad debts transactions; show statement presentation.
(SO 1, 3)

P8–1B At January 1, 2012, Bordeaux Inc. reported the following information on its statement of financial position:

Accounts receivable	$480,000
Allowance for doubtful accounts	35,000

During 2012, the company had the following summary transactions for receivables:

1. Sales on account, $1,600,000
2. Sales returns and allowances, $250,000
3. Collections of accounts receivable, $1,500,000
4. Interest added to overdue accounts, $125,000
5. Write-offs of accounts receivable deemed uncollectible, $45,000
6. Recovery of accounts previously written off as uncollectible, $10,500

Instructions

(a) Prepare the journal entries to record each of the summary transactions.

(b) Enter the January 1 balances in Accounts Receivable and Allowance for Doubtful Accounts, post the entries to the two accounts, and determine the balances.

(c) Prepare the journal entry to record bad debts expense at December 31, assuming that aging the accounts receivable indicates that the amount for estimated uncollectible accounts is $55,000.

(d) Determine the net realizable value of the accounts receivable as at December 31.

(e) Show the statement of financial position presentation of the receivables as at December 31.

(f) Show the income statement presentation of any income statement accounts for the year ended December 31.

Record receivables and bad debts transactions; show statement presentation.
(SO 1, 3)

P8–2B At the beginning of the current period, Huang Ltd. had balances in Accounts Receivable of $200,000 and in Allowance for Doubtful Accounts of $14,000 (credit). During the period, it had net credit sales of $800,000 and collections of $723,000. It wrote off accounts receivable of $21,000. However, a $3,500 account written off as uncollectible was recovered before the end of the current period. Uncollectible accounts are estimated to total $16,000 at the end of the period.

Instructions
(a) Prepare the entries to record the sales and collections during the period.
(b) Prepare the entry to record the write-off of uncollectible accounts during the period.
(c) Prepare the entries to record the recovery of the uncollectible account during the period.
(d) Prepare the entry to record bad debts expense for the period.
(e) Determine the ending balances in Accounts Receivable and Allowance for Doubtful Accounts.
(f) Show the statement of financial position presentation of the receivables at the end of the period.

P8-3B Yasukuni Corporation reported the following information in its general ledger at June 30:

Determine missing amounts.
(SO 1)

Accounts Receivable				Sales	
Beg. bal.	(a)				(d)
	22,500	23,000			
End. bal.	2,250				

Allowance for Doubtful Accounts			Bad Debts Expense	
Beg. bal.		100	(e)	
	25	(b)		
End. bal.		(c)		

All sales were on account. At the end of the year, uncollectible accounts were estimated to total $115 based on an aging schedule.

Instructions
Using your knowledge of receivables transactions, determine the missing amounts. (*Hint:* You may not be able to solve the above items in alphabetical order. In addition, you may find it helpful to reconstruct the journal entries.)

P8-4B Here is information for Zorba Ltd. for the year ended April 30, 2012:

Calculate bad debts amounts.
(SO 1)

Total credit sales	$2,000,000
Accounts receivable at April 30	800,000
Accounts receivable written off during year	35,000
Accounts receivable later recovered (after write-off but before year end)	5,000

At the end of the year, uncollectible accounts were estimated to total $60,000 based on an aging schedule.

Instructions
(a) What amount of bad debts expense will Zorba record if Allowance for Doubtful Accounts has an opening credit balance of $20,000 on May 1, 2011?
(b) Assume the same facts as in (a) except that there is a $40,000 opening credit balance in Allowance for Doubtful Accounts. What amount of bad debts expense will Zorba record?
(c) What are the advantages of using the allowance method of reporting bad debts expense?

P8-5B Imagine Corporation produced the following aging schedule of its accounts receivable at year end:

Prepare aging schedule and record bad debts transactions.
(SO 1)

		Number of Days Outstanding			
	Total	0–30	31–60	61–90	Over 90
Accounts receivable	$192,500	$110,000	$50,000	$20,000	$12,500
Estimated percentage uncollectible		1%	5%	10%	20%

The unadjusted balance in Allowance for Doubtful Accounts is a debit of $5,000.

Instructions
(a) Complete the aging schedule and calculate the estimated allowance for doubtful accounts from the above information.
(b) Prepare the adjusting journal entry to record the bad debts using the information determined in (a). Would your journal entry be different if the unadjusted balance in Allowance for Doubtful Accounts were a credit of $5,000?
(c) In the following year, $3,000 of the outstanding receivables is determined to be uncollectible. Prepare the journal entry to write off the uncollectible amount.
(d) The company subsequently collects $1,500 of the $3,000 that was determined to be uncollectible in (c). Prepare the journal entries to restore the account receivable and record the collection.
(e) Explain why using the allowance method provides more relevant financial information.

(f) Comment on how your answers in (a) to (d) would change if Imagine used a percentage of total accounts receivable of 4%, rather than aging the accounts.

(g) What are the advantages to the company of aging the accounts receivable rather than applying a percentage to total accounts receivable?

Prepare aging schedule; record bad debts transactions.
(SO 1)

P8–6B An aging analysis of Reiko Limited's accounts receivable at December 31, 2012 and 2011 showed the following:

Number of Days Outstanding	Estimated Percentage Uncollectible	December 31	
		2012	2011
0–30 days	3%	$240,000	$220,000
31–60 days	6%	104,000	86,000
61–90 days	12%	62,000	52,000
Over 90 days	20%	34,000	22,000
Total		$440,000	$380,000

1. At December 31, 2011, the unadjusted balance in Allowance for Doubtful Accounts was a credit of $3,000.

2. In 2012, $28,000 of accounts were written off as uncollectible and $3,000 of accounts previously written off were recovered.

Instructions

(a) Prepare an aging schedule to calculate the estimated uncollectible accounts at December 31, 2011 and 2012. Comment on the results.

(b) Record the adjusting entry relating to bad debts on December 31, 2011.

(c) Record the write-off of uncollectible accounts in 2012.

(d) Record the collection of accounts previously written off in 2012.

(e) Prepare the adjusting entry relating to bad debts on December 31, 2012.

(f) Calculate the net realizable value of Reiko accounts receivable at December 31, 2011 and 2012.

(g) Do you think that Reiko was conservative when estimating its bad debts expense? Explain.

Record receivables transactions.
(SO 1, 2)

P8–7B The following selected transactions are for Vu Ltd., which has a September 30 year end and adjusts its accounts annually:

Jan. 1   Loaned Emily Collis, an employee, $6,000 on a four-month, 8% note. Interest is due at maturity.

5   Sold $8,000 of merchandise to Asiz Limited, terms n/15. The merchandise cost $4,800.

20   Accepted Asiz Limited's two-month, 9%, $8,000 note for its balance due. Interest is due monthly. (See January 5 transaction.)

Feb. 18   Sold $4,000 of merchandise costing $2,400 to Swaim Corp. Accepted Swaim's six-month, 7% note in payment. Interest is due at maturity.

20   Collected interest on the Asiz note. (See January 20 transaction.)

Mar. 20   Collected principal and interest for the month on the Asiz note. (See January 20 transaction.)

May 1   Received payment in full from Emily Collis. (See January 1 transaction.)

4   Sold $4,000 of merchandise that cost $3,000 to Paragon Limited. Paragon paid using a bank credit card that has a 3% fee.

25   Accepted Thunderchild Inc.'s three-month, 8%, $3,000 note in settlement of a past-due balance on account. Interest is due at maturity.

Aug. 1   Vu has introduced its own credit card. Pierpont Ltd. used the card to buy merchandise for $6,000 that cost Vu $4,000. Interest on unpaid balances after 30 days is charged at 18% per annum (1.5% per month).

18   Received payment in full from Swaim Corp. on its note due. (See February 18 transaction.)

25   The Thunderchild note was dishonoured. Eventual payment is not expected. (See May 25 transaction.)

Sept. 30   Adjusted any accrued interest on notes and credit cards at year end.

Instructions

Record the transactions. Round your answers to the nearest dollar.

Record notes receivable transactions.
(SO 2)

P8–8B On August 1, 2012, Cappuccitti Company accepted a two-month, 4%, $30,000 note from a customer in settlement of the customer's account. Interest is due on the first day of each month, starting September 1. The company's year end is August 31.

Instructions

(a) Prepare all journal entries for Cappuccitti over the term of the note. Assume that the customer settles the note in full on the maturity date. Round your answers to the nearest dollar.

(b) Assume that instead of honouring the note at maturity, the customer dishonours it. Prepare the necessary journal entry at the maturity date, October 1, 2012, assuming that eventual collection of the note is (1) expected, and (2) not expected.

P8–9B   Sears Canada Inc. reports the following asset accounts (in millions) at January 29, 2011:

Prepare assets section. (SO 3)

Accounts receivable, net	$ 143.2	Income taxes receivable	$ 4.5
Accumulated depreciation—buildings	793.7	Intangible assets	23.5
Accumulated depreciation—equipment		Inventories	953.2
and fixtures	982.4	Land	53.6
Buildings	1,148.1	Other long-term assets	263.2
Cash and equivalents	426.0	Prepaid expenses and other current assets	92.3
Equipment and fixtures	1,151.8	Restricted cash and short-term investments	15.3
Goodwill	11.2		

Instructions
Prepare the assets section of Sears Canada's statement of financial position.

P8–10B   The table below shows, for the three wholesale companies listed, the collection period in days over a three-year period:

Analyze receivables collections. (SO 4)

	2012	2011	2010
Arctic Enterprises Ltd.	22	42	30
Pacific Limited	36	49	29
Maritime Inc.	29	37	11

Instructions
(a) What company had the best receivables turnover ratio in 2010?
(b) In which year did the industry suffer a recession in which customers underwent financial hardship?
(c) One of the companies was investigated in 2012 for improperly recording sales relating to 2013 in 2012. Which company would it have been?
(d) Which company most likely factored its receivables? In what year?
(e) Following the recession, one of the companies tightened its credit-granting policies too much. Which company most likely did this?

P8–11B   Presented here is selected information (in millions) from the 2010 financial statements of Rogers Communications Inc. and Shaw Communications Inc.:

Calculate and evaluate ratios. (SO 4)

	Rogers	Shaw
Net sales	$12,186	$3,718
Allowance for doubtful accounts, Jan. 1	157	17
Allowance for doubtful accounts, Dec. 31	138	19
Accounts receivable (gross), Jan. 1	1,467	166
Accounts receivable (gross), Dec. 31	1,618	212

Instructions
(a) Calculate the receivables turnover and average collection period for both companies, assuming all sales are credit sales. The industry average for the receivables turnover was 14.1 times and the average collection period was 26 days.
(b) Comment on the difference in the companies' collection experiences.

P8–12B   The following ratios are available for Tianjin Inc.:

Evaluate liquidity. (SO 4)

	2012	2011	2010
Current ratio	1.5:1	1.5:1	1.5:1
Receivables turnover	8 times	7 times	6 times
Inventory turnover	6 times	7 times	8 times

Instructions
(a) Is Tianjin's liquidity improving or worsening? Explain.
(b) Do changes in turnover ratios affect profitability? Explain.
(c) Do changes in turnover ratios affect cash flow? Explain.
(d) Identify any steps that the company may wish to consider in order to improve its management of its receivables and inventory.

Broadening Your Perspective

Financial Reporting and Analysis Cases

Financial Reporting: *Eastplats*

Answer questions about receivables. (SO 1, 4)

BYP8-1 The financial statements of Eastern Platinum Limited (Eastplats) are presented in Appendix A at the end of this book.

Instructions

(a) What types of receivables does Eastplats report in its 2010 statement of financial position? (*Hint:* Review Note 7 to the financial statements.)

(b) What is the average collection period of trade receivables in 2010?

(c) Did Eastplats write off any of its accounts as uncollectible in 2009 and 2010? Did it recover any uncollectible accounts?

(d) Is Eastplats likely concerned about any concentration of credit risk? Why or why not? (*Hint*: Review Note 24 (e) (iv) to the financial statements.)

Comparative Analysis: Eastplats and Amplats

Calculate and evaluate ratios. (SO 4)

BYP8-2 The financial statements of Anglo American Platinum Limited (Amplats) are presented in Appendix B following the financial statements for Eastern Platinum Limited (Eastplats) in Appendix A.

Instructions

(a) Calculate the following for each company for its most recent fiscal year. The industry average is shown in parentheses.
1. Current ratio (1:1)
2. Receivables turnover (9.9 times) (Assume all sales were credit sales and use net receivables instead of gross receivables.)
3. Average collection period (37 days)

(b) Given the nature of each company's accounts receivable, what conclusions about each company's liquidity and management of its accounts receivable can be drawn from your calculations in (a)?

Interpreting Financial Information

Determine bad debt expense; calculate and evaluate ratios. (SO 1, 4)

BYP8-3 Li & Fung Limited, based in Hong Kong, is one of the largest suppliers of consumer goods in the world, operating from 70 offices in 40 countries. The company uses IFRS and reported the following information (in millions of HKD) in its financial statements:

	2010	2009	2008
Sales (assume all credit)	$124,115	$104,479	$110,722
Cost of goods sold	107,221	92,406	99,119
Total current assets	32,666	21,579	21,466
Total current liabilities	26,147	17,458	17,848
Accounts receivable (gross)	16,569	12,824	14,994
Allowance for doubtful accounts, end of year	353	263	279
Accounts receivable write-offs	63	164	55
Merchandise inventory	5,996	2,383	2,329

Instructions

(a) Calculate the current ratio, receivables turnover, and inventory turnover for 2010 and 2009. Comment on Li & Fung's liquidity.

(b) Do you anticipate any difficulties in comparing the ratios you calculated in (a) for Li & Fung with those of a Canadian competitor?

(c) Determine the bad debts expense recorded by the company in 2010 and 2009. There were no recoveries of uncollectible accounts.

(d) In 2009, the allowance for doubtful accounts was just slightly lower than it was in the previous year even though its accounts receivable had declined considerably. Comment on the reasons why this could have occurred.

(e) The company, in a note to the financial statements, indicates that its credit risk is not significant. Discuss some reasons why management has made this statement.

(f) On occasion, the company will factor its accounts receivable. Given that the industry average for receivables turnover is 8 times, the company may not use factoring much. Can you explain why?

Comparing IFRS and ASPE

BYP8-4 Assume you are an analyst for Big Bank and you are putting together financial information on two clothing manufacturers, Lava Fashions Inc. and Flow Designs Inc., for your boss, to help her monitor Big Bank's loans with those two companies. Lava Fashions is a public company that follows IFRS and Flow Designs is a private company that follows ASPE.

Understand valuation of accounts receivable and financial statement presentation, and analyze receivables. (SO 1, 3, 4)

One of the most significant assets for both companies is the accounts receivable from retailer customers. You know that your boss will be interested in knowing both the receivables' net realizable value and the receivables' exposure to credit risk (the risk that some of the customers won't ultimately pay for the goods they purchased).

You look at the notes to the financial statements and find that the information provided is considerably different.

LAVA FASHIONS INC.
Extract from Financial Statements

Note 14: Accounts Receivable

	December 31, 2012	December 31, 2011
Trade receivables	$1,854	$1,917
Less: allowance for doubtful accounts	(135)	(124)
Net realizable value	$1,719	$1,793

The aging of gross trade receivables at each reporting date was as follows:

	December 31, 2012	December 31, 2011
Current	$1,322	$1,363
Past due 0–30 days	183	192
Past due 31–60 days	170	167
Past due 61–90 days	50	61
Past due 91–180 days	62	70
Past due > 180 days	67	64
Balance at December 31	$1,854	$1,917

Lava is exposed to normal credit risk with respect to its accounts receivable. It has provisions for potential credit losses. It reduces the potential for such losses because it has no significant exposure to any single customer and because it evaluates a potential customer's creditworthiness before extending credit.

FLOW DESIGNS INC.
Extract from Financial Statements

Note 11: Accounts Receivable

	December 31, 2012	December 31, 2011
Trade receivables	$2,255	$2,378
Less: allowance for doubtful accounts	(535)	(325)
Net realizable value	$1,720	$2,053

Flow provides credit to its customers in the normal course of its operations. It continually conducts credit checks on its customers and has provisions for contingent credit losses. Three major customers represent 30% of the company's accounts receivable as at December 31, 2011.

Instructions

(a) Which company's financial statement note provides more useful information on the carrying value and credit risk for accounts receivable? Why?

(b) Why do you think Lava Fashions provides more information on its accounts receivable than Flow Designs?

(c) What additional information do you think Big Bank would want in order to assess the credit risk in trade receivables for Lava Fashions and Flow Designs?

(d) Where else do you think Big Bank could get information on the credit risk in trade receivables for Lava Fashions and Flow Designs?

Critical Thinking Cases and Activities

Collaborative Learning Activity

Discuss impact of
changes in collection
period.
(SO 4)

BYP8–5   A small construction equipment rental and sales business has customers of two main types: retail consumers who rent equipment on a short-term basis and pay by cash or credit card, and business customers who may rent higher-valued equipment for longer periods of time. These longer-term contracts are more profitable because they minimize nonrental times for the equipment. The company offers sales on account to qualified business customers.

At a monthly management meeting, there are two agenda items that require a decision:

1. The average collection period of accounts receivable is increasing from about 45 days last year to over 60 days this year.
2. The company has the opportunity to bid on a local government equipment supply contract. This contract would increase its overall sales volume by 20%, but the collection period for contract payments could stretch to 120 days.

Instructions

After the class has been divided into groups and you have been assigned one of the two agenda items identified above, do the following:

(a) Discuss the effects on cash flow, the risks for the business, and suggestions to improve the company's financial operations for your assigned item.
(b) Identify any missing information that would be helpful in analyzing the situation.

Communication Activity

Discuss the manage-
ment of receivables.
(SO 4)

BYP8–6   Toys for Big Boys Ltd. sells snowmobiles, personal watercraft, ATVs, and the like. Recently, the company's credit manager retired. The sales staff threw him a big retirement party—they were glad to see him go, because they felt his credit policies restricted their selling ability. The sales staff then convinced management that there was no need to replace the credit manager, since they could handle this responsibility in addition to their sales positions.

Management was thrilled at year end when sales doubled. However, gross accounts receivable also quadrupled and cash flow halved. The average collection period increased from 30 days to 90 days.

Instructions

In a memo to management, explain the internal control and financial impact of allowing the sales staff to manage the credit function. Has the business assumed any additional credit risk? What would you recommend the company do to better manage its increasing accounts receivable?

Ethics Case

Identify issues related
to estimating uncol-
lectible accounts.
(SO 1)

BYP8–7   Sam Wong is the controller of Encounter Limited, a public company. Using a method similar to the one he used in prior years, Sam has completed an aging schedule and determined that the allowance for doubtful accounts should be $100,000 at the end of the current year. Sam has noticed that the age of receivables this year is older than in prior years. The president of the company, Suzanne Chen, is nervous because the bank expects the company to maintain a current ratio of 2:1. After recording the adjustment for bad debts this year, the current assets total $2,000,000 while current liabilities total $1,025,000. Suzanne has demanded that Sam reduce the allowance from $100,000 to $40,000 to reflect current economic conditions.

Instructions

(a) Who are the stakeholders in this case?
(b) Why did Suzanne request the adjustment?
(c) Does the president's request pose an ethical dilemma for the controller?
(d) Is the president's reason for reducing the allowance a valid one?

"All About You" Activity

Identify features
of credit cards for
personal use.
(SO 4)

BYP8–8   As the "All About You" feature in this chapter indicates, credit card use in Canada is substantial. In order to finance their education, some students resort to borrowing on credit cards at high interest rates. Suppose you have one year left of university and you decide you may need to use one or more credit cards to fund the cash shortfall you expect to have in your final year.

Instructions

(a) The Financial Consumer Agency of Canada provides tables comparing the costs and benefits of credit cards available in Canada. Go to the agency's website at www.fcac-acfc.gc.ca/ and search for the Credit Card Comparison Tables. Create a personal list, from most important to least important, of the features that are important to you in selecting a credit card.

(b) Examine the features of your present credit card. If you do not have a credit card, select a likely one on-line for this exercise. Given your analysis above, what are the three major disadvantages of your present (or likely) credit card?

Serial Case

(*Note:* This is a continuation of the serial case from Chapters 1 through 7.)

BYP8–9   The majority of Koebel's Family Bakery's sales are paid by cash, debit card, or credit card. In a few cases, it has extended credit to select customers, including Coffee Beans. To date, Koebel's has been giving Coffee Beans 30 days to pay for the weekly delivery of cupcakes. Generally, Coffee Beans is taking 45 days to pay each invoice issued. As a result, Janet and Brian have had to pay close attention to cash available to purchase additional inventory and pay monthly wages. Although Janet, Brian, and Natalie are happy to have taken on the additional work, they are reconsidering the credit terms they are prepared to offer Coffee Beans. As well, they are attempting to establish a consistent credit policy as they continue to discuss with Biscuits the possibility of a weekly contractual commitment to sell chocolate chip cookies.

Discuss credit policy. (SO 4)

They are meeting with Frank Vosburgh, the president of Coffee Beans, to discuss their ongoing business relationship. Frank has wanted to meet because the demand for cupcakes has increased significantly and it is anticipated that the number of cupcakes required on a weekly basis will double. He would like to continue to have Koebel's prepare the cupcakes on Coffee Beans' behalf and wants to ensure that they can meet the additional demand. Natalie, Janet, and Brian would like to review the terms of sale with Frank. However, before meeting with Frank, they want to consider all of the implications of reducing terms of sale from 30 to 15 days.

Instructions

(a) Identify to Natalie, Janet, and Brian some of the advantages and disadvantages of reducing credit terms to Coffee Beans (and other potential customers) from 30 days to 15 days.
(b) If Koebel's Family Bakery decides to continue providing cupcakes to Coffee Beans and the number of cupcakes to be produced doubles, what are some of the implications for Koebel's cash flow if the credit terms remain at 30 days?
(c) Can you provide other alternatives to Koebel's Family Bakery to encourage Coffee Beans to pay on time?

Answers to Self-Test Questions

1. c	2. c	3. d	4. d	5. b
6. d	7. a	8. a	9. c	10. a

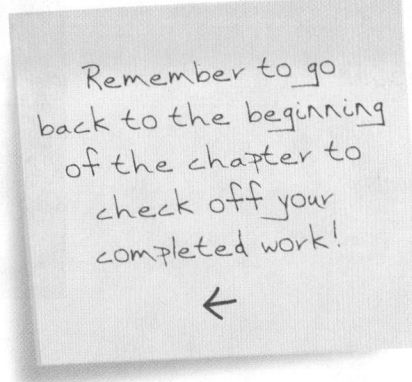

Remember to go back to the beginning of the chapter to check off your completed work!

←

CHAPTER 9

Reporting and Analyzing Long-Lived Assets

study objectives

After studying this chapter, you should be able to:

1. Determine the cost of property, plant, and equipment.
2. Explain and calculate depreciation.
3. Describe other accounting issues related to depreciation.
4. Account for the disposal of property, plant, and equipment.
5. Identify the basic accounting issues for intangible assets and goodwill.
6. Illustrate how long-lived assets are reported in the financial statements.
7. Describe the methods for evaluating the use of assets.

the navigator

ACCOUNTING MATTERS!

WestJet's Assets Are for the Long Haul

WestJet took to the skies in 1996, promoting lower-cost flights and a culture that treats its passengers as guests. From its beginnings with three planes, five destinations, and 220 employees—called WestJetters—the Calgary-based airline has grown to include 91 planes and nearly 8,000 WestJetters, taking their guests to 71 destinations in Canada, the United States, the Caribbean, and Mexico.

Of the fleet of 91 aircraft, WestJet owns 53 (it leases the remaining 38), and these 53 planes account for almost all of the airline's property and equipment, says Robert Palmer, WestJet's Controller. In September 2010, WestJet had over $2.2 billion in property and equipment, of which $1.9 billion was aircraft. Other elements in the property and equipment amount included ground property and equipment, spare engines and parts, buildings, leasehold improvements, and assets under capital leases.

The aircraft's purchase price and any costs required to get it into service are capitalized, as are any costs incurred to add betterments, such as televisions at every seat. Meanwhile, costs incurred to maintain the plane but not increase its useful life or add a benefit, such as to repair damages, are expensed.

Depreciation of the aircraft is based on the plane's economic useful life, which is 20 years, Mr. Palmer explains. The asset's depreciable amount is divided by its useful life to calculate the annual depreciation expense. For example, let's say an aircraft has a cost of $21 million and a residual value of $1 million, for a depreciable cost of $20 million. With a useful life of 20 years, the depreciation on the aircraft will be $1 million each year.

With the move to International Financial Reporting Standards, WestJet's accounting for the depreciation of its aircraft became more complicated. The aircraft are separated into various components—the engine, air frame, and landing gear, for example—and there is also overhaul on those components. Each component is depreciated separately. While the aircraft may have a useful life of 20 years, the engine may need to be overhauled every 10 years. "So we'll depreciate that over 10 years," explains Mr. Palmer.

Determining the aircraft's economic useful life involves consultation with the company's technical operations department, observation of the entire industry, and investigation of various external data sources, says Mr. Palmer. And although WestJet has been operating for less than 20 years, it has disposed of some older planes that had not been purchased brand new. This disposal is accounted for by calculating the carrying amount, which is cost less accumulated depreciation. "So if your selling price is over your carrying amount, a gain is recorded," Mr. Palmer explains. "And if it's less than the carrying amount, then a loss is recorded in the income statement. When we sold those assets in 2004, we had a loss."

WestJet plans to continue to expand its fleet and, with it, the value of its property and equipment. "We have orders up to 2017, which would take our fleet to 135 aircraft—91 owned and 44 leased," says Mr. Palmer.

WestJet does not have any current plans to expand globally, however. Instead, it is seeking partnerships with other airlines. For example, it has a deal with Cathay Pacific in which it will provide the Vancouver to Calgary leg of Cathay's Hong Kong to Vancouver to Calgary flight.

INSIDE CHAPTER

9

- Managing expenditures for plant and equipment (p. 460)

- Nortel patents sold (p. 479)

- Lego trademark dispute resolved (p. 480)

- Are you sure you need a new car? (p. 490)

the navigator

preview of CHAPTER 9

For airlines and many other companies, making the right decisions about long-lived assets is critical because these assets represent huge investments. Among others, these decisions include what assets to acquire and when, how to finance the acquisitions, how to account for the assets, and when to dispose of them.

In this chapter, we address these and other issues surrounding long-lived assets. Our discussion focuses on the following types of long-lived assets: (1) property, plant, and equipment; (2) intangible assets; and (3) goodwill. Long-lived assets can also include natural resources, investment properties, and agricultural assets. The accounting for these assets can be complex so we will leave any detailed coverage of these assets for another accounting course.

The chapter is organized as follows:

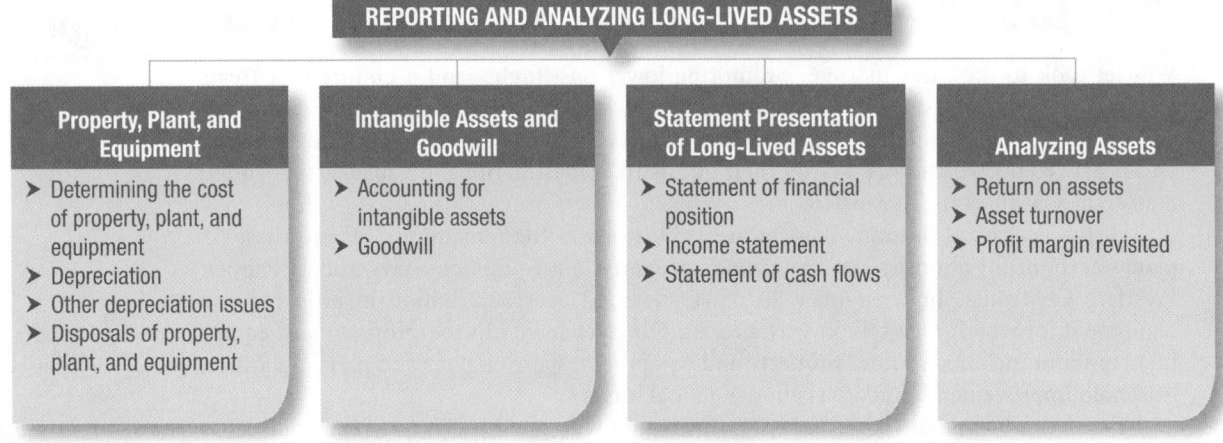

REPORTING AND ANALYZING LONG-LIVED ASSETS

Property, Plant, and Equipment	Intangible Assets and Goodwill	Statement Presentation of Long-Lived Assets	Analyzing Assets
➤ Determining the cost of property, plant, and equipment	➤ Accounting for intangible assets	➤ Statement of financial position	➤ Return on assets
➤ Depreciation	➤ Goodwill	➤ Income statement	➤ Asset turnover
➤ Other depreciation issues		➤ Statement of cash flows	➤ Profit margin revisited
➤ Disposals of property, plant, and equipment			

Property, Plant, and Equipment

STUDY OBJECTIVE 1

Determine the cost of property, plant, and equipment.

Property, plant, and equipment are long-lived resources that a company controls, that have physical substance (a definite size and shape), are used in the operations of a business, and are not intended for sale to customers. Unlike current assets, which are used or consumed in the current accounting period, property, plant, and equipment provide benefits over many years. They are used for the production and sale of goods or services to customers, for rental to others, or for administrative purposes.

Alternative Terminology
Property, plant, and equipment are sometimes called *capital assets* or *fixed assets.*

Property, plant, and equipment are critical to a company's success because they determine the company's production capacity, which in turn affects customer satisfaction. For example, with too few planes, WestJet would lose customers to its competitors. With too many planes, there would be lost revenue from flying planes with empty seats. Management must constantly monitor its needs and adjust the type and number of assets used accordingly. Not doing this can result in lost business opportunities or inefficient use of existing assets, and is a common reason for poor financial results.

Many companies have large investments in property, plant, and equipment. Illustration 9-1 shows the percentages of property, plant, and equipment (PPE) in relation to total assets in several Canadian companies.

▶Illustration 9-1

Property, plant, and equipment (PPE) as a percentage of total assets

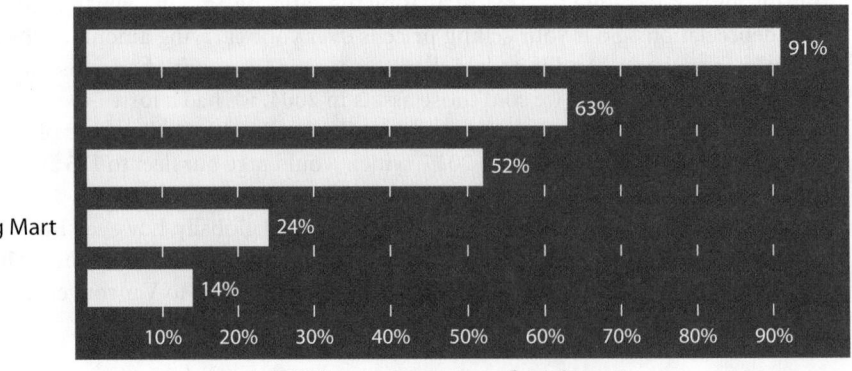

CN Rail	91%
WestJet	63%
PotashCorp	52%
Shoppers Drug Mart	24%
lululemon	14%

PPE as a percentage of total assets

DETERMINING THE COST OF PROPERTY, PLANT, AND EQUIPMENT

As we learned in Chapter 2, most companies record property, plant, and equipment at cost, which includes the following:

1. The purchase price, including certain kinds of taxes and duties, less any discounts or rebates
2. The expenditures necessary to bring the asset to its required location and to make it ready for its intended use

These costs are **capitalized** (recorded as property, plant, and equipment), rather than expensed, if it is probable that the company will receive an economic benefit in the future from the asset and this benefit can be measured. Determining which costs to include in property, plant, and equipment or other long-lived asset accounts and which costs not to include is very important. In general, costs that benefit only the current period are expensed. Such costs are called **operating expenditures**. Costs that benefit future periods are included in a long-lived asset account. These are called **capital expenditures**.

For example, the cost to purchase an asset such as equipment should be recorded as a capital expenditure, because the asset will benefit future periods. In addition, the insurance paid to ship that asset to the company should also be capitalized because the insurance during transit is part of the cost of obtaining the asset. Insurance paid to insure the asset against fire or theft after the asset is situated and in use would be expensed because these costs benefit only the current period. Likewise, any costs incurred to train employees on how to operate the equipment would be expensed and not added to the cost of the equipment because such costs were incurred to get the employees ready not to get the equipment ready for use.

Subsequent to acquisition, the same distinction exists between operating and capital expenditures. Operating expenditures normally benefit only the current period. They are required to maintain an asset in its normal operating condition and often recur, although not always annually. Examples include repainting a building or replacing the tires on a truck. These costs would be debited to an expense account, such as Repairs and Maintenance Expense, rather than being debited to an asset account.

Capital expenditures after acquisition include costs that increase the life of an asset or its productivity or efficiency. These costs are normally larger than operating expenditures and occur less frequently. As was mentioned in our chapter-opening feature story, WestJet capitalizes all refurbishment and upgrading costs if they are incurred to improve the planes' service value or extend their useful lives. Other examples for a different type of business might include the cost to replace the roof on a building or to overhaul an engine in a truck. These costs would be debited to an asset account, such as Buildings or Vehicles.

Property, plant, and equipment are often subdivided into four classes:

1. **Land**, such as a building site
2. **Land improvements**, such as driveways, parking lots, fences, and underground sprinkler systems
3. **Buildings**, such as stores, offices, factories, and warehouses
4. **Equipment**, such as store checkout counters, cash registers, computers, office furniture, factory machinery, and delivery equipment

How to determine the cost of each of the major classes of property, plant, and equipment is explained in the following sections.

Land

All costs related to the purchase of land, including such costs as survey and legal fees, are added to the Land account. If additional work is required to prepare the land for its intended use, such as clearing, grading, and filling, these costs are also recorded as capital expenditures in the Land account. If the land has a building on it that must be removed to make the site suitable for construction of a new building, all demolition and removal costs, less any proceeds from salvaged materials, are added to the Land account. When land has been purchased to construct a building, all costs that are incurred up to the time of excavation for the new building are considered to be part of the costs that are necessary to prepare the land for its intended use.

To illustrate, assume that Brochu Corporation purchases real estate for $100,000 and that the property contains an old warehouse that is torn down at a net cost of $6,000 ($7,500 in costs less $1,500 in proceeds from salvaged materials). Additional expenditures of $1,000 are also incurred for legal fees. Put together, these factors make the cost of the land $107,000, calculated as follows:

Cash price of property	$100,000
Net cost of removing warehouse	6,000
Legal fees	1,000
Cost of land	$107,000

When the acquisition is recorded, Land is debited for $107,000 and Cash is credited for $107,000 (assuming the expenditures were paid in cash). Once the land is ready for its intended use, recurring costs, such as annual property tax, are recorded as operating expenditures—in other words, these costs are matched against the revenues that the land helps generate.

You will recall from Chapter 4 that, because land has an unlimited useful life, the cost of land is not depreciated (allocated over its useful life).

Land Improvements

Land improvements are structural additions made to land, such as driveways, sidewalks, fences, and parking lots. Land improvements, unlike land, decline in service potential over time and require maintenance and replacement. Because of this, land improvements are recorded separately from land and are depreciated over their useful lives.

Many students confuse the cost to get land ready for its intended use with land improvements. They think, for example, that removing an old building or grading are "improving" the land, and thus incorrectly reason that these costs should be considered land improvements. When classifying costs, it is important to remember that one-time costs that are required for getting the land ready to use are always charged to the Land account, while land improvements are typically made after acquisition and can be separately distinguished from the land itself.

Buildings

The cost of a building includes all costs that are directly related to its purchase or construction. When a building is purchased, its cost includes the purchase price, the closing costs, and all costs to make the building ready for its intended use. This can include expenditures for remodelling rooms and offices, and for replacing or repairing the roof, floors, electrical wiring, and plumbing. All of these costs are capitalized (i.e., charged) to the Building account.

When a new building is constructed, its cost consists of the contract price plus payments made for architect fees, building permits, and excavation costs. In addition, interest costs relating to a loan obtained to finance a construction project (i.e., interest that could not be avoided) are also included in the cost of the asset but only up to the date that the asset is ready for use. In these circumstances, interest costs are considered as necessary as materials and labour. There are specific rules for determining the amount of interest costs to capitalize; these are not discussed here as they are normally taught in an intermediate accounting course.

Equipment

The "equipment" classification is a broad one that can include delivery equipment, office equipment, machinery, vehicles, furniture and fixtures, and other similar assets. As with land and buildings, the cost of equipment includes the purchase price and all costs that are necessary to get the equipment ready for its intended use. Thus, freight charges, insurance during transit that is paid by the purchaser, and expenditures that are required in assembling, installing, and testing the equipment are all charged to the Equipment account.

Because they are recurring expenditures that do not benefit future periods, annual costs such as licences and insurance are treated as operating expenditures when they are incurred. To illustrate, assume that Perfect Pizzas Ltd. purchases a delivery van for $32,500. Related expenditures are $500 for painting and lettering, $80 for a motor vehicle licence, and $1,600 for a one-year accident insurance policy. The cost of the delivery van is $33,000, calculated as follows:

Cash price	$32,500
Painting and lettering	500
Cost of delivery van	$33,000

The cost of a motor vehicle licence is treated as a current expense because it is an annual recurring cost. For the same reasons, the cost of the insurance policy is considered a prepaid expense (a current asset). It will be allocated to Insurance Expense throughout the period. The cost of the van and the cost incurred for painting and lettering are capital expenditures because these costs benefit future periods. Painting and lettering are not recorded as separate assets such as a prepaid expense because they are not separate from the van.

The entry to record the purchase of the van and related expenditures, assuming all were paid in cash, is as follows:

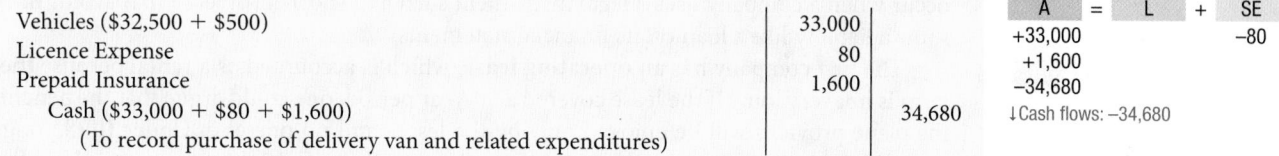

Vehicles ($32,500 + $500)	33,000	
Licence Expense	80	
Prepaid Insurance	1,600	
Cash ($33,000 + $80 + $1,600)		34,680
(To record purchase of delivery van and related expenditures)		

A	=	L	+	SE
+33,000				−80
+1,600				
−34,680				

↓ Cash flows: −34,680

Asset Retirement Costs

The cost of property, plant, and equipment must also include an estimate of the cost of any obligation to dismantle, remove, or restore the long-lived asset when it is retired. For example, if Encana has a natural gas processing plant on which it expects to incur environmental costs to clean up and restore the property at the end of its useful life, these costs, which are known as **asset retirement costs**, are added (debited) to the cost of the plant when it is acquired and depreciated over the life of the plant. Because these costs will not be paid for some time, the offsetting credit is to a long-term liability account called Asset Retirement Obligation. A liability is recorded because as soon as the asset is acquired, the company has an obligation for the related environmental costs. If the use of the asset causes further environmental liabilities to arise, the Asset Retirement Obligation account is adjusted upwards and the related asset account is also increased.

While we will leave a more detailed discussion of asset retirement costs and their associated liabilities to a future accounting course, students should be aware that the cost of many property, plant, and equipment items includes the cost of retiring the asset. We will assume that asset retirement costs equal zero in the examples in this chapter.

Alternative Terminology
Asset retirement costs are also known as *decommissioning* or *restoration* costs.

To Buy or Lease?

In this chapter, we focus on assets that are purchased, but there is an alternative to purchasing, which is leasing. In a lease, a party that owns an asset agrees to allow another party to rent the asset for an agreed period of time at an agreed price. The party that is allowing its asset to be leased is known as the **lessor**, and the party that is paying to use the asset is known as the **lessee**.

Here are some advantages of leasing an asset rather than purchasing it:

1. **Reduced risk of the negative impact of obsolescence.** Obsolescence is the process by which an asset becomes out of date before it physically wears out. Frequently, lease terms allow the lessee to exchange the asset for a more modern or technologically capable asset if it becomes outdated. This is much easier than trying to sell an obsolete asset.
2. **100% financing.** If a company borrows to purchase an asset, it is usually required to make a down payment of at least 20%. Leasing an asset does not require any down payment, which helps to conserve cash. In addition, rent payments are often fixed for the term of the lease so they are predictable, unlike other financing, which often has a floating interest rate.

3. **Income tax advantages.** When a company owns a depreciable asset, it can only deduct the depreciation expense (called *capital cost allowance* for income tax purposes) on its income tax return. (We will learn more about capital cost allowance in a later section of this chapter.) If the company has borrowed to purchase an asset, it can also deduct the interest expense on the borrowed funds. When a company leases an asset, it simply deducts the rent paid on its income tax return. In some years, this deduction may be greater than the deductions taken if the asset was owned.

4. **Off–balance sheet financing.** Let us assume that two companies need to use a plane. The first company rents the plane on a short-term lease of one year. In this case, the only transaction that the company will record is some rent expense. The other company buys the plane by taking out a loan. On the statement of financial position for this company, the plane is listed as an asset along with the related loan. The income statement will show depreciation and interest expense rather than rent expense. The company then sells the plane on the first day of the next year. Both companies used the plane for only one year, yet their financial statements look significantly different. The first company, because it is renting the plane and doesn't have to show any liability because it did not take out a bank loan, is using a technique called off–balance sheet financing. This can occur when a company uses a legal instrument such as a short-term lease that avoids having to show a liability like a loan on its financial statements.

The first company has an **operating lease**, which is accounted as a rental because the lease term is not very long. If the lease covered a 30-year period, one could argue that the benefits that the plane provides will be enjoyed only by the lessee and no one else. Under IFRS, long-term leases like this are known as **finance leases**. Because the definition of an asset is based on the control, not the ownership, of future benefits, for this type of lease, the company would have to show the plane as an asset along with a liability relating to future rent payments. (Under ASPE, a finance lease is called a **capital lease**.) In other words, the plane is treated like a purchase financed with a loan provided by the seller of the asset. In this case, off–balance sheet financing treatment is not achieved and the financial statements would be identical to those prepared by a company that actually owned and operated the plane. For WestJet, most of its leases are for equipment (most of its planes are owned, not leased) and are treated as operating leases.

Determining if a lease is an operating lease or a finance lease goes beyond the scope of this course, but we do want to point out that companies reporting under IFRS may soon be required to treat most leases as finance leases—eliminating the benefits of off–balance sheet financing enjoyed by companies that have short-term leases.

Companies often incur costs when they renovate leased property. These costs are charged to a separate account called Leasehold Improvements. Since the leasehold improvements are attached to a leased property, they belong to the lessor at the end of the lease. Because the benefits of these improvements to the lessee will therefore end when the lease expires, they are depreciated over the remaining life of the lease or the useful life of the improvements, whichever is shorter.

ACCOUNTING MATTERS!   *Investor Perspective*

Managing Expenditures for Plant and Equipment

Crocs Inc. (amounts in U.S. millions)	2010	2009	2008	2007	2006
Revenues	790	646	722	847	355
Property, plant, and equipment	70	71	96	88	35

At the end of 2007, shoes produced by Crocs Inc. were very popular so the company expanded by investing in new plant and equipment, more than doubling capacity throughout the year. But by the end of 2008, demand for the shoes had begun to fall and some equipment was idle. When investors became aware of this, the share price fell from just over $69 per share to just below $39 per share over a two-week period in the fall of 2008. Management did not match asset purchases with demand and was punished with a falling share price.

▶ Do It! **Cost of an Asset**

Assume that $50,000 of factory equipment was purchased on February 4. A $20,000 down payment was made and a bank loan was obtained to pay for the remaining cost of the equipment. Cash expenditures that relate to this purchase include insurance during shipping, $100; an annual insurance policy, $750; installation and testing costs, $500; and staff training costs for the new machinery, $600. (a) What is the cost of the machinery? (b) Record these expenditures.

Action Plan

• Capitalize expenditures that are made to get the machinery ready for its intended use.
• Expense operating costs that benefit only the current period, or which are recurring expenditures.

Solution

(a) The cost of the machinery is $50,600 ($50,000 + $100 + $500).

(b)

Feb. 4	Equipment	50,600	
	Prepaid Insurance	750	
	Salaries Expense	600	
	Cash ($20,000 + $100 + $750 + $500 + $600)		21,950
	Bank Loan Payable ($50,000 − $20,000)		30,000
	(To record purchase of factory machinery and related expenditures)		

DEPRECIATION

STUDY OBJECTIVE 2
Explain and calculate depreciation.

Under International Financial Reporting Standards, companies have two models to choose from when accounting for property, plant, and equipment: the cost model and the revaluation model. The cost model is more commonly used under IFRS, and is the only model allowed for use under ASPE. We will cover the cost model in the following sections of the chapter and refer briefly to the revaluation model in a later section.

ASPE

The **cost model** records property, plant, and equipment at cost when acquired. Subsequent to acquisition, depreciation is recorded each period and the assets are carried at cost less the accumulated depreciation.

As we learned in Chapter 4, **depreciation is the systematic allocation of the cost of property, plant, and equipment (and certain other long-lived assets) over the asset's useful life.** The cost is allocated to expense over the asset's useful life so that expenses are properly matched with the expected use of the asset's future economic benefits.

You will recall that depreciation is recorded in an adjusting journal entry that debits Depreciation Expense and credits Accumulated Depreciation. Depreciation Expense is an income statement account; Accumulated Depreciation appears on the statement of financial position as a contra asset account to the relevant property, plant, or equipment account. The resulting balance, cost less accumulated depreciation, is the carrying amount of a depreciable asset, as was defined in Chapter 4.

It is important to understand that **depreciation is a process of cost allocation, not a process of determining an asset's fair value.** Under the cost model, an increase in the asset's current fair value is not considered relevant, because property, plant, and equipment are not held for resale. (Fair values are only relevant if an impairment loss has occurred, which we will discuss later in this chapter.) As a result, the carrying amount of property, plant, and equipment may be very different from its fair value. In fact, if an asset is fully depreciated, it can have a carrying amount of zero but may still have a large fair value.

Alternative Terminology
An asset's *carrying amount* is also called its *carrying value*, *book value*, or *net book value*.

It is also important to understand that **depreciation neither uses up nor provides cash to replace the asset**. The balance in Accumulated Depreciation only represents the total amount of the asset's cost that has been allocated to expense to date: it is not a cash fund. Cash is neither increased nor decreased by the adjusting entry to record depreciation.

Factors in Calculating Depreciation

In Chapter 4, we learned that depreciation expense is calculated by dividing the cost of the depreciable asset by its useful life. At that time, however, we were assuming that the asset's residual value was zero. In this chapter, we will now include an actual residual value when calculating depreciation. Thus, there are now three factors that affect the calculation of depreciation.

Cost.   Factors that affect the cost of a depreciable asset were explained earlier in this chapter. Remember that the cost of property, plant, and equipment includes the purchase price plus all costs necessary to get the asset ready for use. Cost also includes asset retirement costs, if there are any.

Useful Life.   Useful life is expressed as (a) the period of time over which an asset is expected to be available for use or (b) the number of units of production (such as machine hours) or units of output that are expected to be obtained from an asset. Useful life is an estimate based on such factors as the intended use of the asset and how vulnerable the asset is to wearing out or becoming obsolete. The company's past experience with similar assets is often helpful in estimating a particular asset's useful life.

Residual Value.   **Residual value** is an estimate of the amount that a company would obtain from the disposal of the asset at the end of its useful life. Residual value is not depreciated, since the amount is expected to be recovered at the end of the asset's useful life.

These three factors are summarized in Illustration 9-2.

▸Illustration 9-2
Three factors in calculating depreciation

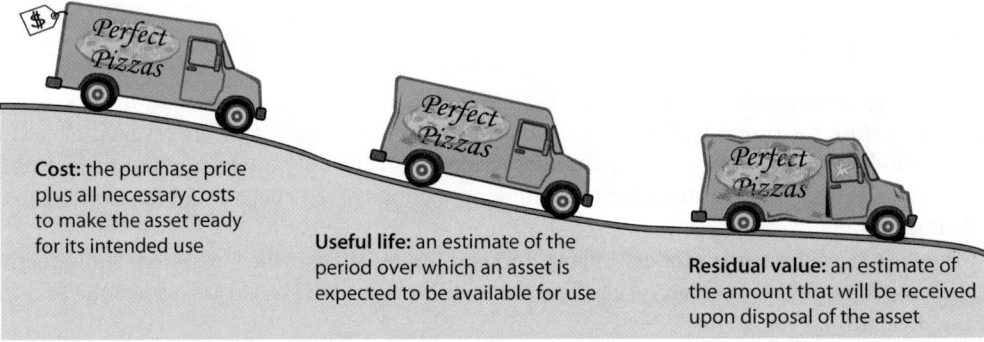

Cost: the purchase price plus all necessary costs to make the asset ready for its intended use

Useful life: an estimate of the period over which an asset is expected to be available for use

Residual value: an estimate of the amount that will be received upon disposal of the asset

ASPE   The difference between a depreciable asset's cost and its residual value is called the **depreciable amount**, which is the total amount to be depreciated over the useful life. Under ASPE, the term *amortization* is often used instead of depreciation, and because of this the depreciable amount is often called the **amortizable cost**.

Depreciation Methods

Depreciation is generally calculated using one of these three methods:

1. Straight-line
2. Diminishing-balance
3. Units-of-production

While all three methods are used, the majority of Canadian publicly traded companies use the straight-line method of depreciation. WestJet, introduced in our feature story, uses the straight-line method to depreciate its property, plant, and equipment.

How do companies choose which method to use? Management must choose the depreciation method that it believes will best reflect the pattern in which the asset's future economic benefits are expected to be consumed. The depreciation method must be reviewed at least once a year. If the expected pattern of consumption of the future economic benefits has changed, the depreciation method must be changed and the change disclosed in notes to the financial statements.

In the sections that now follow, the application of each of these depreciation methods is illustrated using the following data for a delivery van purchased by Perfect Pizzas Ltd. on January 1, 2012:

Cost	$33,000
Estimated residual value	$3,000
Estimated useful life (in years)	5
Estimated useful life (in kilometres)	100,000

Straight-Line. The straight-line method of depreciation was originally defined in Chapter 4. We will define it again here, this time including the impact of the residual amount on this method. The **straight-line method** of calculating depreciation has two steps. First, the depreciable amount is determined by deducting the residual value from the cost of the asset. Second, the depreciable amount is divided by the asset's useful life to calculate the annual depreciation expense. If the asset was in use for only a portion of the year, only a corresponding portion of the annual depreciation expense would be recorded.

The depreciation expense will be the same for each year of the asset's useful life if the cost, the useful life, and the residual value do not change. The calculation of depreciation expense in the first year for Perfect Pizzas' delivery van is shown in Illustration 9-3.

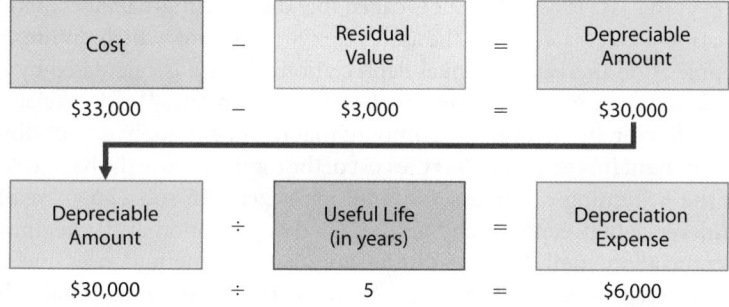

▶Illustration 9-3

Formula for straight-line method

Alternatively, we can calculate a percentage rate to use when determining the delivery van's straight-line annual depreciation expense. First, the depreciation rate is calculated by dividing 100% by the useful life in years. In Perfect Pizzas' case, the depreciation rate is 20% (100% ÷ 5 years). Second, the depreciation expense is calculated by multiplying the asset's depreciable amount by the depreciation rate, as shown in the depreciation schedule in Illustration 9-4.

▶Illustration 9-4

Straight-line depreciation schedule

PERFECT PIZZAS LTD.
Straight-Line Depreciation Schedule

				End of Year	
Year	Depreciable Amount	× Depreciation Rate	= Depreciation Expense	Accumulated Depreciation	Carrying Amount
					$33,000
2012	$30,000	20%	$ 6,000	$ 6,000	27,000
2013	30,000	20%	6,000	12,000	21,000
2014	30,000	20%	6,000	18,000	15,000
2015	30,000	20%	6,000	24,000	9,000
2016	30,000	20%	6,000	30,000	3,000
			$30,000		

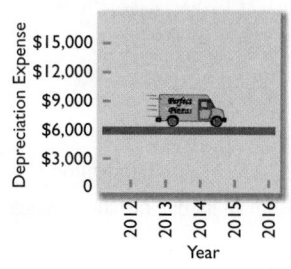

Note that the depreciation expense of $6,000 is the same each year, and that the carrying amount at the end of the useful life is equal to the estimated $3,000 residual value. Because the depreciation expense is the same each year, a graph showing depreciation per year results in a straight-line pattern, as shown in the margin in Illustration 9-4.

What happens when an asset is purchased during the year, rather than on January 1 as in our example? In such cases, it is necessary **to prorate the annual depreciation for the part of the year when the asset is available for use**. If Perfect Pizzas' delivery van was ready to be used on April 1, 2012, the van would be used for nine months in 2012 (April through December). The depreciation for that year would be $4,500 ($30,000 × 20% × 9/12). Note that depreciation is normally rounded to the nearest month. Since depreciation is only an estimate, calculating it to the nearest day gives a false sense of accuracy.

To keep things simple, some companies use a convention for partial-period depreciation rather than calculating depreciation monthly. Companies may choose to allocate a full year's depreciation in the year of acquisition and none in the year of disposal. Other companies record a half-year's depreciation in the year of acquisition, and a half-year's depreciation in the year of disposal. Whatever company policy is used for partial-year depreciation, the impact is not significant in the long run if the policy is used consistently.

Recall that the depreciation method that is used must be consistent with the pattern in which the economic benefits from owning the asset are expected to be consumed. It is therefore appropriate to use the straight-line method when the asset is used uniformly throughout its useful life. Examples of assets that deliver their benefit primarily as a function of time (and therefore uniformly) include office furniture and fixtures, buildings, warehouses, and garages for motor vehicles.

Alternative Terminology
The *diminishing-balance* method is also sometimes called the *declining-balance* method.

Diminishing-Balance.   The **diminishing-balance method** produces a decreasing annual depreciation expense over the asset's useful life. It is called the "diminishing-balance" method because the periodic depreciation is calculated using the asset's carrying amount, which diminishes each year as accumulated depreciation increases. Annual depreciation expense is calculated by multiplying the carrying amount at the beginning of the year by the depreciation rate. The depreciation rate remains constant from year to year, but the carrying amount that the rate is applied to declines each year.

The carrying amount for the first year is the cost of the asset, because the balance in Accumulated Depreciation at the beginning of the asset's useful life is zero. In subsequent years, the carrying amount is the difference between cost and accumulated depreciation at the beginning of the year. Unlike other depreciation methods, the diminishing-balance method uses the asset's carrying amount, not the depreciable amount, to calculate depreciation. **Thus, residual value is not used in determining the amount that the diminishing-balance rate is applied to.** Residual value does, however, limit the total depreciation that can be recorded as care must be taken to ensure that the residual value is not depreciated. Depreciation stops when the asset's carrying amount equals its expected residual value. Since under the diminishing-balance method, a portion of the carrying value remains undepreciated due to the nature of the calculations, care must be taken to ensure that the asset's carrying amount is equal to residual value at the end of its useful life.

Helpful Hint
The straight-line rate is determined by dividing 100% by the estimated useful life. In Perfect Pizzas' case, it is 100% ÷ 5 = 20%.

The diminishing-balance method can be applied using different rates, which result in varying speeds of depreciation. You will find rates such as one time (single), two times (double), and even three times (triple) the straight-line rate of depreciation. A depreciation rate that is often used is double the straight-line rate. This method is referred to as the **double diminishing-balance method**.

If Perfect Pizzas uses double the straight-line rate, the depreciation rate is 40% (2 multiplied by the straight-line rate of 20%). Illustration 9-5 presents the formula and calculation of the first year's depreciation on the delivery van.

▶Illustration 9-5
Formula for diminishing-balance method

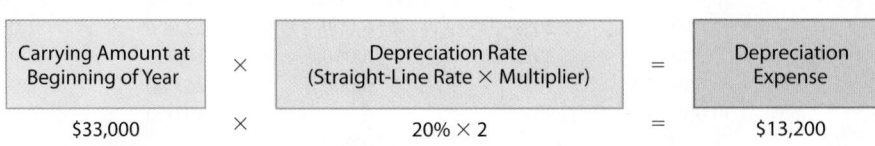

The depreciation schedule under this method is given in Illustration 9-6.

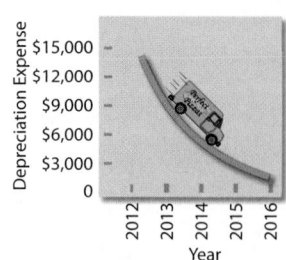

Diminishing-balance depreciation schedule

PERFECT PIZZAS LTD.
Diminishing-Balance Depreciation Schedule

Year	Carrying Amount Beginning of Year	× Depreciation Rate =	Depreciation Expense	End of Year Accumulated Depreciation	Carrying Amount
					$33,000
2012	$33,000	40%	$13,200	$13,200	19,800
2013	19,800	40%	7,920	21,120	11,880
2014	11,880	40%	4,752	25,872	7,128
2015	7,128	40%	2,851	28,723	4,277
2016	4,277	40%	1,277*	30,000	3,000
			$30,000		

*The calculation of $1,711 ($4,277 × 40%) is adjusted to $1,277 so that the carrying amount will equal the residual value.

When an asset is purchased during the year, it is necessary to prorate the diminishing-balance depreciation in the first year, based on time. For example, if Perfect Pizzas had purchased the delivery van on April 1, 2012, depreciation for 2012 would be $9,900 ($33,000 × 40% × 9/12) if depreciation is calculated based on the number of months in a year that it was used. The carrying amount for calculating depreciation in 2013 then becomes $23,100 ($33,000 − $9,900), and the 2013 depreciation is $9,240 ($23,100 × 40%). Future calculations would follow from these amounts until the carrying amount equalled the residual value.

Returning to Illustration 9-6, which assumes that the asset was purchased at the beginning of the year, you can see that the delivery equipment is 64% depreciated ($21,120 ÷ $33,000) at the end of the second year. Under the straight-line method, it would be depreciated 36% ($12,000 ÷ $33,000) at that time.

Regardless of the method that is used, the total amount of depreciation over the life of the delivery van is $30,000—the depreciable amount. In the early years, however, the diminishing-balance depreciation expense will be higher than the straight-line depreciation expense, and in later years it will be less than the straight-line expense. Methods such as the diminishing-balance method that produce higher depreciation expense in the early years than in the later years are known as *accelerated* depreciation methods.

Managers must choose the diminishing-balance, or another accelerated method, if the company receives more economic benefit in the early years of the asset's useful life than in the later years. That is, this method is used if the asset has a higher revenue-producing ability in its early years, or if the asset is expected to become less useful over time.

Units-of-Production.   As indicated earlier, useful life can be expressed in ways other than a time period. In the **units-of-production method**, useful life is expressed using a measure of output such as units produced or a measure of use such as machine hours worked rather than the number of years that the asset is expected to be used. The units-of-production method works well for factory machinery where production can be measured in terms of units produced or machine hours. It is also possible to use the method for such items as motor vehicles (kilometres driven). The units-of-production method is generally not suitable for such assets as buildings or furniture, because activity levels are difficult to measure for these types of assets.

To use the units-of-production method, the units of production in total for the entire useful life are estimated. This amount is divided into the depreciable amount (cost less residual value) to determine the depreciable amount per unit. The depreciable amount per unit is then multiplied by the units of production during the year and the result is the depreciation expense.

To illustrate, assume that Perfect Pizzas' delivery van is driven 15,000 km in the first year of a total estimated useful life of 100,000 km. Using this distance, Illustration 9-7 presents the formula and calculation of depreciation expense in the first year.

Alternative Terminology
The *units-of-production* method is also sometimes called the *units-of-activity* method.

▸Illustration 9-7
Formula for units-of-production method

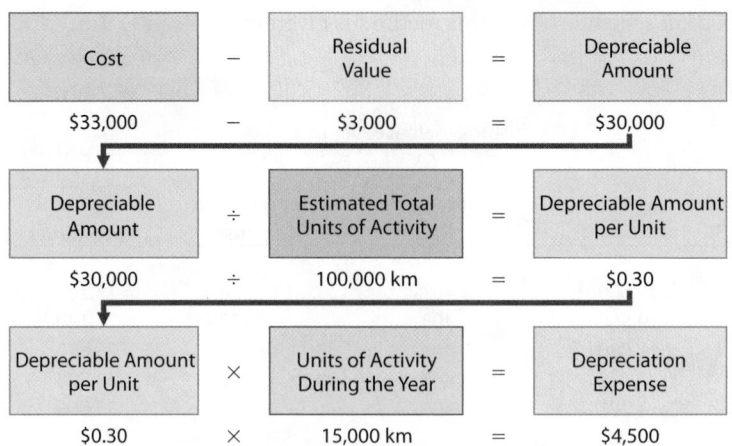

Illustration 9-8 shows the units-of-production depreciation schedule, using assumed distance data for the later years.

▸Illustration 9-8
Units-of-production depreciation schedule

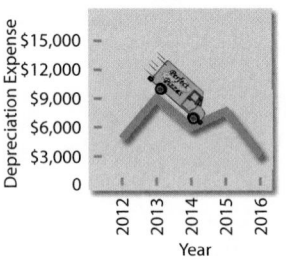

| | | | | End of Year | |
| | Units of | Depreciable | Depreciation | Accumulated | Carrying |
Year	Production	Amount/Unit	Expense	Depreciation	Amount
					$33,000
2012	15,000	$0.30	$ 4,500	$ 4,500	28,500
2013	30,000	0.30	9,000	13,500	19,500
2014	20,000	0.30	6,000	19,500	13,500
2015	25,000	0.30	7,500	27,000	6,000
2016	10,000	0.30	3,000	30,000	3,000
	100,000		$30,000		

PERFECT PIZZAS LTD.
Units-of-Production Depreciation Schedule

This method is easy to apply when assets are purchased during the year. In such cases, the asset's productivity for the partial year is used in calculating depreciation. The units-of-production method, therefore, does not require adjustments for partial periods as the number of units produced already reflects how much the asset was used during the specific period.

Even though it is often difficult to make a reasonable estimate of total activity, it has been reported that about 10% of Canadian companies use this method for assets whose productivity varies significantly from one period to another. In this situation, the units-of-production method results in depreciation amounts that match the benefits consumed as the asset is used.

Alternative Terminology
When natural resources are depreciated, the *units-of-production* method is used and depreciation is referred to as *depletion*.

Comparison of Methods.   The following schedule presents a comparison of annual and total depreciation expense for Perfect Pizzas under the three depreciation methods. In addition, if we assume that profit, before deducting depreciation expense, was $45,000 for each of the five years, we can clearly see the impact of each method on profit.

| | Straight-Line | | Diminishing-Balance | | Units-of-Production | |
| | Depreciation | | Depreciation | | Depreciation | |
Year	Expense	Profit	Expense	Profit	Expense	Profit
2012	$ 6,000	$ 39,000	$13,200	$ 31,800	$ 4,500	$ 40,500
2013	6,000	39,000	7,920	37,080	9,000	36,000
2014	6,000	39,000	4,752	40,248	6,000	39,000
2015	6,000	39,000	2,851	42,149	7,500	37,500
2016	6,000	39,000	1,277	43,723	3,000	42,000
	$30,000	$195,000	$30,000	$195,000	$30,000	$195,000

As discussed earlier, straight-line depreciation results in the same amount of expense each year on the income statement. Diminishing-balance results in higher expenses, and therefore lower profit, in the early years. It also results in lower expenses and higher profit in later years. Results for the units-of-production method vary, depending on the actual usage each year. While periodic depreciation and profit vary each year under the different methods, total depreciation and total profit are the same for the five-year period.

The statement of financial position is also affected because accumulated depreciation is increased by depreciation expense and shareholders' equity is increased by profit. Of course, the choice of depreciation method has no impact on cash flow or the statement of cash flows.

Keeping an Eye on Cash

Depreciation (and amortization) expense is one of the largest differences between accrual-accounting profit and net cash provided by operating activities that is shown in the statement of cash flows. Depreciation expense reduces profit but does not use up cash. Therefore, to determine net cash provided by operating activities, companies must remove any depreciation from profit. For example, if a company reported profit of $175,000 during the year and had depreciation expense of $40,000, net cash provided by operating activities would be $215,000 (assuming no other accrual-accounting differences).

It is therefore important to understand that although a business is profitable, it may actually generate more cash flows than the amount of profit shown on the income statement. For this reason, some companies are able to pay out dividends that are greater than profits, as Boston Pizza did for three consecutive years from 2007 to 2009.

As explained earlier, management should choose the method that best matches the estimated pattern in which the benefits of the asset are expected to be consumed. If the economic benefit following an asset is fairly consistent over time, the straight-line method is appropriate. The diminishing-balance method is appropriate if the company receives more economic benefit in the early years of the asset's useful life than in the later years. The units-of-production method is appropriate for assets where use varies over time. Because companies have more than one type of asset, they often use more than one depreciation method.

DECISION TOOLKIT

 Decision Checkpoints	 Info Needed for Decision	 Tools to Use for Decision	 How to Evaluate Results
What is the impact of the choice of depreciation method?	Depreciation policy	Income statement, statement of financial position, and accounting policy note to the statements	In the early years, straight-line depreciation results in a lower amount of depreciation expense and higher profit on the income statement than the diminishing-balance method. It also results in higher total assets and higher shareholders' equity on the statement of financial position. The opposite is true in the later years. There is no impact on cash flow regardless of method used.

BEFORE YOU GO ON...

▶ Do It! Depreciation

On October 1, 2011, Iron Mountain Ski Corporation purchased a new snow grooming machine for $52,000. The machine was estimated to have a five-year useful life and a $4,000 residual value. It was also estimated to have a total useful life of 6,000 hours. It is used for 1,000 hours in the year ended December 31, 2011, and 1,300 hours in the year ended December 31, 2012. How much depreciation expense should Iron Mountain Ski record in each of 2011 and 2012 under each depreciation method: (a) straight-line, (b) diminishing-balance using twice the straight-line rate, and (c) units-of-production?

Action Plan

- Under straight-line depreciation, annual depreciation expense is equal to the depreciable amount (cost less residual value) divided by the estimated useful life.
- Under diminishing-balance depreciation, annual depreciation expense is equal to twice the straight-line rate of depreciation times the asset's carrying amount at the beginning of the year. Residual values are not used to calculate depreciation in this method, but we must ensure that the carrying amount is not less than residual value.
- Under the straight-line and diminishing-balance methods, the annual depreciation expense must be prorated if the asset is purchased during the year.
- Under units-of-production depreciation, the depreciable amount per unit is equal to the total depreciable amount divided by the total estimated units of production. The annual depreciation expense is equal to the depreciable amount per unit times the actual usage in each year.

Solution

	2011	2012
Straight-line	$2,400	$ 9,600
Diminishing-balance	5,200	18,720
Units-of-production	8,000	10,400

(a) Straight-line: ($52,000 − $4,000) ÷ 5 years = $9,600 per year; for the partial period in 2011:
$9,600 × 3/12 = $2,400

(b) Diminishing-balance: 100% ÷ 5 years = 20% straight-line rate

  20% × 2 = 40% depreciation rate
  2011: $52,000 × 40% × 3/12 = $5,200
  2012:   ($52,000 − $5,200) × 40% = $18,720

(c) Units-of-production: ($52,000 − $4,000) ÷ 6,000 hours = $8 per hour
  2011:   1,000 × $8 = $8,000
  2012:   1,300 × $8 = $10,400

the navigator

OTHER DEPRECIATION ISSUES

STUDY OBJECTIVE 3

Describe other accounting issues related to depreciation.

There are several other issues related to depreciation that we will briefly introduce here. These include how certain assets are separated into their significant components for depreciation purposes, how assets are depreciated for income tax purposes, how the impairment of assets is recorded when the fair value declines, other valuation models, and under what circumstances depreciation is revised.

Significant Components

When an item of property, plant, and equipment includes individual components for which different depreciation methods or rates are appropriate, the cost should be allocated to the asset's significant components and each component should be depreciated separately. For example, an aircraft and its engines may need to be treated as separate depreciable assets if they have different useful lives. WestJet, as we saw in our feature story, records overhauls and engines separately and depreciates each over a different estimated useful life.

Further discussion of calculating depreciation for the different parts of an asset will be left to a later accounting course. For simplicity, we will assume in this text that all of the components of the depreciable asset have the same useful life and we will therefore depreciate each asset as a whole.

Depreciation and Income Tax

For accounting purposes, management determines the method of depreciation to use and estimates the useful life and residual value of assets. The Canada Revenue Agency (CRA) requires that, for income tax purposes, depreciation amounts should not be determined using management estimates but should be determined using tax regulations. For this reason, when preparing a tax return and determining taxable income, companies cannot deduct the depreciation expense used in the income statement. They must deduct the CRA version of depreciation, which is known as **capital cost allowance (CCA)**. In determining CCA, assets are grouped into various classes and the maximum depreciation rates for each asset class are specified. Capital cost allowance is an optional deduction from taxable income, but depreciation expense is not optional for calculating profit. Consequently, you may see some businesses deducting depreciation expense for accounting purposes, while deducting no CCA for income tax purposes.

Impairments

As noted earlier in the chapter, under the cost model, the carrying amount of property, plant, and equipment is the asset's cost less the accumulated depreciation on that asset. As we know, the carrying amount of property, plant, and equipment is rarely the same as its fair value. Remember that the cost model assumes that fair value is not relevant since property, plant, and equipment are not purchased for resale, but rather for use in operations over the long term.

While it is accepted that long-lived assets such as property, plant, and equipment may be undervalued on the statement of financial position, it is not appropriate if they are overvalued. Property, plant, and equipment are considered impaired if the asset's carrying amount exceeds its **recoverable amount**. The recoverable amount can be determined by observing the fair value less selling costs of similar assets in an active market. If this information is not available, the value in use of the asset, which is based on its future cash flows, can be used. If both the fair value less selling costs and the value in use are known, then the greater of these two amounts is used to determine the recoverable amount. When a long-lived asset is impaired, an **impairment loss** is recorded that is equal to the amount by which the asset's carrying amount exceeds its recoverable amount.

Under ASPE, impairment tests are done using a two-step approach, with the second step consisting of the method described above. The first step consists of measuring the cash flows expected to be received from the asset and comparing this with the carrying value. If the cash flows are less than the carrying value, we would calculate the impairment loss in the second step.

ASPE

Companies are required to determine if there are indicators of impairment on a regular basis. If there are no indicators, it is not necessary to test the asset for impairment, but if indicators are present, an impairment test must be done. For example, if a machine has become obsolete, or if the market for a product made by a machine has diminished or has become very competitive, there is a strong possibility that an impairment loss exists. Management is then required to perform an impairment test and this involves determining an estimate of the machine's recoverable amount.

Alternative Terminology
An *impairment loss* is also known as a *writedown*.

To illustrate an impairment loss on a long-lived asset, assume that Piniwa Corporation reviews its equipment for possible impairment. It owns equipment with a cost of $800,000 and accumulated depreciation of $200,000. The equipment's recoverable amount is currently $550,000. The amount of the impairment loss is determined by comparing the asset's carrying amount with its recoverable amount, as follows:

Carrying amount ($800,000 − $200,000)	$600,000
Recoverable amount	550,000
Impairment loss	$ 50,000

The journal entry to record the impairment is:

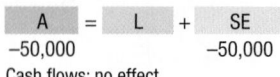

A = L + SE
−50,000   −50,000
Cash flows: no effect

Impairment Loss	50,000	
Accumulated Depreciation—Equipment		50,000
(To record impairment loss on equipment)		

Assuming that the asset will continue to be used in operations, the impairment loss is reported on the income statement as part of operating income from continuing operations and not as a non-operating item in the "other expenses and losses" section. Often the loss is combined and reported with depreciation expense on the income statement. The Accumulated Depreciation account is credited for the impairment loss, rather than an asset account, in order to preserve a record of the asset's original cost. Alternatively, some companies will use an accumulated impairment loss account as well as an accumulated depreciation account.

We had previously defined an asset's carrying amount as its cost less accumulated depreciation. This is still the case, but the Accumulated Depreciation account can now include more than just the depreciation recorded on the asset to date. It will also include impairment losses.

International Financial Reporting Standards allow the reversal of a previously recorded impairment loss but only to the extent that the reversal returns the carrying amount to what it would have been had the impairment never occurred. For example, assume we use straight-line depreciation and purchase equipment costing $100 with no residual value and a five-year useful life. When it is one year old, the equipment would have a carrying amount of $80 and it would have a carrying amount of $60 at the end of its second year. Now assume that the recoverable amount was $68 at the end of the first year. Comparing this with the carrying amount of $80 would require the company to record an impairment loss of $12 at the end of the first year. In its second year of use, depreciation would be based on the impaired carrying amount of $68 and would amount to $17 (the $68 carrying amount divided by the four remaining years) and the carrying amount would be $51 ($68 – $17) at the end of the second year of use. If the recoverable amount at that time was $90, how much of an impairment loss could be reversed? Only enough to return the carrying amount to $60, which is what it would have been had the impairment never occurred. Therefore, an impairment loss reversal of $9 (the difference between the $51 carrying amount with impairment and the $60 carrying amount without impairment) would be recorded as follows:

Accumulated Depreciation—Equipment	9	
Impairment Loss		9
(To record impairment loss reversal on equipment)		

When an impairment loss is reversed, we simply credit the impairment loss account. Did you notice that although the impairment loss was $12, the reversal was only $9? Why? Because part of the impairment loss was reversed through lower depreciation in the second year. Normally depreciation would have been $20 per year but it was only $17 in the second year.

ASPE   Under ASPE, companies are not allowed to reverse impairment losses.

Cost Model versus the Revaluation Model and Valuation Model

As previously mentioned, under International Financial Reporting Standards, companies can choose to account for property, plant, and equipment under either the cost model or the revaluation model. We have been describing the cost model in this chapter because it is used by almost all companies. Only about 3% of companies reporting under IFRS use the revaluation model. The revaluation model is allowed under IFRS mainly because it is particularly useful in countries that experience high rates of inflation and for companies in certain industries, such as real estate, where fair values are more relevant than cost.

Under the **revaluation model**, the carrying amount of property, plant, and equipment is adjusted to reflect its fair value. This model can be applied only to assets whose fair value can be reliably measured, and revaluations must be carried out often enough that the carrying amount is not materially different from the asset's fair value at the statement of financial position date. As we saw when using the cost model, impairment losses or writedowns are recorded in the income statement, as are any reversals of the writedowns. With the revaluation model, **revaluation gains** or write-ups are also recorded, but these must be recorded in Other Comprehensive Income. Any reversals of these revaluation gains or write-ups are also recorded in Other Comprehensive Income. When these gains in Other Comprehensive Income are closed out at the end of the year into Accumulated Other Comprehensive Income, they form a component of the equity account known as the **revaluation surplus**. As application of the revaluation model is relatively complex, and because so few companies will use this model, we will leave further discussion of it to a later accounting course.

Under IFRS, there is an additional category of tangible asset known as **investment properties**. These consist of properties not occupied by the owner and held for the purpose of earning rental income or capital appreciation. Companies can choose to use the cost model or the **valuation model** for investment properties. Although similar to the revaluation model, the valuation model also requires the property's carrying amount to be adjusted to fair value but the entire adjustment is recorded in the income statement with no effect on Other Comprehensive Income. Furthermore, investment properties are not depreciated.

Under ASPE, neither the revaluation model nor the valuation model is used. `ASPE`

DECISION TOOLKIT

 Decision Checkpoints	 Info Needed for Decision	 Tools to Use for Decision	 How to Evaluate Results
Should the company use the cost model or the revaluation model?	Cost and fair value of assets	Compare the cost and fair value amounts, as well as the cost of determining the fair value amounts.	If there is a significant difference and the valuation would make a difference to users' decision-making, consider using the revaluation model. Also consider whether the cost of determining the fair value of assets is worth the information provided to users of the financial statements.
Are the company's long-lived assets over- or undervalued?	Impairment loss; carrying amount of long-lived assets	Compare the carrying and recoverable amounts in light of current business conditions and company performance.	If assets have been adjusted for impairment, expect improved results in subsequent periods, as depreciation will be lower. If assets are substantially undervalued on the statement of financial position, be cautious when interpreting ratios that use carrying amounts, as these ratios may not be comparable to other companies.

Revising Periodic Depreciation

There are several reasons why periodic depreciation may need to be revised during an asset's useful life. These include:

1. **Capital expenditures during the asset's useful life.** While an asset is being used, additional costs relating to it may be incurred. The criteria to determine whether such costs are operating or capital expenditures remain unchanged even if they were not incurred at the acquisition date. As explained earlier in the chapter, if a cost, such as ordinary repairs and maintenance, benefits the company only in the current period, the cost is an operating expenditure and is recorded as an expense in the income statement. If the cost, such as a replacement of a major part or an addition to a building, will benefit future periods, then it is a capital expenditure and is added to the asset's cost. As capital expenditures during the asset's useful life increase the cost of a long-lived asset, the depreciation calculations from that point onward will have to be revised.

2. **Impairment losses.** As described in the previous section, an impairment loss will result in the reduction of the asset's carrying amount. Since the carrying amount is reduced, the depreciation calculations will also be reduced because the depreciable amount is now lower.

3. **Changes in the estimated useful life or residual value.** Management must review its estimates of useful life and residual value each year. For example, wear and tear or obsolescence might indicate that annual depreciation is not enough. Capital expenditures may increase the asset's useful life and/or its residual value. Impairment losses might signal a reduction in useful life and/or residual value. Regardless of the reason for the change, a change in estimated useful life or residual value will cause a revision to the depreciation calculations.

4. **Changes in the pattern in which the asset's economic benefits are consumed.** As discussed earlier, management must review the choice of depreciation method for a long-lived asset at least annually. If the pattern in which the future benefits will be consumed is expected to change, the depreciation method must change as well. A change in methods will obviously result in a revision to depreciation calculations.

Revising depreciation is known as a change in estimate. **Changes in estimates are made in current and future years but not to prior periods.** Thus, when a change in depreciation is made, (1) there is no correction of previously recorded depreciation expense, and (2) depreciation expense for current and future years is revised. The rationale for this treatment is that the original calculations were based on information known at the time when the asset was purchased. The revision is based on new information that should only affect future periods as that information was not available in the past.

A significant change in an estimate must be disclosed in the notes to the financial statements so that financial statement users are aware of the financial impact. For example, extending an asset's useful life will reduce depreciation expense and increase the current period profit. Remember that changes in depreciation result in periodic effects only: total profit over the life of an asset will not be affected by any change in depreciation.

While we will leave the detailed calculation of a change in the depreciation estimate for another accounting course, you should know that many companies need to make revisions to their depreciation. For example, we learned in our feature story that WestJet capitalizes its aircraft refurbishment costs and any other upgrading costs if they were incurred to improve the aircraft's service value or extend their useful lives. This will result in extensive revisions to WestJet's depreciation calculations.

BEFORE YOU GO ON...

▶ Do It! Impairment

Century Satellite Ltd., which reports under IFRS and uses the cost model, tested its property, plant, and equipment for impairment. The company determined that the recoverable amount of equipment was $550,000. The equipment cost $800,000 and had accumulated depreciation of $100,000 at that time. Therefore, an impairment loss was recorded. During the year following the impairment, the company recorded $50,000 of depreciation and at the end of that year the recoverable amount was $580,000. Had the impairment never occurred, the equipment's carrying amount at that time would have been $636,000. (a) Record the impairment loss. (b) Calculate the equipment's carrying amount, after any impairment has been determined in (a). (c) Record the journal entries that would be made in the year following impairment.

Action Plan

- Calculate carrying amount (cost less accumulated depreciation).
- If the recoverable amount is less than the carrying amount, the asset has been impaired.
- If the recoverable amount rises above the carrying amount, an impairment reversal can be recorded as long as it does not increase the carrying amount above the value it would have been had the impairment never occurred.

Solution

(a)

Carrying amount ($800,000 − $100,000)	$700,000
Recoverable amount	550,000
Impairment loss	$150,000

Impairment Loss	150,000	
Accumulated Depreciation—Equipment		150,000
(To record impairment loss on equipment)		

(b) Carrying amount: $800,000 − $100,000 − $150,000 = $550,000

(c) For the next year, depreciation of $50,000 would be recorded as follows:

Depreciation Expense	50,000	
Accumulated Depreciation—Equipment		50,000
(To record depreciation for the year)		

Now the carrying amount is $550,000 − $50,000 = $500,000 and we can reverse $580,000 − $500,000 = $80,000 of the impairment loss as long as it does not make the carrying amount exceed $636,000.

Accumulated Depreciation—Equipment	80,000	
Impairment Loss		80,000
(To record reversal of impairment loss)		

the navigator

DISPOSALS OF PROPERTY, PLANT, AND EQUIPMENT

STUDY OBJECTIVE 4
Account for the disposal of property, plant, and equipment.

Companies dispose of property, plant, and equipment that is no longer useful to them. Illustration 9-9 shows three methods of disposal.

Sale
Equipment is sold

Retirement
Equipment is scrapped or discarded

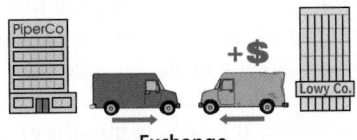

Exchange
Existing equipment is traded for new equipment

►Illustration 9-9
Methods of property, plant, and equipment disposal

Whatever the disposal method, the company must perform the following four steps to record the sale, retirement, or exchange of the property, plant, or equipment:

Step 1: Update depreciation. Depreciation must be recorded over the entire period of time that an asset is available for use. If the disposal occurs in the middle of an accounting period, depreciation must therefore be updated for the fraction of the year that has passed since the last time adjusting entries were recorded up to the date of disposal. Note that the update period will never exceed one year, since adjusting entries are made at least annually.

Step 2: Calculate the carrying amount. Calculate the carrying amount at the time of disposal after updating the accumulated depreciation for any partial-year depreciation recorded in Step 1:

Alternative Terminology
Derecognition is a term used under IFRS to describe the removal of a long-lived asset from the financial statements upon its disposal or when it no longer provides any future benefits.

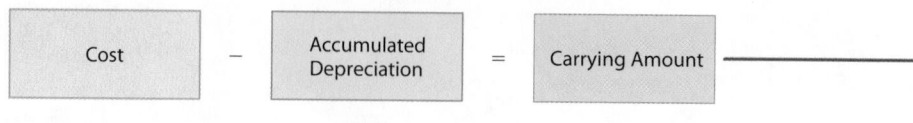

Step 3: Calculate the gain or loss. Determine the amount of the gain or loss on disposal, if any, by comparing the carrying amount with the proceeds received on disposal:

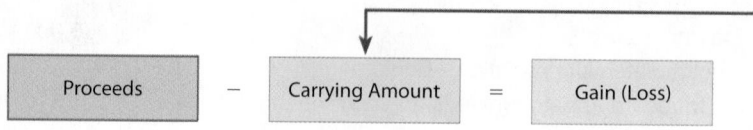

If the proceeds of the sale are more than the carrying amount of the property, plant, or equipment, there is a **gain on disposal**. If the proceeds of the sale are less than the asset's carrying amount, there is a **loss on disposal**.

Step 4: Record the disposal. Record the disposal, removing the cost of the asset disposed of and the accumulated depreciation relating to the disposed asset from each affected account. The asset account is decreased with a credit equal to the cost of the asset disposed. The Accumulated Depreciation account is decreased with a debit for the portion of the account pertaining to the disposed asset, which is the total amount of depreciation and any impairment losses that have been recorded for the asset up to its disposal date. This is the same amount that was used to calculate the carrying amount in Step 2. Record the proceeds (if any), typically with a debit to cash, and record the gain or loss on disposal (if any) by crediting a gain account or debiting a loss account for the difference between the carrying amount of the asset disposed of and the proceeds received.

Sale of Property, Plant, and Equipment

In the following sections, we will illustrate the recording of a sale of equipment, using the straight-line depreciation method, at both a gain and a loss.

Gain on Disposal.   Assume that on July 1, 2012, Wright Ltd. sells equipment for $25,000 cash. The equipment was purchased three and a half years ago, on January 1, 2009, at a cost of $60,000. At that time, it was estimated that the equipment would have a residual value of $5,000 and a useful life of five years.

The first step in recording the sale is to update any unrecorded depreciation. Annual depreciation using the straight-line method is $11,000 [($60,000 − $5,000) ÷ 5]. Note that depreciation would have already been recorded along with other adjusting entries for each of the calendar year ends 2009, 2010, and 2011. The entry to record depreciation expense and update the accumulated depreciation for the first six months of 2012 is as follows:

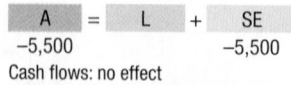

A = L + SE
−5,500   −5,500
Cash flows: no effect

July 1	Depreciation Expense ($11,000 × ⁶/₁₂)	5,500	
	Accumulated Depreciation—Equipment		5,500
	(To record depreciation expense for the first six months of 2012)		

The second step is to calculate the carrying amount on July 1, 2012. As at December 31, 2011, Wright's year end, the equipment had accumulated depreciation of $33,000 ($11,000 × 3 years). After the accumulated depreciation balance is updated on July 1, 2012, to $38,500 ($33,000 + $5,500), the carrying amount is $21,500 (cost of $60,000 − accumulated depreciation of $38,500).

The third step is to calculate the gain or loss on disposal. A $3,500 gain is calculated as follows:

Proceeds from sale	$25,000
Less: Carrying amount at date of disposal	21,500
Gain on disposal	$ 3,500

The fourth step is the entry to record the sale of the equipment, as follows:

July 1	Cash	25,000	
	Accumulated Depreciation—Equipment	38,500	
	Equipment		60,000
	Gain on Disposal		3,500
	(To record sale of equipment at a gain)		

A	=	L	+	SE
+25,000				+3,500
+38,500				
−60,000				
↑Cash flows: +25,000				

A gain on disposal is reported as a reduction of operating expenses in the "Operating Expenses" section of the income statement.

Loss on Disposal. Assume that instead of selling the equipment for $25,000, Wright sells it for $20,000. In this case, a loss of $1,500 is calculated:

Proceeds from sale	$20,000
Less: Carrying amount at date of disposal	21,500
Loss on disposal	$ (1,500)

The entry to record the sale of the equipment is:

July 1	Cash	20,000	
	Accumulated Depreciation—Equipment	38,500	
	Loss on Disposal	1,500	
	Equipment		60,000
	(To record sale of equipment at a loss)		

A	=	L	+	SE
+20,000				−1,500
+38,500				
−60,000				
↑Cash flows: +20,000				

A loss on disposal is reported in the "Operating Expenses" section of the income statement.

Retirement of Property, Plant, and Equipment

Instead of being sold, some assets are simply retired by a company at the end of their useful lives. Because some productive assets may have very specific uses and consequently no ready market when the company no longer needs them, they are simply retired rather than being sold.

Retirement of an asset is recorded just like a sale except that there are no proceeds. As illustrated earlier, depreciation is first updated for any partial period up to the date of retirement. The carrying amount is then calculated. If the asset is retired before it is fully depreciated, there is a loss on disposal that is equal to the asset's carrying amount at the date of retirement. Since no proceeds are received in a retirement, a gain will never occur.

Quite often the carrying amount will equal zero; however, a journal entry is still required to remove all accounts related to the retired asset from the books. The Accumulated Depreciation account is decreased (debited) for the balance in the account related to the retired asset. The retired asset account is reduced (credited) for its balance. Any loss on disposal is recorded as a debit.

What happens if a company is still using a fully depreciated asset? In this case, the asset and its accumulated depreciation continue to be reported on the statement of financial position, without further depreciation, until the asset is retired. Reporting the asset and related depreciation on the statement of financial position informs the reader of the financial statements that the asset is still being used by the company. Once an asset is fully depreciated, even if it is still being used, no additional depreciation should be taken. Accumulated depreciation on an asset can never be more than its cost less residual value.

Exchanges of Property, Plant, and Equipment

In an exchange of assets, a new asset is typically purchased by trading in an old asset, and a **trade-in allowance** is given toward the purchase price of the new asset. An additional cash payment is usually also required for the difference between the trade-in allowance and the purchase price of the new asset.

Instead of being sold for cash, therefore, the old asset is sold for a trade-in allowance on the purchase of the new asset. The new asset is seen as being purchased for cash plus the value of the old asset. Accounting for exchange transactions is complex and further discussion of exchanges is left for future accounting courses.

BEFORE YOU GO ON...

▶ Do It! Disposition of a Vehicle

Overland Trucking Ltd. has a truck that it purchased on January 1, 2008, for $30,000. This purchase was recorded in the Vehicles account at the time. The truck has since been depreciated on a straight-line basis with an estimated residual value of $3,000 and a useful life of six years.

Overland has a December 31 year end. Assume two different situations: (a) the company sells the truck on October 1, 2012, for $10,000 cash, and (b) the truck is determined to be worthless on January 1, 2013, so the company simply retires it. What entry should Overland use to record each scenario?

Action Plan

- Update any unrecorded depreciation for partial periods.
- Calculate the carrying amount.
- Compare the proceeds with the carrying amount to determine whether any gain or loss has occurred.
- Record any proceeds that are received and any gain or loss.
- Recall that a gain is not possible in a retirement of assets and that all accounts related to the retired asset must be removed.

Solution

(a) Sale of the truck for cash:
Annual depreciation expense: ($30,000 − $3,000) ÷ 6 years = $4,500
Accumulated depreciation recorded from Jan. 1, 2008, to Dec. 31, 2011 (the last time adjusting entries were recorded): $4,500 × 4 years = $18,000

Oct. 1, 2012	Depreciation Expense ($4,500 × $9/12$)	3,375	
	Accumulated Depreciation—Vehicles		3,375
	(To record depreciation for nine months)		
	Cash	10,000	
	Accumulated Depreciation—Vehicles ($18,000 + $3,375)	21,375	
	Gain on Disposal [$10,000 − ($30,000 − $21,375)]		1,375
	Vehicles		30,000
	(To record sale of truck at a gain)		

(b) Retirement of the truck:

Jan. 1, 2013	Accumulated Depreciation—Vehicles ($4,500 × 5 years)	22,500	
	Loss on Disposal [$0 − ($30,000 − $22,500)]	7,500	
	Vehicles		30,000
	(To record retirement of truck at a loss)		

the navigator

Intangible Assets and Goodwill

Property, plant, and equipment and intangible assets are similar in that both are long-lived resources that are used in the operations of a business, and are not intended for sale to customers. Both provide economic benefits in future periods. Intangible assets differ from property, plant, and equipment in that they do not have physical substance. The future economic benefits flowing from an intangible asset may include revenue from the sale of products or services, cost savings, or other benefits resulting from the company's use of the asset.

STUDY OBJECTIVE 5
Identify the basic accounting issues for intangible assets and goodwill.

Intangible assets involve rights, privileges, and/or competitive advantages. For example, the use of intellectual property in a production process may reduce future production costs and allow the company to sell the product at a lower price. For some companies, intangible assets are the most valuable assets they have. Some widely known intangibles are Alexander Graham Bell's patent on the telephone, the franchises of Tim Hortons, the trade name of President's Choice, and the trademark of lululemon.

An intangible asset must be identifiable, which means it must meet one of the two following criteria: (1) it can be separated from the company and sold, whether or not the company intends to do so, or (2) it is based on contractual or legal rights, regardless of whether or not it can be separated from the company. Since goodwill cannot be separated from a company and sold, there are differences in the accounting for goodwill compared with other intangible assets.

Although financial statements report many intangibles and goodwill on the statement of financial position, there are many other significant intangibles and goodwill that are not reported. To give an example, according to its 2011 financial statements, lululemon's overall carrying amount (the excess of assets over liabilities—in other words, equity) on its statement of financial position was U.S. $394 million. But its *fair value*—the total market price of all its shares that can be traded on the stock exchange on that same date—was nearly 10 times greater at $3.8 billion. It is not uncommon for a company's reported carrying amount to differ from its fair value because amounts on the statement of financial position are often reported at historical cost. But an extreme difference like this lessens the usefulness of the statement of financial position to decision makers. In the case of lululemon, the difference is primarily due to unrecorded intangibles and goodwill. For many companies with unique products, most of their value is from intangibles and goodwill such as knowledge-based assets, and many of these are not reported under current accounting practices.

ACCOUNTING FOR INTANGIBLE ASSETS

Similar to property, plant, and equipment, **intangible assets are recorded at cost**. Cost includes all the costs of acquisition and other costs that are needed to make the intangible asset ready for its intended use, including legal fees and similar charges.

As with property, plant, and equipment, companies have a choice of following the cost model or the revaluation model when accounting for an intangible asset subsequent to acquisition. The majority of companies use the cost model as it is very difficult and costly to determine the fair value of intangibles. So we will leave further study of the revaluation model as it applies to intangible assets for a later accounting course.

Under the cost model, if an intangible asset has a **finite (limited) life**, its cost must be systematically allocated over its useful life. We called this *depreciation* when discussing property, plant, and equipment. With intangible assets, we will use the term **amortization**. Under ASPE, amortization is often the word used to describe depreciation of property, plant, and equipment *or* amortization of intangible assets.

ASPE

For an intangible asset with a finite life, its **amortizable amount** (its cost less its residual value) should be allocated over the shorter of (1) the estimated useful life and (2) the legal life. Intangible assets, by their nature, rarely have any residual value, so the amortizable amount is normally equal to the cost. In addition, the useful life of an intangible asset is usually shorter than its legal life, so useful life is most often used as the amortization period.

When a company estimates the useful life of an intangible asset, it must consider factors such as how long the company expects to use the asset, when it may become obsolete, the level of demand for products or services it produces, and other factors that can diminish the usefulness of the intangible. For example, suppose a computer hardware manufacturer obtained a patent on a new computer chip that it developed (we will discuss patents in the next section). The legal life of the patent is 20 years. From experience, we know that the useful life of a computer chip is rarely more than three years—and often less—because new, superior chips are developed so rapidly that existing chips quickly become obsolete. Consequently, we would question the amortization expense of a company if it amortized its patent on a computer chip for longer than three years. Amortizing an intangible over a period that is too long will understate amortization expense, overstate the company's profit, and overstate its assets and equity.

Amortization begins when the intangible asset is ready to be used as intended by management. Similar to depreciation, the company must use the amortization method that best matches the pattern in which the asset's future economic benefits are expected to be consumed. If that pattern cannot be reliably determined, the straight-line method should be used. Similar to depreciation, amortization expense is recognized on the income statement as an operating expense. Companies often combine depreciation and amortization expenses in a single amount for reporting purposes.

Just as land is considered to have an indefinite life, there are also intangible assets with an indefinite life. An intangible asset is considered to have an **indefinite (unlimited) life** when, based on an analysis of all of the relevant factors, there is no foreseeable limit to the period over which the intangible asset is expected to generate net cash inflows for the company. If an intangible asset has an indefinite life, it is not amortized.

ASPE As with property, plant, and equipment, companies must determine if there are indicators of impairment on intangible assets with definite lives. If there are indicators, an impairment test is performed. Intangible assets with indefinite lives must be tested annually even if no indications of impairment are present. Under ASPE, this annual test is not required unless indications are present.

Recall from earlier in this chapter that an asset is impaired if its recoverable amount falls below its carrying amount. If any impairment is evident, the asset must be written down to its recoverable amount and an impairment loss recorded in the income statement. Under International Financial Reporting Standards, an impairment can be reversed for intangible assets (with the exception of goodwill), just as it can be reversed for property, plant, and equipment. Under ASPE, reversals are not permitted.

Similar to depreciation, amortization is revised if there is a change in cost or useful life, or an impairment loss, and the revision is treated as a change in estimate.

At disposal, just as with property, plant, and equipment, the intangible asset's carrying amount is eliminated, and a gain or loss, if any, is recorded.

In the next two sections, we will look in more detail at the accounting for intangibles with finite lives and those with indefinite lives.

Intangible Assets with Finite Lives

Examples of intangible assets with finite lives include patents and copyrights. We also include research and development costs in this section because these costs often lead to the creation of patents and copyrights.

Patents. A **patent** is an exclusive right issued by the Canadian Intellectual Property Office of Industry Canada that allows the patent holder to manufacture, sell, or otherwise control an invention for a period of 20 years from the date of the application. A patent cannot be renewed. But a patent's legal life can be extended if the patent holder obtains new patents for improvements or other changes in the basic design.

The initial cost of a patent is the price paid to acquire the patent. Subsequent to acquisition, legal costs to register the patent, along with legal costs incurred to defend the patent in an infringement suit, would also be included in the cost of the patent and amortized over time.

The cost of a patent should be amortized over its 20-year legal life or its useful life, whichever is shorter. As mentioned earlier, the useful life should be carefully assessed by considering whether the patent is likely to become ineffective at contributing to revenue before the end of its legal life.

ACCOUNTING MATTERS! *Management Perspective*

Nortel Patents Sold

Nortel Networks was a major Canadian corporation that filed for bankruptcy in January 2009. Since then, Nortel has raised about $3 billion for its creditors by selling off its business assets. In 2011, the 6,000 patents and patent applications owned by the company went up for sale. The patents allow buyers to control and license some of the technology used in the BlackBerry, Apple iPhone, and devices that that run on Google's Android operating system. The patents ended up selling for U.S. $4.5 billion to a consortium of six software companies, including Research in Motion®, Apple, and Microsoft, amongst others. This is despite the fact that the carrying amount of Nortel's intangibles was only $51 million at the time because many of the initial research costs were expensed prior to the decision to develop the product to the point where a patent could be obtained.

Copyrights. A **copyright** is granted by the Canadian Intellectual Property Office, giving the owner the exclusive right to reproduce and sell an artistic or published work. Copyrights are valid for the life of the creator plus 50 years. Generally, a copyright's useful life is significantly shorter than its legal life, and the copyright is therefore amortized over its useful life.

The cost of the copyright consists of the cost of acquiring and defending it. The cost may be quite low and be composed of only the fee paid, or it may amount to a great deal more if a copyright infringement suit is involved.

Research and Development Costs. When a company develops intangible assets internally rather than acquiring them from another party, two accounting problems arise: (1) It is sometimes difficult to determine the costs related to a specific project, and (2) it is hard to know the extent and timing of future benefits. To help resolve these issues, we look at the three phases a company goes through when developing its own intangibles: research, development, and post-development.

During the research phase, expenditures are made but it is not yet known if these costs will have any future benefit. Consequently, they are recorded in the account **Research Expenses**. Research is more specifically defined as the original planned investigation that is done to gain new knowledge and understanding.

The development phase begins when certain criteria are met that indicate that the project being developed will have future benefit. All of the following criteria must be met: (a) the project is technically feasible, (b) the company has a desire to complete development, (c) the company is able to complete development, and (d) a market exists for the product. Once all of these conditions are met, future expenditures on the project that specifically relate to its development will be recorded in the asset account **Development Costs**. During this phase, if expenditures incurred relate to another specific asset like equipment or a patent, then those costs are recorded in their respective accounts rather than in Development Costs. A development cost can be defined as the application of research to a plan or design for a new or improved product or process for commercial use. Furthermore, during this phase, if costs are incurred that do not really relate to the development of the project, like advertising, these costs should be recorded as expenses.

The post-development phase begins when commercial production of the product or process that was developed begins. During this stage, development costs would be amortized over the useful life of the product or process developed.

Intangible Assets with Indefinite Lives

An intangible asset is considered to have an indefinite life when there is no foreseeable limit to the length of time over which the asset is expected to generate net cash inflows for the company. Examples of intangible assets with indefinite lives include trademarks and trade names, franchises, and licences. Intangible assets do not always fit perfectly in a specific category. Sometimes trademarks, trade names, franchises, or licences do have limited lives. In such cases, they would be amortized over the shorter of their legal life and useful life. It is more usual, however, for these intangible assets to have indefinite lives and, because of this, they are not amortized.

Trademarks, Trade Names, and Brands.   A **trademark (trade name)** or brand is a word, phrase, jingle, or symbol that distinguishes or identifies a particular business or product. Trade names like Blue Jays, Big Mac, Nike, Calgary Stampede, and TSN create immediate brand recognition and generally help the sale of the product or service. Each year, Interbrand ranks the world's best brands. In 2010, the most valuable Canadian brands, in order, were Shoppers Drug Mart, Canadian Tire, and lululemon. However, it was lululemon that had the largest increase in its value that year. The most valuable brand in the world is Walmart.

The creator or original user may obtain the exclusive legal right to the trademark or trade name by registering it with the Canadian Intellectual Property Office. This registration provides continuous protection and may be renewed every 15 years as long as the trademark or trade name is in use. In most cases, companies continuously renew their trademarks or trade names. Consequently, as long as the trademark or trade name continues to be marketable, it will have an indefinite useful life.

If the trademark or trade name is purchased, the cost is the purchase price. If it is developed internally rather than purchased, it cannot be recognized as an intangible asset on the statement of financial position. The reason is that expenditures on internally developed trademarks or brands cannot be distinguished from the cost of developing the business as a whole and consequently cannot be measured.

ACCOUNTING MATTERS!   *Management Perspective*

Lego Trademark Dispute Resolved

More than a decade after the battle began, Montreal-based toy company Mega Brands finally emerged victorious in its legal fight with Danish rival Lego AS over the shape of its building blocks. In a final and binding ruling, the European Court of Justice said that Lego cannot use trademarks to protect the shape of its iconic building blocks, meaning Mega Brands has the right to sell similar bricks in Europe. The two rows of studs on the top of the bricks perform a "technical function" and therefore can't be trademarked, the court said in its decision.

The dispute, which began in the late 1990s, had been moving through the European legal process at a glacial pace, but eventually reached the end of all possible appeals. Lego conceded, saying: "We have no option but to note the court's ruling."

While the win is a morale boost for the troubled Canadian toy maker, Mega Brands must continue clawing its way back from a near disastrous couple of years in which its survival was at risk. Around 2009, the company was heavily in debt, reeling from a recall of a line of magnetic toys that had caused the death of one child and injuries to 27 others, and was still involved in a now-settled legal fight against some former partners. "For a while there, they were left for dead," said analyst Gerrick Johnson of BMO Nesbitt Burns Inc. in New York. Now, "they are on a much better footing."

Source: Richard Blackwell, "Mega Brands Wins Lengthy Legal Battle with Rival Lego," *Globe and Mail,* September 15, 2010, p. B2.

Franchises and Licences. When you purchase a Civic from a Honda dealer, fill up your tank at the corner Irving station, or order a double-double at Tim Hortons, you are dealing with franchises. A **franchise** is a contractual arrangement under which the franchisor grants the franchisee the right to sell certain products, to provide specific services, or to use certain trademarks or trade names, usually within a designated geographic area.

Another type of franchise, granted by a government body, permits the company to use public property in performing its services. Examples are the use of city streets for a bus line or taxi service;

the use of public land for telephone, power, and cable television lines; and the use of airwaves for wireless devices, radio, or TV broadcasting. Such operating rights are referred to as **licences**.

When costs can be identified with the acquisition of the franchise or licence, an intangible asset should be recognized. These rights have indefinite lives and are not amortized.

Annual payments, which are often in proportion to the franchise's total sales, are sometimes required under a franchise agreement. These are called *royalties* and are recorded as operating expenses in the period in which they are incurred.

DECISION TOOLKIT

Decision Checkpoints	 Info Needed for Decision	 Tools to Use for Decision	 How to Evaluate Results
Is the company's amortization of intangibles reasonable?	The estimated useful life of intangibles with finite lives from notes to the financial statements of both the company and its competitors	If the company's estimated useful life is significantly higher than that of its competitors, or does not seem reasonable in light of the circumstances, the reason for the difference should be investigated.	Too high an estimated useful life will result in understating amortization expense and overstating profit and assets.

GOODWILL

Goodwill is an asset representing the future economic benefits arising from the purchase of a business that are not individually identified and separately recognized. In other words, it represents the excess amount paid for a business above the fair market value of the identifiable assets of that business less the fair market value of its liabilities. Goodwill is the extra value relating to a business being acquired because it could have exceptional management, a desirable location, good customer relations, skilled employees, high-quality products, fair pricing policies, and harmonious relations with labour unions. Unlike other assets, which can be sold *individually* in the marketplace—such as investments or property, plant, and equipment—goodwill can be identified only with the business *as a whole*. This is also what differentiates goodwill from other intangible assets. It cannot be separated from the company, nor is it based on legal rights.

If goodwill can only be identified with the business as a whole, how can its value be determined? Certainly a number of businesses have many of the factors cited above (exceptional management, a desirable location, and so on). However, to determine the cost of these items would be difficult and very subjective—and subjective valuations do not contribute to the reliability of financial statements. For this reason, internally generated goodwill is not recognized as an asset. Goodwill is only recorded when it can be measured objectively and this only occurs when the business is actually acquired.

Goodwill is recorded only when there is a purchase of an entire business, at which time an independent valuation can be determined. The cost of the goodwill is measured by comparing the cost paid to acquire the business with the fair value of its net identifiable assets (assets less liabilities). If the cost is greater than the net identifiable assets, then the purchaser has paid for something that is not identifiable. The purchaser has paid for something that cannot be separated and sold—goodwill. In this situation, because a transaction has occurred, the cost of the purchased goodwill can be measured and therefore recorded as an asset.

Because goodwill has an indefinite life, just as the company has an indefinite life, it is not amortized. Since goodwill is measured using a company's fair value—a value that can easily change—IFRS requires goodwill to be tested annually for impairment even if there are no indications of impairment. Under ASPE, impairment tests on goodwill are only conducted if indications of impairment exist.   `ASPE`

Under both IFRS and ASPE, impairment losses on goodwill are never reversed, even if the company's value increases after the impairment loss has been recorded.

DECISION TOOLKIT

Decision Checkpoints	**Info Needed for Decision**	**Tools to Use for Decision**	**How to Evaluate Results**
Is the company's goodwill overvalued?	Impairment loss; carrying amount and fair values of the company	Determine if an impairment loss has been recorded and what circumstances led to the impairment.	If goodwill is significant and values are fluctuating, consider excluding goodwill from ratio analysis.

BEFORE YOU GO ON...

▶ Do It! Accounting for Intangibles

The Dummies R' Us Corporation purchased a copyright on a new book series for $15,000 cash on August 1, 2011. The books are anticipated to have a saleable life of three years. One year later, the company incurs $6,000 of legal costs (paid in cash) to successfully defend this copyright in court. The company's year end is July 31. Record the purchase of the copyright on August 1, 2011; the year-end amortization at July 31, 2012; and the legal costs incurred at August 1, 2012.

Action Plan

- Amortize intangible assets with limited lives over the shorter of their useful life and legal life (the legal life of a copyright is the life of the author plus 50 years).
- Treat costs to successfully defend an intangible asset as capital expenditures because they benefit future periods.

Solution

Aug. 1, 2011	Copyright	15,000	
	Cash		15,000
	(To record purchase of copyright)		
July 31, 2012	Amortization Expense ($15,000 ÷ 3)	5,000	
	Accumulated Amortization—Copyright		5,000
	(To record amortization expense)		
Aug. 1, 2012	Copyright	6,000	
	Cash		6,000
	(To record costs incurred to defend copyright)		

Statement Presentation of Long-Lived Assets

STUDY OBJECTIVE 6

Illustrate how long-lived assets are reported in the financial statements.

Long-lived assets have a major impact on three financial statements: the statement of financial position, income statement, and statement of cash flows. In addition, if a company chooses to use the revaluation model, any valuation gains will affect other comprehensive income on the statement of comprehensive income. This statement will be illustrated in Chapter 12.

STATEMENT OF FINANCIAL POSITION

Long-lived assets are normally reported in the statement of financial position under the headings "Property, Plant, and Equipment," "Intangible Assets," and "Goodwill." Some companies combine property, plant, and equipment and intangible assets, other than goodwill, under a single heading, such as "Capital Assets."

Either on the statement of financial position or in the notes, the cost of each of the major classes of assets is disclosed, as well as the accumulated depreciation pertaining to tangible assets and accumulated amortization relating to intangible assets. In addition, the company must specify which depreciation and amortization methods it uses and the useful lives or rates in the notes to its financial statements.

Under International Financial Reporting Standards, companies also have to disclose if they are using the cost or the revaluation model for each class of assets, and include a reconciliation of the carrying amount at the beginning and end of the period for each class of long-lived assets in the notes to the financial statements. This means they must show all of the following for each class of long-lived assets: (1) additions, (2) disposals, (3) depreciation or amortization, (4) impairment losses, and (5) reversals of impairment losses. If a company uses the revaluation model, it must also disclose any increases or decreases from revaluations, as well as other information about the revaluation.

WestJet reports the following information related to property, plant, and equipment and intangible assets in its statement of financial position (which it calls *balance sheet*). Summary information is reported in the statement of financial position for its property and equipment and detailed in a separate note, as shown in Illustration 9-10.

▶ Illustration 9-10
WestJet's statement of financial position (balance sheet)

WESTJET AIRLINES LTD. Balance Sheet (partial) December 31, 2010 (in millions)			
Property and equipment (Note 5)			$2,227
Intangible assets (Note 6)			13
Note 5. Property and equipment	Cost	Accumulated Depreciation	Net
Aircraft	$2,472	$623	$1,849
Ground property and equipment	122	62	60
Spare engines and parts	106	28	78
Buildings	136	13	123
Leasehold improvements	10	3	7
Assets under capital leases	4	1	3
Development costs and other assets	107	–	107
	$2,957	$730	$2,227

Note 6 to WestJet's statements indicates that its intangible assets consist of computer software. Its accounting policy note reports that the company uses straight-line depreciation and amortization for all of its long-lived assets.

INCOME STATEMENT

Depreciation expense, gains and losses on disposal, and impairment losses are presented in the operating section of the income statement. WestJet reported $133 million for depreciation and amortization in the operating expenses section of its income statement for the year ended December 31, 2010. It also reported a $190-million net gain from the disposal of property and equipment. Companies must disclose their impairment policy in the notes to the financial statements, which WestJet did even though there were no impairment losses recorded.

STATEMENT OF CASH FLOWS

The cash flows from the purchase and sale of long-lived assets are reported in the investing activities section of the statement of cash flows. Illustration 9-11 shows the investing activities section of

WestJet's statement of cash flows. This company is in a growth cycle and it reported purchases of long-lived assets but no significant sale proceeds.

▸Illustration 9-11

WestJet's statement of cash flows presentation of investing activities

WESTJET AIRLINES LTD.
Statement of Cash Flows (partial)
Year Ended December 31, 2010
(in millions)

WESTJET

Investing activities	
Aircraft additions	$(29,884)
Other property and equipment and intangible additions	(18,675)
Cash used in investing activities	(48,559)

BEFORE YOU GO ON...

▸Do It! Statement Presentation

Selkirk Enterprises Ltd. is a newly formed corporation that has prepared its financial statements for its first fiscal year end in accordance with IFRS. It uses the revaluation model for land and buildings and the cost model on all other long-lived assets. For each item listed below, state whether it can be found in profit on the income statement (IS), in other comprehensive income (OCI), or on the statement of financial position (SFP).

Accumulated Amortization—Development Costs	Gain on Disposal
Accumulated Depreciation—Buildings	Goodwill
Accumulated Depreciation—Equipment	Impairment Loss
Accumulated Impairment Loss	Land
Amortization Expense	Loss on Disposal
Buildings	Repairs and Maintenance Expense
Depreciation Expense	Research Expense
Development Costs	Revaluation Gain
Equipment	Revaluation Loss

Action Plan

- Recall how the revaluation model treats any adjustments to fair value that increase the carrying amount of an asset to a value that exceeds what it would have been had the cost model been used. They are recorded in other comprehensive income.
- Reversals of revaluation gains recorded in other comprehensive income are limited to the amount needed to return the carrying amount to what it would have been had the cost model been used. However, because this company is in its first year of operation, there are no reversals occurring.
- Under IFRS, when using the cost model, reversals of impairment losses can be made, but this company is in its first year of operations so reversals will not be occurring.

Solution

Accumulated Amortization—Development Costs	SFP	Gain on Disposal	IS
Accumulated Depreciation—Buildings	SFP	Goodwill	SFP
Accumulated Depreciation—Equipment	SFP	Impairment Loss	IS
Accumulated Impairment Loss	SFP	Land	SFP

Amortization Expense	IS	Loss on Disposal	IS
Buildings	SFP	Repairs and Maintenance Expense	IS
Depreciation Expense	IS	Research Expense	IS
Development Costs	SFP	Revaluation Gain	OCI
Equipment	SFP	Revaluation Loss	IS

Analyzing Assets

The presentation of financial statement information about long-lived assets allows decision makers to analyze a company's use of its total assets. We will use two ratios to analyze assets: the return on assets and asset turnover.

STUDY OBJECTIVE 7
Describe the methods for evaluating the use of assets.

RETURN ON ASSETS

The **return on assets** ratio measures overall profitability. This ratio is calculated by dividing profit by average total assets. The return on assets ratio indicates the amount of profit generated by each dollar invested in assets. The higher the return on assets, the more profitable the company is.

The following data (in millions) are provided for WestJet Airlines Ltd. for the fiscal years 2010 and 2009:

	2010	2009
Net sales	$2,405	$2,068
Profit	137	98
Total assets	3,563	3,494

Total assets at the end of 2008 were $3,269 million.

The return on assets for WestJet is shown in Illustration 9-12. This illustration also shows this ratio for Air Canada, WestJet's major competitor, as well as the industry average.

> Illustration 9-12
> Return on assets

RETURN ON ASSETS = $\dfrac{\text{PROFIT}}{\text{AVERAGE TOTAL ASSETS}}$		
($ in millions)	2010	2009
WestJet	$\dfrac{\$137}{(\$3,563 + \$3,494) \div 2} = 3.9\%$	$\dfrac{\$98}{(\$3,494 + \$3,269) \div 2} = 2.9\%$
Air Canada	1.0%	(0.1)%
Industry average	2.3%	(1.4)%

As the illustration shows, WestJet's return on assets improved in 2010 compared with 2009. In both years, it was above the industry average, while Air Canada's return on assets, although improving, was not above the industry average in 2010. This was mainly attributable to lower occupancy (load factor) on its planes.

ASSET TURNOVER

The **asset turnover** ratio indicates how efficiently a company uses its assets; that is, how many dollars of sales are generated by each dollar invested in assets. It is calculated by dividing net sales by average total assets. When we compare two companies in the same industry, the one with the higher asset turnover ratio is generally perceived to be operating more efficiently because it is generating more sales for every dollar invested in assets. However, with this ratio we are usually assuming that the age of the depreciable assets is about the same for each company. If this assumption is not valid, the company with the newer, less depreciated assets will tend to have a lower turnover. Also, if a company leases rather than owns some of its major assets, this will make the turnover ratio higher because the denominator will have a lower amount for assets. Asset turnover is not expressed in percentage terms like return ratios but in "times per year," like any turnover ratio.

The asset turnover ratios of WestJet, Air Canada, and their industry for 2010 and 2009 are presented in Illustration 9-13.

▸Illustration 9-13
Asset turnover

$$\text{ASSET TURNOVER} = \dfrac{\text{NET SALES}}{\text{AVERAGE TOTAL ASSETS}}$$		
($ in millions)	2010	2009
WestJet	$\dfrac{\$2,405}{(\$3,563 + \$3,494) \div 2} = 0.7 \text{ times}$	$\dfrac{\$2,068}{(\$3,494 + \$3,269) \div 2} = 0.6 \text{ times}$
Air Canada	1.0 times	0.9 times
Industry average	0.8 times	0.7 times

The asset turnover ratios in the illustration indicate that for each dollar invested in assets in 2010, WestJet generated sales of $0.70 and Air Canada $1.00. WestJet's asset turnover was lower than Air Canada's. The major reason for this was due not to a lower numerator but a higher denominator as WestJet's planes are newer and less depreciated than Air Canada's planes.

Asset turnover ratios vary considerably across industries. The average asset turnover for utility companies in Canada in 2010 was 0.3 times, and for retailers it was 1.8 times. Asset turnover ratios, therefore, should only be compared within an industry, not between different industries.

PROFIT MARGIN REVISITED

For a complete picture of the sales-generating ability of assets, it is also important to look at a company's profit margin ratio. In Chapter 5, you learned about profit margin. Profit margin is calculated by dividing profit by net sales. It tells how effective a company is in turning its sales into profits; that is, how much profit is generated by each dollar of sales.

Together, the profit margin and asset turnover explain the return on assets ratio. Illustration 9-14 shows how return on assets can be calculated from the profit margin and asset turnover ratios for WestJet in 2010.

▸Illustration 9-14
Composition of WestJet's 2010 return on assets (in millions)

PROFIT MARGIN	×	ASSET TURNOVER	=	RETURN ON ASSETS
$\dfrac{\text{Profit}}{\text{Net Sales}}$	×	$\dfrac{\text{Net Sales}}{\text{Average Total Assets}}$	=	$\dfrac{\text{Profit}}{\text{Average Total Assets}}$
$\dfrac{\$137}{\$2,405} = 5.7\%$		$\dfrac{\$2,405}{(\$3,563 + \$3,494) \div 2} = 0.7 \text{ times}$		$\dfrac{\$137}{(\$3,563 + \$3,494) \div 2} = 3.9\%$

This relationship has important implications for management. From Illustration 9-14, we can see that if a company wants to increase its return on assets, it can do so either by increasing the margin it generates from each dollar of goods that it sells (profit margin), or by trying to increase the volume of goods or services that it sells (asset turnover).

Let's evaluate WestJet's return on assets for 2010 again, but this time by evaluating the ratio's components: the profit margin and asset turnover ratios. WestJet has a profit margin of 5.7%. Compared with the industry average of 2.8%, WestJet is more profitable. Two possible explanations could be higher ticket prices or better control of costs. Given that WestJet is a discount airline, its superior profitability comes from low costs. This advantage is offset by lower asset turnover. Despite this, WestJet still maintains a higher overall return on assets than its nearest competitor, Air Canada.

DECISION TOOLKIT

Decision Checkpoints	 Info Needed for Decision	 Tools to Use for Decision	 How to Evaluate Results
How efficient is the company at generating profit from its assets?	Profit and average total assets	$\text{Return on assets} = \dfrac{\text{Profit}}{\text{Average total assets}}$	Indicates the profit generated per dollar of assets. A high value suggests that the company is efficient in using its resources to generate profit.
How efficient is the company at generating sales from its assets?	Net sales and average total assets	$\text{Asset turnover} = \dfrac{\text{Net sales}}{\text{Average total assets}}$	Indicates the sales dollars generated per dollar of assets. A high value suggests that the company is efficient in using its resources to generate sales.

BEFORE YOU GO ON...

▶ Do It! Analyze Assets

Saluda Enterprises Ltd. and Unami Corporation are competitors that manufacture various household appliances. Starting in 2012, Saluda's management team embarked on a new corporate strategy. Early that year, they found a Mexican company that could supply some of the components used in their appliances at a reduced cost. They decided to pass some, but not all, of these savings onto customers so they lowered their prices in an effort to boost the number of appliances sold. Unami finally reacted to this strategy in late 2012 when it bought the Mexican company. Listed below are some key amounts taken from the financial statements of these competitors. Calculate (a) the profit margin, (b) the asset turnover, and (c) return on assets. (d) Explain why the ratios changed in 2012. Assume that for both companies, total assets were the same in 2011 and 2010.

	Saluda		Unami	
	2012	2011	2012	2011
Net sales	$1,200	$1,000	$1,800	$2,000
Profit	100	80	170	200
Total assets	520	500	1,200	800

(continued)

Action Plan

- Recall the formulas for each ratio: Profit margin = profit ÷ net sales; asset turnover = net sales ÷ average total assets; return on assets = profit ÷ average total assets.
- If the ratio changed compared with the prior year, determine if the change is a result of the numerator or the denominator changing the most.
- Remember how the profit margin and asset turnover ratios relate to explain the return on assets ratio.
- Relate the change from above to the facts provided about the company's strategies.

Solution

	Saluda		Unami	
	2012	2011	2012	2011
(a) Profit margin	8.3% $\dfrac{\$100}{\$1,200}$	8.0% $\dfrac{\$80}{\$1,000}$	9.4% $\dfrac{\$170}{\$1,800}$	10.0% $\dfrac{\$200}{\$2,000}$
(b) Asset turnover	2.4 times $\dfrac{\$1,200}{(\$520 + \$500) \div 2}$	2.0 times $\dfrac{\$1,000}{(\$500 + \$500) \div 2}$	1.8 times $\dfrac{\$1,800}{(\$1,200 + \$800) \div 2}$	2.5 times $\dfrac{\$2,000}{(\$800 + \$800) \div 2}$
(c) Return on assets	19.6% $\dfrac{\$100}{(\$520 + \$500) \div 2}$	16.0% $\dfrac{\$80}{(\$500 + \$500) \div 2}$	17.0% $\dfrac{\$170}{(\$1,200 + \$800) \div 2}$	25.0% $\dfrac{\$200}{(\$800 + \$800) \div 2}$

(d) Profit margin analysis: Saluda was able to find a cheaper source for components, which enabled it to earn a higher profit while at the same time reducing the components' selling price, which allowed it to sell more products. This hurt Unami, causing its sales to drop. Unami was unable to cut expenses as fast as sales were falling, which caused its profit margin to fall.

Asset turnover analysis: Saluda's increased sales did not create the need for a significant increase in assets, so turnover rose. Unami's asset turnover fell for two reasons: (1) sales volumes dropped because Saluda was taking away customers seeking lower prices, and (2) because of the acquisition of the Mexican company, assets rose with no corresponding increase in revenues because the acquisition was so late in the year.

Return on assets: This ratio is a function of the two preceding ratios. Because Saluda's profit margin and asset turnover ratios rose in 2012, the result was a higher return on assets. For Unami, it was both the lower profit margin and the lower asset turnover that caused the drop in the return on assets.

the
navigator

comparing
IFRS and ASPE

Key Differences	International Financial Reporting Standards (IFRS)	Accounting Standards for Private Enterprises (ASPE)
Models for valuing property, plant, and equipment	Choice of cost model or revaluation model	Only cost model allowed
Models for valuing investment properties	Choice of cost model or valuation model for investment properties	No separate recognition of investment properties—considered to be property, plant, and equipment—so only cost model allowed
Impairment requirements for property, plant, and equipment and intangible assets with finite lives	Must determine each year if indicators of impairment are present and if so perform an impairment test. Reversals of impairment losses are allowed.	No annual requirement to determine if indicators of impairment exist, but when it is apparent they exist, an impairment test must be done. An impairment test occurs in two steps: (1) determine that the cash flows from the asset do not exceed its carrying value, and (2) calculate the impairment loss. Impairment losses cannot be reversed.
Goodwill and intangible assets with indefinite lives	Must perform impairment test annually. Impairment losses can be reversed on intangible assets but not on goodwill.	Same approach used as above.
Terminology	*Depreciation* is used to describe cost allocation for property, plant, and equipment. Long-term leases that are essentially the purchase of an asset are called *finance leases*.	*Amortization* may be used instead of *depreciation* for property, plant, and equipment. Long-term leases that are essentially the purchase of an asset are known as *capital leases*.

the navigator

Are You Sure You Need a New Car?

Rent-A-Wreck holds the number one position in used car rental and sales in Canada. The company has long determined that it can maximize its profitability by buying and renting used cars instead of new cars.

Would you maximize your economic well-being by buying a used car rather than a new one? Buying a new vehicle is a straightforward process. You borrow money from a lending institution, pay for the car, and then make monthly payments on the loan. As you pay off the loan, you gain equity in the vehicle until it is all yours. You can keep the vehicle as long as you like and do whatever you want to it.

Should you consider leasing a car instead of buying one? There are many benefits to leasing, including a low down payment, driving a late-model vehicle that's covered by the manufacturer's warranty, and not having to spend a large amount to obtain use of the vehicle. On the other hand, the disadvantages to leasing include a restriction on the number of kilometres that you can drive without additional charges, and a requirement to maintain the vehicle in good condition. At the end of the lease, you have no equity in the vehicle to put toward a new car.

Monthly lease payments are lower than monthly loan payments, assuming the same costs and interest rates, because with a lease you are only paying off a portion of the cost of the vehicle plus interest. With a loan, your payments cover the entire cost of the vehicle plus interest. Both lease and loan payments include interest on the declining balance of the lease or loan. Buying a car—whether new or used—is more economical than leasing one. However, some people receive a great deal of pleasure from driving a newer car so maybe the extra cost of leasing is worth it.

Some Facts

- If you drive 18,000 km a year in a Chevrolet Cobalt, a typical compact car, it will cost you on average about 12.6 cents a kilometre plus another $6,257 in fixed costs, according to the Canadian Automobile Association. A typical minivan, like a Dodge Grand Caravan, would cost you 16.8 cents per kilometre plus $8,568 in additional fixed costs. A Toyota Prius hybrid would cost you 8.2 cents per kilometre plus $7,333 in fixed costs.
- Depreciation is the largest cost of owning a vehicle. Although most cars are sold before they are 15 years old, they depreciate at different rates and two cars that had the same purchase price may have different values after four years. The Canadian Black Book Company compared the 2011 values of vehicles purchased in 2007 for 17 different vehicle categories. The cars that retained the highest percentage value of the original purchase price included the Volkswagen Beetle for subcompact cars, and the Jeep Wrangler for the compact SUV category.
- There are about 20.7 million vehicles on the roads in Canada. Not all of them are new: about half of these vehicles are from the 2002 vehicle model year or earlier.

What Do You Think?

To save money, you're renting an apartment on the outskirts of the city where you're going to school, and you need a car to get to campus and to your part-time job. Should you buy a new car?

YES I do not want to worry about my car breaking down and, if it does break down, I want it to be covered by a warranty.

NO I am a university student and I want to keep my costs down. Used cars are more dependable than they used to be.

Sources: Canadian Automobile Association, "Driving Costs," 2010 edition, www.caa.ca/documents/CAA_Driving_Costs_Brochure_2010.pdf accessed March 11, 2011. Canadian Black Book 2011, "Best Retained Value Awards," www.canadianblackbook.com/cbb-awards.html, accessed March 11, 2011. Jeremy Cato "What Does Your Car Cost: It's More Than You Think," *The Globe and Mail*, September 2, 2010, page G1. Office of Consumer Affairs, Industry Canada, "Spending Smarter—Car Lease or Buy Calculator," www.ic.gc.ca/eic/site/oca-bc.nsf/eng/ca01851.html accessed March 11, 2011.

Summary of Study Objectives

1. Determine the cost of property, plant, and equipment. The cost of property, plant, and equipment includes all expenditures that are necessary to acquire these assets and make them ready for their intended use. When applicable, cost also includes asset retirement costs.

2. Explain and calculate depreciation. Depreciation is the process of allocating the cost of a long-lived asset over the asset's useful (service) life in a systematic way. Depreciation is not a process of valuation, and it does not result in an accumulation of cash.

There are three commonly used depreciation methods: straight-line, diminishing-balance, and units-of-production.

Method	Annual Depreciation Pattern	Calculation
Straight-line	Constant amount	(Cost – residual value) ÷ estimated useful life (in years)
Diminishing-balance	Diminishing amount	Carrying amount at beginning of year × diminishing-balance rate
Units-of-production	Varying amount	(Cost – residual value) ÷ total estimated units of production × actual production during the year

Each method results in the same amount of total depreciation over the asset's useful life.

3. Describe other accounting issues related to depreciation. When an item of property, plant, and equipment includes individual components for which different depreciation methods or rates are appropriate, the cost should be allocated to the asset's significant components and each component should be depreciated separately.

Depreciation expense for income tax purposes is called capital cost allowance (CCA). The Canada Revenue Agency requires companies to use the single diminishing-balance method on most assets and prescribes the rate of depreciation.

Property, plant, and equipment are tested for impairment whenever circumstances indicate that an asset might be impaired. If the asset is impaired, an impairment loss, equal to the difference between the asset's carrying amount and recoverable amount, is recorded. A previously recorded loss can be reversed under IFRS but not under ASPE.

Under IFRS, companies can account for property, plant, and equipment using the cost or revaluation model. Most use the cost model. Under the revaluation model, revaluation gains and impairment losses are recorded but the revaluation gains (write-ups) must be recorded in other comprehensive income and can be reversed later through other comprehensive income. Also under IFRS, investment properties can be valued using the cost model or valuation model, which allows companies to record valuation gains or losses in the income statement and does not allow for depreciation. Under ASPE, the revaluation and valuation models are not permitted.

When circumstances change the cost, residual value, or useful life of an asset, or the pattern in which the future benefits are consumed, a revision of depreciation is required. Revisions are also necessary if an impairment loss has been recorded or reversed. Revisions are treated as changes in estimates and are adjusted in the present and future periods, not retroactively.

4. Account for the disposal of property, plant, and equipment. The procedure for accounting for the disposal of property, plant, and equipment through sale or retirement is:

Step 1: Update any unrecorded depreciation.

Step 2: Calculate the carrying amount.

Step 3: Calculate any gain (proceeds less carrying amount) or loss (carrying amount less proceeds) on disposal.

Step 4: Remove the asset and accumulated depreciation accounts related to the sold or retired asset and record the proceeds received and the gain or loss (if any).

5. Identify the basic accounting issues for intangible assets and goodwill. Intangible assets are reported at cost, which includes all expenditures that are necessary to prepare the asset for its intended use. An intangible asset with a finite life is amortized over the shorter of its useful life or legal life. Like property, plant, and equipment, intangible assets with finite lives are tested for impairment only if indicators of impairment are present. Intangible assets with indefinite lives are not amortized and must be tested for impairment annually under IFRS but only when indicators of impairment are present under ASPE. Impairment losses can be reversed under IFRS but not under ASPE.

Goodwill, which is the difference between the price paid for a business and the fair value of the identifiable assets less liabilities of the business, is not considered an intangible asset because it is not "identifiable." Goodwill has an indefinite life and is not amortized. It is tested for impairment annually under IFRS but under ASPE it is only tested if indicators of impairment are present. Goodwill impairment losses are never reversed.

6. Illustrate how long-lived assets are reported in the financial statements. In the statement of financial position, land, land improvements, buildings, and equipment are usually combined and shown under the heading "Property, Plant, and Equipment." Intangible assets with finite and indefinite lives are sometimes combined under the heading "Intangible Assets" or are listed separately. Goodwill must be presented separately. Either on the statement of financial position or in the notes, the cost of the major classes of long-lived assets is presented. The accumulated depreciation and amortization, and carrying amount by major classes or in total, are also disclosed. The depreciation and amortization methods and rates must also be indicated.

The company's impairment policy and any impairment losses should be described and reported. The company must disclose whether it is using the cost or revaluation model. If the latter, any valuation gains (or reversals) are reported in other comprehensive income and accumulate in equity in the revaluation surplus component of accumulated other comprehensive income.

Depreciation expense, any gain or loss on disposal, and any impairment losses are reported as operating expenses in the income statement.

In the statement of cash flows, any cash flows from the purchase or sale of long-lived assets are reported as investing activities.

7. **Describe the methods for evaluating the use of assets.** The use of assets may be analyzed using the return on assets and

asset turnover ratios. Return on assets (profit ÷ average total assets) indicates how well assets are used to generate profit. This is really a function of the following two ratios: asset turnover (net sales ÷ average total assets), which indicates how efficiently assets are used to generate revenue, and profit margin (profit ÷ net sales), which measures the profit made on each sale.

Glossary

Amortizable amount   The cost of a finite-life intangible asset less its residual value. (p. 477)

Amortization   The systematic allocation of the amortizable cost of a finite-life intangible asset over the asset's useful life. (p. 477)

Asset retirement costs   The amount added to the cost of an asset that relates to the retirement of that asset. (p. 459)

Asset turnover   A measure of how efficiently a company uses its total assets to generate sales. It is calculated by dividing net sales by average total assets. (p. 486)

Capital cost allowance   (CCA)   A method of depreciation that is used for income tax purposes. Claiming CCA is optional. (p. 469)

Capital expenditures   Expenditures that benefit future periods. They are recorded as long-lived assets. (p. 457)

Copyright   An exclusive right granted by the federal government allowing the owner to reproduce and sell an artistic or published work. (p. 479)

Cost model   A model for accounting for a long-lived asset that carries the asset at its cost less accumulated depreciation or amortization, and less any impairment losses. (p. 461)

Depreciable amount   The cost of a depreciable asset (e.g., property, plant, and equipment) less its residual value. (p. 462)

Development costs   Assets arising from the application of research to a plan or design for a new or improved product or process for commercial use. (p. 479)

Diminishing-balance method   A depreciation method that applies a constant rate (the straight-line rate, which is 100% divided by the useful life) to the carrying amount of an asset. This method produces a decreasing annual depreciation expense over the asset's useful life. (p. 464)

Finance lease   (also known as a capital lease) A long-term agreement allowing one party (the lessee) to use the

asset of another party (the lessor). The arrangement is accounted for as a purchase because the lease term covers a major portion of the asset's life. (p. 460)

Franchise   A contractual arrangement under which the franchisor grants the franchisee the right to sell certain products, to render specific services, or to use certain trademarks or trade names, usually within a designated geographic area. (p. 480)

Gain on disposal   The excess of the proceeds received from the sale of an asset not normally held for resale over the carrying amount of that asset. (p. 474)

Goodwill   The amount paid to acquire another company that exceeds the fair value of the company's net identifiable assets. (p. 481)

Impairment loss   The amount by which the carrying amount of an asset exceeds its recoverable amount. (p. 469)

Investment properties   Land and buildings that are not occupied by the owner and are held for the purpose of earning rental income or capital appreciation. (p. 471)

Lessee   A party that has made contractual arrangements to pay for the use of another party's asset. (p. 459)

Lessor   A party that has agreed contractually to let another party use its asset. (p. 459)

Licences   Operating rights to use property that are granted by a government agency to a company. (p. 480)

Loss on disposal   The excess of the carrying amount of an asset not normally held for resale over the proceeds received from the sale that asset. (p. 474)

Operating expenditures   Expenditures that benefit only the current period. They are immediately matched against revenues as an expense. (p. 457)

Operating lease   An arrangement allowing one party (the lessee) to use the asset of another party (the lessor). The arrangement is accounted for as a rental usually because the lease term is not very long. (p. 460)

Patent An exclusive right issued by the federal government that enables the recipient to manufacture, sell, or otherwise control an invention for a period of 20 years from the date of the application. (p. 478)

Recoverable amount The higher of the asset's fair value, less costs to sell, and its value in use. It is compared with an asset's carrying amount when performing an impairment test. (p. 469)

Research expenses Expenditures on an original planned investigation that is done to gain new knowledge and understanding. These costs are expensed because criteria for recording them as assets have not been met. (p. 479)

Residual value An estimate of the amount that a company would obtain from the disposal of an asset if the asset were already as old as it will be and in the condition it is expected to be in at the end of its useful life. (p. 462)

Return on assets A profitability measure that indicates the amount of profit generated by each dollar invested in assets. It is calculated as profit divided by average total assets. It can also be calculated by multiplying profit margin by asset turnover. (p. 485)

Revaluation gains The amount by which the fair value of an asset exceeds its carrying amount under the revaluation model. (p. 471)

Revaluation model An alternative to the cost model under IFRS that adjusts the carrying amount of property, plant, and equipment and intangible assets to their fair value. (p. 470)

Revaluation surplus The component of accumulated other comprehensive income that has accumulated revaluation gains on assets accounted for using the revaluation model under IFRS. (p. 471)

Trademark (trade name) A word, phrase, jingle, or symbol that distinguishes or identifies a particular business or product. (p. 480)

Units-of-production method A depreciation method in which the useful life is expressed in terms of the total units of production or total use expected from the asset. Depreciation expense is calculated by multiplying the depreciable amount by actual activity during the year divided by the estimated total activity. The method will produce an expense that will vary each period depending on the amount of activity. (p. 465)

Valuation model An alternative to the cost model for investment properties under IFRS. With this model, an investment property is not depreciated but its carrying amount is adjusted to its fair value when it is materially different. (p. 471)

DECISION TOOLKIT—A SUMMARY

 Decision Checkpoints	 Info Needed for Decision	 Tools to Use for Decision	 How to Evaluate Results
What is the impact of the choice of depreciation method?	Depreciation policy	Income statement, statement of financial position, and accounting policy note to the statements	In the early years, straight-line depreciation results in a lower amount of depreciation expense and higher profit on the income statement than the diminishing-balance method. It also results in higher total assets and higher shareholders' equity on the statement of financial position. The opposite is true in the later years. There is no impact on cash flow regardless of method used.
Should the company use the cost model or the revaluation model?	Cost and fair value of assets	Compare the cost and fair value amounts, as well as the cost of determining the fair value amounts.	If there is a significant difference and the valuation would make a difference to users' decision-making, consider using the revaluation model. Also consider whether the cost of determining the fair value of assets is worth the information provided to users of the financial statements.

(continued)

Are the company's long-lived assets over- or undervalued?	Impairment loss; carrying amount of long-lived assets	Compare the carrying and recoverable amounts in light of current business conditions and company performance.	If assets have been adjusted for impairment, expect improved results in subsequent periods, as depreciation will be lower. If assets are substantially undervalued on the statement of financial position, be cautious when interpreting ratios that use carrying amounts, as these ratios will not show the company's potential.
Is the company's amortization of intangibles reasonable?	The estimated useful life of intangibles with finite lives from notes to the financial statements of both the company and its competitors	If the company's estimated useful life is significantly higher than that of its competitors, or does not seem reasonable in light of the circumstances, the reason for the difference should be investigated.	Too high an estimated useful life will result in understating amortization expense and overstating profit.
Is the company's goodwill overvalued?	Impairment loss; carrying amount and fair values of the company	Determine if an impairment loss has been recorded and what circumstances led to the impairment.	If goodwill is significant and values are fluctuating, consider excluding goodwill from ratio analysis.
How efficient is the company at generating profit from its assets?	Profit and average total assets	$$\text{Return on assets} = \frac{\text{Profit}}{\text{Average total assets}}$$	Indicates the profit generated per dollar of assets. A high value suggests that the company is efficient in using its resources to generate profit.
How efficient is the company at generating sales from its assets?	Net sales and average total assets	$$\text{Asset turnover} = \frac{\text{Net sales}}{\text{Average total assets}}$$	Indicates the sales dollars generated per dollar of assets. A high value suggests that the company is efficient in using its resources to generate sales.

the navigator

USING THE DECISION TOOLKIT

Research In Motion® (RIM)® Limited, headquartered in Waterloo, Ontario, manufactures and markets innovative wireless products (including the popular BlackBerry)® for the worldwide mobile communications market.

In the past, many stock analysts have recommended purchasing RIM's shares but, with increased competition from the Apple iPhone and other smart devices, some analysts are no longer in favour of the shares. A friend of yours, Rafik Khan, has an interest in buying RIM's shares and has asked you some questions about its financial statements. Excerpts from RIM's financial statements follow:

RESEARCH IN MOTION LIMITED
Statement of Financial Position (partial)
February 26, 2011
(in U.S. millions)

Assets	
Property, plant and equipment, net	$2,504
Intangible assets, net	1,798
Goodwill	508

RESEARCH IN MOTION LIMITED
Notes to the Consolidated Financial Statements
February 26, 2011

1. Summary of Significant Accounting Policies
<u>Property, plant and equipment, net</u>

Property, plant and equipment is stated at cost less accumulated amortization . . . Amortization is provided using the following rates and methods:

Buildings, leaseholds and other	Straight-line over terms between 5 and 40 years
BlackBerry operations and other information technology	Straight-line over terms between 3 and 5 years
Manufacturing equipment, research and development equipment, and tooling	Straight-line over terms between 2 and 8 years
Furniture and fixtures	20% per annum diminishing balance

<u>Intangible assets, net</u>

Intangible assets are stated at cost less accumulated amortization . . . Intangible assets are amortized as follows:

Acquired technology	Straight-line over 2 to 5 years
Licences	Straight-line over terms of licence agreements or on a per unit basis based upon the anticipated number of units sold during the terms, subject to a maximum of 5 years
Patents	Straight-line over 17 years or over estimated useful life

<u>Goodwill</u>

Goodwill is not amortized, but is tested for impairment annually.

Instructions

Answer the following questions asked by Rafik:

1. Why does RIM report its intangible assets and goodwill separately on its statement of financial position?
2. Why does RIM likely use a different amortization method for its furniture and fixtures than it uses for its buildings and leaseholds?
3. Why does RIM not amortize its goodwill?
4. Rafik was able to get the following information related to RIM:

	RIM	Industry Average
Profit margin	17.1%	2.0%
Return on assets	29.1%	2.8%

Rafik knows that the profit margin and return on assets are somehow related to the asset turnover ratio. He expects that RIM will have an asset turnover that is more than double the industry average because RIM's profit margin and return on assets are so much higher than the industry average. Explain to Rafik if this is true or not.

Solution

1. RIM's intangible assets consist of acquired technology, licences, and patents. All of these can be separated from the company and sold, if the company chooses to do so. Goodwill is similar to an intangible asset in some respects, but cannot be separated from the company and sold.
2. RIM likely uses a different depreciation (which it calls amortization) method (diminishing-balance) for its furniture and fixtures because they produce a different economic benefit pattern than its buildings and leaseholds. In the case of buildings, time is normally the main factor affecting usage and therefore the straight-line method of depreciation is often the most appropriate. In the case of furniture and fixtures, it may be that these are anticipated to be more productive in their early years than in their later years, and so the diminishing-balance method would be the most appropriate.
3. Goodwill is not amortized because it has an indefinite life.

(continued)

4. Rafik is correct that profit margin and return on assets are related to the asset turnover ratio. Asset turnover × profit margin = return on assets. Therefore, asset turnover = return on assets ÷ profit margin. Using this formula to calculate the asset turnover, we find that Rafik was incorrect in thinking that RIM's asset turnover will be significantly higher than the industry average asset turnover. RIM's asset turnover of 1.7 times (29.1% ÷ 17.1%) is just slightly more than the industry average asset turnover of 1.4 times (2.8% ÷ 2.0%).

Comprehensive Do It!

Dulcimer Ltd. purchased a machine at a cost of $35,000 on June 1, 2012. The machine was expected to have a residual value of $3,000 at the end of its four-year useful life. Dulcimer has a December 31 year end.

During its useful life, the machine was expected to be used 10,000 hours. Anticipated annual hourly use was as follows: 1,300 hours in 2012; 2,800 hours in 2013; 3,300 hours in 2014; 1,900 hours in 2015; and 700 hours in 2016.

Instructions
Prepare depreciation schedules showing the expected depreciation expense for 2012 to 2016 using the following methods: (a) straight-line, (b) diminishing-balance using double the straight-line rate, and (c) units-of-production.

Action Plan
- For straight-line depreciation, determine the depreciable amount (cost less residual value) and divide this by the estimated useful life in years or multiply it by one divided by the useful life in years to determine an annual percentage. For years when the machine is not used throughout the year, do not forget to multiply the annual depreciation by a ratio of months used divided by 12 months in the year.
- For the diminishing-balance method, determine the straight-line rate by taking one divided by useful life in years and then double this rate. Multiply the rate by the carrying amount at the beginning of the period. For years when the machine is not used throughout the year, do not forget to multiply the annual depreciation by a ratio of months used divided by 12 months in the year. Make sure that you cease depreciating the machine once its carrying amount is equal to the residual value.
- For the units-of-production method, determine the depreciation rate per unit of production (hours used) by taking the depreciable amount (cost less residual value) and dividing it by the total units that the machine is expected to produce over its useful life. Then multiply that rate by the units produced (hours used). There is no need to prorate this calculation for partial-year use because the proration effect is already reflected in the units produced in the period.

Solution to Comprehensive Do It!
(a)

DULCIMER LTD.
Straight-Line Depreciation Schedule

Year	Depreciable Amount	× Depreciation Rate	= Depreciation Expense	Accumulated Depreciation (End of Year)	Carrying Amount (End of Year)
					$35,000
2012	$32,000[a]	25%[b] × 7/12	$4,667	$ 4,667	30,333
2013	32,000	25%	8,000	12,667	22,333
2014	32,000	25%	8,000	20,667	14,333
2015	32,000	25%	8,000	28,667	6,333
2016	32,000	25% × 5/12	3,333	32,000	3,000

[a] $35,000 − $3,000 = $32,000
[b] 100% ÷ 4 years = 25%

(b)

| | | | | | End of Year | |
| | Carrying Amount | × Depreciation | = Depreciation | Accumulated | Carrying |
Year	Beginning of Year	Rate	Expense	Depreciation	Amount
					$35,000
2012	$35,000	50%[a] × 7/12	$10,208	$10,208	24,792
2013	24,792	50%	12,396	22,604	12,396
2014	12,396	50%	6,198	28,802	6,198
2015	6,198	50%	3,099	31,901	3,099
2016	3,099	50%	99[b]	32,000	3,000

DULCIMER LTD.
Diminishing-Balance Depreciation Schedule

[a] 25% × 2
[b] Adjusted to $99 because the ending carrying amount should not be less than the expected residual value.

(c)

DULCIMER LTD.
Units-of-Production Depreciation Schedule

| | | | | | End of Year | |
| | Units of | × Depreciable | = Depreciation | Accumulated | Carrying |
Year	Activity	Cost/Unit	Expense	Depreciation	Amount
					$35,000
2012	1,300	$3.20[a]	$ 4,160	$ 4,160	30,840
2013	2,800	3.20	8,960	13,120	21,880
2014	3,300	3.20	10,560	23,680	11,320
2015	1,900	3.20	6,080	29,760	5,240
2016	700	3.20	2,240	32,000	3,000

[a]$35,000 − $3,000 = $32,000 ÷ 10,000 total units = $3.20/unit

Self-Test, Brief Exercises, Exercises, Problems: Set A, and many more components are available for practice in WileyPLUS.

Self-Test Questions

Answers are at the end of the chapter.

(SO 1) 1. Corrieten Ltd. purchased equipment and incurred these costs:

Invoice price	$24,000
Freight—FOB shipping point	1,000
Insurance during transit	200
Annual licence fee	350
Training workers on equipment	280
Installation and testing	400
Total costs	$26,230

What amount should be recorded as the cost of the equipment?
(a) $24,000
(b) $24,200
(c) $25,600
(d) $25,950

(SO 2) 2. Kildare Ltd. purchased equipment on January 1, 2011, at a total invoice cost of $800,000. The equipment has an estimated residual value of $20,000 and an estimated useful life of five years. Assuming the straight-line method of depreciation is used, what is the amount of accumulated depreciation at December 31, 2012, the second year of the asset's useful life?
(a) $156,000
(b) $160,000
(c) $312,000
(d) $320,000

(SO 2) 3. Kant Enterprises Ltd. purchased a truck for $32,000 on July 1, 2012. The truck has an estimated residual value of $2,000, an estimated useful life of five years, and an estimated total mileage of 300,000 km. If 50,000 km are driven in 2012, what amount of depreciation expense would Kant record at December 31, 2012, assuming it uses the units-of-production method?
(a) $2,500
(b) $3,000
(c) $5,000
(d) $5,333

(SO 2) 4. Refer to the data provided for Kant Enterprises in question 3. If Kant uses the double diminishing-balance method of depreciation, what amount of depreciation expense would be recorded at December 31, 2012?
(a) $6,000
(b) $6,400
(c) $12,000
(d) $12,800

(SO 2) 5. Which depreciation method would result in the highest profit in the first year of an asset's life if the asset's output was relatively high in its first year of operations?
(a) Straight-line
(b) Double diminishing-balance
(c) Units-of-production
(d) Capital cost allowance

(SO 3) 6. If equipment with an original cost of $125,000, residual value of $5,000, and accumulated depreciation of $25,000 had a recoverable amount of $80,000, an impairment loss would be recorded amounting to:
(a) $0
(b) $20,000
(c) $45,000
(d) $55,000

(SO 4) 7. Oviatt Ltd. sold equipment for $10,000 cash. At the time of disposal, the equipment had a cost

of $45,000 and accumulated depreciation of $30,000. Oviatt should record a:
(a) $5,000 loss on disposal
(b) $5,000 gain on disposal
(c) $15,000 loss on disposal
(d) $15,000 gain on disposal

(SO 5) 8. Pierce Inc. incurred $150,000 of research costs in its laboratory in January 2012 to develop a new product. On February 2, 2012, $20,000 was paid for legal fees to register a patent related to the new product. On July 31, 2012, Pierce paid $15,000 for legal fees in a successful defence of the patent. What is the total amount that should be debited to the Patents account through July 31, 2012?
(a) $15,000
(b) $20,000
(c) $35,000
(d) $185,000

(SO 6) 9. Which of the following statements is true?
(a) Since intangible assets lack physical substance, they need to be disclosed only in the notes to the financial statements.
(b) Goodwill should be combined and reported with other intangible assets on the statement of financial position.
(c) Intangible assets are typically combined with property, plant, and equipment and reported in the "Property, Plant, and Equipment" section of the statement of financial position.
(d) Property, plant, and equipment; intangible assets; and goodwill should be separately reported on the statement of financial position.

(SO 7) 10. Which of the following ratios helps determine how efficiently a company uses its assets?
(a) Current ratio
(b) Profit margin
(c) Debt to total assets
(d) Asset turnover

Questions

(SO 1) 1. (a) Susan Leung is uncertain about how to determine the cost of property, plant, and equipment. Explain this for her. (b) Susan is also wondering what an asset retirement cost is and how that affects the cost of property, plant, and equipment.

(SO 1) 2. Deer Fern Inc. purchases equipment and incurs a number of expenditures before it is ready to use the equipment. Give two examples of operating expenditures and two examples of capital expenditures and explain how these expenditures on new equipment would be recorded and why.

(SO 1) 3. What are land improvements? Should the cost of clearing and grading land be recorded as a land improvement or not? Why or why not?

(SO 1) 4. Explain the difference between an operating lease and a finance lease. What amounts are recorded on the financial statements for each type of lease?

(SO 2) 5. In a recent press release, the president of Anwar Inc. stated that something has to be done about depreciation. The president said, "Depreciation does not come close to accumulating the cash needed to replace the asset at the end of its useful life." What is your response to the president?

(SO 2) 6. Contrast the effects of the three depreciation methods on (1) depreciation expense, (2) profit, (3) accumulated depreciation, and (4) carrying amount in each of the following: (a) the early years of an asset's life, and (b) over the total life of the asset.

(SO 2) 7. Why is the depreciable amount (the asset's cost less residual value) used in the straight-line and units-of-production methods but not in the diminishing-balance method?

(SO 2) 8. Why must the calculation of depreciation be adjusted for any fraction of a year since purchase when the straight-line and diminishing-balance methods are used, but no adjustment is needed when the units-of-production method is used?

(SO 2, 3) 9. What factors should a company consider when choosing a depreciation method? When revising a depreciation method?

(SO 3) 10. Lucien Corporation uses straight-line depreciation for financial reporting purposes but CCA (the single diminishing-balance method) for income tax purposes. (a) What is the major difference between CCA and other forms of depreciation? (b) Is it acceptable to use different methods for financial reporting and income tax purposes? Why is Lucien likely doing this?

(SO 3) 11. (a) What factors could contribute to an impairment loss? (b) In what circumstances, if any, is a company using IFRS allowed to write up its property, plant, and equipment? (c) Would your answers to (a) and (b) change if the company used ASPE rather than IFRS?

(SO 3) 12. How do impairment losses and capital expenditures during a depreciable asset's useful life affect the factors that are used in annual depreciation calculations? What impact might this have on the annual depreciation expense?

(SO 3) 13. Can impairment losses be reversed under IFRS? Can they be reversed under ASPE? Why?

(SO 3) 14. Describe the differences between the revaluation and valuation models allowed under IFRS.

(SO 4) 15. If equipment is sold in the middle of a fiscal year, why does depreciation have to be updated for the partial period? Doesn't the journal entry to record the sale subsequently remove the accumulated depreciation from the books anyway?

(SO 4) 16. How is a gain or loss on the sale of property, plant, or equipment calculated? Is the calculation the same for the retirement of property, plant, or equipment?

(SO 4) 17. Rashid Corporation owns a machine that is fully depreciated but is still being used. How should Rashid account for this asset and report it in the financial statements?

(SO 5) 18. Heflin Corporation has been amortizing its finite-life intangible assets over their legal life. The company's accountant argues that this is appropriate because an intangible asset's legal life is known with certainty, but the useful life of an intangible asset is subjective. Why is this not correct, and what impact might it have on the company's financial statements?

(SO 5) 19. Two years ago, Pesowski Corp. purchased a patent for $5 million that allows the company to produce and sell a special video game controller. During the year, the company determined that Sucha Ltd. was producing and selling an identical game controller. Pesowski spent $500,000 on legal fees to successfully enforce its rights under the patent. How should Pesowski account for the legal fees and why?

(SO 5) 20. Why are intangible assets with a finite life amortized, but intangible assets with an indefinite life are not?

(SO 5) 21. Bob Leno, a business student, is working on a case for one of his classes. The company in the case needs to raise cash to market a new product it has developed. His roommate Saul Cain, an engineering student, takes one look at the company's statement of financial position and says, "This company has an awful lot of goodwill. Why don't you recommend that they sell some of it to raise cash?" How should Bob respond to Saul?

(SO 6) 22. Explain how long-lived assets and transactions relating to them should be reported on (a) the statement of financial position, (b) the income statement, and (c) the statement of cash flows.

(SO 6) 23. What information about long-lived assets should be disclosed in the notes to the financial statements?

(SO 7) 24. Give an example of an industry that would be characterized by (a) a high asset turnover and low profit margin, and (b) a low asset turnover and high profit margin.

(SO 7) 25. How can the profit margin and asset turnover ratios be used to help explain the return on assets?

(SO 7) 26. In 2010, Tim Hortons Inc. reported net sales of U.S. $1,755 million, and average total assets of U.S. $2,288 million. In 2009, its net sales were U.S. $1,704 million and average total assets, U.S. $2,043 million. How effective has the company been at generating sales from its assets over these two years?

Brief Exercises

BE9–1 These expenditures were incurred by Shumway Ltd. in purchasing land: cash price $50,000; legal fees $2,500; clearing and grading $3,500; installation of fence $3,000. What is the cost of the land? Determine cost. (SO 1)

BE9–2 Basler Ltd. incurs these expenditures in purchasing a truck: invoice price $42,000; installation of a trailer hitch $1,000; one-year accident insurance policy $2,000; motor vehicle licence $150; painting and lettering $750. What is the cost of the truck? Determine cost. (SO 1)

Identify operating and capital expenditures.
(SO 1)

BE9–3   Indicate whether each of the following items is an operating expenditure (O) or a capital expenditure (C). If the expenditure is neither, write NA for "not applicable" in the space provided.

(a) _____ Repaired building roof, $1,500
(b) _____ Replaced building roof, $27,500
(c) _____ Purchased building, $480,000
(d) _____ Purchased supplies, $350
(e) _____ Purchased truck, $55,000
(f) _____ Purchased oil and gas for truck, $155

(g) _____ Replaced tires on truck, $500
(h) _____ Anticipated retirement costs for plant, $5,000,000
(i) _____ Added new wing to building, $250,000
(j) _____ Painted interior of building, $1,500
(k) _____ Rebuilt engine on truck, $7,500
(l) _____ Upgraded air conditioning system, $10,000

Calculate straight-line depreciation.
(SO 2)

BE9–4   Buckingham Ltd. purchases a delivery truck on January 1, 2012, at a cost of $86,000. The truck is expected to have a residual value of $6,000 at the end of its four-year useful life. Buckingham has a December 31 year end. Calculate the depreciation using the straight-line method (a) for each year of the truck's life, and (b) in total over the truck's life.

Calculate partial-year straight-line depreciation.
(SO 2)

BE9–5   Depreciation information for Buckingham Ltd. is given in BE9–4. Assuming the delivery truck was purchased on May 3, 2012, calculate the depreciation expense using the straight-line method for 2012, 2013, and 2016.

Calculate diminishing-balance depreciation.
(SO 2)

BE9–6   Depreciation information for Buckingham Ltd. is given in BE9–4. Using the diminishing-balance method and assuming the depreciation rate is equal to one time the straight-line rate, calculate the depreciation (a) for 2012 and 2013, and (b) in total over the truck's life.

Calculate partial-year diminishing-balance depreciation.
(SO 2)

BE9–7   Depreciation information for Buckingham Ltd. is given in BE9–4. Assuming the delivery truck was purchased on May 3, 2012, calculate the depreciation expense using the diminishing-balance method for 2012 and 2013. Assume the depreciation rate is equal to one time the straight-line rate.

Calculate units-of-production depreciation.
(SO 2)

BE9–8   Speedy Taxi Service uses the units-of-production method to calculate depreciation on its taxicabs. Each cab is expected to be driven 325,000 km. Taxi 10 was purchased on March 1, 2011, for $33,000 and is expected to have a residual value of $500. Taxi 10 was driven 125,000 km in 2011 and 105,000 km in 2012. Speedy Taxi Service has a December 31 year end. Calculate the depreciation expense on Taxi 10 for each year.

Record impairment loss.
(SO 3)

BE9–9   Fortune Cookie Corporation owns equipment that cost $90,000 and has accumulated depreciation of $54,000. The equipment's recoverable amount is $30,000. Prepare the journal entry to record the impairment loss.

Explain depreciation revision and impairment.
(SO 3)

BE9–10   Tibble Corporation recently determined that the recoverable value of one of its milling machines is less than its current carrying amount. In addition, the machine's useful life is now expected to be three years less than what the company had originally estimated. Explain how the impairment loss and the reduction in useful life will affect the company's annual depreciation expense calculation and the accumulated depreciation account balance for (a) previous years, (b) the current year, and (c) future years.

Record sale of equipment.
(SO 4)

BE9–11   Johnson Limited sells office equipment on September 30, 2012, for $42,000 cash. The office equipment originally cost $144,000 when purchased on January 1, 2009. It has an estimated residual value of $4,000 and a useful life of five years. Depreciation was last recorded on December 31, 2011, the company's year end. Prepare the journal entries to (a) update depreciation using the straight-line method to September 30, 2012, and (b) record the sale of the equipment.

Record retirement of equipment.
(SO 4)

BE9–12   Ruiz Ltd. retires delivery equipment that cost $42,000. Prepare journal entries to record the transaction if accumulated depreciation is (a) $42,000, and (b) $40,000.

Evaluate goodwill.
(SO 5)

BE9–13   In its unadjusted trial balance, Boxer Limited had assets of $800,000 and liabilities of $200,000. An appraisal of the assets indicated that their fair value was $100,000 more than the carrying amount shown on the trial balance. The liabilities' fair value was equal to their carrying value. Mandrake Inc. made an offer to purchase Boxer Limited. When such offers are made, the purchaser, Mandrake Inc., receives all of the assets and also assumes the liabilities of Boxer. The value of the assets of $900,000 less the value of the liabilities of $200,000 is $700,000 yet Mandrake offered $840,000. Why was the offer so high? What is the difference between the $840,000 and the $700,000 called?

Record patent transactions; show statement presentation.
(SO 5, 6)

BE9–14   Surkis Corporation purchased a patent for $180,000 cash on April 2, 2012. Its legal life is 20 years and its estimated useful life is 10 years. (a) Prepare the journal entry to record the (1) purchase of the patent on January 2, 2012, and (2) amortization for the first year ended December 31, 2012. (b) Show how the patent would be reported on the statement of financial position at December 31.

Classify long-lived assets.
(SO 6)

BE9–15   Indicate whether each of the following items should be recorded as property, plant, and equipment (PPE) or an intangible asset (I) on the statement of financial position. If the asset does not fit either of these categories, write NA for "not applicable" in the space provided.

(a)	___ Building	(i)	___ Operating lease
(b)	___ Franchise	(j)	___ Machinery
(c)	___ Inventory	(k)	___ Parking lot
(d)	___ Common shares	(l)	___ Patent
(e)	___ Land	(m)	___ Research costs
(f)	___ Land held for sale	(n)	___ Trademark
(g)	___ Licence right	(o)	___ Asset retirement cost for a building
(h)	___ Cash		

BE9–16 **Canadian Tire Corporation, Limited** reported the following selected information about long-lived assets at January 1, 2011 (in millions):

Prepare partial statement of financial position.
(SO 6)

Accumulated amortization—asset under finance lease	$ 20.2
Accumulated amortization—buildings	960.2
Accumulated amortization—fixtures and equipment	488.2
Accumulated amortization—leasehold improvements	181.6
Asset under finance lease	60.5
Buildings	2,605.6
Construction in progress	128.4
Fixtures and equipment	736.8
Goodwill	71.9
Land	785.8
Leasehold improvements	552.9
Mark's Work Wearhouse indefinite-life intangibles	58.4

Prepare the property, plant, and equipment section of the statement of financial position for Canadian Tire.

BE9–17 **Gildan Activewear Inc.** reported net sales (in U.S. millions) of $1,311 in 2010 and $1,038 in 2009. The company also reported a profit of $198 in 2010 and $95 in 2009. Assets at the end of 2010 were $1,321; at the end of 2009, $1,074; and at the end of 2008, $1,095. (a) Calculate Gildan's asset turnover, profit margin, and return on assets for 2011 and 2010. (b) Comment on whether the return on assets changed primarily due to a changing asset turnover or a changing profit margin.

Calculate and evaluate ratios.
(SO 7)

Exercises

E9–1 The following expenditures relating to property, plant, and equipment were made by Bachinski Ltd.:

Classify expenditures.
(SO 1)

1. Paid $600,000 for a plant site.
2. Paid $8,000 of legal fees on the purchase of the plant site.
3. Paid $33,000 to demolish an old building on the plant site; residual materials were sold for $5,000.
4. Paid $35,000 for paving the parking lot on the plant site.
5. Paid $37,600 in architect fees for the design of the new plant.
6. Promised to pay $50,000 in restoration costs when the company is finished using the plant site.
7. Paid $90,000 for a new delivery truck.
8. Paid $5,000 to have the company name and advertising slogan painted on the new truck.
9. Paid an $80 motor vehicle licence fee on the new truck.
10. Paid $1,800 for a one-year accident insurance policy on the new truck.

Instructions
(a) Explain what types of expenditures should be included in determining the cost of property, plant, and equipment.
(b) List the numbers of the above transactions, and beside each number write the account title that the expenditure should be debited to.

E9–2 Hohnberger Enterprises purchased equipment on March 15, 2012, for $75,000. The company also paid the following amounts: $1,000 for delivery charges; $200 for insurance while the equipment was in transit; $1,800 for a one-year insurance policy; $2,100 to train employees to use the new equipment; and $2,800 for testing and installation. The equipment was ready for use on April 1, 2012, but the company did not start using it until May 1, 2012.

Calculate cost and depreciation.
(SO 1, 2)

Hohnberger has estimated the equipment will have a 10-year useful life with no residual value. It expects to consume the equipment's future economic benefits evenly over the useful life. The company has a December 31 year end.

Instructions
(a) Calculate the cost of the equipment.
(b) When should the company begin depreciating the equipment: March 15, April 1, or May 1? Why?

(c) Which depreciation method should the company use? Why?

(d) Using the method chosen in (c), calculate the depreciation on the equipment for 2012.

Calculate and compare depreciation under different methods.
(SO 2)

E9–3 Intercity Bus Lines Inc. purchased a bus on January 1, 2011, at a cost of $410,000. The company estimated that the bus will have a residual value of $10,000. The bus is expected to be driven 500,000 km during its 10-year life. The company has a December 31 year end.

Instructions

(a) Calculate the depreciation expense under the straight-line method for 2011 and 2012.

(b) Calculate the depreciation expense under the diminishing-balance method, using double the straight-line rate, for 2011 and 2012.

(c) Calculate the depreciation expense under the units-of-production method, assuming the actual distance driven was 44,800 km for 2011, and 60,300 km for 2012.

(d) Based on this information, which depreciation method should Intercity Bus Lines use? Explain.

Calculate and compare depreciation under different methods.
(SO 2)

E9–4 Cirrus Ltd. purchased a new machine on April 4, 2011, at a cost of $172,000. The company estimated that the machine would have a residual value of $16,000. The machine is expected to be used for 10,000 working hours during its four-year life. Actual machine usage was 500 hours in 2011; 2,800 hours in 2012; 2,900 hours in 2013; 2,600 hours in 2014; and 1,200 hours in 2015. Cirrus Ltd. has a December 31 year end.

Instructions

(a) Calculate depreciation for the machine under each of the following methods: (1) straight-line, (2) diminishing-balance using double the straight-line rate, and (3) units-of-production.

(b) Which method results in the highest depreciation expense over the life of the asset?

(c) Which method results in the highest cash flow over the life of the asset?

Discuss implications of changing depreciation methods.
(SO 2)

E9–5 Solinger Limited has just hired a new CFO. The CFO has reviewed the accounting policies relating to depreciation and has suggested to the audit committee that the straight-line method that is currently in use should be changed to a diminishing-balance approach since most of the depreciable assets are relatively new. The company is considering the possibility of "going public" and selling an issue of new shares on a stock exchange to finance its expansion.

Instructions

Write a short memo to the audit committee explaining:

(a) the effect that this change will have on the income statement and statement of financial position in the current year, prior year, and future years;

(b) your opinion as to whether this change is appropriate;

(c) why the CFO proposed the change; and

(d) whether the committee needs any additional information before making a decision to support or reject the CFO's proposal.

Calculate straight-line depreciation; discuss revision of estimate.
(SO 2, 3)

E9–6 At the beginning of 2012, Lindy Weink, the new controller of Lafrenière Inc., reviewed the expected useful life and residual value of two of the company's machines and proposed changes as follows:

Date Acquired	Cost	Useful Life (in years) Original	Proposed	Residual Value Original	Proposed
Jan. 1, 2002	$800,000	20	25	$40,000	$62,000
Jan. 1, 2010	$120,000	5	4	$ 5,000	$ 3,600

Instructions

(a) Calculate the annual depreciation for each asset using the straight-line method and the original useful life and residual value.

(b) Calculate the accumulated depreciation and carrying amount of each asset on December 31, 2012.

(c) If the company accepts Lindy's proposed changes in useful life and residual value, will depreciation expense for each asset in 2012 be higher or lower than depreciation expense in 2011? Explain.

Record impairment loss; discuss presentation.
(SO 3, 6)

E9–7 Penang Corporation is a public company that purchased some equipment on January 1, 2010, for $850,000. It had an estimated useful life of eight years and a $50,000 residual value. Penang uses straight-line depreciation and has a December 31 year end. At December 31, 2012, management tested the asset for impairment. The equipment's recoverable amount was $320,000.

Instructions·

(a) Calculate the equipment's carrying amount at December 31, 2012, before any impairment loss is recorded.

(b) Record the impairment loss.

(c) How should the impairment loss be reported in the financial statements?

(d) Assuming that the equipment is used throughout 2013, what would the depreciation expense be for that year?

(e) At the end of 2013, could the impairment loss be reversed? Would the amount of the reversal be exactly equal to the answer in (b) above? If not, what would it be?

E9–8 Presented here are selected transactions for Spector Limited for 2012. Spector uses straight-line depreciation.

Jan. 1 Sold a delivery truck for $10,000 cash. The truck cost $62,000 when it was purchased on January 1, 2010, and was depreciated based on a four-year useful life with a $6,000 residual value.

Sept. 1 Sold computers that were purchased on January 1, 2010. They cost $10,980 and had a useful life of three years with no residual value. The computers were sold for $1,500 cash.

Dec. 30 Retired equipment that was purchased on January 1, 2003. The equipment cost $150,000 and had a useful life of 10 years with no residual value.

Instructions
Record the above transactions.

E9–9 Shown below are the T accounts relating to equipment that was purchased in cash by a company on the first day of the current year. The equipment was depreciated on a straight-line basis with an estimated useful life of 10 years and a residual value of $100. Some of the equipment was sold on the last day of the year for cash proceeds while some other equipment not sold became impaired.

Cash		Equipment		Accumulated Depreciation	
	Jan. 1 1,100	Jan. 1 1,100			Dec. 31 100
Dec. 31 450			Dec. 31 440	Dec. 31 40	Dec. 31 55

Depreciation Expense	Gain on Disposal	Impairment Loss
?	?	?

Instructions
Based on the information provided, derive the value of the missing amounts in the income statement accounts.

E9–10 Rahim Corporation purchased a boardroom table for $5,000. The company planned to keep it for four years, after which it was expected to be sold for $500.

Instructions
(a) Calculate the depreciation expense for each of the first three years under (1) the straight-line method, and (2) the double diminishing-balance method.
(b) Assuming Rahim sold the table for $1,225 at the end of the third year, calculate the gain or loss on disposal under each depreciation method.
(c) Determine the impact on profit (total depreciation of the table plus any loss on disposal or less any gain on disposal) of each method over the entire three-year period.

E9–11 Collins Ltd. has these transactions related to intangible assets and goodwill in 2012, its first year of operations:

Jan. 2   Purchased a patent with an estimated useful life of five years and a legal life of 20 years for $40,000.
Apr. 1   Acquired another company and recorded goodwill of $300,000 as part of the purchase.
July 1   Acquired a franchise for $250,000. The franchise agreement expires on July 1, 2019.
Sept. 1 Incurred research costs of $150,000.
30   Incurred development costs of $50,000. No marketable product has been identified as yet.
Dec. 31 Recorded annual amortization.
31   Tested the intangible assets for impairment. Recoverable amounts exceeded carrying amounts in all cases. Also tested goodwill and determined that it had a recoverable amount of $270,000.

Instructions
(a) Prepare the entries to record the above transactions. Assume all costs incurred were for cash.
(b) Show the presentation of the intangible assets and goodwill on the statement of financial position at December 31, 2012.

E9–12 A co-op student, Toni Johnston, encountered the following situations at Chin Chin Corporation, a publicly traded company:

1. Toni learned that Chin Chin is depreciating its buildings and equipment, but not its land. She could not understand why land was omitted, so she prepared journal entries to depreciate all the company's property, plant, and equipment for the current year end.
2. Toni determined that Chin Chin's amortization policy on its intangible assets was wrong. The company was amortizing its patents but not its goodwill. She fixed that for the current year end by adding goodwill to her adjusting entry

for amortization. She told a fellow student that she felt she had improved the consistency of the company's accounting policies by making these changes.

3. Chin Chin has a building still in use that has a zero carrying amount but a substantial fair value. Toni felt that this practice did not benefit the company's users—especially the bank—and wrote the building up to its fair value. After all, she reasoned, you can write down assets if fair values are lower. Writing them up if fair value is higher is yet another example of the improved consistency that her employment has brought to the company's accounting practices.

Instructions

Explain whether or not the accounting treatment in each of the above situations is appropriate. If an accounting principle or assumption has been violated, explain what the appropriate accounting treatment should be.

Classify long-lived accounts; prepare partial statement of financial position. (SO 6)

E9–13   Air Canada reported the following selected information as at December 31, 2010 (in millions):

	Amount
Accumulated depreciation—assets under finance leases	$ 853
Accumulated depreciation—buildings, including leasehold improvements	228
Accumulated depreciation—flight equipment, including spare engines	1,758
Accumulated depreciation—ground and other equipment	76
Accumulated amortization—other finite life intangible assets	276
Accumulated amortization—Star Alliance membership	42
Additions to capital assets	118
Air Canada and other trade names	276
Assets under finance leases	1,959
Buildings, including leasehold improvements	702
Depreciation, amortization and obsolescence expense	679
Flight equipment, including spare engines	5,797
Loss on disposal of assets	7
Ground and other equipment	170
International route rights and slots	310
Other finite life intangible assets	418
Proceeds from the sale of assets	29
Star Alliance membership	125

Instructions

(a) Identify in which financial statement (statement of financial position, income statement, or statement of cash flows) and which section (e.g., property, plant, and equipment) each of the above items should be reported.

(b) Prepare the property, plant, and equipment and intangible assets sections of the statement of financial position as at December 31, 2010.

Calculate and evaluate ratios. (SO 7)

E9–14   Ajax Limited reported the following information (in millions) at December 31, 2012: net sales $14,000; profit $350; total assets at December 31, 2012, $7,200; and total assets at December 31, 2011, $6,800.

Instructions

(a) Calculate the following ratios for the year: (1) return on assets, (2) asset turnover, and (3) profit margin.

(b) By showing the appropriate calculation, prove mathematically how the profit margin and asset turnover work together to explain the return on assets.

(c) On average, the ratio values for Ajax's competitors are: return on assets 4.5%, asset turnover 1.5 times, and profit margin 3.0%. Compare these with those of Ajax and determine if Ajax is performing better than the industry.

Explain effect of events on ratios. (SO 7)

E9–15   Complete the table below by inserting the applicable letter in each box—"I" for increase, "D" for decrease, "N" for no effect, and "CD" for cannot determine—to describe the effect of each isolated event on all of the ratios in the column headings:

Event	Profit Margin	Asset Turnover	Return on Assets
(a) Aging assets are not being replaced.			
(b) Operating expenses have been cut due to efficiencies.			
(c) The company has increased prices of products with no reduction in the number of products sold.			
(d) Depreciation method was changed from straight-line to diminishing balance; assets are quite new.			
(e) The government has raised the income tax rate.			
(f) A major upgrade of assets has occurred.			

Problems: Set A

P9-1A   In 2012, Westlake Ltd. had the following transactions related to the purchase of property. Assume all transactions are for cash unless otherwise stated.

Determine cost; record property transactions.
(SO 1, 2, 3)

Feb. 7	Purchased real estate for $550,000, paying $150,000 cash and signing a mortgage payable for the balance. The site had an old building on it and the fair values of the land and building were $500,000 and $50,000, respectively. Westlake intends to construct an apartment building on the site.
9	Paid legal fees of $11,000 on the real estate purchase of February 7.
15	Paid $30,000 to demolish the old building and make the land ready for the construction of the apartment building.
17	Received $8,000 from the sale of material from the demolished building.
Mar. 2	Paid architect fees on the apartment building of $36,000.
July 5	The full cost for construction of the apartment building was $1.3 million. Paid $340,000 cash and signed a bank loan payable for the balance.
Aug. 22	Paid $24,000 for sidewalks and a parking lot for the building.
Sept. 1	Purchased a one-year insurance policy on the finished building for $5,000.

Instructions
(a) Record the transactions.
(b) Determine the cost of the land, land improvements, and building that will appear on Westlake's December 31, 2012, statement of financial position.
(c) When would depreciation begin on the items recorded above?
(d) Under IFRS, could the company adopt a model that does not require depreciation? Under ASPE?

P9-2A   The transactions that follow are expenditures related to property, plant, and equipment:

Classify expenditures.
(SO 1)

1. Operator controls on equipment were replaced for $7,000, because the original control devices were not adequate.
2. A total of $4,600 was spent for decorative landscaping (planting flowers and shrubs, etc.).
3. A new air conditioning system for the factory office was purchased for $16,000.
4. Windows broken in a labour dispute were replaced for $2,400.
5. A fee of $1,500 was paid for adjusting and testing new machinery before its use.
6. Machinery damaged by a forklift was repaired for $5,000.
7. The transmission in a delivery truck was repaired for $2,500.
8. Expenditures totalling $3,000 were incurred to repaint the exterior of the factory.

Instructions
For each of the transactions listed above, indicate the title of the account that you think should be debited in recording the transaction. Briefly explain your reasoning.

P9-3A   Mazlin Limited purchased a machine on account on April 2, 2012, at an invoice price of $360,000. On April 4, it paid $2,000 for delivery of the machine. A one-year, $4,000 insurance policy on the machine was purchased on April 5. On April 18, Mazlin paid $8,000 for installation and testing of the machine. The machine was ready for use on April 30.

Determine cost; calculate depreciation under different methods.
(SO 1, 2, 3)

   Mazlin estimates the machine's useful life will be five years with a residual value of $80,000. Mazlin has a December 31 year end.

Instructions
(a) Determine the cost of the machine.
(b) Calculate the annual depreciation and total depreciation over the asset's life using (1) straight-line depreciation, (2) double diminishing-balance depreciation, and (3) single diminishing-balance depreciation. Which method causes profit to be lower in the early years of the asset's life?
(c) Assume instead that, when Mazlin Limited purchased the machine, there was no residual value and the company had a legal obligation to ensure that the machine would be recycled at the end of its useful life. The cost of the recycling will be significant. Would this have an impact on the answers to (a) and (b) above? Explain.

P9-4A   Whitley Corporation purchased machinery on January 1, 2012, at a cost of $450,000. The machinery's estimated useful life is four years or 350,000 units, with a residual value of $12,500. The machine actually produces 115,000 units in 2012; 95,000 units in 2013; 75,000 units in 2014; and 65,000 units in 2015. The company is considering which depreciation method should be used for financial reporting purposes.

Calculate and compare depreciation under different methods.
(SO 2)

Instructions
(a) Prepare separate depreciation schedules for the life of the machinery using the straight-line and units-of-production methods.

(b) Which method would result in the lower profit for 2012? In the lower total profit over the four-year period?

(c) Which method would result in the lower carrying amount at the end of 2012? In the lower carrying amount at the end of the four-year period?

(d) Which method would result in the lower cash flow for 2012? In the lower total cash flow over the four-year period?

(e) What factors should management consider when deciding on the appropriate depreciation method?

Calculate and compare depreciation under different methods.
(SO 2)

P9–5A Valmont Limited purchased high-tech equipment on March 27, 2012, at a cost of $122,000. Management is contemplating the merits of using the diminishing-balance or units-of-production method of depreciation instead of the straight-line method, which it currently uses for other equipment. The new equipment has an estimated residual value of $2,000 and an estimated useful life of either three years or 30,000 units. Demand for the products produced by the equipment is sporadic so the equipment will be used in some years more than others. Assume the equipment produces the following number of units each year: 7,400 units in 2012; 10,200 units in 2013; 9,900 units in 2014; and 2,500 units in 2015. Valmont has a December 31 year end.

Instructions

(a) Prepare separate depreciation schedules for the life of the equipment using the straight-line method, the double diminishing-balance method, and the units-of-production method.

(b) Compare the total depreciation expense and accumulated depreciation under each of the three methods over the life of the equipment.

(c) How does each different method of depreciation affect the company's cash flows?

(d) Which method do you recommend? Why?

Determine effect of depreciation method over life of asset.
(SO 2, 4)

P9–6A Yukon Productions Corp. purchased equipment on March 1, 2012, for $70,000. The company estimated the equipment would have a useful life of three years and produce 12,000 units, with a residual value of $10,000. During 2012, the equipment produced 4,900 units. On November 30, 2013, the machine was sold for $18,000 and had produced 5,600 units that year.

Instructions

(a) Record all the necessary entries for the years ended December 31, 2012 and 2013, using the following depreciation methods: (1) straight-line, (2) single diminishing-balance, and (3) units-of-production.

(b) Prepare a schedule to show the overall impact of the total depreciation expense, combined with the gain or loss on sale, for the two-year period, under each method of depreciation (consider the total effect on profit over the two-year period). Comment on your results.

Record property, plant, and equipment transactions; prepare partial statement of financial position.
(SO 2, 4, 6)

P9–7A At January 1, 2012, Youngstown Limited reported the following property, plant, and equipment accounts:

Accumulated depreciation—buildings	$ 62,200,000
Accumulated depreciation—equipment	54,000,000
Buildings	97,400,000
Equipment	150,000,000
Land	20,000,000

The company uses straight-line depreciation for buildings and equipment, and its year end is December 31. The buildings are estimated to have a 40-year useful life and no residual value; the equipment is estimated to have a 10-year useful life and no residual value. Interest on the notes (described below) is due annually on the anniversary date of the issue. During 2012, the following selected transactions occurred:

Apr. 1	Purchased land for $4.4 million. Paid $1.1 million cash and issued a three-year, 6% note for the balance.
May 1	Sold equipment for $300,000 cash. The equipment cost $2.8 million when originally purchased on January 1, 2004.
June 1	Sold land for $3.6 million. Received $900,000 cash and accepted a three-year, 5% note for the balance. The land cost $1.4 million when purchased on June 1, 2006.
July 1	Purchased equipment for $2.2 million cash.
Dec. 31	Retired equipment that cost $1 million when purchased on December 31, 2002.

Instructions

(a) Record the above transactions.

(b) Record any adjusting entries required at December 31.

(c) Prepare the property, plant, and equipment section of the company's statement of financial position at December 31, 2012.

Calculate depreciation; discuss revision of estimate.
(SO 2, 3)

P9–8A On January 1, 2010, Penaji Corporation acquired equipment costing $65,000. It was estimated at that time that this equipment would have a useful life of eight years and a residual value of $3,000. The straight-line method of depreciation is used by the company for its equipment, and its year end is December 31.

At the beginning of 2012 (the beginning of the third year of the equipment's life), the company's engineers reconsidered their expectations. They estimated that the equipment's useful life would more likely be six years in total, instead of the previously estimated eight years.

Instructions

(a) Calculate the equipment's accumulated depreciation and carrying amount at the beginning of 2012 immediately before the change in useful life.

(b) Would you expect Penaji's depreciation expense to increase or decrease in 2012 after the change in useful life? Why?

(c) Should the company treat the change in useful life retroactively or only for current and future periods? Explain.

(d) If Penaji had *not* revised the equipment's remaining useful life at the beginning of 2012, what would its total depreciation expense have been over the equipment's life? What would have been the accumulated depreciation and carrying amount at the end of the equipment's useful life?

(e) Would you expect the company's total depreciation expense to change after the useful life has been revised? Would there be changes to the accumulated depreciation and carrying amount at the end of the equipment's useful life?

P9–9A   Altona Limited purchased delivery equipment on March 1, 2010, for $130,000 cash. At that time, the equipment was estimated to have a useful life of five years and a residual value of $10,000. The equipment was disposed of on September 30, 2012. Altona uses the diminishing-balance method with a 20% rate of depreciation and has an August 31 year end.

Record acquisition, depreciation, and disposal of equipment. (SO 2, 4)

Instructions

(a) Record the acquisition of equipment on March 1, 2010.

(b) Record depreciation at August 31, 2010, 2011, and 2012.

(c) Record the disposal of the equipment on September 30, 2012, under each of the following independent assumptions:
   1. It was sold for $60,000.
   2. It was sold for $80,000.
   3. It was retired.

P9–10A   Sugden Limited purchased land and a building on August 1, 2011, for $595,000. The company paid $200,000 in cash and signed a 5% bank loan payable for the balance. The bank loan is due April 1, 2013. At that time, Sugden estimated that the land was worth $340,000 and the building $255,000. The building was estimated to have a 40-year useful life with a $15,000 residual value. The company has a December 31 year end and uses the straight-line depreciation method for buildings. The following are related transactions and adjustments during the next three years:

Record acquisition, depreciation, impairment, and disposal of equipment. (SO 2, 3, 4)

2011
Dec. 31   Recorded the annual depreciation.
       31   Paid the interest owing on the bank loan.

2012
May   21   Paid $2,000 for repairs to the roof.
Dec. 31   Recorded the annual depreciation.
       31   Paid the interest owing on the bank loan.
       31   The land and building were tested for impairment. The land had a recoverable amount of $280,000 and the building $249,000.

2013
Mar. 31   Sold the land and building for $480,000 cash—$250,000 for the land and $230,000 for the building.
Apr.   1   Paid the bank loan and interest owing.

Instructions

(a) Record the above transactions and adjustments for each year.

(b) What factors may have been responsible for the impairment on December 31, 2012?

(c) Assume instead that the company sold the land and building on March 31, 2013, for $650,000 cash—$390,000 for the land and $260,000 for the building. Record the journal entry (or entries) to record the sale.

(d) Now assume that the land and building were not sold in 2013 and that by the end of December 31, 2013, the fair values of each were $390,000 and $260,000, respectively. Could the impairment loss recorded in 2012 be reversed under IFRS if the cost model were used? Could it be reversed if the revaluation model were used? Could it be reversed under ASPE?

P9–11A   Due to rapid employee turnover in the accounting department, the following transactions involving intangible assets and goodwill were recorded in a questionable way by the Stiles Corporation's accountant, Jim Lowenstein, in the year ended December 31, 2012:

Correct errors in recording intangible asset transactions. (SO 5)

   1. Stiles developed a new manufacturing process in the first quarter of the year, incurring costs of $320,000. Of this amount, 45% was considered to be development costs that could be capitalized while the rest were considered research

costs. The development phase ended on March 31. Jim recorded the entire $320,000 in the Equipment account and depreciated it over a 15-year useful life starting on January 1, 2012.

2. On July 1, 2012, Stiles purchased a small company and Jim recorded goodwill of $800,000 as part of the transaction. This was calculated by taking the purchase price of $4 million less the net carrying amount of the purchased company's assets and liabilities, which was $3.2 million, despite the fact that the fair value of some equipment with a 5-year life was $100,000 higher than their carrying amount. Jim recorded a half-year's amortization for the goodwill in 2012, based on an estimated 40-year life.

3. On March 1, 2012, the company purchased a trademark for $95,000. Shortly thereafter, it was sued for trademark infringement. At the end of the year, Jim determined that the recoverable amount of the trademark was $35,000. He did not record an impairment loss, because he is hopeful that the recoverable amount will rebound next year after the conclusion of the legal case defending the company's right to use this trademark.

4. The company made a $12,000 charitable donation on December 31, 2012, which was recorded with a debit to goodwill.

Instructions

Prepare the necessary journal entries to correct any errors made in recording the above transactions.

Record intangible asset transactions; prepare partial statement of financial position.
(SO 5, 6)

P9–12A   The intangible assets and goodwill reported by Ghani Corporation at December 31, 2011, follow:

Copyrights (#1)	$36,000	
Less: Accumulated amortization	24,000	$ 12,000
Trademark		54,000
Goodwill		125,000
Total		$191,000

The copyright (#1) was acquired on January 1, 2010, and has a useful life of three years. The trademark was acquired on January 1, 2008, and is expected to have an indefinite life. The company has a December 31 year end.

The following cash transactions may have affected intangible assets and goodwill during 2012:

Jan. 5   Paid $7,000 in legal costs to successfully defend the trademark against infringement by another company.

July 1   Developed a new product, incurring $210,000 in research and $50,000 in development costs. The development phase ended on July 1. The product is expected to have a useful life of 20 years.

Sept. 1   Paid $60,000 to a popular hockey player to appear in commercials advertising the company's products. The commercials will air in early September.

Oct. 1   Acquired another copyright (Copyright #2) for $180,000. The new copyright has a useful life of three years.

Dec. 31   Determined the recoverable amount of the trademark and goodwill to be $65,000 and $90,000, respectively. There was no indication that any other assets were impaired.

Instructions

(a) Prepare journal entries to record the transactions.

(b) Prepare any adjusting journal entries required at December 31.

(c) Show the presentation of the intangible assets and goodwill on the statement of financial position at December 31, 2012.

Calculate and evaluate ratios.
(SO 7)

P9–13A   Green Mountain Coffee Roasters, Inc. and Starbucks Corporation reported the following information in 2010 (in U.S. millions):

	Green Mountain	Starbucks
Total assets, 2010	$1,370.5	$ 6,385.9
Total assets, 2009	813.4	5,576.8
Net sales	1,356.7	10,707.4
Profit	79.5	945.6

Industry averages were as follows: profit margin, 4.7%; return on assets, 8.0%; and asset turnover, 1.7 times.

Instructions

(a) For each company, calculate the profit margin, return on assets, and asset turnover ratios for 2010.

(b) Based on your calculations in part (a), comment on how effectively each company is using its assets to generate sales and produce profit.

(c) What, if anything, complicates your ability to compare the two companies in (b)?

Calculate and evaluate ratios.
(SO 7)

P9–14A   Delicious Limited competes in the fast food industry with Scrumptious Limited. Delicious embarked on a major expansion in 2012, borrowing a large amount of money and acquiring a small competitor. The company did this because the price for the competitor was low due to increased competition. The acquisition doubled the number of restaurants that

Delicious has. Scrumptious, on the other hand, took a more conservative approach and did not buy any new assets, focusing instead on a strategy of making existing operations more efficient. Data for the two companies are provided below in millions of dollars:

	Delicious	Scrumptious
Total assets, 2012	$2,000	$ 800
Total assets, 2011	1,100	900
Total assets, 2010	1,000	1,000
Net sales, 2012	3,100	1,900
Net sales, 2011	1,500	1,700
Profit, 2012	350	180
Profit, 2011	150	200

Instructions
(a) Calculate the profit margin, asset turnover, and return on asset ratios for each company in 2011 and 2012.
(b) Provide an explanation for the year-over-year changes in the ratios calculated in (a).
(c) Comment on which company has been more successful in executing its strategy.

Problems: Set B

P9-1B In 2012, Kadmen Ltd. incurred the following transactions related to the purchase of a property. Assume all transactions are for cash unless otherwise stated.

*Determine cost; record property transactions.
(SO 1, 2, 3)*

Jan. 22	Purchased real estate for a future plant site for $440,000, paying $110,000 cash and signing a mortgage payable for the balance. There was an old building on the site. The fair values of the land and building were $340,000 and $100,000, respectively.
24	Paid $9,000 for legal fees on the real estate purchase.
31	Paid $50,000 to demolish the old building to make room for the new plant.
Feb. 13	Graded and filled the land at a cost of $16,000 in preparation for the construction.
28	Received $15,000 for residual materials from the demolished building.
Mar. 14	Paid $68,000 in architect fees for the building plans.
31	Paid the local municipality $10,000 for building permits and $20,000 for the 2012 property taxes.
Apr. 22	Excavation costs for the new building were $34,000.
June 15	Received a bill from the building contractor for half of the cost of the new building, $600,000. Paid $150,000 in cash and signed a bank loan payable for the balance.
Sept. 14	Received a bill for the remaining $600,000 owed to the building contractor for the construction of the new building. Paid $200,000 cash and signed a bank loan payable for the balance.
Oct. 12	Paved the parking lots, driveways, and sidewalks for $84,000.
20	Installed a fence for $16,000.

Instructions
(a) Record the transactions.
(b) Determine the cost of the land, land improvements, and building that will appear on Kadmen's December 31, 2012, statement of financial position.
(c) When will depreciation on the items recorded above begin?
(d) Under IFRS, would the company have the option of not depreciating any of these assets? Under ASPE?

P9-2B The following expenditures are for a forklift:

*Classify expenditures.
(SO 1)*

1. Rebuilding of the diesel engine, $10,000
2. New tires, $4,000
3. New safety cab, $5,000
4. Replacement of the windshield, $800
5. Training a new operator, $1,600
6. New paint job after the company changed its logo and colours, $2,000
7. One-year accident insurance policy, $1,110
8. Payment to an operator to reorganize where items were stored in the warehouse to increase efficiency, $2,400.

Instructions
For each of the transactions listed above, indicate the title of the account that you think should be debited in recording the transaction. Briefly explain your reasoning.

Determine cost; calculate depreciation under different methods.
(SO 1, 2, 3)

P9-3B Mouskori Limited purchased a machine on September 3, 2012, at a cash price of $187,800. On September 4, it paid $1,200 for delivery of the machine. A one-year, $1,950 insurance policy on the machine was purchased on September 6. On September 20, Mouskori paid $7,000 for installation and testing of the machine. The machine was ready for use on September 30.

Mouskori estimates the machine's useful life will be four years, or 40,000 units, with no residual value. Assume the equipment produces the following number of units each year: 2,500 units in 2012; 10,300 units in 2013; 9,900 units in 2014; 8,800 units in 2015; and 8,500 units in 2016. Mouskori has a December 31 year end.

Instructions
(a) Determine the cost of the machine.
(b) Calculate the annual depreciation and the total depreciation over the asset's life using (1) straight-line depreciation, (2) double diminishing-balance depreciation, and (3) units-of-production depreciation. Which method causes profit to be lower in the early years of the asset's life?
(c) Assume instead that, when Mouskori Corporation purchased the machine, the company had a legal obligation to ensure that the machine would be recycled at the end of its useful life and that the cost of this recycling would be significant. Would this have an impact on the answers to (a) and (b) above? Explain.

Calculate and compare depreciation under different methods.
(SO 2)

P9-4B Piper Corporation purchased machinery on January 1, 2012, at a cost of $280,000. The machinery's estimated useful life is five years, with a residual value of $10,000. The company is considering which depreciation method to use for financial reporting purposes.

Instructions
(a) Prepare separate depreciation schedules for the life of the machinery using the straight-line and double diminishing-balance methods.
(b) Which method would result in the higher profit for 2012? In the higher total profit over the five-year period?
(c) Which method would result in the higher carrying amount at the end of 2012? In the higher carrying amount at the end of the five-year period?
(d) Which method would result in the higher cash flow for 2012? In the higher total cash flow over the five-year period?
(e) What factors should management consider when deciding on the appropriate depreciation method?

Calculate and compare depreciation under different methods.
(SO 2)

P9-5B Fast Arrow Ltd. purchased a new bus on October 3, 2012, at a total cost of $130,000 each. Management is contemplating the merits of using the diminishing-balance or units-of-production methods of depreciation instead of the straight-line method, which it currently uses for other buses. The new bus has an estimated residual value of $10,000, and an estimated useful life of either three years or 300,000 km. Use of the bus will be sporadic so it could be much higher in some years than in other years. Assume the new bus is driven as follows: 15,000 km in 2012; 130,000 km in 2013; 65,000 km in 2014; and 90,000 km in 2015. Fast Arrow has an October 31 year end.

Instructions
(a) Prepare separate depreciation schedules for the life of the bus using the straight-line method, the double diminishing-balance method, and the units-of-production method.
(b) Compare the total depreciation expense and accumulated depreciation under each of the three methods over the life of the bus.
(c) How does each different method of depreciation affect the company's cash flows?
(d) Which method do you recommend? Why?

Determine effect of depreciation method over life of asset.
(SO 2, 4)

P9-6B PEI Productions Ltd. purchased equipment on February 1, 2012, for $50,000. The company estimated the equipment would have a useful life of three years and would produce 10,000 units, with a residual value of $10,000. During 2012, the equipment produced 4,000 units. On October 31, 2013, the machine was sold for $12,000; it had produced 5,000 units that year.

Instructions
(a) Record all the necessary entries for the years ended December 31, 2012 and 2013 for the following depreciation methods: (1) straight-line, (2) single diminishing-balance, and (3) units-of-production.
(b) Prepare a schedule to show the overall impact of the total depreciation expense, combined with the gain or loss on sale for the two-year period, under each method of depreciation (consider the total effect on profit over the two-year period). Comment on your results.

Record property, plant, and equipment transactions; prepare partial statement of financial position.
(SO 2, 4, 6)

P9-7B At January 1, 2012, Hammersmith Limited reported the following property, plant, and equipment accounts:

Accumulated depreciation—buildings	$24,200,000
Accumulated depreciation—equipment	30,000,000
Buildings	57,000,000
Equipment	96,000,000
Land	8,000,000

The company uses straight-line depreciation for buildings and equipment, and its year end is December 31. The buildings are estimated to have a 40-year life and no residual value; the equipment is estimated to have a 10-year useful life and no residual value. Interest on all notes is payable or collectible at maturity on the anniversary date of the issue.

During 2012, the following selected transactions occurred:

Apr. 1	Purchased land for $3.8 million. Paid $950,000 cash and issued a 10-year, 6% note for the balance.
May 1	Sold equipment for $700,000 cash. The equipment cost $1.5 million when it was originally purchased on January 1, 2008.
June 1	Sold land for $2.4 million. Received $760,000 cash and accepted a 6% note for the balance. The land cost $600,000 when purchased on June 1, 1996.
July 1	Purchased equipment for $2 million on account, terms n/60.
Sept. 2	Paid amount owing on account for purchase of equipment on July 1.
Dec. 31	Retired equipment that cost $940,000 when purchased on December 31, 2002.

Instructions

(a) Record the above transactions.
(b) Record any adjusting entries required at December 31.
(c) Prepare the property, plant, and equipment section of the company's statement of financial position at December 31, 2012.

P9–8B   On January 1, 2010, Bérubé Ltée acquired equipment costing $60,000. It was estimated at that time that this equipment would have a useful life of five years and a residual value of $4,500. The straight-line method of depreciation is used by Bérubé for its equipment, and its year end is December 31.

At the beginning of 2012 (the beginning of the third year of the equipment's life), the company's engineers reconsidered their expectations. They estimated that the equipment's useful life would more likely be seven years in total, instead of the previously estimated five years.

Calculate depreciation; discuss revision of estimate. (SO 2, 3)

Instructions

(a) Calculate the equipment's accumulated depreciation and carrying amount at the beginning of 2012, immediately before the change in useful life.
(b) Would you expect the company's depreciation expense to increase or decrease in 2012 after the change in useful life? Why?
(c) Should Bérubé treat the change in the useful life retroactively or only for current and future periods? Explain.
(d) If the company had *not* revised the equipment's remaining useful life at the beginning of 2012, what would its total depreciation expense have been over the equipment's life? What would have been the accumulated depreciation and carrying amount at the end of the equipment's useful life?
(e) Would you expect Bérubé's total depreciation expense to change after the useful life has been revised? Would there be changes to the accumulated depreciation and carrying amount at the end of the equipment's useful life?

P9–9B   Balmoral Limited purchased equipment on January 1, 2010, for $170,000 on account. At that time, the equipment was estimated to have a useful life of five years and a $2,000 residual value. The equipment was disposed of on June 1, 2012, when the company relocated to new premises. Walker uses the diminishing-balance method with a 20% rate of depreciation and has a September 30 year end.

Record acquisition, depreciation, and disposal of equipment. (SO 2, 4)

Instructions

(a) Record the acquisition of the equipment on January 1, 2010.
(b) Record the depreciation at September 30, 2010 and 2011.
(c) Record the disposal of the equipment on June 2, 2012, under each of the following independent assumptions:
   1. It was sold for $105,000.
   2. It was sold for $80,000.
   3. It was retired.

P9–10B   Arnison Corp. purchased land and a building on May 1, 2011, for $385,000. The company paid $115,000 in cash and signed a 5% note payable for the balance. The note is due on February 1, 2013. At that time, Arnison estimated that the land was worth $150,000 and the building $235,000. The building was estimated to have a 25-year useful life with a $35,000 residual value. The company has a December 31 year end and uses the single diminishing-balance depreciation method (where the rate is 1 ÷ the life of the asset) for buildings. The following are related transactions and adjustments during the next three years:

Record acquisition, depreciation, impairment, and disposal of equipment. (SO 2, 3, 4)

2011
Dec. 31	Recorded the annual depreciation.
31	Paid the interest owing on the note payable.

<u>2012</u>
Feb. 17 Paid $225 to have the furnace cleaned and serviced.
Dec. 31 Recorded the annual depreciation.
  31 Paid the interest owing on the note payable.
  31 The land and building were tested for impairment. The land had
    a recoverable amount of $120,000 and the building $240,000.

<u>2013</u>
Jan. 31 Sold the land and building for $320,000 cash—$110,000 for the
   land and $210,000 for the building.
Feb. 1 Paid the note payable and interest owing.

Instructions

(a) Record the above transactions and adjustments.

(b) What factors may have been responsible for the impairment?

(c) Assume instead that the company sold the land and building on January 31, 2013, for $400,000 cash—$160,000 for the land and $240,000 for the building. Record the journal entry (or entries) to record the sale.

(d) Now assume that the land and building were not sold in 2013 and that by the end of December 31, 2013, the fair values of each were $160,000 and $240,000, respectively. At the end of the year, could the impairment loss recorded in 2012 be reversed under IFRS if the cost model were used? Could it be reversed if the revaluation model were used? Could it be reversed under ASPE?

Correct errors in recording intangible asset transactions.
(SO 5)

P9–11B Due to rapid employee turnover in the accounting department, the following transactions involving intangible assets and goodwill were recorded in a questionable way by Rachael Summers, a new accountant who was just hired by Balty Ltd. in the year ended December 31, 2012:

1. Balty developed an electronic monitoring device for running shoes which should have a useful life of three years. It incurred research costs of $140,000 and development costs with probable future benefits of $90,000. The development phase ended on May 1, 2012. Rachael recorded all of these costs in the Patent account.

2. The company registered the patent for the "cyber shoe" device developed in transaction 1 above on February 1, 2012. Legal fees and registration costs totalled $44,000. These costs were recorded in the Legal Fees Expense account.

3. During May the company successfully fought off a competitor in court to defend its patent, incurring $76,000 of legal fees. These costs were also debited to the Legal Fees Expense account.

4. The company recorded $11,500 of annual amortization for the patent over its legal life of 20 years [$140,000 + $90,000 = $230,000 ÷ 20 years]. The patent's expected useful life is five years.

5. Balty tested the patent for impairment at the end of 2012 and found that its recoverable amount of $115,000 was less than its carrying amount of $218,500 ($230,000 − $11,500). Rachael recorded an impairment loss of $103,500.

Instructions

Prepare the necessary journal entries to correct any errors made in recording the above transactions.

Record intangible asset transactions; prepare partial statement of financial position.
(SO 5, 6)

P9–12B The intangible assets and goodwill reported by Ip Corp. at December 31, 2011, follow:

Patent #1	$70,000	
Less: Accumulated amortization	14,000	$ 56,000
Copyright #1	$48,000	
Less: Accumulated amortization	28,800	19,200
Goodwill		210,000
Total		$285,200

The patent was acquired in January 2010 and has a useful life of 10 years. Copyright #1 was acquired in January 2007 and also has a useful life of 10 years. The following cash transactions may have affected intangible assets and goodwill during 2012:

Jan. 2 Paid $22,500 in legal costs to successfully defend patent #1 against infringement by another company. Determined that the revised annual amortization for this patent will be $9,812.

July 1 Developed a new product, incurring $220,000 in research costs and $60,000 in development costs. The development phase ended on July 1. The useful life of the new product is equal to 20 years.

Sept. 1 Paid $11,000 to an Olympic rower to appear in commercials advertising the company's products. The commercials will air in September.

Oct. 1 Acquired a second copyright for $16,000. Copyright #2 has a useful life of five years.

Dec. 31 Determined the recoverable amount of the goodwill to be $175,000. There was no indication that any intangible assets were impaired.

Instructions
(a) Prepare the journal entries to record the above transactions.
(b) Prepare any adjusting journal entries required at December 31, the company's year end.
(c) Show the presentation of the intangible assets and goodwill on the statement of financial position at December 31, 2012.

P9–13B Le Château Inc. and Reitmans (Canada) Limited are two competitors in the retail clothing industry. They reported the following information at January 29, 2011 (in millions of dollars):

Calculate and evaluate ratios.
(SO 7)

	Reitmans	Le Château
Total assets, Jan. 29, 2011	$ 657.6	$246.9
Total assets, Jan. 30, 2010	631.4	236.0
Net sales	1,070.3	319.0
Profit	87.0	19.1

Industry averages are as follows: profit margin, 3.2%; return on assets, 3.5%; and asset turnover, 1.1 times.

Instructions
(a) For each company, calculate the profit margin, return on assets, and asset turnover ratios for 2010.
(b) Based on your calculations in part (a), comment on how effectively each company is using its assets to generate sales and produce profit.
(c) What, if anything, complicates your ability to compare the two companies in (b)?

P9–14B Two brewing companies that compete against each other are Northern Ale Ltd. (NAL) and Brew Right Inc. (BRI). The industry is experiencing a slump and each company has undertaken a different strategy to adapt to this new environment. NAL has adopted an expansion strategy by borrowing funds to purchase another company. This has boosted 2012 sales by 67% and 2012 profit by 47%, which the company CEO has mentioned in several press releases. BRI has decided to streamline operations and cut costs by looking at more efficient ways to operate the business. Data for the two companies are listed below in millions of dollars:

Calculate and evaluate ratios.
(SO 7)

	NAL	BRI
Total assets, 2012	$2,500	$1,100
Total assets, 2011	1,100	1,050
Total assets, 2010	1,000	1,000
Net sales, 2012	2,500	1,800
Net sales, 2011	1,500	1,500
Profit, 2012	220	250
Profit, 2011	150	150

Instructions
(a) Calculate the profit margin, asset turnover, and return on asset ratios for each company in 2011 and 2012.
(b) Provide an explanation for the year-over-year changes in the ratios calculated in (a).
(c) Comment on which company has been more successful in executing its strategy.

Broadening Your Perspective

Financial Reporting and Analysis Cases

Financial Reporting: *Eastplats*

BYP9–1 The financial statements of Eastern Platinum Limited (Eastplats) are presented in Appendix A at the end of this textbook.

Answer questions about long-lived assets.
(SO 2, 3)

Instructions
(a) What depreciation method is used by Eastplats for mining properties and for residential properties?
(b) What is the useful life of the company's mine houses and office buildings?
(c) As at December 31, 2010, what percentage of the cost of plant and equipment owned had been depreciated? (*Hint:* See Note 9.)

(d) Why would the company have mineral properties that were not being depleted? (*Hint:* See Note 9.)

(e) Using the statement of cash flows, determine if the company was able to pay for property, plant, and equipment expenditures with its net operating cash flows in 2009 and in 2010.

(f) Did the company have any asset retirement obligations at the end of 2010? Did the company use different terminology to describe this obligation?

(g) Did the company have any impairment losses in 2009 or 2010?

Comparative Analysis: *Eastplats and Amplats*

Calculate and evaluate ratios.
(SO 7)

BYP9–2   The financial statements of Anglo American Platinum Limited (Amplats) are presented in Appendix B, following the financial statements for Eastern Platinum Limited (Eastplats) in Appendix A.

Instructions

(a) Based on the information in these financial statements, calculate the following ratios for each company for 2010, its most recent fiscal year:

1. Profit margin

2. Return on assets

3. Asset turnover

(b) Industry averages for the above three ratios are as follows: profit margin, 6.2%; return on assets, 3.9%; and asset turnover, 0.6 times. What conclusions about the management of assets can be drawn from your results in (a) and these data?

Interpreting Financial Information

Discuss the revaluation model.
(SO 3, 7)

BYP9–3   Brookfield Asset Management Inc., headquartered in Toronto, is a global company focused on property, power, and infrastructure asset management. It was one of the first companies in Canada to prepare its financial statements in accordance with IFRS in 2010. Shown below is an extract from the notes to its financial statements at December 31, 2010:

Note 9: Property, plant and equipment
(in millions at December 31)

	2010	2009	2008
Cost	$12,026	$ 8,911	$ 7,534
Accumulated fair value changes	7,417	8,373	8,063
Accumulated depreciation	(1,295)	(561)	–
Carrying amount	$18,148	$16,723	$ 15,597

Instructions

(a) Do you think that the company has adopted the cost or revaluation model for its property, plant, and equipment?

(b) If the company sold none of these assets in 2010, what do you think depreciation expense on the income statement would be for that year?

(c) During 2010, when adjusting property, plant, and equipment to fair value, was there a revaluation gain or loss?

(d) On which financial statement(s) would the revaluation gain or loss be recorded?

(e) Would the use of the revaluation model for this company improve the return on assets ratio or the asset turnover ratio?

Comparing IFRS and ASPE

Discuss impairment; calculate and evaluate ratios.
(SO 3, 7)

BYP9–4   The Rosewood Resort and the Blaze Mountain Resort are located in Ontario's fastest-growing four-season resort area. Both resorts are owned by privately owned companies. Rosewood, which is owned by a German company, follows IFRS, and Blaze Mountain, which is owned by a small group of Canadian private investors, follows ASPE. Both companies use the cost model when accounting for property, plant, and equipment.

From 2004 to 2006, both resorts experienced a period of decline where the number of visitors to the area dwindled. Because of this, at the end of the 2006 fiscal year, each company recorded an impairment loss of $1,000,000 on its buildings because the recoverable amount of these assets did not exceed their carrying amount at that time.

Since 2006, the number of visitors to each resort has risen steadily. Resort bookings have dramatically increased because the country's largest developer of destination resorts has opened a ski village, chalets, lodges, and a golf resort in the area. As a result, by the end of the 2012 fiscal year, the recoverable amount of the building, of each resort now exceeds their carrying amount, as shown below along with other pertinent information.

	Rosewood	Blaze Mountain
Net sales for the year ended December 31, 2012	$2,250,000	$ 2,500,000
Profit for the year ended December 31, 2012	180,000	200,000
Average total assets	9,000,000	10,000,000
Carrying amount of buildings, December 31, 2012	5,000,000	6,000,000
Recoverable amount of buildings, December 31, 2012	7,000,000	6,500,000
What carrying amount of buildings at December 31, 2012, would have been had impairment not occurred in 2006	5,800,000	6,700,000

Instructions

(a) Ignoring depreciation, at the end of 2012 can Rosewood reverse some or all of the impairment loss recorded in 2006? If so how much? What adjusting entry would be made to record this reversal?

(b) Ignoring depreciation, at the end of 2011 can Blaze Mountain reverse some or all of the impairment loss recorded in 2006? If so how much? What adjusting entry would be made to record this reversal?

(c) Calculate the profit margin, asset turnover, and return on asset ratios for both companies based on the unadjusted amounts provided above. Recalculate each ratio after taking into account any impairment loss reversals if applicable.

(d) Based on the ratios calculated after taking into effect any impairment loss reversals, if applicable, which company is performing better? Why?

(e) If you were a banker deciding whether to provide financing to Rosewood or Blaze Mountain, would you prefer each company to use the same accounting standards? If you could choose which standards each company had to report under, which standards might be the most helpful in making your financing decisions?

(f) If different accounting standards produce different account balances on financial statements, what additional information may users want to have in order to evaluate the nature and performance of long-lived assets?

Critical Thinking Cases and Activities

Collaborative Learning Activity

BYP9–5 The reporting of long-lived assets in the financial statements is often described as the area that is most dependent on management judgement and estimates. The result is that companies with similar performance in their day-to-day operations may report significantly different profits. Areas affecting financial reporting include:

Discuss determination and reporting of long-lived assets. (SO 2, 3, 5, 6)

1. The decision to lease or purchase long-lived assets
2. The decision to use the cost or revaluation model
3. Depreciation of buildings and equipment
4. Determining the impairment of assets
5. Treatment of research and development costs

Instructions

After the class has been divided into groups and you have been assigned one of the five areas listed above, do the following:

(a) Identify where management makes judgements that will affect the reported financial results for your chosen area.

(b) Identify the effect of the judgements you identified in (a) on key financial statement amounts and ratios such as profit margin, asset turnover, and return on assets.

Communication Activity

BYP9–6 John Lacasse, the chief financial officer of a real estate company, has been asked to review International Accounting Standard "IAS 16 *Property, Plant and Equipment*" to see how it would apply to the company. IAS 16 permits two accounting models for the treatment of property, plant, and equipment:

Discuss cost and revaluation models. (SO 3)

- Cost model: Assets are carried at their cost less accumulated depreciation and impairment.
- Revaluation model: Assets are carried at a revalued amount, which is the asset's fair value at the date of revaluation less subsequent depreciation and impairment, provided that the fair value can be measured reliably.

   Under the revaluation model, revaluations should be done regularly so that an asset's carrying amount does not differ materially from its fair value at the statement of financial position date.

Instructions

Write a letter to John that outlines the advantages and disadvantages of increasing the value of property, plant, and equipment in a real estate company. You should discuss in your letter the depreciable amount, and any other points that you wish to make.

Ethics Case

BYP9–7 Imporia Container Ltd. is suffering from declining sales of its main product, non-biodegradable plastic cartons. The president, Benny Benson, instructs his controller, Yeoh Siew Hoon, to change estimates relating to a processing line of automated plastic extruding equipment, purchased for $3 million in January 2010. The equipment was originally estimated to have a useful life of five years and a residual value of $200,000 and depreciation has been recorded for two years on that basis. Benny wants the estimated useful life changed to a total of seven years and the residual value raised to $500,000. Yeoh Siew is hesitant to make the change, believing it inappropriate to "manage profits" in this way. Benny

Discuss revision of estimates. (SO 2, 3, 7)

says, "Hey, the useful life is only an estimate, and I've heard that our competition uses a six-year life on their production equipment. By the way, four of the six buildings we own have probably fallen in value this year. Because of the cost basis of accounting we don't have to write them down but the other two buildings have gone up in value so let's use IFRS rules to record a gain on them."

Instructions

(a) Who are the stakeholders in this situation?

(b) Will Benny Benson's proposed changes increase or decrease profit in 2012?

(c) What impact will the proposed (1) change in useful life, and (2) reporting buildings at fair value have on the company's profit margin and asset turnover?

(d) Discuss whether the proposed changes described above are unethical or simply a good business practice by an astute president.

"All About You" Activity

Examine lease or buy options.
(SO 3)

BYP9–8   The "All About You" feature in this chapter discusses the advantages of buying or leasing a vehicle. You probably have a vehicle in mind that you would like to purchase some day and may have explored everything from the colour to the engine. Now it's time to explore the facts about leasing and buying.

Instructions

Go to the Office of Consumer Affairs on the Industry Canada website (www.ic.gc.ca). Go to the "For Consumers" section and find the "Take Charge of Your Debts" subsection and then locate the "Money, Credit, and Debt" section under which you will find the Vehicle Lease or Buy Calculator. This is an on-line tool that will help you to determine how much it would cost to lease or buy a car. The calculator will give you a comparison of three ownership options over an eight-year time period. Before you use the calculator, you should read "What the calculator can do for you" and "How to use the calculator."

Using the calculator, answer the following questions:

(a) How much interest would you be charged and how much would each monthly payment be if you purchased a car for $25,000 and paid for it with a five-year loan with a financing rate of 6.25% in your home province? (Assume that you have a zero down payment and that you do not have a vehicle to trade.)

(b) If you leased a $25,000 vehicle, using each of the two options offered by the Vehicle Lease or Buy Calculator, how much interest would you pay? How much would your monthly payments be? Why does the calculator use an eight-year time period?

(c) What is the total outlay including maintenance costs for the purchase of the vehicle and for each of the two leasing options explored in (b)?

(d) Which of the options—purchase option or the two leasing options—would you prefer and why?

Serial Case

(*Note*: This is a continuation of the serial case from Chapters 1 through 8.)

Determine cost;
record equipment
transactions.
(SO 1, 4)

BYP 9–9   Janet, Brian, and Natalie have decided to take on the additional work offered by Coffee Beans. Recall that Coffee Beans is doubling the number of cupcakes required on a weekly basis. The Koebels are also reconsidering the Biscuits offer to provide chocolate chip cookies on a weekly basis. Currently, Koebel's Family Bakery has enough capacity to bake all of the cupcakes required by Coffee Beans and, if they accept the Biscuits offer, has enough capacity to bake all of the cookies required on a weekly basis. If, however, any other large orders are received they would have to turn these orders away.

The Koebels would like to buy two new ovens (including one to replace one of their commercial ovens) as well as purchase another refrigerator. The Koebels have discussed the required changes with a contractor, and estimate the costs as follows:

1. Cost of two new ovens, $30,000 (2 at $15,000).
2. The old oven could be sold to the community daycare centre for $100. The oven was originally purchased for $5,000 on January 3, 2008. It has been depreciated on a straight-line basis over a five-year useful life with no residual value.
3. Cost of new refrigerator, $8,000.
4. Cost of plumbing upgrade as a result of the installation of the new refrigerator, $1,500.
5. Cost of electrical panel upgrade as a result of the installation of the two new ovens, $2,500.
6. Shipping costs, $500 per appliance.
7. Additional insurance required on the new equipment, $1,200 per year.
8. Painting of the walls in the bakery to "freshen things up," $3,850.

The Koebels anticipate that the cost of the upgrade can be financed with cash they currently have in the bank. The equipment upgrade could take place during the late summer when the sales at the bakery are a little slower. If all goes smoothly in terms of installation, the new equipment could be ready for use by September 1, 2012.

Natalie is concerned about the recording of these transactions in the accounting records. She is not certain which costs should be capitalized and which should be expensed.

Instructions

(a) Identify which of the above costs should be capitalized and which should be expensed.

(b) Record the journal entry for the disposal of the old oven on September 1, 2012. Assume that the last time depreciation was recorded was on June 30, 2012.

(c) Record the journal entry for the purchase and installation of the new equipment on September 1, 2012.

Answers to Self-Test Questions

1. c	2. c	3. c	4. b	5. a
6. b	7. a	8. c	9. d	10. d

Remember to go back to the beginning of the chapter to check off your completed work!

←

Comprehensive Case: Chapters 3 to 9

Record and post trans-action and adjusting journal entries; prepare adjusted trial balance and financial statements.
(SO 2, 3, 4, 6)

Very Clear Images Ltd. has been in operation for several years. It purchases, customizes, and sells studio sets for its clients. The company's post-closing trial balance at July 31, 2012, the end of its fiscal year, is presented below:

VERY CLEAR IMAGES LTD.
Post-Closing Trial Balance
July 31, 2012

	Debit	Credit
Cash	$ 167,333	
Accounts receivable	2,700,000	
Allowance for doubtful accounts		300,000
Notes receivable	200,000	
Interest receivable	2,667	
Inventory	500,000	
Equipment	194,000	
Accumulated depreciation—equipment		68,750
Vehicles	260,000	
Accumulated depreciation—vehicles		33,000
Accounts payable		1,009,000
Bank loan payable		350,000
Common shares		300,000
Retained earnings		1,963,250
	$4,024,000	$4,024,000

The company had a limited amount of business activity in August 2012 because of holidays for both the company and its major customers. You have been hired on a temporary basis to update the company's records for August. The August transactions and adjustments are presented below:

Aug.   1   Paid $20,000 for office expenses and $36,000 for the August rent.

2   Accepted a 6-month, 8% note in exchange for Chen Enterprises' overdue account receivable of $100,000.

3   Sale on account to Chavier Ltd. for $500,000, terms 2/10, n/30. Cost of goods sold, $190,000. The company uses a perpetual inventory system.

8   Determined that an account receivable from Densmore Ltd. of $70,000 is uncollectible.

9   $300,000 partial payment on account is received from Chavier Ltd.

10   Old equipment was sold to a second-hand dealer for $2,000. The equipment's original cost was $44,000; accumulated depreciation to the date of disposal was $19,250.

14   Paid a $20,000 income tax instalment.

21   Purchased new equipment on account for $24,000. No depreciation is recorded on long-lived assets acquired during the last half of the month.

31   Collected a three-month note receivable and interest from Strombolis Ltd. at maturity. The note was originally issued for $200,000 on June 1, 2012, at an 8% interest rate. Interest was due at maturity.

31   Recorded credit card sales from sales of digital library images for the month, $75,000. Credit card charges are 1.5%. The cost of goods sold is $15,000.

31   The monthly bank statement revealed the following unrecorded items: interest on bank loan, $1,500, and bank charges, $130.

31   Reviewed outstanding accounts receivable. Determined, through an aging of accounts, that doubtful accounts totalled $320,000 at month end.

31   Recorded depreciation for the month on the vehicles. Original cost, $260,000; useful life, five years. It is estimated that the vehicles will be driven for 2 million kilometres over their useful lives. Estimated residual value, $40,000. The units-of-production method of depreciation is used. In August, 16,000 kilometres were driven.

31   Recorded depreciation for the month on the remaining equipment that cost $150,000 and is still in use. Useful life of all equipment is estimated to be three years with no residual value. The diminishing-balance method of depreciation is used at one time the straight-line rate.

31   Paid salaries for the month of $100,000.

31   Accrued interest on the Chen Enterprises note receivable.

31   Because of a recent hail storm, the estimated recoverable amount for the delivery vehicles is only $200,000.

Instructions

(a) Record the August transactions and adjustments.

(b) Set up T accounts, enter the July 31 balances, and post the journal entries from (a) to the accounts.

(c) Prepare an adjusted trial balance at August 31.

(d) Prepare an income statement, statement of changes in equity, and statement of financial position at August 31.

10

Reporting and Analyzing Liabilities

The Navigator
Chapter 10

- Scan *Study Objectives*
- Read *Feature Story*
- Read text and answer *Do It!s*
- Review *Comparing IFRS and ASPE*
- Review *Summary of Study Objectives*
- Review *Decision Toolkit—A Summary*
- Work *Using the Decision Toolkit*
- Work *Comprehensive Do It!'s*
- Answer *Self-Test Questions*
- Complete *assignments*
- Go to *WileyPLUS* for practice and tutorials

study objectives

After studying this chapter, you should be able to:

1. Account for current liabilities.
2. Account for instalment notes payable.
3. Account for bonds payable.
4. Identify the requirements for the financial statement presentation and analysis of liabilities.

the
navigator

Canada Post Borrows for Future Gains

The Canada Post Group—a group of related businesses including Canada Post Corporation and subsidiaries Purolator Courier Ltd., SCI Group Inc., and joint venture Innovapost Inc.—employs approximately 71,000 people. In 2010, Canada Post delivered about 11 billion pieces of mail to 15 million residential and business addresses across the country.

Like any business, Canada Post Corporation's current liabilities include accounts payable and accrued liabilities, as well as salaries payable to its employees. Current liabilities also include income tax payable, unearned (deferred) revenue, outstanding money orders, and the current portion of its non-current debt. The contractual maturities of these liabilities are less than 12 months.

The Crown corporation took on a significant amount of debt for the first time in 2010 by raising $1 billion in the Canadian capital markets. Although it already had about $55 million in non-current debt at the time, this was the first time it had taken on a liability of that size.

There are basically three forms of financing, explains Wayne Cheeseman, Canada Post's chief financial officer. "There's internally generated funds, the equity market, or the debt capital markets. Being a Crown corporation, the equity markets aren't open to us. We do generate funds internally, but it won't be sufficient when we look at our long-term plans. So we looked to the debt capital markets and raised money there, obviously with a plan to pay that off over time."

Canada Post raised $1 billion by issuing two series of bonds—the first series or tranche of $500 million, maturing July 2025 and bearing interest at 4.08%, payable semi-annually; and the second tranche of $500 million, maturing July 2040 and bearing interest at 4.36%, payable semi-annually, explains Mr. Cheeseman.

The decision to raise money through the debt capital markets followed Parliament's approval of a legal amendment that increased Canada Post's borrowing limit from $300 million to $2.5 billion. "We did have to go back to the Department of Finance to get approval on the terms and conditions, but the legislative approval was in place," says Mr. Cheeseman.

Canada Post planned to use the money raised for its Postal Transformation initiative currently under way. "The Postal Transformation involves redoing and upgrading our physical and technological platform," says Mr. Cheeseman. The corporation is working to modernize its operations with several capital projects planned over several years, including new and renovated buildings and updated equipment and systems. The initiative includes building a new processing plant in Winnipeg, replacing part of its current fleet with fuel-efficient, low-emission vehicles, and implementing new sorting equipment in its plants. Once the initiative is completed, the corporation will have a much greater ability to track and trace parcels, and will have more accurate address management systems.

"We basically have two goals—to provide an acceptable level of service to all Canadians while remaining financially self-sufficient," says Mr. Cheeseman. These improvements are expected to save Canada Post approximately $250 million a year. "With the cost savings, we're going to take advantage of the coming attrition in the business. It won't be a situation where people lose their jobs. It's simply that as they retire, we won't replace a number of people."

With these long-term plans, Canada Post hopes to remain viable and relevant in Canada's changing and technologically advancing society.

the navigator

preview of CHAPTER | **10**

The feature story discusses Canada Post's recent decision to raise money by issuing bonds. This decision committed Canada Post to up to 30 years of repaying this debt, in addition to the accompanying interest. Given the obligation and cost, why do companies borrow money? Why do they sometimes borrow for the short term and other times long term? In this chapter, we answer these questions.

This chapter is organized as follows:

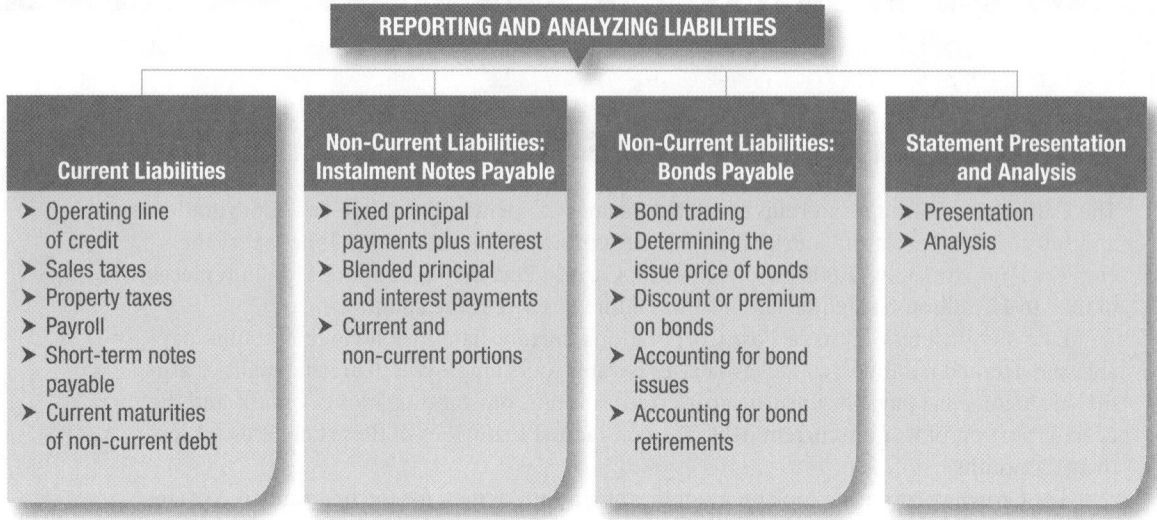

REPORTING AND ANALYZING LIABILITIES

Current Liabilities	**Non-Current Liabilities: Instalment Notes Payable**	**Non-Current Liabilities: Bonds Payable**	**Statement Presentation and Analysis**
➤ Operating line of credit ➤ Sales taxes ➤ Property taxes ➤ Payroll ➤ Short-term notes payable ➤ Current maturities of non-current debt	➤ Fixed principal payments plus interest ➤ Blended principal and interest payments ➤ Current and non-current portions	➤ Bond trading ➤ Determining the issue price of bonds ➤ Discount or premium on bonds ➤ Accounting for bond issues ➤ Accounting for bond retirements	➤ Presentation ➤ Analysis

Current Liabilities

STUDY OBJECTIVE 1

Account for current liabilities.

In Chapter 2, we defined liabilities as present obligations that result from past transactions. These obligations (debts) must be paid sometime in the future by the transfer of assets or services. This future payment date (the maturity date) is the primary reason for the two basic classifications of liabilities: (1) current liabilities, and (2) non-current liabilities.

A **current liability** is a debt that will be paid within one year and from existing current assets or through the creation of other current liabilities. Most companies pay current liabilities out of current assets (e.g., cash) rather than by creating other liabilities (e.g., paying an account payable by issuing a note payable). Debts that do not meet both criteria are classified as **non-current** or **long-term liabilities**.

Financial statement users want to know whether a company's obligations are current or non-current. This is important since a company that has more current liabilities than current assets often lacks liquidity; i.e., short-term debt-paying ability. Users must also look at total (short- and long-term) liabilities in order to assess a company's solvency—its ability to pay its interest and debt when due. Finally, users want to know what types of liabilities a company has.

The different types of current liabilities include bank indebtedness arising from operating lines of credit; accounts payable; accrued liabilities such as taxes, salaries, and interest; unearned revenue; notes or loans payable; and the current portion of non-current debt. Entries for many of these liabilities, including accounts payable and unearned revenue, have been explained in previous chapters. In this section, we discuss in more detail operating lines of credit, sales taxes, property taxes, payroll, notes payable, and current maturities of non-current debt.

OPERATING LINE OF CREDIT

Current assets (such as accounts receivable) do not always turn into cash at the exact time that current liabilities (such as accounts payable) must be paid. Consequently, most companies have an **operating line of credit**, also known as a credit facility, at their bank to help them manage temporary cash shortfalls. This means that the company has been pre-authorized by the bank to borrow money, up to a pre-set limit, when it is needed. Interest is usually charged at a floating interest rate on any amounts used from the line of credit. A **floating** (or **variable**) **interest rate** changes as market rates change and is usually based on the prime borrowing rate. The prime rate is the interest rate that banks charge their best customers. This rate is usually increased by a specified percentage that matches the company's risk profile.

Security, called **collateral**, is often required by banks as protection against a possible default on the loan by the borrower. Collateral normally includes some, or all, of the company's current assets (e.g., accounts receivable or inventories); investments; or property, plant, and equipment.

Line of credit borrowings are normally on a short-term basis, and are repayable immediately upon request—that is, on demand—by the bank. In reality, repayment is rarely demanded without notice. A line of credit makes it very easy for a company to borrow money. It does not have to call or visit its bank to actually arrange the transaction. The bank simply covers any cheques written in excess of the bank account balance, up to the approved credit limit.

Amounts drawn on an operating line of credit result in a negative, or overdrawn, cash balance at year end. No special entry is required to record the overdrawn amount. The normal credits to cash will simply accumulate and are reported as **bank indebtedness** in the current liabilities section of the statement of financial position, with a suitable note disclosure.

It is important to look not only at any amounts drawn on the operating line of credit, but also at any unused capacity. Amounts available to be drawn in the future from an operating line of credit add to a company's liquidity. Canada Post is authorized to borrow up to $250 million from the Government of Canada for short-term cash management purposes. In addition, its subsidiaries have access to operating lines of credit totalling $200 million, of which $149 million is unused at December 31, 2010.

SALES TAXES

As consumers, we are well aware that many of the products and services we purchase are subject to sales tax. Sales tax is expressed as a percentage of the sales price. Sales tax may take the form of the Goods and Services Tax (GST), Provincial Sales Tax (PST), or Harmonized Sales Tax (HST). In Quebec, the PST is known as the Quebec Sales Tax (QST).

At the time of writing this textbook, the federal GST was assessed at a rate of 5% across Canada. Provincial sales tax rates currently vary from 0% to 10% across Canada. In most provinces that are subject to GST and PST, GST is charged on the selling price of the item before PST is applied, thus avoiding GST being charged on PST. However, in the provinces of Quebec and Prince Edward Island, PST is charged on GST. For example, in Quebec a $100 sale would result in $5 of GST ($100 × 5%) and $8.93 of QST [($100 + $5) × 8.5%]. The increased sales tax rate is 13.9% [($5 + $8.93) ÷ $100] rather than 13.5% (5% GST + 8.5% QST).

In several provinces, such as Newfoundland and Labrador, Nova Scotia, New Brunswick, and Ontario the PST and GST have been combined into one Harmonized Sales Tax. In 2011, the HST was 13% in Newfoundland and Labrador, New Brunswick, and Ontario, and 15% in N.S.

When a sale occurs, the retailer collects the sales tax from the customer and periodically (normally monthly) remits (sends) the sales tax collected to the designated federal and provincial collecting authorities. In the case of GST and HST, collections may be offset against payments (i.e., sales tax payments made by the company on its own eligible purchases). Only the net amount owing or recoverable will be paid or refunded.

The amount of the sale and the amount of the sales tax collected are usually rung up separately on the cash register. The cash register readings are then used to credit the two accounts Sales and Sales Tax Payable. For example, assuming that the March 25 cash register readings for the Islander Corporation show sales of $10,000 and Harmonized Sales Tax of $1,300 (where the HST rate is 13%), the entry is:

Mar. 25	Cash	11,300	
	Sales		10,000
	Sales Tax Payable ($10,000 × 13%)		1,300
	(To record sales and sales tax)		

A	=	L	+	SE
+11,300		+1,300		+10,000

↑Cash flows: +11,300

If, instead of being subject to harmonized sales tax, Islander was located in a province subject to federal sales tax of $500 (GST rate of 5%), and provincial sales tax of $700 (PST rate of 7%), the entry would be:

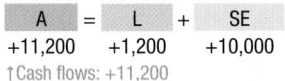

A = L + SE
+11,200 +1,200 +10,000
↑Cash flows: +11,200

Mar. 25	Cash	11,200	
	Sales		10,000
	Sales Tax Payable [($10,000 × 5%) + ($10,000 × 7%)]		1,200
	(To record sales and sales taxes)		

When the sales taxes are remitted, the Sales Tax Payable account is debited and Cash is credited. For simplicity, we use one account—Sales Tax Payable—here, although many companies use separate accounts for GST Payable and PST Payable. Note that Islander does not report sales tax as an expense; it simply forwards the amounts paid by the customers to the respective government. Thus, Islander Corporation is really only a collection agent for the governments.

From the brief introduction provided above, you can already see that sales tax can be complicated. In addition, not all goods and services are taxable. Varying and changing sales tax rates have added complexity to the accounting process. Fortunately, point-of-sale computer programs and accounting software can automatically determine and record the correct sales tax rate, or rates, for each good or service provided. Nonetheless, it is still important to make sure all of the relevant sales tax regulations in your jurisdiction are clearly understood before recording sales tax.

PROPERTY TAXES

Businesses that own property pay property taxes each year. These taxes are charged by the municipal and provincial governments, and are calculated at a specified rate for every $100 of the assessed value of the property (i.e., land and building). Property taxes are generally for a calendar year, although bills are not usually issued until the spring of each year. In other words, even though a property tax bill may cover the period of January through December, it is not usually issued until March—well after the property tax year has begun.

To illustrate, assume that Tantramar Management Ltd. owns land and a building in the city of Regina. Tantramar's year end is December 31 and it makes adjusting entries annually. Tantramar receives its property tax bill of $6,000 for the calendar year on March 1, payable on May 31.

In March, when Tantramar receives the property tax bill, two months have passed in the year. The company records the property tax expense for the months of January and February and the liability owed at that point in time as follows:

A = L + SE
+1,000 −1,000
Cash flows: no effect

Mar. 1	Property Tax Expense ($6,000 × 2/12)	1,000	
	Property Tax Payable		1,000
	(To record property tax expense for January and February)		

In May, when Tantramar records the payment of the liability recorded on March 1, it also records the expense incurred to date for the months of March, April, and May. As at May 31, five months have passed and should be recorded as property tax expense (two months in the entry above and three months in the entry below). The remaining seven months of the year are recorded as a prepayment, as shown in the following entry:

A = L + SE
+3,500 −1,000 −1,500
−6,000
↓Cash flows: −6,000

May 31	Property Tax Payable	1,000	
	Property Tax Expense ($6,000 × 3/12)	1,500	
	Prepaid Property Tax ($6,000 × 7/12)	3,500	
	Cash		6,000
	(To record payment of property tax for January through December)		

After the payment of the property tax, Tantramar has a zero balance in its liability account but still has a prepayment. Since Tantramar only makes adjusting entries annually, it would not adjust the prepaid property tax account until year end, December 31. At that time, it would make the following entry:

Dec. 31	Property Tax Expense		3,500	
	Prepaid Property Tax			3,500
	(To record property tax expense for June through December)			

A	=	L	+	SE
−3,500				−3,500

Cash flows: no effect

There are other acceptable ways to record and adjust property taxes. Some companies would debit Prepaid Property Tax for $6,000 on March 1 and wait until adjusting entries are prepared to record any expense. Other companies would debit Property Tax Expense initially when the bill is recorded on March 1 to save a later adjusting entry. In addition, companies may prepare monthly or quarterly adjusting entries. Regardless, at year end, whatever way is used, the company should have the same ending balances. In this case, the accounts Prepaid Property Tax and Property Tax Payable should each have a zero balance and Property Tax Expense should have a balance of $6,000.

PAYROLL

Every employer incurs three types of liabilities related to employees' salaries or wages: (1) the net pay owed to employees, (2) employee payroll deductions, and (3) employer payroll obligations.

The first type of liability is the amount of salary or wages owed to employees. Management personnel are generally paid **salaries**, which are expressed as a specific amount per week (weekly), per two weeks (biweekly), per month (monthly), or per year (annually). Part-time employees or employees paid on an hourly basis or by the work produced (an amount per unit of product) are normally paid **wages**. The total amount of salaries or wages earned by the employee is called **gross pay**.

Note that an employer's total salaries and wages do not include payments made for services of professionals such as accountants, lawyers, and architects. Such professionals are independent contractors rather than salaried employees. Payments to them are called fees, rather than salaries or wages. This distinction is important, because government regulations for the payment and reporting of payroll apply only to employees.

The second type of liability is the amount of employee **payroll deductions** required by law to be deducted (withheld) from employees' gross, or total, pay. Assume that Linfang Wang works 40 hours this week for Pepitone Inc., earning $10 per hour. Will Linfang receive a cheque for $400 (40 × $10) at the end of the week? Definitely not. The reason: Pepitone has to withhold amounts known as payroll deductions from Linfang's wages, and pay these amounts to various other parties.

Some payroll deductions are mandatory, while others are voluntary. Mandatory payroll deductions include amounts withheld for federal and provincial income taxes, Canada Pension Plan (CPP) contributions, and employment insurance (EI) premiums. Companies might also withhold voluntary deductions for benefits such as health and pension plans, union dues, and charitable contributions, as well as for other purposes.

An employee's gross pay, or total earnings, less any employee payroll deductions withheld from the employee's earnings, is known as **net pay**. This is the amount that the company (the employer) must pay to the employee. As Linfang learned above, gross pay is very different from net pay.

Illustration 10-1 on the following page summarizes the types of payroll deductions that most companies normally have and that are responsible for the difference between gross and net pay.

The third type of liability is employer (not employee) payroll obligations. In addition to the liabilities incurred as a result of employee payroll deductions, the employer is expected to pay various payroll costs that are charged on certain payroll deductions, such as the employer's share of CPP and EI. Furthermore, the provincial governments require employer funding of a workers' compensation plan. All of these contributions, plus items such as employer-sponsored health plans and pensions and compensated absences (e.g., statutory holidays, vacation pay), are referred to together as **employee benefits**. The employer's share of these costs is recorded as an employee benefits expense.

In summary, companies must withhold payroll deductions from their employees on behalf of the government and other third parties. In addition, they also incur various employer payroll costs. Until these payroll deductions and costs are remitted to the third parties that they are collected for, they are reported as a current liability in the statement of financial position.

▸Illustration 10-1
Payroll deductions

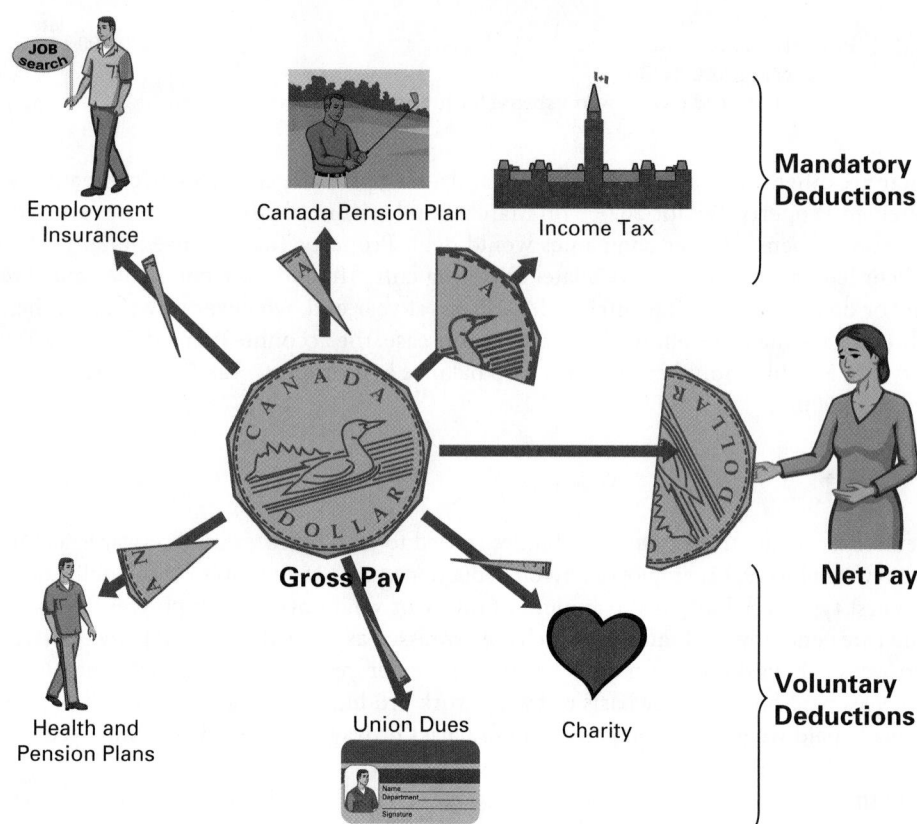

To illustrate the recording of payroll, we will continue to use Pepitone as our example. The accrual of a $100,000 weekly payroll for Pepitone is illustrated in the following journal entry, using assumed amounts:

A	=	L	+	SE
+4,950				−100,000
+1,780				
+20,427				
+2,395				
+1,037				
+69,411				

Cash flows: no effect

Mar. 7	Salaries Expense	100,000	
	CPP Payable		4,950
	EI Payable		1,780
	Income Tax Payable		20,427
	United Way Payable		2,395
	Union Dues Payable		1,037
	Salaries Payable		69,411
	(To record payroll and employee deductions for the week ending March 7)		

In the above journal entry, Pepitone records $100,000—the gross pay amount—as salaries expense. The net pay of $69,411 that is owed to employees is recorded as salaries payable. In addition, Pepitone records as separate liabilities amounts it owes for its employee payroll deductions withheld on behalf of others, such as the CPP, EI, and income tax owed to the government, charitable contributions made on behalf of the United Way, and dues owed to the union.

Note that while the employee payroll deductions are part of salaries expense, employer payroll costs are not. Employer payroll costs are debited to a separate expense account called Employee Benefits Expense. Based on the $100,000 payroll in our Pepitone example, the following entry would be made to record the employer's expense and liability for its share of the payroll costs, or employee benefits:

A	=	L	+	SE
+4,950				−11,947
+2,492				
+1,575				
+2,930				

Cash flows: no effect

Mar. 7	Employee Benefits Expense	11,947	
	CPP Payable		4,950
	EI Payable		2,492
	Workers' Compensation Payable		1,575
	Health Insurance Benefits Payable		2,930
	(To record employer's payroll costs on March 7 payroll)		

In addition to recording the employer's share of CPP and EI in the above journal entry, we have also recorded the employer costs for workers' compensation and health care. In this example, we have assumed that the health care benefits are paid by the employer and not shared between the employer and the employee as is sometimes the case.

On the same day, or on a later day, Pepitone must also pay its employees. The following entry records the payment of the weekly payroll on March 7:

Mar. 7	Salaries Payable	69,411	
	Cash		69,411
	(To record payment of the March 7 payroll)		

A = L + SE
−69,411   −69,411
↓Cash flows: −69,411

Although we have recorded the accrual of the payroll and payment of the payroll in separate journal entries above, they could also be combined and recorded in one compound entry—especially if paid the same day as the accrual is recorded.

Note that Pepitone is only paying its employees in this entry and is not making its payroll deductions. Employee and employer payroll deductions will be remitted later in the month when they are due to government authorities or other third parties. Normally payroll deductions must be remitted no later than the 15th day of the month following the monthly pay period. Depending on the size of the payroll deductions, however, the employer's payment deadline could be different.

ACCOUNTING MATTERS!   *Management Perspective*

Rising Cost of Employee Benefits

The battle over employee benefits has grown as increases in the cost of benefits outpace increases in salaries and wages. A report entitled "Benefits Benchmarking 2009: Balancing Competitiveness and Cost," prepared by the Conference Board of Canada, states that benefit costs represent 20% of gross payroll and the total costs are increasing by an average of 10% per year.

While cutting benefits may be the obvious solution, it is not always the best strategy—especially in a competitive labour market. Consequently, companies are trying to find better ways to communicate the value of benefits to employees and enhance employees' understanding of the cost implications of their actions. A partial solution by employers is a move toward flexible benefit programs, which include employee accounts with prescribed spending limits. Programs such as these help eliminate the uncertainty of increasing benefits as well as meet the needs of a changing workforce.

Source: Karla Thorpe, "Rising Benefit Costs Challenge Employers," *CAmagazine*, June-July 2010, p. 10

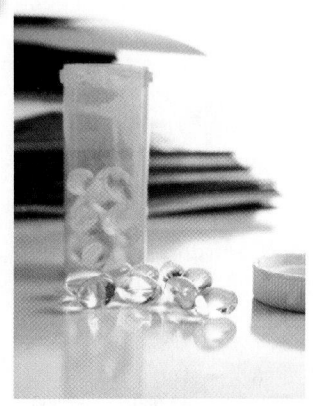

SHORT-TERM NOTES PAYABLE

A promissory note, or note payable, is a promise to repay a specified amount of money, either at a fixed future date or on demand. Notes payable are often used instead of accounts payable because they give the lender written documentation of the obligation, which helps if legal action is needed to collect the debt. Notes payable are also frequently issued to meet short-term financing needs.

Notes can be issued for varying periods. Notes that are due for payment within one year of the statement of financial position date are classified as current liabilities. Most notes are interest-bearing, with interest due monthly or at maturity. While short-term notes can have floating interest rates, similar to that described earlier for an operating line of credit or credit facility, it is more usual for them to have a fixed interest rate. A **fixed interest rate** is a constant rate for the entire term of the note.

Students often have difficulty understanding the difference between a note payable and an account payable. There are differences, however. An account payable is an informal promise to pay, while a note payable is a written promise to pay that gives the payee a stronger legal claim. An account payable arises only from credit purchases (amounts owed to suppliers), while a note payable can be used for credit purchases, extending an account payable beyond normal amounts or due dates, or to borrow money. An account payable is usually due within a short period of time

Alternative Terminology
Notes payable are also commonly referred to as *loans payable*.

Helpful Hint
Notes payable are the opposite of notes receivable, and the accounting is similar.

(e.g., 30 days), while a note payable can extend for longer periods (e.g., 30 days to up to one year, or even several years). Finally, an account payable does not incur interest unless the account is overdue, while a note payable usually bears interest for its entire duration.

To illustrate the accounting for a note payable, assume that HSBC Bank lends $100,000 to Williams Ltd. on March 1, 2012. Because this is a loan from a bank, it is commonly referred to as a bank loan payable. The loan is due in four months, on July 1, and 6% interest, along with the principal amount ($100,000) of the loan, is payable at maturity.

Williams makes the following journal entry when it receives the $100,000:

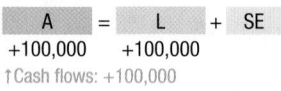

Mar. 1	Cash	100,000	
	Bank Loan Payable		100,000
	(To record receipt of four-month, 6% bank loan from HSBC)		

Interest accrues over the life of the bank loan and must be recorded periodically. If Williams has a March 31 year end, an adjusting entry is required to recognize the interest expense and interest payable of $500 ($100,000 × 6% × $^{1}/_{12}$) at March 31. Recall from Chapter 4 that interest is calculated for short-term notes (loans) by multiplying the principal amount by the annual interest rate by the fraction of the year. That is, the 6% is an annual interest rate and must be adjusted for the period of time—which may be the number of months as we have assumed here, or the number of days.

The adjusting entry is:

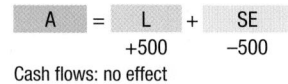

Helpful Hint
Interest rates are always expressed as an annual (one-year) rate, regardless of the term of the note or loan.

Mar. 31	Interest Expense	500	
	Interest Payable		500
	(To accrue interest for March on HSBC bank loan)		

In the March 31 year-end financial statements, the current liabilities section of the statement of financial position will show a bank loan payable of $100,000, and interest payable of $500. In addition, interest expense of $500 will be reported in the "other expenses and losses" section of the income statement.

At maturity (July 1), Williams Ltd. must pay the principal of the loan ($100,000) plus $2,000 interest ($100,000 × 6% × $^{4}/_{12}$). One month, $500 for the month of March, of this interest has already been accrued. Interest must also be updated for $1,500 ($100,000 × 6% × $^{3}/_{12}$) for the three additional months—April through June—since interest was last recorded. This can be done in two separate entries as shown below, or in one compound entry to record the interest and payment of the note.

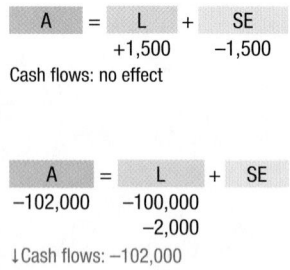

July 1	Interest Expense	1,500	
	Interest Payable		1,500
	(To accrue interest for April, May, and June on HSBC bank loan)		

July 1	Bank Loan Payable	100,000	
	Interest Payable ($500 + $1,500)	2,000	
	Cash ($100,000 + $2,000)		102,000
	(To record payment of HSBC bank loan and interest at maturity)		

CURRENT MATURITIES OF NON-CURRENT DEBT

Companies often have a portion of non-current (long-term) debt that is due in the current year. For example, Canada Post reports $13 million as the "current portion of long-term debt" at December 31, 2010.

To illustrate, assume that Cudini Construction borrows $25,000 on January 1, 2012, for five years. The terms of the loan specify that each January 1, starting January 1, 2013, $5,000 of the note will be repaid. When financial statements are prepared on December 31, 2012, $5,000 should be reported as a current liability and $20,000 as a non-current liability.

It is not necessary to prepare an adjusting entry to recognize the current maturities of non-current debt. The proper statement classification of each statement of financial position account is recognized when the statement of financial position is prepared.

BEFORE YOU GO ON...

▶Do It! Current Liabilities

Prepare the journal entries to record the following transactions:

1. Pre-tax sales on April 2 totalled $256,000. The HST rate is 12%. Record the sales and sales tax.

2. A property tax bill for the calendar year of $12,000 is received on May 1 and is due June 30. Record the entries on May 1 and June 30, assuming the company has a calendar year end.

3. A company's gross salary amounts to $10,000 for the week ended July 11. Amounts deducted from the employees' salaries are CPP of $495, EI of $178, income tax of $3,465, and health insurance of $950. The employer's portion of CPP is $495 and of EI, $249. Record the weekly payroll on July 11, assuming cash is paid to the employees but the payroll amounts withheld are still due.

4. Accrue interest on December 31 (the company's year end) for a three-month, 6%, $10,000 bank loan effective November 1. Interest is payable on the first of each month.

Action Plan

- Record sales separately from the sales tax. Recall that sales tax is a liability until remitted.
- Record the property tax expense and the property tax payable for the amounts incurred to date. Record the prepaid property tax at the time of payment for any amounts paid in advance.
- Record both the employees' portion of the payroll and the benefits owed by the employer. Employee deductions are not an expense for the employer.
- Remember the formula for interest: principal (face) value × annual interest rate × time.

Solution

1.	Apr. 2	Cash ($256,000 + $30,720)	286,720	
		Sales		256,000
		Sales Tax Payable ($256,000 × 12%)		30,720
		(To record sales and sales tax)		
2.	May 1	Property Tax Expense ($12,000 × 4/12)	4,000	
		Property Tax Payable		4,000
		(To record property tax expense for January to April and amount owing)		
	June 30	Property Tax Payable	4,000	
		Property Tax Expense ($12,000 × 2/12)	2,000	
		Prepaid Property Tax ($12,000 × 6/12)	6,000	
		Cash		12,000
		(To record payment of property tax for January through December)		
3.	July 11	Salaries Expense	10,000	
		CPP Payable		495
		EI Payable		178
		Income Tax Payable		3,465
		Health Insurance Payable		950
		Cash		4,912
		(To record payroll and employee deductions)		
	11	Employee Benefits Expense	744	
		CPP Payable		495
		EI Payable		249
		(To record employee benefits)		
4.	Dec. 31	Interest Expense ($10,000 × 6% × 1/12)	50	
		Interest Payable		50
		(To accrue interest for December on bank loan)		

the navigator

Non-Current Liabilities: Instalment Notes Payable

A **non-current liability** is an obligation that is expected to be paid after one year or longer. These obligations are often in the form of instalment notes or bonds. These obligations are also known as financial instruments; more specifically a **financial liability**, which means that there is a contractual obligation to pay cash in the future. Instalment notes payable are explained in this section, followed by bonds in the next section.

Using long-term notes payable in debt financing is common. Long-term notes payable are similar to short-term notes payable except that the terms of the notes are for more than one year. Long-term notes may have fixed or floating interest rates. In periods of unstable interest rates, it is common for notes to have a floating interest rate that changes as the prime borrowing rate changes. For example, a company may have long-term debt on which it pays interest at the Bank of Canada prime rate plus 1%.

A long-term note may be **secured** or **unsecured debt**. A secured note pledges title (gives ownership) to specific assets as collateral or security for the loan. Secured notes are also known as mortgages. A **mortgage payable** is widely used by individuals to purchase homes. It is also used by many companies to acquire property, plant, and equipment. Unsecured notes are issued against the general credit of the borrower. There are no assets used as collateral.

ACCOUNTING MATTERS!   *Investor Perspective*

Increasing Mortgage Debt

The annual report from the Canadian Association of Accredited Mortgage Professionals (CAAMP) noted that there were more than $1 trillion of mortgages payable outstanding by 5.65 million home owners in 2010. This amount owed by mortgage holders was an increase of 7.6% over the prior year and an increase of 194% over the previous 15 years.

This increase was primarily due to low interest rates, which encouraged many home owners to refinance, in addition to higher home prices resulting in increased borrowings. The majority of mortgage holders have fixed interest rate mortgages, which means they are not as vulnerable to increasing interest rates. The CAAMP report states that "There are about 100,000 borrowers who are susceptible to short-term moves of interest rates, which is quite a small share (less than 2 percent) of the 5.65 million mortgage holders in Canada."

Source: Steve Ladurantaye, "Canadian Mortgage Debt Tops $1-Trillion for First Time," *The Globe and Mail*, November 8, 2010, p. B3

While short-term notes are normally repayable in full at maturity, most long-term notes are repayable in a series of periodic payments. These payments are known as **instalments** and are paid monthly, quarterly, semi-annually, or at another defined period.

As with short-term notes, the terms *notes* and *loans* are used interchangeably. Each instalment payment consists of a mix of (1) interest on the unpaid balance of the loan, and (2) a reduction of the loan principal. The actual instalment payments generally take one of two forms: (1) fixed principal payments plus interest, or (2) blended principal and interest payments. Let's look at each of these payment patterns in more detail.

FIXED PRINCIPAL PAYMENTS PLUS INTEREST

Instalment loans with fixed principal payments are repayable in **equal periodic amounts plus interest.** As mentioned earlier, interest may be either fixed or floating. For simplicity, we will assume a fixed interest rate. To illustrate, assume that on January 1, 2012, Belanger Ltée borrows $120,000 from the bank for a five-year period at a 7% interest rate to finance a research laboratory. The entry to record the loan is as follows:

Jan. 1	Cash	120,000	
	Bank Loan Payable		120,000
	(To record receipt of five-year, 7% bank loan)		

A	=	L	+	SE
+120,000		+120,000		

↑Cash flows: +120,000

The terms of the loan provide for equal monthly instalment payments of $2,000 ($120,000 ÷ 60 monthly periods) on the first of each month, plus interest of 7% on the outstanding principal balance.

Monthly interest expense is calculated by multiplying the outstanding principal balance by the interest rate. Because a portion of the principal balance is repaid each month, the outstanding principal balance will change (decrease) each month. This is different from what we observed in the calculation of interest on short-term loans, because the principal balance does not change throughout the term of a short-term loan.

For Belanger, the first payment date is February 1, and the interest expense is $700 ($120,000 × 7% × $\frac{1}{12}$). Similar to short-term loans, the 7% is an annual interest rate and must be adjusted for the monthly time period. The cash payment of $2,700 is the total of the instalment payment of $2,000, which is applied against the principal, plus the interest of $700.

The entry to record the first instalment payment on February 1 is as follows:

Feb. 1	Interest Expense ($120,000 × 7% × $\frac{1}{12}$)	700	
	Bank Loan Payable	2,000	
	Cash ($2,000 + $700)		2,700
	(To record instalment payment on bank loan)		

A	=	L	+	SE
−2,700		−2,000		−700

↓Cash flows: −2,700

An instalment payment schedule is a useful tool to help organize this information and to provide information that helps prepare journal entries. A partial instalment payment schedule for the first few months for Belanger Ltée, with amounts rounded to the nearest dollar, is shown in Illustration 10-2.

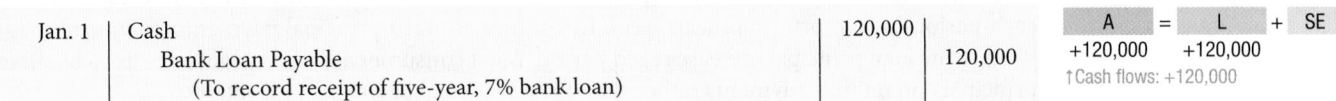

BELANGER LTÉE
Instalment Payment Schedule—Fixed Principal Payments

Interest Period	(A) Cash Payment (B + C)	(B) Interest Expense (D × 7% × $\frac{1}{12}$)	(C) Reduction of Principal ($120,000 ÷ 60)	(D) Principal Balance (D − C)
Jan. 1				$120,000
Feb. 1	$2,700	$700	$2,000	118,000
Mar. 1	2,688	688	2,000	116,000
Apr. 1	2,677	677	2,000	114,000

► Illustration 10-2
Instalment payment schedule—fixed principal payments

Column A, the cash payment, is the total of the principal payment, $2,000, plus the interest. The cash payment changes each period because the interest changes. Column B determines the interest expense, which decreases each period because the principal balance, on which interest is calculated, decreases. Column C is the principal repayment amount of $2,000. This payment is constant each period in a "fixed principal payment plus interest" pattern. Column D is the principal balance, which decreases each period by the amount of the principal repayment.

In summary, with fixed principal payments, the interest decreases each period as the principal decreases. The portion applied to the reduction of the loan principal stays constant, but because of the decreasing interest, the total cash payment decreases.

BLENDED PRINCIPAL AND INTEREST PAYMENTS

Instalment loans with blended principal and interest payments are repayable in **equal periodic amounts, including interest.** Blended principal and interest payments result in changing amounts of interest and principal applied to the loan. As with fixed principal payments, the interest decreases each period (as the principal decreases). In contrast to fixed principal payments, the portion applied to the loan principal increases each period. Most consumer and mortgage loans use a blend of principal and interest payments rather than fixed principal payments plus interest.

To illustrate this option, assume that instead of fixed principal payments, Belanger Ltée repays its bank loan in equal monthly blended principal and interest instalments of $2,376. As with the fixed principal payments illustrated above, monthly interest expense is calculated by multiplying the outstanding principal balance by the interest rate. For the first payment date—February 1—interest expense is $700 ($120,000 × 7% × $\frac{1}{12}$). The instalment payment of $2,376 is fixed for each month, and includes interest and principal amounts that will vary. In February, the principal balance will be reduced by $1,676, which is the difference between the instalment payment of $2,376 and the interest amount of $700.

The entry to record the borrowing of the money from the bank on January 1 is the same as in the previous section. The entry to record the instalment payment uses the same accounts but different amounts (except that interest expense is the same amount for the first month). The first instalment payment on February 1 is recorded as follows:

A	=	L	+	SE
−2,376		−1,676		−700

↓Cash flows: −2,376

Feb. 1	Interest Expense ($120,000 × 7% × $\frac{1}{12}$)	700	
	Bank Loan Payable ($2,376 − $700)	1,676	
	Cash		2,376
	(To record instalment payment on bank loan)		

An instalment payment schedule can also be prepared for blended principal and interest payments. Illustration 10-3 shows a partial instalment payment schedule for the first few months for Belanger Ltée, with amounts rounded to the nearest dollar.

▶ Illustration 10-3

Instalment payment schedule—blended payments

		BELANGER LTÉE		
	Instalment Payment Schedule—Blended Payments			
Interest Period	(A) Cash Payment	(B) Interest Expense (D × 7% × $\frac{1}{12}$)	(C) Reduction of Principal (A − B)	(D) Principal Balance (D − C)
Jan. 1				$120,000
Feb. 1	$2,376	$700	$1,676	118,324
Mar. 1	2,376	690	1,686	116,638
Apr. 1	2,376	680	1,696	114,942

Column A, the cash payment, is specified and is the same for each period. The amount of this cash payment can actually be calculated mathematically. It can also be determined using present value techniques, which are discussed later in the chapter.

Column B determines the interest expense, which decreases each period because the principal balance that the interest is calculated on decreases. Column C is how much the principal is reduced by. This is the difference between the cash payment of $2,376 and the interest for the period. Consequently this amount will increase each period. Column D is the principal balance, which decreases each period by a varying amount; that is, by the reduction of the principal amount from Column C.

In summary, with blended payments, the interest decreases each period as the principal decreases. The total cash payment stays constant, but because of the decreasing interest, the reduction of principal increases.

The following schedule summarizes the differences between the two types of instalment payment patterns:

Instalment Payment Pattern	Principal	Interest	Total Cash Payment
Fixed principal plus interest	Constant: Reduction of principal equal each period	Decreases: Interest expense decreases each period	Decreases: Total cash payment decreases each period
Blended principal and interest	Increases: Reduction of principal increases each period	Decreases: Interest expense decreases each period	Constant: Total cash payment equal each period

CURRENT AND NON-CURRENT PORTIONS

With both types of instalment loans, the reduction in principal for the next year must be reported as a current liability. The remaining unpaid principal is classified as a non-current liability (unless it is expected to be refinanced.

For example, consider the following fixed principal annual instalment payment schedule:

Interest Period	Cash Payment	Interest Expense	Reduction of Principal	Principal Balance
Issue Date				$50,000
2011	$13,500	$3,500	$10,000	40,000
2012	12,800	2,800	10,000	30,000
2013	12,100	2,100	10,000	20,000
2014	11,400	1,400	10,000	10,000
2015	10,700	700	10,000	0

If financial statements were being prepared at the end of 2012, the company would report $30,000 as its total liability for the bank loan, shown in red in the principal balance column. Of this, $10,000 ($30,000 – $20,000)—the amount to be repaid within the next year (2013), which is also highlighted above in red—would be reported as a current liability. The company would report $20,000—the amount to be repaid beyond next year (2014 and 2015)—as a non-current liability. This amount too is highlighted in red in the above table. Note that, when the current portion ($10,000) and the non-current portion ($20,000) are added together, the amount should agree with the total amount owing at the end of 2012, $30,000.

BEFORE YOU GO ON...

▶Do It! Instalment Mortgage Payable

On December 31, 2012, Tian Inc. borrowed $500,000, signing a 15-year, 8% mortgage in return. The terms provide for semi-annual blended instalment payments of $28,915 (principal and interest) on June 30 and December 31. (a) Prepare an instalment payment schedule for the first two years of the mortgage through to December 31, 2014. (b) Prepare the journal entries required to record the receipt of the mortgage loan on December 31, 2012, and the first two instalment payments on June 30, 2013, and December 31, 2013. (c) Show the presentation of the mortgage liability on the statement of financial position at December 31, 2013.

Action Plan

- Prepare an instalment payment schedule. Round all amounts to the nearest dollar.
- Multiply the semi-annual interest rate by the principal balance at the beginning of the period to determine the interest expense. The reduction of principal is the difference between the cash payment and the interest expense.
- Record the instalment payments, recognizing that each payment consists of (1) interest on the unpaid mortgage balance, and (2) a reduction of the mortgage principal.
- The current portion of the mortgage payable is the amount of principal that will be repaid in the next year (2014). The non-current portion is the total liability at the date in question (December 31, 2013) less the current portion.

(continued)

Solution

(a)

Interest Period	Cash Payment	Interest Expense	Reduction of Principal	Principal Balance
Dec. 31, 2012				$500,000
June 30, 2013	$28,915	$20,000	$ 8,915	491,085
Dec. 31, 2013	28,915	19,643	9,272	481,813
June 30, 2014	28,915	19,273	9,642	472,171
Dec. 31, 2014	28,915	18,887	10,028	462,143

(b)

Dec. 31, 2012	Cash	500,000	
	Mortgage Payable		500,000
	(To record receipt of 15-year, 8% mortgage payable)		
June 30, 2013	Interest Expense ($500,000 × 8% × 6/12)	20,000	
	Mortgage Payable ($28,915 – $20,000)	8,915	
	Cash		28,915
	(To record semi-annual instalment payment on mortgage)		
Dec. 31, 2013	Interest Expense [($500,000 – $8,915) × 8% × 6/12)]	19,643	
	Mortgage Payable ($28,915 – $19,643)	9,272	
	Cash		28,915
	(To record semi-annual instalment payment on mortgage)		

(c)

TIAN INC. December 31, 2013 Statement of Financial Position (partial)	
Current liabilities	
Current portion of mortgage payable ($9,642 + $10,028)	$ 19,670
Non-current liabilities	
Mortgage payable	462,143
Total liabilities	481,813

the navigator

Non-Current Liabilities: Bonds Payable

STUDY OBJECTIVE 3
Account for bonds payable.

Alternative Terminology
The *coupon interest rate* is also known as the *contractual interest rate* or the *stated interest rate.*

Like other kinds of non-current debt, a **bond** is a promise to repay a specified amount of money at a fixed future date. A bond is used instead of other types of debt when the amount of financing needed is too large for one lender. A large amount (e.g., $1 million) is typically divided into small denominations (usually $1,000), which makes it possible for more than one lender to participate in the bond offering. Whereas both small and large corporations issue notes, only large corporations issue bonds.

Accounting for notes and bonds is quite similar. Both have a fixed maturity date and pay interest. Although both can have a fixed or floating interest rate, most bonds have a fixed interest rate. This rate, which determines the amount of interest to pay to bondholders, is known as the **coupon interest rate** and is always quoted as an annual rate. Bond interest is normally paid semi-annually although some bonds pay interest monthly or quarterly, similar to notes.

Like notes, bonds may be **unsecured** or **secured.** Unsecured bonds are also known as **debentures.** Both notes and bonds can be payable at maturity or in instalments. Bonds that mature on a single specified future date are known as **term bonds.** The amount of principal due at maturity is usually called the **face value.** Bonds that mature in instalments are known as **serial bonds,** although these are not a common type of bonds. In contrast to most instalment notes and loans, which are repayable in a series of periodic instalment payments, bonds are normally repayable in full at maturity unless they are retired early. If bonds are **redeemable,** they can be retired by the company before they mature.

BOND TRADING

A significant difference between notes and bonds is that bonds can be traded on a stock exchange in the same way as shares are. Notes are seldom traded on the stock exchange. Bonds may also be structured as **convertible bonds** that can be exchanged (converted) into common shares at an agreed-upon price.

As was discussed in the chapter opening feature story, Canada Post has bonds and they are listed on the Toronto Stock Exchange. An illustrative listing for one of its bond issues is shown below:

Issuer	Coupon Rate	Coupon Frequency	Maturity Date	Price	Yield
Canada Post	4.36	S	2040-07-16	107.97	3.90

This bond listing for Canada Post indicates that these particular bonds have a coupon interest rate of 4.36% per year. The coupon frequency states that interest is paid semi-annually (S). This means that Canada Post would pay each $1,000 bondholder interest of $21.80 ($1,000 × 4.36% × $^{6}/_{12}$) twice a year. The bonds mature on July 16, 2040.

Bond prices are quoted as a percentage of the face value of the bonds, which is usually $1,000. For example, if the bond price is stated as 100, this means that the bonds will sell at 100% of the face value. If the face value is $1,000, then the bonds will sell for $1,000 ($1,000 × 100%). You can assume that bonds are issued in $1,000 denominations unless you are told otherwise.

With respect to the Canada Post bonds described in the above listing, the price of 107.97 means that $1,079.70 ($1,000 × 107.97%) was the selling price of each $1,000 bond on the date of the above listing. The yield, or market interest rate, on the bonds was 3.9%. The **market interest rate** is the rate investors demand for lending their money. This rate is also commonly known as the effective interest rate.

As is the case with share transactions, transactions between a bondholder and other investors are not journalized by the issuing corporation. If Vinod Thakkar sells his Canada Post bonds to Julie Tarrel, the issuing corporation—Canada Post in this case—does not record the transaction. While the issuer (or its trustee) does keep records of the names of bondholders, a corporation makes journal entries only when it issues bonds, makes an interest payment, or buys back and retires its bonds.

DETERMINING THE ISSUE PRICE OF BONDS

If you were an investor interested in purchasing a bond, how would you decide how much to pay? To be more specific, assume that Candlestick Inc. issues a zero-interest bond (a bond that pays no interest) with a face value of $1 million due in five years. For this bond, the only cash you receive is $1 million at the end of five years. Would you pay $1 million for this bond? We hope not, because $1 million received five years from now is not the same as $1 million received today.

You should not pay $1 million because of what is called the **time value of money.** If you had $1 million today, you would invest it and earn interest so that after five years your investment could be worth more than $1 million. Thus, if someone is going to pay you $1 million five years from now, you would want to figure out its equivalent today. That amount—how much must be invested today at current interest rates to have $1 million in five years—is called the present value and would be a lower amount than the future or face value of $1 million.

The present value of a bond is the amount at which it sells in the marketplace. The issue price (present value), therefore, depends on three factors: (1) the dollar amounts to be received,

(2) the length of time until the amounts are received, and (3) the market rate of interest. The process of finding the present value is referred to as discounting the future amounts.

To illustrate, assume that on January 1, 2012, Candlestick Inc. issues $1 million of 5% bonds, due in five years, with interest payable semi-annually on January 1 and July 1. The purchaser of the bonds would receive the following two cash inflows: (1) the face or principal amount of $1 million to be paid at maturity, and (2) 10 interest payments of $25,000 ($1,000,000 × 5% × 6/12 months) over the term of the bonds. A time diagram for both cash flows is shown in Illustration 10-4.

▶ **Illustration 10-4**
Time diagram of cash flows

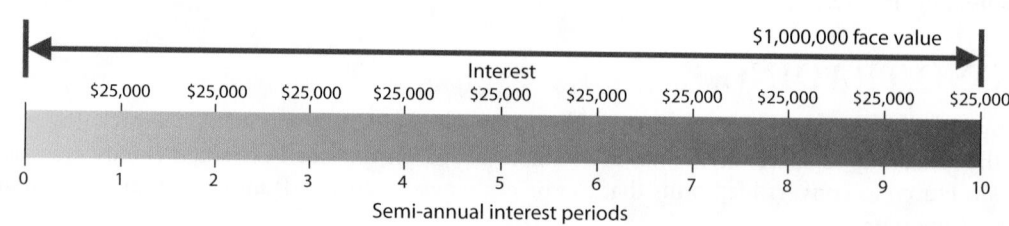

The issue price of a bond is equal to the present value of all the future cash inflows—face value and interest—promised by the bond. There are standardized present value tables available to determine present value factors that can be used to calculate the present value, or issue price, of the bond. We have reproduced present value tables in Appendix C for your reference at the end of the book. You should refer to them now as you review the following procedures for calculating the present value of a bond:

Alternative Terminology
The *issue price* is also called the *selling price, fair value,* or *market value* of the bonds.

1. Face value: Use Table 1 (the present value of $1) to determine the factor to use to calculate the present value of the principal or face value of the bond. In Candlestick's case, this is a single payment of $1 million to be paid at the end of the bond term, five years hence. Locate the appropriate factor at the intersection of the number of periods (n) and the interest rate (i).

   When interest is paid semi-annually, you must double the number of periods and halve the annual interest rate. In the Candlestick example, the five-year term of the bonds means that there are 10 semi-annual interest periods. In addition, the annual market interest rate of 5% becomes 2.5% (5% × 6/12) when adjusted for the semi-annual period. The present value factor to be used for the face value for $n = 10$ and $i = 2.5\%$ is 0.78120.

2. Interest: Use Table 2 (the present value of an annuity of $1) to determine the factor to use to calculate the present value of the bond interest. In Candlestick's case, $25,000 of interest is to be paid every six months for the next five years or 10 semi-annual periods. The present value factor to be used for the interest for $n = 10$ and $i = 2.5\%$ is 8.75206.

Using the above factors, we can calculate the present values of the face value and interest amounts as follows:

Present value of $1,000,000 received in 10 periods
  $1,000,000 × 0.78120 ($n = 10, i = 2.5\%$) $ 781,200
Present value of $25,000 received for each of 10 periods
  $25,000 × 8.75206 ($n = 10, i = 2.5\%$)   218,800
Present value (issue price) of bonds $1,000,000
Where n = number of interest periods and i = interest rate

Note that the bonds' face value and the coupon interest rate are always used to calculate the interest payment—$25,000 in this case. While the coupon interest rate is used to determine the interest payment, the market interest rate is always used to determine the appropriate factor to be used for the present value. When the present value (issue price) of the bond equals the face value, these two rates are the same (both are 5% per annum), as is the case in our Candlestick example above.

The present value can also be determined mathematically using a financial calculator or spreadsheet program. The same principles are involved as described above. First, you need to input the future value (*FV*), the market interest rate per period (*i*), the number of semi-annual interest periods (*n*), and then tell it to calculate the present value of the face value. In the Candlestick example, the future value (*FV*) is $1 million, the interest rate (*i*) is 2.5%, and the number of interest periods (*n*) is 10.

Second, you need to input the interest payment (*PMT*), the interest rate (*i*), the number of interest periods (*n*), and then tell it to calculate the present value of the interest. In the Candlestick example, the interest payment (*PMT*) is $25,000, the market interest rate per period (*i*) is 2.5%, and the number of semi-annual periods (*n*) is 10. Some calculators may require you to enter the payment amount as a minus (e.g., –25000) and you may also have to input information that the payment is at the end (not the beginning) of each period.

We will not illustrate how to use a financial calculator or spreadsheet program here as the methodology for each can vary. You should be aware that the present value amounts calculated with a financial calculator or spreadsheet program will most likely differ by a few dollars from those calculated using the factors in the present value tables as we have illustrated above. This is because the factors in the present value tables are rounded to five decimal places whereas your own calculations are likely not rounded at all, or rounded to the number of decimal places you specify.

DISCOUNT OR PREMIUM ON BONDS

The present value calculations for Candlestick above assumed that the coupon interest rate and the market interest rate were the same. However, market interest rates change daily. They are influenced by the type of bond issued, the company's financial position and performance, the state of the economy, and current industry conditions, among other factors. As a result, the coupon and market interest rates often differ, and bonds therefore sell below or above their face value.

To illustrate, suppose that investors have one of two options: (1) purchase bonds that have just been issued with a coupon interest rate of 6%, or (2) purchase bonds issued at an earlier date with a lower coupon interest rate of 5%. If the bonds are of equal risk, investors will choose the 6% investment. To make the investments equal, and the option 2 bonds worth purchasing, investors would need a higher rate of interest for option 2 than the 5% coupon interest. But investors cannot change the coupon interest rate stated on the bonds. What they can do instead is pay less than the face value for the bonds. By paying less for the bonds, investors can effectively obtain a higher yield, or market interest rate, of 6%. When the market interest rate is higher than the coupon interest rate, the bonds are said to sell at a **discount**.

On the other hand, the market interest rate may be lower than the coupon interest rate. In that case, investors will pay more than face value for the bonds. That is, if the market interest rate is 4% but the coupon interest rate on the bonds is 5%, everyone will want to buy the bonds and the price will rise above the bonds' face value. In these cases, the bonds are said to sell at a **premium**.

The relationship between interest rates and a resulting discount, face value, or premium is shown in Illustration 10-5.

Helpful Hint
Bond prices vary inversely with changes in the market interest rate. For example, as market interest rates increase, bond prices decrease.

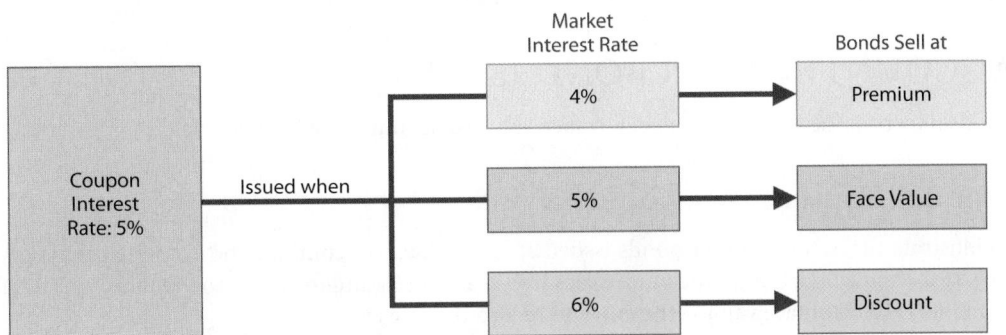

▶Illustration 10-5
Interest rates and bond prices

The Canada Post bonds shown in the bond trading section earlier in this chapter were issued at a premium. In that particular case, the market interest rate (3.9%) was lower than the coupon interest rate (4.36%). That is why the bonds sold for more than their face value (107.97%).

Issuing bonds at an amount different from face value is quite common. By the time a company prints the bond certificates (which provide the legal documentation for the bonds) and markets the bonds, it will be a coincidence if the market rate and the coupon rate are the same. Thus, the issue of bonds at a discount does not mean there is doubt about the financial strength of the issuer. Conversely the sale of bonds at a premium does not indicate that the financial strength of the issuer is exceptional.

Once the bonds are issued, the interest on bonds payable is calculated using the effective-interest method. The **effective-interest method** is an amortization method used to allocate a bond discount or premium to interest expense over the life of the bond. This method results in a periodic interest expense that equals a constant percentage (the market or effective interest rate) of the carrying amount of the bond. The **carrying amount** of a bond is its face value less any unamortized discount, or plus any unamortized premium. At the date of issue, the carrying amount equals the bond's issue price.

The calculation of amortization using the effective-interest method is shown in Illustration 10-6.

▶ **Illustration 10-6**
Calculation of amortization using effective-interest method

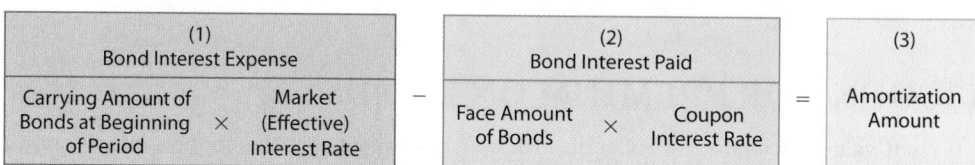

As shown in Illustration 10-6, the following steps are required under the effective-interest method of amortization:

1. Calculate the **bond interest expense:** Multiply the carrying amount of the bonds at the beginning of the interest period by the market (effective) interest rate for the semi-annual (or appropriate) period.
2. Calculate the **bond interest paid** (or accrued): Multiply the face value of the bonds by the coupon interest rate for the semi-annual (or appropriate) period.
3. Calculate the **amortization amount:** Determine the difference between the amounts calculated in steps (1) and (2).

Note that this is similar to the calculation of interest for long-term instalment notes payable, where interest expense was calculated using the carrying (principal) amount of the note multiplied by the interest rate. In the case of the note, there was no "effective" interest rate as there is for bonds. In addition, we did not have to worry about any discount or premium with the notes, although there are circumstances where non–interest-bearing notes can also be issued with a discount or premium.

The effective-interest method is required for companies reporting under IFRS. Private companies reporting using ASPE can choose to use either the effective-interest method or other methods, if they do not differ materially from the effective-interest method. Because the use of the effective-interest method is prevalent, we focus on this method in the chapter.

ACCOUNTING FOR BOND ISSUES

Bonds may be issued at face value, below face value (discount), or above face value (premium).

Issuing Bonds at Face Value

To illustrate the accounting for bonds issued at face value, let's continue the example discussed in the last section where Candlestick Inc. issues five-year, 5%, $1-million bonds on January 1, 2012, for $1 million (100% of face value). The entry to record the sale is:

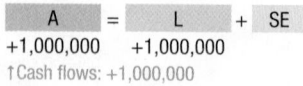

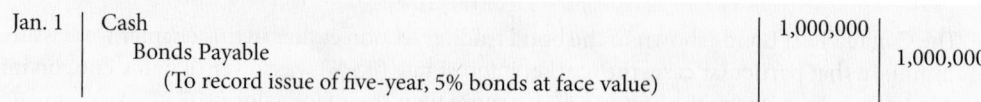

Jan. 1	Cash	1,000,000	
	Bonds Payable		1,000,000
	(To record issue of five-year, 5% bonds at face value)		

Because these bonds were issued at face value, the interest expense and interest paid are the same. Interest expense and interest paid are calculated by multiplying $1,000,000 × 5% × 6/12, which equals $25,000. Interest is payable semi-annually on January 1 and July 1, so the following entry must be made on July 1 to record the interest expense and interest paid:

July 1	Interest Expense	25,000	
	Cash		25,000
	(To record semi-annual bond interest payment)		

A	=	L	+	SE
−25,000				−25,000
↓ Cash flows: −25,000				

At December 31, Candlestick's year end, an adjusting entry is required to recognize the $25,000 of interest expense incurred since July 1 that is due to be paid on January 1. The entry is:

Dec. 31	Interest Expense	25,000	
	Interest Payable		25,000
	(To accrue semi-annual bond interest)		

A	=	L	+	SE
		+25,000		−25,000
Cash flows: no effect				

The interest payable on the bonds is classified as a current liability at December 31, 2012, because it is scheduled for payment within the next year. The bonds payable are reported in the non-current liability section of the statement of financial position because their maturity date is January 1, 2017 (more than one year away). When the interest is paid on January 1, 2013, Interest Payable is decreased (debited) and Cash is also decreased (credited) for $25,000.

Issuing Bonds at a Discount

To illustrate the issue of bonds at a discount, assume that Candlestick sells its bonds to yield a market (effective) interest rate of 6%. When the market interest rate is 6%, the 5% Candlestick bonds are not very attractive to investors, who could earn a higher interest rate (6%) elsewhere. Investors will discount the price of the bonds to result in an effective yield of 6%, which is higher than the 5% coupon interest rate.

Whether using present value tables or a financial calculator or spreadsheet program, the key inputs needed to determine the issue price of the bonds are as follows:

Future value $(FV) = \$1,000,000$
Market interest rate $(i) = 3\%$ (6% × 6/12)
Interest payment $(PMT) = \$25,000$ ($1,000,000 × 5% × 6/12)
Number of semi-annual periods $(n) = 10$ (5 years × 2)

Recall that, while the coupon interest rate (5%) is used to determine the interest payment, it is the market interest rate (6%) that is used to determine the present value factor. Using the present value tables in Appendix C at the end of this textbook, we determine that the bonds will sell for $957,345 (95.7345% of face value):

Present value of $1,000,000 received in 10 periods	
$1,000,000 × 0.74409 ($n = 10, i = 3\%$)	$744,090
Present value of $25,000 received for each of 10 periods	
$25,000 × 8.53020 ($n = 10, i = 3\%$)	213,255
Present value (issue price) of bonds	$957,345

The issue price of $957,345 results in a bond discount of $42,655 ($1,000,000 – $957,345). The entry to record the sale is:

Jan. 1	Cash	957,345	
	Bonds Payable		957,345
	(To record issue of five-year, 5% bonds at a discount)		

A	=	L	+	SE
+957,345		+957,345		
↑ Cash flows: +957,345				

Rather than crediting the Bonds Payable account for the issue price of $957,345, some companies use a separate contra liability account to keep track of the bond discount. That is, they would record bonds payable as a credit of $1 million and record the bond discount in a separate account as a debit of $42,655. For reporting purposes, however, current accounting standards—both IFRS and ASPE—require the presentation of bonds net of any discounts (or premiums, as we will learn in the next section). Consequently, many companies record their journal entries on a net basis as well. Although both ways of *recording* bond transactions are acceptable, we will illustrate the recording of bond journal entries net of any discount or premium in this text, which is what is required for *reporting* purposes.

Helpful Hint
Present value is always less than future value. The difference between present and future value is interest.

Amortizing the Discount. The bond discount must be allocated to interest expense over the life of the bonds. The $25,000 interest payment is recorded as interest expense every semi-annual period for five years (10 semi-annual periods). The bond discount is also allocated to interest expense over the 10 periods—this allocation is referred to as **amortizing the discount**. Consequently, the amortization of the discount increases the amount of interest expense that is reported each period, in addition to increasing the carrying amount in the liability account.

For the first interest period, the bond interest expense is $28,720, calculated by multiplying the carrying amount of the bonds by the market interest rate ($957,345 × 6% × %12). The interest payment, $25,000, is the same whether the bonds are issued at face value, at a discount, or at a premium. It is calculated by multiplying the face value of the bonds by the coupon interest rate ($1,000,000 × 5% × %12). The amortization is the difference between the interest expense and the interest paid ($28,720 – $25,000 = $3,720).

At July 1, the entry to record the payment of interest and amortization of bond discount by Candlestick is as follows:

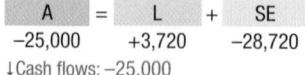

A = L + SE
−25,000 +3,720 −28,720
↓ Cash flows: −25,000

July 1	Interest Expense	28,720	
	Bonds Payable		3,720
	Cash		25,000
	(To record semi-annual bond interest payment and amortization of bond discount)		

We have recorded this in one compound journal entry, but two separate journal entries could be prepared instead to: (1) debit Interest Expense and credit Bonds Payable for the amortization of the discount, $3,720, and (2) debit Interest Expense and credit Cash for the interest payment, $25,000.

At the second interest period, the bonds' carrying amount is now $961,065 ($957,345 + $3,720). The carrying amount will continue to increase by the amount of the discount amortization until, at maturity, the bonds' carrying amount equals their face value.

To calculate the interest expense for the second interest period, we multiply the carrying amount of the bonds by the market interest rate to arrive at $28,832 ($961,065 × 6% × %12). The interest payment is unchanged at $25,000. As before, the amortization is the difference between the interest expense and the interest paid ($28,832 – $25,000 = $3,832).

At December 31, Candlestick's year end, the following adjusting entry is made to record interest and amortization for the second interest period:

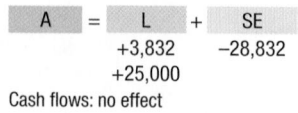

A = L + SE
+3,832 −28,832
+25,000
Cash flows: no effect

Dec. 31	Interest Expense	28,832	
	Bonds Payable		3,832
	Interest Payable		25,000
	(To accrue semi-annual bond interest and record amortization of bond discount)		

A bond discount amortization schedule is useful to organize and track the interest expense, discount amortization, and interest payable amounts, similar to the instalment payment schedules shown earlier in the chapter for notes payable. Such a schedule is especially useful when the amortization of the bond discount is recorded directly in the Bonds Payable account as we have done above, rather than recorded in a separate contra liability account. A complete bond amortization schedule is shown in Illustration 10-7. Note that amounts have been rounded to the nearest dollar for simplicity.

▶ Illustration 10-7
Bond discount amortization schedule

CANDLESTICK INC.
Bond Discount Amortization Schedule

Semi-Annual Interest Period	(A) Interest Payment ($1,000,000 × 5% × 6/12)	(B) Interest Expense (Preceding Bond Carrying Amount × 6% × 6/12)	(C) Discount Amortization (B – A)	(D) Unamortized Discount (D – C)	(E) Bond Carrying Amount ($1,000,000 – D)
Issue date				$42,655	$ 957,345
1	$ 25,000	$ 28,720	$ 3,720	38,935	961,065
2	25,000	28,832	3,832	35,103	964,897
3	25,000	28,947	3,947	31,156	968,844
4	25,000	29,065	4,065	27,091	972,909
5	25,000	29,187	4,187	22,904	977,096
6	25,000	29,313	4,313	18,591	981,409
7	25,000	29,442	4,442	14,149	985,851
8	25,000	29,576	4,576	9,573	990,427
9	25,000	29,713	4,713	4,860	995,140
10	25,000	29,860*	4,860	0	1,000,000
	$250,000	$292,655	$42,655		

*Adjusted for rounding differences.

In Column A of Illustration 10-7, the interest payment is calculated by multiplying the bonds' face value by the semi-annual coupon interest rate. This amount remains constant for each period. Column B determines the interest expense, which increases each period because the carrying amount that the interest is calculated on increases. It is calculated by multiplying the carrying amount by the semi-annual market interest rate.

Column C is the amount of the discount amortization. It is the difference between the interest expense (Column B) and the interest payment (Column A) for each period. Just as the interest expense increases each period, so does the discount amortization. Column D shows the amount of the unamortized discount. It is reduced each period by the discount amortization (Column C) until it reaches zero at maturity.

Column E is the carrying amount of the bond. The face value, $1 million in this case, is decreased each period by the amount of the unamortized discount (Column D). Because the unamortized discount amount will be fully amortized and decline to a zero balance at maturity, the bond carrying amount will increase each period until it finally reaches the face value at maturity. Note that Candlestick must repay $1 million at maturity even though it received only $957,345 from the sale of the bonds on January 1, 2012.

The carrying amount of a bond always equals its present value. Note that at any point in time, you can use present value techniques to determine the carrying amount of the bond—not just at the issue date as we have illustrated in this chapter. So if you were asked what the carrying amount of the Candlestick bond would be at the end of a certain period, you could either prepare a schedule as shown in Illustration 10-7 or calculate the present value of the bond at the end of the specified period where n, the number of interest periods remaining, would be adjusted as required.

Issuing Bonds at a Premium

The issue of bonds at a premium can be illustrated by assuming that the Candlestick bonds described above are instead sold when the market (effective) interest rate is 4%. When the market interest rate is 4%, the 5% Candlestick bonds are very attractive to investors. Investors will pay a premium to obtain bonds that offer a higher coupon interest rate than they could earn elsewhere. If they pay a premium, the effective rate yield becomes 4%, which is lower than the 5% coupon interest rate.

Whether using present value tables or a financial calculator or spreadsheet program, the key inputs needed to determine the issue price of the bonds are as follows:

Future value (FV) = $1,000,000
Market interest rate (i) = 2% (4% × 6/12)
Interest payment (PMT) = $25,000 ($1,000,000 × 5% × 6/12)
Number of semi-annual periods (n) = 10 (5 years × 2)

Note that it is only the market interest rate that has changed from our previous illustration of issuing bonds at a discount to this one issuing bonds at a premium. All other facts remain unchanged.

Using the present value tables in Appendix C at the end of this textbook, we determine that the bonds will sell for $1,044,915 (104.4915% of face value).

Present value of $1,000,000 received in 10 periods	
$1,000,000 × 0.82035 ($n$ = 10, i = 2%)	$ 820,350
Present value of $25,000 received for each of 10 periods	
$25,000 × 8.98259 ($n$ = 10, i = 2%)	224,565
Present value (issue price) of bonds	$1,044,915

This issue price of $1,044,915 results in a premium of $44,915 ($1,044,915 – $1,000,000). The entry to record the sale of the bonds is:

A	=	L	+	SE
+1,044,915		+1,044,915		

↑Cash flows: +1,044,915

Jan. 1	Cash	1,044,915	
	Bonds Payable		1,044,915
	(To record issue of five-year, 5% bonds at a premium)		

Rather than crediting the Bonds Payable account for the issue price of $1,044,915, some companies use a separate adjunct account to keep track of the bond premium. An **adjunct account** is the opposite of a contra account. A contra account reduces a related account while an adjunct account increases, or is added to, a related account. If an adjunct account were used, Bonds Payable would be credited for $1 million and the bond premium would be recorded in a separate account as a credit of $44,915.

As we explained in the Issuing Bonds at a Discount section, both IFRS and ASPE accounting standards require the presentation of bonds net of any premiums (or discounts, as we learned in the previous section). We have chosen to illustrate the recording of bond journal entries net of any premium or discount in this text.

Amortizing the Premium. The bond premium must be allocated to interest expense over the life of the bonds. The $25,000 interest payment is recorded as interest expense every semi-annual period for five years (10 semi-annual periods). The bond premium is also allocated so that it *reduces* the interest expense over the 10 periods—this allocation is called **amortizing the premium**.

For the first interest period, the bond interest expense is $20,898, calculated by multiplying the bonds' carrying amount by the market interest rate ($1,044,915 × 4% × 6/12). The interest payment is unchanged at $25,000. The amortization is the difference between the interest paid and the interest expense ($25,000 – $20,898 = $4,102).

At July 1, the entry to record the payment of interest and amortization of the bond premium by Candlestick is as follows:

Helpful Hint
Whereas amortizing a bond discount *increases* interest expense, amortizing a bond premium *decreases* interest expense.

A	=	L	+	SE
– 25,000		– 4,102		–20,898

↓Cash flows: –25,000

July 1	Interest Expense	20,898	
	Bonds Payable	4,102	
	Cash		25,000
	(To record semi-annual bond interest payment and amortization of bond premium)		

In the above entry, the interest expense account is effectively increased (debited) for the interest payment ($25,000) and decreased (credited) for the bond premium amortization ($4,102).

At the second interest period, the carrying amount of the bonds is now $1,040,813 ($1,044,915 − $4,102). The carrying amount will continue to decrease until, at maturity, the bonds' carrying amount equals their face value.

To calculate the interest expense for the second interest period, we multiply the bonds' carrying amount by the market interest rate to arrive at $20,816 ($1,040,813 × 4% × 6/12). The interest payment is unchanged at $25,000. As before, the amortization is the difference between the interest paid and the interest expense ($25,000 − $20,816 = $4,184).

At December 31, Candlestick's year end, the following adjusting entry is made to record interest and amortization for the second interest period:

Dec. 31	Interest Expense	20,816	
	Bonds Payable	4,184	
	Interest Payable		25,000
	(To accrue semi-annual bond interest and record amortization of bond premium)		

A	=	L	+	SE
		− 4,184		−20,816
		+25,000		

Cash flows: no effect

A bond premium amortization schedule is useful to organize and track the interest expense, premium amortization, and interest payable amounts, similar to the schedule shown above for the amortization of a bond discount. A bond amortization schedule is shown in Illustration 10-8.

CANDLESTICK INC.
Bond Premium Amortization Schedule

Semi-Annual Interest Period	(A) Interest Payment ($1,000,000 × 5% × 6/12)	(B) Interest Expense (Preceding Bond Carrying Amount × 4% × 6/12)	(C) Premium Amortization (A − B)	(D) Unamortized Premium (D − C)	(E) Bond Carrying Amount ($1,000,000 + D)
Issue date				$44,915	$1,044,915
1	$ 25,000	$ 20,898	$ 4,102	40,813	1,040,813
2	25,000	20,816	4,184	36,629	1,036,629
3	25,000	20,733	4,267	32,362	1,032,362
4	25,000	20,647	4,353	28,009	1,028,009
5	25,000	20,560	4,440	23,569	1,023,569
6	25,000	20,471	4,529	19,040	1,019,040
7	25,000	20,381	4,619	14,421	1,014,421
8	25,000	20,288	4,712	9,709	1,009,709
9	25,000	20,194	4,806	4,903	1,004,903
10	25,000	20,097*	4,903	0	1,000,000
	$250,000	$205,085	$44,915		

*Adjusted for rounding differences.

Illustration 10-8

Bond premium amortization schedule

In Column A of Illustration 10-8, the interest payment is calculated by multiplying the bonds' face value by the semi-annual coupon interest rate. This amount remains constant for each period. Column B determines the interest expense, which decreases each period because the carrying amount that the interest is calculated on decreases. It is calculated by multiplying the carrying amount by the semi-annual market interest rate.

Column C is the amount of the premium amortization. It is the difference between the interest payment (Column A) and the interest expense (Column B) for each period. Because the interest expense decreases each period while the interest payment remains constant, the premium amortization increases each period. Column D is the amount of the unamortized premium. It is reduced each period by the premium amortization (Column C) until it reaches zero at maturity.

Column E is the carrying amount of the bond. The face value, $1 million in this case, is increased each period by the amounts of the unamortized premium (Column D). Because the unamortized premium amount will be fully amortized and decline to a zero balance at maturity, the bond carrying amount will decrease each period until it finally reaches the face value at maturity. Note that even though Candlestick received $1,044,915 from the sale of the bonds on January 1, 2012, it is only required to repay the maturity value, $1 million.

Illustration 10-9 compares the different carrying amounts of Candlestick bonds issued at a discount and premium. As you can see, the carrying amount of bonds issued at a discount increases until it reaches the face value, $1 million in this case, at maturity at the end of Year 5 (January 1, 2017). The carrying amount of bonds issued at a premium decreases until it reaches the face value of $1 million at maturity at the end of Year 5 (January 1, 2017).

▶ **Illustration 10-9**

Comparison of bond carrying amounts over time

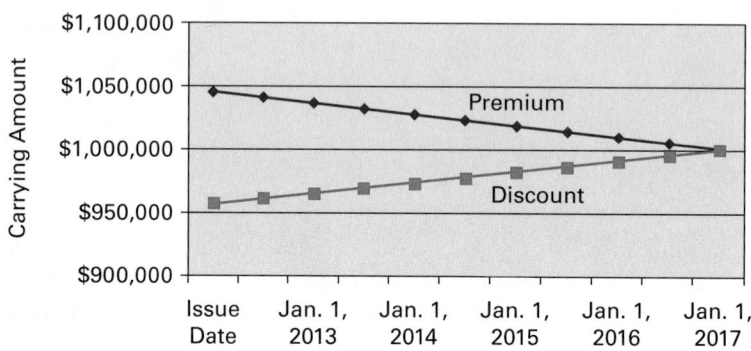

ACCOUNTING FOR BOND RETIREMENTS

Bonds are retired either (1) when they mature, or (2) when the issuing corporation purchases them on the open market before they mature. Some bonds have special redemption provisions that allow them to be retired before they mature. Bonds that can be retired at a specified price before maturity at the option of the company (the issuer) are known as **redeemable (or callable) bonds**.

Why would a company want to have the option to retire its bonds early? If interest rates drop, it can be financially advantageous to retire the bond issue and replace it with a new bond issue at a lower interest rate. Or a company may become financially able to repay its debt earlier than expected. Let's look now at the required entries for redeeming bonds at maturity and before maturity.

Redeeming Bonds at Maturity

Regardless of the issue price of bonds, the bonds' carrying amount at maturity will equal their face value. By the time the bonds mature, any discount or premium will be fully amortized and will have a zero balance.

Assuming that the interest for the last interest payment period is recorded, the entry to record the redemption of the Candlestick bonds at maturity, on January 1, 2017, is:

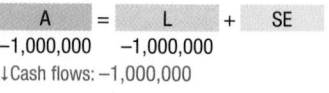

Jan. 1	Bonds Payable	1,000,000	
	Cash		1,000,000
	(To record redemption of bonds at maturity)		

Since no proceeds are received, there is no gain or loss when bonds are retired at maturity.

Redeeming Bonds Before Maturity

Redeeming bonds early is similar to disposing of property, plant, and equipment. To record a redemption of bonds, it is necessary to (1) update any unrecorded interest, including amortization,

(2) eliminate the carrying amount of the bonds at the redemption date, (3) record the cash paid, and (4) recognize the gain or loss on redemption.

For the first step, interest must be updated if the bonds are redeemed between semi-annual interest payment dates. For the second step, the Bonds Payable account must be removed from the books. For the third and fourth steps, the cash paid to repurchase the bonds is recorded. A gain on redemption results when the cash paid is less than the carrying amount of the bonds. A loss on redemption results when the cash paid is more than the carrying amount of the bonds.

To illustrate, assume that Candlestick sells its bonds at a premium, as described in the last section. It redeems the bonds at 101 at the end of the fourth year (eighth period), after paying the semi-annual interest. Assume that the bonds' carrying amount at the redemption date is $1,009,709. Recall that the carrying amount can be determined at any point in time by preparing a bond premium amortization schedule or by using present value techniques.

The entry to record the redemption on January 1, 2016 (end of the eighth period), is:

Jan. 1	Bonds Payable	1,009,709	
	Loss on Bond Redemption ($1,010,000 − $1,009,709)	291	
	Cash ($1,000,000 × 101%)		1,010,000
	(To record redemption of bonds at 101)		

A	=	L	+	SE
−1,010,000		−1,009,709		− 291

↓Cash flows: −1,010,000

The loss of $291 is the difference between the cash paid of $1,010,000 and the carrying amount of the bonds of $1,009,709.

As we mentioned earlier, calculating a loss or a gain on the redemption of bonds is similar to the calculation of a loss or gain on the sale of property, plant, and equipment. In both cases, the proceeds (cash) are compared with the carrying amount. However, the determination of whether there is a loss or a gain is, of course, different. For example, when you sell an asset (such as property, plant, and equipment), you gain when the cash received is greater than the carrying amount. When you retire a liability (such as bonds), you gain when the cash paid is less than the carrying amount.

Losses and gains on bond redemption are reported in the income statement as "other expenses and losses" or "other revenues and gains." Unlike the sale of property, plant, and equipment, which is considered part of profit from operations, the redemption of bonds usually results in large and infrequent amounts, which, because they are unusual, are reported separately.

BEFORE YOU GO ON...

▶ Do It! Bond Transactions

On January 1, 2012, R & B Inc. issued $500,000 of 10-year, 4% bonds to yield a market interest rate of 5%, which resulted in an issue price of 92.2. Interest is paid semi-annually on January 1 and July 1. On July 1, 2016, before maturity and after the interest payment had been made, the carrying amount of the bonds was $476,214. The company redeems the bonds at 95 on this date. (a) Using present value factors from Appendix C at the end of this textbook, prove the bonds' issue price of 92.2. (b) Prepare the entries to record (1) the issue of the bonds on January 1, 2012, (2) the payment of interest and amortization of any bond discount or premium on July 1, 2012, and (3) the redemption of the bonds on July 1, 2016. Round all amounts to the nearest dollar.

Action Plan

- Identify the key inputs required to determine present value, whether using tables or a financial calculator.
- To use present value tables to calculate the present value (issue price), use Table 1 (the present value of $1) in Appendix C to determine the factor to use to calculate the present value of the principal, which is a single sum. Use Table 2 (the present value of an annuity of $1) in Appendix C to calculate the present value of the interest, which recurs periodically (as an annuity). Remember to double the number of periods and halve the annual interest rate when the interest is paid semi-annually.

(continued)

- Apply the issue price as a percentage (e.g., 92.2%) to the face value of the bonds to determine the proceeds received.
- Recall that the amortization of a bond discount results in a debit to Interest Expense and a credit to Bonds Payable, while the amortization of a bond premium results in the reverse.
- To record the redemption, eliminate the carrying amount of the bonds and record the cash paid. Calculate and record the gain or loss (the difference between the cash paid and the carrying amount).

Solution

(a) Key inputs: Future value (FV) = $500,000
Market interest rate (i) = 2.5% (5% $\times$ $^6/_{12}$)
Interest payment (PMT) = $10,000 ($500,000 $\times$ 4% $\times$ $^6/_{12}$)
Number of semi-annual periods (n) = 20 (10 years $\times$ 2)

Present value of $500,000 received in 20 periods
$500,000 $\times$ 0.61027 (n = 20, i = 2.5%) $305,135
Present value of $10,000 received for each of 20 periods
$10,000 $\times$ 15.58916 (n = 20, i = 2.5%)   155,892
Present value (issue price) of bonds $461,027

Issue price = $461,027 $\div$ $500,000 = 92.2%

(b)

I. Jan. 1, 2012	Cash ($500,000 $\times$ 92.2%)	461,027	
	Bonds Payable		461,027
	(To record issue of 10-year, 4% bonds at a discount)		
2. July 1, 2012	Interest Expense ($461,027 $\times$ 5% $\times$ $^6/_{12}$)	11,526	
	Bonds Payable ($11,526 – $10,000)		1,526
	Cash ($500,000 $\times$ 4% $\times$ $^6/_{12}$)		10,000
	(To record semi-annual bond interest payment and amortization of discount)		
3. July 1, 2016	Bonds Payable	476,214	
	Gain on Bond Redemption ($476,214 – $475,000)		1,214
	Cash ($500,000 $\times$ 95%)		475,000
	(To record redemption of 10-year, 4% bonds at 95)		

the navigator

Statement Presentation and Analysis

STUDY OBJECTIVE 4

Identify the requirements for the financial statement presentation and analysis of liabilities.

Liabilities add up to a significant amount on the financial statements of almost all companies and must be disclosed in detail so they can be properly understood by lenders and other creditors as well as investors. These and other users are very interested in assessing a company's liquidity and solvency in regard to its liabilities. We will look at the presentation and analysis of liabilities in the next sections.

PRESENTATION

The presentation of liability-related accounts in the income statement is fairly straightforward. Gains on bond redemptions are reported in the "other revenues and gains" section of the statement and losses on bond redemptions and interest expense are separately reported in the "other expenses and losses" section of the statement. The presentation in the statement of financial position is a bit more involved, so we will look at this in more detail.

Liabilities are usually segregated as current or non-current on the statement of financial position, except in certain industries where not segregating current and non-current liabilities would provide more useful information. This normally occurs in financial institutions and real estate companies.

Current Liabilities

Current liabilities are generally reported as the first category in the liabilities section of the statement of financial position. Each of the primary types of current liabilities can be listed separately within this category or detailed in the notes to the financial statements. In addition, the terms of any operating lines of credit and notes (loans) payable are disclosed in the notes to the financial statements.

Similar to current assets, current liabilities are generally listed in their order of liquidity (by their due date). However, this is not always possible, because of the varying maturity dates that may exist for specific obligations such as short-term notes payable. You will recall from earlier chapters that companies also have the option of presenting current liabilities in order of reverse liquidity. International companies often present their current liabilities following non-current liabilities and order items within each classification in reverse order to what is normally seen in North America. Some international companies also net their current assets and current liabilities.

Illustration 10-10 shows how Canada Post presents its current liabilities in a traditional order in its statement of financial position (which it calls the balance sheet):

Illustration 10-10
Canada Post current liabilities

CANADA POST Balance Sheet (partial) December 31, 2010 (in millions)	
Current liabilities	
Accounts payable and accrued liabilities	$459
Salaries and benefits payable	576
Deferred revenue	120
Outstanding money orders	41
Current portion of long-term debt	13
Total current liabilities	1,209

Non-Current Liabilities

Non-current or long-term liabilities are usually reported separately, immediately following current liabilities if companies follow the traditional North American order or preceding current liabilities if companies use a reverse-liquidity order. There is no generally prescribed order within the non-current liability classification.

The presentation of Canada Post's non-current liabilities is shown in Illustration 10-11.

Illustration 10-11
Canada Post non-current liabilities

CANADA POST Balance Sheet (partial) December 31, 2009 (in millions)	
Non-current liabilities	
Long-term debt	$1,095
Accrued pension, other retirement and post-employment benefit liability	2,950
Future income tax liabilities	40
Other long-term liabilities	37
Total non-current liabilities	4,122

Generally, non-current liabilities are measured and reported at amortized cost. The fair value of the non-current debt should also be disclosed in the notes to the financial statements if it is possible to estimate it. In limited circumstances, there is an option to value financial liabilities at fair value rather than at amortized cost. Valuing financial liabilities at fair value normally applies only to complex financial instruments, which are beyond the scope of an introductory accounting course and are not discussed here.

Full disclosure of non-current debt is very important. Summary data are usually presented in the statement of financial position and detailed data (such as interest rates, maturity dates, conversion privileges, assets pledged as collateral, and fair value if available) are shown in the notes to the financial statements. Canada Post's disclosure about its non-current liabilities fills 11 pages in the notes to its financial statements.

Provisions and Contingent Liabilities

Liabilities can be said to be certain (definitely determinable) or uncertain. Liabilities with a known payee, due date, and amount payable are *certain liabilities*. Examples of these include accounts payable and the other types of liabilities we discussed to date in this chapter.

Liabilities that are uncertain are those for which we may not know who we owe, when we owe, and/or how much we owe. Such *uncertain liabilities* are known as provisions or contingent liabilities. **Provisions** are defined as liabilities of uncertain timing or amount; however, there is no uncertainty about the fact that a charge will result. An example of a provision is a product warranty. A company knows it will incur a charge for returned products for repair or refund under warranty but it doesn't know exactly when or what it will cost. Provisions are recorded in the accounts using reliable estimates based on past experience and future expectations. As we have learned from past chapters, many liabilities are based on reasonable and probable estimates.

Contingent liabilities are existing or possible obligations arising from past events. The liability is contingent (dependent) on whether or not some uncertain future event occurs that will confirm either its existence or the amount payable, or both. Although contingent assets exist, they are rare. Contingent liabilities are far more common and are the focus of this section.

One example of a contingent liability is a loan guarantee. This is when one company (e.g., a parent company) guarantees or promises to assume the loan obligation if the other company (e.g., a subsidiary company) is unable to repay the loan. The guaranteeing company will have an actual liability and a loss only if the borrower does not make the payments on the loan.

Another example of a contingent liability is an unsettled lawsuit. A company may not be able to predict whether it will win or lose a legal case and if it will be required to pay damages if the suit is lost until the case is heard by the courts in the future. *Financial Reporting in Canada* reports that 81% of Canadian companies reported contingencies in a recent year, and of these, litigation was the most common contingency reported.

Accounting rules require that uncertain liabilities be either recorded (accrued) or disclosed in the notes to the financial statements, unless the possibility of occurrence is remote. Whether a liability should be recorded or disclosed depends on the probability of the future event occurring that will confirm if there is a liability and a related loss. For example, if it is probable that a legal case will be lost, the company should record the liability as a provision. The definition of "probability" under IFRS is "more likely than not," which is normally interpreted to mean more than a 50% probability of occurring.

Accounting Standards for Private Enterprises are slightly different in terms of the assessment of probability. The definition of probability under ASPE is "likely," which is a higher level of probability than under IFRS. Under both IFRS and ASPE, the amount must be reasonably estimable before any liability can be accrued regardless of the likelihood of occurrence.

On the other hand, if it is merely possible that the legal case referred to above will be lost, the company should treat the obligation as a contingent liability. Contingent liabilities are not recorded. Instead, information about contingent liabilities is disclosed in the notes to the financial statements and includes disclosure about the uncertainties related to the amount and/or timing of the possible liability. Canada Post has three pages included in the notes to its financial statements disclosing its commitments and contingencies.

In summary, under current accounting standards, contingencies are recorded as provisions in the accounting records if they are probable (or likely for companies using ASPE) and reasonably estimable. Otherwise, they are disclosed as contingent liabilities in the notes to the financial statements unless the probability of occurrence is remote.

DECISION TOOLKIT

Decision Checkpoints	Info Needed for Decision	Tools to Use for Decision	How to Evaluate Results
Does the company have any contingent liabilities?	Knowledge of events with uncertain but possibly negative outcomes	Financial statements and notes to the financial statements	If negative outcomes are possible, determine the likelihood and amount of the loss, and the potential impact on the financial statements.

ANALYSIS

A careful examination of debt obligations makes it easier to assess a company's ability to pay its current obligations. It also helps determine whether a company can obtain long-term financing in order to grow.

Liquidity

Liquidity ratios measure a company's short-term ability to pay its maturing obligations and to meet unexpected needs for cash. You will recall that we learned about the current ratio (current assets ÷ current liabilities) in Chapter 2, the inventory turnover ratio (cost of goods sold ÷ average inventory) in Chapter 6, and the receivables turnover ratio (net credit sales ÷ average gross accounts receivable) in Chapter 8. We will not illustrate these ratios again here.

In recent years, many companies have intentionally reduced their more liquid current assets (such as accounts receivable and inventory) because these assets cost too much to hold. Companies that keep fewer liquid assets on hand must rely on other sources of liquidity. One such source is an **operating line of credit,** as discussed earlier in this chapter. If a low amount of liquid assets causes a cash shortfall, a company can borrow money on its available short-term lines of credit as necessary. Consequently it is important to interpret a company's liquidity ratios in the context of any unused lines of credit, which add to a company's short-term financing flexibility.

You may recall that we discussed Canada Post's operating line of credit earlier in the chapter. It and its subsidiaries have access to $400 million ($250 million from the Government of Canada and $200 million from a line of credit) for short-term financing needs. Only $51 million has been drawn to date so there is still $349 of unused capacity to draw upon should it need it.

DECISION TOOLKIT

Decision Checkpoints	Info Needed for Decision	Tools to Use for Decision	How to Evaluate Results
Can the company obtain short-term financing when necessary?	Liquidity ratios, available lines of credit from notes to the financial statements	Compare available lines of credit with current liabilities. Also evaluate liquidity ratios.	If liquidity ratios are low, lines of credit should be high to compensate.

Solvency

Solvency ratios, such as the debt to total assets and times interest earned ratios, measure a company's ability to repay its long-term debt and survive over a long period of time. As the feature story about Canada Post shows, going into debt is often necessary in order to grow a business. However, debt must be carefully monitored to ensure that it does not hurt a company's solvency. We will review the debt to total assets ratio next, and then introduce a related ratio, the times interest earned ratio.

Debt to Total Assets.   In Chapter 2, you learned that one measure of a company's solvency is **debt to total assets**. It is calculated by dividing total liabilities by total assets. This ratio indicates the extent to which a company's assets are financed by debt.

Using the following selected information (in millions) from Canada Post's statement of financial position, the company's debt to total assets ratios for 2010 and 2009 are calculated in Illustration 10-12. The illustration also shows summary ratios for UPS, Canada Post's closest competitor (recall that Canada Post owns Purolator Courier), as well as industry averages.

	2010	2009
Total assets	$7,600	$6,029
Total liabilities	5,331	4,213

▶Illustration 10-12
Debt to total assets

	DEBT TO TOTAL ASSETS = $\dfrac{\text{TOTAL LIABILITIES}}{\text{TOTAL ASSETS}}$	
(in millions)	**2010**	**2009**
Canada Post	$\dfrac{\$5,331}{\$7,600} = 70.1\%$	$\dfrac{\$4,213}{\$6,029} = 69.9\%$
UPS	76.0%	75.9%
Industry average	33.8%	31.5%

Whereas for liquidity ratios, higher ratios generally indicate improved performance, it is the opposite for the debt to total assets ratio. For this ratio, the lower the better. Less debt is better than more debt.

Canada Post's debt to total assets ratio deteriorated slightly in 2010 from 69.9% to 70.1%. This is because its liabilities, especially with the addition of significant long-term debt in 2010, grew faster than its assets.

Canada Post's debt to total assets is, however, better (lower) than that of UPS in both 2009 and 2010, whose debt to total assets ratio also deteriorated marginally in 2010. It should be noted that it is difficult to compare Canada Post fully with UPS as UPS does not deliver letter mail. Canada Post is the sole mail provider in Canada. Still, a significant portion of both companies' business consists of package delivery. Both companies' debt to total assets ratios are much worse (higher) than that of the industry.

Debt to total assets varies across industries because different financing options are appropriate for different industries. For example, the average debt to total assets ratio for the retail industry was 35% in 2010. The average debt to total assets ratio for the forestry industry for the same period was higher, at 49%.

Times Interest Earned.   The debt to total assets ratio should always be interpreted in light of the company's ability to handle its debt. That is, a company might have a high debt to total assets ratio, but still be able to easily cover its interest payments. Alternatively a company may have a low debt to total assets ratio and struggle to cover its interest payments.

The **times interest earned** ratio gives an indication of a company's ability to meet interest payments as they come due. It is calculated by dividing the sum of profit, interest expense, and income tax expense, by interest expense. It uses profit or earnings before interest and taxes (often abbreviated as **EBIT**) because this number best represents the amount that is available to cover interest.

Alternative Terminology
The *times interest earned ratio* is also known as the *interest coverage ratio.*

EBIT can be found directly on the income statement or calculated by adding interest expense and income tax expense to profit. These are amounts that were originally deducted to determine profit. They are added back now to *remove* them from profit, and give the amount of profit before interest and taxes.

Illustration 10-13 uses the following selected information (in millions) from Canada Post's income statement to calculate its times interest earned ratios for 2010 and 2009. The illustration also shows summary ratios for UPS and industry averages.

	2010	2009
Interest expense	$ 30	$ 7
Income tax (benefit) expense	(136)	95
Profit	439	281

$$\text{TIMES INTEREST EARNED} = \frac{\text{PROFIT} + \text{INTEREST EXPENSE} + \text{INCOME TAX EXPENSE (EBIT)}}{\text{INTEREST EXPENSE}}$$		
(in millions)	2010	2009
Canada Post	$\dfrac{\$439 + \$30 - \$136}{\$30} = 11.1$ times	$\dfrac{\$281 + \$7 + \$95}{\$7} = 54.7$ times
UPS	16.6 times	8.6 times
Industry average	16.3 times	14.1 times

Illustration 10-13
Times interest earned

Contrary to the debt to total assets ratio, the higher the better for the times interest earned ratio. With the large increase in long-term debt, it is not surprising that Canada Post's times interest earned ratio declined (decreased) significantly in 2010 from 54.7 times to 11.1 times, as its interest expense increased. During this same time period, while Canada Post's time interest earned ratio deteriorated, both UPS and the industry average improved.

Canada Post's solvency, although declining, still appears to be reasonable. A times interest ratio of 11.1 times is still a good coverage ratio. In addition, Canada Post has access to unused operating lines of credit and the protection of the Government of Canada as a crown corporation.

Operating Leases.   You will recall that leases were discussed in Chapter 9. For accounting purposes, operating leases are treated as periodic rentals—no assets or liabilities are recorded on the company's books. Finance/capital leases, on the other hand, are treated like a debt-financed purchase—increasing both assets and liabilities.

Operating leases are often short-term, such as the rental of a car or an apartment. If, however, an operating lease covers a long period of time, it may be viewed as "off-balance-sheet financing." Off-balance-sheet financing refers to situations where liabilities are not recorded on the statement of financial position.

Many believe that some companies will choose to structure a lease arrangement as an operating lease rather than a finance lease simply to avoid recording a liability. In their opinion, if an operating lease results in the long-term use of an asset and an unavoidable obligation, it should be recorded as an asset and a liability rather than as a periodic rental expense.

You may also recall from Chapter 9 that standard setters are currently working on a project to reclassify leases. They are suggesting that leases be classified as an asset based on the right to use the property and as a liability based on the related obligation, rather than according to the terms of the lease agreement. Deliberations are not yet finalized.

In the interim, companies are required to report their operating lease obligations in a note to the financial statements. Canada Post reports a total obligation of $730 million of operating leases for its facilities, transportation equipment, and other items in the notes to its financial statements.

This information allows analysts and other financial statement users to adjust a company's ratios for unrecorded debt if they feel that the inclusion of this debt would have a significant effect on the interpretation of a company's solvency. Canada Post's operating leases are about 14 percent of its total liabilities, so they may be considered to be significant to a user's decision-making. As the adjustments required to remove the effects of operating leases from solvency ratios are complex, they are left to a financial statement analysis course.

Credit Ratings.   Credit-rating agencies, such as the Dominion Bond Rating Service (DBRS), provide opinions about a company's ability to make timely payments (of principal and interest) on its short- and long-term debt. Short-term debt is rated using an "R" scale, with R-1 being the highest credit quality. Within this scale, the rating is further divided as R-1 (high), R-1 (middle), and R-1 (low) to further distinguish between high, superior, and satisfactory credit quality. Short-term debt rated as R-4 or higher is considered to be speculative.

Long-term debt is rated using a different letter scale than short-term debt. The highest-quality long-term debt is rated as AAA, superior quality as AA, and good quality as A. The credit scale descends to the D, or default, category. Generally long-term debt rated below BBB is referred to as speculative and non-investment grade, with a higher risk of default. Canada Post's long-term debt is rated AAA—the highest rating possible by DBRS.

ACCOUNTING MATTERS!   *Investor Perspective*

Global Public Debt Problems

It is not just individual company debt that is important to monitor, but also "public" debt. Worldwide, global debt exceeds $40 trillion, or an amount that is two-thirds of global GDP. In Canada, if all types of debt are added together–government debt, corporate debt, and consumer debt–they amount to more than 250% of GDP. This translates to $3.3 trillion of total debt, or over $100,000 of debt for every person in the country.

The Economist magazine warns that massive public debt is a "gathering, global storm." Not only can increasing debt mean higher rates of interest, but "This creates a recurring popularity test for individual governments . . . Fail that vote, as the Greek government did in early 2010, and the country can be plunged into imminent crisis." The magazine goes on to add that the risk of crisis now applies to many of the world's most affluent countries.

Countries, like corporations, have credit ratings. Lenders pay close attention to a country's credit scores. Currently, 55 countries have a debt rating below BBB, as they struggle to decide how much money to borrow (or print) to sustain their economies.

Source: Neil Reynolds, "Death by Debt: Governments Need a Cure–Fast," *The Globe and Mail,* October 20, 2010, p. B2

■ Keeping an Eye on Cash

Cash is critical with respect to debt. Companies must not only be able to generate enough cash to pay their interest charges when due but also to repay any principal amounts due annually and/or at maturity. If a company fails to meet any of its due dates, it can have serious consequences for its credit rating.

Debt covenants help companies reduce their risk of default and also help protect lenders. Most borrowing agreements include restrictions called debt covenants that restrict a company's ability to invest, pay dividends, or make other decisions that might adversely affect the company's ability to pay interest and principal.

As well, the statement of cash flows helps provide information about how much cash is being used for debt purposes. Cash paid for interest expense is usually reported in the operating activities section of the cash flow statement. Information on cash inflows and outflows during the year that resulted from the principal portion of debt transactions is reported in the financing activities section of the statement. We will learn about using the statement of cash flows to calculate debt coverage ratios in Chapter 13.

DECISION TOOLKIT

Decision Checkpoints	Info Needed for Decision	Tools to Use for Decision	How to Evaluate Results
Can the company meet its obligations in the long term?	Total liabilities, total assets, profit, interest expense, and income tax expense	Times interest earned $$= \frac{\text{Profit} + \text{Interest expense} + \text{Income tax expense (EBIT)}}{\text{Interest expense}}$$ Compare the times interest earned ratio with the debt to total assets ratio.	A high times interest earned ratio indicates there is enough profit available to cover annual interest payments. A low debt to total assets ratio is preferable, but a high debt to total assets ratio along with a high times interest earned ratio is acceptable.
Does the company have significant unrecorded obligations, such as operating leases?	Information on unrecorded obligations, such as operating lease payments disclosed in the notes to the financial statements	Compare liquidity and solvency ratios with and without unrecorded obligations included.	If ratios differ significantly after including unrecorded obligations, these obligations should not be ignored in analysis.

BEFORE YOU GO ON...

▶ Do It! Liquidity and Solvency

Markel Corporation reported the following information in its financial statements:

MARKEL CORPORATION
Statement of Financial Position
December 31

	2012	2011
Assets		
Cash	$ 30,000	$20,000
Inventory	30,850	20,750
Prepaid expenses	5,600	6,500
Equipment	38,000	45,600
Total assets	$104,450	$92,850
Liabilities and shareholders' equity		
Accounts payable	$ 13,350	$18,750
Interest payable	2,500	3,500
Bonds payable	50,000	60,000
Common shares	25,000	5,000
Retained earnings	13,600	5,600
Total liabilities and shareholders' equity	$104,450	$92,850

(continued)

MARKEL CORPORATION
Condensed Income Statement
Year Ended December 31

	2012	2011
Revenue	$100,000	$90,000
Operating expenses	85,000	77,000
Profit from operations	15,000	13,000
Interest expense	5,000	6,000
Income tax expense	2,000	1,400
Profit	$ 8,000	$ 5,600

(a) Calculate Markel's current, debt to total assets, and times interest earned ratios for each year.

(b) Identify if the change in each ratio from 2011 to 2012 is an improvement or a deterioration.

Action Plan

- Determine total current assets and total current liabilities. Divide current assets by current liabilities to calculate the current ratio.
- Determine total liabilities. Divide total liabilities by total assets to calculate the debt to total assets ratio.
- Divide the earnings (profit) before interest and income tax expense by the interest expense to calculate the times interest earned ratio. If there are no other revenues or expenses besides interest expense, then EBIT is the same as profit from operations.
- Recall that the higher the better for all ratios except for the debt to total assets ratio.

Solution

	(a)		(b)
	2012	2011	
Current ratio	$\dfrac{\$30,000 + \$30,850 + \$5,600}{\$13,350 + \$2,500}$ $= 4.2:1$	$\dfrac{\$20,000 + \$20,750 + \$6,500}{\$18,750 + \$3,500}$ $= 2.1:1$	Improvement
Debt to total assets	$\dfrac{\$13,350 + \$2,500 + \$50,000}{\$104,450}$ $= 63.0\%$	$\dfrac{\$18,750 + \$3,500 + \$60,000}{\$92,850}$ $= 88.6\%$	Improvement
Times interest earned	$\dfrac{\$15,000}{\$5,000}$ $= 3.0$ times	$\dfrac{\$13,000}{\$6,000}$ $= 2.2$ times	Improvement

comparing
IFRS and ASPE

Key Differences	International Financial Reporting Standards (IFRS)	Accounting Standards for Private Enterprises (ASPE)
Bonds	Must use the effective-interest method to amortize any bond premium or discount.	Normally will use the effective-interest method to amortize any bond premium or discount but permitted to use alternative methods if the results do not differ materially from the effective-interest method.
Contingent liability	The definition of probability used to record a contingent liability (called a provision when recorded) is "more likely than not."	The definition of probability used to record a contingent liability is "likely," which is a higher level of probability than under IFRS.

the navigator

Managing Your Student Loan

When companies need money for operations, they go to lenders, other creditors, or investors. When you, a student, need money for school, you must rely on contributions from parents and other relatives, money from summer or part-time jobs, plus grants, bursaries, and scholarships. If these sources do not cover the cost of post-secondary education, you can also look into student loans. Federal, provincial, and territorial governments offer student loan programs. Private institutions such as banks, trust companies, and credit unions may also offer loan options if you do not qualify for a government student loan.

Student loans are a useful option to consider when you are deciding how to pay for your education. It is important to understand your obligations and responsibilities as a borrower because a student loan is a loan, and you will be required to pay it back. The amount of your student loan is determined based on an assessment of your financial need, which is different for each student. First, your allowable costs (which may include education, living, and transportation costs) and your resources are calculated. The difference between the two is your assessed financial need. For this purpose, and for future personal financial planning, maintenance of your personal financial records is critical. These personal financial records include such records as your income tax return, payroll documents, and other invoices and payments. It is also imperative that you keep your personal financial statements up to date, such as your statement of financial position, which was discussed in the Chapter 2 "All About You."

Financial experts offer the following tips for minimizing the amount of your student loan:

- Be educated about the loan process; know how much interest you will have to pay, and how long it will take you to pay the loan back.
- Get free money whenever you can; grants, bursaries, and scholarships are tax-exempt and don't have to be paid back.
- If you need help in repaying your loans, repayment assistance programs are available in most provinces.
- Make sure you claim all relevant income tax credits (such as the tuition, education, and textbook credits and interest paid on student loans).

Some Facts

- Canadian full-time students were paying an average of $5,138 in tuition fees for the 2010–11 academic year. Full-time graduate students were paying an average of $5,182.
- Many students are also asked to pay additional compulsory fees: the national average was $702 for the 2010–11 academic year. These fees vary by institution and usually cover items such as recreation, student health services, student associations, and the like.
- A 2010 report from Statistics Canada found that the number of students graduating with outstanding student loans, either government-sponsored or from another source, increased from 49% in the 1990s to 57% in the 2000s. According to the Canadian Council on Learning, the average debt for a student graduating from a Canadian university was $26,880 in 2009.
- For students who have loans, the amount of the student loan has also increased (in constant dollars), from an average of $15,200 in the 1990s to $18,800 in the 2000s. Also, the number of students with loans in excess of $50,000 increased from 2% to 6% over the same time period.

What Do You Think?

Suppose you own a car, but your parents use their car to drop you off at university and pick you up later on their way home. You decide to add your parents' car expenses to your list of expenses when applying for a student loan, because you know the more expenses you have, the more likely you are to obtain financial aid. To increase your chances of receiving aid, should you overstate your expenses?

YES You are playing within the rules as you do own a car and how would the government know that you were not commuting to university in your own car?

NO Random audits are conducted each year and, if it were found out that you had lied about your expenses, you would never be able to apply for another government student loan.

Sources: Statistics Canada, "The Financial Impact of Student Loans," *The Daily*, January 29, 2010. Statistics Canada, "University Tuition Fees," *The Daily*, September 16, 2010. Postmedia News, "Student Debt More than Doubled in Last 20 Years," September 4, 2010. Dianne Nice, "Now That's an Expensive Lesson," *Globe and Mail*, February 15, 2011, p. L4.

Summary of Study Objectives

1. **Account for current liabilities.** A current liability is a debt that will be paid (1) from existing current assets or through the creation of other current liabilities, and (2) within one year. An example of a current liability is an operating line of credit that results in bank indebtedness. Current liabilities also include sales taxes, payroll deductions, and employee benefits, all of which the company collects on behalf of third parties. Other examples include property tax and interest on notes or loans payable, which must be accrued until paid. The portion of non-current debt that is due within the next year must be deducted from the non-current debt and reported as a current liability.

2. **Account for instalment notes payable.** Long-term notes payable are usually repayable in a series of instalment payments. Each payment consists of (1) interest on the unpaid balance of the note, and (2) a reduction of the principal balance. These payments can be either (1) fixed principal payments plus interest or (2) blended principal and interest payments. With fixed principal payments plus interest, the reduction of principal is constant but the cash payment and interest expense decrease each period as the principal decreases. With blended principal and interest payments, the reduction of principal increases while the interest expense decreases each period. In total, the cash payment (principal and interest) remains constant each period.

3. **Account for bonds payable.** Bonds are issued at their present (market) value. When they are issued, the Cash account is debited and the Bonds Payable account is credited for the issue price of the bonds.

   Bond discounts and bond premiums represent the difference between a bond's face value and present value. They are amortized to interest expense over the life of the bond using the effective-interest method of amortization. Amortization is calculated as the difference between the interest paid and the interest expense. Interest paid is calculated by multiplying the bonds' face value by the coupon interest rate. Interest expense is calculated by multiplying the bonds' carrying amount (which is equal to their present value at that time) at the beginning of the interest period by the market interest rate. The amortization of a bond discount increases interest expense and the bond's carrying amount. The amortization of a bond premium decreases interest expense and the bond's carrying amount.

   When bonds are retired at maturity, Bonds Payable is debited and Cash is credited. There is no gain or loss at retirement. If bonds are redeemed before maturity, it is necessary to (a) update any unrecorded interest and amortization, (b) eliminate the carrying amount of the bonds at the redemption date, (c) record the cash paid, and (d) recognize any gain or loss on redemption.

4. **Identify the requirements for the financial statement presentation and analysis of liabilities.** Interest expense and any loss on the redemption of bonds is reported as "other expenses and losses" in the income statement. Any gain on redemption is reported as "other revenues and gains."

   In the statement of financial position, current liabilities are usually reported first, followed by non-current liabilities. Contingent liabilities are uncertain liabilities awaiting confirmation by a future event that are not recorded unless probable. The terms and nature of each recorded and contingent liability should be described in the notes accompanying the financial statements.

   The liquidity of a company may be analyzed by calculating the current ratio, in addition to the receivables and inventory turnover ratios. The solvency of a company may be analyzed by calculating the debt to total assets and times interest earned ratios. Another factor to consider is unrecorded debt, such as operating lease obligations.

Glossary

Bond   A type of long-term debt issued by large corporations, universities, and governments that involves a promise to repay a large amount of money at a fixed future date. (p. 534)

Collateral   Assets pledged as security for the payment of a debt. (p. 523)

Contingent liabilities   Existing or possible obligations arising from past events. The liability is contingent (dependent) on whether or not some uncertain future event occurs that will confirm either its existence or the amount payable, or both. (p. 548)

Coupon interest rate   (also known as the contractual or stated interest rate) The rate stated in a bond certificate used to determine the amount of interest the borrower pays and the investor receives. (p. 534)

Discount   The difference between a bond's face value and its issue price when it is sold for less than its face value. This occurs when the market interest rate is higher than the coupon interest rate. (p. 537)

EBIT   Earnings (profit) before interest expense and income tax expense. (p. 551)

Effective-interest method   A method of amortizing a bond discount or premium that results in a periodic interest expense that equals a constant percentage (the market or effective interest rate) of the bond's carrying amount. Amortization is calculated as the difference between the interest expense and the interest paid. (p. 538)

Employee benefits   Payments made by an employer for pension, insurance, health, and/or other benefits paid on behalf of its employees. (p. 525)

Financial liability   A form of financial instrument, represented by a contractual obligation to pay cash in the future. (p. 530)

Fixed interest rate   An interest rate that is constant (unchanged) over the term of the debt. (p. 527)

Floating (variable) interest rate   An interest rate that changes over the term of the debt with fluctuating borrowing rates. (p. 523)

Gross pay   The total compensation (e.g., salaries and wages) earned by an employee. (p. 525)

Market interest rate   (also known as the effective interest rate) The rate that investors demand for loaning funds to a corporation. (p. 535)

Mortgage payable   A long-term loan secured by a mortgage that pledges title to property as collateral for the loan. (p. 530)

Net pay   Gross pay less payroll deductions. (p. 525)

Operating line of credit   (also known as a credit facility) A pre-arranged agreement to borrow money at a bank, up to an agreed-upon amount. (p. 522)

Payroll deductions   Deductions from gross pay to determine the amount of a paycheque. (p. 525)

Premium   The difference between the issue price and the face value of a bond when a bond is sold for more than its face value. This occurs when the market interest rate is less than the coupon interest rate. (p. 537)

Provisions   Liabilities of uncertain timing or amount. They are recorded in the accounts based on reasonable and probable estimates. (p. 548)

Secured debt   Debt, such as notes or bonds, for which specific assets of the issuer have been pledged as collateral. (p. 530)

Times interest earned   A measure of a company's solvency, calculated by dividing profit (earnings) before interest expense and income tax expense (EBIT) by interest expense. (p. 551)

Unsecured debt   (also known as debentures) Debt, such as notes or bonds, that has been issued against the general credit of the borrower. (p. 530)

DECISION TOOLKIT—A SUMMARY

 Decision Checkpoints	 Info Needed for Decision	 Tools to Use for Decision	 How to Evaluate Results
Does the company have any contingent liabilities?	Knowledge of events with uncertain but possibly negative outcomes	Financial statements and notes to the financial statements	If negative outcomes are possible, determine the likelihood and amount of the loss, and the potential impact on the financial statements.
Can the company obtain short-term financing when necessary?	Liquidity ratios, available lines of credit from notes to the financial statements	Compare available lines of credit with current liabilities. Also evaluate liquidity ratios.	If liquidity ratios are low, lines of credit should be high to compensate.
Can the company meet its obligations in the long term?	Total liabilities, total assets, profit, interest expense, and income tax expense	Times interest earned $$= \frac{\text{Profit} + \text{Interest expense} + \text{Income tax expense (EBIT)}}{\text{Interest expense}}$$ Compare the times interest earned ratio with the debt to total assets ratio.	A high times interest earned ratio indicates there is enough profit available to cover annual interest payments. A low debt to total assets ratio is preferable, but a high debt to total assets ratio along with a high times interest earned ratio is acceptable.
Does the company have significant unrecorded obligations, such as operating leases?	Information on unrecorded obligations, such as operating lease payments disclosed in the notes to the financial statements	Compare liquidity and solvency ratios with and without unrecorded obligations included.	If ratios differ significantly after including unrecorded obligations, these obligations should not be ignored in analysis.

the navigator

USING THE DECISION TOOLKIT

Royal Mail Holdings plc is comparable to Canada Post. Royal Mail is the national postal service in the United Kingdom. It also owns Parcelforce, a parcel delivery company, similar to Canada Post's Purolator.

Selected financial information for Royal Mail follows:

ROYAL MAIL HOLDINGS plc
Selected Financial Information
March 31, 2011
(in £ millions)

Statement of financial position	
Non-current assets	3,486
Current assets	2,311
Non-current liabilities	6,313
Current liabilities	2,591
Income statement	
Interest expense	114
Income tax expense	106
Loss	258

Additional information:
The company had an unused operating line of credit of £75 million at March 31, 2011.

Instructions
(a) Canada Post's current ratio is 1.3:1. Calculate Royal Mail's current ratio, and compare its liquidity with that of Canada Post and the industry average of 1.8:1.
(b) Calculate Royal Mail's debt to total assets and times interest earned ratios, and compare its solvency with that of Canada Post and the industry averages of 33.8% and 16.3 times, respectively.
(c) Comment on Royal Mail's operating line of credit.

Solution

(a) Liquidity:

(in millions)	Royal Mail	Canada Post	Industry Average
Current ratio	$\frac{£2,311}{£2,591} = 0.9:1$	1.3:1	1.8:1

Royal Mail's current ratio of 0.9:1 means that it has $0.90 of current assets for each $1 of current liabilities. In other words, its current liabilities exceed its current assets. Although its available line of credit improves its liquidity position, the latter is still not good and significantly below that of Canada Post and the industry. Neither company has inventory nor many receivables, but if they did, these ratios should also be calculated for both companies before reaching a conclusion about the adequacy of their liquidity.

(b) Solvency:

(in millions)	Royal Mail	Canada Post	Industry Average
Debt to total assets	$\frac{£2,591 + £6,313}{£2,311 + £3,486} = 153.6\%$	70.1%	33.8%
Times interest earned	$\frac{£(258) + £114 + £106}{£114} = (0.3)$ times	11.1 times	16.3 times

Royal Mail's debt to total assets ratio of 153.6% is drastically worse (higher) than that of Canada Post and the industry. The Royal Mail's liabilities far exceed its assets. Its times interest earned is negative, primarily due to a loss reported in the current year. It also is significantly worse (lower) than that of Canada Post and the industry.

(c) Royal Mail's unused operating line of credit improves its liquidity and may help reduce concerns its short-term lenders and creditors may have.

the navigator

Comprehensive Do It! #1

(Instalment Note Payable)

Snyder Software Inc. successfully developed a new computer program. To produce and market the program, the company needed to raise $500,000. On December 31, 2011, Snyder borrowed $500,000 from the bank for 15 years at 6%. The terms of the bank loan provide for semi-annual fixed principal plus interest payments on June 30 and December 31.

Instructions

(a) Prepare an instalment payment schedule for the first four instalment payments. Round all amounts to the nearest dollar.

(b) Record the receipt of the bank loan on December 31, 2011.

(c) Record the first instalment payment on June 30, 2012.

(d) Indicate the current, non-current, and total amounts that would be presented in the statement of financial position for the bank loan payable at December 31, 2012.

(e) Explain how the pattern of payments would change if the instalment payments were blended principal and interest rather than fixed principal plus interest.

Action Plan

- Calculate the instalment payment (reduction of principal) by dividing the total loan amount by the number of periods over which it will be repaid.
- Determine the interest expense for the bank loan by multiplying the semi-annual interest rate by the principal balance at the beginning of the period.
- The cash payment is the total of the principal payment and interest expense.
- Record the instalment payments, recognizing that each payment consists of (1) interest on the unpaid loan balance, and (2) a reduction of the loan principal.
- The current portion of the bank loan payable is the amount of principal that will be repaid in the next year. The non-current portion is the total liability at the date in question (December 31, 2012) less the current portion.

Solution to Comprehensive Do It! #1 (Instalment Note Payable)

(a)

Interest Period	(A) Cash Payment (B + C)	(B) Interest Expense (D × 6% × 6/12)	(C) Reduction of Principal ($500,000 ÷ 30)	(D) Principal Balance (D − C)
Issue date (Dec. 31, 2011)				$500,000
1 (June 30, 2012)	$31,667	$15,000	$16,667	483,333
2 (Dec. 31, 2012)	31,167	14,500	16,667	466,666
3 (June 30, 2013)	30,667	14,000	16,667	449,999
4 (Dec. 31, 2013)	30,167	13,500	16,667	433,332

(b)

Dec. 31, 2011	Cash	500,000	
	Bank Loan Payable		500,000
	(To record receipt of 15-year, 6% bank loan)		

(c)

June 30, 2012	Interest Expense ($500,000 × 6% × 6/12)	15,000	
	Bank Loan Payable ($500,000 ÷ 30)	16,667	
	Cash		31,667
	(To record semi-annual instalment payment on bank loan)		

(continued)

(d) The current liability is $33,334 ($16,667 + $16,667).
The non-current liability is $433,332.
The total liability is the balance of $466,666 at the end of the second period, December 31, 2012.

(e) In a fixed principal plus interest situation, the reduction of the principal is constant while the interest expense and total cash payment decreases. In a blended principal and interest situation, the reduction of the principal would increase while the interest expense decreased. The total cash payment would remain constant each period. In both situations, the journal entries are unchanged—it is just the amounts that change.

Comprehensive Do It! #2

(Bonds Payable)

Snyder Software Inc. successfully developed a new computer program. To produce and market the program, the company needed to raise $500,000. Instead of borrowing money from the bank, as illustrated in Comprehensive Do It! #1, assume instead that on December 31, 2011, Snyder issued $500,000 of 10-year, 6% bonds. At the time of issue, the market interest rate was 5%. The terms provide for semi-annual interest payments on June 30 and December 31.

Instructions

(a) Calculate the issue price of the bonds on December 31, 2011. Round all amounts to the nearest dollar.

(b) Prepare a bond amortization schedule using the effective-interest method through to December 31, 2012.

(c) Record the issue of the bonds on December 31, 2011.

(d) Record the first two interest payments on June 30, 2012, and December 31, 2012.

(e) Indicate the current, non-current, and total amounts that would be presented in the statement of financial position for the bonds at December 31, 2012.

Action Plan

- Key inputs: Future value (FV) = $500,000
  Market interest rate (i) = 2.5% (5% × $\frac{6}{12}$)
  Interest payment (PMT) = $15,000 ($500,000 × 6% × $\frac{6}{12}$)
  Number of semi-annual periods (n) = 20 (10 years × 2)
- To calculate the issue price of the bonds using the present value tables in Appendix C, use Table 1 (the present value of $1) to determine the factor to use to calculate the present value of the principal, which is a single sum. Use Table 2 (the present value of an annuity of $1) in Appendix C to calculate the present value of the interest, which recurs periodically (as an annuity). Remember to double the number of periods and halve the annual interest rate for interest paid semi-annually.
- Record and report bonds payable at their present value (carrying amount).
- Use the coupon interest rate to calculate the interest paid and the market interest rate to calculate the interest expense. The amortization amount (adjusted to the Bonds Payable account) is the difference between the interest paid and the interest expense.
- The current portion of the bonds is any interest payable, as well as any bonds that mature (will be repaid) in the next year. The non-current portion is the bonds' total carrying amount at the date in question (December 31, 2012) less the current portion, if any.

Solution to Comprehensive Do It! #2 (Bonds Payable)

(a)

Present value of $500,000 received in 20 periods

$500,000 × 0.61027 ($n = 20, i = 2.5\%$)	$305,135

Present value of $15,000 received for each of 20 periods

$15,000 × 15.58916 ($n = 20, i = 2.5\%$)	233,837
Present value (issue price) of bonds	$538,972

(b)

SNYDER SOFTWARE INC.
Bond Premium Amortization Schedule (partial)

Interest Period	(A) Interest Payment ($500,000 × 6% × 6/12)	(B) Interest Expense (E × 5% × 6/12)	(C) Premium Amortization (A − B)	(D) Unamortized Premium (D − C)	(E) Bond Carrying Amount ($500,000 + D)
Issue date (Dec. 31, 2011)				$38,972	$538,972
1 (June 30, 2012)	$15,000	$13,474	$1,526	37,446	537,446
2 (Dec. 31, 2012)	15,000	13,436	1,564	35,882	535,882

(c)

Dec. 31, 2011	Cash	538,972	
	Bonds Payable		538,972
	(To record issue of 10-year, 5% bonds at a premium)		

(d)

June 30, 2012	Interest Expense ($538,972 × 5% × 6/12)	13,474	
	Bonds Payable ($15,000 − $13,474)	1,526	
	Cash ($500,000 × 6% × 6/12)		15,000
	(To record semi-annual bond interest payment and amortization of bond premium)		
Dec. 31, 2012	Interest Expense ($537,446 × 5% × 6/12)	13,436	
	Bonds Payable ($15,000 − $13,436)	1,564	
	Cash ($500,000 × 6% × 6/12)		15,000
	(To record semi-annual bond interest payment and amortization of bond premium)		

(e) There is no current liability related to the bonds at December 31 because the bonds do not mature until 2021 and the interest is fully paid as at December 31, 2011. The non-current liability is $535,882. The total liability is $535,882.

Self-Test, Brief Exercises, Exercises, Problems: Set A, and many more components are available for practice in WileyPLUS.

Self-Test Questions

Answers are at the end of the chapter.

(SO 1) 1. Restouche Ltd. has $4,515 of pre-tax sales. If Restouche collects 13% HST with each sale, what is the amount to be credited to the Sales account?
(a) $587
(b) $3,996

(c) $4,515
(d) $5,102

(SO 1) 2. On March 1, Swift Current Limited received its property tax assessment in the amount of

$12,000 for the calendar year. The property tax bill is due May 1. If Swift Current prepares quarterly financial statements, how much prepaid property tax should the company report at the end of its second quarter, June 30?

(a) $4,000
(b) $6,000
(c) $8,000
(d) $12,000

(SO 1) 3. Severin works for the Blue Door Corporation at a salary of $550 per week. Canada Pension Plan contributions are $27.23 for the employee and the same for the employer. Income tax is $79.15. Employment insurance premiums are $9.79 for the employee and $13.71 for the employer. How much is Severin's weekly net pay (i.e., take-home pay)?

(a) $392.89
(b) $433.83
(c) $470.85
(d) $550.00

(SO 2) 4. Boudreault Ltée issues a three-year, 7%, $497,000 instalment note payable on January 1. The note will be paid in three annual fixed principal payments of $165,667, plus interest, that are payable at the end of each year. What is the amount of interest expense that should be recognized by Boudreault in the second year?

(a) $17,395
(b) $23,193
(c) $23,968
(d) $34,790

(SO 2) 5. Zhang Inc. borrows $497,000 from the bank at 7% for a three-year period on January 1. The bank loan will be repaid in three annual blended principal and interest payments of $189,383 that are due at the end of each year. What is the amount of interest expense that should be recognized by Zhang in the second year?

(a) $17,395
(b) $23,193
(c) $23,968
(d) $34,790

(SO 3) 6. On January 1, Scissors Corp. issues $200,000 of five-year, 7% bonds at 97. The entry to record the issue of the bonds would include a:

(a) debit to Cash for $200,000.
(b) debit to Interest Expense for $6,000.

(c) debit to Investment in Bonds for $194,000.
(d) credit to Bonds Payable for $194,000.

(SO 3) 7. On January 1, Daigle Corporation issued $2 million of five-year, 7% bonds with interest payable on January 1 and July 1. The bonds sold for $1,918,880 to yield a market interest rate of 8%. The debit entry to the Bond Interest Expense account (rounded to the nearest dollar) on July 1 is for:

(a) $67,161.
(b) $70,000.
(c) $76,755.
(d) $80,000.

(SO 3) 8. Gester Corporation redeems its $100,000 of face value bonds at 105 on January 1. The bonds' carrying amount at the redemption date is $103,745. The entry to record the redemption will include a:

(a) debit of $1,255 to Loss on Bond Redemption.
(b) credit of $1,255 to Gain on Bond Redemption.
(c) credit of $103,745 to Bonds Payable.
(d) debit of $105,000 to Cash.

(SO 4) 9. Which of the following ratio combinations indicates that a company's solvency is improving?

(a) Debt to total assets ratios of 55% in year 2 and 45% in year 1
(b) Times interest earned ratios of 7 times in year 2 and 10 times in year 1
(c) Debt to total assets ratios of 55% in year 2 and 45% in year 1 and times interest earned ratios of 7 times in year 2 and 10 times in year 1
(d) Debt to total assets ratios of 45% in year 2 and 55% in year 1 and times interest earned ratios of 10 times in year 2 and 7 times in year 1

(SO 4) 10. In a recent year, K-Dough Corporation had profit of $150,000, interest expense of $30,000, and income tax expense of $20,000. What was K-Dough's times interest earned ratio?

(a) 5.0 times
(b) 5.7 times
(c) 6.0 times
(d) 6.7 times

Questions

(SO 1) 1. Identify the similarities and differences between accounts payable and notes payable.

(SO 1) 2. What is the difference between an operating line of credit and a short- or long-term bank loan payable?

(SO 1) 3. Your roommate says, "Sales tax is a part of the cost of doing business and should be reported in

the sales revenue section of the income statement." Do you agree? Explain.

(SO 1) 4. Explain how recording property tax can result in an expense (property tax expense), a liability (property tax payable), and an asset (prepaid property tax).

(SO 1)   5. What is the difference between (a) gross and net pay, and (b) employee payroll deductions and employee benefits?

(SO 1, 2) 6. Explain how to determine the current and non-current portions of debt for presentation in the liabilities section of the statement of financial position.

(SO 2)   7. Identify the similarities and differences between short-term notes payable and long-term instalment notes payable.

(SO 2)   8. Distinguish between instalment notes payable with fixed principal payments plus interest and those with blended principal and interest payments.

(SO 2)   9. When students borrow money for their post-secondary education under the Canada Student Loans Program, they sign an instalment note payable. It must be repaid, starting six months after graduation, in equal monthly amounts including principal and interest. Is this a fixed or blended payment pattern?

(SO 2)   10. When students borrow money for their post-secondary education under the Canada Student Loans Program, they can choose a fixed interest rate of prime + 5% or a floating interest rate of prime + 2.5%. (a) Explain the difference be-tween these two types of interest rates. (b) Which interest rate—fixed or variable—do you think you would prefer? Explain.

(SO 2)   11. Doug Bareak, a friend of yours, has recently purchased a home for $200,000. He paid $20,000 down and financed the remainder with a 20-year, 5% mortgage that is payable in blended payments of principal and interest of $1,290 per month. At the end of the first month, Doug received a state-ment from the bank indicating that only $540 of the principal was paid during the month. At this rate, he calculated that it would take over 28 years to pay off the mortgage. Explain why Doug is incorrect.

(SO 3)   12. Identify the similarities and differences between bonds payable and (a) instalment notes payable, and (b) common shares.

(SO 3)   13. La Mi and Jack Dalton are discussing how the issue price of a bond is determined. La believes that the issue price depends only on the amount of the principal payment at the end of the term of a bond. Is she right? Discuss.

(SO 3)   14. Stoney Inc. sold bonds with a face value of $100,000 for $104,000. Was the market interest rate equal to, less than, or greater than the bonds' coupon interest rate? Explain.

(SO 3)   15. Explain how amortization is calculated when bonds are issued (a) at a discount, and (b) at a premium.

(SO 3)   16. How will the total cost of borrowing be affected if a bond is sold (a) at a discount and (b) at a premium? Explain how this cost of borrowing should be recorded over the life of the bonds.

(SO 3)   17. Why is there no gain or loss when bonds are redeemed at maturity, but there usually is a gain or loss when bonds are redeemed before maturity?

(SO 4)   18. In general, what are the requirements for the financial statement presentation of (a) current liabilities, (b) non-current liabilities, and (c) contingent liabilities?

(SO 4)   19. What criterion must be met before a contingent liability can be recorded as a provision? How does this criterion differ depending on whether the company is a public company using IFRS or a private company using ASPE?

(SO 4)   20. Review Note 14 to Eastplats's financial state-ments in Appendix A where it reports a provision for environmental rehabilitation. Why is this accounted for as a provision rather than a contingent liability?

(SO 4)   21. Distinguish between liquidity and solvency. Provide an example of two ratios that can be used to measure each.

(SO 4)   22. Explain how an operating line of credit can help a company's liquidity.

(SO 4)   23. Explain why the debt to total assets ratio should never be interpreted without referring to the times interest earned ratio.

(SO 4)   24. Explain why it is important to know if a company has significant operating lease commitments.

Brief Exercises

BE10–1   Centennial Sales Ltd. reports cash sales of $6,000 on October 1. (a) Record the sales assuming they occurred in Ontario and are subject to 13% HST (charged on selling price only). (b) Record the sales assuming they occurred in Quebec and are subject to 5% GST and 8.5% QST (charged on selling price plus GST).

Record sales taxes.
(SO 1)

BE10–2   Pierce Corp. has a December 31 year end. It received its property tax assessment of $24,000 on April 30 for the calendar year. The property tax bill is payable on July 15. Prepare the journal entries to record the property tax on (a) April 30, (b) July 15, and (c) December 31, assuming the company adjusts its accounts annually.

Record property tax.
(SO 1)

BE10–3   Zerbe Consulting Inc.'s gross salaries for the biweekly period ended August 22 were $15,000. Deductions included $743 for CPP, $267 for EI, and $6,258 for income tax. The employer's payroll costs were $743 for CPP and $374 for EI. Prepare journal entries to record (a) the payment of salaries on August 22, and (b) the employer payroll costs on August 22, assuming they will not be remitted to the government until September.

Record payroll.
(SO 1)

Record short-term loan.
(SO 1)

BE10–4 Romez Limited borrowed $60,000 from the bank on July 1 for three months; 5% interest is payable the first of each month, starting August 1. Romez's year end is August 31. Prepare journal entries to record (a) the receipt of the bank loan on July 1; (b) (1) the payment of interest on August 1, (2) the accrual of interest on August 31, (3) the payment of interest on September 1, and (4) the payment of interest on October 1; and (c) payment of the bank loan at maturity on October 1.

Discuss fixed and floating rates of interest.
(SO 2)

BE10–5 Assume that you qualify for a $25,000 loan from the Canada Student Loans Program to help finance your education. You are considering whether to repay this loan on graduation with a fixed interest rate of prime + 5% or a floating interest rate of prime + 2.5%. Assuming you start repaying your loan immediately upon graduation, information related to your loan options follows:

	Fixed Interest Rate	Floating Interest Rate
Amount of loan	$25,000	$25,000
Prime interest rate assumed	2.75%	2.75%
Number of months to repay loan	120 months	120 months
Monthly instalment payment	$300	$268
Total interest payable over life of loan	$11,003	$7,188

(a) Identify the advantages and disadvantages of each interest rate option. (b) Explain which option you think is best for you and why.

Complete instalment payment schedule; identify current and non-current portions.
(SO 2)

BE10–6 Assad Inc. issued a five-year, 7% instalment note payable, with fixed principal payments plus interest, due annually. The following instalment payment schedule is partially completed:

Interest Period	Cash Payment	Interest Expense	Reduction of Principal	Principal Balance
Issue date				$50,000
1	$13,500	$ [1]	[2]	40,000
2	12,800	2,800	[3]	[4]
3	[5]	2,100	[6]	[7]
4	11,400	1,400	[8]	10,000
5	10,700	700	[9]	[10]

(a) Fill in the missing amounts for items [1] through [10]. Round all amounts to the nearest dollar. (b) What are the current and non-current portions of the note at the end of period 3?

Complete instalment payment schedule; identify current and non-current portions.
(SO 2)

BE10–7 Hyatt Inc. issued a five-year, 7% instalment loan payable, with blended principal and interest payments due annually. The following instalment payment schedule is partially completed:

Interest Period	Cash Payment	Interest Expense	Reduction of Principal	Principal Balance
Issue date				$50,000
1	$12,195	$ [1]	$ 8,695	41,305
2	[2]	2,891	[3]	32,001
3	[4]	[5]	9,955	[6]
4	[7]	1,543	[8]	11,394
5	[9]	801*	11,394	[10]

*Adjusted for rounding differences.

(a) Fill in the missing amounts for items [1] to [10]. Round all amounts to the nearest dollar. (b) What are the current and non-current portions of the loan at the end of period 3?

Record mortgage payable.
(SO 2)

BE10–8 Eyre Inc. signs a 10-year, 7%, $300,000 mortgage payable on November 30, 2011, to obtain financing for a new building. The terms provide for monthly payments. Prepare the entries to record the mortgage on November 30, 2011, and the first two payments on December 31, 2011, and January 31, 2012, assuming the payment is (a) a fixed principal payment of $2,500, plus interest, and (b) a blended principal and interest payment of $3,483. Round all amounts to the nearest dollar.

Calculate present value of bond.
(SO 3)

BE10–9 Carvel Corp. issued $500,000 of five-year, 6% bonds, with interest payable semi-annually. How much would Carvel receive from the sale of these bonds if the market interest rate was (a) 5%, (b) 6%, and (c) 7%?

Record bond issue.
(SO 3)

BE10–10 Keyser Corporation issued $100,000 of five-year, 4% bonds dated May 1, 2012. (a) Prepare the journal entry to record the sale of these bonds on May 1, 2012, assuming that the bonds were issued at (1) 99, (2) 100, and (3) 101. (b) What will the carrying amount be at maturity, May 1, 2017, under each of the three different issue price scenarios?

BE10–11 Keystone Corporation issued $1 million of five-year, 5% bonds dated March 1, 2011, at 100. Interest is payable semi-annually on September 1 and March 1. Keystone has a December 31 year end. (a) Record the issue of these bonds on March 1, 2011. (b) Record the first interest payment on September 1, 2011. (c) Record the adjusting journal entry on December 31, 2011, to accrue the interest. (d) Prepare the journal entry to record the second interest payment on March 1, 2012.

Record bond transactions.
(SO 3)

BE10–12 A partial bond discount amortization schedule for Chiasson Corp. follows:

Complete bond amortization schedule; answer questions.
(SO 3)

Semi-Annual Interest Period	Interest Payment	Interest Expense	Discount Amortization	Unamortized Discount	Bond Carrying Amount
Issue date				$62,311	$937,689
1 (June 30)	$45,000	[1]	$1,884	[2]	939,573
2 (Dec. 31)	45,000	$46,979	[3]	58,448	[4]

(a) Fill in the missing amounts for items [1] to [4].
(b) What is the face value of the bonds?
(c) What is the coupon interest rate on the bonds? The market interest rate?
(d) Explain why interest expense is greater than interest paid.
(e) Prepare the journal entry to record the payments of interest on June 30 and December 31, assuming Chiasson's year end is December 31.

BE10–13 On May 1, 2011, Jianhua Corporation issued $200,000 of five-year, 5% bonds, with interest payable semi-annually on November 1 and May 1. The bonds were issued to yield a market interest rate of 4%. (a) Calculate the bonds' present value (issue price) on May 1. (b) Record the issue of the bonds on May 1. (c) Prepare the journal entry to record the interest on November 1, 2011. (d) Prepare the journal entry to accrue the interest on April 30, 2012, Jianhua's year end.

Calculate present value; record bond transactions.
(SO 3)

BE10–14 Hathaway Ltd.'s general ledger reported a balance in its Bonds Payable account of $950,000 at November 30. The bonds had a face value of $1 million, and were redeemed on November 30, immediately after interest had been paid to the bondholders. Prepare the journal entry to record the redemption, assuming the bonds are redeemed at (a) 99, and (b) 101.

Record bond redemption.
(SO 3)

BE10–15 Identify which of the following transactions would be classified as a current liability and/or which would be classified as a non-current liability. For those that are neither, identify where they should be classified or disclosed.

Identify current and non-current liabilities.
(SO 4)

1. A bank loan payable due in two years, with principal due at maturity and interest due the first of each month
2. Cash received in advance by Air Canada for airline tickets
3. HST collected on sales
4. Unused amount of operating line of credit
5. Obligations due under finance leases
6. Obligations due under operating leases
7. Bonds payable, due in 10 years
8. Payroll deductions withheld from the employees' weekly pay
9. Prepaid property tax
10. A $75,000 mortgage payable, of which $5,000 is due in the next year

BE10–16 For each of the following independent situations, indicate whether it should be recorded as a provision or disclosed as a contingent liability for a publicly traded company reporting under IFRS. Indicate if your answer would change if the company were a private company reporting under ASPE.

Account for contingencies.
(SO 4)

1. A pending lawsuit for which a negative outcome has been estimated and determined to be "likely"
2. A pending lawsuit, about which the outcome cannot be determined
3. A nuisance lawsuit, which the company is not anticipated to lose
4. A loan guarantee for a subsidiary company that has a credit rating of AA

BE10–17 The Molson Coors Brewing Company's 2010 financial statements contain the following selected data (in U.S. millions):

Calculate liquidity and solvency ratios.
(SO 4)

Total current assets	$ 2,220.9
Total current liabilities	1,333.9
Total assets	12,697.6
Total liabilities	4,855.0
Income tax expense	138.7
Interest expense	110.2
Profit	709.9

Calculate Molson Coors's (a) current ratio, (b) debt to total assets ratio, and (c) times interest earned ratio.

Analyze solvency.
(SO 4)

BE10–18   The following solvency ratios are available for Drira Corporation:

	2012	2011
Debt to total assets	50%	45%
Times interest earned	10 times	8 times

(a) Identify whether the change in each ratio is an improvement or deterioration. (b) Did the company's overall solvency improve or deteriorate in 2012?

Exercises

Determine impact
of current liability
transactions.
(SO 1)

E10–1   A list of transactions follows:

1. Purchased inventory (perpetual system) on account.
2. Extended payment terms of the account payable in item 1 by issuing a nine-month, 5% note payable.
3. Recorded accrued interest on the note payable from item 2.
4. Recorded payment of the note and accrued interest from items 2 and 3.
5. Recorded cash received from sale of services, plus HST.
6. Recorded salaries expense, employee payroll deductions, and paid employees.
7. Recorded employer's share of employee benefits.
8. Recorded property tax expense and property tax payable when bill was received.
9. Recorded a receipt of cash for services that will be performed in the future.
10. Recorded the performance of services for item 9.

Instructions
Set up a table using the format that follows. Indicate the effect of each of the above transactions on the financial statement categories in the table: use "+" for increase, "−" for decrease, and "NE" for no effect. The first one has been done for you as an example.

	Assets	Liabilities	Shareholders' Equity	Revenues	Expenses	Profit
1.	+	+	NE	NE	NE	NE

Record current
liabilities.
(SO 1)

E10–2   Jintao Ltd. incurred the following transactions related to current liabilities:

1. Jintao's cash register showed the following totals at the end of the day on April 10: pre-tax sales $25,000; GST $1,250; and PST $1,750.
2. Jintao received its property tax bill for the calendar year for $26,400 on May 1, payable July 1.
3. Jintao's gross payroll for the week of August 15 was $40,500. The company deducted $2,005 for CPP, $721 for EI, $3,200 for pension, and $8,010 for income tax from the employees' pay. Jintao's payroll costs for the week were $2,005 for CPP and $1,009 for EI.
4. On November 1, Jintao borrowed $50,000 from First Bank for a six-month period; 4% interest on the bank loan is payable the first of each month.

Instructions
(a) Record the above transactions.
(b) Assuming that Jintao's year end is December 31 and that it makes adjusting entries annually, prepare any adjusting entries required for the property tax in transaction 2 and the interest in transaction 4.

Record short-term
loans.
(SO 1)

E10–3   Dougald Construction Ltd. borrowed $250,000 from TD Bank on October 1, 2011, for a nine-month period; 5% interest is payable at maturity. Both companies have a December 31 year end and make adjusting entries annually.

Instructions
(a) For Dougald Construction, record (1) the receipt of the bank loan on October 1, 2011; (2) the accrual of interest on December 31, 2011; and (3) the payment of the loan on July 1, 2012.
(b) For the TD Bank, record (1) the issue of the bank loan on October 1, 2011; (2) the accrual of interest on December 31, 2011; and (3) the collection of the loan on July 1, 2012. (*Hint:* The TD Bank uses a Notes Receivable account to record its loans. You might find it helpful to review accounting for notes receivable in Chapter 8.)

Record mortgage
payable.
(SO 2)

E10–4   Ste. Anne Corp. issued a 10-year, 5%, $150,000 mortgage payable to finance the construction of a building at December 31, 2011. The terms provide for semi-annual instalment payments on June 30 and December 31.

Instructions

(a) Record the issue of the mortgage payable on December 31, 2011.
(b) Record the first two instalment payments on June 30, 2012, and December 31, 2012, assuming the payment is (1) a fixed principal payment of $7,500, and (2) a blended principal and interest payment of $9,622. Round all amounts to the nearest dollar.

E10-5 On January 1, 2012, Wolstenholme Corp. borrowed $10,000 by signing a three-year, 7% note payable. The note is payable in three annual blended principal and interest instalments of $3,811 at the end of each year, December 31.

Instructions

(a) Prepare an instalment payment schedule for the term of the note. Round all amounts to the nearest dollar.
(b) Record (1) the issue of the note on January 1, and (2) the first instalment payment on December 31.
(c) What amounts would be reported as current and non-current in the liabilities section of Wolstenholme's statement of financial position on December 31, 2012?

Record instalment note payable; identify current and non-current portions. (SO 2)

E10-6 The following instalment payment schedule is for a long-term bank loan payable:

Interest Period	Cash Payment	Interest Expense	Reduction of Principal	Principal Balance
Issue date				$100,000.00
1	$23,097.48	$5,000.00	$18,097.48	81,902.52
2	23,097.48	4,095.13	19,002.35	62,900.17
3	23,097.48	3,145.01	19,952.47	42,947.70
4	23,097.48	2,147.38	20,950.10	21,997.60
5	23,097.48	1,099.88	21,997.60	0.00

Analyze instalment payment schedule. (SO 2)

Instructions

(a) Is the above schedule a fixed principal or blended principal and interest payment schedule?
(b) Assuming payments are made annually, what is the interest rate on the bank loan?
(c) Prepare the journal entry to record the first instalment payment.
(d) What are the current and non-current portions of the bank loan at the end of period 2?

E10-7 The following information about two independent bond issues was reported in the financial press:

1. Alberta Capital Finance 2.25% bonds, maturing September 15, 2015, were issued at a price of 99.46 to yield a market interest rate of 3.51%.
2. City of Waterloo 2.25% bonds, maturing December 1, 2012, were issued at a price of 100.46 to yield a market interest rate of 2.02%.

Analyze and record bond issue. (SO 3)

Instructions

(a) Were the Alberta Capital Finance bonds issued at a premium or a discount?
(b) Were the City of Waterloo bonds issued at a premium or a discount?
(c) Explain how bonds, both paying the same coupon interest rate (2.25%), could be issued at different prices.
(d) Record the issue of $100,000 of each of these two bonds.

E10-8 On September 1, 2011, Mooney Corporation issued $400,000 of 10-year, 5% bonds at 100. Interest is payable semi-annually on September 1 and March 1. Mooney's year end is December 31.

Record bond transactions; show statement of financial position presentation. (SO 3)

Instructions

(a) Prepare journal entries to record the following:
  1. The issue of the bonds on September 1, 2011
  2. The accrual of interest on December 31, 2011
  3. The payment of interest on March 1, 2012
(b) Identify what amounts, if any, would be reported as a current liability and non-current liability with respect to the bond and bond interest accounts on December 31, 2011.

E10-9 A partial bond amortization schedule follows for Hwee Corporation:

Complete amortization schedule; answer questions. (SO 3)

Semi-Annual Interest Period	Interest Payment	Interest Expense	Discount/Premium Amortization	Unamortized Discount/Premium	Bond Carrying Amount
Issue date				$74,387	$925,613
1 (Apr. 30)	$25,000	[1]	$2,768	[2]	928,381
2 (Oct. 31)	25,000	$27,851	[3]	68,768	[4]
3 (Apr. 30)	[5]	27,937	[6]	[7]	934,169

Instructions

(a) Fill in the missing amounts for items [1] to [7].
(b) What is the face value of the bonds?
(c) Were the bonds issued at a discount or at a premium?
(d) What is the coupon interest rate on the bonds? The market interest rate?
(e) Explain why interest expense is greater than interest paid.
(f) Explain why interest expense will increase each period.
(g) What will be the bonds' carrying amount on their maturity date?

Calculate present
value; record bond
transactions.
(SO 3)

E10–10   Tagawa Corporation issued $500,000 of 10-year, 5% bonds on January 1, 2012, at a price to yield a market interest rate of 6%. Interest is payable semi-annually on July 1 and January 1. Tagawa has a December 31 year end.

Instructions

(a) Calculate the bonds' present value (issue price) on January 1.
(b) Record the issue of the bonds on January 1.
(c) Record the payment of interest on July 1.
(d) Record the accrual of interest on December 31.

Record bond
redemption.
(SO 3)

E10–11   The following independent situations occurred on June 30, 2012:

1. Ernst Corporation redeemed $120,000 of 7% bonds at 101. The bonds' carrying amount at the redemption date was $115,133.

2. Takase Corporation redeemed $150,000 of 8% bonds at 99. The bonds' carrying amount at the redemption date was $156,237.

3. Young, Inc. redeemed $150,000 of 6% bonds at their maturity date, June 30, 2012.

Instructions

Record the transaction for each of the above situations.

Prepare liabilities
section.
(SO 4)

E10–12   Le Château Inc. reported the following liabilities (in thousands) in its January 31, 2010, financial statements:

Accounts payable and accrued liabilities	$ 27,151	Income taxes payable	$ 19	
Current portion of long-term debt	11,752	Long-term debt	21,464	
Dividends payable	4,293	Operating leases	267,263	
Future income taxes	3,910	Other long-term liabilities	10,222	
		Unused operating line of credit	9,653	

Instructions

(a) Identify which of the above liabilities are likely current and which are likely non-current. Say if an item fits in neither category. Explain the reasoning for your selections.
(b) Prepare the liabilities section of Le Château's statement of financial position.

Discuss contingent
liabilities.
(SO 4)

E10–13   Walmart Stores, Inc. is sued about once every two hours every day of the year. These allegations range from falls on icy parking lots to injuries sustained in shoppers' stampedes to a murder with a rifle purchased at one of its stores. The company recently disclosed the following in the notes to its financial statements:

> The company is involved in a number of legal proceedings. The company has made accruals with respect to these matters, where appropriate, which are reflected in the company's Consolidated Financial Statements. For some matters, the amount of liability is not probable or the amount cannot be reasonably estimated and therefore accruals have not been made. However, where a liability is reasonably possible and material, such matters have been disclosed.

Instructions

(a) The above states that "the company has made accruals . . . where appropriate." Explain when it would be appropriate for Walmart to accrue a liability as a provision rather than disclose it as a contingent liability.
(b) Comment on any implications the contingent liabilities might have for analysis of Walmart's solvency.
(c) How might the accrual or disclosure of these legal proceedings change if Walmart were a private company reporting under ASPE?

Analyze liquidity.
(SO 4)

E10–14   The following selected information (in thousands) was taken from Fruition Collections Ltd.'s December 31 statement of financial position:

	2012	2011
Current assets		
Cash	$2,574	$1,021
Accounts receivable	2,147	1,575
Inventories	1,201	1,010
Other current assets	322	192
Total current assets	$6,244	$3,798
Total current liabilities	$4,503	$2,619

Instructions

(a) Calculate the current ratio for each of the two years. (1) Based only on this information, would you say that the company's liquidity is strong or weak? (2) What additional information should you request to complete your assessment of liquidity?

(b) Suppose that Fruition Collections used $1,000,000 of its cash to pay off $1,000,000 of its accounts payable. Would this transaction change the current ratio?

(c) At December 31, 2012, Fruition Collections had an unused operating line of credit of $4 million. Does this information affect the assessment of the company's short-term liquidity that you made in (a) above?

E10–15   Maple Leaf Foods Inc.'s financial statements contain the following selected data (in thousands):

Analyze solvency.
(SO 4)

	2010	2009
Total assets	$2,996,795	$3,057,464
Total liabilities	1,779,418	1,868,414
Profit	25,822	52,147
Income tax expense	17,766	27,296
Interest expense	66,386	81,234

Instructions

(a) Calculate the debt to total assets and times interest earned ratios for 2010 and 2009. Did Maple Leaf's solvency improve or deteriorate in 2010?

(b) The notes to Maple Leaf Foods' financial statements show that the company has future operating lease commitments totalling $344,144 thousand in 2010 and $344,963 thousand in 2009. Discuss how these unrecorded obligations affect the analysis of Maple Leaf Foods' solvency.

Problems: Set A

P10–1A   On February 29, 2012, Molega Ltd.'s general ledger contained the following liability accounts:

Record and present current liabilities.
(SO 1, 4)

Accounts payable	$42,500
CPP payable	2,680
EI payable	1,123
Sales tax payable	5,800
Income tax payable	5,515
Unearned revenue	15,000

The following selected transactions occurred during the month:

Mar. 2   Issued a three-month, 6% note payable in exchange for an account payable in the amount of $10,000. Interest is due at maturity.

5   Sold merchandise for cash totalling $40,000, plus 13% HST. The cost of goods sold was $24,000. Molega uses a perpetual inventory system.

9   Received the property tax bill of $18,000 for the calendar year. It is payable on May 1.

12   Provided services for customers who had made advance payments of $7,500.

13   Paid $5,800 HST to the Receiver General for sales tax collected in February.

16   Paid $9,318 to the Receiver General for amounts owing from the February payroll for employee payroll deductions of $7,323 (CPP $1,340, EI $468, and income tax $5,515) and for employee benefits of $1,995 (CPP $1,340, and EI $655).

27   Paid $30,000 to trade creditors on account.

31   Recorded and paid monthly payroll. Gross salaries totalled $16,000 and payroll deductions included CPP of $792, EI of $285, and income tax of $5,870. Employee benefits included CPP of $792 and EI of $399.

Instructions

(a) Record the above transactions.

(b) Record any required adjusting entries at March 31.

(c) Prepare the current liabilities section of the statement of financial position at March 31.

P10–2A   Cling-on Ltd. sells rock-climbing products and also operates an indoor climbing facility for climbing enthusiasts. On September 1, 2012, the company had a balance of $12,000 in its Bank Loan Payable account, representing a loan borrowed from the local credit union on July 1. The loan and 6% interest are both payable at maturity, on September 30. Note that the company records adjusting entries only annually at its year end, December 31.

Record and present short-term notes.
(SO 1, 4)

During the next four months, Cling-on incurred the following:

Sept.	1	Purchased inventory on account for $15,000 from Black Diamond, terms n/30. The company uses a perpetual inventory system.
	30	Repaid the $12,000 bank loan payable to the credit union (see opening balance), as well as any interest owed.
Oct.	1	Issued a six-month, 7%, $15,000 note payable to Black Diamond in exchange for the account payable (see Sept. 1 transaction). Interest is payable on the first of each month.
	2	Borrowed $25,000 from Montpelier Bank for 12 months at 8% to finance the building of a new climbing area for advanced climbers (use the asset account Climbing Wall). Interest is payable monthly on the first of each month.
Nov.	1	Paid interest on the Black Diamond note and Montpelier Bank loan.
Dec.	1	Paid interest on the Black Diamond note and Montpelier Bank loan.
	2	Purchased a vehicle for $28,000 from Auto Dealer Ltd. to transport clients to nearby climbing sites. Paid $8,000 as a down payment and borrowed the remainder from the Montpelier Bank for 12 months at 7%. Interest is payable quarterly, at the end of each quarter.
	31	Recorded accrued interest for the Black Diamond note and Montpelier Bank loans.

Instructions

(a) Record the above transactions.

(b) Open T accounts for the Interest Expense, Interest Payable, Bank Loans Payable, and Notes Payable accounts. Post the above entries.

(c) Assuming there is no other interest expense than that recorded in the transactions above, show the income statement presentation of interest expense for the year ended December 31.

(d) Show the statement of financial position presentation of the bank loans, notes, and interest payable at December 31.

Record instalment note.
(SO 2)

P10–3A On September 30, 2011, Atwater Corporation purchased a piece of equipment for $550,000. The equipment was purchased with a $50,000 down payment and a three-year, 8%, $500,000 mortgage for the balance. The terms provide for payment of the mortgage with quarterly fixed principal payments of $41,667, plus interest, starting on December 31. Atwater has a December 31 year end.

Instructions

(a) Record the purchase of equipment on September 30, 2011.

(b) Record the first two instalment payments, on December 31, 2011, and March 31, 2012. Round all amounts to the nearest dollar.

(c) Repeat part (b) assuming that the terms provide for quarterly blended principal and interest payments of $47,280, rather than fixed principal payments of $41,667, plus interest.

Prepare instalment payment schedule; record and present instalment note.
(SO 2, 4)

P10–4A Elite Electronics signed a 10-year, 6.5%, $350,000 mortgage on June 30, 2011, to help finance a new research laboratory. The mortgage terms provide for semi-annual blended principal and interest payments of $24,073. Payments are due on December 31 and June 30. The company's year end is June 30.

Instructions

(a) Prepare an instalment payment schedule for the first two years. Round all amounts to the nearest dollar.

(b) Record the receipt of the mortgage loan on June 30, 2011.

(c) Record the first two instalment payments, on December 31, 2011, and June 30, 2012.

(d) Show the statement of financial position presentation of the mortgage payable at June 30, 2012.

Prepare instalment payment schedule; record and present instalment note.
(SO 2, 4)

P10–5A Peter Furlong has just approached a venture capitalist for financing for his sailing school. The lender is willing to loan Peter $100,000 at a high-risk interest rate of 12%. The loan is payable over three years in fixed principal payments each quarter of $8,333, plus interest. Peter signs a note payable and receives the loan on April 30, 2012. He makes the first payment on July 31. The company's year end is October 31.

Instructions

(a) Prepare an instalment payment schedule for the three years. Round all amounts to the nearest dollar.

(b) Record the receipt of the funds from the note on April 30.

(c) Record the first two instalment payments, on July 31 and October 31.

(d) Show the statement of financial position presentation of the note payable at October 31, 2012.

(e) Explain how the quarterly and total cash payments would change if the note had been payable in blended principal and interest payments of $10,046, rather than fixed principal payments plus interest.

Record bond transactions.
(SO 3)

P10–6A On October 1, 2011, PFQ Corp. issued $600,000 of 10-year, 5% bonds at 100. The bonds pay interest semi-annually on April 1 and October 1. PFQ's year end is December 31 and it makes adjusting entries annually.

Instructions

(a) Identify the coupon and market rates of interest on October 1, 2011, when PFQ issued the bonds.

(b) Record the issue of the bonds on October 1, 2011.

(c) Prepare the adjusting entry to record the accrual of interest on December 31, 2011.

(d) Record the first interest payment on April 1, 2012.

(e) Record the second interest payment on October 1, 2012.

(f) Assume that on October 1, 2012, immediately after paying the semi-annual interest, PFQ redeems all of the bonds at 102. Record the redemption of the bonds.

P10–7A The following is from Peppermint Patty Ltd.'s statement of financial position at December 31, 2011:

Record bond transactions.
(SO 3)

PEPPERMINT PATTY LTD.
Statement of Financial Position (partial)
December 31, 2011

Current liabilities	
Interest payable	$ 5,000
Non-current liabilities	
Bonds payable, 5%, due January 1, 2021	186,246

The bonds have a face value of $200,000 and were issued one year ago at a price to yield a market interest rate of 6%. Interest is payable semi-annually on January 1 and July 1.

Instructions

(a) Record the payment of bond interest on January 1, 2012, assuming the accrued interest expense is $5,570 and interest payable is $5,000 at December 31.

(b) Assume that on January 1, 2012, after paying interest, Peppermint Patty redeems bonds having a face value of $50,000 at 98. Record the redemption of the bonds.

(c) Record the payment of bond interest on July 1, 2012, on the remaining bonds.

(d) Prepare the adjusting entry on December 31, 2012, to accrue the interest on the remaining bonds.

P10–8A On July 1, 2011, Global Satellites Corporation issued $1.5 million of 10-year, 7% bonds to yield a market interest rate of 6%. The bonds pay semi-annual interest on July 1 and January 1. Global has a December 31 year end.

Calculate present value; prepare amortization schedule; record and present bond transactions.
(SO 3, 4)

Instructions

(a) Calculate the bonds' present value (issue price) on July 1.

(b) Prepare an amortization table through January 1, 2013 (three interest periods) for this bond issue. Round all amounts to the nearest dollar.

(c) Record the issue of the bonds on July 1.

(d) Prepare the adjusting entry on December 31, 2012, to accrue the interest on the bonds.

(e) Show the statement of financial position presentation of the liabilities at December 31, 2012.

P10–9A The following transactions occurred in Wendell Corporation, which has a December 31 year end:

Classify liabilities.
(SO 4)

1. Property taxes of $40,000 were assessed on March 1 for the calendar year. They are payable by May 1.

2. Wendell signed a five-year, 7%, $200,000 instalment note payable on July 1. The note requires fixed principal payments of $40,000, plus interest annually on each June 30 for the next five years.

3. Wendell purchased merchandise for $120,000 on December 23 on account, terms n/30, FOB shipping point. The merchandise was shipped on December 28 and received by Wendell on January 2.

4. Wendell received $10,000 from customers on December 21 for services to be performed in January.

5. On December 31, Wendell sold merchandise for $8,000, plus 12% HST. The cost of goods sold was $5,000. The company uses a perpetual inventory system.

6. Weekly salaries of $6,000 are paid every Friday for a five-day workweek (Monday to Friday). This year, December 31 is a Wednesday. Payroll deductions for the three days include CPP of $297, EI of $107, and income tax of $1,300. Employee benefits include CPP of $297 and EI of $150.

7. Wendell is the defendant in a negligence lawsuit. Wendell's legal counsel estimates that Wendell may suffer a $75,000 loss if it loses the suit. In legal counsel's opinion, it is not possible at this time to determine whether or not the case will be lost.

8. Wendell made income tax instalments of $45,000 throughout the year. After the preparation of its corporate income tax return at year end, it was determined that total income tax payable for the year was $50,000.

9. Wendell reported non-current debt of $250,000 at December 31, of which $30,000 was due within the next year.

10. Wendell has a $100,000 operating line of credit available, on which no funds have yet been drawn.

Instructions

(a) Identify which of the above transactions should be presented in the current liabilities section and which should be recorded in the non-current liabilities section of Wendell's statement of financial position on December 31. Identify the account title(s) and amount(s) for each reported liability.

(b) Indicate any information that should be disclosed in the notes to Wendell's financial statements.

Analyze liquidity and
solvency.
(SO 4)

P10–10A You have been presented with the following selected information taken from the financial statements of Magna International Inc. (in U.S. millions):

	2010	2009	2008
Statement of financial position			
Accounts receivable	$ 3,645	$ 3,062	$ 2,821
Inventory	1,896	1,721	1,647
Total current assets	7,814	6,303	7,351
Total assets	13,898	12,303	13,189
Current liabilities	5,200	4,299	5,093
Total liabilities	5,833	4,943	5,826
Income statement			
Net sales	24,102	$17,367	$23,704
Cost of goods sold	20,924	15,697	20,982
Interest expense	12	27	51
Income tax expense (recovery)	236	(18)	257
Profit (loss)	973	(493)	71

Instructions

(a) Calculate each of the following ratios for 2010 and 2009. Industry ratios are shown in parentheses.
   1. Current ratio (2010, 1.4:1:1; 2009, 1.4:1)
   2. Receivables turnover (2010, 7.1 times; 2009, 6.9 times)
   3. Inventory turnover (2010, 9.4 times; 2009, 9.8 times)
   4. Debt to total assets (2010, 38.3%; 2009, 41.9%)
   5. Times interest earned (2010, 5.3 times; 2009, 6.3 times)
(b) Based on your results in (a), comment on Magna's liquidity and solvency.
(c) Magna had a U.S. $2-billion operating line of credit, of which U.S. $1.9 billion was unused at the end of 2010 and 2009. Discuss the implications of this information for your analysis.
(d) Magna had operating lease commitments totalling U.S. $1,765 million in 2010 and U.S. $1,699 million in 2009. Discuss the implications of this information for your analysis.

Analyze liquidity and
solvency.
(SO 4)

P10–11A The following selected liquidity and solvency ratios are available for two companies operating in the petroleum industry:

	Petro-Zoom	Sun-Oil	Industry Average
Current ratio	1.3:1	1.2:1	1.4:1
Receivables turnover	12 times	13 times	11 times
Inventory turnover	16 times	10 times	19 times
Debt to total assets	41%	39%	34%
Times interest earned	21 times	24 times	26 times

Instructions

Assume that you are the credit manager of the local bank. Answer the following questions, using relevant ratios to justify your answer:

(a) Both Petro-Zoom and Sun-Oil have applied for a short-term loan from your bank. Which of the two companies is more liquid and should get more consideration for a short-term loan? Explain.
(b) Both Petro-Zoom and Sun-Oil have applied for a long-term loan from your bank. Are you concerned about the solvency of either company? Explain why or why not.

Problems: Set B

Record and present
current liabilities.
(SO 1, 4)

P10–1B On January 1, 2012, Burlington Inc.'s general ledger contained these opening balances for its liability accounts:

Accounts payable	$52,000	Sales tax payable	$18,000
CPP payable	3,810	Income tax payable	7,700
EI payable	1,598	Unearned revenue	16,000

The following selected transactions occurred during the month:

Jan. 5   Sold merchandise for cash totalling $20,000, plus 5% GST and 7% PST. The cost of goods sold was $14,000. Burlington uses a perpetual inventory system.

13   Paid $18,000 ($7,500 GST to the Receiver General and $10,500 PST to the provincial Minister of Finance) for sales taxes collected in December.

14   Paid $13,108 to the Receiver General for amounts owing from the December payroll for the employee payroll deductions of $10,271 (CPP $1,905, EI $666, and income tax $7,700) and employee benefits of $2,837 (CPP $1,905, and EI $932).

15   Borrowed $18,000 from HSBC Bank for three months; 6% interest is payable monthly on the 15th of each month.

19   Provided services for customers who had made advance payments of $7,000.

22   Paid $32,000 to trade creditors on account.

28   Received assessment of property taxes of $4,200 for the calendar year. They are payable on March 1.

29   Paid monthly payroll. Gross salaries totalled $40,000 and payroll deductions include CPP of $1,980, EI of $712, and income tax of $9,474. Employee benefits included CPP of $1,980 and EI of $997.

Instructions

(a) Record the above transactions.

(b) Record any required adjusting entries at January 31.

(c) Prepare the current liabilities section of the statement of financial position at January 31.

P10–2B   MileHi Mountain Bikes Ltd. markets mountain-bike tours to clients vacationing in various locations in the mountains of British Columbia. On March 1, 2012, the company had a balance of $15,000 in Notes Payable for a six-month, 7% note issued to Eifert Corp. on October 1, with interest payable at maturity. Note that the company records adjusting entries only annually at its year end, June 30.

Record and present short-term notes. (SO 1, 4)

In preparation for the upcoming summer biking season, MileHi engaged in the following transactions:

Mar. 2   Purchased Mongoose bikes for use as rentals by borrowing $8,000 from the Western Bank for a three-month period; 8% interest is payable at maturity.

31   Paid the $15,000 note payable to Eifert Corp. (see opening balance), as well as any interest owed.

Apr. 1   Issued a nine-month, 6%, $25,000 note to Mountain Real Estate for the purchase of mountain property on which to build bike trails. Interest is payable at the first of each month.

May 1   Paid interest on the Mountain Real Estate note (see April 1 transaction).

2   Borrowed $18,000 from Western Bank for a four-month period. The funds will be used for working capital for the beginning of the season. 7% interest is payable at maturity.

June 1   Paid interest on the Mountain Real Estate note (see April 1 transaction).

2   Paid principal and interest to the Western Bank (see March 2 transaction).

29   Purchased a trailer for $5,000 to transport the bikes from one location to another. Paid $500 as a down payment and borrowed the remainder from the Western Bank for a 12-month period; 6% interest is payable quarterly, at the end of each quarter starting September 30.

30   Recorded accrued interest for the Mountain Real Estate note and Western Bank loan at MileHi's year end.

Instructions

(a) Record the above transactions.

(b) Open T accounts for the Interest Expense, Interest Payable, Notes Payable, and Bank Loans Payable accounts. Post the above entries.

(c) Assuming there is no other interest expense than that recorded in the transactions above, show the income statement presentation of the interest expense for the year ended June 30.

(d) Show the statement of financial position presentation of the notes, bank loans, and interest payable at June 30.

P10–3B   On July 31, 2012, Myron Corporation purchased a piece of equipment for $750,000. The equipment was purchased with a $50,000 down payment and through the issue of a four-year, 6%, $700,000 mortgage payable for the balance. The terms provide for the mortgage to be repaid with monthly blended principal and interest instalment payments of $16,440 starting on August 31. Myron has a September 30 year end.

Record instalment note. (SO 2)

Instructions

(a) Record the purchase of equipment and issue of the mortgage on July 31.

(b) Record the first two instalment payments, on August 31 and September 30. Round all amounts to the nearest dollar.

(c) Repeat part (b) assuming that the terms provide for monthly fixed principal payments of $14,583, plus interest, rather than blended payments of $16,440.

P10–4B   Kinyae Electronics Limited signed a 10-year, 8%, $500,000 mortgage on December 31, 2011, to help finance a plant expansion. The terms of the mortgage provide for semi-annual fixed principal payments of $25,000, plus interest. Payments are due on June 30 and December 31.

Prepare instalment payment schedule; record and present instalment note. (SO 2, 4)

Instructions

(a) Prepare an instalment payment schedule for the first two years. Round all amounts to the nearest dollar.
(b) Record the issue of the mortgage payable on December 31, 2011.
(c) Record the first two instalment payments, on June 30, 2012, and December 31, 2012.
(d) Show the statement of financial position presentation of the mortgage payable at December 31, 2012.

Prepare instalment payment schedule; record and present instalment note.
(SO 2, 4)

P10–5B   A local ski hill has just approached a venture capitalist for financing for its new business venture, the development of another local ski hill. On April 1, 2010, the venture capitalist loaned the company $100,000 at an interest rate of 13%. The loan is payable over four years in annual blended principal and interest instalments of $33,619, due each March 31. The first payment is due March 31, 2011. The ski hill's year end is March 31.

Instructions

(a) Prepare an instalment payment schedule for the loan period. Round all amounts to the nearest dollar.
(b) Record the receipt of the loan on April 1, 2010.
(c) Record the first two instalment payments, on March 31, 2011, and March 31, 2012.
(d) Show the statement of financial position presentation of the loan payable as at March 31, 2012.
(e) Explain how the annual and total interest expense would change if the loan had been payable in fixed principal payments of $25,000, plus interest, rather than in blended principal and interest payments.

Record bond transactions.
(SO 3)

P10–6B   On May 1, 2011, MEM Corp. issued $800,000 of five-year, 6% bonds at 100. The bonds pay interest semi-annually on November 1 and May 1. MEM's year end is December 31 and it makes adjusting entries annually.

Instructions

(a) Identify the coupon and market rates of interest on May 1, 2011, when MEM issued the bonds.
(b) Record the issue of the bonds on May 1, 2011.
(c) Record the first interest payment on November 1, 2011.
(d) Prepare the adjusting entry to record the accrual of interest on December 31, 2011.
(e) Record the second interest payment on May 1, 2012.
(f) Assume that on May 1, 2012, immediately after paying the semi-annual interest, MEM redeems all of the bonds at 98. Record the redemption of the bonds.

Record bond transactions.
(SO 3)

P10–7B   The following is from Disch Corp.'s statement of financial position at December 31, 2011:

DISCH CORP.	
Statement of Financial Position (partial)	
December 31, 2011	
Current liabilities	
Interest payable	$ 45,000
Non-current liabilities	
Bonds payable, 6%, due January 1, 2021	1,607,650

The bonds have a face value of $1.5 million and were issued on January 1, 2011 at a price to yield a market interest rate of 5%. Interest is payable semi-annually on January 1 and July 1.

Instructions

(a) Record the payment of bond interest on January 1, 2012, assuming the accrued interest expense is $40,309 and the interest payable is $45,000 at December 31.
(b) Assume that on January 1, 2012, after paying interest, Disch redeems bonds having a face value of $500,000 at 102. Record the redemption of the bonds.
(c) Record the payment of bond interest on July 1, 2012, on the remaining bonds.
(d) Prepare the adjusting entry on December 31, 2012, to accrue the interest on the remaining bonds.

Calculate present value; prepare amortization schedule; record and present bond transactions.
(SO 3, 4)

P10–8B   On July 1, 2011, Ponasis Corporation issued $1 million of 10-year, 6% bonds at a price to yield a market interest rate of 7%. The bonds pay semi-annual interest on July 1 and January 1. Ponasis has a December 31 year end.

Instructions

(a) Calculate the bonds' present value (issue price) on July 1.
(b) Prepare an amortization table through January 1, 2013 (three interest periods) for this bond issue. Round all amounts to the nearest dollar.
(c) Record the issue of the bonds on July 1, 2011.
(d) Prepare the adjusting entry on December 31, 2012, to accrue the interest on the bonds.
(e) Show the statement of financial position presentation of the liabilities at December 31, 2012.

P10–9B The following transactions are for Iqaluit Ltd., which has an April 30 year end:

Classify liabilities.
(SO 4)

1. Received property taxes assessment of $12,000 on March 1 for the calendar year. They are payable by May 1.
2. Purchased equipment for $35,000 on April 1 by making a $5,000 down payment and borrowing the remainder from the bank for a six-month period; 6% interest is payable on the first of each month.
3. Purchased merchandise for $7,000 on April 27 on account, terms 2/10, n/30.
4. Sold merchandise on April 28 for $15,000, plus 5% GST (there is no PST in Nunavut, where Iqaluit Ltd. is based). The cost of the goods sold was $10,500. The company uses a perpetual inventory system.
5. Received $25,000 from customers on April 29 for services to be performed in May.
6. Weekly salaries of $10,000 are paid every Friday for a five-day workweek (Monday to Friday). This year, April 30 is a Thursday. Payroll deductions for the four days include CPP of $495, EI of $178, and income tax of $3,710. Employee benefits include CPP of $495 and EI of $249.
7. Iqaluit was named in a lawsuit alleging negligence for an oil spill that leaked into the neighbouring company's water system. Iqaluit's legal counsel estimates that the company will likely lose the suit but the amount of the loss cannot be determined as yet.
8. Iqaluit paid income tax instalments of $60,000 throughout the year. After the preparation of its year-end corporate income tax return, it was determined that the total income tax payable for the year was $55,000.
9. Iqaluit reported non-current liabilities of $150,000 at April 30, of which $15,000 was due within the next year.
10. Iqaluit has a $50,000 operating line of credit available, on which no funds have yet been drawn.

Instructions
(a) Identify which of the above transactions should be presented in the current liabilities section and which should be recorded in the non-current liabilities section of Iqaluit's statement of financial position on April 30. Identify the account title(s) and amount(s) for each reported liability.
(b) Indicate any information that should be disclosed in the notes to Iqaluit's financial statements.

P10–10B The following selected information was taken from Barrick Gold Corporation's financial statements (in U.S. millions):

Analyze liquidity
and solvency.
(SO 4)

	2010	2009	2008
Statement of financial position			
Accounts receivable	$ 346	$ 251	$ 197
Inventory	1,852	1,540	1,278
Total current assets	7,113	4,938	4,112
Total assets	33,322	27,075	24,161
Current liabilities	2,489	1,773	1,844
Total liabilities	12,588	11,528	8,707
Income statement			
Net sales	10,924	$8,136	$7,613
Cost of goods sold	4,201	3,807	3,706
Interest expense	121	57	21
Income tax expense	1,370	648	594
Profit (loss)	3,274	(4,274)	785

Instructions
(a) Calculate each of the following ratios for 2010 and 2009. Industry ratios are shown in parentheses.
    1. Current ratio (2010 2.4:1:1; 2009, 1.9:1)
    2. Receivables turnover (2010, 17.6 times; 2009, 19.5 times)
    3. Inventory turnover (2010, 3.6 times; 2009, 4.0 times)
    4. Debt to total assets (2010, 16.0%; 2009, 17.4%)
    5. Times interest earned (2010, 4.6 times; 2009, 16.3 times)
(b) Based on your results in (a), comment on Barrick Gold's liquidity and solvency.
(c) Barrick Gold has three pages of disclosure in the notes to its statements about pending litigation. Discuss the implications of this information for your analysis.

P10–11B The following selected liquidity and solvency ratios are available for two companies operating in the fast food industry:

Analyze liquidity
and solvency.
(SO 4)

	Grab 'N Gab	Chick 'N Lick	Industry Average
Current ratio	0.8:1	0.7:1	0.9:1
Receivables turnover	46 times	38 times	34 times
Inventory turnover	39 times	45 times	31 times
Debt to total assets	49%	40%	39%
Times interest earned	10 times	5 times	7 times

Instructions

Assume that you are the credit manager of the local bank. Answer the following questions, using relevant ratios to justify your answer:

(a) Both Grab 'N Gab and Chick 'N Lick have applied for a short-term loan from your bank. Which of the two companies is more liquid and should get more consideration for a short-term loan? Explain.

(b) Both Grab 'N Gab and Chick 'N Lick have applied for a long-term loan from your bank. Are you concerned about the solvency of either company? Explain why or why not.

Broadening Your Perspective

Financial Reporting and Analysis Cases

Financial Reporting: *Eastplats*

Answer questions about financial statements. (SO 4)

BYP10–1 The financial statements of Eastern Platinum Limited are presented in Appendix A at the end of the book.

Instructions

(a) What types of current and non-current liabilities were reported in Eastplats's statement of financial position at December 31, 2010?

(b) Eastplats reports finance leases but no operating leases. Explain what impact this would have, if any, on a solvency analysis of the company.

(c) In Note 25, Events After the Reporting Period, Eastplats reports that it has arranged for a U.S. $100 million loan. Assuming total assets and total liabilities remain unchanged except for the impact of this loan, what impact do you expect the U.S. $100 million loan is to have on the company's debt to total assets ratio? That is, would you expect this ratio to increase, decrease, or remain unchanged. Explain.

Comparative Analysis: *Eastplats and Amplats*

Analyze liquidity and solvency. (SO 4)

BYP10–2 The financial statements of Anglo American Platinum Limited are presented in Appendix B following the financial statements for Eastern Platinum Limited in Appendix A.

Instructions

(a) Based on the information contained in the financial statements, calculate the following ratios for each company for 2010. Industry ratios are shown in parentheses.

1. Current ratio (2.3:1)
2. Receivables turnover (7.9 times)
3. Inventory turnover (3.0 times). For Eastplats, production costs represent the cost of goods sold during the period.
4. Debt to total assets (23.7%)
5. Times interest earned (19.9 times)

(b) What conclusions about the companies' liquidity and solvency can be drawn from the ratios calculated in (a)?

Interpreting Financial Information

Discuss contingent liabilities. (SO 4)

BYP10–3 British American Tobacco (BAT) plc is the second largest tobacco company in the world, after U.S.-based Philip Morris International Inc. Its contingent liabilities note runs 12 pages long in its financial statements.

The following selected information about contingent liabilities has been extracted from the notes to its financial statements:

> In cases where the Group has an obligation as a result of a past event existing at the balance sheet date, it is probable that an outflow of economic resources will be required to settle the obligation and the amount of the obligation can be reliably estimated, a provision would be recognised based on best estimates and management judgment....
>
> While it is impossible to be certain of the outcome of any particular case or of the amount of any possible adverse verdict, the Group believes that the defences of the Group's companies to all these various claims are meritorious on both the law and the facts, and a vigorous defence is being made everywhere....
>
> Having regard to all these matters, the Group (i) does not consider it appropriate to make any provision in respect of any pending litigation and (ii) does not believe that the ultimate outcome of this litigation will significantly impair the Group's financial condition.

Instructions

(a) British American Tobacco is a defendant in thousands of cases against tobacco companies. Management holds the view that there are good defences against all the claims and states that it will defend each case vigorously. Given that the tobacco industry is the target of so many lawsuits, does it make sense to you that BAT only discloses information about its legal disputes rather than accruing the amounts of the lawsuits as liabilities? Explain.

(b) British American Tobacco's debt to total assets ratio is 65.7% and its times interest earned is 9.7 times. What implications do the contingent liabilities reported in BAT's financial statements have for an analysis of its solvency?

(c) Two of BAT's top competitors are Philip Morris International Inc., headquartered in the United States, and Japan Tobacco, headquartered in Japan. What general areas related to the recording and reporting of liabilities might you want to check regarding each country's financial reporting standards before you compare BAT's results with those of Philip Morris and Japan Tobacco?

Comparing IFRS and ASPE

BYP10–4 Matthew Munk, a venture capitalist, is considering investing in Fly Fast Airlines Limited, a private company that owns and operates a small airline business. Fly Fast Airlines operates out of the major centres in Canada and competes directly with the larger airlines on short-haul flights. One of its major competitors is East Jet Airlines Limited.

Calculate and evaluate solvency; compare IFRS and ASPE. (SO 3, 4)

Fly Fast prepares its financial statements in accordance with ASPE, while East Jet is a publicly traded company that prepares its financial statements in accordance with IFRS.

The following is an excerpt of selected financial amounts (in thousands) from Fly Fast's and East Jet's financial statements:

	East Jet	Fly Fast
Statement of Financial Position		
Current assets	$1,268,710	$317,178
Non-current assets	2,294,134	573,533
Current liabilities	832,172	120,000
Non-current liabilities	1,222,993	270,000
Income Statement		
Revenue	$2,609,261	$652,315
Profit	136,720	34,180
Income tax expense	59,947	14,986
Interest expense	60,164	9,876

The major capital expenditure in the airline industry is the purchase of aircraft and supporting equipment. These are typically acquired by way of lease obligations and other forms of debt.

As Matthew considers investing in Fly Fast, he would like to evaluate its solvency and ability to pay interest on its liabilities.

Instructions

(a) Identify two financial ratios that Matthew can use to assess the solvency of Fly Fast in contrast to that of its main competitor, East Jet. Calculate the recommended ratios for both Fly Fast and East Jet. Which company has better solvency?

(b) What is the main difference between IFRS and ASPE that Matthew should consider when comparing the two companies? How could Matthew resolve these discrepancies in order to improve the comparability of these two companies?

(c) Both Fly Fast and East Jet have bond liabilities that were originally issued at a discount. Fly Fast uses the straight-line method to amortize the discount and East Jet uses the effective-interest method. Would the use of two different methods to amortize the discount on bonds payable impact Matthew's assessment of Fly Fast?

Critical Thinking Cases and Activities

Collaborative Learning Activity

BYP10–5 Your local supermarket recently introduced a customer loyalty program. For each dollar you spend on groceries, you get one point. If you earn 800 points and redeem them, the supermarket will give you a $5 rebate when you pay for your groceries. If you wait a bit longer and accumulate 2,000 points, you will get a $15 rebate when you redeem the points. Or, if you can accumulate 6,500 points and redeem them, you would get a $50 rebate.

Discuss criteria for liability recognition. (SO 1)

Instructions

With the class divided into groups, assign a debate position for each of the following issues:

(a) Should unredeemed customer loyalty points be recorded as a current liability by the supermarket—yes or no? Refer to the conceptual framework and elements of financial statements in your answer.

(b) Assuming your answer to (a) is "yes," identify the factors the supermarket would need to consider when calculating the cost of the customer loyalty points. If your answer to (a) is "no," identify where unredeemed customer loyalty points should be recorded, if at all.

(c) Discuss whether a company should administer a customer loyalty program or not. Identify the advantages and disadvantages. What other alternatives are there?

Communication Activity

Discuss changing definition of liabilities. (SO 4)

BYP10–6   International accounting standards require that a liability be recognized in the accounting records when (1) there is a present obligation, (2) it is probable (more likely than not) that an outflow of resources will be required to settle the obligation, and (3) a reliable estimate can be made of the amount of the obligation.

Accounting standard setters are currently debating whether to remove the second criterion, on probability. That is, companies would recognize all present obligations that can be measured reliably.

Instructions

Write a memorandum to the standard setters stating whether you agree with this proposed approach or not. Include in your memo any advantages and disadvantages you can think of from the perspective of (a) management, and (b) the external users of the financial statements.

Ethics Case

Discuss impact of lease structure. (SO 4)

BYP10–7   Crown Point Inc. is in the process of arranging a long-term lease for the company's equipment. The company has dismissed the option of borrowing money from the bank and buying the equipment and is now trying to decide between structuring the lease as an operating lease or a finance lease. Ms. Ranier, the company's CEO, strongly urges the controller to structure the lease as an operating lease. "That way," she says, "we won't add debt that might create problems with our existing debt covenants at the bank."

Instructions

(a) Who are the stakeholders in this situation?

(b) Explain generally how an operating lease affects the financial statements of a company, compared with a finance lease.

(c) Is it unethical to deliberately structure a lease as an operating lease just to keep the debt off the financial statements?

(d) Do you think analysts will be able to distinguish among the financial impacts of purchasing equipment by borrowing from a bank compared with leasing it on an operating lease or a finance lease?

"All About You" Activity

Identify options for Canada Student Loan. (SO 2)

BYP10–8   As indicated in the "All About You" feature in this chapter, a student loan is a loan that must be repaid. Assume that when you have completed your studies you have a student loan of $25,000.

Instructions

Go to the Government of Canada's CanLearn website at www.canlearn.ca and search for the Loan Repayment Estimator. Use the estimator and the information about it to answer the following questions.

(a) What options do you have about when you must start to make repayments on your loan and what options do you have regarding the length of time you can take to repay the loan?

(b) What is the monthly loan repayment for each option in (a) using a fixed interest rate?

(c) What is the monthly loan payment for each option in (a) using a floating interest rate?

(d) Assume that you want to pay off the loan in five years, how much would that change your payments, assuming (1) a fixed interest rate, and (2) a floating interest rate?

Serial Case

(*Note:* This is a continuation of the serial case from Chapters 1 through 9.)

Prepare instalment payment schedule; record and present an instalment note. (SO 2, 4)

BYP10–9   The equipment upgrade that Koebel's Family Bakery decided to undertake proved to be a little more expensive than initially budgeted. Natalie, Janet, and Brian had originally thought that the project could be paid for with cash in the bank. Instead, an operating line of credit was obtained. At November 25, 2012, the balance used on the line of credit, and recorded in the Bank Indebtedness account, was $25,000.

At June 25, 2012, the balance of the 6% mortgage payable was $48,216. Monthly blended principal and interest instalment payments are $670 paid on the 25th of each month.

The mortgage is up for renewal on November 25, 2012, and Janet, Brian, and Natalie would like the mortgage term to be five years, instead of the seven years remaining. Current interest rates are at 5%. Brian and Natalie are considering transferring the balance of the line of credit onto the mortgage payable balance outstanding instead of trying to pay the balance outstanding from cash generated from operations. The bank is happy to accommodate this request and has estimated the monthly blended principal and interest instalment payments to be $1,341 for the combined amounts, commencing December 25, 2012.

Instructions

(a) If the amount of mortgage owing was $48,216 on June 25, and blended payments are $670 per month as indicated above, what is the amount of the mortgage owing at November 25, 2012, immediately before it is renegotiated? Round all amounts to the nearest dollar.

(b) Assume that the Koebels increase the mortgage payable amount you determined in (a) by $25,000, the amount of the line of credit outstanding at November 25, 2012. What is the revised amount of the mortgage payable at November 26? Record the increase in the mortgage payable on November 26.

(c) Prepare a revised instalment payment schedule using the blended instalment payments of $1,341, from December 25, 2012, to June 25, 2014. Round all amounts to the nearest dollar.

(d) Record the first two instalment payments for December 25, 2012, and January 25, 2013.

(e) From information provided in (c), show the presentation of the current and non-current portions of the mortgage payable on the statement of financial position at June 30, 2013.

Answers to Self-Study Questions

1. c   2. b   3. b   4. b   5. c
6. d   7. c   8. a   9. d   10. d

Remember to go back to the beginning of the chapter to check off your completed work!

←

The Navigator
Chapter 11

- ☐ Scan *Study Objectives*
- ☐ Read *Feature Story*
- ☐ Read text and answer *Do It!s*
- ☐ Review *Comparing IFRS and ASPE*
- ☐ Review *Summary of Study Objectives*
- ☐ Review *Decision Toolkit—A Summary*
- ☐ Work *Using the Decision Toolkit*
- ☐ Work *Comprehensive Do It!*
- ☐ Answer *Self-Test Questions*
- ☐ Complete *assignments*
- ☐ Go to *WileyPLUS* for practice and tutorials

study objectives

After studying this chapter, you should be able to:

1. Identify and discuss the major characteristics of a corporation.
2. Record common share transactions.
3. Record preferred share transactions.
4. Prepare the entries for cash dividends, stock dividends, and stock splits, and understand their financial impact.
5. Indicate how shareholders' equity is presented in the financial statements.
6. Evaluate dividend and earnings performance.

the navigator

lululemon Stretches to Success

lululemon athletica inc. sells not only fashionable yoga-inspired athletic apparel, but also the philosophy of living a longer, healthier, and more fun life. The idea has certainly caught on. A simple step inside a yoga or fitness class anywhere across the country will provide evidence of the company's success—its logo will no doubt be on the backs and hips of a good number of those in attendance.

In just over a decade, the company has grown from a combined design studio and retail outlet sharing space with a Vancouver yoga studio to one of the fastest growing athletic apparel companies in the world. lululemon's first store opened in November 2000 in Vancouver's hip beach area of Kitsilano. Although there was no official plan at that point to open more locations, the store's popularity called for expansion. By January 2010, lululemon had 124 stores located in Canada, the United States, and Australia.

Such rapid expansion resulted in a need for equity financing. At the end of 2005, company founder Chip Wilson sold a 48% stake in the company for U.S. $100 million to a group of private investors. In July 2007, the company went public with an initial public offering.

Since then, lululemon's share price has stretched up, bent down, and then stretched up again, as the company experienced some bad press about claims of healthy benefits made about its seaweed-infused clothing, then went through the financial turmoil of 2008 and 2009, and subsequent economic recovery. lululemon's share price fell from a high of $57 per share in 2007 to a low of $6 per share in 2009. By the end of 2010, the shares had rebounded and were trading around $68 per share. The company does not issue dividends to shareholders, but instead retains any available funds for use in the operation and expansion of the business.

Despite the volatility in its share price, sales continue to grow. The company also expanded on-line, with the addition of an e-commerce option on its website. Christine Day, the company's chief executive officer, comments: "We are very pleased with the growing sales momentum in our business, which has accelerated as the economy has improved, and with some of our key initiatives which have taken hold, such as expanding our running line, elevated product to give more value to our customers, and our e-commerce launch. Our . . . sales increase reflects the strength of the lululemon brand driven by our quality, design, product innovation, and unique positioning."

With robust sales and resulting profits, the company's share price continued to grow. In July 2011, lululemon's shares split two-for-one, increasing its authorized number of common shares from 200 million to 400 million and reducing its share price from $114 to $57.

The company is now tapping into the younger market with the introduction of its ivivva athletic brand, geared toward 6- to 12-year-old girls. First tested at three stores in Vancouver, Victoria, and Calgary, ivivva apparel is designed for gymnastics, dance, figure skating, and team sports.

No better endorsement of lululemon could come than from Oprah Winfrey, when, in November 2010, she named lululemon athletica apparel as one of her "ultimate favourite things."

the navigator

Many companies start out small and grow into large corporations, just as lululemon in our feature story has. It should not be surprising, then, that corporations are the dominant form of business organization. In this chapter, we look at the essential features of a corporation. The accounting for, and reporting of, the different components that make up shareholders' equity are explained. We conclude by reviewing dividend and earnings measures of performance.

The chapter is organized as follows:

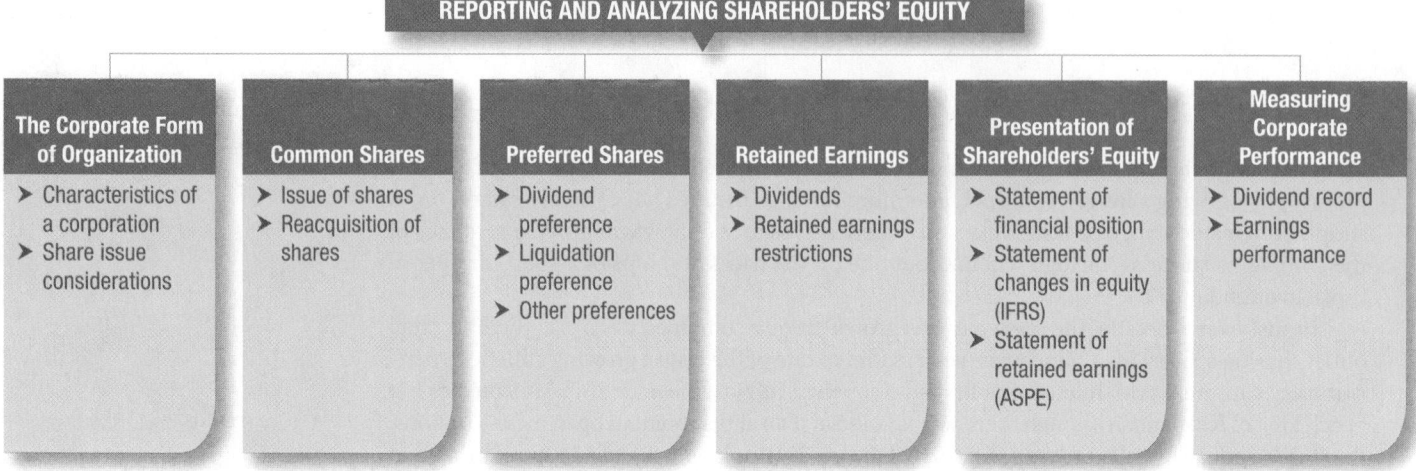

The Corporate Form of Organization

A **corporation** is a legal entity that is separate and distinct from its owners, who are known as shareholders. Corporations may be classified in a variety of ways. Two common classifications are by purpose and by ownership. A corporation may be organized for the purpose of making a **profit** (such as lululemon), or it may be **not-for-profit** (such as the Canadian Cancer Society).

In classification by ownership, there is also a distinction between public and private corporations. A **public corporation** may have thousands of shareholders, and its shares are regularly traded on a securities market, such as the Toronto Stock Exchange. Most of the largest Canadian companies are publicly held. Examples are the Royal Bank, George Weston Ltd., Magna International Inc., and Imperial Oil Ltd. Our textbook feature companies, Eastern Platinum Limited and Anglo American Platinum Limited, are also publicly held.

In contrast, a **private corporation**—often called a privately held corporation—usually has only a few shareholders. It does not offer its shares for sale to the general public. Private companies are generally much smaller than public companies, although there are some exceptions, such as McCain Foods, The Jim Pattison Group, and the Irving companies. lululemon, in our feature story, was a privately held corporation until it offered its shares for sale to the public in 2007, after which it became a publicly traded company.

CHARACTERISTICS OF A CORPORATION

Many characteristics distinguish corporations—whether public or private—from proprietorships and partnerships. Recall from Chapter 1 that a proprietorship is a business owned by one person, and a partnership is owned by two or more people who are associated as partners. We also discussed some of the distinguishing characteristics of a corporation in Chapter 1, and we review them again here.

Separate Legal Existence

As a legal entity that is separate and distinct from its owners, the corporation acts under its own name rather than in the name of its shareholders. lululemon, for example, may buy, own, and sell property, borrow money, and enter into legally binding contracts in its own name. It may also sue or be sued. And it pays income tax as a separate entity.

In contrast to a proprietorship or partnership, where the owners' actions bind the proprietorship or partnership, the acts of a corporation's owners (shareholders) do not bind the corporation unless these owners are also agents of the corporation. For example, if you owned lululemon shares, you would not have the right to purchase a new production facility for the company unless you were designated as an agent of the corporation.

Limited Liability of Shareholders

The liability of shareholders is limited to their investment in the shares of the corporation. This means that creditors only have access to corporate assets to satisfy their claims: in other words, shareholders cannot be made to pay for the company's liabilities out of their personal assets. They may lose their investment, but they will not lose *more* than their investment.

Limited liability is a significant advantage for the corporate form of organization. However, in certain situations, creditors may demand a personal guarantee from a controlling shareholder. This has the effect of making the controlling shareholder's personal assets available, if required, to satisfy the creditor's claim—which, of course, eliminates or reduces the advantage of limited liability.

Transferable Ownership Rights

Ownership of a corporation is held in shares of capital, which are transferable units. Shareholders can dispose of part or all of their interest in a corporation simply by selling their shares. The transfer of shares is entirely up to the shareholder. It does not require the approval of either the corporation or other shareholders.

In addition, the transfer of ownership rights among shareholders has no effect on the corporation's financial position. It does not affect the corporation's assets, liabilities, or shareholders' equity. The transfer of ownership rights is a transaction between individual shareholders. The corporation does not participate in the transfer of these ownership rights; it is only involved in the original sale of the share capital.

Ability to Acquire Capital

It is fairly easy for a corporation to obtain capital by issuing shares. Buying shares in a corporation is often attractive to an investor because a shareholder has limited liability and shares are readily transferable. Also, because only small amounts of money need to be invested, many individuals can become shareholders. A successful corporation's ability to obtain capital is almost unlimited.

Note that the "almost unlimited" ability to acquire capital is only true for large, publicly traded corporations. Small, or closely held, corporations can have as much difficulty in acquiring capital as do proprietorships or partnerships.

Continuous Life

Corporations have an unlimited life. Since a corporation is a separate legal entity, its continuance as a going concern is not affected by the withdrawal, death, or incapacity of a shareholder, employee, or officer. As a result, a successful corporation can have a continuous and indefinite life. For example, Hudson's Bay Company, the oldest commercial corporation in North America, was founded in 1670 and is still going strong. Its ownership has changed over the years from a publicly traded corporation to a private corporation, but the corporation itself still continues. In contrast, proprietorships end if anything happens to the proprietor and partnerships normally re-form if anything happens to one of the partners.

Corporation Management

Shareholders can invest in a corporation without having to manage it personally. Although shareholders legally own the corporation, they manage it indirectly through a board of directors they elect. The board, in turn, sets the broad strategic objectives for the company. The board also selects officers, such as a president and one or more vice-presidents, to execute policy and to perform daily management functions. Chip (Dennis) Wilson is the chair of lululemon's board of directors. Christine Day is lululemon's president and chief executive officer. She and the chief financial officer also sit on lululemon's board of directors, as do seven independent (outside) directors.

Government Regulations

Canadian companies may be incorporated federally, under the terms of the *Canada Business Corporations Act,* or provincially, under the terms of a provincial business corporations act. Federal and provincial laws usually state the requirements for issuing and reacquiring shares and distributing profits. Similarly, the regulations of provincial securities commissions control the sale of share capital to the general public. When a corporation's shares are listed and traded on foreign securities markets, the corporation must also respect the reporting requirements of these exchanges. For example, lululemon's shares are listed on both the Toronto Stock Exchange in Canada and the Nasdaq Stock Market in the United States. Complying with federal, provincial, and securities regulations in multiple jurisdictions increases the cost and complexity of the corporate form of organization.

Income Tax

Proprietorships and partnerships do not pay income tax as separate entities. Instead, each owner's (or partner's) share of profit from these organizations is reported on his or her personal income tax return. Income tax is then paid on this amount by the individual. Corporations, on the other hand, must pay federal and provincial income taxes as separate legal entities. Income tax rates vary based on the type of income and by province. In general, however, corporate income tax rates are lower than the rate individuals would pay on the same amount of income, and especially so for small businesses.

In addition to the potential for reduced income tax, another advantage of incorporation is being able to delay personal income tax. The shareholders of a corporation do not pay tax on corporate profit until the profit is distributed to them as dividends. Some people argue that corporate profit is taxed twice (double taxation)—once at the corporate level and again at the individual level when the dividend is received. This is not completely true, however, as individuals receive a dividend tax credit to offset most of the tax paid at the corporate level.

It is wise to get expert advice to determine whether incorporating will result in more or less income tax than operating as a proprietorship or partnership. Income tax laws are complex and tax rates are subject to change. Careful tax planning is essential for any business venture.

DECISION TOOLKIT

Decision Checkpoints	Info Needed for Decision	Tools to Use for Decision	How to Evaluate Results
Should the company incorporate?	Capital needs, growth expectations, type of business, income tax status	Corporations have limited liability, greater ability to raise capital, and professional managers. In addition, there is a potential for reduced income tax. There is increased cost and complexity from additional government regulations.	Carefully weigh the costs and benefits in light of the particular circumstances.

SHARE ISSUE CONSIDERATIONS

After incorporation, a corporation sells ownership rights as shares. The shares of the company are divided into different classes, such as Class A, Class B, and so on. The rights and privileges for each class of shares are stated in articles of incorporation, which form the "constitution" of the company. The different classes are usually identified by the generic terms *common shares* and *preferred shares*. When a corporation has only one class of shares, that class has the rights and privileges of common shares. As mentioned in Chapter 2, common shares are also known internationally as *ordinary shares*.

Each common share gives the shareholder the ownership rights shown in Illustration 11-1.

Vote Shareholders have the right to vote on certain matters, such as the election of the board of directors. Each shareholder normally has one vote for each common share owned.

▶Illustration 11-1
Ownership rights of shareholders

Dividends Shareholders share in the distribution of the corporate profit through dividends, in proportion to the number of shares owned.

Liquidation Shareholders share in any assets that remain after liquidation, in proportion to the number of shares owned. This is known as a residual claim because shareholders are paid only if any cash remains after all the assets have been sold and all liabilities paid.

When lululemon issued common shares to the public for the first time in 2007, it had to make several decisions. How many shares should be authorized for sale? At what price should the shares be issued? What value should be assigned to the shares? These questions are discussed in the following sections.

Authorized Share Capital

The amount of share capital that a corporation is authorized to sell is indicated in its articles of incorporation. It may be specified as either an unlimited amount or a specific number (e.g., 500,000 shares authorized). Most companies in Canada have an unlimited amount of authorized shares. If a number is specified, the amount of **authorized shares** normally anticipates a company's initial and later capital needs.

lululemon has an authorized number of shares specified. At the end of its 2010 fiscal year, it had 5 million preferred shares and 200 million common shares authorized. The authorization of share capital does not result in a formal accounting entry, because the event has no immediate effect on either corporate assets or shareholders' equity. It is the issue (sale) of shares that results in a transaction, not the authorization of shares. For example, lululemon has never issued preferred shares even though it is authorized to do so. Consequently, no journal entry has been made by lululemon to record the issue of preferred shares.

Issue of Shares

The first time a corporation's shares are offered for sale to the public, the offer is called an **initial public offering (IPO)**. lululemon issued 18.2 million common shares at U.S. $18 each in an IPO in July 2007. When a company issues shares through an IPO, it receives the cash (less any financing or issue fees) from the sale of the shares. The company's assets (cash) increase, and its shareholders' equity (share capital) also increases. **Issued shares** are authorized shares that have been sold. lululemon had 51,126,000 common shares issued at the end of its 2010 fiscal year.

Once the shares have been issued and sold, they then trade on the secondary market. That is, investors buy and sell shares from each other rather than from the company, using a stock exchange such as the Toronto Stock Exchange. As mentioned earlier in the chapter, when shares are sold among investors, there is no impact on the company's financial position. The company receives no additional assets, and it issues no additional shares. The only change in the company records is the name of the shareholder, not the number of shares issued.

For example, when Chip Wilson sold some common shares he owned in 2005 to a group of private investors, no journal entry was made by lululemon. The sale of shares was a personal transaction between Chip Wilson and the new shareholders who purchased the shares. In contrast, when an initial public offering of new shares was sold by lululemon in 2007, a journal entry was made by lululemon to record the cash received from the sale of these shares and the new common shares issued.

ACCOUNTING MATTERS! *Investor Perspective*

IPO Market

The value of IPOs issued in Canada in 2010 totalled $5 billion, a significant amount of new share issues but below the $6-billion-a-year average of the previous decade. The best-performing Canadian IPO was Calgary's Secure Energy Services Inc., whose IPO share price increased 87% from $3 to $5.61 in 2010.

Another Calgary-based company issuing shares in 2010 for the first time was Smart Technologies Inc., a maker of electronic whiteboards. Unfortunately, its performance was disappointing for its IPO investors. Smart Technologies listed its shares on the U.S. Nasdaq Stock Exchange, where the company's share price slid from its IPO price of U.S. $17 to a low of U.S. $8.06 in 2010. It had the embarrassing distinction of being one of the five worst-performing IPOs in 2010.

Source: David Milstead, "Investors Find IPO Market Full of Land Mines," *The Globe and Mail*, November 23, 2010, p. B12.

Fair Value of Shares

After the initial issue of new shares, the share price changes according to the interaction between buyers and sellers. In general, the price follows the trend of a company's profits and dividends. Factors that are beyond a company's control (such as an embargo on oil, an economic recession, changes in interest rates, the outcome of an election, and war) also influence share prices.

For each listed security, the financial press reports the highest and lowest prices that the share sold at for the year, the annual dividend rate, the high and low prices for the day, and the net change over the previous day. The total volume of shares traded on a particular day, the dividend yield, and the price-earnings ratio are also reported. A recent listing for lululemon's common shares on the Toronto Stock Exchange follows:

| 365-day | | stock | sym | div | high | low | close | chg | vol (000) | yld | p/e ratio |
high	low										
115.16	33.11	lululemon athletica	LLL	0.00	58.77	57.17	58.58	+1.38	181,325	0.00	63.54

lululemon's shares have traded as high as $115.16 and as low as $33.11 during the past year. The stock's ticker symbol is "LLL." lululemon does not pay an annual dividend, which is indicated by the "0.00" amount in the "div" column. The high and low share prices for the date shown were $58.77 and $57.17 per share, respectively. The closing share price was $58.58, in increase of $1.38 from the previous day. The trading volume was 181,325,000 shares.

Since lululemon does not pay dividends, there is no dividend yield ("yld"). The dividend yield reports the rate of return an investor earned from dividends, calculated by dividing the dividend per share by the share price. We will learn more about this ratio later in the chapter. lululemon's shares are currently trading at a price-earnings ("p/e") ratio (share price divided by earnings per share) of

63.54 times earnings. The dividend yield and price-earnings ratios are often interpreted together to determine how much investors favour a company.

One commonly reported measure of the fair value of a company's total equity is its market capitalization. The **market capitalization** of a company is calculated by multiplying the number of shares issued by the share price at any given date. lululemon's market capitalization was nearly $8.5 billion at the time of writing. The largest market capitalization for any company in Canada is that of the Royal Bank, whose market capitalization at the end of 2010 was just over $74 billion.

Legal Capital

When shares are issued, they form the **share capital** of the corporation. You will recall that the shareholders' equity section of a corporation's statement of financial position includes both share capital and retained earnings, in addition to other possible items such as accumulated other comprehensive income. The distinction between retained earnings and share capital is important from both a legal and an economic point of view. Retained earnings can be distributed to shareholders as dividends or retained in the company for operating needs. On the other hand, share capital is **legal capital** that cannot be distributed to shareholders. It must remain invested in the company for the protection of corporate creditors.

Some countries, notably the United States, assign a par or stated value to shares to predetermine the amount of legal capital. lululemon was originally incorporated in Delaware, and its common shares have a $0.01 par value. The use of par values for shares is rare in Canada. In fact, companies that are incorporated federally and companies incorporated in some provinces are not allowed to issue shares with par values.

Instead, **no par value shares**, which are shares that have not been assigned a predetermined value, are issued. When no par value shares are issued, all of the proceeds received are considered to be legal capital. Whenever shares are issued in this chapter, you can assume that they are no par value shares.

BEFORE YOU GO ON...

▶ Do It! Corporation Characteristics

Indicate whether each of the following statements is true or false:

_____ 1. Shareholders of a corporation have unlimited liability.

_____ 2. It is relatively easy for a large, publicly traded corporation to obtain capital through the issue of shares.

_____ 3. The journal entry to record the authorization of share capital includes a credit to the appropriate preferred or common share account.

_____ 4. The journal entry to record the sale of common shares from one shareholder to another involves a credit to the Common Shares account.

_____ 5. The proceeds received from the sale of no par value shares equal the company's legal capital.

Action Plan

• Review the characteristics of a corporation.
• Understand the difference between authorized and issued share capital.

Solution

1. False. The liability of shareholders is normally limited to their investment in the corporation.

2. True.

3. False. The authorization of share capital does not result in a formal accounting entry; only the actual issue of shares results in a journal entry.

4. False. The company makes no journal entry to record the sale of common shares owned by one shareholder to another.

5. True.

the navigator

Common Shares

STUDY OBJECTIVE 2
Record common share transactions.

Contributed capital is the amount shareholders paid, or contributed, to the corporation in exchange for shares of ownership. This includes **share capital**, in addition to other sources of capital affected by share transactions. Recall that share capital can consist of both common shares and preferred shares. All corporations must issue common shares, whereas they can choose whether or not to issue preferred shares. We will look at common shares in this section and preferred shares in the next.

Alternative Terminology
Contributed capital is also known as contributed surplus.

ISSUE OF SHARES

Common shares may be issued (sold) to investors, who then become shareholders of the corporation. To illustrate the issue of common shares, assume that Hydro-Slide, Inc. is authorized to issue an unlimited number of no par value common shares and that it issues 1,000 of these shares for $2 per share on January 12.

As mentioned earlier, when no par value common shares are issued, the entire proceeds from the sale become legal capital. That means that the proceeds of the share issue are credited to the Common Shares account. The entry to record this transaction is:

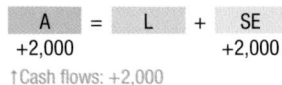

A	=	L	+	SE
+2,000				+2,000

↑Cash flows: +2,000

Jan. 12	Cash	2,000	
	Common Shares		2,000
	(To record issue of 1,000 common shares)		

Common shares are most commonly issued in exchange for cash, especially in large corporations. However, they may also be issued for a consideration other than cash, such as services (e.g., compensation to lawyers or consultants) or noncash assets (e.g., land, buildings, or equipment). When shares are issued for a noncash consideration, they should be recorded at the **fair value of the consideration (e.g., goods or services) received**. If the fair value of the consideration received cannot be reliably determined, then the fair value of the consideration given up would be used instead.

For example, assume that 5,000 common shares were issued by Hydro-Slide in exchange for a parcel of land on January 27. The shares were trading at $3.50 per share and the land was valued at $20,000 on the date of the acquisition. The transaction is recorded using the value of the land ($20,000)—the consideration received—rather than the value of the common shares ($17,500 = 5,000 × $3.50)—the consideration given up.

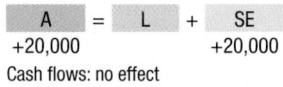

A	=	L	+	SE
+20,000				+20,000

Cash flows: no effect

Jan. 27	Land	20,000	
	Common Shares		20,000
	(To record issue of 5,000 common shares in exchange for land)		

> *ASPE*   Noncash considerations can also occur in private companies, where they tend to be found even more often than they are in large publicly traded companies. When shares are issued for a noncash consideration in a private company following ASPE, the valuation of the shares can be slightly different than that described above for a publicly traded company following IFRS. The shares of a private company should be recorded at the most reliable of the two values—the fair value of the consideration (e.g., goods or services) received or fair value of the consideration given up. Quite often the fair value of the consideration received is the most reliable value because a private company's shares seldom trade and therefore do not have a ready market value.

REACQUISITION OF SHARES

Companies can purchase their own shares on the open market. A corporation may acquire its own shares to meet any of the following objectives, among others:

1. To increase trading of the company's shares in the securities market in the hope of enhancing the company's value. If a company feels that its shares are trading at a price that is less than what they are worth, it may buy back the shares. When the number of shares available for sale in the stock market decreases, the share price should increase.
2. To reduce the number of shares issued. By reducing the number of shares issued and reducing shareholders' equity, earnings per share and return on equity will increase. We first introduced earnings per share in Chapter 2 and will discuss both earnings per share and return on equity later in this chapter.
3. To eliminate hostile shareholders by buying them out.
4. To have additional shares available for issue to employees under bonus and stock compensation plans, or for use in acquiring other companies.

For federally incorporated companies, and most provincially incorporated companies, the repurchased shares must be retired (cancelled). This effectively restores the shares to the status of authorized but unissued shares. In some Canadian provinces, in the United States, and internationally, reacquired shares can be held in the "treasury" for subsequent reissue rather than retired. We will look at each of these options in the next two sections.

> **Alternative Terminology**
> The terms *reacquired* and *repurchased* are used interchangeably with respect to stock purchases.

Reacquisition of Shares—Retired (Cancelled)

The reacquisition and retirement of shares is a common practice and the financial press often contains announcements of "normal course issuer bids," which inform the public that a company plans to repurchase its shares. To record a reacquisition and retirement of common shares (or preferred shares, which we will discuss in the next section), the following steps are required:

1. **Remove the cost of the shares from the share capital account:** Recall that when a long-lived asset is retired, the cost of the asset must be deleted (credited) from the appropriate asset account. Similarly, the cost of the common shares that are reacquired and retired must be determined and this amount is then deleted (debited) from the Common Shares account.

   In order to determine the cost of the common shares reacquired, it is necessary to calculate an **average cost per share**. It is impractical, and often impossible, to determine the original issue cost of each individual common share that is reacquired. An average cost per common share is therefore calculated by dividing the balance in the Common Shares account by the number of shares issued at the transaction date.
2. **Record the cash paid:** The Cash account is credited for the amount paid to reacquire the shares. Note that a company has little choice in *what* it has to pay to reacquire the shares. It must purchase the shares on the secondary market by paying whatever the current share price is on the date of purchase. It can only decide *when* to make the reacquisition.
3. **Record the "gain" or "loss" on reacquisition:** The difference between the price paid to reacquire the shares and their original (or average) cost is basically a "gain" or "loss" on reacquisition. However, because companies cannot realize a gain or suffer a loss from share transactions with their own shareholders, these amounts are not reported on the income statement. They are seen instead as an excess or deficiency that belongs to the original shareholders. As a result, the amount is reported as an increase or decrease in the shareholders' equity section of the statement of financial position.

The accounting for the reacquisition and retirement of shares is different depending on whether the shares are reacquired by paying less than average cost or more than average cost. Although there is no specific guidance given on this subject under IFRS, the common practice is as described in the next two sections.

Reacquisition below Average Cost.   To illustrate the reacquisition of common shares at a price less than their average cost, assume that Hydro-Slide, Inc. now has a total of 25,000 common shares issued and a balance in its Common Shares account of $50,000. The average cost of Hydro-Slide's common shares, immediately before the reacquisition, is $2 per share ($50,000 ÷ 25,000).

On September 23, Hydro-Slide reacquired and retired 5,000 of its common shares at a price of $1.50 per share. Since the average cost of the shares was $2 per share, a $0.50 ($2.00 − $1.50) addition to a separate contributed capital account results, as shown on the next page:

A	=	L	+	SE
−7,500				−10,000
				+2,500

↓Cash flows: −7,500

Sept. 23	Common Shares (5,000 × $2)	10,000	
	Contributed Capital—Reacquisition of Common Shares		2,500
	Cash (5,000 × $1.50)		7,500
	(To record reacquisition and retirement of 5,000 common shares)		

After this entry, Hydro-Slide still has an unlimited number of shares authorized, but only 20,000 (25,000 − 5,000) shares issued, and a balance of $40,000 ($50,000 − $10,000) in its Common Shares account. The difference between the average cost of the shares and the amount paid to repurchase them is credited to a new account, one that is specifically for the contributed capital realized from the reacquisition of shares. Contributed capital is a shareholders' equity account with a normal credit balance. The cash in the entry was paid to the shareholders from whom the shares were repurchased.

Reacquisition above Average Cost. If Hydro-Slide had paid $2.50 per share to reacquire and retire 5,000 of its common shares, rather than the $1.50 per share assumed above, it would result in a debit for the difference between the price paid to reacquire the shares and their average cost. If there is any balance in the contributed capital account from previous transactions related to the same class of shares, this amount would first be reduced (debited). However, contributed capital cannot be reduced beyond any existing balance. In other words, contributed capital can never have a negative, or debit, balance. Instead, any excess deficiency amount would be debited to Retained Earnings.

The journal entry to record the reacquisition and retirement of Hydro-Slide's common shares at a price of $2.50 per share is as follows:

A	=	L	+	SE
−12,500				−10,000
				−2,500

↓Cash flows: −12,500

Sept. 23	Common Shares (5,000 × $2)	10,000	
	Retained Earnings	2,500	
	Cash (5,000 × $2.50)		12,500
	(To record reacquisition and retirement of 5,000 common shares)		

In this entry, Hydro-Slide is assumed to have no previous balance in the contributed capital account. After this entry, Hydro-Slide still has 20,000 (25,000 − 5,000) shares issued and a balance of $40,000 ($50,000 − $10,000) in its Common Shares account.

In summary, the only difference in the accounting for reacquisitions at prices below or above the average cost has to do with recording the difference between the amount paid to repurchase the shares and their average cost. If the shares are reacquired at a price below their average cost, the difference is credited to a contributed capital account. If the shares are reacquired at a price above the average cost, the difference is debited first to the contributed capital account used in prior reacquisitions, and second, to the Retained Earnings account if there is no credit balance remaining in the contributed capital account.

Reacquisition of Shares—Held in Treasury

Alternative Terminology
Treasury shares are also known as *treasury stock*.

In most cases, when shares are reacquired, they are retired. In a few provinces in Canada, they may be held in the "treasury" for future resale. **Treasury shares** consist of a company's own shares that have been reacquired and are being held for future reissue.

As illustrated above, when shares are reacquired and retired, the Common (or Preferred) Shares account is debited for the cost of the shares. In contrast, when shares are reacquired and held for future reissue, the account Treasury Shares is debited for the price paid to acquire the shares. When the shares are later reissued, the Treasury Shares account will be credited for the same amount. The Treasury Shares account has a normal debit balance and is a contra shareholders' equity account.

We chose not to illustrate the accounting entries for treasury shares in this chapter as treasury share transactions do not occur very often in Canada. Only 4% of Canadian companies reported holding treasury shares in a recent year. Treasury shares are not permitted for federally incorporated companies in Canada, although they are common in other countries where the law permits.

BEFORE YOU GO ON...

▶ Do It! Common Share Transactions

On March 1, Assiniboia Corporation had 100,000 common shares issued, with a balance in the Common Shares account of $1.2 million and a balance in the Contributed Capital—Reacquisition of Shares account of $25,000. On March 15, Assiniboia issued an additional 20,000 common shares at $15 per share. On June 1, it reacquired and retired 10,000 of its own common shares at $16 per share. Record the share transactions.

Action Plan

- Credit the common shares account for the entire proceeds received in a share issue.
- Keep a running total of the number of shares issued to date.
- Calculate the average cost per share by dividing the balance in the shares account by the number of shares issued.
- Debit the shares account for the average cost of the reacquired shares. If the reacquisition cost is below the average cost, credit the difference to a contributed capital account. If the reacquisition cost is above the average cost, debit the difference to Retained Earnings unless there is already a balance in a contributed capital account from previous reacquisitions and retirements.

Solution

Mar. 15	Cash (20,000 × $15)	300,000	
	Common Shares		300,000
	(To record issue of 20,000 common shares)		

Mar. 15: Balance in Common Shares account: $1,200,000 + $300,000 = $1,500,000
Number of common shares issued: 100,000 + 20,000 = 120,000
Average cost: $1,500,000 ÷ 120,000 = $12.50

June 1	Common Shares (10,000 × $12.50)	125,000	
	Contributed Capital—Reacquisition of Shares	25,000	
	Retained Earnings	10,000	
	Cash (10,000 × $16)		160,000
	(To record reacquisition and retirement of 10,000 common shares)		

June 1: Balance in Common Shares account: $1,200,000 + $300,000 − $125,000 = $1,375,000
Number of common shares issued: 100,000 + 20,000 − 10,000 = 110,000
Average cost: $1,375,000 ÷ 110,000 = $12.50

the navigator

Preferred Shares

To appeal to a larger segment of potential investors, a company may issue an additional class of shares, called preferred shares. **Preferred shares** have contractual provisions that give them a preference, or priority, over common shares in certain areas. Typically, preferred shareholders have priority over the payment of dividends and, in the event of liquidation, over the distribution of assets. However, they do not usually have the voting rights that the common shares have.

Like common shares, preferred shares may be issued for cash or for noncash considerations. They can also be reacquired. The entries for these transactions are similar to the entries for common shares, so they are not repeated here. When a company has more than one class of shares, separate account titles should be used (e.g., Preferred Shares, Common Shares).

We will discuss the key features of preferred shares, including dividend and liquidation preferences, in the next sections.

STUDY OBJECTIVE 3
Record preferred share transactions.

DIVIDEND PREFERENCE

As indicated above, **preferred shareholders have the right to share in the distribution of dividends before common shareholders do**. For example, if the annual dividend rate on preferred shares is $5 per share, common shareholders will not receive any dividends in the current year until preferred shareholders have received $5 per share. Preferred shares such as these would be called "$5 preferred." The $5 indicates the dividend rate, which, similar to interest rates, is always stated as an annual rate. Even though dividends are reported as an annual dollar amount per share, it is usual to pay dividends quarterly. For example, in 2010, BCE Inc. had an annual dividend rate of $1.20 on one of its classes (A) of preferred shares. This dividend is paid quarterly at a rate of $0.30 ($1.20 ÷ 4) per share.

Preferred shares may contain a **cumulative** dividend feature. This right means that when dividends are declared, preferred shareholders must be paid both current-year dividends and any unpaid prior-year dividends before common shareholders receive dividends. Preferred shares without this feature are called **noncumulative**. A dividend that is not paid on noncumulative preferred shares in any particular year is lost forever.

When preferred shares are cumulative, preferred dividends that are not declared in a period are called **dividends in arrears**. No distribution can be made to common shareholders until this entire cumulative preferred dividend is paid. In other words, dividends cannot be paid to common shareholders while any preferred share dividends are in arrears. It is unusual for a company to have any dividends in arrears. At the time of writing, no Canadian company reported dividends in arrears for its most recent fiscal year.

It is important to understand that, if a company does have dividends in arrears, they would not be considered a liability. No obligation exists until a dividend is declared by the board of directors. However, the amount of dividends in arrears should be disclosed in the notes to the financial statements. This allows investors to evaluate the potential impact of this commitment on the corporation's financial position.

Even though there is no requirement to pay an annual dividend, companies that are unable to meet their dividend obligations—whether cumulative or noncumulative—are not looked upon favourably by the investment community. As a chief financial officer noted in discussing one company's failure to pay its preferred dividend for a period of time, "Not meeting your obligations on something like that is a major black mark on your record."

LIQUIDATION PREFERENCE

In addition to having a priority claim over common shares on any distribution of dividends, preferred shares also have a priority claim over common shares on corporate assets if the corporation fails. This means that if the company is bankrupt, preferred shareholders will get money back before common shareholders do. The preference on assets may be for the legal value of the shares or for a specified liquidating value. So, while creditors still rank above all shareholders in terms of preference in liquidations, preferred shareholders rank above common shareholders. This is important as the money usually runs out before everyone gets paid.

Because of these two preferential rights—the right to dividends and the right to assets in the event of liquidation—preferred shareholders generally do not mind that they do not have the voting right that common shareholders have.

OTHER PREFERENCES

The attractiveness of preferred shares as an investment is sometimes increased by adding a conversion privilege. **Convertible preferred shares** allow the exchange of preferred shares for common shares at a specified ratio. Nearly half of the companies in Canada that have preferred shares also have this conversion privilege. Convertible preferred shares are purchased by investors who want the greater security of preferred shares, but who also desire the added option of conversion if the value of the common shares increases significantly.

Most preferred shares are also issued with a redemption or call feature. **Redeemable (or callable) preferred shares** give the issuing corporation the right to purchase the shares from shareholders at specified future dates and prices. The redemption feature offers some flexibility to a corporation by enabling it to eliminate this type of equity security when it is advantageous to do so. While most preferred shares have a fixed dividend rate, some callable preferred shares offer a floating rate option. These are known as **rate-reset preferred shares** and offer shareholders the option of locking in a fixed dividend rate at each call date (reset date) or changing to a floating rate.

Retractable preferred shares are similar to redeemable or callable preferred shares, except that it is at the *shareholder's* option, rather than the corporation's option, that the shares are redeemed. This usually occurs at an arranged price and date.

When preferred shares are retractable, the distinction between equity and debt is not clear. Similar to debt, retractable preferred shares offer a rate of return (dividend income) to the investor, and with the redemption of the shares, a repayment of the principal investment. Because of this, retractable preferred shares are considered to be an example of a financial liability, which we first discussed in Chapter 10. Consequently, retractable preferred shares are presented in the *liabilities* section of the statement of financial position rather than in the equity section.

Companies are issuing an increasing number of shares with innovative preferences. Some have the attributes of both debt and equity; others have the attributes of both common and preferred shares. Accounting for such financial instruments presents unique challenges for accountants. Further detail is left for an intermediate accounting course.

BEFORE YOU GO ON...

▶ Do It! Preferred Share Transactions

At January 1, 2011, MasterMind Corporation had 100,000 shares of $2, cumulative, no par value preferred shares authorized, of which 10,000 shares were issued for $250,000. On July 1, 2012, the company issued an additional 2,500 shares for $30 per share. (a) Record the issue of preferred shares on July 1, 2012. (b) Assuming dividends are paid quarterly, calculate the total dividend that MasterMind could pay for the calendar year 2012. (c) Assuming MasterMind has not declared a dividend in 2011 or in 2012 because of a cash shortfall, calculate any dividends in arrears at the end of 2012.

Action Plan

- Credit the preferred share account for the entire proceeds received in a share issue.
- Keep a running total of the number of shares issued to date.
- Recall that the dividend rate given on preferred shares is always expressed as an annual amount. Divide the dividend rate by 4 to determine the quarterly dividend rate.
- Determine dividends on preferred shares by multiplying the quarterly dividend rate by the number of preferred shares for each quarter.
- Understand the cumulative feature: If preferred shares are cumulative, then any missed dividend (dividends in arrears) must be paid to the preferred shareholders before dividends can be paid to the common shareholders.

Solution

(a)

July 1	Cash (2,500 × $30)		75,000	
	Preferred Shares			75,000
	(To record issue of 2,500 preferred shares)			

(b) 2012 dividend = ($2 × 4/4 quarters × 10,000) + ($2 × 2/4 quarters × 2,500)
= $22,500

(c) Dividends in arrears = 2011 dividend ($2 × 10,000) + 2012 dividend ($22,500)
= $42,500

Retained Earnings

STUDY OBJECTIVE 4

Prepare the entries for cash dividends, stock dividends, and stock splits, and understand their financial impact.

As we have learned in past chapters, retained earnings are the cumulative profits since incorporation that have been retained in the company (i.e., that have not been distributed to shareholders). Each year, profit is added to (or a loss is deducted from) the opening Retained Earnings account balance and dividends are then deducted from this balance: the result is the ending retained earnings amount. We have looked at the components of profit in prior chapters. We will focus on the impact of dividends on retained earnings in this section and identify other items that affect retained earnings in the next section.

DIVIDENDS

A **dividend** is a pro rata (equal) distribution of a portion of a corporation's retained earnings to its shareholders. "Pro rata" means that if you own, say, 10% of the common shares, you will receive 10% of the dividend.

Many high-growth companies, such as lululemon in our feature story, do not pay dividends. Their policy is to retain all of their profit to make it easier for the company to grow. Investors purchase shares in companies like lululemon with the hope that the share price will increase in value and they will realize a profit when they sell their shares. Other investors purchase shares of established companies with the hope of earning dividends (and maybe also of profiting from some share price appreciation when they sell their shares).

Cash dividends are the most common in practice but stock dividends are also declared on occasion. We will look at each of these types of dividends in the next two sections.

Cash Dividends

A **cash dividend** is a distribution of cash to shareholders. Cash dividends can be paid to preferred or common shareholders. If dividends are paid to both the preferred and common shareholders, remember that the preferred shareholders have to be paid first.

For a corporation to pay a cash dividend, it must meet a two-part solvency test under the *Canada Business Corporations Act*:

1. It must have sufficient cash or resources to be able to pay its liabilities as they become due after the dividend is declared and paid, and
2. The net realizable value of its assets must exceed the total of its liabilities and share capital.

Under some provincial legislation, a company must also have enough retained earnings before it can pay a dividend although this is not a requirement for federally incorporated companies.

In addition, a company cannot pay dividends unless its board of directors decides to do so, at which point the board "declares" (i.e., officially states) the dividend to be payable. The board of directors has full authority to determine the amount of retained earnings to be distributed in the form of dividends and the amount to be retained in the company. Dividends do not accrue like interest on a loan, and they are not a liability until they are declared.

Entries for Cash Dividends.   Three dates are important in connection with dividends: (1) the declaration date, (2) the record date, and (3) the payment date. Normally, there are several weeks between each date and the next one. For example, on October 26, 2010 (the declaration date),

■ Keeping an Eye on Cash

We mentioned above that a company has to have sufficient cash in order to pay its liabilities before it can pay a dividend. How much cash is enough? That is hard to say but a company must keep enough cash on hand to pay for its ongoing operations and to pay its bills as they come due.

Before paying a cash dividend, a company's board of directors must carefully consider current and future demands on the company's cash resources. In some cases, current (or planned future) liabilities may make a cash dividend inappropriate.

In order to remain in business, companies *must* honour their interest payments to creditors, bankers, and debt holders. But the payment of dividends to shareholders is discretionary (i.e., a choice). Consequently, investors must keep an eye on the company's dividend policy and understand what it may mean. For many companies, regular increases in the amount of dividends paid when the company has irregular profits can be a warning signal. For example, companies with high dividends and rising debt may be borrowing money to pay shareholders.

In 2008 and 2009, many banks and other companies froze their dividend rates and some companies even reduced their dividend rates. This was because, with the credit crisis and declining economy, there was less cash to share. By not making dividend increases, "banks are giving you a message that things are not as good, and that paying out a higher dividend is not the best use of their money right now," said Norman Levine, the managing director of Portfolio Management Corp. By 2010 and 2011, increases in dividend rates were becoming more common once again.

Canadian National Railway declared a quarterly dividend of $0.27 per share payable to its common shareholders. These dividends were paid on December 31, 2010 (the payment date), to the shareholders of record at the close of business on December 10, 2010 (the record date).

On the **declaration date**, the board of directors formally authorizes the cash dividend and announces it to shareholders. The declaration of a cash dividend commits the corporation to a binding legal obligation. An entry is therefore required to recognize the increase in Cash Dividends (which results in a decrease in retained earnings) and the increase in the liability Dividends Payable.

In prior chapters, we often assumed that the dividend was declared and paid on the same day for simplicity. In this chapter, we illustrate the separation of the declaration of the dividend and the payment of the dividend and record accounting entries on two different dates—the declaration date and the payment date. We also used an account called "Dividends" to record a cash dividend. Here, we use the more specific title "Cash Dividends" to differentiate from other types of dividends, such as stock dividends.

To illustrate a cash dividend to preferred shareholders, assume that on December 1, 2012, the directors of IBR Inc. declare a $0.50 per share cash dividend on the company's 100,000 preferred shares, payable on January 20 to shareholders of record on December 22. The dividend is $50,000 (100,000 × $0.50), and the entry to record the declaration is:

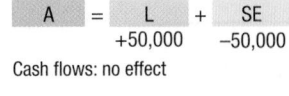

	Declaration Date		
Dec. 1	Cash Dividends	50,000	
	Dividends Payable		50,000
	(To record declaration of cash dividend)		

The Cash Dividends account will be closed into, and reduce, the Retained Earnings account at the end of the year. Dividends Payable is a current liability: it will normally be paid within the next month or so—on January 20 in this particular example.

On the **record date**, ownership of the shares is determined. As discussed earlier, individual share owners may change as shares are bought and sold on the secondary market. Although transactions between shareholders do not affect the company's financial position, the company does have to maintain shareholder records identifying individual owners so it knows who to pay the dividend to. In the interval between the declaration date and the record date, the company updates its share ownership record. For IBR, the record date is December 22. No journal entry is required on the record date, because the corporation's liability that was recognized on the declaration date is unchanged.

On the **payment date**, dividends are paid to the shareholders. The journal entry on January 20, the payment date, is:

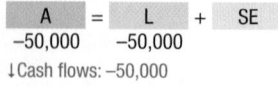

A = L + SE
−50,000 −50,000
↓Cash flows: −50,000

	Payment Date		
Jan. 20	Dividends Payable	50,000	
	Cash		50,000
	(To record payment of cash dividend)		

As shown below, the declaration of a cash dividend increases liabilities and reduces shareholders' equity. There is no effect on the record date. The payment of a dividend reduces both assets and liabilities, but it has no effect on shareholders' equity. The cumulative effect of the declaration and payment of a cash dividend on a company's financial statements is to decrease both assets (through cash) and shareholders' equity (through retained earnings). In the illustration below, "+" means increase, "−" means decrease, and "NE" means "no effect."

	Assets	Liabilities	Shareholders' Equity	
			Share Capital	Retained Earnings
Declaration of cash dividend	NE	+	NE	−
Record date	NE	NE	NE	NE
Payment of cash dividend	−	−	NE	NE
Cumulative effect of declaration and payment of cash dividend	−	NE	NE	−

Stock Dividends

A **stock dividend** is a distribution of the corporation's own shares to shareholders. Whereas a cash dividend is paid in cash, a stock dividend is distributed (paid) in shares. And, while a cash dividend decreases assets (through the Cash account) and shareholders' equity (through the Retained Earnings account), a stock dividend does not change either assets, liabilities, or total shareholders' equity. No cash has been paid, and no liabilities have been assumed. Two accounts in shareholders' equity are affected, but the changes offset each other. A stock dividend results in a decrease in retained earnings and an increase in share capital but it does not change *total* shareholders' equity.

What, then, are the purposes and benefits of a stock dividend? A corporation generally issues a stock dividend for one or more of the following reasons:

1. To satisfy shareholders' dividend expectations while conserving cash.
2. To increase the marketability of the shares. When the number of shares increases, the share price decreases on the stock market. Decreasing the market price of the shares makes it easier for investors to purchase them.
3. To emphasize that a portion of shareholders' equity has been permanently reinvested in the legal capital of the business and is unavailable for cash dividends.

Similar to a cash dividend, there is a declaration date, record date, and distribution (payment) date for a stock dividend. The size of the stock dividend and the value to be assigned to each dividend share are determined by the board of directors when the dividend is declared. The *Canada Business Corporations Act* requires that stock dividends be recorded at **fair value** (market price per share) at the declaration date because this is what the corporation would have received if the shares had been issued for cash rather than as a stock dividend.

Entries for Stock Dividends.   To illustrate the accounting for stock dividends, assume that IBR Inc. has 50,000 common shares with a balance of $500,000 in Common Shares and $300,000 in Retained Earnings. On June 30, it declares a 10% stock dividend to shareholders of record at July 20, to be distributed to shareholders on August 5. The share price on June 30 is $15 per share.

The number of shares to be issued is 5,000 (50,000 × 10%). The total amount to be debited to the Stock Dividends account is $75,000 (5,000 × $15). Note that it is the fair value at the declaration date that is relevant for this transaction, and not the fair value on the record date or distribution date.

The entry to record the declaration of the stock dividend is as follows:

June 30	Stock Dividends	75,000	
	Common Stock Dividends Distributable		75,000
	(To record declaration of 10% stock dividend)		

A	=	L	+	SE
				−75,000
				+75,000

Cash flows: no effect

Stock Dividends Distributable is a shareholders' equity account. It is not a liability, because assets will not be used to pay the dividend. Instead, it will be "paid" with common shares. If a statement of financial position is prepared before the dividend shares are issued, the distributable account is reported as share capital in the shareholders' equity section of the statement of financial position. As was the case with cash dividends, the Stock Dividends account will be closed into, and reduce, the Retained Earnings account at the end of the year.

Helpful Hint
Note that the credit entry uses the word *Distributable*, not *Payable*, in the account title.

Similar to cash dividends, there is no entry at the record date. When the dividend shares are issued on August 5, the account Stock Dividends Distributable is decreased (debited) and the account Common Shares is increased (credited), as follows:

Aug. 5	Stock Dividends Distributable	75,000	
	Common Shares		75,000
	(To record issue of 5,000 common shares in a 10% stock dividend)		

A	=	L	+	SE
				−75,000
				+75,000

Cash flows: no effect

Note that neither of the above entries changes shareholders' equity in total. However, the composition of shareholders' equity changes because a portion of retained earnings is transferred to the common shares account. These effects are shown below for IBR Inc.:

	Before Stock Dividend	Change	After Stock Dividend
Shareholders' equity			
Common shares	$500,000	+$75,000	$575,000
Retained earnings	300,000	−75,000	225,000
Total shareholders' equity	$800,000	$ 0	$800,000
Number of shares	50,000	+5,000	55,000

In this example, the Common Shares account increased by $75,000—the fair value of the shares—and Retained Earnings decreased by the same amount. Note also that total shareholders' equity remains unchanged at $800,000, the total both before and after the stock dividend. The number of shares also increases by 5,000 (50,000 × 10%).

Stock Splits

Although stock splits are not dividends, we discuss them in this section because of their similarities to stock dividends. A **stock split**, like a stock dividend, involves the issue of additional shares to shareholders according to their percentage ownership. However, a stock split is usually much larger than a stock dividend. For example, a stock dividend might result in an additional 10% of common shares issued, whereas a stock split could result in 100% more common shares issued. This is because the main purpose of a stock split is to increase the marketability of the shares by lowering the share price. Because most investors buy shares in multiples of 100, reducing the price per share through stock splits makes a company's shares more affordable for the average investor. Consequently, a lower stock market price increases investors' interest in a company and makes it easier for a corporation to issue additional shares.

The effect of a stock split on the share price is generally inversely proportional to the size of the split—i.e., the larger the split, the lower the price per share. For example, after lululemon's 2-for-1 stock split, the fair value of its shares fell from $114 to $57. Sometimes, due to increased investor interest, the share price then rises more rapidly beyond its original split value.

In a stock split, the number of shares is increased by a specified proportion. For example, in a 2-for-1 split, a company that has 100,000 shares issued before the split will issue an additional 100,000 shares and have a total of 200,000 shares (100,000 × 2) issued after the split. A stock split does not have any effect on total share capital, retained earnings, or total shareholders' equity. Only the number of shares increases.

These effects are shown below for IBR Inc., assuming that instead of issuing a 10% stock dividend, it split its 50,000 common shares on a 2-for-1 basis:

	Before Stock Split	Change	After Stock Split
Shareholders' equity			
Common shares	$500,000	$0	$500,000
Retained earnings	300,000	0	300,000
Total shareholders' equity	$800,000	$0	$800,000
Number of shares	50,000	+50,000	100,000

Because a stock split does not affect the balances in any shareholders' equity accounts, **it is not necessary to journalize a stock split**. Only a memo entry explaining the effect of the split (e.g., the change in the number of shares) is needed.

ACCOUNTING MATTERS!   *Investor Perspective*

Rewarding Shareholders

Magna International Inc., a Canadian auto parts giant, announced an increase in its dividend, a stock split, and a share buyback program in response to strong profit and cash flow, even at historically low levels of vehicle production. Optimistic about its future, the company increased its dividend 20% to U.S. $0.18 per share, split its shares 2-for-1, and announced plans to reacquire and retire as many as 4 million common shares.

After the stock split, Magna's share price dropped by about half and then immediately rose 6% on the Toronto Stock Exchange—its highest level since 2007. "It shows that they're paying more attention to shareholders now," said Michael Willemse, an analyst with CIBC World Markets Inc.

Source: Greg Keenan, "Magna Boosts Dividend as Profit Soars Fourfold," *The Globe and Mail*, November 5, 2010, p. B1.

Comparison of Effects

A cash dividend, stock dividend, and stock split have differing impacts on a company's financial position. The cumulative effect of these differences is shown in Illustration 11-2. In the illustration, "+" means increase, "−" means decrease, and "NE" means "no effect."

Illustration 11-2

Effects of cash dividends, stock dividends, and stock splits

	Assets	=	Liabilities	+	Share Capital	+	Retained Earnings	Number of Shares
					Shareholders' Equity			
Cash dividend	−		NE		NE		−	NE
Stock dividend	NE		NE		+		−	+
Stock split	NE		NE		NE		NE	+

Cash dividends reduce assets (the Cash account) when paid and reduce retained earnings (the Cash Dividends account). Stock dividends increase share capital (the Common or Preferred Shares account) when distributed and decrease retained earnings (the Stock Dividends account). Stock splits do not affect any of the accounts. However, both a stock dividend and stock split increase the number of shares issued.

RETAINED EARNINGS RESTRICTIONS

The balance in Retained Earnings is generally available for dividend declarations. In some cases, however, there may be **retained earnings restrictions**. These make a portion of the balance unavailable for dividends. Restrictions result from one or more of the following causes:

1. **Legal restrictions.** You will recall that treasury shares are a company's own shares that have been reacquired and held for later reissue. In some jurisdictions, a portion of retained earnings equal to the cost of any treasury shares purchased must be restricted from being paying dividends.
2. **Contractual restrictions.** Long-term debt contracts may restrict retained earnings as a condition for the loan. These restrictions are known as **debt covenants**, which, among other things, can limit the use of corporate assets for the payment of dividends. Such restrictions make it more likely that a corporation will be able to meet its required loan payments.
3. **Voluntary restrictions.** The board of directors may voluntarily create retained earnings restrictions for specific purposes. For example, the board may authorize a restriction because of a future plant expansion. By reducing the amount of retained earnings available for dividends, the company makes more cash available for the planned expansion.

Remember that retained earnings are part of the shareholders' claim on the corporation's total assets. The balance in Retained Earnings does not, however, represent a claim on any one specific asset. For example, restricting $100,000 of retained earnings does not necessarily mean that there will be $100,000 of cash set aside. All that a restriction does is to inform users that a portion of retained earnings is not available for dividend payments.

No journal entry is necessary to record a retained earnings restriction, but they are disclosed in the notes to the financial statements.

Alternative Terminology
Restrictions are sometimes called *reserves*.

BEFORE YOU GO ON...

▶ Do It! Dividends and Split Effects

Sing CD Corporation has had five years of record profits. Due to this success, the price of its 500,000 common shares tripled from $15 per share to $45. During this period, the Common Shares account remained the same at $2 million. Retained Earnings increased from $1.5 million to $10 million. President Bill McGrath is considering either (1) a 10% stock dividend or (2) a 2-for-1 stock split. He asks you to show the before-and-after effects of each option on the corporation's shareholders' equity and on the number of shares.

Action Plan

- Calculate the stock dividend effects by multiplying the stock dividend percentage by the number of existing shares to determine the number of new shares to be issued. Multiply the number of new shares by the price (fair value) of each share.
- A stock dividend increases the number of shares and affects both the Common Shares and Retained Earnings accounts.
- A stock split increases the number of shares but does not affect the Common Shares or Retained Earnings accounts.

Solution

1. With a 10% stock dividend, the stock dividend amount is $2,250,000 (500,000 × 10% = 50,000 × $45). The new balance in Common Shares is $4,250,000 ($2,000,000 + $2,250,000) and Retained Earnings is now $7,750,000 ($10,000,000 − $2,250,000).

2. With a stock split, the account balances in Common Shares and Retained Earnings after the stock split are the same as they were before: $2 million and $10 million, respectively.

The effects on the shareholders' equity accounts of each option are as follows:

	Original Balances	After Stock Dividend	After Stock Split
Common shares	$ 2,000,000	$ 4,250,000	$ 2,000,000
Retained earnings	10,000,000	7,750,000	10,000,000
Total shareholders' equity	$12,000,000	$12,000,000	$12,000,000
Number of shares	500,000	550,000	1,000,000

the navigator

Presentation of Shareholders' Equity

STUDY OBJECTIVE 5

Indicate how shareholders' equity is presented in the financial statements.

Shareholders' equity transactions are reported in the statement of financial position and statement of changes in equity for companies using International Financial Reporting Standards. Companies using Accounting Standards for Private Enterprises can prepare a statement of retained earnings rather than a statement of changes in equity. Equity transactions are not reported in the income statement, although the income statement is linked to shareholders' equity through retained earnings.

STATEMENT OF FINANCIAL POSITION

In the shareholders' equity section of the statement of financial position, the following are reported: (1) contributed capital, (2) retained earnings, and (3) accumulated other comprehensive income. These categories have been introduced in past chapters. We will review each of them briefly here.

Contributed Capital

Within contributed capital, two classifications are recognized:

1. **Share capital.** This category consists of preferred and common shares. Because of the additional rights they give, preferred shares are shown before common shares. Information about the legal capital, number of shares authorized, number of shares issued, and any particular share preferences (e.g., a dividend rate) is reported for each class of shares either directly in the shareholders' equity section of the statement of financial position or in a note to the financial statements. Note also that any stock dividends distributable that exist at year end are also reported under share capital.

   ASPE — Private companies reporting under ASPE are not required to disclose the number of shares authorized, only the number issued along with their related rights and privileges.

2. **Additional contributed capital.** This category includes amounts contributed from reacquiring and retiring shares. If shares have been issued with a par or stated value, then amounts paid for the shares in excess of the par or stated value are recorded as additional contributed capital. Other situations not discussed in this textbook can also result in additional contributed capital. If a company has a variety of sources of additional contributed capital, it is important to distinguish each one by source. For many companies, however, there is no additional contributed capital. The caption "share capital" is therefore used more often than "contributed capital."

Retained Earnings

Retained earnings are the cumulative profits (or losses) since incorporation that have been retained in the company (i.e., not distributed to shareholders). Each year, profit is added (or a loss is deducted) and dividends declared are deducted from the opening retained earnings balance to determine the ending retained earnings amount.

Other additions or deductions from retained earnings can also occur, most notably from changes in accounting policies. We will learn more about this type of adjustment to retained earnings in Chapter 14. Recall that it is only the end-of-period balance of retained earnings that is presented in the shareholders' equity section of the statement of financial position, not the detailed changes that are presented in the statement of changes in equity.

Retained Earnings is a shareholders' equity account whose normal balance is a credit. If a deficit (debit balance) exists, it is reported as a deduction from shareholders' equity, rather than as the usual addition. Notes to the financial statements are required to explain any restricted retained earnings and any dividends that may be in arrears.

Accumulated Other Comprehensive Income (IFRS)

Most revenues, expenses, gains, and losses are included in profit. However, certain gains and losses bypass profit and are recorded as direct adjustments to shareholders' equity. These are known as **other comprehensive income** (or loss, if negative).

There are several examples of other comprehensive income or loss. These include unrealized gains and losses from cash flow hedges; translation gains and losses on certain types of foreign currency transactions; revaluations of property, plant, and equipment accounted for using the revaluation model; actuarial gains and losses on defined-benefit pension plans, and other examples we will learn about in the next chapter. These are all topics for more advanced accounting courses.

Comprehensive income (loss) or total comprehensive income (loss) includes both profit and other comprehensive income. This means that it includes (1) the revenues, expenses, gains, and losses included in profit, *and* (2) the gains and losses that bypass profit but affect shareholders' equity as shown in Illustration 11-3.

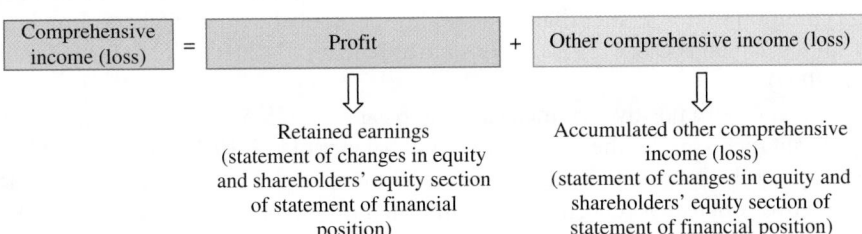

▶ Illustration 11-3
Comprehensive income

You will recall that profit—a period figure—is included in the retained earnings reported on the statement of changes in equity and shareholders' equity section of the statement of financial position. This is because retained earnings is the cumulative total of profits retained in the business. Similarly, other comprehensive income—also a period figure—is included in the accumulated other comprehensive income reported on the same statements. And, just as retained earnings can be negative (i.e., a deficit), other comprehensive income and comprehensive income can also be negative and reported as a loss rather than as income.

Similar to retained earnings, **accumulated other comprehensive income (loss)** is the *cumulative* change in shareholders' equity that results from the gains and losses that bypass profit but affect shareholders' equity. In other words, it starts with the balance at the beginning of the period and is increased by other comprehensive income and decreased by other comprehensive losses during the period, to arrive at the ending balance. It is this ending balance that is reported in the shareholders' equity section of the statement of financial position.

Only companies reporting using IFRS have to report other comprehensive income. Companies reporting using ASPE do not. Of course, not all companies using IFRS will have examples of other comprehensive income. However, if they do, they must report comprehensive income in a statement of comprehensive income, and accumulated other comprehensive income in the statement of changes in equity and the shareholders' equity section of the statement of financial position. We will learn about the preparation of the statement of comprehensive income for companies using IFRS in the next chapter.

`ASPE`

Presentation of Shareholders' Equity

lululemon reports common shares, retained earnings, and accumulated other comprehensive income in the shareholders' equity section of its balance sheet (statement of financial position), as shown in Illustration 11-4.

▶Illustration 11-4

lululemon statement of financial position—shareholders' equity section

LULULEMON ATHLETICA INC.
Balance Sheet (partial)
January 31, 2010
(in U.S. thousands)

lululemon ⟳ athletica

	2010	2009
Shareholders' equity		
Contributed capital		
Common shares, $0.01 par value, 200,000 shares authorized and 51,126 shares issued in 2010 (50,422 in 2009)	$ 511	$ 504
Additional paid-in capital	158,921	155,961
Total contributed capital	159,432	156,465
Retained earnings	67,809	9,528
Accumulated other comprehensive income (loss)	5,867	(11,151)
	$233,108	$154,842

lululemon has 200 million common shares authorized, with 51,126 thousand issued at January 31, 2010 (50,422 thousand as at February 1, 2009). It also has a significant amount of additional paid-in capital. This is an additional contributed capital account that arises because of the low legal capital (par) value of lululemon's shares. If the shares had been of no par value, which is the norm in Canada, this entire amount would have been credited directly to a share capital account (e.g., common shares) rather than to an additional contributed capital account. lululemon's total contributed capital is U.S. $159,432 thousand at January 31, 2010 (U.S. $156,465 thousand at February 1, 2009).

lululemon reported a positive retained earnings balance of U.S. $67,809 thousand at January 31, 2010, a significant increase over the retained earnings balance of U.S. $9,528 thousand at February 1, 2009. The company also reported accumulated other comprehensive income of U.S. $5,867 thousand at the end of 2010, whereas it reported an accumulated other comprehensive loss of U.S. $11,151 thousand at the end of 2009. lululemon's total shareholders' equity is U.S. $233,108 thousand at January 31, 2010, a significant increase over U.S. $154,842 thousand at February 1, 2009.

If lululemon also had treasury shares (which it does not), they would be presented as a deduction from the subtotal of all the other components reported in the shareholders' equity section of the statement of financial position. That is, treasury stock is normally the last item listed (deducted) in the shareholders' equity section.

STATEMENT OF CHANGES IN EQUITY (IFRS)

Alternative Terminology
The *statement of changes in equity* is also known as the *statement of shareholders' equity.*

As we learned in Chapter 1, the **statement of changes in equity** discloses changes in total shareholders' equity for the period, as well as changes in each shareholders' equity account, including contributed capital, retained earnings, and accumulated other comprehensive income. It is a required statement for companies reporting under IFRS.

lululemon's statement of shareholders' equity (statement of changes in equity) is shown in Illustration 11-5. lululemon has prepared its statement in tabular form, but other formats are also acceptable.

LULULEMON ATHLETICA INC.
Statement of Shareholders' Equity (partial)
Year Ended January 31, 2010
(in U.S. thousands)

lululemon ⟳ athletica

	Common Shares		Additional Paid-In Capital	Retained Earnings	Accumulated Other Comprehensive Income (Loss)	Total
	Number of Shares	Legal Capital				
Bal., February 1, 2009	50,422	$504	$155,961	$ 9,528	$(11,151)	$154,842
Comprehensive income						
Net income				58,281		58,281
Foreign currency translation adjustment					17,018	17,018

Stock-based compensation			1,758			1,758
Common shares	134	1	(1)			
Restricted share issuance	15					
Stock option exercises	555	6	1,203			1,209
Bal., January 31, 2010	51,126	$511	$158,921	$67,809	$ 5,867	$233,108

▶Illustration 11-5
lululemon statement of changes in equity

lululemon details the changes in its equity accounts starting with the account balances at the beginning of the fiscal year (February 1, 2009) and ending with the account balances at the end of the fiscal year (January 31, 2010). While we have included the changes for only one year in Illustration 11-5, lululemon actually includes the changes for the last three fiscal years in its published statement.

In the above statement, you can see both the number of shares issued and the dollar amount of the changes in the year in the legal capital (par value, in lululemon's case) and additional contributed (paid-in) capital received for the shares. In the statement of changes of equity demonstrated previously in this textbook, we did not include a column for the number of shares. We will now include this column in our statements going forward for additional information, as has lululemon.

You can also see how net income (profit) increases retained earnings. Finally, the accumulated other comprehensive loss is reduced by a positive foreign currency translation adjustment, which results in an accumulated other comprehensive income amount at the end of the year.

Note that all of the dollar amounts as at January 31, 2010, that are shown in the above illustration were reported in the shareholders' equity section of lululemon's statement of financial position shown in Illustration 11-4. We recommend that you now trace these opening and ending balances, and the total shareholders' equity amounts, to those shown in Illustration 11-4.

STATEMENT OF RETAINED EARNINGS (ASPE)

Private companies that report using Accounting Standards for Private Enterprises usually have a much simpler capital structure. In addition, they often have few share transactions that can be detailed in the notes to the financial statements. Consequently, private companies are not required to prepare a statement of changes in equity but instead prepare a statement of retained earnings. This statement can be prepared as a separate statement or combined with the income statement.

ASPE

A **statement of retained earnings** shows the amounts and causes of changes in retained earnings during the period. Similar to the statement of changes in equity, a statement of retained earnings must be prepared after the income statement is prepared, as profit is a key component of retained earnings. In contrast to the statement of changes in equity, which shows the amounts and causes of changes in all of the shareholders' equity accounts, the statement of retained earnings shows only the changes in the Retained Earnings account.

The beginning retained earnings amount is shown on the first line of the statement. Then profit is added and dividends (if any) are deducted to calculate the retained earnings at the end of the period. If a company has a loss, it is deducted (rather than added) in the statement of retained earnings. This statement covers the same period of time as the income statement.

A sample statement of retained earnings is shown in Illustration 11-6 for Graber Inc., using assumed data:

▶Illustration 11-6
Statement of retained earnings

GRABER INC. Statement of Retained Earnings Year Ended December 31, 2012	
Balance, January 1	$1,068,000
Add: Profit	262,800
	1,330,800
Less: Cash dividends	58,000
Balance, December 31	$1,272,800

BEFORE YOU GO ON...

▶ Do It! Statement of Changes in Equity

Grand Lake Corporation had the following shareholders' equity balances at January 1, 2012:

Common shares, unlimited number authorized, no par value, 500,000 issued	$1,000,000
Retained earnings	600,000
Accumulated other comprehensive income	100,000

The following selected information is available for the year ended December 31, 2012:

1. Issued 100,000 common shares for $300,000.

2. Declared and paid dividends of $0.10 per share.

3. Reported profit of $360,000.

4. Reported other comprehensive income of $25,000.

Prepare a statement of changes in equity.

Action Plan

• The statement of changes in equity covers a period of time, starting with the opening balances and ending with the ending balances for the period.
• Explain the changes in each shareholders' equity account, as well as total shareholders' equity.
• Recall that comprehensive income consists of both profit and any other comprehensive income.

Solution

GRAND LAKE CORPORATION Statement of Changes in Equity Year Ended December 31, 2012					
	Common Shares			Accumulated	
	Number of Shares	Legal Capital	Retained Earnings	Other Comprehensive Income	Total
Balance, January 1	500,000	$1,000,000	$600,000	$100,000	$1,700,000
Issued common shares	100,000	300,000			300,000
Cash dividends			(60,000)		(60,000)
Comprehensive income					
Profit			360,000		360,000
Other comprehensive income				25,000	25,000
Balance, December 31	600,000	$1,300,000	$900,000	$125,000	$2,325,000

Measuring Corporate Performance

STUDY OBJECTIVE 6

Evaluate dividend and earnings performance.

Investors are interested in both a company's dividend record and its earnings performance. Although they are often parallel, sometimes they are not. Each item should therefore be investigated separately.

DIVIDEND RECORD

One way that companies reward investors for their investment is to pay them dividends. The **payout ratio** measures the percentage of profit distributed as cash dividends. It is calculated by dividing the cash dividends by profit.

We are unable to calculate a payout ratio for lululemon because it does not pay dividends. To illustrate the calculation of the payout ratio, we will use Canadian National (CN) Railway Company. We will look at the payout ratios for its common shares for the years ended December 31, 2010 and 2009. The following selected information (in millions, except for per share information) is used in the calculation of the payout ratio shown in Illustration 11-7:

	2010	2009
Profit	$2,104	$1,854
Cash dividends	503	474
Dividends per common share	1.30	1.01
Common share price	66.35	57.34

> Illustration 11-7
> CN Railway payout ratio

PAYOUT RATIO = $\dfrac{\text{CASH DIVIDENDS}}{\text{PROFIT}}$		
(in millions)	2010	2009
Payout ratio	$\dfrac{\$503}{\$2,104} = 23.9\%$	$\dfrac{\$474}{\$1,854} = 25.6\%$
Industry average	28.9%	n/a

In 2010, CN paid 23.9% of its profit back to its common shareholders, a slight decrease from 2009 when it paid 25.6% and lower than the industry average. Note that the industry average was not available for 2009.

Another dividend measure that interests shareholders is the dividend yield. The **dividend yield** is calculated by dividing the dividend per share by the market price per share, as shown in Illustration 11-8.

> Illustration 11-8
> CN Railway dividend yield

DIVIDEND YIELD = $\dfrac{\text{DIVIDEND PER SHARE}}{\text{MARKET PRICE PER SHARE}}$		
	2010	2009
Dividend yield	$\dfrac{\$1.30}{\$66.35} = 2.0\%$	$\dfrac{\$1.01}{\$57.34} = 1.8\%$
Industry average	1.4%	2.8%

The dividend yield is a measure of the profit generated for the shareholder by each share, and is based on the market price of the shares. CN's dividend yield was 2% at the end of 2010 and 1.8% at the end of 2009. It is notable that, while CN's dividend yield was lower than the industry average in 2009, it surpassed the industry average in 2010.

The dividend yield is, in essence, a measure of a shareholder's return on his or her investment. In CN's case, an investor who purchased common shares at the end of 2010 would have paid $66.35 to purchase each share. Based on the annual dividend of $1.30 per share, the investor is earning a return of 2% on this investment.

Of course, dividend income is only one part of an investor's return on an investment in shares. Investors hope to also earn a return from increases in the market price of their shares when they are ready to sell them. In general, however, investors tend to buy shares with high payout ratios and dividend yields if they are looking to earn a regular income (dividend). They tend to buy shares with low payout ratios and dividend yields if they are looking for more capital appreciation (growth) from their shares.

Companies that have high growth rates tend to be characterized by low payout ratios and dividend yields because they reinvest most of the profit back into the business. For example, lululemon clearly states its dividend policy in its annual report: "We have never declared or paid any cash dividends on our common stock and do not anticipate paying any cash dividends on our common stock in the foreseeable future. We anticipate that we will retain all of our available funds for use in the operation and expansion of our business."

Illustration 11-9 shows the payout ratios and dividend yields of selected companies in a recent year.

▶ Illustration 11-9
Payout ratios and dividend yields

	Payout Ratio (%)	Dividend Yield (%)
BCE	23.3	5.5
Eastern Platinum	0.0	0.0
Empire	8.6	1.4
Google	0.0	0.0
Kimberly-Clark	39.3	4.3
Royal Bank	34.0	5.0

ACCOUNTING MATTERS!   *Investor Perspective*

Are High Dividend Yields and Payout Ratios Good or Bad?

Dividend yields generally move inversely to share prices. Some people believe that a high dividend yield should encourage investors to consider selling their shares rather than hanging on to them for the income potential. Vaughn Warrington, an investment advisor with RBC Dominion Securities who has published a book called *Dividends Rule*, considers a 6% dividend yield "pretty much a ceiling." Of course, there are exceptions. In 2009, for example, the Bank of Montreal's dividend yield rose to 11%. Investors who bought Bank of Montreal shares then have seen the share price more than double. But this is not the rule.

Payout ratios are also an important consideration. Mr. Warrington believes a payout ratio under 40% is the right number for a company to have. Other experts say up to 50% is ideal but they can live with as much as 70% for solid, well-established companies.

Choosing reliable dividend stocks should involve more than looking at guidelines for yield and payout ratios, though. Investors should look at the company's underlying business and make sure its dividend policy makes sense for its business strategy.

Source: Bob Carrick, "Don't Be Distracted by High Dividend Yields," *The Globe and Mail*, August 15, 2010, p. B10.

DECISION TOOLKIT

Decision Checkpoints	 Info Needed for Decision	 Tools to Use for Decision	 How to Evaluate Results
What portion of its profit does the company pay out in dividends?	Profit and total cash dividends	$$\text{Payout ratio} = \frac{\text{Cash dividends}}{\text{Profit}}$$	A low ratio suggests that the company is retaining its profit for investment in future growth.
What percentage of the share price is the company paying in dividends?	Dividends and share price	$$\text{Dividend yield} = \frac{\text{Dividend per share}}{\text{Market price per share}}$$	A high dividend yield is considered desirable for investors. It also means that the company is paying out, rather than retaining, its profit.

EARNINGS PERFORMANCE

The earnings performance, or profitability, of a company is measured in several different ways. In an earlier chapter, we learned about the earnings per share ratio. In this section, we will revisit the calculation of this ratio and introduce a new profitability ratio, the return on common shareholders' equity.

Earnings per Share

You will recall that we learned how to calculate earnings per share in Chapter 2. In that chapter, the formula for earnings per share was presented in Illustration 2-17. At that time, we gave the information for you to calculate the earnings per share and said that you would learn how to calculate the numerator (profit available to common shareholders) and the denominator (weighted average number of common shares) in Chapter 11. To further what we learned in Chapter 2, we have added to Illustration 11-10 below the information that is needed for calculating earnings per share for lululemon (in U.S. thousands).

Profit Available to Common Shareholders (Profit – Preferred Dividends)	÷	Weighted Average Number of Common Shares	=	Earnings per Share
$58,281 – $0	÷	70,251	=	$0.83

▸Illustration 11-10
lululemon earnings per share

The numerator, **profit available to common shareholders**, is calculated by subtracting any preferred dividends from profit. This is because preferred shareholders have preferential rights to receive these dividends before the common shareholders can share in any remaining amounts. In lululemon's case, no preferred shares have been issued so its profit available to common shareholders is the same as its profit.

For the denominator of the earnings per share calculation, the weighted average number of shares is used. Note that lululemon's weighted average number of common shares, 70,251 thousand, is not the same as the ending balance of its common shares, 51,126 thousand, that was reported earlier in Illustration 11-5. You will recall that, whenever we calculate a ratio with a period figure (e.g., profit) and an end-of-period figure (e.g., the number of common shares), we always average the end-of-period figure so that the numerator and denominator in the calculation are for the same period of time. However, we do not use a straight average in the calculation of the number of common shares as we do in some other ratio calculations. For example, we do not take the beginning and ending balances of the number of common shares, add them together, and divide the result by two.

Instead, we use a **weighted average number of common shares** as this considers the impact of shares issued at different times throughout the year. This is done because the issue of shares changes the amount of assets on which profit can be generated. Consequently, shares issued or purchased during each current period must be weighted by the fraction of the year (or period) that they have been issued. If there is no change in the number of common shares issued during the year, the weighted average number of shares will be the same as the ending balance. If new shares are issued or existing shares are reacquired throughout the year, then these shares are adjusted for the fraction of the year they are outstanding to determine the weighted average number of shares.

To illustrate the calculation of the weighted average number of common shares, assume that a company had 100,000 common shares on January 1. It reacquired and retired 7,500 shares on July 1 and issued an additional 10,000 shares on October 1. The weighted average number of shares for the year would be calculated as follows:

Date	Actual Number		Weighted Average
Jan. 1	100,000	$\times\,^{12}/_{12} =$	100,000
July 1	(7,500)	$\times\,^{6}/_{12} =$	(3,750)
Oct. 1	10,000	$\times\,^{3}/_{12} =$	2,500
	102,500		98,750

As illustrated, 102,500 shares were actually issued by the end of the year. Of these, 100,000 were issued for the full year and are allocated a full weight, or 12 months of 12 months. The 7,500 reacquired shares were only issued for six months (January 1 to June 30) and are weighted for $^6/_{12}$ of the year. Consequently, the portion of the year (July 1 to December 31) when they were no longer issued, 3,750 weighted shares, has to be deducted to determine the weighted average. The other 10,000 shares have only been issued for three months (from October 1 to December 31) and are weighted for $^3/_{12}$ of the year, to result in 2,500 weighted shares. In total, the company's weighted average number of shares is 98,750 for the year. In the next calendar year, the 102,500 shares would receive full weight (unless new shares are issued or others repurchased) because all 102,500 shares would be issued for the entire year.

Complex Capital Structure.   When a corporation has securities that may be converted into common shares, it has what is called a complex capital structure. One example of a convertible security is convertible preferred shares. When the preferred shares are converted into common shares, the additional common shares will result in a reduced, or diluted, earnings per share figure.

Two earnings per share figures are calculated when a corporation has a complex capital structure. The first earnings per share figure is called **basic earnings per share**. The earnings per share amount we calculated in Illustration 11-10, $0.83, is known as basic earnings per share, which is what lululemon reported on its income statement for 2010.

The second earnings per share figure is called **diluted earnings per share**. This figure calculates *hypothetical* earnings per share as though *all* securities that can be converted into, or exchanged for, common shares have actually been converted or exchanged (even though they really have not). lululemon, which has other securities that can be converted into common shares (stock options, in this case), is considered to have a complex capital structure. It also reports diluted earnings per share of $0.82 for the year ended January 31, 2010. Note that diluted earnings per share will never be higher than basic earnings per share.

The calculation of diluted earnings per share is complex. In addition, the determination of the weighted average number of shares for both basic and diluted earnings per share becomes more complicated when there are stock dividends and stock splits during the year. Further discussion of diluted earnings per share and other complexities is left to an intermediate accounting course.

ASPE   The disclosure of earnings per share is required for companies reporting using IFRS. This ratio is considered to be so important that it must be reported directly on the income statement (or the statement of comprehensive income, which will be illustrated in the next chapter). As we mentioned in Chapter 2, companies reporting using ASPE do not have to report earnings per share.

Return on Equity

A widely used ratio that measures profitability from the common shareholders' viewpoint is the **return on common shareholders' equity**. This ratio shows how many dollars were earned for each dollar invested by common shareholders. It is calculated by dividing profit available to common shareholders by average common shareholders' equity. As we just learned, the profit available to common shareholders is profit less any preferred dividends. Common shareholders' equity is total shareholders' equity less the legal capital of any preferred shares. Recall that everything else belongs to the common, or residual, shareholders.

We can calculate a return on common shareholders' equity for lululemon using the information presented below. In lululemon's particular case, its common shareholders' equity is the same as its total shareholders' equity since it does not have any preferred shares.

(in U.S. thousands)	2010	2009	2008
Profit	$ 58,281	$ 39,363	$ 30,843
Shareholders' equity	233,108	154,842	112,034

lululemon's return on common shareholders' equity ratios are calculated for 2010 and 2009 in Illustration 11-11.

Illustration 11-11
lululemon return on common shareholders' equity

RETURN ON COMMON SHAREHOLDERS' EQUITY = $\dfrac{\text{PROFIT} - \text{PREFERRED DIVIDENDS}}{\text{AVERAGE COMMON SHAREHOLDERS' EQUITY}}$		
(in U.S. thousands)	2010	2009
Return on common shareholders' equity	$\dfrac{\$58,281 - \$0}{(\$233,108 + \$154,842) \div 2} = 30.0\%$	$\dfrac{\$39,363 - \$0}{(\$154,842 + \$112,034) \div 2} = 29.5\%$
Industry average	22.2%	20.4%

In 2010, lululemon's return on common shareholders' equity was 30%, a slight increase over 2009. Both years' returns exceeded the industry average by quite a margin.

DECISION TOOLKIT

Decision Checkpoints	Info Needed for Decision	Tools to Use for Decision	How to Evaluate Results
How does the company's profit compare with previous years?	Profit available to common shareholders and weighted average number of common shares	Earnings per share = $\dfrac{\text{Profit} - \text{Preferred dividends}}{\text{Weighted average number of common shares}}$	A higher measure suggests improved performance. Values should not be compared across companies.
What is the company's return on its common shareholders' investment?	Profit available to common shareholders and average common shareholders' equity	Return on common shareholders' equity = $\dfrac{\text{Profit} - \text{Preferred dividends}}{\text{Average common shareholders' equity}}$	A high measure suggests a strong earnings performance from the common shareholders' perspective.

BEFORE YOU GO ON...

▶ Do It! Earnings Per Share

The Shoten Corporation reported profit of $249,750 for the year ended October 31, 2012. The shareholders' equity section of its statement of financial position reported 3,000 $2 cumulative preferred shares and 50,000 common shares issued. Of the common shares, 40,000 had been issued since the beginning of the year, 15,000 were issued on March 1, and 5,000 were reacquired and retired on August 1. Calculate Shoten's earnings per share.

Action Plan

- Subtract any preferred dividends from profit to determine the profit available for common shareholders.
- Note that cumulative preferred dividends are deducted from profit whether declared or not; noncumulative preferred dividends are deducted only if declared.
- Adjust the shares for the fraction of the year issued to determine the weighted average number of common shares.
- Divide the profit available for common shareholders by the weighted average number of common shares to calculate earnings per share.

(continued)

Solution

Preferred dividends: $3,000 \times \$2 = \$6,000$

Weighted average number of common shares

Date	Actual Number		Weighted Average
Nov. 1	40,000	$\times\ ^{12}/_{12} =$	40,000
Mar. 1	15,000	$\times\ ^{8}/_{12} =$	10,000
Aug. 1	(5,000)	$\times\ ^{3}/_{12} =$	(1,250)
	50,000		48,750

Earnings per share $\dfrac{\$249,750 - \$6,000}{48,750} = \$5$

comparing
IFRS and ASPE

Key Differences	International Financial Reporting Standards (IFRS)	Accounting Standards for Private Enterprises (ASPE)
Issue of shares for a noncash consideration	When shares are issued for a noncash consideration, they should be recorded at the fair value of the consideration (e.g., goods or services) received. If the fair value of the consideration received cannot be reliably determined, then the fair value of the consideration given up would be used instead.	When shares are issued for a noncash consideration, they should be recorded at the most reliable of the two values—the fair value of the consideration (e.g., goods or services) received or the fair value of the consideration given up.
Authorized share capital	Must present the number of shares authorized, in addition to the number of shares issued, along with their related rights and privileges in the financial statements.	Not required to disclose the number of shares authorized in the financial statements, only the number issued along with their related rights and privileges.
Comprehensive income	Must present accumulated other comprehensive income in statement of financial position and detail changes in other comprehensive income in the statement of changes in equity.	Disclosure of comprehensive income is not required.
Statement of changes in equity/retained earnings	Changes in all shareholders' equity accounts are presented in a statement of changes in equity.	Changes in retained earnings are presented in a statement of retained earnings. Changes in share capital and other accounts are presented in the notes to the financial statements.
Earnings per share	Required to present in the income statement (or statement of comprehensive income).	Not required to present in the income statement.

Should I Play the Market?

When companies need additional financing, they raise this money by issuing shares (equity financing) or borrowing money (debt financing).

Suppose you have some extra cash and would like to buy some shares (equity) in a public company. An equity investment carries neither a promise that your investment will be returned to you nor a guarantee that your investment will earn income. Buying a company's common shares rather than preferred shares represents a decision to take a greater risk. With preferred shares, a shareholder will often receive dividend income. While a common shareholder can also receive dividend income, usually dividends are not paid on common shares. Common shareholders earn income if they can sell their shares at a price higher than what they paid for them (which is known as share price appreciation).

Share prices are determined by the interaction of buyers and sellers. Share prices can be influenced by both objective factors, such as a company's profits, and subjective factors, such as future expectations, including unverified information or rumours. Nevertheless, if a company prospers, the price of its common shares will typically rise. If the company doesn't prosper, or if external factors such as the economy or the Canadian dollar exchange rate are negative or expected to be negative, the share price will likely decline.

If you plan to invest in shares, you need to consider the following:

- How will you decide which companies to invest in? Do you plan to purchase shares for dividend income or for growth (share price appreciation)?
- How will you manage your investment portfolio? What is your time frame, how will you evaluate performance, and how will you determine the right time to sell and the right time to buy?

Some Facts

- The largest stock exchange in Canada is the Toronto Stock Exchange (TSX). It was established in 1852 and is owned by TMX Group Inc.
- Canadian markets are small compared with the number of listed companies in the world. In 2011, there were 45,595 listed companies worldwide, of which 3,743 were listed with the TMX Group.
- The TMX Group is third in North America and eighth in the world by total listed market capitalization. In the first two quarters of 2010, it was the stock exchange with the second-highest number of initial public offerings (IPOs) of new shares.
- Research is ongoing to establish whether men and women have different investing styles. Studies in the United States have suggested that men of all ages have higher levels of financial literacy than women of the same age. But men are more prone to over-confidence than women, and their stock market behaviour is riskier, resulting in higher trading costs and lower returns. Women tend to prefer a slow and steady approach.
- A recent poll conducted for BMO Nesbitt Burns found that 29% of Canadians do not hold any investments. The poll also confirmed that men were more likely than women to invest in equities (25% men, 13% women), more likely to make changes to their investment account (41% men, 34% women), and more optimistic about the future of the stock market (69% men, 55% women).

What Do You Think?

Jemima Djeric has a good salary with excellent potential for advancement in the newly listed public company where she works. She has accumulated $10,000 in savings, which is sitting in a bank savings account earning very little interest. She has decided to use $5,000 of her savings to buy shares in her employer. Should Jemima make this investment?

YES She has a good income, and purchasing shares will align her interests with those of the company she works for. She will also have an opportunity to earn dividends if any are paid, as well as sell her shares for more than she paid for them if the price increases in the future.

NO There is more risk with a stock investment. She might make money if the share price increases but she could also lose her savings if the share price decreases and she has to sell her shares before it recovers.

Sources: World Federation of Exchanges, "Statistics: Number of Listed Companies," "Domestic Market Capitalization," www.world-exchanges.org/, accessed March 14, 2011. Noreen Rasbach, "Invest Like a Man or a Woman?," *Globe and Mail*, November 16, 2010, p. L2. Investopedia.com.

Summary of Study Objectives

1. **Identify and discuss the major characteristics of a corporation.** The major characteristics of a corporation are separate legal existence, limited liability of shareholders, transferable ownership rights, the ability to acquire capital, continuous life, corporation management, government regulations, and corporate income tax.

    Corporations issue shares for sale to investors. The proceeds received from the issue of no par value shares—the most common type of shares—becomes the company's legal capital. After the initial public offering (IPO), the shares trade among investors on the secondary stock market and do not affect the company's financial position.

2. **Record common share transactions.** If only one class of shares is issued, they are considered to be common shares. Common shares have the right to vote on certain matters, such as the election of the board of directors, in addition to other rights.

    When no par value common shares are issued for cash, the entire proceeds are debited to the Cash account and credited to the Common Shares account. When shares are issued for non-cash goods or services in a company following IFRS, the fair value of the goods or services received is used to record the transaction if it can be reliably determined. If not, the fair value of the common shares is used. For a private company following ASPE, the most reliable of the two fair values should be used.

    A company can also reacquire its own shares from investors. It normally must then retire (cancel) the shares, although provisions exist in certain jurisdictions to hold the shares in treasury for future reissue.

    When shares are reacquired and retired, the average cost is debited to the Common Shares account. If the shares are reacquired at a price below the average cost, the difference is credited to a contributed capital account created from prior reacquisitions. If the shares are reacquired at a price above the average cost, the difference is debited first to a contributed capital account if it has a balance, and second to the Retained Earnings account.

3. **Record preferred share transactions.** The accounting for preferred shares is similar to the accounting for common shares. Preferred shares have contractual provisions that give them preference over common shares for dividends and assets in the event of liquidation. Dividends are quoted as an annual rate (e.g., $5 preferred), but are normally paid quarterly.

    In addition, preferred shares may have other preferences, such as the right to convert, redeem, reset rates, and/or retract.

However, preferred shares do not have the right to vote—only common shares have voting rights.

4. **Prepare the entries for cash dividends, stock dividends, and stock splits, and understand their financial impact.** Entries for both cash and stock dividends are required at the declaration date and the payment or distribution date. There is no entry (other than a memo entry) for a stock split. Cash dividends reduce assets (cash) and shareholders' equity (retained earnings). Stock dividends increase common shares and decrease retained earnings but do not affect assets, liabilities, or shareholders' equity in total. Stock splits also have no impact on assets, liabilities, or shareholders' equity. The number of shares increases with both stock dividends and stock splits.

5. **Indicate how shareholders' equity is presented in the financial statements.** In the shareholders' equity section of the statement of financial position for companies using IFRS, share capital, retained earnings, and accumulated other comprehensive income are reported separately. If additional contributed capital exists, then the caption "Contributed capital" is used for share capital (preferred and common shares) and additional contributed capital that may have been created from the reacquisition of shares or from other sources. A statement of changes in equity explains the changes in each shareholders' equity account, and in total, for the reporting period. Notes to the financial statements explain details about authorized and issued shares, restrictions on retained earnings and dividends in arrears, if there are any.

    For private companies reporting using ASPE, the number of authorized shares need not be disclosed. In addition, comprehensive income is not reported and a statement of changes in equity is not required. Instead, a statement of retained earnings is prepared that explains the changes in the retained earnings account for the reporting period.

6. **Evaluate dividend and earnings performance.** A company's dividend record can be evaluated by looking at what percentage of profit it chooses to pay out in dividends, as measured by the dividend payout ratio (dividends divided by profit) and the dividend yield ratio (dividends per share divided by the share price).

    Earnings performance can be measured by two profitability ratios: earnings per share (profit less preferred dividends divided by the weighted average number of common shares) and the return on common shareholders' equity ratio (profit available to common shareholders divided by average common shareholders' equity).

Glossary

Authorized shares   The amount of share capital that a corporation is authorized to sell. The amount may be unlimited or specified. (p. 585)

Cash dividend   A pro rata (proportional) distribution of cash to shareholders. (p. 594)

Contributed capital   The total amount contributed by shareholders, or reacquired from them, in exchange for shares of ownership. It consists of share capital and additional contributed capital, if any. (p. 588)

Corporation A company organized as a separate legal entity, with most of the rights and privileges of a person. Shares are evidence of ownership. (p. 582)

Cumulative A feature of preferred shares that entitles the shareholder to receive current-year and unpaid prior-year dividends when dividends are declared before common shareholders receive any dividends. (p. 592)

Declaration date The date the board of directors formally declares (approves) a dividend and announces it to shareholders. (p. 595)

Dividend yield A measure of the percentage of the share price that is paid in dividends. It is calculated by dividing dividends per share by the share price. (p. 605)

Dividends in arrears Dividends that were not declared on cumulative preferred shares during a period. (p. 592)

Initial public offering (IPO) The initial offering of a corporation's shares to the public. (p. 585)

Issued shares The portion of authorized shares that has been sold. (p. 585)

Legal capital The amount per share that must be retained in the business for the protection of corporate creditors. Equal to the proceeds received from the issue of no par value shares. (p. 587)

Market capitalization A measure of the fair value of a company's equity. It is calculated by multiplying the number of shares by the share price at any given date. (p. 587)

Noncumulative Preferred shares that are entitled to the current dividend, if declared, but not to any undeclared and unpaid amounts from prior years. (p. 592)

No par value shares Share capital that has not been pre-assigned a legal capital value. The total proceeds from the sale of no par value shares become the legal capital. (p. 587)

Payment date The date dividends are paid to shareholders. (p. 596)

Payout ratio A measure of the percentage of the profit distributed in the form of cash dividends to common shareholders. It is calculated by dividing cash dividends by profit. (p. 604)

Preferred shares Share capital that has contractual preferences over common shares in certain areas. (p. 591)

Profit available to common shareholders Profit less the annual preferred dividend. (p. 607)

Record date The date when ownership of shares is determined for dividend purposes. (p. 595)

Retained earnings restrictions Circumstances that make a portion of retained earnings currently unavailable for dividends. (p. 599)

Return on common shareholders' equity A measure of profitability from the shareholders' point of view. It is calculated by dividing profit minus preferred dividends by average common shareholders' equity (total shareholders' equity minus preferred shares). (p. 608)

Share capital The amount paid, or contributed, to the corporation by shareholders in exchange for shares of ownership. It can consist of preferred and common shares. (p. 587, 588)

Statement of retained earnings A statement that summarizes the changes in the Retained Earnings account during the period. This statement is issued only by private companies reporting using ASPE. (p. 603)

Stock dividend A pro rata (proportional) distribution of the corporation's own shares to shareholders. (p. 596)

Stock split The issue of additional shares to shareholders accompanied by a reduction in the legal capital per share. (p. 597)

Treasury shares A corporation's own shares that have been reacquired and not retired (cancelled). They are held in the "treasury" for later reissue. (p. 590)

Weighted average number of common shares A weighted average of the number of common shares issued during the year. Shares issued or purchased during the year are weighted by the fraction of the year for which they have been issued. (p. 607)

DECISION TOOLKIT—A SUMMARY

 Decision Checkpoints	 Info Needed for Decision	 Tools to Use for Decision	 How to Evaluate Results
Should the company incorporate?	Capital needs, growth expectations, type of business, income tax status	Corporations have limited liability, greater ability to raise capital, and professional managers. In addition, there is a potential for reduced income tax. There is increased cost and complexity from additional government regulations.	Carefully weigh the costs and benefits in light of the particular circumstances.

(continued)

What portion of its profit does the company pay out in dividends?	Profit and total cash dividends	$$\text{Payout ratio} = \frac{\text{Cash dividends}}{\text{Profit}}$$	A low ratio suggests that the company is retaining its profit for investment in future growth.
What percentage of the share price is the company paying in dividends?	Dividends and share price	$$\text{Dividend yield} = \frac{\text{Dividend per share}}{\text{Market price per share}}$$	A high dividend yield is considered desirable for investors. It also means that the company is paying out, rather than retaining, its profit.
How does the company's profit compare with previous years?	Profit available to common shareholders and weighted average number of common shares	$$\text{Earnings per share} = \frac{\text{Profit} - \text{Preferred dividends}}{\text{Weighted average number of common shares}}$$	A higher measure suggests improved performance. Values should not be compared across companies.
What is the company's return on its common shareholders' investment?	Profit available to common shareholders and average common shareholders' equity	$$\text{Return on common shareholders' equity} = \frac{\text{Profit} - \text{Preferred dividends}}{\text{Average common shareholders' equity}}$$	A high measure suggests a strong earnings performance from the common shareholders' perspective.

the navigator

USING THE DECISION TOOLKIT

Many companies, including La Senza and Victoria's Secret, have added high-performance yoga clothing in an attempt to compete with lululemon. The following selected information (in U.S. millions, except per share information) is available for Limited Brands, Inc., parent company to La Senza and Victoria's Secret. Note that Limited Brands has no preferred shares.

	2010	2009
Profit	$ 448.0	$ 220.0
Cash dividends	193.4	193.4
Shareholders' equity	2,184.0	1,874.0
Weighted average number of common shares	322.3	322.1
Dividends per share	0.60	0.60
Market price per share	19.02	7.87

Instructions

Calculate the (a) payout ratio, (b) dividend yield, (c) earnings per share, (d) price-earnings ratio, and (e) return on common shareholders' equity for Limited Brands for 2010. Contrast the company's earnings performance, where available, with that of lululemon and the industry, which is given in the chapter and below.

lululemon's price-earnings ratio was 36.3 times in 2010. Industry averages were 28.9% for the payout ratio, 2.4% for the dividend yield, 16.8 times for the price-earnings ratio, and 22.2% for the return on common shareholders' equity. There is no industry average available for earnings per share.

Solution

(in U.S. millions, except per share information)	Limited Brands	lululemon	Industry
(a) Payout ratio	$$\frac{\$193.4}{\$448.0} = 43.2\%$$	n/a	28.9%
(b) Dividend yield	$$\frac{\$0.60}{\$19.02} = 3.2\%$$	n/a	2.4%
(c) Earnings per share	$$\frac{\$448.0 - \$0}{322.3} = \$1.39$$	$0.83	n/a
(d) Price-earnings ratio	$$\frac{\$19.02}{\$1.39} = 13.7 \text{ times}$$	36.3 times	16.8 times
(e) Return on common shareholders' equity	$$\frac{\$488 - \$0}{(\$2,184.0 + \$1,874.0) \div 2} = 24.1\%$$	30.0%	22.2%

You will recall that lululemon paid no dividends in 2010, so it has no payout ratio or dividend yield. Limited Brands' payout ratio and dividend yield are higher than that of its competitors in the industry.

It is not possible to compare earnings per share between companies, because of the differing capital structures. However, it is possible to compare the price-earnings ratios. Investors appear to favour lululemon much more than Limited Brands. This could be because of lululemon's rapid growth, or anticipated future performance. Limited Brands' price-earnings ratio is also below that of the industry, so it is not as well favoured by investors as other companies. This is interesting because Limited Brands' dividend yield is above that of the industry.

Both companies have a return on common shareholders' equity in excess of that of the industry. lululemon's return is significantly above that of both Limited Brands and the industry, which may be one of the factors driving its high price-earnings ratio.

Comprehensive Do It!

Rolman Corporation is authorized to issue an unlimited number of no par value common shares and 100,000 no par value $6 cumulative preferred shares. At January 1, 2012, it had the following selected opening balances: Preferred shares, nil; Common Shares, 300,000 issued, $1.8 million; Retained Earnings, $1,150,000; and Accumulated Other Comprehensive Income, $50,000.

During the year ended December 31, 2012, the company had the following share transactions:

Jan. 10   Issued 100,000 common shares at $8 per share.

July 1   Issued 20,000 preferred shares at $50 per share.

Sept. 1   Declared a 5% stock dividend to common shareholders of record on September 15, distributable September 30. The price of the common shares on September 1 was $10 per share. On September 15, the share price was $12 per share and on September 30, it was $11 per share.

Nov. 1   Reacquired 5,000 preferred shares at $40 per share.

Dec. 24   Declared an annual preferred cash dividend to shareholders of record on January 15, payable January 31.

     31   A loan agreement entered into on December 31 contains a restrictive covenant that limits the payment of future dividends to 15% of profit.

In addition, Rolman reported profit of $392,000 and other comprehensive income of $5,000 for the year.

Instructions

(a) Record the above transactions.

(b) Prepare the statement of changes in equity and the shareholders' equity section of the statement of financial position.

Action Plan

- Keep a running total of the number of shares issued to date.
- Apply the stock dividend percentage to the number of common shares issued. Multiply the new shares to be issued by the fair value of the shares.
- Record the reacquisition of shares at the average cost. Calculate the average cost per share by dividing the balance in the share account by the number of shares issued.
- Recall that the statement of changes in equity explains the changes for the period in the beginning and ending balances of each shareholders' equity account.
- The statement of financial position reports shareholders' equity at the end of the period. Disclose the share details in the shareholders' equity section of the statement of financial position.

(continued)

Solution to Comprehensive Do It!

(a)

Jan.	10	Cash (100,000 × $8)
		    Common Shares
		        (To record issue of 100,000 common shares)
			800,000	800,000

July	1	Cash (20,000 × $50)
		    Preferred Shares
		        (To record issue of 20,000 preferred shares)
			1,000,000	1,000,000

Sept.	1	Stock Dividends (300,000 + 100,000 = 400,000 × 5% =
		20,000 × $10)
		    Stock Dividends Distributable
		        (To record declaration of 5% stock dividend)
			200,000	200,000

	15	Record date—no entry required		

	30	Stock Dividends Distributable
		    Common Shares
		        (To record issue of 20,000 common shares in a 5% stock
		        dividend)
			200,000	200,000

Nov.	1	Preferred Shares (5,000 × $50)
		    Cash (5,000 × $40)
		    Contributed Capital—Reacquisition of Preferred Shares
		        (To record reacquisition of 5,000 preferred shares at an
		        average cost of $50 [$1,000,000 ÷ 20,000] per share)
			250,000	200,000
				50,000

Dec.	24	Cash Dividends (20,000 − 5,000 = 15,000 × $6)
		    Dividends Payable
		        (To record declaration of annual preferred cash
		        dividend)
			90,000	90,000

	31	No entry required—disclosure only		

(b)

ROLMAN CORPORATION
Statement of Changes in Equity
Year Ended December 31, 2012

	Preferred Shares		Common Shares				Accumulated	
	Number of Shares	Legal Capital	Number of Shares	Legal Capital	Additional Contributed Capital	Retained Earnings	Other Comprehensive Income	Total
Balance, Jan. 1			300,000	$1,800,000		$1,150,000	$50,000	$3,000,000
Issued common shares			100,000	800,000				800,000
Issued preferred shares	20,000	$1,000,000						1,000,000
Declared and issued stock dividend			20,000	200,000		(200,000)		0
Reacquired preferred shares	(5,000)	(250,000)			$50,000			(200,000)
Declared dividends						(90,000)		(90,000)
Comprehensive income								
Profit						392,000		392,000
Other comprehensive income							5,000	5,000
Balance, Dec. 31	15,000	$ 750,000	420,000	$2,800,000	$50,000	$1,252,000	$55,000	$4,907,000

ROLMAN CORPORATION
Statement of Financial Position (partial)
December 31, 2012

Shareholders' equity
  Contributed capital
    Share capital
      Preferred shares, 100,000 no par value $6 cumulative
        authorized, 15,000 shares issued $ 750,000
      Common shares, unlimited number of no par value shares
        authorized, 420,000 shares issued   2,800,000 $3,550,000
    Additional contributed capital
      Contributed capital—reacquisition of preferred shares   50,000
    Total contributed capital   3,600,000
  Retained earnings (Note x)   1,252,000
  Accumulated other comprehensive income   55,000
Total shareholders' equity $4,907,000

Note x: A loan agreement contains a restrictive covenant that limits the payment of future dividends to 15% of profit.

Self-Test, Brief Exercises, Exercises, Problems—Set A, and many more components are available for practice in WileyPLUS.

Self-Test Questions

Answers are at the end of the chapter.

(SO 1)   1. Saint Simeon Corporation has 100,000 common shares authorized and 75,000 common shares issued. How many more common shares can Saint Simeon sell?
    (a) 0
    (b) 25,000
    (c) 75,000
    (d) 100,000

(SO 2)   2. Which of the following statements is *false?*
    (a) Ownership of common shares gives the owner a voting right.
    (b) If a company's shares are sold by one shareholder to another, this transaction must be recorded by the company.
    (c) The authorization of share capital does not result in a transaction that is recorded by the company.
    (d) Legal capital cannot be distributed to shareholders.

(SO 2)   3. A company will buy back its own shares:
    (a) to force the share price up.
    (b) to force the share price down.
    (c) to increase the number of shares available for dividends.
    (d) to save cash.

(SO 3)   4. ABC Corporation issues 1,000 preferred shares at $12 per share. In recording the transaction, a credit of $12,000 is made to:
    (a) Investment in ABC Corporation
    (b) Preferred Shares
    (c) Accumulated Other Comprehensive Income
    (d) Contributed Capital—Reacquisition of Preferred Shares

(SO 3)   5. Flood Limited had 25,000 of preferred shares issued at $1,250,000 at the beginning of the year. It issued 10,000 preferred shares at $60 per share on July 1 and reacquired 5,000 preferred shares on December 31 for $55 per share. The December 31 reacquisition transaction would result in:
    (a) a debit to the Preferred Shares account for $264,286.
    (b) a debit to the Preferred Shares account for $275,000.
    (c) a credit to the Contributed Capital—Reacquisition of Preferred Shares account for $10,714.
    (d) a credit to the Cash account for $264,286.

(SO 4)   6. Entries for cash dividends are required on the:
    (a) declaration date and record date.
    (b) record date and payment date.

(c) declaration date, record date, and payment date.

(d) declaration date and payment date.

(SO 4)   7. Which of the following statements about stock dividends and stock splits is *true*?
(a) A stock dividend and stock split increase total shareholders' equity.
(b) A stock dividend and stock split decrease total shareholders' equity.
(c) A stock dividend and stock split have no effect on total shareholders' equity.
(d) A stock dividend and stock split have no effect on the number of common shares.

(SO 5)   8. Which of the following is *not* reported in a statement of changes in equity?
(a) Legal capital of common shares
(b) Fair value of common shares
(c) Dividends
(d) Accumulated other comprehensive income

(SO 6)   9. If a company's profit is $50,000, its total assets $1 million, its average common shareholders' equity $500,000, and its net sales $800,000, its return on common shareholders' equity is:
(a) 3.3%.
(b) 5.0%.
(c) 6.2%.
(d) 10.0%.

(SO 6)   10. For the year ended June 30, 2012, Dupuis Inc. reported profit of $90,000. It had 5,000 common shares issued since the beginning of the year, July 1, 2011, and 2,000 shares issued on January 1, 2012. In addition, it paid dividends of $3 per common share at the end of the year and had a share price of $60. It had no preferred shares. What were its earnings per share and dividend yield?
(a) $12.86 and 5%
(b) $12.86 and 23%
(c) $15 and 5%
(d) $15 and 20%

Questions

(SO 1)   1. Corporations can be classified by purpose (e.g., profit or not-for-profit) or by ownership (e.g., public or private). Explain the difference between each of these types of classifications.

(SO 1)   2. Pat Kabza, a student, asks for your help in understanding the different corporation characteristics. Explain the following characteristics to Pat and identify whether they are an advantage or a disadvantage of the corporate form of organization: (a) separate legal existence, (b) limited liability of shareholders, (c) transferable ownership rights, (d) ability to acquire capital, (e) continuous life, (f) separation of management and ownership, (g) government regulations, and (h) income taxation.

(SO 1)   3. Richard Boudreault purchased 100 lululemon athletica common shares for $18 a share from the company's initial public offering. A year later, Richard purchased 200 more lululemon shares for $30 each on the Toronto Stock Exchange. Explain the impact of each of these transactions on lululemon's (a) assets, (b) liabilities, and (c) shareholders' equity.

(SO 1)   4. What is legal capital? How is the value of the legal capital determined? Why is legal capital reported separately from retained earnings in the shareholders' equity section of the statement of financial position?

(SO 1)   5. The market capitalization of Plazacorp Retail Properties Limited was $146 million at the end of 2009 and $207 million at the end of 2010. Explain what "market capitalization" means and describe the effect of this increase in market capitalization between 2009 and 2010 on Plazacorp's assets, liabilities, and shareholders' equity.

(SO 1, 2) 6. Letson Corporation is authorized to issue 100,000 common shares. During its first two years of operation, Letson issued 60,000 shares and reacquired and retired 10,000 of these shares. (a) After these transactions, how many shares are authorized and issued? (b) Are both authorized and issued shares recorded in the general journal?

(SO 1, 3) 7. What are the basic ownership rights of common shareholders? How are they similar to, and different from, those of preferred shareholders?

(SO 2)   8. (a) Why would a company reacquire some of its own shares? (b) Under what circumstances can the reacquired shares be (1) retired, or (2) held as treasury shares?

(SO 2)   9. Explain how the accounting for the reacquisition of shares changes depending on whether the reacquisition price is greater or lower than average cost.

(SO 2)   10. Ciana Chiasson is confused. She says, "I don't understand why sometimes, when the price paid to reacquire shares is greater than their average cost, the 'loss on reacquisition' is debited to a contributed capital account. But at other times, it is debited to the Retained Earnings account. And sometimes it is even debited to both!" Help Ciana understand.

(SO 2, 3) 11. When common and preferred shares are issued for a consideration other than cash (e.g., goods or services), at what value should the shares be recorded for a publicly traded company following IFRS? Would your answer change if it were a private company following ASPE?

(SO 3)   12. The Royal Bank of Canada has a noncumulative class of preferred shares with a dividend rate of $1.125. Assad David owns 1,000 of these shares. If the Royal Bank declares and pays a dividend on these shares, how much dividend can Assad expect to receive each quarter?

(SO 3) 13. What is the difference between cumulative and noncumulative preferred shares? Can dividends in arrears arise for both types of preferred shares? Explain.

(SO 4) 14. What conditions must be met before a cash dividend is paid?

(SO 4) 15. Contrast the effects of the (a) declaration date, (b) record date, and (c) payment date for a cash dividend on a company's (1) assets, (2) liabilities, (3) share capital, (4) retained earnings, and (5) total shareholders' equity.

(SO 4) 16. Contrast the effects of a (a) cash dividend, (b) stock dividend, and (c) stock split on a company's (1) assets, (2) liabilities, (3) share capital, (4) retained earnings, (5) total shareholders' equity, and (6) number of shares.

(SO 4) 17. Bella Corporation has 10,000 common shares issued when it announces a 2-for-1 split. Before the split, the shares were trading for $140 per share. (a) After the split, how many shares will be issued? (b) After the split, what will be the approximate share price?

(SO 4) 18. Why are cash and stock dividends recorded in the general journal but stock splits are not?

(SO 4) 19. For what reasons might a company restrict its retained earnings? How are they reported in the financial statements?

(SO 5) 20. Indicate how each of the following should be reported in (a) the statement of changes in equity and (b) the shareholders' equity section of the statement of financial position: (1) common shares, (2) preferred shares, (3) stock dividends distributable, (4) contributed capital—reacquisition of shares, (5) retained earnings, (6) treasury shares, and (7) accumulated other comprehensive income.

(SO 5) 21. What is comprehensive income? Distinguish between other comprehensive income and accumulated other comprehensive income.

(SO 5) 22. What is the difference between a statement of changes in equity and statement of retained earnings? How do each of these relate to the shareholders' equity section of the statement of financial position?

(SO 5) 23. Distinguish between the content of the (a) shareholders' equity sections and (b) financial statements of a publicly traded company using IFRS and a private company using ASPE.

(SO 6) 24. Indicate whether each of the following is generally considered favourable or unfavourable by a potential investor:
(a) A decrease in the payout ratio
(b) An increase in the dividend yield
(c) A decrease in the return on common shareholders' equity
(d) An increase in earnings per share

(SO 6) 25. Coca-Cola recently reported dividends per share of U.S. $1.76 and a dividend yield of 2.7%. Pepsi reported dividends per share of U.S. $1.92 and a dividend yield of 2.9% for the same period. Which company had the higher share price?

(SO 6) 26. In the calculation of earnings per share, why is the weighted average number of common shares used instead of the number of common shares at the end of the year?

(SO 6) 27. Why do the earnings per share and return on common shareholders' equity ratios use profit available to common shareholders in their numerator rather than profit?

(SO 6) 28. Company A has a price-earnings ratio of 10 times and a payout ratio of 4%. Company B has a price-earnings ratio of 40 times and a payout ratio of 0%. (a) Which company's shares would be of more interest to an investor wanting a steady dividend income? (b) Which company's shares would be of more interest to an investor wanting to sell her shares for a profit?

Brief Exercises

BE11–1 In July 2010, the Agricultural Bank (AgBank) of China Limited issued an IPO of 172 billion HKD (Hong Kong dollars) on the Shanghai and Hong Kong stock markets that set the record for the world's largest IPO to date. Shares purchased under the IPO were sold at 3.20 HKD per share. If a shareholder were to purchase AgBank's shares at the end of 2010, they would pay 3.83 HKD per share. Explain the impact of the shares sold (a) under the IPO in July 2010 for 3.20 HKD and (b) on the Hong Kong stock market in December 2010 for 3.83 HKD on AgBank's financial position. *Evaluate impact of share issue. (SO 1)*

BE11–2 On May 1, Armada Corporation incorporated and authorized 100,000 preferred shares and an unlimited number of common shares. On May 2, Armada issued 1,000 common shares for $15 per share. On June 15, it issued an additional 500 common shares for $17 per share. On November 1, Armada issued 100 preferred shares for $30 per share. On December 15, it issued an additional 100 preferred shares for $35 per share. (a) Record the share transactions. (b) What is the average cost (rounded to the nearest cent) of each of the common and preferred shares? *Record issue of shares. (SO 2, 3)*

BE11–3 On June 12, Dieppe Corporation commenced operations and issued 60,000 common shares for $300,000. On July 11, it issued an additional 15,000 common shares for $90,000. On November 28, it reacquired and retired 25,000 shares. Record the share transactions assuming the company paid (a) $125,000 to reacquire the shares, and (b) $135,000 to reacquire the shares. *Record issue and reacquisition of shares. (SO 2)*

Discuss share reacquisition.
(SO 2)

BE11–4   The TD Bank reacquired 30.6 million of its own common shares for $2,158 million in fiscal 2010 and held them as treasury shares until they were later resold. (a) What are some of the likely reasons the TD Bank reacquired its own shares? (b) How would the TD Bank report any treasury shares in the shareholders' equity section of its statement of financial position at year end? (c) Would your answer in (b) change if the TD Bank had reacquired and retired the shares instead of holding them in its treasury? Explain.

Record issue of shares for cash and noncash.
(SO 2, 3)

BE11–5   On March 8, Daschen Inc., a publicly traded company, issued 5,000 preferred shares for cash of $30 per share. On April 20, when the shares were trading at $35, the company issued an additional 3,000 preferred shares in exchange for land with a fair value of $110,000. (a) Prepare the journal entries for each transaction. (b) Would your answer change if you were unable to determine the land's fair value on April 20?

Determine dividends in arrears.
(SO 3)

BE11–6   Canaan Limited had 20,000 $2 cumulative preferred shares issued. It was unable to pay any dividend to the preferred shareholders in the current year. (a) What are the dividends in arrears? (b) How would the dividends in arrears be reported in the financial statements? (c) Would your answer to (a) change if the preferred shares were noncumulative rather than cumulative?

Record cash dividend.
(SO 4)

BE11–7   The Seabee Corporation has 30,000 $2 noncumulative preferred shares. It declares a quarterly cash dividend on November 15 to shareholders of record on December 10. The dividend is paid on December 31. Prepare the entries on the appropriate dates to record the cash dividend.

Record stock dividend.
(SO 4)

BE11–8   Satina Corporation has 100,000 common shares. It declares a 5% stock dividend on December 1 to shareholders of record on December 20. The shares are issued on January 10. The share price is $15 on December 1, $14.50 on December 20, and $14.75 on January 10. Prepare the entries on the appropriate dates to record the stock dividend.

Analyze impact of stock split.
(SO 4)

BE11–9   In May 2010, Canadian Natural Resources Limited, one of Canada's largest natural gas producers, completed a 2-for-1 stock split. Immediately before the split, Canadian Natural had 542,327,000 common shares trading at $70.78 per share. (a) How many shares did it have after the stock split? (b) What was the most likely price of the shares after the stock split? (c) How would Canadian Natural record this stock split?

Compare cash dividend, stock dividend, and stock split.
(SO 4)

BE11–10   Indicate whether each of the following transactions would increase (+), decrease (−), or have no effect (NE) on total assets, total liabilities, total shareholders' equity, and the number of shares:

	Assets	Liabilities	Shareholders' Equity	Number of Shares
(a) Declared cash dividend.				
(b) Paid cash dividend declared in (a).				
(c) Declared stock dividend.				
(d) Distributed stock dividend declared in (c).				
(e) Split stock 2-for-1.				

Determine missing amounts in statement of changes in equity.
(SO 5)

BE11–11   Canning Corporation reported the following statement of changes in equity accounts for the year ended December 31, 2012.

CANNING CORPORATION
Statement of Changes in Equity
Year Ended December 31, 2012

	Common Shares		Additional Contributed Capital	Retained Earnings	Accumulated Other Comprehensive Income	Total
	Number of Shares	Legal Capital				
Bal., Jan. 1	500,000	$1,500,000	$500,000	$3,000,000	$100,000	$5,100,000
Issued common shares	40,000	[2]				440,000
Declared and issued stock dividend	10,000	110,000		[5]		[7]
Reacquired and retired common shares	[1]	(74,600)	$[3]			(200,000)
Declared dividends				(135,000)		(135,000)
Comprehensive income						
Profit				750,000		[8]
Other comprehensive income					[6]	25,000
Bal., Dec. 31	530,000	$1,975,400	$[4]	$3,505,000	$125,000	$5,980,000

Determine the missing amounts [1] to [8].

BE11–12 Refer to the data given in BE11–11 for Canning Corporation. Canning had an unlimited number of no par value common shares authorized. Prepare the shareholders' equity section of its statement of financial position at December 31, 2012.

Prepare shareholders' equity section.
(SO 5)

BE11–13 For the year ended December 31, 2012, Stirling Farms Limited, a private company, reported a profit of $150,000. The company declared dividends of $90,000 and paid $80,000 of these dividends during the year. (a) Prepare a statement of retained earnings for the year, assuming the balance in Retained Earnings on January 1, 2012, was $490,000. (b) How might this statement change if Stirling Farms were a publicly traded company?

Prepare statement of retained earnings.
(SO 5)

BE11–14 Paul Schwartz, president of Schwartz Corporation, believes that it is good practice to maintain a constant payout of dividends relative to profit. Last year, profit was $600,000, and the company paid $60,000 in dividends. This year, due to some unusual circumstances, the company had a profit of $2 million. Paul expects next year's profit to be about $700,000. What was Schwartz's payout ratio last year? If it is to maintain the same payout ratio, what amount of dividends would it pay this year? Is this a good idea? In other words, what are the pros and cons of maintaining a constant payout ratio?

Evaluate payout ratio.
(SO 6)

BE11–15 Messier Inc. has 34,000 common shares on January 1, 2012. On July 1, 8,000 shares were reacquired and retired. On August 31 and November 30, 9,000 and 6,000 shares were issued, respectively. Calculate (a) the number of common shares issued at December 31, 2012, and (b) the weighted average number of common shares for 2012.

Calculate weighted average number of shares.
(SO 6)

BE11–16 Refer to the data for Messier Inc. given in BE11–15. Messier reported a profit of $370,000. Messier also had 10,000 $2 cumulative preferred shares, on which the dividend for the current year was declared and paid. Calculate the earnings per share.

Calculate earnings per share.
(SO 6)

BE11–17 Salliq Ltd. reported the following selected information for the year ended January 31, 2012: profit, $14,000; beginning shareholders' equity, $104,000; and ending shareholders' equity, $122,000. Salliq has no preferred shares. (a) Calculate the return on common shareholders' equity. (b) Explain how your calculation in (a) would change if Salliq had preferred shares and had paid the preferred shareholders a dividend.

Calculate return on common shareholders' equity.
(SO 6)

Exercises

E11–1 The following is a recent stock market listing for Bombardier Inc. Class B (common) shares:

Interpret stock market listing.
(SO 1)

365-day		stock	sym	div	high	low	close	chg	vol (000)	yld	p/e ratio
high	low										
6.24	4.25	Bombardier	BBD.B	0.10	4.82	4.79	4.81	−0.01	347,197	2.10	13.74

Instructions
(a) What is the highest price Bombardier's shares traded for during the year? The lowest?
(b) What is the annual per share dividend paid on these shares?
(c) If you had purchased 1,000 common shares at Bombardier's closing price of the day in the above listing, what would be the total cost of your share purchase?
(d) What was the closing price of Bombardier's common shares on the previous day?
(e) How many Bombardier common shares were sold on the trading day of the listing?
(f) What would be your likely motivation for purchasing these shares—dividend income or capital appreciation? Explain.

E11–2 Santiago Corp., a publicly traded company, had 2,500 preferred shares issued with a balance of $55,000 and 140,000 common shares issued with a balance of $700,000 at the beginning of the year. The following share transactions occurred during the year:

Record issue of shares.
(SO 2, 3)

June 12   Issued 50,000 common shares for $5 per share.
July 11   Issued 1,000 preferred shares for $25 per share.
Oct.   1   Issued 10,000 common shares in exchange for land. The common shares were trading for $6 per share on that date. The fair value of the land was estimated to be $65,000.
Nov. 15   Issued 1,500 preferred shares for $30 per share.

Instructions
(a) Record the above transactions.
(b) Calculate the average cost (rounded to the nearest cent) for each of the preferred and common shares.

Record reacquisition of shares.
(SO 2)

E11–3   Enviro Corporation reported having 35,000 common shares issued for a total share capital of $140,000 on its December 31, 2011, statement of financial position. On February 15, 2012, it reacquired 5,000 of these shares. This is the first time Enviro has reacquired any of its shares.

Instructions
(a) Record the reacquisition of the shares, assuming the company paid $18,000 to reacquire them.
(b) Repeat part (a), assuming instead that the company paid $21,500 to reacquire the shares.

Record issue and reacquisition of shares.
(SO 2, 3)

E11–4   Moosonee Ltd. was incorporated on January 5, 2012, and is authorized to issue an unlimited number of preferred and common shares. The company had the following share transactions in its first month of operations:

Jan.	6	Issued 200,000 common shares for $1.50 per share.
	12	Issued 50,000 common shares for $1.75 per share.
	17	Issued 10,000 preferred shares for $25 per share.
	18	Issued 500,000 common shares for $2 per share.
	24	Reacquired 200,000 common shares for $1.90 per share.
	27	Reacquired 5,000 preferred shares for $22 per share.

Instructions
(a) Record the above transactions.
(b) What is the number of preferred shares remaining, and their average cost, at the end of January?
(c) What is the number of common shares remaining, and their average cost, at the end of January?

Determine dividends in arrears.
(SO 3)

E11–5   Marsh Corporation issued 400,000 $1 cumulative preferred shares. In its first year of operations, it paid $300,000 of dividends to its preferred shareholders. In its second year, the company paid dividends of $500,000 to its preferred shareholders.

Instructions
(a) What is the total annual preferred dividend supposed to be for the preferred shareholders?
(b) Calculate any dividends in arrears in years 1 and 2.
(c) Explain how dividends in arrears should be reported in the financial statements.
(d) If the preferred shares were noncumulative rather than cumulative, how much dividend would the company have been obligated to pay its preferred shareholders in each year?

Record and post share and dividend transactions.
(SO 2, 4)

E11–6   On January 1, Tarow Corporation had 80,000 common shares, recorded at $600,000, and retained earnings of $1,000,000. During the year, the following transactions occurred:

Apr.	1	Issued 5,000 common shares at $10 per share.
June	15	Declared a cash dividend of $0.25 per share to common shareholders of record on June 30, payable on July 10.
Aug.	21	Declared a 5% stock dividend to common shareholders of record on September 5, distributable on September 20. The shares were trading for $12 a share on August 21.
Nov.	1	Issued 3,000 common shares at $12 per share.
Dec.	20	Reacquired 10,000 common shares for $11 per share. This was the first time Tarow had reacquired its own shares. Round the average cost to the nearest cent.

Instructions
(a) Record the above transactions.
(b) Open T accounts and post to the shareholder equity accounts journalized in (a).

Compare cash dividend, stock dividend, and stock split.
(SO 4)

E11–7   Laine Inc. is considering one of three following courses of action: (1) paying a $0.50 cash dividend, (2) distributing a 5% stock dividend, or (3) effecting a 2-for-1 stock split. The current share price is $14 per share.

Instructions
Help Laine make its decision by completing the following chart (treat each possibility independently):

	Before Action	After Cash Dividend	After Stock Dividend	After Stock Split
Total assets	$1,250,000			
Total liabilities	$ 250,000			
Shareholders' equity				
Common shares	600,000			
Retained earnings	400,000			
Total shareholders' equity	1,000,000			
Total liabilities and shareholders' equity	$1,250,000			
Number of common shares	100,000			

E11-8 Before preparing financial statements for the current year, the auditors for Koo Ltd. discovered the following possible errors in the accounts:

1. Koo has 10,000 $5 noncumulative preferred shares issued. Because of a cash shortage late in the year, it did not declare the last quarter's dividend for the year. The accountant debited Cash Dividends and credited Dividends Payable for the liability owed to the preferred shareholders.
2. A 5% common stock dividend (1,000 shares) was declared when the shares were trading for $5. To record the declaration, the account Long-Term Investments was debited and Dividends Payable was credited for the fair value of the shares. The shares have not yet been distributed.
3. A 3-for-1 stock split involving the issue of 200,000 new common shares (for a total of 300,000 common shares) was recorded as a debit to Stock Splits and a credit to Common Shares for the fair value of the shares. The shares were trading for $5 on the date of the split.

Instructions
Prepare any correcting entries that are required.

E11-9 The general ledger of Val d'Or Corporation contains the following selected accounts and information:

1. Cash	6. Retained earnings
2. Common shares	7. Contributed capital—reacquisition of common shares
3. Revaluation gain from revaluing property, plant, and equipment to fair value	8. Cash dividend
4. Long-term investments	9. Treasury shares
5. Preferred shares	10. Common stock dividend distributable

Instructions
Using the table headings below, indicate whether or not each of the above accounts should be reported in the statement of changes in equity. If yes, indicate whether the account should be reported in the share capital, additional contributed capital, retained earnings, accumulated other comprehensive income, or another section of the statement. If not, indicate in which financial statement (statement of financial position or income statement) and in which section the account should be reported. The first account has been done for you as an example.

		Statement of Changes in Equity					
Account	Share Capital	Additional Contributed Capital	Retained Earnings	Accumulated Other Comprehensive Income	Other	Financial Statement	Classification
1. Cash						Statement of financial position	Current assets

E11-10 The following accounts appear in the ledger of Ozabal Inc. after the books are closed at December 31, 2012:

Accumulated other comprehensive loss	$ 50,000
Common shares (no par value, unlimited number of shares authorized, 250,000 shares issued)	500,000
Common stock dividends distributable	50,000
Contributed capital—reacquisition of common shares	25,000
Preferred shares ($1.25 noncumulative, no par value, 100,000 shares authorized, 10,000 shares issued)	250,000
Retained earnings	900,000

Instructions
Prepare the shareholders' equity section of Ozabal's statement of financial position, assuming $100,000 of retained earnings is restricted for a plant expansion.

E11-11 The Blue Canoe Limited reported the following changes to its shareholders' equity accounts for the year ended December 31, 2012.

Accumulated other comprehensive income:		Retained earnings:	
Balance, Jan. 1	$ 40,000	Balance, Jan. 1	$ 1,500,000
Balance, Dec. 31	65,000	Balance, Dec. 31	1,830,000
Foreign currency		Profit	400,000
translation gain	25,000	Dividends	(70,000)
Other contributed capital:		Share capital:	
Balance, Jan. 1	540,000	Balance, Jan. 1 (32,000)	800,000
Balance, Dec. 31	485,000	Balance, Dec. 31 (33,000)	955,000
Reacquisition of shares	(55,000)	Reacquisition and retirement of shares (1,000)	(25,000)
		Shares issued (2,000)	180,000

Instructions

(a) Prepare a statement of shareholders' equity for the year.

(b) Prepare the shareholders' equity section of the balance sheet at December 31.

Prepare statement
of retained earnings.
(SO 5)

E11–12 Sobeys Inc. is a private company. It reported beginning retained earnings at May 2, 2009, of $1,068.2 million. During the year ended May 1, 2010, it reported a profit of $262.8 million and declared and paid dividends on its common shares of $58 million.

Instructions

(a) Prepare a statement of retained earnings for the year ended May 1, 2010.

(b) If Sobeys were a publicly traded company, would it still have to prepare a statement of retained earnings? Explain.

Calculate and
evaluate ratios.
(SO 6)

E11–13 The following selected information is available for two competitors, Nike, Inc. and Adidas AG:

	Nike (in U.S. $)	Adidas (in EUR)
Share price	$86.05	€49.46
Dividends per share	1.24	0.35
Earnings per share	4.15	1.25

Instructions

(a) Calculate the payout, dividend yield, and price-earnings ratios for each company.

(b) Which company would investors favour for dividend income purposes? For capital appreciation purposes?

Calculate earnings
per share.
(SO 6)

E11–14 Chinook Corporation started the year ended November 30, 2012, with 60,000 common shares and no preferred shares issued. The following changes in share capital occurred during the year:

Feb.	28	Issued 15,000 common shares for $225,000.
May	31	Reacquired and retired 5,000 common shares for $90,000.
Sept.	1	Issued 20,000 $1 cumulative preferred shares for $500,000.
Nov.	1	Issued 6,000 common shares in exchange for land. The shares were trading for $20 on this date and the fair value of the land was $115,000.
	30	Reported profit of $351,250.
	30	Declared the quarterly cash dividend to the preferred shareholders of record on December 16, payable on December 31.

Instructions

(a) Calculate the profit available for the common shareholders.

(b) Calculate the weighted average number of common shares for the year.

(c) Calculate the earnings per share for the year.

(d) Why is it necessary to calculate a weighted average number of shares? Why not use the number of shares at the end of the year?

Calculate and
evaluate ratios.
(SO 6)

E11–15 Selected financial information (in millions, except per share information) is available for CIBC at October 31:

	2010	2009	2008
Total cash dividends paid to common shareholders	$1,350	$1,328	$1,285
Cash dividends per common share	$3.48	$3.48	$3.48
Profit (loss) available to common shareholders	$2,114	$850	$(2,298)
Common shareholders' equity	$12,634	$11,119	$11,200
Market price per common share	$78.23	$62.00	$54.66
Weighted average number of common shares	388	382	370

Instructions

Calculate the dividend yield, payout, earnings per share, and return on common shareholders' equity ratios for the common shareholders for 2010 and 2009. Comment on your findings.

Problems: Set A

Record and post
equity transactions;
prepare shareholders'
equity section.
(SO 2, 3, 4, 5)

P11–1A Remmers Corporation, a publicly traded company, was organized on January 1, 2012. It is authorized to issue an unlimited number of no par value $3 noncumulative preferred shares and an unlimited number of no par value common shares. The following share transactions were completed during the company's first year of operations:

Jan.	10	Issued 100,000 common shares for $2 per share.
Mar.	1	Issued 10,000 preferred shares for $52 per share.

May 1 Issued 75,000 common shares for $3 per share.

July 24 Issued 16,800 common shares for $60,000 cash and used equipment. The equipment originally cost $15,000. It now has a carrying amount of $7,500 and a fair value of $8,000. The common shares were trading for $4 per share on this date.

Sept. 1 Issued 5,000 common shares for $5 per share.

Nov. 1 Issued 2,000 preferred shares for $55 per share.

Dec. 15 Declared a $36,000 dividend to the preferred shareholders, to shareholders of record on December 31, payable on January 10.

31 Reported profit of $650,000 for the year.

Instructions
(a) Record the above transactions for 2012, including any required closing entries.
(b) Open T accounts and post to the shareholders' equity accounts.
(c) Prepare the shareholders' equity section of the statement of financial position at December 31.

P11–2A The following shareholders' equity accounts are reported by Talty Inc. on January 1, 2012:

Common shares (500,000 issued)	$4,000,000
Preferred shares ($6 cumulative, 9,000 issued)	600,000
Contributed capital—reacquisition of preferred shares	2,000
Retained earnings	1,958,000
Accumulated other comprehensive income	25,000

Show impact of trans-
actions on accounts.
(SO 2, 3, 4, 5)

The following selected transactions, given in chronological order, occurred during the year:

1. Issued 10,000 common shares for $12 per share.
2. Issued 5,000 common shares in exchange for equipment. The fair value of the shares was $12 per share. The fair value of the equipment could not be reliably determined.
3. Issued 1,000 preferred shares for $60 per share.
4. Reacquired and retired 500 preferred shares for $50 each.
5. The annual preferred share dividend was declared and paid during the year.
6. Determined that the company had an other comprehensive loss of $5,000 from the revaluation of land.

Instructions
For each of the above transactions, indicate its impact on the items in the table that follows. Indicate if the item will increase (+) or decrease (−), and by how much, or if it will not be affected (n/a). The first transaction has been done for you as an example.

					Shareholders' Equity		
							Accumulated
					Additional		Other
			Preferred	Common	Contributed	Retained	Comprehensive
	Assets	Liabilities	Shares	Shares	Capital	Earnings	Income
1.	+$120,000	n/a	n/a	+$120,000	n/a	n/a	n/a

P11–3A Largent Corporation, a publicly traded company, is authorized to issue 200,000 no par value $4 cumulative preferred shares and an unlimited number of no par value common shares. On January 1, 2012, the general ledger contained the following shareholders' equity accounts:

Record and post
equity transactions;
prepare statements.
(SO 2, 3, 4, 5)

Preferred shares (8,000 shares issued)	$ 440,000
Common shares (70,000 shares issued)	1,050,000
Contributed capital—reacquisition of preferred shares	25,000
Retained earnings	800,000
Accumulated other comprehensive income	10,000

The following equity transactions occurred in 2012:

Jan. 10 Reacquired and retired 10,000 common shares for $240,000.

Feb. 6 Issued 10,000 preferred shares for $600,000.

Apr. 6 Issued 20,000 common shares for $560,000.

May 29 Declared a semi-annual dividend to the preferred shareholders of record at June 12, payable July 1.

Aug. 22 Issued 5,000 common shares in exchange for a building. At the time of the exchange, the building was valued at $165,000 and the common shares at $150,000.

Dec. 15 The board decided there were insufficient funds to declare the semi-annual dividend to the preferred shareholders.

31 Profit for the year was $582,000.

Instructions

(a) Record the above transactions, including any required closing entries.
(b) Open T accounts and post to the shareholders' equity accounts.
(c) Prepare the statement of changes in equity for the year.
(d) Prepare the shareholders' equity section of the statement of financial position at December 31, including any required note disclosure.

Record and post equity transactions; prepare statements under ASPE.
(SO 2, 3, 4, 5)

P11–4A   On January 1, 2012, Conway Ltd., a private company, had the following shareholders' equity accounts:

Preferred shares, $5 noncumulative, no par value, unlimited number authorized, none issued	
Common shares, no par value, unlimited number authorized, 1.5 million issued	$1,500,000
Retained earnings	1,900,000

The following selected transactions occurred during 2012:

Jan.	2	Issued 100,000 preferred shares at $100 per share.
Feb.	8	Issued 50,000 common shares in exchange for land. On this date, the value of the land was $105,000. The common shares have not recently traded but the last time they were issued, they were sold for $2 per share.
Mar.	5	Declared the quarterly cash dividend to preferred shareholders of record on March 20, payable April 1.
Apr.	18	Issued 200,000 common shares at $2.50 per share.
June	5	Declared the quarterly cash dividend to preferred shareholders of record on June 20, payable July 1.
Sept.	5	Declared the quarterly cash dividend to preferred shareholders of record on September 20, payable October 1.
Dec.	5	Declared the quarterly cash dividend to preferred shareholders of record on December 20, payable January 1.
	14	Declared a cash dividend of $0.50 per share to the common shareholders of record on December 29, payable January 10.
	31	Profit for the year was $1.6 million.

Instructions

(a) Record the above transactions for 2012, including any required closing entries.
(b) Open T accounts and post to the shareholders' equity accounts.
(c) Prepare a statement of retained earnings for the year.
(d) Prepare the shareholders' equity section of the statement of financial position at December 31.
(e) Conway is a private company following ASPE. If it followed IFRS instead, how might your answers in (a) through (d) change?

Reproduce equity accounts; prepare shareholders' equity section.
(SO 2, 3, 4, 5)

P11–5A   The general ledger of Robichaud Corporation, a publicly traded company, contained the following shareholders' equity accounts in 2012:

	January 1	December 31
Preferred shares (10,000 and 20,000 shares issued, respectively)	$ 500,000	$1,000,000
Common shares (320,000 and 370,000 shares issued, respectively)	2,700,000	3,700,000
Common stock dividends distributable	0	407,000
Retained earnings	2,980,000	3,345,000

A review of the accounting records for the year ended December 31, 2012, reveals the following information:

1. On January 1, 10,000 no par value $5 noncumulative preferred shares were issued for $50 each. An unlimited number are authorized.
2. On October 1, 50,000 no par value common shares were sold for cash at $20 per share. An unlimited number are authorized.
3. The annual preferred shareholders' dividend was declared and paid in cash in 2012.
4. On December 31, a 5% common stock dividend was declared on common shares when the share price was $22. The stock dividend is distributable on January 20.
5. Profit for the year was $872,000.
6. On December 31, the board of directors authorized a $500,000 restriction on retained earnings for a plant expansion.

Instructions

(a) Reproduce the Preferred Shares, Common Shares, Common Stock Dividends Distributable, and Retained Earnings general ledger accounts for the year.
(b) Prepare the shareholders' equity section of the statement of financial position at December 31, including any required note disclosure.

P11-6A The condensed statement of financial position of Laporte Corporation reports the following amounts:

Compare impact of cash dividend, stock dividend, and stock split. (SO 4)

LAPORTE CORPORATION
Statement of Financial Position (partial)
June 30, 2012

Total assets		$16,000,000
Total liabilities		$ 6,000,000
Shareholders' equity		
Common shares, no par value, unlimited number authorized, 400,000 issued	$2,000,000	
Retained earnings	8,000,000	10,000,000
Total liabilities and shareholders' equity		$16,000,000

The common shares are currently trading for $30 per share. Laporte wants to assess the impact of three possible alternatives:

1. Payment of a $1.50 per share cash dividend
2. Distribution of a 5% stock dividend
3. A 3-for-2 stock split

Instructions
(a) Determine the impact of each alternative on (1) assets, (2) liabilities, (3) common shares, (4) retained earnings, (5) total shareholders' equity, and (6) the number of shares.
(b) Identify the advantages and disadvantages of each alternative for the company.

P11-7A Cameco Corporation reported the following changes to its shareholders' equity accounts (in thousands) for the year ended December 31, 2010:

Prepare statements. (SO 5)

Accumulated other comprehensive		Retained earnings:	
income (loss):		Balance, Jan. 1	$3,158,506
Balance, Jan. 1	$ 41,284	Balance, Dec. 31	3,563,089
Balance, Dec. 31	(24,995)	Profit	514,749
Other comprehensive loss	(66,279)	Dividends	110,166
Other contributed capital:		Share capital:	
Balance, Jan. 1	131,577	Balance, Jan. 1 (392,839)	1,512,461
Balance, Dec. 31	142,376	Balance, Dec. 31 (394,351)	1,535,857
Other	10,799	Shares issued (1,512)	23,396

Additional information:
Cameco has an unlimited number of common shares authorized. The number of shares issued is shown in parentheses in the share capital section of the above table, and is also in thousands.

Instructions
(a) Prepare a statement of changes in equity for the year ended December 31, 2010.
(b) Prepare the shareholders' equity section of the statement of financial position at December 31, 2010.

P11-8A On January 1, 2012, Wirth Corporation, a publicly traded company, had these shareholders' equity accounts:

Record and post dividend transactions; prepare statements. (SO 4, 5)

Common shares (no par value, unlimited number of shares authorized, 110,000 shares issued)	$1,100,000
Retained earnings	540,000
Accumulated other comprehensive income	60,000

During the year, the following transactions occurred:

Jan. 15 Declared a $1 per share cash dividend to shareholders of record on January 31, payable February 15.

Apr. 15 Declared a 10% stock dividend to shareholders of record on April 30, distributable May 15. On April 15, April 30, and May 15, the share prices were $15, $13.50, and $14, respectively.

Oct. 1 Effected a 2-for-1 stock split. On October 1, the share price was $20.

Dec. 31 Determined that profit for the year was $350,000.

Instructions

(a) Record the above transactions, including any required closing entries.
(b) Open T accounts as required and post to the shareholders' equity accounts.
(c) Prepare a statement of changes in equity for the year.
(d) Prepare the shareholders' equity section of the statement of financial position at December 31.

Calculate earnings
per share.
(SO 6)

P11–9A Gualtieri Inc.'s shareholders' equity accounts were as follows at the beginning of the current fiscal year, August 1, 2011:

$5 noncumulative preferred shares (25,000 shares issued)	$2,500,000
Common shares (350,000 shares issued)	3,750,000
Retained earnings	2,250,000
Total shareholders' equity	$8,500,000

During the year, the following selected transactions occurred:

Dec.	1	Issued 60,000 common shares for $20 per share.
Feb.	1	Reacquired and retired 10,000 common shares for $21 per share.
June	20	Declared the annual preferred dividend to shareholders of record on July 10, payable on July 31.
July	31	Profit for the year ended July 31, 2012, was $1,280,000.

Instructions

(a) Calculate the weighted average number of common shares for the year.
(b) Calculate the earnings per share.
(c) Why is it important to use a weighted average number of shares in the calculation of earnings per share? Why not just use the number of shares issued at year end?

Evaluate ratios.
(SO 6)

P11–10A The following summary of the earnings per share (in U.S. $), price-earnings (P-E), payout, and dividend yield ratios is available for five years ended December 31 for Barrick Gold Corporation:

	Earnings per Share	P-E Ratio	Payout Ratio	Dividend Yield
2006	$1.44	21.1 times	13%	0.7%
2007	1.29	26.8	23	0.9
2008	0.90	39.6	44	1.1
2009	(4.73)	n/a	(9)	1.1
2010	3.32	16.0	13	0.9

Instructions

(a) What are some possible reasons that Barrick Gold's dividend payout ratio improved from 23% in 2007 to 44% in 2008 while its dividend yield ratio changed very little from 0.9% in 2007 to 1.1% in 2008?
(b) Why do you think Barrick Gold's price-earnings ratio was higher in 2008 than in 2007 even though its earnings per share was lower?
(c) If you were an investor looking for dividend income, would you be happy with Barrick Gold's dividend policy? Explain.
(d) If you were one of Barrick Gold's creditors, what would you think about the company continuing to pay dividends (e.g., in 2009) regardless of whether it reports profit or a loss? Explain.

Calculate and
evaluate ratios.
(SO 6)

P11–11A The following selected information (in millions, except for per share information) is available for the National Bank of Canada for the year ended October 31:

	2010	2009
Weighted average number of common shares	162.1	160.3
Profit available to common shareholders	$971	$795
Common cash dividends per share	2.48	2.48
Total common cash dividends	402	398
Average common shareholders' equity	5,754	5,062
Market price per common share	67.13	60.13
Industry averages were as follows:		
Payout ratio	11.8%	n/a
Dividend yield	3.8%	4.9%
Earnings per share	n/a	n/a
Price-earnings ratio	12.0 times	12.8 times
Return on common shareholders' equity	15.5%	12.0%

Instructions

(a) Calculate the following ratios for the common shareholders for each fiscal year:
   1. Payout ratio
   2. Dividend yield
   3. Earnings per share
   4. Price-earnings ratio
   5. Return on common shareholders' equity
(b) Comment on the above ratios for 2010 in comparison with the prior year, and in comparison with the industry.

P11–12A Selected ratios for two companies operating in the petroleum industry follow, along with the industry averages:

Evaluate profitability ratios.
(SO 6)

Ratio	Petro-Boost	World Oil	Industry Average
Profit margin	10.0%	8.4%	5.7%
Return on common shareholders' equity	15.1%	29.6%	18.1%
Return on assets	11.0%	12.6%	6.3%
Asset turnover	1.1 times	1.5 times	1.1 times
Earnings per share	$4.06	$4.38	n/a
Price-earnings ratio	14.2 times	17.1 times	11.8 times
Payout ratio	12.3%	9.9%	17.0%
Dividend yield	1.9%	0.7%	n/a

Instructions

(a) Compare the profitability of Petro-Boost with that of World Oil, and with the industry average. Which company is more profitable? Explain.
(b) You would like to invest in the shares of one of the two companies. Your goal is to have regular income from your investment that will help pay your tuition fees for the next few years. Which of the companies is a better choice for you? Explain.
(c) Assume that instead of looking for regular income, you are looking for growth in the share value so that you can resell the shares at a gain in the future. Now which of the two companies is better for you? Explain.

Problems: Set B

P11–1B Wetland Corporation, a publicly traded company, was organized on June 1, 2011. It is authorized to issue an unlimited number of no par value $4 cumulative preferred shares and an unlimited number of no par value common shares. The following share transactions were completed during the company's first year of operations:

Record and post equity transactions; prepare shareholders' equity section.
(SO 2, 3, 4, 5)

June	5	Issued 80,000 common shares for $4 per share.
Aug.	21	Issued 5,000 preferred shares for $55 per share.
Sept.	15	Issued 22,000 common shares in exchange for land. The asking price of the land was $100,000 and the fair value was $95,000. The common shares were trading for $4.25 per share on this date.
Nov.	20	Issued 78,000 common shares for $4.50 per share.
Jan.	12	Reacquired and retired 80,000 common shares for $4 per share. (Round the average cost per share to the nearest cent).
Mar.	9	Issued 10,000 common shares for $5 per share.
Apr.	16	Issued 2,000 preferred shares for $60 per share.
May	15	Declared the annual preferred dividend to the preferred shareholders, to shareholders of record on May 30, payable on June 10.
	31	Reported profit of $250,000 for the year.

Instructions

(a) Record the above transactions for the year ended May 31, 2012, including any required closing entries.
(b) Open T accounts and post to the shareholders' equity accounts.
(c) Prepare the shareholders' equity section of the statement of financial position at May 31, 2012.

P11–2B The following shareholders' equity accounts are reported by Branch Inc. on January 1, 2012:

Show impact of transactions on accounts.
(SO 2, 3, 4, 5)

Common shares (150,000 issued)	$2,400,000
Preferred shares ($4 noncumulative, 5,000 issued)	350,000
Contributed capital—reacquisition of common shares	50,000
Retained earnings	1,276,000
Accumulated other comprehensive income	15,000

The following selected transactions, given in chronological order, occurred during the year:

1. Issued 10,000 common shares for $25 per share.
2. Issued 100 preferred shares for $75 per share.
3. Reacquired and retired 25,000 common shares for $24 per share. (Round the average cost per share to the nearest cent.)
4. Issued 1,000 common shares in exchange for land. The fair value of the shares was $25 per share. The fair value of the land was not able to be reliably determined.
5. Declared and paid the preferred shareholders a $2 per share dividend.
6. Determined that the company had other comprehensive income of $5,000 from the revaluation of land.

Instructions

For each of the above transactions, indicate its impact on the items in the table below. Indicate if the item will increase (+) or decrease (−), and by how much, or if it will not be affected (n/a). The first transaction has been done for you as an example.

			Shareholders' Equity				
	Assets	Liabilities	Preferred Shares	Common Shares	Additional Contributed Capital	Retained Earnings	Accumulated Other Comprehensive Income
1.	+$250,000	n/a	n/a	+$250,000	n/a	n/a	n/a

Record and post equity transactions; prepare statements. (SO 2, 3, 4, 5)

P11–3B Ujjal Corporation, a publicly traded company, is authorized to issue an unlimited number of no par value $5 noncumulative preferred shares and an unlimited number of no par value common shares. On February 1, 2011, the general ledger contained the following shareholders' equity accounts:

Preferred shares (8,000 shares issued)	$ 440,000
Common shares (70,000 shares issued)	1,050,000
Contributed capital—reacquisition of common shares	75,000
Retained earnings	1,000,000
Accumulated other comprehensive income	65,000

The following equity transactions occurred during the year ended January 31, 2012:

Feb. 28 Issued 2,500 preferred shares for $150,000.
Apr. 12 Issued 100,000 common shares for $3.2 million.
May 25 Issued 2,500 common shares in exchange for land. At the time of the exchange, the land was valued at $75,000 and the common shares at $80,000.
Sept. 12 Reacquired and retired 45,000 common shares for $1,275,000. (Round the average cost per share to the nearest cent.)
Dec. 29 Declared a $2.50 per share dividend to the preferred shareholders of record at January 15, payable February 1.
Jan. 31 A loss of $5,000 was incurred for the year.

Instructions

(a) Record the above transactions for the year ended January 31, 2012, including any required closing entries.
(b) Open T accounts and post to the shareholders' equity accounts.
(c) Prepare the statement of changes in equity for the year.
(d) Prepare the shareholders' equity section of the statement of financial position at January 31, 2012.

Record and post equity transactions; prepare statements under ASPE. (SO 2, 3, 4, 5)

P11–4B On January 1, 2012, Schipper Ltd., a private company, had the following shareholders' equity accounts:

Preferred shares, $2 noncumulative, no par value, unlimited number authorized, none issued	
Common shares, no par value, unlimited number authorized, 100,000 issued	$150,000
Retained earnings	580,000

The following selected transactions occurred during 2012:

Jan. 2 Issued 10,000 preferred shares for $50 per share.
Mar. 10 Declared the quarterly cash dividend to preferred shareholders of record on March 22, payable April 1.
June 10 Declared the quarterly cash dividend to preferred shareholders of record on June 22, payable July 1.
Aug. 12 Issued 10,000 common shares for $3.30 per share.
Sept. 1 Declared the quarterly cash dividend to preferred shareholders of record on September 22, payable October 1.

Oct. 15 Issued 5,000 common shares in exchange for equipment. The common shares had not traded recently but were valued at $3.50 per share on the last date they had traded. The value of the equipment was $15,000 on October 15.

Nov. 1 Declared a $0.50 cash dividend per share to the common shareholders of record on November 22, payable December 10. The fourth quarter cash dividend to preferred shareholders was not declared nor paid.

Dec. 31 A loss of $50,000 was reported for the year.

Instructions

(a) Record the above transactions, including any required closing entries.
(b) Open T accounts and post to the shareholders' equity accounts.
(c) Prepare a statement of retained earnings for the year.
(d) Prepare the shareholders' equity section of the statement of financial position at December 31.
(e) Schipper is a private company following ASPE. If it followed IFRS instead, how might your answers in (a) through (d) change?

P11–5B The general ledger of Maggio Corporation, a publicly traded company, contained the following shareholders' equity accounts in 2012:

(margin note) Reproduce equity accounts; prepare shareholders' equity section. (SO 2, 3, 4, 5)

	Jan. 1	Dec. 31
Preferred shares (15,000 and 15,000 shares issued, respectively)	$ 750,000	$ 750,000
Common shares (255,000 and 291,500 issued, respectively)	3,210,000	3,857,000
Contributed capital—reacquisition of common shares	200,000	200,000
Retained earnings	980,000	1,373,000

A review of the accounting records for the year ended December 31, 2012, reveals the following information:

1. On March 1, 20,000 no par value common shares were sold for $17.50 per share. An unlimited number are authorized.
2. On August 18, a 6% common stock dividend was declared for 16,500 shares when the share price was $18. The stock dividend was distributed on September 25.
3. The preferred shares are $4 cumulative no par value. An unlimited number of preferred shares are authorized. The quarterly preferred shareholders' dividend was declared and paid in 2012 for each quarter.
4. Profit for the year was $750,000.
5. On December 31, the directors authorized a $200,000 restriction on retained earnings in accordance with a debt covenant.

Instructions

(a) Reproduce the Preferred Shares, Common Shares, Contributed Capital, and Retained Earnings general ledger accounts for the year.
(b) Prepare the shareholders' equity section of the statement of financial position at December 31, including any required note disclosure.

P11–6B The condensed statement of financial position of Erickson Corporation reports the following amounts:

(margin note) Compare impact of cash dividend, stock dividend, and stock split. (SO 4)

ERICKSON CORPORATION
Statement of Financial Position (partial)
January 31, 2012

Total assets		$9,000,000
Total liabilities		$2,500,000
Shareholders' equity		
Common shares, unlimited number authorized, 500,000 issued	$3,000,000	
Retained earnings	3,500,000	6,500,000
Total liabilities and shareholders' equity		$9,000,000

The common shares are currently trading for $15 per share. Erickson wants to assess the impact of three possible alternatives on the corporation and its shareholders:

1. Payment of a $1 per share cash dividend
2. Distribution of a 5% stock dividend
3. A 2-for-1 stock split

Instructions

(a) Determine the impact of each alternative on (1) assets, (2) liabilities, (3) common shares, (4) retained earnings, (5) total shareholders' equity, and (6) the number of shares.
(b) Identify the advantages and disadvantages of each alternative for the company.

Prepare statements.
(SO 5)

P11–7B **Tim Hortons Inc.** reported the following changes to its shareholders' equity accounts (in thousands) for the year ended January 2, 2011.

Accumulated other comprehensive loss:		Share capital:	
Balance, Jan. 3, 2010	$ 120,061	Balance, Jan. 3, 2010 (177,040)	$493,435
Balance, Jan. 2, 2011	143,589	Balance, Jan. 2, 2011 (170,386)	474,508
Other comprehensive loss	23,528	Reacquisition of shares (6,746)	(22,074)
Retained earnings:		Shares issued (92)	3,147
Balance, Jan. 3, 2010	796,235		
Balance, Jan. 2, 2011	1,105,882		
Profit	623,959		
Dividends	(90,304)		
Reacquisition of common shares	(223,773)		
Other	(235)		

Additional information:
Tim Hortons has an unlimited number of common shares authorized with a stated value of $2.84 per share. The number of shares issued is shown in parentheses in the share capital section of the above table, and are also in thousands.

Instructions
(a) Prepare a statement of changes in equity for the year ended January 2, 2011.
(b) Prepare the shareholders' equity section of the statement of financial position at January 2, 2011.

Record and post
dividend transactions;
prepare statements.
(SO 4, 5)

P11–8B On January 1, 2012, Stengel Corporation, a publicly traded company, had these shareholders' equity accounts:

Common shares (no par value, unlimited number of shares authorized, 75,000 issued)	$1,700,000
Retained earnings	900,000
Accumulated other comprehensive loss	125,000

During the year, the following transactions occurred:

Feb. 1 Declared a $1 per share cash dividend to shareholders of record on February 15, payable March 1.
Apr. 1 Effected a 3-for-1 stock split. On April 1, the share price was $36.
July 1 Declared a 5% stock dividend to shareholders of record on July 15, distributable July 31. On July 1,
July 15, and July 31, the share prices were $14, $13.50, and $13.75, respectively.
Dec. 31 Determined that profit for the year was $400,000.

Instructions
(a) Record the above transactions, including any required closing entries.
(b) Open T accounts as required and post to the shareholders' equity accounts.
(c) Prepare a statement of changes in equity for the year.
(d) Prepare the shareholders' equity section of the statement of financial position at December 31.

Calculate earnings
per share.
(SO 6)

P11–9B Blue Bay Logistics Ltd.'s shareholders' equity accounts were as follows at the beginning of the current fiscal year, April 1, 2011:

$6 cumulative preferred shares (20,000 shares issued)	$1,800,000
Common shares (500,000 shares issued)	3,750,000
Contributed capital—reacquisition of common shares	50,000
Retained earnings	1,500,000
Total shareholders' equity	$7,100,000

During the year, the following selected transactions occurred:

June 1 Reacquired and retired 2,000 common shares for $10 per share.
July 1 Issued 50,000 common shares for $11 per share.
Feb. 28 Declared the annual preferred dividend to shareholders of record on March 12, payable on
April 1.
Mar. 31 Profit for the year ended March 31, 2012, was $1,016,750.

Instructions
(a) Calculate the weighted average number of common shares for the year.
(b) Calculate the earnings per share.
(c) Why is it important to use profit available to common shareholders in the calculation of earnings per share? Why not just use profit?

P11–10B The following summary of the earnings per share, price-earnings (P-E), payout, and dividend yield ratios is available for five years ended December 31 for TransAlta Corporation:

Evaluate ratios.
(SO 6)

	Earnings per Share	P-E Ratio	Payout Ratio	Dividend Yield
2006	$0.22	121.1 times	447.7%	4.1%
2007	1.53	21.8	65.6	3.4
2008	1.18	20.6	91.5	4.4
2009	0.90	26.1	129.8	4.9
2010	1.00	21.2	146.3	5.5

Instructions

(a) What are some possible reasons that TransAlta's price-earnings and dividend payout ratios fell from 121.1 times and 447.7%, respectively, in 2006 to 21.8 times and 65.5% in 2007? What does this mean?

(b) Why do you think TransAlta's price-earnings ratio declined to 21.8 times while its earnings per share improved to $1.53 in 2007?

(c) What are some possible reasons that TransAlta's payout ratio increased in 2010 at a time when its price-earnings ratio declined?

(d) If you were an investor looking for dividend income, would you be happy with TransAlta's dividend policy? Explain.

P11–11B The following selected information (in millions, except for per share information) is available for The Bank of Nova Scotia for the year ended October 31:

Calculate and
evaluate ratios.
(SO 6)

	2010	2009
Weighted average number of common shares	1,032	1,013
Profit available for common shareholders	$4,038	$3,361
Common cash dividends per share	1.96	1.96
Total common cash dividends	2,023	1,990
Average common shareholders' equity	22,359	19,922
Market price per common share	54.50	45.25
Industry averages were as follows:		
Payout ratio	11.8%	n/a
Dividend yield	3.8%	4.9%
Earnings per share	n/a	n/a
Price-earnings ratio	12.0 times	12.8 times
Return on common shareholders' equity	15.5%	12.0%

Instructions

(a) Calculate the following ratios for the common shareholders for each fiscal year:
   1. Payout ratio
   2. Dividend yield
   3. Earnings per share
   4. Price-earnings ratio
   5. Return on common shareholders' equity

(b) Comment on the above ratios for 2010 in comparison with the prior year and in comparison with the industry.

P11–12B Selected ratios for two retailers follow, along with the industry averages:

Evaluate profitability
ratios.
(SO 6)

Ratio	Bargain Hunters	Discount Paradise	Industry Average
Profit margin	6.8%	3.5%	3.7%
Return on common shareholders' equity	24.9%	22.4%	20.8%
Return on assets	10.2%	8.8%	9.2%
Asset turnover	1.5 times	2.5 times	2.5 times
Earnings per share	$3.30	$2.49	$2.33
Price-earnings ratio	12.3 times	17.0 times	16.3 times
Payout ratio	9.4%	25.0%	19.3%
Dividend yield	0.8%	2.5%	1.2%

Instructions

(a) Compare the profitability of Bargain Hunters with that of Discount Paradise, and with the industry average. Which company is more profitable? Explain.

(b) You would like to invest in the shares of one of the two companies. Your goal is to have regular income from your investment that will help pay your tuition fees for the next few years. Which of the two companies is a better choice for you? Explain.

(c) Assume that instead of looking for regular income, you are looking for growth in the share value so that you can resell the shares at a gain in the future. Now which of the two companies is better for you? Explain.

Broadening Your Perspective

Financial Reporting and Analysis Cases

Financial Reporting: *Eastplats*

Answer questions about shareholders' equity.
(SO 1, 2, 3, 4, 5)

BYP11–1   The financial statements of Eastern Platinum Limited (Eastplats) are presented in Appendix A at the end of this book.

Instructions

(a) How many common shares and preferred shares has Eastplats authorized? What value (e.g., no par value, par value, stated value) are these shares? (*Hint*: See Note 17.)

(b) Using the statement of changes in equity, (1) determine how many common shares were issued, and (2) calculate the average cost of Eastplats's common shares at the end of 2010 and 2009.

(c) Did Eastplats declare any dividends in 2010 and 2009? If so, how much?

(d) Did Eastplats report a positive retained earnings amount or a deficit in 2010 and 2009?

Comparative Analysis: *Eastplats and Amplats*

Calculate ratios and comment on liquidity, solvency, and profitability.
(SO 6)

BYP11–2   The financial statements of Anglo American Platinum Limited (Amplats) are presented in Appendix B following the financial statements for Eastern Platinum Limited (Eastplats) in Appendix A.

Instructions

(a) Calculate or find the earnings per share for each company for 2010. Is there a difference between basic and diluted earnings per share for either company?

(b) Calculate the asset turnover, return on assets, and return on common shareholders' equity ratios for each company for 2010.

(c) Can you determine which company is more profitable based on your answers in (a) and (b)?

Interpreting Financial Information

Calculate and evaluate ratios.
(SO 6)

BYP11–3   Germany-based sportswear retailer PUMA AG Rudolf Dassler Sport reported the following selected information (in EUR millions, except per share data) for the years ended December 31, 2010 and 2009:

	2010	2009
Net sales	2,706.4	2,447.3
Average total assets	2,145.8	1,880.1
Average shareholders' equity	1,259.8	1,126.3
Total dividends	27.1	41.5
Profit	202.2	77.3
Weighted average number of shares	15.0	15.1
Cash dividend per share	1.80	1.80
Price per share	248.00	231.84

PUMA has no preferred shares.

Instructions

(a) Calculate the asset turnover, return on assets, and return on common shareholders' equity ratios for each year. Evaluate PUMA's change in profitability.

(b) Calculate the earnings per share, price-earnings, payout, and dividend yield ratios for each year. Discuss the implications of your findings for investors.

(c) Discuss the implications of comparing Germany-based PUMA with its key competitors, Adidas, also headquartered in Germany, and Nike, headquartered in the United States.

(d) If you wished to compare PUMA's profitability with that of a private company following ASPE, what considerations should you keep in mind? Explain.

Comparing IFRS and ASPE

Compare ownership structure, issue of shares, and earnings per share for public and private company.
(SO 1, 2, 6)

BYP11-4   Prime Restaurants Inc. (PRI) is a Canadian public company that operates casual dining restaurants, including East Side Mario's and Casey's, in addition to restaurants, pubs, and Belgian-style brasseries called Bier Markt.

Service Inspired Restaurants (SIR Corp.) is a privately held Canadian company that owns and operates full-service restaurants, including Alice Fazooli's, Jack Astor's, and Loose Moose Tap & Grill.

Instructions

(a) Although the companies are similar, PRI has chosen to be a public company while SIR Corp. is privately held. Why do you think the two companies chose different types of ownership structure?

(b) When PRI or SIR purchases new restaurants, part of the payment may be in shares of PRI or SIR. How would PRI determine the fair value of its shares for this purpose? How would SRI Corp. determine the fair value of its shares? Which fair value measure would be the more reliable?

(c) Since PRI is a public company, it uses IFRS and is required to disclose earnings per share. SIR uses ASPE and is not required to report earnings per share. Why do you think the standard setters do not require private companies to disclose their earnings per share?

(d) For public companies, earnings per share is one of the key performance measures used by investors to evaluate their investment. What types of performance measures would SIR Corp.'s investors use to evaluate their investment?

Critical Thinking Cases and Activities

Collaborative Learning Activity

BYP11–5 The senior management of Rodart Corporation Ltd. has just returned from a series of meetings with the investment dealers who cover the industry for the investing public. The analysts expressed concern about the lack of growth in Rodart's dividend even though the company's profits have been steadily increasing. The company's capital budget will require it to raise funds next year and management is concerned that a poor review from the investment analysts will make it more difficult to raise money in the stock market.

Distinguish between issuing shares or increasing dividend. (SO 2, 3, 4)

Management is considering the following alternatives:

1. Issue new shares (preferred or common).
2. Increase Rodart's dividend above the industry average, in the hope that the market will respond to the improved dividend yield by increasing the market price of the shares.

Instructions

After the class has been divided into groups and your group has been assigned one of the two alternatives for analysis, do the following:

(a) Identify the risks and benefits of the alternative. Identify the measurements (ratios, share prices, and so on) that will be used to determine the success or failure of your option if it is implemented.

(b) Present your analysis to a group that has been assigned the other alternative.

(c) In the combined group, vote on a course of action.

Communication Activity

BYP11–6 Earnings per share is the most commonly cited financial ratio. Indeed, share prices rise and fall in reaction to a company's earnings per share. The price-earnings ratio is also published in many newspapers' stock market listings.

Discuss earnings per share and price-earnings ratios. (SO 6)

Instructions

Write a memo explaining why earnings per share and the price-earnings ratio are so important to investors. Explain how both ratios are calculated and how they relate to each other. Include in your memo an explanation of how to interpret a high or low price-earnings ratio. Also comment on any reporting differences for publicly traded companies following IFRS and private companies following ASPE.

Ethics Case

BYP11–7 Flambeau Corporation has paid 60 consecutive quarterly cash dividends (15 years' worth). The last six months have been a real cash drain on the company, however, as profit margins have been greatly narrowed by increasing competition. With a cash balance that is only enough to meet day-to-day operating needs, the president, Vince Ramsey, has decided that a stock dividend instead of a cash dividend should be declared. He tells Flambeau's financial vice-president, Janice Rahn, to issue a press release stating that the company is extending its consecutive dividend record with the declaration of a 5% stock dividend. "Write the press release convincing the shareholders that the stock dividend is just as good as a cash dividend," he orders. "Just watch our share price rise when we announce the stock dividend; it must be a good thing if that happens."

Discuss impact of stock dividend. (SO 4)

Instructions

(a) Who are the stakeholders in this situation?

(b) What is the effect of a stock dividend on a corporation's shareholders' equity accounts?

(c) Will the share price rise if a stock dividend is declared, as the president expects?

(d) Is there anything unethical about President Ramsey's intentions or actions?

"All About You" Activity

Distinguish between equity and debt investments and their effect on ratios.
(SO 2, 3, 6)

BYP11–8   In this chapter, you learned about equity financing and in Chapter 10 you learned about debt financing.

Instructions

(a) Distinguish among investments in common shares, preferred shares, and bonds in terms of their risk and return to an investor.

(b) Identify the likely effect of each alternative—equity financing versus debt financing—on the following ratios: debt to total assets, earnings per share, and return on common shareholders' equity.

Serial Case

(*Note:* This is a continuation of the serial case from Chapters 1 through 10.)

Record equity transactions; prepare shareholders' equity section.
(SO 2, 4, 5)

BYP11–9   Natalie, Janet, and Brian are thrilled with the success of Koebel's Family Bakery Ltd. That success, however, has meant that the Koebels have had no time to enjoy personal interests. When Natalie was hired, Janet and Brian believed that they would have a little more time to take a holiday, leaving Natalie in charge. Because of the weekly cupcake contract with Coffee Beans, that has not happened.

Coffee Beans has increased the volume of cupcakes required on a weekly basis, and the bakery is desperately trying to keep up with the demand. Natalie, Janet, and Brian recognize that more help is needed with running the business. Currently, each of them owns 100 shares of the 300 common shares issued.

Natalie's brother, Daniel, has been operating a trucking business in a major Canadian city for a number of years. After being away for over a decade, he has returned with a keen interest in helping his family out at the bakery. He believes that the experience he has obtained operating his trucking business will prove to be a great resource that Koebel's can rely upon as it continues to experience significant growth. Daniel would like to purchase a 25% interest in the company in exchange for cash and one of the delivery trucks he has kept.

The share capital and retained earnings of Koebel's Family Bakery Ltd. at July 1, 2011, are as follows:

Share capital
  $6 cumulative preferred shares, no par value, 10,000 shares authorized, none issued
  Common shares, no par value, unlimited number of shares authorized, 300 shares issued $ 300
  Retained earnings   214,957

Profit for the year ended June 30, 2012, was $216,069. In addition, a dividend of $90,000 was declared on June 15, 2012, to common shareholders of record on June 20, 2012, payable on June 30, 2012.

Based on the bakery's success, the Koebels would like to issue 100 common shares to Daniel for $1,200 per share. The fair value of the delivery truck is estimated at $45,000. The sale of shares to Daniel is expected to take place on June 30, 2012. After the sale of the shares to Daniel, each member of the Koebel family will hold a 25% interest in the common shares of Koebel's Family Bakery.

Instructions

(a) Prepare the journal entries required for the dividend declared on June 15 and paid on June 30, 2012. Who will receive the dividend to be paid on June 30, 2012, and for what amount?

(b) Assume Daniel purchases a total of 100 common shares on June 30, 2012, in exchange for his delivery truck and cash of $75,000. Prepare the journal entries required.

(c) Prepare a statement of retained earnings for the year ended June 30, 2012. If Koebel's followed IFRS rather than ASPE, would it still have to prepare a statement of retained earnings?

(d) Prepare the shareholders' equity section of the statement of financial position at June 30, 2012.

(e) Calculate the average cost per common share before and after shares are issued to Daniel. Why do you think there has been an increase in the value of the common shares?

Answers to Self-Test Questions

1. b	2. b	3. a	4. b	5. a
6. d	7. c	8. b	9. d	10. c

Remember to go back to the beginning of the chapter to check off your completed work!

←

Comprehensive Case: Chapters 10 and 11

QFR Inc. is a fast-growing real estate company owned 100% by Flip Roberts. Flip sees significant opportunities to acquire properties, fix them up, and sell them for a profit. Flip has identified properties with great potential for resale that can be bought for $2.5 million. He is confident that he will be able to resell them within two to three years for $3.5 million. Flip has identified two possible financing options for QFR to consider: (1) Issue 10% bonds for $2.5 million or, (2) issue 50,000 additional common shares for $50 each (for a total of $2.5 million).

Compare financing options, revise financial statements, and evaluate performance.
(SO 2, 5, 6)

Flip believes the properties will generate an additional $375,000 of rent revenue with additional expenses of $100,000 for depreciation, $37,500 for repairs and maintenance, and $12,500 for other expenses. The income tax rate will remain at 30%. The company will have to pay additional interest of $250,000 if bonds are issued, whereas Flip will have to give up 50% of his equity ownership if common shares are issued.

The company's statement of financial position and income statement follow:

QFR INC.
Statement of Financial Position
December 31, 2012

Assets			Liabilities and Shareholders' Equity			
Current assets			Current liabilities			
Cash	$ 100,000		Payables and accruals	$ 8,000		
Accounts receivable	10,000		Current portion of long-term debt	142,000	$ 150,000	
	110,000		Non-current liabilities		3,850,000	
			Shareholders' equity			
Property, plant, and equipment			Common shares, unlimited			
(net of accumulated depreciation)	4,890,000		number authorized, 50,000 issued	$500,000		
Total assets	$5,000,000		Retained earnings	500,000	1,000,000	
			Total liabilities and shareholders' equity		$5,000,000	

QFR INC.
Income Statement
Year Ended December 31, 2012

Rent revenue		$750,000
Expenses		
Interest	$300,000	
Depreciation	200,000	
Repairs and maintenance	112,500	
Other expenses	37,500	650,000
Profit before income tax		100,000
Income tax expense (30%)		30,000
Profit		$ 70,000
Earnings per share		$1.40

Instructions

(a) Record the purchase of the properties for $2.5 million, assuming the purchase is completed on January 1, 2012, under each of the two financing options identified above. Of the $2.5 million purchase price, $0.5 million should be allocated to land and $2 million to buildings.

(b) For option 1 (issue of bonds), do the following:

  1. Record the accrual of 10% interest on the bonds on December 31, 2012, assuming the bonds were issued at face value and that interest is paid annually each January 1.

  2. Calculate the revised revenue and expense amounts for 2012, using the income statement data provided above and the additional revenue and expense information given in the case and recorded in (b).

  3. Prepare the revised 2012 income statement, using the information calculated in (b) (2).

(c) For option 2 (issue of shares), do the following:

  1. Calculate the revised number of common shares issued at December 31, 2012.

  2. Calculate the revised revenue and expense amounts for 2012, using the income statement data provided above and the additional revenue and expense information given in the case.

  3. Prepare the revised 2012 income statement, using the information calculated in (c) (2).

(d) Calculate the revised shareholders' equity (common shares and retained earnings) amounts for 2012 for each option.

(e) Calculate earnings per share and return on common shareholders' equity (using ending equity rather than average equity) before and after each of the two financing options.

(f) Which financing option would you recommend? Explain.

12

Reporting and Analyzing Investments

The Navigator
Chapter 12

- ☐ Scan *Study Objectives*
- ☐ Read *Feature Story*
- ☐ Read text and answer *Do It!s*
- ☐ Review *Comparing IFRS and ASPE*
- ☐ Review *Summary of Study Objectives*
- ☐ Review *Decision Toolkit—A Summary*
- ☐ Work *Using the Decision Toolkit*
- ☐ Work *Comprehensive Do It!*
- ☐ Answer *Self-Test Questions*
- ☐ Complete *assignments*
- ☐ Go to *WileyPLUS* for practice and tutorials

study objectives

After studying this chapter, you should be able to:

1. Identify reasons to invest, and classify investments.
2. Account for non-strategic investments.
3. Account for strategic investments.
4. Indicate how investments are reported in the financial statements.
5. Compare the accounting for a bond investment and a bond payable (Appendix 12A).

the navigator

Managing Money for Clients and the Company

Like all large organizations, Scotiabank manages its money through a number of investment vehicles. It has two main areas of investments: its regular banking operations and strategic acquisitions.

"In banks, we're always changing the mix of financial assets, looking for different opportunities," says Sean McGuckin, Senior Vice President and Head, Risk Policy & Capital Markets, "whereas for non-financial institutions, financial assets may not be their primary assets. It could be property, plant, and equipment, oil in the ground, what have you. So they may take a longer-term view on some of their investments." Scotiabank is like an individual investor who reviews and rebalances his or her portfolio regularly, rather than one who buys stocks and holds them over time with little adjustment.

In its regular banking operations, Scotiabank holds investments in trading portfolios and treasury portfolios. In its trading environment, Scotiabank buys and sells securities primarily to facilitate customer requests and invests in certain securities to adjust its trading risk profile. These may be debt instruments such as bonds, or equity instruments such as common and preferred shares. Scotiabank's treasury investments strengthen the organization's liquidity profile by having some assets on hand that it could quickly convert into cash if needed. The bank also uses various investments in fixed-term securities or variable-rate securities to help adjust its interest rate exposure. These investments can be held for a few days or longer. As well, the bank may also invest in long-term instruments, for example, five-year government bonds.

Scotiabank also invests strategically by acquiring all or a portion of other companies. "Our strategy, like most companies, is to grow," Mr. McGuckin explains. "You can grow either organically over time by continuing to build out your business, or you can acquire growth, i.e., buy a company." If a business fits within Scotiabank's overall strategy, it may buy shares in that company.

For example, several years ago Scotiabank had bought 19% of the shares in DundeeWealth Inc. Then, in 2011, it bought all the remaining common shares that it did not already own. "The acquisition of DundeeWealth demonstrates our strong commitment to build our wealth management presence in Canada and aligns to our global wealth management strategy," said Scotiabank President and CEO Rick Waugh, at the time the acquisition was announced.

These strategic investments have additional benefits in allowing Scotiabank to diversify into different revenue streams and leverage its existing business since the acquired company may have products that would be of interest to existing customers.

In fact, there are many reasons and ways by which organizations make investments, whether they are non-strategic investments to earn a higher return on extra cash than from a bank account, or strategic investments to influence or control another company, such as a competitor, supplier, or complementary business that their customers may benefit from.

the navigator

preview of
CHAPTER 12

Investments can be made by purchasing equity securities issued by corporations or by purchasing debt securities issued by corporations or governments. Investments can be either non-strategic, where the goal is to generate investment income, or strategic, where the goal is to influence the decisions made by the company invested in. As you will see in the chapter, the way in which a company accounts for each of its investments is determined by several factors, including whether the investment is non-strategic or strategic.

The chapter is organized as follows:

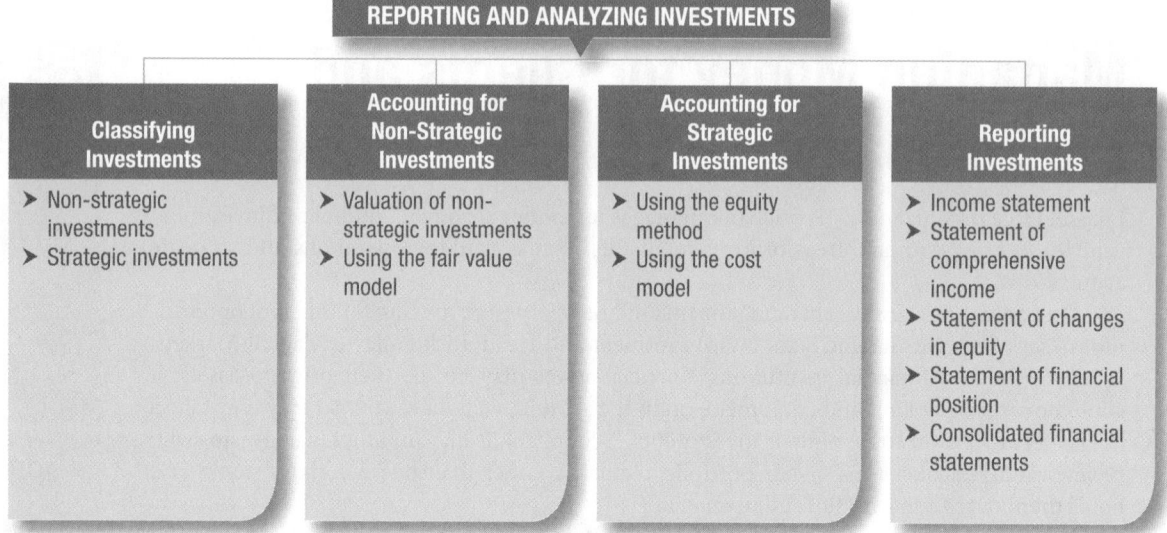

Classifying Investments

STUDY OBJECTIVE 1

Identify reasons to invest, and classify investments.

Recall that in Chapter 8 you were introduced to the concept of financial assets. These are assets that consist of cash, receivables, and investments that have a contractual right to receive cash. It is common practice for corporations to purchase financial assets for investment purposes, such as debt and equity investments. **Debt investments** are made by purchasing low-risk guaranteed investment certificates or term deposits, as well as investments in bonds, commercial paper, and a large variety of other debt securities available for purchase. They earn interest revenue over time and in most cases, the borrower has an obligation to return the original amount (principal) of the investment on a fixed maturity date. **Equity investments**, on the other hand, have no such obligations and are therefore riskier as there is no requirement to receive any form of revenue over time or to receive back the original amount invested. They are usually made by buying either preferred or common shares of other corporations in the expectation of generating revenue from dividend income or a gain on future sale.

These investments may be made for one of two reasons: as a **non-strategic investment** to generate investment income, as noted above, or as a **strategic investment** to influence or control the operations of another company in some way. While either debt or equity securities can be purchased as non-strategic investments, companies may purchase equity securities (normally common shares) for strategic purposes. This is because, for most companies, only common shareholders have voting rights and the ability to influence or control the company's major decisions. Usually each common share has one vote at an annual general meeting of shareholders so investors with large blocks of common shares can influence decisions made by the company through their voting power. Preferred shareholders generally do not have voting rights, and therefore they have no influence or control. The reasons corporations make these types of investments are shown in Illustration 12-1.

Reason	Purpose	Type of Investment
Non-strategic investment	To generate investment income (interest, dividends, appreciation in share prices)	Debt securities (guaranteed investment certificates, term deposits, bonds, commercial paper) and equity securities (preferred and common shares)
Strategic investment	To influence or control another company	Equity securities (common shares)

▶Illustration 12-1
Why corporations invest

NON-STRATEGIC INVESTMENTS

There are several reasons for a company to purchase debt or equity securities of another company as a non-strategic investment. A corporation may have **excess cash** that it does not immediately need. For example, many companies have seasonal fluctuations in their sales levels, which can lead to idle cash until purchases are made for the next busy season. Until the cash is needed, the excess funds may be invested to earn a greater return than would be realized by just holding the funds in the company's chequing account.

When investing excess cash for short periods of time, corporations generally invest in debt securities that have low risk and high liquidity. Examples include guaranteed investment certificates, bankers' acceptances, term deposits, and treasury bills. It is usually not wise to invest short-term excess cash in equity securities. If the share price drops just before the company needs the cash again, the company will be forced to sell its investment at a loss. Most debt instruments do not change significantly in value and are purchased for the interest they generate.

If a company has excess cash for a prolonged period of time, and wants a low-risk investment, bonds or preferred shares may be purchased as their values do not fluctuate very much. Although a company is not required to pay out a dividend, as discussed in Chapter 11, it is common to do so for preferred shares. Investments of this nature usually generate steady amounts of dividend revenue over time.

A company can also invest in debt and equity securities with the hope of selling them later at a higher price and benefiting from their price appreciation. The resulting gain is called a capital gain, which receives preferential income tax treatment in Canada because only half of the gain is usually taxed. Non-strategic investments that are held for the purpose of earning capital gains are called **trading investments**.

Non-strategic investments can be further classified as **short-term investments** or **long-term investments** depending on how liquid the investment is and how long management wants to hold the investment.

The following sections discuss the classification and methods of accounting for non-strategic investments.

STRATEGIC INVESTMENTS

Although both debt and equity securities can be purchased as non-strategic investments, only equity securities (normally common shares) can be purchased for the strategic purpose of influencing relationships between companies. For example, a company may acquire common shares of another company in order to use the shares' voting rights to exercise some influence or control.

The degree of influence determines how a strategic investment is classified. More details about the degree of influence and how it affects the accounting for that investment will be discussed later in this chapter. Note also that, while non-strategic investments can be either short- or long-term, strategic investments can only be long-term.

BEFORE YOU GO ON...

▶ Do It! Investment Classifications

For each investment below, determine:

(a) whether the investment is a debt or equity instrument.

(b) whether the investment is non-strategic or strategic.

(c) the purpose for making the investment.

1. Investment in 90-day treasury bills, purchased with excess cash after the Christmas season

2. Investment in Microsoft common shares, intended to be sold when the price rises 10% above cost

3. Investment in Bombardier 20-year bonds, intended to be held for 20 years

4. Investment in 40% of the shares of Ajax Limited, a supplier

Action Plan

- Distinguish between debt and equity investments:
  - Debt investments are securities that have fixed due dates to receive interest revenue and a maturity date on which the investment's original amount is returned.
  - Equity investments give the owner a portion of equity in a company and are usually made by buying preferred or common shares.
- Distinguish between non-strategic and strategic investments:
  - Non-strategic investments are debt or equity investments that are purchased to earn interest or dividend revenue and/or to earn gains from the appreciation in the value of the investment.
  - Strategic investments are equity investments that represent a sizeable amount of a company's common shares so that the investor can influence or control the decisions made by that company.

Solution

	(a)	(b)	(c)
1.	Debt	Non-strategic	Interest revenue for 90 days
2.	Equity	Non-strategic	Share price appreciation (capital gain)
3.	Debt	Non-strategic	Interest revenue over the long term
4.	Equity	Strategic	Influence the company or other shareholders with a large block of voting common shares

Accounting for Non-Strategic Investments

STUDY OBJECTIVE 2
Account for non-strategic investments.

At acquisition, debt and equity investments are recorded at their purchase cost. Although the investment's fair value is equal to its cost when purchased, this value may rise and fall greatly during the time debt and equity investments are held. Bond and share prices may jump dramatically with favourable economic events and drop drastically with unfavourable conditions. For example, in August 2011,

Agrium Inc.'s common share price was at $74 but it rose to $87 in early September 2011. Scotiabank, which was mentioned in our feature story, often invests in companies like Agrium for the purpose of trading their shares for a profit. Volatility of share prices presents investors with an opportunity for trading profits. If prices can change so much, an important question arises: how should non-strategic investments be valued at the statement of financial position date—at fair value or at cost or at some other value? The next sections will discuss the valuation models for non-strategic investments.

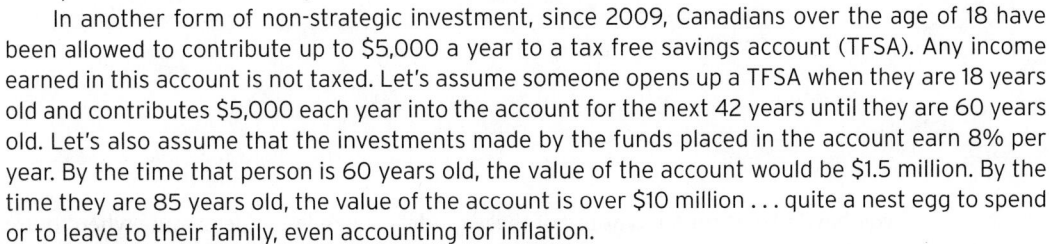

ACCOUNTING MATTERS!   *Investor Perspective*

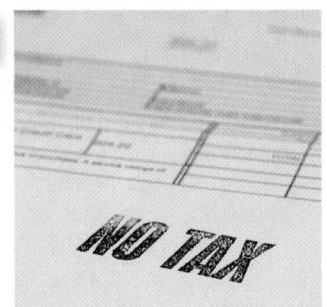

Non-Strategic Investments for Individuals

Most individual Canadians, when they invest in the shares of public companies, are buying non-strategic investments rather than strategic ones. These individuals may trade these shares frequently or not, depending on their investment strategies. Studies have shown that investors with smaller portfolios of non-strategic investments usually have a higher return on their investments if they resist the urge to frequently trade them. One reason for this is the cost of brokers' commissions, which increase with trading activity. Another reason is the fact that income tax is only paid on gains once the investment is sold, so delaying the sale of an investment also delays the payment of any income tax on these gains.

In another form of non-strategic investment, since 2009, Canadians over the age of 18 have been allowed to contribute up to $5,000 a year to a tax free savings account (TFSA). Any income earned in this account is not taxed. Let's assume someone opens up a TFSA when they are 18 years old and contributes $5,000 each year into the account for the next 42 years until they are 60 years old. Let's also assume that the investments made by the funds placed in the account earn 8% per year. By the time that person is 60 years old, the value of the account would be $1.5 million. By the time they are 85 years old, the value of the account is over $10 million . . . quite a nest egg to spend or to leave to their family, even accounting for inflation.

VALUATION OF NON-STRATEGIC INVESTMENTS

Accounting standards relating to investments have been in a state of transition. A new standard has been issued under IFRS to simplify accounting for investments. It's mandatory effective date is still under discussion at the time of writing this textbook, although early application is permitted, and the coverage that follows in this text assumes this standard has been applied. Under ASPE, there are some different approaches taken in certain areas of investment accounting, which will be highlighted when applicable.

Before we determine how to value different types of non-strategic investments, let's examine the three major models that are to be used for valuing investments and then discuss under what circumstances each model would be used for various types of non-strategic investments.

1. **Fair value model**. Under this model, investments are adjusted upwards or downwards to reflect their fair value at year end. Fair value, for this purpose, means the price that would be received to sell an asset in an orderly transaction between market participants at the measurement date. This adjustment (the difference between the investment's fair value and carrying amount) to reflect fair value is known as an **unrealized gain or loss**. It is recorded in the income statement along with any interest or dividend revenue. When the investment is sold, any resulting gain or loss is known as a **realized gain or loss** and is also shown in the income statement.

2. **Amortized cost model**. Under this model, the investment's carrying amount is not adjusted to reflect fair value (unless it is impaired, similar to the way we would record impairment on property). Consequently, no unrealized gains and losses are recorded. The term *amortized* is used because if the investment was purchased at a discount or a premium, as is often the case when purchasing bond investments, the discount or premium would be gradually amortized over the period of time until the bond matures. You learned about bond premium and discount amortization in Chapter 10 when accounting for bond liabilities and you will review this concept again with regard to bond investments in the appendix to this chapter. Because this model requires amortization over the remaining term of the investment, it is used for debt investments rather

than equity investments. Any interest revenue or realized gains and losses on this type of investment are reported in the income statement.

3. **Cost model**. This model (often referred to as the cost method) is very similar to the amortized cost model except that it is used for equity investments. Because this type of investment does not give rise to a discount or premium (because there is no period to maturity for an equity investment), the concept of amortization does not apply to this model. Investment revenue under this model arises from dividend revenue along with realized gains and losses that would be reported in the income statement.

A summary of these three models is shown Illustration 12-2.

Illustration 12-2

Summary of valuation models for non-strategic investments

Valuation Model	Fair Value	Amortized Cost	Cost
Type of investment usually using this model	Debt and equity	Debt	Equity
Basis on which investment is carried after being acquired	Fair value	Amortized cost	Cost
Dividend revenue or interest revenue; realized gains and losses	Recorded on income statement as other revenues and gains or other expenses and losses	Recorded on income statement as other revenues and gains or other expenses and losses	Recorded on income statement as other revenues and gains or other expenses and losses
Unrealized gains and losses	Recorded on income statement as other revenues and gains or other expenses and losses	Not recorded	Not recorded

Now that you have a basic understanding of these models, you need to determine when to use them. In general, the fair value model is used for all non-strategic investments unless either of the following two exceptions is present:

1. **The investment is held to earn cash flows (a business model test) with payments of only principal and interest specified in a contract (a characteristic of asset test).** In most cases, investments held to earn cash flows on fixed payment dates would be debt instruments that make interest payments and are not purchased for the purpose of earning realized gains through trading activities. Because they are intended to be held until the investment matures, the amortized cost model is used to account for these investments. If a debt investment is purchased for the purpose of trading, it would be accounted for like any other non-strategic investment, using the fair value model.

2. **The investment is not held to earn cash flows and there is no fair value available because the security does not trade in an active market.** In this case, the fair value model cannot be used so the cost model is adopted. The use of this model is rare in practice, as most equity and debt investments that are non-strategic and held for trading purposes are made in investments that can easily be sold. After all, if the investment is non-strategic in nature, the investor is usually not planning to hold on to an equity investment for an extended period of time and will want to invest in securities that can readily be sold. However, if an investor is planning to hold a debt security for an extended period of time, the amortized cost model is used.

Illustration 12-3 summarizes some of the concepts mentioned above.

Illustration 12-3

Recognition and measurement criteria for non-strategic investments

Type of Non-Strategic Investment	Purpose	Valuation Model
Debt investment	Held to earn interest revenue	Amortized cost
	Held for trading purposes	Fair value
Equity investment	Equity investments quoted in an active market	Fair value
	Equity investments not quoted in an active market	Cost

As stated above, the fair value model is to be used to value non-strategic investments, with two exceptions. With regard to these exceptions, the amortized cost model will be covered in the appendix to this chapter and the cost model will be covered later in this chapter when discussing strategic investments, as this model is also used for these types of investments. We will now take a closer look at how to account for investments under the fair value model.

USING THE FAIR VALUE MODEL

Non-strategic debt and equity investments that are purchased for the purpose of trading (selling) in the near term in order to earn gains are the types of investments that are accounted for using the fair value model.

When investments are valued at their fair value, any increase or decrease in the market price changes the asset value reported on the statement of financial position, with a corresponding unrealized gain or loss recorded in the income statement. An unrealized gain or loss is recorded rather than a realized gain or loss because the investment has not actually been sold and the gain or loss "realized." Rather, the change in value is said to be "unrealized." When recording unrealized gains and losses, this is often referred to as a fair value adjustment.

To illustrate the valuation of trading investments accounted for under the fair value model, assume that on December 31, 2012, Plano Corporation has the following costs and fair values for its debt and equity securities:

Trading Investments	Cost	Fair Value	Unrealized Gain (Loss)
BCE shares	$ 50,000	$ 48,000	$(2,000)
Norbord bonds	90,000	95,000	5,000
Total	$140,000	$143,000	$ 3,000

Plano has an overall unrealized gain of $3,000 because the total fair value of $143,000 is $3,000 greater than the total cost of $140,000. Its trading investments would be reported at $143,000 at December 31 in the current assets section of the statement of financial position. In addition, Plano would report a net unrealized gain of $3,000 as other revenues and gains in its income statement. **Note that unrealized gains and losses for trading investments under the fair value model are reported in exactly the same way as realized gains and losses.**

The adjustment of the trading investments to fair value and the recognition of any unrealized gain or loss is usually done through an adjusting journal entry at year end. The adjusting entry for Plano is:

Dec. 31	Trading Investments—Norbord Bonds	5,000	
	Trading Investments—BCE Shares		2,000
	Unrealized Gain on Trading Investments		3,000
	(To record unrealized gain on trading investments)		

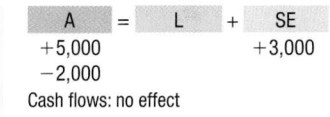

A = L + SE
+5,000   +3,000
−2,000
Cash flows: no effect

Note that this entry assumes that it is individual securities that are adjusted, not the aggregate portfolio. It would be equally correct to combine the BCE shares and Norbord bonds into a single account in the above journal entry and maintain a subsidiary ledger containing the details of individual investments. Furthermore, if the company had only one trading investment, it would not be necessary to specify the name of the investee in the account name. This entry also nets an unrealized loss of $2,000 on the BCE shares with an unrealized gain of $5,000 on the Norbord bonds. Although we have chosen to net the gain and loss here, it would also be correct to record these separately.

If, early in January, Plano sells its BCE shares for $48,000, the following journal entry would be recorded:

Jan. 5	Cash	48,000	
	Trading Investments—BCE Inc. Shares		48,000
	(To record sale of BCE shares)		

A = L + SE
+48,000
−48,000
↑Cash flows: +48,000

Although the BCE shares originally cost $50,000, because they were written down to their fair value of $48,000 on December 31, the new carrying amount is $48,000. Consequently, the investment account is credited for that amount. Although it could be argued that the $2,000 unrealized loss recorded in the prior year has now been realized, for simplicity we are not going to reclassify an unrealized loss from one period into a realized loss in another period, as such a reclassification has no impact on the profit reported in either period.

If the shares had been sold for $47,000 instead of $48,000, then a realized loss of $1,000 ($48,000 − $47,000) would have been recorded. In other words, a loss of $2,000 ($50,000 − $48,000) would have been recorded in the last period, when that loss occurred, on December 31. A further loss of $1,000 would then be recorded in this period, again in the same period as when the loss occurs. This would be done as follows:

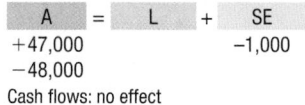

A   =   L   +   SE
+47,000   −1,000
−48,000
Cash flows: no effect

Jan. 5	Cash	47,000	
	Realized Loss on Trading Investments	1,000	
	Trading Investments—BCE Shares		48,000
	(To record a realized loss on trading investments)		

Available-for-Sale Investments

The discussion of non-strategic equity investments has thus far indicated that the fair value approach is used to value an investment unless it is a debt investment held to earn interest revenue (when the amortized cost model is used) or an equity investment where fair value could not be determined (when the cost model is used). These are the general requirements expressed in the new IFRS standard. However, if an investor has an equity investment that is non-strategic and is also not held for trading or not capable of prompt liquidation, should it be accounted for using the fair value model? The answer is yes. However, investors are allowed to make an election so they can account for this type of equity investment using a modified fair value approach known as the **fair value through other comprehensive income (OCI) model**. This model is exactly like the fair value model described above with one exception: unrealized gains and losses are not recorded in the income statement but are instead recorded in other comprehensive income. In this way, unrealized gains and losses can be excluded from the evaluation of management because they are not included in the determination of profit. When the investment is sold, these unrealized gains and losses are then reversed out of other comprehensive income and placed directly in retained earnings. Because companies will have to make a specific election to use this modified approach, it remains to be seen how widely it will be used. Consequently, detailed coverage of this topic is left for an intermediate accounting course.

The fair value through other comprehensive income model is currently in use and investments accounted for under this method are known as **available-for-sale investments**. This term is expected to be discontinued with the adoption of the new IFRS standard.

ASPE   The fair value through other comprehensive income model is not used under ASPE because these standards do not provide for the use of other comprehensive income.

DECISION TOOLKIT

Decision Checkpoints	Info Needed for Decision	Tools to Use for Decision	How to Evaluate Results
Should a company reporting under IFRS make an election to use the fair value through OCI model for non-strategic equity investments?	Need to know how management is evaluated on the performance of an investment and whether the investment is to be held on a short- or long-term basis.	If an investment is to be held on a longer-term basis, management is less likely to be evaluated on unrealized gains and losses. Excluding these investments from the income statement makes sense, especially if management receives bonuses based on profit.	Review the financial statements to see the extent to which investments are recorded using the fair value through OCI model. This will give an indication of how the company views the importance of measuring short-term fluctuations in the fair value of investments in the income statement and may provide some insight into the relationship between investment performance and bonus calculations.

▶Do It! Non-Strategic Investments

Wang Corporation had the following transactions:

Sept.	2	Purchased an investment in Hillary Corp. shares for $30,400 with the intention of trading it soon.
Oct.	12	Received a dividend on the Hillary shares, $750.
	22	Sold half of the investment in Hillary shares for $14,250.
Dec.	31	The remaining Hillary shares are worth $15,000 on this date.

(a) Record the above transactions.

(b) Prepare the adjusting entry for the valuation of the investment on December 31, Wang's year end.

(c) Identify where each account would be reported and on what financial statement.

Action Plan

- Use the fair value model for trading investments.
- Record the trading investment initially at cost and adjust for changes in fair value.
- When the investment is adjusted for any change in value, record any difference between the shares' carrying amount and fair value as an unrealized gain or loss.
- Report dividend revenue and both realized and unrealized gains (losses) as other revenues and gains (or other expenses and losses) on the income statement.
- When the investment is sold, record any difference between the cost of the shares and the proceeds as a realized gain or loss.

Solution

(a)

Sept.	2	Trading Investments	30,400	
		Cash		30,400
		(To record purchase of Hillary Corp. shares)		
Oct.	12	Cash	750	
		Dividend Revenue		750
		(To record receipt of dividend on Hillary shares)		
	22	Cash	14,250	
		Realized Loss on Trading Investments	950	
		Trading Investments ($30,400 × ½)		15,200
		(To record sale of half of Hillary shares)		

(b)

Dec.	31	Unrealized Loss on Trading Investments	200	
		($15,200 − $15,000)		
		Trading Investments		200
		(To record unrealized loss on trading investments)		

(c) The Cash and Trading Investments accounts would be reported as current assets on the statement of financial position. Dividend Revenue would be reported as other revenues and gains on the income statement. The Realized Loss and Unrealized Loss accounts would be reported as other expenses and losses on the income statement.

the navigator

Accounting for Strategic Investments

An **investor** is the company that purchases (owns) securities. An **investee** is the company that issues (sells) the securities. An investor that owns common shares has the potential to strategically influence the investee. The accounting for equity investments in common shares is based on how much influence the investor has over the investee's operating, investing, and financial affairs.

STUDY OBJECTIVE 3
Account for strategic investments.

> Illustration 12-4
Accounting guidelines for strategic investments

Investor's Ownership Interest in Investee's Common Shares	Presumed Influence over Investee	Method to Account for Investment
Less than 20%	Insignificant	Fair value
20% to 50%	Significant	Equity method
More than 50%	Control	Consolidation of financial statements

As noted in Illustration 12-4, if the investor owns less than 20% of the investee's common shares, the investment is accounted for under the fair value model. Remember that, although the fair value model is normally used, an election can be made to account for the investment using the fair value through OCI model, as discussed earlier in this chapter. When an investor owns 20% or more of the common shares of another company, the investor is generally presumed to have a **significant influence** over the decisions of the investee company. When an investee can be significantly influenced, it is known as an **associate**.

The presumption of significant influence may not be valid if other evidence exists to refute it. For example, a company that purchases a 25% interest in another company in a "hostile" acquisition may not have any significant influence over the investee. If less than 20% ownership is held, there is a presumption that significant influence does not exist but evidence could suggest otherwise. For example, if a highly respected investor with 18% ownership has board membership and plays a key role in forming company strategy, then significant influence could exist.

Among the questions that should be considered in determining an investor's influence are (1) whether the investor has representation on the investee's board of directors, (2) whether the investor participates in the investee's policy-making process, (3) whether there are material transactions between the investor and the investee, (4) whether the investor and investee are exchanging managerial personnel, and (5) whether the investor is providing key technical information to the investee. Companies are required to use judgement instead of blindly following the guidelines.

ACCOUNTING MATTERS!   *Investor Perspective*

ACE Holdings and Its Investment in Air Canada

Over time the percentage of ownership that an investor has in an investee can be reduced for a number of reasons. Sometimes, the investor will simply sell all or a portion of the investee's shares but sometimes, the investor's percentage of ownership can be diluted if the investee sells newly issued shares to other investors.

For example, ACE Aviation Holdings Inc. was formed in 2004 to hold a controlling interest in Air Canada as it emerged from bankruptcy protection. At that time, ACE held 75% of Air Canada's shares and because it exercised control, it prepared consolidated financial statements including all of Air Canada's results within their statements.

In October 2009, Air Canada sought additional financing by issuing new shares to an investment syndicate. After the issue of these shares, ACE owned only 27% of Air Canada's shares and commencing at that time began to account for its investment using the equity method. Although ACE no longer controlled Air Canada, it continued to exercise significant influence.

Over one year later in December 2010, ACE decided to sell some of its Air Canada shares to other investors. It sold 16% of Air Canada's shares for $156 million and recorded a gain on the sale of these shares of $43 million. Since this reduced ACE's stake in Air Canada to 11%, the investment was no longer accounted for using the equity method. The company now accounts for its investment using the fair value through other comprehensive income option.

If the investor has more than 50% of the investee's voting shares, we generally consider that investee to be a **subsidiary company** of the investor. In this case, the investor is referred to as the **parent company**. Even though the investee is a separate legal entity, it is part of a group of corporations controlled by the parent. In order to show shareholders and other users of the parent's financial statements the full extent of the group's operations, the financial statements of all entities within the group are combined resulting in **consolidated financial statements**. The process of consolidating financial statements is quite complex and will be left for an advanced accounting course, but in essence, the investment account is replaced with all of the subsidiary's assets and liabilities.

USING THE EQUITY METHOD

When an investor exercises significant influence over an associate, the investee company, to some extent, becomes an extension of the investor company. Consequently, such an investment is recorded using the equity method.

Under the **equity method**, the investment is initially recorded at cost in an account called Investment in Associates. After that, the Investment in Associates account is adjusted annually to show how the investor's equity in the associate has changed. In this way, the movement in the investment account reflects the changes that are occurring to the associate's retained earnings. When the associate has a profit, the investor will increase the investment account for its share of the profit. When the associate declares a dividend, resulting in the reduction of its retained earnings, the investor's investment account will be decreased. It would be wrong to delay recognizing the investor's share of profit until a cash dividend is received or declared, as that approach would ignore the fact that the investor and associate are, in some sense, one company, and that the investor therefore benefits from, and can influence the timing of, the distribution of the associate's profit.

> **Helpful Hint**
> Under the equity method, revenue is recognized on the accrual basis; i.e., when it is earned by the investee.

To keep its records up to date, each year the investor adjusts the investment account to:

1. **Record its share of the associate's profit (loss):** When the associate has a profit, the investor records its share of the profit by increasing (debiting) the investment account and increasing (crediting) a revenue account. Conversely, when the associate has a loss, the investor increases (debits) a loss account and decreases (credits) the investment account for its share of the associate's loss.
2. **Record the dividends received:** This is done by decreasing (crediting) the investment account for the amount of any dividends received. The investment account is reduced for dividends received because the associate's net assets are decreased when a dividend is paid.

We will now illustrate the equity method, using two fictitious companies, Milar Corporation and Beck Inc.

Recording Acquisition of Shares

Beck Inc. has 10,000 common shares issued in total. Assume that on January 1, 2012, Milar Corporation (the investor) acquires 30%, or 3,000 common shares, of Beck (the associate) for $120,000 cash or $40 per share. Milar is assumed to have significant influence over Beck and will use the equity method to account for this transaction. If Milar had more than one associate, we would add the associate's name to the investment account name, or maintain a subsidiary ledger of associates similar to that discussed in the Using the Fair Value Model section with respect to trading investments. The entry to record this investment is:

Jan. 1	Investment in Associates	120,000	
	Cash		120,000
	(To record purchase of Beck common shares)		

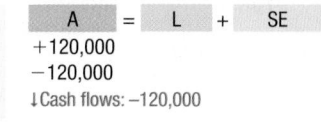

A = L + SE
+120,000
−120,000
↓ Cash flows: −120,000

Recording Investment Revenue

Now assume that for the year ended December 31, 2012, Beck reports profit of $100,000 and declares and pays a $40,000 cash dividend. At December 31, 2012, Beck's common shares were trading at $42 each. Milar is required to record (1) its share of Beck's profit, $30,000 (30% × $100,000), and

(2) the reduction in the investment account for the dividends received, $12,000 ($40,000 × 30%). If Milar had only owned the Beck shares for a portion of the year, the revenue recorded from the Beck investment would be prorated for that portion. The entries are as follows:

A	=	L	+	SE
+30,000				+30,000

Cash flows: no effect

(1)			
Dec. 31	Investment in Associates	30,000	
	Revenue from Investment in Associates		30,000
	(To record 30% equity in Beck's profit)		

A	=	L	+	SE
+12,000				
−12,000				

↑Cash flows: +12,000

(2)			
Dec. 31	Cash	12,000	
	Investment in Associates		12,000
	(To record dividends received from Beck)		

No entry is required under the equity method for the increase in the shares' fair value (from $40 to $42 per share). After the above transactions are posted, the investment and revenue accounts show the following:

Investment in Associates				Revenue from Investment in Associates	
Jan. 1	120,000	Dec. 31	12,000	Dec. 31	30,000
Dec. 31	30,000				
Bal. Dec. 31	138,000				

During the year, the investment account has increased by $18,000 ($30,000 − $12,000). This $18,000 is Milar's 30% share of the $60,000 increase in Beck's retained earnings ($100,000 − $40,000). In addition, Milar will report $30,000 of revenue from its investment, which is 30% of Beck's profit of $100,000.

The revenue recorded under the equity method can be significant. Illustration 12-5 compares the journal entries recorded above under the equity method with the journal entries that would have been recorded if significant influence did not exist and the fair value model were used to account for the investment assuming that it was held for trading. This is done on the left-hand side of the illustration. On the right-hand side of the illustration, we assume that Milar did have significant influence over Beck and used the equity method (as just illustrated in this section).

▶Illustration 12-5
Comparison of fair value and equity methods

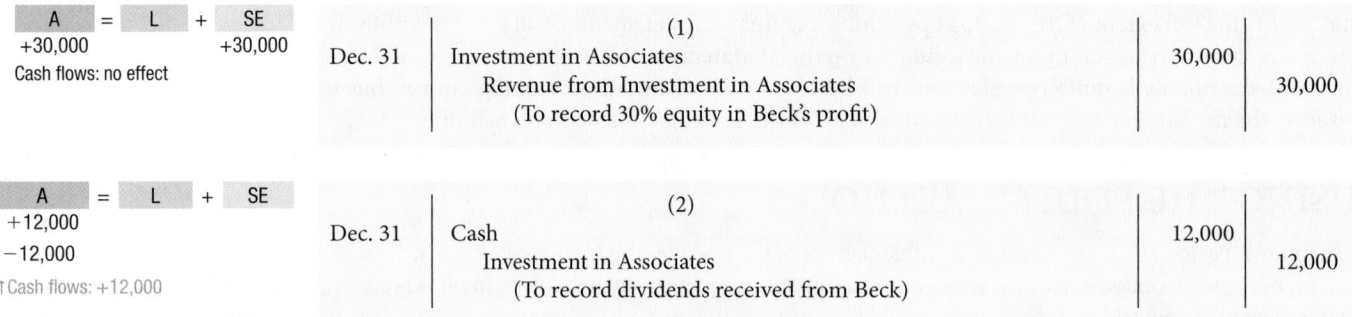

Fair Value Model			Equity Method		
Acquisition			*Acquisition*		
Trading Investments	120,000		Investment in Associates	120,000	
Cash		120,000	Cash		120,000
Investee reports profit			*Associate reports profit*		
No entry			Investment in Associates	30,000	
			Revenue from Investment in Associates		30,000
Investee pays dividends			*Associate pays dividends*		
Cash	12,000		Cash	12,000	
Dividend Revenue		12,000	Investment in Associates		12,000
Adjustment to fair value			*Adjustment to fair value*		
Trading Investments	6,000		No entry		
Unrealized Gain on Trading Investments		6,000			

Using the fair value method, the investment is reported as a short-term investment of $120,000. Dividend revenue of $12,000 is recognized in the income statement, as is an unrealized gain of $6,000 (3,000 shares × $2 [$42 fair value less $40 purchase price] per share). Using the equity method of accounting, the investment account is reported as $138,000 and revenue of $30,000 is recognized on the income statement. Notice how the use of different methods can affect profit and the carrying amount of assets. The decision as to whether an investee can be significantly influenced is therefore a very critical one.

Canadian Tire Scores a Deal with Forzani

In a highly strategic move, Canadian Tire Corporation acquired sports retailer Forzani Group Ltd. in what analysts think was a play to stave off potential competition from the United States.

In 2011, Canadian Tire made a $771-million all-cash bid to acquire all of Forzani's common (Class A) shares. Forzani has more than 500 retail outlets in major urban shopping malls across Canada.

The share purchase not only gives Canadian Tire a greater access to the 18-to-34-year-old demographic, analysts say it gives the retail giant a stronghold in the sporting goods segment, which could come under fire from U.S. sports retailer Dick's Sporting Goods, which has been rumoured to be eyeing a presence in Canada.

"Canadian Tire has always been strong in youth and adult segments, but the customer that eludes us is the younger demographic that shops in malls and urban centres," said Stephen Wetmore, Canadian Tire chief executive.

Share prices of both Forzani and Canadian Tire rose after the deal was announced.

Source: Eric Lam and John Shmuel, "Canadian Tire Naps Up Forzani," *National Post*, May 10, 2011, p. FP1.

USING THE COST MODEL

You saw earlier that non-strategic investments that are actively traded are recorded at fair value. However, if a fair value cannot be determined because there is no active market for these investments, the cost model is used.

Alternative Terminology
The *cost model* is also known as the *cost method*.

When it comes to strategic investments, those that constitute control of an investee require the consolidation of financial statements. To perform a consolidation, we do not need to know the current fair value of the subsidiary's shares. Likewise, if a strategic investment is one with significant influence, we do not need to know the fair value of the associate's shares to properly use the equity method.

Under ASPE, investors have a choice of using either the equity method or the cost model when accounting for significantly influenced investments that are not actively traded. This choice is allowed because private companies that use ASPE often prepare financial statements primarily for tax purposes and revenue arising from the recording of a portion of the associate's profit is not taxable. It therefore makes sense not to record this revenue as required under the equity method. This choice between the equity or cost method assumes that the shares of the associate are not quoted in an active market. If they are, companies can choose between the equity and fair value models.

`ASPE`

In summary, the cost model is used for non-strategic investments not held for the purpose of earning interest revenue and is also used when fair value cannot be determined.

Under the cost model, the investment is recorded initially at cost and is not subsequently adjusted until sold. When the investee declares a dividend, the investor will record dividend revenue. The equity investment is reported on the statement of financial position at cost. Details regarding these transactions are covered below.

Recording Acquisition of Shares

At acquisition, the cost of the investment is the price paid to acquire the equity securities. Assume, for example, that on July 1, 2012, Passera Corporation (the investor) acquires 1,000 common shares of Beal Corporation (the investee) at $40 per share. Beal is a private corporation and its shares are held by only two individuals and Passera. If Beal has a total of 10,000 common shares, then Passera has a 10% (1,000 ÷ 10,000) ownership interest in Beal. Assume also that Passera does not plan to trade these securities. Because the shares of this company are not actively traded, assume that a fair value for the shares is not readily obtainable. This investment would thus be recorded using the cost model. If Passera was able to significantly influence Beal by acquiring more than 20% of the outstanding shares and reported under ASPE, it could account for this investment using the cost model or the equity method. As you saw above, if the investor has significant influence, the investment account used is named Investment in Associates, but if no significant influence exists, we will use the account name Long-Term Investments. The assumption here is that the Beal shares are the only long-term investment held by Passera. If there were others, we would distinguish them by adding the name of the investee to the account name or maintaining a subsidiary ledger.

The entry to record the acquisition of the Beal shares is as follows:

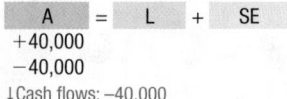

July 1	Long-Term Investments	40,000	
	Cash		40,000
	(To record purchase of 1,000 common shares of Beal)		

This investment would be reported as a non-current asset on the statement of financial position.

Recording Dividend Revenue

During the time the shares are held, entries are required for any cash dividends that the investee declares. If a $2-per-share dividend is declared and paid by Beal Corporation on October 1, the entry that Passera would record is:

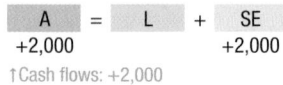
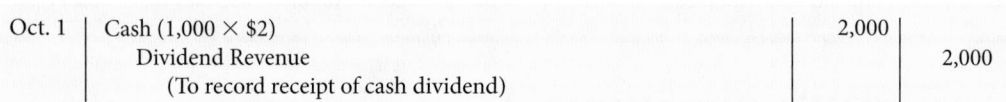

Oct. 1	Cash (1,000 × $2)	2,000	
	Dividend Revenue		2,000
	(To record receipt of cash dividend)		

Dividend revenue is reported as other revenue in the income statement.

Recording Sales of Shares

When shares are sold, the difference between the net proceeds from the sale and the cost of the shares is recognized as a realized gain or realized loss. Assume that Passera Corporation receives net proceeds of $39,000 on the sale of its Beal Corporation shares on December 10. Because the shares cost $40,000, a loss of $1,000 has been realized. The entry to record the sale is:

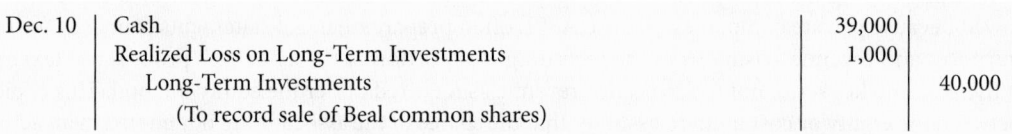

Dec. 10	Cash	39,000	
	Realized Loss on Long-Term Investments	1,000	
	Long-Term Investments		40,000
	(To record sale of Beal common shares)		

The loss is reported in the other expenses and losses section of the income statement. A gain on sale would have been reported in the other revenues and gains section of the income statement.

DECISION TOOLKIT

 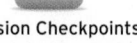 Decision Checkpoints	 Info Needed for Decision	 Tools to Use for Decision	 How to Evaluate Results
Should a company reporting under ASPE use the cost model or the equity method when accounting for its strategic investments in associates when the shares are not actively traded?	Need to know what the users of the financial statements are using the information regarding these investments for.	If the financial statements of the investor are used primarily to evaluate the performance of the associate, then recording a portion of the associate's income is critical to this evaluation. On the other hand, if the financial statements are used primarily for tax purposes, then recording a share of the associate's income is not necessary as the investor does not pay tax on this income, the associate does.	Review the financial statements to see the extent to which investments are recorded using the cost model. This will give an indication of how the company views the importance of measuring the performance of the investment in the associate relative to the importance of having information in the income statement that is consistent with the information needed to complete the company's income tax return.

BEFORE YOU GO ON...

▶ Do It! Strategic Investments

CJW Inc., a private company using IFRS, purchased 20% of North Sails Ltd.'s 60,000 common shares for $10 per share on January 2, 2012. On April 15, North Sails paid a cash dividend of $45,000. On December 31, North Sails reported profit of $120,000 for the year and had a share value of $10.25. Prepare all necessary journal entries assuming (a) CJW could not obtain significant influence in the investee so it plans to trade the shares as a non-strategic investment; (b) this is a strategic investment under IFRS in which there is significant influence; and (c) this is a strategic investment in which there is significant influence, but CJW reports under ASPE and North Sails shares do not trade actively so CJW has chosen to use the cost model.

Action Plan

- Fair value model
  - Under IFRS use this model when there is no significant influence.
  - Recognize dividend revenue when dividends are declared.
  - Adjust the investment's carrying amount to fair value, thereby recognizing an unrealized gain or unrealized loss at year end that is recorded in the income statement.
- Equity method
  - Under IFRS use the equity method when there is significant influence (normally 20% or more ownership of the common shares of another corporation).
  - Under the equity method, recognize revenue when the associate reports profit. The declaration of dividends is not revenue; rather, it reduces the equity investment.
- Cost model
  - Use the cost model when the investment's fair value cannot be determined. In this case, the investment still pertains to an associate and will still be referred to as an investment in an associate even though the cost model will be used.
  - Under the cost model, only dividend revenue and realized gains and losses are recognized in the income statement.

Solution

(a) Fair value model

Jan.	2	Trading Investments (20% × 60,000 × $10)	120,000	
		Cash		120,000
		(To record purchase of 12,000		
		[20% × 60,000] North Sails shares)		
Apr.	15	Cash	9,000	
		Dividend Revenue (20% × $45,000)		9,000
		(To record receipt of cash dividend)		
Dec.	31	Trading Investments	3,000	
		Unrealized Gain on Trading Investments		3,000
		(12,000 × $0.25 [$10.25 − $10])		
		(To record unrealized gain on trading investment)		

(b) Equity method

Jan.	2	Investment in Associates (20% × 60,000 × $10)	120,000	
		Cash		120,000
		(To record purchase of 12,000		
		[20% × 60,000] North Sails shares)		
Apr.	15	Cash	9,000	
		Investment in Associates (20% × $45,000)		9,000
		(To record receipt of cash dividend)		

(continued)

Dec.	31	Investment in Associates (20% × $120,000)	24,000	
		Revenue from Investment in Associates		24,000
		(To record 20% equity in North Sails' profit)		

(c) Cost model

Jan.	2	Investment in Associates (20% × 60,000 × $10)	120,000	
		Cash		120,000
		(To record purchase of 12,000		
		[20% × 60,000] North Sails shares)		

Apr.	15	Cash	9,000	
		Dividend Revenue (20% × $45,000)		9,000
		(To record receipt of cash dividend)		

| Dec. | 31 | No entry | | |

Reporting Investments

STUDY OBJECTIVE 4
Indicate how investments
are reported in the financial
statements.

This section will review the presentation of investments in the income statement, statement of comprehensive income, statement of changes in equity, and statement of financial position.

INCOME STATEMENT

Gains and losses on investments, whether they are realized or unrealized, must be presented in the financial statements. Realized gains and losses are presented in the income statement. Unrealized gains and losses from trading investments are also presented in the income statement. These gains and losses, as well as other investment-related accounts such as those for interest and dividend revenue, are reported as other revenues and gains or other expenses and losses in the non-operating section of the income statement.

Scotiabank, introduced in our chapter-opening feature story, reported realized gains and other investment income on trading investments of $1,371 million in its income statement for the year ended October 31, 2010, as shown in Illustration 12-6.

▶Illustration 12-6
Income statement

BANK OF NOVA SCOTIA	
Income Statement (partial)	
Year Ended October 31, 2010	
(in millions)	
Other income	
Trading revenues	$1,016
Net gain (loss) on securities other than trading	355
	$1,371

STATEMENT OF COMPREHENSIVE INCOME

You learned in Chapter 11 that the **statement of comprehensive income** includes not only profit reported on the income statement but also "other comprehensive income" transactions. You learned about other comprehensive income in past chapters. You will recall that sources of other comprehensive income include certain translation gains and losses on foreign currency and revaluations of property, plant, and equipment under the revaluation model. A new source of other comprehensive income introduced in this chapter occurs when unrealized gains and losses are recorded using the fair value through OCI model.

Companies can present the items included in other comprehensive income in a separate statement or at the bottom of the income statement in a combined statement of comprehensive income.

Scotiabank presents its profit in an income statement and then prepares a separate statement of comprehensive income by listing profit and then adding other comprehensive income (or subtracting other comprehensive loss) elements to profit to arrive at comprehensive income. It reported comprehensive income of $3,988 million in 2010, as Illustration 12-7 shows.

Illustration 12-7
Statement of comprehensive income

BANK OF NOVA SCOTIA Statement of Comprehensive Income (partial) Year Ended October 31, 2010 (in millions)		
Profit		$4,239
Other comprehensive income (loss), net of tax		
Change in unrealized loss on available-for-sale securities	$278	
Unrealized foreign currency losses	(591)	
Other	62	(251)
Comprehensive income		$3,988

The bank's profit of $4,239 million was reduced by the other comprehensive loss of $251 million, resulting in overall comprehensive income of $3,988 million. Note that adjustments to comprehensive income are reported net of income tax. For simplicity, we are ignoring the income tax implications of comprehensive income in this chapter.

STATEMENT OF CHANGES IN EQUITY

As you learned in Chapter 11, the statement of changes in equity presents the changes in each component of shareholders' equity each period. This includes changes in share capital, retained earnings, accumulated other comprehensive income (loss), and any other equity items that a company might report. While profit increases retained earnings, other comprehensive income (loss) increases (decreases) accumulated other comprehensive income.

An extract from the bank's statement of changes in equity, detailing the determination of accumulated other comprehensive income, is shown below in Illustration 12-8. Note that detailed calculations of the changes in share capital have been omitted in the following illustration for simplicity. Shown below are the movements in retained earnings and accumulated other comprehensive income only.

Illustration 12-8
Statement of changes in equity

BANK OF NOVA SCOTIA Statement of Changes in Equity (partial) Year Ended October 31, 2010 (in millions)		
Share capital (not detailed)		$ 9,750
Retained earnings		
Balance at beginning of year	$19,916	
Profit	4,239	
Dividends	(2,223)	
Balance at end of year		21,932
Accumulated other comprehensive loss		
Balance at beginning of year	$ (3,800)	
Other comprehensive income (loss)	(251)	
Balance at end of year		(4,051)
Total shareholders' equity		$27,631

It is important to understand that the other comprehensive loss of $251 million shown in Illustration 12-8 is not the same amount reported as the ending comprehensive income amount on the bank's statement of comprehensive income, which was $3,988 million. This is because comprehensive income shown in Illustration 12-7 comprises both profit ($4,239 million) and the other comprehensive loss ($251 million). Similar to how ending retained earnings is determined, the current period's other comprehensive loss of $251 million is added to the opening accumulated other comprehensive loss balance to determine the ending balance. This resulted in an ending accumulated other comprehensive loss of $4,051 million, as shown above. It is this amount that is reported in the shareholders' equity section of the statement of financial position.

STATEMENT OF FINANCIAL POSITION

In the statement of financial position presentation, investments are classified as short-term or long-term.

Short-Term Investments

If we show assets from most to least liquid, cash is listed first in the current assets section of the statement of financial position. Scotiabank also views its highly liquid investments that are near maturity (usually less than three months) as cash equivalents. You will recall in Chapter 7 that consideration is currently being given to combining cash equivalents with short-term investments rather than with cash for presentation purposes in the future.

Other short-term investments rank next in order of liquidity. As you learned earlier, trading investments are always classified as current assets, whereas available-for-sale investments may be either current or long-term, depending on whether the investment is capable of reasonably prompt liquidation and when management intends to sell it. Regardless of their classification, these types of investments are carried at fair value. No distinction is usually made between debt and equity securities on the face of the statement of financial position. These securities are often combined and reported as one portfolio amount on that statement. Most companies will then provide further details in notes to the financial statements.

Illustration 12-9 shows how Scotiabank reports its short-term investments.

▶ **Illustration 12-9**	**BANK OF NOVA SCOTIA**
Presentation of short-term investments	Statement of Financial Position (partial)
	October 31, 2010
	(in millions)

Current assets	
Trading securities	$64,684
Available-for-sale securities	8,890

In the notes to its statements, Scotiabank details its mix of trading and available-for-sale securities.

Long-Term Investments

Long-term investments include debt securities held to earn interest revenue until they mature, and consequently they are reported at amortized cost. Any portion that is expected to mature within the year is classified as a current asset. Long-term investments would include equity securities that are purchased to have significant influence or control. If an investment is not large enough to exercise either significant influence or control, but is still being held for long-term purposes, it will typically be accounted for using the fair value model unless the option to use the fair value through other comprehensive income model is taken. As noted earlier, investments recorded using the latter approach are currently called available-for-sale securities.

Scotiabank reports its long-term investments as shown in Illustration 12-10.

▶ **Illustration 12-10**	**BANK OF NOVA SCOTIA**
Presentation of long-term investments	Statement of Financial Position (partial)
	October 31, 2010
	(in millions)

Assets	
Long-term investments	
Available-for-sale investments	$38,338
Equity accounted investments	4,651

In the notes to its financial statements, Scotiabank provides further detail about these investments.

Illustration 12-3, in the non-strategic investments section of this chapter, summarized the classification and valuation of debt and equity investments. Illustration 12-11 expands on Illustration 12-3 by summarizing the reporting of both non-strategic and strategic investments and how they relate to short- and long-term investment sections on the statement of financial position.

Statement of Financial Position Classification	Strategy	Type of Investment	Valuation Model
Short-term investments (current assets)	Non-strategic	Trading investments (debt or equity)	Fair value
Long-term investments (non-current assets)	Non-strategic	Equity investments without significant influence or control, with determinable fair values	Fair value
		Debt investments held to earn interest revenue	Amortized cost
	Strategic	Investments in associates (equity investment with significant influence)	Equity method (with option under ASPE to use cost model if shares are not quoted in an active market or fair value if they are quoted)

Illustration 12-11
Reporting and valuation of short- and long-term investments

For the non-strategic equity investments above, if the investment is supposed to be reported at fair value and this value cannot be determined, the cost model would be used. Furthermore, for a non-strategic equity investment that is not held for trading, an election can be taken to use the fair value through OCI model. As menioned previously in this chapter, we do not cover the details of this model in this text.

Accumulated Other Comprehensive Income (Loss)

Accumulated other comprehensive income (or loss) is presented in the shareholders' equity section of the statement of financial position. Scotiabank reports an accumulated other comprehensive loss of $4,051 million, as shown earlier in Illustration 12-8.

Illustration 12-12 reviews the interrelationships among the income statement, statement of comprehensive income, statement of changes in equity, and statement of financial position. Note that changes in share capital have not been detailed in the illustration shown below but the statement of changes in equity would include this information as well as changes in retained earnings, accumulated other comprehensive income, and any other equity items.

Illustration 12-12
Financial statement interrelationships

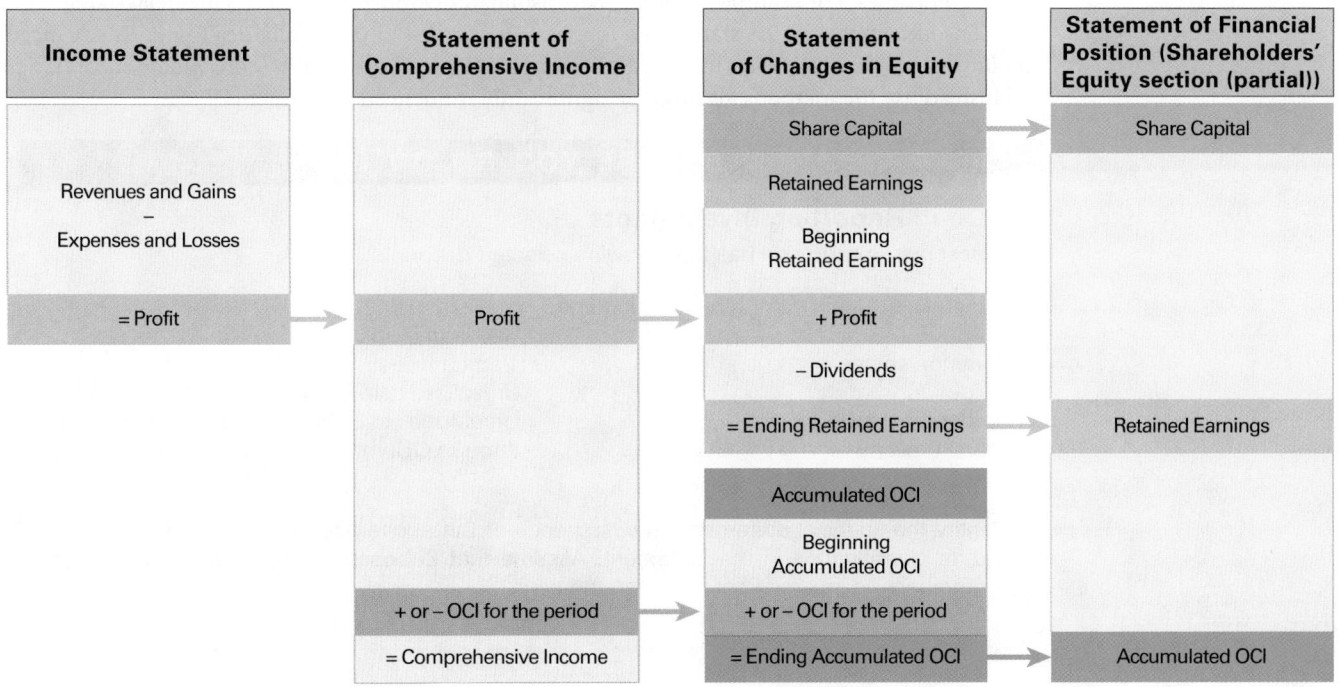

Although we have chosen not to illustrate the statement of cash flows, you will recall from earlier chapters that the purchase and sale of investments is generally reported in the investing activities section of the statement. You will learn more about this in the next chapter.

■ Keeping an Eye on Cash

You have seen so far how various transactions relating to investments affect the statement of financial position and the income statement, but how do these transactions affect the statement of cash flows? The table below shows items arising from investment transactions and how they are shown on the statement of cash flows. You will learn more about the preparation of the statement of cash flows in Chapter 13.

Transaction	Impact on Statement of Cash Flows
Purchase of investment	Investing cash outflow, unless the investment purchased was a current asset, in which case the payment is treated as an operating outflow as the investment is treated like inventory.
Dividends and interest received recorded as revenue	Operating or investing cash inflow (under ASPE shown only as an operating cash flow)
Dividends recorded under the equity method as a reduction in the investment account	Operating or investing cash inflow (under ASPE shown only as an operating cash flow)
Realized and unrealized gains and losses	Not shown because gains and losses do not constitute a cash flow
Proceeds received from the sale of an investment	Can be shown as an investing cash inflow unless the investment when purchased was a current asset, in which case the proceeds are shown as an operating inflow as the investment is treated like inventory

CONSOLIDATED FINANCIAL STATEMENTS

Earlier in the chapter, you learned that when one company controls another, consolidated financial statements are prepared that show the combined assets and liabilities of both the parent and subsidiary companies. For example, Scotiabank consolidates DundeeWealth Inc.'s financial statements.

ASPE

Consolidating financial statements is a complex topic that is usually dealt with in advanced accounting courses. However, under ASPE, companies can choose not to consolidate subsidiaries and instead use the methods allowed for significantly influenced investments.

BEFORE YOU GO ON...

▶ Do It! Reporting Investments

Zaboschuk Corporation has the following selected accounts:

Accumulated other comprehensive income	Realized gain or loss
Cash	Revenue from investments in associates
Common shares	Trading investments
Dividends	Unrealized gain or loss under fair value model
Dividend revenue	Unrealized gain or loss under fair value
Interest revenue	through OCI model
Investment in associates	

Identify the financial statement on which each of the above accounts would be reported and its classification in the statement. Assume that Zaboschuk reports profit and other comprehensive income in separate statements.

Action Plan

- Determine whether each account belongs on the income statement, statement of other comprehensive income, statement of changes in equity, and/or statement of financial position.
- Organize each account into its proper classification on each statement.

Solution

Account	Financial Statement	Classification
Accumulated other comprehensive income	Statement of changes in equity; statement of financial position	Accumulated OCI; shareholders' equity
Cash	Statement of financial position	Current assets
Common shares	Statement of changes in equity; statement of financial position	Share capital; shareholders' equity
Dividends	Statement of changes in equity	Retained earnings section (deduction from retained earnings)
Dividend revenue	Income statement	Other revenues and gains
Interest revenue	Income statement	Other revenues and gains
Investment in associates	Statement of financial position	Non-current assets
Realized gain or loss	Income statement	Other revenues and gains or other expenses and losses
Revenue from investments in associates	Income statement	Other revenues and gains
Trading investments	Statement of financial position	Current assets
Unrealized gain or loss under fair value model	Income statement	Other revenues and gains or other expenses and losses
Unrealized gain or loss under fair value through OCI model	Statement of other comprehensive income	Other comprehensive income

the navigator

APPENDIX 12A—INVESTMENTS IN BONDS WITH DISCOUNTS AND PREMIUMS

Chapter 10 discussed bonds from the issuer's perspective where the bonds were liabilities. Corporations and governments are the major issuers of bonds that are purchased by investors. The issuer of the bonds is known as the investee. The purchaser of the bonds, or the bondholder, is known as the investor. For the investor, short-term investments in bonds, because they are not held for the purposes of earning interest until the bond matures, are accounted for using the fair value model. Long-term investments in bonds, on the other hand, are typically accounted for using the amortized cost model.

You will recall from Chapter 10 that premiums or discounts on long-term bonds payable must be amortized using the effective-interest method of amortization. Similarly, premiums or discounts on bond investments must be amortized using the effective-interest method. However, under ASPE,

STUDY OBJECTIVE 5

Compare the accounting for a bond investment and a bond payable.

ASPE

companies have the choice of amortizing premiums and discounts on a straight-line basis over the period to maturity if the results do not differ materially from the effective-interest method. The effective interest rate method will be illustrated in this chapter.

If a bond investment is held for trading purposes, there is no requirement to amortize any premium or discount because it is not held to earn interest. Any misstatement of interest that might result would not be significant.

While the amortization of discounts and premiums on bonds payable was recorded in an Interest Expense account, the amortization of discounts and premiums on a bond investment is recorded in an Interest Revenue account. If there is a bond premium on a long-term bond investment, the Interest Revenue account and carrying amount of the investment is *reduced* by the amortization amount. If there is a bond discount, the Interest Revenue account and carrying amount of the investment is *increased* by the amortization amount.

RECORDING A BOND INVESTMENT FOR THE INVESTOR

This section will illustrate the recording of a bond investment using an example for Kuhl Corporation (the bond purchaser). It will then compare Kuhl's recording to Doan Inc.'s (the bond issuer's) recording of its bond liability. Assume that Kuhl Corporation acquires $50,000 of Doan 10-year, 6% bonds on January 1, 2012, for $49,000. This means that the bonds sold at a discount of $1,000 ($50,000 − $49,000). The price of $49,000 was based on a market, or effective, rate of interest of 6.272%. The bonds pay interest semi-annually, on July 1 and January 1. We will use the account Long-Term Investments because this investment is not held for trading purposes nor is it an investment in an associate. If more than one such investment were held, we would add the company's specific name to the end of the account name or use a subsidiary ledger to track each individual investment. Assuming that Kuhl is intending to hold these bonds until maturity and is therefore using the amortized cost model, the entry to record the investment is as follows:

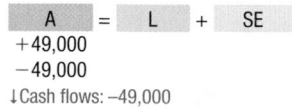

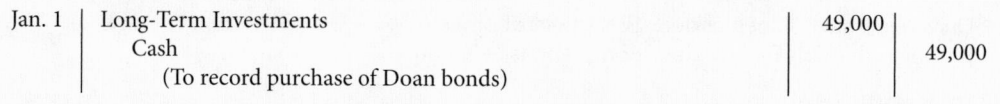

	Jan. 1	Long-Term Investments	49,000	
		Cash		49,000
		(To record purchase of Doan bonds)		

In the above entry, the bonds are recorded at their acquisition cost of $49,000. Similar to a bond liability, the $1,000 discount on the bonds is not recorded separately but rather is netted with the cost in the investment account. Therefore the balance in the Long-Term Investments account really consists of a credit relating to the discount of $1,000 and a debit relating to the bond's maturity value of $50,000. Over time, the credit pertaining to the discount will be amortized. This process transfers a portion of this credit into the interest revenue account in the income statement and increases it to reflect the benefit of buying the bond at a discount.

Interest to be received in cash is calculated by multiplying the face value of the bond investment by the coupon (stated) interest rate per semi-annual period. Kuhl will collect interest of $1,500 ($50,000 × 6% × $^6/_{12}$) semi-annually on July 1 and January 1.

Interest revenue will differ from the cash received by the amount of discount that is to be amortized. The interest revenue is calculated by multiplying the carrying amount of the bond investment by the market (effective) rate of interest per semi-annual interest period. Kuhl's interest revenue is $1,537 ($49,000 × 6.272% × $^6/_{12}$) for the first interest period. Interest revenue is then compared with the interest received to determine the amount by which to amortize the discount (i.e., the portion of the $1,000 discount that is amortized in this six-month period). The amortization is $37 ($1,537 − $1,500) in this case, and is debited to the bond investment account. Notice that the interest revenue of $1,537 is higher than the interest received in cash of $1,500 because the company is recognizing the benefit of purchasing the bond at a discount over the period that it intends to hold the bond.

The entry to record the receipt of interest on July 1 is:

July 1	Cash ($50,000 × 6% × $^6/_{12}$)	1,500	
	Long-Term Investments	37	
	Interest Revenue ($49,000 × 6.272% × $^6/_{12}$)		1,537
	(To record receipt of interest on Doan bonds)		

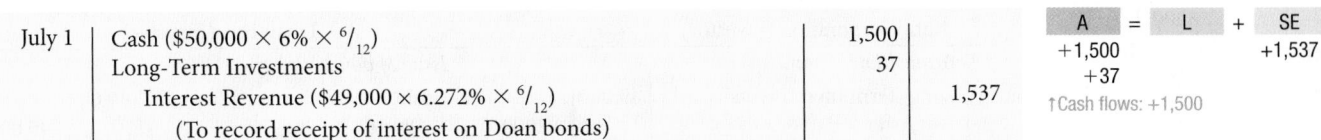

After amortization, the investment's carrying amount will increase to $49,037, which is the bond's present value on July 1. This is shown in the following T account:

Long-Term Investments		
Jan. 1	49,000	
July 1	37	
Bal. July 1	49,037	

If the bonds are later sold before their maturity date, it is necessary to (1) update any unrecorded interest, (2) debit Cash for the proceeds received, (3) credit the investment account for the cost of the bonds, and (4) record any gain or loss realized on the sale. Any difference between the proceeds from the sale and their original cost is recorded as a realized gain or loss.

Assume, for example, that Kuhl receives proceeds of $50,500 plus accrued interest on the sale of the Doan bonds on September 1, 2012. First, record the interest entry for the two months from July 1 to September 1.

Sept. 1	Cash ($50,000 × 6% × $^2/_{12}$)	500	
	Long-Term Investments	13	
	Interest Revenue ($49,037 × 6.272% × $^2/_{12}$)		513
	(To record receipt of interest on Doan bonds)		

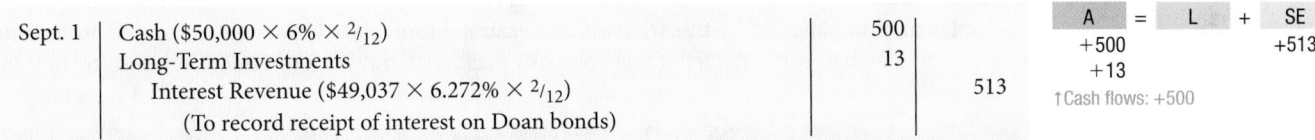

The difference between the cash, $500, and the interest revenue, $513, is the amortization of the discount, $13 ($513 − $500). The investment's carrying amount is now $49,050, as shown here:

Long-Term Investments		
Jan. 1	49,000	
July 1	37	
Sept. 1	13	
Bal. Sept. 1	49,050	

Since the investment has been sold for $50,500, a gain of $1,450 has been realized ($50,500 − $49,050). The entry to record the sale is:

Sept. 1	Cash	50,500	
	Long-Term Investments		49,050
	Realized Gain on Long-Term Investments		1,450
	(To record sale of Doan bonds)		

Note that a gain on the sale of debt investments is reported as other revenues and gains in the income statement.

RECORDING A BOND FOR INVESTOR AND INVESTEE

With a few exceptions, recording a debt investment in bonds (an asset) for an investor is essentially the opposite of recording bonds payable (a liability) for an investee, which was discussed in Chapter 10. Using the Kuhl Corporation example, Illustration 12A-1 compares the recording of the bonds as an investment for Kuhl and as a liability for Doan.

▶Illustration 12A-1
Comparison of a bond investment using the amortized cost model and a bond liability

Kuhl Corporation (Investor)			Doan Inc. (Investee)		
Acquisition of bonds			*Issue of bonds*		
Jan. 1	Long-Term Investments	49,000	Cash	49,000	
	Cash		49,000	Bonds Payable		49,000
Receipt of interest and amortization of discount			*Payment of interest and amortization of discount*		
July 1	Cash	1,500	Interest Expense	1,537	
	Long-Term Investments	37	Bonds Payable		37
	Interest Revenue		1,537	Cash		1,500
Sale of investment					
Sept. 1	Cash	500	No entry as the interest that Kuhl		
	Long-Term Investments	13	receives is paid by the party that		
	Interest Revenue		513	purchases the bond from Kuhl		
1	Cash	50,500			
	Long-Term Investments		49,050			
	Realized Gain on Long-Term Investments		1,450			

Recording an investment in bonds (an asset) for an investor differs from the recording of bonds payable (a liability) for an investee in the following two ways. First, any premium or discount is not amortized by the investor as it is by the investee if the bonds are held for trading purposes and accounted for under the fair value model. Second, assuming that Kuhl sold its bonds on the open market, the issuer, Doan, is not affected by this transaction because it took place between Kuhl and another company. Doan would only be affected if that company decided to buy back (redeem) its bonds from Kuhl.

BEFORE YOU GO ON...

▶Do It! Investments in Bonds with Discounts and Premiums

Gemini Limited purchased a 6%, 5-year, $100,000 Dynex bond on January 1, 2012, for $104,000 with the intention of holding it until maturity. At that time, market interest rates were 5.08%. The bond matures on December 31, 2016, and pays interest on June 30 and December 31 each year. Gemini has a December 31 year end.

(a) Explain why the bond was purchased by Gemini Limited at a premium.

(b) Record the journal entries that Gemini would make on January 1, June 30, and December 31, 2012.

(c) Explain why a different amount of interest revenue is recorded on June 30 and December 31, 2012.

(d) If market interest rates rise, will bond prices fall? Why?

(e) Assume that the market value of the bond on December 31, 2012, was $105,000 and because of this, Gemini decided to sell the bond immediately after receiving the interest payment that day. Record the journal entry that the company would make to record this sale.

Action Plan

- Record bond investments at their cost when acquired.
- Calculate the interest revenue on a bond by multiplying the carrying amount of the bond at the beginning of the period by the market interest rate when the bond was purchased.
- Calculate the cash payment received for interest on the bond by multiplying the face or maturity value of the bond by the coupon interest rate.
- If the bond is to be held until maturity, any premium or discount is amortized over time. The amount to be amortized is the difference between the interest revenue earned and the interest revenue received. Over time, the carrying amount of a bond investment will move toward its maturity value as the discount or premium on the bond is amortized.
- When a bond investment is sold, the difference between its carrying amount and the proceeds received from its sale is the gain or loss on the sale of the bond.

Solution

(a) A bond will typically sell at a price that is equal to its present value determined by using market interest rates on the date that the investment is acquired. In this case, since the bond offers a coupon interest rate that is greater than the market interest rate, the bond is more attractive to investors, who will bid the price of the bond up to a value where its effective interest rate will then be equal to the market rate. A bond premium can be considered an additional cost to obtain the investment, which is amortized over time until maturity through reductions in interest revenue.

(b) Journal entries for the events described above are shown below:

Jan. 1	Long-Term Investments	104,000	
	Cash		104,000
	(To record purchase of Dynex bond)		
June 30	Cash ($6\% \times \$100{,}000 \times {}^{6}/_{12}$)	3,000	
	Long-Term Investments		358
	Interest Revenue ($5.08\% \times \$104{,}000 \times {}^{6}/_{12}$)		2,642
	(To record interest revenue on Dynex bond)		
Dec. 31	Cash ($6\% \times \$100{,}000 \times {}^{6}/_{12}$)	3,000	
	Long-Term Investments		367
	Interest Revenue ($5.08\% \times (\$104{,}000 - \$358) \times {}^{6}/_{12}$)		2,633
	(To record interest revenue on Dynex bond)		

(c) Every time interest revenue is recorded, the premium on the bond is amortized. This in turn lowers the carrying amount of the bond, as a portion of the cost of the bond is allocated to interest revenue. Since the interest revenue earned is a function of the carrying amount, which is falling each period, the interest revenue in turn will fall each period.

(d) If market interest rates rise, the bond becomes less attractive to potential investors as its interest rate is locked in at 6%. Consequently, the bond price will fall. Therefore, bond prices are inversely related to changes in market interest rates.

(e) The journal entry that would be recorded for the sale of this bond would be:

Dec. 31	Cash	105,000	
	Long-Term Investments ($\$104{,}000 - \$358 - \$367$)		103,275
	Realized Gain on Long-Term Investments		1,725

comparing
IFRS and ASPE

Key Differences	International Financial Reporting Standards (IFRS)	Accounting Standards for Private Enterprises (ASPE)
Fair value through OCI model	Allowed	Not allowed because other comprehensive income is not reported
Accounting for investments in associates	Must use the equity method	Choice of using the equity method or cost model if shares do not have quoted prices. If they are quoted, the equity method or the fair value model can be chosen
Investments in bonds	Must use the effective-interest method to amortize any bond premium or discount	Normally will use the effective-interest method to amortize any bond premium or discount but permitted to use alternative methods if the results do not differ materially from the effective-interest method
Consolidation of financial statements	Consolidation required if investor controls investee	Consolidation is optional. If consolidation is not used, there is a choice of using the equity method or cost model if shares do not have quoted prices. If they are quoted, the equity method or the fair value model can be chosen

A Good Day to Start Saving

Savings are an essential part of personal financial planning. Without savings, you cannot purchase investments, afford major purchases, deal with emergencies, or retire in comfort. To become a successful saver, you should: (1) set a goal for saving a certain amount each month, (2) make a plan for accomplishing this goal, and (3) save regularly.

Some people may be good savers but have little idea of how to invest. There are two basic ways to invest: (1) by lending money to others by buying debt instruments such as Canada Savings Bonds or guaranteed investment certificates (GICs), or (2) by investing in equity instruments such as the shares of a publicly traded company. A debt investment is usually safer and the goal is to earn interest revenue over a period of time. An equity investment is riskier and the goal is to earn a gain from the appreciation in the value of the investment and perhaps some dividend revenue.

Canadians aged 18 and over are allowed to put up to $5,000 of their savings each year into a tax free savings account (TFSA). Investment income and capital gains earned by investments inside a TFSA are not taxed, which can save you thousands of dollars. You can set up a TFSA at most financial institutions.

Experts recommend that, if you will need to access your savings within the near future, you should have more debt investments because of their lower risk. If you do not need cash from your investments, consider investing in equities.

Some Facts

- Some 71% of respondents in a recent poll conducted by CIBC said that it was important to set financial goals for themselves and their family, but only 51% of respondents had financial goals in place.
- At the end of 2010, the personal savings rate in Canada was 4%, which was 0.5 of a percentage point higher than a year before, but considerably lower than the 10% achieved in the 1980s and early 1990s. Increases in real estate wealth have contributed to non-strategic saving by Canadians. As the rate of growth in the value of homes has decreased, Canadians have returned to "active" saving—putting money aside and not spending it.
- Two-thirds of Canadians say the first investment they ever owned was a Canada Savings Bond (CSB). In the 1980s and 1990s, they were very popular as a safe and higher-return investment. In recent years, the rates offered by these bonds have not kept up with those offered on other low-risk investments. The number of CSBs sold has declined from $17 billion per year in the 1980s to $2 billion in 2010.

What Do You Think?

You are entering the first year of university and have recently inherited $30,000. This $30,000 will help you fund your education. Your parents want you to invest some of the money in a TFSA and GICs, but you know you could get a greater return by purchasing shares in a public company.

YES You know that you will use all this money for your education, so it should be invested in a low-risk savings vehicle with a steady predictable return. If the money goes into a TFSA account where bonds are held or a GIC or some combination, you know it will be there when you need it.

NO Savings accounts and GICs pay very little interest and you can earn a higher return by buying shares in a public company.

Sources: Kim Covert, "Setting Goals and Making Plans Key to Financial Confidence: Poll," *Financial Post*, January 20, 2011; Rob Carrick, "For the Young, A Better Way to Retire Well," *The Globe and Mail*, January 13, 2011, p. B14; Statistics Canada, "Economic Indicators by Province and Territory, December 2010," *The Daily*, February 28, 2010; CIBC World Markets, "Economic Insights," February 28, 2011; Tim Kiladze, "The Long, Slow Death of a Once-Loved Way to Save," *The Globe and Mail*, March 24, 2011, p. B1.

Summary of Study Objectives

1. Identify reasons to invest, and classify investments. Corporations generally purchase investments in debt and equity securities for one of two reasons. The investment may be purchased as a non-strategic investment to generate investment income or it might be purchased as a strategic investment to influence or control the operations of another company. Non-strategic investments may include debt securities that are purchased to earn investment income through the receipt of interest payments. Sometimes, though, a debt security may be held for trading purposes. Non-strategic equity investments can be held for trading purposes or to earn dividend revenue and can be held for any length of time.

2. Account for non-strategic investments. Non-strategic investments include investments in debt and equity securities. All debt investments are non-strategic and those intended to be held to maturity are accounted for using the amortized cost model, whereby interest revenue and realized gains and losses are reported in the income statement. If the investment, whether debt or equity, is instead held for trading purposes, it is accounted for using the fair value model. This model recognizes unrealized gains and losses that result from adjusting the carrying amount of the investment to fair value. These amounts, along with any realized gains and losses and interest and dividend revenue, are reported in the income statement. In limited circumstances, an election to use the fair value through OCI model can be made instead of choosing to use the fair value model for equity investments that are non-strategic and not held for trading purposes. Under ASPE, the fair value method is used when fair value is determinable. If the fair value of a non-strategic investment cannot be determined, the cost model is used. Under this method, an investment is recorded at cost and remains at this amount unless impaired. Dividend and interest revenue is recorded along with realized gains and losses in the income statement.

3. Account for strategic investments. When an investor company makes a strategic investment, it is usually done to influence or control the investee. Significant influence is usually achieved when at least 20% of the investee's shares are acquired, although qualitative factors should also be evaluated to determine the existence of significant influence. If the investor is not able to exert significant influence over the investee company, the investment is accounted for using the fair value model just like other non-strategic equity investments.

When significant influence exists (share ownership of usually 20% or more along with qualitative evidence of influence), the equity method should be used. The equity method records investment revenue from an associate (a significantly influenced investee) based on the investor's proportion of the associate's income. If the investor receives dividends from the associate, they reduce the carrying amount of the investment account because that company's equity has fallen. These investments are not adjusted to fair value unless there is a permanent decline in value below cost. Under ASPE, the investor has the choice of accounting for a significantly influenced investment using either the equity method or the cost model if the shares of the associate are not quoted in an active market. If they are quoted, the investor can choose to use the equity method or the fair value model.

When the investor obtains control (usually more than 50% of the shares) of the investee, the subsidiary's financial statements are consolidated into those of the parent company.

4. Indicate how investments are reported in the financial statements. Non-strategic equity investments are usually held for trading purposes and would be shown in the current assets section of the statement of financial position. If a non-strategic equity investment is not held for trading purposes (currently known as available-for-sale or AFS investments), it may be shown as a long-term investment on the statement of financial position. However, AFS securities may also be classified as short-term depending on management's intention and ability to liquidate the investment. Debt-related non-strategic investments that are held to earn interest revenue until maturity may be shown as current assets or long-term investments, depending on their maturity date. Strategic investments in significantly influenced associates are shown as long-term investments.

Accumulated other comprehensive income is presented in the shareholders' equity section of the statement of financial position.

Realized gains and losses are presented as other revenues and gains or other expenses and losses in the income statement. Unrealized gains and losses under the fair value model are also presented in this manner but unrealized gains and losses under the fair value through OCI model are presented as other comprehensive income (loss) in the statement of comprehensive income.

Changes in share capital, retained earnings, and accumulated comprehensive income are shown in the statement of changes in equity.

When a company controls the common shares of another company (ownership of usually greater than 50%) consolidated financial statements that detail the financial position of the combined entity must also be prepared.

5. Compare the accounting for a bond investment and a bond payable (Appendix 12A). The accounting for a bond investment is similar to that of a bond payable in that any premium or discount is amortized using the effective-interest method of amortization. Companies using ASPE can choose to use the straight-line method instead if the results do not materially differ from the effective-interest method. Premiums and discounts are not amortized for non-strategic investments that are held for trading purposes and accounted for under the fair value model.

Glossary

Amortized cost model   A method of valuing debt investments that are held to earn cash flows with specified payment dates in a contract. (p. 643)

Associate   An investee that is significantly influenced by an investor. (p. 648)

Available-for-sale investments Non-strategic equity securities that are not classified as trading investments. They are reported at fair value on the statement of financial position using the fair value through other comprehensive income model. This category will soon no longer be used, and although some equity investments may be valued using the fair value through other comprehensive income model, no debt investments will be allowed to use this model. (p. 646)

Consolidated financial statements Financial statements that present the assets and liabilities controlled by the parent company and the total profitability of the combined companies (the parent company and the subsidiary companies). (p. 649)

Cost model (also known as the cost method) An accounting model in which an equity investment is recorded at cost because a fair value for the investment cannot be readily determined. This model is also a choice allowed under ASPE for investments in associates. Investment revenue is recognized only when cash dividends are earned. (p. 644)

Debt investments Investments in money-market instruments, bonds, commercial paper, or similar items. (p. 640)

Equity investments Investments in the share capital (common and/or preferred shares) of other corporations. (p. 640)

Equity method An accounting method in which the investment in common shares is initially recorded at cost. The investment account is then adjusted (increased for the investor's share of the investee's profit and decreased for dividends received) to show the investor's equity in the investee. (p. 649)

Fair value model A valuation method that reports non-strategic debt or equity investments that are held for trading at their fair values, resulting in the recording of unrealized gains and losses in the income statement. (p. 643)

Fair value through other comprehensive income (OCI) model A fair value model for equity investments that can be used only with an election under IFRS (not used under ASPE). It allows investors to record unrealized gains and losses in other comprehensive income rather than in profit. (p. 646)

Investee The corporation that issues (sells) the debt or equity securities. (p. 647)

Investor The corporation that buys (owns) the debt or equity securities. (p. 647)

Non-strategic investment A debt or equity investment that is purchased mainly to generate investment income. (p. 640)

Parent company A company that controls (usually owns more than 50% of) the common shares of another company. (p. 649)

Realized gain or loss The difference between fair value and cost (carrying amount) when an investment is actually sold. (p. 643)

Significant influence An ability of an investor to influence decisions made by an investee, which is assumed to exist when more than 20% but less than 50% of an investee's shares are owned. (p. 648)

Statement of comprehensive income A financial statement that presents the profit (loss) and other comprehensive income (loss) for a specific period of time. Other comprehensive income items, such as unrealized gains and losses from available-for-sale securities, are not reported on the income statement because they are not considered critical to the evaluation of management's performance, but are included in comprehensive income. (p. 654)

Strategic investment An equity investment that is purchased to influence or control another company. (p. 640)

Subsidiary company A company whose common shares are controlled (usually more than 50% of the common shares are owned) by another company. (p. 649)

Trading investments Non-strategic debt or equity investments that are bought to generate profits from short-term price fluctuations. Reported at fair value on the statement of financial position. (p. 641)

Unrealized gain or loss The difference between the fair value and cost (carrying amount) of an investment still held (owned) by the investor. (p. 643)

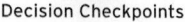

DECISION TOOLKIT—A SUMMARY

 Decision Checkpoints	 Info Needed for Decision	Tools to Use for Decision	 How to Evaluate Results
Should a company reporting under IFRS make an election to use the fair value through OCI model for non-strategic equity investments?	Need to know how management is evaluated on the performance of an investment and whether the investment is to be held on a short- or long-term basis.	If an investment is to be held on a longer-term basis, management is less likely to be evaluated on unrealized gains and losses, so excluding these from the income statement makes sense, especially if management receives bonuses based on profit.	Review the financial statements to see the extent to which investments are recorded using the fair value through OCI model. This will give an indication of how the company views the importance of measuring short-term fluctuations in the fair value of investments in the income statement and may provide some insight into the relationship between investment performance and bonus calculations.

| Should a company reporting under ASPE use the cost model or the equity method when accounting for its strategic investments in associates when the shares are not actively traded? | Need to know what the users of the financial statements are using the information regarding these investments for. | If the financial statements of the investor are used primarily to evaluate the performance of the associate, then recording a portion of the associate's income is critical to this evaluation. On the other hand, if the financial statements are used primarily for tax purposes, then recording a share of the associate's income is not necessary as the investor does not pay tax on this income, the associate does. | Review the financial statements to see the extent to which investments are recorded using the cost model. This will give an indication of how the company views the importance of measuring the performance of the investment in the associate relative to the importance of having information in the income statement that is consistent with the information needed to complete the company's income tax return. |

USING THE DECISION TOOLKIT

The Simmons Foundation was established to hold a number of investments on behalf of a publicly funded university and allocate the investment income to a number of worthy projects undertaken by the university. The foundation reports under IFRS, given its high public profile, and consults with several financial advisors who ensure that it has an appropriate mix of debt and equity investments in its portfolio. Some of the debt investments mature in less than a few years while others mature in 10 or 20 years. All of the debt investments are typically held to maturity. Other investments include non-strategic equity investments, some of which are actively traded while others are not.

Instructions

(a) What reasons does the foundation have for purchasing both debt and equity investments?

(b) Why would debt investments with different maturities be purchased?

(c) What do you think are the criteria that the foundation would use to evaluate the performance of the financial advisors? Should different criteria be used for different types of investments?

(d) Given the criteria discussed in (c) above, how should each type of investment be accounted for?

(e) The foundation is considering a strategic investment without achieving control. How would this be accounted for and presented on the statement of financial position? How would the profit and dividends relating to this investment be reported?

(f) If the foundation were using ASPE instead of IFRS, would it have more or less choice when it came to presenting information in its financial statements?

Solution

(a) When the foundation purchases debt investments, they are held to maturity and this is done for the purpose of earning interest revenue. These types of investments on average are less risky than equity investments and typically earn a lower return. The equity investments are held for trading purposes so as to earn dividend income and realize gains on the sale of these investments.

(b) Debt investments, such as bonds, with shorter periods to maturity are chosen so that, if interest rates change, the foundation will not be "locked in" and earn a specific interest rate that may now be too low. Debt investments, such as bonds, with longer terms are purchased so that interest revenue will be stable for a number of years, which makes it easier to prepare budgets.

(c) Investment portfolios are used to achieve two major objectives: the earning of investment income through periodic receipts of cash from interest and dividends and/or price appreciation in the value of the investments held. Measuring how effectively these objectives were achieved serves as the criterion for evaluating the advisor's performance. For example, if a debt investment such as a bond was chosen by an advisor for the purpose of earning interest revenue for the next 10 years, fluctuations in the bond price are irrelevant to the evaluation of the advisor so his or her performance should be measured based on the amount of interest revenue earned. On the other hand, if an advisor chose an equity or debt investment for the purpose of trading it, they should be evaluated based on the amount of price appreciation through either realized or unrealized gains achieved by the investment.

(d) If the criterion to measure the performance of a debt investment is the interest revenue it will earn to maturity, the amortized cost model should be used when accounting for such an investment. This model does not measure unrealized gains and losses, as these are not relevant to the objectives for investing in such a security. On the other hand, if the investment was purchased for its potential price appreciation, then the fair value model should be used, as this model recognizes unrealized gains and losses and carries the investment at its fair value. Knowing this information allows users of the financial statements to better evaluate the investment's performance.

(e) A strategic investment is an equity investment where the investor obtains a significant portion of the voting shares of an investee or associate, usually 20% or more of the shares. Undertaking such an investment requires the investor's commitment to become more involved with the associate's operations and the foundation must take this into consideration before making the investment. If 20% to 50% of the shares are purchased, it is likely that significant influence is achieved, although other qualitative factors may have to be considered. Given that the foundation uses IFRS, an investment of this size would be accounted for using the equity method. It would be reported as a non-current asset that would be increased by the foundation's share of the associate's profit (with a corresponding increase in investment revenue) and decreased by its share of the associate's dividends (with a corresponding increase in cash).

(f) Under IFRS, an election could be made to use the fair value through OCI approach rather than the fair value approach for non-strategic, non-trading investments. This election is not available under ASPE so there is less choice with respect to this type of investment. On the other hand, if the investment was large enough to attain significant influence over the investee, under ASPE a choice would exist to account for the investment using either the equity method or cost model, if the shares did not have a quoted fair value, or a choice between the equity method or the fair value model if the shares did have a quoted fair value. Under IFRS, only the equity method could be used.

Comprehensive Do It!

In 2012, its first year of operations, Northstar Finance Corporation, which reports under IFRS, had the following transactions regarding its investments:

May	1	Purchased 600 Sandburg Ltd. common shares for $60 per share. This investment is held for trading purposes.
June	1	Purchased 1,000 bonds of Gladstone Inc. at $100 each. These bonds bear interest at 6%, which is paid semi-annually on November 30 and May 31 each year. They are also purchased for trading purposes.
July	1	Purchased 4,000 Cey Corporation common shares for $70 per share. This represents 25% of the issued common shares. Because of this investment, the directors of Cey have invited a Northstar executive to sit on their board.
Sept.	1	Received a $1-per-share cash dividend from Cey.
Nov.	1	Sold 200 Sandburg common shares for $63 per share.
	30	Interest on the Gladstone bonds is received.
Dec.	15	Received a $0.50-per-share cash dividend on Sandburg common shares.
	31	On this date, the fair values per share were $55 for Sandburg and $73 for Cey. The fair value of the Gladstone bonds was $101 each. Cey reported a profit for the year ended December 31, 2012, of $100,000.

Instructions

(a) Record the above transactions.

(b) Prepare the adjusting entries required to report the investments at their fair value and accrue any investment revenue.

(c) Show the presentation of each investment and the related investment income in the statement of financial position and income statement.

(d) Without recording any entries or presenting financial statements, discuss how your answer could change if Northstar used ASPE.

Action Plan

- Keep a running balance of the number of shares and bonds purchased and sold for each investment.
- Calculate the realized gains or losses by subtracting the cost of any investments sold from the proceeds received from their sale.
- Determine the adjustment to fair value based on the difference between the carrying amount (cost) and fair value of the securities.

Solution to Comprehensive Do It!

(a) Journal entries for the following transactions are shown below:

May 1	Trading Investments—Sandburg shares	36,000	
	Cash (600 × $60)		36,000
	(To record purchase of 600 Sandburg common shares)		
June 1	Trading Investments—Gladstone bonds	100,000	
	Cash (1,000 × $100)		100,000
	(To record purchase of 1,000 Gladstone bonds)		
July 1	Investment in Associates	280,000	
	Cash (4,000 × $70)		280,000
	(To record purchase of Cey common shares)		
Sept. 1	Cash (4,000 × $1)	4,000	
	Investment in Associates		4,000
	(To record dividend received from associate, Cey, of $1 per share)		
Nov. 1	Cash (200 × $63)	12,600	
	Trading Investments—Sandburg shares (200 × $60)		12,000
	Realized Gain on Trading Investments		600
	(To record sale of 200 Sandburg shares)		
30	Cash (6% × $100,000 × $^6/_{12}$)	3,000	
	Interest Revenue		3,000
	(To record interest received on Gladstone bonds)		
Dec. 15	Cash [(600 − 200) × $0.50]	200	
	Dividend Revenue		200
	(To record dividend received of $0.50 per share from Sandburg)		

(b) Adjusting entries that would be recorded on December 31 are shown below:

Dec. 31	Unrealized Loss on Trading Investments	1,000	
	Trading Investments—Gladstone bonds	1,000	
	[1,000 × ($101 − $100)]		
	Trading Investments—Sandburg shares		2,000
	[400 × ($55 − $60)]		
	(To record net unrealized loss on Sandburg shares and Gladstone bonds)		
31	No entry is made for the change in the fair value of Cey shares as the equity method is used for this investment.		
31	Interest Receivable (6% × $100,000 × $^1/_{12}$)	500	
	Interest Revenue		500
	(To accrue interest revenue on Gladstone bonds)		

(*continued*)

31	Investment in Associates	12,500	
	Revenue from Investment in Associates		12,500
	(25% × $100,000 × ⁶/₁₂)		
	(To record Northstar's share of Cey's profit since the date of acquisition of July 1, which was six months ago)		

Supporting calculations:

	Trading Investment— Sandburg Shares	Trading Investment— Gladstone Bonds	Total Trading Investments	Investment in Associates
At acquisition	$36,000	$100,000	$136,000	$280,000
Dividends received				(4,000)
Carrying amount of shares sold	(12,000)		(12,000)	
Adjustment to fair value	(2,000)	1,000	(1,000)	
Share of associate's profit				12,500
Carrying amount, December 31	$22,000	$101,000	$123,000	$288,500

(c) Financial statement presentation would appear as follows:

> **NORTHSTAR FINANCE CORPORATION**
> Statement of Financial Position (partial)
> December 31, 2012
>
> Assets

Current assets	
Trading investments	$123,000
Interest receivable	500
Non-current assets	
Investment in associates	288,500

Note: Details of the adjustment from carrying amount to fair value would be disclosed in the notes to the financial statements.

> **NORTHSTAR FINANCE CORPORATION**
> Income Statement (partial)
> Year Ended December 31, 2012

Other revenue and gains	
Revenue from investment in associates	$12,500
Interest revenue	3,500
Realized gain on trading investments	600
Dividend revenue	200
	16,800
Other expenses and losses	
Unrealized loss on trading investments	1,000

(d) If Northstar reported using ASPE, it could account for the investment in Cey Corporation using either the equity method or the fair value model. If the fair value model were used, other revenue would be increased from the $12,500 share of Cey's income to $16,000 consisting of dividend revenue of $4,000 and an unrealized gain of $12,000 arising from the difference in the fair value of the investment of $292,000 (4,000 shares at $73 each) and the carrying amount of $280,000. Therefore the total change to profit would be an increase of $3,500. On the statement of financial position, the investment would be shown at its fair value of $292,000 rather than the amount shown above of $288,500 under the equity method. So in summary, both profit and the carrying amount of the investment account would be higher by $3,500.

the navigator

Self-Test, Brief Exercises, Exercises, Problems: Set A, and many more components are available for practice in WileyPLUS.

Note: All questions, exercises, and problems below with an asterisk (*) relate to material in Appendix 12A.

Self-Test Questions

Answers are at the end of the chapter.

(SO 1) 1. Which of the following is the best reason for a corporation's managers to purchase equity securities as a strategic investment?
(a) They want to exert influence over the decisions of the investee company.
(b) They want to invest excess cash for short periods of time to earn a greater return than would be earned if the funds were simply held in the company's chequing account.
(c) They want to invest excess cash for the long term to generate investment income.
(d) They speculate that the investment will increase in value and result in a gain when sold.

(SO 1) 2. Which of the following is a strategic investment?
(a) Equity investment held for the purpose of trading
(b) Debt investment held for the purpose of trading
(c) Debt investment intended to be held to maturity
(d) Equity investment representing 30% of the issued common shares

(SO 1) 3. Which statement does *not* apply to an investment that is being held until it matures in three years?
(a) The company is speculating that a debt investment will increase in value and it will therefore be able to sell it at a gain.
(b) The company is more interested in earning interest revenue than in realizing gains from the investment.
(c) The company has the ability to hold the investment to maturity.
(d) The investment is classified as a non-current asset.

(SO 2) 4. Which statement is *incorrect* with respect to the valuation models used for non-strategic investments?
(a) Unrealized gains and losses are not reported when the amortized cost model is used.
(b) Realized gains and losses are not reported in the income statement when using the amortized cost model.
(c) Both unrealized and realized gains and losses are reported in the income statement under the fair value model.
(d) The cost model is used only for equity investments.

(SO 2) 5. Boisclair Ltée sells investments reported under the fair value model that cost $28,000 for $26,000 in the same year as they were purchased. The entry to record this sale would include a:
(a) debit to a realized loss account of $2,000.
(b) debit to an unrealized loss account of $2,000.
(c) debit to OCI of $2,000.
(d) debit to a Trading Investments account of $26,000.

(SO 2) 6. A company purchased an equity investment for trading purposes for $20,000 in April 2011 and determined that its fair value was $23,000 on its year-end date of December 31, 2011. In 2012, the investment was sold for $24,000. Based on these facts, the company will record:
(a) a realized gain of $3,000 in 2011 and a realized gain of $1,000 in 2012.
(b) no gain or loss in 2011 and a $1,000 realized gain in 2012.
(c) an unrealized gain of $3,000 in 2011 and a realized gain of $1,000 in 2012.
(d) no gain or loss in 2011 and a $3,000 realized gain in 2012.

(SO 3) 7. The equity method of accounting for strategic equity investments should be used when the investor:
(a) owns less than 20% of the investee's common shares, because there is no significant influence.
(b) owns more than 20% of the investee's common shares but not more than 50%, because this indicates that significant influence has been achieved.
(c) owns 50% or more of the common shares, and has achieved control.
(d) has purchased debt investments that will be held until maturity.

(SO 3) 8. Big K Ranch owns 20% of Little L Ranch. Little L Ranch reported profit of $150,000 and paid dividends of $40,000 this year. How much investment revenue would Big K Ranch report if it used the equity method to account for this investment?
(a) $8,000
(b) $22,000
(c) $30,000
(d) $110,000

(SO 4)   9. Athabasca Holdings Ltd. has owned 40% of the shares of Mackenzie Ltd. for a number of years. Athabasca reports under ASPE and uses the cost model. For the year just ended, Mackenzie earned $100,000 of profit and declared and paid dividends of $20,000. Athabasca would report how much investment revenue for the year pertaining to its investment in Mackenzie?
  (a) $8,000
  (b) $20,000
  (c) $32,000
  (d) $40,000

(SO 4)   10. Accumulated other comprehensive income is reported on which of the following statements?
  (a) Income statement
  (b) Statement of financial position
  (c) Statement of changes in equity
  (d) Both (b) and (c)

(SO 5)   *11. Which of the following statements is *incorrect* with regard to recording bonds under the amortized cost model?
  (a) Unrealized gains and losses are recorded through adjusting entries at the end of the period.

the navigator

  (b) A bond purchased at a premium will result in interest revenue recorded exceeding the amount of interest received.
  (c) Premiums and discounts are usually not recorded separately for the investor.
  (d) The investor records the bonds initially at acquisition cost rather than at their maturity value.

(SO 5)   *12. Bonds with a face value of $100,000 were purchased for $90,000 with the intention of holding the bonds to maturity. The following entry would be made by the investor when the semi-annual interest is received (assuming no previous accrual of interest):
  (a) Debit Cash, Credit Interest Revenue
  (b) Debit Cash, Credit Long-Term Investment, Credit Interest Revenue
  (c) Debit Cash, Debit Long-Term Investment, Credit Interest Revenue
  (d) Debit Cash, Debit Interest Revenue, Credit Long-Term Investment

Questions

(SO 1)   1. What are the reasons why corporations invest in debt and equity securities?

(SO 1)   2. Explain the differences between non-strategic and strategic investments.

(SO 1, 4)   3. Cumby Corporation is a golf equipment retailer that owns 1,000 common shares of Suncor Energy Inc. It intends to sell these shares if it needs cash. (a) Is the investment in Suncor considered a non-strategic investment or a strategic investment? Explain your reasoning. (b) Would the investment be classified as a current asset or a non-current asset on Cumby's statement of financial position?

(SO 2, 4)   4. At what amount—cost, amortized cost, or fair value—are each of the following reported on a statement of financial position: (a) common shares in a publicly traded company that will probably be sold within a year, (b) bond investments that will be held until maturity, and (c) shares in a private company that do not have a determinable fair value?

(SO 2)   5. What is the difference between realized gains/losses and unrealized gains/losses?

(SO 2)   6. Communications Inc. reported trading investments at their fair value of $255 million on its year-end statement of financial position. These securities were purchased earlier in the year at a cost of $245 million. (a) How should the difference between these two amounts be recorded and reported? (b) Would your answer differ if the fair value of these securities could not be determined?

(SO 2)   7. Timmerman Ltd. purchased $1 million of 10-year bonds at face value (100) in 2012. The bonds were trading at 105 on December 31, 2012. (a) At what amount would the bonds be reported in the December 31, 2012, statement of financial position if management intended to hold the bonds until maturity? (b) How would your answer differ if management were holding the bonds for trading purposes? Explain why the investment is reported differently depending on management's intentions.

(SO 2)   8. Music Makers Ltd. reported trading investments with an original cost of $115,000 and a fair value of $130,000 at December 31, 2011. It also reported an unrealized gain of $15,000 relating to the investment. During 2012, the investment was sold for $125,000. Describe how the sale of the investment would be recorded and reported in the 2012 financial statements.

(SO 3)   9. What constitutes "significant influence"? Is it safe to conclude that there is significant influence when a company owns 20% of the common shares of another company?

(SO 3)   10. When should a strategic equity investment in a publicly traded company be accounted for using (a) the cost model and (b) the equity method? Would your answer change if the investee was a private company?

(SO 3)   11. Identify what is included in the carrying amount of a strategic equity investment using the (a) cost model and (b) equity method.

(SO 3)　12. Explain how, and why, the investment revenue differs when a strategic long-term equity investment is accounted for using the (a) cost model and (b) equity method.

(SO 4)　13. Indicate how (a) trading investments, (b) investments in associates, and (c) debt investments held to maturity are classified on the statement of financial position.

(SO 4)　14. Identify the proper statement presentation of the following accounts: (a) Unrealized Gain on Trading Investments, (b) Realized Loss on Trading Investments, (c) Revenue from Investment in Associates, and (d) Realized Loss on Long-Term Investments.

(SO 4)　15. Distinguish between other comprehensive income and accumulated other comprehensive income. Indicate how each is reported in the financial statements.

(SO 4)　16. Explain how the income statement, statement of comprehensive income, statement of changes in equity, and statement of financial position are interrelated.

(SO 3, 4)　17. George Weston Ltd. owns 63% of the common shares of Loblaw Cos. Ltd. (a) What method should George Weston Ltd. use to account for this investment? (b) Which company is the parent? The subsidiary? (c) What kind of financial statements should George Weston Ltd. prepare to properly present this investment?

(SO 5)　*18. Compare the accounting for a debt investment in bonds to the accounting for a bond liability.

(SO 2, 5)　*19. Explain why premiums and discounts on bond investments must be amortized when using the amortized cost model and why no amortization occurs when using the fair value model.

(SO 5)　*20. When bonds mature, a journal entry is recorded on the books of both the investor and the investee (issuer). However, when bonds are sold by the investor prior to maturity on the open market, the sale of the bond investment results in a journal entry on the books of the investor, but not on the books of the investee (issuer). Explain why.

Brief Exercises

BE12–1　Identify whether each of the following is most likely (a) a debt or equity investment, and (b) a non-strategic or strategic investment. (c) Identify the most likely reason (in terms of gains or income) for making the investment.

Classify investments. (SO 1)

		(a) Debt or Equity Investment?	(b) Non-Strategic or Strategic Investment?	(c) Reason for Making the Investment?
1.	120-day treasury bill			
2.	Common shares of Manulife purchased with a temporary surplus of cash			
3.	30% of the common shares of a company purchased in order to obtain a position on the board of directors			
4.	Bonds purchased with a temporary cash surplus			
5.	100% of the common shares of a company purchased to amalgamate its operations with those of the investor			
6.	Five-year bonds intended to be held for the entire term of the bonds			

BE12–2　On January 1, 2012, Columbia Ltd. purchased $200,000 of 10%, 10-year bonds at face value (100) with the intention of selling the bonds early next year. Interest is received semi-annually on July 1 and January 1. At December 31, 2012, which is the company's fiscal year end, the bonds were trading in the market at 97. Prepare the journal entries to record (a) the purchase of the bonds on January 1, (b) the receipt of the interest on July 1, and (c) any adjusting entries required at December 31.

Record trading investment. (SO 2)

BE12–3　Using the data presented in BE12–2, assume that Columbia Ltd. intended to hold the investment until it matures. Prepare the journal entries to record (a) the purchase of the bonds on January 1, (b) the receipt of the interest on July 1, and (c) any adjusting entries required at December 31.

Record investment held to maturity. (SO 2)

Record trading investment. (SO 2)

BE12–4   Using the data presented in BE12-2, assume that the bonds were sold for $194,000 on January 2, 2013. Record the sale of the bonds.

Record trading investment. (SO 2)

BE12–5   On August 1, 2012, McLellan Ltd. purchased 1,000 Datawave common shares for $45,000 cash with the intention of trading the shares. On December 31, 2012, McLellan's year end, the shares' fair value was $49,000. Prepare the journal entry to record (a) the purchase of this investment on August 1, and (b) any adjusting journal entry required at December 31.

Record trading investment. (SO 2)

BE12–6   Using the data presented in BE12–5, assume that the shares were sold for $47,000 on February 1, 2013. Record the sale.

Record strategic investment, using equity method. (SO 3)

BE12–7   On January 1, Rook Corporation, a publicly traded company, purchased 25% of Hook Ltd. common shares for $400,000. At December 31, Hook paid a $32,000 dividend (Rook received its share that day) and reported profit of $800,000. The shares' fair value at December 31 was $420,000. Record each of these transactions, assuming Rook has significant influence over Hook. How much revenue would be reported by Rook because of its share of Hook?

Record strategic investment, using cost model. (SO 3)

BE12–8   Using the data presented in BE12–7, assume that Rook Corporation reports under ASPE and has chosen to account for its investment in Hook Ltd. using the cost model assuming that the shares do not trade in an active market. Record each of the transactions and any necessary adjusting journal entries under this assumption. How much revenue would be reported by Rook in this situation? Explain why this differs from your answer in BE12–7.

Record strategic investment, using fair value model. (SO 3)

BE12–9   Using the data presented in BE12–7, assume that Rook Corporation is not able to exercise significant influence over Hook Ltd. Record each of the transactions and any necessary adjusting journal entries under this assumption and also assume that management intends to hold the investment for a long time. How much revenue would be reported by Rook in this situation? Explain why this differs from your answers in BE12–7.

Determine investment account balances and indicate statement presentation. (SO 3, 4)

BE12–10   Chan Inc., a publicly traded company, purchased 20% of Dong Ltd.'s common shares for $225,000 on January 1. During the year, Dong reported profit of $350,000 and paid a dividend of $40,000. The investment's fair value at December 31 was $275,000. (a) Assuming there is significant influence, indicate the balance in the investment account at year end and where it would be reported in the statement of financial position. (b) Assuming Chan does not have significant influence, determine the balance in the investment account at year end and where it would be reported in the statement of financial position. (c) Assuming Chan reports under ASPE and chooses to use the cost model, determine the balance in the investment account at year end and where it would be reported in the statement of financial position.

Adjust trading investments; show statement presentation. (SO 2, 4)

BE12–11   Cost and fair value for the trading investments of Kootenay Ltd. at December 31, 2012, are $102,000 and $118,000, respectively. (a) Prepare the adjusting entry to record the investments at fair value. (b) Show the financial statement presentation of the investments and any related accounts.

Indicate statement presentation. (SO 4)

BE12–12   Indicate on which financial statement (i.e., the statement of financial position, income statement, or statement of changes in equity) each of the following accounts would be reported. Also give the appropriate financial statement classification (e.g., current assets, non-current assets, shareholders' equity, other revenues and gains, etc.).

	Financial Statement	Classification
A bond investment that will mature next year	_____	_____
Dividend revenue	_____	_____
Investment in associate	_____	_____
Investment of a few hundred common shares in a large publicly traded company that is held for trading purposes	_____	_____
A bond investment that management intends to hold for 10 years	_____	_____
Realized gain on a trading investment	_____	_____
Unrealized gain on a trading investment	_____	_____
Dividends received from a non-strategic investment	_____	_____
Interest earned on a trading investment	_____	_____

Classify items as profit or OCI. (SO 4)

BE12–13   Rosewater Corporation, which reports under IFRS, reported a realized gain on the sale of long-term bond investments and an unrealized loss of $28,000 on its trading investments for the year ended April 30, 2012. The corporation also has $17,000 of revenue relating to its share of the profit of an associate. The accountant wasn't absolutely sure if these items should have been included in profit or in other comprehensive income. Identify whether each of the above items should be included in profit or OCI. Would your answer change if the equity investment was not a trading investment?

BE12–14 Sabre Corporation, which reports under IFRS, has the following investments at December 31, 2012:

1. Trading investments: common shares of National Bank, cost $25,000, fair value $29,000
2. Investment in an associate (40% ownership): common shares of Sword Corp., cost $110,000, fair value cannot be determined as the shares do not trade publicly. Investment was purchased on January 1, 2012. For the year ended December 31, 2012, Sword Corp. reported profit of $25,000 and paid out dividends of $8,000.
3. Equity investment: common shares of Epee Inc. (18% ownership) purchased on July 1, 2012, cost $210,000, fair value at December 31, 2012, $275,000. Management intends to purchase more shares of Epee in two years. Epee earned $21,000 for the year ended December 31, 2012, and paid out dividends of $1,000 which were received at the end of each quarter in 2012.
4. Bond investment that is to be held to maturity: bonds of Ghoti Ltd., amortized cost $160,000, fair value $172,000

Prepare a partial statement of financial position for Sabre Corporation at December 31, 2012.

Prepare partial statement of financial position.
(SO 4)

BE12–15 Brookfield Asset Management Inc., a publicly traded company, reported in note 8 to its financial statements for the year ended December 31, 2010, the following information: purchases of investments in associates: $1,738 million; share of profit of associates: $765 million; dividends received from associates: $374 million; investment in associates at year end: $6,629 million. Explain how each of these amounts should be reported in Brookfield's financial statements.

Indicate statement presentation.
(SO 4)

*BE12–16 On June 30, $150,000 of five-year, 10% Plaza bonds are issued at $138,960 to yield a market interest rate of 12%. Interest is payable semi-annually each June 30 and December 31. (a) Record the purchase of these bonds on June 30 and the receipt of the first interest payment on December 31 on the books of the investor assuming the bonds are to be held to maturity. (b) Record the issue of the bonds on June 30 and the first interest payment on December 31 on the books of the investee (issuer).

Record bonds for investor and investee.
(SO 5)

Exercises

E12–1 Gleason Telecommunications Ltd. has several investments in debt and equity securities of other companies:

1. 15% of the common shares of Morrison Telecommunications Inc., with the intent of purchasing at least 10% more of the common shares and requesting a seat on Morrison's board of directors
2. 100% of the 15-year bonds issued by Li Internet Ltd., intended to be held for 15 years
3. 95% of the common shares of Barlow Internet Services Inc.
4. 120-day treasury bills, purchased for interest income
5. 10% of the common shares of Talk to Us Ltd., to be sold if the share price increases

Classify investments.
(SO 1)

Instructions
Indicate whether each of the above investments is a (a) debt or equity investment, and (b) non-strategic or strategic investment.

E12–2 Kroshka Holdings Corporation has several investments in debt and equity securities of other companies:

1. 10-year BCE bonds, intended to be held until the bonds mature
2. 10-year GE bonds, intended to be sold if interest rates go down
3. 5-year Government of Canada bonds, intended to be sold if cash is needed
4. 180-day treasury bill
5. Bank of Montreal preferred shares, purchased for the dividend income
6. TMX common shares, purchased to sell in the near term at a profit. These shares are part of an investment portfolio that is actively traded.

Classify investments.
(SO 1, 4)

Instructions
(a) Indicate whether each of the above investments is a non-strategic or strategic investment.
(b) For each investment that you classified as non-strategic in part (a), indicate whether it is a trading investment, an investment that will be held until maturity, or an investment that does not relate to these two categories.
(c) Indicate whether each of the above investments would be classified as a short-term (current asset) or long-term investment on Kroshka Holdings' statement of financial position.

E12–3 Matthews Ltd. purchased $700,000 of 10-year, 10% bonds on July 1, 2012, at 106.5. The purchase price was based on a market interest rate of 9%. Interest is received semi-annually on January 1 and July 1. The bonds were trading at 107 at December 31, 2012. Matthews intends to trade the bonds in the near future.

Record trading investment.
(SO 2)

Instructions

(a) Record the purchase of the bonds.

(b) Record any required adjusting journal entries at December 31.

Record trading investment.
(SO 2)

E12–4 During the year ended December 31, 2012, McCormick Inc. had the following transactions for its trading investments:

Jan.	1	Purchased 2,000 Starr Corporation $5, preferred shares for $210,000 cash.
Apr.	1	Received quarterly cash dividend.
July	1	Received quarterly cash dividend.
	2	Sold 500 Starr shares for $57,000 cash.
Oct.	1	Received quarterly cash dividend.
Nov.	22	Starr declared the quarterly dividend on November 22, to preferred shareholders of record on December 15, payable on January 1.
Dec.	31	Starr's shares were trading at $115 per share.

Instructions

(a) Record the above transactions.

(b) Prepare any required adjusting entries at December 31. If no adjusting entries are required, explain why.

(c) On February 15, 2013, McCormick sold 500 Starr shares for $117 per share. Record the sale of the shares.

Adjust trading investment for multiple years.
(SO 2)

E12–5 Kouchibouguac Inc. reports the following costs and fair values for its trading investment portfolio of multiple years at June 30:

	2010	2011	2012
Cost	$269,000	$269,000	$269,000
Fair value	260,500	275,400	281,200

Instructions

Prepare the required adjusting entry to report the investment portfolio at its fair value at June 30 of each year.

Record trading investments; indicate statement presentation.
(SO 2, 4)

E12–6 At December 31, 2012, the trading investments for Yanik Inc. are as follows:

Security	Cost	Fair Value
A	$18,500	$21,000
B	12,500	14,000
C	21,000	19,000
Totals	$52,000	$54,000

Instructions

(a) Prepare the adjusting entry at December 31 to report the trading investment portfolio at fair value.

(b) Show the financial statement presentation of the trading investments and any related accounts at December 31, 2012.

(c) On March 22, 2013, Yanik sold security A for $22,000 cash. Record the sale of the security.

Record strategic investment, using cost and fair value models.
(SO 3)

E12–7 Aurora Cosmetics Ltd., which reports under IFRS, acquired 40% of Diner Corporation's 30,000 common shares for $16 per share on January 1, 2012. On June 15, Diner paid a cash dividend of $70,000 and Aurora received its share of the dividend on the same day. On December 31, Diner reported profit of $150,000 for the year. At December 31, Diner's shares were trading at $20 per share.

   Aurora Cosmetics also acquired 15% of the 200,000 common shares of Bell Fashion Ltd. for $28 per share on March 18, 2012. On June 30, Bell paid a $150,000 dividend. On December 31, Bell reported profit of $320,000 for the year. At December 31, Bell's shares were trading at $26 per share. Aurora intends to hold on to the Bell shares as a long-term investment for the dividend income.

Instructions

Record the above transactions for the year ended December 31, 2012.

Identify method of accounting for strategic investments.
(SO 3)

E12–8 Cameco Corp., the world's largest producer of uranium concentrates, has several long-term investments, including a 100% investment in Cameco Europe, a 23.3% investment in UEX Corporation (a publicly traded company that Cameco does not want to trade), and a 24% interest in Global Laser Enrichment LLC (a private corporation with no determinable fair value that Cameco does not wish to trade).

Instructions

(a) Indicate whether each of the above investments should be accounted for using the cost model, the fair value model, or the equity method, and explain why.

(b) Which of the above investments, if any, should be consolidated with Cameco's operations?

E12–9 Lovell Corporation purchased 200,000 of the 1 million common shares of Abacus Ltd. on October 1, 2012, at $2.50 per share. Near the end of the fourth quarter, Abacus declared and paid dividends on its common shares of $80,000. Lovell received its share of the dividends on December 29. Abacus also announced that it had profit for the quarter ending December 31, 2012, of $200,000. At the end of the year, the Abacus common share price had risen to $3 per share.

Account for investment in associates.
(SO 3, 4)

Instructions
Record the journal entries that Lovell would make during the last quarter ending December 31, 2012, under the following assumptions:
(a) Lowell reports under IFRS and has significant influence over Abacus.
(b) Lowell reports under IFRS but does not have significant influence over Abacus.
(c) Lowell reports under ASPE and has significant influence over Abacus but has chosen to use the cost model for this investment under the assumption that the fair value of Abacus shares cannot be obtained.

E12–10 Grimsby Holdings Ltd. reports under IFRS and has two portfolios of investments: trading investments and investments in associates. Information regarding these two portfolios is shown below:

Determine investment account balances and indicate statement presentation.
(SO 2, 3, 4)

Account	Trading Investments	Investments in Associates
Balance, beginning of year	$100,000	$300,000
Purchases of investments during the year	30,000	40,000
Proceeds from sale of investments during the year	55,000	32,000
Realized gain (loss) on sale of investments	12,000	(10,000)
Dividends received	3,000	8,000
Share of associates' profit		43,000
Fair value of portfolio, end of year	94,000	350,000

Instructions
(a) Calculate the ending balance for each investment category at the end of the year.
(b) Record the journal entries for each event described in the table above.
(c) Present the amounts that would be reported on the income statement and statement of financial position at year end.

*E12–11 On June 30, 2012, Imperial Inc. purchased $500,000 of Acme Corp. 5% bonds at a price to yield a market interest rate of 6%. The bonds pay interest semi-annually on June 30 and December 31, and mature on June 30, 2022. Imperial plans to hold this investment until it matures. At December 31, 2012, which is the year end for both companies, the bonds were trading at 93.

Record bonds for investor and investee.
(SO 5)

Instructions
(a) Calculate the present value (issue price) of the bonds on June 30, 2012.
(b) For Imperial, the investor, record
   1. the purchase of the bonds on June 30, 2012,
   2. the receipt of interest on December 31, 2012, and
   3. the receipt of interest on June 30, 2013.
(c) For Acme, the investee (issuer), record
   1. the issue of the bonds on June 30, 2012,
   2. the payment of interest on December 31, 2012, and
   3. the payment of interest on June 30, 2013.
(d) Explain how your responses to (a) and (b) would differ if Imperial classified the bond investment as a trading investment instead of one that would be held until maturity.

Problems: Set A

P12–1A The following Givarz Corporation transactions are for bonds that were purchased as trading investments for the year ended December 31, 2012:

Record trading investments; show statement presentation.
(SO 2, 4)

Feb.	1	Purchased $100,000 of Leslye Corporation 9% bonds at 104. Interest is received semi-annually on August 1 and February 1. The bonds mature on February 1, 2014.
Aug.	1	Received interest on Leslye bonds.
	2	Sold $40,000 of the Leslye bonds at 102.
Dec.	31	Accrued interest on the remaining bonds.
	31	The fair value of the remaining bonds was 100 on this date.

Instructions

(a) Record the above transactions, including required adjusting entries (if any).
(b) Show how the investments would be presented on the statement of financial position at December 31, 2012.
(c) Determine the balance in each of the income statement accounts that are affected in the transactions above and indicate how they would be presented on the income statement for the year ended December 31, 2012.

Record trading invest-
ments; show statement
presentation.
(SO 2, 4)

P12–2A   During 2012, Kakisa Financial Corporation had the following trading investment transactions:

Feb.	1	Purchased 600 CBF common shares for $36,000.
Mar.	1	Purchased 800 RSD common shares for $24,000.
Apr.	1	Purchased 7% MRT bonds at face value, for $60,000. Interest is received semi-annually on April 1 and October 1.
July	1	Received a cash dividend of $3 per share on the CBF common shares.
Aug.	1	Sold 200 CBF common shares at $58 per share.
Sept.	1	Received a cash dividend of $1.50 per share on the RSD common shares.
Oct.	1	Received the semi-annual interest on the MRT bonds.
	1	Sold the MRT bonds for $62,000.
Dec.	31	The market prices of the CBF and RSD common shares were $55 and $31 per share, respectively.

Instructions

(a) Record the above transactions, including required adjusting entries (if any).
(b) Show how the investments would be presented on the statement of financial position at December 31, 2012.
(c) Determine the balance in each of the income statement accounts that are affected in the transactions above and indicate how they would be presented on the income statement for the year ended December 31, 2012.

Record trading
investments; show
statement presentation.
(SO 2, 4)

P12–3A   Data for Kakisa Financial's trading investment transactions in 2012 are presented in P12–2A. Kakisa had the following trading investment transactions in 2013:

Mar.	1	Sold 400 CBF common shares for $23,600.
June	1	Purchased 2,000 KEF common shares for $28,000.
Sept.	1	Received a cash dividend of $1.50 per share on the RSD common shares.
Oct.	1	Sold 400 RSD common shares for $12,500.
Dec.	1	The market prices of the RSD and KEF common shares were $33 and $11 per share, respectively.

Instructions

(a) Record the above transactions, including required adjusting entries (if any).
(b) Show how the investments would be presented on the statement of financial position at December 31, 2013.
(c) Determine the balance in each of the income statement accounts that are affected in the transactions above and indicate how they would be presented on the income statement for the year ended December 31, 2013.

Record trading
investments; show
statement presentation.
(SO 2, 4)

P12–4A   On December 31, 2010, Chartwell Financial Corporation's portfolio of trading investments consisted of the following securities:

	Quantity	Carrying Amount	Fair Value
Alpha Ltd. common shares	1,000	$ 50,000	$ 50,000
Bravo Ltd. common shares	1,400	98,000	98,000
Hicks Ltd. preferred shares	800	32,000	32,000
		$180,000	$180,000

The following transactions occurred in 2011:

Jan.	7	Sold all of the Alpha common shares at $48 per share.
	10	Purchased 800 Miranda Limited common shares at $90 per share.
Feb.	2	Received a cash dividend of $2.50 per share on the Hicks preferred shares.
	10	Sold all the Hicks preferred shares at $35 per share.
Mar.	15	Received 70 Bravo common shares as a result of a 5% stock dividend when the price was $66 per share.
June	23	Received 1,600 additional Miranda common shares as a result of a 3-for-1 stock split.
Sept.	1	Purchased an additional 600 Miranda common shares at $28 per share.
Dec.	15	Received a cash dividend of $0.50 per share on the Miranda common shares.
	31	The market prices of the Bravo and Miranda common shares were $60 per share and $32 per share, respectively.

Instructions

(a) Record the above transactions, including required adjusting entries (if any).
(b) Show how the investments would be presented on the statement of financial position at December 31, 2011.
(c) Determine the balance in each of the income statement accounts that are affected in the transactions above and indicate how they would be presented on the income statement for the year ended December 31, 2011.
(d) How would your answers to (b) and (c) change if the fair values of the securities in the portfolio could not be obtained?

P12–5A Data for Chartwell Financial's trading investment transactions in 2011 were presented in P12–4A. The following data relate to trading investment activity during 2012:

Record trading investments; show statement presentation.
(SO 2, 4)

1. Sold all of the Bravo common shares for $58 per share.
2. The market price of the Miranda common shares at December 31, 2012, was $34 per share.

Instructions

(a) Record the sale of the Bravo common shares and any adjusting entries required at year end.
(b) Show how the investments would be presented on the statement of financial position at December 31, 2012.
(c) Determine the balance in each of the income statement accounts that are affected in the transactions above and indicate how they would be presented on the income statement for the year ended December 31, 2012.
(d) How would your answers to (b) and (c) change if the fair values of the securities in the portfolio could not be obtained?

P12–6A On December 31, 2012, Val d'Or Ltée, a publicly traded company, held the following debt and equity investments:

Determine valuation of investments; indicate statement presentation.
(SO 2, 4)

	Quantity	Cost per Unit	Fair Value per Unit
Debt Securities			
CIBC bonds	2,000	$100	$ 97
Government of Canada bonds	1,000	100	135
Equity Securities			
Bank of Montreal	2,000	55	61
Fortis Inc.	5,000	29	32
TransCanada Corp.	5,000	36	40

Instructions

(a) Calculate the cost and fair value of Val d'Or's investment portfolio at December 31.
(b) If Val d'Or considers its entire portfolio to be trading investments, at what value should the investments be reported on the statement of financial position at December 31? At what amount, and where, should any unrealized gains or losses on the debt securities be reported?
(c) If Val d'Or intends to hold the debt securities until maturity, at what value should the investments be reported on the statement of financial position at December 31? At what amount, and where, should any unrealized gains or losses be reported?
(d) If all of the investments held by Val d'Or related to private companies and no fair value information relating to these securities could be obtained, what would be the impact on the income statement and on the statement of financial position?

P12–7A Lai Inc., which reports under IFRS, had the following investment transactions:

Identify impact of investment transactions.
(SO 2, 3, 4)

1. Purchased Chang Corporation preferred shares as a trading investment.
2. Received a stock dividend on the Chang preferred shares.
3. Purchased Government of Canada bonds for cash, intending to hold them until maturity.
4. Accrued interest on the Government of Canada bonds.
5. Sold half of the Chang preferred shares at a price less than originally paid.
6. On the first day of the year, purchased 25% of Xing Ltd.'s common shares, which was enough to achieve significant influence.
7. Received Xing's financial statements, which reported a net loss for the year.
8. Received a cash dividend from Xing.
9. The fair value of Chang's preferred shares was lower than cost at year end.
10. The fair value of the Government of Canada bonds was higher than cost at year end.

Instructions

(a) Using the following table format, indicate whether each of the above transactions would result in an increase (+), a decrease (−), or no effect (NE) on the specific element in the statement. The first one has been done for you as an example.

Statement of Financial Position			Income Statement		
Assets	Liabilities	Shareholders' Equity	Revenues and Gains	Expenses and Losses	Profit
1. (+/−) NE	NE	NE	NE	NE	NE

(b) Which of your answers in the table above would change if Lai reported under ASPE and chose to use the cost model to account for its investments in associates?

Record strategic investment using various models.
(SO 3)

P12–8A   Drummond Services Ltd., which reports under IFRS, acquired 25% of the common shares of Bella Roma Ltd. on January 1, 2012, by paying $1.8 million for 100,000 shares. Bella Roma paid a $0.50-per-share cash dividend in each quarter that was received on March 15, June 15, September 15, and December 15. Bella Roma reported profit of $1.1 million for the year. At December 31, the market price of the Bella Roma shares was $17 per share.

Instructions
(a) Prepare the journal entries for Drummond Services for 2012, assuming Drummond cannot exercise significant influence over Bella Roma but intends to hold the shares for a number of years.
(b) Prepare the journal entries for Drummond Services for 2012, assuming Drummond can exercise significant influence over Bella Roma.
(c) What factors help determine whether a company has significant influence over another company?
(d) Prepare the journal entries for Drummond Services for 2012, assuming that the company reports under ASPE and has chosen to account for its investment using the cost model.
(e) Under ASPE, why do you think companies can choose to use the cost model?
(f) For (a), (b), and (d) above, track the movement in all accounts affected by this investment throughout 2012 in columnar format, showing the balance in the accounts at the beginning of the year and the amount of each transaction affecting the accounts during the year to arrive at the balance in the accounts at the end of the year.

Record strategic investment using various models; indicate statement presentation.
(SO 3, 4)

P12–9A   Hat Limited has a total of 200,000 common shares issued. On October 3, 2011, CT Inc., a publicly traded company, purchased a block of these shares in the open market at $50 per share to hold as a long-term equity investment. Hat reported profit of $575,000 for the year ended September 30, 2012, and CT received a $0.25-per-share dividend on that date. Hat's shares were trading at $53 per share at September 30, 20012.
   This problem assumes three independent situations related to the accounting for this investment by CT:

   Situation 1: CT purchased 25,000 Hat common shares.
   Situation 2: CT purchased 70,000 Hat common shares.
   Situation 3: CT purchased 200,000 Hat common shares.

Instructions
(a) For each situation, identify whether CT should use the cost model, fair value model, equity method or consolidation to account for its investment in Hat.
(b) For situations 1 and 2, record in CT's books all transactions related to the investment for the year ended September 30, 2012.
(c) Track the movement throughout the year in the investment account and any related investment revenue account for situations 1 and 2 in columnar format, showing the balance in these accounts at the beginning of the fiscal year and the amount of any transactions affecting the accounts during the year to arrive at the balance in the accounts at the end of the fiscal year on September 30, 2012.
(d) In situation 3, what kind of financial statements should be prepared to report the combined operations of CT and Hat? Whose name will be on the financial statements?
(e) In situation 2, what other method could CT use if it was reporting under ASPE rather than IFRS and the shares did not trade in an active market? Why do you think this option exists?

Analyze strategic investment.
(SO 3)

P12–10A   Sandhu Travel Agency Ltd. has 400,000 common shares authorized and 120,000 shares issued on December 31, 2011. On January 2, 2012, Kang Inc., which reports under IFRS, purchased shares of Sandhu Travel Agency for $40 per share. Kang intends to hold these shares as a long-term investment.
   Kang's accountant prepared a trial balance as at December 31, 2012, under the assumption that Kang could not exercise significant influence over Sandhu Travel Agency. Under this assumption, the trial balance included the following accounts and amounts related to the Sandhu investment:

Long-term investment	$1,320,000
Dividend revenue	90,000
Unrealized gain on long-term investment	120,000

Instructions
(a) How many shares of Sandhu Travel Agency did Kang purchase on January 2? (*Hint:* Subtract the unrealized gain from the investment account.)
(b) What percentage of Sandhu Travel Agency's shares does Kang own?
(c) What was the amount of the cash dividend per share that Kang received from Sandhu Travel Agency in 2012?
(d) What was the fair value per share of the Sandhu Travel Agency shares at December 31, 2012?
(e) Assume that, after closely examining the situation, Kang's auditors determine that Kang does have significant influence over Sandhu Travel Agency. Accordingly, the investment account balance is adjusted to $1,400,000 at December 31, 2012. What was the profit reported by Sandhu Travel Agency for the year ended December 31, 2012?

(f) Assuming that Kang does have significant influence over Sandhu Travel Agency, what amount will Kang report on its income statement for 2012 with regard to this investment?

(g) How would your answer to (f) change if Kang reported under ASPE and chose to use the cost model when accounting for its investment in Sandhu because the shares did not trade in an active market?

*P12–11A   On January 1, 2012, Jackson Corp. purchased $1.6 million of 10-year, 7% bonds for $1,658,157. The purchase price was based on a market interest rate of 6.5%. Interest is received semi-annually on July 1 and January 1. Jackson's year end is September 30. Jackson intends to hold the bonds until January 1, 2022, the date the bonds mature. The bonds' trading value was $1,660,000 on September 30, 2012.

Record bond investment; show statement presentation. (SO 4, 5)

Instructions

(a) Record the purchase of the bonds on January 1, 2012.

(b) Prepare a bond amortization schedule for the term of the bonds.

(c) Prepare the entry to record the receipt of interest on July 1, 2012.

(d) Prepare any adjusting entries required at September 30, 2012.

(e) Prepare the entry to record the repayment of the bonds on January 1, 2022.

(f) Show the financial statement presentation of the bonds at September 30, 2012.

(g) How would your answer to (d) change if the bonds were held for trading purposes?

*P12–12A   The following bond transactions occurred during 2012 for the University of Higher Learning (UHL) and Otutye Ltd.:

Record bonds for investor and investee. (SO 5)

Feb.   1   UHL issued $10 million of five-year, 8% bonds at 98. The bonds pay interest semi-annually on August 1 and February 1 and were sold at a discount because the market interest rate was 8.5%.

       1   Otutye Ltd. purchased $3 million of UHL's bonds at 98 as a long-term investment that was to be held to maturity.

Aug.   1   The semi-annual interest on the bonds was paid.

       1   After paying the semi-annual interest on the bonds on this date, UHL decided to repurchase $3 million of its bonds and retire them. UHL repurchased all $3 million of the bonds from Otutye at 99.

Instructions

(a) Prepare all required journal entries for Otutye Ltd., the investor, to record the above transactions.

(b) How would the journal entries for Otutye Ltd. change if the investment had been purchased for trading purposes?

(c) Prepare all required entries for UHL, the investee, to record the above transactions.

(d) Comment on the differences in recording that you observe between the investor and the investee.

Problems: Set B

P12–1B   The following Liu Corporation transactions are for bonds that were purchased as trading investments for the year ended December 31, 2012:

Record trading investments; show statement presentation. (SO 2, 4)

Jan.   1   Purchased $100,000 of RAM Corporation 8% bonds at 96. Interest is received semi-annually on July 1 and January 1. The bonds mature on January 1, 2014.

July   1   Received interest on the RAM bonds.

       2   Sold $25,000 of RAM bonds at 100.

Dec.   31   Accrued interest on the remaining bonds.

       31   The fair value of the remaining bonds was 101 on this date.

Instructions

(a) Record the above transactions, including required adjusting entries (if any).

(b) Show how the investments would be presented on the statement of financial position at December 31, 2012.

(c) Determine the balance in each of the income statement accounts that are affected in the transactions above and indicate how they would be presented on the income statement for the year ended December 31, 2012.

P12–2B   During 2012, Cheque Mart Ltd. had the following trading investment transactions:

Record trading investments; show statement presentation. (SO 2, 4)

Feb.   1   Purchased 1,000 IBF common shares for $30,000.

Mar.   1   Purchased 500 RST common shares for $29,000.

Apr.   1   Purchased 6% CRT bonds at face value, for $90,000. Interest is received semi-annually on April 1 and October 1

July   1   Received a cash dividend of $2 per share on the IBF common shares.

Aug.   1   Sold 350 IBF common shares at $33 per share.

Sept. 1 Received a cash dividend of $1.50 per share on the RST common shares.
Oct.   1 Received the semi-annual interest on the CRT bonds.
       1 Sold the CRT bonds for $86,000.
Dec. 31 The market prices of the IBF and RST common shares were $28 and $62 per share, respectively.

Instructions

(a) Record the above transactions, including required adjusting entries (if any).
(b) Show how the investments would be presented on the statement of financial position at December 31, 2012.
(c) Determine the balance in each of the income statement accounts that are affected in the transactions above and indicate how they would be presented on the income statement for the year ended December 31, 2012.

Record trading investments; show statement presentation. (SO 2, 4)

P12–3B Data for Cheque Mart's trading investment transactions in 2012 are presented in P12–2B. Cheque Mart had the following trading investment transactions in 2013:

Mar.   1 Sold 650 IBF common shares for $22,100.
June   1 Purchased 2,000 DEF common shares for $18,000.
Sept. 1 Received a cash dividend of $1.50 per share on the RST common shares.
Oct.   1 Sold 250 RST common shares for $14,250.
Dec. 31 The market prices of the RST and DEF common shares were $56 and $12 per share, respectively.

Instructions

(a) Record the above transactions, including required adjusting entries (if any).
(b) Show how the investments would be presented on the statement of financial position at December 31, 2013.
(c) Determine the balance in each of the income statement accounts that are affected in the transactions above and indicate how they would be presented on the income statement for the year ended December 31, 2013.

Record trading investments; show statement presentation. (SO 2, 4)

P12–4B On December 31, 2010, Cantech Limited's portfolio of trading investments was as follows:

	Quantity	Carrying Amount	Fair Value
Elana Ltd. common shares	1,000	$ 56,000	$ 56,000
Haley Ltd. common shares	1,400	98,000	98,000
Renda Corp. preferred shares	800	36,000	36,000
		$190,000	$190,000

The following transactions occurred in 2011:

Jan.   7 Sold all of the Elana common shares at $59 per share.
      10 Purchased 400 Melinda Corporation common shares at $65 per share.
      26 Received a cash dividend of $1.20 per share on the Haley common shares.
Feb.   2 Received a cash dividend of $1 per share on the Renda preferred shares.
      10 Sold all of the Renda preferred shares at $42 per share.
Apr. 30 Received 1,400 additional Haley common shares as a result of a 2-for-1 stock split.
July   1 Received a cash dividend of $0.60 per share on the Haley common shares.
Aug. 23 Received 20 Melinda common shares as a result of a 5% stock dividend when the price was $62 per share.
Sept. 1 Purchased an additional 400 Melinda common shares at $62 per share.
Dec. 31 The market price of Haley common shares was $37 per share and the market price of Melinda common shares was $43 per share.

Instructions

(a) Record the above transactions, including required adjusting entries (if any).
(b) Show how the investments would be presented on the statement of financial position at December 31, 2011.
(c) Determine the balance in each of the income statement accounts that are affected in the transactions above and indicate how they would be presented on the income statement for the year ended December 31, 2011.
(d) How would your answers to (b) and (c) change if the fair values of the securities in the portfolio could not be obtained?

Record trading investments; show statement presentation. (SO 2, 4)

P12–5B Data for Cantech's trading investment transactions in 2011 were presented in P12–4B. The following data relate to trading investment activity during 2012:

1. Sold all of the Haley common shares for $39 a share.
2. The market price of the Melinda common shares at December 31, 2012, was $41 per share.

Instructions

(a) Record the sale of the Haley common shares and any adjusting entries required at year end.
(b) Show how the investments would be presented on the statement of financial position at December 31, 2012.

(c) Determine the balance in each of the income statement accounts that are affected in the transactions above and indicate how they would be presented on the income statement for the year ended December 31, 2012.

(d) How would your answers to (b) and (c) change if the fair values of the securities in the portfolio could not be obtained?

P12–6B On January 1, 2012, Sturge Enterprises Inc., a publicly held company, held the following debt and equity investments:

Security	Quantity	Cost per Unit
Ajax Ltd. shares	1,500	$12
Beta Corp. shares	2,000	7

Determine valuation of investments; indicate statement presentation.
(SO 2, 4)

During the year, Sturge made the following purchases:

Security	Quantity	Cost per Unit
Ajax Ltd. shares	1,200	$ 11
Ajax Ltd. shares	1,000	9
Ajax Ltd. shares	1,000	10
Beta Corp. shares	500	8
Citrus Inc. bonds	300	100

There were no differences between cost and fair value at January 1, 2012. The market prices of the various securities at year end, December 31, 2012, were as follows: Ajax shares $6; Beta shares $9; and Citrus bonds $107.

Instructions

(a) Calculate the cost and fair value of Sturge Enterprises' investment portfolio at December 31.

(b) If Sturge Enterprises considers its entire portfolio to be trading investments, at what value should these investments be reported on the statement of financial position at December 31? At what amount, and where, should any unrealized gains or losses be reported?

(c) If Sturge Enterprises intends to hold the Citrus bonds until they mature, at what value should these bonds be reported on the statement of financial position at December 31? At what amount, and where, should any unrealized gains or losses on the bonds be reported?

(d) If all of the investments held by Sturge Enterprises related to private companies and no fair value information related to these securities could be obtained, what would be the impact on the income statement and on the statement of financial position?

P12–7B Olsztyn Inc., which reports under IFRS, had the following investment transactions:

1. Purchased Arichat Corporation common shares as trading investment.
2. Received a cash dividend on Arichat common shares.
3. Purchased Bombardier bonds intending to hold them to maturity.
4. Received interest on Bombardier bonds.
5. Sold half of the Bombardier bonds at a price greater than originally paid.
6. On the first day of the year, purchased 40% of LaHave Ltd.'s common shares, which was enough to achieve significant influence.
7. Received LaHave's financial statements, which reported profit for the year.
8. Received a cash dividend from LaHave.
9. The fair value of Arichat's common shares was higher than cost at year end.
10. The fair value of Bombardier's bonds was lower than their amortized cost at year end.

Identify impact of investment transactions.
(SO 2, 3, 4)

Instructions

(a) Using the following table format, indicate whether each of the above transactions would result in an increase (+), a decrease (−), or no effect (NE) on the specific element on the statement. The first one has been done for you as an example.

Statement of Financial Position			Income Statement		
Assets	Liabilities	Shareholders' Equity	Revenues and Gains	Expenses and Losses	Profit
1. (+/−) NE	NE	NE	NE	NE	NE

(b) Which of your answers in the table above would change if Olsztyn reported under ASPE and chose to use the cost model to account for its investments in associates because the shares did not trade in an active market?

P12–8B Cassidy Concrete Corp., which reports under IFRS, acquired 20% of Enda Inc.'s common shares on January 1, 2012, by paying $3 million for 100,000 shares. Enda paid a $0.50-per-share cash dividend which Cassidy received on June 30 and again on December 31. Enda reported profit of $1,680,000 for the year. At December 31, the market price of the Enda shares was $31 per share.

Record strategic investment using various models.
(SO 3)

Instructions

(a) Prepare the journal entries for Cassidy Concrete for 2012, assuming Cassidy cannot exercise significant influence over Enda.

(b) Prepare the journal entries for Cassidy Concrete for 2012, assuming Cassidy can exercise significant influence over Enda.

(c) What factors help determine whether a company has significant influence over another company?

(d) Prepare the journal entries for Cassidy Concrete for 2012, assuming that the company reports under ASPE and has chosen to account for its investment using the cost model because the shares did not trade in an active market.

(e) Under ASPE, why do you think companies can choose to use the cost model?

(f) For (a), (b), and (d) above, track the movement in all accounts affected by this investment throughout 2012 in columnar format, showing the balance in the accounts at the beginning of the year and the amount of each transaction affecting the accounts during the year to arrive at the balance in the accounts at the end of the year.

Record strategic investment using various models; indicate statement presentation.
(SO 3, 4)

P12–9B   Sub Corporation has a total of 500,000 common shares issued. On January 2, 2012, Partridge Inc., a publicly traded company, purchased a block of these shares in the open market at $10 per share to hold as a long-term equity investment. At the end of 2012, Sub Corporation reported profit of $350,000 and Partridge received a $0.50-per-share dividend from Sub. Sub Corporation's shares were trading at $12 per share at December 31, 2012.

This problem assumes three independent situations related to the accounting for this investment by Partridge:

Situation 1: Partridge purchased 60,000 Sub common shares.
Situation 2: Partridge purchased 125,000 Sub common shares.
Situation 3: Partridge purchased 500,000 Sub common shares.

Instructions

(a) For each situation, identify whether Partridge should use the cost model, the fair value model, the equity method or consolidation to account for its investment in Sub.

(b) For situations 1 and 2, record in Partridge's books all transactions related to the investment for the year ended December 31, 2012.

(c) Track the movement throughout the year in the investment account and any related investment revenue account for situations 1 and 2 in columnar format, showing the balance in these accounts at the beginning of the fiscal year and the amount of any transactions affecting the accounts during the year to arrive at the balance in these accounts at the end of the fiscal year on December 31, 2012.

(d) In situation 3, what kind of financial statements should be prepared to report the combined operations of Partridge and Sub? Whose name will be on the financial statements?

(e) In situation 2, what other method could Partridge use if it was reporting under ASPE rather than IFRS and the shares did not trade in an active market? Why do you think this option exists?

Analyze strategic investment.
(SO 3)

P12–10B   On January 2, 2012, Hadley Inc., which reports under IFRS, purchased shares of Letourneau Cycles Corp. for $10 per share. Hadley intends to hold these shares as a long-term investment. During 2012, Letourneau Cycles reported profit of $1 million and paid cash dividends of $200,000. The investment's fair value at December 31, 2012, was $950,000.

Hadley's accountant prepared a trial balance as at December 31, 2012, under the assumption that Hadley could exercise significant influence over Letourneau Cycles. Under this assumption, the trial balance included the following accounts and amounts:

Investment in associates	$960,000
Investment revenue	200,000

Instructions

(a) What percentage of the Letourneau Cycles' shares does Hadley own? (*Hint:* The ownership percentage can be determined using the investment revenue and Letourneau's profit.)

(b) What was the amount of the cash dividend that Hadley received from Letourneau Cycles during 2012?

(c) How many shares of Letourneau Cycles did Hadley purchase on January 2?

(d) What questions need to be asked to determine if Hadley has significant influence over Letourneau Cycles?

(e) Assume that, after closely examining the situation, Hadley's auditors determine that Hadley does not have significant influence over Letourneau Cycles. What amount should be reported on Hadley's statement of financial position at December 31 for its investment in Letourneau Cycles? What will be reported on Hadley's income statement for 2012?

(f) How would your answer to (e) change if Hadley reported under ASPE and chose to use the cost model when accounting for its investment in Letourneau assuming that the shares did not trade in an active market?

Record bond investment; show statement presentation.
(SO 4, 5)

*P12–11B   On January 1, 2012, Morissette Inc. purchased $800,000 of 10-year, 6% bonds for $770,921. The purchase price was based on a market interest rate of 6.5%. Interest is received semi-annually on July 1 and January 1. Morissette's year end is October 31. Morissette intends to hold the bonds until January 1, 2022, the date the bonds mature. The bonds' fair value on October 31, 2012, was $790,000.

Instructions

(a) Record the purchase of the bonds on January 1, 2012.
(b) Prepare a bond amortization schedule for the term of the bonds.
(c) Prepare the entry to record the receipt of interest on July 1, 2012.
(d) Prepare any adjusting entries required at October 31, 2012.
(e) Prepare the entry to record the repayment of the bonds on January 1, 2022.
(f) Show the financial statement presentation of the bonds at October 31, 2012.
(g) How would your answer to (d) change if the bonds were held for trading purposes?

*P12–12B On January 1, 2012, CASB Incorporated issued $1 million of 10-year, 8% bonds at 102. They were sold at a premium because the market interest rate was 7.7%. The bonds pay interest semi-annually on June 30 and December 31. On January 1, Densmore Consulting Ltd. purchased $200,000 of CASB bonds at 102 as a trading investment. On July 1, after receiving the bond interest, Densmore Consulting sold its CASB bonds at 103. Both companies have a December 31 year end.

Record bonds for investor and investee. (SO 5)

Instructions

(a) Prepare all required entries for Densmore Consulting, the investor, to record the above transactions.
(b) How would the journal entries for Densmore Consulting change if the investment had been purchased with the intent of holding it to maturity?
(c) Prepare all required entries for CASB, the investee, to record the above transactions.
(d) Comment on the differences in recording that you observe between the investor and the investee.

Broadening Your Perspective

Financial Reporting and Analysis Cases

Financial Reporting: *Eastplats*

BYP12–1   The financial statements of Eastern Platinum Limited (Eastplats) are presented in Appendix A at the end of this textbook.

Identify investments. (SO 1, 4)

Instructions

(a) Does Eastplats report any investments on its statement of financial position? If so, are they debt or equity investments? Are they current or non-current?
(b) Does Eastplats report any investment income on its income statement? On its statement of comprehensive income? Indicate what type of investment income is reported, if any.
(c) Note 5 to the financial statements lists a number of subsidiaries owned by the company. Why aren't investment accounts relating to these subsidiaries shown on the statement of financial position?
(d) What section of the statement of cash flows would you look at to determine if investments were purchased or sold? What amount of investments, if any, did Eastplats purchase or sell during 2011?

Comparative Analysis: *Eastplats and Amplats*

BYP12–2   The financial statements of Anglo American Platinum Limited (Amplats) are presented in Appendix B, following the financial statements for Eastern Platinum Limited (Eastplats) in Appendix A.

Compare investments. (SO 1, 2, 3, 4)

Instructions

(a) Compare the statements of financial positions of the two companies. Which one tends to make more investments in associates? Which one tends to make more short-term investments? What is the most likely reason for this?
(b) Compare the statements of cash flows of the two companies. Did either company receive dividends from its investees? How did each company show the interest received on its investments?
(c) On Amplats's statement of cash flows, what is the largest item that caused a cash inflow relating to investments? Do you think that this item related to a significantly influenced investment?
(d) Compare the income statements of the two companies. Which one records the most income (losses) from its associates?

Interpreting Financial Information

BYP12–3   Bank of Montreal (BMO) is Canada's fourth-largest bank. In 2011, it acquired a 100% interest in Marshall & Ilsley Corp., a mid-sized U.S. bank, for U.S. $4.1 billion.

Analyze strategic investment. (SO 3, 4)

Instructions

(a) BMO paid for this acquisition by issuing new BMO common shares to the current shareholders of Marshall & Illsley Corp. Prepare the journal entry that BMO made when it acquired Marshall & Ilsley Corp.

(b) When the acquisition was announced, the shares of BMO fell by over 6% while the shares of Marshall & Ilsley rose by 18%. Why do you think this happened?

(c) Will the investment in Marshall & Ilsley appear on BMO's consolidated statement of financial position? Why or why not?

(d) If BMO had purchased only 25% of Marshall & Ilsley for $1 billion and you found that the investment was being carried on the statement of financial position one year later at $1.1 billion, what would be the most likely reason for the increase in the investment account balance?

Comparing IFRS and ASPE

Compare strategic equity investment under IFRS and ASPE. (SO 3)

BYP12-4 Two brothers, Adam and Robert Merkle, began A&R Plumbing Ltd. (ARP), a private company, approximately five years ago. At the time, Adam had recently graduated from a business program with a specialization in accounting and Robert had just completed a plumbing apprenticeship. Adam performed all administrative tasks (inventory ordering, accounting, payroll, etc.) while Robert provided the skills of the trade. ARP had a very slow start and for the first two years all revenues were generated by providing emergency plumbing services. ARP operated at a loss for the first two years of operations. In the third year, ARP landed several large subcontractor deals with various home builders and began installing plumbing in new homes. ARP began to be profitable. In June 2011, Adam and Robert's business relationship started to deteriorate and they were having trouble agreeing on any business decisions. Adam decided that it would be best if he left the business and Robert agreed to purchase Adam's share of ARP. The company shares were privately held and were not traded actively on the market so Adam agreed to sell his shares in the business for an amount equal to 10 times the profit of the business for the year ended December 31, 2011.

The company prepares its financial statements in accordance with Accounting Standards for Private Enterprises. In January 2011, ARP purchased 20,000 common shares of Canadian Plumbing Supplies Ltd (CPS). CPS is a plumbing supply distributor and its shares were acquired for $100,000. The shares represented a 20% ownership holding of CPS and the shares are traded actively on the Toronto Stock Exchange. Since the purchase, neither Adam nor Robert has been actively involved in any decisions related to CPS's operations. However, once Robert obtains full control of ARP, he plans on using ARP's 20% share to obtain a seat on the CPS board of directors. He wants to use his board position to develop a referral system whereby CPS will refer customers to ARP for plumbing services. At December 31, 2011, CPS's shares were trading for $4.50 each.

CPS's year end is December 31. For the year ended December 31, 2011, CPS reported a loss of $30,000. CPS did not declare any dividends. Adam had accounted for the investment in ARP using the cost model.

Instructions

(a) Robert has come to you, an independent public accountant, for advice. He would like you to assess the accounting choice that Adam has made for the investment in CPS.

  1. Describe the acceptable accounting policy choices available under ASPE to account for ARP's investment in CPS. Is the cost model an acceptable method under ASPE for this investment?

  2. Discuss whether Adam's selection of the cost model is an indication of any bias he may have. Explain.

  3. Which accounting policy choice do you think Robert would prefer? Why?

(b) Explain how the accounting policy choices available to ARP for its investment in CPS might be different if it reported its financial results in accordance with IFRS.

Critical Thinking Cases and Activities

Collaborative Learning Activity

Classify, and determine valuation of, investments. (SO 1, 2, 3)

BYP12-5 Marham Roynold Ltd., a publicly traded company, owns and manages commercial and construction projects with a focus on environmentally friendly buildings. Marham Roynold needs advice on the proper way to value and account for investments on its December 31, 2011, financial statements.

Investment #1: A $3.5-million investment in the common shares of an oil company purchased early in the year. By December 31, the shares' fair value had risen to $4.2 million. Marham Roynold's senior management has noted that the recent, rapid increase in the market value of these shares is due to the rise in oil prices, but, given the international situation, they are not sure that the increase in value will be sustained. The managers are considering the sale of the investment to realize the gain, but they are concerned that if they sell now, an opportunity to earn further gains on this investment could be lost.

Investment #2: A $2.5-million investment in the bonds of an alternative energy company that were acquired five years ago, with a current fair market value of $1.5 million. Although the common shares of this alternative energy company have fallen in market value, the company remains solvent and the senior management of Marham Roynold are of the opinion that this is a good long-term investment. Marham Roynold will be facing a significant income tax liability next year when a major construction project comes to a profitable close. If it sold this investment, it would consider a similar purchase in the future.

Instructions

After the class has been divided into groups and you have been assigned one of the two investments for analysis, do the following:

(a) Identify the classification options (debt or equity; short-term or long-term) that are available for the investments described above. Discuss the appropriateness of each option and recommend the best classification.

(b) Based on your recommendation in (a), determine the valuation model that should be used for each investment at December 31, 2011.

(c) Assuming the two investments are sold in 2012, identify the impact of this sale on the financial statements.

Communication Activity

BYP12–6   In this chapter, you have learned about three models under IFRS that can be used to account for equity investments after they are acquired: fair value, cost, and equity.

Instructions

Write a memo explaining when each model should be used for equity investments and the impact that each of these has on the income statement and the statement of financial position. Is it possible for management to influence or manipulate the choice of model to be used? Under ASPE is there more choice?

Identify method of accounting for equity investments and impact on statements.
(SO 2, 3, 4)

Ethics Case

BYP12–7   Kreiter Financial Services Ltd. recently purchased a portfolio of debt and equity securities. Financial vice-president Vicki Lemke and controller Ula Greenwood are in the process of classifying the securities in the portfolio.

Lemke suggests accounting for both debt and equity securities expected to increase in value during the year using the fair value model in order to increase profit. She wants to account for all securities that are expected to decline in value using the cost model for equity securities and the amortized cost model for debt securities so that no decline in the value of the investment will ever be shown.

Greenwood disagrees. She recommends accounting for all equity securities that are expected to increase in value using the equity method and using the amortized cost model for all debt securities and the cost model for equity securities expected to fall in value to avoid recording the decline. Greenwood argues that the fair value of an equity investment is more volatile and if the equity method were used instead, there would be a "smoother" buildup in the value of the investment.

Compare valuation models; identify impact on statements.
(SO 2, 3, 4)

Instructions

(a) Prepare arguments against the position taken by Lemke. What flaws are there in her arguments? Are any of her proposals reasonable? Does she understand the implications that each method has for the financial statements?

(b) Prepare arguments against the position taken by Greenwood. What flaws are there in her arguments? Are any of her proposals reasonable? Does she understand the implications that each method has for the financial statements?

(c) Assume that Lemke and Greenwood classify the portfolio properly. If Kreiter sold all of its trading investments that had risen in value just prior to year end and sold all of its trading investments that declined in value immediately after year end, would these decisions allow the company to manipulate profit?

"All About You" Activity

BYP12–8   In this chapter, you learned that saving is an important part of personal financial planning and that without savings you cannot make investments. One way to invest your savings is to open a tax free savings account (TFSA) and make a contribution. Let's assume that you have $5,000 to invest in your TFSA and are considering one of the following: savings account, guaranteed investment certificate (GIC), or units of a Canadian equity mutual fund that holds common shares of large corporations.

Compare personal savings options.
(SO 1)

Instructions

For each of the savings account, GIC, and mutual fund alternatives:

(a) Go to the website of your Canadian financial institution and find the current rates of return that each investment is providing.

(b) If you invested the $5,000 in a savings account, a GIC, or a mutual fund, how much would each of these alternatives be worth after two years if the present rate of return continued?

Hint: Use the investment savings calculator under Tools at www.ingdirect.ca or an equivalent site.

Serial Case

(*Note:* This is a continuation of the serial case from Chapters 1 through 11.)

BYP 12–9   The year ended June 30, 2013, has been another successful one for Koebel's Family Bakery Ltd. The success, however, has meant that Natalie, Daniel, Janet, and Brian have spent many long hours in the bakery accommodating their customers. Janet and Brian have still not had time to enjoy any of their successes and are considering retirement from the bakery.

Compare strategic equity investments.
(SO 3)

The Koebel family has come to know the executives at Biscuits, a public corporation, and Coffee Beans, a private corporation. Both of these organizations have been thrilled with the products that Koebel's Family Bakery has provided over the year.

Frank Vosburgh, the president of Biscuits, wishes to strengthen the relationship between Koebel's Family Bakery and Biscuits. He recognizes that Janet and Brian are considering retirement. He has put forward an offer for Biscuits to purchase all of the shares that are currently held by the Koebel family. He has also guaranteed employment to both Natalie and Daniel for the next 10 years.

Bruce Anderson, the president of Coffee Beans, has found out about the offer put forward by Biscuits and is concerned that the great relationship he has developed with Koebel's Bakery will be not be maintained if Koebel's is taken over by Biscuits. As a result, he has also offered to purchase the shares held by Janet and Brian, leaving Natalie and Daniel with their 50% ownership interest and the responsibility for running the bakery. Natalie and Daniel would maintain control of the company. You will recall from Chapter 11 that 100 common shares are owned by each family member, for a total of 400 common shares.

Instructions

(a) If Biscuits were to succeed in the offer to purchase all of the shares of Koebel's Family Bakery Ltd., describe how this investment would be accounted for in the accounting records of Biscuits. Would a change in the manner in which Koebel's accounting records are maintained have to be undertaken? Why or why not?

(b) If Coffee Beans were to succeed in the offer to purchase Janet and Brian's shares (50%) of Koebel's Family Bakery Ltd., describe how this investment would be accounted for in the accounting records of Coffee Beans. Would a change in the manner in which Koebel's accounting records are maintained have to be undertaken? Why or why not?

(c) Identify some of the advantages and disadvantages to Janet, Brian, Natalie, and Daniel of each of these offers.

Answers to Self-Test Questions

1. a   2. d   3. a   4. b   5. a   6. c
7. b   8. c   9. a   10. d   *11. a   *12. c

Remember to go
back to the beginning
of the chapter to
check off your
completed work!

←

Statement of Cash Flows

study objectives

After studying this chapter, you should be able to:

1. Describe the purpose and content of the statement of cash flows.
2. Prepare the operating activities section of a statement of cash flows using one of two approaches: (a) the indirect method or (b) the direct method.
3. Prepare the investing activities section of a statement of cash flows.
4. Prepare the financing activities section of a statement of cash flows.
5. Complete the statement of cash flows.
6. Use the statement of cash flows to evaluate a company's liquidity and solvency.

ACCOUNTING MATTERS!

Cash Flow Can Be a Rocky Road

What a difference a few years can make! In 2006, metal prices were riding high on the stock markets, creating a swell of cash for mining companies like Teck Resources, headquartered in Vancouver. At the time Teck, a world leader in the production of zinc and metallurgical coal, as well as a significant producer of copper, gold, and specialty metals, was busy trying to decide how best to spend its money. It took part in a bidding war for Inco Ltd., which it lost, then invested a significant amount of cash in the purchase of Aur Resources Inc. in 2007.

The investment in Aur Resources resulted in a large drop in cash on the statement of financial position—$1.4 billion in 2007 compared with $5 billion in 2006. However, profit figures that year still represented "the second best earnings year in our history," Don Lindsay, President and CEO, reported in the 2007 Annual Report.

The first eight months of 2008 were also quite good for the company. In July, it announced plans to acquire the assets of the Fording Canadian Coal Trust, taking on $11.2 billion of debt to finance the acquisition. In late 2008, "unprecedented volatility for the world economy and for the mining sector" resulted, as described by Mr. Lindsay. Because of this, the timing of the Fording transaction created "very significant short-term challenges," according to Mr. Lindsay.

During this economic turmoil in late 2008 and early 2009, Teck had to implement a multi-step program to manage its debt, including suspending dividends, reducing planned capital expenditures, withdrawing from a copper project in Panama, reducing refined zinc production, selling its interest in a gold property in Chile, selling other assets, and reducing its global workforce by 13%.

Any free cash flow went toward servicing the company's debt. Teck was able to repay a bridge loan for the Fording project in July 2009 entirely from cash flow generated by its operating activities. By the end of 2009, Teck's cash flow had returned to 2006 levels at $5 billion.

Teck's financial position continued to improve in 2010 as a result of strong commodity markets, resulting in significantly higher prices in its copper and coal business units. When the company generated cash flow from operating activities of more than $2.7 billion, it was able to further reduce its debt in 2010, which resulted in annual interest savings of $225 million. In addition, it refinanced some of its debt to spread the maturities of its debt over a longer time period. As a result, Teck's credit rating was upgraded by the major credit-rating agencies in 2010 to "BBB"—an investment-grade rating—from what previously was considered to be a junk rating.

Standard & Poor's (S&P) Rating Services said that the rating change reflected Teck's recent moves to reduce debt. However, S&P also noted that the company's coal, zinc, and copper production businesses are vulnerable to volatile prices for metals, which is why its rating is still at the B level, unlike some of its competitors that have a cost structure better suited to weather the cyclicality that defines the mining industry.

The statement of financial position, income statement, statement of comprehensive income, and statement of changes in equity do not show the whole picture of a company's financial condition. In fact, looking at the financial statements of some organizations, a thoughtful investor might ask questions like these: How did Global Energy Services purchase equipment in a year when it had no cash but only bank indebtedness? Why did the Wilfrid Laurier University Students' Union spend $632,000 of cash in a year in which it earned only $345,000? Where did the Bank of Montreal get the $4.1 billion it spent to purchase U.S. bank Marshall & Ilsley? This chapter presents the statement of cash flows, which answers these and similar questions.

The chapter is organized as follows:

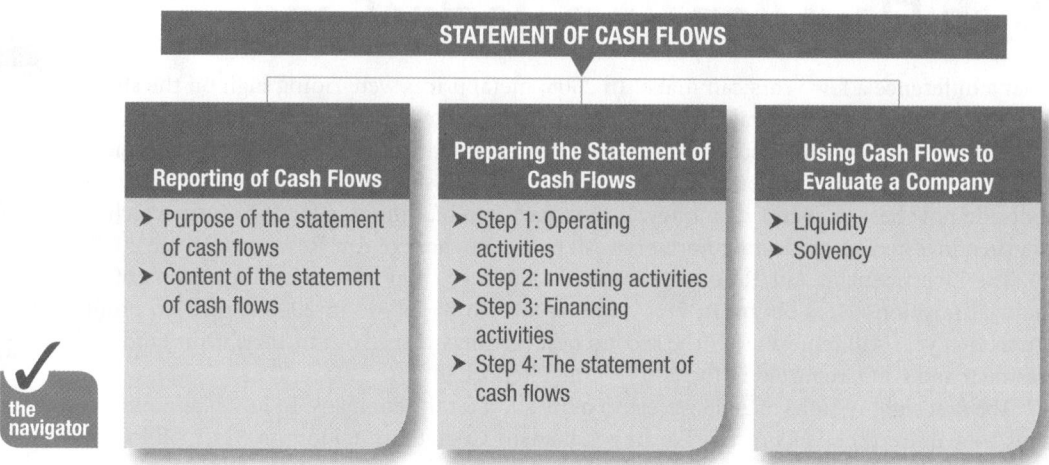

Reporting of Cash Flows

STUDY OBJECTIVE 1
Describe the purpose and content of the statement of cash flows.

The financial statements that we have studied so far present only partial information about a company's cash flows (cash receipts and cash payments). For example, comparative statements of financial position show the increase in property, plant, and equipment during the year, but they do not show how the additions were financed or paid for. The income statement reports profit for the year, but it does not indicate the amount of cash generated or used by operating activities. The statement of changes in equity shows cash dividends declared, but not the cash dividends paid during the year.

As our chapter-opening feature story about Teck demonstrates, it is essential to understand a company's cash flows in order to determine its financial capabilities and options to wisely use (or obtain) cash. In order to do so, we will begin by examining the purpose and content of the statement of cash flows.

PURPOSE OF THE STATEMENT OF CASH FLOWS

Alternative Terminology
The *statement of cash flows* is also commonly known as the *cash flow statement*.

The main purpose of the statement of cash flows is to provide information that enables users to assess a company's ability to generate cash, and the company's needs in using these cash flows. For example, a statement of cash flows, when used in conjunction with the other financial statements, provides information about a company's investing and financing activities that enables users to evaluate the changes in a company's assets and liabilities and in its financial structure (including its liquidity and solvency). Cash flow information is also useful in assessing a company's ability to generate future cash flows. From this assessment, users are in a better position to predict the company's ability to affect the amounts and timing of cash flows in order to adapt to changing circumstances and opportunities. The statement of cash flows can also enhance the comparability of different companies because it eliminates the accrual-based effects of using different accounting treatments for similar transactions and events.

Because of the importance of this information to users, the statement of cash flows is a required financial statement for both publicly traded and private corporations.

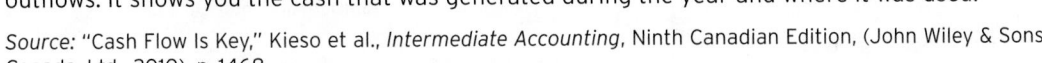

ACCOUNTING MATTERS!   *Management Perspective*

Cash Flow Is Key

Clearwater Seafoods, headquartered in Nova Scotia, harvests, processes, and distributes fresh and frozen fish and shellfish worldwide. It has managed to stay afloat in a tough business for more than 30 years, and has done so in part because it understands the importance of cash flows. "The ability to sustain and grow cash flows is key," says Tyrone Cotie, director of corporate finance and investor relations. "The statement of cash flows ties together the information contained on the statement of financial position and income statement," Mr. Cotie explains. "It provides an accurate picture of the cash flows of the business by removing the noncash items from the income statement and by adding the investments noted on the balance sheet to cash outflows. It shows you the cash that was generated during the year and where it was used."

Source: "Cash Flow Is Key," Kieso et al., *Intermediate Accounting*, Ninth Canadian Edition, (John Wiley & Sons Canada, Ltd., 2010), p. 1468.

CONTENT OF THE STATEMENT OF CASH FLOWS

Before we can start preparing the statement of cash flows, we must first understand what it includes and why. We will begin by reviewing the definition of cash used in the statement of cash flows and then discuss how cash receipts and payments are classified within the statement.

Definition of Cash

The statement of cash flows is often prepared using **cash and cash equivalents** as its basis rather than just cash. You will recall from Chapter 7 that cash equivalents are short-term, highly liquid investments that are readily convertible to cash within a very short period of time. Generally, only debt investments due within three months qualify by this definition. Bank overdrafts that are repayable on demand are included in (deducted from) cash and cash equivalents.

As mentioned earlier in this text, the International Accounting Standards Board and the Financial Accounting Standards Board are currently working on a joint project to improve the presentation of information in the financial statements. While this project is still under way, one of the proposed recommendations is to exclude "cash equivalents" from the definition of cash in the statement of cash flows. In other words, this statement would present information about the changes in cash only, and not cash and cash equivalents. Given this intended direction, we have chosen to present the statement of cash flows in this chapter using cash only, although you will see different companies using different definitions over the next few years until this recommendation is finalized.

Classification of Cash Flows

The statement of cash flows classifies cash receipts and cash payments into three types of activities: (1) operating, (2) investing, and (3) financing. The transactions that are found within each type of activity include the following:

1. **Operating activities** include the cash effects of transactions that create revenues and expenses. They affect profit.
2. **Investing activities** include (a) purchasing and disposing of investments and long-lived assets and (b) lending money and collecting the loans. Investing activities generally affect non-current asset accounts.

3. **Financing activities** include (a) obtaining cash from issuing debt and repaying the amounts borrowed and (b) obtaining cash from shareholders and paying them dividends. Financing activities generally affect non-current liability and shareholders' equity accounts.

Illustration 13-1 lists typical cash receipts and cash payments in each of the three activities.

▶Illustration 13-1

Cash receipts and payments classified by activity

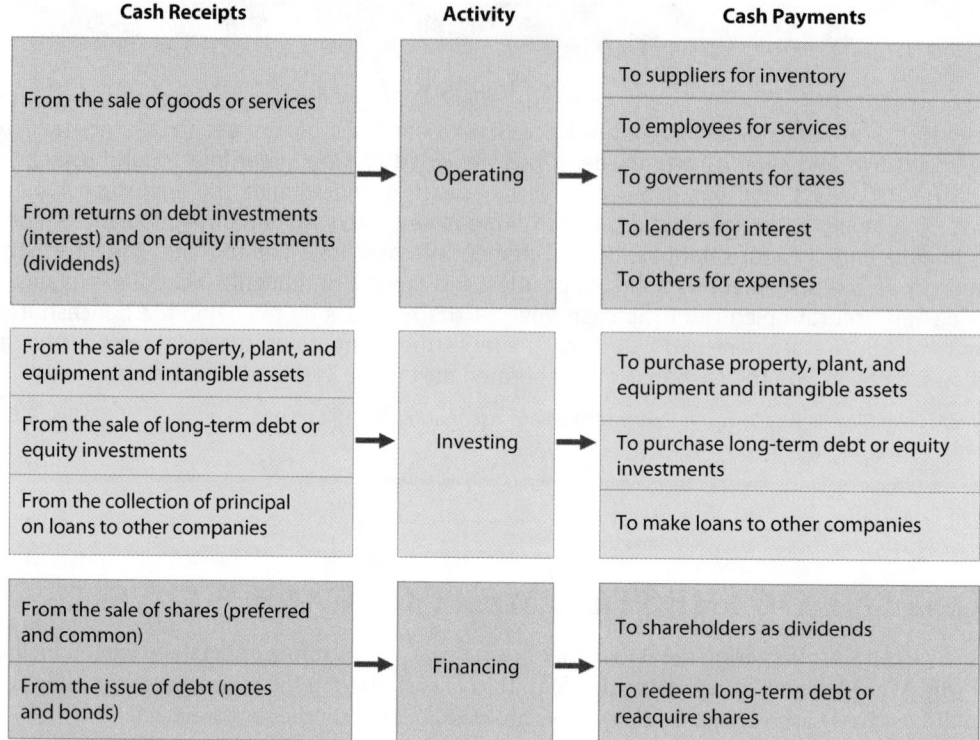

As you can see above, some cash flows relating to investing or financing activities are classified as operating activities. For example, receipts of investment revenue (interest and dividends) are classified in the above illustration as operating activities. So are payments of interest to lenders. Why are these considered operating activities? Because these items are reported in the income statement, where results of operations are shown.

ASPE   Companies reporting under IFRS have a choice as to where to classify interest and dividends. For example, interest and dividends received may be classified as either an operating or investing activity. Interest and dividends paid may be classified as either an operating or financing activity. Once the choice is made, it must be applied consistently. Private companies reporting under ASPE classify interest received and paid and dividends received as operating activities and dividends paid as financing activities. This is the most common practice for both publicly traded and private companies. Because of this, this classification is the one illustrated above in Illustration 13-1 and the one we recommend you use when completing assignments in this text.

Significant Noncash Activities

It is important to recognize that not all of a company's significant activities involve cash. The following are examples of noncash activities:

1. Issue of debt to purchase assets
2. Issue of shares to purchase assets
3. Conversion of debt into equity
4. Exchange of property, plant, and equipment

Significant investing and financing activities that do not affect cash are not reported in the body of the statement of cash flows. However, these activities are reported in a note to the financial statements. Note that this disclosure requirement also includes the noncash portion of a partial cash transaction, as the following example shows. Assume that a building is purchased for $10 million. A $1-million down payment was made and the remainder was financed with a mortgage payable. Transactions such as these should not be netted. The acquisition of the building (a $10-million investing activity) by a mortgage payable (a $9-million financing activity) would be separately disclosed in the notes and cross-referenced to the $1-million cash outflow reported in the investing activities section of the statement of cash flows.

BEFORE YOU GO ON...

▶ Do It! Cash Flow Activities

Plano Moulding Corp. had the following cash transactions:

(a) Issued common shares.

(b) Sold a long-term debt investment.

(c) Purchased a tractor-trailer truck. Made a cash down payment and financed the remainder with a mortgage payable.

(d) Paid interest on the mortgage payable.

(e) Collected cash for services provided.

(f) Acquired equipment by issuing common shares.

Classify each of these transactions by type of cash flow activity. Indicate whether the transaction would be reported as a cash inflow or cash outflow, or as a noncash activity.

Action Plan
- Report as operating activities the cash effects of transactions that create revenues and expenses and are used to determine profit.
- Report as investing activities the transactions that (a) acquire and dispose of investments and long-lived assets, and (b) lend money and collect loans.
- Report as financing activities the transactions that (a) obtain cash by issuing debt or repay the amounts borrowed, and (b) obtain cash from shareholders or pay them dividends.

Solution

(a) Financing activity, cash inflow

(b) Investing activity, cash inflow

(c) Investing activity, cash outflow for down payment. The remainder is a noncash investing activity for truck and noncash financing activity for mortgage payable.

(d) Operating activity, cash outflow

(e) Operating activity, cash inflow

(f) Noncash activity (noncash investing activity for equipment and noncash financing activity for common shares)

the navigator

STUDY OBJECTIVE 2

Prepare the operating activities section of a statement of cash flows using one of two approaches: (a) the indirect method or (b) the direct method.

Preparing the Statement of Cash Flows

We first introduced the statement of cash flows in Chapter 1. You will recall that the general format of the statement is as shown in Illustration 13-2.

► Illustration 13-2

Format of the statement of cash flows

COMPANY NAME Statement of Cash Flows Period Covered		
Operating activities		
(Prepared using indirect or direct method)	XX	
Net cash provided (used) by operating activities		XXX
Investing activities		
(List of individual inflows and outflows)	XX	
Net cash provided (used) by investing activities		XXX
Financing activities		
(List of individual inflows and outflows)	XX	
Net cash provided (used) by financing activities		XXX
Net increase (decrease) in cash		XXX
Cash, beginning of period		XXX
Cash, end of period		XXX

The statement covers the same period of time as the income statement, statement of comprehensive income, and statement of changes in equity (e.g., for the year ended). Cash inflows and outflows are reported in three separate sections: operating, investing, and financing. The section that reports cash flows from operating activities always appears first. When we introduced the statement of cash flows in Chapter 1, we used the direct method of preparing the operating activities section for simplicity although we did not call it the "direct method" at the time. As we will learn, there are two acceptable ways to prepare the operating activities section: the indirect method and the direct method.

The operating activities section is followed by the investing activities section and then the financing activities section. Each of these sections report a subtotal showing net cash either provided or used by each activity. These subtotals are totalled to determine the net increase or decrease in cash for the period. This amount is then added to (if a net increase) or subtracted from (if a net decrease) the beginning-of-period cash balance to obtain the end-of-period cash balance. The end-of-period cash balance should agree with the cash balance reported on the statement of financial position.

When we illustrated the statement of cash flows in Chapter 1, and in subsequent chapters, we did so without explaining how to prepare it. Let's return to basics now and learn how to prepare the statement of cash flows. Where do we find the information to prepare this statement?

There are no specific accounts in the general ledger for the types of operating activities, investing activities, or financing activities shown in Illustration 13-1. This is because the statement of cash flows is prepared differently from the other financial statements in that it is not prepared from an adjusted trial balance. The statement of cash flows requires detailed information about the changes in account balances that occurred between two periods of time. An adjusted trial balance will not provide the necessary data. The information to prepare this statement usually comes from three sources:

1. The **comparative statement of financial position** is examined to determine the amounts of the changes in assets, liabilities, and shareholders' equity from the beginning of the period to its end.
2. The **income statement** and related noncash current asset and current liability accounts from the statement of financial position are used to determine the amount of cash provided or used by operating activities during the period.
3. **Additional information** includes transaction data that are needed to determine how cash was provided or used during the period. We will also use selected information from the statement of changes in equity to help us complete the statement of cash flows and the notes to the financial statements.

There are four steps to prepare the statement of cash flows from these data sources, as shown in Illustration 13-3.

Step 1: Prepare operating activities section.
Determine the net cash provided (used) by operating activities by converting profit from an accrual basis to a cash basis. To do this, analyze the current year's income statement, relevant current asset and current liability accounts from the comparative statement of financial position, and selected information.

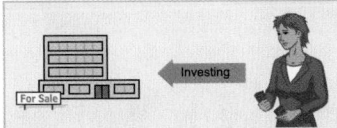

Step 2: Prepare investing activities section.
Determine the net cash provided (used) by investing activities by analyzing changes in non-current asset accounts from the comparative statement of financial position, and selected information.

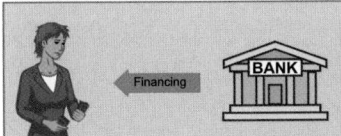

Step 3: Prepare financing activities section.
Determine the net cash provided (used) by financing activities by analyzing changes in non-current liability and equity accounts from the comparative statement of financial position, and selected information.

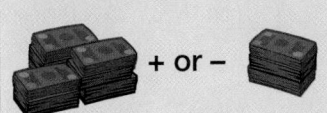

Step 4: Complete the statement of cash flows.
Determine the net increase (decrease) in cash. Compare the net change in cash reported on the statement of cash flows with the change in cash reported on the statement of financial position to make sure the amounts agree.

▸Illustration 13-3
Steps in preparing the statement of cash flows

To explain and illustrate the preparation of a statement of cash flows, we will use financial information from Computer Services Corporation. Illustration 13-4 presents Computer Services' current- and previous-year statement of financial position, its current-year income statement, and related financial information.

▸Illustration 13-4
Financial information for Computer Services Corporation

COMPUTER SERVICES CORPORATION
Statement of Financial Position
December 31

	2012	2011	Increase (Decrease)
Assets			
Current assets			
Cash	$ 55,000	$ 33,000	$ 22,000
Accounts receivable	20,000	30,000	(10,000)
Merchandise inventory	15,000	10,000	5,000
Prepaid expenses	5,000	1,000	4,000
Property, plant, and equipment			
Land	140,000	30,000	110,000
Building	160,000	40,000	120,000
Accumulated depreciation—building	(11,000)	(5,000)	6,000
Equipment	27,000	10,000	17,000
Accumulated depreciation—equipment	(3,000)	(1,000)	2,000
Total assets	$408,000	$148,000	
Liabilities and Shareholders' Equity			
Liabilities			
Current liabilities			
Accounts payable	$ 28,000	$ 12,000	16,000
Income tax payable	6,000	8,000	(2,000)

(continued)

Non-current liabilities			
Bonds payable	130,000	20,000	110,000
Shareholders' equity			
Common shares	70,000	50,000	20,000
Retained earnings	164,000	48,000	116,000
Accumulated other comprehensive income	10,000	10,000	0
Total liabilities and shareholders' equity	$408,000	$148,000	

COMPUTER SERVICES CORPORATION Income Statement Year Ended December 31, 2012		
Sales revenue		$507,000
Cost of goods sold		150,000
Gross profit		357,000
Operating expenses		
Other operating expenses	$141,000	
Depreciation expense	9,000	
Loss on sale of equipment	3,000	153,000
Profit from operations		204,000
Other expenses and losses		
Interest expense		12,000
Profit before income tax		192,000
Income tax expense		47,000
Profit		$145,000

Additional information for 2012:

1. The company uses a perpetual inventory system.
2. Assume that prepaid expenses relate to other operating expenses and accounts payable relate to purchases of merchandise inventory on account.
3. The company acquired land by issuing $110,000 of long-term bonds.
4. Equipment costing $25,000 was purchased for cash.
5. The company sold equipment with a carrying amount of $7,000 (cost of $8,000, less accumulated depreciation of $1,000) for $4,000 cash.
6. Depreciation expense consists of $6,000 for the building and $3,000 for equipment.
7. The company paid a $29,000 cash dividend.
8. The bonds were issued at face value.
9. There was no other comprehensive income reported in 2012.

We will now apply the four steps shown in Illustration 13-3 using the above information for Computer Services Corporation, starting with the operating activities section.

STEP 1: OPERATING ACTIVITIES

Determine the Net Cash Provided (Used) by Operating Activities by Converting Profit from an Accrual Basis to a Cash Basis

In order to perform step 1 and determine the cash provided (used) by operating activities, profit must be converted from an accrual basis to a cash basis. Note that it is *profit* that is used for operating activities and not total comprehensive income.

Why does profit have to be converted to the cash basis of accounting? Under generally accepted accounting principles, companies use the accrual basis of accounting. As you have learned in past chapters, revenue recognition guidelines do not await the collection of cash, as long as collection is reasonably assured. For example, sales revenues are recorded for both cash sales and sales on account. Similarly, under expense recognition guidelines, many expenses are recorded that have not been paid in cash. Some will never be paid in cash, to use depreciation as but one example. Thus, under the accrual basis of accounting, profit is not the same as net cash provided (used) by operating activities. Teck Resources, introduced in our chapter-opening feature story, reported profit of $1,975 million for the year ended December 31, 2010, yet its cash flow provided by operating activities was $2,743 million.

Profit can be converted to net cash provided (used) by operating activities by one of two methods: (1) the indirect method or (2) the direct method. The **indirect method** converts total profit from an accrual basis to a cash basis. The **direct method** converts each individual revenue and expense account from an accrual basis to a cash basis, identifying specific cash receipts and payments. **Both methods arrive at the same total amount** for "Net cash provided (used) by operating activities." The only difference is which items they disclose.

To expand on the general format of the statement of cash flows shown in Illustration 13-2, the indirect and direct methods would look somewhat like the following:

Indirect Method			Direct Method		
Operating activities			Operating activities		
Profit		XX	Cash receipts from customers		XX
Adjustments to reconcile profit to net cash			Cash payments		
provided (used) by operating activities			To suppliers	XX	
(List of individual adjustments)	XX	XX	For operating expenses	XX	
Net cash provided (used) by operating		XX	To employees	XX	
activities			For interest	XX	
			For income tax	XX	XX
			Net cash provided (used) by operating		XX
			activities		

While both the indirect and direct methods are acceptable choices to determine cash flows from operating activities, the direct method is preferred by standard setters. It is considered to be more informative to users and is easier to compare with other financial statements. Despite this preference, most companies use the indirect method because it is easier to prepare and reveals less company information to competitors. For example, more than 90% of international companies use the indirect method. Teck, introduced in our chapter-opening story, uses the indirect method, as does Eastplats, our textbook feature company.

ACCOUNTING MATTERS! *Investor Perspective*

Why Does the Indirect Method Persist?

The statement of cash flows should be one of the most important tools for any user across the organization, whether internal or external. But, all too often, this statement adds little insight into a company's operations. Take, for example, Sears Canada. Sears's business is pretty simple. It buys clothes, housewares, and other products, puts them in its stores, and sells them.

When you look at the operating activities section of Sears's statement of cash flows, prepared using the indirect method, you find references to noncash items such as depreciation and changes in noncash current asset and current liability account balances. Nowhere does it tell you how much cash Sears received from shoppers or how much it paid its suppliers.

The joint financial statement presentation project under way by standard setters has tentatively recommended that the direct method for presenting operating activities be used in preparing the statement of cash flows since it would provide data that are more informative to users. Although analysts and academics agree with this proposal, preparers strongly oppose any requirement to use the direct method. In their view, the benefits provided by the direct method do not outweigh the costs to prepare that type of statement—in particular, the costs required for systems modification to capture the transaction data required in the direct method.

On this and subsequent pages, in two separate sections, we describe the use of the two methods. Section 1 explains the indirect method. Section 2 explains the direct method. Both methods are included because they are acceptable choices for both publicly traded and private companies. These sections are independent of each other in case your instructor wishes to assign only one section. When you have finished the section(s) assigned by your instructor, turn to the next topic after these sections, "Step 2: Investing Activities."

Section 1: Indirect Method

STUDY OBJECTIVE 2 (a)

Prepare the operating activities section of the statement of cash flows using the indirect method.

To determine the net cash provided (used) by operating activities under the indirect method, profit is adjusted for items that did not affect cash. Illustration 13-5 shows three common types of adjustments that are made to adjust profit for items that affect accrual-based profit but do not affect cash. The first two types of adjustments—noncash expenses and revenues and losses and gains—are found on the income statement. The last type of adjustment—changes (increases or decreases) in certain current asset and current liability accounts—is found on the statement of financial position.

▶Illustration 13-5

Adjustments to convert profit to net cash provided (used) by operating activities

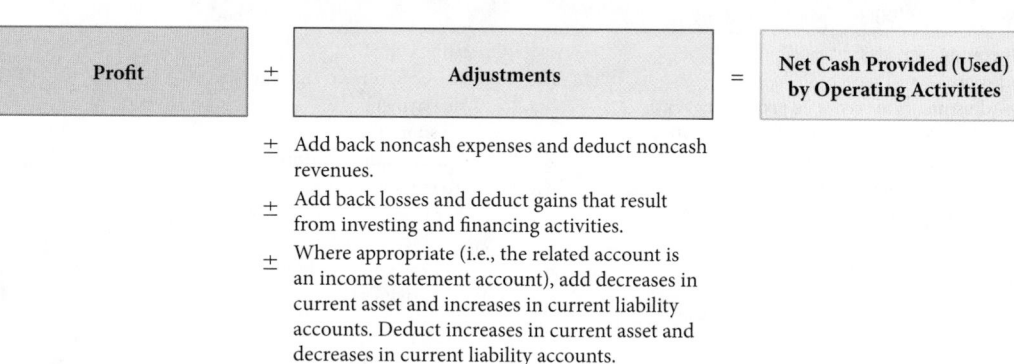

± Add back noncash expenses and deduct noncash revenues.

± Add back losses and deduct gains that result from investing and financing activities.

± Where appropriate (i.e., the related account is an income statement account), add decreases in current asset and increases in current liability accounts. Deduct increases in current asset and decreases in current liability accounts.

The next three sections explain each type of adjustment.

NONCASH EXPENSES AND REVENUES

The income statement includes expenses that do not use cash, such as depreciation and amortization expense. For example, Computer Services' income statement reports depreciation expense of $9,000. Although depreciation expense reduces profit, it does not reduce cash. Recall that the entry to record depreciation is:

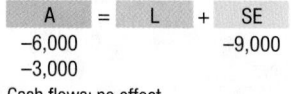

A	=	L	+	SE
−6,000				−9,000
−3,000				

Cash flows: no effect

Depreciation Expense	9,000	
Accumulated Depreciation—Building		6,000
Accumulated Depreciation—Equipment		3,000

This entry has no effect on cash, so depreciation expense is added back to profit in order to arrive at net cash provided (used) by operating activities. It is important to understand that depreciation expense is not added to operating activities as if it were a source of cash. As shown in the journal entry above, depreciation does not involve cash. It is added to cancel the deduction that was created by the depreciation expense when profit was determined.

The following is a partial operating activities section of the statement of cash flows for Computer Services. The addition of the noncash expense to profit is highlighted in red.

Operating activities	
Profit	$145,000
Adjustments to reconcile profit to net cash provided (used) by operating activities	
Depreciation expense	9,000

Similar to depreciation expense, amortization expense for intangible assets is also added to profit to arrive at net cash provided (used) by operating activities. Another example of a noncash expense is the amortization of bond discounts and premiums. Recall from Chapter 10 that the journal entry made by a bond issuer to amortize a bond discount results in a debit to the Interest Expense account and a credit to the Bonds Payable account. So any portion of interest expense that is related to the amortization of a bond discount must be added to profit to determine the net cash provided (used) by operating activities.

Just as the amortization of a bond discount by a bond issuer increases interest expense but does not use cash, the amortization of a bond premium reduces interest expense but does not reduce cash. The journal entry to amortize a bond premium results in a debit to the Bonds Payable account and a credit to the Interest Expense account. So any portion of interest expense that is related to the amortization of a bond premium must be deducted from profit to determine the net cash provided (used) by operating activities.

Just as a bond issuer can incur amortization for a bond discount or premium, so can a bond investor who is holding the bonds as a long-term investment. You will recall that we learned about amortizing bond discounts and premiums for investors in Chapter 12. Adjusting profit for the effects of the amortization on bond discounts and premiums for investors is similar except that amortization of a bond discount increases interest revenue and the amortization of a bond premium decreases interest revenue.

LOSSES AND GAINS

Cash received from the sale of long-lived assets should be reported in the investing activities section of the statement of cash flows. In order to do this, all losses and gains from investing activities must first be eliminated from profit to arrive at cash from operating activities. Why is this necessary? Perhaps it will help if we review the accounting for the sale of property, plant, and equipment.

The sale of property, plant, and equipment is recorded by (1) recognizing the cash proceeds that are received, (2) removing the asset and accumulated depreciation accounts from the books, and (3) recognizing any loss or gain on the sale.

To illustrate, recall that Computer Services' income statement reported a $3,000 loss on the sale of equipment. With the additional information provided in Illustration 13-4, we can reconstruct the journal entry to record the sale of equipment:

			A	=	L	+	SE
Cash	4,000		+4,000				−3,000
Accumulated Depreciation	1,000		+1,000				
Loss on Sale of Equipment	3,000		−8,000				
Equipment		8,000	↑Cash flows: +4,000				

The cash proceeds of $4,000 that are received are not considered part of operating activities; rather, they are part of investing activities. Selling equipment is not part of a company's primary activities. **There is therefore no cash inflow (or outflow) from operating activities.** Logically, then, to calculate the net cash provided (used) by operating activities, we have to eliminate the loss or gain on the sale of an asset from profit.

To eliminate the $3,000 loss on the sale of the equipment, we have to add the loss back to profit to cancel the original deduction in the income statement. We can then arrive at net cash provided (used) by operating activities, as shown in the following partial statement of cash flows for Computer Services:

Operating activities	
Profit	$145,000
Adjustments to reconcile profit to net cash	
provided (used) by operating activities	
Depreciation expense	9,000
Loss on sale of equipment	3,000

If a gain on sale occurs, the gain is deducted from profit in order to determine net cash provided (used) by operating activities. For both a loss and a gain, the actual amount of cash received from the sale is reported as a source of cash in the investing activities section of the statement of cash flows.

Losses and gains are also possible in other circumstances, such as when debt is retired. The same adjustment guidelines apply as described for losses and gains on the sale of assets, except that the other side of the transaction is reported in financing activities, rather than investing activities.

CHANGES IN CURRENT ASSET AND CURRENT LIABILITY ACCOUNTS

Another type of adjustment in converting profit to net cash provided (used) by operating activities involves examining the changes (increases or decreases) in certain noncash current asset and current liability accounts, also known as working capital accounts. You will recall that working capital is the difference between current assets and current liabilities.

Not all current asset and current liability, or working capital, accounts affect operating activities, however. One such example is short-term loans or notes receivable that have been issued for lending purposes rather than for trade. The issue and repayment of loans or notes such as these are shown instead in the investing section of the statement of cash flows. Similarly, short-term loans or notes payable that have been incurred for lending purposes rather than trade are shown in the financing section of the statement of cash flows.

So what types of working capital accounts affect operating activities? You learned in Chapter 4 that accruals affect a noncash current asset and a revenue account or a current liability and an expense account. An example of an accrual account that must be examined is the Accounts Receivable account, which includes amounts owed to the company for sales that have been made but for which cash collections have not yet been received. You also learned in Chapter 4 that prepayments affect a noncash current asset and an expense account or a current liability and a revenue account. An example of a prepayment is the Prepaid Insurance account, which reflects insurance that has been paid in advance but has not yet expired. Because accruals and prepayments affect revenue and expense accounts in the income statement but do not involve cash, we need to adjust profit to determine the net cash provided (used) by operating activities.

Changes in Current Assets

We will analyze the changes in Computer Services' current asset accounts to determine each change's impact on profit and cash. The adjustments that are required for changes in noncash current asset accounts that affect operating activities are as follows: increases in current asset accounts are deducted from profit, and decreases in current asset accounts are added to profit, to arrive at net cash provided (used) by operating activities.

Accounts Receivable. Computer Services' accounts receivable decreased by $10,000 (from $30,000 to $20,000) during the year. When accounts receivable decrease during the year, revenues on an accrual basis are lower than revenues on a cash basis. In other words, more cash was collected during the period than was recorded as revenue. For Computer Services, this means that cash receipts were $10,000 higher than revenues.

Illustration 13-4 shows that Computer Services had $507,000 in sales revenue reported on its income statement. To determine how much cash was collected in connection with this revenue, it is useful to analyze the Accounts Receivable account:

			Accounts Receivable			
Jan.	1	Balance	30,000			
		Sales on account	507,000	Receipts from customers		517,000
Dec.	31	Balance	20,000			

$10,000 net decrease (add to profit)

If sales revenue (assumed to be sales on account) recorded during the period was $507,000 (Dr. Accounts Receivable; Cr. Sales Revenue), and the change in Accounts Receivable during the period was a decrease of $10,000, then cash receipts from customers must have been $517,000 (Dr. Cash; Cr. Accounts Receivable).

Consequently, revenues reported on the accrual-based income statement were $10,000 lower than cash collections. To convert profit to net cash provided (used) by operating activities, the $10,000 decrease in accounts receivable must be added to profit because $10,000 more cash was collected than was reported as accrual-based revenue in the income statement.

What happens if accounts receivable increase rather than decrease? When the Accounts Receivable account increases during the year, this means that revenues on an accrual basis are higher than cash receipts. Therefore, the amount of the increase in accounts receivable is deducted from profit to arrive at net cash provided (used) by operating activities.

Merchandise Inventory. Computer Services' merchandise inventory increased by $5,000 (from $10,000 to $15,000) during the year. When inventory increases during the year, the cost of goods purchased is greater than the cost of goods sold expense recorded in the income statement. In other words, Computer Services must have purchased $5,000 more inventory than it sold. To determine how much cash it paid for purchases of its merchandise, it is useful to analyze the Merchandise Inventory account:

		Merchandise Inventory			
Jan.	1	Balance	10,000		
		Purchases	155,000	Cost of goods sold	150,000
Dec.	31	Balance	15,000		

$5,000 net increase (deduct from profit)

In a perpetual inventory system, the Merchandise Inventory account is increased by the cost of goods purchased (debit Merchandise Inventory and credit Accounts Payable) and decreased by the cost of goods sold (debit Cost of Goods Sold and credit Merchandise Inventory). Because Computer Services reported $150,000 of cost of goods sold on its income statement (as shown in Illustration 13-4), purchases of merchandise during the year must have been $155,000.

To convert profit to net cash provided (used) by operating activities, the $5,000 increase in the Merchandise Inventory must be deducted from profit. As explained above, the increase in inventory means that the cash-based expense must be increased, which has the effect of reducing profit. If inventory decreases rather than increases, the opposite would occur.

The deduction of an increase in inventory from profit does not completely convert an accrual-based figure to a cash-based figure. It does not tell us how much cash was paid for the goods purchased. It just converts the cost of goods sold to the cost of goods purchased during the year. The analysis of accounts payable—shown later in this section—completes this analysis by converting the cost of goods purchased from an accrual basis to a cash basis.

Prepaid Expenses. Computer Services' prepaid expenses increased by $4,000 (from $1,000 to $5,000) during the year. When prepaid expenses increase during the year, expenses reported on the accrual-based income statement are lower than expenses would be on a cash basis. This means that cash payments were made in the current period, but expenses have been deferred to future periods.

Computer Services' other operating expenses, other than its depreciation expense and loss from the sale of equipment, have been combined in one summary account in Illustration 13-4. These other operating expenses would include administrative and selling expenses, among other types of expenses. To determine how much cash was paid relative to these expenses, the Prepaid Expenses account must be analyzed. Other operating expenses, as reported on the income statement, are $141,000. Accordingly, payments for expenses must have been $145,000:

		Prepaid Expenses			
Jan.	1	Balance	1,000		
		Payments for expenses	145,000	Other operating expenses	141,000
Dec.	31	Balance	5,000		

$4,000 net increase (deduct from profit)

To adjust profit to net cash provided (used) by operating activities, the $4,000 increase in prepaid expenses must be deducted from profit to determine the cash paid for expenses. If prepaid expenses decrease during the year, rather than increasing, expenses reported on an accrual-based income statement would be higher than expenses on a cash basis. Decreases in prepaid expenses would be added to profit rather than deducted as we did above for an increase in prepaid expenses.

If Computer Services Corporation had any accrued liabilities (e.g., for property tax or utility bills), these would also have to be considered before we could completely determine the amount of cash paid for other operating expenses.

Changes in Current Liabilities

We will now look at the changes in Computer Services' current liability accounts to determine each change's impact on profit and cash. The adjustments that are required for changes in current liability accounts are as follows: increases in current liability accounts are added to profit, and decreases in current liability accounts are deducted from profit, to arrive at net cash provided (used) by operating activities.

Accounts Payable. In some companies, the Accounts Payable account is used only to record purchases of merchandise on account. An accrued liability account is used to record the credit entry for other expenditures made on account. In other companies, the Accounts Payable account is used to record all credit purchases. For simplicity in this chapter, we have assumed that Accounts Payable is used only to record purchases of merchandise on account.

Computer Services' accounts payable increased by $16,000 (from $12,000 to $28,000) during the year. When accounts payable increase during the year, expenses on an accrual basis are higher than expenses on a cash basis. For Computer Services, this means that it received $16,000 more in goods than it actually paid for.

To illustrate, recall that Computer Services' Accounts Payable account is increased by purchases of merchandise (Dr. Merchandise Inventory; Cr. Accounts Payable) and decreased by payments to suppliers (Dr. Accounts Payable; Cr. Cash). We determined the amount of purchases made by Computer Services in the analysis of the Merchandise Inventory account earlier: $155,000. Using this figure, we can now determine that payments to suppliers must have been $139,000.

		Accounts Payable			
		Jan.	1	Balance	12,000
Payments to suppliers	139,000			Purchases	155,000
		Dec.	31	Balance	28,000

$16,000 net increase (add to profit)

To convert profit to net cash provided (used) by operating activities, the $16,000 increase in accounts payable must be added to profit. The increase in accounts payable means that less cash was paid for the purchases than was deducted in the accrual-based expenses section of the income statement. The addition of $16,000 completes the adjustment required to convert the cost of goods purchased to the cash paid for these goods.

Decreases in accounts payable mean that more cash was paid for purchases than recorded as an expense. As a result, decreases in accounts payable are deducted from profit.

In summary, the conversion of the cost of goods sold on the accrual-based income statement to the cash paid for goods purchased involves two steps: (1) The change in the Merchandise Inventory account adjusts the cost of goods sold to the accrual-based cost of goods purchased. (2) The change in the Accounts Payable account adjusts the accrual-based cost of goods purchased to the cash-based payments to suppliers.

Income Tax Payable. A change in the Income Tax Payable account reflects the difference between the income tax expense incurred and the income tax actually paid during the year.

Computer Services' Income Tax Payable account decreased by $2,000 (from $8,000 to $6,000) during the year. This means that the $47,000 of income tax expense reported on the income statement in Illustration 13-4 was $2,000 less than the $49,000 of taxes paid during the period, as shown in the following T account:

Income Tax Payable					
		Jan.	1	Balance	8,000
Payments for income tax	49,000			Income tax expense	47,000
		Dec.	31	Balance	6,000

$2,000 net decrease (deduct from profit)

To adjust profit to net cash provided (used) by operating activities, the $2,000 decrease in income tax payable must be deducted from profit. If the amount of income tax payable had increased during the year, the increase would be added to profit to reflect the fact that income tax expense deducted on the accrual-based income statement was higher than the cash paid during the period.

The partial statement of cash flows in Illustration 13-6 shows the impact on operating activities of the changes in the current asset and current liability accounts (the changes are highlighted in red). It also shows the adjustments that were described earlier for noncash expenses and revenues and losses and gains. The operating activities section of the statement of cash flows is now complete.

COMPUTER SERVICES CORPORATION Statement of Cash Flows—Indirect Method (partial) Year Ended December 31, 2012		
Operating activities		
Profit		$145,000
Adjustments to reconcile profit to net cash provided (used) by operating activities		
Depreciation expense	$ 9,000	
Loss on sale of equipment	3,000	
Decrease in accounts receivable	10,000	
Increase in merchandise inventory	(5,000)	
Increase in prepaid expenses	(4,000)	
Increase in accounts payable	16,000	
Decrease in income tax payable	(2,000)	27,000
Net cash provided by operating activities		172,000

► Illustration 13-6
Net cash provided (used) by operating activities—indirect method

Helpful Hint
Whether the indirect or direct method (Section 2) is used, net cash provided (used) by operating activities will be the same.

In summary, the operating activities section of Computer Services' statement of cash flows shows that the accrual-based profit of $145,000 resulted in net cash provided by operating activities of $172,000, after adjustments for noncash items.

SUMMARY OF CONVERSION TO NET CASH PROVIDED (USED) BY OPERATING ACTIVITIES—INDIRECT METHOD

As shown in the previous pages, the statement of cash flows prepared by the indirect method starts with profit. It then adds or deducts items from profit to arrive at net cash provided (used) by operating activities. Selected adjustments to profit to determine cash provided (used) by operating activities are summarized here:

Noncash expenses	Depreciation expense (property and equipment)	Add
	Amortization expense (intangible assets)	Add
	Amortization of a bond discount for a bond issuer (interest expense)	Add
	Amortization of a bond premium for a bond issuer (interest expense)	Deduct

Noncash revenues	Amortization of a bond discount for a bond investor (interest revenue)	Deduct
	Amortization of a bond premium for a bond investor (interest revenue)	Add
Losses and gains	Losses	Add
	Gains	Deduct
Changes in certain noncash current asset and current liability accounts	Increase in current asset account	Deduct
	Decrease in current asset account	Add
	Increase in current liability account	Add
	Decrease in current liability account	Deduct

BEFORE YOU GO ON...

▶ Do It! Net Cash Provided (Used) by Operating Activities

Selected financial information follows for Reynolds Ltd. at December 31. Prepare the operating activities section of the statement of cash flows using the indirect method.

	2012	2011	Increase (Decrease)
Current assets			
Cash	$29,000	$37,000	$(8,000)
Accounts receivable	68,000	26,000	42,000
Merchandise inventory	54,000	10,000	44,000
Prepaid expenses	4,000	6,000	(2,000)
Current liabilities			
Accounts payable	35,000	55,000	(20,000)
Accrued liabilities	4,000	5,000	(1,000)
Salaries payable	6,000	4,000	2,000
Income tax payable	20,000	10,000	10,000

REYNOLDS LTD.
Income Statement
Year Ended December 31, 2012

Sales revenue		$890,000
Cost of goods sold		465,000
Gross profit		425,000
Operating expenses		
Salaries expense	$150,000	
Administrative expenses	46,000	
Depreciation expense	33,000	
Loss on sale of equipment	4,000	233,000
Profit from operations		192,000
Other expenses and losses		
Interest expense		12,000
Profit before income tax		180,000
Income tax expense		36,000
Profit		$144,000

Action Plan

- Start with profit to determine the net cash provided (used) by operating activities.
- Examine the income statement: Add noncash expenses like depreciation that increase expense; deduct noncash expenses like amortization of a bond premium for an issuer. Add losses and deduct gains.
- Analyze the current portion of the statement of financial position: Add decreases in related noncash current asset accounts and increases in related noncash current liability accounts. Deduct increases in related noncash current asset accounts and decreases in related noncash current liability accounts.

Solution

REYNOLDS LTD. Statement of Cash Flows (partial) Year Ended December 31, 2012		
Operating activities		
Profit		$144,000
Adjustments to reconcile profit to net cash provided (used) by operating activities		
Depreciation expense	$33,000	
Loss on sale of equipment	4,000	
Increase in accounts receivable	(42,000)	
Increase in merchandise inventory	(44,000)	
Decrease in prepaid expenses	2,000	
Decrease in accounts payable	(20,000)	
Decrease in accrued liabilities	(1,000)	
Increase in salaries payable	2,000	
Increase in income tax payable	10,000	(56,000)
Net cash provided by operating activities		88,000

the navigator

Section 2: Direct Method

Similar to the indirect method, net cash provided (used) by operating activities is determined by adjusting the income statement from the accrual basis of accounting to the cash basis of accounting. Whereas the indirect method adjusts total profit, the direct method adjusts each individual revenue and expense item in the income statement.

We will analyze the accrual-based revenues and expenses reported in Computer Services' income statement in the following sections. The cash receipts and cash payments that relate to these revenues and expenses will be determined by adjusting for changes (increases or decreases) in the related current asset and current liability accounts.

To simplify and condense the operating activities section, only major classes of operating cash receipts and cash payments are reported. The difference between the cash receipts and cash payments for these major classes is the net cash provided (used) by operating activities.

These relationships are shown in Illustration 13-7 on the following page.

CASH RECEIPTS

We will now look at Computer Services' cash receipts. Note that it has only one source of cash receipts—from the sale of goods to its customers.

STUDY OBJECTIVE 2 (b)
Prepare the operating activities section of the statement of cash flows using the direct method.

►Illustration 13-7

Major classes of cash receipts
and payments

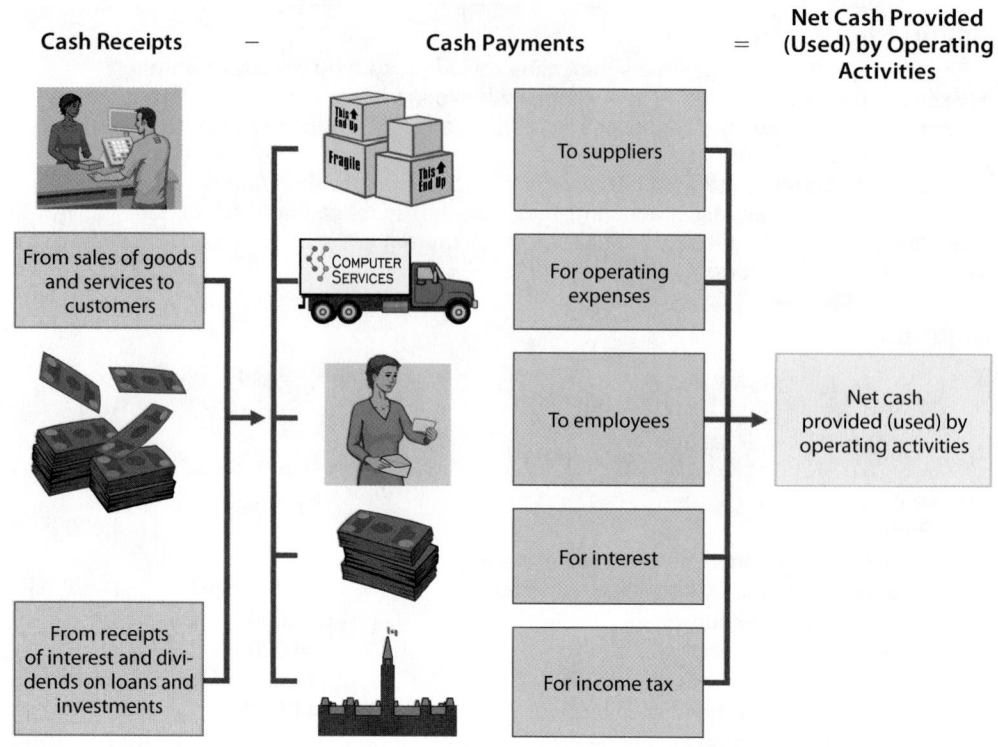

Cash Receipts — **Cash Payments** = **Net Cash Provided (Used) by Operating Activities**

Cash Receipts from Customers

The income statement shown in Illustration 13-4 for Computer Services reported sales revenue from customers of $507,000. How much of that was received in cash? To answer that, it is necessary to look at the change in accounts receivable during the year.

Computer Services' accounts receivable decreased by $10,000 (from $30,000 to $20,000) during the year. When accounts receivable decrease during the year, revenues on an accrual basis are lower than revenues on a cash basis. In other words, more cash was collected during the period than was recorded as revenue. To determine the amount of cash receipts, the decrease in accounts receivable is added to sales revenue.

For Computer Services, cash receipts from customers were $517,000, or $10,000 higher than revenues, as shown as in Illustration 13-8.

►Illustration 13-8

Formula to calculate cash receipts
from customers

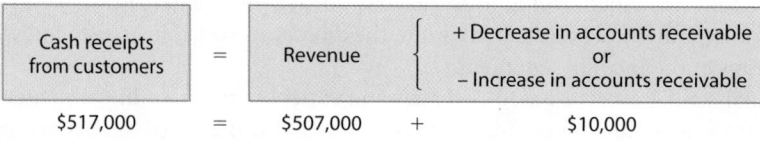

Cash receipts from customers	=	Revenue	{ + Decrease in accounts receivable or − Increase in accounts receivable
$517,000	=	$507,000 +	$10,000

Alternatively, when the Accounts Receivable account balance increases during the year, revenues on an accrual basis are higher than cash receipts. In other words, revenues have increased, but not all of these revenues resulted in cash receipts. Therefore, the amount of the increase in accounts receivable is deducted from sales revenues to arrive at cash receipts from customers.

Cash Receipts from Interest

Computer Services does not have cash receipts from any source other than customers. If an income statement details other revenue, such as interest revenue, these amounts must be adjusted for any receivable amounts to determine the actual cash receipts.

Interest is the most common source of other revenue. Similar to the adjustments shown in Illustration 13-8, decreases in interest receivable would be added to interest revenue. Increases in interest receivable would be deducted from interest revenue.

Sometimes interest revenue may include noncash amounts for the amortization of discounts and premiums on long-term investments in bonds. Recall from Chapter 12 that the amortization of a bond discount for an investor increases interest revenue but does not affect cash. The journal entry debits the Long-Term Investment account and credits the Interest Revenue account. The amortization of a bond premium reduces interest revenue but does not affect cash. The journal entry debits the Interest Revenue account and credits the Long-Term Investment account. So any portion of interest revenue that is related to the amortization of a bond discount or premium must also be removed from interest revenue to determine cash receipts from interest.

CASH PAYMENTS

Computer Services has many sources of cash payments: suppliers, operating expenses, interest, and income taxes. We will analyze each of these in the next sections.

Cash Payments to Suppliers

Using the perpetual inventory system, Computer Services reported a cost of goods sold of $150,000 on its income statement as shown in Illustration 13-4. How much of that was paid in cash to suppliers (also known as creditors)? To answer that, it is necessary to first calculate the cost of goods purchased for the year. After the cost of goods purchased is calculated, cash payments to suppliers can be determined.

1. **Cost of goods purchased:** To calculate the cost of goods purchased, the cost of goods sold must be adjusted for any change in merchandise inventory. When the Merchandise Inventory account increases during the year, the cost of goods purchased is higher than the cost of goods sold. To determine the cost of goods purchased, the increase in inventory is added to the cost of goods sold. Computer Services' inventory increased by $5,000 so its cost of goods purchased is $155,000.

Cost of goods sold	$150,000
Add: Increase in merchandise inventory	5,000
Cost of goods purchased	155,000

Any decrease in inventory would be deducted from the cost of goods sold.

2. **Cash payments to suppliers:** After the cost of goods purchased is calculated, cash payments to suppliers can be determined. This is done by adjusting the cost of goods purchased for the change in accounts payable. In some companies, the Accounts Payable account is used only to record purchases of merchandise on account. An accrued liability account such as Accrued Expenses Payable or some similar account is used to record other credit purchases. In other companies, the Accounts Payable account is used to record all credit purchases. For simplicity, we have assumed in this chapter that Accounts Payable is used only to record purchases of merchandise on account.

Consequently, when accounts payable increase during the year, purchases on an accrual basis are higher than they are on a cash basis. To determine cash payments to suppliers, an increase in accounts payable is deducted from the cost of goods purchased. For Computer Services, cash payments to suppliers were $139,000.

Cost of goods purchased (from [1] above)	$155,000
Less: Increase in accounts payable	16,000
Cash payments to suppliers	139,000

On the other hand, there may be a decrease in accounts payable. That would occur if cash payments to suppliers amounted to more than purchases. In that case, the decrease in accounts payable is added to the cost of goods purchased.

The narrative above is shown in formula format in Illustration 13-9.

▸Illustration 13-9
Formula to calculate cash payments
to suppliers

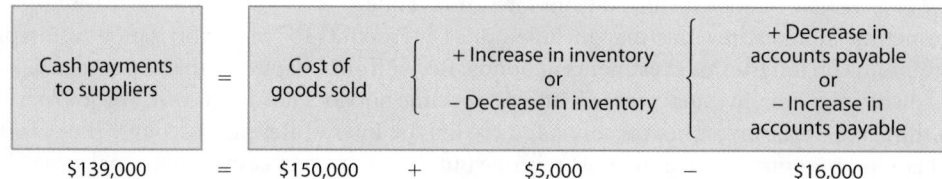

Cash Payments for Operating Expenses

Computer Services' income statement shown in Illustration 13-4 includes $141,000 of other operating expenses. In this particular case, other operating expenses are total operating expenses exclusive of the noncash depreciation expense and loss on the sale of equipment, which have been reported separately for our convenience. If these amounts had been combined, we would have first had to remove the noncash expenses before determining how much of the $141,000 of other operating expenses was paid in cash. Then, we then need to adjust this amount for any changes in prepaid expenses and accrued liabilities.

If prepaid expenses increase during the year, the cash paid for operating expenses will be higher than the operating expenses reported on the income statement. To adjust operating expenses to cash payments for services, any increase in prepaid expenses must be added to operating expenses. On the other hand, if prepaid expenses decrease during the year, the decrease must be deducted from operating expenses.

Operating expenses must also be adjusted for changes in accrued liability accounts (e.g., accrued expenses payable). While for simplicity we have assumed in this chapter that accrued liabilities are recorded separately from accounts payable, some companies do combine them with accounts payable. This is one reason that using the direct method can be difficult in real life. If accrued liabilities and accounts payable are combined and recorded in one account, you have to figure out what proportion of accounts payable relate to purchases of merchandise, and what relates to other payables, in order to determine the cash payments to suppliers and cash payments for operating expenses.

At this point in time, Computer Services does not have any accrued liabilities related to its operating expenses. If it did, any changes in these accounts would affect operating expenses as follows: When an accrued liability account increases during the year, operating expenses on an accrual basis are higher than they are on a cash basis. To determine cash payments for operating expenses, an increase in the accrued liability account is deducted from operating expenses. On the other hand, a decrease in an accrued liability account is added to operating expenses because the cash payments are greater than the operating expenses.

Computer Services' cash payments for operating expenses were $145,000, calculated as in Illustration 13-10.

▸Illustration 13-10
Formula to calculate cash payments
for operating expenses

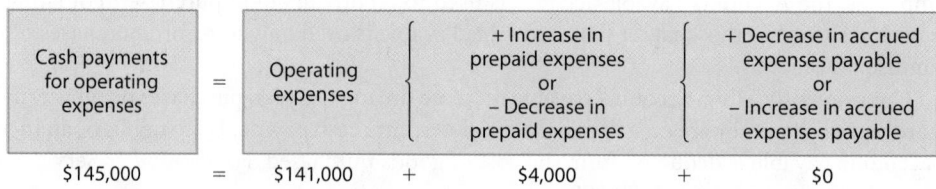

Cash Payments to Employees

Some companies report payments to employees separately, removing these payments from their operating expenses. To determine payments to employees, you would have to know the salaries expense amount on the income statement and any salaries payable on the comparative statement of financial position. Cash payments to employees would equal the salaries expense plus any decrease (or less any increase) during the period in the amount of salaries payable.

Other companies condense their income statement in such a way that cash payments to suppliers and employees cannot be separated from cash payments for operating expenses (i.e., they do not disclose their salaries expense separately). Although the disclosure will not be as informative, for reporting purposes it is acceptable to combine these sources of cash payments.

Cash Payments for Interest

Computer Services reported $12,000 of interest expense on its income statement in Illustration 13-4. This amount equals the cash paid, since the comparative statement of financial position indicated no interest payable at the beginning or end of the year. If there was any interest payable, decreases in the interest payable account would be added to, or increases would be deducted from, the interest expense account to determine cash payments for interest.

Sometimes interest expense may include noncash amounts for the amortization of bond discounts and premiums by a bond issuer. The amortization of a bond discount increases interest expense but does not use cash. Recall from Chapter 10 that the journal entry to amortize a bond discount results in a debit to the Interest Expense account and a credit to the Bonds Payable account. The amortization of a bond premium reduces interest expense but does not reduce cash. The journal entry to amortize a bond premium results in a debit to the Bonds Payable account and a credit to the Interest Expense account. So any portion of interest expense that is related to the amortization of a bond discount or premium must also be removed from interest expense to determine cash payments for interest.

Cash Payments for Income Tax

Computer Services reported income tax expense of $47,000 on its income statement shown in Illustration 13-4. Income tax payable, however, decreased by $2,000 (from $8,000 to $6,000) during the year. This means that income tax paid was more than the income tax reported in the income statement. Decreases in income tax payable are added to income tax expense, to determine the cash payments for income tax. This would be $49,000 for Computer Services.

The relationship among cash payments for income tax, income tax expense, and changes in income tax payable is shown in Illustration 13-11.

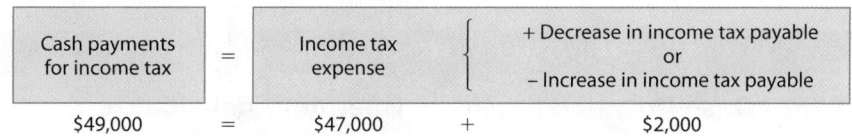

▶ Illustration 13-11
Formula to calculate cash payments for income tax

All of the revenues and expenses in Computer Services' income statement have now been adjusted to a cash basis. The operating activities section of the statement of cash flows is shown in Illustration 13-12. Note that positive numbers in the statement of cash flows prepared using the direct method indicate cash inflows (receipts) and negative numbers, shown in parentheses, indicate cash outflows (payments).

COMPUTER SERVICES CORPORATION
Statement of Cash Flows (partial)
Year Ended December 31, 2012

Operating activities		
Cash receipts from customers		$517,000
Cash payments		
To suppliers	$(139,000)	
For operating expenses	(145,000)	
For interest	(12,000)	
For income tax	(49,000)	(345,000)
Net cash provided by operating activities		172,000

▶ Illustration 13-12
Net cash provided (used) by operating activities—direct method

Helpful Hint
Whether the direct or indirect method (Section 1) is used, net cash provided (used) by operating activities will be the same.

SUMMARY OF CONVERSION TO NET CASH PROVIDED (USED) BY OPERATING ACTIVITIES—DIRECT METHOD

As shown on the previous pages, revenues and expenses reported on the income statement are reviewed to determine if any cash receipts and cash payments relate to them. Noncash revenues and expenses are excluded. Any revenue and expense accounts with cash effects are included, after adjusting them for changes (increases or decreases) in the related current asset and current liability accounts to determine cash receipts and cash payments in the operating activities section.

The adjustments that are required to convert individual revenues and expenses from an accrual basis of accounting to a cash basis of accounting are summarized here:

	Cash Receipts (Revenues)	Cash Payments (Expenses)
Current assets		
Increase in account balance	Deduct (−)	Add (+)
Decrease in account balance	Add (+)	Deduct (−)
Current liabilities		
Increase in account balance	Add (+)	Deduct (−)
Decrease in account balance	Deduct (−)	Add (+)

Note that while the adjustments to revenues shown above are in the same direction as those we discussed in the indirect section, the adjustments to expenses move in the opposite direction. This is because in the indirect method, we are adjusting profit (in which expenses are deductions). In the direct method, we are adjusting each individual expense account, which will later be deducted in the calculation of operating activities.

BEFORE YOU GO ON...

▶ Do It! Net Cash Provided (Used) by Operating Activities

Selected financial information follows for Reynolds Ltd. at December 31. Prepare the operating activities section of the statement of cash flows using the indirect method.

	2012	2011	Increase (Decrease)
Current assets			
Cash	$29,000	$37,000	$(8,000)
Accounts receivable	68,000	26,000	42,000
Merchandise inventory	54,000	10,000	44,000
Prepaid expenses	4,000	6,000	(2,000)
Current liabilities			
Accounts payable	35,000	55,000	(20,000)
Accrued expenses payable	4,000	5,000	(1,000)
Salaries payable	6,000	4,000	2,000
Income tax payable	20,000	10,000	10,000

REYNOLDS LTD.
Income Statement
Year Ended December 31, 2012

Sales revenue		$890,000
Cost of goods sold		465,000
Gross profit		425,000
Operating expenses		
Salaries expense	$150,000	
Administrative expenses	46,000	
Depreciation expense	33,000	
Loss on sale of equipment	4,000	233,000
Profit from operations		192,000
Other expenses and losses		
Interest expense		12,000
Profit before income tax		180,000
Income tax expense		36,000
Profit		$144,000

Action Plan

- Determine the net cash provided (used) by operating activities by adjusting each individual revenue and expense item for changes in the related current asset and current liability account.
- Remove any noncash revenues and expenses.
- To adjust revenues for changes in related working capital accounts, add decreases in current asset accounts and increases in current liability accounts. Deduct increases in current asset accounts and decreases in current liability accounts. To adjust expenses, add increases in current asset accounts and decreases in current liability accounts. Deduct decreases in current asset accounts and increases in current liability accounts.
- Assume that the accounts payable relate to suppliers.
- Assume that the prepaid expenses and accrued expenses payable relate to administrative expenses.
- Report cash receipts and cash payments by major sources and uses: (1) cash receipts from customers, and (2) cash payments to suppliers, for administrative expenses, to employees, for interest, and for income tax.

Solution

REYNOLDS LTD.
Statement of Cash Flows (partial)
Year Ended December 31, 2012

Operating activities		
Cash receipts from customers		$848,000[1]
Cash payments		
To suppliers	$(529,000)[2]	
For administrative expenses	(45,000)[3]	
To employees	(148,000)[4]	
For interest	(12,000)	
For income tax	(26,000)[5]	(760,000)
Net cash provided by operating activities		88,000

Calculations:

[1] Cash receipts from customers: $890,000 − $42,000 (accounts receivable) = $848,000

(continued)

[2] Payments to suppliers: $465,000 + $44,000 (inventory) + $20,000 (accounts payable) = $529,000

[3] Payments for administrative expenses: $46,000 − $2,000 (prepaid expenses) + $1,000 (accrued expenses payable) = $45,000

[4] Payments to employees: $150,000 − $2,000 (salaries payable) = $148,000

[5] Payments for income tax: $36,000 − $10,000 (income tax payable) = $26,000

STEP 2: INVESTING ACTIVITIES

STUDY OBJECTIVE 3

Prepare the investing activities section of a statement of cash flows.

Determine the Net Cash Provided (Used) by Investing Activities by Analyzing Changes in Non-Current Asset Accounts

Regardless of whether the indirect or direct method is used to calculate operating activities, investing and financing activities are measured and reported in the same way. We will look first at investing activities in this section, and financing activities in the next.

Investing activities affect non-current asset accounts, such as long-term investments; property, plant, and equipment; and intangible assets. Note that not all types of investments are classified as investing activities, only cash flows from the purchase and sale of long-term investments. For example, investments in debt or equity securities of other companies that are held specifically for trading purposes are classified as operating activities rather than as investing activities. This is because they relate to revenue-producing activities of the company, similar to inventory purchased for resale. You will recall that trading investments were discussed in Chapter 12.

Although it is primarily non-current asset accounts that give rise to investing activities, there is one current asset account that may also be classified as investing activities. For example, short-term notes receivable issued for loans rather than for trade transactions would be classified as an investing activity rather than an operating activity. The point of mentioning exceptions such as this is to advocate caution about applying general guidelines too widely.

We will use the statement of financial position and additional information provided in Illustration 13-4 to determine what effect, if any, the change in each relevant current asset and non-current asset account had on cash. Computer Services did not have any affected current asset accounts but does have three non-current asset accounts that must be analyzed: Land, Building, and Equipment.

LAND

Land increased by $110,000 during the year, as reported in Computer Services' statement of financial position in Illustration 13-4. The additional information provided states that this land was purchased by issuing long-term bonds. Issuing bonds for land has no effect on cash, but it is a significant noncash investing activity (acquisition of land), as well as a noncash financing activity (issue of bonds), that must be disclosed in a note to the statement of cash flows.

BUILDING

The Building account increased by $120,000 during the year, as reported in Illustration 13-4. What caused this increase? No additional information has been provided regarding this change. Whenever unexplained differences in non-current accounts occur, we assume the transaction was for cash. That is, we would assume in this case that a building was acquired, or expanded, for $120,000 cash and report this cash outflow as an investing activity.

Accumulated Depreciation—Building

Accumulated Depreciation increased by $6,000 during the year, as shown in Illustration 13-4. As explained in the additional information, this increase resulted from the $9,000 of depreciation expense reported on the income statement, of which $6,000 related to the building:

Accumulated Depreciation—Building				
	Jan.	1	Balance	5,000
			Depreciation expense	6,000
	Dec.	31	Balance	11,000

$6,000 net increase

Depreciation expense is a noncash charge and does not affect the statement of cash flows.

EQUIPMENT

Computer Services' Equipment account increased by $17,000, as reported in Illustration 13-4. The additional information provided in this illustration explains that this was a net increase resulting from two different transactions: (1) a purchase of equipment for $25,000 cash, and (2) a sale of equipment that cost $8,000 for $4,000 cash. The following entries reproduce these two equipment transactions:

Equipment	25,000	
Cash		25,000

A	=	L	+	SE
+25,000				
−25,000				

↓ Cash flows: −25,000

Cash	4,000	
Accumulated Depreciation	1,000	
Loss on Sale of Equipment	3,000	
Equipment		8,000

A	=	L	+	SE
+4,000				−3,000
+1,000				
−8,000				

↑ Cash flows: +4,000

The T account that follows summarizes the changes in the Equipment account during the year:

Equipment					
Jan.	1	Balance	10,000		
		Purchase of equipment	25,000	Cost of equipment sold	8,000
Dec.	31	Balance	27,000		

$17,000 net increase

In the above example, you were given information about both the purchase and the sale of equipment. Often, in analyzing accounts, you will be given just one piece of information and will have to figure out the information that is missing. For example, if you knew the beginning and ending balances of the Equipment account as well as the fact that the cost of the equipment sold was $8,000, you could determine that the cost of the equipment purchased must have been $25,000.

Each transaction should be reported separately on the statement of cash flows. If a company did not report cash inflows and outflows from investing (and financing) activities separately, it would make it difficult for the user to assess future cash flows. Consequently, when a net change in a non-current statement of financial position account has occurred during the year, the individual items that caused the net change should be reported separately. In this particular case, the purchase of equipment should be reported as a $25,000 outflow of cash. The sale of equipment should be reported as a $4,000 inflow of cash. Note that it is the cash proceeds that are reported on the statement of cash flows, not the cost of the equipment sold.

Accumulated Depreciation—Equipment

The accumulated depreciation for equipment increased by $2,000. This change does not represent the overall depreciation expense for the year. The additional information in Illustration 13-4 reported that depreciation expense was $9,000 in total, of which $3,000 related to the equipment.

We can use the journal entry shown earlier for the sale of the equipment and the information about the amount of the depreciation expense recorded for the year to help us understand why the Accumulated Depreciation account increased by $2,000, and not $3,000:

$2,000 net increase

Accumulated Depreciation—Equipment					
		Jan.	1	Balance	1,000
Sale of equipment	1,000			Depreciation expense	3,000
		Dec.	31	Balance	3,000

The $2,000 net increase is composed of two different amounts: (1) a reduction in accumulated depreciation of $1,000 as a result of the sale of equipment described above, and (2) an increase in accumulated depreciation of $3,000 as a result of depreciation expense for the current period.

As we have seen, the sale of the equipment affected a number of accounts: one account on Computer Services' income statement (Loss on Sale of Equipment) and three accounts on its statement of financial position (Cash, Equipment, and Accumulated Depreciation). In the statement of cash flows, it is important to combine the effects of this sale in one place: the investing activities section. The overall result, then, is that the loss on the sale of the equipment is removed from the operating activities section of the statement of cash flows and the cash proceeds received from the sale of the equipment are shown in their entirety in the investing activities section.

INVESTMENTS

Although Computer Services has no investment accounts, it is important to remember to remove any noncash transactions when analyzing changes in any long-term investment and investment-related accounts. These would include the amortization of bond discounts and premiums as well as both realized and unrealized gains and losses on investments carried at fair value through profit and loss. Similar to the sale of equipment discussed above, items reported for investments in a statement of cash flows should consist only of amounts paid when purchasing long-term investments and amounts received when selling long-term investments.

The investing activities section of Computer Services' statement of cash flows is shown in Illustration 13-13. It reports the purchase of a building as well as the purchase and sale of equipment.

▶ Illustration 13-13
Net cash provided (used) by investing activities

COMPUTER SERVICES CORPORATION		
Statement of Cash Flows (partial)		
Year Ended December 31, 2012		
Investing activities		
Purchase of building	$(120,000)	
Purchase of equipment	(25,000)	
Sale of equipment	4,000	
Net cash used by investing activities		$(141,000)
Note x: Significant noncash investing and financing activities		
Issue of bonds to purchase land		$110,000

It also reports in the accompanying notes to the statement the significant noncash investing and financing activity.

As a company grows, you can expect to see it *use* cash for its investing activities as it purchases property, plant, and equipment. Typically, you do not see cash *provided* by investing activities unless a company sells off excess assets. Obtaining cash by selling off non-current assets could mean that a company may be in the midst of restructuring its business activities, or even in financial difficulties. Understanding the pattern of a company's cash flows over time can provide important information for users.

BEFORE YOU GO ON...

▶ Do It! Net Cash Provided (Used) by Investing Activities

Umiujaq Corporation reported an opening balance of $146,000 and an ending balance of $135,000 in its Equipment account; and an opening balance of $47,000 and an ending balance of $62,000 in its Accumulated Depreciation—Equipment account. During the year, it sold equipment for cash with a cost of $21,000, a carrying amount of $5,000, and a gain on the sale of $1,000. It also purchased equipment for cash. It recorded depreciation expense on the equipment of $31,000. Calculate the cash received from the sale of equipment and the cash paid for equipment.

Action Plan

- Use journal entries and T accounts, and your knowledge of account relationships, to reconstruct the transactions affecting the Equipment account. Fill in the information given and use this to determine any missing information (e.g., the cost of equipment purchased).
- Use journal entries and T accounts, and your knowledge of account relationships, to reconstruct the transactions affecting the Accumulated Depreciation account. Fill in the information given and use this to determine any missing information (e.g., the accumulated depreciation on the equipment sold).
- Remember that the carrying amount of equipment is its cost less accumulated depreciation and that gains result when the cash proceeds exceed the carrying amount.

Solution

Cash received from sale of equipment = $6,000

Cash	6,000	
Accumulated Depreciation ($21,000 – $5,000)	16,000	
Gain on Sale of Equipment		1,000
Equipment		21,000

Cash paid for equipment = $10,000

Equipment	10,000	
Cash		10,000

Equipment

Opening balance	146,000		
Purchase of equipment	10,000	Sale of equipment	21,000
Ending balance	135,000		

Accumulated Depreciation—Equipment

		Opening balance	47,000
Sale of equipment	16,000	Depreciation expense	31,000
		Ending balance	62,000

the navigator

STEP 3: FINANCING ACTIVITIES

Determine the Net Cash Provided (Used) by Financing Activities by Analyzing Changes in Non-Current Liability and Equity Accounts

The third step in preparing a statement of cash flows is to analyze the changes in non-current liability and equity accounts. In addition, changes involving short-term loans (including notes) payable should also be reported in the financing activities section if they have been incurred for lending purposes rather than for trade.

To determine the financing activities, we need to examine any short-term loans payable, non-current liability, and shareholders' equity accounts on the statement of financial position and statement of changes in equity, and any additional information. Computer Services has one non-current liability account (Bonds Payable) and three shareholders' equity accounts (Common Shares, Retained Earnings, and Accumulated Other Comprehensive Income), as shown in Illustration 13-4.

BONDS PAYABLE

Bonds Payable increased by $110,000, as shown in Illustration 13-4. As indicated earlier, land was acquired by issuing these bonds. This noncash transaction is reported as a note to the statement of cash flows because it is a significant noncash financing activity, (issue of bonds) as well as a noncash investing activity (acquisition of land).

The Bonds Payable account may also increase or decrease due to the amortization of a bond discount or premium. Recall that the amortization of a bond discount increases the Bonds Payable account while the amortization of a bond premium decreases the Bonds Payable account. Amortization does not affect cash and must be considered when analyzing any changes in the account before determining the amount of bonds purchased or sold during the period. Computer Services' bonds were issued at face value so there is no bond discount or premium amortization to consider in its case.

SHARE CAPITAL

Share capital can include both preferred and common shares. Computer Services does not have any preferred shares, but does have a balance of $70,000 in common shares at the end of 2012. According to Illustration 13-4, the company's Common Shares account increased by $20,000. Since no additional information is provided about any reacquisition of shares, we assume that this change relates solely to the issue of additional common shares for cash. The cash inflow from the issue of shares is reported in the financing activities section of the statement of cash flows.

If the company had reacquired shares, the amount of cash paid to reacquire the shares would be reported as a cash outflow in the financing activities section of the statement of cash flows. This is the case regardless of whether the company retired the reacquired shares or held them in treasury for later reissue.

RETAINED EARNINGS

What caused the net increase of $116,000 in Retained Earnings reported in Illustration 13-4? This increase can be explained by two factors. First, profit increased retained earnings by $145,000. Second, the additional information provided in Illustration 13-4 indicates that a cash dividend of $29,000 was paid.

This information could also have been determined by analyzing the T account:

Retained Earnings					
		Jan.	1	Balance	48,000
Cash dividend	29,000			Profit	145,000
		Dec.	31	Balance	164,000

$116,000 net increase {

As we noted in the investing activities section, these two changes must be reported separately. The profit is therefore reported, albeit indirectly, in the operating activities section of the statement of cash flows (after the revenue and expense components have been adjusted to a cash basis using either the indirect or direct method).

The cash dividend paid is reported as a cash outflow in the financing activities section of the statement. Note that the Retained Earnings account above only reports the dividend declared. This amount must be adjusted to determine the dividend paid, if there is any balance in the Dividends Payable account reported in the current liabilities section of the statement of financial position. Computer Services did not have any dividends payable.

ACCUMULATED OTHER COMPREHENSIVE INCOME

Computer Services had no change in its accumulated other comprehensive income between 2011 and 2012. That is why it did not prepare a statement of comprehensive income, only an income statement, in 2012. If accumulated other comprehensive income had increased or decreased in the current year, it would not affect the statement of cash flows as there are no cash effects in any of the sources of other comprehensive income. That is why the starting point for the operating activities of the statement of cash flows is profit and not comprehensive income.

The financing activities section of Computer Services' statement of cash flows is shown below and reports the issue of common shares and payment of a dividend. It also reports in the accompanying notes to the statement the significant noncash investing and financing activity. This is the same note shown in Illustration 13-13. It is not a new note; it has been included here for completeness only.

▶ Illustration 13-14

Net cash provided (used) by financing activities

COMPUTER SERVICES CORPORATION Statement of Cash Flows (partial) Year Ended December 31, 2012		
Financing activities		
Issue of common shares	$20,000	
Payment of cash dividend	(29,000)	
Net cash used by financing activities		$(9,000)
Note x: Significant noncash investing and financing activities		
Issue of bonds to purchase land		$110,000

As a company grows, you can expect to see cash *provided* by its financing activities. Most companies are not able to generate sufficient cash from their operating activities as they are growing to pay for their investing activities, so they have to borrow for any shortfall. Growing companies must invest in productive assets, such as buildings and equipment. To finance these purchases, the company will have to issue debt or shares.

Typically you do not see cash *used* by financing activities as we see in Illustration 13-14 for Computer Services unless a company is mature and able to start to repay its debt. As we mentioned in the investing activities section, understanding the pattern of a company's cash flows over time can provide important information for users.

BEFORE YOU GO ON...

▶ Do It! Net Cash Provided (Used) by Financing Activities

La Tuque Corporation reported an opening balance of $80,000 and an ending balance of $95,000 in its Common Shares account, an opening balance of $15,000 and an ending balance of $20,000 in its Contributed Capital—Reacquisition of Common Shares account, and an opening balance of $250,000 and an ending balance of $325,000 in its Retained Earnings account. During the year, it issued $50,000 of common shares for cash and reacquired common shares for cash. It also reported a profit of $100,000 and paid a cash dividend during the year. Assuming there were no other transactions affecting the common shares, contributed capital, and retained earnings accounts, and that there were no dividends payable, calculate the cash paid to reacquire the common shares and the cash paid for the dividend.

(continued)

Action Plan

- Use journal entries and T accounts, and your knowledge of account relationships, to reconstruct the transactions affecting the Common Shares and Contributed Capital accounts. Fill in the information given and use this to determine any missing information (e.g., the average cost of the reacquired shares).
- Use journal entries and T accounts, and your knowledge of account relationships, to reconstruct the transactions affecting the Retained Earnings account. Fill in the information given and use this to determine any missing information (e.g., the dividend declared).

Solution

Cash paid to reacquire shares = $30,000

Common Shares	35,000	
Contributed Capital—Reacquisition of Common Shares		5,000
Cash		30,000

Common Shares

		Opening balance	80,000
Reacquisition of shares	35,000	Issue of shares	50,000
		Ending balance	95,000

Contributed Capital—Reacquisition of Common Shares

		Opening balance	15,000
		Reacquisition of shares	5,000
		Ending balance	20,000

Cash paid for dividend = $25,000

Cash Dividends	25,000	
Cash		25,000

Retained Earnings

		Opening balance	250,000
Cash dividend	25,000	Profit	100,000
		Ending balance	325,000

STEP 4: THE STATEMENT OF CASH FLOWS

STUDY OBJECTIVE 5

Complete the statement of cash flows.

Complete the Statement of Cash Flows and Determine the Net Increase (Decrease) in Cash

Using the partial information shown in Illustration 13-12 for operating activities, in Illustration 13-13 for investing activities, and in Illustration 13-14 for financing activities, we can now combine the sections and present a complete statement of cash flows for Computer Services Corporation, as shown in Illustration 13-15.

The statement of cash flows starts with the operating activities section. Because it is preferred by standard setters, we have chosen to illustrate the direct method of preparing the operating activities section in Illustration 13-15. The operating activities section prepared using the indirect method was shown in Illustration 13-6, and could be substituted in this illustration if desired. Both methods report cash provided by operating activities of $172,000. As mentioned earlier in the chapter, while the operating activities sections differ in format between the indirect and direct methods, the investing and financing activities sections are exactly the same.

▸Illustration 13-15
Statement of cash flows—
direct method

COMPUTER SERVICES CORPORATION
Statement of Cash Flows
Year Ended December 31, 2012

Operating activities		
Cash receipts from customers		$517,000
Cash payments		
To suppliers	$(139,000)	
For operating expenses	(145,000)	
For interest	(12,000)	
For income tax	(49,000)	(345,000)
Net cash provided by operating activities		172,000
Investing activities		
Purchase of building	$(120,000)	
Purchase of equipment	(25,000)	
Sale of equipment	4,000	
Net cash used by investing activities		(141,000)
Financing activities		
Issue of common shares	$ 20,000	
Payment of cash dividend	(29,000)	
Net cash used by financing activities		(9,000)
Net increase in cash		22,000
Cash, January 1		33,000
Cash, December 31		$ 55,000
Note x: Significant noncash investing and financing activities		
Issue of bonds to purchase land		$110,000

The statement continues with investing activities, reporting that investing activities used $141,000 of cash. Financing activities follow, and used $9,000 of cash. The statement concludes with the net change in cash, reconciled to the beginning- and end-of-period cash balances. The comparative statement of financial position in Illustration 13-4 indicates that the net change in cash during the period was an increase of $22,000. The $22,000 net increase in cash reported in the statement of cash flows above agrees with this change.

Notice how the statement of cash flows links the different financial statements. For example, income statement accounts are explained in the operating activities section of the statement of cash flows in terms of their impact on cash. This incorporates changes from current asset and current liability accounts on the statement of financial position to help convert accrual-based income statement items (profit in the case of the indirect method and individual revenue and expense items in the case of the direct method) to cash-based items. The investing and financing activities on the statement of cash flows explain the remaining changes between assets and liabilities on the statement of financial position. In addition, the statement of changes in equity and the shareholders' equity section of the statement of financial position help determine information about the issue and reacquisition of shares or payment of dividends shown in the financing activities section. The overall effect of all the activities shown on the statement of cash flows leads to the end-of-period cash balances reported on it and the statement of financial position.

Additional disclosures are required to complete the statement of cash flows. As we previously discussed, significant noncash investing and financing activities must be reported in the notes to the financial statements. In addition, if a company has combined cash equivalents with its cash, it must disclose the components of its cash equivalents along with a reconciliation of the amounts reported on the statement of cash flows with those reported on the statement of financial position. There are other disclosures required, but we will leave discussion of these to a future accounting course.

■ Keeping an Eye on Cash

Just as products have a life cycle, so too do companies. The "corporate" life cycle can be said to consist of four phases: introductory, growth, maturity, and decline. Each phase, as indicated in the following graph, can help us understand what to expect for a company's cash flow from its operating, investing, and financing activities.

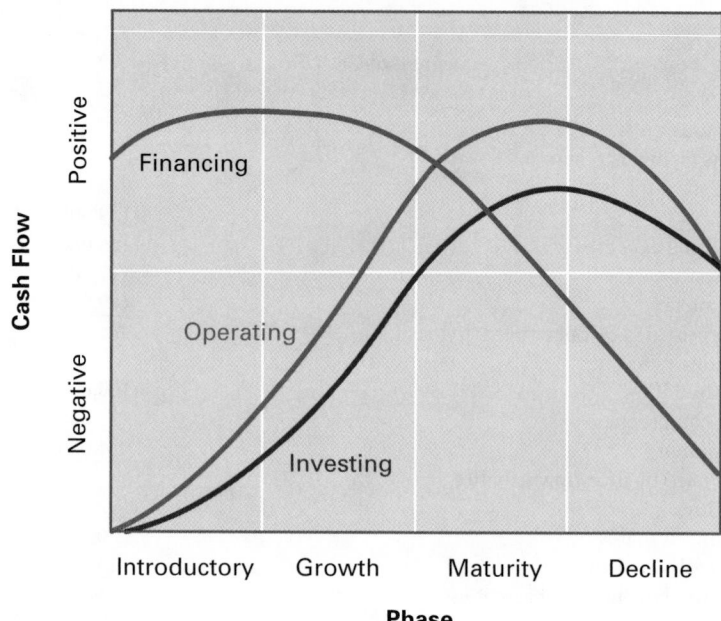

In the introductory and growth phases, we don't usually expect to see a company generate positive cash from its operating activities. Because the company is making significant investments in its long-lived assets, cash generated by investing activities is also negative. In contrast, cash generated by financing activities is usually positive as debt and equity are issued to pay for the investments and cover the operating activities shortfall.

As companies move to the maturity and decline phases of their life cycle, these patterns tend to reverse. The company is usually able to generate positive cash from its operating activities as it reaches maturity, which is used to cover its investing activities. At this point in their life cycle, companies can start to pay dividends, retire debt, and/or buy back shares so their cash flows from financing activities move toward the negative. In the decline phase, cash from operating activities decreases. Cash from investing activities is positive as the company sells off its excess assets, before starting to decline. Cash is used for financing activities as the company continues to pay off its debt.

BEFORE YOU GO ON...

▶ Do It! Statement of Cash Flows

Selected information follows for Reynolds Ltd. at December 31:

	2012	2011	Increase (Decrease)
Cash	$ 61,000	$ 37,000	$24,000
Property, plant, and equipment			
Land	45,000	70,000	(25,000)
Buildings	200,000	200,000	0
Accumulated depreciation—buildings	(21,000)	(11,000)	10,000
Equipment	193,000	68,000	125,000
Accumulated depreciation—equipment	(28,000)	(10,000)	18,000
Liabilities and shareholders' equity			
Bonds payable	110,000	150,000	(40,000)
Common shares	200,000	60,000	140,000
Retained earnings	201,000	112,000	89,000

Additional information:

1. Cash provided by operating activities was $88,000 for the year, whether calculated using the indirect or direct method as shown in the Before You Go On—Do It! examples in the Operating Activities section of the chapter.

2. Equipment was purchased for cash. Equipment with a cost of $41,000 and a carrying amount of $36,000 was sold at a loss of $4,000.

3. Bonds of $40,000, originally issued at face value, were redeemed at their face value for cash.

4. Common shares were issued for cash; no shares were reacquired during the year.

5. Profit was $144,000.

6. A cash dividend was paid.

Prepare a statement of cash flows, excluding the detail normally required for the operating activities section.

Action Plan

- Begin with the operating activities section.
- Determine the net cash provided (used) by investing activities. Investing activities generally relate to changes in non-current asset accounts.
- Determine the net cash provided (used) by financing activities. Financing activities generally relate to changes in non-current liabilities and shareholders' equity accounts.
- Determine the net increase (decrease) in cash. Reconcile to the end-of-period cash balance reported on the statement of financial position ($61,000 in this case).

Solution

REYNOLDS LTD.		
Statement of Cash Flows		
Year Ended December 31, 2012		
Operating activities		
Net cash provided by operating activities		$ 88,000
Investing activities		
Sale of land	$ 25,000	
Sale of equipment	32,000[1]	
Purchase of equipment	(166,000)[2]	
Net cash used by investing activities		(109,000)
Financing activities		
Redemption of bonds	$(40,000)	
Issue of common shares	140,000	
Payment of dividends	(55,000)[3]	
Net cash provided by financing activities		45,000
Net increase in cash		24,000
Cash, January 1		37,000
Cash, December 31		$ 61,000

[1] Sale of equipment: $36,000 (carrying amount) − $4,000 (loss) = $32,000

[2] Purchase of equipment: $68,000 (opening account balance) − $41,000 (sale of equipment) + $166,000 (purchase of equipment) = $193,000 (ending account balance)

[3] Payment of dividends: $112,000 (opening account balance) + $144,000 (profit) − $55,000 (dividends) = $201,000 (ending account balance)

Using Cash Flows to Evaluate a Company

Previous chapters have presented ratios that are used to analyze a company's liquidity and solvency. Most of those ratios used accrual-based numbers from the income statement and statement of financial position. In this section, we focus on ratios that are *cash-based* rather than accrual-based. That is, instead of only using numbers from the income statement and statement of financial position, these ratios also use numbers from the statement of cash flows. Analysts often find it helpful to supplement and compare accrual-based measures with cash-based measures.

In this section, we will use the following selected information (in millions) to introduce cash-based liquidity and solvency ratios for Teck, featured in our chapter-opening story:

	2010	2009
Net cash provided by operating activities	$ 2,743	$ 2,983
Net capital expenditures	810	590
Cash dividends	118	0
Current assets	3,306	3,676
Total assets	29,209	29,873
Current liabilities	1,740	2,363
Total liabilities	13,033	15,282

LIQUIDITY

Liquidity is the ability of a company to pay obligations expected to become due within the next year. In Chapter 2, you learned that one measure of liquidity is the current ratio (current assets divided by current liabilities). One disadvantage of the current ratio is that it uses year-end balances of current asset and current liability accounts. These year-end balances may not be representative of the company's position during most of the year. Another disadvantage is that current assets and current liabilities include accrual-based numbers.

A ratio that partially corrects this problem is the **cash current debt coverage** ratio. It is calculated by dividing net cash provided or used by operating activities by average current liabilities. We say it "partially corrects this problem" because, even though the numerator uses cash-based numbers, the denominator, current liabilities, does not.

The cash current debt coverage ratio for Teck is shown in Illustration 13-16 for 2010, along with comparative results for Freeport-McMoRan Copper & Gold Inc. Freeport-McMoRan, a key competitor to Teck, is an international mining company headquartered in Arizona. We have also provided each company's current ratio for comparative purposes. Unfortunately, although there are industry averages for the more commonly used accrual-based measures, no industry averages are available for cash-based measures.

▶Illustration 13-16
Cash current debt coverage ratio

CASH CURRENT DEBT COVERAGE = $\dfrac{\text{NET CASH PROVIDED (USED) BY OPERATING ACTIVITIES}}{\text{AVERAGE CURRENT LIABILITIES}}$		
(in millions)	**Cash Current Debt Coverage Ratio**	**Current Ratio**
Teck	$\dfrac{\$2,743}{(\$1,740 + \$2,363) \div 2} = 1.3 \text{ times}$	$\dfrac{\$3,306}{\$1,740} = 1.9{:}1$
Freeport-McMoRan	1.9 times	2.6:1

Teck's cash provided by operating activities is 1.3 times more than its average current liabilities. In other words, it is generating $1.30 of cash flow from operating activities to cover each dollar of current liabilities. The higher the cash current debt coverage ratio, the better a company's liquidity.

Teck's current ratio is much stronger than its cash current debt coverage ratio. However, with the amount of the difference between the two measures, it is likely that Teck's current assets include some amount of accruals (e.g., from revenue billed but not yet collected or from merchandise purchased on account). This is not a problem, however, as long as the receivables are collectable and the inventory is saleable.

Teck's cash current debt coverage ratio is lower than that of Freeport-McMoRan, as is its current ratio. This is not surprising given Teck's use of its cash generated by operating activities to reduce its debt over the last few years.

DECISION TOOLKIT

 Decision Checkpoints	 Info Needed for Decision	 Tools to Use for Decision	 How to Evaluate Results
Is the company generating sufficient cash from operating activities to meet its current obligations?	Net cash provided or used by operating activities and average current liabilities	Cash current debt coverage = $\dfrac{\text{Net cash provided (used) by operating activities}}{\text{Average current liabilities}}$	A high value suggests good liquidity. Since the numerator contains a cash flow measure, it provides a useful supplement to the current ratio.

SOLVENCY

Solvency is the ability of a company to survive over the long term. We will introduce two cash-based measures of solvency: the cash total debt coverage ratio and free cash flow.

Cash Total Debt Coverage

The cash total debt coverage ratio is similar to the cash current debt coverage ratio except that it uses total liabilities instead of current liabilities. The **cash total debt coverage** ratio is calculated by dividing net cash provided or used by operating activities by average total liabilities. This ratio indicates a company's ability to repay its liabilities from cash generated from operating activities; that is, without having to liquidate productive assets such as property, plant, and equipment. The higher the cash total debt coverage ratio is, the more solvent a company is.

The cash total debt coverage ratios for Teck and Freeport-McMoRan are given in Illustration 13-17 for 2010. For comparative purposes, the accrual-based counterpart, the debt to total assets ratio, is also provided for each company. You will recall from Chapter 2 that the debt to total assets ratio is calculated by dividing total liabilities by total assets.

▶ Illustration 13-17
Cash total debt coverage ratio

$$\text{CASH TOTAL DEBT COVERAGE} = \frac{\text{NET CASH PROVIDED (USED) BY OPERATING ACTIVITIES}}{\text{AVERAGE TOTAL LIABILITIES}}$$

(in millions)	Cash Total Debt Coverage Ratio	Debt to Total Assets
Teck	$\dfrac{\$2,743}{(\$13,033 + \$15,282) \div 2} = 0.2$ times	$\dfrac{\$13,033}{\$29,209} = 44.6\%$
Freeport-McMoRan	0.4 times	50.5%

Teck's cash total debt coverage ratio of 0.2 times means that it is generating $0.20 to cover each dollar of total liabilities. This ratio is significantly less than its cash current debt coverage ratio of 1.3 times, so we know that Teck has a considerable amount of non-current liabilities.

Although Freeport-McMoRan's cash total debt coverage ratio is better than that of Teck, the inverse is true for the debt to total assets ratio. Recall that the higher the cash total debt coverage ratio, the better, while the lower the debt to total assets ratio, the better. Since both ratios are moving in different directions (i.e., the cash total debt coverage ratio is worse while the debt to total assets ratio is better), we can conclude that there is likely some difference between the cash and accrual measures for the two companies.

It is difficult to reach a conclusion about either company's solvency position without also knowing more about each company's ability to handle its debt (e.g., its times interest earned ratio). However, a low cash total debt coverage ratio could signal a long-term solvency problem if the company is not able to generate enough cash internally to repay its debt.

Free Cash Flow

Cash provided by operating activities is often adjusted to take into account the fact that a company must invest in new assets just to maintain its current level of operations. In addition, if a company pays dividends, it must also have cash available so that it can continue paying dividends to satisfy investors. Free cash flow is a solvency-based measure that helps creditors and investors understand how much discretionary cash flow a company has left from its operating activities available to use to expand operations, reduce debt, go after new opportunities, or pay additional dividends, among other alternatives. You may recall that free cash flow was briefly introduced in Chapter 2 in the Keeping an Eye on Cash feature.

Although there are different definitions of free cash flow, a commonly used one is to deduct net capital expenditures and dividends from cash provided or used by operating activities to determine **free cash flow**. Net capital expenditures—representing amounts paid for the acquisition of property, plant, and equipment less any recoveries from the sale of these assets—can be found in the investing activities section of the statement of cash flows. Dividends paid, if any, are reported in the financing activities section of the statement of cash flows.

Illustration 13-18 presents the free cash flow numbers for Teck and Freeport-McMoRan for both 2010 and 2009.

▶Illustration 13-18
Free cash flow

FREE CASH FLOW =	NET CASH PROVIDED (USED) BY OPERATING ACTIVITIES	− NET CAPITAL EXPENDITURES	− DIVIDENDS PAID
(in millions)	2010		2009
Teck (in CAD millions)	$2,743 − $810 − $118 = $1,815		$2,983 − $590 − $0 = $2,393
Freeport-McMoRan (in USD millions)	$3,881		$2,581

Teck's free cash flow declined in 2010, although it is still a very healthy $1,815 million. Recall that we discussed Teck's use of its free cash flow to reduce its debt in our chapter-opening feature story. Freeport-McMoRan's free cash flow was higher than Teck's, especially in 2010 when it increased by U.S. $1.3 billion over 2009. Freeport-McMoRan generated sufficient cash from its operating activities to cover capital expenditures and dividends and still have U.S. $3,881 million remaining for other uses.

DECISION TOOLKIT

Decision Checkpoints	Info Needed for Decision	Tools to Use for Decision	How to Evaluate Results
Is the company generating sufficient cash from operating activities to meet its total obligations?	Net cash provided or used by operating activities and average total liabilities	Cash total debt coverage = $\dfrac{\text{Net cash provided (used) by operating activities}}{\text{Average total liabilities}}$	A high value suggests the company is solvent; that is, it will meet its obligations in the long term. Since the numerator contains a cash flow measure, it provides a useful supplement to the debt to total assets ratio.
Can the company meet its long-term obligations?	Net cash provided or used by operating activities, net capital expenditures, and cash dividends	Free cash flow = Net cash provided (used) by operating activities − Net capital expenditures − Dividends paid	Free cash flow indicates the potential to finance new investments, reduce debt, or pay more dividends.

ACCOUNTING MATTERS!   *Investor Perspective*

Saving Cash for a Rainy Day

Facing an uncertain economic environment in 2009 and 2010, companies hoarded their cash, amassing a rainy-day fund the likes of which hadn't been seen in over 40 years. The stores of cash were the result of drastic cost-cutting measures during the recession, followed by a slow recovery in the economy, which increased both profit and cash. Free cash flow was said to be at its highest level since the 1960s for the average company.

Howard Silverblatt, a senior analyst at Standard & Poor's, said that companies were holding an "amazing amount of cash, considering if they're lucky they are getting a percent [interest] on it." The levels of cash were becoming too much of a good thing for most shareholders, given the razor-thin interest rates. They started demanding that the money be put to better use or returned to shareholders.

Source: Joanna Slater, "Corporate America Sits on Cash Hoard," *The Globe and Mail*, July 4, 2010, p. B1.

BEFORE YOU GO ON...

▶ Do It! Cash-Based Measures

Speyside Inc. reported the following selected information:

	2012	2011	2010
Net cash provided by operating activities	$ 72,000	$ 62,000	
Net capital expenditures	24,000	20,000	
Cash dividends	10,000	10,000	
Current liabilities	32,000	30,000	$ 34,000
Total liabilities	240,000	220,000	250,000

(a) Calculate the company's cash current debt coverage ratio, cash total debt coverage ratio, and free cash flow for 2012 and 2011. (b) Indicate whether the company's liquidity and solvency have improved, deteriorated, or did not change in 2012 based on these three measures.

Action Plan:

- Recall the formula for cash current debt coverage, a measure of liquidity: Net cash provided (used) by operating activities ÷ average current liabilities.
- Recall the formula for cash total debt coverage, a measure of solvency: Net cash provided (used) by operating activities ÷ average total liabilities.
- Recall the formula for free cash flow, a measure of solvency: Net cash provided (used) by operating activities − net capital expenditures − cash dividends.

Solution:

	(a)		(b)
	2012	2011	
Cash current debt coverage	$\dfrac{\$72,000}{(\$32,000 + \$30,000) \div 2}$ = 2.3 times	$\dfrac{\$62,000}{(\$30,000 + \$34,000) \div 2}$ = 1.9 times	Improvement
Cash total debt coverage	$\dfrac{\$72,000}{(\$240,000 + \$220,000) \div 2}$ = 0.3 times	$\dfrac{\$62,000}{(\$220,000 + \$250,000) \div 2}$ = 0.3 times	Unchanged
Free cash flow	$72,000 − $24,000 − $10,000 = $38,000	$62,000 − $20,000 − $10,000 = $32,000	Improvement

the navigator

comparing
IFRS and ASPE

Key Differences	International Financial Reporting Standards (IFRS)	Accounting Standards for Private Enterprises (ASPE)
Classification of activities	Interest and dividends received may be classified as operating or investing activities.	Interest and dividends received are classified as operating activities.
	Interest and dividends paid may be classified as operating or financing activities.	Interest paid is classified as an operating activity. Dividends paid are classified as a financing activity.
	Once the choice is made, it must be applied consistently.	

the navigator

Where Does All the Money Go?

As you learned in this chapter, the statement of cash flows provides vital information to a company about the cash generated or used by operating, investing, and financing activities. If a company's cash flow from operating activities does not cover its investing and financing cash needs, it must find additional cash. A company should always have a cash budget that shows anticipated cash flows, ideally covering more than one year.

A cash budget is a good idea for individuals as well as for companies. Do you know how you spend your cash? Your personal statement of cash flows can help you track the relationship between your cash inflows and cash outflows. Most of us know approximately how much we spend on recurring items such as rent, transit or car payments, cell phone bills, or tuition fees, but we don't really know how much we spend on incidentals such as snacks, coffee, or music downloads. If you were able to reduce your cash expenditure by an average of $5 per day, that would be $35 a week or $1,820 per year that you could save.

Some Facts

- The average Canadian household spent $71,117 on goods and services in 2009, down 0.3% from 2008. The largest share of the budget went to personal taxes (20%), shelter (20%), and transportation (14%). Food accounted for 10% of the budget. Household spending on cell phone and other wireless services was up more than 13% from 2008 to an average of $620 in 2009. At the same time, spending for conventional land-line telephone service continued to fall, dropping 4.5% to $550.
- A Harris Decima poll, sponsored by the CICA, found that 84% of respondents thought that young people were not prepared to manage their finances. The Canadian parents interviewed thought that the most important financial skills they should teach their children were first, to minimize income tax, and second, to manage their finances efficiently. But 78% of the respondents had tried to teach their own children these skills and 60% of them did not think they had been successful.
- Mint.com is a free on-line finance tracking service. Set-up is easy: you create an anonymous Mint account, then add your bank account details and information about your credit cards, loans, and other debts. You can set up a budget and Mint will track every transaction and let you know when you are about to go over your limit. Mint Canada is required to comply with Canadian privacy laws and cannot share your personal financial information without your consent.

What Do You Think?

You live on campus and own a car. You use the car for pleasure and to drive to a job that is 10 km away. Suppose your personal statement of cash flows includes the following items for the current year:

- Cash inflows of $20,000
- Cash outflows for tuition, board, and books $16,000; vehicle costs $3,000; vacation $2,000; cell phone service $600; and snacks and beverages $500.

Should you get rid of your car and cell phone, stop eating snacks, and give up the idea of a vacation?

YES Because the cash outflows ($16,000 + $3,000 + $2,000 + $600 + $500 = $22,100) are greater than the cash inflows ($20,000), you will accumulate debt that you will have to pay back when you finish university. While you need your car for work, you should consider reducing the cost of your cell phone, snacks, and beverages, and defer your vacation to help reduce the amount of money you will have to borrow.

NO A person has to have a bit of fun. Life would be boring if you couldn't call and get together with your friends and get away once in awhile.

Sources: Statistics Canada, "Survey of Household Spending," *The Daily*, December 17, 2010. Nora Underwood, "Early Adopters Are Breezy about Online Money-Trackers," *Globe and Mail*, January 11, 2011, p. L3. Canadian Institute of Chartered Accountants, "Canadians Signal Strong Need for Financial Literacy Education at All Ages," January 5, 2011.

Summary of Study Objectives

1. **Describe the purpose and content of the statement of cash flows.** The statement of cash flows provides information about the cash receipts and cash payments resulting from the operating, investing, and financing activities of a company during a specific period.

   Operating activities include the cash effects of transactions that are used in the determination of profit. Operating activities are affected by noncash items in the income statement and changes in certain noncash current asset and current liability accounts in the statement of financial position. Investing activities involve cash flows resulting from changes in non-current asset items. Financing activities involve cash flows resulting from non-current liabilities and shareholders' equity items. These are general guidelines, to which there are a few exceptions.

2. **Prepare the operating activities section of a statement of cash flows using one of two approaches: (a) the indirect method or (b) the direct method.** The first step in the preparation of a statement of cash flows is to determine the net cash provided (used) by operating activities using either the indirect or direct method (preferred). In the indirect method, this is done by converting profit from an accrual basis to a cash basis. In the direct method, this is done by converting each individual revenue and expense account from an accrual basis to a cash basis.

3. **Prepare the investing activities section of a statement of cash flows.** The second step in the preparation of a statement

   of cash flows is to analyze the changes in non-current asset accounts and record them as investing activities, or as significant noncash transactions.

4. **Prepare the financing activities section of a statement of cash flows.** The third step in the preparation of a statement of cash flows is to analyze the changes in non-current liability and equity accounts and record them as financing activities, or as significant noncash transactions.

5. **Complete the statement of cash flows.** The fourth and final step in the preparation of a statement of cash flows is to complete the statement of cash flows and determine the net increase or decrease in cash.

6. **Use the statement of cash flows to evaluate a company's liquidity and solvency.** Liquidity can be measured by the cash-based cash current debt coverage ratio (net cash provided or used by operating activities divided by average current liabilities) and compared with the accrual-based current ratio (current assets divided by current liabilities). Solvency can be measured by the cash-based cash total debt coverage ratio (net cash provided or used by operating activities divided by average total liabilities) and compared with the accrual-based debt to total assets ratio (total liabilities divided by total assets). Free cash flow (net cash provided or used by operating activities minus net capital expenditures minus dividends) is another measure of solvency.

Glossary

Cash current debt coverage   A cash-based ratio used to evaluate liquidity. It is calculated by dividing net cash provided (used) by operating activities by average current liabilities. (p. 724)

Cash total debt coverage   A cash-based ratio used to evaluate solvency. It is calculated by dividing net cash provided (used) by operating activities by average total liabilities. (p. 725)

Direct method   A method of determining net cash provided (used) by operating activities by adjusting each item in the income statement from the accrual basis to the cash basis. (p. 699)

Financing activities   Cash flow activities from non-current liability and equity accounts. These include (a) obtaining cash by issuing debt and repaying the amounts borrowed and (b) obtaining cash from shareholders and providing them with a return on their investment. (p. 694)

Free cash flow   A cash-based measure used to evaluate solvency. It is calculated by deducting net capital

expenditures and cash dividends from net cash provided (used) by operating activities. (p. 726)

Indirect method   A method of determining net cash provided (used) by operating activities in which profit is adjusted for items that do not affect cash. (p. 699)

Investing activities   Cash flow activities from non-current asset accounts. These include (a) purchasing and disposing of long-term investments and long-lived assets and (b) lending money and collecting on those loans. (p. 693)

Operating activities   Cash flow activities from transactions that create revenues and expenses and therefore are included in the determination of profit. They are affected by noncash items in the income statement and changes (increases or decreases) in related noncash current asset and liability accounts in the statement of financial position. (p. 693)

DECISION TOOLKIT-A SUMMARY

Decision Checkpoints	Info Needed for Decision	Tools to Use for Decision	How to Evaluate Results
Is the company generating sufficient cash from operating activities to meet its current obligations?	Net cash provided or used by operating activities and average current liabilities	Cash current debt coverage = $\dfrac{\text{Net cash provided (used) by operating activities}}{\text{Average current liabilities}}$	A high value suggests good liquidity. Since the numerator contains a cash flow measure, it provides a useful supplement to the current ratio.
Is the company generating sufficient cash from operating activities to meet its total obligations?	Net cash provided or used by operating activities and average total liabilities	Cash total debt coverage = $\dfrac{\text{Net cash provided (used) by operating activities}}{\text{Average total liabilities}}$	A high value suggests the company is solvent; that is, it will meet its obligations in the long term. Since the numerator contains a cash flow measure, it provides a useful supplement to the debt to total assets ratio.
Can the company meet its long-term obligations?	Net cash provided or used by operating activities, net capital expenditures, and cash dividends	Free cash flow = Net cash provided (used) by operating activities − Net capital expenditures − Dividends paid	Free cash flow indicates the potential to finance new investments, reduce debt, or pay more dividends.

USING THE DECISION TOOLKIT

Stantec Inc., headquartered in Edmonton, is a professional consulting services company with more than 10,500 employees in more than 160 offices throughout North America. Stantec's statement of cash flows for the most recent three years follows:

STANTEC INC.
Statement of Cash Flows
Years Ended December 31
(in thousands)

	2010	2009	2008
Operating activities			
Cash receipts from clients	$1,499,392	$1,564,415	$1,222,566
Cash paid to suppliers	(510,410)	(545,671)	(276,862)
Cash paid to employees	(821,360)	(852,459)	(737,931)
Dividends received	2,852	1,283	150
Interest received	3,111	2,192	1,857
Interest paid	(16,775)	(12,383)	(6,597)
Income taxes paid	(51,548)	(65,731)	(50,037)
Income taxes recovered	9,522	8,331	6,884
Net cash provided by operating activities	114,784	99,977	160,030
Investing activities			
Business acquisitions	(66,989)	(73,078)	(92,087)
Increase in investments held for self-insured liabilities	(7,301)	(11,040)	(358)
Proceeds on sale of investments	11,263		9
Purchase of intangible assets	(3,262)	(3,062)	(2,846)
Purchase of property and equipment	(25,725)	(17,366)	(32,791)
Proceeds on disposition of property and equipment	412	1,331	410
Net cash used by investing activities	(91,602)	(103,215)	(127,663)

(*continued*)

Financing activities			
Repayment of long-term debt	(183,301)	(152,498)	(166,390)
Proceeds from long-term borrowings	216,948	68,771	228,337
Repayment of finance lease obligations	(5,356)	(2,759)	(438)
Repurchase of shares for cancellation	(4,887)		(8,914)
Proceeds from issue of share capital	3,044	2,346	1,199
Net cash provided (used) by financing activities	26,448	(84,140)	53,794
Other (foreign exchange gain [loss])	(1,589)	(1,911)	3,643
Net increase (decrease) in cash and cash equivalents	48,041	(89,289)	89,804
Cash and cash equivalents, beginning of the year	14,690	103,979	14,175
Cash and cash equivalents, end of the year	$ 62,731	$ 14,690	$ 103,979

Additional information:

1. Current liabilities were $331,342 thousand, $283,811 thousand, and $300,009 thousand at the end of 2010, 2009, and 2008, respectively.
2. Total liabilities were $697,930 thousand, $575,965 thousand, and $605,911 thousand at the end of 2010, 2009, and 2008, respectively.
3. Profit was $93,595 thousand, $55,940 thousand, and $29,017 thousand in 2010, 2009, and 2008, respectively.

Instructions

(a) Does Stantec use the indirect or direct method to prepare its operating activities section?
(b) Calculate Stantec's cash current debt coverage ratio, cash total debt coverage ratio, and free cash flow for 2010 and 2009.
(c) Comment on any significant changes in Stantec's cash flows over the last three years.

Solution

(a) Stantec uses the direct method to prepare the operating activities section of its statement of cash flows.
(b) (in thousands)

	2010	2009
Cash current debt coverage	$\dfrac{\$114,784}{(\$331,342 + \$283,811) \div 2}$ = 0.4 times	$\dfrac{\$99,977}{(\$283,811 + \$300,009) \div 2}$ = 0.3 times
Cash total debt coverage	$\dfrac{\$114,784}{(\$697,930 + \$575,965) \div 2}$ = 0.2 times	$\dfrac{\$99,977}{(\$575,965 + \$605,911) \div 2}$ = 0.2 times
Free cash flow	$\$114,784 - (\$25,725 - \$412) - \$0$ = $\$89,471$	$\$99,977 - (\$17,366 - \$1,331) - \$0$ = $\$83,942$

(c) Cash provided by operating activities increased between 2009 and 2010 and declined significantly between 2008 and 2009 despite increases in Stantec's profit year over year. In 2009, its cash receipts from clients increased but the cash paid to suppliers and employees increased faster. In 2010, Stantec's cash receipts declined, but its cash paid to suppliers and employees declined even faster, contributing to the improvement in cash provided by operating activities. Stantec's cash current debt coverage increased during the same period while its cash total debt coverage ratio remained unchanged.

During the past three years, Stantec spent considerable cash on business acquisitions although the cash outflows have declined each year. It also purchased property and equipment during this same period. Its free cash flow increased by $5,529 ($89,471 − $83,942) thousand in 2010, even after covering these capital expenditures.

Stantec obtained a significant amount of new long-term financing in 2010 and 2008. In both of these years, its debt borrowings exceeded its debt repayments. In 2009, it was able to repay more debt than it borrowed. This was the primary reason that net cash from financing activities decreased in 2009.

Overall, Stantec has seen a decrease in its cash position. At the beginning of 2008, it had $14,175 thousand in cash and cash equivalents, which increased to $103,979 thousand at the end of 2008. By the end of 2009, its cash and cash equivalents balance had declined to $14,690 thousand, primarily because its debt repayments exceeded its borrowings, as mentioned above. In 2010, this balance improved somewhat to $62,731 thousand, but was still only 60% of the 2008 year-end level of $103,979 thousand.

the navigator

Comprehensive Do It!

The comprehensive income statement for Kosinski Inc. contains the following condensed information:

KOSINSKI INC.
Statement of Comprehensive Income
Year Ended December 31, 2012

Sales	$6,583,000
Cost of goods sold	3,427,000
Gross profit	3,156,000
Operating expenses	2,349,000
Profit from operations	807,000
Interest expense	124,000
Profit before income tax	683,000
Income tax expense	203,000
Profit	480,000
Other comprehensive loss	10,000
Total comprehensive income	$ 470,000

The following selected current asset and current liability balances are reported on Kosinski's comparative statement of financial position at December 31:

	2012	2011	Increase (Decrease)
Cash	$150,000	$ 30,000	$120,000
Accounts receivable	775,000	610,000	165,000
Merchandise inventory	834,000	867,000	(33,000)
Accounts payable	521,000	501,000	20,000
Income tax payable	53,000	25,000	28,000

Additional information:
1. The company uses a perpetual inventory system.
2. Operating expenses include salaries expense of $1,000,000, depreciation expense of $300,000, amortization expense of $80,000, and a loss on the sale of machinery of $24,000.
3. The other comprehensive loss resulted from a revaluation of the fair value of land, which decreased from $500,000 to $490,000 during the year.
4. Machinery was sold for $270,000, at a loss of $24,000.
5. New machinery was purchased during the year for $1,250,000. It was partially financed by a bank loan payable issued for $400,000.
6. Dividends paid in 2012 totalled $100,000.

Instructions
(a) Prepare the statement of cash flows using the indirect method.
(b) Prepare the statement of cash flows using the direct method.
(c) Identify the similarities and differences between your answers in (a) and (b).

Action Plan
- Determine the net cash provided (used) by operating activities. Operating activities generally relate to revenues and expenses shown on the income statement, which are affected by noncash items in the income statement and changes in noncash current assets and current liabilities in the statement of financial position.
- Recall that profit is used to determine the net cash provided (used) by operating activities and not total comprehensive income.
- Determine the net cash provided (used) by investing activities. Investing activities generally relate to changes in non-current asset accounts.
- Determine the net cash provided (used) by financing activities. Financing activities generally relate to changes in non-current liability and shareholders' equity accounts.
- Determine the net increase (decrease) in cash. Verify that this amount agrees with the end-of-period cash balance reported on the statement of financial position.

(continued)

Solution to Comprehensive Do It!

(a)

KOSINSKI Inc.
Statement of Cash Flows—Indirect Method
Year Ended December 31, 2012

Operating activities		
Profit		$480,000
Adjustments to reconcile profit to net cash provided by operating activities		
Depreciation expense	$ 300,000	
Amortization expense	80,000	
Loss on sale of machinery	24,000	
Increase in accounts receivable	(165,000)	
Decrease in merchandise inventory	33,000	
Increase in accounts payable	20,000	
Increase in income tax payable	28,000	320,000
Net cash provided by operating activities		800,000
Investing activities		
Sale of machinery	$ 270,000	
Purchase of machinery (see Note x)	(850,000)	
Net cash used by investing activities		(580,000)
Financing activities		
Payment of cash dividends	$(100,000)	
Net cash used by financing activities		(100,000)
Net increase in cash		120,000
Cash, January 1		30,000
Cash, December 31		$150,000

Note x: Machinery was purchased for $1,250,000 and partially financed by the issue of a $400,000 bank loan payable.

(b)

KOSINSKI INC.
Statement of Cash Flows—Direct Method
Year Ended December 31, 2012

Operating activities		
Cash receipts from customers	$6,418,000[1]	
Cash payments		
To suppliers	(3,374,000)[2]	
For operating expenses	(945,000)[3]	
To employees	(1,000,000)	
For interest	(124,000)	
For income tax	(175,000)[4]	
Net cash provided by operating activities		$800,000
Investing activities		
Sale of machinery	$ 270,000	
Purchase of machinery (see Note x)	(850,000)	
Net cash used by investing activities		(580,000)
Financing activities		
Payment of cash dividends	$ (100,000)	
Net cash used by financing activities		(100,000)
Net increase in cash		120,000
Cash, January 1		30,000
Cash, December 31		$150,000

Note x: Machinery was purchased for $1,250,000 and partially financed by the issue of a $400,000 bank loan payable.

Calculations:

[1] Cash receipts from customers: $6,583,000 − $165,000 (accounts receivable) = $6,418,000
[2] Cash payments to suppliers: $3,427,000 − $33,000 (merchandise inventory) − $20,000 (accounts payable) = $3,374,000
[3] Cash payments for operating expenses: $2,349,000 − $1,000,000 (salaries: shown separately as cash payments to employees) − $300,000 (depreciation) − $80,000 (amortization) − $24,000 (loss) = $945,000
[4] Cash payments for income tax: $203,000 − $28,000 (income tax payable) = $175,000

(c) Both the indirect and direct methods report the same net cash provided by operating activities, but they report different detail within each section. Both methods report the same totals and detail for the investing and financing activities section. Both methods arrive at the same change in cash for the period and ending cash balances.

 **Self-Test, Brief Exercises, Exercises, Problems: Set A, and many more components are available for practice in WileyPLUS.**

Self-Test Questions

Answers are at the end of the chapter.

(SO 1, 2) 1. Which is an example of a cash flow from an operating activity?
(a) A payment of cash to lenders for interest
(b) A receipt of cash from the sale of common shares
(c) A payment of dividends to shareholders
(d) A purchase of merchandise inventory on account

(SO 1, 3) 2. Which is an example of a cash flow from an investing activity?
(a) A receipt of cash from the issue of bonds payable
(b) A payment of cash to repurchase common shares
(c) A receipt of cash from the sale of equipment
(d) A purchase of a building, fully financed by a mortgage payable

(SO 1, 4) 3. Which is an example of a cash flow from a financing activity?
(a) A receipt of cash from the sale of land
(b) A payment of dividends to shareholders
(c) A payment of cash for income tax
(d) A receipt of cash for interest on an investment

(SO 2a) 4. Profit for the year is $132,000. During the year, accounts payable increased by $10,000, merchandise inventory decreased by $6,000, and accounts receivable increased by $12,000. Under the indirect method, what is the net cash provided (used) by operating activities?
(a) $116,000
(b) $128,000
(c) $136,000
(d) $148,000

(SO 2a) 5. In determining net cash provided (used) by operating activities under the indirect method, noncash items that are added back to profit do *not* include:
(a) depreciation expense.
(b) amortization of a bond discount by a bond issuer.
(c) a gain on the sale of equipment.
(d) a loss on the sale of equipment.

(SO 2b) 6. The beginning balance in Accounts Receivable is $44,000. The ending balance is $42,000. Sales on account during the period are $129,000. What are the cash receipts from customers?
(a) $127,000
(b) $129,000
(c) $131,000
(d) $141,000

(SO 2b) 7. Which of the following items is reported in the operating activities section of a statement of cash flows prepared by the direct method?
(a) A loss on the sale of a building
(b) An increase in accounts receivable
(c) Depreciation expense
(d) Cash payments to suppliers

(SO 3, 4) 8. The following data relate to cash received or paid from various transactions for Orange Corporation:

Sale of land	$100,000
Issue of common shares	70,000
Sale of a long-term investment	50,000
Payment of cash dividends	40,000
Purchase of equipment	30,000

Orange's net cash provided by investing and financing activities is as follows:

(a) $120,000 provided by investing activities and $30,000 provided by financing activities.

(b) $70,000 provided by investing activities and $80,000 provided by financing activities.

(c) $50,000 provided by investing activities and $100,000 provided by financing activities.

(d) $180,000 provided by investing activities and $110,000 provided by financing activities.

(SO 6) 9. Which of the following statements is *not* true?
(a) The higher the cash current debt coverage and current ratios, the better.
(b) The higher the cash total debt coverage and debt to total assets ratios, the better.
(c) The higher the free cash flow, the better.
(d) The cash current debt coverage ratio is a liquidity ratio.

(SO 6) 10. The cash current debt coverage ratio is a cash-based counterpart to the accrual-based:
(a) current ratio.
(b) receivables turnover.
(c) debt to total assets.
(d) free cash flow.

Questions

(SO 1) 1. What is a statement of cash flows and why is it useful?

(SO 1) 2. What are "cash equivalents"? Should a company combine cash equivalents with cash when preparing the statement of cash flows? Explain why or why not.

(SO 1) 3. Explain the differences among the three categories of activities—operating, investing, and financing—reported in the statement of cash flows.

(SO 1) 4. Private companies following ASPE can classify interest and dividends differently than can companies following IFRS. Explain how these classifications can differ and identify the most commonly used classification(s).

(SO 1) 5. Masood and Adriana were discussing where they should report significant noncash investing and financing transactions in Rock Candy Corp.'s statement of cash flows. Give two examples of noncash transactions and describe where they should be reported.

(SO 2) 6. (a) Identify whether each of the following is used in the preparation of a statement of cash flows: (1) the adjusted trial balance, (2) the statement of financial position, (3) the income statement, (4) the statement of comprehensive income, and (5) the statement of changes in equity. (b) Explain how each of the items identified in (a) is used in the preparation of the statement of cash flows.

(SO 2) 7. Goh Corporation changed its method of reporting operating activities from the indirect method to the direct method in order to make its statement of cash flows more informative to its readers. Will this change increase, decrease, or not affect the net cash provided (used) by operating activities?

(SO 2) 8. In 2010, The Brick Ltd., one of Canada's largest retailers of household furniture, reported $39 million of profit. During the same period of time, its cash provided by operating activities,

of $61 million, was more than one and a half times the amount of profit. Explain how this could occur.

(SO 2a) 9. Describe the indirect method for determining net cash provided (used) by operating activities.

(SO 2a) 10. Why and how is depreciation and amortization expense reported in the operating activities section of a statement of cash flows prepared using the indirect method?

(SO 2a) 11. The sale of equipment at a gain is deducted from profit when calculating net cash provided (used) by operating activities in the indirect method. Jacques doesn't understand why gains aren't added, rather than deducted, on the statement of cash flows since they result in an increase in profit on the income statement. He also doesn't understand why only the gain and not the proceeds from the entire sale of the equipment is reported in the operating activities section. Help Jacques understand the reporting of the sale of equipment on the statement of cash flows.

(SO 2b) 12. Describe the direct method for determining net cash provided (used) by operating activities.

(SO 2b) 13. Under the direct method, why is depreciation and amortization expense not reported in the operating activities section?

(SO 2, 3) 14. Denis says, "I understand that operating activities are affected by changes in current asset and current liability accounts. I also know that trading investments are current assets and that the purchase and sale of trading investments are recorded as operating activities. What I don't understand is why the purchase and sale of investments–whether current or non-current–are not always classified as investing activities." Help Denis understand the classification of investments.

(SO 2b, 3, 4) 15. Explain how (a) the sale of equipment at a gain, and (b) the redemption of bonds payable at a loss are reported on a statement of cash flows using the direct method.

(SO 2, 4)   16. Laurel says, "I understand that operating activities are affected by changes in current asset and current liability accounts. I also know that short-term loans payable are current liabilities. What I don't understand is why short-term loans are not always classified as operating activities. Occasionally they are classified as operating activities but mostly they are classified as financing activities." Help Laurel understand the classification of short-term loans payable.

(SO 2, 3, 4)   17. In general, would you expect a growing company to report positive or negative cash flows from its operating, investing, and financing activities? Explain.

(SO 5)   18. Explain how the statement of cash flows interrelates to the other financial statements.

(SO 6)   19. Give examples of cash- and accrual-based ratios that measure (a) liquidity, and (b) solvency.

(SO 6)   20. In 2010, Leon's Furniture Limited reported a current ratio of 2.6:1 and a cash current debt coverage ratio of 0.6 times. Explain why Leon's cash current debt coverage is likely so much lower than its current ratio.

(SO 6)   21. In 2010, Rogers Communications Inc. reported a debt to total assets ratio of 77% and a cash total debt coverage ratio of 0.3 times. Its competitor, Shaw Communications Inc., reported a debt to total assets ratio of 73% and a cash total debt coverage ratio of 0.2 times in the same year. Based only on this information, which company is more solvent?

(SO 6)   22. A company's cash total debt coverage ratio and free cash flow have been declining steadily over the last five years. What does this decline likely mean to creditors and investors?

(SO 6)   23. How is it possible for a company to report positive net cash provided by operating activities but have a negative free cash flow?

Brief Exercises

BE13–1 For each of the following transactions, indicate whether it will result in an increase (+), decrease (−), or have no effect (NE) on cash flows:

(a) _____ Repayment of mortgage payable
(b) _____ Payment of interest on mortgage
(c) _____ Purchase of land in exchange for common shares
(d) _____ Reacquisition of preferred shares
(e) _____ Purchase of a trading investment

(f) _____ Collection of accounts receivable
(g) _____ Declaration of cash dividend
(h) _____ Payment of a cash dividend (see item [g] above)
(i) _____ Purchase of merchandise inventory
(j) _____ Recording of depreciation expense

Indicate impact of transactions on cash.
(SO 1)

BE13–2 Classify each of the transactions listed in BE13–1 as an operating (O), investing (I), financing (F), or significant noncash investing and financing (NC) activity. If a transaction does not belong in any of these classifications, explain why.

Classify activities.
(SO 1)

BE13–3 Mega Brands Inc. reported the following items on its statement of cash flows:

1. _____ Repayment of long-term debt
2. _____ Income tax expense
3. _____ Acquisition of property, plant, and equipment
4. _____ Issue of common shares
5. _____ Issue of debentures (bonds)
6. _____ Interest expense
7. _____ Changes in noncash operating working capital items

Classify activities.
(SO 1, 2a)

(a) Indicate where each of the above items was reported in Mega Brands' statement of cash flows—as an operating activity (O), investing activity (I), or financing activity (F). (b) Does Mega Brands use the indirect or direct method of preparing the operating activities section of its statement of cash flow? Explain how you came to your conclusion.

BE13–4 Indicate whether each of the following transactions would be added to (i) or subtracted from (−) profit to calculate net cash provided (used) by operating activities using the indirect method. If a transaction is not an operating activity, indicate that it is NA (not applicable).

(a) _____ Depreciation expense
(b) _____ Increase in accounts receivable
(c) _____ Decrease in merchandise inventory in the perpetual inventory system
(d) _____ Increase in accounts payable
(e) _____ Decrease in income tax payable

(f) _____ Gain on sale of equipment
(g) _____ Loss on sale of long-term investment
(h) _____ Revaluation of land upward to current fair value
(i) _____ Amortization of a discount on a bond investment
(j) _____ Impairment loss for goodwill

Indicate impact on operating activities—indirect method.
(SO 2a)

Calculate operating
activities—indirect
method.
(SO 2a)

BE13–5 The comparative statement of financial position for Dupigne Corporation shows the following noncash current asset and liability accounts at March 31:

	2012	2011
Accounts receivable	$60,000	$40,000
Merchandise inventory	75,000	70,000
Prepaid expenses	6,000	4,000
Accounts payable	35,000	40,000
Interest payable	5,000	7,500
Income tax payable	17,000	12,000

Dupigne's income statement reported the following selected information for the year ended March 31, 2012: profit was $275,000, depreciation expense was $60,000, and a loss on the sale of land was $15,000. Dupigne uses a perpetual inventory system. Calculate net cash provided (used) by operating activities using the indirect method.

Calculate cash receipts
from customers—
direct method.
(SO 2b)

BE13–6 Idol Corporation has accounts receivable of $14,000 at January 1, and of $24,000 at December 31. Sales revenues were $170,000 for the year. What amount of cash was received from customers?

Calculate cash
payments to suppliers—
direct method.
(SO 2b)

BE13–7 Columbia Sportswear Company reported cost of goods sold of U.S. $854,120 million on its 2010 income state-ment. It also reported an increase in merchandise inventory of U.S. $87,265 million and an increase in accounts payable of U.S. $60,252 million. What amount of cash was paid to suppliers, assuming that the company uses a perpetual inventory system and that accounts payable relate to merchandise creditors?

Calculate cash pay-
ments for operating
expenses—direct
method.
(SO 2b)

BE13–8 Excellence Corporation reports operating expenses of $100,000, including depreciation expense of $15,000, amortization expense of $2,500, and a gain of $500 on the disposal of equipment during the current year. During this same period, prepaid expenses increased by $6,600 and accrued expenses payable decreased by $2,400. Calculate the cash pay-ments for operating expenses.

Calculate cash pay-
ments for income
tax—direct method.
(SO 2b)

BE13–9 Home Grocery Limited reported income tax expense of $90,000 for the year. (a) Calculate the cash payments for income tax assuming income tax payable increased by $2,000 during the year. (b) Repeat part (a), assuming income tax payable decreased by $2,000 during the year.

Calculate operating
activities—direct
method.
(SO 2b)

BE13–10 The comparative statement of financial position for Baird Corporation shows the following noncash current asset and liability accounts at March 31:

	2012	2011
Accounts receivable	$60,000	$40,000
Merchandise inventory	64,000	70,000
Prepaid expenses	6,000	4,000
Accounts payable	35,000	40,000
Interest payable	4,000	5,000
Income tax payable	10,000	5,000

Baird's income statement reported the following selected information for the year ended March 31, 2012: sales were $850,000, cost of goods sold was $475,000, operating expenses were $230,000 (which included depreciation expense of $20,000), interest expense was $50,000, and income tax expense was $15,000. Calculate net cash provided (used) by operat-ing activities using the direct method.

Calculate cash received
from sale of equipment.
(SO 3)

BE13–11 The T accounts for equipment and accumulated depreciation for Trevis Ltd. are shown here:

Equipment				Accumulated Depreciation—Equipment			
Beg. bal.	80,000	Disposals	20,000	Disposals	5,500	Beg. bal.	44,500
Acquisitions	40,000					Depreciation	20,000
End bal.	100,000					End bal.	59,000

In addition, Trevis's income statement reported a $1,500 loss on the sale of equipment. (a) What amount was reported on the statement of cash flows as "cash provided by sale of equipment"? (b) In what section of the statement of cash flows would this transaction be reported?

Prepare investing
activities section.
(SO 3)

BE13–12 Holmes Corporation reported the following information (in thousands) at December 31, 2012:

	2012	2011
Long-term investments	$ 150	$ 100
Land	200	200
Buildings	300	300

Accumulated depreciation—buildings	90	75
Equipment	500	400
Accumulated depreciation—equipment	200	200

Additional information:

1. Long-term investments were purchased during the year; none were sold.
2. Equipment was purchased during the year. In addition, equipment with a cost of $100 and a carrying amount of $50 was sold at a gain of $10.

Prepare the investing activities section of Holmes's statement of cash flows for the year.

BE13–13 Canadian Tire Corporation, Limited reported a profit of $453.6 million for the year ended January 1, 2011. Its retained earnings were $3,013.7 million at the beginning of the year and $3,393.5 million at the end of the year. It had no dividends payable at the beginning or end of the year. What amount of dividends did Canadian Tire pay during the year?

Calculate cash paid for dividends.
(SO 4)

BE13–14 Nicoloff Corporation reported the following information (in thousands) at December 31, 2012:

Prepare financing activities section.
(SO 4)

	2012	2011
Dividends payable	$ 15	$ 10
Bank loan payable—current portion	200	200
Bank loan payable—non-current portion	400	300
Common shares	600	400
Retained earnings	700	500

Additional information:

1. The bank loan was increased by additional borrowings of $300 to partially finance the purchase of new equipment that cost $500. The bank loan was decreased by repayments.
2. Common shares were issued during the year. None were reacquired.
3. Dividends were paid during the year.
4. Profit for the year was $400.

Prepare the financing activities section of Nicoloff's statement of cash flows for the year.

BE13–15 Jain Corporation reported net cash provided by operating activities of $325,000, net cash used by investing activities of $250,000, and net cash provided by financing activities of $70,000. In addition, cash spent for net capital expenditures during the period was $200,000, and $25,000 of dividends were paid. Average current liabilities were $215,000 and average total liabilities were $360,000. Calculate these values: (a) cash current debt coverage, (b) cash total debt coverage, and (c) free cash flow.

Calculate cash-based ratios.
(SO 6)

BE13–16 Big Rock Brewery reported the following selected liquidity ratios:

Evaluate liquidity.
(SO 6)

	2010	2009
Current ratio	1.7:1	1.8:1
Cash current debt coverage	1.7 times	2.0 times

Both the current and cash current debt coverage ratios declined in 2010. What does this mean?

BE13–17 Bombardier Inc. reported the following selected solvency ratios:

Evaluate solvency.
(SO 6)

	2010	2009
Debt to total assets	82.6%	88.1%
Cash total debt coverage	0.7 times	0.9 times

Based on the above, has Bombardier's solvency improved or deteriorated? Explain.

Exercises

E13–1 A list of cash transactions (except for item 10) follows:

Classify activities.
(SO 1)

	(a) Cash	(b) Noncash Account	(c) Classification
1. Provided services to a customer.	+	Service Revenue	O
2. Repaid a bank loan.			
3. Paid interest on the bank loan.			

4. Purchased equipment.
5. Collected one of the accounts receivable.
6. Paid employees.
7. Paid dividends previously declared.
8. Issued common shares.
9. Sold merchandise to a customer.
10. Purchased land by issuing common shares.

Instructions

Complete the above table indicating (a) whether each transaction increases (+), decreases (−), or has no effect (NE) on cash; (b) what other account beside Cash is affected in the transaction; and (c) whether the transaction should be classified as an operating activity (O), investing activity (I), financing activity (F), or noncash investing and financing activity (NC). The first one has been done for you as an example.

Classify activities.
(SO 1)

E13–2   Eng Corporation had the following transactions:

	(a)	(b)
	Cash Effect	Classification

1. Issued common shares for $50,000.
2. Purchased a machine for $30,000. Made a $5,000 down payment and issued a long-term note payable for the remainder.
3. Collected $16,000 of accounts receivable.
4. Paid a $25,000 cash dividend.
5. Sold a long-term investment with a carrying amount of $15,000 for $18,000.
6. Sold merchandise inventory for $1,000.
7. Paid $18,000 on accounts payable.
8. Purchased a trading investment for $100,000.
9. Purchased merchandise inventory for $28,000 on account.
10. Collected $1,000 in advance from customers.

Instructions

(a) In the above table, indicate by how much each transaction increases (+) or decreases (−) cash. If the transaction has no effect (NE) on cash, say so.

(b) Identify whether the transaction should be classified as an operating activity (O), investing activity (I), financing activity (F), or noncash investing and financing activity (NC).

Discuss noncash items.
(SO 1)

E13–3   Crown Point Limited reports the following noncash transactions:

1. Recorded an impairment loss on goodwill
2. Recorded depreciation expense
3. Recorded amortization of a bond premium for a bond investor
4. Recorded an unrealized gain on long-term equity investment carried at fair value
5. Purchased a new vehicle by signing a note payable
6. Declared and distributed a stock dividend
7. Effected a 2-for-1 stock split
8. Converted an account receivable to a note receivable
9. Recorded a revaluation adjustment of property, plant, and equipment to current fair value
10. Acquired equipment by issuing common shares

Instructions

For each of the above transactions, explain why it does not involve cash and where it should be reported, if at all, on the statement of cash flows or accompanying notes.

Indicate impact of transactions on profit and operating activities.
(SO 2)

E13–4   He Corporation had the following transactions:

	(a)	(b)
	Profit	Cash Provided (Used) by Operating Activities

1. Sold merchandise inventory for cash at a higher price than its cost.   +   +
2. Collected cash in advance from a customer for a service to be provided in the future.
3. Purchased merchandise inventory on account in a perpetual inventory system.
4. Declared and paid dividends.
5. Recorded and paid salaries.
6. Recorded income tax payable.

7. Accrued interest receivable.
8. Recorded depreciation expense.
9. Paid an amount owing on account to a supplier.
10. Collected an amount owing from a customer.

Instructions
Complete the above table indicating whether each transaction will increase (+), decrease (−), or have no effect (NE) on (a) profit and (b) cash provided (used) by operating activities. The first one has been done for you as an example.

E13–5 The following is a list of transactions that occurred during the year.

Classify activities—indirect method. (SO 2a)

	Operating Activities	Investing Activities	Financing Activities	Noncash Activities
1. Purchased merchandise inventory for cash.	−	NE	NE	NE
2. Sold merchandise inventory on account.				
3. Sold equipment for cash at a loss.				
4. Recorded depreciation on equipment.				
5. Paid dividends.				
6. Recorded an unrealized loss on a long-term equity investment carried at fair value.				
7. Collected an account from a customer.				
8. Issued bonds payable at a discount.				
9. Reacquired and retired common shares at a price less than the average cost.				
10. Purchased land by issuing common shares.				

Instructions
Complete the above table indicating in which classification(s) each transaction would appear in a statement of cash flows prepared using the indirect method, and whether the transaction would be added to (+), deducted from (−), or have no effect (NE) on the category you have chosen. The first one has been done for you as an example.

E13–6 Selected information from Juno Ltd.'s statement of financial position and income statement is shown below:

Prepare operating activities section—indirect method. (SO 2a)

JUNO LTD.
Statement of Financial Position (partial)
December 31

	2012	2011
Current assets		
Accounts receivable	$7,000	$12,000
Merchandise inventory	5,900	4,500
Prepaid expenses	3,000	2,500
Current liabilities		
Accounts payable	3,750	2,500
Income tax payable	1,200	800
Accrued liabilities	2,500	1,500
Bank loan payable—current portion	5,000	10,000

JUNO LTD.
Income Statement
Year Ended December 31, 2012

Net sales	$190,000
Cost of goods sold	114,000
Gross profit	76,000
Operating expenses	50,000
Profit from operations	26,000
Interest expense	1,200
Profit before income tax	24,800
Income tax expense	3,800
Profit	$ 21,000

Additional information:

1. The bank loan was issued to finance the purchase of equipment.
2. Operating expenses included depreciation expense of $11,000 and a loss of $5,000 on the sale of equipment.

Instructions
Prepare the operating activities section of the statement of cash flows, using the indirect method.

Convert operating activities from accrual to cash basis—direct method.
(SO 2b)

E13–7 The following is a list of income statement accounts that must be converted from the accrual basis to the cash basis in order to calculate cash provided (used) by operating activities using the direct method:

Income Statement Account	Change in Current Asset/ Current Liability Account	(a) Add to (+) or Deduct from (−) Income Statement Account	(b) Related Cash Receipt or Payment
1. Sales revenue	Increase in accounts receivable	−	Cash receipts from customers
2. Dividend revenue	Decrease in dividends receivable		
3. Interest revenue	Increase in interest receivable		
4. Rent revenue	Increase in unearned rent		
5. Cost of goods sold	Increase in merchandise inventory		
6. Cost of goods sold	Increase in accounts payable		
7. Insurance expense	Increase in prepaid insurance		
8. Salaries expense	Increase in salaries payable		
9. Interest expense	Decrease in interest payable		
10. Income tax expense	Increase in income tax payable		

Instructions

For each of the above changes in a current asset or current liability account listed beside the related income statement account, identify if (a) the change should be added to (+) or deducted from (−) the income statement account in order to convert the accrual-based number to a cash-based number; and (b) the title of the resulting cash receipt or payment on the statement of cash flows. The first one has been done for you as an example.

Calculate cash flows—direct method.
(SO 2b)

E13–8 The following selected information is taken from the general ledger of Carnival Limited:

(a) Sales revenue	$160,000
Accounts receivable, January 1	16,000
Accounts receivable, December 31	14,000
(b) Cost of goods sold	$ 96,000
Merchandise inventory, January 1	9,200
Merchandise inventory, December 31	10,900
Accounts payable, January 1	11,500
Accounts payable, December 31	10,700
(c) Salaries expense	$ 35,000
Salaries payable, January 1	500
Salaries payable, December 31	675
(d) Interest expense	$ 57,552
Bonds payable, January 1	957,345
Bonds payable, December 31	964,897

Note: The interest relates solely to the bonds. There were no transactions other than amortization in the bonds payable account.

Instructions

Using the above information and the direct method, calculate the (a) cash receipts from customers, (b) cash payments to suppliers, (c) cash payments to employees, and (d) cash payments for interest.

Prepare operating activities section—direct method.
(SO 2b)

E13–9 Selected information from Juno Ltd.'s statement of financial position and income statement is found in E13–6. In addition to the information contained in these statements, please note the following:

1. Prepaid expenses and accrued liabilities relate to operating expenses.
2. Accounts payable relate to purchases of merchandise.
3. Operating expenses included depreciation expense of $11,000 and a loss of $5,000 on the sale of equipment.

Instructions

Prepare the operating activities section of the statement of cash flows, using the direct method.

Calculate investing and financing activities.
(SO 3, 4)

E13–10 The following selected accounts are from Dupré Corp.'s general ledger:

		Land	
Jan. 1	Bal.	500,000	
Dec. 31		6,000	
Dec. 31	Bal.	506,000	

Equipment

Jan.	1	Bal.	160,000			
July	31		70,000			
Sept.	2		53,000	Nov. 10		39,000
Dec.	31	Bal.	244,000			

Accumulated Depreciation—Equipment

				Jan.	1	Bal.	71,000
Nov. 10			30,000	Dec.	31		48,000
				Dec.	31	Bal.	89,000

Bank Loan Payable

			Jan.	1	Bal.	0
			Sept.	2		43,000
			Dec.	31	Bal.	43,000

Retained Earnings

			Jan.	1	Bal.	105,000
Aug. 23		4,000	Dec.	31		60,000
			Dec.	31	Bal.	161,000

Accumulated Other Comprehensive Income

	Jan.	1	Bal.	10,000
	Dec.	31		6,000
	Dec.	31	Bal.	16,000

Additional information:

July 31	Equipment with a cost of $70,000 was purchased for cash.
Sept. 2	Equipment with a cost of $53,000 was purchased and partially financed through the issue of a long-term bank loan payable.
Aug. 23	A $4,000 cash dividend was paid.
Nov. 10	A loss of $3,000 was incurred on the sale of equipment.
Dec. 31	Depreciation expense of $48,000 was recorded for the year.
31	Profit for the year was $60,000.
31	Other comprehensive income for the year, from the revaluation of land to fair value, was $6,000.

Instructions

From the postings in the above accounts and additional information provided, indicate what information would be reported in the investing and/or financing activities sections of, and notes to, the statement of cash flows.

E13–11 The comparative statement of financial position for Puffy Ltd. follows:

Prepare statement of cash flows—indirect and direct methods. (SO 2a, 2b, 3, 4, 5)

PUFFY LTD.
Statement of Financial Position
December 31

	2012	2011
Assets		
Cash	$ 53,000	$ 22,000
Accounts receivable	80,000	76,000
Inventories	185,000	189,000
Land	70,000	100,000
Equipment	265,000	200,000
Accumulated depreciation	(66,000)	(32,000)
Total assets	$587,000	$555,000
Liabilities and Shareholders' Equity		
Accounts payable	$ 39,000	$ 47,000
Bank loan payable	150,000	200,000
Common shares	199,000	174,000
Retained earnings	199,000	134,000
Total liabilities and shareholders' equity	$587,000	$555,000

Additional information:

1. Profit was $115,000.
2. Sales were $978,000.
3. Cost of goods sold was $751,000.
4. Operating expenses were $43,000, exclusive of depreciation expense.
5. Depreciation expense was $34,000.
6. Interest expense was $14,000.
7. Income tax expense was $26,000.
8. Land was sold at a gain of $5,000.
9. No equipment was sold during the year.
10. $50,000 of the bank loan was repaid during the year.
11. Common shares were issued for $25,000.

Instructions

Prepare a statement of cash flows using (a) the indirect method, or (b) the direct method, as assigned by your instructor.

Compare cash flows for three companies.
(SO 2, 3, 4, 6)

E13–12   Condensed profit and cash flow information follow for three companies operating in the same industry:

	Company A	Company B	Company C
Profit	$ 75,000	$ 25,000	$(50,000)
Net cash provided (used) by operating activities	100,000	(25,000)	(25,000)
Net cash provided (used) by investing activities	(50,000)	(25,000)	35,000
Net cash provided (used) by financing activities	(25,000)	75,000	15,000
Net increase in cash	25,000	25,000	25,000

Instructions

Which company is in better financial condition? Explain the reasoning behind your decision.

Calculate and evaluate liquidity and solvency.
(SO 6)

E13–13   Information for two companies in the same industry, Ria Corporation and Les Corporation, is presented here:

	Ria Corporation	Les Corporation
Net cash provided by operating activities	$200,000	$200,000
Average current liabilities	50,000	150,000
Average total liabilities	200,000	200,000
Net capital expenditures	20,000	35,000
Dividends paid	24,000	18,000

Instructions

(a) Calculate the cash current debt coverage ratio, cash total debt coverage ratio, and free cash flow for each company.
(b) Compare the liquidity and solvency of the two companies.

Evaluate liquidity and solvency.
(SO 6)

E13–14   Presented here are selected ratios for PepsiCo, Inc. and The Coca-Cola Company:

	PepsiCo	Coca-Cola
Current ratio	1.1:1	1.2:1
Cash current debt coverage	0.7 times	0.6 times
Debt to total assets	68.5%	57.1%
Cash total debt coverage	0.2 times	0.3 times
Free cash flow (in U.S. millions)	$2,298	$3,383

Instructions

Evaluate the liquidity and solvency of the two companies.

Problems: Set A

Classify activities.
(SO 1)

P13–1A   The following is a list of transactions that took place during the year:

	(a) Classification	(b) Cash Flow	(c) Profit
1. Paid salaries to employees.	O	—	—
2. Sold land for cash, at a gain.			
3. Purchased a building by making a down payment in cash and signing a mortgage payable for the balance.			
4. Made a principal repayment on the mortgage.			

(a)   (b)   (c)

5. Paid interest on the mortgage.
6. Issued common shares for cash.
7. Purchased shares of another company to be held as a long-term non-strategic investment.
8. Paid dividends to shareholders.
9. Sold merchandise inventory on account, at a price greater than cost. The company uses a perpetual inventory system.
10. Wrote down the cost of the remaining inventory to its net realizable value.

Instructions
(a) Classify each of the above transactions as an operating activity (O), investing activity (I), financing activity (F), or noncash investing and financing activity (NC). If it does not fit into one of these classifications, indicate that there is no effect (NE). The first one has been done for you as an example.
(b) Specify if the transaction will result in a cash inflow (+), cash outflow (−), or have no effect on cash (NE).
(c) Indicate if the transaction will increase (+), decrease (−), or have no effect (NE) on profit.
(d) Explain how it is possible for the same transaction to affect cash and profit differently.

P13–2A   The income statement for Whistler Ltd., a publicly traded company following IFRS, is presented here:

Prepare operating activities section—indirect and direct methods.
(SO 2a, 2b)

WHISTLER LTD.
Income Statement
Year Ended November 30, 2012

Sales	$8,000,000
Cost of goods sold	5,000,000
Gross profit	3,000,000
Operating expenses	2,000,000
Profit from operations	1,000,000
Interest expense	100,000
Profit before income tax	900,000
Income tax expense	300,000
Profit	$ 600,000

Additional information:

1. Operating expenses include $75,000 of depreciation expense and a $100,000 impairment loss on property, plant, and equipment.
2. Accounts receivable increased by $190,000.
3. Merchandise inventory decreased by $50,000.
4. Prepaid expenses related to operating expenses increased by $40,000.
5. Accounts payable to suppliers of merchandise decreased by $180,000.
6. Accrued liabilities related to operating expenses decreased by $90,000.
7. Interest payable decreased by $10,000.
8. Income tax payable increased by $20,000.

Instructions
(a) Prepare the operating activities section of the statement of cash flows, using either (1) the indirect method or (2) the direct method, as assigned by your instructor.
(b) Would your answer in (a) change if Whistler were a private company following ASPE?

P13–3A   The income statement for Tremblant Limited is presented here:

Prepare operating activities section—indirect and direct methods—and discuss methods.
(SO 2a, 2b)

TREMBLANT LIMITED
Income Statement
Year Ended December 31, 2012

Service revenue	$925,000
Operating expenses	701,000
Profit from operations	224,000
Interest expense	75,000
Profit before income tax	149,000
Income tax expense	37,250
Profit	$111,750

Tremblant's statement of financial position contained these comparative data at December 31:

	2012	2011
Accounts receivable	$57,000	$47,000
Prepaid expenses	12,000	15,000
Accounts payable	36,000	41,000
Salaries payable	19,500	20,000
Unearned revenue	12,000	9,000
Interest payable	6,250	5,000
Income tax payable	4,000	9,250

Additional information:

1. Operating expenses include depreciation expense, $50,000; amortization expense, $15,000; administrative expenses, $110,000; salaries expense, $500,000; and loss on the sale of equipment, $26,000.
2. Interest expense includes $10,000 related to the amortization of a bond premium on bonds payable.
3. Prepaid expenses, accounts payable, and unearned revenue relate to operating (administrative) expenses.

Instructions
(a) Prepare the operating activities section of the statement of cash flows, using either (1) the indirect method or (2) the direct method, as assigned by your instructor.
(b) Which method—indirect or direct—do you recommend this company use to prepare its operating activities section? Explain your reasoning.

Calculate and classify cash flows for property, plant, and equipment. (SO 3)

P13–4A The following selected account balances relate to the property, plant, and equipment accounts of Katewill Inc.:

	2012	2011
Accumulated depreciation—buildings	$337,500	$300,000
Accumulated depreciation—equipment	144,000	96,000
Depreciation expense—buildings	37,500	37,500
Depreciation expense—equipment	60,000	48,000
Land	100,000	60,000
Buildings	750,000	750,000
Equipment	300,000	240,000
Gain on sale of equipment	5,000	0

Additional information:

1. Purchased $40,000 of land for cash.
2. Purchased $75,000 of equipment for a $10,000 down payment, financing the remainder with a bank loan. Equipment was also sold during the year.

Instructions
(a) Calculate any cash inflows or outflows related to the property, plant, and equipment accounts in 2012.
(b) Indicate where each of the cash inflows or outflows identified in (a) would be classified on the statement of cash flows or accompanying notes.
(c) Would you expect a growing company to be generating or using cash for its investing activities? Explain.

Calculate and classify cash flows for shareholders' equity. (SO 4)

P13–5A The following selected account balances relate to the shareholders' equity accounts of Valerio Corp.:

	2012	2011
Preferred shares, 2,250 shares in 2012; 2,750 in 2011	$225,000	$275,000
Common shares, 50,000 shares in 2012; 40,000 in 2011	600,000	400,000
Contributed capital—reacquired preferred shares	35,000	50,000
Retained earnings	500,000	300,000
Accumulated other comprehensive income	40,000	50,000
Cash dividends—preferred	11,250	13,750
Dividends payable	2,812	3,438

Additional information:

1. The company reacquired and retired 500 preferred shares in 2012. The preferred shares were originally issued at an average cost of $50,000.
2. During the year, 10,000 common shares were issued. No common shares were repurchased.
3. The company reported an other comprehensive loss of $10,000 in 2012 from the revaluation of land to fair value.

Instructions

(a) Determine the amounts of any cash inflows or outflows related to the shareholders' equity accounts in 2012.

(b) Indicate where each of the cash inflows or outflows identified in (a) would be classified on the statement of cash flows or accompanying notes.

(c) Would you expect a growing company to be generating or using cash for its financing activities? Explain.

P13–6A Financial statements for E-Perform, Inc. follow:

Prepare statement of cash flows—indirect and direct methods.
(SO 2a, 2b, 3, 4, 5)

E-PERFORM, INC.
Statement of Financial Position
December 31

	2012	2011
Assets		
Cash	$ 97,800	$ 48,400
Trading investments	128,000	114,000
Accounts receivable	75,800	43,000
Inventories	122,500	92,850
Prepaid expenses	18,400	26,000
Property, plant, and equipment	270,000	242,500
Accumulated depreciation	(50,000)	(52,000)
Total assets	$662,500	$514,750
Liabilities and Shareholders' Equity		
Accounts payable	$ 93,000	$ 77,300
Accrued liabilities	11,500	7,000
Bank loan payable	110,000	150,000
Common shares	200,000	175,000
Retained earnings	248,000	105,450
Total liabilities and shareholders' equity	$662,500	$514,750

E-PERFORM, INC.
Income Statement
Year Ended December 31, 2012

Sales		$492,780
Cost of goods sold		185,460
Gross profit		307,320
Operating expenses		116,410
Profit from operations		190,910
Other revenues and gains and other expenses and losses		
Unrealized gain on trading investments	$14,000	
Interest expense	(4,730)	9,270
Profit before income tax		200,180
Income tax expense		45,000
Profit		$155,180

Additional information:

1. Prepaid expenses and accrued liabilities relate to operating expenses.
2. An unrealized gain on trading investments of $14,000 was recorded.
3. New equipment costing $85,000 was purchased for $25,000 cash and a $60,000 long-term bank loan payable.
4. Old equipment having an original cost of $57,500 was sold for $1,500.
5. Accounts payable relate to merchandise creditors.
6. Some of the bank loan was repaid during the year.
7. A dividend was paid during the year.
8. Operating expenses include $46,500 of depreciation expense and a $7,500 loss on sale of equipment.

Instructions

(a) Prepare the statement of cash flows, using either (1) the indirect method or (2) the direct method, as assigned by your instructor.

(b) E-Perform's cash position doubled between 2011 and 2012. Identify the primary reason(s) for this significant increase.

Prepare statement of
cash flows—indirect
and direct methods.
(SO 2a, 2b, 3, 4, 5)

P13–7A   The financial statements of Resolute Inc. are presented here:

RESOLUTE INC.
Statement of Financial Position
December 31

	2012	2011
Assets		
Cash	$ 13,000	$ 5,000
Accounts receivable	38,000	24,000
Merchandise inventory	27,000	20,000
Property, plant, and equipment	80,000	78,000
Accumulated depreciation	(30,000)	(24,000)
Goodwill	5,000	16,000
Total assets	$133,000	$119,000
Liabilities and Shareholders' Equity		
Accounts payable	$ 17,000	$ 15,000
Salaries payable	1,900	2,100
Income tax payable	1,000	4,000
Bank loan payable	34,100	50,650
Common shares	18,000	14,000
Retained earnings	56,000	28,250
Accumulated other comprehensive income	5,000	5,000
Total liabilities and shareholders' equity	$133,000	$119,000

RESOLUTE INC.
Income Statement
Year Ended December 31, 2012

Sales	$256,000
Cost of goods sold	140,000
Gross profit	116,000
Operating expenses	78,250
Profit from operations	37,750
Interest expense	4,000
Profit before income tax	33,750
Income tax expense	6,000
Profit	$ 27,750

Additional information:

1. Equipment was sold during the year for $8,500 cash. The equipment originally cost $12,000 and had a carrying amount of $8,500 at the time of sale.
2. Equipment costing $14,000 was purchased in exchange for $4,000 cash and a $10,000 long-term bank loan.
3. Accounts payable relate to merchandise creditors.
4. Some of the bank loan was repaid during the year.
5. Operating expenses are composed of $9,500 of depreciation expense, $7,750 of administrative expenses, $50,000 of salaries expense, and an $11,000 impairment loss on goodwill.

Instructions

(a) Prepare the statement of cash flows, using either (1) the indirect method or (2) the direct method, as assigned by your instructor.
(b) Resolute's cash position more than doubled between 2011 and 2012. Identify the primary reason(s) for this significant increase.

Discuss operating cash
flows and profit.
(SO 1, 2, 5)

P13–8A   The TJX Companies, Inc., parent company of Winners, HomeSense, and StyleSense, among other companies, reported cash provided by operating activities of U.S. $1,976 million for the year ended January 30, 2011 (fiscal 2010), a decrease of U.S. $296 million over the U.S. $2,272 million reported for fiscal 2009. The company also reported profit of U.S. $1,343 million in fiscal 2010, an increase of U.S. $129 million over profit of U.S. $1,214 million reported for fiscal 2009. Its cash and cash equivalents increased by U.S. $127 million during fiscal 2010, from U.S. $1,615 million to U.S. $1,742 million. TJX includes its highly liquid investments, with a maturity date of three months or less, as cash equivalents.

Instructions

(a) How is it possible that TJX can generate U.S. $1,976 million of cash provided by operating activities in fiscal 2010 but earn only U.S. $1,343 million of profit in the same year?

(b) Explain how TJX decreased its cash provided by operating activities by U.S. $296 million in fiscal 2010 while profit increased by U.S. $129 million over the same period.

(c) Explain how TJX can have a decrease of U.S. $296 million in its cash provided by operating activities in fiscal 2010 while reporting an increase of U.S. $127 million in the ending balance of its cash and cash equivalents over the same period.

P13–9A Selected information (in thousands) for Reitmans (Canada) Limited and Le Château Inc. for fiscal 2010 follows:

Calculate and evaluate liquidity and solvency.
(SO 6)

	Reitmans	Le Château
Net cash provided by operating activities	$146,139	$41,643
Average current liabilities	77,798	42,691
Average total liabilities	115,926	76,414
Net capital expenditures	33,185	20,075
Dividends paid	49,351	17,010

Instructions

(a) Calculate the cash current debt coverage ratio, cash total debt coverage ratio, and free cash flow for each company.

(b) Using the ratios calculated in (a), compare the liquidity and solvency of the two companies.

P13–10A Selected ratios for two companies are as follows:

Evaluate liquidity and solvency.
(SO 6)

	Grenville	Portage
Current ratio	1.7:1	1.2:1
Receivables turnover	10 times	20 times
Inventory turnover	4 times	2 times
Cash current debt coverage	0.4 times	0.3 times
Debt to total assets	60%	20%
Times interest earned	5 times	20 times
Cash total debt coverage	0.2 times	0.1 times

Instructions

(a) Which company is more liquid? Explain.

(b) Which company is more solvent? Explain.

P13–11A Condensed profit and cash flow information follow for three coffee companies: Tim Hortons Inc., The Second Cup Ltd., and Starbucks Corporation:

Compare cash flows for three companies.
(SO 2, 3, 4, 5)

	Tim Hortons (in CAD millions)	Second Cup (in CAD millions)	Starbucks (in USD millions)
Profit	$624.0	$ 9.3	$ 948.3
Net cash provided by operating activities	$525.5	$11.2	$1,704.9
Net cash provided (used) by investing activities	296.0	(1.7)	(789.5)
Net cash used by financing activities	(368.8)	(8.7)	(351.2)
Net increase in cash	452.7	0.8	564.2
Cash, beginning of year	121.7	4.6	599.8
Cash, end of year	$574.4	$ 5.4	$1,164.0

Instructions

(a) Compare the provision and use of cash in each of the three activities by each company.

(b) Based on the information provided above, which company appears to be in the strongest position? Explain the reasoning behind your decision.

Problems: Set B

P13–1B The following is a list of transactions that took place during the year:

Classify activities.
(SO 1)

	(a) Classification	(b) Cash Flow	(c) Profit
1. Collected an account receivable.	O	+	NE
2. Sold equipment for cash, at a loss.			
3. Recorded an unrealized gain on a trading investment.			

(a)   (b)   (c)

4. Acquired land by issuing common shares.
5. Reacquired and retired common shares at a price in excess of average cost.
6. Paid dividends to preferred shareholders.
7. Recorded depreciation expense.
8. Issued preferred shares for cash.
9. Purchased inventory for cash. The company uses a perpetual inventory system.
10. Provided services on account.

Instructions

(a) Classify each of the above transactions as an operating activity (O), investing activity (I), financing activity (F), or noncash investing and financing activity (NC). If it does not fit into one of these classifications, indicate that there is no effect (NE). The first one has been done for you as an example.
(b) Specify if the transaction will result in a cash inflow (+), cash outflow (−), or have no effect on cash (NE).
(c) Indicate if the transaction will increase (+), decrease (−), or have no effect (NE) on profit.
(d) Explain how it is possible for the same transaction to affect cash and profit differently.

Prepare operating activities section—indirect and direct methods.
(SO 2a, 2b)

P13–2B The income statement for Gum San Ltd., a publicly traded company following IFRS, is presented here:

GUM SAN LTD.	
Income Statement	
Year Ended December 31, 2012	
Sales	$4,500,000
Cost of goods sold	2,390,000
Gross profit	2,110,000
Operating expenses	1,070,000
Profit before income tax	1,040,000
Interest revenue	12,000
Profit before income tax	1,052,000
Income tax expense	260,000
Profit	$ 792,000

Additional information:

1. Operating expenses include $150,000 of depreciation expense and a $12,000 gain on sale of equipment.
2. Accounts receivable increased by $500,000.
3. Merchandise inventory decreased by $220,000.
4. Prepaid expenses related to operating expenses increased by $170,000.
5. Accounts payable to suppliers of merchandise increased by $50,000.
6. Accrued liabilities related to operating expenses decreased by $165,000.
7. Income tax payable decreased by $16,000.

Instructions

(a) Prepare the operating activities section of the statement of cash flows, using either (1) the indirect method or (2) the direct method, as assigned by your instructor.
(b) Would your answer in (a) change if Gum San were a private company following ASPE?

Prepare operating activities section—indirect and direct methods—and discuss methods.
(SO 2a, 2b)

P13–3B The income statement for Hanalei International Inc. is presented here:

HANALEI INTERNATIONAL INC.	
Income Statement	
Year Ended December 31, 2012	
Fee revenue	$565,000
Operating expenses	365,000
Profit from operations	200,000
Interest expense	10,000
Profit before income tax	190,000
Income tax expense	47,500
Profit	$142,500

Hanalei's statement of financial position contained these comparative data at December 31:

	2012	2011
Accounts receivable	$50,000	$60,000
Prepaid insurance	5,000	8,000
Accounts payable	40,000	31,000

Unearned revenue	$10,000	$14,000
Salaries payable	10,000	7,500
Interest payable	1,000	1,750
Income tax payable	4,000	3,500

Additional information:

1. Operating expenses include depreciation expense, $45,000; amortization expense, $5,000; administrative expenses, $40,000; salaries expense, $300,000; and gain on sale of equipment, $25,000.
2. Interest expense includes $500 related to the amortization of a bond discount on bonds payable.
3. Prepaid insurance, accounts payable, and unearned revenue relate to operating (administrative) expenses.

Instructions

(a) Prepare the operating activities section of the statement of cash flows, using either (1) the indirect method or (2) the direct method, as assigned by your instructor.
(b) Which method—indirect or direct—do you recommend this company use to prepare its operating activities section? Explain your reasoning.

P13–4B The following selected account balances relate to the property, plant, and equipment accounts of Bird Corp.:

Calculate and classify cash flows for property, plant, and equipment. (SO 3)

	2012	2011
Accumulated depreciation—buildings	$ 675,000	$ 600,000
Accumulated depreciation—equipment	288,000	192,000
Depreciation expense—buildings	75,000	75,000
Depreciation expense—equipment	128,000	96,000
Land	250,000	200,000
Buildings	1,250,000	1,250,000
Equipment	500,000	480,000
Loss on sale of equipment	4,000	0

Additional information:

1. Purchased land for $50,000, making a $20,000 down payment and financing the remainder with a mortgage payable.
2. Equipment was purchased for $80,000 cash. Equipment was also sold during the year.

Instructions

(a) Calculate any cash inflows or outflows related to the property, plant, and equipment accounts in 2012.
(b) Indicate where each of the cash inflows or outflows identified in (a) would be classified on the statement of cash flows or accompanying notes.
(c) Would you expect a growing company to be generating or using cash for its investing activities? Explain.

P13–5B The following selected account balances relate to the shareholders' equity accounts of Mathur Corp. at year end:

Calculate and classify cash flows for shareholders' equity. (SO 4)

	2012	2011
Preferred shares, 5,000 shares	$125,000	$125,000
Common shares, 9,000 shares in 2012, 10,000 in 2011	148,800	136,000
Contributed capital—reacquired common shares	0	40,000
Retained earnings	240,000	250,000
Accumulated other comprehensive income	15,000	10,000
Cash dividends—preferred	6,250	6,250
Stock dividends—common	40,000	0

Additional information:

1. The company reacquired and retired 2,000 common shares in 2012 for $40 per share. The average cost of the shares was $13.60 per share.
2. All cash dividends were declared and paid during the same year. There were no dividends payable at the end of 2011 or 2012.
3. During the year, 1,000 common shares were issued as a stock dividend. The fair value of the shares at the time of declaration was $40 per share.
4. Profit was $49,050 in 2012.
5. The company reported other comprehensive income of $5,000 in 2012 from the revaluation of land to fair value.

Instructions

(a) Determine the amounts of any cash inflows or outflows related to the shareholders' equity accounts in 2012.
(b) Indicate where each of the cash inflows or outflows identified in (a) would be classified on the statement of cash flows or accompanying notes.
(c) Would you expect a growing company to be generating or using cash for its financing activities? Explain.

Prepare statement of
cash flows—indirect
and direct methods.
(SO 2a, 2b, 3, 4, 5)

P13–6B   Financial statements for Nackawic Inc. follow:

NACKAWIC INC.
Statement of Financial Position
December 31

	2012	2011
Assets		
Cash	$ 82,700	$ 47,250
Accounts receivable	80,800	37,000
Inventories	131,900	102,650
Long-term investments	94,500	107,000
Property, plant, and equipment	290,000	205,000
Accumulated depreciation	(49,500)	(40,000)
Total assets	$630,400	$458,900
Liabilities and Shareholders' Equity		
Accounts payable	$ 62,700	$ 48,280
Accrued liabilities	12,100	18,830
Bank loan payable	140,000	70,000
Common shares	240,000	200,000
Retained earnings	175,600	121,790
Total liabilities and shareholders' equity	$630,400	$458,900

NACKAWIC INC.
Income Statement
Year Ended December 31, 2012

Sales		$317,500
Cost of goods sold		99,460
Gross profit		218,040
Operating expenses		82,120
Profit from operations		135,920
Other expenses and losses		
Interest expense	$12,940	
Realized loss on sale of long-term investments	7,500	20,440
Profit before income tax		115,480
Income tax expense		27,670
Profit		$ 87,810

Additional information:

1. Long-term investments were sold for $5,000, resulting in a realized loss of $7,500.
2. New equipment costing $141,000 was purchased for $71,000 cash and a $70,000 bank loan payable.
3. Equipment costing $56,000 was sold for $15,550, resulting in a gain of $8,750.
4. Accounts payable relate to merchandise creditors; accrued liabilities relate to operating expenses.
5. A dividend was paid during the year.
6. Operating expenses include $58,700 of depreciation expense and an $8,750 gain on sale of equipment.

Instructions
(a) Prepare the statement of cash flows, using either (1) the indirect method or (2) the direct method, as assigned by your instructor.
(b) Nackawic's cash position increased by 75 percent between 2011 and 2012. Identify the primary reason(s) for this significant increase.

Prepare statement of
cash flows—indirect
and direct methods.
(SO 2a, 2b, 3, 4, 5)

P13–7B   The financial statements of Wetaskiwin Limited are presented here:

WETASKIWIN LIMITED
Statement of Financial Position
December 31

	2012	2011
Assets		
Cash	$ 9,000	$ 10,000
Trading investments	14,000	23,000
Accounts receivable	28,000	14,000
Merchandise inventory	29,000	25,000

Property, plant, and equipment	73,000	78,000
Accumulated depreciation	(30,000)	(24,000)
Total assets	$123,000	$126,000

Liabilities and Shareholders' Equity

Accounts payable	$ 32,000	$ 58,000
Income tax payable	2,000	10,000
Bank loan payable	15,000	20,000
Common shares	25,000	25,000
Retained earnings	64,000	28,000
Accumulated other comprehensive loss	(15,000)	(15,000)
Total liabilities and shareholders' equity	$123,000	$126,000

WETASKIWIN LIMITED
Income Statement
Year Ended December 31, 2012

Sales		$286,000
Cost of goods sold		154,000
Gross profit		132,000
Operating expenses		74,000
Profit from operations		58,000
Other expenses and losses		
Unrealized loss on trading investments	$9,000	
Interest expense	3,000	12,000
Profit before income tax		46,000
Income tax expense		10,000
Profit		$ 36,000

Additional information:

1. Recorded an unrealized loss of $9,000 on trading investments.
2. Equipment was sold during the year for $8,000 cash. This equipment originally cost $15,000 and had a carrying amount of $10,000 at the time of sale.
3. Equipment costing $10,000 was purchased in exchange for $5,000 cash and a bank loan for the balance.
4. Accounts payable relate to merchandise creditors.
5. Operating expenses are composed of $11,000 of depreciation expense, $12,000 of administrative expenses, $49,000 of salaries expense, and a $2,000 loss on the sale of equipment.

Instructions
(a) Prepare the statement of cash flows, using either (1) the indirect method or (2) the direct method, as assigned by your instructor.
(b) Wetaskiwin's cash position declined by $1,000 between 2011 and 2012. Identify the reason(s) for this decrease.

P13–8B   Ontario Power Generation (OPG) Inc.'s statement of cash flows reported cash provided by operating activities of $816 million in 2010, a $517 million increase over the $299 million reported in 2009. It reported profit of $649 million in 2010, a $26 million increase over profit of $623 million reported in 2009. Cash and cash equivalents reported on the statement of financial position also increased, by $209 million, from $71 million in 2009 to $280 million in 2010. OPG includes its money market securities, with a maturity date of three months or less, as cash equivalents.

Discuss operating cash flows and profit.
(SO 1, 2, 5)

Instructions
(a) How is it possible that OPG can have only $649 million of profit in 2010 but generate $816 million of cash provided by operating activities in the same year?
(b) Explain how OPG increased its profit by only $26 million from 2009 to 2010, while its cash provided by operating activities increased by $517 million over the same period.
(c) Explain how OPG can have an increase of $517 million in its cash provided by operating activities in 2010 while reporting an increase of only $209 million in its cash and cash equivalents over the same period.

P13–9B   Selected information (in USD millions) for Google Inc. and Yahoo! Inc. for 2010 follows:

Calculate and evaluate liquidity and solvency.
(SO 6)

	Google	Yahoo!
Net cash provided by operating activities	$11,081.0	$1,240.2
Average current liabilities	6,371.5	1,671.8
Average total liabilities	8,051.5	2,374.5
Net capital expenditures	4,108.0	714.1
Dividends paid	0	0

Instructions

(a) Calculate the cash current debt coverage ratio, cash total debt coverage ratio, and free cash flow for each company.

(b) Using the ratios calculated in (a), compare the liquidity and solvency of the two companies.

Evaluate liquidity and
solvency.
(SO 6)

P13–10B   Selected ratios for two companies are as follows:

	Barrington	Ste-Croix
Current ratio	1:1	0.8:1
Receivables turnover	6 times	4 times
Inventory turnover	5 times	4 times
Cash current debt coverage	0.5 times	0.4 times
Debt to total assets	75%	50%
Times interest earned	6 times	2 times
Cash total debt coverage	0.4 times	0.3 times

Instructions

(a) Which company is more liquid? Explain.

(b) Which company is more solvent? Explain.

Compare cash flows for
three companies.
(SO 2, 3, 4, 5)

P13–11B   Condensed profit and cash flow information (in USD millions) follow for three fast food companies: McDonald's Corporation, Burger King Holdings, Inc., and Wendy's/Arby's Group, Inc.:

	McDonald's	Burger King	Wendy's
Profit	$4,946.3	$ 186.8	$ (2.6)
Net cash provided by operating activities	$6,341.6	$ 310.4	$231.3
Net cash used by investing activities	(2,056.0)	(134.9)	(144.2)
Net cash used by financing activities	(3,728.7)	(96.9)	(428.9)
Other (foreign exchange gain [loss])	34.1	(12.7)	1.6
Net increase in cash and cash equivalents	591.0	65.9	(340.2)
Cash and cash equivalents, beginning of year	1,796.0	121.7	538.9
Cash and cash equivalents, end of year	$2,387.0	$ 187.6	$198.7

Instructions

(a) Compare the provision and use of cash in each of the three activities by each company.

(b) Based on the information provided above, which company appears to be in the strongest position? Explain.

Broadening Your Perspective

Financial Reporting and Analysis Cases

Financial Reporting: *Eastplats*

Answer questions
about the statement of
cash flows.
(SO 1, 2, 3, 4, 5)

BYP13–1   The financial statements of Eastern Platinum Limited (Eastplats) are presented in Appendix A at the end of this book.

Instructions

(a) Does Eastplats use the indirect or direct method of calculating operating activities?

(b) What was the amount of net operating cash flows reported for 2010? For 2009?

(c) From your analysis of the 2010 statement of cash flows, what was the most significant investing activity? Financing activity?

(d) What amount was reported as the increase or decrease in cash and cash equivalents on the statement of cash flows for 2010? 2009?

(e) How does Eastplats define cash and cash equivalents? Do the cash and cash equivalents reported on the statement of cash flows reconcile to the statement of financial position amounts that are reported? Provide details of the reconciliation.

(f) Did Eastplats report any significant noncash investing and financing activities in 2010 or 2009?

Comparative Analysis: *Eastplats and Amplats*

Calculate and evaluate
liquidity and solvency.
(SO 2, 6)

BYP13–2   The financial statements of Anglo American Platinum Limited (Amplats) are presented in Appendix B, following the financial statements for Eastern Platinum Limited (Eastplats) in Appendix A.

Instructions

(a) Calculate the following ratios for Amplats and Eastplats for 2010

    1. Cash current debt coverage   4. Debt to total assets

    2. Current ratio   5. Times interest earned

    3. Cash total debt coverage   6. Free cash flow

(b) Compare the liquidity and solvency of each company from the ratios calculated in (a).

(c) Amplats uses the direct method of reporting operating activities while Eastplats uses the indirect method. Does this difference affect your comparison in (b)? Explain.

Interpreting Financial Information

BYP13–3 **PaperlinX Limited**, an Australian paper manufacturer using IFRS, reported the following in the operating activities section of its statement of cash flows:

Discuss indirect and direct methods and calculate ratios.
(SO 2, 6)

PAPERLINX LIMITED
Statement of Cash Flows (partial)
Year Ended June 30
(in AUD millions)

	2010	2009
Operating activities		
Receipts from customers	$5,226.7	$7,315.0
Payments to suppliers and employees	(5,169.9)	(7,214.1)
Dividends received	0.1	0.8
Interest received	2.8	3.6
Interest paid	(36.4)	(98.3)
Income tax paid	(0.2)	(13.0)
Net cash provided (used) by operating activities	23.1	(6.0)

Additional information:

	2010	2009
Net capital expenditures	$ 11.5	$ 26.9
Dividends paid	0	10.3
Average current liabilities	1,261.6	1,519.4
Average total liabilities	1,541.1	2,064.8

Instructions

(a) Is PaperlinX using the direct or indirect method when preparing its operating activities? Explain why you named the method you did.

(b) Does IFRS require or recommend the use of one method over another when preparing the operating activities section of a statement of cash flows?

(c) Identify any possible classification differences that an analyst should be aware of before comparing PaperlinX's statement of cash flows with that of another company, whether in Australia or any other country.

(d) Calculate PaperlinX's cash current debt coverage, cash total debt coverage, and free cash flow for 2010 and 2009. Comment on any changes in the company's liquidity and solvency based on these measures.

Comparing IFRS and ASPE

BYP13–4 **Bayer AG**, best known for its line of Bayer Aspirin, is a publicly traded company with operations worldwide. It reported the following selected data (in € millions) for the six months ended June 30, 2011:

Adjust and compare liquidity and solvency with different classifications.
(SO 1, 6)

BAYER GROUP
Selected Financial Information
Six Months Ended June 30, 2011
(€ millions)

Net cash provided by operating activities	€ 2,331
Net cash used by investing activities	(1,540)
Net cash used by financing activities	(1,759)
Average current liabilities	12,548
Average total liabilities	67,810

Included in its calculation of net cash used by investing activities are €28 million of interest and dividends received and €471 of net capital expenditures. Included in its calculation of net cash used by financing activities are €1,241 million of dividend payments and €473 million of interest payments.

John Allman, controller of a private health care company, Baxter Healthcare Inc., would like to compare Baxter's cash ratios with those of Bayer's. However, he realizes that there are certain differences in the classification of activities between companies like Bayer, which uses IFRS, and companies like Baxter, which uses ASPE.

Instructions

(a) Using Bayer's data, calculate its cash current debt coverage, cash total debt coverage, and free cash flow ratios.

(b) Adjust Bayer's net cash provided (used) by operating activities, investing activities, and/or financing activities for any IFRS/ASPE classification differences so that they are comparable with the classifications used under ASPE.

(c) Using the adjusted cash provided by operating activities data calculated in (b), recalculate Bayer's cash current debt coverage, cash total debt coverage, and free cash flow ratios.

(d) Compare and comment upon the results of your calculations in (a) and (c).

Critical Thinking Cases and Activities

Collaborative Learning Activity

Calculate and evaluate liquidity and solvency. (SO 6)

BYP13–5   You have been given the following condensed financial data for two companies from different industries:

	Utility Corp.		Retail Co. Ltd.	
	2012	2011	2012	2011
Net cash provided by operating activities	$ 637	$ 661	$ 71	$ 63
Current assets	1,126	1,150	219	208
Total assets	12,160	11,166	424	414
Current liabilities	1,594	1,697	95	88
Total liabilities	8,620	7,773	181	178

Instructions

Divide the class into groups. Assign half your group members to Utility Corp. and the remaining group members to Retail Co. Ltd. Then do the following:

(a) Calculate the following ratios for 2012: (1) current ratio, (2) cash current debt coverage, (3) debt to total assets, and (4) cash total debt coverage.

(b) Assess the company's liquidity and solvency, including the answers to the following questions in your analysis:

  1. What liquidity and solvency risk is there for your company?

  2. What additional information would you need to make a more detailed analysis?

(c) As a group, compare the results of your analysis for each company.

Communication Activity

Discuss analysis using accrual- and cash-based ratios. (SO 6)

BYP13–6   Some analysts believe cash-based numbers are more reliable than accrual-based numbers because they feel the adjustment process allows management too much discretion to manipulate the results. One analyst was overheard to say: "You can't always trust the profit figure reported, because of all the estimates and judgement that go into its determination. That's why I always compare accrual-based ratios with cash-based ratios when analyzing a company."

Instructions

Write a memo explaining the advantages and disadvantages of accrual-based ratios and cash-based ratios. Include in your answer a discussion of whether you think it is possible to manipulate cash-based figures, or only accrual-based figures.

Ethics Case

Discuss dividend policy and classification of interest. (SO 1)

BYP13–7   Onwards and Upwards Corporation has paid cash dividends to its shareholders for eight consecutive years. The board of directors' policy requires that in order for a dividend to be declared, cash provided by operating activities as reported in the current year's statement of cash flows must exceed $1 million. The job of president Phil Monat is secure so long as Phil produces annual operating cash flows to support the usual dividend.

At the end of the current year, controller Leland Yee informs president Monat of some disappointing news. The net cash provided by operating activities is only $970,000. The president says to Leland, "We must get that amount above $1 million. Isn't there some way to increase this amount?" Leland answers, "These figures were prepared by my assistant. I'll go back to my office and see what I can do." The president replies, "I know you won't let me down, Leland."

Upon close scrutiny of the statement of cash flows, Leland concludes that he can get net cash provided by operating activities above $1 million by reclassifying interest paid from the operating activities section, where it has been classified in the past, to the financing activities section. The company is a publicly traded company using IFRS. Leland knows that under IFRS companies have a choice between classifying interest paid as an operating or financing activity. He returns to the president and exclaims, "You can tell the board to declare their usual dividend. Our cash flow provided by operating activities is $1,030,000." Excited, the president exclaims, "Good job, Leland! I knew I could count on you."

Instructions

(a) Should any other factors, besides net cash provided by operating activities, be considered by the board in setting the company's dividend policy?

(b) Who are the stakeholders in this situation?

(c) Was there anything unethical about the president's actions? Was there anything unethical about the controller's actions?

(d) Would your answers to (b) and (c) change if Onwards and Upwards were a private company using ASPE?

"All About You" Activity

BYP13–8 In this chapter, you learned about cash flow and the important decisions that must be made when cash inflow does not cover cash outflow.

Calculate and assess cash flow.
(SO 5)

Instructions

Go to the Investor Education website at www.getsmarteraboutmoney.ca. Go to the Calculators/Worksheets and Tools section and complete the student budget worksheet. Is your cash outflow greater than your cash inflow? Can you find three discretionary expenses that you could reduce or live without?

Serial Case

(Note: This is a continuation of the serial problem from Chapters 1 through 12.)

BYP13–9 The Koebels have met with representatives of Biscuits, a public company, and Coffee Beans, a private company. Both companies have offered to purchase the shares of Koebel's Family Bakery Ltd. The financial statements, including the statement of cash flows, for Koebel's Family Bakery have been prepared for analysis and the Koebels are meeting to discuss these financial statements with representatives of both of these companies. These meetings will enable Janet and Brian to decide upon the best alternative as they move forward with their decision to sell their shares. Natalie and Daniel have been offered employment at each one of these companies and want to ensure each company has the ability to continue to operate.

Compare cash flows for three companies; evaluate liquidity and solvency.
(SO 2, 3, 4, 5, 6)

Selected information for Koebel's Family Bakery, Biscuits, and Coffee Beans for 2013 follows:

	Koebel's Family Bakery Ltd.	Biscuits Ltd.	Coffee Beans Ltd.
Profit	$199,629	$ 2,628,000	$ 699,000
Net cash provided by operating activities	$235,279	$ 6,821,000	$1,594,000
Net cash used by investing activities	(157,833)	(3,397,000)	(1,448,000)
Net cash used by financing activities	(37,071)	(1,762,000)	(890,000)
Net (decrease) increase in cash	40,375	1,662,000	(744,000)
Cash, beginning of year	159,068	2,252,000	776,000
Cash, end of year	$199,443	$ 3,914,000	$ 32,000
Average current liabilities	$ 31,121	$16,233,000	$3,759,000
Average total liabilities	81,551	27,758,500	8,879,000
Net capital expenditures	144,000	3,414,000	1,448,000
Dividends paid	120,000	580,000	0

Instructions

(a) Calculate the cash current debt coverage ratio, cash total debt coverage ratio, and free cash flow for each company.

(b) Compare the provision and use of cash in each of the three activities—operating, investing, and financing—by company.

(c) Based on the information provided in (a) and (b), identify why Biscuits and Coffee Beans are likely pursuing an investment in Koebel's Family Bakery.

(d) Based on the information provided in (a) and (b), identify for the Koebels some of the issues they should consider before making the decision to sell their shares and/or to be employed by one of these companies.

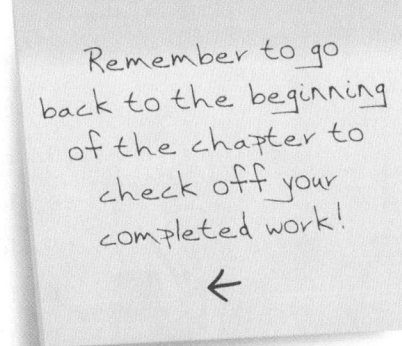

Remember to go back to the beginning of the chapter to check off your completed work!

Answers to Self-Test Questions

1. a   2. c   3. b   4. c   5. c
6. c   7. d   8. a   9. b   10. a

Performance Measurement

study objectives

After studying this chapter, you should be able to:

1. Understand the concept of sustainable income and indicate how irregular items are presented.

2. Explain and apply horizontal analysis.

3. Explain and apply vertical analysis.

4. Identify and calculate ratios that are used to analyze liquidity.

5. Identify and calculate ratios that are used to analyze solvency.

6. Identify and calculate ratios that are used to analyze profitability.

7. Understand the limitations of financial analysis.

the navigator

Corporate Reporting Proves to Be Fertile Ground

With the ever-increasing size of the global population, demands on the world's food and agricultural resources are also increasing. As the world's largest producer of primary plant nutrients—nitrogen, phosphate, and potassium—as well as fertilizers, animal feed supplements, and industrial products, Potash Corporation of Saskatchewan Inc. (PotashCorp) is helping to address these demands.

Launched as a Crown corporation by the Province of Saskatchewan in 1975, PotashCorp became a publicly traded company in 1989. Today, with operations and business interests throughout the world, PotashCorp serves customers in five regions—China, India, Brazil, Southeast Asia, and North America—that account for more than half the world's population and consume nearly two-thirds of the world's fertilizer. In 2010, the Saskatoon-based company successfully fought off a takeover bid by BHP Billiton Limited, an international resource company based in Australia.

PotashCorp takes the transparency and accountability that come with being a public company very seriously. And it has been rewarded for its efforts. In November 2010, the company received four of the Canadian Institute of Chartered Accountants (CICA) Corporate Reporting Awards, including the Award of Excellence for Corporate Reporting in the Mining Sector. This was the eighth consecutive year in which the company received multiple honours at the event. PotashCorp also won the Award of Excellence in the financial reporting and electronic disclosure categories and received honourable mention for sustainable development reporting.

"Every year, we look for ways to expand and enhance the way we deliver information to our stakeholders, with a belief that accountability and transparency make us a stronger and more valuable company," said Denita Stann, Vice President, Investor and Public Relations at PotashCorp.

CICA judges said PotashCorp "produced a report designed to engage readers while conveying a clear investment proposition." Like all annual reports, the company's document for the 2009 fiscal year presented the financial results and management discussion and analysis (MD&A). The judges noted that PotashCorp presented well-laid-out financial statements, a well-organized MD&A, and clear definitions of the financial reporting terms included in the report. In addition, the annual report described what the company's goals for 2009 were and how well it met them, and listed targets for 2010. As well, it presented "excellent disclosure around IFRS," the judges commented.

The judges were particularly impressed by PotashCorp's electronic disclosure. "The company continues to make improvements to its website by incorporating social media and interactivity, in addition to providing practical information that is easy to navigate and download," the judges said. They also commended PotashCorp on its corporate governance processes and accountability to its stakeholders. The company commented, in its annual report, "By listening to and being accountable to our shareholders, we build trust and support, which enhances our ability to execute our strategies."

The annual report is the most important financial document a public company produces. It is a crucial tool for investors, lenders, other creditors, regulators, and many other users to gather the information they require to make important decisions about a company. In taking care to communicate effectively with its shareholders and other parties so that they can make well-informed decisions, PotashCorp demonstrates its commitment to keeping its stakeholders informed—one of the most important issues in corporate governance today.

the navigator

preview of
CHAPTER 14

An important lesson can be learned from PotashCorp's annual report, described in our feature story. Effective communication is the key to helping users make decisions. The purpose of this chapter is to give you a comprehensive review of the financial analysis tools a company's stakeholders use to help them make decisions. We will also examine the impact of certain irregular items on financial results and analyses. In addition, we will identify factors that can impose limits on the analysis of financial information.

The chapter is organized as follows:

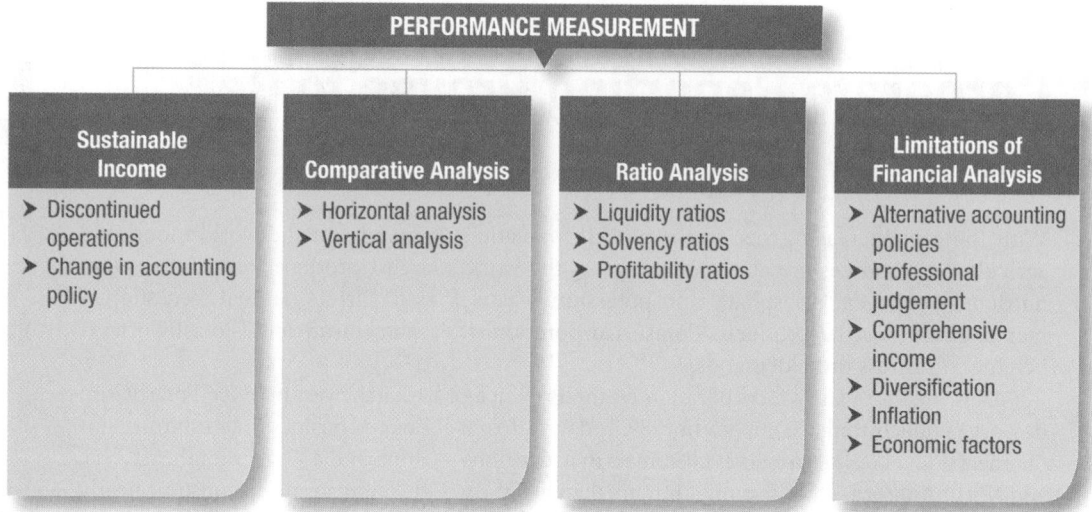

Sustainable Income

STUDY OBJECTIVE 1
Understand the concept of sustainable income and indicate how irregular items are presented.

We learned about the objective of financial reporting in Chapter 2: to provide information about a company that is useful to existing and potential investors, lenders, and other creditors in making decisions about providing resources to the company. This financial information is provided by general purpose financial statements, which are used to assess the financial position and performance—past, current, and future—of a company. For example, investors, lenders, and other creditors often use profit reported on the income statement to help estimate future cash flows and, in particular, their timing and certainty. When they do this, they must make sure that profit does not include irregular (i.e., out of the ordinary) items that are not likely to recur.

Profit adjusted for irregular items is known as **sustainable income**—the level of profit that is most likely to be obtained in the future. Sustainable income differs from actual profit by the amount of irregular revenues, expenses, gains, and losses that are included in profit. For example, suppose Rye Corporation reports that this year's profit is $500,000, but this amount includes a once-in-a-lifetime gain of $400,000. In estimating next year's profit for Rye Corporation, we would likely ignore this $400,000 gain and estimate that next year's profit will be in the neighbourhood of $100,000, plus or minus any expected changes. That is, based on this year's results, the company's sustainable income is roughly $100,000.

To help determine sustainable income, irregular items are reported separately on the financial statements. We will discuss two common types of irregular items in this chapter: discontinued operations and changes in accounting policy.

DISCONTINUED OPERATIONS

The term **discontinued operations** refers to the disposal, or availability for sale, of a component of an entity. A **component of an entity**, for the purpose of discontinued operations, represents a separate major line of business or major geographical area of operations that has been disposed of or is held for sale. It must be clearly distinguishable operationally and financially from the rest of the company.

Most large corporations have major lines of business, many in different geographic areas. For example, PotashCorp has three separate major lines of business differentiated by type of chemical nutrient: potash, phosphate, and nitrogen. It also operates in five different geographical regions as was mentioned in the feature story, three of which are considered to be major.

PotashCorp did not report any discontinued operations in any recent year. However, SunOpta Inc. did and we will illustrate the presentation of discontinued operations in the statement of financial position and income statement using SunOpta. SunOpta is an Ontario-based natural and organic food products company, with operations in Canada, the United States, and Europe, as well as other countries. As a result of falling sales, the company decided to shed its non-core assets, including its Canadian food distribution business and its fibre preparation and pretreatment business, both of which are considered components of an entity for the purpose of discontinued operations.

Statement of Financial Position

Assets and liabilities of a discontinued operation that are held for sale are reported separately on the statement of financial position. They are valued and reported at the lower of their carrying amount and fair value (less any anticipated costs of selling) as current or non-current assets or liabilities. Of course, assets or liabilities that have already been disposed of are no longer recorded or reported on the statement of financial position.

Illustration 14-1 shows how SunOpta presented its discontinued operations on its fiscal 2010 and 2009 statements of financial position (which it calls balance sheet).

SUNOPTA INC. Balance Sheet (partial) January 1, 2011, and December 31, 2009 (in U.S. thousands)		
	2010	2009
Current assets held for sale (note 3)	—	$56,140
Non-current assets held for sale (note 3)	—	33,120
Current liabilities held for sale (note 3)	—	19,135
Non-current liabilities held for sale (note 3)	—	487

▶ Illustration 14-1
Presentation of discontinued operations on statement of financial position

SunOpta did not have any discontinued assets held for sale at the end of fiscal 2010 as the sales were completed in that year. In Note 3 to its financial statements, SunOpta explains the details of this decision and presents financial information about each of the specific assets and liabilities that were affected in 2009.

Income Statement

Discontinued operations are segregated from continuing operations and reported separately on the income statement. Because companies want readers of the financial statements to understand that discontinued operations are not likely to recur, they are shown near the bottom of the income statement immediately following the profit or loss from continuing operations. Any income tax relating to discontinued operations is also segregated from the income tax expense relating to continuing operations and shown within the discontinued operations section of the income statement.

Discontinued operations on the income statement can consist of two parts: (1) the profit (loss) from the discontinued operations, net of any income tax expense or savings, and (2) the gain (loss) on the disposal of the component, net of any income tax expense or savings. Of course, if the component of an entity has not yet been disposed of and is being held for sale, only the first part (the profit or loss from the discontinued operations) will be reported on the income statement until the actual disposal occurs.

Illustration 14-2 shows the information that SunOpta reported on its income statement (which it calls statement of operations) regarding the discontinuation of its operations.

SUNOPTA INC.
Statement of Operations (partial)
Years Ended January 1, 2011, and December 31, 2009
(in U.S. thousands)

	2010	2009
Profit (loss) from continuing operations before income tax	$19,029	$(12,718)
Income tax (expense) recovery	(5,463)	3,201
Profit (loss) from continuing operations	13,566	(9,517)
Discontinued operations (note 3)		
Loss from discontinued operations, net of income tax	(14,569)	(273)
Gain on sale of discontinued operations, net of income tax	62,950	
Profit (loss) from discontinued operations, net of income tax	48,381	(273)
Profit (loss)	$61,947	$ (9,790)

Expenses are deducted from revenues on SunOpta's income statement to calculate profit or loss from continuing operations before income tax, although it is not detailed in the above illustration. Income tax expense applicable to continuing operations is then deducted (or added in the case of income tax savings) to arrive at profit or loss from continuing operations. Note that the caption "profit (loss) from continuing operations" is used and "discontinued operations" are separately reported. Within the discontinued operations section, both the operating loss and the gain on disposal are reported net of applicable income tax.

In addition, although not illustrated here, earnings per share must be reported separately for continuing operations and for discontinued operations so that investors can clearly see the impact of this decision on the company. The impact of the discontinued operations on cash flow must also be reported separately on the statement of cash flows.

Discontinued operations are not uncommon and can have a significant impact on a company's financial position and profit. In general, in evaluating a company, it makes sense to eliminate irregular items such as discontinued operations from the analysis.

CHANGE IN ACCOUNTING POLICY

Alternative Terminology
Accounting policies are also known as *accounting standards* and *accounting principles*.

Another type of irregular item, one that affects profits of prior periods, is a change in accounting policy. A **change in accounting policy** occurs when the accounting policy used in the current year is different from the one used in the preceding year. To ensure the comparability of financial statements from year to year, accounting policies should be applied consistently from period to period. This does not mean, however, that changes can never be made. When a change is made, it is classified as either voluntary or mandatory.

A voluntary change in accounting policy is allowed when management can show that the new accounting policy results in a more reliable and relevant presentation of events or transactions in the financial statements. An example of a voluntary change in accounting policy is a change in inventory cost formula (e.g., from average cost to FIFO) if the new formula better corresponds to the physical use and flow of goods and is a comparable practice with that used by other companies in the same industry. Voluntary changes in accounting policy are rare.

A mandatory change in accounting policy is one that is required by standard setters, such as the transition to IFRS and ASPE from Canadian GAAP in 2011. We will continue to see these in the next few years as more standards are updated and converged.

Changes in accounting policies affect financial reporting in four ways:

ASPE

1. The cumulative effect of the change in accounting policy relating to prior years should be reported (net of any income tax expense or savings) as an adjustment to opening retained earnings because the restated income of those prior years is now closed into retained earnings. Since prior-period profits are affected, a change in accounting policy must be reported in the retained earnings section of the statement of changes in equity (or in the statement of retained earnings for private companies following ASPE), rather than in the current period's income statement.

2. The new policy should be used for reporting the results of operations in the current year.
3. All prior-period financial statements should be restated to make comparisons easier.
4. The effects of the change should be detailed and disclosed in a note.

Ideally, all accounting changes are applied retrospectively. This means that a financial statement from any prior year that is presented for comparative purposes must be restated as if the new accounting policy had been used in the past. At times, especially with accounting changes that are mandated, it is impractical to do this and the change is only reported prospectively; that is, for the current and future years.

Alternative Terminology
Retrospectively is also known as *retroactively*.

To illustrate the presentation of a retrospective change in accounting policy, we will use Rozek Inc., a hypothetical company that changed its inventory cost formula from FIFO to average cost at the beginning of 2012. It decided to make this change because industry best practice dictated that the average cost formula was the most appropriate choice for the type of inventory and industry to which Rozek belongs.

The cumulative effect on prior-year income statements of this change in inventory policy is to increase cost of goods sold and decrease profit before income tax by an assumed amount of $24,000. If the company has a 30% income tax rate, the income tax savings are $7,200 ($24,000 × 30%) and the net effect on prior-period profits after income tax is a decrease of $16,800 ($24,000 − $7,200).

The effect of this change on opening retained earnings, using assumed data, is shown in Rozek's statement of changes in equity in Illustration 14-3.

▶Illustration 14-3
Presentation of change in accounting policy

ROZEK INC.
Statement of Changes in Equity
Year Ended December 31, 2012

	Common Shares	Retained Earnings	Accumulated Other Comprehensive Income	Total Equity
Balance, January 1, as previously reported	$250,000	$500,000	$29,000	$ 779,000
Less: Cumulative effect on prior years of change in inventory cost formula (net of $7,200 income tax savings)		(16,800)		(16,800)
Balance, January 1, as restated	250,000	483,200	29,000	762,200
Issued common shares	35,000			35,000
Profit		301,000		301,000
Balance, December 31	$285,000	$784,200	$29,000	$1,098,200

As you can see from Illustration 14-3, it is only opening retained earnings in the statement of changes of equity that is affected by this retrospective change in accounting policy. In addition to retained earnings, Rozek's merchandise inventory account on its 2011 statement of financial position would also be restated for this change. A note to the financial statements would detail the impact of the change and the fact that the prior year's statements have been restated.

 **ACCOUNTING MATTERS!** *Investor Perspective*

Transition to IFRS and ASPE

One of the most daunting changes in accounting policy that public and private companies have faced was the adoption of International Financial Reporting Standards and Accounting Standards for Private Enterprises in 2011. In many cases, companies were required to apply these new standards retrospectively. This meant that the opening statement of financial position and the comparative financial statements had to be prepared in accordance with the recognition, measurement, presentation, and disclosure requirements of IFRS or ASPE.

Fortunately, standard setters were aware of the practical difficulties of applying these standards retrospectively, and provided limited exemptions—some mandatory and some optional. In general, the exemptions related to areas where it was considered to be inappropriate to apply hindsight (e.g., for estimates) or where the cost outweighed the benefits of applying the standard. In such cases, the change only required prospective application.

DECISION TOOLKIT

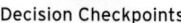 Decision Checkpoints	 Info Needed for Decision	 Tools to Use for Decision	 How to Evaluate Results
Has the company sold, or is it holding for sale, a component of an entity?	Discontinuation of, or plans to discontinue, a component of an entity	Discontinued operations section of the statement of financial position, income statement, and/or statement of cash flows	If a component of an entity has been discontinued, its results in the current period should not be included in assessing the company's financial position or in estimating its future profit or cash flows.
Has the company changed any of its accounting policies?	Change in accounting policy	Cumulative effect of a change in accounting policy in the statement of changes in equity (or statement of retained earnings for private company using ASPE) and notes to the financial statements	Where possible, financial statements are restated using the new policy to make them easier to compare.

BEFORE YOU GO ON...

▶ Do It! Discontinued Operations

AIR Corporation reported profit from continuing operations before income tax of $150 million and a loss on disposal of a paper facility of $99 million before income tax for the year ended October 31, 2012. The company had an income tax rate of 25% and a weighted average of 85 million common shares. Prepare a partial income statement, starting with profit from continuing operations before income tax, including earnings per share information.

Action Plan

- Separately calculate and report the income tax effect of continuing operations and discontinued operations.
- Separately calculate and report earnings per share for continuing operations and discontinued operations.

Solution

AIR CORPORATION Income Statement (partial) Year Ended October 31, 2012 (in thousands)	
Profit from continuing operations before income tax	$150,000
Income tax expense	37,500[1]
Profit from continuing operations	112,500
Loss on disposal of paper facility, net of $24,750[2] income tax savings	74,250[3]
Profit	$ 38,250
Earnings per share from continuing operations	$ 1.32[4]
Loss per share from discontinued operations	(0.87)[5]

Calculations:
[1] $150,000 × 25% = $37,500
[2] $99,000 × 25% = $24,750
[3] $99,000 − $24,750 = $74,250
[4] $112,500 ÷ 85,000 = $1.32
[5] $74,250 ÷ 85,000 = $(0.87)

Comparative Analysis

As mentioned earlier, investors, lenders, and other creditors are interested in a company's sustainable income. They will use this information, in addition to information found in the other financial statements, to make comparisons in order to evaluate a company's past and current financial performance and position, and help determine future expectations.

STUDY OBJECTIVE 2
Explain and apply horizontal analysis.

Various tools are available to help users make comparisons of a company's financial data. In the following two sections, we will explain and illustrate horizontal and vertical analysis, two commonly used tools in comparative analysis. But first, we should note that, while a company's financial statement data are usually the starting point in any analysis, it is important to review non-financial information as well. Non-financial information includes information found in a company's annual report such as its mission, strategy, goals and objectives, and management discussion and analysis (MD&A). Understanding a company's business strategy and its goals and objectives is important when interpreting financial performance, as we learned in our feature story about PotashCorp.

HORIZONTAL ANALYSIS

Horizontal analysis, also called **trend analysis**, is a technique to determine the change (increase or decrease) that has taken place in a series of financial statement data over time. This change can be expressed as either an amount or a percentage.

Horizontal analysis is used in intracompany comparisons. You will recall from earlier chapters that intracompany comparisons involve financial data *within* a company, comparing current financial data with that of one or more prior years. Comparisons within a company are often useful to detect significant trends. For example, net sales for the last five years for PotashCorp are shown in Illustration 14-4 in dollars (in U.S. millions) and percentages:

Helpful Hint
The term *horizontal analysis* means that we view financial statement data from left to right (or right to left) across time.

	2010	2009	2008	2007	2006
Net sales	$6,051.0	$3,657.6	$8,989.2	$4,764.0	$3,376.8
% of base-year amount	179.2%	108.3%	266.2%	141.1%	100.0%
% change for year	65.4%	(59.3)%	88.7%	41.1%	—

▸**Illustration 14-4**
Horizontal analysis for PotashCorp's sales

If we assume that 2006 is the base year, we can express net sales in each year as a percentage of the base-year (or period) amount (i.e., as a percentage of the amount from 2006). We call this a **horizontal percentage of a base-period amount**. This percentage is calculated by dividing the amount for the specific period we are analyzing by the base-period amount, as shown in Illustration 14-5.

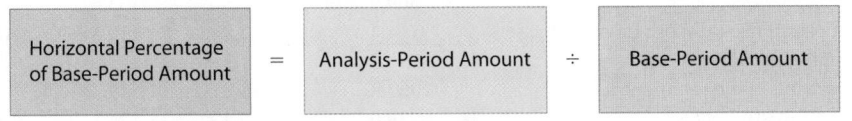

▸**Illustration 14-5**
Horizontal percentage of a base-period amount formula

We can use horizontal analysis on the PotashCorp's sales shown in Illustration 14-4 to determine that net sales in 2010 are 179.2% of net sales in 2006 by dividing U.S. $6,051.0 million by U.S. $3,376.8 million. In other words, sales in 2010 are 179.2% greater than sales five years earlier in 2006.

Reviewing the percentages of base-year amounts shown in the second row of Illustration 14-4, we can easily see the trend of PotashCorp's net sales. Sales increased in 2007 and 2008, before dropping substantially in 2009. Sales started recovering in 2010. It is important to understand the economic circumstances that a company is operating in before one can fully interpret changes in sales, or changes in any financial amount. For example, in late 2008 and 2009, much of the industrialized world entered into a global recession and resulting financial crisis. Sales declined in every sector of the economy, affecting fertilizer companies like PotashCorp. It would be difficult to properly interpret PotashCorp's past performance over this time period without fully understanding the economy and resulting effects of demand and supply on potash prices in the period under analysis.

We can also use horizontal analysis to measure the percentage change for any one specific period by calculating a **horizontal percentage change for the period**. This is calculated by dividing the dollar amount of the change between the specific year under analysis and the base year by the base-year amount, as shown in Illustration 14-6.

▶Illustration 14-6
Horizontal percentage change for period formula

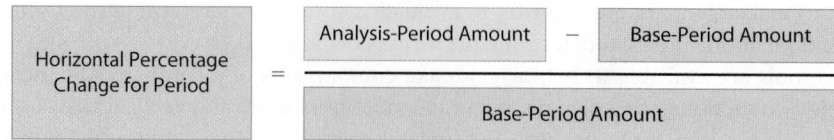

For example, if we set each prior year as our base year, we can see that sales increased by U.S. $2,393.4 million ($6,051.0 − $3,657.6) between 2009 and 2010. This increase can then be expressed as a percentage by dividing the amount of the change between the two years, U.S. $2,393.4 million, by the amount in 2009, U.S. $3,657.6 million. Thus, in 2010 sales increased by 65.4% compared with 2009. The horizontal percentage change in sales for each year is presented in the last row of Illustration 14-4. Note that no change can be calculated for the first year in our example, 2006.

We will use horizontal analysis (percentage change for period) to compare PotashCorp's statement of financial position and income statement in the next sections. We will also use other financial and non-financial information found in PotashCorp's annual report to help us understand some of the reasons for the changes we will observe by comparing these statements.

Statement of Financial Position

Condensed statements of financial position for PotashCorp for 2010 and 2009, showing dollar and percentage changes for the two-year period, are shown in Illustration 14-7.

▶Illustration 14-7
Horizontal analysis of statement of financial position (percentage change for period)

POTASH CORPORATION OF SASKATCHEWAN INC.
Statement of Financial Position
December 31
(in U.S. millions)

	2010	2009	Increase (Decrease) Amount	Increase (Decrease) Percentage
Assets				
Current assets				
Cash and cash equivalents	$ 411.9	$ 385.4	$ 26.5	6.9%
Accounts receivable	1,043.7	1,137.9	(94.2)	(8.3)%
Inventories	569.9	623.5	(53.6)	(8.6)%
Prepaid expenses and other current assets	114.4	124.9	(10.5)	(8.4)%
Total current assets	2,139.9	2,271.7	(131.8)	(5.8)%
Property, plant, and equipment	8,062.7	6,413.3	1,649.4	25.7%
Long-term investments	4,938.0	3,760.3	1,177.7	31.3%
Intangible assets	18.6	20.0	(1.4)	(7.0)%
Goodwill	97.0	97.0	0	0.0%
Other assets	363.1	359.9	3.2	0.9%
Total assets	$15,619.3	$12,922.2	$2,697.1	20.9%
Liabilities and Shareholders' Equity				
Liabilities				
Current liabilities				
Payables and accrued charges	$ 1,245.7	$ 796.8	$ 448.9	56.3%
Short-term debt and current portion of long-term debt	1,946.1	780.6	1,165.5	149.3%
Total current liabilities	3,191.8	1,577.4	1,614.4	102.3%
Non-current liabilities	5,623.3	4,905.0	718.3	14.6%
Total liabilities	8,815.1	6,482.4	2,332.7	36.0%
Shareholders' equity	6,804.2	6,439.8	364.4	5.7%
Total liabilities and shareholders' equity	$15,619.3	$12,922.2	$2,697.1	20.9%

Note that in a horizontal analysis, while the amount column of the increase or decrease is additive (the total change is an increase of U.S. $2,697.1 million), the percentage column is not additive (20.9% is not a total).

The horizontal analysis of PotashCorp's comparative statement of financial position shows that several changes occurred between 2009 and 2010. In the current assets section, cash and cash equivalents increased by 6.9%. It is helpful to look at the statement of cash flows to determine the cause of key changes in cash during the year. After reviewing this statement (not illustrated here), we learn that the increase in cash is primarily because of increased sales and reduced expenses.

The analysis also shows that accounts receivable decreased by U.S. $94.2 million, or 8.3%. We will look at the income statement in the next section to determine if sales changed proportionately to the receivables decrease. If not, this may be an indicator of improved or deteriorating receivables. Inventories also decreased by U.S. $53.6 million, or 8.6%, because of a strong recovery in demand in 2010 following 2009's record decline in potash markets. Overall, current assets decreased by U.S. $131.8 million, or 5.8%.

With respect to non-current assets, there are two significant changes: property, plant, and equipment increased by U.S. $1,649.4 million, or 25.7%, and long-term investments increased by U.S. $1,177.7 million, or 31.3%. In 2010, PotashCorp added to its property, plant, and equipment as it expanded its potash capacity. Its investments increased primarily because of the purchase of additional shares in Israel Chemicals Ltd., the world's sixth-largest potash producer, and an increase in the fair value of these shares.

PotashCorp's total current liabilities increased by U.S. $1,614.4 million, or 102.3%. You will see that accounts payable and accrued liabilities increased significantly as did the short-term debt and current portion of long-term debt. Accounts payable and accrued liabilities increased primarily due to higher income tax payable. The significant increase in short-term debt and the current portion of long-term debt was a result of debt coming due in 2011. Despite this reclassification of long-term debt as current, total non-current liabilities still increased by U.S. $718.3 million, or 14.6%. This occurred because of the issue of new long-term debt in the fourth quarter of 2010.

In the shareholders' equity section (not detailed in Illustration 14-7), increased accumulated other comprehensive income accounted for most of the U.S. $364.4-million, or 5.7%, increase. Because total liabilities increased by 36% while total shareholders' equity increased by only 5.7%, we can see that PotashCorp is financing the growth of its business by assuming additional debt rather than by issuing equity.

Income Statement

Illustration 14-8 presents a horizontal analysis of PotashCorp's condensed income statement for the years 2010 and 2009.

POTASH CORPORATION OF SASKATCHEWAN INC. Income Statement Year Ended December 31 (in U.S. millions) 𝐑 **Potash**Corp				
			Increase (Decrease)	
	2010	2009	Amount	Percentage
Net sales	$6,051.0	$3,657.6	$2,393.4	65.4%
Cost of goods sold	3,426.0	2,643.0	783.0	29.6%
Gross profit	2,625.0	1,014.6	1,610.4	158.7%
Selling and administrative expenses	228.1	183.6	44.5	24.2%
Other operating income	(151.2)	(349.8)	(198.6)	(56.8)%
Profit from operations	2,548.1	1,180.8	1,367.3	115.8%
Interest expense	99.1	120.9	(21.8)	(18.0)%
Profit before income tax	2,449.0	1,059.9	1,389.1	131.1%
Income tax expense	642.8	79.2	563.6	711.6%
Profit	$1,806.2	$ 980.7	$ 825.5	84.2%

Illustration 14-8

Horizontal analysis of income statement (percentage change for period)

A horizontal analysis of the income statement shows that net sales increased by U.S. $2,393.4 million, or 65.4%. PotashCorp noted in its management discussion and analysis that its sales volume was up as "customers globally responded to favourable crop economics and the need to address potash-depleted soils." This is significant given the decrease in accounts receivable we noted in the statement of financial position. Normally, if sales increase, it is not surprising to also have an increase in receivables. The fact there was a decrease in accounts receivable during a period of increased sales reassures us about how collectible the receivables are.

Interestingly, while net sales increased by 65.4%, cost of goods sold increased by only 29.6%. PotashCorp appears to have been able to command higher sales prices because of the resurgence in potash demand while still controlling its costs. Taken together, these activities have resulted in an increase in gross profit of U.S. $1,610.4 million, or 158.7%.

PotashCorp's selling and administrative expenses increased by U.S. $44.5 million, or 24.2%, which is significantly less than the increase in net sales. However, other operating income decreased by U.S. $198.6 million, or 56.8%. Overall, PotashCorp reported a notable increase in its profit from operations of U.S. $1,367.3, or 115.8%. Interest expense was down by U.S. $21.8 million, or 18%, because of lower interest rates in 2010. PotashCorp noted that "Rates on short-term debt obligations were higher in 2009 [than in 2010] as a result of the global financial crisis, which reduced market liquidity and increased the cost of short-term borrowings." With the increase in profit before income tax, PotashCorp also reported a significant increase in its income tax expense.

The measurement of changes from period to period in percentages is fairly straightforward and quite useful. However, the calculations can be affected by complications. For example, if an item has a small value in a base year and a large value in the next year, the percentage change, although large, may not be meaningful. Look at the 711.6% increase in income tax in Illustration 14-8. This is because the base year amount was relatively low. In addition, if an item has no value in a base year and a value in the next year, no percentage change can be determined. Finally, if a negative amount appears in the base year and a positive amount in the following year, or vice versa, no percentage change can be calculated.

We have not done a horizontal analysis of PotashCorp's statement of comprehensive income (which it presents separately from its income statement), statement of changes in equity, and statement of cash flows as analyses of these statements are not as useful as horizontal analyses done on the statement of financial position and income statement. The amounts presented in these other statements already give details of the changes between two periods.

DECISION TOOLKIT

 Decision Checkpoints	 Info Needed for Decision	 Tools to Use for Decision	How to Evaluate Results
How do the company's financial position and operating results compare with those of previous periods?	Statement of financial position and income statement	Comparative financial statements should be prepared over at least two years, with the first year reported as the base year. Changes in each line item relative to the base year should be presented both by amount and by percentage. This is called horizontal analysis.	A significant change should be investigated to determine what caused it.

BEFORE YOU GO ON...

▶ Do It! Horizontal Analysis

Selected condensed information (in thousands) from Bonora Ltd.'s income statement for four years ended June 30 follows:

	2012	2011	2010	2009
Net sales	$37,600	$36,500	$38,700	$40,500
Cost of goods sold	14,900	14,200	13,800	15,300
Gross profit	22,700	22,300	24,900	25,200

Operating expenses	18,500	17,400	16,200	17,600
Profit from operations	4,200	4,900	8,700	7,600
Income tax expense	1,050	1,225	2,175	1,900
Profit	$ 3,150	$ 3,675	$ 6,525	$ 5,700

Using horizontal analysis, calculate (a) the percentage of the base-year amount for each year, assuming that 2009 is the base year, and (b) the percentage change between each year and the next.

Action Plan

- Horizontal percentage of the base-year amount: Set the base-year (2009) dollar amounts at 100%. Express each subsequent year's amount as a percentage of the base period by dividing the dollar amount for the year under analysis by the base-year amount.
- Horizontal percentage change between two periods: Divide the dollar amount of the change between the prior and current years by the prior-year amount.

Solution

(a) Percentage of base-year amount

	2012	2011	2010	2009
Net sales	93%	90%	96%	100%
Cost of goods sold	97%	93%	90%	100%
Gross profit	90%	88%	99%	100%
Operating expenses	105%	99%	92%	100%
Profit from operations	55%	64%	114%	100%
Income tax expense	55%	64%	114%	100%
Profit	55%	64%	114%	100%

(b) Percentage change for each year

	2012	2011	2010	2009
Net sales	3%	(6)%	(4)%	—
Cost of goods sold	5%	3%	(10)%	—
Gross profit	2%	(10)%	(1)%	—
Operating expenses	6%	7%	(8)%	—
Profit from operations	(14)%	(44)%	14%	—
Income tax expense	(14)%	(44)%	14%	—
Profit	(14)%	(44)%	14%	—

the navigator

STUDY OBJECTIVE 3
Explain and apply vertical analysis.

VERTICAL ANALYSIS

Vertical analysis, also called **common size analysis**, is a technique that expresses each item in a financial statement as a percentage of a base amount in the same financial statement. Note that while horizontal analysis compares data across more than one year, vertical analysis compares data within the same year.

The **vertical percentage of a base amount** is calculated by dividing the financial statement amount under analysis by the base amount in that particular financial statement, as shown in Illustration 14-9.

Helpful Hint
The term *vertical analysis* means that we view financial statement data from up to down (or down to up) within the same period of time.

▶ Illustration 14-9
Vertical percentage of a base amount formula

Vertical Percentage of Base Amount	=	Analysis Amount	÷	Base Amount

The base amount commonly used for the statement of financial position is *total assets* (or total liabilities and shareholders' equity which equals total assets). For example, we might say that current assets are 13.7% of total assets (total assets being the base amount). The base amount for the income statement is usually *revenues* for a service company and *net sales* for a merchandising company. We might say that cost of goods sold is 56.6% of net sales (net sales being the base amount). The base amount is usually the largest amount on each statement.

Vertical analysis is used in both intracompany and intercompany comparisons. Vertical analysis is helpful to compare financial data both *within* a company and *between* one or more competitor companies. We will use vertical analysis to compare PotashCorp's statement of financial position and income statement for two years as well as with one of its competitors, in the next sections.

Statement of Financial Position

Illustration 14-10 presents a vertical analysis of PotashCorp's comparative statement of financial position.

▶ Illustration 14-10
Vertical analysis of statement of financial position

POTASH CORPORATION OF SASKATCHEWAN INC.
Statement of Financial Position
December 31
(in U.S. millions)

℞ PotashCorp

	2010		2009	
	Amount	Percentage	Amount	Percentage
Assets				
Current assets				
Cash and cash equivalents	$ 411.9	2.6%	$ 385.4	3.0%
Accounts receivable	1,043.7	6.7%	1,137.9	8.8%
Inventories	569.9	3.7%	623.5	4.8%
Prepaid expenses and other current assets	114.4	0.7%	124.9	1.0%
Total current assets	2,139.9	13.7%	2,271.7	17.6%
Property, plant, and equipment	8,062.7	51.7%	6,413.3	49.6%
Long-term investments	4,938.0	31.6%	3,760.3	29.1%
Intangible assets	18.6	0.1%	20.0	0.2%
Goodwill	97.0	0.6%	97.0	0.7%
Other assets	363.1	2.3%	359.9	2.8%
Total assets	$15,619.3	100.0%	$12,922.2	100.0%
Liabilities and Shareholders' Equity				
Liabilities				
Current liabilities				
Payables and accrued charges	$ 1,245.7	8.0%	$ 796.8	6.2%
Short-term debt and current portion of long-term debt	1,946.1	12.4%	780.6	6.0%
Total current liabilities	3,191.8	20.4%	1,577.4	12.2%
Non-current liabilities	5,623.3	36.0%	4,905.0	38.0%
Total liabilities	8,815.1	56.4%	6,482.4	50.2%
Shareholders' equity	6,804.2	43.6%	6,439.8	49.8%
Total liabilities and shareholders' equity	$15,619.3	100.0%	$12,922.2	100.0%

Vertical analysis shows the relative size of each item in the statement of financial position compared with a base amount. It can be prepared for one or more years, as we've shown in Illustration 14-10. It is also useful to compare vertically prepared information for multiple periods with similar information provided earlier in our horizontal analysis. It is interesting to note that all the current assets declined slightly as a vertical percentage of total assets when compared with the prior year.

Property, plant, and equipment increased by 25.7% between 2009 and 2010 according to our horizontal analysis in Illustration 14-7. We won't repeat the reason for this increase given in the horizontal analysis section; however, it is interesting that it only increased as a percentage of total assets by 2.1% (51.7% − 49.6%) over the two years. Long-term investments increased by 31.3% in our horizontal analysis, but they only increased slightly as a percentage of total assets, from 29.1% in 2009 to 31.6% in 2010.

Total current liabilities increased from 12.2% to 20.4% as a percentage of total liabilities and shareholders' equity (or total assets) from 2009 to 2010, compared with showing a 102.3% horizontal increase in Illustration 14-7. Non-current liabilities decreased from 38% in 2009 to 36% in 2010 as a percentage of total liabilities and shareholders' equity. While shareholders' equity increased in absolute dollar terms, it decreased from 49.8% in 2009 to 43.6% in 2010 as a percentage of total liabilities and shareholders' equity.

Income Statement

Illustration 14-11 presents a vertical analysis of PotashCorp's comparative income statement.

> **Illustration 14-11**
> Vertical analysis of income statement

POTASH CORPORATION OF SASKATCHEWAN INC.
Income Statement
Year Ended December 31
(in U.S. millions)

R PotashCorp

	2010 Amount	2010 Percentage	2009 Amount	2009 Percentage
Net sales	$6,051.0	100.0%	$3,657.6	100.0%
Cost of goods sold	3,426.0	56.6%	2,643.0	72.3%
Gross profit	2,625.0	43.4%	1,014.6	27.7%
Selling and administrative expenses	228.1	3.8%	183.6	5.0%
Other operating income	(151.2)	(2.5)%	(349.8)	(9.6)%
Profit from operations	2,548.1	42.1%	1,180.8	32.3%
Interest expense	99.1	1.6%	120.9	3.3%
Profit before income tax	2,449.0	40.5%	1,059.9	29.0%
Income tax expense	642.8	10.6%	79.2	2.2%
Profit	$1,806.2	29.9%	$ 980.7	26.8%

Although cost of goods sold increased by 29.6% in 2010 in our horizontal analysis shown in Illustration 14-8, it actually had a significant decline as a percentage of net sales from 72.3% in 2009 to 56.6% in 2010, as shown in Illustration 14-11. The resulting gross profit margin is up substantially. In our horizontal analysis, we also found fairly significant changes in other income statement accounts. However, in the vertical analysis, these changes appear less dramatic when expressed as a percentage of net sales.

Although vertical analysis can also be performed on the other period statements—comprehensive income, changes in equity, and cash flows—this is seldom done. As mentioned earlier, the value of these statements comes from the analysis of the changes during the year, and not from percentage comparisons of these changes against a base amount.

■ Keeping an Eye on Cash

While a common size analysis of the statement of cash flows is not always productive, a detailed review of this statement is a useful starting point to understand where the company's cash comes from and what it is used for. When reviewing the contents of the operating, investing, and financing activities sections, it may be helpful to calculate the total of the major sources and uses of cash over several years since annual reporting periods are often too short for decision-making. For example, financing of asset replacements, major expansions, or business acquisitions often spans several years.

The types of questions that analyzing the statement of cash flows can help answer include:

- Is cash generated from, or used by, each classification of activity growing or declining?
- Is the company generating enough cash from its operating activities to pay for asset replacements or is it relying on debt to finance them?
- What is the company's dependence on debt financing versus equity financing?
- What types of cash sources are available for financing activities?
- Does the company pay dividends using cash generated from operating activities, from selling assets (investing activities), or from issuing debt (financing activities)?
- What is the company's cash flexibility to meet unexpected demands?

Intercompany Comparisons

Vertical analysis also makes it easier to compare different companies. For example, one of PotashCorp's main competitors is Agrium Inc. Using vertical analysis, we can make a more meaningful comparison of the condensed income statements of PotashCorp and Agrium, as shown in Illustration 14-12.

Illustration 14-12

Intercompany comparison by vertical analysis

POTASHCORP AND AGRIUM Income Statement Year Ended December 31, 2010 (in U.S. millions)	PotashCorp		Agrium	
	Amount	Percentage	Amount	Percentage
Net sales	$6,051.0	100.0%	$ 10,520	100.0%
Cost of goods sold	3,426.0	56.6%	7,869	74.8%
Gross profit	2,625.0	43.4%	2,651	25.2%
Selling and administrative expenses	228.1	3.8%	1,274	12.1%
Other operating (income) expenses	(151.2)	(2.5)%	274	2.6%
Profit from operations	2,548.1	42.1%	1,103	10.5%
Interest expense	99.1	1.6%	107	1.0%
Profit from continuing operations before income tax	2,449.0	40.5%	996	9.5%
Income tax expense	642.8	10.6%	265	2.5%
Profit from continuing operations	1,806.2	29.9%	731	7.0%
Loss from discontinued operations			17	0.2%
Profit	$1,806.2	29.9%	$ 714	6.8%

At 56.6%, PotashCorp's cost of goods sold is a lower percentage of net sales than Agrium's at 74.8%. This results in a much higher gross profit margin of 43.4% for PotashCorp than Agrium's gross profit margin of 25.2%.

It is interesting to note that PotashCorp's selling and administrative expenses are also significantly lower than Agrium's. As a result, PotashCorp's profit is correspondingly higher at 29.9% of net sales compared with Agrium's profit from continuing operations at 7% of net sales.

Agrium reports a loss from discontinued operations of a commodity management business of U.S. $17 million in 2010. PotashCorp has no discontinued operations. Which profit line do you think is most useful for comparative purposes: profit from continuing operations or profit? If you answered profit from continuing operations, you are correct. Users are most interested in sustainable income, as we learned early in the chapter. While it is important to still consider the impact of the discontinued operations on Agrium's financial position and performance, comparable figures for analysis purposes would be the profit from continuing operations line.

Despite Agrium being a much larger company than PotashCorp in absolute dollars, vertical analysis clearly shows the differences between the two companies as it reduces each financial statement item to a percentage that can be compared more easily than large differences in dollar amounts. Vertical analysis can also be used to compare two companies' statements of financial position, although we have not done so here.

DECISION TOOLKIT

Decision Checkpoints	 Info Needed for Decision	 Tools to Use for Decision	 How to Evaluate Results
How do the relationships between items in this year's financial statements compare with last year's relationships or those of competitors?	Statement of financial position and income statement	Each line item on the statement of financial position should be presented as a percentage of total assets (total liabilities and shareholders' equity). Each line item on the income statement should be presented as a percentage of revenue (or net sales). This is called vertical analysis.	Any difference, either across years or between companies, should be investigated to determine the cause.

BEFORE YOU GO ON...

▶ Do It! Vertical Analysis

Selected condensed information (in thousands) from Bonora Ltd.'s income statement for four years ended June 30 follows:

	2012	2011	2010	2009
Net sales	$37,600	$36,500	$38,700	$40,500
Cost of goods sold	14,900	14,200	13,800	15,300
Gross profit	22,700	22,300	24,900	25,200
Operating expenses	18,500	17,400	16,200	17,600
Profit from operations	4,200	4,900	8,700	7,600
Income tax expense	1,050	1,225	2,175	1,900
Profit	$ 3,150	$ 3,675	$ 6,525	$ 5,700

Using vertical analysis, calculate the percentage of a base amount for each year.

Action Plan

- Set the base amount as net sales in an income statement.
- Vertical percentage of a base amount: divide the specific asset amount by the base amount for each year.

Solution

	2012	2011	2010	2009
Net sales	100%	100%	100%	100%
Cost of goods sold	40%	39%	36%	38%
Gross profit	60%	61%	64%	62%
Operating expenses	49%	48%	42%	43%
Profit from operations	11%	13%	22%	19%
Income tax expense	3%	3%	5%	5%
Profit	8%	10%	17%	14%

Ratio Analysis

The first step in any comprehensive analysis is to perform a horizontal and vertical analysis. This helps users understand some of the reasons for changes in financial position and performance, as well as identify further areas for investigation. Ratio analysis completes the analysis. Similar to horizontal and vertical analyses, ratio analysis is also a comparative tool used to evaluate the significance of financial data for a company. However, ratio analysis is much broader than the other tools, as it can be used in all three types of comparisons (intracompany, intercompany, and industry) discussed in this text.

In the next three sections, we provide an example of a comprehensive ratio analysis using the liquidity, solvency, and profitability ratios presented in past chapters. This analysis uses three categories of comparisons: (1) intracompany, comparing two years of data for PotashCorp for 2010 and 2009; (2) intercompany, comparing PotashCorp and Agrium for 2010 and 2009; and (3) industry, comparing both companies with fertilizer industry averages for 2010 and 2009.

You will recall that PotashCorp's statement of financial position was presented earlier in the chapter in Illustration 14-7 and its income statement in Illustration 14-8. We will use the information in these two financial statements, in addition to the following data, to calculate PotashCorp's ratios:

STUDY OBJECTIVE 4

Identify and calculate ratios that are used to analyze liquidity.

(in U.S. millions, except for share information)	2010	2009
Net cash provided by operating activities	$ 2,999.0	$ 923.9
Net capital expenditures	$ 1,978.3	$ 1,763.8
Total cash dividends	$ 117.7	$ 118.0
Dividend per share	$ 0.13	$ 0.13
Market price per share	$ 154.36	$ 113.91
Weighted average number of shares (in thousands)	886,371	886,740

Detailed calculations of the ratios are not shown in the ratios that follow, but you can use the above data and the statement of financial position and income statement data shown earlier in the chapter to recalculate the ratios for PotashCorp to make sure you understand where the numbers came from.

LIQUIDITY RATIOS

Liquidity ratios measure a company's short-term ability to pay its maturing obligations and to meet unexpected needs for cash. Short-term lenders and other creditors, such as bankers and suppliers, are particularly interested in assessing liquidity. Liquidity ratios include working capital, the current ratio, cash current debt coverage, receivables turnover, average collection period, inventory turnover, and days in inventory. Cash provided by operating activities, reported on the statement of cash flows, is also useful in assessing liquidity.

Working Capital

Working capital is the difference between current assets and current liabilities. It is one measure of liquidity. However, as we learned in Chapter 2, the current ratio—which expresses current assets and current liabilities as a ratio rather than as an amount—is a more useful indicator of liquidity. Consequently, we will not illustrate working capital again here, and will focus instead on the current ratio.

Current Ratio

The current ratio expresses the relationship of current assets to current liabilities, and is calculated by dividing current assets by current liabilities. It is widely used for evaluating a company's liquidity and short-term debt-paying ability.

The 2010 and 2009 current ratios for PotashCorp, Agrium, and the industry are shown below. Note that in the following ratio comparison, and in all ratios that follow, there is a column titled Comparison, indicating whether the 2010 result is better or worse than the 2009 result shown for each of PotashCorp, Agrium, and the industry.

CURRENT RATIO = $\dfrac{\text{CURRENT ASSETS}}{\text{CURRENT LIABILITIES}}$			
	2010	2009	Comparison
PotashCorp	0.7:1	1.4:1	Worse
Agrium	1.6:1	2.0:1	Worse
Industry average	1.8:1	2.1:1	Worse

What does the current ratio actually mean? The 2010 ratio of 0.7:1 means that for every dollar of current liabilities, PotashCorp has $0.70 of current assets. PotashCorp's current ratio decreased between 2010 and 2009, mainly because of a significant increase in its current liabilities, primarily its short-term debt and the current portion of its long-term debt. Recall from Illustration 14-7 that current assets decreased by 5.8%, while current liabilities increased by 102.3%.

PotashCorp's current ratio is significantly less than both Agrium's and that of the industry. It is noteworthy that both Agrium and the industry experienced declines in their current ratios as well in 2010. However, it is too early in our analysis to draw any conclusions about PotashCorp's liquidity, because the current ratio is only one measure of liquidity. It does not take into account the composition of the company's current assets or operating cash flows.

Cash Current Debt Coverage

One disadvantage of the current ratio is that it uses year-end balances of current asset and current liability accounts. These year-end balances may not reflect the company's position during most of the year. A ratio that partially corrects this problem is the cash current debt coverage ratio. It is calculated by dividing net cash provided (or used) by operating activities (from the statement of cash flows) by average current liabilities. Because it uses cash provided (or used) by operating activities from the statement of cash flows that covers a period of time, rather than current assets that represent a balance at a point in time, the cash current debt coverage ratio may be a better indicator of liquidity.

The 2010 and 2009 cash current debt coverage ratios for PotashCorp and Agrium are shown below. Industry averages are not available (n/a) for cash-based ratios.

CASH CURRENT DEBT COVERAGE =	$\dfrac{\text{NET CASH PROVIDED (USED) BY OPERATING ACTIVITIES}}{\text{AVERAGE CURRENT LIABILITIES}}$		
	2010	**2009**	**Comparison**
PotashCorp	1.3:1	0.4:1	Better
Agrium	0.2:1	0.5:1	Worse
Industry average	n/a	n/a	n/a

PotashCorp's cash provided by operating activities increased significantly, from U.S. $923.9 million in 2009 to U.S. $2,999 million in 2010. This represents an increase of 225%! Given the significant increase in profits and the resulting increase in cash provided by operating activities during the period, we would expect an increase in the cash current debt coverage. Thus the increase to 1.3:1 is not surprising.

PotashCorp's cash current debt coverage is significantly higher than Agrium's and increased in 2010 while Agrium's cash current debt coverage ratio decreased.

Receivables Turnover

We mentioned earlier that a high current ratio is not always a good indication of liquidity. The high result could be because of increased receivables resulting from uncollectible accounts. The ratio that is used to assess the liquidity of the receivables is the receivables turnover. It measures the number of times, on average, that receivables are collected during the period. The receivables turnover is calculated by dividing net credit sales (sales on account less sales returns and allowances and discounts) by average gross accounts receivable (before the allowance for doubtful accounts is deducted) during the year.

The 2010 and 2009 receivables turnover ratios for PotashCorp, Agrium, and the industry are shown below.

RECEIVABLES TURNOVER =	$\dfrac{\text{NET CREDIT SALES}}{\text{AVERAGE GROSS ACCOUNTS RECEIVABLE}}$		
	2010	**2009**	**Comparison**
PotashCorp	5.6 times	3.1 times	Better
Agrium	6.8 times	7.1 times	Worse
Industry average	6.4 times	6.5 times	Worse

Since companies do not normally disclose the proportion of their sales that were made for cash and for credit, we normally assume that all sales are credit sales. In addition, not all companies report gross and net accounts receivable separately. In such cases, it is appropriate to use net accounts receivable. The important thing is to be consistent in your input data to ensure that the resulting ratios are comparable.

PotashCorp's receivables turnover improved substantially in 2010, from 3.1 times to 5.6 times. PotashCorp states in its annual report that its goal is to become "the supplier of choice to high-volume, high margin customers with the lowest credit risk." While PotashCorp has improved its receivables turnover, it is still lower than both Agrium's and the industry average for 2010 despite the decline in both Agrium's and the industry's turnover ratios in 2010.

Average Collection Period.   A variant of the receivables turnover is calculated by converting it into a collection period stated in days. This is done by dividing 365 days by the receivables turnover. The 2010 and 2009 average collection period for PotashCorp, Agrium, and the industry are shown below.

AVERAGE COLLECTION PERIOD $= \dfrac{\text{365 DAYS}}{\text{RECEIVABLES TURNOVER}}$			
	2010	2009	Comparison
PotashCorp	65 days	118 days	Better
Agrium	54 days	51 days	Worse
Industry average	57 days	56 days	Worse

Analysts frequently use the average collection period to assess the effectiveness of a company's credit and collection policies. The general rule is that the collection period should not greatly exceed the credit period (i.e., the time allowed for payment). While we do not know PotashCorp's credit period, it appears to have been much better at collecting its accounts receivable in 2010 than in 2009.

Although PotashCorp's collection period has improved in 2010, it is still not quite as good as that of Agrium and of the industry.

Inventory Turnover

Slow-moving inventory can also distort the current ratio. The liquidity of a company's inventory is measured by the inventory turnover ratio. This ratio measures the number of times on average that the inventory is sold during the period, and is calculated by dividing the cost of goods sold by the average inventory.

The 2010 and 2009 inventory turnover ratios for PotashCorp, Agrium, and the industry are shown below.

INVENTORY TURNOVER $= \dfrac{\text{COST OF GOODS SOLD}}{\text{AVERAGE INVENTORY}}$			
	2010	2009	Comparison
PotashCorp	5.7 times	3.9 times	Better
Agrium	3.4 times	2.8 times	Better
Industry average	3.4 times	2.7 times	Better

PotashCorp's inventory turnover improved in 2010. PotashCorp's strategy is to match supply to demand to minimize excess inventory, something that is easier to do during a period of high demand, as was the case in 2010. Its inventory turnover is significantly better than both Agrium's and the industry average, both of which improved in 2010 but not by as much as that of PotashCorp. One explanation for PotashCorp's much higher inventory turnover than that of Agrium is that Agrium operates retail outlets, which require more stockpiling of inventory. PotashCorp does not operate any retail outlets.

Days in Inventory.   A variant of the inventory turnover ratio is days in inventory, which measures the average number of days it takes to sell the inventory. It is calculated by dividing 365 days by the inventory turnover.

The 2010 and 2009 days in inventory for PotashCorp, Agrium, and the industry are shown below.

DAYS IN INVENTORY $= \dfrac{365\ DAYS}{INVENTORY\ TURNOVER}$			
(in U.S. millions)	2010	2009	Comparison
PotashCorp	64 days	94 days	Better
Agrium	107 days	130 days	Better
Industry average	107 days	135 days	Better

PotashCorp's 64 days in inventory means that in 2010, on average, it took PotashCorp 64 days from the time raw materials were started in the production process until they were sold. This average is much better than that of Agrium and the industry. Generally, the faster inventory is sold, the less cash there is tied up in inventory and the less chance there is of inventory becoming obsolete.

It appears safe to conclude that PotashCorp's current ratio, even though it decreased, still indicates good liquidity, since we have learned through our analysis that both the receivables and inventory turnover ratios are strong and have contributed to increased operating cash flows and cash on hand.

It is worth noting here that the above interpretations are based not only on the financial data, but also on the knowledge gained from an understanding of PotashCorp and Agrium, their businesses, and their activities by reading their annual reports. As mentioned earlier in the chapter, non-financial information is important in interpreting the financial results.

Liquidity Conclusion

In an intracompany comparison, except for the current ratio, all of PotashCorp's liquidity ratios improved from 2009 to 2010, as would be expected given the general improvement in the overall economy. In an intercompany and industry comparison, all of PotashCorp's liquidity ratios, with the exception of the current, receivables turnover, and average collection period ratios, were better than both Agrium's and the industry average in 2010. In addition, PotashCorp also has access to an unused credit facility (operating line of credit), which gives it a source of additional liquidity if needed.

Summary of Liquidity Ratios

Illustration 14-13 summarizes the liquidity ratios we have used in this chapter, and throughout the textbook. We have included the chapter number where each ratio was discussed in detail for your review. In addition to the ratio formula and what it measures, the desired direction (higher or lower) of the ratio result is included.

▶Illustration 14-13
Liquidity ratios

Chapter	Ratio	Formula	What the Ratio Measures	Desired Result
2	Working capital	Current assets − Current liabilities	Short-term debt-paying ability	Higher
2	Current ratio	$\dfrac{\text{Current assets}}{\text{Current liabilities}}$	Short-term debt-paying ability	Higher
13	Cash current debt coverage	$\dfrac{\text{Net cash provided (used) by operating activities}}{\text{Average current liabilities}}$	Short-term debt-paying ability (cash basis)	Higher
8	Receivables turnover	$\dfrac{\text{Net credit sales}}{\text{Average gross accounts receivable}}$	Liquidity of receivables	Higher
8	Average collection period	$\dfrac{\text{365 days}}{\text{Receivables turnover}}$	Number of days receivables are outstanding	Lower
6	Inventory turnover	$\dfrac{\text{Cost of goods sold}}{\text{Average inventory}}$	Liquidity of inventory	Higher
6	Days in inventory	$\dfrac{\text{365 days}}{\text{Inventory turnover}}$	Number of days inventory is on hand	Lower

To summarize, a higher result is generally considered to be better for the working capital, current, cash current debt coverage, receivables turnover, and inventory turnover ratios. For those ratios that use turnover ratios in their denominators—the average collection period and days in inventory—a lower result is better. That is, you want to take fewer days to collect receivables and have fewer days of inventory on hand than the opposite situation.

Of course, there are exceptions. A current ratio can be high at times because of higher balances of receivables and inventory included in current assets that are the result of uncollectible receivables or slow-moving inventory. This is why it is important never to conclude an assessment of liquidity based only on one ratio. In the case of the current ratio, it should always be interpreted along with the receivables and inventory turnover ratios.

BEFORE YOU GO ON...

▶Do It! Liquidity Analysis

Liquidity ratios for two companies follow:

	Wasis Corporation	Rita Limited
Current ratio	1.6:1	1.9:1
Receivables turnover	27.0 times	22.6 times
Inventory turnover	6.8 times	5.6 times

(a) For each company, calculate the average collection period and days in inventory ratios.

(b) Identify whether Wasis or Rita has the "better" current ratio, receivables turnover ratio, average collection period, inventory turnover ratio, and days in inventory.

(c) Which company is more liquid? Explain.

Action Plan

• Review the formula for each ratio so you understand how it is calculated and how to interpret it.
• The current ratio should always be interpreted along with the receivables and inventory turnover ratios.
• Remember that for liquidity ratios, a higher result is usually better unless the current ratio has been artificially inflated by slow-moving receivables or inventory.

Solution

(a)

Wasis	Rita

Average collection period

$$\frac{365 \text{ days}}{27.0} = 14 \text{ days} \qquad \frac{365 \text{ days}}{22.6} = 16 \text{ days}$$

Days in inventory

$$\frac{365 \text{ days}}{6.8} = 54 \text{ days} \qquad \frac{365 \text{ days}}{5.6} = 65 \text{ days}$$

(b) Rita has the better (higher) current ratio, ignoring any potential inflation due to slow-moving receivables and inventory. Wasis has the better (higher) receivables and inventory turnover ratios. It also has the better (lower) average collection period and days in inventory ratios.

(c) Wasis is the more liquid of the two companies, as it collects its receivables and sells its inventory sooner than does Rita. This could help explain Rita's higher current ratio, although this is unlikely given the small differential between both companies' liquidity ratios. In addition, it is noteworthy that, even though Wasis has a better receivables turnover and average collection period than does Rita, both companies are collecting their receivables in a very timely fashion—far less than 30 days. It is safe to assume that neither company has a large proportion of receivables and they most likely sell their goods for cash more often than on account.

the navigator

SOLVENCY RATIOS

While liquidity ratios measure a company's ability to pay its current liabilities, solvency ratios measure the ability to pay total liabilities. The debt to total assets, times interest earned, and cash total debt coverage ratios give information about debt-paying ability. In addition, free cash flow gives information about the company's discretionary cash flow that is available to expand operations, go after new opportunities, or pay additional dividends, among other alternatives.

STUDY OBJECTIVE 5
Identify and calculate ratios that are used to analyze solvency.

Debt to Total Assets

The debt to total assets ratio measures the percentage of the total assets that is provided by creditors. It is calculated by dividing total liabilities (both current and non-current) by total assets. This ratio indicates the company's reliance on debt. The higher the percentage of debt to total assets, the greater the risk that the company may be unable to meet its maturing obligations. The lower the ratio, the more equity "buffer" there is for creditors if the company becomes insolvent. So, from the creditors' point of view, a low ratio of debt to total assets is good. However, if the ratio is too low, it may indicate that management is not trying to grow the business by obtaining financing from lenders.

The 2010 and 2009 debt to total assets ratios for PotashCorp, Agrium, and the industry are shown below.

DEBT TO TOTAL ASSETS = $\dfrac{\text{TOTAL LIABILITIES}}{\text{TOTAL ASSETS}}$			
	2010	2009	Comparison
PotashCorp	56.4%	50.2%	Worse
Agrium	58.0%	53.1%	Worse
Industry average	28.1%	26.5%	Worse

PotashCorp's debt to total assets ratio of 56.4% in 2010 means that creditors have provided financing to cover 56.4% of the company's total assets. The inverse means that shareholders have provided financing to cover 43.6% (100% − 56.4%) of the company's total assets.

PotashCorp's solvency, as measured by the debt to total assets ratio, deteriorated between 2009 and 2010, by increasing from 50.2% to 56.4%. According to Illustration 14-7, presented earlier in the chapter, total assets increased by 20.9% in 2010 and total liabilities increased by 36.0%. PotashCorp is financing its additional assets by adding debt during a period of relatively low interest rates. This means that the company is borrowing more money at a low interest rate and using those funds to grow the business when potash prices are rising. This is an effective financing strategy but it does increase risk.

PotashCorp's debt to total assets ratio is slightly better than Agrium's but much worse than the industry average. Note that the debt to total assets ratios of all three worsened slightly in 2010.

Another ratio with a similar meaning to the debt to total assets ratio is the debt to equity ratio. It shows the use of borrowed funds relative to the investments by shareholders. The debt to equity ratio is calculated by dividing total liabilities by total shareholders' equity. When the debt to total assets ratio equals 50%, the debt to equity ratio is 100% (because total liabilities plus shareholders' equity equals total assets).

Using this definition, PotashCorp's debt to equity ratio for 2010 is 129.6% (U.S. $8,815.1 million ÷ U.S. $6,804.2 million). This means that PotashCorp has financed its operations with 1.3 times as much debt as equity.

Times Interest Earned

While a company's debt level is important, its ability to service the debt—that is, pay the interest—is of equal or greater importance. The times interest earned ratio (also called interest coverage) indicates the company's ability to meet interest payments as they come due. It is calculated by dividing profit (earnings) before interest expense and income tax by interest expense. This is often abbreviated as EBIT, which stands for earnings before interest and tax. EBIT represents the amount that is available to cover interest.

The 2010 and 2009 times interest earned ratios for PotashCorp, Agrium, and the industry are shown below.

TIMES INTEREST EARNED = $\dfrac{\text{PROFIT + INTEREST EXPENSE + INCOME TAX EXPENSE (EBIT)}}{\text{INTEREST EXPENSE}}$			
	2010	2009	Comparison
PotashCorp	25.7 times	9.8 times	Better
Agrium	10.1 times	5.3 times	Better
Industry average	10.2 times	16.2 times	Worse

PotashCorp's 2010 times interest earned was 25.7 times. That is, its profit before interest and taxes was 25.7 times the amount needed for interest expense. PotashCorp's times interest earned ratio increased more than 2.5 times between 2009 to 2010. It is now much more than Agrium's times interest earned ratio of 10.1 times and the industry average of 10.2 times. PotashCorp's increase in corporate profit in 2010 had a significant impact on this ratio.

Times interest earned should always be interpreted along with the debt to total assets ratio. Even though PotashCorp's debt to total assets ratio deteriorated in 2010, because of the significant increase in its ability to handle the interest on this debt, its solvency would appear to be in good shape. It is interesting that, although the times interest earned ratio improved for both PotashCorp and Agrium, it declined for the industry at the same time as its debt to assets ratio also worsened.

Cash Total Debt Coverage

A cash-based equivalent to the debt to total assets ratio is the cash total debt coverage ratio. This ratio indicates a company's ability to repay its liabilities from cash provided by operating activities, without having to liquidate the assets used in its operations. It is calculated by dividing net cash provided (or used) by operating activities (from the statement of cash flows) by average total liabilities.

The 2010 and 2009 cash total debt coverage ratios for PotashCorp and Agrium are shown below.

CASH TOTAL DEBT COVERAGE =	NET CASH PROVIDED (USED) BY OPERATING ACTIVITIES / AVERAGE TOTAL LIABILITIES		
	2010	2009	Comparison
PotashCorp	0.4 times	0.2 times	Better
Agrium	0.1 times	0.3 times	Worse
Industry average	n/a	n/a	n/a

An industry ratio for this measure is not available, but PotashCorp's cash total debt coverage ratio doubled from 0.2 times in 2009 to 0.4 times in 2010. One way of interpreting the cash total debt coverage ratio is to say that cash provided by PotashCorp's 2010 operating activities would be enough to pay off 40% of its total liabilities. If 40% of liabilities were retired each year, it would take approximately two and a half more years to retire all debt. PotashCorp's cash total debt coverage ratio was higher than Agrium's 0.1 times in 2010, although it was lower in 2009.

PotashCorp's cash total debt coverage ratio improved in 2010, even though the debt to total assets ratio deteriorated. This is because of the significant increase in cash generated by operating activities in 2010 that was used to repurchase common shares rather than reducing debt.

Free Cash Flow

Another indication of a company's solvency is the amount of excess cash that it generates after investing to maintain its current productive capacity and after paying current dividends. This amount is referred to as free cash flow.

Free cash flow for 2010 and 2009 for PotashCorp and Agrium are shown below.

FREE CASH FLOW = NET CASH PROVIDED (USED) BY OPERATING ACTIVITIES − NET CAPITAL EXPENDITURES − DIVIDENDS PAID			
(in U.S. millions)	2010	2009	Comparison
PotashCorp	$903.0	$(957.9)	Better
Agrium	$117.0	$1,069.0	Worse
Industry average	n/a	n/a	n/a

PotashCorp's free cash flow improved considerably from 2009 to 2010. Cash provided by operating activities increased in 2010 by U.S. $2,075.1 million, which was the primary reason that free cash flow increased by U.S. $1,860.9 million ($903.0 + $957.9). This huge increase, discussed in the management discussion and analysis section of the company's annual report, was attributed to improved profitability.

PotashCorp's free cash flow was significantly higher than Agrium's U.S. $117 million. There is no amount available for the industry.

Solvency Conclusion

In an intracompany comparison, except for the debt to total assets ratio, all of PotashCorp's other solvency ratios improved in 2010. The increase in PotashCorp's times interest earned ratio, taken together with its debt to total assets ratio, leads to the conclusion that its overall solvency improved in 2010. On an intercompany comparison, all of Potashcorp's 2010 solvency ratios were far better than those of Agrium. On an industry comparison, although its debt to total assets ratio was not as good as the industry, its 2010 times interest earned ratio proved that it could handle the interest on its debt easily.

Summary of Solvency Ratios

Illustration 14-14 summarizes the solvency ratios discussed above, and throughout this textbook.

▶Illustration 14-14

Solvency ratios

Chapter	Ratio	Formula	What the Ratio Measures	Desired Result
2, 10	Debt to total assets	$\dfrac{\text{Total liabilities}}{\text{Total assets}}$	Percentage of total assets provided by creditors	Lower
10	Times interest earned	$\dfrac{\text{Profit} + \text{Interest expense} + \text{Income tax expense (EBIT)}}{\text{Interest expense}}$	Ability to meet interest payments	Higher
13	Cash total debt coverage	$\dfrac{\text{Net cash provided (used) by operating activities}}{\text{Average total liabilities}}$	Long-term debt-paying ability (cash basis)	Higher
13	Free cash flow	Net cash provided (used) by operating activities − Net capital expenditures − Dividends paid	Cash available from operating activities for discretionary purposes	Higher

For the debt to total assets ratio, a lower result is generally considered to be better. Having less debt reduces a company's dependence on debt financing and offers more flexibility for future financing alternatives. For times interest earned, cash total debt coverage, and free cash flow, a higher result is better.

It is important to interpret the debt to total assets and times interest earned ratios together. For example, a company may have a high debt to total assets ratio and a high times interest earned ratio, which indicates that it is able to handle a high level of debt. Or, it may have a low debt to total assets ratio and a low times interest earned ratio, indicating it has difficulty in paying its interest even for a low amount of debt. Consequently, one should always interpret a company's solvency after considering the interrelationship of these two ratios.

BEFORE YOU GO ON...

▼

▶Do It! Solvency Analysis

Selected information from the financial statement of the Home Affairs Corporation follows:

	2012	2011
Total assets	$1,000,000	$1,015,000
Total liabilities	737,700	809,000
Interest expense	59,000	40,500
Income tax expense	48,400	50,500
Profit	193,600	202,000

(a) For each company, calculate the debt to total assets and times interest earned ratios.

(b) Comment on whether Home Affairs' overall solvency has improved or deteriorated in 2012.

Action Plan

- Review the formula for each ratio so you understand how it is calculated and how to interpret it.
- The debt to total assets ratio should always be interpreted together with the times interest earned ratio.
- Remember that for debt to total assets, a lower result is better. For other solvency ratios, a higher result is better.

Solution

(a)

	2012	2011	Comparison
Debt to total assets	$\dfrac{\$737,700}{\$1,000,000} = 73.8\%$	$\dfrac{\$809,000}{\$1,015,000} = 79.7\%$	Better
Times interest earned	$\dfrac{\$193,600 + \$59,000 + \$48,400}{\$59,000}$ $= 5.1 \text{ times}$	$\dfrac{\$202,000 + \$40,500 + \$50,500}{\$40,500}$ $= 7.2 \text{ times}$	Worse

(b) Overall, solvency has deteriorated in 2012. While the debt to total assets ratio has improved in 2012, total liabilities are still a very high percentage of total assets. Of greater concern is the proportionally greater decline in the times interest earned ratio in 2012. The company is no longer able to handle its interest payments as well as in the past, even though it is still able to cover its interest payments 5.1 times. Taken together, this leads us to conclude that overall solvency has deteriorated.

the navigator

PROFITABILITY RATIOS

Profitability ratios measure the company's earnings or operating success for a specific period of time. For a company to have operating success, assets must be used to efficiently generate revenue and expenses must be effectively controlled. Consequently, profitability ratios focus mainly on the relationships between income statement items and statement of financial position items. Understanding these relationships can help management determine where to focus efforts on improving profitability.

Illustration 14-15 diagrams these relationships and will guide our discussion of PotashCorp's profitability. Profitability ratios include the return on common shareholders' equity, return on assets, profit margin, asset turnover, and gross profit margin ratios, as shown in Illustration 14-15.

STUDY OBJECTIVE 6
Identify and calculate ratios that are used to analyze profitability.

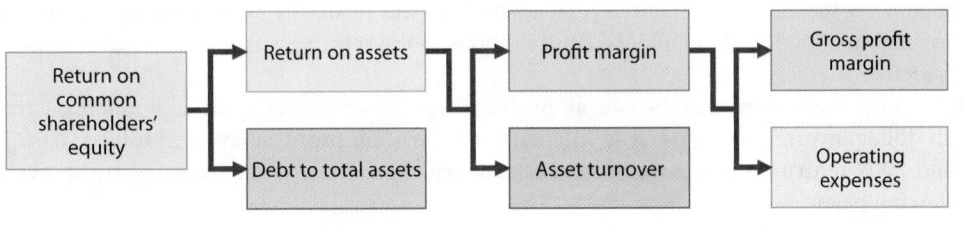

▶ Illustration 14-15
Relationship among profitability measures

As shown in the above illustration, the return on common shareholders' equity ratio is affected by the return on assets and debt to total assets ratios. If a company wants to increase its return on common shareholders' equity, it can either increase its return on assets or increase its reliance on debt financing. In fact, as long as the return on assets is higher than the interest rate paid on debt, the return on common shareholders' equity will always be increased by the use of debt.

The return on assets ratio is affected by the profit margin and asset turnover. If a company wants to increase its return on assets, it can do this by either increasing its operating efficiency (profit margin), or trying to increase its asset utilization (asset turnover).

And, of course, the profit margin is affected by the gross profit margin and the amount, or percentage, of operating expenses (assuming there are no other revenues and gains or other expenses and losses). If a company wants to increase its profit margin, it can increase its gross profit margin (by either raising selling prices or reducing its cost of goods sold), or reduce its operating expenses.

We will now look at each of these ratios in turn and examine their relationships. In addition, before we conclude this section, we will also review the earnings per share, price-earnings, payout, and dividend yield ratios.

Return on Common Shareholders' Equity

A widely used measure of profitability from the common shareholders' viewpoint is the return on common shareholders' equity. This ratio shows how many dollars of profit were earned for each dollar invested by the shareholders. It is calculated by dividing profit available to common shareholders (profit − preferred dividends) by average common shareholders' equity (total shareholders' equity − preferred shares).

The 2010 and 2009 return on common shareholders' equity ratios for PotashCorp, Agrium, and the industry are shown below.

RETURN ON COMMON SHAREHOLDERS' EQUITY = $\dfrac{\text{PROFIT} - \text{PREFERRED DIVIDENDS}}{\text{AVERAGE COMMON SHAREHOLDERS' EQUITY}}$			
	2010	2009	Comparison
PotashCorp	27.3%	17.8%	**Better**
Agrium	14.4%	8.4%	**Better**
Industry average	14.6%	26.9%	**Worse**

PotashCorp's return on common shareholders' equity increased significantly in 2010. It is better than both Agrium's and the industry average. It is interesting that PotashCorp and Agrium's returns improved in 2010 while those of their industry counterparts declined.

Return on Assets

The return on common shareholders' equity is affected by two factors: the return on assets ratio and the debt to total assets ratio. We looked earlier in this chapter at PotashCorp's debt to total assets ratio and noted an increase (deterioration) in this ratio. We will now look at the return on assets to determine if the increase in the debt to total assets ratio was primarily responsible for the increase in the return on common shareholders' equity ratio or if the return on assets ratio was responsible for this increase.

Return on assets measures the overall profitability of assets in terms of how much is earned on each dollar invested in assets. It is calculated by dividing profit by average total assets. The 2010 and 2009 return on assets ratios for PotashCorp, Agrium, and the industry are shown on the following page.

RETURN ON ASSETS $= \dfrac{\text{PROFIT}}{\text{AVERAGE TOTAL ASSETS}}$			
	2010	2009	Comparison
PotashCorp	12.7%	8.5%	Better
Agrium	6.3%	3.7%	Better
Industry average	7.6%	15.1%	Worse

PotashCorp's return on assets of 12.7% in 2010 is higher than its return of 8.5% in 2009. This change is once again influenced by the increase in profit. Its return on assets is higher than both Agrium's and the industry average in 2010. Once again, we see that PotashCorp's and Agrium's returns increased in 2010 at a time when the industry's decreased.

Note that PotashCorp's 2010 rate of return on common shareholders' equity (27.3%) is much higher than its rate of return on assets (12.7%). The reason is that PotashCorp has made effective use of leverage. **Leveraging or trading on the equity** means that the company has borrowed money at a lower rate of interest than the rate of return it earns on the assets it purchased with the borrowed funds. Leverage enables management to use money supplied by non-shareholders (non-owners) to increase the return to shareholders.

Profit Margin

The profit margin is one of two factors that affect the return on assets. The other factor is asset turnover, which we will look at immediately following this section. The profit margin measures the percentage of profit that each dollar of sales produces. It is calculated by dividing profit by net sales for the period.

The 2010 and 2009 profit margin ratios for PotashCorp, Agrium, and the industry are shown below.

PROFIT MARGIN $= \dfrac{\text{PROFIT}}{\text{NET SALES}}$			
	2010	2009	Comparison
PotashCorp	29.8%	26.8%	Better
Agrium	6.8%	4.0%	Better
Industry average	11.8%	19.7%	Worse

PotashCorp reported a 29.8% profit margin in 2010. This profit margin was of course greater than that of 2009, given the increase in profit between the two years. It also exceeded Agrium's and the industry average by a considerable amount. As we saw with other profitability ratios, the industry average declined while PotashCorp and Agrium's profit margin improved.

Asset Turnover

The asset turnover ratio measures how efficiently a company uses its assets to generate sales. It is calculated by dividing net sales by average total assets for the period. The resulting number shows the dollars of sales produced by each dollar invested in assets.

The 2010 and 2009 asset turnover ratios for PotashCorp, Agrium, and the industry are shown below.

ASSET TURNOVER $= \dfrac{\text{NET SALES}}{\text{AVERAGE TOTAL ASSETS}}$			
	2010	2009	Comparison
PotashCorp	0.4 times	0.3 times	Better
Agrium	0.9 times	0.9 times	No change
Industry average	0.7 times	0.8 times	Worse

The asset turnover ratio shows that PotashCorp generated $0.40 of sales in 2010 for each dollar it had invested in assets. The asset turnover was up slightly from 2009; however, it is lower than Agrium's and that of the industry. While PotashCorp's asset turnover improved in 2010, Agrium's remained unchanged, and the industry's deteriorated.

From the analysis in this and the previous section, we can see that the significant driver of PotashCorp's return on assets was its profit margin, which improved far more than did its asset turnover.

Gross Profit Margin

We saw above that the profit margin increased in 2010 from 26.8% to 29.8%. Two factors influence the profit margin: one is the gross profit margin, the other is the company's ability to control its operating expenses.

The gross profit margin is calculated by dividing gross profit (net sales less cost of goods sold) by net sales. This ratio indicates a company's ability to maintain an adequate selling price above its cost of goods sold. The 2010 and 2009 gross profit margin ratios for PotashCorp, Agrium, and the industry are shown below.

GROSS PROFIT MARGIN $= \dfrac{\text{GROSS PROFIT}}{\text{NET SALES}}$			
	2010	2009	Comparison
PotashCorp	43.4%	27.7%	Better
Agrium	25.2%	21.3%	Better
Industry average	37.4%	41.4%	Worse

PotashCorp's gross profit margin increased from 27.7% in 2009 to 43.4% in 2010. This gross profit margin is higher than Agrium's 25.2% and the industry average of 37.4%.

There were several reasons for the increased gross profit in 2010 for PotashCorp. First, there was a significant increase in sales revenue. Second, while the cost of goods sold increased on an absolute dollar basis, it declined as a vertical percentage of net sales, as we saw in Illustration 14-11.

PotashCorp's increase in its gross profit margin was a significant factor that contributed to the increase in its profit margin. The other factor affecting the profit margin is operating expenses. In 2010, PotashCorp had 43.4% of each dollar of sales remaining to cover its operating and non-operating expenses and generate a profit.

The company was reasonably effective in controlling its operating expenses in 2010. As shown in Illustration 14-8, selling and administrative expenses increased by 24.2%, which was far less than the percentage increase in sales. The gross profit margin less the operating expenses resulted in an increase in profit from operations of 115.8% for 2010.

The ratios we just reviewed—return on common shareholders' equity, return on assets, profit margin, asset turnover, and gross profit margin—focus on the company's profitability and the interrelationships among the various profitability measures. The next four ratios—earnings per share, price-earnings, payout ratio, and dividend yield—are of more interest to investors analyzing the prospects of a publicly traded company's shares.

Earnings per Share

Earnings per share is a measure of the profit realized on each common share. It is calculated by dividing profit available to common shareholders (profit − preferred dividends) by the weighted average number of common shares. Earnings per share is widely used by current and potential investors. It is the only ratio that must be presented on the income statement or statement of comprehensive income by companies following IFRS. As we mentioned earlier in this text, earnings per share is not required to be reported by companies following ASPE.

ASPE

Earnings per share for 2010 and 2009 for PotashCorp, Agrium, and the industry are shown below.

EARNINGS PER SHARE $= \dfrac{\text{PROFIT} - \text{PREFERRED DIVIDENDS}}{\text{WEIGHTED AVERAGE NUMBER OF COMMON SHARES}}$			
(in U.S. $)	2010	2009	Comparison
PotashCorp	$2.04	$1.11	Better
Agrium	$4.53	$2.33	Better
Industry average	n/a	n/a	n/a

Note that no industry average is included above. Comparisons with the industry average, or with Agrium's earnings per share, are not meaningful, because of the different financing structures (e.g., debt or equity) used by different companies, as well as the wide variations in numbers of shares issued by companies. The only meaningful earnings per share comparison is an intracompany one. PotashCorp's earnings per share increased significantly, from $1.11 in 2009 to $2.04 in 2010, as did Agrium's.

Price-Earnings (P-E) Ratio

The price-earnings ratio is an often-quoted statistic that measures the ratio of the market price of each common share to the earnings per share. It is commonly known as a market measure because it uses a company's share price, which reflects the stock market's (investors') expectations for the company.

The 2010 and 2009 price-earnings ratios for PotashCorp, Agrium, and the industry are shown below.

PRICE-EARNINGS $= \dfrac{\text{MARKET PRICE PER SHARE}}{\text{EARNINGS PER SHARE}}$			
	2010	2009	Comparison
PotashCorp	75.7 times	102.6 times	Worse
Agrium	20.3 times	26.4 times	Worse
Industry average	29.2 times	13.6 times	Better

At the end of 2010, each PotashCorp common share sold for 75.7 times the amount of profit that was earned by each share. In 2009, each share sold for 102.6 times profit. In general, a higher price-earnings ratio means investors favour the company. They are willing to pay more for the shares because they believe the company has good prospects for growth and profit in the future.

Why did PotashCorp's price-earnings ratio drop so significantly in 2010? Recall that its earnings per share nearly doubled in 2010. This alone, with a constant share price, would cause the price-earnings ratio to drop by nearly half. In PotashCorp's case, its share price increased about 36% while its earnings per share increased about 84%. These combined to result in the decline in the price-earnings ratio. Note that PotashCorp's price-earnings ratio is still much higher than both Agrium's and the industry average.

Some investors carefully study price-earnings ratios over time to help them determine when to buy or sell shares. If the highs and lows of a particular share's price-earnings ratio remain constant over several operating cycles, then these highs and lows can indicate selling and buying points for the shares. They could also mean other things, however, including that the share is over- or under-priced. Investors should be very cautious in interpreting price-earnings ratios.

ACCOUNTING MATTERS!   *Investor Perspective*

Netflix on a Roll

Netflix, Inc., a popular Internet movie and television service, expected its profit to grow 33% in 2011. Its share price skyrocketed to more than U.S. $200 in early 2011, up four times from what it was worth a year before. High future expectations have translated into a high price-earnings ratio for Netflix: 78 times at the end of 2010. Its P-E ratio was much higher than those of Apple and Google, both of which were building on-line entertainment delivery services themselves. "There is no denying that Netflix is on a roll, with accelerating subscriber growth coupled with declining cost of customer acquisition," noted Steve Frankel, an analyst with Dougherty & Co. However, he worried that the high price-to-earnings valuation left no room for error as the company faced increased competition and challenges.

Source: Simon Avery, "Netflix Sky-High Valuation Leaves No Room for Error," *The Globe and Mail*, December 1, 2010, page B16.

Payout Ratio

The payout ratio measures the percentage of profit that is distributed as cash dividends. It is calculated by dividing cash dividends by profit. Companies that have high growth rates usually have low payout ratios because they reinvest most of their profit back into the company.

The 2010 and 2009 payout ratios for PotashCorp, Agrium, and the industry are shown below.

$$\text{PAYOUT RATIO} = \frac{\text{CASH DIVIDENDS}}{\text{PROFIT}}$$			
	2010	2009	Comparison
PotashCorp	6.5%	12.0%	Worse
Agrium	2.4%	4.6%	Worse
Industry average	11.9%	n/a	n/a

With a relatively constant dividend and an increase in profit, PotashCorp could be expected to experience a declining payout ratio. PotashCorp's payout ratio did reduce to 6.5% in 2010. Its payout ratio was significantly higher than Agrium's; however, it is less than the industry average. Corporate directors have control over the amount of dividends paid each year, and are generally reluctant to reduce a dividend below the amount paid in a previous year. Therefore, the payout ratio will actually decrease if a company's profit increases but the company keeps its total dividend payment the same or more. PotashCorp has historically paid quarterly dividends, and it held these dividends constant over the last two years.

Dividend Yield

The dividend yield supplements the payout ratio. The dividend yield reports the rate of return a shareholder earned from dividends during the year. It is calculated by dividing the dividend per share by the market price per share. Similar to the price-earnings ratio, this ratio is also known as a market measure, because of the use of the stock market price in its calculation.

The dividend yields for 2010 and 2009 for PotashCorp, Agrium, and the industry are shown below.

$$\text{DIVIDEND YIELD} = \frac{\text{DIVIDEND PER SHARE}}{\text{MARKET PRICE PER SHARE}}$$			
(in U.S. millions)	2010	2009	Comparison
PotashCorp	0.1%	0.1%	No change
Agrium	0.1%	0.2%	Worse
Industry average	1.5%	1.3%	Better

PotashCorp's dividend yield remained relatively unchanged in 2010. PotashCorp's dividend yield was the same as Agrium's in 2010, both of which were significantly below that of the industry. As with the payout ratio, companies that are expanding rapidly can be expected to have lower dividend yields as shareholders are often looking for growth in the share value.

Profitability Conclusion

In an intracompany comparison, PotashCorp's profitability measures have all improved from 2009 to 2010, with two exceptions: its price-earnings and payout ratios declined. When profits rise faster than share prices and dividend payments, these ratios will decline.

In an intercompany comparison, PotashCorp's profitability exceeds that of Agrium and the industry in 2010, except for three ratios: asset turnover, payout, and dividend yield. PotashCorp's asset turnover ratio is lower than both Agrium's and the industry's. Its payout ratio and dividend yield, while better than or the same as those of Agrium, are lower than those of the industry.

Based on the price-earnings ratio, investors appear to be favouring PotashCorp over Agrium, likely because of its improved profitability and anticipated future growth. Both companies would likely be purchased by investors for capital appreciation (future profitable resale as the share price increases) rather than for the dividend income.

Summary of Profitability Ratios

Illustration 14-16 summarizes the profitability ratios discussed above, and throughout this textbook.

▶ Illustration 14-16
Profitability ratios

Chapter	Ratio	Formula	What the Ratio Measures	Desired Result
11	Return on common share-holders' equity	$\dfrac{\text{Profit} - \text{Preferred dividends}}{\text{Average common shareholders' equity}}$	Profitability of share-holders' investment	Higher
9	Return on assets	$\dfrac{\text{Profit}}{\text{Average total assets}}$	Overall profitability of assets	Higher
5	Profit margin	$\dfrac{\text{Profit}}{\text{Net sales}}$	Profit generated by each dollar of sales	Higher
9	Asset turnover	$\dfrac{\text{Net sales}}{\text{Average total assets}}$	How efficiently assets are used to generate sales	Higher
5	Gross profit margin	$\dfrac{\text{Gross profit}}{\text{Net sales}}$	Margin between selling price and cost of goods sold	Higher
2, 11	Earnings per share	$\dfrac{\text{Profit} - \text{Preferred dividends}}{\text{Weighted average number of common shares}}$	Profit earned on each common share	Higher
2	Price-earnings ratio	$\dfrac{\text{Market price per share}}{\text{Earnings per share}}$	Relationship between market price per share and earnings per share	Higher
11	Payout ratio	$\dfrac{\text{Cash dividends}}{\text{Profit}}$	Percentage of profit distributed as cash dividends	Higher
11	Dividend yield	$\dfrac{\text{Dividend per share}}{\text{Market price per share}}$	Income generated for the shareholder by each share, based on the market price per share	Higher

For the profitability ratios shown above, a higher result is generally considered to be better. However, there are some user-related considerations with respect to the price-earnings and pay-out ratios that must be understood. A higher price-earnings ratio generally means that investors favour that company and have high expectations of future profitability. However, some investors avoid shares with high P-E ratios in the belief that they are overpriced, so not everyone prefers a high P-E ratio.

Investors interested in purchasing a company's shares for income purposes (in the form of a dividend) are interested in companies with a high payout ratio. Investors more interested in pur-chasing a company's shares for growth purposes (for the share price's appreciation) are interested in a low payout ratio. They would prefer to see the company retain its profit rather than pay it out.

This ends our comprehensive analysis illustration using PotashCorp. What can be practically covered in a textbook shows only the tip of the iceberg when it comes to the types of financial infor-mation available and the ratios that are used by various industries. The availability of information is not a problem. The real challenge is to be discriminating enough to choose pertinent data for comparisons and do relevant analyses.

We have shown liquidity, solvency, and profitability ratios in separate sections above. However, it is important to recognize that analysis should not focus on one section in isolation of the others. Liquidity, solvency, and profitability are closely interrelated in most companies. For example, a com-pany's profitability is affected by the availability of financing and its liquidity. Similarly, a company's solvency not only requires satisfactory liquidity but is also affected by its profitability.

It is also important to recognize that the ratios shown in Illustrations 14-13, 14-14, and 14-16 are only examples of commonly used ratios. There are many different and additional ratios and groupings that financial analysts use. Users should therefore determine which ratios best suit the decisions they need to make.

Finally, it is important to remember that ratios give clues about underlying conditions that may not be seen from an inspection of the individual components of a particular ratio. But a single ratio by itself is not very meaningful. Accordingly, ratios must be interpreted alongside information that has been gained from a detailed review of the financial information, including horizontal and verti-cal analyses, as well as relevant non-financial information.

BEFORE YOU GO ON...

▶ **Do It! Profitability Analysis**

Selected information from the financial statements of two companies competing in the same industry follows:

	De Marchi Corporation	Bear Limited
Total assets, beginning of year	$388,000	$372,000
Total assets, end of year	434,000	536,000
Total liabilities, beginning of year	119,000	76,000
Total liabilities, end of year	97,000	135,000
Total common shareholders' equity, beginning of year	269,000	296,000
Total common shareholders' equity, end of year	337,000	401,000
Net sales	660,000	780,000
Gross profit	175,000	248,000
Profit	68,000	105,000

(a) For each company, calculate the following ratios: return on common shareholders' equity, return on assets, debt to total assets, profit margin, asset turnover, and gross profit margin.

(b) Which company is more profitable? Explain.

(c) What is the key driver of Bear Limited's return on common shareholders' equity ratio, when compared with that of De Marchi Corporation?

Action Plan

- Review the formula for each ratio so you understand how it is calculated and how to interpret it.
- Remember that for profitability ratios, a higher result is usually better.
- Recall that the return on assets and debt to total assets ratios combine to explain the return on common shareholders' equity ratio. The profit margin and the asset turnover ratios combine to explain the return on assets ratio.

Solution

(a)

	De Marchi	Bear

Return on common shareholders' equity

$$\frac{\$68,000}{(\$269,000 + \$337,000) \div 2} = 22.4\% \qquad \frac{\$105,000}{(\$296,000 + \$401,000) \div 2} = 30.1\%$$

Return on assets

$$\frac{\$68,000}{(\$388,000 + \$434,000) \div 2} = 16.5\% \qquad \frac{\$105,000}{(\$372,000 + \$536,000) \div 2} = 23.1\%$$

Debt to total assets $\dfrac{\$97,000}{\$434,000} = 22.4\%$ $\qquad \dfrac{\$135,000}{\$536,000} = 25.2\%$

Profit margin $\dfrac{\$68,000}{\$660,000} = 10.3\%$ $\qquad \dfrac{\$105,000}{\$780,000} = 13.5\%$

Asset turnover

$$\frac{\$660,000}{(\$388,000 + \$434,000) \div 2} = 1.6 \text{ times} \qquad \frac{\$780,000}{(\$372,000 + \$536,000) \div 2} = 1.7 \text{ times}$$

Gross profit margin $\dfrac{\$175,000}{\$660,000} = 26.5\%$ $\qquad \dfrac{\$248,000}{\$780,000} = 31.8\%$

(b) Bear is more profitable than De Marchi on all profitability ratios.

(continued)

(c) Bear has the higher return on common shareholders' equity ratio, primarily because of its higher return on assets ratio as there is not a large difference between the two companies' debt to total assets ratios. The factor most influencing the higher return on assets ratio is the profit margin. Bear has the higher profit margin of the two companies, much higher than its asset turnover. Drilling down, this particular ratio—profit margin—is the key driver of Bear's significantly higher return on common shareholders' equity ratio.

Limitations of Financial Analysis

STUDY OBJECTIVE 7

Understand the limitations of financial analysis.

Before relying on the information you have gathered through your horizontal, vertical, and ratio analyses, you must understand the limitations of these tools and of the financial statements they are based on. Some of the factors that can limit the usefulness of your analysis include alternative accounting policies, professional judgement, comprehensive income, diversification, inflation, and economic factors.

ALTERNATIVE ACCOUNTING POLICIES

Variations among companies in their use of generally accepted accounting principles may lessen the comparability of their statements. Companies may choose from a large number of acceptable accounting policies, such as different inventory cost formulas (FIFO or average) or depreciation methods (straight-line, diminishing-balance, or units-of-production). Different choices can result in differing financial positions, which again affect how easily their results can be compared.

For example, PotashCorp uses two depreciation methods to allocate the cost of different components of its property, plant, and equipment: straight-line and units-of-production. Agrium uses the straight-line method for all of its property, plant, and equipment. You can therefore expect to have variations in the carrying amounts of property, plant, and equipment on the statement of financial position and in depreciation expense and profit on the income statement just because of these differing choices. That is, they result in ratio numbers whose comparative increase or decrease may be attributable solely to an accounting policy choice. Note that although depreciation may be different because of the choice of accounting policy, this is really just an "artificial," or timing, difference. Although there may be differences year by year, in total, over the life of the asset, there is no difference.

In more and more industries, competition is global and this too can present a challenge. For example, although both PotashCorp and Agrium are Canadian, other competitors include Yara International of Norway and the Mosaic Company in the United States. The United States uses a different set of accounting standards than do Canadian publicly traded companies like PotashCorp and Agrium. And what if we wanted to compare PotashCorp and Agrium to a private company using ASPE rather than IFRS? Although differences in accounting policies might be detectable from reading the notes to the financial statements, adjusting the financial data to compensate for the different policies is difficult, if not impossible, in some cases.

 ACCOUNTING MATTERS!   *Investor Perspective*

How Comparable Are IFRS Financial Statements?

The conversion to IFRS by Canadian companies was driven by the long-run objective of enhancing global comparability of financial statements. But in the short run, a number of differences arose from the conversion process itself. For example, there were a number of optional exemptions available to companies to assist in the conversion process. Some companies in the same industry chose different combinations of exemptions. This resulted in a significant variation in the measurement of selected opening balances of those companies.

CGA-Canada warned that "comparability of ratios based on IFRS figures with those based on pre-changeover Canadian GAAP may naturally be impaired and the trend analysis misleading," in its report, *The Effects of IFRS on Financial Ratios: Early Evidence in Canada*. The report also discussed increased volatility that arises when a company uses fair value accounting. Incremental adjustments to certain accounts for fair value changes can significantly impact the comparability of ratios within a company as well as an industry.

Source: Michel Blanchette, François-Érik Racicot, and Jean-Yves Girard, *The Effects of IFRS on Financial Ratios: Early Evidence in Canada*, Certified General Accountants (CGA) Association of Canada, 2011.

PROFESSIONAL JUDGEMENT

We must accept that management has to use professional judgement in choosing the most appropriate accounting policy for the circumstances. Because judgement is required, management's choices may be biased in favour of a presentation that furthers certain company objectives. In addition, many estimates are required in preparing financial information. Estimates are used, for example, in determining the allowance for uncollectible receivables, estimated useful lives and residual values for depreciation, and fair values of certain investment securities and properties. To the extent that these estimates are inaccurate or biased, ratios and percentages that are based on such information will also be inaccurate or biased.

To help ensure that the quality of information is as high as possible, audit committees are held responsible for quizzing management on the degree of aggressiveness or conservatism that has been applied and on the quality of underlying accounting policies, estimates, and judgements. In addition, CEOs and CFOs of Canadian public companies are required to certify that the financial statements, together with other financial information, "present fairly" and do not misrepresent in all material respects the company's financial condition, financial performance, and cash flows.

COMPREHENSIVE INCOME

Most financial ratios exclude total comprehensive income, or other comprehensive income, from the analysis. Profitability ratios, including industry averages, generally use data from the income statement and not from the statement of comprehensive income, which includes both profit and other comprehensive income. In addition, there are no standard ratio formulas incorporating comprehensive income.

Nonetheless, it is important to review a company's sources of comprehensive income in any financial analysis. For example, PotashCorp reported a profit of U.S. $1,806.2 million for the year ended December 31, 2010. During the same year, it reported other comprehensive income of U.S. $595.5 million, which resulted in total comprehensive income of U.S. $2,401.7 million ($1,806.2 + $595.5). PotashCorp's profit margin in 2010 was 29.8%. However, if a profit margin were calculated using total comprehensive income rather than just profit, it would have been 39.7% ($2,401.7 ÷ $6,051.0) instead of 29.8% ($1,806.2 ÷ $6,051.0).

In cases like this, where other comprehensive income is significant, and depending on the source of the income, some analysts will adjust profitability ratios to incorporate the effect of total comprehensive income. Of course, you will recall from past chapters that private companies following ASPE do not report comprehensive income so this limitation would apply only to private and public companies following IFRS.

ASPE

DIVERSIFICATION

Diversification in Canadian industry can also limit the usefulness of financial analysis. Many companies today are so diversified that they cannot be classified by industry. Canadian Tire, for example, sells selected grocery, home, car, clothing, sports, and leisure products. In addition, it is the country's largest independent gasoline retailer. Consequently, deciding what industry a company like Canadian Tire is in can actually be one of the main challenges to an effective evaluation of its results.

Other companies may appear to be comparable but are not. McCain Foods and Irving-owned Cavendish Farms compete in the frozen potato product field. Yet McCain produces other food products besides french fries, and Irving has many other interests, including oil, newspapers, tissue products, transportation, and shipbuilding.

Because of this diversification, analysts must be careful in interpreting consolidated financial statements. You will recall that we learned about consolidated financial statements in Chapter 12. Consolidated statements include financial information about the parent company and each of its subsidiaries. The parent company may have a strong debt to total assets ratio, and the subsidiary a weak one. However, because these statements are consolidated, the combined results may show that the debt to total assets ratio is close to the industry average. The fact that the subsidiary may have solvency problems is hidden from the general public because of the consolidated reporting of the financial information. Of course, such a situation would not be hidden from management as it has access to the individual statements of each subsidiary company even though the general public does not.

When companies have significant operations in different lines of business, they are required to report additional disclosures in a segmented information note to their financial statements. IFRS has specific revenue, profit, and asset tests to determine if a company is required to report segmented information or not (you will learn more about this in an intermediate accounting course). If a company has reportable segments, it must disclose relevant information about revenues, operating income, and/or identifiable assets by products and services, by geographic area, and by major customer.

ASPE Note that segments are not as common in private companies as they are in large public companies and consequently there are no requirements for the disclosure of segments in ASPE.

INFLATION

Our accounting information system does not adjust data for price-level changes. For example, a five-year comparison of PotashCorp's net sales shows growth of 179.2%. But this growth trend would be misleading if the general price level had increased or decreased greatly during the same period. In actuality, inflation was 9.4% during this same period, so while PotashCorp's sales have indeed increased, they have not increased as much as it first appears. Still, our comparisons are relevant because data that have not been adjusted for inflation are being used consistently for both revenues and expenses, and for each period.

In Canada, inflation was not very significant at the time of writing. In the 1990s and 2000s, Canada's inflation rate was quite low, averaging 2%. In the early 1980s, by comparison, the inflation rate exceeded 10%. Today, the Bank of Canada tries to maintain an inflation rate within the 1% to 3% range.

ECONOMIC FACTORS

We cannot properly interpret a financial analysis without also considering the economic circumstances in which a company operates. Economic measures such as the rate of interest, unemployment, and changes in demand and supply can have a significant impact on a company's performance.

For example, as we noted earlier in this chapter, much of the industrialized world entered into a global recession in late 2008 and 2009. During times like an economic recession, horizontal analyses and ratios compared across years lose much of their relevance. When losses result in negative numbers, it is difficult to calculate percentages and ratios, much less interpret them. Vertical analyses become more useful in such times. If a company has losses, they must be assessed based on the factors driving the loss in the current period. Less attention should be paid to comparing the losses with results from prior periods.

One must use this information, along with non-financial information, to try to assess what changes relate to the economic situation and what changes relate to factors that management can, or should be able to, control. For example, have operating expenses increased faster than revenues? Why? Are consumers not spending? Are prices too high? Have expenses not been adequately controlled or adjusted for the current marketplace? Particular attention must be paid to the company's results compared with those of its competitors and the entire industry.

DECISION TOOLKIT

Decision Checkpoints	**Info Needed for Decision**	**Tools to Use for Decision**	**How to Evaluate Results**
Does the company report other comprehensive income?	Statement of income and comprehensive income	Determine source and amount of other comprehensive income	If other comprehensive income is significant, selected profitability ratios should be recalculated using total comprehensive income rather than profit.
Are efforts to evaluate the company hampered by alternative accounting policies, professional judgement, diversification, inflation, and economic factors?	Financial statements as well as other information that is disclosed	Review accounting policies and estimates for comparability and reasonableness. Assess the strength of corporate governance processes. Review segmented information. Check that inflation is in a reasonable range. Understand significant economic factors.	If there are any comparability issues or irregularities, the analysis should be relied on with caution.

BEFORE YOU GO ON...

▶ Do It! Other Comprehensive Income

HSBC Bank Canada reported the following selected information (in millions) for the year ended December 31, 2010:

Average total assets	$71,416
Total revenue	2,493
Profit	490
Other comprehensive income (loss)	(11)
Total comprehensive income	479

(a) Calculate the return on assets and profit margin ratios using (1) profit as the numerator, and (2) total comprehensive income as the numerator.

(b) Do you think other comprehensive income is a significant factor in the analysis of HSBC Bank's profitability?

Action Plan

- Recall the formula for return on assets: Profit ÷ Average total assets. Substitute total comprehensive income instead of profit to determine the impact of other comprehensive income on profitability.
- Recall the formula for profit margin: Profit ÷ Net sales. Substitute total comprehensive income instead of profit to determine the impact of other comprehensive income on profitability.
- To determine the significance of other comprehensive income, compare the ratios with and without other comprehensive income and assess whether the change in the ratio is significant enough to affect decision-making.

Solution

(a) ($ in millions)

	(1)	(2)
Return on assets	$\dfrac{\$490}{\$71,416} = 0.7\%$	$\dfrac{\$479}{\$71,416} = 0.7\%$
Profit margin	$\dfrac{\$490}{\$2,493} = 19.7\%$	$\dfrac{\$479}{\$2,493} = 19.2\%$

(b) The inclusion of other comprehensive income in the calculation of the profitability ratios is not significant enough to make a difference in a user's decision-making.

the navigator

comparing
IFRS and ASPE

Key Differences	International Financial Reporting Standards (IFRS)	Accounting Standards for Private Enterprises (ASPE)
Change in accounting policy	The cumulative effect of a change in accounting policy is reported retrospectively as an adjustment to opening retained earnings in the statement of changes of equity.	The cumulative effect of a change in accounting policy is reported retrospectively as an adjustment to opening retained earnings in the statement of retained earnings.
Earnings per share	Must be reported on the face of the income statement or statement of comprehensive income.	Earnings per share is not required to be reported.
Comprehensive income	If other comprehensive income is significant, selected profitability ratios should be recalculated using total comprehensive income rather than profit.	Comprehensive income is not reported.
Segmented reporting	There are specific revenue, profit, and asset tests to determine if information must be reported in the notes to the financial statements for segments.	There are no disclosure requirements for reporting segment information.

the navigator

Should I Invest in the Stock Market?

As you have seen throughout this textbook, both individuals and companies use ratios to help them make decisions about investing in the stock market. Some of the ratios they use to make decisions include the earnings per share, price-earnings, payout, and dividend yield ratios. The motive for investing can be either to have a steady source of income through dividends or to have the possibility of the investment appreciating in value over time as the share price rises.

Financial planners recommend that, before you make personal investments in the stock market, you first ensure that you are in control of your personal finances by not spending more money than you are making and eliminating any student loan and credit card debt. Personal financial planning goals will help you set your priorities.

The type of savings or investment vehicle to use will likely vary according to your age and family situation, income, savings goals, and other factors. In addition, you should try to take advantage of any tax-free savings opportunities by holding investments within a Tax Free Savings Account (TFSA) or Registered Retirement Savings Plan (RRSP), whenever possible.

If you decide that now is the time to invest in the market, how do you start? Most investors start by buying units of a mutual fund or they purchase units in an exchange-traded fund (ETF), rather than purchasing shares of an individual company. Both of these investment vehicles will help diversify the risk for an individual investor.

In a mutual fund, the investors' monies are pooled together and a manager selects the investments and manages the pooled funds on behalf of individual investors. The value of the fund is determined by the value of the investments held in the fund at the end of each day. Each mutual fund holds different investments and you must select the fund with the objectives that best fit your financial goals.

Similar to a mutual fund, an ETF holds a basket of shares. However, there is no selection process; it simply mirrors a particular market index. The share holdings are not actively managed. The advantage of an ETF is that the fund generally charges lower fees to invest your money.

Some Facts

- During February 2011, an average of 488 million shares, valued at $7 billion, were traded daily, in over 850,000 transactions on the TSX.
- Canadians had invested over $658 billion in mutual funds at the end of the 2011 RRSP season. The most popularly held mutual funds were in the broad categories of equity funds (38% of net assets invested), balanced funds (43%), and bond funds (13%).
- According to the 2010 financial reports of the five major Canadian banks, Canadians held a total of over $750 billion in chequing accounts, savings accounts, guaranteed investment certificates (GICs), and other savings instruments.
- ETFs are gaining in popularity with Canadian investors. The first ETF was launched in 1989 with a fund that tracked the TSE 35 and later the TSE 100 indices. In September 2010, there were over 150 ETFs listed on the TSX with $35 billion of assets under management.

What Do You Think?

Your grandparents have given you $50,000 to put toward your post-secondary education. You would like to invest the $50,000 in a dividend income fund. Is this a good idea?

YES A dividend income fund will likely include shares with high payout and dividend yield ratios, so you will earn a regular income. If you choose a fund with a good track record, it won't matter if the price fluctuates: you will still make money because of the dividend income and the unit value may even increase over time.

NO Just because a company within a fund declared dividends in the past, that does not guarantee dividends will be distributed at the same rate in the future. There is also a risk that the unit value may decline. If loss of capital is an issue, you may want to consider a less risky investment such as a GIC.

Sources: TMX Group, "Consolidated Trading Statistics, February 2011," and "Equity Financing Statistics, December 2010," www.tmx.com, accessed March 17, 2011. Investment Funds Institute of Canada, "Highlights for February 2011," www.ifac.ca, accessed March 17, 2011. Bank of Montreal, "History of ETFs," www.bmo.com, accessed March 17, 2011.

Summary of Study Objectives

1. **Understand the concept of sustainable income and indicate how irregular items are presented.** Sustainable income is the level of profit likely to be obtained in the future. It excludes irregular revenues and expenses that may be included in profit.

   Irregular items are presented separately from continuing operations to highlight their infrequent nature. Discontinued operations are reported separately on the statement of financial position, income statement, and statement of cash flows, net of income tax. The cumulative effect on prior-period profits of a change in accounting policy is presented on the statement of changes in equity (or retained earnings in the case of a private company following ASPE), net of income tax, as an adjustment to opening retained earnings. For comparability, all prior-period financial statements that are presented should be restated, if possible, using the new accounting policy.

2. **Explain and apply horizontal analysis.** Horizontal analysis is a technique for evaluating a series of data over time to determine the increase or decrease that has taken place, expressed as either an amount or a percentage. The horizontal percentage of a base-period amount is calculated by dividing the amount in a specific period by a base-period amount. The horizontal percentage change for the period is calculated by dividing the dollar amount of the change between periods by a base-period amount.

3. **Explain and apply vertical analysis.** Vertical analysis is a technique that expresses each item in a financial statement as a percentage of a relevant total (base amount) in that same financial statement. For example, the vertical percentage of a base amount can be determined by expressing each item on the income statement as a percentage of revenue (or net sales) or each item on the statement of financial position as a percentage of total assets by dividing the financial statement amount under analysis by the base amount for that particular financial statement.

4. **Identify and calculate ratios that are used to analyze liquidity.** Liquidity ratios include working capital, the current ratio, cash current debt coverage, receivables turnover and average collection period, and inventory turnover and days in inventory. The formula, what it measures, and desired result of each ratio are presented in Illustration 14-13.

5. **Identify and calculate ratios that are used to analyze solvency.** Solvency ratios include debt to total assets, times interest earned, cash total debt coverage, and free cash flow. The formula, what it measures, and desired result of each ratio are presented in Illustration 14-14.

6. **Identify and calculate ratios that are used to analyze profitability.** Profitability ratios include return on common shareholders' equity, return on assets, profit margin, asset turnover, gross profit margin, earnings per share, price-earnings, payout, and dividend yield. The formula, what it measures, and desired result of each ratio are presented in Illustration 14-16.

7. **Understand the limitations of financial analysis.** The usefulness of financial analysis can be limited by (1) the use of alternative accounting policies, (2) professional judgement affecting the quality of the information, (3) the existence of a large amount of other comprehensive income, (4) diversification within a company or industry, (5) significant inflation, and (6) variable economic factors.

Glossary

Change in accounting policy　Use of a different accounting policy in the current year compared with what was used in the preceding year. Changes can be mandatory or voluntary. (p. 762)

Component of an entity　A separate major line of business or major geographic area of operations that can be clearly distinguished operationally and financially from the rest of the company. (p. 760)

Discontinued operations　The disposal, or availability for sale, of a separate component of an entity. (p. 760)

Horizontal analysis　(also known as trend analysis) A technique for evaluating a series of financial statement data over a period of time to determine the increase (decrease) that has taken place. This increase (decrease) is expressed as either an amount or a percentage. (p. 765)

Horizontal percentage change for the period　A percentage measuring the change from one period to the next period. It is calculated by dividing the dollar amount of the change between the specific period under analysis and the base (prior) period by the base-period amount. (p. 766)

Horizontal percentage of a base-period amount　A percentage measuring the change since a base period, normally involving more than one period. It is calculated by dividing the amount for the specific period under analysis by the base-period amount. (p. 765)

Sustainable income　The most likely level of profit to be obtained in the future, determined by adjusting profit for irregular items such as discontinued operations. (p. 760)

Vertical analysis (also known as common size analysis) A technique for evaluating financial statement data that expresses each item in a financial statement as a percentage of a base amount. The base amount is usually net sales in the income statement and total assets in the statement of financial position. (p. 769)

Vertical percentage of a base amount A percentage measuring the proportion of an amount in a financial statement within a period. It is calculated by dividing the financial statement amount under analysis by the base amount for that particular financial statement (such as net sales for the income statement or total assets for the statement of financial position). (p. 769)

DECISION TOOLKIT—A SUMMARY

Decision Checkpoints	Info Needed for Decision	Tools to Use for Decision	How to Evaluate Results
Has the company sold, or is it holding for sale, a component of an entity?	Discontinuation of, or plans to discontinue, a component of an entity	Discontinued operations section of the statement of financial position, income statement, and/or statement of cash flows	If a component of an entity has been discontinued, its results in the current period should not be included in assessing the company's financial position or in estimating its future profit or cash flows.
Has the company changed any of its accounting policies?	Change in accounting policy	Cumulative effect of a change in accounting policy in the statement of changes in equity (or statement of retained earnings for private company using ASPE) and notes to the financial statements	Where possible, financial statements are restated using the new policy to make them easy to compare.
How do the company's financial position and operating results compare with those of previous periods?	Statement of financial position and income statement	Comparative financial statements should be prepared over at least two years, with the first year reported as the base year. Changes in each line item relative to the base year should be presented both by amount and by percentage. This is called horizontal analysis.	A significant change should be investigated to determine what caused it.
How do the relationships between items in this year's financial statements compare with last year's relationships or those of competitors?	Statement of financial position and income statement	Each line item on the statement of financial position should be presented as a percentage of total assets (total liabilities and shareholders' equity). Each line item on the income statement should be presented as a percentage of revenue (or net sales). This is called vertical analysis.	Any difference, either across years or between companies, should be investigated to determine the cause.
Does the company report other comprehensive income?	Statement of income and comprehensive income	Determine source and amount of other comprehensive income	If other comprehensive income is significant, selected profitability ratios should be recalculated using total comprehensive income rather than profit.
Are efforts to evaluate the company hampered by alternative accounting policies, professional judgement, diversification, inflation, and economic factors?	Financial statements as well as other information that is disclosed	Review accounting policies and estimates for comparability and reasonableness. Assess the strength of corporate governance processes. Review segmented information. Check that inflation is in a reasonable range. Understand significant economic factors.	If there are any comparability issues or irregularities, the analysis should be relied on with caution.

USING THE DECISION TOOLKIT

Goldcorp Inc. and Yamana Gold Inc. are two Canadian competitors in the gold industry. Selected liquidity, solvency, and profitability ratios follow for the two companies and their industry for a recent year:

	Goldcorp	Yamana Gold	Industry
Liquidity			
Current ratio	2.2:1	1.8:1	2.4:1
Average collection period	28 days	20 days	21 days
Days in inventory	61 days	58 days	102 days
Solvency			
Debt to total assets	44.2%	44.4%	56.0%
Times interest earned	9.6 times	10.2 times	8.6 times
Profitability			
Return on common shareholders' equity	1.6%	2.9%	5.2%
Return on assets	0.9%	1.6%	2.3%
Profit margin	8.8%	16.3%	7.6%
Asset turnover	0.1 times	0.1 times	0.3 times
Gross profit margin	37.1%	39.5%	47.8%

Instructions

(a) Which company is more liquid? Explain.
(b) Which company is more solvent? Explain.
(c) Which company is more profitable? Explain.

Solution

(a) Yamana Gold is more liquid than Goldcorp. Although Goldcorp appears to have a stronger current ratio than Yamana Gold, it is slower at collecting its receivables and selling its inventory. Yamana Gold is slightly better than the industry at collecting its receivables, while Goldcorp lags behind the industry average. Nonetheless, Goldcorp's average collection period is still a good one at less than 30 days. The higher inventory may be artificially increasing Goldcorp's current ratio, making it appear better than it really is. This could also be the case with the industry average for the current ratio.

(b) Yamana Gold is more solvent than Goldcorp. Although its debt to total assets ratio is slightly higher (worse) than that of Goldcorp, its times interest earned ratio is also higher, indicating its ability to handle its debt. Both companies' solvency is better than that of their industry counterparts.

(c) Yamana Gold is more profitable than Goldcorp on all profitability measures. Both companies are generally behind the industry averages with the exception of their profit margins. This is interesting because the industry's gross profit margin is higher than both companies while the profit margin is lower. This indicates that Goldcorp and Yamana Gold were able to keep their operating costs lower than the industry, especially Yamana Gold.

the navigator

Comprehensive Do It!

A vertical analysis of the condensed financial statements of Mukhin Inc. for the years 2009 to 2012 follows:

MUKHIN INC.
Vertical Analysis of Statement of Financial Position
May 31

	2012	2011	2010	2009
Assets				
Current assets	11.1%	11.1%	13.9%	11.4%
Current assets of discontinued operations	0.2%	2.1%	0.6%	4.2%
Non-current assets	88.0%	77.0%	84.8%	81.2%
Non-current assets of discontinued operations	0.7%	9.8%	0.7%	3.2%
Total assets	100.0%	100.0%	100.0%	100.0%

(*continued*)

Liabilities and Shareholders' Equity

	2012	2011	2010	2009
Liabilities				
Current liabilities	19.3%	17.5%	19.0%	15.0%
Current liabilities of discontinued operations	0.0%	1.4%	0.2%	4.1%
Non-current liabilities	52.4%	52.1%	46.0%	45.3%
Non-current liabilities of discontinued operations	2.3%	4.8%	1.8%	3.4%
Total liabilities	74.0%	75.8%	67.0%	67.8%
Shareholders' equity	26.0%	24.2%	33.0%	32.2%
Total liabilities and shareholders' equity	100.0%	100.0%	100.0%	100.0%

MUKHIN INC.
Vertical Analysis of Income Statement
Year Ended May 31

	2012	2011	2010	2009
Revenues	100.0%	100.0%	100.0%	100.0%
Expenses	87.8%	89.5%	104.0%	96.0%
Profit (loss) from continuing operations before income tax	12.2%	10.5%	(4.0%)	4.0%
Income tax expense (recovery)	3.8%	3.1%	(0.3%)	2.3%
Profit (loss) from continuing operations	8.4%	7.4%	(3.7%)	1.7%
Profit (loss) from discontinued operations	0.0%	(0.2%)	1.4%	9.0%
Profit (loss)	8.4%	7.2%	(2.3%)	10.7%

Instructions

(a) How should discontinued operations be treated in a financial analysis?

(b) Discuss the significant changes between 2009 and 2012 for the company with and without the impact of discontinued operations.

Action Plan

- Exclude the impact of irregular items in your analysis.
- Look at the percentage comparisons both vertically (within the year) and horizontally (across the years).

Solution to Comprehensive Do It!

(a) Irregular items, such as discontinued operations, should be excluded from any comparative analysis because these items are not expected to recur and do not represent sustainable income going forward.

(b) Current assets increased in 2010, declined in 2011, and remained stable in 2012. Mukhin's current liabilities are a higher percentage of total assets than are its current assets. Current liabilities have generally been increasing, except for in 2011. Except for during that same year, 2011, Mukhin's non-current assets have also been increasing as a percentage of total assets. Non-current liabilities have been increasing steadily. The company likely increased its long-term liabilities to help finance increasing purchases of non-current assets.

Mukhin's liquidity and solvency appear to be declining over recent years, with increasing percentages of liabilities (exclusive of discontinued operations). We would have to perform further analyses (e.g., ratio analysis) to determine the reasons for this decline.

In terms of profitability, Mukhin appears to be controlling its expenses, which have declined, except in 2010. Except for this same year, its profitability (based on profit from continuing operations) also appears to be on the increase.

It is interesting to note the impact that discontinued operations have on Mukhin's financial position. These should be excluded from our comparative analysis. However, except in 2009, the discontinued operations have not significantly affected Mukhin's profitability.

the navigator

Self-Test Questions

Answers are at the end of the chapter.

(SO 1)   1. Discontinued operations
   (a) are reported as part of other revenues and gains or other expenses and losses on the income statement.
   (b) are segregated and reported on the income statement after profit from continuing operations.
   (c) are segregated and reported on the statement of changes in equity as an adjustment to opening retained earnings.
   (d) are disclosed only in the notes to the financial statements.

(SO 1)   2. On which of the following financial statements is a change in accounting policy, applied retrospectively, reported by a publicly traded company?
   (a) Statement of financial position
   (b) Statement of changes in equity
   (c) Statement of cash flows
   (d) All of the above

(SO 2)   3. Rankin Inlet Corporation reported profit of $300,000, $330,000, and $360,000 in the years 2010, 2011, and 2012, respectively. If 2010 is the base year, what is the horizontal percentage of the base-year amount for 2012?
   (a) 36%
   (b) 100%
   (c) 110%
   (d) 120%

(SO 2)   4. Rankin Inlet Corporation reported profit of $300,000, $330,000, and $360,000 in the years 2010, 2011, and 2012, respectively. What is the horizontal percentage change for each period?
   (a) 10% for 2010 to 2011 and 9% for 2011 to 2012
   (b) 110% for 2010 to 2011 and 109% for 2011 to 2012
   (c) 10% for 2010 to 2011 and 20% for 2011 to 2012
   (d) 110% for 2010 to 2011 and 120% for 2011 to 2012

(SO 3)   5. What type of analysis does the following schedule show?

	Amount	Percentage
Current assets	$200,000	25%
Non-current assets	600,000	75%
Total assets	$800,000	100%

   (a) Horizontal analysis
   (b) Differential analysis
   (c) Vertical analysis
   (d) Ratio analysis

(SO 4)   6. A company reported an increasing current ratio and decreasing inventory turnover and receivables turnover ratios. This means the
   (a) company may be experiencing liquidity problems.
   (b) company has improved its overall liquidity position.
   (c) company's sales of its inventory are improving while its collection of receivables is deteriorating.
   (d) company has fewer current assets.

(SO 5)   7. Which of the following situations would be the most likely indicator that Wang Corporation might have a solvency problem?
   (a) Increasing debt to total assets and times interest earned ratios
   (b) Increasing debt to total assets and decreasing times interest earned ratios
   (c) Decreasing debt to total assets and times interest earned ratios
   (d) Decreasing debt to total assets and increasing times interest earned ratios

(SO 6)   8. Which of the following situations is the most likely indicator of corporate profitability?
   (a) Increasing price-earnings ratio
   (b) Increasing return on assets, asset turnover, and profit margin ratios
   (c) Decreasing return on common shareholders' equity and increasing asset turnover
   (d) Decreasing gross profit margin and increasing profit margin

(SO 7)   9. Torstar Corporation, a publicly traded company, has two reportable segments: a newspaper and digital division and a book publishing division. Which of the following statements is true?
   (a) Torstar must report segmented information in the notes to its financial statements.
   (b) The reporting of segmented information is optional.
   (c) Torstar must report its primary operations from its newspapers and digital division in its financial statements, and report financial information about its book publishing division in the notes to its financial statements.
   (d) Torstar should report its financial results in individual subsidiary financial statements for each division, rather than in consolidated financial statements.

(SO 7) 10. Which of the following situations might indicate that a financial analysis should be used with caution?
    (a) Different inventory cost formulas are being used by competing companies with similar types of inventory.
    (b) A company had no reportable segments.
    (c) The company has no other comprehensive income.
    (d) Inflation is low.

Questions

(SO 1)   1. Explain the concept of sustainable income.

(SO 1)   2. Identify two irregular items and indicate which financial statement(s) they affect and how.

(SO 1)   3. (a) What are discontinued operations?
(b) Explain how they are reported on the statement of financial position and income statement.

(SO 1)   4. What is a change in accounting policy? Distinguish between voluntary and mandatory changes.

(SO 1)   5. Changes in accounting policies can affect financial reporting in four ways. (a) Identify each way. (b) Would your answer in (a) change if the company followed ASPE instead of IFRS?

(SO 2)   6. Explain how a horizontal analysis is affected if an account (a) has no value in a base year and a value in the next year, or (b) has a negative value in the base year and a positive value in the next year.

(SO 2)   7. The Forzani Group Ltd. reported a profit of $35,418 thousand for the year ended January 30, 2011. It experienced a 23.1% increase in profit over the year ended January 31, 2010. What was its profit for the year ended January 31, 2010?

(SO 3)   8. Can vertical analysis be used to compare two companies of different sizes and using different currencies, such as Anheuser-Busch InBev SA/NV, the world's largest brewer, headquartered in Belgium, and SABMiller plc, the second-largest brewer, headquartered in the United Kingdom? Explain.

(SO 3)   9. Tim Hortons Inc. reported $2,536,495 thousand of revenue for the year ended January 2, 2011. If its cost of goods sold is 60.2% in a vertical analysis, what is the dollar amount of its cost of goods sold?

(SO 2, 3) 10. Two methods of financial statement analysis are horizontal analysis and vertical analysis. Explain the difference between these two methods.

(SO 2, 3) 11. Explain how the (a) horizontal percentage of a base-period amount, (b) horizontal percentage change for a period, and (c) vertical percentage of a base amount is calculated.

(SO 2, 3, 4) 12. (a) Distinguish among the following bases of comparison: intracompany, intercompany, and industry average. (b) Explain which analysis technique(s)—horizontal analysis, vertical analysis, or ratio analysis—is normally used with each base of comparison.

(SO 4) 13. Is a high current ratio always a good indicator of a company's liquidity? Describe two situations in which a high current ratio might be hiding liquidity problems.

(SO 5) 14. Starbucks Corporation reported a debt to total assets ratio of 42.3% and times interest earned ratio of 49.6 times in 2010. The industry averages were 44.8% and 11.4 times, respectively. Is Starbucks' solvency better or worse than that of the industry?

(SO 6) 15. CIBC's return on assets was 0.7%. During the same year, CIBC reported a return on common shareholders' equity of 19.2%. Has CIBC made effective use of leverage? Explain.

(SO 6) 16. Explain how the profit margin, asset turnover, and debt to total assets ratios help explain the return on common shareholders' equity ratio.

(SO 1, 6) 17. In 2011, Lai Inc. reported a profit margin of 5% before discontinued operations and a profit margin of 8% after discontinued operations. In 2012, the company had no discontinued operations and reported a profit margin of 6.5%. Has Lai's profitability improved or weakened? Explain.

(SO 6) 18. (a) If you were an investor interested in buying the shares of a company with growth potential, what ratios would you look at to help you make your decision? (b) How would your answer change if you were interested in buying shares with an income potential?

(SO 4, 5, 6) 19. What does each of the following types of ratios measure: (a) liquidity, (b) solvency, and (c) profitability?

(SO 4, 5, 6) 20. Which ratio(s) should be used to help answer each of these questions?
    (a) How efficient is the company in using its assets to produce sales?
    (b) How near to sale is the inventory on hand?
    (c) How many dollars were earned for each dollar invested by shareholders?
    (d) How able is the company to pay interest charges as they come due?
    (e) How able is the company to repay a short-term loan?

(SO 6, 7) 21. In 2010, Yum Brands Inc. reported a profit margin of 10.4% using profit in the numerator. Had the profit margin been based on total comprehensive income, instead of profit, the revised profit margin would have remained unchanged at 10.4%. In 2009, its profit margin was 10.0% using profit and 11.7% using total comprehensive income. Has Yum Brands' profitability improved or deteriorated in 2010?

(SO 7) 22. Identify and explain the factors that can limit the usefulness of financial analysis.

(SO 7) 23. Explain how changing from one accounting policy to another can affect financial analysis.

(SO 7) 24. Explain how management must use professional judgement in financial reporting and how this can affect financial analysis.

(SO 7) 25. McCain Foods and Cavendish Farms are close competitors in the frozen potato product field. Yet, McCain produces other frozen food products besides french fries, such as pizzas, vegetables, desserts, juices, and dinner entrees. Assuming you were able to access each company's financial statements, in what way(s) would their differing lines of business affect your financial analysis?

(SO 7) 26. McCain Foods and Cavendish Farms are both private companies. McCain Foods uses IFRS and Cavendish Farms uses ASPE. What impact do these differing standards have for financial analysis purposes?

Brief Exercises

Calculate sustainable income.
(SO 1)

BE14–1 Avondale Inc. reported the following information from its income statement for the current year:

Profit from continuing operations before income tax	$1,040,000
Interest expense	125,000
Income tax expense	260,000
Loss on operations of discontinued chemical division, net of $60,000 income tax savings	140,000
Loss on disposal of chemical division, net of $30,000 income tax savings	70,000

Based on the above information, what is Avondale's sustainable income?

Determine effects of change in accounting policy.
(SO 1)

BE14–2 Pason Systems Inc. changed its component depreciation policy for its rental equipment. In the notes to its financial statements, it commented that "Rental equipment, which was previously depreciated on a unit-of-use method, is now depreciated on the declining-balance method at an annual rate of 20% with no residual value. Management believes that because of the nature of the Company's rental systems, which are comprised of a significant number of component parts, that the declining balance method is most appropriate as it treats all of the parts as a pool of assets rather than discrete rental units." Explain how this change in accounting policy would have affected Pason Systems' financial statements.

Classify regular and irregular income statement items.
(SO 1)

BE14–3 A numbered list of income statement classifications for a merchandising company follows. Write the number of the appropriate classification beside each item in the lettered list below to show in what section the item would be reported:

1. Gross profit section
2. Operating expenses section
3. Other revenues and gains section
4. Other expenses and losses section
5. Discontinued operations section
6. Not reported on income statement

(a) _____ A realized gain on the sale of trading investments
(b) _____ Sales revenue
(c) _____ A change in accounting policy
(d) _____ Salaries expense
(e) _____ Cost of goods sold
(f) _____ Dividend revenue
(g) _____ A loss from operations of a discontinued wholesale business
(h) _____ Interest expense
(i) _____ A writedown of obsolete inventory
(j) _____ A gain on the sale of assets of a discontinued wholesale business

Prepare horizontal analysis.
(SO 2)

BE14–4 Selected data from the comparative statement of financial position of Rioux Ltd. are shown below:

	2012	2011	2010
Cash	$ 150,000	$ 175,000	$ 75,000
Accounts receivable	600,000	400,000	450,000
Inventory	780,000	600,000	700,000
Property, plant, and equipment	3,130,000	2,800,000	2,850,000
Intangible assets	90,000	100,000	0
Total assets	$4,750,000	$4,075,000	$4,075,000

(a) Calculate the horizontal percentage of a base-year amount, assuming 2010 is the base year.
(b) Calculate the horizontal percentage change for each year.

BE14–5 Selected horizontal percentages of a base-period amount from Coastal Ltd.'s income statement are listed here:

	2012	2011	2010
Net sales	110%	101%	100%
Cost of goods sold	105%	111%	100%
Operating expenses	99%	112%	100%
Income tax expense	136%	60%	100%

Use horizontal analysis to determine change in profit.
(SO 2)

Assuming that Coastal did not have any non-operating or irregular items, did its profit increase, decrease, or remain unchanged over the three-year period? Explain.

BE14–6 Prepare a vertical analysis using the following data (in thousands) from the comparative income statement of JTI Inc.:

	2012	2011
Net sales	$1,914	$2,073
Cost of goods sold	1,612	1,674
Gross profit	302	399
Operating expenses	218	210
Profit before income tax	84	189
Income tax expense	17	38
Profit	$ 67	$ 151

Prepare vertical analysis.
(SO 3)

BE14–7 Vertical analysis percentages from Waubon Corp.'s income statement are listed here:

	2012	2011	2010
Net sales	100.0%	100.0%	100.0%
Cost of goods sold	59.4%	60.5%	60.0%
Operating expenses	19.6%	20.4%	20.0%
Income tax expense	4.2%	3.8%	4.0%

Use vertical analysis to determine change in profit.
(SO 3)

Assuming that Waubon did not have any non-operating or irregular items, did its profit as a percentage of sales increase, decrease, or remain unchanged over the three-year period? Explain.

BE14–8 For each of the following independent situations, indicate whether the change would generally be viewed as an improvement or deterioration:

(a) An increase in the profit margin
(b) A decrease in inventory turnover
(c) A decrease in days in inventory
(d) An increase in the current ratio
(e) A decrease in free cash flow
(f) An increase in cash current debt coverage
(g) An increase in debt to total assets
(h) A decrease in times interest earned
(i) A decrease in the asset turnover
(j) An increase in the average collection period

Interpret changes in ratios.
(SO 4, 5, 6)

BE14–9 Selected financial data for Shumway Ltd. are shown below. (a) Calculate for each of 2011 and 2010 the (1) current ratio, (2) receivables turnover ratio, and (3) inventory turnover ratio. (b) Based on these ratios, what conclusion(s) can be drawn about the company's liquidity?

Calculate and evaluate liquidity.
(SO 4)

	2012	2011	2010
Accounts receivable (gross)	$ 850,000	$ 750,000	$ 650,000
Merchandise inventory	1,020,000	980,000	840,000
Total current assets	2,100,000	2,000,000	1,700,000
Total current liabilities	1,000,000	1,100,000	1,250,000
Net credit sales	6,420,000	6,240,000	5,430,000
Cost of goods sold	4,540,000	4,550,000	3,950,000

BE14–10 Holysh Inc. reported a current ratio of 1.5:1 in the current fiscal year, which is higher than its current ratio last year of 1.2:1. It also reported a receivables turnover of 9 times, which is less than last year's receivables turnover of 12 times, and an inventory turnover of 6 times, which is less than last year's inventory turnover of 9 times. Is Holysh's liquidity improving or deteriorating? Explain.

Evaluate liquidity.
(SO 4)

Evaluate solvency.
(SO 5)

BE14–11   Manulife Financial Corporation reported the following measures for 2010 and 2009:

	2010	2009
Debt to total assets	85.5%	83.6%
Times interest earned	(0.1) times	0.9 times
Cash total debt coverage	0.1 times	0.1 times
Free cash flow (in millions)	$10,871	$10,873

Is Manulife's solvency improving or deteriorating? Explain.

Evaluate profitability.
(SO 6)

BE14–12   The Second Cup Ltd. reported the following ratios for 2010 and 2009:

	2010	2009
Return on common shareholders' equity	13.4%	16.8%
Return on assets	9.1%	12.1%
Debt to total assets	13.8%	13.8%
Profit margin	37.0%	58.8%
Asset turnover	0.2 times	0.2 times

(a) Is Second Cup's profitability improving or deteriorating? (b) What is the key reason driving the change in Second Cup's return on common shareholders' equity in 2010? Explain.

Evaluate market
measures.
(SO 6)

BE14–13   Recently, the price-earnings ratio of Loblaws was 15.7 times, and the price-earnings ratio of Bank of Montreal was 12.8 times. The dividend yield of each company was 0.8% and 2.8%, respectively. Which company's shares would you purchase for growth? For income? Explain.

Determine impact of
other comprehensive
income on profitability.
(SO 6, 7)

BE14–14   Thomson Reuters Corporation reported the following selected information (in U.S. millions):

	2010	2009	2008
Profit	$ 933	$ 867	$ 1,321
Other comprehensive income (loss)	(117)	793	(2,658)
Total comprehensive income (loss)	816	1,660	(1,337)

Explain whether, and if so how, the above information would affect your analysis of Thomson Reuters' profitability.

Exercises

Indicate reporting of
regular and irregular
items.
(SO 1)

E14–1   The following independent events occurred at Ike Inc. during the year:

1. A realized gain on the sale of long-term investments
2. A loss caused by a labour strike
3. A mandatory change in accounting policy
4. Current assets of a discontinued component of an entity being held for immediate and probable sale
5. An operating loss from a discontinued component of an entity, held for immediate and probable sale
6. An impairment loss on goodwill

Instructions
(a) Identify which of the above items are sustainable (regular) items and which are irregular items.
(b) Indicate on which financial statement each of the above items would be reported, and where.

Identify reporting of
discontinued
operations and effect
on sustainable income.
(SO 1)

E14–2   On May 25, 2010, Homburg Invest Inc. sold its portfolio of Canadian income-producing investment properties. For the year ended December 31, 2010, it reported a loss of $88,054 thousand, which included a loss from its discontinued operations of $106,377 thousand. For the same year, Homburg reported current assets classified as held for sale of $144,247 thousand and current liabilities associated with these assets classified as held for sale of $91,989 thousand. All amounts are net of income tax.

Instructions
(a) Based on the information provided above, what is Homburg's sustainable income?

(b) Indicate where, and how, the loss, assets, and liabilities from the discontinued operations would be reported on Homburg's financial statements.

E14–3   Canada Paste Inc. reported a $1-million charge in the current year, net of income tax, after adopting new accounting policies mandated by the International Accounting Standards Board. For the same year, Canada Paste reported $54 million in profit (after income tax).

Identify reporting of change in accounting policy and effect on sustainable income. (SO 1)

Instructions
(a) Indicate where, and how, this $1-million charge would be reported on Canada Paste's financial statements.
(b) Based on the information provided above, what is Canada Paste's sustainable income?

E14–4   Condensed data from the comparative statement of financial position of Dressaire Inc. follow:

Prepare horizontal analysis. (SO 2)

	2012	2011	2010
Current assets	$120,000	$ 80,000	$100,000
Non-current assets	400,000	350,000	300,000
Current liabilities	70,000	90,000	65,000
Non-current liabilities	165,000	105,000	150,000
Common shares	150,000	115,000	100,000
Retained earnings	135,000	120,000	85,000

Instructions
(a) Calculate the horizontal percentage of a base-year amount, using 2010 as the base year.
(b) Calculate the horizontal percentage change for each year.

E14–5   Condensed data from the income statement for Fleetwood Corporation follow:

Prepare vertical analysis. (SO 3)

	2012	2011
Net sales	$800,000	$600,000
Cost of goods sold	550,000	375,000
Gross profit	250,000	225,000
Operating expenses	175,000	125,000
Profit before income tax	75,000	100,000
Income tax expense	15,000	20,000
Profit	$ 60,000	$ 80,000

Instructions
Prepare a vertical analysis for each year.

E14–6   The income statement for Talisman Energy Inc. follows:

Prepare horizontal and vertical analyses of income statement. (SO 2, 3)

TALISMAN ENERGY INC.
Income Statement
Year Ended December 31
(in millions)

	2010	2009	2008
Net sales	$6,802	$5,946	$8,442
Other revenue	110	115	112
Total revenue	6,912	6,061	8,554
Operating expenses	5,613	6,558	4,052
Profit (loss) from continuing operations before income tax	1,299	(497)	4,502
Income tax expense	891	161	1,623
Profit (loss) from continuing operations	408	(658)	2,879
Income from discontinued operations, net of income tax	240	1,095	640
Profit	$ 648	$ 437	$3,519

Instructions
(a) Calculate the horizontal percentage of a base-year amount, assuming 2008 is the base year.
(b) Prepare a vertical analysis for each year, using total revenue as the base.
(c) Identify any significant changes from 2008 to 2010, including the impact of discontinued operations on your analysis.

Classify ratios.
(SO 4, 5, 6)

E14–7   The following is a list of the ratios and values we have calculated in this text:

(a)	(b)	
_____	_____	Asset turnover
_____	_____	Average collection period
_____	_____	Cash current debt coverage
_____	_____	Cash total debt coverage
_____	_____	Current ratio
_____	_____	Days in inventory
_____	_____	Debt to total assets
_____	_____	Dividend yield
_____	_____	Earnings per share
_____	_____	Free cash flow
_____	_____	Gross profit margin
_____	_____	Inventory turnover
_____	_____	Payout ratio
_____	_____	Price-earnings ratio
_____	_____	Profit margin
_____	_____	Receivables turnover
_____	_____	Return on assets
_____	_____	Return on common shareholders' equity
_____	_____	Times interest earned
_____	_____	Working capital

Instructions
(a) Classify each of the above ratios as a liquidity (L), solvency (S), or profitability (P) ratio.
(b) For each of the above ratios, indicate whether a higher result is generally considered better (B) or worse (W).

Evaluate liquidity.
(SO 4)

E14–8   The following selected ratios are available for Pampered Pets Inc. for the three most recent years:

	2012	2011	2010
Current ratio	2.7:1	2.4:1	2.1:1
Receivables turnover	6.7 times	7.4 times	8.2 times
Inventory turnover	7.7 times	8.6 times	9.9 times

Instructions
(a) Has the company's collection of its receivables improved or deteriorated over the last three years?
(b) Is the company selling its inventory faster or slower than in past years?
(c) Overall, has the company's liquidity improved or deteriorated over the last three years? Explain.

Evaluate solvency.
(SO 5)

E14–9   The following selected ratios are available for Ackabe Inc. for the three most recent years:

	2012	2011	2010
Debt to total assets	50.0%	45.5%	40.3%
Times interest earned	1.8 times	1.4 times	1.0 times
Cash total debt coverage	0.7 times	0.5 times	0.3 times

Instructions
(a) Has the debt to total assets improved or deteriorated over the last three years?
(b) Has the times interest earned improved or deteriorated over the last three years?
(c) Overall, has the company's solvency improved or deteriorated over the last three years? Explain.

Evaluate profitability.
(SO 6)

E14–10   The following selected profitability ratios are available for two companies, BetaCom Corporation and Top Corporation, for a recent fiscal year:

	BetaCom	Top	Industry
Gross profit margin	37.5%	48.2%	37.9%
Profit margin	5.2%	4.9%	4.8%
Return on common shareholders' equity	9.5%	6.4%	6.0%
Return on assets	5.7%	5.4%	4.8%
Asset turnover	1.1 times	1.1 times	1.0 times

Instructions
Which company is more profitable? Explain, making sure to refer to the industry ratios where appropriate.

E14–11 Selected information for Teck Resources Limited for the most recent three years is as follows:

	2010	2009	2008
Return on common shareholders' equity	12.9%	13.8%	7.3%
Return on assets	8.0%	7.5%	3.8%
Debt to total assets	23.7%	35.5%	53.9%
Asset turnover	0.3 times	0.3 times	0.2 times
Profit margin	21.1%	23.7%	11.0%

Instructions

(a) What was the main driver of the company's return on assets over the last three years? Explain.

(b) What was the main driver of the company's return on common shareholders' equity over the last three years? Explain.

E14–12 Live Ltd. reported the following comparative statement of financial position data:

LIVE LTD.
Statement of Financial Position
December 31

	2012	2011
Assets		
Cash	$ 25,000	$ 30,000
Accounts receivable (net)	70,000	60,000
Merchandise inventory	70,000	65,000
Property, plant, and equipment (net)	180,000	165,000
Total assets	$345,000	$320,000
Liabilities and Shareholders' Equity		
Accounts payable	$ 70,000	$ 75,000
Mortgage payable—current portion	5,000	5,000
Mortgage payable—non-current portion	115,000	120,000
Common shares	90,000	80,000
Retained earnings	65,000	40,000
Total liabilities and shareholders' equity	$345,000	$320,000

Additional information for 2012:

1. Profit was $25,000.
2. Gross sales on account were $420,000. Sales returns and allowances on account amounted to $20,000.
3. Cost of goods sold was $198,000.
4. The allowance for doubtful accounts was $8,000 at the end of 2011, and $8,500 at the end of 2012.
5. Net cash provided by operating activities was $5,000.

Instructions

(a) Calculate the following ratios for 2012:
   1. Current ratio
   2. Receivables turnover
   3. Average collection period
   4. Inventory turnover
   5. Days in inventory
   6. Cash current debt coverage
   7. Debt to total assets
   8. Cash total debt coverage
   9. Return on common shareholders' equity
   10. Return on assets

(b) Indicate whether each of the above ratios is a measure of liquidity (L), solvency (S), or profitability (P).

E14–13 The following selected ratios are available for a recent year for Rogers Communications Inc. and TELUS Corporation:

	Rogers	TELUS	Industry Average
Liquidity			
Current ratio	0.8:1	0.6:1	1.0:1
Receivables turnover	8.7 times	10.4 times	15.2 times
Inventory turnover	6.7 times	29.9 times	65.3 times

	Solvency			
	Debt to total assets	66.7%	59.0%	68.9%
	Times interest earned	4.1 times	3.4 times	3.6 times
	Profitability			
	Return on common shareholders' equity	32.8%	16.2%	4.6%
	Return on assets	8.7%	3.9%	1.0%
	Profit margin	12.6%	11.2%	2.0%
	Gross profit margin	88.2%	45.2%	55.8%
	Price-earnings ratio	13.8 times	20.6 times	26.5 times

Instructions

(a) Which company is more liquid? Explain.

(b) Which company is more solvent? Explain.

(c) Which company is more profitable? Explain.

(d) Which company do investors favour? Is this consistent with your findings in (a) to (c)?

Determine effect of different situations on ratios.
(SO 4, 6, 7)

E14–14 Several different situations are outlined below that may affect the financial results of two different companies operating in the same industry.

Situation	Ratio
1. Company A sells most of its merchandise for cash; Company B sells most of its merchandise on account.	Receivables turnover
2. Company A reported a loss from discontinued operations; Company B had no discontinued operations.	Return on assets
3. Company A uses the straight-line depreciation method and an estimated useful life of 5 years; Company B uses the straight-line depreciation method and an estimated useful life of 8 years for similar equipment.	Asset turnover
4. Company A is experiencing a high level of inflation in its primary country of operation; Company B is operating in a country with no or little inflation.	Return on common shareholders' equity
5. Company A reported other comprehensive income; Company B was a private company and reported no comprehensive income.	Profit margin

Instructions

(a) For each of the situations described above, explain how it would affect the ratio given beside it. For example, in item 1, cash sales would not affect the numerator (net credit sales) or the denominator (average accounts receivable) in the calculation of the receivables turnover ratio, whereas sales on account would affect both.

(b) Explain how each of the above situations would affect a comparative financial analysis.

Problems: Set A

Discuss impact of change in accounting policy, comprehensive income, and segment information on analysis.
(SO 1, 7)

P14–1A **Canadian Tire Corporation, Limited** adopted a new accounting policy to measure goodwill and other intangible assets during fiscal 2009 (year ended January 2, 2010). This was a mandated change in accounting policy, with a net impact after income tax of $3.1 million.

On its statement of comprehensive income, Canadian Tire reported profit of $335 million and an other comprehensive loss of $141.1 million for fiscal 2009. It reported a profit of $453.6 million and other comprehensive income of $7.7 million for fiscal 2010.

Canadian Tire also reported revenue, profit before income tax, and total assets, in addition to other selected information, for four reportable segments—Canadian Tire retail, financial services, petroleum, and Mark's Work Wearhouse—in the notes to its financial statements.

Instructions

(a) Explain how the change in accounting policy would affect Canadian Tire's comparative financial statements presented for the year ended January 2, 2010 (fiscal 2009) and January 1, 2011 (fiscal 2010).

(b) Explain how the (1) change in accounting policy, (2) other comprehensive income, and (3) segmented information would affect your analysis of Canadian Tire's financial position and performance in fiscal 2009 and 2010.

Prepare horizontal analysis.
(SO 2)

P14–2A **ClubLink Enterprises Limited** is Canada's largest golf course and resort owner. The following selected information is available for three recent fiscal years:

CLUBLINK ENTERPRISES LIMITED
Statement of Financial Position
December 31
(in thousands)

	2010	2009	2008
Assets			
Current assets	$ 11,731	$ 28,516	$ 27,429
Non-current assets	599,681	599,237	613,871
Total assets	$611,412	$627,753	$641,300
Liabilities and Shareholders' Equity			
Liabilities			
Current liabilities	$ 48,631	$ 80,276	$ 77,885
Non-current liabilities	406,984	392,917	453,790
Total liabilities	455,615	473,193	531,675
Shareholders' equity	155,797	154,560	109,625
Total liabilities and shareholders' equity	$611,412	$627,753	$641,300

CLUBLINK ENTERPRISES LIMITED
Income Statement
Year Ended December 31
(in thousands)

	2010	2009	2008
Revenue	$205,195	$204,996	$210,497
Operating expenses	167,630	167,287	168,091
Profit from operations	37,565	37,709	42,406
Interest expense	22,108	23,397	25,283
Other expense (income)	(344)	1,155	1,290
Profit before income tax	15,801	13,157	15,833
Income tax expense	3,959	2,002	9,708
Profit	$ 11,842	$ 11,155	$ 6,125

ClubLink had 18,917, 17,049, and 16,647 golf club members as at December 31, 2010, 2009, and 2008, respectively.

Instructions
(a) Calculate the horizontal percentage of the base-year amount for each of the statement of financial position and income statement, assuming 2008 is the base year.
(b) Identify the key components in ClubLink's statement of financial position and income statement that are primarily responsible for the change in the company's financial position and performance over the three-year period.

P14–3A The following condensed information is available for the former Big Rock Brewery Income Trust, known as Big Rock Brewery Inc. effective January 1, 2011:

Prepare vertical analysis.
(SO 3)

BIG ROCK BREWERY
Statement of Financial Position
December 31
(in thousands)

	2010	2009	2008
Assets			
Current assets	$ 7,426	$ 8,380	$ 6,684
Non-current assets	27,035	27,985	29,216
Total assets	$34,461	$36,365	$35,900
Liabilities and Unitholders' Equity			
Liabilities			
Current liabilities	$ 4,322	$ 4,725	$ 4,676
Non-current liabilities	4,786	5,939	6,228
Total liabilities	9,108	10,664	10,904
Unitholders' equity	25,353	25,701	24,996
Total liabilities and unitholders' equity	$34,461	$36,365	$35,900

BIG ROCK BREWERY
Income Statement
December 31
(in thousands)

	2010	2009	2008
Net sales	$45,130	$46,232	$37,633
Cost of sales	19,418	20,216	14,905
Gross profit	25,712	26,016	22,728
Operating expenses	20,054	19,038	18,345
Profit from operations	5,658	6,978	4,383
Interest expense	147	142	178
Other income	(327)	(304)	(219)
Profit before income tax	5,838	7,140	4,424
Income tax recovery	(279)	(289)	(531)
Profit	$ 6,117	$ 7,429	$ 4,955

Instructions

(a) Prepare a vertical analysis of the statement of financial position and income statement for each year.

(b) Identify the key components in Big Rock's statement of financial position and income statement that are primarily responsible for the change in the company's financial position and performance over the three-year period.

(c) How has Big Rock primarily financed its assets—through debt or equity—over the last three years?

Interpret horizontal and vertical analysis. (SO 2, 3)

P14–4A   A horizontal and vertical analysis of the income statement for a service company providing consulting services is shown below:

SERVICE CORPORATION
Horizontal Income Statement
Year Ended December 31

	2012	2011	2010	2009
Revenue	120.0%	110.0%	114.0%	100.0%
Operating expenses	118.6%	111.4%	114.3%	100.0%
Profit from operations	123.3%	106.7%	113.3%	100.0%
Interest expense	40.0%	60.0%	80.0%	100.0%
Other revenue	240.0%	140.0%	200.0%	100.0%
Profit before income tax	166.8%	130.2%	131.7%	100.0%
Income tax expense	166.8%	130.2%	131.7%	100.0%
Profit	166.8%	130.2%	131.7%	100.0%

SERVICE CORPORATION
Vertical Income Statement
Year Ended December 31

	2012	2011	2010	2009
Revenue	100.0%	100.0%	100.0%	100.0%
Operating expenses	69.2%	70.9%	70.2%	70.0%
Profit from operations	30.8%	29.1%	29.8%	30.0%
Interest expense	3.3%	5.4%	7.0%	10.0%
Other revenue	(1.0)%	(0.6)%	(0.9)%	(0.5)%
Profit before income tax	28.5%	24.3%	23.7%	20.5%
Income tax expense	5.7%	4.9%	4.8%	4.1%
Profit	22.8%	19.4%	18.9%	16.4%

Instructions

(a) How effectively has the company controlled its operating expenses over the four-year period?

(b) In a horizontal analysis, the company's income tax expense has changed exactly the same as profit (66.8%) over the four-year period. Yet, in a vertical analysis, the income tax percentage is different than that of the profit percentage in each period. Explain how this is possible.

(c) Identify any other key financial statement components that have changed over the four-year period for the company.

(d) Identify any additional information that might be helpful to you in your analysis of this company over the four-year period.

P14–5A   Nexen Inc. reported the following selected information for the last five years (in millions, except earnings per share):

Calculate and evaluate profitability ratios with discontinued operations.
(SO 1, 6)

	2010	2009	2008	2007	2006
Net sales	$ 5,411	$ 4,203	$ 7,424	$ 5,583	$ 3,936
Average common shareholders' equity	8,218	7,418	6,374	5,123	4,316
Average total assets	22,404	22,528	20,115	17,616	15,873
Profit from continuing operations	572	512	1,715	1,086	601
Profit from discontinued operations	625	24	—	—	—
Profit	1,197	536	1,715	1,086	601
Earnings per share from continuing operations	1.09	0.98	3.26	2.06	1.15
Total earnings per share	2.28	1.03	3.26	2.06	1.15

Instructions
(a) Calculate Nexen's return on common shareholders' equity (for this calculation, note that the company has no preferred shares), return on assets, and profit margin ratios before and after discontinued operations for each of the last five years.
(b) Evaluate Nexen's profitability over the last five years before and after discontinued operations.
(c) Which analysis—before or after discontinued operations—is more relevant to investors? Explain.

P14–6A   Condensed statement of financial position and income statement data for Pitka Corporation follow:

Calculate and evaluate ratios.
(SO 4, 5, 6)

PITKA CORPORATION
Statement of Financial Position
December 31

	2012	2011	2010
Assets			
Current assets			
Cash	$ 25,000	$ 20,000	$ 18,000
Accounts receivable (net)	55,000	45,000	48,000
Inventory	100,000	85,000	64,000
Total current assets	180,000	150,000	130,000
Long-term investments	55,000	70,000	45,000
Property, plant, and equipment (net)	500,000	370,000	258,000
Total assets	$735,000	$590,000	$433,000
Liabilities and Shareholders' Equity			
Liabilities			
Current liabilities	$ 85,000	$ 80,000	$ 30,000
Non-current liabilities	155,000	85,000	20,000
Total liabilities	240,000	165,000	50,000
Shareholders' equity			
Common shares	330,000	300,000	300,000
Retained earnings	165,000	125,000	83,000
Total shareholders' equity	495,000	425,000	383,000
Total liabilities and shareholders' equity	$735,000	$590,000	$433,000

PITKA CORPORATION
Income Statement
Year Ended December 31

	2012	2011
Sales	$740,000	$500,000
Less: Sales returns and allowances	40,000	50,000
Net sales	700,000	450,000
Cost of goods sold	450,000	300,000
Gross profit	250,000	150,000
Operating expenses	150,000	84,000
Profit from operations	100,000	66,000
Interest expense	10,000	4,000
Profit before income tax	90,000	62,000
Income tax expense	18,000	12,400
Profit	$ 72,000	$ 49,600

Additional information:

1. The allowance for doubtful accounts was $4,800 in 2010, $4,500 in 2011, and $5,000 in 2012.
2. All sales were credit sales.
3. Net cash provided by operating activities was $119,600 in 2011 and $102,000 in 2012.

Instructions

(a) Calculate the following ratios for each of 2011 and 2012:
   1. Current ratio
   2. Receivables turnover
   3. Inventory turnover
   4. Debt to total assets
   5. Times interest earned
   6. Cash total debt coverage
   7. Return on assets
   8. Profit margin
   9. Asset turnover
   10. Gross profit margin

(b) Identify whether the change in each ratio from 2011 to 2012 was favourable, unfavourable, or unchanged.

Calculate and evaluate ratios.
(SO 4, 5, 6)

P14–7A Condensed statement of financial position and comprehensive income statement data for Click and Clack Ltd. follow:

CLICK AND CLACK LTD.
Statement of Financial Position
December 31

	2012	2011
Assets		
Cash	$ 70,000	$ 65,000
Accounts receivable (net)	95,000	90,000
Merchandise inventory	130,000	125,000
Prepaid expenses	24,000	23,000
Long-term investments	45,000	40,000
Property, plant, and equipment (net)	390,000	305,000
Total assets	$754,000	$648,000
Liabilities and Shareholders' Equity		
Liabilities		
Accounts payable	$ 45,000	$ 42,000
Accrued liabilities	30,000	40,000
Bank loan payable (current)	110,000	100,000
Bonds payable, due 2022	200,000	150,000
Total liabilities	385,000	332,000
Shareholders' equity		
Common shares (20,000 shares issued)	200,000	200,000
Retained earnings	172,000	116,000
Accumulated other comprehensive loss	(3,000)	
Total shareholders' equity	369,000	316,000
Total liabilities and shareholders' equity	$754,000	$648,000

CLICK AND CLACK LTD.
Statement of Comprehensive Income
Year Ended December 31

	2012	2011
Sales	$900,000	$840,000
Cost of goods sold	600,000	575,000
Gross profit	300,000	265,000
Operating expenses	184,000	160,000
Profit from operations	116,000	105,000
Interest expense	30,000	20,000

Profit before income tax	86,000	85,000
Income tax expense	22,000	20,000
Profit	64,000	65,000
Other comprehensive loss	(3,000)	
Total comprehensive income	$ 61,000	$ 65,000

Additional information:

1. The allowance for doubtful accounts was $4,000 in 2011 and $5,000 in 2012.
2. Accounts receivable at the beginning of 2011 were $88,000, net of an allowance for doubtful accounts of $3,000.
3. Merchandise inventory at the beginning of 2011 was $115,000.
4. Total assets at the beginning of 2011 were $630,000.
5. Total current liabilities at the beginning of 2011 were $180,000.
6. Total liabilities at the beginning of 2011 were $371,000.
7. Shareholders' equity at the beginning of 2011 was $259,000.
8. Seventy-five percent of the sales were on account.
9. Net cash provided by operating activities was $85,000 in 2011 and $96,000 in 2012.
10. Net capital expenditures were $50,000 in 2011 and $125,000 in 2012.
11. In each of 2011 and 2012, $8,000 of dividends were paid to the common shareholders.

Instructions
(a) Calculate all possible liquidity, solvency, and profitability ratios for each of 2011 and 2012.
(b) Discuss the changes in Click and Clack's liquidity, solvency, and profitability from 2011 to 2012 with reference to the relevant ratios calculated in (a).

P14–8A Selected ratios for the current year for two companies in the office supplies industry, Bureau Nouveau Inc. and Supplies Unlimited Corp., follow: *Evaluate ratios.* (SO 4, 5, 6)

	Bureau Nouveau	Supplies Unlimited	Industry Average
Asset turnover	2.6 times	2.2 times	2.5 times
Average collection period	31 days	35 days	36 days
Cash current debt coverage	0.3 times	0.1 times	0.2 times
Current ratio	1.7:1	2.0:1	1.6:1
Days in inventory	61 days	122 days	73 days
Debt to total assets	50%	30%	50%
Dividend yield	0.3%	0.5%	1.0%
Earnings per share	$3.50	$2.40	n/a
Gross profit margin	23%	30%	27%
Payout ratio	8%	22%	10%
Price-earnings ratio	29 times	45 times	38 times
Profit margin	5%	4%	4%
Return on assets	13%	9%	10%
Return on common shareholders' equity	26%	13%	20%
Times interest earned	4.2 times	8.6 times	7.1 times

Instructions
(a) Both companies offer their customers credit terms of net 30 days. Indicate which ratio(s) should be used to assess how well the accounts receivable are managed. Comment on how well each company appears to be at managing its accounts receivable.
(b) How well does each company appear to be managing its inventory? Indicate the ratio(s) used to assess inventory management.
(c) Which company is more solvent? Identify the ratio(s) used to determine this, and defend your choice.
(d) You notice that Supplies Unlimited's profit margin is less than that of Bureau Nouveau. Identify two possible reasons for this.
(e) What is mostly responsible for Bureau Nouveau's higher return on common shareholders' equity: return on assets or use of debt? Explain.
(f) What is mostly responsible for Bureau Nouveau's higher return on assets: profit margin or asset turnover? Explain.
(g) Bureau Nouveau's payout ratio is lower than Supplies Unlimited's and the industry average. Indicate one possible reason for this.
(h) What is the market price per share of each company's common shares?
(i) Which company do investors appear to believe has greater prospects for growing in future? Indicate the ratio(s) you used to reach this conclusion, and explain your reasoning.

Evaluate liquidity, solvency, and profitability.
(SO 4, 5, 6)

P14–9A   The following ratios are available for fast-food competitors McDonald's Corporation and Burger King Holdings, Inc., and their industry, for a recent year:

	McDonald's	Burger King	Industry Average
Liquidity			
Current ratio	1.5:1	0.9:1	1.2:1
Receivables turnover	21.5 times	18.3 times	54.8 times
Inventory turnover	133.6 times	n/a	33.2 times
Solvency			
Debt to total assets	44.6%	40.1%	44.8%
Times interest earned	16.5 times	6.7 times	11.4 times
Profitability			
Return on common shareholders' equity	34.5%	17.8%	2.4%
Return on assets	15.9%	6.8%	1.0%
Profit margin	20.6%	7.5%	0.8%
Asset turnover	0.8 times	0.9 times	1.2 times
Gross profit margin	40.0%	33.1%	36.9%
Price-earnings ratio	16.6 times	17.6 times	19.9 times
Dividend yield	3.0%	1.0%	1.6%

Instructions
(a) Which company is more liquid? Explain.
(b) Which company is more solvent? Explain.
(c) Which company is more profitable? Explain.
(d) Which company do investors favour? Is your answer consistent with your findings in (a) to (c)?

Determine effect of transactions on ratios.
(SO 4, 5, 6)

P14–10A   The following ratios are available for Yami Corporation:

Current ratio	1.5:1
Inventory turnover	10 times
Debt to total assets	40%
Profit margin	10%
Asset turnover	2 times

Instructions
(a) Indicate whether each of the above ratios would increase, decrease, or remain unchanged as a result of each of the following independent transactions:
   1. Yami pays an account payable.
   2. Yami collects an account receivable.
   3. Yami purchases a long-term non-strategic equity investment.
   4. Yami sells merchandise for cash at a profit.
   5. Yami buys equipment for cash.
(b) Would your answers to any of the above change if the current ratio were 0.5:1 instead of 1.5:1?

Discuss impact of accounting policies on financial analysis.
(SO 4, 5, 6, 7)

P14–11A   You are in the process of analyzing two similar companies in the same industry. You learn that they have different accounting practices and policies, as follows:

1. Company A, which has the same type of inventory as Company B, uses the FIFO cost formula while Company B uses average. Prices have been generally rising in this industry.
2. Company A uses operating leases for most of its buildings, while Company B uses finance leases for its buildings.

Instructions
(a) Considering only the impact of the choice of inventory cost formula, determine which company will report a higher (1) current ratio, (2) debt to total assets ratio, and (3) profit margin ratio, or if the choice of cost formula will have no impact.
(b) Considering only the impact of the choice of lease accounting, determine which company will report a higher (1) current ratio, (2) debt to total assets ratio, and (3) profit margin ratio, or if the choice of lease will have no impact.
(c) Will the use of different accounting practices and policies affect your analysis? Explain.
(d) Identify two other limitations of financial analysis that an analyst should watch for when analyzing financial statements.

Problems: Set B

P14–1B China Southern Airlines Limited changed its IFRS accounting policy from the revaluation model to the cost model during fiscal 2009 (year ended December 31) to improve the comparability of its financial results with other airlines. This was a voluntary change in accounting policy that was accounted for retrospectively.

On its statement of comprehensive income, China Southern Airlines reported a profit of renminbi (RMB) 6,415 million and an other comprehensive loss of RMB 15 million for 2010. It reported a profit of RMB 527 million and other comprehensive income of RMB 30 million for 2009.

China Southern Airlines also reported revenue, profit before income tax, and total assets, in addition to other selected information, for two segments—airline business (comprising passenger and cargo operations) and other (comprising aviation repair services, aviation training services, ground services, and catering services)—in the notes to its financial statements.

Discuss impact of change in accounting policy, comprehensive income, and segment information on analysis. (SO 1, 7)

Instructions
(a) Explain how the change in accounting policy would affect China Southern Airlines' comparative financial statements presented for the years ended December 31, 2009 and 2010.
(b) Explain how the (1) change in accounting policy, (2) other comprehensive income, and (3) segmented information would affect your analysis of China Southern Airlines' financial position and performance in 2009 and 2010.

P14–2B lululemon athletica inc. has seen a significant amount of growth over the last three years. The following selected information is available for three recent fiscal years:

Prepare horizontal analysis, with discontinued operations. (SO 1, 2)

LULULEMON ATHLETICA INC.
Statement of Financial Position
January 31
(in U.S. thousands)

	2011	2010	2009
Assets			
Current assets	$389,279	$216,410	$116,988
Non-current assets	110,023	90,848	94,648
Total assets	$499,302	$307,258	$211,636
Liabilities and Shareholders' Equity			
Liabilities			
Current liabilities	$ 85,364	$ 58,678	$ 45,335
Non-current liabilities	19,645	15,472	11,459
Total liabilities	105,009	74,150	56,794
Shareholders' equity	394,293	233,108	154,842
Total liabilities and shareholders' equity	$499,302	$307,258	$211,636

LULULEMON ATHLETICA INC.
Income Statement
Year Ended January 31
(in U.S. thousands)

	2011	2010	2009
Net revenue	$711,704	$452,898	$353,488
Cost of goods sold	316,757	229,812	174,421
Gross profit	394,947	223,086	179,067
Operating expenses	214,556	136,540	122,503
Profit from operations	180,391	86,546	56,564
Other income	2,536	164	821
Profit before income tax	182,927	86,710	57,385
Income tax expense	61,080	28,429	16,884
Profit from continuing operations	121,847	58,281	40,501
Net loss from discontinued operations			1,138
Profit	$121,847	$ 58,281	$ 39,363

Instructions
(a) Calculate the horizontal percentage of the base-year amount for each of the statement of financial position and income statement, assuming 2009 is the base year.
(b) Identify the key components in lululemon's statement of financial position and income statement that are primarily responsible for the change in the company's financial position and performance over the three-year period.

Prepare vertical analysis.
(SO 3)

P14–3B The following condensed information is available for Yellow Media Inc., Canada's largest Internet media and marketing company:

YELLOW MEDIA INC.
Statement of Financial Position
December 31
(in thousands)

	2010	2009	2008
Assets			
Current assets	$ 443,370	$ 417,662	$ 470,900
Fixed assets	112,445	95,425	104,642
Intangible assets	2,123,776	2,008,499	2,102,466
Goodwill	6,508,984	6,342,580	6,648,667
Other assets	111,673	77,440	39,544
Total assets	$9,300,248	$8,941,606	$9,366,219
Liabilities and Shareholders' Equity			
Liabilities			
Current liabilities	$ 478,562	$ 385,525	$ 376,164
Non-current liabilities	2,871,617	2,534,434	2,930,947
Total liabilities	3,350,179	2,919,959	3,307,111
Shareholders' equity	5,950,069	6,021,647	6,059,108
Total liabilities and shareholders' equity	$9,300,248	$8,941,606	$9,366,219

YELLOW MEDIA INC.
Income Statement
Year Ended December 31
(in thousands)

	2010	2009	2008
Revenues	$1,679,860	$1,639,884	$1,696,713
Operating expenses	1,164,104	1,244,176	986,297
Profit from operations	515,756	395,708	710,416
Other revenues and gains	(4,712)		
Other expenses and losses	185,906	144,116	170,525
Profit before income tax	334,562	251,592	539,891
Income tax expense	60,527	42,710	30,664
Profit	$ 274,035	$ 208,882	$ 509,227

Instructions

(a) Prepare a vertical analysis of the statement of financial position and income statement for each year.

(b) Identify the key components in Yellow Media's statement of financial position and income statement that are primarily responsible for the change in the company's financial position and performance over the three-year period.

(c) How has Yellow Media primarily financed its assets—through debt or equity—over the last three years?

Interpret horizontal and vertical analysis.
(SO 2, 3)

P14-4B A horizontal and vertical analysis of the income statement for a retail company selling a wide variety of general merchandise is shown below:

RETAIL CORPORATION
Horizontal Income Statement
Year Ended January 30

	2012	2011	2010	2009
Revenue	140.0%	111.0%	114.0%	100.0%
Cost of goods sold	148.3%	113.3%	116.7%	100.0%
Gross profit	127.5%	107.5%	110.0%	100.0%
Operating expenses	171.4%	133.1%	126.9%	100.0%
Profit from operations	93.3%	87.6%	96.9%	100.0%
Interest expense	40.0%	60.0%	80.0%	100.0%
Other revenue	240.0%	140.0%	200.0%	100.0%
Profit before income tax	140.0%	110.8%	113.8%	100.0%
Income tax expense	160.0%	116.0%	124.0%	100.0%
Profit	135.2%	109.5%	111.4%	100.0%

RETAIL CORPORATION Vertical Income Statement Year Ended January 30				
	2012	2011	2010	2009
Revenue	100.0%	100.0%	100.0%	100.0%
Cost of goods sold	63.6%	61.2%	61.4%	60.0%
Gross profit	36.4%	38.8%	38.6%	40.0%
Operating expenses	21.4%	21.0%	19.5%	17.5%
Profit from operations	15.0%	17.8%	19.1%	22.5%
Interest expense	(2.9%)	(5.4%)	(7.0%)	(10.0%)
Other revenue	0.9%	0.6%	0.9%	0.5%
Profit before income tax	13.0%	13.0%	13.0%	13.0%
Income tax expense	2.9%	2.6%	2.7%	2.5%
Profit	10.1%	10.4%	10.3%	10.5%

Instructions

(a) How effectively has the company controlled its cost of goods sold over the four-year period?

(b) In a vertical analysis, the company's profit before income tax has remained unchanged at 13% of revenue over the four-year period. Yet, in a horizontal analysis, profit before income tax has grown 40% over that period of time. Explain how this is possible.

(c) Identify any other key financial statement components that have changed over the four-year period for the company.

(d) Identify any additional information that might be helpful to you in your analysis of this company over the four-year period.

P14–5B The Home Depot Inc. reported the following selected information for the last five years (in U.S. millions, except earnings per share):

Calculate and evaluate profitability ratios with discontinued operations.
(SO 1, 6)

	2011	2010	2009	2008	2007
Net sales	$67,997	$66,176	$71,288	$77,349	$79,022
Average common shareholders' equity	19,141	18,585	17,746	21,372	25,970
Average total assets	40,501	41,020	24,244	48,294	48,334
Profit from continuing operations	3,338	2,620	2,312	4,210	5,266
Net loss (gain) from discontinued operations	—	41	(52)	185	495
Profit	3,338	2,661	2,260	4,395	5,761
Earnings per share from continuing operations	2.01	1.55	1.37	2.28	2.56
Total earnings per share	2.01	1.57	1.34	2.38	2.80

Instructions

(a) Calculate Home Depot's return on common shareholders' equity (for this calculation, note that the company has no preferred shares), return on assets, and profit margin ratios before and after discontinued operations for each of the last five years.

(b) Evaluate Home Depot's profitability over the last five years before and after discontinued operations.

(c) Which analysis—before or after discontinued operations—is more relevant to investors? Explain.

P14–6B Condensed statement of financial position and income statement data for Colinas Corporation appear on the following page.

Calculate and evaluate ratios.
(SO 4, 5, 6)

Instructions

(a) Calculate the following ratios for each of 2011 and 2012:
   1. Current ratio
   2. Receivables turnover
   3. Inventory turnover
   4. Debt to total assets
   5. Times interest earned
   6. Cash total debt coverage
   7. Return on assets
   8. Profit margin
   9. Asset turnover
   10. Gross profit margin

(b) Indicate whether the change in each ratio from 2011 to 2012 was favourable, unfavourable, or unchanged.

COLINAS CORPORATION
Statement of Financial Position
December 31

	2012	2011	2010
Assets			
Cash	$ 30,000	$ 24,000	$ 10,000
Accounts receivable (net)	80,000	50,000	53,000
Inventory	85,000	45,000	50,000
Other current assets	70,000	75,000	62,000
Long-term investments	100,000	76,000	50,000
Property, plant, and equipment (net)	595,000	345,000	315,000
Total assets	$960,000	$615,000	$540,000
Liabilities and Shareholders' Equity			
Liabilities			
Current liabilities	$ 63,500	$ 51,000	$ 65,000
Non-current liabilities	245,000	65,000	70,000
Total liabilities	308,500	116,000	135,000
Shareholders' equity			
Common shares	416,500	319,000	275,000
Retained earnings	235,000	180,000	130,000
Total shareholders' equity	651,500	499,000	405,000
Total liabilities and shareholders' equity	$960,000	$615,000	$540,000

COLINAS CORPORATION
Income Statement
Year Ended December 31

	2012	2011
Sales	$950,000	$840,000
Less: Sales returns and allowances	60,000	40,000
Net sales	890,000	800,000
Cost of goods sold	490,000	450,000
Gross profit	400,000	350,000
Operating expenses	266,000	260,000
Profit from operations	134,000	90,000
Interest expense	27,750	8,750
Profit before income taxes	106,250	81,250
Income tax expense	21,250	16,250
Profit	$ 85,000	$ 65,000

Additional information:

1. The allowance for doubtful accounts was $2,400 in 2010, $2,750 in 2011, and $3,650 in 2012.
2. Assume all sales were credit sales.
3. Net cash provided by operating activities was $91,000 in 2011 and $107,500 in 2012.

Calculate and evaluate ratios.
(SO 4, 5, 6)

P14–7B Condensed statement of financial position and comprehensive income statement data for Star Track Ltd. follow:

STAR TRACK LTD.
Statement of Financial Position
December 31

	2012	2011
Assets		
Cash	$ 50,000	$ 42,000
Accounts receivable (net)	100,000	87,000
Inventories	400,000	300,000
Prepaid expenses	25,000	31,000
Long-term investments	80,000	50,000
Land	125,000	75,000
Buildings and equipment (net)	560,000	400,000
Total assets	$1,340,000	$985,000

Liabilities and Shareholders' Equity
Liabilities

Notes payable	$ 150,000	$ 50,000
Accounts payable	245,000	190,000
Current portion of mortgage payable	48,750	25,000
Mortgage payable, due 2022	200,000	125,000
Total liabilities	643,750	390,000
Shareholders' equity		
Common shares (100,000 shares issued)	400,000	400,000
Retained earnings	292,250	195,000
Accumulated other comprehensive income	4,000	—
Total shareholders' equity	696,250	595,000
Total liabilities and shareholders' equity	$1,340,000	$985,000

STAR TRACK LTD.
Statement of Comprehensive Income
Year Ended December 31

	2012	2011
Net sales	$1,100,000	$950,000
Cost of goods sold	650,000	635,000
Gross profit	450,000	315,000
Operating expenses	285,000	215,000
Profit from operations	165,000	100,000
Interest expense	30,000	10,000
Profit before income tax	135,000	90,000
Income tax expense	33,750	22,500
Profit	101,250	67,500
Other comprehensive income	4,000	—
Total comprehensive income	$ 105,250	$ 67,500

Additional information:

1. The allowance for doubtful accounts was $5,000 in 2011 and $10,000 in 2012.
2. Accounts receivable at the beginning of 2011 were $80,000, net of an allowance for doubtful accounts of $3,000.
3. Inventories at the beginning of 2011 were $320,000.
4. Total assets at the beginning of 2011 were $1,075,000.
5. Current liabilities at the beginning of 2011 were $250,000.
6. Total liabilities at the beginning of 2011 were $543,500.
7. Total shareholders' equity at the beginning of 2011 was $531,500.
8. All sales were on account.
9. Net cash provided by operating activities was $135,500 in 2011 and $223,000 in 2012.
10. Net capital expenditures were $50,000 in 2011 and $92,000 in 2012.
11. In each of 2011 and 2012, $4,000 of dividends were paid to the common shareholders.

Instructions
(a) Calculate all possible liquidity, solvency, and profitability ratios for each of 2011 and 2012.
(b) Discuss the changes in Star Track's liquidity, solvency, and profitability from 2011 to 2012 with reference to the relevant ratios calculated in (a).

P14–8B Selected ratios for the current year for two companies in the beverage industry, Refresh Corp. and Flavour Limited, follow:

Evaluate ratios.
(SO 4, 5, 6)

	Refresh	Flavour	Industry Average
Asset turnover	1.0 times	1.0 times	0.9 times
Cash total debt coverage	30%	20%	n/a
Current ratio	0.7:1	1.1:1	0.8:1
Debt to total assets	56%	72%	81%
Dividend yield	0.2%	1.1%	2.0%
Earnings per share	$0.98	$1.37	$1.08
Gross profit margin	74%	60%	58%
Inventory turnover	6.8 times	7.9 times	8.3 times

	Refresh	Flavour	Industry Average
Payout ratio	10%	25%	30%
Price-earnings ratio	50.3 times	24.3 times	32.2 times
Profit margin	12%	9%	8%
Receivables turnover	11.4 times	9.8 times	9.3 times
Return on assets	12%	9%	7%
Return on common shareholders' equity	27%	32%	38%
Times interest earned	15.3 times	7.9 times	5.3 times

Instructions

(a) Both companies offer their customers credit terms of net 30 days. Indicate which ratio(s) should be used to assess how well the accounts receivable are managed. Comment on how well each company appears to be at managing its accounts receivable.

(b) How well does each company appear to be managing its inventory? Indicate the ratio(s) used to assess inventory management.

(c) Which company, Refresh or Flavour, is more solvent? Identify the ratio(s) used to determine this, and defend your choice.

(d) You notice that Refresh's profit margin is higher than Flavour's and the industry average. Identify two possible reasons for this.

(e) What is mostly responsible for Flavour's higher return on common shareholders' equity: return on assets or use of debt? Explain.

(f) What is mostly responsible for Refresh's higher return on assets: profit margin or asset turnover? Explain.

(g) Refresh's payout ratio is lower than Flavour's and the industry average. Indicate one possible reason for this.

(h) What is the market price per share of each company's common shares?

(i) Which company, Refresh or Flavour, do investors appear to believe has greater prospects for future growth? Indicate the ratio(s) you used to reach this conclusion, and explain your reasoning.

Evaluate liquidity, solvency, and profitability.
(SO 4, 5, 6)

P14–9B   The following ratios are available for toolmakers Stanley Black & Decker, Inc. and Snap-On Incorporated, and their industry, for a recent year:

	Stanley Black & Decker	Snap-On	Industry Average
Liquidity			
Current ratio	1.8:1	2:1	2.6:1
Receivables turnover	8.7 times	6.1 times	7.4 times
Inventory turnover	6.7 times	4.8 times	3.9 times
Solvency			
Debt to total assets	32.9%	45.7%	22.5%
Times interest earned	3.2 times	6.1 times	7.6 times
Profitability			
Return on common shareholders' equity	4.4%	13.9%	4.9%
Return on assets	2.0%	5.2%	2.6%
Profit margin	2.4%	7.0%	3.0%
Asset turnover	0.8 times	0.7 times	0.9 times
Gross profit margin	35.1%	45.7%	33.3%
Price-earnings ratio	58.1 times	19.2 times	33.9 times
Payout ratio	101.5%	38.2%	17.4%
Dividend yield	1.8%	2.0%	1.2%

Instructions

(a) Which company is more liquid? Explain.

(b) Which company is more solvent? Explain.

(c) Which company is more profitable? Explain.

(d) Which company do investors favour? Is your answer consistent with your findings in (a) to (c)? Explain.

Determine effect of transactions on ratios.
(SO 4, 5, 6)

P14–10B   The following ratios and measures are available for Hubei Corporation:

Receivables turnover	10 times
Debt to total assets	40%
Free cash flow	$25,000
Profit margin	10%
Earnings per share	$2

Instructions

(a) Indicate whether each of the above would increase, decrease, or remain unchanged by each of the following independent transactions:
   1. Hubei issues common shares.
   2. Hubei collects an account receivable.
   3. Hubei issues a mortgage payable.
   4. Hubei sells equipment at a loss.
   5. Hubei's share price increases from $10 to $12.
(b) Would your answers to any of the above change if the profit margin were negative and the earnings per share were a loss per share?

P14–11B You are in the process of analyzing two similar companies in the same industry. You learn that they have different accounting practices and policies, as follows:

Discuss impact of accounting policies on financial analysis. (SO 4, 5, 6, 7)

   1. Company A, which has the same type of equipment as Company B, uses the straight-line method of depreciation while Company B uses diminishing-balance. This is the first year of operations for both companies.
   2. Company A is a private company and does not report other comprehensive income. Company B is a publicly traded company that generates and reports other comprehensive income.

Instructions

(a) Considering only the impact of the choice of depreciation method, determine which company will report a higher (1) current ratio, (2) debt to total assets ratio, and (3) profit margin ratio, or if the depreciation method will have no impact.
(b) Considering only the impact of total comprehensive income, determine which company will report a higher (1) current ratio, (2) debt to total assets ratio, and (3) profit margin ratio, or if the other comprehensive income will have no impact.
(c) Will the use of different accounting practices and policies affect your analysis? Explain.
(d) Identify two other limitations of financial analysis that an analyst should watch for when analyzing financial statements.

Broadening Your Perspective

Financial Reporting and Analysis Cases

Financial Reporting: *Eastplats*

BYP14–1 The financial statements of Eastern Platinum Limited (Eastplats) are presented in Appendix A at the end of this book. The following selected information (in U.S. thousands) has been taken from these, and the prior year's, financial statements:

Prepare horizontal and vertical analysis. (SO 2, 3)

	2010	2009	2008
Income statement			
Revenue	$ 155,000	$111,365	$ 114,681
Cost of operations	132,408	99,993	94,623
Mine operating earnings	22,592	11,372	20,058
Operating expenses	13,569	11,110	321,351
Profit (loss) from operations	9,023	262	(301,293)
Statement of financial position			
Current assets	392,911	55,621	74,375
Non-current assets	734,064	651,229	518,983
Current liabilities	30,220	23,845	40,597
Non-current liabilities	55,576	53,493	44,226
Shareholders' equity	1,041,179	629,512	508,535

Instructions

(a) Calculate the horizontal percentage of the base-year amount for the selected information shown above, assuming 2008 is the base year.

(b) Calculate the vertical percentage of a base amount for each of the (1) income statement data, using revenue as the base amount, and (2) statement of financial position data, using total assets as the base amount, shown above for each year.

(c) Comment on any significant changes you observe from your calculations in (a) and (b).

Comparative Analysis: *Eastplats and Amplats*

Calculate and evaluate liquidity, solvency, and profitability.
(SO 4, 5, 6)

BYP14–2   The financial statements of Anglo American Platinum Limited (Amplats) are presented in Appendix B following the financial statements for Eastern Platinum Limited (Eastplats) in Appendix A.

Instructions

(a) Calculate liquidity ratios for 2010 that you believe are relevant for each company. Which company is more liquid?

(b) Calculate solvency ratios for 2010 that you believe are relevant for each company. Which company is more solvent?

(c) Calculate profitability ratios for 2010 that you believe are relevant for each company. For the return on common shareholders' equity ratio, note that neither company has any preferred shares. Which company is more profitable?

(d) What information that is not included in the financial statements might also be useful for comparing Eastplats and Amplats?

Interpreting Financial Information

Calculate and evaluate liquidity, solvency, and profitability.
(SO 4, 5, 6)

BYP14–3   The following data were taken from the 2010 financial statements of tire manufacturers Compagnie Générale des Établissements Michelin (Michelin) and The Goodyear Tire & Rubber Company:

	Michelin (in euro millions)	Goodyear (in USD millions)
Average accounts receivable	€ 2,542	$ 2,638
Average inventory	3,382	2,710
Total current assets	9,665	8,045
Total assets	19,663	15,630
Average total assets	13,475	15,020
Total current liabilities	4,845	5,307
Average current liabilities	10,682	4,701
Total liabilities	11,536	14,125
Average total liabilities	11,280	13,478
Average total common shareholders' equity	6,811	954
Net sales	17,891	18,832
Cost of goods sold	12,403	15,452
Gross profit	5,488	3,380
Interest expense	10	316
Income tax expense	449	172
Profit (loss)	1,049	(216)
Net cash provided by operating activities	1,322	924
Net capital expenditures	903	944
Cash dividends	760	0

Instructions

Where available, industry averages are shown in parentheses next to each ratio below.

(a) Calculate the following liquidity ratios for each company and discuss the relative liquidity of the two companies and the tire manufacturing industry:

1. Current ratio (1.6:1)
2. Cash current debt coverage (n/a)
3. Receivables turnover (6.4 times)
4. Inventory turnover (6.1 times)

(b) Calculate the following solvency ratios for each company and discuss the relative solvency of the two companies and of the tire manufacturing industry:

1. Debt to total assets (34.2%)
2. Times interest earned (1.8 times)
3. Cash total debt coverage (n/a)
4. Free cash flow (n/a)

(c) Calculate the following profitability ratios for each company and discuss the relative profitability of the two companies and the tire manufacturing industry:
1. Return on common shareholders' equity (−3.1%)
2. Return on assets (−0.5%)
3. Profit margin (−0.4%)
4. Asset turnover (1.3 times)
5. Gross profit margin (17.3%)

(d) Identify the key differences between each company and their industry. What factors might be causing the differences you found?

Comparing IFRS and ASPE

BYP14–4 **InterRent Real Estate Investment Trust** is a publicly traded company, headquartered in Ontario, generating revenue from rental operations and the sale of revenue-producing properties. The following are excerpts from its 2010 and 2009 financial statements, during which time it used Canadian GAAP prior to adopting IFRS on January 1, 2011.

Compare and adjust discontinued operations; evaluate profitability.
(SO 1, 2, 3, 6)

INTERRENT REAL ESTATE INVESTMENT TRUST
Income Statement
Year Ended December 31
(in thousands)

	2010	2009
Rental revenue	$31,922	$ 31,773
Rental expenses	16,945	16,599
Profit before the under-noted	14,977	15,174
Financing costs	11,381	11,325
Administrative costs	3,508	6,957
Depreciation expense	7,113	6,697
	22,002	24,979
Loss from continuing operations	(7,025)	(9,805)
Profit (loss) from discontinued operations (Note 10)	29	(272)
Loss	$(6,996)	$(10,077)

Note 10—Discontinued Operations

In 2010, InterRent disposed of four properties (35 suites) (2009–one property, 22 suites) and classified seventeen income producing properties (482 suites) as discontinued operations as a result of InterRent initiating an active program to dispose of these properties.

The following table sets forth the results of operations associated with the properties reported as discontinued operations:

(in thousands)	2010	2009
Rental revenue	$3,431	$3,646
Rental expenses	3,472	3,871
Loss	(41)	(225)
Gain (loss) on disposal	596	(47)
Loss on write-down of properties held for sale	(526)	-
Discontinued operations	$ 29	$ (272)

Instructions

Assume you are a financial analyst and have been asked to perform a comprehensive analysis of InterRent's performance. This requires you do the following: evaluate InterRent's accounting policies, perform a vertical and horizontal analysis, and calculate key ratios for InterRent.

(a) In its 2010 and 2009 financial statements, InterRent classified its discontinued operations according to Canadian GAAP prior to the transition to IFRS. Do you think InterRent's properties would meet the definition of discontinued operations under IFRS in 2011? Why or why not?

(b) When performing vertical and horizontal analyses, if companies follow different accounting policies, it may be necessary to make adjustments to the financial statements so that they are comparable with other companies. Based upon your answer in part (a), what adjustments (if any) would you have to make to InterRent's 2010 and 2009 income statements in order to make InterRent comparable with other companies in the real estate industry that follow IFRS? Will these adjustments result in a change in the overall 2010 and 2009 loss?

(c) One of the key ratios for real estate companies such as InterRent is the net rental ratio (which is the same as the gross profit margin). Calculate the net rental ratio, using profit before the under-noted as a proxy for gross profit, for each of the unadjusted 2010 and 2009 figures and the adjusted 2010 and 2009 figures. What is the impact of your adjustments on the net rental ratio?

Critical Thinking Cases and Activities

Collaborative Learning Activity

Determine effect of investment on ratios.
(SO 4, 6)

BYP14–5 As the general manager of operations for a regional division of a construction materials manufacturing company, you are seeking ways to make your operation more efficient, while being constantly aware of how your operation is evaluated by head office.

Ratios for the most recent year reported to head office for its evaluation included:

Current ratio	2.2:1
Receivables turnover	10 times
Inventory turnover	8 times
Gross profit margin	25%
Profit margin	10%
Return on assets	8%

The management team is reviewing a proposal to develop an Internet-based electronic marketplace. With an investment in internal IT infrastructure modification and connective technology, your operation could expect benefits in:

- Materials sourcing and purchasing, resulting in lower product costs and lower levels of in-stock inventory requirements
- Shipping and logistics planning, resulting in faster order-to-delivery cycles for customers, more efficient billing, and faster collection of customer accounts
- Market intelligence data, resulting in the identification and pursuit of new customers and markets.

While all of these benefits are desirable, they must weighed against the significant expenditure over the next three years on IT infrastructure, business process redesign, and staff training. As general manager, you expect to work at this plant for only another two to three years. After that, you hope to be promoted to a senior position at head office.

Instructions
With the class divided into groups, do the following:
(a) Considering the expected benefits described above, state whether you would expect each of the above ratios to improve or deteriorate in the short term, if an Internet-based electronic marketplace is developed. Justify your answer.
(b) The VP of Sales is enthusiastic about developing an electronic marketplace because she is confident that customers will reward the better service with loyalty to the company. If this is true, what could be the long-term effect on the key ratios given above?
(c) Could your two- to three-year time horizon as the general manager affect your decision on this project? Explain.

Communication Activity

Identify limitations of financial analysis.
(SO 7)

BYP14–6 You are a new member of the board of directors and audit committee of Rad Corp., a high-tech company. Rad Corp was a private company using ASPE until last year, when it became a publicly traded company using IFRS. You are preparing for your first meeting of the audit committee, at which the year-end financial results, including key ratios, will be presented.

Instructions
Identify any of the limitations of financial statement analysis that you believe may apply to Rad Corp. Prioritize your list and prepare questions that you should raise at the audit committee meeting to help you better understand the financial results and ratios.

Ethics Case

Identify ethical issues in the presentation of ratios.
(SO 2, 4, 5, 6)

BYP14–7 Vern Fairly, president of Flex Industries Inc., wants to issue a press release to boost the company's image and its share price, which has been gradually falling. As controller, you have been asked to provide a list of horizontal percentages and financial ratios for Flex Industries' first-quarter operations.

Two days after you provide the ratios and data requested, you are asked by Anne Saint-Onge, Flex's vice-president of communications, to review the accuracy of the financial and operating data contained in the press release written by the president and edited by Anne. In the news release, the president highlights the sales increase of 10% over last year's first quarter and the positive change in the current ratio from 1.1:1 last year to 1.5:1 this year. He also emphasizes that production was up 15% over last year's first quarter.

You note that the release contains only positive or improved ratios and none of the negative or worsening ratios. For instance, there is no mention of the fact that although the current ratio improved, the cash current debt coverage ratio fell from 0.2% to 0.1%, or that the debt to total assets ratio has increased from 35% to 45%. Nor is there any mention that the reported profit for the quarter would have been a loss if excess machinery had not been sold at a gain.

Instructions

(a) Who are the stakeholders in this situation?

(b) Is there anything unethical in President Fairly's actions?

(c) As controller, should you remain silent? Why or why not? Does Anne have any responsibility?

"All About You" Activity

BYP14–8   Jo Trembley, who has a small portfolio of shares of publicly traded Canadian corporations, is concerned about missing out on hot stock picks, like RIM or Celestica.

Jo's stock evaluation method includes comparing the price-earnings ratio of a potential investment with the industry average for that sector. Because companies like RIM and Celestica reported losses, rather than profits, in their early years, price-earnings ratio calculations were not possible. Therefore, these shares were excluded from Jo's analysis.

Discuss the price-earnings ratio and other factors assessed in making an investment. (SO 6, 7)

Instructions

(a) When you purchase a company's shares, should you look for a high or low price-earnings ratio? Explain.

(b) Can an industry average for the price-earnings ratio be a meaningful benchmark for a particular industry? Consider industries that are stable versus those that are undergoing rapid expansion and/or technological change.

(c) What other factors besides the price-earnings ratio should you consider in making your share purchase decision?

Serial Case

(*Note*: This is a continuation of the serial case from Chapters 1 through 13.)

BYP 14-9   Janet, Brian, Natalie, and Daniel have sold their shares of Koebel's Family Bakery Ltd. to Biscuits Ltd., a public company. One of the terms of the sale agreement was that Natalie and Daniel had to become and remain employees of Biscuits for the next two years and continue to operate the bakery. Natalie and Daniel are now operating Koebel's Bakery as a wholly owned subsidiary of Biscuits.

Evaluate liquidity, solvency, and profitability. (SO 4, 5, 6)

Daniel and Natalie have received a sizeable amount of cash from the sale of their shares of Koebel's Family Bakery. As a result, they are considering where next to make an investment. They recognize how profitable Koebel's continues to be as a subsidiary of Biscuits and are considering investing some of their excess cash in Biscuits. They have accumulated a number of ratios for Biscuits, Cookies Are for Us (a publicly traded competitor of Biscuits), and the overall industry to enable them to make a decision on whether or not they should invest in Biscuits.

Ratio	Biscuits Ltd.	Cookies Are for Us Ltd.	Industry Ratio
Current ratio	1.9:1	1.2:1	1.9:1
Receivables turnover	37.2 times	28.4 times	17.3 times
Inventory turnover	25.3 times	23.6 times	18.0 times
Debt to total assets	54.8%	52.5%	50.0% times
Times interest earned	23.8 times	21.7 times	17.4 times
Return on common shareholders' equity	11.9%	6.9%	9.5%
Return on assets	5.3%	5.0%	6.6%
Profit margin	3.9%	3.0%	5.2%
Gross profit margin	23.0%	21.0%	19.9%
Price-earnings ratio	32.5 times	23.8 times	27.5 times

Instructions

(a) Which company is more liquid? Explain.

(b) Which company is more solvent? Explain.

(c) Which company is more profitable? Explain.

(d) Which company do investors favour? Explain.

(e) Natalie and Daniel are familiar with ASPE from their previous experience with Koebel's as a private company. Biscuits and Cookies Are for Us use IFRS. Are there any particular differences Natalie and Daniel should be aware of that might affect their analysis of these two companies?

(f) What other considerations must Natalie and Daniel consider before making an investment in any public company?

Remember to go back to the beginning of the chapter to check off your completed work!

←

Answers to Self-Test Questions

1. b   2. b   3. d   4. a   5. c   6. a   7. b   8. b   9. a   10. a

Comprehensive Case: Chapters 13–14

Prepare vertical analysis; calculate and evaluate ratios; prepare statement of cash flows.
(SO 3, 4, 5, 6)

Manutech Ltd.'s industrial product sales were down in 2011. Fortunately, after investing in a customer relationship management system, it was able to turn its operations around in 2012. Selected financial statement data follow:

MANUTECH LTD.
Income Statement
Year Ended December 31

	2012	2011
Net sales	$1,470,000	$1,100,000
Cost of goods sold	735,000	655,000
Gross profit	735,000	445,000
Operating expenses	313,500	270,000
Profit from operations	421,500	175,000
Interest expense	61,500	53,600
Profit before income tax	360,000	121,400
Income tax expense	90,000	30,350
Profit	$ 270,000	$ 91,050

MANUTECH LTD.
Statement of Financial Position
December 31

	2012	2011
Assets		
Current assets		
Cash	$ 30,000	$ 79,500
Accounts receivable (gross)	150,000	105,000
Inventories	112,000	90,000
Total current assets	292,000	274,500
Property, plant, and equipment (net)	1,100,000	965,000
Intangible assets	120,000	120,000
Total assets	$1,512,000	$1,359,500
Liabilities and Shareholders' Equity		
Liabilities		
Current liabilities		
Accounts payable	$ 65,000	$ 72,500
Accrued liabilities	15,000	20,000
Bank loan payable	85,000	
Total current liabilities	165,000	92,500
Bonds payable	650,000	670,000
Total liabilities	815,000	762,500
Shareholders' equity		
Common shares, 10,000 shares issued	100,000	100,000
Retained earnings	597,000	497,000
Total shareholders' equity	697,000	597,000
Total liabilities and shareholders' equity	$1,512,000	$1,359,500

Additional information for 2012:

1. Assume all sales were credit sales.
2. Manutech has no bad debts and no allowance for doubtful accounts.
3. Property, plant, and equipment increased in 2012 by the $300,000 cost of a new customer relationship management system and decreased by additional accumulated depreciation for the year of $165,000.
4. The bonds payable were originally issued at face value. $20,000 of the bonds were repaid in 2012.
5. Cash dividends paid during the year amounted to $170,000.

Instructions

(a) Prepare a vertical analysis of the income statements for 2011 and 2012. Use the results to answer the following question from management: "We know that sales volume has increased, but we don't know if the profit margin is also increasing. If the profit margin is increasing, what are some of the likely reasons for this increase?"

(b) Calculate the following liquidity ratios for 2012 and compare the company's results with the industry average:

	Industry Average
Current ratio	3.0:1
Average collection period	28 days
Days in inventory	30 days

(c) Calculate the following solvency ratios for 2012 and compare the company's results with the industry average:

	Industry Average
Debt to total assets	50.0%
Times interest earned	3.0 times

(d) Calculate the following profitability ratios for 2012 and compare the company's results with the industry average:

	Industry Average
Return on assets	8.5%
Profit margin	10.1%
Asset turnover	0.8 times
Gross profit margin	44.5%

(e) After a review of the financial statements, the vice-president is surprised that the cash balance reported on the statement of financial position at year end is not higher, since financial performance improved and net cash provided by operating activities was determined to be $355,500. Prepare the investing and financing activities sections of the statement of cash flows for 2012 to explain where the cash has been used.

Specimen Financial Statements: Eastern Platinum Limited (Eastplats)

In this appendix, and the next, we illustrate current financial reporting with two different sets of corporate financial statements that are prepared in accordance with international financial reporting standards (IFRS). We are grateful for permission to use the actual financial statements of Eastern Platinum Limited (Eastplats) in Appendix A and Anglo American Platinum Limited (Amplats) in Appendix B. We should note that Anglo American Platinum added the "American" to its official name immediately after the release of its year-end statements, which are still titled Anglo Platinum in Appendix B.

The financial statement package for Eastplats includes the independent auditor's report, consolidated income statement, statement of comprehensive income, statement of financial position, statement of changes in equity, statement of cash flows, and notes to the financial statements.

We encourage students to use these financial statements in conjunction with relevant material in the textbook. In particular, these statements can be used to solve the Financial Reporting and Comparative Analysis cases in the Broadening Your Perspective section of the end of chapter material.

The complete annual report for Eastplats can be found on the companion website to this textbook in the Annual Reports section and under the Additional Resources tab in the read, study and practice section of WileyPLUS.

Deloitte.

Deloitte & Touche LLP
2800 - 1055 Dunsmuir Street
4 Bentall Centre
P.O. Box 49279
Vancouver BC V7X 1P4
Canada

Tel: 604-669-4466
Fax: 604-685-0395
www.deloitte.ca

Independent Auditor's Report
To the Shareholders of
Eastern Platinum Limited

We have audited the accompanying consolidated financial statements of Eastern Platinum Limited (the "Company"), which comprise the consolidated statements of financial position as at December 31, 2010 and 2009, and the consolidated statements of income, comprehensive income, changes in equity, and cash flows for the years then ended, and a summary of significant accounting policies and other explanatory information.

Management's Responsibility for the Consolidated Financial Statements

Management is responsible for the preparation and fair presentation of these consolidated financial statements in accordance with International Financial Reporting Standards, and for such internal control as management determines is necessary to enable the preparation of consolidated financial statements that are free from material misstatement, whether due to fraud or error.

Auditor's Responsibility

Our responsibility is to express an opinion on these consolidated financial statements based on our audits. We conducted our audits in accordance with Canadian generally accepted auditing standards. Those standards require that we comply with ethical requirements and plan and perform the audit to obtain reasonable assurance about whether the consolidated financial statements are free from material misstatement.

An audit involves performing procedures to obtain audit evidence about the amounts and disclosures in the consolidated financial statements. The procedures selected depend on the auditor's judgment, including the assessment of the risks of material misstatement of the consolidated financial statements, whether due to fraud or error. In making those risk assessments, the auditor considers internal control relevant to the entity's preparation and fair presentation of the consolidated financial statements in order to design audit procedures that are appropriate in the circumstances, but not for the purpose of expressing an opinion on the effectiveness of the entity's internal control. An audit also includes evaluating the appropriateness of accounting policies used and the reasonableness of accounting estimates made by management, as well as evaluating the overall presentation of the consolidated financial statements.

We believe that the audit evidence we have obtained in our audits is sufficient and appropriate to provide a basis for our audit opinion.

Opinion

In our opinion, the consolidated financial statements present fairly, in all material respects, the financial position of the Company as at December 31, 2010 and 2009, and its financial performance and its cash flows for the years then ended in accordance with International Financial Reporting Standards.

(Signed) Deloitte & Touche LLP

Chartered Accountants
Vancouver, British Columbia
March 21, 2011

Eastern Platinum Limited
Consolidated income statements
(Expressed in thousands of U.S. dollars, except per share amounts)

	Note	Year ended December 31, 2010	Year ended December 31, 2009
Revenue		$ **155,000**	$ 111,365
Cost of operations			
Production costs		**109,901**	82,839
Depletion and depreciation	9	**22,507**	17,154
		132,408	99,993
Mine operating earnings		**22,592**	11,372
Expenses			
General and administrative		**12,117**	10,528
Share-based payments	17(c)	**1,452**	582
		13,569	11,110
Operating profit		**9,023**	262
Other income (expense)			
Interest income		**1,797**	1,786
Finance costs	19	**(1,807)**	(1,691)
Foreign exchange loss		**(160)**	(758)
Profit (loss) before income taxes		**8,853**	(401)
Deferred income tax recovery	15	**924**	1,623
Net profit for the year		$ **9,777**	$ 1,222
Attributable to			
Non-controlling interest	18	$ **(3,575)**	$ (4,428)
Equity shareholders of the Company		**13,352**	5,650
Net profit for the year		$ **9,777**	$ 1,222
Earnings per share			
Basic	20	$ **0.02**	$ 0.01
Diluted	20	$ **0.02**	$ 0.01
Weighted average number of common shares outstanding in thousands			
Basic	20	**683,177**	680,577
Diluted	20	**694,839**	687,790

Eastern Platinum Limited
Consolidated statements of comprehensive income
(Expressed in thousands of U.S. dollars)

	Year ended December 31, 2010	Year ended December 31, 2009
Net profit for the year	$ 9,777	$ 1,222
Other comprehensive income		
Exchange differences on translating foreign operations	70,355	116,678
Exchange differences on translating non-controlling interest	762	2,467
Comprehensive income for the year	$ 80,894	$ 120,367
Attributable to		
Non-controlling interest	(2,813)	(1,961)
Equity shareholders of the Company	83,707	122,328
Comprehensive income for the year	$ 80,894	$ 120,367

Eastern Platinum Limited
Consolidated statements of financial position as at
December 31, 2010 and 2009
(Expressed in thousands of U.S. dollars)

	Note	December 31, 2010	December 31, 2009
Assets			
Current assets			
Cash and cash equivalents	6	$ 107,846	$ 7,249
Short-term investments		242,446	14,409
Trade and other receivables	7	33,787	29,138
Inventories	8	8,832	4,825
		392,911	55,621
Non-current assets			
Property, plant and equipment	9	715,976	634,778
Refining contract	10	14,265	14,169
Other assets	11	3,823	2,282
		$ 1,126,975	$ 706,850
Liabilities			
Current liabilities			
Accounts payable and accrued liabilities	12	$ 27,009	$ 22,919
Current portion of finance leases	13	3,211	926
		30,220	23,845
Non-current liabilities			
Provision for environmental rehabilitation	14	8,934	8,152
Finance leases	13	–	2,850
Deferred tax liabilities	15	46,642	42,491
		85,796	77,338
Equity			
Issued capital	17	1,219,869	890,150
Equity-settled employee benefits reserve		33,390	32,336
Currency translation adjustment		17,456	(52,899)
Deficit		(236,764)	(250,116)
Capital and reserves attributable to equity shareholders of the Company		1,033,951	619,471
Non-controlling interest	18	7,228	10,041
		1,041,179	629,512
		$ 1,126,975	$ 706,850

Approved and authorized for issue by the Board on March 21, 2011.

"David Cohen"
David Cohen, Director

"Robert Gayton"
Robert Gayton, Director

Eastern Platinum Limited
Consolidated statements of changes in equity
(Expressed in thousands of U.S. dollars, except number of shares)

	Issued capital		Equity-settled employee benefits reserve	Currency translation adjustment	Deficit	Capital and reserves attributable to equity shareholders of the Company	Non-controlling interest	Equity
	Shares	Amount						
Balance,								
December 31, 2008	680,526,454	$ 890,049	$ 31,827	$ (169,577)	$ (255,766)	$ 496,533	$ 12,002	$ 508,535
Stock options exercised	366,871	101	(73)	-	-	28	-	28
Share-based payments	-	-	582	-	-	582	-	582
Net profit	-	-	-	-	5,650	5,650	(4,428)	1,222
Currency translation adjustment	-	-	-	116,678	-	116,678	2,467	119,145
Balance,								
December 31, 2009	680,893,325	$ 890,150	$ 32,336	$ (52,899)	$ (250,116)	$ 619,471	$ 10,041	$ 629,512
Public offering	224,250,000	345,391	-	-	-	345,391	-	345,391
Share issuance costs	-	(16,501)	-	-	-	(16,501)	-	(16,501)
Stock options exercised	2,446,242	829	(398)	-	-	431	-	431
Share-based payments	-	-	1,452	-	-	1,452	-	1,452
Net profit	-	-	-	-	13,352	13,352	(3,575)	9,777
Currency translation adjustment	-	-	-	70,355	-	70,355	762	71,117
Balance,								
December 31, 2010	907,589,567	$ 1,219,869	$ 33,390	$ 17,456	$ (236,764)	$ 1,033,951	$ 7,228	$ 1,041,179

Eastern Platinum Limited
Consolidated statements of cash flows
(Expressed in thousands of U.S. dollars)

	Note	Year ended December 31, 2010	Year ended December 31, 2009
Operating activities			
Profit (loss) before income taxes		$ 8,853	$ (401)
Adjustments to net profit (loss) for non-cash items			
Depletion and depreciation	9	22,507	17,154
Refining contract amortization	10	1,513	1,332
Share-based payments	17	1,452	582
Interest income		(1,797)	(1,786)
Finance costs	19	1,807	1,691
Foreign exchange loss		160	758
Environmental expense		-	301
Net changes in non-cash working capital items			
Trade and other receivables		(2,318)	(13,169)
Inventories		(3,040)	22
Accounts payable and accrued liabilities		1,322	(15,135)
Cash generated from (utilized in) operations		30,459	(8,651)
Adjustments to net profit (loss) for cash items			
Interest income received		1,767	1,855
Finance costs paid		(252)	(69)
Acquisition related dividend taxes paid		-	(2,422)
Net operating cash flows		31,974	(9,287)
Investing activities			
(Purchase) maturity of short-term investments		(223,118)	22,647
Purchase of other assets		(1,129)	(929)
Property, plant and equipment expenditures		(32,991)	(28,955)
Sale of property, plant and equipment		-	1,552
Net investing cash flows		(257,238)	(5,685)
Financing activities			
Common shares issued for cash, net of share issue costs -public financing		328,890	-
Common shares issued for cash - exercise of stock options		423	32
Repayment of current loans		-	(3,065)
Payment of finance leases		(2,161)	(1,223)
Net financing cash flows		327,152	(4,256)
Effect of exchange rate changes on cash and cash equivalents		(1,291)	671
Increase (decrease) in cash and cash equivalents		100,597	(18,557)
Cash and cash equivalents, beginning of year		7,249	25,806
Cash and cash equivalents, end of year		$ 107,846	$ 7,249

Eastern Platinum Limited
Notes to the consolidated financial statements – years ended December 31, 2010 and 2009
(Expressed in thousands of U.S. dollars, except number of shares and per share amounts)

1. **Nature of operations**

   Eastern Platinum Limited (the "Company") is a platinum group metal ("PGM") producer engaged in the mining, exploration and development of PGM properties located in various provinces in South Africa.

   Eastern Platinum Limited is a publicly listed company incorporated in Canada with limited liability under the legislation of the Province of British Columbia. The Company's shares are listed on the Toronto Stock Exchange, Alternative Investment Market, and the Johannesburg Stock Exchange.

   The head office, principal address and records office of the Company are located at 1075 West Georgia Street, Suite 250, Vancouver, British Columbia, Canada, V6E 3C9. The Company's registered address is 1055 West Georgia Street, Suite 1500, Vancouver, British Columbia, Canada, V6E 4N7.

2. **Basis of preparation**

   In February 2009, the British Columbia and Ontario Securities Commissions granted the Company exemptive relief to adopt International Financial Reporting Standards ("IFRS") with an adoption date of January 1, 2009 and a transition date of January 1, 2008. These consolidated financial statements, including comparatives, have been prepared using accounting policies in compliance with International Financial Reporting Standards ("IFRS") as issued by the International Accounting Standards Board ("IASB").

   The preparation of financial statements requires management to make judgments, estimates and assumptions that affect the application of policies and reported amounts of assets and liabilities, and revenue and expenses. The estimates and associated assumptions are based on historical experience and various other factors that are believed to be reasonable under the circumstances, the results of which form the basis of making the judgments about carrying values of assets and liabilities that are not readily apparent from other sources. Actual results may differ from these estimates.

   The estimates and underlying assumptions are reviewed on an ongoing basis. Revisions to accounting estimates are recognized in the period in which the estimate is revised if the revision affects only that period or in the period of the revision and further periods if the review affects both current and future periods.

   Judgments made by management in the application of IFRS that have a significant effect on the financial statements and estimates with a significant risk of material adjustment in the current and following fiscal years are discussed in Notes 4(v) and 4(w).

3. **Application of new and revised International Financial Reporting Standards**

   Effective January 1, 2010, the Company adopted new and revised International Financial Reporting Standards ("IFRSs") that were issued by the International Accounting Standards Board ("IASB"). The application of these new and revised IFRSs has not had any material impact on the amounts reported for the current and prior years but may affect the accounting for future transactions or arrangements.

   (a) *Amendments to IFRS 2 Share-based Payment – Group Cash-settled Share-based Payment Transactions*

   The amendments clarify the scope of IFRS 2, as well as the accounting for group cash-settled share-based payment transactions in the separate (or individual) financial statements of an entity receiving the goods or services when another group entity or shareholder has the obligation to settle the award.

Eastern Platinum Limited
Notes to the consolidated financial statements – years ended December 31, 2010 and 2009
(Expressed in thousands of U.S. dollars, except number of shares and per share amounts)

3.   **Application of new and revised IFRSs (continued)**

  (b)   *Amendments to IFRS 3 Business Combinations*

    The main amendments to IFRS 3 *Business Combinations* are as follows:

    (i)   The revised standard also applies to business combinations involving only mutual entities and to business combinations achieved by contract alone.

    (ii)   The definition of a business has been amended to clarify that it can include a set of activities and assets that are not being operated as a business, as long as an acquirer is capable of operating the set of activities and assets as a business.

    (iii) All business combinations are accounted for by applying the acquisition method (previously the purchase method).

    (iv)   The acquirer can elect to measure any non-controlling interest at fair value at the acquisition date, or at its proportionate interest in the fair value of the identifiable assets and liabilities of the acquiree, on a transaction-by-transaction basis.

    (v)   Subsequent recognition of deferred tax assets acquired in a business combination that did not satisfy the criteria for recognition at the acquisition date would be recognized in profit or loss.

    This standard applies prospectively to acquisitions with a date on or after the beginning of the first annual period beginning on or after July 1, 2009.

  (c)   *Amendments to IFRS 8 Operating Segments*

    The amendments clarify that disclosing segment information with respect to total assets is only required if such information is regularly reported to the chief operating decision maker.

  (d)   *Amendments to IAS 7 Statement of Cash Flows*

    The amendments clarify that only expenditures that result in the recognition of an asset can be classified as a cash flow from investing activities.

  (e)   *Amendments to IAS 17 Leases*

    The IASB deleted guidance stating that a lease of land with an indefinite economic life normally is classified as an operating lease, unless at the end of the lease term title is expected to pass to the lessee. The amendments also clarify that when a lease includes both the land and building elements, an entity should determine the classification of each element taking into account the fact that land normally has an indefinite economic life.

  (f)   *Amendments to IAS 27 Consolidated and Separate Financial Statements*

    The main amendments to IAS 27 *Consolidated and Separate Financial Statements* are as follows:

    (i)   Changes in a parent's ownership interest that do not result in the loss of control of a controlled subsidiary are accounted for as equity transactions. Accordingly, acquisitions of additional non-controlling interests are accounted for as equity transactions. Disposals of equity interests while retaining control are accounted for as equity transactions.

Eastern Platinum Limited
Notes to the consolidated financial statements – years ended December 31, 2010 and 2009
(Expressed in thousands of U.S. dollars, except number of shares and per share amounts)

3.   **Application of new and revised IFRSs (continued)**

(f)   *Amendments to IAS 27 Consolidated and Separate Financial Statements (continued)*

(ii)   Transactions resulting in a loss of control would cause a gain or loss to be recognized in profit or loss.

(iii)   Losses applicable to the non-controlling interests, including negative other comprehensive income, are allocated to non-controlling interests even if doing so causes the non-controlling interests to have a negative balance.

(g)   *Amendments to IAS 36 Impairment of Assets*

The amendments clarify that the largest unit to which goodwill should be allocated is the operating segments level. This amendment applies prospectively.

(h)   *Amendments to IAS 38 Intangible Assets*

The amendments clarify that an intangible asset that is separable only together with a related contract, identifiable asset or liability is recognized separately from goodwill together with the related item, and that complementary intangible assets with similar useful lives may be recognized as a single asset. The amendments also describe valuation techniques commonly used by entities when measuring the fair value of intangible assets acquired in a business combination for which no active market exists. These amendments are applied prospectively.

(i)   *Amendments to IAS 39 Financial Instruments: Recognition and Measurement*

The main amendments consist of:

(i)   Additional guidance provided to help determine whether loan prepayment penalties result in an embedded derivative that needs to be separated.

(ii)   Clarification that the scope exemption is restricted to forward contracts between an acquirer and a selling shareholder to buy or sell an acquiree that will result in a business combination at a future acquisition date within a reasonable period normally necessary to obtain any required approvals and to complete the transaction.

(iii)   Clarification that the gains or losses on a cash flow hedge should be reclassified from other comprehensive income to profit or loss during the period that the hedged forecast cash flows impact profit or loss.

The amendments apply prospectively to all unexpired contracts from the date of adoption.

Eastern Platinum Limited
Notes to the consolidated financial statements – years ended December 31, 2010 and 2009
(Expressed in thousands of U.S. dollars, except number of shares and per share amounts)

4.   **Summary of significant accounting policies**

The consolidated financial statements have been prepared under the historical cost convention, except for the revaluation of certain financial instruments. The Company's principal accounting policies are outlined below:

(a)   Basis of consolidation

These consolidated financial statements incorporate the financial statements of the Company and the entities controlled by the Company (its subsidiaries, including special purpose entities). Control exists when the Company has the power, directly or indirectly, to govern the financial and operating policies of an entity so as to obtain benefits from its activities. The financial statements of subsidiaries are included in the consolidated financial statements from the date that control commences until the date that control ceases. All significant intercompany transactions and balances have been eliminated.

Non-controlling interest in the net assets of consolidated subsidiaries are identified separately from the Company's equity. Non-controlling interest consists of the non-controlling interest at the date of the original business combination plus the non-controlling interest's share of changes in equity since the date of acquisition.

Special Purpose Entities ("SPE's") as defined in SIC 12 *Consolidation – Special Purpose Entities* are entities which are created to accomplish a narrow and well-defined objective (e.g. to act as a Black Economic Empowerment ("BEE") partner). SPE's are subject to consolidation when there is an indication that an entity controls the SPE. The Company has determined that its investment in Gubevu Consortium Investment Holdings (Pty) Ltd. ("Gubevu") is a SPE that the Company controls. The accounts of Gubevu are consolidated with those of the Company.

(b)   Business combinations

Acquisitions of subsidiaries and businesses are accounted for using the acquisition method. The consideration for each acquisition is measured as the aggregate of the fair values (at the date of exchange) of assets given, liabilities incurred or assumed, and equity instruments issued by the Company in exchange for control of the acquiree. Any costs directly attributable to the business combination are generally recognized in profit or loss as incurred.

The acquiree's identifiable assets, liabilities and contingent liabilities that meet the conditions for recognition under IFRS 3 *Business Combinations* are recognized at their fair values at the acquisition date, except for non-current assets (or disposal groups) that are classified as held for sale in accordance with IFRS 5 *Non-current Assets Held for Sale and Discontinued Operations,* which are recognized and measured at fair value less costs to sell.

Goodwill arising on acquisition is recognized as an asset and initially measured at cost, being the excess of the cost of the acquisition over the Company's interest in the net fair value of the identifiable assets, liabilities and contingent liabilities recognized. If the Company's interest in the net fair value of the acquiree's identifiable assets, liabilities and contingent liabilities exceeds the cost of the acquisition, the excess is recognized immediately in profit or loss.

The interest of non-controlling shareholders in the acquiree is initially measured at the non-controlling shareholders' proportion of the net fair value of the assets, liabilities and contingent liabilities recognized.

Eastern Platinum Limited
Notes to the consolidated financial statements – years ended December 31, 2010 and 2009
(Expressed in thousands of U.S. dollars, except number of shares and per share amounts)

4. **Summary of significant accounting policies (continued)**

(c) Presentation currency

The Company's presentation currency is the U.S. dollar ("$"). The functional currencies of Eastern Platinum Limited and its South African subsidiaries are the Canadian Dollar and South African Rand ("ZAR"), respectively. These consolidated financial statements have been translated to the U.S. dollar in accordance with IAS 21 *The Effects of Changes in Foreign Exchange Rates*. This standard requires that assets and liabilities be translated using the exchange rate at period end, and income, expenses and cash flow items are translated using the rate that approximates the exchange rates at the dates of the transactions (i.e. the average rate for the period).

(d) Foreign currency translation

In preparing the financial statements of the individual entities, transactions in currencies other than the entity's functional currency (foreign currencies) are recorded at the rates of exchange prevailing at the dates of the transactions. At each statement of financial position date, monetary assets and liabilities are translated using the period end foreign exchange rate. Non-monetary assets and liabilities are translated using the historical rate on the date of the transaction. Non-monetary assets and liabilities that are stated at fair value are translated using the historical rate on the date that the fair value was determined. All gains and losses on translation of these foreign currency transactions are included in profit or loss.

(e) Revenue recognition

Revenue is measured at the fair value of the consideration received or receivable. The following specific criteria must be met before revenue is recognized:

(i) Sale of goods

Revenue from the sale of platinum group and other metals is recognized when all of the following conditions are satisfied:

- the specific risks and rewards of ownership have been transferred to the purchaser;
- the Company does not retain continuing managerial involvement to the degree usually associated with ownership or effective control over the metals sold;
- the amount of revenue can be measured reliably;
- it is probable that the economic benefits associated with the transaction will flow to the Company; and
- the costs incurred or to be incurred in respect of the sale can be measured reliably.

The sale of platinum group metals is provisionally priced such that the price is not settled until a predetermined future date based on the market price at that time. Revenue on these sales is initially recognized (when the conditions above are met) at the current market price. The difference between the present value and the future value of the current market price is recognized as interest income over the term of settlement. Subsequent to initial recognition but prior to settlement, sales are marked to market at each reporting date using the forward price for the period equivalent to that outlined in the contract. This mark to market adjustment is recorded in revenue.

Eastern Platinum Limited
Notes to the consolidated financial statements – years ended December 31, 2010 and 2009
(Expressed in thousands of U.S. dollars, except number of shares and per share amounts)

4. **Summary of significant accounting policies (continued)**

(e) *Revenue recognition (continued)*

(ii) *Rental income*

Rental income from residential properties is recognized on a straight-line basis over the term of the lease.

(iii) *Interest income*

Interest income is recognized in profit or loss as it accrues, using the effective interest method.

(f) *Share-based payments*

The Company grants stock options to buy common shares of the Company to directors, officers and employees. The board of directors grants such options for periods of up to ten years, with vesting periods determined at its sole discretion and at prices equal to or greater than the closing market price on the day preceding the date the options were granted.

The fair value of the options is measured at grant date, using the Black-Scholes option pricing model, and is recognized over the period that the employees earn the options. The fair value is recognized as an expense with a corresponding increase in equity. The amount recognized as an expense is adjusted to reflect the number of share options expected to vest.

(g) *Finance costs*

Finance costs comprise interest payable on revenue advances, finance leases, provision for environmental rehabilitation and other borrowings. Interest payable on borrowings is calculated using the effective interest method and foreign exchange gains and losses on foreign currency borrowings.

(h) *Income taxes*

Income tax expense consists of current and deferred tax expense. Income tax expense is recognized in profit or loss.

Current tax expense is the expected tax payable on the taxable income for the year, using tax rates enacted or substantively enacted at period end, adjusted for amendments to tax payable with regards to previous years.

Deferred tax assets and liabilities are recognized for deferred tax consequences attributable to unused tax loss carry forwards, unused tax credits and differences between the financial statement carrying amounts of existing assets and liabilities and their respective tax bases. Deferred tax assets and liabilities are measured using the enacted or substantively enacted tax rates expected to apply when the asset is realized or the liability settled.

The effect on deferred tax assets and liabilities of a change in tax rates is recognized in profit or loss in the period that substantive enactment occurs.

A deferred tax asset is recognized to the extent that it is probable that future taxable profits will be available against which the asset can be utilized. To the extent that the Company does not consider it probable that a deferred tax asset will be recovered, the deferred tax asset is reduced.

Eastern Platinum Limited
Notes to the consolidated financial statements – years ended December 31, 2010 and 2009
(Expressed in thousands of U.S. dollars, except number of shares and per share amounts)

4. **Summary of significant accounting policies (continued)**

(h) *Income taxes (continued)*

The following temporary differences do not result in deferred tax assets or liabilities:
- the initial recognition of assets or liabilities, not arising in a business combination, that does not affect accounting or taxable profit
- goodwill
- investments in subsidiaries, associates and jointly controlled entities where the timing of reversal of the temporary differences can be controlled and reversal in the foreseeable future is not probable.

Deferred tax assets and liabilities are offset when there is a legally enforceable right to set off current tax assets against current tax liabilities and when they relate to income taxes levied by the same taxation authority and the Company intends to settle its current tax assets and liabilities on a net basis.

(i) *Earnings (loss) per share*

Basic earnings (loss) per share is computed by dividing the net earnings (loss) attributable to common shareholders by the weighted average number of shares outstanding during the reporting period. Diluted earnings (loss) per share is computed similar to basic earnings (loss) per share except that the weighted average shares outstanding are increased to include additional shares for the assumed exercise of stock options and warrants, if dilutive. The number of additional shares is calculated by assuming that outstanding stock options and warrants were exercised and that the proceeds from such exercises were used to acquire common stock at the average market price during the reporting periods.

(j) *Comprehensive income (loss)*

Comprehensive income (loss) is the change in the Company's net assets that results from transactions, events and circumstances from sources other than the Company's shareholders and includes items that are not included in net profit such as unrealized gains or losses on available-for-sale investments, gains or losses on certain derivative instruments and foreign currency gains or losses related to translation of the financial statements of foreign operations. The Company's comprehensive income (loss), components of other comprehensive income, and cumulative translation adjustments are presented in the consolidated statements of comprehensive income (loss) and the consolidated statements of changes in equity.

(k) *Property, plant and equipment*

(i) *Mining assets*

Assets owned and mineral properties being depleted are recorded at cost less accumulated depreciation and accumulated impairment losses. Mineral properties not being depleted are recorded at cost less accumulated impairment losses. All direct costs related to the acquisition, exploration and development of mineral properties are capitalized until the properties to which they relate are ready for their intended use, sold, abandoned or management has determined there to be impairment. If economically recoverable ore reserves are developed, capitalized costs of the related property are reclassified as mineral properties being depleted and amortized using the units-of-production method following commencement of production. Interest on borrowings incurred to finance mining assets is capitalized until the asset is capable of carrying out its intended use.

Eastern Platinum Limited
Notes to the consolidated financial statements – years ended December 31, 2010 and 2009
(Expressed in thousands of U.S. dollars, except number of shares and per share amounts)

4. **Summary of significant accounting policies (continued)**

   (k) *Property, plant and equipment (continued)*

      (i) *Mining assets (continued)*

         Mining properties and mining and process facility assets are amortized on a units-of-production basis which is measured by the portion of the mine's proven and probable ore reserves recovered during the period. Capital work-in-progress, which is included in mining assets, is not depreciated until the assets are ready for their intended use.

         Although the Company has taken steps to verify title to the properties in which it has an interest, in accordance with industry standards for properties in the exploration stage, these procedures do not guarantee the Company's title. Property title may be subject to unregistered prior agreements and non-compliance with regulatory requirements.

      (ii) *Residential properties and other property, plant and equipment*

         Residential properties and other property, plant and equipment are recorded at cost less accumulated depreciation and impairment losses. These assets are depreciated using the straight-line method based on estimated useful lives, which generally range from 5 to 7 years, with the exception of residential properties and mine houses whose estimated useful lives are 50 years and office buildings whose estimated useful lives are 20 years. Land is not depreciated.

         Where an item of plant and equipment comprises significant components with different useful lives, the components are accounted for as separate items of plant and equipment.

         Expenditures incurred to replace a component of an item of property, plant and equipment that is accounted for separately, including major inspection and overhaul expenditures, are capitalized. Directly attributable expenses incurred for major capital projects and site preparation are capitalized until the asset is brought to a working condition for its intended use. These costs include dismantling and site restoration costs to the extent these are recognized as a provision.

         The cost of self-constructed assets includes the cost of materials, direct labour and an appropriate portion of normal overheads.

         The costs of day-to-day servicing are recognized in profit or loss as incurred. These costs are more commonly referred to as "maintenance and repairs."

         Financing costs directly associated with the construction or acquisition of qualifying assets are capitalized at interest rates relating to loans specifically raised for that purpose, or at the weighted average borrowing rate where the general pool of group borrowings is utilized. Capitalization of borrowing costs ceases when the asset is substantially complete.

         The depreciation method, useful life and residual values are assessed annually.

Eastern Platinum Limited

Notes to the consolidated financial statements – years ended December 31, 2010 and 2009
(Expressed in thousands of U.S. dollars, except number of shares and per share amounts)

4. **Summary of significant accounting policies (continued)**

(k) *Property, plant and equipment (continued)*

(iii) *Leased assets*

Leases in which the Company assumes substantially all risks and rewards of ownership are classified as finance leases. Assets held under finance leases are recognized at the lower of the fair value of the leased property and the present value of the minimum lease payments at inception of the lease, less accumulated depreciation and impairment losses. Lease payments are accounted for as discussed in Note 4(r).

(iv) *Subsequent Costs*

The cost of replacing part of an item within property, plant and equipment is recognized when the cost is incurred if it is probable that the future economic benefits will flow to the group and the cost of the item can be measured reliably. The carrying amount of the part that has been replaced is expensed. All other costs are recognized as an expense as incurred.

(v) *Impairment*

The Company's tangible and intangible assets are reviewed for indications of impairment at each statement of financial position date. If indication of impairment exists, the asset's recoverable amount is estimated.

An impairment loss is recognized when the carrying amount of an asset, or its cash-generating unit, exceeds its recoverable amount. A cash-generating unit is the smallest identifiable group of assets that generates cash inflows that are largely independent of the cash inflows from other assets or groups of assets. Impairment losses are recognized in profit and loss for the period. Impairment losses recognized in respect of cash-generating units are allocated first to reduce the carrying amount of any goodwill allocated to cash-generating units and then to reduce the carrying amount of the other assets in the unit on a pro-rata basis.

The recoverable amount is the greater of the asset's fair value less costs to sell and value in use. In assessing value in use, the estimated future cash flows are discounted to their present value using a pre-tax discount rate that reflects current market assessments of the time value of money and the risks specific to the asset. For an asset that does not generate largely independent cash inflows, the recoverable amount is determined for the cash-generating unit to which the asset belongs.

(vi) *Reversal of impairment*

An impairment loss is reversed if there is an indication that there has been a change in the estimates used to determine the recoverable amount. An impairment loss is reversed only to the extent that the asset's carrying amount does not exceed the carrying amount that would have been determined, net of depreciation or amortization, if no impairment loss had been recognized. An impairment loss with respect to goodwill is never reversed.

Eastern Platinum Limited
Notes to the consolidated financial statements – years ended December 31, 2010 and 2009
(Expressed in thousands of U.S. dollars, except number of shares and per share amounts)

4. Summary of significant accounting policies (continued)

(l) Refining contract

The Company sells substantially all its PGM concentrate to one customer under the terms of an off-take or refining contract. The refining contract is amortized over the original life of the contract, estimated to be fifteen years, commencing in mid 2004. An evaluation of the carrying value of the contract is undertaken whenever events or changes in circumstances indicate that the carrying amount may not be recoverable.

(m) Inventories

Inventories, comprising stockpiled ore, concentrate awaiting further processing and sale, and chrome inventory are valued at the lower of cost and net realizable value. Consumables are valued at the lower of cost and net realizable value, with replacement cost used as the best available measure of net realizable value. Cost is determined using the weighted average method and includes direct mining expenditures and an appropriate portion of normal overhead expenditure. In the case of concentrate, direct concentrate costs are also included. Net realizable value is the estimated selling price in the ordinary course of business, less the estimated costs of completion and selling expenses. Obsolete, redundant and slow moving stores are identified and written down to net realizable values.

(n) Short-term investments

Short-term investments are investments which are transitional or current in nature, with an original maturity greater than three months.

(o) Cash and cash equivalents

Cash and cash equivalents consist of cash on hand, deposits in banks and highly liquid investments with an original maturity of three months or less.

(p) Financial assets

Financial assets are classified into one of four categories:
- fair value through profit or loss ("FVTPL");
- held-to-maturity ("HTM");
- available for sale ("AFS"); and,
- loans and receivables.

The classification is determined at initial recognition and depends on the nature and purpose of the financial asset.

(i) FVTPL financial assets

Financial assets are classified as FVTPL when the financial asset is held for trading or it is designated as FVTPL.

A financial asset is classified as held for trading if:
- it has been acquired principally for the purpose of selling in the near future;
- it is a part of an identified portfolio of financial instruments that the Company manages and has an actual pattern of short-term profit-taking; or
- it is a derivative that is not designated and effective as a hedging instrument.

Eastern Platinum Limited
Notes to the consolidated financial statements – years ended December 31, 2010 and 2009
(Expressed in thousands of U.S. dollars, except number of shares and per share amounts)

4. **Summary of significant accounting policies (continued)**

(p) *Financial assets (continued)*

(i) *FVTPL financial assets (continued)*

Financial assets classified as FVTPL are stated at fair value with any resultant gain or loss recognized in profit or loss. The net gain or loss recognized incorporates any dividend or interest earned on the financial asset. The Company does not have any assets classified as FVTPL financial assets.

(ii) *HTM investments*

HTM investments are recognized on a trade-date basis and are initially measured at fair value, including transaction costs. The Company does not have any assets classified as HTM investments.

(iii) *AFS financial assets*

Short-term investments and other assets held by the Company are classified as AFS and are stated at fair value. Gains and losses arising from changes in fair value are recognized in other comprehensive income and are accumulated in the investments revaluation reserve. To date, these gains and losses have not been significant due to the nature of the underlying investment. Impairment losses, interest calculated using the effective interest method and foreign exchange gains and losses on monetary assets, are recognized directly in profit or loss rather than equity. When an investment is disposed of or is determined to be impaired, the cumulative gain or loss previously recognized in the investments revaluation reserve is included in profit or loss for the period.

The fair value of AFS monetary assets denominated in a foreign currency is translated at the spot rate at the statement of financial position date. The change in fair value attributable to translation differences on amortized cost of debt instruments is recognized in profit or loss, while other changes are recognized in equity.

(iv) *Loans and receivables*

Trade receivables, loans, and other receivables that have fixed or determinable payments that are not quoted in an active market are classified as loans and receivables.

Loans and receivables are initially recognized at the transaction value and subsequently carried at amortized cost less impairment losses. The impairment loss of receivables is based on a review of all outstanding amounts at period end. Bad debts are written off during the year in which they are identified. Interest income is recognized by applying the effective interest rate, except for short-term receivables when the recognition of interest would be immaterial.

(v) *Effective interest method*

The effective interest method calculates the amortized cost of a financial asset and allocates interest income over the corresponding period. The effective interest rate is the rate that discounts estimated future cash receipts over the expected life of the financial asset, or, where appropriate, a shorter period, to the net carrying amount on initial recognition.

Eastern Platinum Limited
Notes to the consolidated financial statements – years ended December 31, 2010 and 2009
(Expressed in thousands of U.S. dollars, except number of shares and per share amounts)

4. **Summary of significant accounting policies (continued)**

(p) *Financial assets (continued)*

(v) *Effective interest method (continued)*

Income is recognized on an effective interest basis for debt instruments other than those financial assets classified as FVTPL.

(vi) *Impairment of financial assets*

Financial assets, other than those at FVTPL, are assessed for indicators of impairment at each period end. Financial assets are impaired when there is objective evidence that, as a result of one or more events that occurred after the initial recognition of the financial asset, the estimated future cash flows of the investment have been impacted.

Objective evidence of impairment could include the following:
- significant financial difficulty of the issuer or counterparty;
- default or delinquency in interest or principal payments; or
- it has become probable that the borrower will enter bankruptcy or financial reorganization.

For financial assets carried at amortized cost, the amount of the impairment is the difference between the asset's carrying amount and the present value of the estimated future cash flows, discounted at the financial asset's original effective interest rate.

The carrying amount of all financial assets, excluding trade receivables, is directly reduced by the impairment loss. The carrying amount of trade receivables is reduced through the use of an allowance account. When a trade receivable is considered uncollectible, it is written off against the allowance account. Subsequent recoveries of amounts previously written off are credited against the allowance account. Changes in the carrying amount of the allowance account are recognized in profit or loss.

With the exception of AFS equity instruments, if, in a subsequent period, the amount of the impairment loss decreases and the decrease relates to an event occurring after the impairment was recognized, the previously recognized impairment loss is reversed through profit or loss. On the date of impairment reversal, the carrying amount of the financial asset cannot exceed its amortized cost had impairment not been recognized.

(vii) *Derecognition of financial assets*

A financial asset is derecognized when:
- the contractual right to the asset's cash flows expire; or
- if the Company transfers the financial asset and substantially all risks and rewards of ownership to another entity.

Eastern Platinum Limited
Notes to the consolidated financial statements – years ended December 31, 2010 and 2009
(Expressed in thousands of U.S. dollars, except number of shares and per share amounts)

4. **Summary of significant accounting policies (continued)**

(q) *Environmental rehabilitation*

The Company recognizes liabilities for statutory, contractual, constructive or legal obligations associated with the retirement of property, plant and equipment, when those obligations result from the acquisition, construction, development or normal operation of the assets. The net present value of future rehabilitation cost estimates arising from the decommissioning of plant and other site preparation work is capitalized to mining assets along with a corresponding increase in the rehabilitation provision in the period incurred. Discount rates using a pre-tax rate that reflect the time value of money are used to calculate the net present value. The rehabilitation asset is depreciated on the same basis as mining assets.

The Company's estimates of reclamation costs could change as a result of changes in regulatory requirements, discount rates and assumptions regarding the amount and timing of the future expenditures. These changes are recorded directly to mining assets with a corresponding entry to the rehabilitation provision. The Company's estimates are reviewed annually for changes in regulatory requirements, discount rates, effects of inflation and changes in estimates.

Changes in the net present value, excluding changes in the Company's estimates of reclamation costs, are charged to profit and loss for the period.

The net present value of restoration costs arising from subsequent site damage that is incurred on an ongoing basis during production are charged to profit or loss in the period incurred.

The costs of rehabilitation projects that were included in the rehabilitation provision are recorded against the provision as incurred. The cost of ongoing current programs to prevent and control pollution is charged against profit and loss as incurred.

(r) *Leases*

(i) *The Company as lessor*

Rental income from operating leases is recognized on a straight-line basis over the term of the corresponding lease. Initial direct costs incurred in negotiating and arranging an operating lease are added to the carrying amount of the leased asset and recognized on a straight-line basis over the lease term.

(ii) *The Company as lessee*

Assets held under finance leases are recognized as assets of the Company at the lower of the fair value at the inception of the lease or the present value of the minimum lease payments. The corresponding liability is recognized as a finance lease obligation. Lease payments are apportioned between finance charges and reduction of the lease obligation to achieve a constant rate of interest on the remaining liability. Finance charges are charged to profit or loss, unless they are directly attributable to qualifying assets, in which case they are capitalized.

Operating lease payments are expensed on a straight-line basis over the term of the relevant lease. Incentives received upon entry into an operating lease are recognized straight-line over the lease term.

Eastern Platinum Limited
Notes to the consolidated financial statements – years ended December 31, 2010 and 2009
(Expressed in thousands of U.S. dollars, except number of shares and per share amounts)

4. **Summary of significant accounting policies (continued)**

(s) *Provisions*

Provisions are recorded when a present legal or constructive obligation exists as a result of past events where it is probable that an outflow of resources embodying economic benefits will be required to settle the obligation, and a reliable estimate of the amount of the obligation can be made.

The amount recognized as a provision is the best estimate of the consideration required to settle the present obligation at the statement of financial position date, taking into account the risks and uncertainties surrounding the obligation. Where a provision is measured using the cash flows estimated to settle the present obligation, its carrying amount is the present value of those cash flows. When some or all of the economic benefits required to settle a provision are expected to be recovered from a third party, the receivable is recognized as an asset if it is virtually certain that reimbursement will be received and the amount receivable can be measured reliably.

(t) *Employee benefits*

(i) *Employee post-retirement obligations – defined contribution retirement plan*

The Company's South African subsidiaries operate a defined contribution retirement plan for its employees. The pension plan is funded by payments from the employees and the subsidiaries and payments are charged to profit and loss for the period as incurred. The assets of the different plans are held by independently managed trust funds. The South African Pension Funds Act of 1956 governs these funds.

(ii) *Leave pay*

Employee entitlements to annual leave are recognized as they are earned by the employees. A provision, stated at current cost, is made for the estimated liability at period end.

(u) *Financial liabilities and equity*

Debt and equity instruments are classified as either financial liabilities or as equity in accordance with the substance of the contractual arrangement.

An equity instrument is any contract that evidences a residual interest in the assets of an entity after deducting all of its liabilities. Equity instruments issued by the Company are recorded at the proceeds received, net of direct issue costs.

Financial liabilities are classified as either financial liabilities at FVTPL or other financial liabilities.

(i) *Other financial liabilities*

Other financial liabilities are initially measured at fair value, net of transaction costs, and are subsequently measured at amortized cost using the effective interest method, with interest expense recognized on an effective yield basis.

The effective interest method is a method of calculating the amortized cost of a financial liability and of allocating interest expenses over the corresponding period. The effective interest rate is the rate that exactly discounts estimated future cash payments over the expected life of the financial liability, or, where appropriate, a shorter period, to the net carrying amount on initial recognition.

Eastern Platinum Limited
Notes to the consolidated financial statements – years ended December 31, 2010 and 2009
(Expressed in thousands of U.S. dollars, except number of shares and per share amounts)

4.   Summary of significant accounting policies (continued)

(u)   Financial liabilities and equity (continued)

(i)   Other financial liabilities (continued)

The Company has classified trade and other payables, short-term financial liabilities and long-term financial liabilities as other financial liabilities.

(ii)   Derecognition of financial liabilities

The Company derecognizes financial liabilities when, and only when, the Company's obligations are discharged, cancelled or they expire.

(v)   Critical accounting estimates

Critical accounting estimates are estimates and assumptions made by management that may result in material adjustments to the carrying amount of assets and liabilities within the next financial year.

(i)   Impairment of property, plant and equipment

Please refer to Note 4(k)(v).

(ii)   Rehabilitation provision

The future value of the provision for environmental rehabilitation was determined using an inflation rate of 5.49% (December 31, 2009 – 7.00%) and an estimated life of mine of 20 years for Zandfontein (December 31, 2009 – 18 years), 11 years for Maroelabult (December 31, 2009 – 18 years), 14 years for Crocette (December 31, 2009 – Nil), 1 year for Kennedy's Vale (December 31, 2009 – 1 year) and 22 years for Spitzkop (December 31, 2009 – 26 years). The provision has been discounted to present value at a discount rate of 8.29% (December 31, 2009 – 8.39%).

(w)   Critical accounting judgments

Critical accounting judgements are accounting policies that have been identified as being complex or involving subjective judgments or assessments.

(i)   Determination of functional currency

In accordance with IAS 21 *The Effects of Changes in Foreign Exchange Rates*, management determined that the functional currencies of Eastern Platinum Limited and its South African subsidiaries are the Canadian Dollar and South African Rand ("ZAR"), respectively, as these are the currencies of the primary economic environment in which the companies operate.

(ii)   Useful life of assets

At December 31, 2010 the remaining LOM for Zandfontein, Maroelabult, Crocette and Kennedy's Vale was assessed at 244 months, 133 months, 163 months and 12 months respectively (December 31, 2009 – 211 months, 211 months, 211 months and 12 months, respectively) based on proven and probable ore reserves. The change in remaining mine life will be evaluated each year as the reserves move to the proven and probable category.

Eastern Platinum Limited
Notes to the consolidated financial statements – years ended December 31, 2010 and 2009
(Expressed in thousands of U.S. dollars, except number of shares and per share amounts)

4.   **Summary of significant accounting policies (continued)**

(w)   *Critical accounting judgments (continued)*

(iii)   *Depreciation rates*

The estimated maximum useful lives of property, plant and equipment are:

Mining assets owned	
Underground and other assets	Life of mine
Mine houses	50 years
Office buildings	20 years
Plant	Life of mine
Computer equipment	3 years
Mining assets leased	5 years
Mineral properties being depleted	Life of mine
Residential properties	50 years
Properties and land	50 years

(x)   *Accounting standards issued but not yet effective*

(i)   *Effective for annual periods beginning on or after February 1, 2010*

- Amendment to IAS 32 *Financial Instruments: Presentation*

Rights, options or warrants to acquire a fixed number of the Company's equity instruments for a fixed amount of any currency will be allowed to be classified as equity instruments so long as the Company offers the rights, options or warrants pro rata to all of the Company's existing owners of the same class of the Company's non-derivative equity instruments.

(ii)   *Effective for annual periods beginning on or after July 1, 2010*

- Amendments to IFRS 3 *Business Combinations*

Clarification that the contingent consideration arising in a business combination previously accounted for in accordance with IFRS 3 that is outstanding at the adoption date continues to be accounted for in accordance with IFRS 3.

Limiting the accounting policy choice to measure non-controlling interests upon initial recognition at fair value or at the non-controlling interest's proportionate share of the acquiree's identifiable net assets to instruments that give rise to a present ownership interest and that currently entitle the holder to a share of net assets in the event of liquidation.

Expansion of the guidance with regards to the attribution of the market-based measure of an acquirer's share-based payment awards issued in exchange for acquiree awards.

- Amendments to IAS 27 *Consolidated and Separate Financial Statements*

Clarification that the amendments to IAS 21 *The Effects of Changes in Foreign Exchange Rates*, IAS 28 *Investments in Associates*, and IAS 31 *Interests in Joint Ventures* resulting from IAS 27 should be applied prospectively, except for amendments resulting from renumbering.

Eastern Platinum Limited
Notes to the consolidated financial statements – years ended December 31, 2010 and 2009
(Expressed in thousands of U.S. dollars, except number of shares and per share amounts)

4. **Summary of significant accounting policies (continued)**

(x) *Accounting standards issued but not yet effective (continued)*

(iii) *Effective for annual periods beginning on or after January 1, 2011*

- Amendments to IFRS 7 *Financial Instruments: Disclosures*

  Amendment to disclosure requirements, specifically, ensuring qualitative disclosures are made in close proximity to quantitative disclosures in order to better enable financial statement users to evaluate an entity's exposure to risks arising from financial instruments.

- Amendments to IAS 1 *Presentation of Financial Statements*

  Clarification that the breakdown of changes in equity resulting from transactions recognized in other comprehensive income is required to be presented in the statement of changes in equity or in the notes to the financial statements.

- Amendments to IAS 24 *Related Party Disclosures*

  Amendment of the definition for related parties.

- Amendments to IAS 34 *Interim Financial Reporting*

  Addition of further examples of events or transactions that require disclosure and removal of references to materiality when discussing other minimum disclosures.

(iv) *Effective for annual periods beginning on or after July 1, 2011*

- Amendments to IFRS 7 *Financial Instruments: Disclosures*

  Increase in disclosure with regards to the transfer of financial assets, especially if there is a disproportionate amount of transfer transactions that take place around the end of a reporting period.

(v) *Effective for annual periods beginning on or after January 1, 2013*

- New standard IFRS 9 *Financial Instruments*

  Partial replacement of IAS 39 *Financial Instruments: Recognition and Measurement*

The Company has not early adopted these revised standards and is currently assessing the impact that these standards will have on the consolidated financial statements.

Eastern Platinum Limited

Notes to the consolidated financial statements – years ended December 31, 2010 and 2009

(Expressed in thousands of U.S. dollars, except number of shares and per share amounts)

5. Subsidiaries and associates

(a) Subsidiaries

Details of the Company's subsidiaries at December 31, 2010 are as follows:

Name of subsidiary	Principal activity	Place of incorporation and operation	Proportion of ownership interest and voting power held	
			December 31, 2010	December 31, 2009
Eastern Platinum Holdings Limited	Holding company	BVI (i)	100%	100%
Eastplats Holdings Limited	Holding company	BVI (i)	100%	100%
Eastplats Acquisition Co. Ltd.	Holding company	BVI (i)	100%	100%
Eastplats International Incorporated	Holding company	Barbados	100%	100%
Royal Anthem Investments 134 (Pty) Ltd.	Holding company	South Africa	100%	100%
Spitzkop Joint Venture	Mining	South Africa	93.37%	93.37%
Barplats Investments Limited	Mining	South Africa	87.49%	87.49%
Spitzkop Platinum (Pty) Ltd.	Mining	South Africa	86.74%	86.74%
Mareesburg Joint Venture	Mining	South Africa	75.5%	75.5%
Lion's Head Platinum (Pty) Ltd.	Holding company	South Africa	51%	51%
Gubevu Consortium Investment Holdings (Pty) Ltd. (ii)	Holding company	South Africa	49.99%	49.99%

(i) British Virgin Islands ("BVI")

(ii) The Company has determined that its investment in Gubevu Consortium Investment Holdings (Pty) Ltd. is a Special Purpose Entity.

(b) Associates

Details of the Company's associates at December 31, 2010 are as follows:

Name of associate	Principal activity	Place of incorporation and operation	Proportion of ownership interest and voting power held	
			December 31, 2010	December 31, 2009
Afrimineral Holdings (Pty) Ltd.	Holding company	South Africa	49%	49%

Eastern Platinum Limited
Notes to the consolidated financial statements – years ended December 31, 2010 and 2009
(Expressed in thousands of U.S. dollars, except number of shares and per share amounts)

6.   Cash and cash equivalents

Cash and cash equivalents are comprised of:

	December 31, 2010	December 31, 2009
Cash in bank	$ 102,654	$ 7,249
Short-term money market instruments	5,192	-
	$ 107,846	$ 7,249

7.   Trade and other receivables

Trade and other receivables are comprised of the following:

	December 31, 2010	December 31, 2009
Trade receivables	$ 30,142	$ 25,839
Current tax receivable	1,283	1,057
Other receivables	2,556	2,316
Allowance for doubtful debts for other receivables	(194)	(74)
	$ 33,787	$ 29,138

(a)   *Aging of past due, but not impaired*

The average credit period of PGM sales is 4 months. The Company has the right to request up to a 90% advance on payment, payable 1 month subsequent to sale. The Company has financial risk management policies in place to ensure that all receivables are received within the pre-agreed credit terms.

Included in trade and other receivables are receivables with a carrying value of $152 (December 31, 2009 - $276) that are past due but have not been provided for. For the years ended December 31, 2010 and 2009, substantially all of the Company's PGM production was sold to one customer and there was no significant change in the credit quality of this customer over that time. The past due amounts are considered recoverable.

	December 31, 2010	December 31, 2009
Less than 5 months	$ -	$ 276
5 months and greater	152	-
	$ 152	$ 276

Eastern Platinum Limited
Notes to the consolidated financial statements – years ended December 31, 2010 and 2009
(Expressed in thousands of U.S. dollars, except number of shares and per share amounts)

7. **Trade and other receivables (continued)**

(b) *Movement in the allowance for doubtful debts*

	December 31, 2010	December 31, 2009
Opening balance	$ 74	$ 85
Impairment losses recognized on receivables	116	42
Amounts written off during the year as uncollectible	(16)	(26)
Amounts recovered during the year	-	(43)
Foreign exchange translation gains and losses	20	16
Closing balance	$ 194	$ 74

(c) *Aging of impaired receivables*

	December 31, 2010	December 31, 2009
Less than 4 months	46	6
Greater than 4 months	148	68
	$ 194	$ 74

At December 31, 2010, other receivables of $194 (December 31, 2009 - $74) were impaired and provided for. These receivables were for rental income, and impairment was determined based on payment history.

8. **Inventories**

	December 31, 2010	December 31, 2009
Consumables	$ 6,607	$ 4,549
Ore and concentrate	477	276
Chrome inventory	1,748	-
	$ 8,832	$ 4,825

Production costs for the year ended December 31, 2010 was $109,901 (December 31, 2009 - $82,839). Production costs represent the cost of inventories sold during the period. For the years ended December 31, 2010 and 2009 production costs did not include any amounts with regards to the write-down of inventory to net realizable value or with regards to the reversal of write-downs.

At December 31, 2010 and 2009, no inventories have been pledged as security for liabilities.

Eastern Platinum Limited

Notes to the consolidated financial statements – years ended December 31, 2010 and 2009
(Expressed in thousands of U.S. dollars, except number of shares and per share amounts)

9. Property, plant and equipment

	Plant and equipment owned	Plant and equipment leased	Mineral properties being depleted	Mineral properties not being depleted	Residential properties	Properties and land	TOTAL
Cost							
Balance as at December 31, 2008	$ 315,547	$ 4,892	$ 108,680	$ 444,115	$ 7,954	$ 5,299	$ 886,487
Assets acquired	27,593	-	(186)	921	88	331	28,747
Disposals	(1,510)	-	-	-	-	-	(1,510)
Foreign exchange movement	84,593	1,240	27,606	101,086	2,029	1,348	217,902
Balance as at December 31, 2009	$ 426,223	$ 6,132	$ 136,100	$ 546,122	$ 10,071	$ 6,978	$ 1,131,626
Assets acquired	32,444	-	-	261	286	-	32,991
Foreign exchange movement	56,520	768	17,040	58,901	1,275	874	135,378
Balance as at December 31, 2010	$ 515,187	$ 6,900	$ 153,140	$ 605,284	$ 11,632	$ 7,852	$ 1,299,995
Accumulated depreciation and impairment losses							
Balance as at December 31, 2008	$ 91,179	$ 1,966	$ 12,397	$ 273,084	$ 1,726	$ 662	$ 381,014
Depreciation	11,298	1,092	4,646	-	118	-	17,154
Foreign exchange movement	24,467	633	3,722	69,238	452	168	98,680
Balance as at December 31, 2009	$ 126,944	$ 3,691	$ 20,765	$ 342,322	$ 2,296	$ 830	$ 496,848
Depreciation	15,452	1,244	5,676	-	135	-	22,507
Foreign exchange movement	17,574	598	3,224	42,862	302	104	64,664
Balance as at December 31, 2010	$ 159,970	$ 5,533	$ 29,665	$ 385,184	$ 2,733	$ 934	$ 584,019
Carrying amounts							
At December 31, 2008	$ 224,368	$ 2,926	$ 96,283	$ 171,031	$ 6,228	$ 4,637	$ 505,473
At December 31, 2009	$ 299,279	$ 2,441	$ 115,335	$ 203,800	$ 7,775	$ 6,148	$ 634,778
At December 31, 2010	$ 355,217	$ 1,367	$ 123,475	$ 220,100	$ 8,899	$ 6,918	$ 715,976

Eastern Platinum Limited
Notes to the consolidated financial statements
(Expressed in thousands of U.S. dollars, except number of shares and per share amounts)

9. Property, plant and equipment

	Crocodile River Mine (a)	Kennedy's Vale Project (b)	Spitzkop PGM Project (c)	Mareesburg Project (c)	Other property plant and equipment	TOTAL
Cost						
Balance as at December 31, 2008	$ 442,262	$ 319,109	$ 101,712	$ 23,294	$ 110	$ 886,487
Assets acquired	27,826	-	826	95	-	28,747
Disposals	(1,510)	-	-	-	-	(1,510)
Foreign exchange movement	116,798	80,908	16,456	3,722	18	217,902
Balance as at December 31, 2009	$ 585,376	$ 400,017	$ 118,994	$ 27,111	$ 128	$ 1,131,626
Assets acquired	32,728	-	47	214	2	32,991
Foreign exchange movement	76,470	50,082	7,316	1,503	7	135,378
Balance as at December 31, 2010	$ 694,574	$ 450,099	$ 126,357	$ 28,828	$ 137	$ 1,299,995
Accumulated depreciation and impairment losses						
Balance as at December 31, 2008	$ 107,855	$ 273,084	$ -	$ -	$ 75	$ 381,014
Depreciation	17,130	-	-	-	24	17,154
Foreign exchange movement	29,432	69,238	-	-	10	98,680
Balance as at December 31, 2009	$ 154,417	$ 342,322	$ -	$ -	$ 109	$ 496,848
Depreciation	22,500	-	-	-	7	22,507
Foreign exchange movement	21,796	42,861	-	1	6	64,664
Balance as at December 31, 2010	$ 198,713	$ 385,183	$ -	$ 1	$ 122	$ 584,019
Carrying amounts						
At December 31, 2008	$ 334,407	$ 46,025	$ 101,712	$ 23,294	$ 35	$ 505,473
At December 31, 2009	$ 430,959	$ 57,695	$ 118,994	$ 27,111	$ 19	$ 634,778
At December 31, 2010	$ 495,861	$ 64,916	$ 126,357	$ 28,827	$ 15	$ 715,976

Eastern Platinum Limited
Notes to the consolidated financial statements – years ended December 31, 2010 and 2009
(Expressed in thousands of U.S. dollars, except number of shares and per share amounts)

9. Property, plant and equipment (continued)

(a) *Crocodile River Mine ("CRM")*

The Company holds directly and indirectly 87.5% of CRM, which is located on the eastern portion of the western limb of the Bushveld Complex. The Maroelabult and Zandfontein sections are currently in production. Development of the Crocette section recommenced on April 4, 2010.

(b) *Kennedy's Vale Project ("KV")*

The Company holds directly and indirectly 87.5% of KV, which is located on the eastern limb of the Bushveld Complex, near Steelpoort in the Province of Mpumalanga. It comprises PGM mineral rights on five farms in the Steelpoort Valley. The development of this project was on hold as at December 31, 2010.

(c) *Spitzkop PGM Project and Mareesburg Project*

The Company holds directly and indirectly a 93.4% interest in the Spitzkop PGM Project and a 75.5% interest in the Mareesburg Project. The Company currently acts as the operator of both the Mareesburg Platinum Project and Spitzkop PGM Project, both located on the eastern limb of the Bushveld Complex. Planning for the development of these projects commenced in late 2010.

10. Refining Contract

During the year ended June 30, 2006, the Company acquired a 69% interest in Barplats and assigned a portion of the purchase price to the off-take contract governing the sales of Barplats' PGM concentrate production. The initial value of the contract was $17,939. During the year ended June 30, 2007, the Company acquired an additional 5% interest in Barplats resulting in an additional allocation to the contract of $4,802 for a total aggregate value of $22,741. During the year ended December 31, 2008, the Company acquired an additional 2.47% interest in Barplats. The acquisition did not affect the aggregate value of the contract. The value of the contract is amortized over the remaining term of the contract which is 8.5 years as at December 31, 2010.

Cost

Balance as at December 31, 2008	$	16,850
Foreign exchange movement		4,272
Balance as at December 31, 2009	$	21,122
Foreign exchange movement		2,645
Balance as at December 31, 2010	$	**23,767**

Accumulated amortization

Balance as at December 31, 2008	$	4,357
Amortization		1,332
Foreign exchange movement		1,264
Balance as at December 31, 2009	$	6,953
Amortization		1,513
Foreign exchange movement		1,036
Balance as at December 31, 2010	$	**9,502**

Carrying amounts

At December 31, 2008	$	12,493
At December 31, 2009	$	14,169
At December 31, 2010	$	**14,265**

Eastern Platinum Limited
Notes to the consolidated financial statements
(Expressed in thousands of U.S. dollars, except number of shares and per share amounts)

11. Other assets

Other assets consists of a money market fund investment that is classified as available-for-sale and serves as security for a guarantee issued to the Department of Mineral Resources of South Africa in respect of the environmental rehabilitation liability (Note 14). Changes to other assets for the year ended December 31, 2010 are as follows:

Balance, December 31, 2008	$	1,017
Additional investment	$	811
Service fees		(6)
Interest income		123
Foreign exchange movement		337
Balance, December 31, 2009	$	2,282
Additional investment		955
Service fees		(8)
Interest income		185
Foreign exchange movement		409
Balance, December 31, 2010	$	**3,823**

12. Accounts payable and accrued liabilities

	December 31, 2010		December 31, 2009
Trade payables	$ 10,604	$	9,932
Accrued liabilities	10,240		6,849
Other	6,165		6,138
	$ 27,009	$	22,919

The average credit period of purchases is 1 month. The Company has financial risk management policies in place to ensure that all payables are paid within the pre-agreed credit terms.

13. Finance leases

Finance leases relate to mining vehicles with lease terms of 5 years payable half yearly in advance. The Company has the option to purchase the vehicles for a nominal amount at the conclusion of the lease agreements. The Company's obligations under finance leases are secured by the lessor's title to the leased assets. Interest is calculated at the South African prime rate plus 1%. At December 31, 2010, the finance leases are repayable in 1 semiannual installment (December 31, 2009 – 3) of $667 (December 31, 2009 - $611) and a top-up payment of $2,738 in December 2011. The fair value of the finance lease liabilities approximated carrying value.

(a) Minimum lease payments

	December 31, 2010		December 31, 2009
No later than 1 year	$ 3,405	$	1,221
Later than 1 year, but no later than 5 years	-		3,061
	3,405	$	4,282
Less: future finance charges	(194)		(506)
Present value of minimum lease payments	$ 3,211		3,776

Eastern Platinum Limited
Notes to the consolidated financial statements
(Expressed in thousands of U.S. dollars, except number of shares and per share amounts)

13. Finance leases (continued)

(b)   Present value of minimum lease payments

	December 31, 2010	December 31, 2009
No later than 1 year	$ 3,211	$ 926
Later than 1 year, but no later than 5 years	-	2,850
	$ 3,211	$ 3,776

14. Provision for environmental rehabilitation

Although the ultimate amount of the environmental rehabilitation provision is uncertain, the fair value of these obligations is based on information currently available, including closure plans and applicable regulations. Significant closure activities include land rehabilitation, demolition of buildings and mine facilities and other costs.

The liability for the environmental rehabilitation provision at December 31, 2010 is approximately ZAR 58.9 million ($8,934). The liability was determined using an inflation rate of 5.49% (December 31, 2009 – 7.00%) and an estimated life of mine of 20 years for Zandfontein (December 31, 2009 – 18 years), 11 years for Maroelabult (December 31, 2009 – 18 years), 14 years for Crocette (December 31, 2009 – Nil), 1 year for Kennedy's Vale (December 31, 2009 – 1 year) and 22 years for Spitzkop (December 31, 2009 – 26 years). A discount rate of 8.29% was used (December 31, 2009 – 8.39%). A guarantee of $3,823 (December 31, 2009 - $2,282) has been issued to the Department of Mineral Resources (Note 11). The guarantee will be utilized to cover expenses incurred to rehabilitate the mining area upon closure of the mine. The undiscounted value of this liability is approximately ZAR 215.4 million ($32,694).

Changes to the environmental rehabilitation provision are as follows:

Balance, December 31, 2008	$ 5,598
Revision in estimates	629
Interest expense (Note 19)	443
Foreign exchange movement	1,482
Balance, December 31, 2009	$ 8,152
Revision in estimates	(961)
Interest expense (Note 19)	694
Foreign exchange movement	1,049
Balance, December 31, 2010	$ **8,934**

15. Income taxes

The income tax recognized in profit or loss comprises of:

	December 31, 2010	December 31, 2009
Deferred tax recovery relating to the origination and reversal of temporary differences	$ 924	$ 1,623
Total deferred income tax recovery	$ 924	$ 1,623

Eastern Platinum Limited
Notes to the consolidated financial statements
(Expressed in thousands of U.S. dollars, except number of shares and per share amounts)

15. Income taxes (continued)

The provision for income taxes reported differs from the amounts computed by applying the cumulative Canadian federal and provincial income tax rates to the loss before tax provision due to the following:

	December 31, 2010	December 31, 2009
Statutory tax rate	28.50%	30.00%
Expected tax expense (recovery) on (profit) loss before income tax	$ 2,523	$ (120)
Difference in tax rates between foreign jurisdictions and Canada	(9,365)	(9,057)
Items not deductible for income tax purposes	534	1,986
Tax losses not recognized	4,572	5,568
Change in tax estimates	812	-
Deferred income tax recovery	$ (924)	$ (1,623)

The approximate tax effect of each item that gives rise to the Company's deferred tax liabilities are as follows:

	December 31, 2010	December 31, 2009
Non-capital loss carry forwards	$ 12,031	$ 5,175
Share issue costs	3,582	1,013
Accumulated cost base difference on assets and other	(43,517)	(36,877)
Deferred receipts	(6,102)	(5,461)
Deferred tax liabilities before valuation allowance	$ (34,006)	$ (36,150)
Less valuation allowance	(12,636)	(6,341)
Total deferred tax liabilities	$ (46,642)	$ (42,491)

The movement between the opening and closing balances was recognized in profit or loss.

Eastern Platinum Limited
Notes to the consolidated financial statements
(Expressed in thousands of U.S. dollars, except number of shares and per share amounts)

15. Income taxes (continued)

At December 31, 2010, the Company has non-capital losses of approximately Cdn$20,679 available to apply against future Canadian income for tax purposes. In South Africa, the Company has unredeemed capital expenditures available for utilization against future mining taxable income of approximately R3.2 billion, and estimated assessable tax losses of approximately R103 million. The South African losses do not expire unless the Company's mining activities cease. The Canadian non-capital losses will expire as follows (in thousands of Canadian dollars):

	2010 Cdn$ (000's)
2012	272
2013	1,592
2014	916
2025	3,224
2026	6,105
2027	3,393
2028	4,217
2029	75
2030	885
	$ 20,679

At December 31, 2010, the Company has capital losses of Cdn$1,569 available to apply against future capital gains in Canada.

The Company's operations are conducted in a number of countries with complex tax legislation and regulations pertaining to the Company's activities. Any reassessment of the Company's tax filings by the tax authorities may result in material adjustments to net profit or loss, tax assets and operating loss carry-forwards. The Company provides for such reassessments when it is probable that a taxation authority will not sustain the Company's filing position and the amount of the tax exposure can be reasonably estimated. As at December 31, 2010, no provisions have been made in the financial statements for any estimated tax liability.

16. Commitments

The Company has committed to capital expenditures on projects of approximately ZAR 86 million ($13,056) as at December 31, 2010 (December 31, 2009 – ZAR 37 million, $4,959).

17. Issued capital

(a) *Authorized*

- Unlimited number of preferred redeemable, voting, non-participating shares without nominal or par value,

- Unlimited number of common shares with no par value.

(b) *December 30, 2010 Public Offering*

On December 30, 2010, the Company completed a public offering (the "Public Offering"). The Public Offering consisted of 224,250,000 common shares, of which 195,361,476 common shares were sold at a price of Cdn$1.55 and 28,888,524 common shares were sold at a price of £0.9568. Share issue costs of Cdn$16,501 were incurred.

Eastern Platinum Limited
Notes to the consolidated financial statements
(Expressed in thousands of U.S. dollars, except number of shares and per share amounts)

17. Issued capital (continued)

(c) *Share options*

The Company has an incentive plan (the "2008 Plan"), approved by the Company's shareholders at its annual general meeting held on June 4, 2008, under which options to purchase common shares may be granted to its directors, officers, employees and others at the discretion of the Board of Directors. Under the terms of the 2008 Plan:

-   75 million common shares are reserved for issuance upon the exercise of options.

-   All outstanding options at June 4, 2008 granted under the Company's previous plan (the "2005 Plan") will continue to exist under the 2008 plan provided that the fundamental terms governing such options will be deemed to be those under the 2005 Plan.

-   Each option granted shall be for a term not exceeding five years from the date of being granted and the vesting period is determined based on the discretion of the Board of Directors. Vesting is dependent on continued employment with the Company.

-   The option exercise price is set at the date of the grant and cannot be less than the closing market price of the Company's common shares on the Toronto Stock Exchange on the day immediately preceding the day of the grant of the option.

-   The 2008 Plan includes share appreciation rights providing for an optionee to elect to exercise options and to receive an amount in common shares equal to the difference between fair market value at the time of exercise and the exercise price for the options exercised.

(i)   *Movements in share options during the year*

The changes in share options during the years ended December 31, 2010 and 2009 were as follows:

	December 31, 2010		December 31, 2009	
	Number of options	Weighted average exercise price	Number of options	Weighted average exercise price
		Cdn$		Cdn$
Balance outstanding, beginning of year	59,575,834	1.48	64,746,000	1.52
Options granted	2,231,000	1.30	695,000	0.57
Options exercised	(2,794,995)	0.33	(535,999)	0.32
Options forfeited	(1,035,003)	1.82	(5,329,167)	2.00
Balance outstanding, end of year	57,976,836	1.52	59,575,834	1.48

2,794,995 share options were exercised during the year ended December 31, 2010. The weighted average closing share price at the date of exercise was Cdn$1.50.

Eastern Platinum Limited
Notes to the consolidated financial statements
(Expressed in thousands of U.S. dollars, except number of shares and per share amounts)

17. Issued capital (continued)

(c)   *Share options (continued)*

(ii)   *Fair value of share options granted in the year*

The fair value of each option granted is estimated at the time of the grant using the Black-Scholes option pricing model with weighted average assumptions for grants as follows:

	2010
	January 18
Exercise price	**Cdn$1.30**
Closing market price on day preceding date of grant	**Cdn$1.30**
Grant date share price	**Cdn$1.42**
Risk-free interest rate	**1.73%**
Expected life	**3 years**
Annualized volatility	**83%**
Dividend rate	**0%**
Grant date fair value	**Cdn$0.80**

	2009			
	February 11	June 30	November 3	Weighted average
Exercise price	Cdn$0.32	Cdn$0.52	Cdn$0.76	Cdn$0.57
Closing market price on day preceding date of grant	Cdn$0.32	Cdn$0.52	Cdn$0.76	Cdn$0.57
Grant date share price	Cdn$0.38	Cdn$0.52	Cdn$0.81	Cdn$0.59
Risk-free interest rate	1.69%	1.84%	1.86%	1.83%
Expected life	3 years	3 years	3 years	3 years
Annualized volatility	78%	79%	82%	80%
Dividend rate	0%	0%	0%	0%
Grant date fair value	Cdn$0.21	Cdn$0.27	Cdn$0.45	Cdn$0.32

Exercise price is the closing market price on the day preceding the date the options were granted, as defined by the 2008 Plan.

Grant date share price is the closing market price on the day the options were granted.

Expected volatility is based on the historical share price volatility since Eastern Platinum Limited completed its acquisition of Barplats Investment Limited on May 2, 2006, or for 3 years prior to the date of grant, whichever is shorter.

Eastern Platinum Limited
Notes to the consolidated financial statements
(Expressed in thousands of U.S. dollars, except number of shares and per share amounts)

17. Issued capital (continued)

(c) *Share options (continued)*

(iii) *Share options outstanding at the end of the year*

The following table summarizes information concerning outstanding and exercisable options at December 31, 2010:

Options outstanding	Options exercisable	Exercise price	Remaining Contractual Life (Years)	Expiry date
		Cdn$		
6,725,000	6,725,000	1.70	0.40	May 24, 2011
250,000	250,000	1.70	0.91	November 27, 2011
19,987,500	19,987,500	1.82	1.19	March 7, 2012
14,573,334	14,573,334	0.32	2.97	December 18, 2013
20,000	-	0.32	3.12	February 11, 2014
400,000	400,000	0.52	3.50	June 30, 2014
95,002	45,000	0.76	3.84	November 3, 2014
2,226,000	2,226,000	1.30	4.06	January 18, 2015
13,070,000	13,070,000	2.31	6.77	October 5, 2017
460,000	460,000	3.38	7.15	February 20, 2018
170,000	170,000	3.38	7.24	March 27, 2018
57,976,836	57,906,834		3.00	

The weighted average exercise price of options exercisable at December 31, 2010 is Cdn$1.53.

(d) *Share purchase warrants*

The changes in warrants during the years ended December 31, 2010 and 2009 were as follows:

	December 31, 2010		December 31, 2009	
	Number of warrants	**Weighted average exercise price**	Number of warrants	Weighted average exercise price
		Cdn$		Cdn$
Balance outstanding, beginning of year	-	-	58,485,996	1.80
Warrants exercised	-	-	-	-
Warrants expired	-	-	(58,485,996)	1.80
Balance outstanding, end of year	-	-	-	-

Eastern Platinum Limited
Notes to the consolidated financial statements
(Expressed in thousands of U.S. dollars, except number of shares and per share amounts)

18. Non-controlling interest

The non-controlling interests are comprised of the following:

Balance, December 31, 2008	$	12,002
Non-controlling interests' share of loss in Barplats		(1,908)
Non-controlling interests' share of interest on advances to Gubevu		(2,520)
Foreign exchange movement		2,467
Balance, December 31, 2009	$	10,041
Non-controlling interests' share of loss in Barplats		(866)
Non-controlling interests' share of interest on advances to Gubevu		(2,709)
Foreign exchange movement		762
Balance, December 31, 2010	$	**7,228**

19. Finance costs

	December 31, 2010	December 31, 2009
Interest on revenue advances	$ 614	$ 482
Interest on finance leases	277	377
Interest on provision for environmental rehabilitation	694	443
Interest on tax	209	2
Other interest	13	387
	$ 1,807	$ 1,691

20. Earnings per share

The weighted average number of ordinary shares for the purposes of diluted earnings per share reconciles to the weighted average number of ordinary shares used in the calculation of basic earnings per share as follows:

	December 31, 2010	December 31, 2009
	(in thousands)	
Weighted average number of ordinary shares used in the calculation of basic earnings per share	683,177	680,577
Shares deemed to be issued for no consideration in respect of options	11,662	7,213
Weighted average number of ordinary shares used in the calculation of diluted earnings per share	694,839	687,790

The earnings used to calculate basic and diluted earnings per share for the year ended December 31, 2010 was $13,352 (December 31, 2009 – $5,650).

Eastern Platinum Limited
Notes to the consolidated financial statements
(Expressed in thousands of U.S. dollars, except number of shares and per share amounts)

20. Earnings per share (continued)

The following potential ordinary shares, outstanding at December 31, 2010, are anti-dilutive and are therefore excluded from the weighted average number of ordinary shares for the purposes of diluted earnings per share:

	December 31, 2010	December 31, 2009
	(in thousands)	
Options	40,663	41,434

21. Retirement benefit plans

The Barplats Provident Fund is an independent, defined contribution plan administered by Liberty Life Limited in South Africa. The costs associated with the defined contribution plan included in net profit were $3,894 (December 31, 2009 - $2,705). The total number of employees in the plan at December 31, 2010 was 1,762 (December 31, 2009 – 1,800).

22. Related party transactions

Balances and transactions between the Company and its subsidiaries have been eliminated on consolidation and are not disclosed in this note. Details of the transactions between the Company and other related parties are disclosed below.

(a) Trading transactions

The Company's related parties consist of companies owned by executive officers and directors as follows:

	Nature of transactions
Andrews PGM Consulting	Consulting
Buccaneer Management Inc.	Management
Jazz Financial Ltd.	Management
Maluti Services Limited	General and administrative
Xiste Consulting Ltd.	Management

The Company incurred the following fees and expenses in the normal course of operations in connection with companies owned by key management and directors. Expenses have been measured at the exchange amount which is determined on a cost recovery basis.

	Note	December 31, 2010	December 31, 2009
Consulting fees	(i)	$ 304	$ 232
General and administrative expenses		193	48
Management fees		2,253	1,429
		$ 2,750	$ 1,709

(i)   The Company paid fees to a private company controlled by a director of the Company for consulting services performed outside of his capacity as a director.

Amounts due to related parties are unsecured, non-interest bearing and due on demand. Accounts payable at December 31, 2010 included $1,089 (December 31, 2009 - $510) which were due to private companies controlled by officers of the Company.

Eastern Platinum Limited
Notes to the consolidated financial statements
(Expressed in thousands of U.S. dollars, except number of shares and per share amounts)

22. Related party transactions (continued)

(b) *Compensation of key management personnel*

The remuneration of directors and other members of key management personnel during the years ended December 31, 2010 and 2009 were as follows:

	Note	December 31, 2010	December 31, 2009
Salaries and directors' fees	(i)	$ 3,758	$ 2,695
Share-based payments	(ii)	1,627	93
		$ 5,385	$ 2,788

(i)   Salaries and directors' fees include consulting and management fees disclosed in Note 22(a).

(ii) Share-based payments are the fair value of options granted to key management personnel.

(iii) Key management personnel were not paid post-employment benefits, termination benefits, or other long-term benefits during the years ended December 31, 2010 and 2009.

23. Segmented information

(a) Operating segment - The Company's operations are primarily directed towards the acquisition, exploration and production of platinum group metals in South Africa.

(b) Geographic segments - The Company's assets, revenues and expenses by geographic areas for the years ended December 31, 2010 and 2009 are as follows:

Eastern Platinum Limited

Notes to the consolidated financial statements – years ended December 31, 2010 and 2009
(Expressed in thousands of U.S. dollars, except number of shares and per share amounts)

23. Segmented Information (continued)

(b) *Geographic segments (continued)*

December 31, 2010

	Crocodile River Mine	Kennedy's Vale	Spitzkop	Mareesburg	Other	Total South Africa	Barbados and BVI	Canada	TOTAL
Current assets	$ 45,787	$ 445	$ 1,669	$ 61	$ 997	$ 48,959	$ -	$ 343,952	$ 392,911
Property, plant and equipment	495,861	64,916	126,357	28,827	-	715,961	-	15	715,976
Refining contract	14,265	-	-	-	-	14,265	-	-	14,265
Other Assets	3,823	-	-	-	-	3,823	-	-	3,823
	$ 559,736	$ 65,361	$ 128,026	28,888	$ 997	$ 783,008	$ -	$ 343,967	$ 1,126,975
Property, plant and equipment expenditures	$ 32,728	$ -	$ 47	$ 214	$ -	$ 32,989	$ -	$ 2	$ 32,991
Revenue	$ 155,000	$ -	$ -	$ -	$ -	$ 155,000	$ -	$ -	$ 155,000
Production costs	(109,901)	-	-	-	-	(109,901)	-	-	(109,901)
Depletion and depreciation	(22,499)	-	-	-	-	(22,499)	-	(8)	(22,507)
General and administrative expenses	(4,591)	(1,396)	(118)	(114)	(16)	(6,235)	(60)	(5,822)	(12,117)
Share-based payment	(79)	-	-	-	-	(79)	-	(1,373)	(1,452)
Interest income	1,635	-	-	8	-	1,643	-	154	1,797
Finance costs	(1,027)	(752)	(28)	-	-	(1,807)	-	-	(1,807)
Foreign exchange (loss) gain	(827)	-	-	-	-	(827)	-	667	(160)
Profit (loss) before income taxes	17,711	(2,148)	(146)	(106)	(16)	15,295	(60)	(6,382)	8,853
Deferred income tax recovery (expense)	2,240	-	-	-	-	2,240	(1,316)	-	924
Net profit (loss)	$ 19,951	$ (2,148)	$ (146)	(106)	$ (16)	$ 17,535	$ (1,376)	$ (6,382)	$ 9,777

Eastern Platinum Limited
Notes to the consolidated financial statements
(Expressed in thousands of U.S. dollars, except number of shares and per share amounts)

23. Segmented Information (continued)

(b) *Geographic segments (continued)*

December 31, 2009

	Crocodile River Mine	Kennedy's Vale	Spitzkop	Mareesburg	Other	Total South Africa	Canada	TOTAL
Current assets	$ 36,749	$ 176	$ 1,509	$ 45	$ 1,003	$ 39,482	$ 16,139	$ 55,621
Property, plant and equipment	430,959	57,695	118,994	27,111	-	634,759	19	634,778
Refining contract	14,169	-	-	-	-	14,169	-	14,169
Other assets	2,282	-	-	-	-	2,282	-	2,282
	$ 484,159	$ 57,871	$ 120,503	$ 27,156	$ 1,003	$ 690,692	$ 16,158	$ 706,850
Property, plant and equipment expenditures	$ 27,826	$ -	$ 826	$ 95	$ -	$ 28,747	$ -	$ 28,747
Sale of property, plant and equipment	(1,510)	-	-	-	-	(1,510)	-	(1,510)
Revenue	$ 111,365	$ -	$ -	$ -	$ -	$ 111,365	$ -	$ 111,365
Production costs	(82,839)	-	-	-	-	(82,839)	-	(82,839)
Depreciation and amortization	(17,130)	-	-	-	-	(17,130)	(24)	(17,154)
General and administrative expenses	(3,397)	(2,286)	(510)	(157)	(26)	(6,376)	(4,152)	(10,528)
Share-based payment	(489)	-	-	-	-	(489)	(93)	(582)
Interest income	1,388	-	38	-	-	1,426	360	1,786
Finance costs	(1,547)	-	-	-	-	(1,547)	(144)	(1,691)
Foreign exchange gain (loss)	28	-	-	-	-	28	(786)	(758)
Profit (loss) before income taxes	7,379	(2,286)	(472)	(157)	(26)	4,438	(4,839)	(401)
Deferred income tax recovery	1,623	-	-	-	-	1,623	-	1,623
Net profit (loss)	$ 9,002	$ (2,286)	$ (472)	$ (157)	$ (26)	$ 6,061	$ (4,839)	$ 1,222

For the years ended December 31, 2010 and 2009, substantially all of the Company's PGM production was sold to one customer.

Eastern Platinum Limited
Notes to the consolidated financial statements
(Expressed in thousands of U.S. dollars, except number of shares and per share amounts)

24. Financial instruments

(a) *Management of capital risk*

The capital structure of the Company consists of equity attributable to common shareholders, comprising issued capital, equity-settled employee benefits reserve, deficit and currency translation adjustment. The Company's objectives when managing capital are to: (i) preserve capital, (ii) obtain the best available net return, and (iii) maintain liquidity.

The Company manages the capital structure and makes adjustments to it in light of changes in economic conditions and the risk characteristics of the underlying assets. To maintain or adjust the capital structure, the Company may attempt to issue new shares.

The Company is not subject to externally imposed capital requirements.

(b) *Categories of financial instruments*

	December 31, 2010		December 31, 2009	
Financial assets				
Cash and cash equivalents	$	107,846	$	7,249
Loans and receivables				
Trade receivables		33,787		29,138
Available for sale financial assets				
Short-term investments		242,446		14,409
Other assets		3,823		2,282
	$	387,902	$	53,078
Financial liabilities				
Other financial liabilities				
Accounts payable and accrued liabilities	$	27,009	$	22,919
Current portion of finance leases		3,211		926
Long-term portion of finance leases		-		2,850
	$	30,220	$	26,695

(c) *Fair value of financial instruments*

(i) *Fair value estimation of financial instruments*

The fair value of financial instruments traded in active markets is based on quoted market prices at the balance sheet date.

The fair values of cash and cash equivalents, short-term investments, trade receivables and accounts payable approximate their carrying values due to the short-term to maturities of these financial instruments.

The fair value of short-term debt was determined using discounted cash flows at prevailing market rates and the fair value is considered to approximate carrying value.

Eastern Platinum Limited
Notes to the consolidated financial statements
(Expressed in thousands of U.S. dollars, except number of shares and per share amounts)

24. Financial instruments (continued)

(c) *Fair value of financial instruments (continued)*

   (ii) *Fair value measurements recognized in the statement of financial position*

   Financial instruments that are measured subsequent to initial recognition at fair value are grouped into a hierarchy based on the degree to which the fair value is observable. Level 1 fair value measurements are derived from unadjusted, quoted prices in active markets for identical assets or liabilities. Level 2 fair value measurements are derived from inputs other than quoted prices included within Level 1 that are observable for the asset or liability directly or indirectly. Level 3 fair value measurements are derived from valuation techniques that include inputs for the asset or liability that are not based on observable market data.

   The Company's short-term investments and other assets are measured subsequent to initial recognition at fair value and are Level 2 financial instruments at December 31, 2010. There were no transfers between levels during the year ended December 31, 2010.

(d) *Reclassification of financial assets*

   There was no reclassification of financial assets during the years ended December 31, 2010 and 2009.

(e) *Financial risk management*

   The Company's financial instruments are exposed to certain financial risks, including currency risk, interest rate risk, price risk, credit risk and liquidity risk. The Company's exposure to these risks and its methods of managing the risks remain consistent.

   (i) *Currency risk*

   The Company is exposed to the financial risk related to the fluctuation of foreign exchange rates. The Company's revenues are based on US dollar PGM prices, but the Company receives revenues in South African Rand. A significant change in the currency exchange rates between the South African Rand relative to the US dollar could have an effect on the Company's results of operations, financial position and cash flows. The Company has not entered into any derivative financial instruments to manage exposures to currency fluctuations.

   The carrying amount of the Company's subsidiary's foreign-currency denominated monetary assets at December 31, 2010, is as follows:

	December 31, 2010	December 31, 2009
Financial assets		
Loans and receivables	**30,142**	25,839

Eastern Platinum Limited
Notes to the consolidated financial statements
(Expressed in thousands of U.S. dollars, except number of shares and per share amounts)

24. Financial instruments (continued)

(e) *Financial risk management (continued)*

(i) *Currency risk (continued)*

The sensitivity of the Company's net earnings due to changes in the exchange rate between the South African Rand and the United States dollar is summarized in the table below. This sensitivity is based on loans and receivables not denominated in the functional currency of the subsidiary. The increase (decrease) in net earnings is due to the effect of the exchange rate on financial instruments.

	Year ended Dec. 31, 2010	
	10% weakening of ZAR in relation to USD FX rate	10% strengthening of ZAR in relation to USD FX rate
Increase (decrease) in net earnings	3,014	(3,014)

The carrying amount of the Company's head office foreign-currency denominated monetary assets at December 31, 2010 is as follows:

	December 31, 2010	December 31, 2009
Financial assets		
Cash and cash equivalents	43,110	-

The sensitivity of the Company's net earnings due to changes in the exchange rate between the U.K. Pound Sterling and the United States dollar is summarized in the table below. This sensitivity is based on cash and cash equivalents not denominated in the functional currency of head office. The (decrease) increase in net earnings is due to the effect of the exchange rate on financial instruments.

	Year ended Dec. 31, 2010	
	10% weakening of GBP in relation to USD FX rate	10% strengthening of GBP in relation to USD FX rate
(Decrease) increase in net earnings	(4,311)	4,311

Eastern Platinum Limited
Notes to the consolidated financial statements
(Expressed in thousands of U.S. dollars, except number of shares and per share amounts)

24. Financial instruments (continued)

   (e)   *Financial risk management (continued)*

       (ii)   *Interest rate risk*

Interest rate risk is the risk that the fair value or future cash flows of a financial instrument will fluctuate because of changes in market interest rates. The Company is exposed to interest rate risk on its short-term investments. The risk that the Company will realize a loss as a result of a decline in the fair value of short-term investments is limited because these investments, although available for sale, are generally not sold before maturity. The Company monitors its exposure to interest rates and has not entered into any derivative financial instruments to manage this risk.

The Company has not included a sensitivity analysis of interest rate risk at year-end as it does not reflect the exposure experienced during the twelve months ended December 31, 2010. The Company's financial assets as at December 31, 2010 were significantly higher than throughout the year due to the closing of the Company's public offering on December 30, 2010. Presenting such an analysis would be misleading.

      (iii)   *Price risk*

The Company is exposed to price risk with respect to fluctuations in the prices of platinum group metals. These fluctuations directly affect revenues and trade receivables. As at December 31, 2010, the Company's financial assets subject to metal price risk consist of trade receivables of $30,142 (December 31, 2009 - $25,839). Historically, the Company has not entered into any derivative financial instruments to manage exposures to price fluctuations. No such derivative financial instruments existed at December 31, 2010 and 2009.

The Company has not included a sensitivity analysis of price risk at year-end as it does not reflect the exposure experienced during the twelve months ended December 31, 2010. Presenting such an analysis would be misleading.

      (iv)   *Credit risk*

Credit risk is the risk of an unexpected loss if a customer or third party to a financial instrument fails to meet its contractual obligations, and arises principally from the Company's trade receivables. The carrying value of the financial assets represents the maximum credit exposure.

The Company currently sells substantially all of its PGM concentrate production to one customer under an off-take contract. At December 31, 2010, the Company had receivable balances associated with this one customer of $30,142 (December 31, 2009 - $25,839). The loss of this customer or unexpected termination of the off-take contract could have a material adverse effect on the Company's results of operations, financial condition and cash flows. The Company has not experienced any bad debts with this customer.

The Company minimizes credit risk by reviewing the credit risk of the counterparty to the arrangement and has made any necessary provisions related to credit risk at December 31, 2010.

Eastern Platinum Limited
Notes to the consolidated financial statements
(Expressed in thousands of U.S. dollars, except number of shares and per share amounts)

24. Financial instruments (continued)

(e)   *Financial risk management (continued)*

(v)   *Liquidity risk*

Liquidity risk is the risk that the Company will not be able to meet its financial obligations as they fall due. The Company has a planning and budgeting process in place to help determine the funds required to support the Company's normal operating requirements on an ongoing basis and its expansionary plans. The Company ensures that there are sufficient funds to meet its short-term business requirements, taking into account its anticipated cash flows from operations and its holdings of cash and cash equivalents.

The Company's policy is to invest its excess cash in highly liquid, fully guaranteed, bank-sponsored instruments. The Company staggers the maturity dates of its investments over different time periods and dates to minimize exposure to interest rate changes. This strategy remains unchanged from 2009.

In the normal course of business, the Company enters into contracts that give rise to commitments for future minimum payments. The following table summarizes the Company's significant commitments and corresponding maturities.

	December 31, 2010 Total	<1 year
Accounts payable	$ 27,009	$ 27,009
Finance leases	3,405	3,405
Commitments	13,056	13,056
	$ 43,470	$ 43,470

	December 31, 2009 Total	<1 year	1-3 years
Accounts payable	$ 22,919	$ 22,919	$ -
Finance leases	4,282	1,221	3,061
Purchase commitments	881	881	-
Capital expenditures	4,078	4,078	-
	$ 32,160	$ 29,099	$ 3,061

Eastern Platinum Limited
Notes to the consolidated financial statements
(Expressed in thousands of U.S. dollars, except number of shares and per share amounts)

25. Events after the reporting period

From January 1, 2011 to March 21, 2011:

(a) 550,000 stock options were exercised by way of stock appreciation rights at a weighted average exercise price of Cdn$0.32.

(b) The Company received formal letters of commitment to underwrite a US$100 million financing package. The mandated lead arrangers are UniCredit Bank AG, London Branch and The Standard Bank of South Africa Limited. The terms and conditions of the financing package include:

- Scheduled tenor of 5.5 years with an 18 month grace period
- Separate amortizing term loan (US$70 million) and revolving loan facilities (US$30 million)
- Initial interest rate of US LIBOR + 3.85% rising to US LIBOR + 4.15% for the last three years of the loan.

Specimen Financial Statements: Anglo American Platinum Limited (Amplats)

In this appendix, we illustrate current financial reporting using the financial statements of Anglo American Platinum Limited (commonly known as Amplats), the world's largest miner of platinum group metals.

The financial statement package includes the independent auditor's report, consolidated statement of comprehensive income, statement of financial position, statement of cash flows, and statement of changes in equity—all denominated in the South African rand (R). We should note that Anglo American Platinum added the "American" to its official name immediately after the release of its year-end statements, which are still titled Anglo Platinum in this appendix.

These statements, along with the accompanying notes to the financial statements, are also available converted to their U.S. dollar equivalents in Amplats's complete annual report, which can be found on the companion website to this textbook in the Annual Reports section and under the Additional Resources tab in the read, study, and practice section of WileyPLUS.

We encourage you to use these financial statements in conjunction with relevant material in the textbook, and to solve the Comparative Analysis cases in the Broadening Your Perspective section at the end of every chapter.

Deloitte.

Pnvate Bag ×6
Gallo Manor 2052
South Africa

Deloitte & Touche
Registered Auditors
Audit - Johannesburg
Buildings 1 and 2
Deloitte Place
The Woodlands
Woodlands Drive
Woodmead Sandton
Docex 10 Johannesburg

Tel: +.27 (0)11 806 5000
Fax: +27 (0)11 806 5111
www.deloitte.com

INDEPENDENT AUDITOR'S REPORT TO THE MEMBERS OF ANGLO PLATINUM LIMITED

Report on the Financial Statements

We have audited the annual financial statements and group annual financial statements of Anglo Platinum Limited, which comprise the statement of financial position and the consolidated statement of financial position as at 31 December 2010, the statement of comprehensive income and the consolidated statement of comprehensive income, the statement of changes in equity and the consolidated statement of changes in equity, statement of cash flows and consolidated statement of cash flows for the year then ended, and a summary of significant accounting policies and other explanatory notes, and the directors' report, as set out on pages 174 to 271.

Directors' Responsibility for the Financial Statements

The company's directors are responsible for the preparation and fair presentation of these financial statements in accordance with International Financial Reporting Standards and South African General Accepted Accounting Practice and in the manner required by the Companies Act of South Africa. This responsibility includes: designing, implementing and maintaining internal control relevant to the preparation and fair presentation of financial statements that are free from material misstatement, whether due to fraud or error; selecting and applying appropriate accounting policies; and making accounting estimates that are reasonable in the circumstances.

Auditor's Responsibility

Our responsibility is to express an opinion on these financial statements based on our audit. We conducted our audit in accordance with International Standards on Auditing. Those standards require that we comply with ethical requirements and plan and perform the audit to obtain reasonable assurance whether the financial statements are free from material misstatement.

An audit involves performing procedures to obtain audit evidence about the amounts and disclosures in the financial statements. The procedures selected depend on the auditor's judgement, including the assessment of the risks of material misstatement of the financial statements, whether due to fraud or error. In making those risk assessments, the auditor considers internal control relevant to the entity's preparation and fair presentation of the financial statements in order to design audit procedures that are appropriate in the circumstances, but not for the purpose of expressing an opinion on the effectiveness of the entity's internal control. An audit also includes evaluating the appropriateness of accounting principles used and the reasonableness of accounting estimates made by management, as well as evaluating the overall presentation of the financial statements.

We believe that the audit evidence we have obtained is sufficient and appropriate to provide a basis for our audit opinion.

Opinion

In our opinion, the annual financial statements present fairly, in all material respects, the financial position of the company and of the group as at 31 December 2010, and their financial performance and cash flows for the year then ended in accordance with International Financial Reporting Standards and South African General Accepted Accounting Practice, and in the manner required by the Companies Act of South Africa.

Deloitte & Touche

Per Graeme Berry
Partner
4 February 2011

National Executive: GG Gelink Chief Executive AE Swiegers Chief Operating Officer GM Pinnock Audit
DL Kennedy Risk Advisory NB kader Tax & Legal Services L Geeringh Consulting L Bam Corporate Finance
JK Mazzocco Human Resources CR Beukman Finance TJ Brown Clients NT Mtoba Chairman of the Board
MJ Comber Deputy Chairman of the Board

A full list of partners and directors is available on request

B-BBEE rating: Level 2 contributor/AAA (certified by Empowerdex)

Member of Deloitte Touche Tohmatsu Limited

ANNUAL FINANCIAL STATEMENTS

CONSOLIDATED STATEMENT OF COMPREHENSIVE INCOME
for the year ended 31 December

	Notes	2010 Rm	2009 Rm
Gross sales revenue	1	46,352	36,947
Commissions paid		(327)	(260)
Net sales revenue	2	46,025	36,687
Cost of sales		(37,991)	(34,715)
Gross profit on metal sales	3	8,034	1,972
Other net expenditure	7	(405)	(659)
Market development and promotional expenditure		(376)	(392)
Operating profit		7,253	921
Profit on disposal of 37% interest in Western Bushveld Joint Venture		788	–
Gain on listing of Bafokeng-Rasimone Platinum Mine (BRPM)	40	4,466	–
Profit on disposal of investment in Booysendal Joint Venture		–	1,982
Profit on disposal of 51% interest in Bokoni Platinum Mines	41	–	536
Interest expensed	8	(318)	(532)
Interest received	8	248	296
Remeasurements of loan and receivables	8	302	(93)
Dividends received	8	–	64
Loss from associates	17	(426)	(199)
Profit before taxation	9	12,313	2,975
Taxation	10	(2,197)	153
Profit for the year		10,116	3,128
Other comprehensive income			
Deferred foreign exchange translation losses		(240)	(85)
Share of other comprehensive income/(losses) of associates		14	(19)
Gain on available for sale investments		129	–
Total comprehensive income for the year		10,019	3,024
Profit attributable to:			
Owners of the company		9,959	3,012
Non-controlling interests		157	116
		10,116	3,128
Total comprehensive income attributable to:			
Owners of the company		9,862	2,908
Non-controlling interests		157	116
		10,019	3,024
Headline earnings	12	4,931	710
Attributable to ordinary shareholders		4,931	705
Attributable to preference shareholders		–	5
Number of ordinary shares in issue (millions)		261.6	236.8
Weighted average number of ordinary shares in issue (millions)		254.8	243.7*
Earnings per ordinary share (cents)	11		
– Basic		3,909	1,234*
– Diluted		3,896	1,230*

*Refer to note 50.

CONSOLIDATED STATEMENT OF FINANCIAL POSITION
as at 31 December

	Notes	2010 Rm	2009 Rm
ASSETS			
Non-current assets		65,408	57,778
Property, plant and equipment	14	37,438	35,283
Capital work-in-progress	15	17,065	18,074
Investment in associates	17	7,339	3,301
Investments held by environmental trusts	19	569	78
Other financial assets	20	2,904	941
Other non-current assets	21	93	101
Current assets		18,393	18,043
Inventories	22	12,558	11,292
Trade and other receivables	23	2,988	2,891
Other assets	24	305	328
Other current financial assets	25	8	–
Cash and cash equivalents	26	2,534	3,532
Total assets		83,801	75,821
EQUITY AND LIABILITIES			
Share capital and reserves			
Share capital	27	26	24
Share premium		21,381	9,143
Foreign currency translation reserve		(499)	(138)
Available for sale reserve		129	–
Retained earnings		33,521	23,109
Non-controlling interests		460	495
Shareholders' equity		55,018	32,633
Non-current liabilities		19,774	34,830
Interest-bearing borrowings	28	6,622	22,773
Obligations due under finance leases	29	1	2
Other financial liabilities	30	148	175
Environmental obligations	31	1,388	1,196
Employees' service benefit obligations	32	–*	6
Deferred taxation	33	11,615	10,678
Current liabilities		9,009	8,358
Current interest-bearing borrowings	28	22	18
Trade and other payables	34	6,190	5,409
Other liabilities	35	2,042	2,119
Other current financial liabilities	30	183	158
Share-based payment provision	32	108	162
Taxation	38	464	492
Total equity and liabilities		83,801	75,821

*Less than R500,000.

ANNUAL FINANCIAL STATEMENTS

CONSOLIDATED STATEMENT OF CASH FLOWS
for the year ended 31 December

	Notes	2010 Rm	2009 Rm
Cash flows from operating activities			
Cash receipts from customers		45,617	36,763
Cash paid to suppliers and employees		(34,261)	(31,246)
Cash generated from operations	37	11,356	5,517
Interest paid (net of interest capitalised)		(220)	(424)
Taxation paid	38	(905)	(396)
Net cash from operating activities		10,231	4,697
Cash flows used in investing activities			
Purchase of property, plant and equipment (includes interest capitalised)	39	(7,989)	(11,301)
Proceeds from sale of plant and equipment		29	16
Net proceeds on disposal of 13% of Royal Bafokeng Platinum Limited (RB Plat)	40	1,323	–
Proceeds on disposal of interest in Western Bushveld Joint Venture		186	
Subscription for 'N' preference shares in Newshelf 848 (Proprietary) Limited		(273)	–
Proceeds on disposal of interest in Sichuan Anglo Platinum Exploration Company Limited		14	
Investment in associates	17	–	(38)
Disposal of subsidiary (net of cash disposed)		–	(170)
Disposal of 51% interest in Bokoni Platinum Mines (net of cash disposed)	41	–	27
Proceeds on redemption of 'A' preference shares in Plateau Resources (Proprietary) Limited (Plateau)		–	7
Acquisition of Unki Mines Zimbabwe (net of cash acquired)	42	–	(174)
Repayment by Plateau		–	72
Loans to associates	17	(260)	(181)
Advances made to Plateau for the operating cash shortfall facility		(141)	(190)
Repayment by/(advances made to) ARM Mining Consortium Limited		17	(132)
Proceeds on sale of mining rights and other investments		–	35
Receipt of funds in escrow regarding the Booysendal deal		537	–
Proceeds on rights in preference shares		–	1,610
Disposal of cash and cash equivalents relating to 17% of BRPM		–	(11)
Increase in investments held by environmental trusts		(507)	(27)
Interest received		33	86
Growth in environmental trusts	19	22	43
Dividends received		–	64
Other advances		(32)	–
Net cash used in investing activities		(7,041)	(10,264)
Cash flows (used in)/from financing activities			
Proceeds from the issue of ordinary share capital		18	28
Proceeds from the rights offer (net of costs)		12,404	–
Redemption of preference shares		–	(84)
Purchase of treasury shares for the Bonus Share Plan (BSP)		(270)	(185)
(Repayment of)/proceeds on interest-bearing borrowings		(16,147)	6,971
Repayment of finance lease obligation		(1)	(507)
Preference dividends paid		–	(6)
Cash distributions to minorities		(192)	(82)
Net cash (used in)/from financing activities		(4,188)	6,135
Net (decrease)/increase in cash and cash equivalents		(998)	568
Cash and cash equivalents at beginning of year		3,532	2,870
Transfer from assets held for sale		–	94
Cash and cash equivalents at end of year	26	2,534	3,532
Movement in net debt			
Net debt at beginning of year		(19,261)	(13,459)
Net cash from operating activities		10,231	4,697
Net cash used in investing activities		(7,041)	(10,264)
Other		11,960	(235)
Net debt at end of year		(4,111)	(19,261)
Made up as follows:			
Cash and cash equivalents	26	2,534	3,532
Obligations due under finance leases	29	(1)	(2)
Interest-bearing borrowings	28	(6,622)	(22,773)
Current interest-bearing borrowings	28	(22)	(18)
		(4,111)	(19,261)

CONSOLIDATED STATEMENT OF CHANGES IN EQUITY

for the year ended 31 December

	Share capital Rm	Share premium Rm	Foreign currency translation reserve Rm	Available for sale reserve Rm	Retained earnings Rm	Non-controlling interests Rm	Total Rm
Balance at 31 December 2008	**24**	**9,373**	**(53)**	**–**	**19,691**	**461**	**29,496**
Total comprehensive income for the year			(85)		2,993	116	3,024
Deferred tax charged directly to equity					31		31
Preference dividends paid in cash					(6)		(6)
Excess of net asset value over purchase price on acquisition of Unki Mines from fellow subsidiary					69		69
Cash distributions to minorities						(82)	(82)
Ordinary share capital issued	– *	34					34
Conversion of preference shares	(–)*	(6)					(6)
Redemption of preference shares	(–)*	(84)					(84)
Shares acquired in terms of the BSP – treated as treasury shares	(–)*	(185)					(185)
Shares vested in terms of the BSP		11			(11)		–
Equity-settled share-based compensation					363		363
Shares purchased for employees					(21)		(21)
Balance at 31 December 2009	**24**	**9,143**	**(138)**	**–**	**23,109**	**495**	**32,633**
Total comprehensive income for the year			(240)	129	9,973	157	10,019
Deferred tax charged directly to equity					(28)		(28)
Proceeds of rights offer (net of transaction costs)	2	12,402					12,404
Transfer of prior year translation differences on net investment in foreign subsidiary			(121)		121		–
Rights offer shares subscribed for by the Group ESOP		(30)			30		–
Cash distributions to minorities						(192)	(192)
Issue of shares to certain former preference shareholders (Note 49)	– *	88			(88)		–
Ordinary share capital issued	– *	18					18
Shares acquired in terms of the BSP – treated as treasury shares	(–)*	(270)					(270)
Shares vested in terms of the BSP	– *	30			(30)		–
Equity-settled share-based compensation					475		475
Shares purchased for employees					(41)		(41)
Balance at 31 December 2010	**26**	**21,381**	**(499)**	**129**	**33,521**	**460**	**55,018**

* Less than R500,000.

Present Value Tables

TABLE 1: PRESENT VALUE OF $1 $\left(PV = \dfrac{1}{(1+i)^n}\right)$

(n) Periods	1%	1.5%	2%	2.5%	3%	3.5%	4%	4.5%	5%	6%	7%	8%	9%	10%
1	0.99010	0.98522	0.98039	0.97561	0.97087	0.96618	0.96154	0.95694	0.95238	0.94340	0.93458	0.92593	0.91743	0.90909
2	0.98030	0.97066	0.96117	0.95181	0.94260	0.93351	0.92456	0.91573	0.90703	0.89000	0.87344	0.85734	0.84168	0.82645
3	0.97059	0.95632	0.94232	0.92860	0.91514	0.90194	0.88900	0.87630	0.86384	0.83962	0.81630	0.79383	0.77218	0.75131
4	0.96098	0.94218	0.92385	0.90595	0.88849	0.87144	0.85480	0.83856	0.82270	0.79209	0.76290	0.73503	0.70843	0.68301
5	0.95147	0.92826	0.90573	0.88385	0.86261	0.84197	0.82193	0.80245	0.78353	0.74726	0.71299	0.68058	0.64993	0.62092
6	0.94205	0.91454	0.88797	0.86230	0.83748	0.81350	0.79031	0.76790	0.74622	0.70496	0.66634	0.63017	0.59627	0.56447
7	0.93272	0.90103	0.87056	0.84127	0.81309	0.78599	0.75992	0.73483	0.71068	0.66506	0.62275	0.58349	0.54703	0.51316
8	0.92348	0.88771	0.85349	0.82075	0.78941	0.75941	0.73069	0.70319	0.67684	0.62741	0.58201	0.54027	0.50187	0.46651
9	0.91434	0.87459	0.83676	0.80073	0.76642	0.73373	0.70259	0.67290	0.64461	0.59190	0.54393	0.50025	0.46043	0.42410
10	0.90529	0.86167	0.82035	0.78120	0.74409	0.70892	0.67556	0.64393	0.61391	0.55839	0.50835	0.46319	0.42241	0.38554
11	0.89632	0.84893	0.80426	0.76214	0.72242	0.68495	0.64958	0.61620	0.58468	0.52679	0.47509	0.42888	0.38753	0.35049
12	0.88745	0.83639	0.78849	0.74356	0.70138	0.66178	0.62460	0.58966	0.55684	0.49697	0.44401	0.39711	0.35553	0.31863
13	0.87866	0.82403	0.77303	0.72542	0.68095	0.63940	0.60057	0.56427	0.53032	0.46884	0.41496	0.36770	0.32618	0.28966
14	0.86996	0.81185	0.75788	0.70773	0.66112	0.61778	0.57748	0.53997	0.50507	0.44230	0.38782	0.34046	0.29925	0.26333
15	0.86135	0.79985	0.74301	0.69047	0.64186	0.59689	0.55526	0.51672	0.48102	0.41727	0.36245	0.31524	0.27454	0.23939
16	0.85282	0.78803	0.72845	0.67362	0.62317	0.57671	0.53391	0.49447	0.45811	0.39365	0.33873	0.29189	0.25187	0.21763
17	0.84438	0.77639	0.71416	0.65720	0.60502	0.55720	0.51337	0.47318	0.43630	0.37136	0.31657	0.27027	0.23107	0.19784
18	0.83602	0.76491	0.70016	0.64117	0.58739	0.53836	0.49363	0.45280	0.41552	0.35034	0.29586	0.25025	0.21199	0.17986
19	0.82774	0.75361	0.68643	0.62553	0.57029	0.52016	0.47464	0.43330	0.39573	0.33051	0.27651	0.23171	0.19449	0.16351
20	0.81954	0.74247	0.67297	0.61027	0.55368	0.50257	0.45639	0.41464	0.37689	0.31180	0.25842	0.21455	0.17843	0.14864

TABLE 2: PRESENT VALUE OF AN ANNUITY OF $1 $\left(PV = \dfrac{1-\dfrac{1}{(1+i)^n}}{i}\right)$

(n) Periods	1%	1.5%	2%	2.5%	3%	3.5%	4%	4.5%	5%	6%	7%	8%	9%	10%
1	0.99010	0.98522	0.98039	0.97561	0.97087	0.96618	0.96154	0.95694	0.95238	0.94340	0.93458	0.92593	0.91743	0.90909
2	1.97040	1.95588	1.94156	1.92742	1.91347	1.89969	1.88609	1.87267	1.85941	1.83339	1.80802	1.78326	1.75911	1.73554
3	2.94099	2.91220	2.88388	2.85602	2.82861	2.80164	2.77509	2.74896	2.72325	2.67301	2.62432	2.57710	2.53129	2.48685
4	3.90197	3.85438	3.80773	3.76197	3.71710	3.67308	3.62990	3.58753	3.54595	3.46511	3.38721	3.31213	3.23972	3.16987
5	4.85343	4.78264	4.71346	4.64583	4.57971	4.51505	4.45182	4.38998	4.32948	4.21236	4.10020	3.99271	3.88965	3.79079
6	5.79548	5.69719	5.60143	5.50813	5.41719	5.32855	5.24214	5.15787	5.07569	4.91732	4.76654	4.62288	4.48592	4.35526
7	6.72819	6.59821	6.47199	6.34939	6.23028	6.11454	6.00205	5.89270	5.78637	5.58238	5.38929	5.20637	5.03295	4.86842
8	7.65168	7.48593	7.32548	7.17014	7.01969	6.87396	6.73274	6.59589	6.46321	6.20979	5.97130	5.74664	5.53482	5.33493
9	8.56602	8.36052	8.16224	7.97087	7.78611	7.60769	7.43533	7.26879	7.10782	6.80169	6.51523	6.24689	5.99525	5.75902
10	9.47130	9.22218	8.98259	8.75206	8.53020	8.31661	8.11090	7.91272	7.72173	7.36009	7.02358	6.71008	6.41766	6.14457
11	10.36763	10.07112	9.78685	9.51421	9.25262	9.00155	8.76048	8.52892	8.30641	7.88687	7.49867	7.13896	6.80519	6.49506
12	11.25508	10.90751	10.57534	10.25776	9.95400	9.66333	9.38507	9.11858	8.86325	8.38384	7.94269	7.53608	7.16073	6.81369
13	12.13374	11.73153	11.34837	10.98318	10.63496	10.30274	9.98565	9.68285	9.39357	8.85268	8.35765	7.90378	7.48690	7.10336
14	13.00370	12.54338	12.10625	11.69091	11.29607	10.92052	10.56312	10.22283	9.89864	9.29498	8.74547	8.24424	7.78615	7.36669
15	13.86505	13.34323	12.84926	12.38138	11.93794	11.51741	11.11839	10.73955	10.37966	9.71225	9.10791	8.55948	8.06069	7.60608
16	14.71787	14.13126	13.57771	13.05500	12.56110	12.09412	11.65230	11.23402	10.83777	10.10590	9.44665	8.85137	8.31256	7.82371
17	15.56225	14.90765	14.29187	13.71220	13.16612	12.65132	12.16567	11.70719	11.27407	10.47726	9.76322	9.12164	8.54363	8.02155
18	16.39827	15.67256	14.99203	14.35336	13.75351	13.18968	12.65930	12.15999	11.68959	10.82760	10.05909	9.37189	8.75563	8.20141
19	17.22601	16.42617	15.67846	14.97889	14.32380	13.70984	13.13394	12.59329	12.08532	11.15812	10.33560	9.60360	8.95011	8.36492
20	18.04555	17.16864	16.35143	15.58916	14.87747	14.21240	13.59033	13.00794	12.46221	11.46992	10.59401	9.81815	9.12855	8.51356

Photo Credits

Chapter 1 Opener: Photo courtesy of Eastern Platinum Limited. Page 6: © Phil Date/iStockphoto. Page 10: PhotoDisc Inc. Page 14: © David Freund/iStockphoto. Page 26: © Chris Schmidt/iStockphoto.

Chapter 2 Opener: Photo courtesy of Plazacorp Retail Properties Ltd.. Page 54: BlackBerry®, RIM®, Research In Motion® and related trademarks, names and logos are the property of Research In Motion Limited and are registered and/or used in the U.S. and countries around the world. Used under license from Research In Motion Limited. Page 58: TELUS materials at page 58, used with permission. © 2011 TELUS. All rights reserved. Page 61: © Plesea Petre/iStockphoto. Page 66: © Wavebreakmedia/iStockphoto. Page 72: Frank Gunn/The Canadian Press

Chapter 3 Opener: Photo courtesy of Beavertails. Page 107: © Nicole Waring/iStockphoto. Page 118: © Skynesher/iStockphoto. Page 129: Mario Beauregard/The Canadian Press.

Chapter 4 Opener: Photo courtesy of The University of Western Ontario. Page 166: © Gergana Valcheva/iStockphoto. Page 174: AP Photo/Richard Drew/The Canadian Press. Page 190: © Porcorex/iStockphoto.

Chapter 5 Opener: Steve White/The Canadian Press. Page 232: © Bunhill/iStockphoto. Page 240: Image courtesy of Liquidation World Inc. Page 251: Jeff Chiu/The Canadian Press.

Chapter 6 Opener: Photo courtesy of The Forzani Group Ltd. Page 297: © CW03070/iStockphoto. Page 313: © Zentilia/iStockphoto. Page 318: Photo courtesy of ALDO Group.

Chapter 7 Opener: Photo courtesy of Nick's Steakhouse and Pizza. Page 354: AFP PHOTO/Timothy A. Clary/NewsCom.

Chapter 8 Opener: Steve White/The Canadian Press. Page 419: © Turner Johnson/iStockphoto. Page 430: AP/Charles Krupa/ The Canadian Press.

Chapter 9 Opener: Jeff McIntosh/The Canadian Press. Page 460: © Yen Teoh/iStockphoto. Page 480: © Skip ODonnell/iStockphoto.

Chapter 10 Opener: Photo courtesy of Canada Post. Page 527: © Pamela Moore/iStockphoto. Page 530: © Pgiam/iStockphoto. Page 552: QMI Agency. Page 558: Royal Mail Cruciform (Standard) © and Trade Marks of Royal Mail Group Ltd reproduced by kind permission of Royal Mail Group Ltd. All rights reserved.

Chapter 11 Opener: Richard Lam/The Canadian Press. Page 586: © Rudyanto Wijaya/iStockphoto. Page 598: Adrian Wyld/The Canadian Press. Page 606: © H-Gall/iStockphoto.

Chapter 12 Opener: Kevin Frayer/The Canadian Press. Page 643: © Maria Toutoudaki/iStockphoto. Page 651: Photo courtesy of Canadian Tire Corporation.

Chapter 13 Opener: Photo courtesy of Teck Resources Limited. Page 693: © Robert Linton/iStockphoto. Page 699: © Carmen Martínez Banús/iStockphoto. Page 727: © DNY59/iStockphoto.

Chapter 14 Opener: Photo courtesy of Potash Corporation of Saskatchewan Inc. Page 763: © Günay Mutlu/iStockphoto. Page 788: Photo courtesy of Netflix. Page 792: © Emilijan Sekulovski/iStockphoto.

Company Index

Subject Index *Boldface indicates key terms and definitions*

Comparison of Long-Term Bond Investment and Liability Journal Entries

Transaction	Investor (amortized cost model)	Investee
Purchase/issue of bonds	Dr. Long-Term Investments 　Cr. Cash	Dr. Cash 　Cr. Bonds Payable
Interest receipt/payment and amortization of discount or premium	Dr. Cash Dr. Long-Term Investments (dr. for discount; cr. for premium) 　Cr. Interest Revenue	Dr. Interest Expense 　Cr. Bonds Payable 　(dr. for premium; 　cr. for discount) 　Cr. Cash
Sale of investment	Dr. Cash Dr. Realized Loss (or credit Gain) 　Cr. Long-Term Investments	No entry

STATEMENT OF CASH FLOWS　(Chapter 13)

Business Activities

1. Operating activities: Include cash effects of transactions that create revenues and expenses. They affect profit.
2. Investing activities: Include (a) purchasing and disposing of long-term investments and long-lived assets and (b) lending money and collecting the loans. Investing activities generally affect non-current asset accounts.
3. Financing activities: Include (a) obtaining cash from issuing debt and repaying the amounts borrowed and (b) obtaining cash from shareholders and paying them dividends. Financing activities generally affect non-current liability and shareholders' equity accounts.

Steps in Preparing the Statement of Cash Flows

1. Prepare operating activities section: Determine net cash provided (used) by operating activities by converting profit from accrual basis to cash basis using either indirect or direct method (preferred). To do this, analyze the current year's income statement, relevant current asset and current liability accounts from comparative statement of financial position, and selected information. In the indirect method, this is done by converting total profit from accrual basis to cash basis. In the direct method, this is done by converting each individual revenue and expense account from accrual basis to cash basis.
2. Prepare investing activities section: Determine net cash provided (used) by investing activities by analyzing changes in non-current asset accounts from comparative statement of financial position and selected information.
3. Prepare financing activities section: Determine net cash provided (used) by financing activities by analyzing changes in non-current liability and equity accounts from comparative statement of financial position and selected information.
4. Complete statement of cash flows: Determine net increase (decrease) in cash. Compare net change in cash reported on statement of cash flows with change in cash reported on statement of financial position to make sure amounts agree.

PERFORMANCE MEASUREMENT　(Chapter 14)

Irregular Items

Discontinued operations	Income statement (presented separately, net of income tax, after profit from continuing operations)
Changes in accounting policy	Statement of changes in equity (adjustment, net of income tax, of beginning retained earnings)

Horizontal (Trend) Analysis

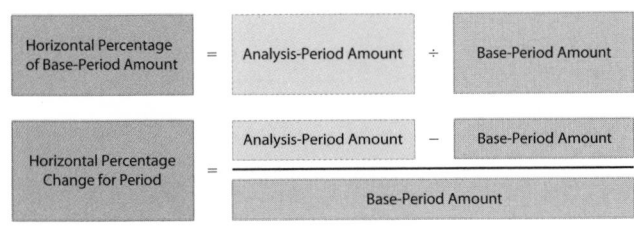

Horizontal Percentage of Base-Period Amount = Analysis-Period Amount ÷ Base-Period Amount

Horizontal Percentage Change for Period = (Analysis-Period Amount − Base-Period Amount) / Base-Period Amount

Vertical (Common-Size) Analysis

Vertical Percentage of Base Amount = Analysis Amount ÷ Base Amount

Liquidity Ratios

Chapter	Ratio	Formula	What the Ratio Measures	Desired Result
2	Working capital	Current assets − Current liabilities	Short-term debt-paying ability	Higher
2	Current ratio	$\dfrac{\text{Current assets}}{\text{Current liabilities}}$	Short-term debt-paying ability	Higher
13	Cash current debt coverage	$\dfrac{\text{Net cash provided (used) by operating activities}}{\text{Average current liabilities}}$	Short-term debt-paying ability (cash basis)	Higher
8	Receivables turnover	$\dfrac{\text{Net credit sales}}{\text{Average gross accounts receivable}}$	Liquidity of receivables	Higher
8	Average collection period	$\dfrac{365 \text{ days}}{\text{Receivables turnover}}$	Number of days receivables are outstanding	Lower
6	Inventory turnover	$\dfrac{\text{Cost of goods sold}}{\text{Average inventory}}$	Liquidity of inventory	Higher
6	Days in inventory	$\dfrac{365 \text{ days}}{\text{Inventory turnover}}$	Number of days inventory is on hand	Lower

Solvency Ratios

Chapter	Ratio	Formula	What the Ratio Measures	Desired Result
2, 10	Debt to total assets	$\dfrac{\text{Total liabilities}}{\text{Total assets}}$	Percentage of total assets provided by creditors	Lower
10	Times interest earned	$\dfrac{\text{Profit + Interest expense + Income tax expense (EBIT)}}{\text{Interest expense}}$	Ability to meet interest payments	Higher
13	Cash total debt coverage	$\dfrac{\text{Net cash provided (used) by operating activities}}{\text{Average total liabilities}}$	Long-term debt-paying ability (cash basis)	Higher
13	Free cash flow	Net cash provided (used) by operating activities − Net capital expenditures − Dividends paid	Cash available from operating activities for discretionary purposes	Higher

Profitability Ratios

Chapter	Ratio	Formula	What the Ratio Measures	Desired Result
11	Return on common shareholders' equity	$\dfrac{\text{Profit − Preferred dividends}}{\text{Average common shareholders' equity}}$	Profitability of shareholders' investment	Higher
9	Return on assets	$\dfrac{\text{Profit}}{\text{Average total assets}}$	Overall profitability of assets	Higher
5	Profit margin	$\dfrac{\text{Profit}}{\text{Net sales}}$	Profit generated by each dollar of sales	Higher
9	Asset turnover	$\dfrac{\text{Net sales}}{\text{Average total assets}}$	How efficiently assets are used to generate sales	Higher
5	Gross profit margin	$\dfrac{\text{Gross profit}}{\text{Net sales}}$	Margin between selling price and cost of goods sold	Higher
2, 11	Earnings per share	$\dfrac{\text{Profit − Preferred dividends}}{\text{Weighted average number of common shares}}$	Profit earned on each common share	Higher
2	Price-earnings ratio	$\dfrac{\text{Market price per share}}{\text{Earnings per share}}$	Relationship between market price per share and earnings per share	Higher
11	Payout ratio	$\dfrac{\text{Cash dividends}}{\text{Profit}}$	Percentage of profit distributed as cash dividends	Higher
11	Dividend yield	$\dfrac{\text{Dividend per share}}{\text{Market price per share}}$	Income generated for the shareholder by each share, based on the market price per share	Higher

SAMPLE FINANCIAL STATEMENTS

Multiple-Step Income Statement (perpetual inventory system)

Name of Company **Income Statement** **Period Ended**		
Sales revenues		
Sales		$X
Less: Sales returns and allowances	$X	
Sales discounts	X	X
Net sales		X
Cost of goods sold		X
Gross profit		X
Operating expenses		
(Examples: salaries, advertising, freight, rent, depreciation, utilities, insurance)		X
Profit from operations		X
Other revenues and gains		
(Examples: interest)	$X	
Other expenses and losses		
(Examples: interest)	X	X
Profit before income tax		X
Income tax expense		X
Profit		$X

Income Statement (cost of goods sold detail in periodic inventory system)

Cost of goods sold		
Beginning inventory		$X
Purchases	$X	
Less: Purchase returns and allowances	X	
Net purchases	X	
Add: Freight in	X	
Cost of goods purchased		X
Cost of goods available for sale		X
Less: Ending inventory		X
Cost of goods sold		$X

Statement of Comprehensive Income

Name of Company **Statement of Comprehensive Income** **Period Ended**	
Profit	$X
Other comprehensive income (loss)	
(Examples: revaluations of property, plant, and equipment; foreign currency translation adjustment)	X
Comprehensive income (loss)	$X

Statement of Changes in Equity

	Common Shares		Additional		Accumulated Other	
	Number of Shares	Legal Capital	Contributed Capital	Retained Earnings	Comprehensive Income (Loss)	Total
Balance, beginning of period	X	$X	$X	$X	$X	$X
Issued shares	X	X				X
Reacquisition of shares	(X)	(X)	(X)	(X)		(X)
Cash dividends				(X)		(X)
Stock dividends	X	X		(X)		
Comprehensive income						
Profit				X		X
Other comprehensive income (loss)					X	X
Balance, end of period	X	$X	$X	$X	$X	$X

Statement of Financial Position

Name of Company **Statement of Financial Position** **End of the Period**		
Assets		
Current assets		
(Examples: cash, short-term (trading) investments, accounts receivable, merchandise inventory, supplies, prepaids)		$X
Long-term investments		
(Examples: equity investments, debt investments)		X
Property, plant, and equipment		
(Examples: land, land improvements, buildings, equipment, natural resources)	$X	
Less: Accumulated depreciation	X	X
Intangible assets		
Limited life intangibles (Examples: patents, copyrights) (net of accumulated amortization)	$X	
Indefinite life intangibles (Examples: trademarks, franchise)	X	X
Goodwill		X
Total assets		$X
Liabilities and Shareholders' Equity		
Liabilities		
Current liabilities		
(Examples: accounts payable, accruals, unearned revenues, bank loan payable, current portion of non-current liabilities)		$X
Non-current liabilities		
(Examples: mortgage payable, bonds payable)		X
Total liabilities		X
Shareholders' equity		
Contributed capital		
Preferred shares	$X	
Common shares	X	
Contributed capital—reacquisition of shares	X	$X
Retained earnings (deficit)		X
Accumulated other comprehensive income (loss)		X	X
Total liabilities and shareholders' equity		$X

STOP AND CHECK: (1) Total assets on the statement of financial position must equal total liabilities and shareholders' equity, and (2) ending shareholders' equity on the statement of financial position must equal ending shareholders' equity on the statement of changes in equity.

Note: The classifications and ordering within the classifications have been presented in order of liquidity in the above statement of financial position. They may be presented in alternate orders, such as a reverse order of liquidity, as well.

Order of Liquidity	Order of Reverse Liquidity
Current assets	Non-current assets
Non-current assets	Current assets
Current liabilities	Shareholders' equity
Non-current liabilities	Non-current liabilities
Shareholders' equity	Current liabilities